Pro WPF in C# 2008

Windows Presentation Foundation with .NET 3.5

SECOND EDITION

Matthew MacDonald

Apress®

Pro WPF in C# 2008: Windows Presentation Foundation with .NET 3.5, Second Edition

Copyright © 2008 by Matthew MacDonald

ISBN-13 (paperback): 978-1-59059-955-6

ISBN-13 (electronic): 978-1-4302-0576-0

Printed and bound in the United States of America 9 8

Trademarked names may appear in this book. Rather than use a trademark symbol with every occurrence of a trademarked name, we use the names only in an editorial fashion and to the benefit of the trademark owner, with no intention of infringement of the trademark.

Lead Editor: Matt Moodie
Technical Reviewer: Christophe Nasarre
Editorial Board: Clay Andres, Steve Anglin, Ewan Buckingham, Tony Campbell, Gary Cornell,
    Jonathan Gennick, Kevin Goff, Matthew Moodie, Joseph Ottinger, Jeffrey Pepper, Frank Pohlmann,
    Ben Renow-Clarke, Dominic Shakeshaft, Matt Wade, Tom Welsh
Project Manager: Sofia Marchant
Copy Editor: Kim Wimpsett
Associate Production Director: Kari Brooks-Copony
Production Editor: Laura Esterman
Compositor: Diana Van Winkle
Proofreader: Nancy Sixsmith
Indexer: Broccoli Information Management
Artists: Diana Van Winkle, April Milne
Cover Designer: Kurt Krames
Manufacturing Director: Tom Debolski

Distributed to the book trade worldwide by Springer-Verlag New York, Inc., 233 Spring Street, 6th Floor, New York, NY 10013. Phone 1-800-SPRINGER, fax 201-348-4505, e-mail orders-ny@springer-sbm.com, or visit http://www.springeronline.com.

For information on translations, please e-mail info@apress.com, or visit http://www.apress.com.

Apress and friends of ED books may be purchased in bulk for academic, corporate, or promotional use. eBook versions and licenses are also available for most titles. For more information, reference our Special Bulk Sales–eBook Licensing web page at http://www.apress.com/info/bulksales.

The information in this book is distributed on an "as is" basis, without warranty. Although every precaution has been taken in the preparation of this work, neither the author(s) nor Apress shall have any liability to any person or entity with respect to any loss or damage caused or alleged to be caused directly or indirectly by the information contained in this work.

The source code for this book is available to readers at http://www.apress.com.

For my wonderful family,
Faria and Maya

Contents at a Glance

About the Author xxii

About the Technical Reviewer xxiii

Acknowledgments xxiv

Introduction xxv

■CHAPTER 1   Introducing WPF 1
■CHAPTER 2   XAML 21
■CHAPTER 3   The Application 57
■CHAPTER 4   Layout 75
■CHAPTER 5   Content 117
■CHAPTER 6   Dependency Properties and Routed Events 137
■CHAPTER 7   Classic Controls 179
■CHAPTER 8   Windows 215
■CHAPTER 9   Pages and Navigation 245
■CHAPTER 10   Commands 289
■CHAPTER 11   Resources 317
■CHAPTER 12   Styles 349
■CHAPTER 13   Shapes, Transforms, and Brushes 367
■CHAPTER 14   Geometries, Drawings, and Visuals 409
■CHAPTER 15   Control Templates 445
■CHAPTER 16   Data Binding 491
■CHAPTER 17   Data Templates, Data Views, and Data Providers 551
■CHAPTER 18   Lists, Trees, Toolbars, and Menus 597
■CHAPTER 19   Documents 643
■CHAPTER 20   Printing 697
■CHAPTER 21   Animation 729
■CHAPTER 22   Sound and Video 783
■CHAPTER 23   3-D Drawing 809
■CHAPTER 24   Custom Elements 855
■CHAPTER 25   Interacting with Windows Forms 903
■CHAPTER 26   Multithreading and Add-Ins 927
■CHAPTER 27   ClickOnce Deployment 965
■INDEX 983

Contents

About the Author xxii

About the Technical Reviewer xxiii

Acknowledgments xxiv

Introduction xxv

■CHAPTER 1   **Introducing WPF** 1

Understanding Windows Graphics 1

    DirectX: The New Graphics Engine 2

    Hardware Acceleration and WPF 2

WPF: A Higher-Level API 4

    Resolution Independence 6

    The Evolution of WPF 11

    Windows Forms Lives On 13

    DirectX Also Lives On 14

    Silverlight 14

The Architecture of WPF 15

    The Class Hierarchy 17

The Last Word 20

■CHAPTER 2   **XAML** 21

Understanding XAML 22

    Graphical User Interfaces Before WPF 22

    The Variants of XAML 24

    XAML Compilation 24

XAML Basics 25

    XAML Namespaces 26

    The Code-Behind Class 27

Properties and Events in XAML 30

    Simple Properties and Type Converters 31

    Complex Properties 32

    Markup Extensions 35

    Attached Properties 36

    Nesting Elements 37

    Special Characters and Whitespace 40

Events 42
The Full Eight Ball Example 43
Using Types from Other Namespaces 44
Loading and Compiling XAML 46
Code-Only 47
Code and Uncompiled XAML 49
Code and Compiled XAML 51
XAML Only 53
The Last Word 54

■CHAPTER 3   **The Application** 57
The Application Life Cycle 57
Creating an Application Object 57
Deriving a Custom Application Class 58
Application Shutdown 60
Application Events 61
Application Tasks 64
Handling Command-Line Arguments 64
Accessing the Current Application 65
Interacting Between Windows 66
Single-Instance Applications 68
The Last Word 74

■CHAPTER 4   **Layout** 75
Understanding Layout in WPF 75
The WPF Layout Philosophy 76
The Layout Process 77
The Layout Containers 77
Simple Layout with the StackPanel 79
Layout Properties 81
Alignment 82
Margin 83
Minimum, Maximum, and Explicit Sizes 84
The WrapPanel and DockPanel 86
The WrapPanel 86
The DockPanel 88
Nesting Layout Containers 90
The Grid 91
Fine-Tuning Rows and Columns 94
Spanning Rows and Columns 96
Split Windows 97

Shared Size Groups 101
The UniformGrid 104
Coordinate-Based Layout with the Canvas 104
Z-Order 106
The InkCanvas 106
Layout Examples 109
A Column of Settings 109
Dynamic Content 111
A Modular User Interface 112
The Last Word 114

■CHAPTER 5   **Content** 117
Understanding Content Controls 117
The Content Property 119
Aligning Content 121
The WPF Content Philosophy 122
Specialized Containers 123
The ScrollViewer 123
The GroupBox and TabItem: Headered Content Controls 127
The Expander 129
Decorators 133
The Border 133
The Viewbox 134
The Last Word 136

■CHAPTER 6   **Dependency Properties and Routed Events** 137
Understanding Dependency Properties 137
Defining and Registering a Dependency Property 138
How WPF Uses Dependency Properties 147
Understanding Routed Events 149
Defining and Registering a Routed Event 149
Attaching an Event Handler 151
Event Routing 153
WPF Events 163
Lifetime Events 163
Input Events 165
Keyboard Input 166
Mouse Input 171
The Last Word 177

■**CHAPTER 7**   **Classic Controls** 179

The Control Class 179
     Background and Foreground Brushes 179
     Fonts 184
     Mouse Cursors 189
Content Controls 190
     Labels 190
     Buttons 191
     Tooltips 194
Text Controls 202
     Multiple Lines of Text 202
     Text Selection 203
     Miscellaneous TextBox Features 204
     The PasswordBox 205
List Controls 206
     The ListBox 206
     The ComboBox 210
Range-Based Controls 211
     The Slider 212
     The ProgressBar 213
The Last Word 214

■**CHAPTER 8**   **Windows** 215

The Window Class 215
     Showing a Window 218
     Positioning a Window 219
     Saving and Restoring Window Location 220
Window Interaction 222
     Window Ownership 224
     The Dialog Model 225
     Common Dialog Boxes 226
Nonrectangular Windows 227
     A Simple Shaped Window 227
     A Transparent Window with Shaped Content 231
     Moving Shaped Windows 232
     Resizing Shaped Windows 233
Vista-Style Windows 235
     Using the Windows Vista Glass Effect 236
     The Task Dialog and File Dialog Boxes 241
The Last Word 243

■CHAPTER 9   Pages and Navigation 245

Understanding Page-Based Navigation 245

Page-Based Interfaces 246

    A Simple Page-Based Application with Nav 247

    The Page Class 248

    Hyperlinks 249

    Hosting Pages in a Frame 252

    Hosting Pages in Another Page 254

    Hosting Pages in a Web Browser 256

The Page History 257

    A Closer Look at URIs in WPF 257

    Navigation History 258

    Maintaining Custom Properties 259

The Navigation Service 260

    Programmatic Navigation 261

    Navigation Events 262

    Managing the Journal 263

    Adding Custom Items to the Journal 265

    Page Functions 270

XAML Browser Applications 273

    XBAP Requirements 273

    Creating an XBAP 274

    Deploying an XBAP 276

    Updating an XBAP 277

    XBAP Security 278

    Full-Trust XBAPs 280

    Combination XBAP/Stand-Alone Applications 280

    Coding for Different Security Levels 281

    Embedding an XBAP in a Web Page 286

The Last Word 287

■CHAPTER 10   Commands 289

Understanding Commands 289

The WPF Command Model 291

    The ICommand Interface 291

    The RoutedCommand Class 292

    The RoutedUICommand Class 293

    The Command Library 294

Executing Commands 295

    Command Sources 295

Command Bindings 296
Using Multiple Command Sources 299
Fine-Tuning Command Text 300
Invoking a Command Directly 300
Disabling Commands 301
Controls with Built-in Commands 304
Advanced Commands 306
Custom Commands 306
Using the Same Command in Different Places 308
Using a Command Parameter 310
Tracking and Reversing Commands 310
The Last Word 315

■CHAPTER 11   **Resources** 317
Assembly Resources 317
Adding Resources 318
Retrieving Resources 319
Pack URIs 321
Content Files 322
Localization 323
Building Localizable User Interfaces 324
Preparing an Application for Localization 325
The Translation Process 326
Object Resources 333
The Resources Collection 333
The Hierarchy of Resources 335
Static and Dynamic Resources 337
Nonshared Resources 339
Accessing Resources in Code 339
Application Resources 340
System Resources 341
Organizing Resources with Resource Dictionaries 342
Sharing Resources Between Assemblies 344
The Last Word 347

■CHAPTER 12   **Styles** 349
Style Basics 349
Creating a Style Object 353
Setting Properties 354
Attaching Event Handlers 356

The Many Layers of Styles 357

Automatically Applying Styles by Type 359

Triggers 360

A Simple Trigger 361

An Event Trigger 363

Last Word 365

█CHAPTER 13   **Shapes, Transforms, and Brushes** 367

Understanding Shapes 367

The Shape Classes 368

Rectangle and Ellipse 370

Sizing and Placing Shapes 371

Sizing Shapes Proportionately with a Viewbox 374

Line 376

Polyline 378

Polygon 379

Line Caps and Line Joins 381

Dashes 382

Pixel Snapping 384

Transforms 385

Transforming Shapes 386

Transforming Elements 388

Better Brushes 390

The LinearGradientBrush 390

The RadialGradientBrush 393

The ImageBrush 395

A Tiled ImageBrush 397

The VisualBrush 399

Opacity Masks 401

Bitmap Effects 403

Blurs 404

Beveled Edges 405

Embossed Edges 406

Glows and Shadows 407

The Last Word 408

█CHAPTER 14   **Geometries, Drawings, and Visuals** 409

Paths and Geometries 409

Line, Rectangle, and Ellipse Geometries 410

Combining Shapes with GeometryGroup 411

Fusing Geometries with CombinedGeometry 413

Curves and Lines with PathGeometry 417
The Geometry Mini-Language 422
Clipping with Geometry 424
Drawings 425
Displaying a Drawing 427
Exporting Clip Art 429
Visuals 431
Drawing Visuals 431
Wrapping Visuals in an Element 433
Hit Testing 437
Complex Hit Testing 439
The Last Word 443

■CHAPTER 15   **Control Templates** 445
Understanding Logical Trees and Visual Trees 445
Understanding Templates 451
The Chrome Classes 454
Dissecting Controls 455
Creating Control Templates 458
A Simple Button 458
Template Bindings 460
Template Triggers 462
Organizing Template Resources 465
Refactoring the Button Control Template 466
Applying Templates with Styles 468
Applying Templates Automatically 470
User-Selected Skins 471
Building More Complex Templates 474
Multipart Templates 474
Control Templates in an ItemsControl 475
Modifying the Scroll Bar 477
Creating a Custom Window 483
The Simple Styles 488
The Last Word 490

■CHAPTER 16   **Data Binding** 491
Data Binding Basics 491
Binding to the Properties of an Element 491
Creating Bindings with Code 495
Multiple Bindings 496

Binding Direction 499
Binding Updates 502
Binding to Objects That Aren't Elements 503
Binding to a Database with Custom Objects 507
Building a Data Access Component 507
Building a Data Object 510
Displaying the Bound Object 511
Updating the Database 513
Change Notification 514
Binding to a Collection of Objects 516
Displaying and Editing Collection Items 516
Inserting and Removing Collection Items 520
Binding to the ADO.NET Objects 521
Binding to a LINQ Expression 523
Data Conversion 526
Formatting Strings with a Value Converter 527
Creating Objects with a Value Converter 531
Applying Conditional Formatting 533
Evaluating Multiple Properties 535
Validation 536
Validation in the Data Object 536
Custom Validation Rules 540
Reacting to Validation Errors 543
Getting a List of Exceptions 544
Showing a Different Error Indicator 545
The Last Word 548

■**CHAPTER 17**   **Data Templates, Data Views, and Data Providers** 551
Data Binding Redux 551
Data Templates 552
Separating and Reusing Templates 554
More Advanced Templates 556
Varying Templates 559
Template Selectors 560
Templates and Selection 565
Style Selectors 570
Changing Item Layout 573
Data Views 574
Retrieving a View Object 575
Filtering Collections 575
Filtering the DataTable 578

Sorting 580
Grouping 581
Creating Views Declaratively 585
Navigating with a View 587
Data Providers 590
The ObjectDataProvider 592
The XmlDataProvider 594
The Last Word 596

■CHAPTER 18   **Lists, Trees, Toolbars, and Menus** 597
The ItemsControl Class 598
The ComboBox 600
A ListBox with Check Boxes or Radio Buttons 604
The ListView 607
Creating Columns with the GridView 608
Resizing Columns 610
Cell Templates 610
Creating a Custom View 613
The TreeView 621
A Data-Bound TreeView 622
Binding a DataSet to a TreeView 626
Just-in-Time Node Creation 627
Menus 630
The Menu Class 630
Menu Items 632
The ContextMenu Class 634
Menu Separators 635
Toolbars and Status Bars 636
The ToolBar 636
The StatusBar 640
The Last Word 641

■CHAPTER 19   **Documents** 643
Understanding Documents 643
Flow Documents 644
The Flow Elements 645
Formatting Content Elements 647
Constructing a Simple Flow Document 648
Block Elements 650
Inline Elements 656
Interacting with Elements Programmatically 663

Text Justification 667
Read-Only Flow Document Containers 668
    Zooming 669
    Pages and Columns 670
    Loading Documents from a File 672
    Printing 673
Editing a Flow Document 674
    Loading a File 674
    Saving a File 676
    Formatting Selected Text 678
    Getting Individual Words 680
Fixed Documents 681
Annotations 683
    The Annotation Classes 684
    Enabling the Annotation Service 685
    Creating Annotations 687
    Examining Annotations 690
    Reacting to Annotation Changes 694
    Storing Annotations in a Fixed Document 694
    Customizing the Appearance of Sticky Notes 695
Last Word 696

■CHAPTER 20   **Printing** 697
Basic Printing 697
    Printing an Element 698
    Transforming Printed Output 701
    Printing Elements Without Showing Them 703
    Printing a Document 704
    Manipulating the Pages in a Document Printout 708
Custom Printing 710
    Printing with the Visual Layer Classes 711
    Custom Printing with Multiple Pages 714
Print Settings and Management 719
    Maintaining Print Settings 720
    Printing Page Ranges 720
    Managing a Print Queue 721
Printing Through XPS 724
    Creating an XPS Document for a Print Preview 725
    Printing Directly to the Printer via XPS 726
    Asynchronous Printing 727
The Last Word 728

■**CHAPTER 21 Animation** 729

Understanding WPF Animation 729
    Timer-Based Animation 730
    Property-Based Animation 731
Basic Animation 731
    The Animation Classes 732
    Animations in Code 735
    Simultaneous Animations 740
    Animation Lifetime 741
    The Timeline Class 742
Declarative Animation and Storyboards 746
    The Storyboard 746
    Event Triggers 747
    Overlapping Animations 752
    Simultaneous Animations 753
    Controlling Playback 754
    Monitoring Progress 759
    Desired Frame Rate 760
Animation Types Revisited 763
    Animating Transforms 764
    Animating Brushes 769
    Key Frame Animation 772
    Path-Based Animation 775
    Frame-Based Animation 778
The Last Word 782

■**CHAPTER 22 Sound and Video** 783

Playing WAV Audio 783
    The SoundPlayer 784
    The SoundPlayerAction 786
    System Sounds 786
The MediaPlayer 787
The MediaElement 789
    Playing Audio Programmatically 789
    Handling Errors 791
    Playing Audio with Triggers 791
    Playing Multiple Sounds 794
    Changing Volume, Balance, Speed, and Position 795
    Synchronizing an Animation with Audio 797
    Playing Video 799
    Video Effects 800

Speech 804
    Speech Synthesis 804
    Speech Recognition 806
The Last Word 808

■CHAPTER 23   **3-D Drawing** 809
3-D Drawing Basics 810
    The Viewport 810
    3-D Objects 811
    The Camera 819
Deeper into 3-D 823
    Shading and Normals 825
    More Complex Shapes 829
    Model3DGroup Collections 830
    Materials Revisited 832
    Texture Mapping 834
Interactivity and Animations 838
    Transforms 838
    Rotations 840
    A Fly Over 841
    The Trackball 843
    Hit Testing 845
    2-D Elements on 3-D Surfaces 849
The Last Word 853

■CHAPTER 24   **Custom Elements** 855
Understanding Custom Elements in WPF 856
Building a Basic User Control 858
    Defining Dependency Properties 859
    Defining Routed Events 862
    Adding Markup 863
    Using the Control 866
    Command Support 866
    A Closer Look at User Controls 869
Lookless Controls 870
    Refactoring the Color Picker Code 871
    Refactoring the Color Picker Markup 871
    Streamlining the Control Template 874
    Theme-Specific Styles and the Default Style 876
Extending an Existing Control 879
    Understanding Masked Edit Controls 879

Mask Syntax 879

The MaskedTextProvider 880

Implementing a WPF Masked Text Box 881

Improving the MaskedTextBox 885

Custom Panels 887

The Two-Step Layout Process 887

The Canvas Clone 891

A Better Wrapping Panel 892

Custom-Drawn Elements 895

The OnRender() Method 896

Evaluating Custom Drawing 897

A Custom-Drawn Element 898

A Custom Decorator 901

The Last Word 902

■CHAPTER 25   **Interacting with Windows Forms** 903

Assessing Interoperability 903

Missing Features in WPF 904

Mixing Windows and Forms 906

Adding Forms to a WPF Application 906

Adding WPF Windows to a Windows Forms Application 907

Showing Modal Windows and Forms 907

Showing Modeless Windows and Forms 908

Visual Styles for Windows Forms Controls 909

Windows Forms Classes That Don't Need Interoperability 909

Creating Windows with Mixed Content 914

WPF and Windows Forms "Airspace" 914

Hosting Windows Forms Controls in WPF 916

WPF and Windows Forms User Controls 918

Hosting WPF Controls in Windows Forms 919

Access Keys, Mnemonics, and Focus 921

Property Mapping 923

The Last Word 925

■CHAPTER 26   **Multithreading and Add-Ins** 927

Multithreading 927

The Dispatcher 928

The DispatcherObject 928

The BackgroundWorker 931

Application Add-Ins 940

The Add-in Pipeline 941

An Application That Uses Add-Ins 946

Interacting with the Host 955

Visual Add-Ins 960

The Last Word 963

■CHAPTER 27   **ClickOnce Deployment** 965

Application Deployment 965

Understanding ClickOnce 966

The ClickOnce Installation Model 967

ClickOnce Limitations 968

A Simple ClickOnce Publication 969

Choosing a Location 970

Deployed Files 974

Installing a ClickOnce Application 975

Updating a ClickOnce Application 977

ClickOnce Options 977

Publish Version 978

Updates 979

Publish Options 980

The Last Word 981

■INDEX 983

About the Author

MATTHEW MACDONALD is an author, educator, and Microsoft MVP in Windows client development. He's a regular contributor to programming journals and the author of more than a dozen books about .NET programming, including *Pro .NET 2.0 Windows Forms and Custom Controls in C#* (Apress, 2005) and *Pro ASP.NET 3.5 in C# 2008* (Apress, 2007). He lives in Toronto with his wife and daughter.

About the Technical Reviewer

 **CHRISTOPHE NASARRE** is a software architect and development lead for Business Objects, a multinational software company focused on business intelligence solutions. During his spare time, Christophe writes articles for *MSDN Magazine*, MSDN, and ASPToday. Since 1996, he has also worked as a technical editor on numerous books on Win32, COM, MFC, .NET, and WPF. In 2007, he wrote his first book, *Windows via C/C++* from MSPress.

Acknowledgments

No author can complete a book without a small army of helpful individuals. I'm deeply indebted to the whole Apress team, including Sofia Marchant and Laura Esterman, who shepherded this second edition through production, Kim Wimpsett, who speedily performed the copy edit, and many other individuals who worked behind the scenes indexing pages, drawing figures, and proofreading the final copy. I also owe a special thanks to Gary Cornell, who always offers invaluable advice about projects and the publishing world.

Christophe Nasarre deserves my sincere thanks for his unfailingly excellent and insightful tech review comments—they've helped me to fill gaps and improve the overall quality of this book. I'm also thankful for the legions of die-hard bloggers on the various WPF teams, who never fail to shed light on the deepest recesses of WPF. I encourage anyone who wants to learn more about the future of WPF to track them down. Finally, I'd never write any book without the support of my wife and these special individuals: Nora, Razia, Paul, and Hamid. Thanks, everyone!

Introduction

When .NET first appeared, it introduced a small avalanche of new technologies. There was a whole new way to write web applications (ASP.NET), a whole new way to connect to databases (ADO.NET), new typesafe languages (C# and VB .NET), and a managed runtime (the CLR). Not least among these new technologies was Windows Forms, a library of classes for building Windows applications.

Although Windows Forms is a mature and full-featured toolkit, it's hardwired to essential bits of Windows plumbing that haven't changed much in the past ten years. Most significantly, Windows Forms relies on the Windows API to create the visual appearance of standard user interface elements such as buttons, text boxes, check boxes, and so on. As a result, these ingredients are essentially uncustomizable.

For example, if you want to create a stylish glow button you need to create a custom control and paint every aspect of the button (in all its different states) using a lower-level drawing model. Even worse, ordinary windows are carved up into distinct regions, with each control getting its own piece of real estate. As a result, there's no good way for the painting in one control (for example, the glow effect behind a button) to spread into the area owned by another control. And don't even think about introducing animated effects such as spinning text, shimmering buttons, shrinking windows, or live previews because you'll have to paint every detail by hand.

The Windows Presentation Foundation (WPF) changes all this by introducing a new model with entirely different plumbing. Although WPF includes the standard controls you're familiar with, it draws every text, border, and background fill *itself*. As a result, WPF can provide much more powerful features that let you alter the way any piece of screen content is rendered. Using these features, you can restyle common controls such as buttons, often without writing any code. Similarly, you can use transformation objects to rotate, stretch, scale, and skew anything in your user interface, and you can even use WPF's baked-in animation system to do it right before the user's eyes. And because the WPF engine renders the content for a window as part of a single operation, it can handle unlimited layers of overlapping controls, even if these controls are irregularly shaped and partially transparent.

Underlying the new features in WPF is a powerful new infrastructure based on DirectX, the hardware-accelerated graphics API that's commonly used in cutting-edge computer games. This means that you can use rich graphical effects without incurring the performance overhead that you'd suffer with Windows Forms. In fact, you even get advanced features such as support for video files and 3-D content. Using these features (and a good design tool), it's possible to create eye-popping user interfaces and visual effects that would have been all but impossible with Windows Forms.

Although the cutting-edge video, animation, and 3-D features often get the most attention in WPF, it's important to note that you can use WPF to build an ordinary Windows application with standard controls and a straightforward visual appearance. In fact, it's just as easy to use common controls in WPF as it is in Windows Forms. Even better, WPF enhances features that appeal directly to business developers, including a vastly improved data binding model, a new set of classes for printing content and managing print queues, and a document feature for displaying large amounts of formatted text. You'll even get a new model for building page-based applications that run seamlessly in Internet Explorer and can be launched from a website, all without the usual security warnings and irritating installation prompts.

Overall, WPF combines the best of the old world of Windows development with new innovations for building modern, graphically rich user interfaces. Although Windows Forms applications will continue to live on for years, developers embarking on new Windows development projects should consider WPF.

▪Tip If you've done a substantial amount of work creating a Windows Forms application, you don't need to migrate it wholesale to WPF to get access to new features such as animation. Instead, you can add WPF content to your existing Windows Forms application, or you can create a WPF application that incorporates your legacy Windows Forms content. Chapter 25 discusses all your interoperability options.

About This Book

This book is an in-depth exploration of WPF for professional developers who know the .NET platform, the C# language, and the Visual Studio development environment. Previous experience with Windows Forms is useful but not required to get the most out of this book.

This book provides a complete description of every major WPF feature, from XAML (the markup language used to define WPF user interfaces) to 3-D drawing and animation. Along the way, you'll occasionally work with code that involves other features of the .NET Framework, such as the ADO.NET classes you use to query a database. These features aren't discussed here. Instead, if you want more information about .NET features that aren't specific to WPF, you can refer to one of the many dedicated .NET titles from Apress.

Chapter Overview

This book includes 26 chapters. If you're just starting out with WPF, you'll find it's easiest to read them in order, as later chapters often draw on the techniques demonstrated in earlier chapters.

The following list gives you a quick preview of each chapter:

Chapter 1: Introducing WPF describes the architecture of WPF, its DirectX plumbing, and the new device-independent measurement system that resizes user interfaces automatically.

Chapter 2: XAML describes the XAML standard that you use to define user interfaces. You'll learn why it was created and how it works, and you'll create a basic WPF window using different coding approaches.

Chapter 3: The Application introduces the WPF application model. You'll see how to create single-instance and document-based WPF applications.

Chapter 4: Layout delves into the layout panels that allow you to organize elements in a WPF window. You'll consider different layout strategies, and you'll build some common types of windows.

Chapter 5: Content describes the WPF content control model, which allows you to place elements *inside* other elements to customize the look of common controls such as buttons and labels.

Chapter 6: Dependency Properties and Routed Events describes how WPF extends .NET's property and event system. You'll see how WPF uses dependency properties to provide support for key features such as data binding and animation, and how it uses event routing to send events bubbling or tunneling through the elements in your user interface.

Chapter 7: Classic Controls considers some of the common controls every Windows developer is familiar with, such as buttons, text boxes, and labels—and their WPF twists.

Chapter 8: Windows examines how windows work in WPF. You'll also learn how to create irregularly shaped windows and use Vista glass effects.

Chapter 9: Pages and Navigation describes how you can build pages in WPF and keep track of navigation history. You'll also see how to build a browser-hosted WPF application that can be launched from a website without a tedious installation step.

Chapter 10: Commands introduces the WPF command model, which allows you to wire multiple controls to the same logical action.

Chapter 11: Resources describes how resources let you embed binary files in your assembly and reuse important objects throughout your user interface.

Chapter 12: Styles explains the WPF style system, which lets you apply a set of common property values to an entire group of controls.

Chapter 13: Shapes, Transforms, and Brushes introduces the 2-D drawing model in WPF. You'll learn to create shapes, alter elements with transforms, and paint exotic effects with gradients, tiles, and images.

Chapter 14: Geometries, Drawings, and Visuals delves deeper into 2-D drawing. You'll learn to create complex paths that incorporate arcs and curves, how to use complex graphics efficiently, and how to use the lower-level visual layer for optimized drawing.

Chapter 15: Control Templates shows you how you can give any WPF control a dramatic new look (and new behavior) by plugging in a customized template. You'll also see how templates allow you to build a skinnable application.

Chapter 16: Data Binding introduces WPF data binding. You'll see how to bind any type of object to your user interface, whether it's an instance of a custom data class or the full-fledged ADO.NET DataSet. You'll also learn how to convert, format, and validate data.

Chapter 17: Data Templates, Data Views, and Data Providers shows some of the tricks for designing professional data-driven interfaces. Along the way, you'll build rich data lists that incorporate pictures, controls, and selection effects.

Chapter 18: Lists, Trees, Toolbars, and Menus considers WPF's family of list controls. You'll see data-oriented controls such as grids and trees, and command-oriented controls such as toolbars and menus.

Chapter 19: Documents introduces WPF's rich document support. You'll learn to use flow documents to present large amounts of text in the most readable way possible, and you'll use fixed documents to show print-ready pages. You'll even use the RichTextBox to provide document editing.

Chapter 20: Printing demonstrates WPF's new printing model, which lets you draw text and shapes in a print document. You'll also learn how to manage page settings and print queues.

Chapter 21: Animation explores WPF's animation framework, which lets you integrate dynamic effects into your application using straightforward, declarative markup.

Chapter 22: Sound and Video describes WPF's media support. You'll see how to control playback for sound and video, and how to throw in synchronized animations and live effects.

Chapter 23: 3-D Drawing explores the support for drawing 3-D shapes in WPF. You'll learn how to create, transform, and animate 3-D objects. You'll even see how to place interactive 2-D controls on 3-D surfaces.

Chapter 24: Custom Elements explores how you can extend the existing WPF controls and create your own. You'll see several examples, including a template-based color picker, a masked text box, and a decorator that performs custom drawing.

Chapter 25: Interacting with Windows Forms examines how you can combine WPF and Windows Forms content in the same application—and even in the same window.

Chapter 26: Multithreading and Add-Ins describes two advanced topics. You'll use multi-threading to create responsive WPF applications that perform time-consuming work in the background. You'll use the add-in model to create an extensible application that can dynamically discover and load separate components.

Chapter 27: ClickOnce Deployment shows how you can deploy WPF applications using the ClickOnce setup model introduced in .NET 2.0.

What You Need to Use This Book

WPF exists in two versions. The original version was released with .NET 3.0 and shipped with Windows Vista. The second (slightly improved) version was released with .NET 3.5. Incidentally, the second version of WPF is named WPF 3.5 to match the version of the .NET Framework.

This book assumes you're using the latest-and-greatest version, .NET 3.5. All the downloadable examples use Visual Studio 2008 projects and target .NET 3.5. However, most of the concepts you'll learn apply equally well to .NET 3.0. For more information about the refinements that were added to WPF in .NET 3.5, refer to the section "The Evolution of WPF" in Chapter 1.

In order to *run* a WPF 3.5 application, your computer must have Microsoft Windows Vista or Microsoft Windows XP with Service Pack 2. You also need the .NET Framework 3.5.

■**Note** In this book, frequent mention is made to Windows Vista and Windows XP—the two client operating systems that WPF supports. It's easy to overlook that WPF actually runs on two related server versions of Windows: Windows Server 2003 and Windows Server 2008.

In order to *create* a WPF 3.5 application (and open the sample projects included with this book), you need Visual Studio 2008, which includes the .NET Framework 3.5.

There's one other option. Instead of using any version of Visual Studio, you can use Expression Blend—a graphically oriented design tool—to build and test WPF applications. Overall, Expression Blend is intended for graphic designers who spend their time creating serious eye candy, while Visual Studio is ideal for code-heavy application programmers. This book assumes you're using Visual Studio. If you'd like to learn more about Expression Blend, you can consult one of many dedicated books on the subject.

Some of the examples in this book use ADO.NET data access code to query a SQL Server database. To try out these examples, you can use the script file that's included with the sample code to install the database (on SQL Server version 2000 or later). Alternatively, you can use a file-based database component that's also included with the sample code. This component retrieves the same data from an XML file, simulating the work of the full database component without requiring a live instance of SQL Server.

Code Samples and URLs

It's a good idea to check the Apress website or http://www.prosetech.com to download the most recent up-to-date code samples. You'll need to do this to test most of the more sophisticated code examples described in this book because the less significant details are usually left out. This book focuses on the most important sections so that you don't need to wade through needless extra pages to understand a concept.

To download the source code, surf to http://www.prosetech.com and look for the page for this book. You'll also find a list of links that are mentioned in this book, so you can find important tools and examples without needless typing.

Feedback

This book has the ambitious goal of being the best tutorial and reference for programming WPF. Toward that end, your comments and suggestions are extremely helpful. You can send complaints, adulation, and everything in between directly to apress@prosetech.com. I can't solve your .NET problems or critique your code, but I will benefit from information about what this book did right and wrong (or what it may have done in an utterly confusing way).

CHAPTER 1

■ ■ ■

Introducing WPF

The Windows Presentation Foundation (WPF) is an entirely new graphical display system for Windows. WPF is designed for .NET, influenced by modern display technologies such as HTML and Flash, and hardware-accelerated. It's also the most radical change to hit Windows user interfaces since Windows 95.

In this chapter you'll peer into the architecture of WPF. You'll get your first look at how it works, and you'll see what it promises for the next generation of Windows applications.

Understanding Windows Graphics

It's hard to appreciate how dramatic WPF is without realizing that Windows developers have been using essentially the same display technology for more than 15 years. A standard Windows application relies on two well-worn parts of the Windows operating system to create its user interface:

- **User32** provides the familiar Windows look and feel for elements such as windows, buttons, text boxes, and so on.

- **GDI/GDI+** provides drawing support for rendering shapes, text, and images at the cost of additional complexity (and often lackluster performance).

Over the years, both technologies have been refined, and the APIs that developers use to interact with them have changed dramatically. But whether you're crafting an application with .NET and Windows Forms, or lingering in the past with Visual Basic 6 or MFC-based C++ code, behind the scenes the same parts of the Windows operating system are at work. Newer frameworks simply deliver better wrappers for interacting with User32 and GDI/GDI+. They can provide improvements in efficiency, reduce complexity, and add prebaked features so you don't have to code them yourself; but they can't remove the fundamental limitations of a system component that was designed more than a decade ago.

■Note The basic division of labor between User32 and GDI/GDI+ was introduced more than 15 years ago and was well established in Windows 3.0. Of course, User32 was simply User at that point, because software hadn't yet entered the 32-bit world.

DirectX: The New Graphics Engine

Microsoft created one way around the limitations of the User32 and GDI/GDI+ libraries: *DirectX*. DirectX began as a cobbled-together, error-prone toolkit for creating games on the Windows platform. Its design mandate was speed, and so Microsoft worked closely with video card vendors to give DirectX the hardware acceleration needed for complex textures, special effects such as partial transparency, and three-dimensional graphics.

Over the years since it was first introduced (shortly after Windows 95), DirectX has matured. It's now an integral part of Windows, with support for all modern video cards. However, the programming API for DirectX still reflects its roots as a game developer's toolkit. Because of its raw complexity, DirectX is almost never used in traditional types of Windows applications (such as business software).

WPF changes all this. In WPF, the underlying graphics technology isn't GDI/GDI+. Instead, it's DirectX. Remarkably, WPF applications use DirectX no matter what type of user interface you create. That means that whether you're designing complex three-dimensional graphics (DirectX's forté) or just drawing buttons and plain text, all the drawing work travels through the DirectX pipeline. As a result, even the most mundane business applications can use rich effects such as transparency and anti-aliasing. You also benefit from hardware acceleration, which simply means DirectX hands off as much work as possible to the GPU (graphics processing unit), which is the dedicated processor on the video card.

■**Note** DirectX is more efficient because it understands higher-level ingredients such as textures and gradients, which can be rendered directly by the video card. GDI/GDI+ doesn't, so it needs to convert them to pixel-by-pixel instructions, which are rendered much more slowly by modern video cards.

One component that's still in the picture (to a limited extent) is User32. That's because WPF still relies on User32 for certain services, such as handling and routing input and sorting out which application owns which portion of screen real estate. However, all the drawing is funneled through DirectX.

■**Note** This is the most significant change in WPF. WPF is *not* a wrapper for GDI/GDI+. Instead, it's a replacement—a separate layer that works through DirectX.

Hardware Acceleration and WPF

You're probably aware that video cards differ in their support for specialized rendering features and optimizations. When programming with DirectX, that's a significant headache. With WPF, it's a much smaller concern, because WPF has the ability to perform everything it does using software calculations rather than relying on built-in support from the video card.

■**Note** There's one exception to WPF's software support. Due to poor driver support, WPF only performs anti-aliasing for 3-D drawings if you're running your application on Windows Vista (and you have a native Windows Vista driver for your video card). That means that if you draw three-dimensional shapes on a Windows XP computer, you'll end up with slightly jagged edges rather than nicely smoothed lines. Anti-aliasing is always provided for 2-D drawings, regardless of the operating system and driver support.

Having a high-powered video card is not an absolute guarantee that you'll get fast, hardware-accelerated performance in WPF. Software also plays a significant role. For example, WPF can't provide hardware acceleration to video cards that are using out-of-date drivers. (If you're using an older video card, these out-of-date drivers are quite possibly the only ones that were provided in the retail package.) WPF also provides better performance under the Windows Vista operating system, where it can take advantage of the new Windows Vista Display Driver Model (WDDM). WDDM offers several important enhancements beyond the Windows XP Display Driver Model (XPDM). Most importantly, WDDM allows several GPU operations to be scheduled at once, and it allows video card memory to be paged to normal system memory if you exceed what's available on the video card.

As a general rule of thumb, WPF offers some sort of hardware acceleration to all WDDM (Windows Vista) drivers and to XPDM (Windows XP) drivers that were created after November 2004, which is when Microsoft released new driver development guidelines. Of course, the level of support differs. When the WPF infrastructure first starts up, it evaluates your video card and assigns it a rating from 0 to 2, as described in the sidebar "WPF Tiers."

Part of the promise of WPF is that you don't need to worry about the details and idiosyncrasies of specific hardware. WPF is intelligent enough to use hardware optimizations where possible, but it has a software fallback for everything. So if you run a WPF application on a computer with a legacy video card, the interface will still appear the way you designed it. Of course, the software alternative may be much slower, so you'll find that computers with older video cards won't run rich WPF applications very well, especially ones that incorporate complex animations or other intense graphical effects. In practice, you might choose to scale down complex effects in the user interface, depending on the level of hardware acceleration that's available in the client (as indicated by the RenderCapability.Tier property).

■**Note** The goal of WPF is to offload as much of the work as possible on the video card so that complex graphics routines are *render-bound* (limited by the GPU) rather than *processor-bound* (limited by your computer's CPU). That way, you keep the CPU free for other work, you make the best use of your video card, and you are able to take advantage of performance increases in newer video cards as they become available.

WPF TIERS

Video cards differ significantly. When WPF assesses a video card, it considers a number of factors, including the amount of RAM on the video card, support for pixel shaders (built-in routines that calculate per-pixel effects such as transparency), and support for vertex shaders (built-in routines that calculate values at the vertexes of a triangle, such as the shading of a 3-D object). Based on these details, it assigns a *rendering tier* value.

WPF recognizes three rendering tiers. They are as follows:

- **Rendering Tier 0.** The video card will not provide any hardware acceleration. This corresponds to a DirectX version level of less than 7.0.

- **Rendering Tier 1.** The video card can provide partial hardware acceleration. This corresponds to a DirectX version level greater than 7.0 but less than 9.0.

- **Rendering Tier 2.** All features that can be hardware accelerated will be. This corresponds to a DirectX version level greater than or equal to 9.0.

In some situations, you might want to examine the current rendering tier programmatically, so you can selectively disable graphics-intensive features on lesser-powered cards. To do so, you need to use the static Tier property of the System.Windows.Media.RenderCapability class. But there's one trick. To extract the tier value from the Tier property, you need to shift it 16 bits, as shown here:

```
int renderingTier = (RenderCapability.Tier >> 16);

if (renderingTier == 0)
{ ... }
else if (renderingTier == 1)
{ ... }
```

This design allows extensibility. In future versions of WPF, the other bits in the Tier property might be used to store information about support for other features, thereby creating subtiers.

For more information about what WPF features are hardware-accelerated for tier 1 and tier 2, and for a list of common tier 1 and tier 2 video cards, refer to http://msdn2.microsoft.com/en-gb/library/ms742196.aspx.

WPF: A Higher-Level API

If the only thing WPF offered was hardware acceleration through DirectX, it would be a compelling improvement, but not a revolutionary one. But WPF actually includes a basket of high-level services designed for application programmers.

Here's a list with some of the most dramatic changes that WPF ushers into the Windows programming world:

- **A web-like layout model.** Rather than fix controls in place with specific coordinates, WPF emphasizes flexible flow layout that arranges controls based on their content. The result is a user interface that can adapt to show highly dynamic content or different languages.

- **A rich drawing model.** Rather than painting pixels, in WPF you deal with *primitives*—basic shapes, blocks of text, and other graphical ingredients. You also have new features, such as true transparent controls, the ability to stack multiple layers with different opacities, and native 3-D support.

■Note The 3-D support in WPF is not as mature as Direct3D or OpenGL. If you are planning to design an application that makes heavy use of three-dimensional drawing (such as a real-time game), WPF probably won't provide the features and performance you need.

- **A rich text model.** After years of substandard text handling with feeble controls such as the classic Label, WPF finally gives Windows applications the ability to display rich, styled text anywhere in a user interface. You can even combine text with lists, floating figures, and other user interface elements. And if you need to display large amounts of text, you can use advanced document display features such as wrapping, columns, and justification to improve readability.

- **Animation as a first-class programming concept.** Yes, you could use a timer to force a form to repaint itself. But in WPF, animation is an intrinsic part of the framework. You define animations with declarative tags, and WPF puts them into action automatically.

- **Support for audio and video media.** Previous user interface toolkits, such as Windows Forms, were surprisingly limited when dealing with multimedia. But WPF includes support for playing any audio or video file supported by Windows Media Player, and it allows you to play more than one media file at once. Even more impressively, it gives you the tools to integrate video content into the rest of your user interface, allowing you to pull off exotic tricks such as placing a video window on a spinning 3-D cube.

- **Styles and templates.** Styles allow you to standardize formatting and reuse it throughout your application. Templates allow you to change the way any element is rendered, even a core control such as the button. It's never been easier to build modern skinned interfaces.

- **Commands.** Most users realize that it doesn't matter whether they trigger the Open command through a menu or a toolbar; the end result is the same. Now that abstraction is available to your code, you can define an application command in one place and link it to multiple controls.

- **Declarative user interface.** Although you can construct a WPF window with code, Visual Studio takes a different approach. It serializes each window's content to a set of XML tags in a XAML document. The advantage is that your user interface is completely separated from your code, and graphic designers can use professional tools to edit your XAML files and refine your application's front end. (*XAML* is short for Extensible Application Markup Language, and it's described in detail in Chapter 2.)

- **Page-based applications.** Using WPF, you can build a browser-like application that lets you move through a collection of pages, complete with forward and back navigation buttons. WPF handles the messy details, such as the page history. You can even deploy your project as a browser-based application that runs right inside Internet Explorer.

Resolution Independence

Traditional Windows applications are bound by certain assumptions about resolution. Developers usually assume a standard monitor resolution (such as 1024 by 768 pixels), design their windows with that in mind, and try to ensure reasonable resizing behavior for smaller and larger dimensions.

The problem is that the user interface in traditional Windows applications isn't scalable. As a result, if you use a high monitor resolution that crams pixels in more densely, your application windows become smaller and more difficult to read. This is particularly a problem with newer monitors that have high pixel densities and run at correspondingly high resolutions. For example, it's common to find consumer monitors (particularly on laptops) that have pixel densities of 120 dpi or 144 dpi (dots per inch), rather than the more traditional 96 dpi. At their native resolution, these displays pack the pixels in much more tightly, creating eye-squintingly small controls and text.

Ideally, applications would use higher pixel densities to show more detail. For example, a high-resolution monitor could display similarly sized toolbar icons but use the extra pixels to render sharper graphics. That way you could keep the same basic layout but offer increased clarity and detail. For a variety of reasons, this solution hasn't been possible in the past. Although you can resize graphical content that's drawn with GDI/GDI+, User32 (which generates the visuals for common controls) doesn't support true scaling.

WPF doesn't suffer from this problem because it renders all user interface elements itself, from simple shapes to common controls such as buttons. As a result, if you create a button that's 1 inch wide on your computer monitor, it can remain 1 inch wide on a high-resolution monitor—WPF will simply render it in greater detail and with more pixels.

Note Resolution independence also has advantages when printing the contents of a window, as you'll see in Chapter 20.

This is the big picture, but it glosses over a few details. Most importantly, you need to realize that WPF bases its scaling on the *system* DPI setting, not the DPI of your physical display device. This makes perfect sense—after all, if you're displaying your application on a 100-inch projector, you're probably standing several feet back and expecting to see a jumbo-size version of your windows. You don't want WPF to suddenly scale down your application to "normal" size. Similarly, if you're using a laptop with a high-resolution display, you probably expect to have slightly smaller windows—it's the price you pay to fit all your information onto a smaller screen. Furthermore, different users have different preferences. Some want richer detail, while others prefer to cram in more content.

So how does WPF determine how big an application window *should* be? The short answer is that WPF uses the system DPI setting when it calculates sizes. But to understand how this really works, it helps to take a closer look at the WPF measurement system.

WPF Units

A WPF window and all the elements inside it are measured using *device-independent units.* A single device-independent unit is defined as 1/96 of an inch. To understand what this means in practice, you'll need to consider an example.

Imagine that you create a small button in WPF that's 96 by 96 units in size. If you're using the standard Windows DPI setting (96 dpi), each device-independent unit corresponds to one real, physical pixel. That's because WPF uses this calculation:

```
[Physical Unit Size] = [Device-Independent Unit Size] × [System DPI]
                     = 1/96 inch × 96 dpi
                     = 1 pixel
```

Essentially, WPF assumes it takes 96 pixels to make an inch because Windows tells it that through the system DPI setting. However, the reality depends on your display device.

For example, consider a 20-inch LCD monitor with a maximum resolution of 1600 by 1200 pixels. Using a dash of Pythagoras, you can calculate the pixel density for this monitor, as shown here:

$$[\text{Screen DPI}] = \frac{\sqrt{1600^2 + 1200^2} \text{ pixels}}{19 \text{ inches}}$$

$$= 100 \text{ dpi}$$

In this case, the pixel density works out to 100 dpi, which is slightly higher than what Windows assumes. As a result, on this monitor a 96-by-96-pixel button will be slightly smaller than 1 inch.

On the other hand, consider a 15-inch LCD monitor with a resolution of 1024 by 768. Here, the pixel density drops to about 85 dpi, so the 96-by-96 pixel button appears slightly *larger* than 1 inch.

In both these cases, if you reduce the screen size (say, by switching to 800 by 600 resolution), the button (and every other screen element) will appear proportionately larger. That's because the system DPI setting remains at 96 dpi. In other words, Windows continues to assume it takes 96 pixels to make an inch, even though at a lower resolution it takes far fewer pixels.

■**Tip** As you no doubt know, LCD monitors are designed with a single resolution, which is called the *native resolution.* If you lower the resolution, the monitor must use interpolation to fill in the extra pixels, which can cause blurriness. To get the best display, it's always best to use the native resolution. If you want larger windows, buttons, and text, consider modifying the system DPI setting instead (as described next).

System DPI

So far, the WPF button example works exactly the same as any other user interface element in any other type of Windows application. The difference is the result if you change the system DPI setting. In the previous generation of Windows, this feature was sometimes called *large fonts*. That's because the system DPI affects the system font size, but often leaves other details unchanged.

Note Many Windows applications don't fully support higher DPI settings. At worst, increasing the system DPI can result in windows that have some content that's scaled up, and other content that isn't, which can lead to obscured content and even unusable windows.

This is where WPF is different. WPF respects the system DPI setting natively and effortlessly. For example, if you change the system DPI setting to 120 dpi (a common choice for users of large high-resolution screens), WPF assumes that it needs 120 pixels to fill an inch of space. WPF uses the following calculation to figure out how it should translate its logical units to physical device pixels:

```
[Physical Unit Size] = [Device-Independent Unit Size] × [System DPI]
                     = 1/96 inch × 120 dpi
                     = 1.25 pixels
```

In other words, when you set the system DPI to 120 dpi, the WPF rendering engine assumes one device-independent unit equals 1.25 pixels. If you show a 96-by-96 button, the physical size will actually be 120 by 120 pixels (because 96 × 1.25 = 120). This is the result you expect—a button that's 1 inch on a standard monitor remains 1 inch in size on a monitor with a higher pixel density.

This automatic scaling wouldn't help much if it only applied to buttons. But WPF uses device-independent units for everything it displays, including shapes, controls, text, and any other ingredient you put in a window. As a result, you can change the system DPI to whatever you want, and WPF will adjust the size of your application seamlessly.

Note Depending on the system DPI, the calculated pixel size may be a fractional value. You might assume that WPF simply rounds off your measurements to the nearest pixel. (In fact, WPF supports a pixel-snapping feature that does exactly this, and you'll learn how to enable it for specific bits of content in Chapter 13.) However, by default, WPF does something different. If an edge of an element falls between pixels, it uses anti-aliasing to blend that edge into the adjacent pixels. This might seem like an odd choice, but it actually makes a fair bit of sense. Your controls won't necessarily have straight, clearly defined edges if you use custom-drawn graphics to skin them; so some level of anti-aliasing is already necessary.

The steps for adjusting the system DPI depend on the operating system. In Windows XP, you follow these steps:

1. Right-click your desktop and choose Display.

2. Choose the Settings tab and click Advanced.

3. On the General tab, choose Normal Size (96 dpi), or Large Size (120 dpi). These are the two recommended options for Windows XP, because custom DPI settings are less likely to be supported by older programs. To try out a custom DPI setting, choose Custom Setting. You can then specify a specific percentage value. (For example, 175% scales the standard 96 dpi to 168 dpi.)

Here's what to do to change system DPI in Windows Vista:

1. Right-click your desktop and choose Personalize.

2. In the list of links on the left, choose Adjust Font Size (DPI).

3. Choose between 96 or 120 dpi. Or click Custom DPI to use a custom DPI setting. You can then specify a percentage value, as shown in Figure 1-1. (For example, 175% scales the standard 96 dpi to 168 dpi.) In addition, when using a custom DPI setting, you have an option named Use Windows XP Style DPI Scaling, which is described in the sidebar "DPI Scaling with Windows Vista."

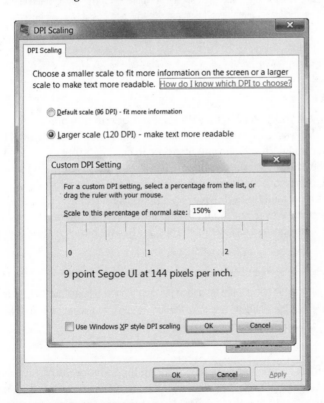

Figure 1-1. *Changing the system DPI*

DPI SCALING WITH WINDOWS VISTA

Because older applications are notoriously lacking in their support for high DPI settings, Windows Vista uses a new technique: *bitmap scaling.*

If you run an application that doesn't appear to support high DPI settings, Windows Vista resizes the contents of the window to the desired DPI, just as if it were an image. The advantage is that the application still believes it's running at the standard 96 dpi. Windows seamlessly translates input (such as mouse clicks) and routes them to the right place in the application's "real" coordinate system.

The scaling algorithm that Windows Vista uses is a fairly good one—it respects pixel boundaries to avoid blurry edges and uses the video card hardware where possible to increase speed—but it inevitably leads to a fuzzier display. It also has a serious limitation in that Windows can't recognize older applications that *do* support high DPI settings. That's because applications need to include a manifest or call SetProcessDPIAware (in User32) to advertise their high DPI support. Although WPF applications handle this step correctly, applications prior to Windows Vista won't use either approach and will be stuck with the less than ideal bitmap scaling.

There are two possible solutions. If you have a few specific applications that support high DPI settings, but don't indicate it, you can configure that detail manually. To do so, right-click the shortcut that starts the application (in the Start menu) and choose Properties. In the Compatibility tab, switch on the option named Disable Display Scaling on High DPI Settings. If you have a lot of applications to configure, this gets tiring fast.

The other possible solution is to disable bitmap scaling altogether. To do so, choose the Use Windows XP Style DPI Scaling option in the Custom DPI Setting dialog box shown in Figure 1-1. The only limitation of this approach is that there may be some applications that won't display properly (and possibly won't be usable) at high DPI settings. By default, Use Windows XP Style DPI Scaling is checked for DPI sizes of 120 or less but unchecked for DPI sizes that are greater.

Bitmap and Vector Graphics

When you work with ordinary controls, you can take WPF's resolution independence for granted. WPF takes care of making sure that everything has the right size automatically. However, if you plan to incorporate images into your application you can't be quite as casual. For example, in traditional Windows applications, developers use tiny bitmaps for toolbar commands. In a WPF application, this approach is not ideal because the bitmap may display artifacts (becoming blurry) as it's scaled up or down according to the system DPI. Instead, when designing a WPF user interface even the smallest icon is generally implemented as a vector graphic. *Vector graphics* are defined as a set of shapes, and as such they can be easily scaled to any size.

■**Note** Of course, drawing a vector graphic takes more time than painting a basic bitmap, but WPF includes optimizations that are designed to lessen the overhead to ensure that drawing performance is reasonable for any business application and most consumer-oriented ones as well.

It's difficult to overestimate the importance of resolution independence. At first glance, it seems like a straightforward, elegant solution to a time-honored problem (which it is). However, in order to design interfaces that are fully scalable, developers need to embrace a new way of thinking.

The Evolution of WPF

Although WPF is a relatively new technology, it already exists in two versions:

- **WPF 3.0.** The first version of WPF was released with two other new technologies: Windows Communication Foundation (WCF) and Windows Workflow Foundation (WF). Together, these three technologies were called the .NET Framework 3.0 (even though the core bits of .NET weren't changed).

- **WPF 3.5.** A year later, a new version of WPF was released as part of the .NET Framework 3.5. The new features in WPF are mostly minor refinements. Some of these bug fixes and performance improvements are available to .NET Framework 3.0 applications through the .NET Framework 3.0 Service Pack 1.

From a developer standpoint, the most significant difference between WPF 3.0 and 3.5 is design-time support. The .NET Framework 3.0 was released without a corresponding version of Visual Studio. Developers could get basic support for Visual Studio 2005 by installing a free Community Technology Preview (CTP). Although these extensions made it possible to create and develop WPF applications in Visual Studio 2005, they didn't provide a drag-and-drop designer for WPF windows.

The .NET Framework 3.5 was released in conjunction with Visual Studio 2008, and as a result, it offers much better design-time support for building WPF applications. This book assumes you are using WPF 3.5 and Visual Studio 2008. However, if you're using WPF 3.0, virtually all of the same concepts apply.

New Features in WPF 3.5

If you've programmed with the first version of WPF, you might be interested in tracking down the changes. Aside from bug fixes, performance tune-ups, and better design support, WPF 3.5 introduces the following enhancements (listed in order of their appearance in this book):

- **Firefox support for XBAPs.** It's now possible to run WPF browser-hosted applications (known as XBAPs) in Firefox as well as in Internet Explorer. Chapter 9 has more.

- **Data binding support for LINQ.** LINQ is a set of language extensions that allow developers to write queries. These queries can pull data out of various data sources, including in-memory collections, XML files, and databases, all without requiring a line of low-level code. (To learn more about LINQ, you can refer to http://msdn.microsoft.com/data/ref/linq or a dedicated book on the subject.) WPF now fully supports using LINQ in data binding scenarios, such as the ones you'll explore in Chapter 16.

- **Data binding support for IDataErrorInfo.** The IDataErrorInfo interface is a key linchpin for business developers who want to build rich data objects with built-in validation. Now, the data binding infrastructure can catch these validation errors and display them in the user interface.

- **Support for placing interactive controls (such as buttons) inside a RichTextBox control.** This feature previously required an obscure workaround. It now works through a simple property that's described in Chapter 19.

- **Support for placing 2-D elements on 3-D surfaces.** This feature previously required a separate download. Now, it's incorporated into the framework, along with better support for 3-D objects that can raise mouse and keyboard events. You'll learn to use these features in Chapter 23.

- **An add-in model.** The add-in model allows an application to host third-party components in a limited security context. Technically, this feature isn't WPF-specific, because it can be used in any .NET 3.5 application. You'll learn how it works with WPF in Chapter 26.

Multitargeting

Previous versions of Visual Studio were tightly coupled to specific versions of .NET. You used Visual Studio .NET to create .NET 1.0 applications, Visual Studio .NET 2003 to create .NET 1.1 applications, and Visual Studio 2005 to create .NET 2.0 applications. Visual Studio 2008 partially removes this restriction. It allows you to create applications that are specifically designed to work with .NET 2.0, .NET 3.0, or .NET 3.5.

Although it's obviously not possible to create a WPF application with .NET 2.0, both .NET 3.0 and .NET 3.5 have WPF support. You may choose to target .NET 3.0 for slightly broader compatibility (because .NET 3.0 applications can run on both the .NET 3.0 and .NET 3.5 runtimes). Or, you may choose to target .NET 3.5 to get access to newer features in WPF or in the .NET platform itself. (One common reason for targeting .NET 3.5 is to support LINQ, the set of technologies that allow .NET languages to access different data sources using a tightly integrated query syntax.)

When you create a new project in Visual Studio (by choosing File ➤ New ➤ Project), you can choose the version of the .NET Framework that you're targeting from a drop-down list in the top-right corner of the New Project dialog box (see Figure 1-2). You can also change the version you're targeting at any point afterward by double-clicking the Properties node in the Solution Explorer and changing the selection in the Target Framework list.

To really understand how the Visual Studio multitargeting system works, you need to know a bit more about how .NET 3.5 is structured. Essentially, .NET 3.5 is built out of three separate pieces—a copy of the original .NET 2.0 assemblies, a copy of the assemblies that were added in .NET 3.0 (for WPF, WCF, and WF), and the new assemblies that were added in .NET 3.5 (for LINQ and a number of miscellaneous features). However, when you create and test an application in Visual Studio, you are always using the .NET 3.5 assemblies. When you choose to target an earlier version of .NET, Visual Studio simply uses a subset of the .NET 3.5 assemblies.

For example, when you choose to target .NET 3.0, you effectively configure Visual Studio to use a *portion* of .NET 3.5—just those assemblies that were available in .NET 2.0 and .NET 3.0. There's a potential stumbling block in this system. Although these assemblies are treated as though they haven't changed in .NET 3.5, they aren't completely identical to the .NET 2.0 versions. For example, they may include performance tweaks, bug fixes, and (very rarely) a new public member in a class. For that reason, if you build an assembly that targets an earlier version of .NET, you should still test it with that version of .NET to make absolutely sure there are no backward compatibility quirks.

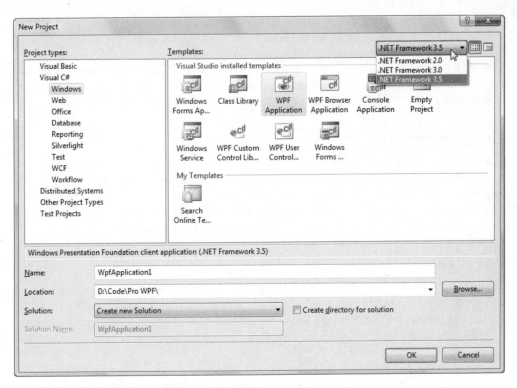

Figure 1-2. *Choosing the target version of the .NET Framework*

■**Note** Visual Studio 2008 doesn't provide a way to build applications that specifically target .NET 3.0 with SP1. Thus, if there's an added feature in the .NET Framework 3.0 Service Pack 1, you won't be able to use it (unless you compile your project by hand at the command line). The only solution is to step up all the way to .NET 3.5.

Windows Forms Lives On

WPF is the platform for the future of Windows user interface development. However, it won't displace Windows Forms overnight. Windows Forms is in many ways the culmination of the display technology built on GDI/GDI+ and User32. It's more mature than WPF and still includes features that haven't made their way into the WPF toolkit (such as the WebBrowser control, the DataGridView control, and the HelpProvider component).

So which platform should you choose when you begin designing a new Windows application? If you're starting from the ground up, WPF is an ideal choice and it offers the best prospects for future enhancements and longevity. Similarly, if you need one of the features that WPF provides and Windows Forms does not—such as 3-D drawing or page-based applications—it makes sense to make the shift. On the other hand, if you have a considerable investment in a Windows Forms–based business application, there's no need to recode your application for WPF. The Windows Forms platform will continue to be supported for years to come.

Perhaps the best part of the story is the fact that Microsoft has invested considerable effort in building an interoperability layer between WPF and Windows Forms (which plays a similar role to the interoperability layer that allows .NET applications to continue to use legacy COM components). In Chapter 25, you'll learn how to use this support to host Windows Forms controls inside a WPF application, and vice versa. WPF offers similarly robust support for integrating with older Win32-style applications.

DirectX Also Lives On

There's one area where WPF isn't a good fit: when creating applications with demanding real-time graphics, such as complex physics-based simulators or cutting-edge action games. If you want the best possible video performance for these types of applications, you'll need to program at a much lower level and use raw DirectX. You can download the managed .NET libraries for DirectX programming at http://msdn.microsoft.com/directx.

Silverlight

Like the .NET Framework itself, WPF is a *Windows-centric technology*. That means that WPF applications can only be used on computers running the Windows operating system (specifically, Windows XP or Windows Vista). Browser-based WPF applications are similarly limited—they can run only on Windows computers, although they support both the Internet Explorer and Firefox browsers.

These restrictions won't change—after all, part of Microsoft's goal with WPF is to take advantage of the rich capabilities of Windows computers and its investment in technologies such as DirectX. However, there is a separate technology named Silverlight that's designed to take a subset of the WPF platform, host it in any modern browser using a plug-in (including Firefox, Opera, and Safari), and open it up to other operating systems (such as Linux and Mac OS). This is an ambitious project that's attracted considerable developer interest.

To make matters more interesting, Silverlight currently exists in two versions:

- **Silverlight 1.0.** This first release includes 2-D drawing features, animation, and media playback features that are similar to those in WPF. However, Silverlight 1.0 has no support for the .NET Framework or the C# and Visual Basic languages—instead, you must use JavaScript code.

- **Silverlight 2.0.** This second release adds a pared-down version of the .NET Framework, complete with a miniature CLR that's hosted by the browser plug-in and a small subset of essential .NET Framework classes. Because Silverlight 2.0 allows you to write code in a .NET language such as C# and Visual Basic, it's a far more compelling technology than Silverlight 1.0. However, at the time of this writing it's still in beta.

Although both Silverlight 1.0 and Silverlight 2.0 are based on WPF and incorporate many of its conventions (such as the XAML markup you'll learn about in the next chapter), they leave out certain feature areas. For example, neither version supports true three-dimensional drawing or rich document display. New features may appear in future Silverlight releases, but the more complex ones might never make the leap.

The ultimate goal of Silverlight is to provide a powerful developer-oriented competitor for Adobe Flash. However, Flash has a key advantage—it's used throughout the Web, and the Flash plug-in is installed just about everywhere. In order to entice developers to switch to a new, less-established technology, Microsoft will need to make sure Silverlight has next-generation features, rock-solid compatibility, and unrivaled design support.

■Note Although the Silverlight programming model is best understood as a dramatically scaled-down version of WPF, it's probably more useful to web developers than rich client developers. That's because web developers can use Silverlight content to enhance ordinary websites or web applications built with ASP.NET. In other words, Silverlight has two potential audiences: web developers who are seeking to create more interactive applications and Windows developers who are seeking to get a broader reach for their applications. To learn more about Silverlight, refer to a dedicated book such as *Pro Silverlight 2.0*, or surf to `http://silverlight.net`.

The Architecture of WPF

WPF uses a multilayered architecture. At the top, your application interacts with a high-level set of services that are completely written in managed C# code. The actual work of translating .NET objects into Direct3D textures and triangles happens behind the scenes, using a lower-level unmanaged component called milcore.dll.

■Note milcore.dll is implemented in unmanaged code because it needs tight integration with Direct3D and because it's extremely performance-sensitive.

Figure 1-3 shows the layers at work in a WPF application.

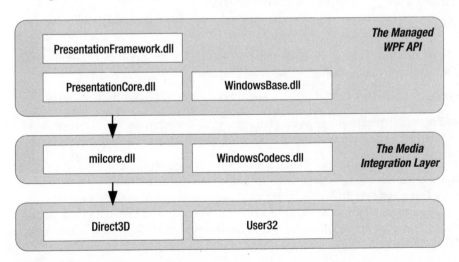

Figure 1-3. *The architecture of WPF*

Figure 1-3 includes these key components:

- **PresentationFramework.dll** holds the top-level WPF types, including those that represent windows, panels, and other types of controls. It also implements higher-level programming abstractions such as styles. Most of the classes you'll use directly come from this assembly.

- **PresentationCore.dll** holds base types, such as UIElement and Visual, from which all shapes and controls derive. If you don't need the full window and control abstraction layer, you can drop down to this level and still take advantage of WPF's rendering engine.

- **WindowsBase.dll** holds even more basic ingredients that have the potential to be reused outside of WPF, such as DispatcherObject and DependencyObject, which introduces the plumbing for dependency properties (a topic you'll explore in detail in Chapter 6).

- **milcore.dll** is the core of the WPF rendering system and the foundation of the Media Integration Layer (MIL). Its composition engine translates visual elements into the triangle and textures that Direct3D expects. Although milcore.dll is considered a part of WPF, it's also an essential system component for Windows Vista. In fact, the Desktop Window Manager (DWM) in Windows Vista uses milcore.dll to render the desktop.

■**Note** milcore.dll is sometimes referred to as the engine for "managed graphics." Much as the common language runtime (CLR) manages the lifetime of a .NET application, milcore.dll manages the display state. And just as the CLR saves you from worrying about releasing objects and reclaiming memory, milcore.dll saves you from thinking about invalidating and repainting a window. You simply create the objects with the content you want to show, and milcore.dll paints the appropriate portions of the window as it is dragged around, covered and uncovered, minimized and restored, and so on.

- **WindowsCodecs.dll** is a low-level API that provides imaging support (for example, processing, displaying, and scaling bitmaps and JPEGs).

- **Direct3D** is the low-level API through which all the graphics in a WPF are rendered.

- **User32** is used to determine what program gets what real estate. As a result, it's still involved in WPF, but it plays no part in rendering common controls.

The most important fact that you should realize is the Direct3D renders *all* the drawing in WPF. It doesn't matter whether you have a modest video card or a much more powerful one, whether you're using basic controls or drawing more complex content, or whether you're running your application on Windows XP or Windows Vista. Even two-dimensional shapes and ordinary text are transformed into triangles and passed through the 3-D pipeline. There is no fallback to GDI+ or User32.

The Class Hierarchy

Throughout this book, you'll spend most of your time exploring the WPF namespaces and classes. But before you begin, it's helpful to take a first look at the hierarchy of classes that leads to the basic set of WPF controls.

Figure 1-4 shows a basic overview with some of the key branches of the class hierarchy. As you continue through this book, you'll dig into these classes (and their relatives) in more detail.

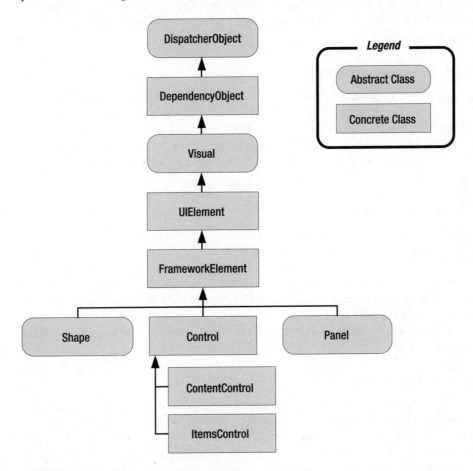

Figure 1-4. *The fundamental classes of WPF*

The following sections describe the core classes in this diagram. Many of these classes lead to whole branches of elements (such as shapes, panels, and controls).

■**Note** The core WPF namespaces begin with System.Windows (for example, System.Windows, System.Windows.Controls, and System.Windows.Media). The sole exception is namespaces that begin with System.Windows.Forms, which are part of the Windows Forms toolkit.

System.Threading.DispatcherObject

WPF applications use the familiar single-thread affinity (STA) model, which means the entire user interface is owned by a single thread. It's not safe to interact with user interface elements from another thread. To facilitate this model, each WPF application is governed by a *dispatcher* that coordinates messages (which result from keyboard input, mouse movements, and framework processes such as layout). By deriving from DispatcherObject, every element in your user interface can verify whether code is running on the correct thread and access the dispatcher to marshal code to the user interface thread. You'll learn more about the WPF threading model in Chapter 3.

System.Windows.DependencyObject

In WPF, the central way of interacting with onscreen elements is through properties. Early on in the design cycle, the WPF architects decided to create a more powerful property model that baked in features such as change notification, inherited default values, and more economical property storage. The ultimate result is the *dependency property* feature, which you'll explore in Chapter 6. By deriving from DependencyObject, WPF classes get support for dependency properties.

System.Windows.Media.Visual

Every element that appears in a WPF is, at heart, a Visual. You can think of the Visual class as a single drawing object, which encapsulates drawing instructions, additional details about how the drawing should be performed (such as clipping, opacity, and transformation settings), and basic functionality (such as hit testing). The Visual class also provides the link between the managed WPF libraries and the milcore.dll that renders your display. Any class that derives from Visual has the ability to be displayed on a window. If you prefer to create your user interface using a lightweight API that doesn't have the higher-level framework features of WPF, you can program directly with Visual objects, as described in Chapter 14.

System.Windows.UIElement

UIElement adds support for WPF essentials such as layout, input, focus, and events (which the WPF team refers to by the acronym *LIFE*). For example, it's here that the two-step measure and arrange layout process is defined, which you'll learn about in Chapter 4. It's also here that raw mouse clicks and key presses are transformed to more useful events such as MouseEnter. As with properties, WPF implements an enhanced event-passing system called *routed events*. You'll learn how it works in Chapter 6. Finally, UIElement adds supports for commands (Chapter 10).

System.Windows.FrameworkElement

FrameworkElement is the final stop in the core WPF inheritance tree. It implements some of the members that are merely defined by UIElement. For example, UIElement sets the foundation for the WPF layout system, but FrameworkElement includes the key properties (such as HorizontalAlignment and Margin) that support it. UIElement also adds support for data binding, animation, and styles, all of which are core features.

System.Windows.Shapes.Shape

Basic shapes classes, such as Rectangle, Polygon, Ellipse, Line, and Path, derive from this class. These shapes can be used alongside more traditional Windows widgets, such as buttons and text boxes. You'll start building shapes in Chapter 13.

System.Windows.Controls.Control

A *control* is an element that can interact with the user. It obviously includes classes such as TextBox, Button, and ListBox. The Control class adds additional properties for setting the font and the foreground and background colors. But the most interesting detail it provides is template support, which allows you to replace the standard appearance of a control with your own stylish drawing. You'll learn about control templates in Chapter 15.

■**Note** In Windows Forms programming, every visual item in a form is referred to as a *control*. In WPF, this isn't the case. Visual items are called *elements*, and only some elements are actually controls (those that can receive focus and interact with the user). To make this system even more confusing, many elements are defined in the System.Windows.Controls namespace, even though they don't derive from System.Windows.Controls.Control and aren't considered controls. One example is the Panel class.

System.Windows.Controls.ContentControl

This is the base class for all controls that have a single piece of content. This includes everything from the humble Label to the Window. The most impressive part of this model (which is described in more detail in Chapter 5) is the fact that this single piece of content can be anything from an ordinary string to a layout panel with a combination of other shapes and controls.

System.Windows.Controls.ItemsControl

This is the base class for all controls that show a collection of items, such as the ListBox and TreeView. List controls are remarkably flexible—for example, using the features that are built into the ItemsControl class you can transform the lowly ListBox into a list of radio buttons, a list of check boxes, a tiled display of images, or a combination of completely different elements that you've chosen. In fact, in WPF menus, toolbars, and status bars are actually specialized lists, and the classes that implement them all derive from ItemsControl. You'll start using lists in Chapter 16 when you consider data binding. You'll learn to enhance them in Chapter 17, and you'll consider the most specialized list controls in Chapter 18.

System.Windows.Controls.Panel

This is the base class for all layout containers—elements that can contain one or more children and arrange them according to specific layout rules. These containers are the foundation of the WPF layout system, and using them is the key to arranging your content in the most attractive, flexible way possible. Chapter 4 explores the WPF layout system in more detail.

The Last Word

In this chapter, you took your first look at WPF and the promise it holds. You considered the underlying architecture and briefly considered the core classes.

WPF is the beginning of the future of Windows development. In time, it will become a system like User32 and GDI/GDI+, on top of which more enhancements and higher-level features are added. Eventually, WPF will allow you to design applications that would be impossible (or at least thoroughly impractical) using Windows Forms.

Clearly, WPF introduces many dramatic changes. However, there are five key principles that immediately stand out because they are so different from previous Windows user interface toolkits such as Windows Forms. These principles are the following:

- **Hardware acceleration.** All WPF drawing is performed through DirectX, which allows it to take advantage of the latest in modern video cards.

- **Resolution independence.** WPF is flexible enough to scale up or down to suit your monitor and display preferences, depending on the system DPI setting.

- **No fixed control appearance.** In traditional Windows development, there's a wide chasm between controls that can be tailored to suit your needs (which are known as *owner-drawn* controls) and those that are rendered by the operating system and essentially fixed in appearance. In WPF, everything from a basic Rectangle to a standard Button or more complex Toolbar is drawn using the same rendering engine and completely customizable. For this reason, WPF controls are often called *lookless controls*—they define the functionality of a control, but they don't have a hard-wired "look."

- **Declarative user interfaces.** In the next chapter, you'll consider XAML, the markup standard you use to define WPF user interfaces. XAML allows you to build a window without using code. Impressively, XAML doesn't limit you to fixed, unchanging user interfaces. You can use tools such as data binding and triggers to automate basic user interface behavior (such as text boxes that update themselves when you page through a record source, or labels that glow when you hover overtop with the mouse), all without writing a single line of C#.

- **Object-based drawing.** Even if you plan to work at the lower-level visual layer (rather than the higher-level element layer), you won't work in terms of painting and pixels. Instead, you'll create shape objects and let WPF maintain the display in the most optimized manner possible.

You'll see these principles at work throughout this book. But before you go any further, it's time to learn about a complementary standard. The next chapter introduces XAML, the markup language used to define WPF user interfaces.

■■■

CHAPTER 2

XAML

XAML (short for Extensible Application Markup Language, and pronounced "zammel") is a markup language used to instantiate .NET objects. Although XAML is a technology that can be applied to many different problem domains, its primary role in life is to construct WPF user interfaces. In other words, XAML documents define the arrangement of panels, buttons, and controls that make up the windows in a WPF application.

It's unlikely that you'll write XAML by hand. Instead, you'll use a tool that generates the XAML you need. If you're a graphic designer, that tool is likely to be a graphical design and drawing program such as Microsoft Expression Blend. If you're a developer, you'll probably start with Visual Studio. Because both tools are equally at home with XAML, you can create a basic user interface with Visual Studio and then hand it off to a crack design team that can polish it up with custom graphics in Expression Blend. In fact, this ability to integrate the workflow between developers and designers is one of the key reasons that Microsoft created XAML.

In this chapter, you'll get a detailed introduction to XAML. You'll consider its purpose, its overall architecture, and its syntax. Once you understand the broad rules of XAML, you'll know what is and isn't possible in a WPF user interface—and how to make changes by hand when it's necessary. More importantly, by exploring the tags in a WPF XAML document you can learn a bit about the object model that underpins WPF user interfaces and get ready for the deeper exploration to come.

CREATING XAML WITH VISUAL STUDIO

In this chapter, you'll take a look at all the details of XAML markup. Of course, when you're designing an application, you won't write all your XAML by hand. Instead, you'll use a tool such as Visual Studio to drag and drop your windows into existence. Based on that, you might wonder whether it's worth spending so much time studying the syntax of XAML.

The answer is a resounding *yes*. Understanding XAML is critical to WPF application design. WPF applications are quite different from Windows Forms applications in this respect—with Windows Forms applications, you could safely ignore the automatically generated UI code, while in WPF applications the XAML often takes center stage. Understanding XAML will help you learn key WPF concepts, such as attached properties (in this chapter), layout (Chapter 4), the content model (Chapter 5), routed events (Chapter 6), and so on. More important, there is a whole host of tasks that are only possible—or are far easier to accomplish—with handwritten XAML. They include the following:

- **Wiring up event handlers.** Attaching event handlers in the most common places—for example, to the Click event of a Button—is easy to do in Visual Studio. However, once you understand how events are wired up in XAML, you'll be able create more sophisticated connections. For example, you can set up an event handler that responds to the Click event of every button in a window. Chapter 6 has more about this technique.

- **Defining resources.** Resources are objects that you define once in your XAML and in a special section of your XAML and then reuse in various places in your markup. Resources allow you to centralize and standardize formatting, and create nonvisual objects such as templates and animations. Chapter 11 shows how to create and use resources.

- **Defining control templates.** WPF controls are designed to be *lookless*, which means you can substitute your custom visuals in place of the standard appearance. To do so, you must create your own control template, which is nothing more than a block of XAML markup. Chapter 15 tackles control templates.

- **Writing data binding expressions.** Data binding allows you to extract data from an object and display it in a linked element. To set up this relationship and configure how it works, you must add a data binding expression to your XAML markup. Chapter 16 introduces data binding.

- **Defining animations.** Animations are a common ingredient in XAML applications. Usually, they're defined as resources, constructed using XAML markup, and then linked to other controls (or triggered through code). Currently, Visual Studio has no design-time support for crafting animations. Chapter 21 delves into animation.

Most WPF developers use a combination of techniques, laying out some of their user interface with a design tool (Visual Studio or Expression Blend) and then fine-tuning it by editing the XAML markup by hand. However, you'll probably find that it's easiest to write all your XAML by hand until you learn about layout containers in Chapter 4. That's because you need to use a layout container to properly arrange multiple controls in a window.

Understanding XAML

Developers realized long ago that the most efficient way to tackle complex, graphically rich applications is to separate the graphical portion from the underlying code. That way, artists can own the graphics and developers can own the code. Both pieces can be designed and refined separately, without any versioning headaches.

Graphical User Interfaces Before WPF

With traditional display technologies, there's no easy way to separate the graphical content from the code. The key problem with Windows Forms application is that every form you create is defined entirely in C# code. As you drop controls onto the design surface and configure them, Visual Studio quietly adjusts the code in the corresponding form class. Sadly, graphic designers don't have any tools that can work with C# code.

Instead, artists are forced to take their content and export it to a bitmap format. These bitmaps can then be used to skin windows, buttons, and other controls. This approach works well for straightforward interfaces that don't change much over time, but it's extremely limiting in other scenarios. Some of its problems include the following:

- Each graphical element (background, button, and so on) needs to be exported as a separate bitmap. That limits the ability to combine bitmaps and use dynamic effects such as antialiasing, transparency, and shadows.

- A fair bit of user interface logic needs to be embedded in the code by the developer. This includes button sizes, positioning, mouse-over effects, and animations. The graphic designer can't control any of these details.

- There's no intrinsic connection between the different graphical elements, so it's easy to end up with an unmatched set of images. Tracking all these items adds complexity.

- Bitmaps can't be resized without compromising their quality. For that reason, a bitmap-based user interface is resolution-dependent. That means it can't accommodate large monitors and high-resolution displays, which is a major violation of the WPF design philosophy.

If you've ever been through the process of designing a Windows Forms application with custom graphics in a team setting, you've put up with a lot of frustration. Even if the interface is designed from scratch by a graphic designer, you'll need to re-create it with C# code. Usually, the graphic designer will simply prepare a mock-up that you need to translate painstakingly into your application.

WPF solves this problem with XAML. When designing a WPF application in Visual Studio, the window you're designing isn't translated into code. Instead, it's serialized into a set of XAML tags. When you run the application, these tags are used to generate the objects that compose the user interface.

Note It's important to understand that WPF doesn't require XAML. There's no reason Visual Studio couldn't use the Windows Forms approach and create code statements that construct your WPF windows. But if it did, your window would be locked into the Visual Studio environment and available to programmers only.

In other words, WPF doesn't require XAML. However, XAML opens up worlds of possibilities for collaboration, because other design tools understand the XAML format. For example, a savvy designer can use a tool such as Expression Design to fine-tune the graphics in your WPF application or a tool such as Expression Blend to build sophisticated animations for it. After you've finished this chapter, you may want to read a Microsoft white paper at http://windowsclient.net/wpf/white-papers/thenewiteration.aspx that reviews XAML and explores some of the ways the developers and designers can collaborate on a WPF application.

Tip XAML plays the same role for Windows applications as control tags do for ASP.NET web applications. The difference is that the ASP.NET tagging syntax is designed to look like HTML, so designers can craft web pages using ordinary web design applications such as FrontPage and Dreamweaver. As with WPF, the actual code for an ASP.NET web page is usually placed in a separate file to facilitate this design.

The Variants of XAML

There are actually several different ways people use the term *XAML*. So far, we've used it to refer to the entire language of XAML, which is an all-purpose XML-based syntax for representing a tree of .NET objects. (These objects could be buttons and text boxes in a window, or custom classes you've defined. In fact, XAML could even be used on other platforms to represent non-.NET objects.)

There are also several subsets of XAML:

- **WPF XAML** encompasses the elements that describe WPF content, such as vector graphics, controls, and documents. Currently, it's the most significant application of XAML, and it's the subset we'll explore in this book.

- **XPS XAML** is the part of WPF XAML that defines an XML representation for formatted electronic documents. It's been published as the separate XML Paper Specification (XPS) standard. You'll explore XPS in Chapter 19.

- **Silverlight XAML** is a subset of WPF XAML that's intended for Silverlight applications. Silverlight is a cross-platform browser plug-in that allows you to create rich web content with two-dimensional graphics, animation, and audio and video. Chapter 1 has more about Silverlight, or you can visit `http://silverlight.net` to learn about it in detail.

- **WF XAML** encompasses the elements that describe Windows Workflow Foundation (WF) content. You can learn more about WF at `http://wf.netfx3.com`.

XAML Compilation

The creators of WPF knew that XAML needed to not just solve the problem of design collaboration—it also needed to be fast. And though XML-based formats such as XAML are flexible and easily portable to other tools and platforms, they aren't always the most efficient option. XML was designed to be logical, readable, and straightforward—not compact.

WPF addresses this shortcoming with BAML (Binary Application Markup Language). BAML is really nothing more than a binary representation of XAML. When you compile a WPF application in Visual Studio, all your XAML files are converted into BAML and that BAML is then embedded as a resource into the final DLL or EXE assembly. BAML is *tokenized*, which means lengthier bits of XAML are replaced with shorter tokens. Not only is BAML significantly smaller, it's also optimized in a way that makes it faster to parse at runtime.

Most developers won't worry about the conversion of XAML to BAML because the compiler performs it behind the scenes. However, it is possible to use XAML without compiling it first. This might make sense in scenarios that require some of the user interface to be supplied just in time (for example, pulled out of a database as a block of XAML tags). You'll see how this works later in this chapter, in the section "Loading and Compiling XAML."

XAML Basics

The XAML standard is quite straightforward once you understand a few ground rules:

- Every element in a XAML document maps to an instance of a .NET class. The name of the element matches the name of the class *exactly*. For example, the element <Button> instructs WPF to create a Button object.

- As with any XML document, you can nest one element inside another. As you'll see, XAML gives every class the flexibility to decide how it handles this situation. However, nesting is usually a way to express *containment*—in other words, if you find a Button element inside a Grid element, your user interface probably includes a Grid that contains a Button inside.

- You can set the properties of each class through attributes. However, in some situations an attribute isn't powerful enough to handle the job. In these cases, you'll use nested tags with a special syntax.

■**Tip** If you're completely new to XML, you'll probably find it easier to review the basics before you tackle XAML. To get up to speed quickly, try the free web-based tutorial at `http://www.w3schools.com/xml`.

Before continuing, take a look at this bare-bones XAML document, which represents a new blank window (as created by Visual Studio). The lines have been numbered for easy reference:

```
1  <Window x:Class="WindowsApplication1.Window1"
2      xmlns="http://schemas.microsoft.com/winfx/2006/xaml/presentation"
3      xmlns:x="http://schemas.microsoft.com/winfx/2006/xaml"
4      Title="Window1" Height="300" Width="300">
5
6      <Grid>
7      </Grid>
8  </Window>
```

This document includes only two elements—the top-level Window element, which represents the entire window, and the Grid, in which you can place all your controls. Although you could use any top-level element, WPF applications rely on just a few:

- Window

- Page (which is similar to Window, but used for navigable applications)

- Application (which defines application resources and startup settings)

As in all XML documents, there can only be one top-level element. In the previous example, that means that as soon as you close the Window element with the </Window> tag, you end the document. No more content can follow.

Looking at the start tag for the Window element you'll find several interesting attributes, including a class name and two XML namespaces (described in the following sections). You'll also find the three properties shown here:

```
4      Title="Window1" Height="300" Width="300">
```

Each attribute corresponds to a separate property of the Window class. All in all, this tells WPF to create a window with the caption Window1 and to make it 300 by 300 units large.

■**Note** As you learned in Chapter 1, WPF uses a relative measurement system that isn't what most Windows developers expect. Rather than letting you set sizes using physical pixels, WPF uses *device-independent units* that can scale to fit different monitor resolutions and are defined as 1/96 of an inch. That means the 300-by-300-unit window in the previous example will be rendered as a 300-by-300-*pixel* window if your system DPI setting is the standard 96 dpi. However, on a system with a higher system DPI, more pixels will be used. Chapter 1 has the full story.

XAML Namespaces

Clearly, it's not enough to supply just a class name. The XAML parser also needs to know the .NET namespace where this class is located. For example, the Window class could exist in several places—it might refer to the System.Windows.Window class, or it could refer to a Window class in a third-party component, or one you've defined in your application. To figure out which class you really want, the XAML parser examines the XML namespace that's applied to the element.

Here's how it works. In the sample document shown earlier, two namespaces are defined:

```
2      xmlns="http://schemas.microsoft.com/winfx/2006/xaml/presentation"
3      xmlns:x="http://schemas.microsoft.com/winfx/2006/xaml"
```

■**Note** XML namespaces are declared using attributes. These attributes can be placed inside any element start tag. However, convention dictates that all the namespaces you need to use in a document should be declared in the very first tag, as they are in this example. Once a namespace is declared, it can be used anywhere in the document.

The xmlns attribute is a specialized attribute in the world of XML that's reserved for declaring namespaces. This snippet of markup declares two namespaces that you'll find in every WPF XAML document you create:

- `http://schemas.microsoft.com/winfx/2006/xaml/`presentation is the core WPF namespace. It encompasses all the WPF classes, including the controls you use to build user interfaces. In this example, this namespace is declared without a namespace prefix, so it becomes the default namespace for the entire document. In other words, every element is automatically placed in this namespace unless you specify otherwise.

- `http://schemas.microsoft.com/winfx/2006/xaml` is the XAML namespace. It includes various XAML utility features that allow you to influence how your document is interpreted. This namespace is mapped to the prefix *x*. That means you can apply it by placing the namespace prefix before the element name (as in **<x:**ElementName>).

As you can see, the XML namespace name doesn't match any particular .NET namespace. There are a couple of reasons the creators of XAML chose this design. By convention, XML namespaces are often URIs (as they are here). These URIs look like they point to a location on the Web, but they don't. The URI format is used because it makes it unlikely that different organizations will inadvertently create different XML-based languages with the same namespace. Because the domain `schemas.microsoft.com` is owned by Microsoft, only Microsoft will use it in an XML namespace name.

The other reason that there isn't a one-to-one mapping between the XML namespaces used in XAML and .NET namespaces is because it would significantly complicate your XAML documents. The problem here is that WPF encompasses well over a dozen namespaces (all of which start with System.Windows). If each .NET namespace had a different XML namespace, you'd need to specify the right namespace for each and every control you use, which quickly gets messy. Instead, the creators of WPF chose to combine all of these .NET namespaces into a single XML namespace. This works because within the different .NET namespaces that are a part of WPF, there aren't any classes that have the same name.

The namespace information allows the XAML parser to find the right class. For example, when it looks at the Window and Grid elements, it sees that they are placed in the default WPF namespace. It then searches the corresponding .NET namespaces, until it finds System.Windows.Window and System.Windows.Controls.Grid.

The Code-Behind Class

XAML allows you to construct a user interface, but in order to make a functioning application you need a way to connect the event handlers that contain your application code. XAML makes this easy using the Class attribute that's shown here:

```
1   <Window x:Class="WindowsApplication1.Window1"
```

The *x* namespace prefix places the Class attribute in the XAML namespace, which means this is a more general part of the XAML language. In fact, the Class attribute tells the XAML parser to generate a new class with the specified name. That class derives from the class that's named by the XML element. In other words, this example creates a new class named Window1, which derives from the base Window class.

The Window1 class is generated automatically at compile time. But here's where things get interesting. You can supply a piece of the Window1 class that will be merged into the automatically generated portion. The piece you specify is the perfect container for your event handling code.

■**Note** This magic happens through the C# feature known as *partial classes*. Partial classes allow you to split a class into two or more separate pieces for development and fuse them together in the compiled assembly. Partial classes can be used in a variety of code management scenarios, but they're most useful in situations like these, where your code needs to be merged with a designer-generated file.

Visual Studio helps you out by automatically creating a partial class where you can place your event handling code. For example, if you create an application named WindowsApplication1, which contains a window named Window1 (as in the previous example), Visual Studio will start you out with this basic skeleton of a class:

```
namespace WindowsApplication1
{
    /// <summary>
    /// Interaction logic for Window1.xaml
    /// </summary>
    public partial class Window1 : Window
    {
        public Window1()
        {
            InitializeComponent();
        }
    }
}
```

When you compile your application, the XAML that defines your user interface (such as Window1.xaml) is translated into CLR type declaration that is merged with the logic in your code-behind class file (such as Window1.xaml.cs) to form one single unit.

The InitializeComponent() Method

Currently, the Window1 class code doesn't include any real functionality. However, it does include one important detail—the default constructor, which calls InitializeComponent() when you create an instance of the class.

■**Note** The InitializeComponent()method plays a key role in WPF applications. For that reason, you should never delete the InitializeComponent() call in your window's constructor. Similarly, if you add another constructor, make sure it also calls InitializeComponent().

The InitializeComponent() method isn't visible in your source code because it's automatically generated when you compile your application. Essentially, all InitializeComponent() does is call the LoadComponent() method of the System.Windows.Application class. The LoadComponent() method extracts the BAML (the compiled XAML) from your assembly and uses it to build your user interface. As it parses the BAML, it creates each control object, sets its properties, and attaches any event handlers.

■**Note** If you can't stand the suspense, jump ahead to the end of the chapter. You'll see the code for the automatically generated InitializeComponent() method in the section "Code and Compiled XAML."

Naming Elements

There's one more detail to consider. In your code-behind class, you'll often want to manipulate controls programmatically. For example, you might want to read or change properties or attach and detach event handlers on the fly. To make this possible, the control must include a XAML Name attribute. In the previous example, the Grid control does not include a Name attribute, so you won't be able to manipulate it in your code-behind file.

Here's how you can attach a name to the Grid:

```
6    <Grid x:Name="grid1">
7    </Grid>
```

You can make this change by hand in the XAML document, or you can select the grid in the Visual Studio designer and set the Name property using the Properties window.

Either way, the Name attribute tells the XAML parser to add a field like this to the automatically generated portion of the Window1 class:

```
private System.Windows.Controls.Grid grid1;
```

Now you can interact with the grid in your Window1 class code by using the name grid1:

```
MessageBox.Show(String.Format("The grid is {0}x{1} units in size.",
  grid1.ActualWidth, grid1.ActualHeight));
```

This technique doesn't add much for the simple grid example, but it becomes much more important when you need to read values in input controls such as text boxes and list boxes.

The Name property shown previously is part of the XAML language, and it's used to help integrate your code-behind class. Somewhat confusingly, many classes define their own Name property. (One example is the base FrameworkElement class from which all WPF elements derive.) XAML parsers have a clever way of handling this. You can set either the XAML Name property (using the x: prefix) or the Name property that belongs to the actual element (by leaving out the prefix). Either way, the result is the same—the name you specify is used in the automatically generated code file *and* it's used to set the Name property.

That means the following markup is equivalent to what you've already seen:

```
<Grid Name="grid1">
</Grid>
```

This bit of magic only works if the class that includes the Name property decorates itself with the RuntimeNameProperty attribute. The RuntimeNameProperty indicates which property should be treated as the name for instances of that type. (Obviously, it's usually the property that's named Name.) The FrameworkElement class includes the RuntimeNameProperty attribute, so there's no problem.

Tip In a traditional Windows Forms application, every control has a name. In a WPF application, there's no such requirement. However, if you create a window by dragging and dropping elements onto the Visual Studio design surface, each element will be given an automatically generated name. This is simply a convenience. If you don't want to interact with an element in your code, you're free to remove its Name attribute from the markup. The examples in this book usually omit element names when they aren't needed, which makes the markup more concise.

By now, you should have a basic understanding of how to interpret a XAML document that defines a window and how that XAML document is converted into a final compiled class (with the addition of any code you've written). In the next section, you'll look at the property syntax in more detail and learn to wire up event handlers.

Properties and Events in XAML

So far, you've considered a relatively unexciting example—a blank window that hosts an empty Grid control. Before going any further, it's worth introducing a more realistic window that includes several controls. Figure 2-1 shows an example with an automatic question answerer.

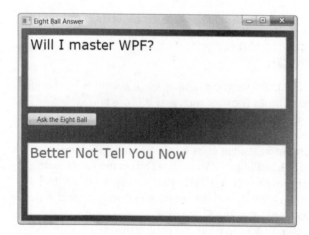

Figure 2-1. *Ask the eight ball and all will be revealed.*

The eight ball window includes four controls: a Grid (the most common tool for arranging layout in WPF), two TextBox objects, and a Button. The markup that's required to arrange and configure these controls is significantly longer than the previous examples. Here's an abbreviated listing that replaces some of the details with an ellipsis (…) to expose the overall structure:

```
<Window x:Class="EightBall.Window1"
    xmlns="http://schemas.microsoft.com/winfx/2006/xaml/presentation"
    xmlns:x="http://schemas.microsoft.com/winfx/2006/xaml"
    Title="Eight Ball Answer" Height="328" Width="412">
```

```
<Grid Name="grid1">
  <Grid.Background>
    ...
  </Grid.Background>
  <Grid.RowDefinitions>
    ...
  </Grid.RowDefinitions>

  <TextBox Name="txtQuestion" ... >
    ...
  </TextBox>

  <Button Name="cmdAnswer" ... >
    ...
  </Button>

  <TextBox Name="txtAnswer" ... >
    ...
  </TextBox>
</Grid>
</Window>
```

In the following sections, you'll explore the parts of this document—and learn the syntax of XAML along the way.

■**Note** XAML isn't limited to the classes that are a part of WPF. You can use XAML to create an instance of any class that meets a few ground rules. You'll learn how to use your own classes with XAML later in this chapter.

Simple Properties and Type Converters

As you've already seen, the attributes of an element set the properties of the corresponding object. For example, the text boxes in the eight ball example configure the alignment, margin, and font:

```
<TextBox Name="txtQuestion"
  VerticalAlignment="Stretch" HorizontalAlignment="Stretch"
  FontFamily="Verdana" FontSize="24" Foreground="Green" ... >
```

In order for this to work, the System.Windows.Controls.TextBox class must provide the following properties: VerticalAlignment, HorizontalAlignment, FontFamily, FontSize, and Foreground. You'll learn the specific meaning for each of these properties in the following chapters.

To make this system work, the XAML parser needs to perform a bit more work than you might initially realize. The value in an XML attribute is always a plain text string. However, object properties can be any .NET type. In the previous example, there are two properties that use enumerations (VerticalAlignment and HorizontalAlignment), one string (FontFamily), one integer (FontSize), and one Brush object (Foreground).

In order to bridge the gap between string values and nonstring properties, the XAML parser needs to perform a conversion. The conversion is performed by *type converters*, a basic piece of .NET infrastructure that's existed since .NET 1.0.

Essentially, a type converter has one role in life—it provides utility methods that can convert a specific .NET data type to and from any other .NET type, such as a string representation in this case. The XAML parser follows two steps to find a type converter:

1. It examines the property declaration, looking for a TypeConverter attribute. (If present, the TypeConverter attribute indicates what class can perform the conversion.) For example, when you use a property such as Foreground, .NET checks the declaration of the Foreground property.

2. If there's no TypeConverter attribute on the property declaration, the XAML parser checks the class declaration of the corresponding data type. For example, the Foreground property uses a Brush object. The Brush class (and its derivatives) use the BrushConverter because the Brush class is decorated with the Type-Converter(typeof(BrushConverter)) attribute declaration.

If there's no associated type converter on the property declaration or the class declaration, the XAML parser generates an error.

This system is simple but flexible. If you set a type converter at the class level, that converter applies to every property that uses that class. On the other hand, if you want to fine-tune the way type conversion works for a particular property, you can use the TypeConverter attribute on the property declaration instead.

It's technically possible to use type converters in code, but the syntax is a bit convoluted. It's almost always better to set a property directly—not only is it faster, it also avoids potential errors from mistyping strings, which won't be caught until runtime. (This problem doesn't affect XAML, because the XAML is parsed and validated at compile time.) Of course, before you can set the properties on a WPF element, you need to know a bit more about the basic WPF properties and data types—a job you'll tackle in the next few chapters.

■**Note** XAML, like all XML-based languages, is *case-sensitive*. That means you can't substitute <button> for <Button>. However, type converters usually aren't case-sensitive, which means both Foreground="White" and Foreground="white" have the same result.

Complex Properties

As handy as type converters are, they aren't practical for all scenarios. For example, some properties are full-fledged objects with their own set of properties. Although it's possible to create a string representation that the type converter could use, that syntax might be difficult to use and prone to error.

Fortunately, XAML provides another option: *property-element syntax*. With property-element syntax, you add a child element with a name in the form Parent.PropertyName. For example, the Grid has a Background property that allows you to supply a brush that's used to paint the area behind the controls. If you want to use a complex brush—one more advanced than a solid color fill—you'll need to add a child tag named Grid.Background, as shown here:

```
<Grid Name="grid1">
  <Grid.Background>
    ...
  </Grid.Background>
  ...
</Grid>
```

The key detail that makes this work is the period (.) in the element name. This distinguishes properties from other types of nested content.

This still leaves one detail—namely, once you've identified the complex property you want to configure, how do you set it? Here's the trick. Inside the nested element, you can add another tag to instantiate a specific class. In the eight ball example (shown in Figure 2-1), the background is filled with a gradient. To define the gradient you want, you need to create a LinearGradientBrush object.

Using the rules of XAML, you can create the LinearGradientBrush object using an element with the name LinearGradientBrush:

```
<Grid Name="grid1">
  <Grid.Background>
    <LinearGradientBrush>
    </LinearGradientBrush>
  </Grid.Background>
  ...
</Grid>
```

The LinearGradientBrush is part of the WPF set of namespaces, so you can keep using the default XML namespace for your tags.

However, it's not enough to simply create the LinearGradientBrush—you also need to specify the colors in that gradient. You do this by filling the LinearGradientBrush.GradientStops property with a collection of GradientStop objects. Once again, the GradientStops property is too complex to be set with an attribute value alone. Instead, you need to rely on the property-element syntax:

```
<Grid Name="grid1">
  <Grid.Background>
    <LinearGradientBrush>
      <LinearGradientBrush.GradientStops>
      </LinearGradientBrush.GradientStops>
    </LinearGradientBrush>
  </Grid.Background>
  ...
</Grid>
```

Finally, you can fill the GradientStops collection with a series of GradientStop objects. Each GradientStop object has an Offset and Color property. You can supply these two values using the ordinary property-attribute syntax:

```
<Grid Name="grid1">
  <Grid.Background>
    <LinearGradientBrush>
      <LinearGradientBrush.GradientStops>
        <GradientStop Offset="0.00" Color="Red" />
        <GradientStop Offset="0.50" Color="Indigo" />
        <GradientStop Offset="1.00" Color="Violet" />
      </LinearGradientBrush.GradientStops>
    </LinearGradientBrush>
  </Grid.Background>
  ...
</Grid>
```

Note You can use property-element syntax for any property. But usually you'll use the simpler property-attribute approach if the property has a suitable type converter. Doing so results in more compact code.

Any set of XAML tags can be replaced with a set of code statements that performs the same task. The tags shown previously, which fill the background with a gradient of your choice, are equivalent to the following code:

```
LinearGradientBrush brush = new LinearGradientBrush();

GradientStop gradientStop1 = new GradientStop();
gradientStop1.Offset = 0;
gradientStop1.Color = Colors.Red;
brush.GradientStops.Add(gradientStop1);

GradientStop gradientStop2 = new GradientStop();
gradientStop2.Offset = 0.5;
gradientStop2.Color = Colors.Indigo;
brush.GradientStops.Add(gradientStop2);

GradientStop gradientStop3 = new GradientStop();
gradientStop3.Offset = 1;
gradientStop3.Color = Colors.Violet;
brush.GradientStops.Add(gradientStop3);

grid1.Background = brush;
```

Markup Extensions

For most properties, the XAML property syntax works perfectly well. But in some cases, it just isn't possible to hard-code the property value. For example, you may want to set a property value to an object that already exists. Or you may want to set a property value *dynamically*, by binding it to a property in another control. In both of these cases, you need to use a *markup extension*—specialized syntax that sets a property in a nonstandard way.

Markup extensions can be used in nested tags or in XML attributes, which is more common. When they're used in attributes, they are always bracketed by curly braces {}. For example, here's how you can use the StaticExtension, which allows you to refer to a static property in another class:

```
<Button ... Foreground="{x:Static SystemColors.ActiveCaptionBrush}" >
```

Markup extensions use the syntax {MarkupExtensionClass Argument}. In this case, the markup extension is the StaticExtension class. (By convention, you can drop the final word *Extension* when referring to an extension class.) The x: prefix indicates that the StaticExtension is found in one of the XAML namespaces. You'll also encounter markup extensions that are a part of the WPF namespaces and don't have the x: prefix.

All markup extensions are implemented by classes that derive from System.Windows.Markup.MarkupExtension. The base MarkupExtension class is extremely simple—it provides a single ProvideValue() method that gets the value you want. In other words, when the XAML parser encounters the previous statement, it creates an instance of the StaticExtension class (passing in the string "SystemColors.ActiveCaptionBrush" as an argument to the constructor) and then calls ProvideValue() to get the object returned by the SystemColors.ActiveCaption.Brush static property. The Foreground property of the cmdAnswer button is then set with the retrieved object.

The end result of this piece of XAML is the same as if you'd written this:

```
cmdAnswer.Foreground = SystemColors.ActiveCaptionBrush;
```

Because markup extensions map to classes, they can also be used as nested properties, as you learned in the previous section. For example, you can use the StaticExtension with the Button.Foreground property like this:

```
<Button ... >
  <Button.Foreground>
    <x:Static Member="SystemColors.ActiveCaptionBrush"></x:Static>
  </Button.Foreground>
</Button>
```

Depending on the complexity of the markup extension and the number of properties you want to set, this syntax is sometimes simpler.

Like most markup extensions, the StaticExtension needs to be evaluated at runtime because only then can you determine the current system colors. Some markup extensions can be evaluated at compile time. These include the NullExtension (which represents a null value) and the TypeExtension (which constructs an object that represents a .NET type). Throughout this book, you'll see many examples of markup extensions at work, particularly with resources and data binding.

Attached Properties

Along with ordinary properties, XAML also includes the concept of *attached properties*—properties that may apply to several controls but are defined in a different class. In WPF, attached properties are frequently used to control layout.

Here's how it works. Every control has its own set of intrinsic properties. (For example, a text box has a specific font, text color, and text content as dictated by properties such as FontFamily, Foreground, and Text.) When you place a control inside a container it gains additional features, depending on the type of container. (For example, if you place a text box inside a grid, you need to be able to choose the grid cell where it's positioned.) These additional details are set using attached properties.

Attached properties always use a two-part name in this form: DefiningType.PropertyName. This two-part naming syntax allows the XAML parser to distinguish between a normal property and an attached property.

In the eight ball example, attached properties allow the individual controls to place themselves on separate rows in the (invisible) grid:

```
<TextBox ... Grid.Row="0">
  [Place question here.]
</TextBox>

<Button ... Grid.Row="1">
  Ask the Eight Ball
</Button>

<TextBox ... Grid.Row="2">
  [Answer will appear here.]
</TextBox>
```

Attached properties aren't really properties at all. They're actually translated into method calls. The XAML parser calls the static method that has this form: *DefiningType*.Set*PropertyName*(). For example, in the previous XAML snippet, the defining type is the Grid class, and the property is Row, so the parser calls Grid.SetRow().

When calling SetPropertyName(), the parser passes two parameters: the object that's being modified, and the property value that's specified. For example, when you set the Grid.Row property on the TextBox control, the XAML parser executes this code:

```
Grid.SetRow(txtQuestion, 0);
```

This pattern (calling a static method of the defining type) is a convenience that conceals what's really taking place. To the casual eye, this code implies that the row number is stored in the Grid object. However, the row number is actually stored in the object that it *applies to*—in this case, the TextBox object.

This sleight of hand works because the TextBox derives from the DependencyObject base class, as do all WPF controls. And as you'll learn in Chapter 6, the DependencyObject is designed to store a virtually unlimited collection of dependency properties. (The attached properties that were discussed earlier are a special type of dependency property.)

In fact, the Grid.SetRow() method is actually a shortcut that's equivalent to calling DependencyObject.SetValue() method, as shown here:

```
txtQuestion.SetValue(Grid.RowProperty, 0);
```

Attached properties are a core ingredient of WPF. They act as an all-purpose extensibility system. For example, by defining the Row property as an attached property, you guarantee that it's usable with any control. The other option, making it a part of a base class such as FrameworkElement, complicates life. Not only would it clutter the public interface with properties that only have meaning in certain circumstances (in this case, when an element is being used inside a Grid), it also makes it impossible to add new types of containers that require new properties.

■**Note** Attached properties are very similar to *extender providers* in a Windows Forms application. Both allow you to add "virtual" properties to extend another class. The difference is that you must create an instance of an extender provider before you can use it, and the extended property value is stored in the extender provider, not the extended control. The attached property design is a better choice for WPF because it avoids lifetime management issues (for example, deciding when to dispose of an extender provider).

Nesting Elements

As you've seen, XAML documents are arranged as a heavily nested tree of elements. In the current example, a Window element contains a Grid element, which contains TextBox and Button elements.

XAML allows each element to decide how it deals with nested elements. This interaction is mediated through one of four mechanisms that are evaluated in this order:

- If the parent implements IList, the parser calls IList.Add() and passes in the child.

- If the parent implements IDictionary, the parser calls IDictionary.Add() and passes in the child. When using a dictionary collection, you must also set the x:Key attribute to give a key name to each item.

- If the parent is decorated with the ContentProperty attribute, the parser uses the child to set that property.

For example, earlier in this chapter you saw how a LinearGradientBrush can hold a collection of GradientStop objects using syntax like this:

```
<LinearGradientBrush>
  <LinearGradientBrush.GradientStops>
    <GradientStop Offset="0.00" Color="Red" />
    <GradientStop Offset="0.50" Color="Indigo" />
    <GradientStop Offset="1.00" Color="Violet" />
  </LinearGradientBrush.GradientStops>
</LinearGradientBrush>
```

The XAML parser recognizes the LinearGradientBrush.GradientStops element is a complex property because it includes a period. However, it needs to process the tags inside (the three GradientStop elements) a little differently. In this case, the parser recognizes that the GradientStops property returns a GradientStopCollection object, and the GradientStopCollection implements the IList interface. Thus, it assumes (quite rightly) that each GradientStop should be added to the collection using the IList.Add() method:

```
GradientStop gradientStop1 = new GradientStop();
gradientStop1.Offset = 0;
gradientStop1.Color = Colors.Red;
IList list = brush.GradientStops;
list.Add(gradientStop1);
```

Some properties might support more than one type of collection. In this case, you need to add a tag that specifies the collection class, like this:

```
<LinearGradientBrush>
  <LinearGradientBrush.GradientStops>
    <GradientStopCollection>
      <GradientStop Offset="0.00" Color="Red" />
      <GradientStop Offset="0.50" Color="Indigo" />
      <GradientStop Offset="1.00" Color="Violet" />
    </GradientStopCollection>
  </LinearGradientBrush.GradientStops>
</LinearGradientBrush>
```

Note If the collection defaults to null, you need to include the tag that specifies the collection class, thereby creating the collection object. If there's a default instance of the collection and you simply need to fill it, you can omit that part.

Nested content doesn't always indicate a collection. For example, consider the Grid element, which contains several other controls:

```
<Grid Name="grid1">
  ...
  <TextBox Name="txtQuestion" ... >
    ...
  </TextBox>
  <Button Name="cmdAnswer" ... >
    ...
  </Button>
  <TextBox Name="txtAnswer" ... >
    ...
  </TextBox>
</Grid>
```

These nested tags don't correspond to complex properties because they don't include the period. Furthermore, the Grid control isn't a collection and so it doesn't implement IList or IDictionary. What the Grid *does* support is the ContentProperty attribute, which indicates the property that should receive any nested content. Technically, the ContentProperty attribute is applied to the Panel class, from which the Grid derives, and looks like this:

```
[ContentPropertyAttribute("Children")]
public abstract class Panel
```

This indicates that any nested elements should be used to set the Children property. The XAML parser treats the content property differently depending on whether or not it's a collection property (in which case it implements the IList or IDictionary interface). Because the Panel.Children property returns a UIElementCollection, and because UIElementCollection implements IList, the parser uses the IList.Add() method to add nested content to the grid.

In other words, when the XAML parser meets the previous markup, it creates an instance of each nested element and passes it to the Grid using the Grid.Children.Add() method:

```
txtQuestion = new TextBox();
...
grid1.Children.Add(txtQuestion);

cmdAnswer = new Button();
...
grid1.Children.Add(cmdAnswer);

txtAnswer = new TextBox();
...
grid1.Children.Add(txtAnswer);
```

What happens next depends entirely on how the control implements the content property. The Grid displays all the controls it holds in an invisible layout of rows and columns, as you'll see in Chapter 4.

The ContentProperty attribute is frequently used in WPF. Not only is it used for container controls (such as Grid) and controls that contain a collection of visual items (such as the List-Box and TreeView), it's also used for controls that contain singular content. For example, the TextBox and Button are only able to hold a single element or piece of text, but they both use a content property to deal with nested content like this:

```
<TextBox Name="txtQuestion" ... >
  [Place question here.]
</TextBox>
<Button Name="cmdAnswer" ... >
  Ask the Eight Ball
</Button>
<TextBox Name="txtAnswer" ... >
  [Answer will appear here.]
</TextBox>
```

The TextBox class uses the ContentProperty attribute to flag the TextBox.Text property. The Button class uses the ContentProperty attribute to flag the Button.Content property. The XAML parser uses the supplied text to set these properties.

The TextBox.Text property only allows strings. However, Button.Content is much more interesting. As you'll learn in Chapter 5, the Content property accepts any element. For example, here's a button that contains a shape object:

```
<Button Name="cmdAnswer" ... >
  <Rectangle Fill="Blue" Height="10" Width="100" />
</Button>
```

Because the Text and Content properties don't use collections, you can't include more than one piece of content. For example, if you attempt to nest multiple elements inside a Button, the XAML parser will throw an exception. The parser also throws an exception if you supply nontext content (such as a Rectangle).

■**Note** As a general rule of thumb, all controls that derive from ContentControl allow a single nested element. All controls that derive from ItemsControl allow a collection of items that map to some part of the control (such as a list of items or a tree of nodes). All controls that derive from Panel are containers that are used to organize groups of controls. The ContentControl, ItemsControl, and Panel base classes all use the ContentProperty attribute.

Special Characters and Whitespace

XAML is bound by the rules of XML. For example, XML pays special attention to a few specific characters, such as & and < and >. If you try to use these values to set the content of an element, you'll run into trouble because the XAML parser assumes you're trying to do something else—such as create a nested element.

For example, imagine you want to create a button that contains the text <Click Me>. The following markup won't work:

```
<Button ... >
  <Click Me>
</Button>
```

The problem here is that it looks like you're trying to create an element named Click with an attribute named Me. The solution is to replace the offending characters with entity references—specific codes that the XAML parser will interpret correctly. Table 2-1 lists the character entities you might choose to use. Note that the quotation mark character entity is only required when setting values using an attribute because the quotation mark indicates the beginning and ending of an attribute value.

Table 2-1. *XML Character Entities*

Special Character	Character Entity
Less than (<)	&lt;
Greater than (>)	&gt;
Ampersand (&)	&amp;
Quotation mark (")	&quot;

Here's the corrected markup that uses the appropriate character entities:

```
<Button ... >
  &lt;Click Me&gt;
</Button>
```

When the XAML parser reads this, it correctly understands that you want to add the text <Click Me> and it passes a string with this content, complete with angled brackets, to the Button.Content property.

■Note This limitation is a XAML detail and it won't affect you if you want to set the Button.Content property in code. Of course, C# has its own special character (the backslash) that must be escaped in string literals for the same reason.

Special characters aren't the only stumbling block you'll run into with XAML. Another issue is whitespace handling. By default, XML collapses all whitespace, which means a long string of spaces, tabs, and hard returns is reduced to a single space. Furthermore, if you add whitespace before or after your element content, this space is ignored completely. You can see this in the EightBall example. The text in the button and the two text boxes is separated from the XAML tags using a hard return and tab to make the markup more readable. However, this extra space doesn't appear in the user interface.

Sometimes this isn't what you want. For example, you may want to include a series of several spaces in your button text. In this case, you need to use the xml:space="preserve" attribute on your element.

The xml:space attribute is a part of the XML standard, and it's an all-or-nothing setting. Once you switch it on, all the whitespace inside that element is retained. For example, consider this markup:

```
<TextBox Name="txtQuestion" xml:space="preserve" ...>
    [There is a lot of space inside these quotation marks "        ".]
</TextBox>
```

In this example, the text in the text box will include the hard return and tab that appear before the actual text. It will also include the series of spaces inside the text and the hard return that follows the text.

If you just want to keep the spaces inside, you'll need to use this less-readable markup:

```
<TextBox Name="txtQuestion" xml:space="preserve" ...
 >[There is a lot of space inside these quotation marks "          ".]</TextBox>
```

The trick here is to make sure no whitespace appears between the opening > and your content, or between your content and the closing <.

Once again, this issue only applies to XAML markup. If you set the text in a text box programmatically, all the spaces you include are used.

Events

So far, all the attributes you've seen map to properties. However, attributes can also be used to attach event handlers. The syntax for this is EventName="EventHandlerMethodName".

For example, the Button control provides a Click event. You can attach an event handler like this:

```
<Button ... Click="cmdAnswer_Click">
```

This assumes that there is a method with the name cmdAnswer_Click in the code-behind class. The event handler must have the correct signature (that is, it must match the delegate for the Click event). Here's the method that does the trick:

```
private void cmdAnswer_Click(object sender, RoutedEventArgs e)
{
    this.Cursor = Cursors.Wait;

    // Dramatic delay...
    System.Threading.Thread.Sleep(TimeSpan.FromSeconds(3));

    AnswerGenerator generator = new AnswerGenerator();
    txtAnswer.Text = generator.GetRandomAnswer(txtQuestion.Text);
    this.Cursor = null;
}
```

As you may have noticed from the signature of this event handler, the event model in WPF is different than in earlier versions of .NET. It supports a new model that relies on *event routing*. You'll learn more in Chapter 6.

In many situations, you'll use attributes to set properties and attach event handlers on the same element. WPF always follows the same sequence: first it sets the Name property (if set), then it attaches any event handlers, and lastly it sets the properties. This means that any event handlers that respond to property changes will fire when the property is set for the first time.

■**Note** It's possible to embed code (such as event handlers) directly in a XAML document using the Code element. However, this technique is thoroughly discouraged and it doesn't have any practical application in WPF. This approach isn't supported by Visual Studio and it isn't discussed in this book.

Visual Studio helps you out with IntelliSense when you add an event handler attribute. Once you enter the equals sign (for example, after you've typed **Click=** in the <Button> element), it shows a drop-down list with all the suitable event handlers in your code-behind class, as shown in Figure 2-2. If you need to create a new event handler to handle this event, you simply need to choose <New Event Handler> from the top of the list.

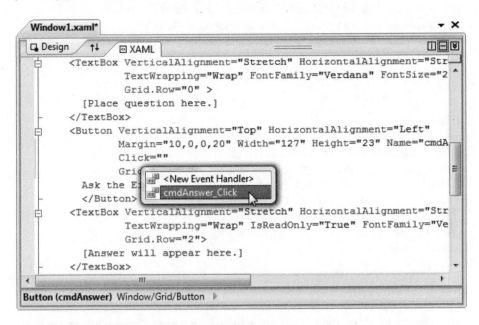

Figure 2-2. *Attaching an event with Visual Studio IntelliSense*

The Full Eight Ball Example

Now that you've considered the fundamentals of XAML, you know enough to walk through the definition for the window in Figure 2-1. Here's the complete XAML markup:

```
<Window x:Class="EightBall.Window1"
 xmlns="http://schemas.microsoft.com/winfx/2006/xaml/presentation"
 xmlns:x="http://schemas.microsoft.com/winfx/2006/xaml"
 Title="Eight Ball Answer" Height="328" Width="412" >
  <Grid Name="grid1">
    <Grid.RowDefinitions>
      <RowDefinition Height="*" />
      <RowDefinition Height="Auto" />
      <RowDefinition Height="*" />
    </Grid.RowDefinitions>
    <TextBox VerticalAlignment="Stretch" HorizontalAlignment="Stretch"
     Margin="10,10,13,10" Name="txtQuestion"
     TextWrapping="Wrap" FontFamily="Verdana" FontSize="24"
     Grid.Row="0">
      [Place question here.]
    </TextBox>
```

```
<Button VerticalAlignment="Top" HorizontalAlignment="Left"
 Margin="10,0,0,20" Width="127" Height="23" Name="cmdAnswer"
 Click="cmdAnswer_Click" Grid.Row="1">
  Ask the Eight Ball
</Button>
<TextBox VerticalAlignment="Stretch" HorizontalAlignment="Stretch"
 Margin="10,10,13,10" Name="txtAnswer" TextWrapping="Wrap"
 IsReadOnly="True" FontFamily="Verdana" FontSize="24" Foreground="Green"
 Grid.Row="2">
  [Answer will appear here.]
</TextBox>

<Grid.Background>
  <LinearGradientBrush>
    <LinearGradientBrush.GradientStops>
      <GradientStop Offset="0.00" Color="Red" />
      <GradientStop Offset="0.50" Color="Indigo" />
      <GradientStop Offset="1.00" Color="Violet" />
    </LinearGradientBrush.GradientStops>
  </LinearGradientBrush>
</Grid.Background>
  </Grid>
</Window>
```

Remember, you probably won't write the XAML for an entire user interface by hand—doing so would be unbearably tedious. However, you might have good reason to edit the XAML code to make a change that would be awkward to accomplish in the designer. You might also find yourself reviewing XAML to get a better idea of how a window works.

Using Types from Other Namespaces

So far, you've seen how to create a basic user interface in XAML using the classes that are a part of WPF. However, XAML is designed as an all-purpose way to instantiate .NET objects, including ones that are in other non-WPF namespaces and those you create yourself.

It might seem odd to consider creating objects that aren't designed for onscreen display in a XAML window, but there are a number of scenarios where it makes sense. One example is when you use data binding and you want to draw information from another object to display in a control. Another example is if you want to set the property of a WPF object using a non-WPF object.

For example, you can fill a WPF ListBox with data objects. The ListBox will call the ToString() method to get the text to display for each item in the list. (Or for an even better list you can create a *data template* that extracts multiple pieces of information and formats them appropriately. This technique is described in Chapter 17.)

In order to use a class that isn't defined in one of the WPF namespaces, you need to map the .NET namespace to an XML namespace. XAML has a special syntax for doing this, which looks like this:

```
xmlns:Prefix="clr-namespace:Namespace;assembly=AssemblyName"
```

Typically, you'll place this namespace mapping in the root element of your XAML document, right after the attributes that declare the WPF and XAML namespaces. You'll also fill in the three italicized bits with the appropriate information, as explained here:

- **Prefix** is the XML prefix you want to use to indicate that namespace in your XAML markup. For example, the XAML language uses the x: prefix.

- **Namespace** is the fully qualified .NET namespace name.

- **AssemblyName** is the assembly where the type is declared, without the .dll extension. This assembly must be referenced in your project. If you want to use your project assembly, leave this out.

For example, here's how you would gain access to the basic types in the System namespace and map them to the prefix sys:

```
xmlns:sys="clr-namespace:System;assembly=mscorlib"
```

Here's how you would gain access to the types you've declared in the MyProject namespace of the current project and map them to the prefix local:

```
xmlns:local="clr-namespace:MyNamespace"
```

Now, to create an instance of a class in one of these namespaces, you use the namespace prefix:

```
<local:MyObject ...></local:MyObject>
```

■Tip Remember, you can use any namespace prefix you want, as long as you are consistent throughout your XAML document. However, the sys and local prefixes are commonly used when importing the System namespace and the namespace for the current project. You'll see them used throughout this book.

Ideally, every class you want to use in XAML will have a no-argument constructor. If it does, the XAML parser can create the corresponding object, set its properties, and attach any event handlers you supply. XAML doesn't support parameterized constructors, and all the elements in WPF elements include a no-argument constructor. Additionally, you need to be able to set all the details you want using public properties. XAML doesn't allow you to set public fields or call methods.

If the class you want to use doesn't have a no-argument constructor, you're in a bit of a bind. If you're trying to create a simple primitive (such as a string, date, or numeric type), you can supply the string representation of your data as content inside your tag. The XAML parser will then use the type converter to convert that string into the appropriate object. Here's an example with the DateTime structure:

```
<sys:DateTime>10/30/2010 4:30 PM</sys:DateTime>
```

This works because the DateTime class uses the TypeConverter attribute to link itself to the DateTimeConverter. The DateTimeConverter recognizes this string as a valid DateTime

object and converts it. When you're using this technique you can't use attributes to set any
properties for your object.

If you want to create a class that doesn't have a no-argument constructor and there isn't a
suitable type converter to use, you're out of luck.

Note Some developers get around these limitations by creating custom wrapper classes. For example,
the FileStream class doesn't include a no-argument constructor. However, you could create a wrapper class
that does. Your wrapper class would create the required FileStream object in its constructor, retrieve the
information it needs, and then close the FileStream. This type of solution is seldom ideal because it invites
hard-coding information in your class constructor and it complicates exception handling. In most cases, it's a
better idea to manipulate the object with a little event handling code and leave it out of your XAML entirely.

The following example puts it all together. It maps the sys: prefix to the System namespace and uses the System namespace to create three DateTime objects, which are used to fill
a list:

```
<Window x:Class="WindowsApplication1.Window1"
    xmlns="http://schemas.microsoft.com/winfx/2006/xaml/presentation"
    xmlns:x="http://schemas.microsoft.com/winfx/2006/xaml"
    xmlns:sys="clr-namespace:System;assembly=mscorlib"
    Width="300" Height="300"
    >
  <ListBox>
    <ListBoxItem>
      <sys:DateTime>10/13/2010 4:30 PM</sys:DateTime>
    </ListBoxItem>
    <ListBoxItem>
      <sys:DateTime>10/29/2010 12:30 PM</sys:DateTime>
    </ListBoxItem>
    <ListBoxItem>
      <sys:DateTime>10/30/2010 2:30 PM</sys:DateTime>
    </ListBoxItem>
  </ListBox>
</Window>
```

Loading and Compiling XAML

As you've already learned, XAML and WPF are separate, albeit complementary, technologies. As
a result, it's quite possible to create a WPF application that doesn't use the faintest bit of XAML.

Altogether, there are three distinct coding styles that you can use to create a WPF application:

- **Code-only.** This is the traditional approach used in Visual Studio for Windows Forms
  applications. It generates a user interface through code statements.

- **Code and uncompiled markup (XAML).** This is a specialized approach that makes sense in certain scenarios where you need highly dynamic user interfaces. You load part of the user interface from a XAML file at runtime using the XamlReader class from the System.Windows.Markup namespace.

- **Code and compiled markup (BAML).** This is the preferred approach for WPF, and the one that Visual Studio supports. You create a XAML template for each window and this XAML is compiled into BAML and embedded in the final assembly. At runtime the compiled BAML is extracted and used to regenerate the user interface.

In the following sections, you'll dig deeper into these three models and how they actually work.

Code-Only

Code-only development is a less common (but still fully supported) avenue for writing a WPF application without any XAML. The obvious disadvantage to code-only development is that it has the potential to be extremely tedious. WPF controls don't include parameterized constructors, so even adding a simple button to a window takes several lines of code. One potential advantage is that code-only development offers unlimited avenues for customization. For example, you could generate a form full of input controls based on the information in a database record, or you could conditionally decide to add or substitute controls depending on the current user. All you need is a sprinkling of conditional logic. By contrast, when you use XAML documents they're embedded in your assembly as fixed unchanging resources.

Note Even though you probably won't create a code-only WPF application, you probably will use the code-only approach to creating a WPF control at some point when you need an adaptable chunk of user interface.

Following is the code for a modest window with a single button and an event handler (see Figure 2-3). When the window is created, the constructor calls an InitializeComponent() method that instantiates and configures the button and the form and hooks up the event handler.

Note To create this example, you must code the Window1 class from scratch (right-click the Solution Explorer, and choose Add ➤ Class to get started). You can't choose Add ➤ Window, because that will add a code file *and* a XAML template for your window, complete with an automatically generated Initialize-Component() method.

```
using System.Windows;
using System.Windows.Controls;
using System.Windows.Markup;
```

```
public class Window1 : Window
{
    private Button button1;

    public Window1()
    {
        InitializeComponent();
    }

    private void InitializeComponent()
    {
        // Configure the form.
        this.Width = this.Height = 285;
        this.Left = this.Top = 100;
        this.Title = "Code-Only Window";

        // Create a container to hold a button.
        DockPanel panel = new DockPanel();

        // Create the button.
        button1 = new Button();
        button1.Content = "Please click me.";
        button1.Margin = new Thickness(30);

        // Attach the event handler.
        button1.Click += button1_Click;

        // Place the button in the panel.
        IAddChild container = panel;
        container.AddChild(button1);

        // Place the panel in the form.
        container = this;
        container.AddChild(panel);
    }

    private void button1_Click(object sender, RoutedEventArgs e)
    {
        button1.Content = "Thank you.";
    }
}
```

Conceptually, the Window1 class in this example is a lot like a form in a traditional Windows Forms application. It derives from the base Window class and adds a private member variable for every control. For clarity, this class performs its initialization work in a dedicated InitializeComponent() method.

Figure 2-3. *A single-button window*

To get this application started, you can use a Main() method with code like this:

```
public class Program : Application
{
    [STAThread()]
    static void Main()
    {
        Program app = new Program();
        app.MainWindow = new Window1();
        app.MainWindow.ShowDialog();
    }
}
```

Code and Uncompiled XAML

One of the most interesting ways to use XAML is to parse it on the fly with the XamlReader. For example, imagine you start with this XAML content in a file named Window1.xml:

```
<DockPanel xmlns="http://schemas.microsoft.com/winfx/2006/xaml/presentation">
  <Button Name="button1" Margin="30">Please click me.</Button>
</DockPanel>
```

At runtime, you can load this content into a live window to create the same window shown in Figure 2-3. Here's the code that does it:

```
using System.Windows;
using System.Windows.Controls;
using System.Windows.Markup;
using System.IO;

public class Window1 : Window
{
```

```
    private Button button1;

    public Window1()
    {
        InitializeComponent();
    }

    private void InitializeComponent()
    {
        // Configure the form.
        this.Width = this.Height = 285;
        this.Left = this.Top = 100;
        this.Title = "Dynamically Loaded XAML";

        // Get the XAML content from an external file.
        FileStream s = new FileStream("Window1.xml", FileMode.Open);
        DependencyObject rootElement = (DependencyObject)XamlReader.Load(s);
        this.Content = rootElement;

        // Find the control with the appropriate name.
        button1 = (Button)LogicalTreeHelper.FindLogicalNode(rootElement, "button1");

        // Wire up the event handler.
        button1.Click += button1_Click;
    }

    private void button1_Click(object sender, RoutedEventArgs e)
    {
        button1.Content = "Thank you.";
    }
}
```

Here, the InitializeComponent() method opens a FileStream on the Window1.xml file.
It then uses the Load() method of the XamlReader to convert the content in this file into a
DependencyObject, which is the base from which all WPF controls derive. This Dependency-
Object can be placed inside any type of container (for example, a Panel), but in this example
it's used as the content for the entire form.

■**Note** In this example, you're loading an element—the DockPanel object—from the XAML file. Alternatively, you could load an entire XAML window (like the eight ball example). In this case, you would cast the
object returned by XamlReader.Load() to the Window type and then call its Show() or ShowDialog() method to
show it.

To manipulate the button, you need to find the corresponding control object in the dynamically loaded content. The LogicalTreeHelper serves this purpose because it has the ability to search an entire tree of control objects, digging down as many layers as necessary until it finds the object with the name you've specified. An event handler is then attached to the Button.Click event.

Another alternative is to use the FrameworkElement.FindName() method. In this example, the root element is a DockPanel object. Like all the controls in a WPF window, DockPanel derives from FrameworkElement. That means you can replace this code:

```
button1 = (Button)LogicalTreeHelper.FindLogicalNode(rootElement, "button1");
```

with this equivalent approach:

```
FrameworkElement frameworkElement = (FrameworkElement)rootElement;
button1 = (Button)frameworkElement.FindName("button1");
```

Obviously, loading XAML dynamically won't be as efficient as compiling the XAML to BAML and then loading the BAML at runtime, particularly if your user interface is complex. However, it opens up a number of possibilities for building dynamic user interfaces.

For example, you could create an all-purpose survey application that reads a form file from a web service and then displays the corresponding survey controls (labels, text boxes, check boxes, and so on). The form file would be an ordinary XML document with WPF tags, which you load into an existing form using the XamlReader. To collect the results once the survey is filled out, you simply need to enumerate over all the input controls and grab their content.

Code and Compiled XAML

You've already seen the most common way to use XAML with the eight ball example shown in Figure 2-1 and dissected throughout this chapter. This is the method used by Visual Studio, and it has several advantages that this chapter has touched on already:

- Some of the plumbing is automatic. There's no need to perform ID lookup with the LogicalTreeHelper or wire up event handlers in code.

- Reading BAML at runtime is faster than reading XAML.

- Deployment is easier. Because BAML is embedded in your assembly as one or more resources, there's no way to lose it.

- XAML files can be edited in other programs, such as design tools. This opens up the possibility for better collaboration between programmers and designers. (You also get this benefit when using uncompiled XAML, as described in the previous section.)

Visual Studio uses a two-stage compilation process when you're compiling a WPF application. The first step is to compile the XAML files into BAML using the xamlc.exe compiler. For example, if your project includes a file name Window1.xaml, the compiler will create a temporary file named Window1.baml and place it in the obj\Debug subfolder (in your project folder). At the same time, a partial class is created for your window, using the language of your choice. For example, if you're using C#, the compiler will create a file named Window1.g.cs in the obj\Debug folder. The *g* stands for *generated*.

The partial class includes three things:

- Fields for all the controls in your window.

- Code that loads the BAML from the assembly, thereby creating the tree of objects. This happens when the constructor calls InitializeComponent().

- Code that assigns the appropriate control object to each field and connects all the event handlers. This happens in a method named Connect(), which the BAML parser calls every time it finds a named object.

The partial class does *not* include code to instantiate and initialize your controls because that task is performed by the WPF engine when the BAML is processed by the Application.LoadComponent() method.

■**Note** As part of the XAML compilation process, the XAML compiler needs to create a partial class. This is only possible if the language you're using supports the .NET Code DOM model. C# and VB support Code DOM, but if you're using a third-party language you'll need to make sure this support exists before you can create compiled XAML applications.

Here's the (slightly abbreviated) Window1.g.cs file from the eight ball example shown in Figure 2-1:

```
public partial class Window1 : System.Windows.Window,
    System.Windows.Markup.IComponentConnector
{
    // The control fields.
    internal System.Windows.Controls.TextBox txtQuestion;
    internal System.Windows.Controls.Button cmdAnswer;
    internal System.Windows.Controls.TextBox txtAnswer;

    private bool _contentLoaded;

    // Load the BAML.
    public void InitializeComponent()
    {
        if (_contentLoaded) {
            return;
        }
        _contentLoaded = true;

        System.Uri resourceLocater = new System.Uri("window1.baml",
            System.UriKind.RelativeOrAbsolute);
        System.Windows.Application.LoadComponent(this, resourceLocater);
    }
```

```
// Hook up each control.
void System.Windows.Markup.IComponentConnector.Connect(int connectionId,
  object target)
{
    switch (connectionId)
    {
        case 1:
            txtQuestion = ((System.Windows.Controls.TextBox)(target));
            return;
        case 2:
            cmdAnswer = ((System.Windows.Controls.Button)(target));
            cmdAnswer.Click += new System.Windows.RoutedEventHandler(
              cmdAnswer_Click);
            return;
        case 3:
            txtAnswer = ((System.Windows.Controls.TextBox)(target));
            return;
    }
    this._contentLoaded = true;
}
}
```

When the XAML-to-BAML compilation stage is finished, Visual Studio uses the appropriate language compiler to compile your code and the generated partial class files. In the case of a C# application, it's the csc.exe compiler that handles this task. The compiled code becomes a single assembly (EightBall.exe) and the BAML for each window is embedded as a separate resource.

XAML Only

The previous sections show you how to use XAML from a code-based application. As a .NET developer, this is what you'll spend most of your time doing. However, it's also possible to use a XAML file without creating any code. This is called a *loose* XAML file. Loose XAML files can be opened directly in Internet Explorer. (Assuming you've installed the .NET Framework 3.0 or are running Windows Vista, which has it preinstalled.)

■**Note** If your XAML file uses code, it can't be opened in Internet Explorer. However, you can build a browser-based application that breaks through this boundary. Chapter 9 describes how.

At this point, it probably seems relatively useless to create a loose XAML file—after all, what's the point of a user interface with no code to drive it? However, as you explore XAML you'll discover several features that are entirely declarative. These include features such as animation, triggers, data binding, and links (which can point to other loose XAML files). Using these features, you can build a few very simple no-code XAML files. They won't seem like complete applications, but they can accomplish quite a bit more than static HTML pages.

To try out a loose XAML page, take a .xaml file and make these changes:

- Remove the Class attribute on the root element.

- Remove any attributes that attach event handlers (such as the Button.Click attribute).

- Change the name of the opening and closing tag from Window to Page. Internet Explorer can only show hosted pages, not stand-alone windows.

You can then double-click your .xaml file to load it up in Internet Explorer. Figure 2-4 shows a converted EightBall.xaml page, which is included with the downloadable code for this chapter. You can type in the top text box, but because the application lacks the code-behind file, nothing happens when you click the button. If you want to create a more capable browser-based application that can include code, you'll need to use the techniques described in Chapter 9.

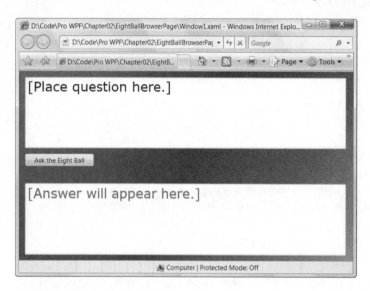

Figure 2-4. *A XAML page in a browser*

The Last Word

In this chapter, you took a tour through a simple XAML file and learned its syntax at the same time. Here's what you saw:

- You considered key XAML ingredients, such as type converters, markup extensions, and attached properties.

- You learned how to wire up a code-behind class that can handle the events raised by your controls.

- You considered the compilation process that takes a standard WPF application into a compiled executable file. At the same time, you took a look at three variants: creating a WPF application through code alone, creating a WPF page with nothing but XAML, and loading XAML manually at runtime.

Although you haven't had an exhaustive look at every detail of XAML markup, you've learned enough to reap all its benefits. Now, your attention can shift to the WPF technology itself, which holds some of the most interesting surprises. In the next chapter you'll start out by considering the core of the WPF application model: the Application class.

CHAPTER 3

■ ■ ■

The Application

While it's running, every WPF application is represented by an instance of the System.Windows.Application class. This class tracks all the open windows in your application, decides when your application shuts down, and fires application events that you can handle to perform initialization and cleanup.

The Application class isn't one of the more fascinating parts of WPF. However, because every WPF application uses the Application class, learning how it works is required reading. In this chapter, you'll quickly get the essentials.

Note The System.Windows.Application class plays the same role in a WPF application as the System.Windows.Forms.Application class plays in a Windows Forms application. But Microsoft, always happy to reinvent the wheel, has given each one subtly different members and functionality.

The Application Life Cycle

In WPF, applications go through a straightforward life cycle. Shortly after your application begins, the application object is created. As your application runs, various application events fire, which you may choose to monitor. Finally, when the application object is released, your application ends.

Creating an Application Object

The simplest way to use the Application class is to create it by hand. The following example shows the bare minimum: an application entry point (a Main() method) that creates a window named Window1 and fires up a new application:

```
using System;
using System.Windows;

public class Startup
{
    [STAThread()]
    static void Main()
    {
```

```
        // Create the application.
        Application app = new Application();

        // Create the main window.
        Window1 win = new Window1();

        // Launch the application and show the main window.
        app.Run(win);
    }
}
```

When you pass a window to the Application.Run() method, that window is set as the main window and exposed to your entire application through the Application.MainWindow property. The Run() method then fires the Application.Startup event and shows the main window.

You could accomplish the same effect with this more long-winded code:

```
// Create the application.
Application app = new Application();

// Create, assign, and show the main window.
Window1 win = new Window1();
app.MainWindow = win;
win.Show();

// Keep the application alive.
app.Run();
```

Both approaches give your application all the momentum it needs. When started in this way, your application continues running until the main window *and every other window* is closed. At that point, the Run() method returns, and any additional code in your Main() method is executed before the application winds down.

■**Note** If you want to start your application using a Main() method, you need to designate the class that contains the Main() method as the startup object in Visual Studio. To do so, double-click the Properties node in the Solution Explorer, and change the selection in the Startup Object list. Ordinarily, you don't need to take this step, because Visual Studio creates the Main() method for you based on the XAML application template. You'll learn about the application template in the next section.

Deriving a Custom Application Class

Although the approach shown in the previous section (instantiating the base Application class and calling the Run() method) works perfectly well, it's not the pattern that Visual Studio uses when you create a new WPF application.

Instead, Visual Studio derives a custom class from the Application class. In a simple application, this approach has no meaningful effect. However, if you're planning to handle application events, it provides a neater model, because you can place all your event handling code in the Application-derived class.

The model Visual Studio uses for the Application class is essentially the same as the model it uses for the windows. The starting point is a XAML template, which is named App.xaml by default. Here's what it looks like (without the resources section, which you'll learn about in Chapter 11):

```
<Application x:Class="TestApplication.App"
    xmlns="http://schemas.microsoft.com/winfx/2006/xaml/presentation"
    xmlns:x="http://schemas.microsoft.com/winfx/2006/xaml"
    StartupUri="Window1.xaml"
    >
</Application>
```

As you might remember from Chapter 2, the Class attribute is used in XAML to create a class derived from the element. Thus, this class creates a class that derives from Application, with the name TestApplication.App. (TestApplication is the name of the project, which is the same as the namespace where the class is defined, and App is the name that Visual Studio uses for the custom class that derives from Application. If you want, you can change the class name to something more exciting.)

The Application tag not only creates a custom application class, but it also sets the StartupUri property to identify the XAML document that represents the main window. As a result, you don't need to explicitly instantiate this window using code—the XAML parser will do it for you.

As with windows, the application class is defined in two separate portions that are fused together at compile time. The automatically generated portion isn't visible in your project, but it contains the Main() entry point and the code for starting the application. It looks something like this:

```
using System;
using System.Windows;

public partial class App : Application
{
    [STAThread()]
    public static void Main()
    {
        TestApplication.App app = new TestApplication.App();
        app.InitializeComponent();
        app.Run();
    }

    public void InitializeComponent()
    {
        this.StartupUri = new Uri("Window1.xaml", System.UriKind.Relative);
    }
}
```

If you're really interested in seeing the custom application class that the XAML template creates, look for the App.g.cs file in the obj\Debug folder inside your project directory.

The only difference between the automatically generated code shown here and a custom application class that you might create on your own is that the automatically generated class uses the StartupUri property instead of setting the MainWindow property or passing the main window as a parameter to the Run() method. You're free to create a custom application class that uses this approach, so long as you use the same URI format. You need to create a relative Uri object that names a XAML document that's in your project. (This XAML document is compiled and embedded in your application assembly as a BAML resource. The resource name is the name of the original XAML file. In the previous example, the application contains a resource named Window1.xaml with the compiled XAML.)

■Note The URI system you see here is an all-purpose way to refer to resources in your application. You'll learn more about how it works in Chapter 11.

The second portion of the custom application class is stored in your project in a file like App.xaml.cs. It contains the event handling code you add. Initially, it's empty:

```
public partial class App : Application
{
}
```

This file is merged with the automatically generated application code through the magic of partial classes.

Application Shutdown

Ordinarily, the Application class keeps your application alive as long as at least one window is still open. If this isn't the behavior you want, you can adjust the Application.ShutdownMode. If you're instantiating your Application object by hand, you need to set the ShutdownMode property before you call Run(). If you're using the App.xaml file, you can simply set the ShutdownMode property in the XAML markup.

You have three choices for the shutdown mode, as listed in Table 3-1.

Table 3-1. *Values from the ShutdownMode Enumeration*

Name	Description
OnLastWindowClose	This is the default behavior—your application keeps running as long as there is at least one window in existence. If you close the main window, the Application.MainWindow property still refers to the object that represents the closed window. (Optionally, you can use code to reassign the MainWindow property to point to a different window.)
OnMainWindowClose	This is the traditional approach—your application stays alive only as long as the main window is open.
OnExplicitShutdown	The application never ends (even if all the windows are closed) unless you call Application.Shutdown(). This approach might make sense if your application is a front end for a long-running background task or if you just want to use more complex logic to decide when your application should close (at which point you'll call the Application.Shutdown() method).

For example, if you want to use the OnMainWindowClose approach and you're using the App.xaml file, you need to make this addition:

```
<Application x:Class="TestApplication.App"
    xmlns="http://schemas.microsoft.com/winfx/2006/xaml/presentation"
    xmlns:x="http://schemas.microsoft.com/winfx/2006/xaml"
    StartupUri="Window1.xaml" ShutdownMode="OnMainWindowClose"
    >
</Application>
```

No matter what shutdown method you choose, you can always use the Application.Shutdown() method to end your application immediately. (Of course, when you call the Shutdown() method, your application doesn't necessarily stop running right away. Calling Application.Shutdown() causes the Application.Run() method to return immediately, but there may be additional code that runs in the Main() method or responds to the Application.Exit event.)

■**Note** When ShutdownMode is OnMainWindowClose and you close the main window, the Application object will automatically close all the other windows before the Run() method returns. The same is true if you call Application.Shutdown(). This is significant, because these windows may have event handling code that fires when they are being closed.

Application Events

Initially, the App.xaml.cs file doesn't contain any code. Although no code is required, you can add code that handles application events. The Application class provides a small set of useful events. Table 3-2 lists the most important ones. It leaves out the events that are used solely for navigation applications (which are discussed in Chapter 9).

Table 3-2. *Application Events*

Name	Description
Startup	Occurs after the Application.Run() method is called and just before the main window is shown (if you passed the main window to the Run() method). You can use this event to check for any command-line arguments, which are provided as an array through the StartupEventArgs.Args property. You can also use this event to create and show the main window (instead of using the StartupUri property in the App.xaml file).
Exit	Occurs when the application is being shut down for any reason, just before the Run() method returns. You can't cancel the shutdown at this point, although the code in your Main() method could relaunch the application. You can use the Exit event to set the integer exit code that's returned from the Run() method.
SessionEnding	Occurs when the Windows session is ending—for example, when the user is logging off or shutting down the computer. (You can find out which one it is by examining the SessionEndingCancelEventArgs.ReasonSessionEnding property.) You can also cancel the shutdown by setting SessionEndingCancelEventArgs.Cancel to true. If you don't, WPF will call the Application.Shutdown() method when your event handler ends.

Continued

Table 3-2. *Continued*

Name	Description
Activated	Occurs when one of the windows in the application gets activated. This occurs when you switch from another Windows program to this application. It also occurs the first time you show a window.
Deactivated	Occurs when a window in the application gets deactivated. This occurs when you switch to another Windows program.
DispatcherUnhandledException	Occurs when an unhandled exception occurs anywhere in your application (on the main application thread). (The application dispatcher catches these exceptions.) By responding to this event, you can log critical errors, and you can even choose to neutralize the exception and continue running your application by setting the DispatcherUnhandledExceptionEventArgs.Handled property to true. You should take this step only if you can be guaranteed that the application is still in a valid state and can continue.

You have two choices for handling events: you can attach an event handler, or you can override the corresponding protected method. If you choose to handle application events, you don't need to use delegate code to wire up your event handler. Instead, you can attach it using an attribute in the App.xaml file. For example, if you have this event handler:

```
private void App_DispatcherUnhandledException(object sender,
  DispatcherUnhandledExceptionEventArgs e)
{
    MessageBox.Show("An unhandled " + e.Exception.GetType().ToString() +
      " exception was caught and ignored.");
    e.Handled = true;
}
```

you can connect it with this XAML:

```
<Application x:Class="PreventSessionEnd.App"
    xmlns="http://schemas.microsoft.com/winfx/2006/xaml/presentation"
    xmlns:x="http://schemas.microsoft.com/winfx/2006/xaml"
    StartupUri="Window1.xaml"
    DispatcherUnhandledException="App_DispatcherUnhandledException"
    >
</Application>
```

For each application event (as listed in Table 3-2), a corresponding method is called to raise the event. The method name is the same as the event name, except it's prefixed with the word *On*, so Startup becomes OnStartup(), Exit becomes OnExit(), and so on. This pattern is extremely common in .NET (and Windows Forms programmers will recognize it well). The only exception is the DispatcherExceptionUnhandled event—there's no OnDispatcherExceptionUnhandled() method, so you always need to use an event handler.

Here's a custom application class that overrides OnSessionEnding and prevents both the system and itself from shutting down if a flag is set:

```
public partial class App : Application
{
    private bool unsavedData = false;
    public bool UnsavedData
    {
        get { return unsavedData; }
        set { unsavedData = value; }
    }

    protected override void OnStartup(StartupEventArgs e)
    {
        base.OnStartup(e);
        UnsavedData = true;
    }

    protected override void OnSessionEnding(SessionEndingCancelEventArgs e)
    {
        base.OnSessionEnding(e);

        if (UnsavedData)
        {
            e.Cancel = true;
            MessageBox.Show(
              "The application attempted to be closed as a result of " +
              e.ReasonSessionEnding.ToString() +
              ". This is not allowed, as you have unsaved data.");
        }
    }
}
```

When overriding application methods, it's a good idea to begin by calling the base class implementation. Ordinarily, the base class implementation does little more than raise the corresponding application event.

Obviously, a more sophisticated implementation of this technique wouldn't use a message box—it would show some sort of confirmation dialog box that would give the user the choice of continuing (and quitting both the application and Windows) or canceling the shutdown.

Application Tasks

Now that you understand how the Application object fits into a WPF application, you're ready to take a look at how you can apply it to a few common scenarios. In the following sections, you'll consider how you can process command-line arguments, support interaction between windows, add document tracking, and create a single-instance application.

Handling Command-Line Arguments

To process command-line arguments, you react to the Application.Startup event. The arguments are provided as an array of strings through the StartupEventArgs.Args property.

For example, imagine you want to load a document when its name is passed as a command-line argument. In this case, it makes sense to read the command-line arguments and perform the extra initialization you need. The following example implements this pattern by responding to the Application.Startup event. It doesn't set the Application.StartupUri property at any point—instead the main window is instantiated using code.

```
public partial class App : Application
{
    private static void App_Startup(object sender, StartupEventArgs e)
    {
        // Create, but don't show the main window.
        FileViewer win = new FileViewer();

        if (e.Args.Length > 0)
        {
            string file = e.Args[0];
            if (System.IO.File.Exists(file))
            {
                // Configure the main window.
                win.LoadFile(file);
            }
        }
        else
        {
            // (Perform alternate initialization here when
            //  no command-line arguments are supplied.)
        }

        // This window will automatically be set as the Application.MainWindow.
        win.Show();
    }
}
```

This method initializes the main window, which is then shown when the App_Startup() method ends. This code assumes that the FileViewer class has a public method (that you've added) named LoadFile(). Here's one possible example, which simply reads (and displays) the text in the file you've identified:

```
public partial class FileViewer : Window
{
    ...

    public void LoadFile(string path)
    {
        this.Content = File.ReadAllText(path);
        this.Title = path;
    }
}
```

You can try an example of this technique with the sample code for this chapter.

> **Note** If you're a seasoned Windows Forms programmer, the code in the LoadFile() method looks a little strange. It sets the Content property of the current Window, which determines what the window displays in its client area. Interestingly enough, WPF windows are actually a type of content control (meaning they derive from the ContentControl class). As a result, they can contain (and display) a single object. It's up to you whether that object is a string, a control, or (more usefully) a panel that can host multiple controls. You'll learn much more about the WPF content model in the following chapters.

Accessing the Current Application

You can get the current application instance from anywhere in your application using the static Application.Current property. This allows rudimentary interaction between windows, because any window can get access the current Application object and through that obtain a reference to the main window.

```
Window main = Application.Current.MainWindow;
MessageBox.Show("The main window is " + main.Title);
```

Of course, if you want to access any methods, properties, or events that you've added to your custom main window class, you need to cast the window object to the right type. If the main window is an instance of a custom MainWindow class, you can use code like this:

```
MainWindow main = (MainWindow)Application.Current.MainWindow;
main.DoSomething();
```

A window can also examine the contents of the Application.Windows collection, which provides references to *all* the currently open windows:

```
foreach (Window window in Application.Current.Windows)
{
    MessageBox.Show(window.Title + " is open.");
}
```

In practice, most applications prefer to use a more structured form of interaction between windows. If you have several long-running windows that are open at the same time and they need to communicate in some way, it makes more sense to hold references to these windows in a custom application class. That way you can always find exactly the window you need. Similarly, if you have a document-based application, you might choose to create a collection that tracks document windows but nothing else. The next section considers this technique.

■**Note** Windows (including the main window) are added to the Windows collection as they're shown, and they're removed when they're closed. For this reason, the position of windows in the collection may change, and you can't assume you'll find a specific window object at a specific position.

Interacting Between Windows

As you've seen, the custom application class is a great place to put code that reacts to different application events. There's one other purpose that an Application class can fill quite nicely: storing references to important windows so one window can access another.

■**Tip** This technique makes sense when you have a modeless window that lives for a long period of time and might be accessed in several different classes (not just the class that created it). If you're simply showing a modal dialog box as part of your application, this technique is overkill. In this situation, the window won't exist for very long, and the code that creates the window is the only code that needs to access it. (To brush up on the difference between modal windows, which interrupt application flow until they're closed, and modeless windows, which don't, refer to Chapter 8.)

For example, imagine you want to keep track of all the document windows that your application uses. To that end, you might create a dedicated collection in your custom application class. Here's an example that uses a generic List collection to hold a group of custom window objects. In this example, each document window is represented by an instance of a class named Document:

```
public partial class App : Application
{
    private List<Document> documents = new List<Document>();

    public List<Document> Documents
    {
        get { return documents; }
        set { documents = value; }
    }
}
```

Now, when you create a new document, you simply need to remember to add it to the Documents collection. Here's an event handler that responds to a button click and does the deed:

```
private void cmdCreate_Click(object sender, RoutedEventArgs e)
{
    Document doc = new Document();
    doc.Owner = this;
    doc.Show();
    ((App)Application.Current).Documents.Add(doc);
}
```

Alternatively, you could respond to an event like Window.Loaded in the Document class to make sure the document object always registers itself in the Documents collection when it's created.

Note This code also sets the Window.Owner property so that all the document windows are displayed "on top" of the main window that creates them. You'll learn more about the Owner property when you consider windows in detail in Chapter 8.

Now you can use that collection elsewhere in your code to loop over all the documents and use public members. In this case, the Document class includes a custom SetContent() method that updates its display:

```
private void cmdUpdate_Click(object sender, RoutedEventArgs e)
{
    foreach (Document doc in ((App)Application.Current).Documents)
    {
        doc.SetContent("Refreshed at " + DateTime.Now.ToLongTimeString() + ".");
    }
}
```

Figure 3-1 demonstrates this application. The actual end result isn't terribly impressive, but the interaction is worth noting—it demonstrates a safe, disciplined way for your windows to interact through a custom application class. It's superior to using the Windows property, because it's strongly typed, and it holds only Document windows (not a collection of all the windows in your application). It also gives you the ability to categorize the windows in another, more useful way—for example, in a Dictionary collection with a key name for easy lookup. In a document-based application, you might choose to index windows in a collection by file name.

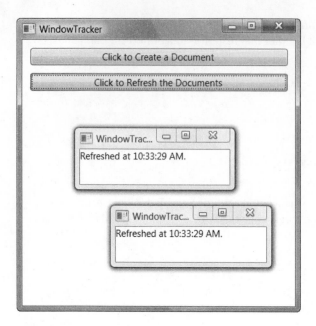

Figure 3-1. *Allowing windows to interact*

■**Note** When interacting between windows, don't forget your object-oriented smarts—always use a layer of custom methods, properties, and events that you've added to the window classes. Never expose the fields or controls of a form to other parts of your code. If you do, you'll quickly wind up with a tightly coupled interface where one window reaches deep into the inner workings of another, and you won't be able to enhance either class without breaking the murky interdependencies between them.

Single-Instance Applications

Ordinarily, you can launch as many copies of a WPF application as you want. In some scenarios, this design makes perfect sense. However, in other cases it's a problem, particularly when building document-based applications.

For example, consider Microsoft Word. No matter how many documents you open (or how you open them), only a single instance of winword.exe is loaded at a time. As you open new documents, they appear in the new windows, but a single application remains in control of all the document windows. This design is the best approach if you want to reduce the overhead of your application, centralize certain features (for example, create a single print queue manager), or integrate disparate windows (for example, offer a feature that tiles all the currently open document windows next to each other).

WPF doesn't provide a native solution for single-instance applications, but you can use several workarounds. The basic technique is to check whether another instance of your application is already running when the Application.Startup event fires. The simplest way to do this is to use a systemwide *mutex* (a synchronization object provided by the operating system that allows for interprocess communication). This approach is simple but limited—most significantly, there's no way for the new instance of an application to communicate with the existing instance. This is a problem in a document-based application, because the new instance may need to tell the existing instance to open a specific document, if it's passed on the command line. (For example, when you double-click a .doc file in Windows Explorer and Word is already running, you expect Word to load the requested file.) This communication is more complex, and it's usually performed through remoting or Windows Communication Foundation (WCF). A proper implementation needs to include a way to discover the remoting server and use it to transfer command-line arguments.

But the simplest approach, and the one that's currently recommended by the WPF team, is to use the built-in support that's provided in Windows Forms and originally intended for Visual Basic applications. This approach handles the messy plumbing behind the scenes.

So, how can you use a feature that's designed for Windows Forms and Visual Basic to manage a WPF application in C#? Essentially, the old-style application class acts as a wrapper for your WPF application class. When your application is launched, you'll create the old-style application class, which will then create the WPF application class. The old-style application class handles the instance management, while the WPF application class handles the real application. Figure 3-2 shows how these parts interact.

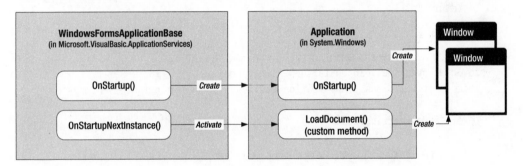

Figure 3-2. *Wrapping the WPF application with a WindowsFormsApplicationBase*

The first step to use this approach is to add a reference to the Microsoft.VisualBasic.dll assembly and derive a custom class from the Microsoft.VisualBasic.ApplicationServices.WindowsFormsApplicationBase class. This class provides three important members that you use for instance management:

- The IsSingleInstance property enables a single-instance application. You set this property to true in the constructor.

- The OnStartup() method is triggered when the application starts. You override this method and create the WPF application object at this point.

- The OnStartupNextInstance() method is triggered when another instance of the application starts up. This method provides access to the command-line arguments. At this point, you'll probably call a method in your WPF application class to show a new window but not create another application object.

Here's the code for the custom class that's derived from WindowsFormsApplicationBase:

```
public class SingleInstanceApplicationWrapper :
  Microsoft.VisualBasic.ApplicationServices.WindowsFormsApplicationBase
{
    public SingleInstanceApplicationWrapper()
    {
        // Enable single-instance mode.
        this.IsSingleInstance = true;
    }

    // Create the WPF application class.
    private WpfApp app;
    protected override bool OnStartup(
      Microsoft.VisualBasic.ApplicationServices.StartupEventArgs e)
    {
        app = new WpfApp();
        app.Run();

        return false;
    }

    // Direct multiple instances.
    protected override void OnStartupNextInstance(
      Microsoft.VisualBasic.ApplicationServices.StartupNextInstanceEventArgs e)
    {
        if (e.CommandLine.Count > 0)
        {
            app.ShowDocument(e.CommandLine[0]);
        }
    }
}
```

When the application starts, this class creates an instance of WpfApp, which is a custom WPF application class (a class that derives from System.Windows.Application). The WpfApp class includes some startup logic that shows a main window, along with a custom ShowDocument() window that loads a document window for a given file. Every time a file name is passed to SingleInstanceApplicationWrapper through the command line, SingleInstanceApplication-Wrapper calls WpfApp.ShowDocument().

Here's the code for the WpfApp class:

```
public class WpfApp : System.Windows.Application
{
    protected override void OnStartup(System.Windows.StartupEventArgs e)
    {
        base.OnStartup(e);
        WpfApp.current = this;

        // Load the main window.
```

```
        DocumentList list = new DocumentList();
        this.MainWindow = list;
        list.Show();

        // Load the document that was specified as an argument.
        if (e.Args.Length > 0) ShowDocument(e.Args[0]);
    }

    public void ShowDocument(string filename)
    {
        try
        {
            Document doc = new Document();
            doc.LoadFile(filename);
            doc.Owner = this.MainWindow;
            doc.Show();

            // If the application is already loaded, it may not be visible.
            // This attempts to give focus to the new window.
            doc.Activate();
        }
        catch
        {
            MessageBox.Show("Could not load document.");
        }
    }
}
```

The only missing detail now (aside from the DocumentList and Document windows) is the entry point for the application. Because the application needs to create the SingleInstanceApplicationWrapper class before the App class, the application needs to start with a traditional Main() method, rather than an App.xaml file. Here's the code you need:

```
public class Startup
{
    [STAThread]
    public static void Main(string[] args)
    {
        SingleInstanceApplicationWrapper wrapper =
          new SingleInstanceApplicationWrapper();
        wrapper.Run(args);
    }
}
```

These three classes—SingleInstanceApplicationWrapper, WpfApp, and Startup—form the basis for a single-instance WPF application. Using these bare bones, it's possible to create a more sophisticated example. For example, the downloadable code for this chapter modifies the WpfApp class so it maintains a list of open documents (as demonstrated earlier). Using

WPF data binding (a feature described in Chapter 16), the DocumentList window displays the currently open documents. Figure 3-3 shows an example with three open documents.

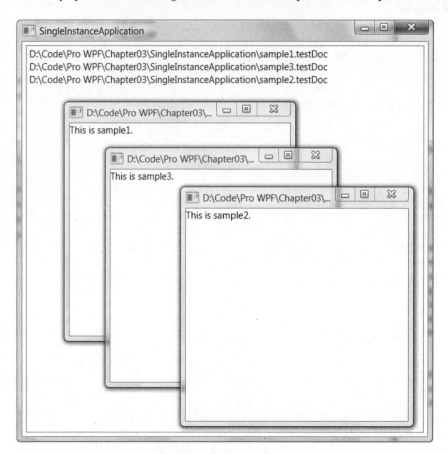

Figure 3-3. *A single-instance application with a central window*

Finally, the SingleInstanceApplication example includes a FileRegistrationHelper class that registers a file extension using the classes in the Microsoft.Win32 namespace:

```
string extension = ".testDoc";
string title = "SingleInstanceApplication";
string extensionDescription = "A Test Document";
FileRegistrationHelper.SetFileAssociation(
  extension, title + "." + extensionDescription);
```

This code needs to be executed only once. After the registration is in place, every time you double-click a file with the extension .testDoc, the SingleInstanceApplication is started, and the file is passed as a command-line argument. If the SingleInstanceApplication is already running, the SingleInstanceApplicationWrapper.OnStartupNextInstance() method is called, and the new document is loaded by the existing application.

■**Note** Single-instance application support will eventually make its way to WPF in a future version. For now, this workaround provides the same functionality with only a little more work required.

WINDOWS VISTA AND UAC

File registration is a task that's usually performed by a setup program. One problem with including it in your application code is that it requires elevated permissions that the user running the application might not have. This is particularly a problem with the User Account Control (UAC) feature in Windows Vista. In fact, by default this code will fail with a security-related exception.

In the eyes of UAC, all applications have one of three *run levels*:

- **asInvoker.** The application inherits the process token of the parent process (the process that launched it). The application won't get administrator privileges unless the user specifically requests them, even if the user is logged on as an administrator. This is the default.

- **requireAdministrator.** If the current user is a member of the Administrators group, a UAC confirmation dialog box appears. Once the user accepts this confirmation, the application gets administrator privileges. If the user is not a member of the Administrators group, a dialog box appears where the user can enter the user name and password of an account that does have administrator privileges.

- **highestAvailable.** The application gets the highest privileges according to its group membership. For example, if the current user is a member of the Administrators group, the application gets administrator privileges (once the user accepts the UAC confirmation). The advantage of this run level is that the application will still run if administrator privileges aren't available, unlike requireAdministrator.

Ordinarily, your application runs with the asInvoker run level. To request administrator privileges, you must right-click the application EXE file and choose Run As Administrator when you start it. To get administrator privileges when testing your application Visual Studio, you must right-click the Visual Studio shortcut and choose Run As Administrator.

If your application needs administrator privileges, you can choose to require them with the requireAdministrator run level or request them with the highestAvailable run level. Either way, you need to create a *manifest*—a file with a block of XML that will be embedded in your compiled assembly. To add a manifest, right-click your project in the Solution Explorer, and choose Add ➤ New Item. Pick the Application Manifest File template, and click Add.

The content of the manifest file is the relatively simple block of XML shown here:

```xml
<?xml version="1.0" encoding="utf-8"?>
<asmv1:assembly manifestVersion="1.0"
 xmlns="urn:schemas-microsoft-com:asm.v1"
 xmlns:asmv1="urn:schemas-microsoft-com:asm.v1"
 xmlns:asmv2="urn:schemas-microsoft-com:asm.v2">
  <assemblyIdentity version="1.0.0.0" name="MyApplication.app"/>
  <trustInfo xmlns="urn:schemas-microsoft-com:asm.v2">
    <security>
      <requestedPrivileges xmlns="urn:schemas-microsoft-com:asm.v3">
        <requestedExecutionLevel level="asInvoker" />
```

```
            </requestedPrivileges>
         </security>
      </trustInfo>
</asmv1:assembly>
```

To change the run level, simply modify the level attribute of the <requestedExcutionLevel> element. Valid values are asInvoker, requireAdministrator, and highestAvailable.

In some cases, you might want to request administrator privileges in specific scenarios. In the file registration example, you might choose to request administrator privileges only when the application is run for the first time and needs to create the registration. This allows you to avoid unnecessary UAC warnings. The easiest way to implement this pattern is to put the code that requires higher privileges in a separate executable, which you can then call when necessary.

The Last Word

In this chapter, you took a quick look at the WPF application model. To manage a simple WPF application, you need to do nothing more than create an instance of the Application class and call the Run() method. However, most applications go further and derive a custom class from the Application class. And as you saw, this custom class is an ideal tool for handling application events and an ideal place to track the windows in your application or implement a single-instance pattern.

You haven't quite plumbed the full reaches of the Application class—there's still a Resources collection to consider, where you can define objects you want to reuse throughout your application, like styles that can be applied to controls in multiple windows. However, it's safe to leave these details to Chapter 11, when you explore the WPF resource model in more detail. Instead, in the next chapter you'll consider how controls are organized into realistic windows using the WPF layout panels.

CHAPTER 4

■ ■ ■

Layout

Half the battle in any user interface design is organizing the content in a way that's attractive, practical, and flexible. But the real challenge is making sure that your layout can adapt itself gracefully to different window sizes.

In WPF, you shape layout using different *containers*. Each container has its own layout logic—some stack elements, others arrange them in a grid of invisible cells, and so on. If you've programmed with Windows Forms, you'll be surprised to find that coordinate-based layout is strongly discouraged in WPF. Instead, the emphasis is on creating more flexible layouts that can adapt to changing content, different languages, and a variety of window sizes. For most developers moving to WPF, the new layout system is a great surprise—and the first real challenge.

In this chapter, you'll see how the WPF layout model works, and you'll begin using the basic layout containers. You'll also consider several common layout examples—everything from a basic dialog box to a resizable split window—in order to learn the fundamentals of WPF layout.

Understanding Layout in WPF

The WPF layout model represents a dramatic shift in the way Windows developers approach user interfaces. In order to understand the new WPF layout model, it helps to take a look at what's come before.

In .NET 1.x, Windows Forms provided a fairly primitive layout system. Controls were fixed in place using hard-coded coordinates. The only saving grace was *anchoring* and *docking*—two features that allowed controls to move or resize themselves along with their container. Anchoring and docking were great for creating simple resizable windows—for example, keeping OK and Cancel buttons stuck to the bottom-right corner of a window, or allowing a TreeView to expand to fill an entire form—but they couldn't handle serious layout challenges. For example, anchoring and docking couldn't implement bi-pane proportional resizing (dividing extra space equally among two regions). They also weren't much help if you had highly dynamic content, such as a label that might expand to hold more text than anticipated, causing it to overlap other nearby controls.

In .NET 2.0, Windows Forms filled the gaps with two new layout containers: the FlowLayoutPanel and TableLayoutPanel. Using these controls, you could create more sophisticated web-like interfaces. Both layout containers allowed their contained controls to grow and bump other controls out of the way. This made it easier to deal with dynamic content, create modular interfaces, and localize your application. However, the layout panels still felt like an add-on to the core Windows Forms layout system, which used fixed coordinates. The layout panels were an elegant solution, but you could see the duct tape holding it all together.

WPF introduces a new layout system that's heavily influenced by the developments in Windows Forms. This system reverses the .NET 2.0 model (coordinate-based layout with optional flow-based layout panels) by making flow-based layout the standard and giving only rudimentary support for coordinate-based layout. The benefits of this shift are enormous. Developers can now create resolution-independent, size-independent interfaces that scale well on different monitors, adjust themselves when content changes, and handle the transition to other languages effortlessly. However, before you can take advantage of these changes, you'll need to start thinking about layout a little differently.

The WPF Layout Philosophy

A WPF window can hold only a single element. To fit in more than one element and create a more practical user interface, you need to place a container in your window and then add other elements to that container.

■**Note** This limitation stems from the fact that the Window class is derived from ContentControl, which you'll study more closely in Chapter 5.

In WPF, layout is determined by the container that you use. Although there are several containers to choose from, the "ideal" WPF window follows a few key principles:

- **Elements (like controls) should not be explicitly sized.** Instead, they grow to fit their content. For example, a button expands as you add more text. You can limit controls to acceptable sizes by setting a maximum and minimum size.

- **Elements do not indicate their position with screen coordinates.** Instead, they are arranged by their container based on their size, order, and (optionally) other information that's specific to the layout container. If you need to add whitespace between elements, you use the Margin property.

■**Tip** Hard-coded sizes and positions are evil because they limit your ability to localize your interface, and they make it much more difficult to deal with dynamic content.

- **Layout containers "share" the available space among their children.** They attempt to give each element its preferred size (based on its content) if the space is available. They can also distribute extra space to one or more children.

- **Layout containers can be nested.** A typical user interface begins with the Grid, WPF's most capable container, and contains other layout containers that arrange smaller groups of elements, such as captioned text boxes, items in a list, icons on a toolbar, a column of buttons, and so on.

Although there are exceptions to these rules, they reflect the overall design goals of WPF. In other words, if you follow these guidelines when you build a WPF application, you'll create a better, more flexible user interface. If you break these rules, you'll end up with a user interface that isn't well suited to WPF and is much more difficult to maintain.

The Layout Process

WPF layout takes place in two stages: a *measure* stage and an *arrange* stage. In the measure stage, the container loops through its child elements and asks them to provide their preferred size. In the arrange stage, the container places the child elements in the appropriate position.

Of course, an element can't always get its preferred size—sometimes the container isn't large enough to accommodate it. In this case, the container must truncate the offending element to fit the visible area. As you'll see, you can often avoid this situation by setting a minimum window size.

■**Note** Layout containers don't provide any scrolling support. Instead, scrolling is provided by a specialized content control—the ScrollViewer—that can be used just about anywhere. You'll learn about the ScrollViewer in Chapter 5.

The Layout Containers

All the WPF layout containers are panels that derive from the abstract System.Windows. Controls.Panel class (see Figure 4-1). The Panel class adds a small set of members, including the three public properties that are detailed in Table 4-1.

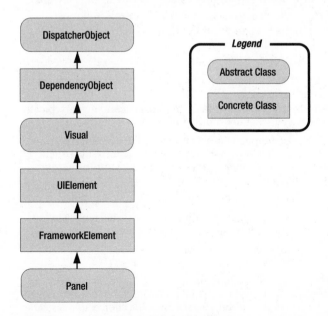

Figure 4-1. *The hierarchy of the Panel class*

Table 4-1. *Public Properties of the Panel Class*

Name	Description
Background	The brush that's used to paint the panel background. You must set this property to a non-null value if you want to receive mouse events. (If you want to receive mouse events but you don't want to display a solid background, just set the background color to Transparent.) You'll learn more about basic brushes in Chapter 7 (and more advanced brushes in Chapter 13).
Children	The collection of items that's stored in the panel. This is the first level of items—in other words, these items may themselves contain more items.
IsItemsHost	A Boolean value that's true if the panel is being used to show the items that are associated with an ItemsControl (such as the nodes in a TreeView or the list entries in a ListBox). Most of the time you won't even be aware that a list control is using a behind-the-scenes panel to manage the layout of its items. However, this detail becomes more important if you want to create a customized list that lays out children in a different way (for example, a ListBox that tiles images). You'll use this technique in Chapter 17.

Note The Panel class also has a bit of internal plumbing you can use if you want to create your own layout container. Most notably, you can override the MeasureOverride() and ArrangeOverride() methods inherited from FrameworkElement to change the way the panel handles the measure stage and the arrange stage when organizing its child elements. You'll learn how to create a custom panel in Chapter 24.

On its own, the base Panel class is nothing but a starting point for other more specialized classes. WPF provides a number of Panel-derived classes that you can use to arrange layout. The most fundamental of these are listed in Table 4-2. As with all WPF controls and most visual elements, these classes are found in the System.Windows.Controls namespace.

Table 4-2. *Core Layout Panels*

Name	Description
StackPanel	Places elements in a horizontal or vertical stack. This layout container is typically used for small sections of a larger, more complex window.
WrapPanel	Places elements in a series of wrapped lines. In horizontal orientation, the WrapPanel lays items out in a row from left to right and then onto subsequent lines. In vertical orientation, the WrapPanel lays out items in a top-to-bottom column and then uses additional columns to fit the remaining items.
DockPanel	Aligns elements against an entire edge of the container.
Grid	Arranges elements in rows and columns according to an invisible table. This is one of the most flexible and commonly used layout containers.
UniformGrid	Places elements in an invisible table but forces all cells to have the same size. This layout container is used infrequently.
Canvas	Allows elements to be positioned absolutely using fixed coordinates. This layout container is the most similar to traditional Windows Forms, but it doesn't provide anchoring or docking features. As a result, it's an unsuitable choice for a resizable window unless you're willing to do a fair bit of work.

Along with these core containers, there are several more specialized panels that you'll encounter in various controls. These include panels that are dedicated to holding the child items of a particular control—such as TabPanel (the tabs in a TabControl), ToolbarPanel (the buttons in a Toolbar), and ToolbarOverflowPanel (the commands in a Toolbar's overflow menu). There's also a VirtualizingStackPanel, which databound list controls use to minimize their overhead, and an InkCanvas, which is similar to the Canvas but has support for handling stylus input on the TabletPC. (For example, depending on the mode you choose, the InkCanvas supports drawing with the pointer to select onscreen elements. And although it's a little counterintuitive, you can use the InkCanvas with an ordinary computer and a mouse.)

Simple Layout with the StackPanel

The StackPanel is one of the simplest layout containers. It simply stacks its children in a single row or column.

For example, consider this window, which contains a stack of three buttons:

```
<Window x:Class="Layout.SimpleStack"
    xmlns="http://schemas.microsoft.com/winfx/2006/xaml/presentation"
    xmlns:x="http://schemas.microsoft.com/winfx/2006/xaml"
    Title="Layout" Height="223" Width="354"
    >
  <StackPanel>
    <Label>A Button Stack</Label>
    <Button>Button 1</Button>
    <Button>Button 2</Button>
    <Button>Button 3</Button>
    <Button>Button 4</Button>
  </StackPanel>
</Window>
```

Figure 4-2 shows the window that results.

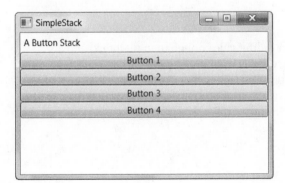

Figure 4-2. *The StackPanel in action*

USING THE STACKPANEL IN VISUAL STUDIO

It's relatively easy to create this example using the designer in Visual Studio. Begin by deleting the root Grid element (if it's there). Then, drag a StackPanel into the window. Next, drag the other elements (the label and four buttons) into the window, in the top-to-bottom order you want.

If you want to rearrange the elements in the StackPanel, you can't simply drag and drop them. Instead, right-click the element you want to move, and choose an option from the Order submenu. The ordering options correspond to the order of the elements in the markup, with the first element occupying the back position and the last element occupying the front position. Thus, you can move an element down to the bottom of the StackPanel (using Bring to Front), up to the top (using Send to Back), or one position down or up (using Bring Forward and Send Backward).

You need to consider a few quirks when you create a user interface with Visual Studio. When you drag elements from the Toolbox to a window, Visual Studio adds certain details to your markup. Visual Studio automatically assigns a name to every new control (which is harmless but unnecessary). It also adds hard-coded Width and Height values, which is much more limiting.

As discussed earlier, explicit sizes limit the flexibility of your user interface. In many cases, it's better to let controls size themselves to fit their content or size themselves to fit their container. In the current example, fixed sizes are a reasonable approach to give the buttons a consistent width. However, a better approach would be to let the largest button size itself to fit its content and have all smaller buttons stretch themselves to match. (This design, which requires the use of a Grid, is described later in this chapter.) And no matter what approach you use with the button, you almost certainly want to remove the hard-coded Width and Height values for the StackPanel, so it can grow or shrink to fit the available space in the window.

By default, a StackPanel arranges elements from top to bottom, making each one as tall as is necessary to display its content. In this example, that means the labels and buttons are sized just large enough to comfortably accommodate the text inside. All elements are stretched to the full width of the StackPanel, which is the width of the window. If you widen the window, the StackPanel widens as well, and the buttons stretch themselves to fit.

The StackPanel can also be used to arrange elements horizontally by setting the Orientation property:

```
<StackPanel Orientation="Horizontal">
```

Now elements are given their minimum width (wide enough to fit their text) and are stretched to the full height of the containing panel. Depending on the current size of the window, this may result in some elements that don't fit, as shown in Figure 4-3.

Clearly, this doesn't provide the flexibility real applications need. Fortunately, you can fine-tune the way the StackPanel and other layout containers work using layout properties, as described next.

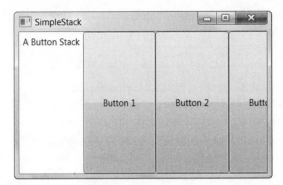

Figure 4-3. *The StackPanel with horizontal orientation*

Layout Properties

Although layout is determined by the container, the child elements can still get their say. In fact, layout panels work in concert with their children by respecting a small set of layout properties, as listed in Table 4-3.

Table 4-3. *Layout Properties*

Name	Description
HorizontalAlignment	Determines how a child is positioned inside a layout container when there's extra horizontal space available. You can choose Center, Left, Right, or Stretch.
VerticalAlignment	Determines how a child is positioned inside a layout container when there's extra vertical space available. You can choose Center, Top, Bottom, or Stretch.
Margin	Adds a bit of breathing room around an element. The Margin property is an instance of the System.Windows.Thickness structure, with separate components for the top, bottom, left, and right edges.
MinWidth and MinHeight	Sets the minimum dimensions of an element. If an element is too large for its layout container, it will be cropped to fit.
MaxWidth and MaxHeight	Sets the maximum dimensions of an element. If the container has more room available, the element won't be enlarged beyond these bounds, even if the HorizontalAlignment and VerticalAlignment properties are set to Stretch.
Width and Height	Explicitly sets the size of an element. This setting overrides a Stretch value for the HorizontalAlignment or VerticalAlignment properties. However, this size won't be honored if it's outside of the bounds set by the MinWidth, MinHeight, MaxWidth, and MaxHeight.

All of these properties are inherited from the base FrameworkElement class and are therefore supported by all the graphical widgets you can use in a WPF window.

■**Note** As you learned in Chapter 2, different layout containers can provide *attached properties* to their children. For example, all the children of a Grid object gain Row and Column properties that allow them to choose the cell where they're placed. Attached properties allow you to set information that's specific to a particular layout container. However, the layout properties in Table 4-3 are generic enough that they apply to many layout panels. Thus, these properties are defined as part of the base FrameworkElement class.

This list of properties is just as notable for what it *doesn't* contain. If you're looking for familiar position properties, such as Top, Right, and Location, you won't find them. That's because most layout containers (all except for the Canvas) use automatic layout and don't give you the ability to explicitly position elements.

Alignment

To understand how these properties work, take another look at the simple StackPanel shown in Figure 4-2. In this example—a StackPanel with vertical orientation—the VerticalAlignment property has no effect because each element is given as much height as it needs and no more. However, the HorizontalAlignment *is* important. It determines where each element is placed in its row.

Ordinarily, the default HorizontalAlignment is Left for a label and Stretch for a Button. That's why every button takes the full column width. However, you can change these details:

```
<StackPanel>
  <Label HorizontalAlignment="Center">A Button Stack</Label>
  <Button HorizontalAlignment="Left">Button 1</Button>
  <Button HorizontalAlignment="Right">Button 2</Button>
  <Button>Button 3</Button>
  <Button>Button 4</Button>
</StackPanel>
```

Figure 4-4 shows the result. The first two buttons are given their minimum sizes and aligned accordingly, while the bottom two buttons are stretched over the entire StackPanel. If you resize the window, you'll see that the label remains in the middle and the first two buttons stay stuck to either side.

■**Note** The StackPanel also has its own HorizontalAlignment and VerticalAlignment properties. By default, both of these are set to Stretch, and so the StackPanel fills its container completely. In this example, that means the StackPanel fills the window. If you use different settings, the StackPanel will be made just large enough to fit the widest control.

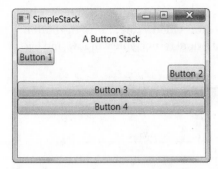

Figure 4-4. *A StackPanel with aligned buttons*

Margin

There's an obvious problem with the StackPanel example in its current form. A well-designed window doesn't just contain elements—it also includes a bit of extra space in between the elements. To introduce this extra space and make the StackPanel example less cramped, you can set control margins.

When setting margins, you can set a single width for all sides, like this:

```
<Button Margin="5">Button 3</Button>
```

Alternatively, you can set different margins for each side of a control in the order *left, top, right, bottom*:

```
<Button Margin="5,10,5,10">Button 3</Button>
```

In code, margins are set using the Thickness structure:

```
cmd.Margin = new Thickness(5);
```

Getting the right control margins is a bit of an art because you need to consider how the margin settings of adjacent controls influence one another. For example, if you have two buttons stacked on top of each other, and the topmost button has a bottom margin of 5, and the bottommost button has a top margin of 5, you have a total of 10 units of space between the two buttons.

Ideally, you'll be able to keep different margin settings as consistent as possible and avoid setting distinct values for the different margin sides. For instance, in the StackPanel example it makes sense to use the same margins on the buttons and on the panel itself, as shown here:

```
<StackPanel Margin="3">
  <Label Margin="3" HorizontalAlignment="Center">
  A Button Stack</Label>
  <Button Margin="3" HorizontalAlignment="Left">Button 1</Button>
  <Button Margin="3" HorizontalAlignment="Right">Button 2</Button>
  <Button Margin="3">Button 3</Button>
  <Button Margin="3">Button 4</Button>
</StackPanel>
```

This way, the total space between two buttons (the sum of the two button margins) is the same as the total space between the button at the edge of the window (the sum of the button margin and the StackPanel margin). Figure 4-5 shows this more respectable window, and Figure 4-6 shows how the margin settings break down.

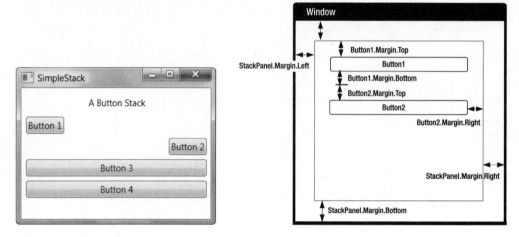

Figure 4-5. *Adding margins between elements*   **Figure 4-6.** *How margins are combined*

Minimum, Maximum, and Explicit Sizes

Finally, every element includes Height and Width properties that allow you to give it an explicit size. However, it's rarely a good idea to take this step. Instead, use the maximum and minimum size properties to lock your control into the right range, if necessary.

■**Tip** Think twice before setting an explicit size in WPF. In a well-designed layout, it shouldn't be necessary. If you do add size information, you risk creating a more brittle layout that can't adapt to changes (such as different languages and window sizes) and truncates your content.

For example, you might decide that the buttons in your StackPanel should stretch to fit the StackPanel but be made no larger than 200 units wide and no smaller than 100 units wide. (By default, buttons start with a minimum width of 75 units.) Here's the markup you need:

```
<StackPanel Margin="3">
  <Label Margin="3" HorizontalAlignment="Center">
   A Button Stack</Label>
  <Button Margin="3" MaxWidth="200" MinWidth="100">Button 1</Button>
  <Button Margin="3" MaxWidth="200" MinWidth="100">Button 2</Button>
  <Button Margin="3" MaxWidth="200" MinWidth="100">Button 3</Button>
  <Button Margin="3" MaxWidth="200" MinWidth="100">Button 4</Button>
</StackPanel>
```

Tip At this point, you might be wondering if there's an easier way to set properties that are standardized across several elements, such as the button margins in this example. The answer is *styles*—a feature that allows you to reuse property settings and even apply them automatically. You'll learn about styles in Chapter 12.

When the StackPanel sizes a button, it considers several pieces of information:

- **The minimum size.** Each button will always be at least as large as the minimum size.

- **The maximum size.** Each button will always be smaller than the maximum size (unless you've incorrectly set the maximum size to be smaller than the minimum size).

- **The content.** If the content inside the button requires a greater width, the StackPanel will attempt to enlarge the button. (You can find out the size that the button wants by examining the DesiredSize property, which returns the minimum width or the content width, whichever is greater.)

- **The size of the container.** If the minimum width is larger than the width of the Stack-Panel, a portion of the button will be cut off. Otherwise, the button will not be allowed to grow wider than the StackPanel, even if it can't fit all its text on the button surface.

- **The horizontal alignment.** Because the button uses a HorizontalAlignment of Stretch (the default), the StackPanel will attempt to enlarge the button to fill the full width of the StackPanel.

The trick to understanding this process is to realize that the minimum and maximum size set the absolute bounds. Within those bounds, the StackPanel tries to respect the button's desired size (to fit its content) and its alignment settings.

Figure 4-7 sheds some light on how this works with the StackPanel. On the left is the window at its minimum size. The buttons are 100 units each, and the window cannot be resized to be narrower. If you shrink the window from this point, the right side of each button will be clipped off. (You can prevent this possibility by applying the MinWidth property to the window itself, so the window can't go below a minimum width.)

As you enlarge the window, the buttons grow with it until they reach their maximum of 200 units. From this point on, if you make the window any larger the extra space is added to either side of the button (as shown on the right).

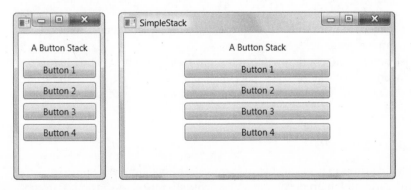

Figure 4-7. *Constrained button sizing*

■**Note** In some situations, you might want to use code that checks how large an element is in a window. The Height and Width properties are no help because they indicate your desired size settings, which might not correspond to the actual rendered size. In an ideal scenario, you'll let your elements size to fit their content, and the Height and Width properties won't be set at all. However, you can find out the actual size used to render an element by reading the ActualHeight and ActualWidth properties. But remember, these values may change when the window is resized or the content inside it changes.

AUTOMATICALLY SIZED WINDOWS

In this example, there's still one element that has hard-coded sizes: the top-level window that contains the StackPanel (and everything else inside). For a number of reasons, it still makes sense to hard-code window sizes:

- In many cases, you want to make a window *smaller* than the desired size of its child elements. For example, if your window includes a container of scrollable text, you'll want to constrain the size of that container so that scrolling is possible. You *don't* want to make the window ridiculously large so that no scrolling is necessary, which is what the container will request. (You'll learn more about scrolling in Chapter 5.)

- The minimum window size may be usable, but it might not give you the most attractive proportions. Some window dimensions just look better.

- Automatic window sizing isn't constrained by the display size of your monitor. So an automatically sized window might be too large to view.

However, automatically sized windows are possible, and they do make sense if you are constructing a simple window with dynamic content. To enable automatic window sizing, remove the Height and Width properties and set the Window.SizeToContent property to WidthAndHeight. The window will make itself just large enough to accommodate all its content. You can also allow a window to resize itself in just one dimension by using a SizeToContent value of Width or Height.

The WrapPanel and DockPanel

Obviously, the StackPanel alone can't help you create a realistic user interface. To complete the picture, the StackPanel needs to work with other more capable layout containers. Only then can you assemble a complete window.

The most sophisticated layout container is the Grid, which you'll consider later in this chapter. But first, it's worth looking at the WrapPanel and DockPanel, which are two more of the simple layout containers provided by WPF. They complement the StackPanel by offering different layout behavior.

The WrapPanel

The WrapPanel lays out controls in the available space, one line or column at a time. By default, the WrapPanel.Orientation property is set to Horizontal; controls are arranged from left to right, and then on subsequent rows. However, you can use Vertical to place elements in multiple columns.

■**Tip** Like the StackPanel, the WrapPanel is really intended for control over small-scale details in a user interface, not complete window layouts. For example, you might use a WrapPanel to keep together the buttons in a toolbar-like control.

Here's an example that defines a series of buttons with different alignments and places them into the WrapPanel:

```
<WrapPanel Margin="3">
  <Button VerticalAlignment="Top">Top Button</Button>
  <Button MinHeight="60">Tall Button 2</Button>
  <Button VerticalAlignment="Bottom">Bottom Button</Button>
  <Button>Stretch Button</Button>
  <Button VerticalAlignment="Center">Centered Button</Button>
</WrapPanel>
```

Figure 4-8 shows how the buttons are wrapped to fit the current size of the WrapPanel (which is determined by the size of the window that contains it). As this example demonstrates, a WrapPanel in horizontal mode creates a series of imaginary rows, each of which is given the height of the tallest contained element. Other controls may be stretched to fit or aligned according to the VerticalAlignment property. In the example on the left in Figure 4-8, all the buttons fit into one tall row and are stretched or aligned to fit. In the example on the right, several buttons have been bumped to the second row. Because the second row does not include an unusually tall button, the row height is kept at the minimum button height. As a result, it doesn't matter what VerticalAlignment setting the various buttons in this row use.

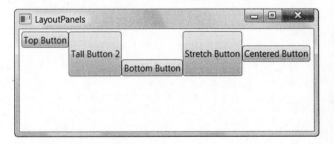 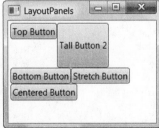

Figure 4-8. *Wrapped buttons*

■**Note** The WrapPanel is the only panel that can't be duplicated with a crafty use of the Grid.

The DockPanel

The DockPanel is a more interesting layout option. It stretches controls against one of its out-side edges. The easiest way to visualize this is to think of the toolbars that sit at the top of many Windows applications. These toolbars are docked to the top of the window. As with the StackPanel, docked elements get to choose one aspect of their layout. For example, if you dock a button to the top of a DockPanel, it's stretched across the entire width of the DockPanel but given whatever height it requires (based on the content and the MinHeight property). On the other hand, if you dock a button to the left side of a container, its height is stretched to fit the container, but its width is free to grow as needed.

The obvious question is this: How do child elements choose the side where they want to dock? The answer is through an attached property named Dock, which can be set to Left, Right, Top, or Bottom. Every element that's placed inside a DockPanel automatically acquires this property.

Here's an example that puts one button on every side of a DockPanel:

```
<DockPanel LastChildFill="True">
  <Button DockPanel.Dock="Top">Top Button</Button>
  <Button DockPanel.Dock="Bottom">Bottom Button</Button>
  <Button DockPanel.Dock="Left">Left Button</Button>
  <Button DockPanel.Dock="Right">Right Button</Button>
  <Button>Remaining Space</Button>
</DockPanel>
```

This example also sets the LastChildFill to true, which tells the DockPanel to give the remaining space to the last element. Figure 4-9 shows the result.

Figure 4-9. *Docking to every side*

Clearly, when docking controls, the order is important. In this example, the top and bottom buttons get the full edge of the DockPanel because they're docked first. When the left and right buttons are docked next, they fit between these two buttons. If you reversed this order, the left and right buttons would get the full sides, and the top and bottom buttons would become narrower because they'd be docked between the two side buttons.

You can dock several elements against the same side. In this case, the elements simply stack up against the side in the order they're declared in your markup. And, if you don't like the spacing or the stretch behavior, you can tweak the Margin, HorizontalAlignment, and VerticalAlignment properties, just as you did with the StackPanel. Here's a modified version of the previous example that demonstrates:

```
<DockPanel LastChildFill="True">
  <Button DockPanel.Dock="Top">A Stretched Top Button</Button>
  <Button DockPanel.Dock="Top" HorizontalAlignment="Center">
   A Centered Top Button</Button>
  <Button DockPanel.Dock="Top" HorizontalAlignment="Left">
   A Left-Aligned Top Button</Button>
  <Button DockPanel.Dock="Bottom">Bottom Button</Button>
  <Button DockPanel.Dock="Left">Left Button</Button>
  <Button DockPanel.Dock="Right">Right Button</Button>
  <Button>Remaining Space</Button>
</DockPanel>
```

The docking behavior is still the same. First the top buttons are docked, then the bottom button, and finally the remaining space is divided between the side buttons and a final button in the middle. Figure 4-10 shows the resulting window.

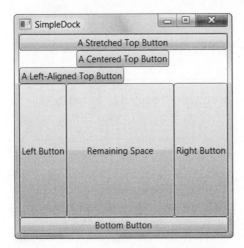

Figure 4-10. *Docking multiple elements to the top*

Nesting Layout Containers

The StackPanel, WrapPanel, and DockPanel are rarely used on their own. Instead, they're used to shape portions of your interface. For example, you could use a DockPanel to place different StackPanel and WrapPanel containers in the appropriate regions of a window.

For example, imagine you want to create a standard dialog box with OK and Cancel buttons in the bottom right-hand corner, and a large content region in the rest of the window. There are several ways to model this interface with WPF, but the easiest option that uses the panels you've seen so far is as follows:

1. Create a horizontal StackPanel to wrap the OK and Cancel buttons together.

2. Place the StackPanel in a DockPanel and use that to dock it to the bottom of the window.

3. Set DockPanel.LastChildFill to true, so you can use the rest of the window to fill in other content. You can add another layout control here, or just an ordinary TextBox control (as in this example).

4. Set the margin properties to give the right amount of whitespace.

Here's the final markup:

```
<DockPanel LastChildFill="True">
  <StackPanel DockPanel.Dock="Bottom" HorizontalAlignment="Right"
   Orientation="Horizontal">
    <Button Margin="10,10,2,10" Padding="3">OK</Button>
    <Button Margin="2,10,10,10" Padding="3">Cancel</Button>
  </StackPanel>
  <TextBox DockPanel.Dock="Top" Margin="10">This is a test.</TextBox>
</DockPanel>
```

Figure 4-11 shows the rather pedestrian dialog box this creates.

■Note In this example, the Padding adds some minimum space between the button border and the content inside (the word "OK" or "Cancel"). You'll learn more about Padding when you consider content controls in Chapter 5.

At first glance, this seems like a fair bit more work than placing controls in precise positions using coordinates in a traditional Windows Forms application. And in many cases, it is. However, the longer setup time is compensated by the ease with which you can change the user interface in the future. For example, if you decide you want the OK and Cancel buttons to be centered at the bottom of the window, you simply need to change the alignment of the StackPanel that contains them:

```
<StackPanel DockPanel.Dock="Bottom" HorizontalAlignment="Center" ... >
```

Figure 4-11. *A basic dialog box*

This design—a simple window with centered buttons—already demonstrates an end result that wasn't possible with Windows Forms in .NET 1.x (at least not without writing code) and required the specialized layout containers with Windows Forms in .NET 2.0. And if you've ever looked at the designer code generated by the Windows Forms serialization process, you'll realize that the markup used here is cleaner, simpler, and more compact. If you add a dash of styles to this window (Chapter 12), you can improve it even further and remove other extraneous details (such as the margin settings) to create a truly adaptable user interface.

■**Tip** If you have a densely nested tree of elements, it's easy to lose sight of the overall structure. Visual Studio provides a handy feature that shows you a tree representation of your elements and allows you to click your way down to the element you want to look at (or modify). This feature is the Document Outline window, and you can show it by choosing View ➤ Other Windows ➤ Document Outline from the menu.

The Grid

The Grid is the most powerful layout container in WPF. Much of what you can accomplish with the other layout controls is also possible with the Grid. The Grid is also an ideal tool for carving your window into smaller regions that you can manage with other panels. In fact, the Grid is so useful that when you add a new XAML document for a window in Visual Studio, it automatically adds the Grid tags as the first-level container, nested inside the root Window element.

The Grid separates elements into an invisible grid of rows and columns. Although more than one element can be placed in a single cell (in which case they overlap), it generally makes sense to place just a single element per cell. Of course, that element may itself be another layout container that organizes its own group of contained controls.

■**Tip** Although the Grid is designed to be invisible, you can set the Grid.ShowGridLines property to true to take a closer look. This feature isn't really intended for prettying up a window. Instead, it's a debugging convenience that's designed to help you understand how the Grid has subdivided itself into smaller regions. This feature is important because you have the ability to control exactly how the Grid chooses column widths and row heights.

Creating a Grid-based layout is a two-step process. First, you choose the number of columns and rows that you want. Next, you assign the appropriate row and column to each contained element, thereby placing it in just the right spot.

You create grids and rows by filling the Grid.ColumnDefinitions and Grid.RowDefinitions collections with objects. For example, if you decide you need two rows and three columns, you'd add the following tags:

```
<Grid ShowGridLines="True">
  <Grid.RowDefinitions>
    <RowDefinition></RowDefinition>
    <RowDefinition></RowDefinition>
  </Grid.RowDefinitions>
  <Grid.ColumnDefinitions>
    <ColumnDefinition></ColumnDefinition>
    <ColumnDefinition></ColumnDefinition>
    <ColumnDefinition></ColumnDefinition>
  </Grid.ColumnDefinitions>

  ...
</Grid>
```

As this example shows, it's not necessary to supply any information in a RowDefinition or ColumnDefinition element. If you leave them empty (as shown here), the Grid will share the space evenly between all rows and columns. In this example, each cell will be exactly the same size, depending on the size of the containing window.

To place individual elements into a cell, you use the attached Row and Column properties. Both these properties take 0-based index numbers. For example, here's how you could create a partially filled grid of buttons:

```
<Grid ShowGridLines="True">
  ...

  <Button Grid.Row="0" Grid.Column="0">Top Left</Button>
  <Button Grid.Row="0" Grid.Column="1">Middle Left</Button>
  <Button Grid.Row="1" Grid.Column="2">Bottom Right</Button>
  <Button Grid.Row="1" Grid.Column="1">Bottom Middle</Button>
</Grid>
```

Each element must be placed into its cell explicitly. This allows you to place more than one element into a cell (which rarely makes sense) or leave certain cells blank (which is often useful). It also means you can declare your elements out of order, as with the final two buttons in this example. However, it makes for clearer markup if you define your controls row by row, and from right to left in each row.

There is one exception. If you don't specify the Grid.Row property, the Grid assumes that it's 0. The same behavior applies to the Grid.Column property. Thus, you leave both attributes off of an element to place it in the first cell of the Grid.

■**Note** The Grid fits elements into predefined rows and columns. This is different than layout containers such as the WrapPanel and StackPanel that create implicit rows or columns as they lay out their children. If you want to create a grid that has more than one row and one column, you must define your rows and columns explicitly using RowDefinition and ColumnDefinition objects.

Figure 4-12 shows how this simple grid appears at two different sizes. Notice that the ShowGridLines property is set to true so that you can see the separation between each column and row.

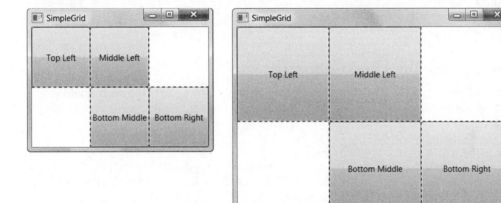

Figure 4-12. *A simple grid*

As you would expect, the Grid honors the basic set of layout properties listed in Table 4-3. That means you can add margins around the content in a cell, you can change the sizing mode so an element doesn't grow to fill the entire cell, and you can align an item along one of the edges of a cell. If you force an element to have a size that's larger than the cell can accommodate, part of the content will be chopped off.

USING THE GRID IN VISUAL STUDIO

When you use a Grid on the Visual Studio design surface, you'll find that it works a bit differently than other layout containers. As you drag an element into a Grid, Visual Studio allows you to place it in a precise position. Visual Studio works this magic by setting the Margin property of your element.

When setting margins, Visual Studio uses the closest corner. For example, if your element is nearest to the top-left corner of the Grid, Visual Studio pads the top and left margins to position the element (and leaves the right and bottom margins at 0). If you drag your element down closer to the bottom-left corner, Visual Studio sets the bottom and left margins instead and sets the VerticalAlignment property to Bottom. This obviously affects how the element will move when the Grid is resized.

Visual Studio's margin-setting process seems straightforward enough, but most of the time it won't create the results you want. Usually, you'll want a more flexible flow layout that allows some elements to expand dynamically and push others out of the way. In this scenario, you'll find that hard-coding position with the Margin property is extremely inflexible. The problems get worse when you add multiple elements, because Visual Studio won't automatically add new cells. As a result, all the elements will be placed in the same cell. Different elements may be aligned to different corners of the Grid, which will cause them to move with respect to one another (and even overlap each other) as the window is resized.

Once you understand how the Grid works, you can correct these problems. The first trick is to configure your Grid before you begin adding elements by defining its rows and columns. (You can edit the RowDefinitions and ColumnDefinitions collections using the Properties window.) Once you've set up the Grid, you can drag and drop the elements you want into the Grid and configure their margin and alignment settings in the Properties window or by editing the XAML by hand.

Fine-Tuning Rows and Columns

If the Grid were simply a proportionately sized collection of rows and columns, it wouldn't be much help. Fortunately, it's not. To unlock the full potential of the Grid, you can change the way each row and column is sized.

The Grid supports three sizing strategies:

- **Absolute sizes.** You choose the exact size using device-independent units. This is the least useful strategy because it's not flexible enough to deal with changing content size, changing container size, or localization.

- **Automatic sizes.** Each row or column is given exactly the amount of space it needs, and no more. This is one of the most useful sizing modes.

- **Proportional sizes.** Space is divided between a group of rows or columns. This is the standard setting for all rows and columns. For example, in Figure 4-12 you'll see that all cells increase in size proportionately as the Grid expands.

For maximum flexibility, you can mix and match these different sizing modes. For example, it's often useful to create several automatically sized rows and then let one or two remaining rows get the leftover space through proportional sizing.

You set the sizing mode using the Width property of the ColumnDefinition object or the Height property of the RowDefinition object to a number. For example, here's how you set an absolute width of 100 device-independent units:

```
<ColumnDefinition Width="100"></ColumnDefinition>
```

To use automatic sizing, you use a value of Auto:

```
<ColumnDefinition Width="Auto"></ColumnDefinition>
```

Finally, to use proportional sizing, you use an asterisk (*):

```
<ColumnDefinition Width="*"></ColumnDefinition>
```

This syntax stems from the world of the Web, where it's used with HTML frames pages. If you use a mix of proportional sizing and other sizing modes, the proportionally sized rows or columns get whatever space is left over.

If you want to divide the remaining space unequally, you can assign a *weight*, which you must place before the asterisk. For example, if you have two proportionately sized rows and you want the first to be half as high as the second, you could share the remaining space like this:

```
<RowDefinition Height="*"></RowDefinition>
<RowDefinition Height="2*"></RowDefinition>
```

This tells the Grid that the height of the second row should be twice the height of the first row. You can use whatever numbers you like to portion out the extra space.

■Note It's easy to interact with ColumnDefinition and RowDefinition objects programmatically. You simply need to know that the Width and Height properties are GridLength objects. To create a GridLength that represents a specific size, just pass the appropriate value to the GridLength constructor. To create a GridLength that represents a proportional (*) size, pass the number to the GridLength constructor, and pass GridUnitType. Start as the second constructor argument. To indicate automatic sizing, use the static property GridLength.Auto.

Using these size modes, you can duplicate the simple dialog box example shown in Figure 4-11 using a top-level Grid container to split the window into two rows, rather than a DockPanel. Here's the markup you'd need:

```
<Grid ShowGridLines="True">
  <Grid.RowDefinitions>
    <RowDefinition Height="*"></RowDefinition>
    <RowDefinition Height="Auto"></RowDefinition>
  </Grid.RowDefinitions>
  <TextBox Margin="10" Grid.Row="0">This is a test.</TextBox>
  <StackPanel Grid.Row="1" HorizontalAlignment="Right" Orientation="Horizontal">
    <Button Margin="10,10,2,10" Padding="3">OK</Button>
    <Button Margin="2,10,10,10" Padding="3">Cancel</Button>
  </StackPanel>
</Grid>
```

■Tip This Grid doesn't declare any columns. This is a shortcut you can take if your Grid uses just one column and that column is proportionately sized (so it fills the entire width of the Grid).

This markup is slightly longer, but it has the advantage of declaring the controls in the order they appear, which makes it easier to understand. In this case, the approach you take is simply a matter of preference. And if you want, you could replace the nested StackPanel with a one-row, two-column Grid.

■**Note** You can create almost any interface using nested Grid containers. (One exception is wrapped rows or columns that use the WrapPanel.) However, when you're dealing with small sections of user interface or laying out a small number of elements, it's often simpler to use the more specialized StackPanel and Dock-Panel containers.

Spanning Rows and Columns

You've already seen how you place elements in cells using the Row and Column attached properties. You can also use two more attached properties to make an element stretch over several cells: RowSpan and ColumnSpan. These properties take the number of rows or columns that the element should occupy.

For example, this button will take all the space that's available in the first and second cell of the first row:

```
<Button Grid.Row="0" Grid.Column="0" Grid.RowSpan="2">Span Button</Button>
```

And this button will stretch over four cells in total by spanning two columns and two rows:

```
<Button Grid.Row="0" Grid.Column="0" Grid.RowSpan="2" Grid.ColumnSpan="2">
  Span Button</Button>
```

Row and column spanning can achieve some interesting effects and is particularly handy when you need to fit elements in a tabular structure that's broken up by dividers or longer sections of content.

Using column spanning, you could rewrite the simple dialog box example from Figure 4-11 using just a single Grid. This Grid divides the window into three columns, spreads the text box over all three, and uses the last two columns to align the OK and Cancel buttons.

```
<Grid ShowGridLines="True">
  <Grid.RowDefinitions>
    <RowDefinition Height="*"></RowDefinition>
    <RowDefinition Height="Auto"></RowDefinition>
  </Grid.RowDefinitions>
  <Grid.ColumnDefinitions>
    <ColumnDefinition Width="*"></ColumnDefinition>
    <ColumnDefinition Width="Auto"></ColumnDefinition>
    <ColumnDefinition Width="Auto"></ColumnDefinition>
  </Grid.ColumnDefinitions>
  <TextBox Margin="10" Grid.Row="0" Grid.Column="0" Grid.ColumnSpan="3">
```

```
    This is a test.</TextBox>
  <Button Margin="10,10,2,10" Padding="3"
    Grid.Row="1" Grid.Column="1">OK</Button>
  <Button Margin="2,10,10,10" Padding="3"
    Grid.Row="1" Grid.Column="2">Cancel</Button>
</Grid>
```

Most developers will agree that this layout isn't clear or sensible. The column widths are determined by the size of the two buttons at the bottom of the window, which makes it difficult to add new content into the existing Grid structure. If you make even a minor addition to this window, you'll probably be forced to create a new set of columns.

As this shows, when you choose the layout containers for a window, you aren't simply interested in getting the correct layout behavior—you also want to build a layout structure that's easy to maintain and enhance in the future. A good rule of thumb is to use smaller layout containers such as the StackPanel for one-off layout tasks, such as arranging a group of buttons. On the other hand, if you need to apply a consistent structure to more than one area of your window (as with the text box column shown later in Figure 4-20), the Grid is an indispensable tool for standardizing your layout.

Split Windows

Every Windows user has seen *splitter bars*—draggable dividers that separate one section of a window from another. For example, when you use Windows Explorer, you're presented with a list of folders (on the left) and a list of files (on the right). You can drag the splitter bar in between to determine what proportion of the window is given to each pane.

In WPF, splitter bars are represented by the GridSplitter class and are a feature of the Grid. By adding a GridSplitter to a Grid, you give the user the ability to resize rows or columns. Figure 4-13 shows a window where a GridSplitter sits between two columns. By dragging the splitter bar, the user can change the relative widths of both columns.

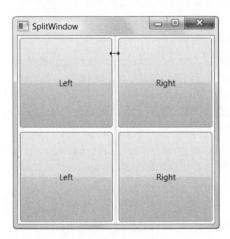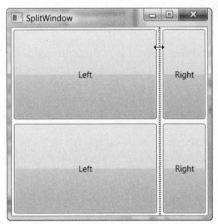

Figure 4-13. *Moving a splitter bar*

Most programmers find that the GridSplitter isn't the most intuitive part of WPF. Understanding how to use it to get the effect you want takes a little experimentation. Here are a few guidelines:

- The GridSplitter must be placed in a Grid cell. You can place the GridSplitter in a cell with existing content, in which case you need to adjust the margin settings so it doesn't overlap. A better approach is to reserve a dedicated column or row for the GridSplitter, with a Height or Width value of Auto.

- The GridSplitter always resizes entire rows or columns (not single cells). To make the appearance of the GridSplitter consistent with this behavior, you should stretch the GridSplitter across an entire row or column, rather than limit it to a single cell. To accomplish this, you use the RowSpan or ColumnSpan properties you considered earlier. For example, the GridSplitter in Figure 4-13 has a RowSpan of 2. As a result, it stretches over the entire column. If you didn't add this setting, it would only appear in the top row (where it's placed), *even though* dragging the splitter bar would resize the entire column.

- Initially, the GridSplitter is invisibly small. To make it usable, you need to give it a minimum size. In the case of a vertical splitter bar (like the one in Figure 4-13), you need to set the VerticalAlignment to Stretch (so it fills the whole height of the available area) and the Width to a fixed size (such as 10 device-independent units). In the case of a horizontal splitter bar, you need to set HorizontalAlignment to Stretch, and Height to a fixed size.

- The GridSplitter alignment also determines whether the splitter bar is horizontal (used to resize rows) or vertical (used to resize columns). In the case of a horizontal splitter bar, you should set VerticalAlignment to Center (which is the default value) to indicate that dragging the splitter resizes the rows that are above and below. In the case of a vertical splitter bar (like the one in Figure 4-13), you should set HorizontalAlignment to Center to resize the columns on either side.

■Note You can change the resizing behavior using the ResizeDirection and ResizeBehavior properties of the GridSplitter. However, it's simpler to let this behavior depend entirely on the alignment settings, which is the default.

Dizzy yet? To reinforce these rules, it helps to take a look at the actual markup for the example shown in Figure 4-13. In the following listing, the GridSplitter details are highlighted:

```
<Grid>
  <Grid.RowDefinitions>
    <RowDefinition></RowDefinition>
    <RowDefinition></RowDefinition>
  </Grid.RowDefinitions>
  <Grid.ColumnDefinitions>
    <ColumnDefinition MinWidth="100"></ColumnDefinition>
```

```
  <ColumnDefinition Width="Auto"></ColumnDefinition>
  <ColumnDefinition MinWidth="50"></ColumnDefinition>
</Grid.ColumnDefinitions>

<Button Grid.Row="0" Grid.Column="0" Margin="3">Left</Button>
<Button Grid.Row="0" Grid.Column="2" Margin="3">Right</Button>
<Button Grid.Row="1" Grid.Column="0" Margin="3">Left</Button>
<Button Grid.Row="1" Grid.Column="2" Margin="3">Right</Button>

<GridSplitter Grid.Row="0" Grid.Column="1" Grid.RowSpan="2"
  Width="3" VerticalAlignment="Stretch" HorizontalAlignment="Center"
  ShowsPreview="False"></GridSplitter>
</Grid>
```

■Tip To create a successful GridSplitter, make sure you supply values for the VerticalAlignment, HorizontalAlignment, and Width (or Height) properties.

This markup includes one additional detail. When the GridSplitter is declared, the ShowsPreview property is set to false. As a result, when the splitter bar is dragged from one side to another, the columns are resized immediately. But if you set ShowsPreview to true, when you drag you'll see a gray shadow follow your mouse pointer to show you where the split will be. The columns won't be resized until you release the mouse button. It's also possible to use the arrow keys to resize a GridSplitter once it receives focus.

The ShowsPreview isn't the only GridSplitter property that you can set. You can also adjust the DragIncrement property if you want to force the splitter to move in coarser "chunks" (such as 10 units at a time). If you want to control the maximum and minimum allowed sizes of the columns, you simply make sure the appropriate properties are set in the ColumnDefinitions section, as shown in the previous example.

■Tip You can change the fill that's used for the GridSplitter so that it isn't just a shaded gray rectangle. The trick is to use the Background property, which accepts simple colors and more complex brushes. You'll learn more in Chapter 7.

A Grid usually contains no more than a single GridSplitter. However, you can nest one Grid inside another, and if you do, each Grid may have its own GridSplitter. This allows you to create a window that's split into two regions (for example, a left and right pane), and then further subdivide one of these regions (say, the pane on the right) into more sections (such as a resizable top and bottom portion). Figure 4-14 shows an example.

Figure 4-14. *Resizing a window with two splits*

Creating this window is fairly straightforward, although it's a chore to keep track of the three Grid containers that are involved: the overall Grid, the nested Grid on the left, and the nested Grid on the right. The only trick is to make sure the GridSplitter is placed in the correct cell and given the correct alignment. Here's the complete markup:

```
<!-- This is the Grid for the entire window. -->
<Grid>
  <Grid.ColumnDefinitions>
    <ColumnDefinition></ColumnDefinition>
    <ColumnDefinition Width="Auto"></ColumnDefinition>
    <ColumnDefinition></ColumnDefinition>
  </Grid.ColumnDefinitions>

  <!-- This is the nested Grid on the left.
       It isn't subdivided further with a splitter. -->
  <Grid Grid.Column="0" VerticalAlignment="Stretch">
    <Grid.RowDefinitions>
      <RowDefinition></RowDefinition>
      <RowDefinition></RowDefinition>
    </Grid.RowDefinitions>
    <Button Margin="3" Grid.Row="0">Top Left</Button>
    <Button Margin="3" Grid.Row="1">Bottom Left</Button>
  </Grid>

  <!-- This is the vertical splitter that sits between the two nested
       (left and right) grids. -->
  <GridSplitter Grid.Column="1"
   Width="3" HorizontalAlignment="Center" VerticalAlignment="Stretch"
   ShowsPreview="False"></GridSplitter>

  <!-- This is the nested Grid on the right. -->
```

```
<Grid Grid.Column="2">
  <Grid.RowDefinitions>
    <RowDefinition></RowDefinition>
    <RowDefinition Height="Auto"></RowDefinition>
    <RowDefinition></RowDefinition>
  </Grid.RowDefinitions>

  <Button Grid.Row="0" Margin="3">Top Right</Button>
  <Button Grid.Row="2" Margin="3">Bottom Right</Button>

  <!-- This is the horizontal splitter that subdivides it into
       a top and bottom region.. -->
  <GridSplitter Grid.Row="1"
   Height="3" VerticalAlignment="Center" HorizontalAlignment="Stretch"
   ShowsPreview="False"></GridSplitter>
  </Grid>
</Grid>
```

■Tip Remember, if a Grid has just a single row or column, you can leave out the RowDefinitions section. Also, elements that don't have their row position explicitly set are assumed to have a Grid.Row value of 0 and are placed in the first row. The same holds true for elements that don't supply a Grid.Column value.

Shared Size Groups

As you've seen, a Grid contains a collection of rows and columns, which are sized explicitly, proportionately, or based on the size of their children. There's one other way to size a row or a column—to match the size of another row or column. This works through a feature called *shared size groups*.

The goal of shared size groups is to keep separate portions of your user interface consistent. For example, you might want to size one column to fit its content and size another column to match that size exactly. However, the real benefit of shared size groups is to give the same proportions to separate Grid controls.

To understand how this works, consider the example shown in Figure 4-15. This window features two Grid objects—one at the top of the window (with three columns) and one at the bottom (with two columns). The leftmost column of the first Grid is sized proportionately to fit its content (a long text string). The leftmost column of the second Grid has exactly the same width, even though it contains less content. That's because it shares the same size group. No matter how much content you stuff in the first column of the first Grid, the first column of the second Grid stays synchronized.

As this example demonstrates, a shared column can be used in otherwise different grids. In this example, the top Grid has an extra column, and so the remaining space is divided differently. Similarly, the shared columns can occupy different positions, so you could create a relationship between the first column in one Grid and the second column in another. And obviously, the columns can host completely different content.

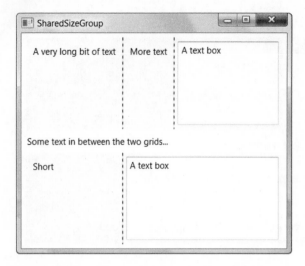

Figure 4-15. *Two grids that share a column definition*

When you use a shared size group, it's as if you've created one column (or row) definition, which is reused in more than one place. It's not a simple one-way copy of one column to another. You can test this out with the previous example by changing the content in the shared column of the second Grid. Now, the column in the first Grid will be lengthened to match (Figure 4-16).

You can even add a GridSplitter to one of the Grid objects. As the user resizes the column in one Grid, the shared column in the other Grid will follow along, resizing itself at the same time.

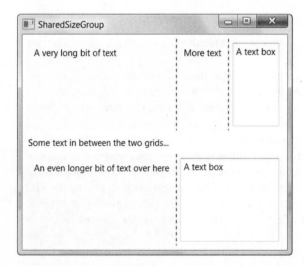

Figure 4-16. *Shared-size columns remain synchronized.*

Creating a shared group is easy. You simply need to set the SharedSizeGroup property on both columns, using a matching string. In the current example, both columns use a group named TextLabel:

```
<Grid Margin="3" Background="LightYellow" ShowGridLines="True">
  <Grid.ColumnDefinitions>
    <ColumnDefinition Width="Auto" SharedSizeGroup="TextLabel"></ColumnDefinition>
    <ColumnDefinition Width="Auto"></ColumnDefinition>
    <ColumnDefinition></ColumnDefinition>
  </Grid.ColumnDefinitions>

  <Label Margin="5">A very long bit of text</Label>
  <Label Grid.Column="1" Margin="5">More text</Label>
  <TextBox Grid.Column="2" Margin="5">A text box</TextBox>
</Grid>
...
<Grid Margin="3" Background="LightYellow"  ShowGridLines="True">
  <Grid.ColumnDefinitions>
    <ColumnDefinition Width="Auto" SharedSizeGroup="TextLabel"></ColumnDefinition>
    <ColumnDefinition></ColumnDefinition>
  </Grid.ColumnDefinitions>

  <Label Margin="5">Short</Label>
  <TextBox Grid.Column="1" Margin="5">A text box</TextBox>
</Grid>
```

There's one other detail. Shared size groups aren't global to your entire application because more than one window might inadvertently use the same name. You might assume that shared size groups are limited to the current window, but WPF is even more stringent than that. To share a group, you need to explicitly set the attached Grid.IsSharedSizeScope property to true on a container somewhere upstream that holds the Grid objects with the shared column. In the current example, the top and bottom Grid are wrapped in another Grid that accomplishes this purpose, although you could just as easily use a different container such as a DockPanel or StackPanel.

Here's the markup for the top-level Grid:

```
<Grid Grid.IsSharedSizeScope="True" Margin="3">
  <Grid.RowDefinitions>
    <RowDefinition></RowDefinition>
    <RowDefinition Height="Auto"></RowDefinition>
    <RowDefinition></RowDefinition>
  </Grid.RowDefinitions>

  <Grid Grid.Row="0" Margin="3" Background="LightYellow" ShowGridLines="True">
    ...
  </Grid>
  <Label Grid.Row="1" >Some text in between the two grids...</Label>
  <Grid Grid.Row="2" Margin="3" Background="LightYellow" ShowGridLines="True">
    ...
  </Grid>
</Grid>
```

■Tip You could use a shared size group to synchronize a separate Grid with column headers. The width of each column can then be determined by the content in the column, which the header will share. You could even place a GridSplitter in the header, which the user could drag to resize the header and the entire column underneath.

The UniformGrid

There is a grid that breaks all the rules you've learned about so far: the UniformGrid. Unlike the Grid, the UniformGrid doesn't require (or even support) predefined columns and rows. Instead, you simply set the Rows and Columns properties to set its size. Each cell is always the same size because the available space is divided equally. Finally, elements are placed into the appropriate cell based on the order in which you define them. There are no attached Row and Column properties, and no blank cells.

Here's an example that fills a UniformGrid with four buttons:

```
<UniformGrid Rows="2" Columns="2">
  <Button>Top Left</Button>
  <Button>Top Right</Button>
  <Button>Bottom Left</Button>
  <Button>Bottom Right</Button>
</UniformGrid>
```

The UniformGrid is used far less frequently than the Grid. The Grid is an all-purpose tool for creating window layouts from the simple to the complex. The UniformGrid is a much more specialized layout container that's primarily useful when quickly laying out elements in a rigid grid (for example, when building a playing board for certain games). Many WPF programmers will never use the UniformGrid.

Coordinate-Based Layout with the Canvas

The only layout container you haven't considered yet is the Canvas. It allows you to place elements using exact coordinates, which is a poor choice for designing rich data-driven forms and standard dialog boxes, but a valuable tool if you need to build something a little different (such as a drawing surface for a diagramming tool). The Canvas is also the most lightweight of the layout containers. That's because it doesn't include any complex layout logic to negotiate the sizing preferences of its children. Instead, it simply lays them all out at the position they specify, with the exact size they want.

To position an element on the Canvas, you set the attached Canvas.Left and Canvas.Top properties. Canvas.Left sets the number of units between the left edge of your element and the left edge of the Canvas. Canvas.Top sets the number of units between the top of your element and the top of the Canvas. As always, these values are set in device-independent units, which line up with ordinary pixels exactly when the system DPI is set to 96 dpi.

> **Note** Alternatively, you can use Canvas.Right instead of Canvas.Left to space an element from the right edge of the Canvas, and Canvas.Bottom instead of Canvas.Top to space it from the bottom. You just can't use both Canvas.Right and Canvas.Left at once, or both Canvas.Top and Canvas.Bottom.

Optionally, you can size your element explicitly using its Width and Height properties. This is more common when using the Canvas than it is in other panels because the Canvas has no layout logic of its own. (And often, you'll use the Canvas when you need precise control over how a combination of elements is arranged.) If you don't set the Width and Height properties, your element will get its desired size—in other words, it will grow just large enough to fit its content.

Here's a simple Canvas that includes four buttons:

```
<Canvas>
  <Button Canvas.Left="10" Canvas.Top="10">(10,10)</Button>
  <Button Canvas.Left="120" Canvas.Top="30">(120,30)</Button>
  <Button Canvas.Left="60" Canvas.Top="80" Width="50" Height="50">
  (60,80)</Button>
  <Button Canvas.Left="70" Canvas.Top="120" Width="100" Height="50">
  (70,120)</Button>
</Canvas>
```

Figure 4-17 shows the result.

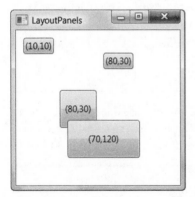

Figure 4-17. *Explicitly positioned buttons in a Canvas*

If you resize the window, the Canvas stretches to fill the available space, but none of the controls in the Canvas moves or changes size. The Canvas doesn't include any of the anchoring or docking features that were provided with coordinate layout in Windows Forms. Part of the reason for this gap is to keep the Canvas lightweight. Another reason is to prevent people from using the Canvas for purposes for which it's not intended (such as laying out a standard user interface).

Like any other layout container, the Canvas can be nested inside a user interface. That means you can use the Canvas to draw some detailed content in a portion of your window, while using more standard WPF panels for the rest of your elements.

Tip If you use the Canvas alongside other elements, you may want to consider setting its ClipToBounds to true. That way, elements inside the Canvas that stretch beyond its bounds are clipped off at the edge of the Canvas. (This prevents them from overlapping other elements elsewhere in your window.) All the other layout containers always clip their children to fit, regardless of the ClipToBounds setting.

Z-Order

If you have more than one overlapping element, you can set the attached Canvas.ZIndex property to control how they are layered.

Ordinarily, all the elements you add have the same ZIndex—0. When elements have the same ZIndex, they're displayed in the same order that they exist in Canvas.Children collection, which is based on the order that they're defined in the XAML markup. Elements declared later in the markup—such as button (70,120)—are displayed overtop of elements that are declared earlier—such as button (120,30).

However, you can promote any element to a higher level by increasing its ZIndex. That's because higher ZIndex elements *always* appear over lower ZIndex elements. Using this technique, you could reverse the layering in the previous example:

```
<Button Canvas.Left="60" Canvas.Top="80" Canvas.ZIndex="1" Width="50" Height="50">
  (60,80)</Button>
<Button Canvas.Left="70" Canvas.Top="120" Width="100" Height="50">
  (70,120)</Button>
```

Note The actual values you use for the Canvas.ZIndex property have no meaning. The important detail is how the ZIndex value of one element compares to the ZIndex value of another. You can set the ZIndex using any positive or negative integer.

The ZIndex property is particularly useful if you need to change the position of an element programmatically. Just call Canvas.SetZIndex() and pass in the element you want to modify and the new ZIndex you want to apply. Unfortunately, there is no BringToFront() or SendToBack() method—it's up to you to keep track of the highest and lowest ZIndex values if you want to implement this behavior.

The InkCanvas

WPF also includes an InkCanvas element that's similar to the Canvas in some respects (and wholly different in others). Like the Canvas, the InkCanvas defines four attached properties that you can apply to child elements for coordinate-based positioning (Top, Left, Bottom, and

Right). However, the underlying plumbing is quite a bit different—in fact, the InkCanvas doesn't derive from Canvas, or even from the base Panel class. Instead, it derives directly from FrameworkElement.

The primary purpose of the InkCanvas is to allow *stylus* input. The stylus is the penlike input device that's used in tablet PCs. However, the InkCanvas works with the mouse in the same way as it works with the stylus. Thus, a user can draw lines or select and manipulate elements in the InkCanvas using the mouse.

The InkCanvas actually holds two collections of child content. The familiar Children collection holds arbitrary elements, just as with the Canvas. Each element can be positioned based on the Top, Left, Bottom, and Right properties. The Strokes collection holds System.Windows.Ink.Stroke objects, which represent graphical input that the user has drawn in the InkCanvas. Each line or curve that the user draws becomes a separate Stroke object. Thanks to these dual collections, you can use the InkCanvas to let the user annotate content (stored in the Children collection) with strokes (stored in the Strokes collection).

For example, Figure 4-18 shows an InkCanvas that contains a picture that has been annotated with extra strokes. Here's the markup for the InkCanvas in this example, which defines the image:

```
<InkCanvas Name="inkCanvas" Background="LightYellow"
 EditingMode="Ink">
  <Image Source="office.jpg" InkCanvas.Top="10" InkCanvas.Left="10"
   Width="287" Height="319"></Image>
</InkCanvas>
```

The strokes are drawn at runtime by the user.

Figure 4-18. *Adding strokes in an InkCanvas*

The InkCanvas can be used in some significantly different ways, depending on the value you set for the InkCanvas.EditingMode property. Table 4-4 lists all your options.

Table 4-4. *Values of the InkCanvasEditingMode Enumeration*

Name	Description
Ink	The InkCanvas allows the user to draw annotations. This is the default mode. When the user draws with the mouse or stylus, a stroke is drawn.
GestureOnly	The InkCanvas doesn't allow the user to draw stroke annotations but pays attention to specific predefined *gestures* (such as dragging the stylus in one direction, or scratching out content). The full list of recognized gestures is listed by the System.Windows.Ink.ApplicationGesture enumeration.
InkAndGesture	The InkCanvas allows the user to draw stroke annotations and also recognizes predefined gestures.
EraseByStroke	The InkCanvas erases a stroke when it's clicked. If the user has a stylus, he can switch to this mode by using the back end of the stylus. (You can determine the current mode using the read-only ActiveEditingMode property, and you can change the mode used for the back end of the stylus by changing the EditingModeInverted property.)
EraseByPoint	The InkCanvas erases a portion of a stroke (a point in a stroke) when that portion is clicked.
Select	The InkCanvas allows the user to select elements that are stored in the Children collection. To select an element, the user must click it or drag a selection "lasso" around it. Once an element is selected, it can be moved, resized, or deleted.
None	The InkCanvas ignores mouse and stylus input.

The InkCanvas raises events when the editing mode changes (ActiveEditingModeChanged), a gesture is detected in GestureOnly or InkAndGesture mode (Gesture), a stroke is drawn (StrokeCollected), a stroke is erased (StrokeErasing and StrokeErased), and an element is selected or changed in Select mode (SelectionChanging, SelectionChanged, SelectionMoving, SelectionMoved, SelectionResizing, and SelectionResized). The events that end in *ing* represent an action that is about to take place but can be canceled by setting the Cancel property of the EventArgs object.

In Select mode, the InkCanvas provides a fairly capable design surface for dragging content around and manipulating it. Figure 4-19 shows a Button control in an InkCanvas as it's being selected (on the left) and then repositioned and resized (on the right).

Figure 4-19. *Moving and resizing an element in the InkCanvas*

As interesting as Select mode is, it isn't a perfect fit if you're building a drawing or diagramming tool. You'll see a better example of how to create a custom drawing surface in Chapter 14.

Layout Examples

You've now spent a considerable amount of time poring over the intricacies of the WPF layout containers. With this low-level knowledge in mind, it's worth looking at a few complete layout examples. Doing so will give you a better sense of how the various WPF layout concepts (such as size-to-content, stretch, and nesting) work in real-world windows.

A Column of Settings

Layout containers such as the Grid make it dramatically easier to create an overall structure to a window. For example, consider the window with settings shown in Figure 4-20. This window arranges its individual components—labels, text boxes, and buttons—into a tabular structure.

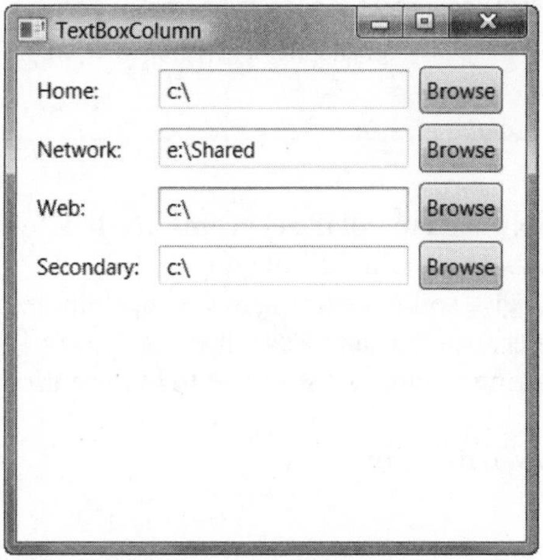

Figure 4-20. *Folder settings in a column*

To create this table, you begin by defining the rows and columns of the grid. The rows are easy enough—each one is simply sized to the height of the containing content. That means the entire row will get the height of the largest element, which in this case is the Browse button in the third column.

```
<Grid Margin="3,3,10,3">
  <Grid.RowDefinitions>
    <RowDefinition Height="Auto"></RowDefinition>
    <RowDefinition Height="Auto"></RowDefinition>
    <RowDefinition Height="Auto"></RowDefinition>
    <RowDefinition Height="Auto"></RowDefinition>
  </Grid.RowDefinitions>
  ...
```

Next, you need to create the columns. The first and last columns are sized to fit their content (the label text and the Browse button, respectively). The middle column gets all the remaining room, which means it grows as the window is resized larger, giving you more room to see the selected folder. (If you want this stretching to top out at some extremely wide maximum value, you can use the MaxWidth property when defining the column, just as you do with individual elements.)

```
...
<Grid.ColumnDefinitions>
  <ColumnDefinition Width="Auto"></ColumnDefinition>
  <ColumnDefinition Width="*"></ColumnDefinition>
  <ColumnDefinition Width="Auto"></ColumnDefinition>
</Grid.ColumnDefinitions>
...
```

■Tip The Grid needs some minimum space—enough to fit the full label text, the browse button, and a few pixels in the middle column to show the text box. If you shrink the containing window to be smaller than this, some content will be cut off. As always, it makes sense to use the MinWidth and MinHeight properties on the window to prevent this from occurring.

Now that you have your basic structure, you simply need to slot the elements into the right cells. However, you also need to think carefully about margins and alignment. Each element needs a basic margin (a good value is 3 units) to give some breathing room. In addition, the label and text box need to be centered vertically because they aren't as tall as the Browse button. Finally, the text box needs to use automatic sizing mode, so it stretches to fit the entire column.

Here's the markup you need to define the first row in the grid:

```
...
<Label Grid.Row="0" Grid.Column="0" Margin="3"
  VerticalAlignment="Center">Home:</Label>
<TextBox Grid.Row="0" Grid.Column="1" Margin="3"
  Height="Auto" VerticalAlignment="Center"></TextBox>
<Button Grid.Row="0" Grid.Column="2" Margin="3" Padding="2">Browse</Button>
...
</Grid>
```

You can repeat this markup to add all your rows by simply incrementing the value of the Grid.Row attribute.

One fact that's not immediately obvious is how flexible this window is because of the use of the Grid control. None of the individual elements—the labels, text boxes, and buttons—have hard-coded positions or sizes. As a result, you can quickly make changes to the entire grid simply by tweaking the ColumnDefinition elements. Furthermore, if you add a row that has longer label text (necessitating a wider first column), the entire grid is adjusted to be consistent, including the rows that you've already added. And if you want to add elements in between the rows—such as separator lines to divide different sections of the window—you can keep the same columns but use the ColumnSpan property to stretch a single element over a larger area.

Dynamic Content

As the column of settings demonstrates, windows that use the WPF layout containers are easy to change and adapt as you revise your application. This flexibility doesn't just benefit you at design time. It's also a great asset if you need to display content that changes dramatically.

One example is *localized text*—text that appears in your user interface and needs to be translated into different languages for different geographic regions. In old-style coordinate-based applications, changing the text can wreak havoc in a window, particularly because a short amount of English text becomes significantly larger in many languages. Even if elements are allowed to resize themselves to fit larger text, doing so often throws off the whole balance of a window.

Figure 4-21 demonstrates how this isn't the case when you use the WPF layout containers intelligently. In this example, the user interface has a short text and a long text option. When the long text is used, the buttons that contain the text are resized automatically and other content is bumped out of the way. And because the resized buttons share the same layout container (in this case, a table column), that entire section of the user interface is resized. The end result is that all buttons keep a consistent size—the size of the largest button.

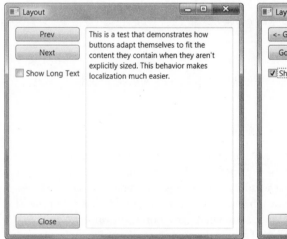

Figure 4-21. *A self-adjusting window*

To make this work, the window is carved into a table with two columns and two rows. The column on the left takes the resizable buttons, while the column on the right takes the text box. The bottom row is used for the Close button. It's kept in the same table so that it resizes along with the top row.

Here's the complete markup:

```
<Grid>
  <Grid.RowDefinitions>
    <RowDefinition Height="*"></RowDefinition>
    <RowDefinition Height="Auto"></RowDefinition>
  </Grid.RowDefinitions>
  <Grid.ColumnDefinitions>
    <ColumnDefinition Width="Auto"></ColumnDefinition>
    <ColumnDefinition Width="*"></ColumnDefinition>
  </Grid.ColumnDefinitions>

  <StackPanel Grid.Row="0" Grid.Column="0">
    <Button Name="cmdPrev" Margin="10,10,10,3">Prev</Button>
    <Button Name="cmdNext" Margin="10,3,10,3">Next</Button>
    <CheckBox Name="chkLongText" Margin="10,10,10,10"
     Checked="chkLongText_Checked" Unchecked="chkLongText_Unchecked">
     Show Long Text</CheckBox>
  </StackPanel>
  <TextBox Grid.Row="0" Grid.Column="1" Margin="0,10,10,10"
   TextWrapping="WrapWithOverflow" Grid.RowSpan="2">This is a test that demonstrates
    how buttons adapt themselves to fit the content they contain when they aren't
    explicitly sized. This behavior makes localization much easier.</TextBox>
  <Button Grid.Row="1" Grid.Column="0" Name="cmdClose"
    Margin="10,3,10,10">Close</Button>
</Grid>
```

The event handlers for the CheckBox aren't shown here. They simply change the text in the two buttons.

A Modular User Interface

Many of the layout containers gracefully "flow" content into the available space, like the StackPanel, DockPanel, and WrapPanel. One advantage of this approach is that it allows you to create truly modular interfaces. In other words, you can plug in different panels with the appropriate user interface sections you want to show and leave out those that don't apply. The entire application can shape itself accordingly, somewhat like a portal site on the Web.

Figure 4-22 demonstrates. It places several separate panels into a WrapPanel. The user can choose which of these panels are visible using the check boxes at the top of the window.

■**Note** Although you can set the background of a layout panel, you can't set a border around it. This example overcomes that limitation by wrapping each panel in a Border element that outlines the exact dimensions. You'll learn how to use the Border and other similarly specialized containers in the next chapter.

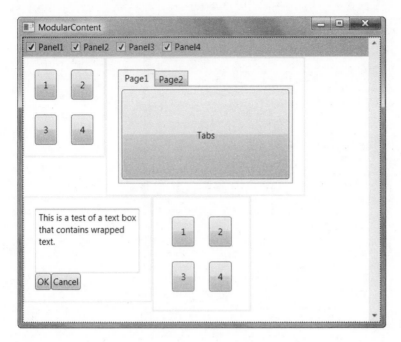

Figure 4-22. *A series of panels in a WrapPanel*

As different panels are hidden, the remaining panels reflow themselves to fit the available space (and the order in which they're declared). Figure 4-23 shows a different permutation of panels.

To hide and show the individual panels, a small bit of code handles check box clicks. Although you haven't considered the WPF event handling model in any detail (Chapter 6 has the full story), the trick is to set the Visibility property:

```
panel.Visibility = Visibility.Collapsed;
```

The Visibility property is a part of the base UIElement class and is therefore supported by just about everything you'll put in a WPF window. It takes one of three values, from the System.Windows.Visibility enumeration, as listed in Table 4-5.

Table 4-5. *Values of the Visibility Enumeration*

Value	Description
Visible	The element appears as normal in the window.
Collapsed	The element is not displayed and doesn't take up any space.
Hidden	The element is not displayed, but the space it would otherwise use is still reserved. (In other words, there's a blank space where it would have appeared). This setting is handy if you need to hide and show elements without changing the layout and the relative positioning of the elements in the rest of your window.

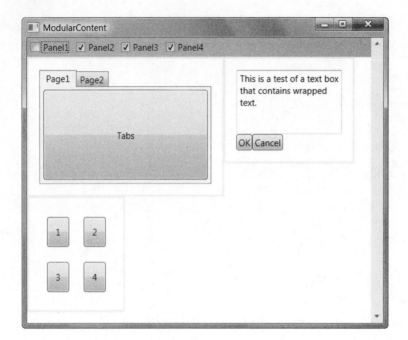

Figure 4-23. *Hiding some panels*

■**Tip** You can use the Visibility property to dynamically tailor a variety of interfaces. For example, you could make a collapsible pane that can appear at the side of your window. All you need to do is wrap all the contents of that pane in some sort of layout container and set its Visibility property to suit. The remaining content will be rearranged to fit the available space.

The Last Word

In this chapter, you took a detailed tour of the new WPF layout model and learned how to place elements in stacks, grids, and other arrangements. You built more complex layouts using nested combinations of the layout containers, and you threw the GridSplitter into the mix to make resizable split windows. And all along, you kept close focus on the reasons for this dramatic change—namely, the benefits you'll get when maintaining, enhancing, and localizing your user interface.

The layout story is still far from over. In the following chapters, you'll see many more examples that use the layout containers to organize groups of elements. You'll also learn about a few additional features that let you arrange content in a window:

- **Specialized containers.** The Border, ScrollViewer, and Expander give you the ability to create content that has borders, can be scrolled, and can be collapsed out of sight. Unlike the layout panels, these containers can only hold a single piece of content. However, you can easily use them in concert with a layout panel to get exactly the effect you need. You'll try out these containers in Chapter 5.

- **The Viewbox.** Need a way to resize graphical content (such as images and vector drawings)? The Viewbox is yet another specialized container that can help you out, and it has built in scaling. You'll take your first look at the Viewbox in Chapter 5.

- **Text layout.** WPF adds new tools for laying out large blocks of styled text. You can use floating figures and lists, and use paging, columns, and sophisticated wrapping intelligence to get remarkably polished results. You'll see how in Chapter 19.

CHAPTER 5

■ ■ ■

Content

In the previous chapter you explored the WPF layout system, which lets you arrange a window by placing elements into specialized layout containers. With this system, even a simple window breaks down to a nested series of Grid, StackPanel, and DockPanel containers. Dig deep enough and you'll eventually find the visible elements (widgets such as buttons, labels, and text boxes) inside the various containers.

However, the layout containers aren't the only example of nested elements. In fact, WPF is designed with a new content model that lets you place elements inside other elements that are otherwise ordinary. Using this technique, you can take many simple controls—such as buttons—and place pictures, vector shapes, and even layout containers inside. This content model is one of the details that make WPF so remarkably flexible.

In this chapter, you'll explore the base ContentControl class that supports this model. You'll also learn how to use more specialized ContentControl descendants to make your panels scrollable and collapsible.

Understanding Content Controls

In Chapter 1, you took a look at the class hierarchy that's at the core of WPF. You also considered the difference between *elements* (which include everything you'll place in a WPF window) and *controls* (which are more specialized elements that derive from the System.Windows.Controls.Control class).

In the world of WPF, a control is generally described as an element that can receive focus and accept user input, such as a text box or a button. However, the distinction is sometimes a bit blurry. The ToolTip is considered to be a control because it appears and disappears depending on the user's mouse movements. The Label is considered to be a control because of its support for *mnemonics* (shortcut keys that transfer the focus to related controls).

Content controls are a still more specialized type of controls that are able to hold (and display) a piece of content. Technically, a content control is a control that can contain a *single* nested element. The one-child limit is what differentiates content controls from layout containers, which can hold as many nested elements as you want.

■**Tip** Of course, you can still pack in a lot of content in a single content control—the trick is to wrap every-thing in a single container, such as a StackPanel or a Grid. For example, the Window class is itself a content control. Obviously, windows often hold a great deal of content, but it's all wrapped in one top-level container. (Typically, this container is a Grid.)

As you learned last chapter, all WPF layout containers derive from the abstract Panel class, which gives the support for holding multiple elements. Similarly, all content controls derive from the abstract ContentControl class. Figure 5-1 shows the class hierarchy.

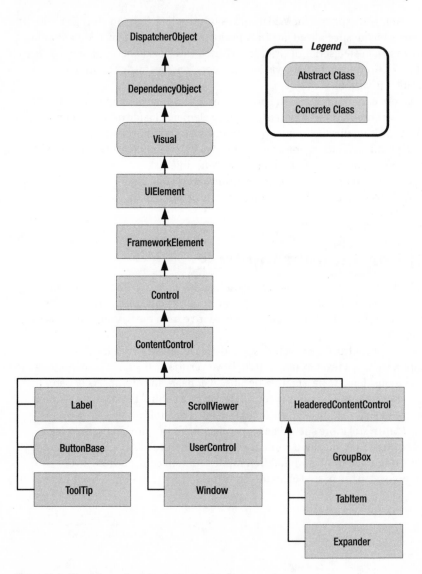

Figure 5-1. *The hierarchy of content controls*

As Figure 5-1 shows, several common controls are actually content controls, including the Label and the ToolTip. Additionally, all types of buttons are content controls, including the familiar Button, the RadioButton, and the CheckBox. There are also a few more specialized content controls, such as ScrollViewer (which allows you to create a scrollable panel), and UserControl class (which allows you to reuse a custom grouping of controls). The Window class, which is used to represent each window in your application, is itself a content control.

Finally, there is a subset of content controls that goes through one more level of inheritance by deriving from the HeaderedContentControl class. These controls have both a content region and a header region, which can be used to display some sort of title. These controls include GroupBox, TabItem (a page in a TabControl), and Expander.

Note Figure 5-1 leaves out very little. It doesn't show the Frame element that's used for content navigation (Chapter 9), and it omits a few elements that are used inside other controls (such as list box and status bar items).

The Content Property

Whereas the Panel class adds the Children collection to hold nested elements, the Content-Control class adds a Content property, which accepts a single object. The Content property supports any type of object, but it separates objects into two groups and gives each group different treatment:

- **Objects that don't derive from UIElement.** The content control calls ToString() to get the text for these controls and then displays that text.

- **Objects that derive from UIElement.** These objects (which include all the visual elements that are a part of WPF) are displayed inside the content control using the UIElement.OnRender() method.

Note Technically, the OnRender() method doesn't draw the object immediately—it simply generates a graphical representation that WPF paints on the screen as needed.

To understand how this works, consider the humble button. So far, the examples that you've seen that include buttons have simply supplied a string:

```
<Button Margin="3">Text content</Button>
```

This string is set as the button content and displayed on the button surface. However, you can get more ambitious by placing other elements inside the button. For example, you can place an image inside using the Image class:

```
<Button Margin="3">
  <Image Source="happyface.jpg" Stretch="None" />
</Button>
```

Or you could combine text and images by wrapping them all in a layout container like the StackPanel:

```
<Button Margin="3">
  <StackPanel>
    <TextBlock Margin="3">Image and text button</TextBlock>
    <Image Source="happyface.jpg" Stretch="None" />
    <TextBlock Margin="3">Courtesy of the StackPanel</TextBlock>
  </StackPanel>
</Button>
```

You'll notice that this example uses the TextBlock instead of a Label control (although either one would work). The TextBlock is a lightweight text element that supports wrapping but doesn't support shortcut keys. Unlike the Label, the TextBlock is not a content control. Chapter 7 describes both the TextBlock and Label in more detail.

Note It's acceptable to place text content inside a content control because the XAML parser converts that to a string object and uses that to set the Content property. However, you can't place string content directly in a layout container. Instead, you need to wrap it in a class that derives from UIElement, such as TextBlock or Label.

If you want to create a truly exotic button, you could even place other content controls such as text boxes and buttons inside (and still nest elements inside these). It's doubtful that such an interface would make much sense, but it is possible. Figure 5-2 shows some sample buttons.

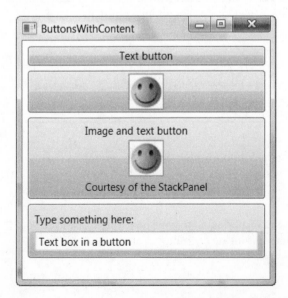

Figure 5-2. *Buttons with different types of nested content*

This is the exact same content model you saw with windows. Just like the Button class, the Window class allows a single nested element, which can be a piece of text, an arbitrary object, or an element.

■Note One of the few elements that is *not* allowed inside a content control is the Window. When you create a Window, it checks to see if it's the top-level container. If it's placed inside another element, the Window throws an exception.

Aside from the Content property, the ContentControl class adds very little. It includes a HasContent property that returns true if there is content in the control, and a ContentTemplate that allows you to build a template telling the control how to display an otherwise unrecognized object. Using ContentTemplate, you can display non-UIElement-derived objects more intelligently. Instead of just calling ToString() to get a string, you can take various property values and arrange them into more complex markup. You'll learn more about WPF data binding in Chapter 16, and data templates in Chapter 17.

Aligning Content

In Chapter 4, you learned how to align different controls in a container using the HorizontalAlignment and VerticalAlignment properties, which are defined in the base FrameworkElement class. However, once a control contains content there's another level of organization to think about. You need to decide how the content inside your content control is aligned with its borders. This is accomplished using the HorizontalContentAlignment and VerticalContentAlignment properties.

HorizontalContentAlignment and VerticalContentAlignment support the same values as HorizontalAlignment and VerticalAlignment. That means you can line content up on the inside of any edge (Top, Bottom, Left, or Right), you can center it (Center), or you can stretch it to fill the available space (Stretch). These settings are applied directly to the nested content element, but you can use multiple levels of nesting to create a sophisticated layout. For example, if you nest a StackPanel in a Label element, the Label.HorizontalContentAlignment determines where the StackPanel is placed, but the alignment and sizing options of the StackPanel and its children will determine the rest of the layout.

In Chapter 4, you also learned about the Margin property, which allows you to add whitespace between adjacent elements. Content controls use a complementary property named Padding, which inserts space between the edges of the control and the edges of the content. To see the difference compare the following two buttons:

```
<Button>Absolutely No Padding</Button>
<Button Padding="3">Well Padded</Button>
```

The button that has no padding (the default) has its text crowded up against the button edge. The button that has a padding of 3 units on each side gets a more respectable amount of breathing space. Figure 5-3 highlights the difference.

Figure 5-3. *Padding the content of the button*

■**Note** The HorizontalContentAlignment, VerticalContentAlignment, and Padding properties are all defined as part of the Control class, not the more specific ContentControl class. That's because there may be controls that aren't content controls but still have some sort of content. One example is the TextBox—its contained text (stored in the Text property) is adjusted using the alignment and padding settings you've applied.

The WPF Content Philosophy

At this point, you might be wondering if the WPF content model is really worth all the trouble. After all, you might choose to place an image inside a button but you're unlikely to embed other controls and entire layout panels. However, there are a few important reasons driving the shift in perspective.

Consider the example shown in Figure 5-2, which includes a simple image button that places an Image element inside the Button control. This approach is less than ideal, because bitmaps are not resolution independent. On a high-dpi display, the bitmap may appear blurry because WPF must add more pixels by interpolation to make sure the image stays the correct size. More sophisticated WPF interfaces avoid bitmaps and use a combination of vector shapes to create custom-drawn buttons and other graphical frills (as you'll see in Chapter 13).

This approach integrates nicely with the content control model. Because the Button class is a content control, you aren't limited to filling it with a fixed bitmap—instead, you can include other content. For example, you can use the classes in the System.Windows.Shapes namespace to draw a vector image inside a button. Here's an example that creates a button with two diamond shapes (as shown in Figure 5-4):

```
<Button Margin="3">
  <Grid>
    <Polygon Points="100,25 125,0 200,25 125,50"
     Fill="LightSteelBlue" />
    <Polygon Points="100,25 75,0 0,25 75,50"
     Fill="White"/>
  </Grid>
</Button>
```

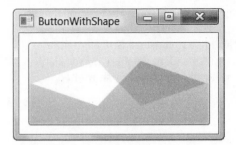

Figure 5-4. *A button with shape content*

Clearly, in this case the nested content model is simpler than adding extra properties to the Button class to support the different types of content. Not only is the nested content model more flexible, it also allows the Button class to expose a simpler interface. And because all content controls support content nesting in the same way, there's no need to add different content properties to multiple classes. (Windows Forms ran into this issue in .NET 2.0, while enhancing the Button and Label class to better support images and mixed image-and-text content.)

In essence, the nested content model is a trade. It simplifies the class model for elements because there's no need to use additional layers of inheritance to add properties for different types of content. However, you need to use a slightly more complex *object* model—elements that can be built out of other nested elements.

■Note You can't always get the effect you want by changing the content of a control. For example, even though you can place any content in a button, a few details never change, such as the button's shaded background, its rounded border, and the mouse-over effect that makes it glow when you move the mouse pointer over it. However, there's another way to change these built-in details—by applying a new control template. Chapter 15 shows how you can change all aspects of a control's look and feel using a control template.

Specialized Containers

In Chapter 7, you'll consider all the control basics and look at simple content controls such as the Label and Button in more detail. But first, it's worth taking a detour to consider a few more sophisticated content controls: ScrollViewer, GroupBox, TabItem, and Expander. All of these controls are designed to help you shape large portions of your user interface. However, because these controls can only hold a single element, you'll usually use them in conjunction with a layout container.

The ScrollViewer

In the previous chapter, you tried out several containers. However, none of them provided support for *scrolling*, which is a key feature if you want to fit large amounts of content in a limited amount of space. In WPF, scrolling support is easy to get, but it requires another ingredient: the ScrollViewer content control.

In order to get scrolling support, you need to wrap the content you want to scroll inside a ScrollViewer. Although the ScrollViewer can hold anything, you'll typically use it to wrap a layout container. For example, in Chapter 4 you saw an example that used a Grid element to create a three-column display of texts, text boxes, and buttons. To make this Grid scrollable, you simply need to wrap the Grid in a ScrollViewer, as shown in this slightly shortened markup:

```
<ScrollViewer>
  <Grid Margin="3,3,10,3">
    <Grid.RowDefinitions>
      ...
    </Grid.RowDefinitions>
    <Grid.ColumnDefinitions>
      ...
    </Grid.ColumnDefinitions>

    <Label Grid.Row="0" Grid.Column="0" Margin="3"
      VerticalAlignment="Center">Home:</Label>
    <TextBox Grid.Row="0" Grid.Column="1" Margin="3"
      Height="Auto" VerticalAlignment="Center"></TextBox>
    <Button Grid.Row="0" Grid.Column="2" Margin="3" Padding="2">
      Browse</Button>

    ...

  </Grid>
</ScrollViewer>
```

The result is shown in Figure 5-5.

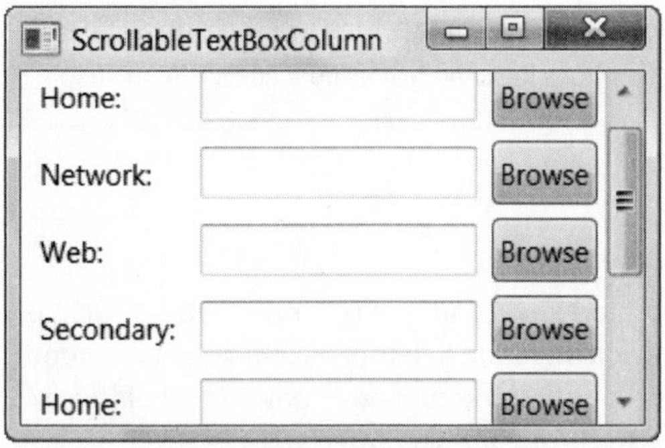

Figure 5-5. *A scrollable window*

If you resize the window in this example so that it's large enough to fit all its content, the scroll bar becomes disabled. However, the scroll bar will still be visible. You can control this behavior by setting the VerticalScrollBarVisibility property, which takes a value from the ScrollBarVisibility enumeration. The default value of Visible makes sure the vertical scroll bar is always present. Use Auto if you want the scroll bar to appear when it's needed and disappear when it's not. Or use Disabled if you don't want the scroll bar to appear at all.

Note You can also use Hidden, which is similar to Disabled but subtly different. First, content with a hidden scroll bar is still scrollable. (For example, you can scroll through the content using the arrow keys.) Second, the content in a ScrollViewer is laid out differently. When you use Disabled, you tell the content in the ScrollViewer that it has only as much space as the ScrollViewer itself. On the other hand, if you use Hidden you tell the content that it has an infinite amount of space. That means it can overflow and stretch off into the scrollable region. Ordinarily, you'll only use Hidden if you plan to allow scrolling by another mechanism (such as the custom scrolling buttons described next). You'll only use Disabled if you want to temporarily prevent the ScrollViewer from doing anything at all.

The ScrollViewer also supports horizontal scrolling. However, the HorizontalScrollBarVisibility property is Hidden by default. To use horizontal scrolling, you need to change this value to Visible or Auto.

Programmatic Scrolling

To scroll through the window in Figure 5-5, you can click the scroll bar with the mouse, you can move over the grid and use a mouse scroll wheel, you can tab through the controls, or you can click somewhere on the blank surface of the grid and use the up and down arrow keys. If this still doesn't give you the flexibility you crave, you can use the methods of the ScrollViewer class to scroll your content programmatically:

- The most obvious are LineUp() and LineDown(), which are equivalent to clicking the arrow buttons on the vertical scroll bar to move up or down once.

- You can also use PageUp() and PageDown(), which scroll an entire screenful up or down and are equivalent to clicking the surface of the scroll bar, above or below the scroll bar thumb.

- Similar methods allow horizontal scrolling, including LineLeft(), LineRight(), PageLeft(), and PageRight().

- Finally, you can use the ScrollTo*Xxx*() methods to go somewhere specific. For vertical scrolling, they include ScrollToEnd() and ScrollToHome(), which take you to the top or bottom of the scrollable content, and ScrollToVerticalOffset(), which takes you to a specific position. There are horizontal versions of the same methods, including ScrollToLeftEnd(), ScrollToRightEnd(), and ScrollToHorizontalOffset().

Figure 5-6 shows an example where several custom buttons allow you to move through the ScrollViewer. Each button triggers a simple event handler that uses one of the methods in the previous list.

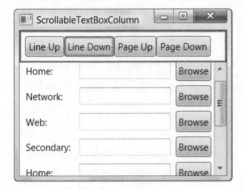

Figure 5-6. *Programmatic scrolling*

Custom Scrolling

The built-in scrolling in the ScrollViewer is quite useful. It allows you to scroll slowly through any content, from a complex vector drawing to a grid of elements. However, one of the most intriguing features of the ScrollViewer is its ability to let its content participate in the scrolling process. Here's how it works:

- You place a scrollable element inside the ScrollViewer. This is any element that implements IScrollInfo.

- You tell the ScrollViewer that the content knows how to scroll itself by setting the ScrollViewer.CanContentScroll property to true.

- When you interact with the ScrollViewer (by using the scroll bar, the mouse wheel, the scrolling methods, and so on), the ScrollViewer calls the appropriate methods on your element using the IScrollInfo interface. The element then performs its own custom scrolling.

■**Note** The IScrollInfo defines a set of methods that react to different scrolling actions. For example, it includes many of the scrolling methods exposed by the ScrollViewer, such as LineUp(), LineDown(), PageUp(), and PageDown(). It also defines methods that handle the mouse wheel.

Very few elements implement IScrollInfo. One element that does is the StackPanel container. Its implementation of IScrollInfo implements *logical scrolling*, scrolling that moves from element to element rather than from line to line.

If you place a StackPanel in a ScrollViewer and you don't set the CanContentScroll property, you get the ordinary behavior. Scrolling up and down moves you a few pixels at a time. However, if you set CanContentScroll to true, each time you click down you scroll to the beginning of the next element:

```
<ScrollViewer CanContentScroll="True">
  <StackPanel>
    <Button Height="100">1</Button>
    <Button Height="100">2</Button>
    <Button Height="100">3</Button>
    <Button Height="100">4</Button>
  </StackPanel>
</ScrollViewer>
```

You may or may not find that the StackPanel's logical scrolling system is useful in your application. However, it's indispensable if you want to create a custom panel with specialized scrolling behavior.

The GroupBox and TabItem: Headered Content Controls

One of the classes that derive from ContentControl is HeaderedContentControl. Its role is simple—it represents a container that has both single-element content (as stored in the Content property) and a single-element header (as stored in the Header property).

There are three classes that derive from ContentControl: GroupBox, TabItem, and Expander. The GroupBox is the simplest of the three. It's displayed as a box with rounded corners and a title. Here's an example (shown in Figure 5-7):

```
<GroupBox Header="A GroupBox Test" Padding="5"
  Margin="5" VerticalAlignment="Top">
  <StackPanel>
    <RadioButton Margin="3">One</RadioButton>
    <RadioButton Margin="3">Two</RadioButton>
    <RadioButton Margin="3">Three</RadioButton>
    <Button Margin="3">Save</Button>
  </StackPanel>
</GroupBox>
```

Figure 5-7. *A basic group box*

Notice that the GroupBox still requires a layout container (such as a StackPanel) to arrange its contents. The GroupBox is often used to group small sets of related controls, such as radio buttons. However, the GroupBox has no built-in functionality, so you can use it how-ever you want. (RadioButton objects are grouped by placing them into any panel. A GroupBox is not required, unless you want the rounded, titled border.)

The TabItem represents a page in a TabControl. The only significant member that the TabItem class adds is the IsSelected property, which indicates whether the tab is currently being shown in the TabControl. Here's the markup that's required to create the simple example that's shown in Figure 5-8:

```
<TabControl Margin="5">
  <TabItem Header="Tab One">
    <StackPanel Margin="3">
      <CheckBox Margin="3">Setting One</CheckBox>
      <CheckBox Margin="3">Setting Two</CheckBox>
      <CheckBox Margin="3">Setting Three</CheckBox>
    </StackPanel>
  </TabItem>
  <TabItem Header="Tab Two">
    ...
  </TabItem>
</TabControl>
```

■**Tip** You can use the TabStripPlacement property to make the tabs appear on the side of the tab control, rather than their normal location at the top.

Figure 5-8. *A set of tabs*

As with the Content property, the Header property can accept any type of object. It dis-plays UIElement-derived classes by rendering them and uses the ToString() method for inline text and all other objects. That means you can create a group box or a tab with graphical content or arbitrary elements in its title. Here's an example:

```
<TabControl Margin="5">
  <TabItem>
    <TabItem.Header>
      <StackPanel>
        <TextBlock Margin="3" >Image and Text Tab Title</TextBlock>
        <Image Source="happyface.jpg" Stretch="None" />
      </StackPanel>
    </TabItem.Header>

    <StackPanel Margin="3">
      <CheckBox Margin="3">Setting One</CheckBox>
      <CheckBox Margin="3">Setting Two</CheckBox>
      <CheckBox Margin="3">Setting Three</CheckBox>
    </StackPanel>
  </TabItem>

  <TabItem Header="Tab Two"></TabItem>
</TabControl>
```

Figure 5-9 shows the somewhat garish result.

Figure 5-9. *An exotic tab title*

The Expander

The most exotic headered content control is the Expander. It wraps a region of content that the user can show or hide by clicking a small arrow button. This technique is used frequently in online help and on web pages to allow them to include large amounts of content without overwhelming users with information they don't want to see.

Figure 5-10 shows two views of a window with three expanders. In the version on the left, all three expanders are collapsed. In the version on the right, all the regions are expanded. (Of course, users are free to expand or collapse any combination of expanders individually.)

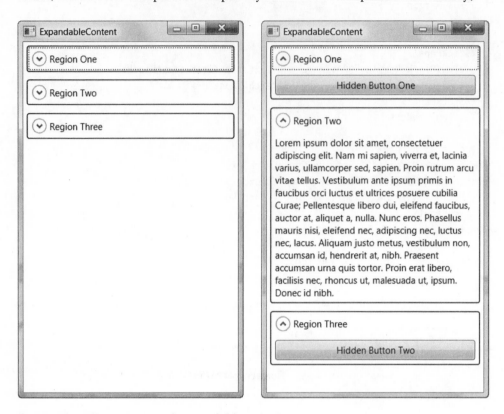

Figure 5-10. *Hiding content with expandable regions*

Using an Expander is extremely simple—you simply need to wrap the content you want to make collapsible inside. Ordinarily, each Expander begins collapsed, but you can change this in your markup (or in your code) by setting the IsExpanded property. Here's the markup that creates the example shown in Figure 5-10:

```
<StackPanel>
  <Expander Margin="5" Padding="5" Header="Region One">
    <Button Padding="3">Hidden Button One</Button>
  </Expander>
  <Expander Margin="5" Padding="5" Header="Region Two" >
    <TextBlock TextWrapping="Wrap">
      Lorem ipsum dolor sit amet, consectetuer adipiscing elit ...
    </TextBlock>
  </Expander>
  <Expander Margin="5" Padding="5" Header="Region Three">
    <Button Padding="3">Hidden Button Two</Button>
  </Expander>
</StackPanel>
```

You can also choose which direction the expander "expands" in. In Figure 5-10, the standard value (Down) is used, but you can also set the ExpandDirection property to Up, Left, or Right. When the Expander is collapsed, the arrow always points in the direction where it will expand.

Life gets a little interesting when using different ExpandDirection values because the effect on the rest of your user interface depends on the type of container. Some containers, such as the WrapPanel, simply bump other elements out of the way. Others, such as Grid, have the option of using proportional or automatic sizing. Figure 5-11 shows an example with a four-cell grid in various degrees of expansion. In each cell is an Expander with a different ExpandDirection. The columns are sized proportionately, which forces the text in the Expander to wrap. (An autosized column would simply stretch to fit the text, making it larger than the window.) The rows are set to automatic sizing, so they expand to fit the extra content.

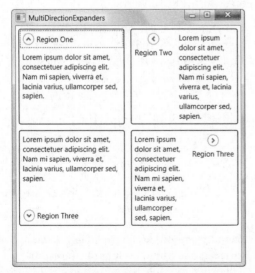

Figure 5-11. *Expanding in different directions*

The Expander is a particularly nice fit in WPF because WPF encourages you to use a flowing layout model that can easily handle content areas that grow or shrink dynamically.

If you need to synchronize other controls with an Expander, you can handle the Expanded and Collapsed events. Contrary to what the naming of these events implies, they fire just *before* the content appears or disappears. This gives you a useful way to implement a lazy load. For example, if the content in an Expander is expensive to create, you might wait until it's shown to retrieve it. Or perhaps you want to update the content just before it's shown. Either way, you can react to the Expanded event to perform your work.

■Note If you like the functionality of the Expander but aren't impressed with the built-in appearance, don't worry. Using the template system in WPF, you can completely customize the expand and collapse arrows so they match the style of the rest of your application. You'll learn how in Chapter 15.

Ordinarily, when you expand an Expander it grows to fit its content. This may create a problem if your window isn't large enough to fit all the content when everything is expanded. There are several strategies for handling this problem:

- You can set a minimum size for the window (using MinWidth and MinHeight) to make sure it will fit everything even at its smallest.

- You can set the SizeToContent property of the window so that it expands automatically to fit the exact dimensions you need when you open or close an Expander. Ordinarily, SizeToContent is set to Manual, but you can use Width or Height to make it expand or contract in either dimension to accommodate its content.

- You can limit the size of the Expander by hard-coding its Height and Width. Unfortunately, this is likely to truncate the content that's inside if it's too large.

- You can create a scrollable expandable region using the ScrollViewer.

For the most part, these techniques are quite straightforward. The only one that requires any further exploration is the combination of an Expander and a ScrollViewer. In order for this approach to work, you need to hard-code the size for the ScrollViewer. Otherwise, it will simply expand to fit its content.

Here's an example:

```
<Expander Margin="5" Padding="5" Header="Region Two">
  <ScrollViewer Height="50">
    <TextBlock TextWrapping="Wrap">
    ...
    </TextBlock>
  </ScrollViewer>
</Expander>
```

It would be nice to have a system in which an Expander could set the size of its content region based on the available space in a window. However, this would present obvious complexities. (For example, how would space be shared between multiple regions when an

Expander expands?) The Grid layout container might seem like a potential solution, but unfortunately it doesn't integrate well with the Expander. If you try it out you'll end up with oddly spaced rows that don't update their heights properly when an Expander is collapsed.

Decorators

You've now seen several containers that are designed to help you manage other bits of content, including the ScrollViewer, GroupBox, and Expander. That makes this a good point to pause and consider another branch of container-like elements that *aren't* content controls. These are *decorators*, and they're typically used to add some sort of graphical embellishment around an object.

All decorators derive from System.Windows.Controls.Decorator. Most decorators are designed for use with specific controls. For example, the Button uses a ButtonChrome decorator to get its trademark rounded corner and shaded background, while the ListBox uses the ListBoxChrome decorator. Changing the appearance of these controls involves replacing their decorator with something else, as you'll see in Chapter 15.

There are also two more general decorators that are useful when composing user interfaces: the Border and the Viewbox.

The Border

The Border class is pure simplicity. It takes a single piece of nested content (which is often a layout panel) and adds a background or border around it.

To master the Border, you need nothing more than the properties listed in Table 5-1.

Table 5-1. *Properties of the Border Class*

Name	Description
Background	Sets a background that appears behind all the content in the border using a Brush object. You can use a solid color or something more exotic.
BorderBrush and BorderThickness	Set the color of the border that appears at the edge of the Border object, using a Brush object, and set the width of the border, respectively. To show a border, you must set both properties.
CornerRadius	Allows you to gracefully round the corners of your border. The greater the CornerRadius, the more dramatic the rounding effect is.
Padding	Adds spacing between the border and the content inside. (By contrast, margin adds spacing outside the border.)

Here's a straightforward, slightly rounded border around a group of buttons in a StackPanel:

```
<Border Margin="5" Padding="5" Background="LightYellow"
 BorderBrush="SteelBlue" BorderThickness="3,5,3,5" CornerRadius="3"
 VerticalAlignment="Top">
  <StackPanel>
    <Button Margin="3">One</Button>
```

```
    <Button Margin="3">Two</Button>
    <Button Margin="3">Three</Button>
  </StackPanel>
</Border>
```

Figure 5-12 shows the result.

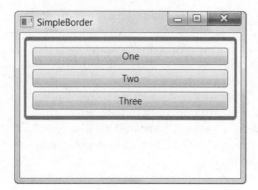

Figure 5-12. *A basic border*

Chapter 7 has more details about brushes and the colors you can use to set BorderBrush and Background.

■**Note** Content controls already have border properties. For example, the Expander controls shown in Figure 5-10 and Figure 5-11 use them to draw a nice outline around the expandable region. (The only exception is the Button control, which doesn't use its border properties because it relies on the ButtonChrome decorator instead.) The Border element is intended to add a border around elements that *don't* have this functionality—namely the layout containers you explored in Chapter 4.

The Viewbox

The Viewbox is a more exotic decorator. Its full use won't become apparent until you learn more about custom drawing in Chapter 13. However, the basic principle behind the Viewbox is easy enough to grasp. Basically, any content you place inside the Viewbox is scaled up or down to fit the bounds of the Viewbox.

The Viewbox scaling process is much more dramatic than the stretch alignment settings you learned about in Chapter 4. When you stretch an element, you simply change the space that's available to that element. This change doesn't have an effect on most vector content because vector drawings usually use fixed coordinates.

For example, consider the button-with-a-shape example that you saw earlier. This shape is placed inside a Grid, and the Grid sizes itself just big enough to fit all the polygons inside. If you enlarge the button, the shape doesn't change—it's just centered inside the button (see Figure 5-13). That's because the size of each polygon is set in absolute coordinates.

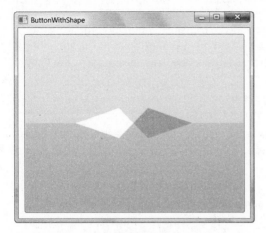

Figure 5-13. *A resized graphical button*

The scaling that the Viewbox does is similar to the scaling you see in WPF if you increase the system DPI setting. It changes every onscreen element proportionately, including images, text, lines and shapes, and the borders on common elements such as the button. If you revise the button-with-a-shape example by wrapping the Grid in a Viewbox, you'll see the resizing behavior that's shown in Figure 5-14:

```
<Button Margin="3">
  <Viewbox>
    <Grid>
      <Polygon Points="100,25 125,0 200,25 125,50"
        Fill="LightSteelBlue" />
      <Polygon Points="100,25 75,0 0,25 75,50"
        Fill="White"/>
    </Grid>
  </Viewbox>
</Button>
```

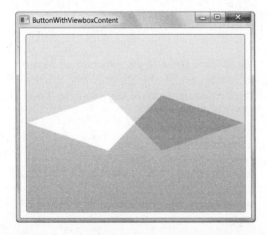

Figure 5-14. *A resized graphical button that uses a Viewbox*

Even though the polygons in the Grid use hard-coded coordinates, the Viewbox is clever enough to transform these coordinates. It decides how to transform them by comparing the Grid's desired size—the size it wants to make itself based on the shape content—against the available size. For example, if the Viewbox is twice as large as the Grid's desired size, the Viewbox scales all its content by a factor of 2.

■Note Usually, you'll only want to use the Viewbox for vector graphics, not ordinary elements and controls.

By default, the Viewbox performs proportional scaling that preserves the aspect ratio of its contents. That means that even if the shape of the button changes, the shape inside won't. (Instead, the Viewbox uses the largest scaling factor that fits inside the available space.) However, you can change this behavior using the Viewbox.Stretch property. By default, it's set to Uniform. Change it to Fill, and the content inside the Viewbox is stretched in both directions to fit the available space exactly, even if it mangles your original drawing.

You can also get more control with the StretchDirection property. By default, this property is set to Both, but you can use UpOnly to create content that can grow but won't shrink beyond its original size and DownOnly to create content that can shrink but not grow.

■Tip If you need more control, such as the ability to set a maximum upper bound and lower bound for the size of your content, consider limiting the size of the Viewbox (or its container) using properties such as MaxHeight, MinHeight, MaxWidth, and MinWidth.

The Last Word

As you've seen, WPF supports more than one content model. In the previous chapter, you learned about panels, which can wrap multiple elements and apply layout logic. In this chapter you considered content controls, which hold a single element and can range from basics (labels and buttons) to specialized containers that create scrollable and collapsible regions. You also took a quick detour to consider decorators, which allow you to add borders and provide dynamic scaling.

WPF still has more in store. In later chapters, you'll learn about items controls that have yet another content model—they can hold multiple items, each of which is displayed in a specific way (in a list box, a tree, a menu, and so on). But first, in the next chapter you'll consider the changes in the WPF event system and a new type of property.

CHAPTER 6

■■■

Dependency Properties and Routed Events

Every .NET programmer is familiar with properties and events, which are a core part of .NET's object abstraction. Few would expect WPF, a user interface technology, to change either of these fundamentals. But surprisingly enough, that's exactly what WPF does.

First, WPF replaces ordinary .NET properties with a higher-level *dependency property* feature. Dependency properties use more efficient storage and support higher-level features such as change notification and property value inheritance (the ability to propagate default values down the element tree). Dependency properties are also the basis for a number of key WPF features, including animation, data binding, and styles. Fortunately, even though the plumbing has changed, you can read and set dependency properties in code in exactly the same way as traditional .NET properties.

The second shift replaces ordinary .NET events with a higher-level *routed event* feature. Routed events are events with more traveling power—they can tunnel down or bubble up the element tree and be processed by event handlers along the way. Routed events allow an event to be handled on one element (such as a label) even though it originates on another (such as an image inside that label). As with dependency properties, routed events can be consumed in the traditional way—by connecting an event handler with the right signature—but you need to understand how they work to unlock all their features.

In this chapter, you'll start by taking a look at dependency properties. You'll see how they're defined and what features they support. Then you'll explore the WPF event system and learn how to fire and handle routed events. Finally, you'll consider the essential WPF events for dealing with mouse and keyboard actions.

Understanding Dependency Properties

Dependency properties are a completely new implementation of properties—one that has a significant amount of added value. You need dependency properties to plug into core WPF features, such as animation, data binding, and styles.

Most of the properties that are exposed by WPF elements are dependency properties. In all the examples you've seen up to this point, you've been using dependency properties without realizing it. That's because dependency properties are designed to be consumed in the same way as normal properties.

However, dependency properties are *not* normal properties. It's comforting to think of a dependency property as a normal property (defined in the typical .NET fashion) with a set of WPF features added on. Conceptually, dependency features behave this way, but that's not how they're implemented behind the scenes. The simple reason why is performance. If the designers of WPF simply added extra features on top of the .NET property system, they'd need to create a complex, bulky layer for your code to travel through. Ordinary properties could not support all the features of dependency properties without this extra overhead.

Dependency properties are a WPF-specific creation. However, the dependency properties in the WPF libraries are always wrapped by ordinary .NET property procedures. This makes them usable in the normal way, even with code that has no understanding of the WPF dependency property system. It seems odd to think of an older technology wrapping a newer one, but that's how WPF is able to change a fundamental ingredient such as properties without disrupting the rest of the .NET world.

Defining and Registering a Dependency Property

You'll spend much more time using dependency properties than creating them. However, there are still many reasons that you'll need to create your own dependency properties. Obviously, they're a key ingredient if you're designing a custom WPF element. However, they're also required in some cases if you want to add data binding, animation, or another WPF feature to a portion of code that wouldn't otherwise support it. For example, you'll see your first required use of dependency properties in Chapter 9, when persisting custom information in a page-based application.

Creating a dependency property isn't difficult, but the syntax takes a little getting used to. It's thoroughly different than creating an ordinary .NET property.

The first step is to define an object that *represents* your property. This is an instance of the DependencyProperty class. The information about your property needs to be available all the time, and possibly even shared among classes (as is common with WPF elements). For that reason, your DependencyProperty object must be defined as a static field in the associated class.

For example, the FrameworkElement class defines a Margin property that all elements share. Unsurprisingly, Margin is a dependency property. That means it's defined in the FrameworkElement class like this:

```
public class FrameworkElement: UIElement, ...
{
    public static readonly DependencyProperty MarginProperty;


    ...
}
```

By convention, the field that defines a dependency property has the name of the ordinary property, plus the word *Property* at the end. That way, you can separate the dependency property definition from the name of the actual property. The field is defined with the readonly keyword, which means it can only be set in the static constructor for the FrameworkElement.

Defining the DependencyProperty object is just the first step. In order for it to become usable, you need to register your dependency property with WPF. This step needs to be completed before any code uses the property, so it must be performed in a static constructor for the associated class.

WPF ensures that DependencyProperty objects can't be instantiated directly, because the DependencyObject class has no public constructor. Instead, a DependencyObject instance can be created only using the static DependencyProperty.Register() method. WPF also ensures that DependencyProperty objects can't be changed after they're created, because all DependencyProperty members are read-only. Instead, their values must be supplied as arguments to the Register() method.

The following code shows an example of how a DependencyPropery must be created. Here, the FrameworkElement class uses a static constructor to initialize the MarginProperty:

```
static FrameworkElement()
{
    FrameworkPropertyMetadata metadata = new FrameworkPropertyMetadata(
        new Thickness(), FrameworkPropertyMetadataOptions.AffectsMeasure);

    MarginProperty = DependencyProperty.Register("Margin",
        typeof(Thickness), typeof(FrameworkElement), metadata,
        new ValidateValueCallback(FrameworkElement.IsMarginValid));
    ...
}
```

There are two steps involved in registering a dependency property. First, you create a FrameworkPropertyMetadata object that indicates what services you want to use with your dependency property (such as support for data binding, animation, and journaling). Next, you register the property by calling the static DependencyProperty.Register() method. At this point, you are responsible for supplying a few key ingredients:

- The property name (Margin in this example)

- The data type used by the property (the Thickness structure in this example)

- The type that owns this property (the FrameworkElement class in this example)

- Optionally, a FrameworkPropertyMetadata object with additional property settings

- Optionally, a callback that performs validation for the property

The first three details are all straightforward. The FrameworkPropertyMetadata object and the validation callback are more interesting. You'll take a look at these details in the following two sections.

Property Validation

The validation callback allows you to enforce the validation that you'd normally add in the set portion of a property procedure. The callback you supply must point to a method that accepts an object parameter and returns a Boolean value. You return true to accept the object as valid and false to reject it.

The validation of the FrameworkElement.Margin property isn't terribly interesting because it relies on an internal Thickness.IsValid() method. This method makes sure the Thickness object is valid for its current use (representing a margin). For example, it may be possible to construct a perfectly acceptable Thickness object that isn't acceptable for setting the margin. One example is a Thickness object with negative dimensions. If the supplied Thickness object isn't valid for a margin, the IsMarginValid property returns false:

```
private static bool IsMarginValid(object value)
{
    Thickness thickness1 = (Thickness) value;
    return thickness1.IsValid(true, false, true, false);
}
```

There's one limitation with validation callbacks: they are static methods that don't have access to the object that's being validated. All you get is the newly applied value. While that makes them easier to reuse, it also makes it impossible to create a validation routine that takes other properties into account. The classic example is an element with a Maximum and Minimum property. Clearly, it should not be possible to set the Maximum to a value that's less than the Minimum. However, you can't enforce this logic with a validation callback because you'll only have access to one property at a time.

■**Note** The preferred approach to solve this problem is to use value *coercion*. Coercion is a step that occurs just before validation, and it allows you to modify a value to make it more acceptable (for example, raising the Maximum so it's at least equal to the Minimum) or disallow the change altogether. The coercion step is handled through another callback, but this one's attached to the FrameworkPropertyMetadata object, which is described in the next section.

The Property Wrapper

The final step is to wrap your WPF property in traditional .NET property. However, whereas typical property procedures retrieve or set the value of a private field, the property procedures for a WPF property use the GetValue() and SetValue() methods that are defined in the base DependencyObject class. Here's an example:

```
public Thickness Margin
{
    set { SetValue(MarginProperty, value); }
    get { return (Thickness)GetValue(MarginProperty); }
}
```

When you create the property wrapper, you should include nothing more than a call to SetValue() and a call to GetValue(), as in the previous example. You should *not* add any extra code to validate values, raise events, and so on. That's because other features in WPF may bypass the property wrapper and call SetValue() and GetValue() directly. (One example is when a compiled XAML file is parsed at runtime.) Both SetValue() and GetValue() are public.

■Note The property wrapper isn't the right place to validate data or raise an event. However, WPF does provide a place for this code—the trick is to use dependency property callbacks. Validation should be performed through the DependencyProperty.ValidateValueCallback shown previously, while events can be raised from the FrameworkPropertyMetadata.PropertyChangedCallback shown in the next section.

You now have a fully functioning dependency property, which you can set just like any other .NET property using the property wrapper:

```
myElement.Margin = new Thickness(5);
```

There's one extra detail. Dependency properties follow strict rules of precedence to determine their current value. Even if you don't set a dependency property directly, it may already have a value—perhaps one that's applied by a binding, style, or animation, or one that's inherited through the element tree. (You'll learn more about these rules of precedence a bit later in the section "How WPF Uses Dependency Properties.") However, as soon as you set the value directly, it overrides all these other influences.

At some point later, you may want to remove your local value setting and let the property value be determined as though you never set it. Obviously, you can't accomplish this by setting a new value. Instead, you need to use another method that's inherited from DependencyObject: the ClearValue() method. Here's how it works:

```
myElement.ClearValue(FrameworkElement.MarginProperty);
```

Property Metadata

Technically, you don't need to create a FrameworkPropertyMetadata object because there's an overload of the Dependency.Register() method that doesn't require one. However, you need the FrameworkPropertyMetadata object if you want to configure any one of a number of dependency property features.

■Note In the Windows Forms platform, the same function is provided using ordinary .NET attributes from several namespaces. Although you'll still use some attributes with WPF elements (for example, to attach custom type converters), the system is clearer because several important options are grouped into the FrameworkPropertyMetadata class.

Most of these features are configured through simple Boolean flags. (The default value for each Boolean flag is false.) A few are callbacks that point to custom methods that you create to perform a specific task. Table 6-1 lists the available properties.

Table 6-1. *Properties of the FrameworkPropertyMetadata Class*

Name	Description
AffectsArrange, AffectsMeasure, AffectsParentArrange, and AffectsParentMeasure	If true, the dependency property may affect how adjacent elements (or the parent element) are placed during the measure pass and the arrange pass of a layout operation. For example, the Margin dependency property sets AffectsMeasure to true, signaling that if the margin of an element changes, the layout container needs to repeat the measure step to determine the new placement of elements.
AffectsRender	If true, the dependency property may affect something about the way an element is drawn, requiring that the element be repainted.
BindsTwoWayByDefault	If true, this dependency property will use two-way data binding instead of one-way data binding by default. However, you can specify the binding behavior you want explicitly when you create the binding.
Inherits	If true, the dependency property value propagates through the element tree and can be inherited by nested elements. For example, Font is an inheritable dependency property—if you set it on a higher-level element, it's inherited by nested elements, unless they explicitly override it with their own font settings.
IsAnimationProhibited	If true, the dependency property can't be used in an animation.
IsNotDataBindable	If true, the dependency property can't be set with a binding expression.
Journal	If true, this dependency property will be persisted to the journal (the history of visited pages) in a page-based application.
SubPropertiesDoNotAffectRender	If true, WPF will not rerender an object if one of its subproperties (the property of a property) changes.
DefaultUpdateSourceTrigger	This sets the default value for the Binding.UpdateSourceTrigger property when this property is used in a binding expression. The UpdateSourceTrigger determines when a databound value applies its changes. You can set the UpdateSourceTrigger property manually when you create the binding.
DefaultValue	This sets the default value for the dependency property.
CoerceValueCallback	This provides a callback that attempts to "correct" a property value before it's validated.
PropertyChangedCallback	This provides a callback that is called when a property value is changed.

Property Coercion

It's important to understand the relationship between the ValidateValueCallback (which you can supply as an argument to the DependencyProperty.Register() method) and the PropertyChangedCallback and CoerceValueCallback (which you can supply as constructor arguments when creating the FrameworkPropertyMetadata object). Here's how all the pieces come into play:

- First, the CoerceValueCallback method has the opportunity to modify the supplied value (usually, to make it consistent with other properties) or return DependencyProperty.UnsetValue, which rejects the change altogether.

- Next, the ValidateValueCallback is fired. This method returns true to accept a value as valid, or false to reject it. Unlike the CoerceValueCallback, the ValidateValueCallback does not have access to the actual object on which the property is being set, which means you can't examine other property values.

- Finally, if both these previous stages succeed, the PropertyChangedCallback is triggered. At this point, you can raise a change event if you want to provide notification to other classes.

The CoerceValueCallback is the preferred way to deal with interrelated properties. For example, the ScrollBar provides Maximum, Minimum, and Value properties, all of which are inherited from the RangeBase class. When the Maximum is set, it's coerced so that it can't be less than the Minimum:

```
private static object CoerceMaximum(DependencyObject d, object value)
{
    RangeBase base1 = (RangeBase)d;
    if (((double) value) < base1.Minimum)
    {
        return base1.Minimum;
    }
    return value;
}
```

In other words, if the value that's applied to the Maximum property is less than the Minimum, the Minimum value is used instead to cap the Maximum. Notice that the CoerceValueCallback passes two parameters—the value that's being applied, *and* the object to which it's being applied.

When the Value is set, a similar coercion takes place. The Value property is coerced so that it can't fall outside of the range defined by the Minimum and Maximum, using this code:

```
internal static object ConstrainToRange(DependencyObject d, object value)
{
    double newValue = (double)value;
    RangeBase base1 = (RangeBase)d;

    double minimum = base1.Minimum;
    if (newValue < minimum)
    {
        return minimum;
    }
    double maximum = base1.Maximum;
    if (newValue > maximum)
    {
        return maximum;
    }
    return newValue;
}
```

The Minimum property doesn't use value coercion at all. Instead, once it has been changed, it triggers a PropertyChangedCallback that forces the Maximum and Value properties to follow along by manually triggering *their* coercion:

```
private static void OnMinimumChanged(DependencyObject d,
  DependencyPropertyChangedEventArgs e)
{
    RangeBase base1 = (RangeBase)d;
    ...
    base1.CoerceValue(RangeBase.MaximumProperty);
    base1.CoerceValue(RangeBase.ValueProperty);
}
```

Similarly, once the Maximum has been set and coerced, it manually coerces the Value property to fit:

```
private static void OnMaximumChanged(DependencyObject d,
  DependencyPropertyChangedEventArgs e)
{
    RangeBase base1 = (RangeBase)d;
    ...
    base1.CoerceValue(RangeBase.ValueProperty);
    base1.OnMaximumChanged((double) e.OldValue, (double)e.NewValue);
}
```

The end result is that if you set conflicting values, the Minimum takes precedence, the Maximum gets its say next (and may possibly be coerced by the Minimum), and then the Value is applied (and may be coerced by both the Maximum and Minimum).

The goal of this somewhat confusing sequence of steps is to ensure that the ScrollBar properties can be set in various orders without causing an error. This is an important consideration for initialization, such as when a window is being created for a XAML document. All WPF controls guarantee that their properties can be set in any order, without causing any change in behavior.

A careful review of the previous code calls this goal into question. For example, consider this code:

```
ScrollBar bar = new ScrollBar();
bar.Value = 100;
bar.Minimum = 1;
bar.Maximum = 200;
```

When the ScrollBar is first created, Value is 0, Minimum is 0, and Maximum is 1.

After the second line of code, the Value property is coerced to 1 (because initially the Maximum property is set to the default value 1). But something remarkable happens when you reach the fourth line of code. When the Maximum property is changed, it triggers coercion on both the Minimum and Value properties. This coercion acts on the values you specified *originally*. In other words, the local value of 100 is still stored by the WPF dependency property system, and now that it's an acceptable value, it can be applied to the Value property. Thus, after this single line of code executes, two properties have changed. Here's a closer look at what's happening:

```
ScrollBar bar = new ScrollBar();
bar.Value = 100;
// (Right now bar.Value returns 1.)
bar.Minimum = 1;
// (bar.Value still returns 1.)
bar.Maximum = 200;
// (Now now bar.Value returns 100.)
```

This behavior persists no matter when you set the Maximum property. For example, if you set a Value of 100 when the window loads, and set the Maximum property later when the user clicks a button, the Value property is still restored to its rightful value of 100 at that point. (The only way to prevent this from taking place is to set a different value or remove the local value that you've applied using the ClearValue() method that all elements inherit from DependencyObject.)

This behavior is due to WPF's property resolution system, which stores the exact local value you've set internally but *evaluates* what the property should be (using coercion and a few other considerations) when you read the property. More information about this system is in the section "How WPF Uses Dependency Properties" later in this chapter.

■**Note** Long-time Windows Forms programmers may remember the ISupportInitialize interface, which was used to solve similar problems in property initialization by wrapping a series of property changes into a batch process. Although you can use ISupportInitialize with WPF (and the XAML parser respects it), few of the WPF elements use this technique. Instead, it's encouraged to resolve these problems using value coercion. There are a number of reasons that coercion is preferred. For example, coercion solves other problems that can occur when an invalid value is applied through a data binding or animation, unlike the ISupportInitialize interface.

Shared Dependency Properties

Some classes share the same dependency property, even though they have separate class hierarchies. For example, both TextBlock.FontFamily and Control.FontFamily point to the same static dependency property, which is actually defined in the TextElement class and TextElement.FontFamilyProperty. The static constructor of TextElement registers the property, but the static constructors of TextBlock and Control simply reuse it by calling the DependencyProperty.AddOwner() method:

```
TextBlock.FontFamilyProperty =
  TextElement.FontFmamilyProperty.AddOwner(typeof(TextBlock));
```

You can use the same technique when you create your own custom classes (assuming the property is not already provided in the class you're inheriting from, in which case you get it for free). You can also use an overload of the AddOwner() method that allows you to supply a validation callback and a new FrameworkPropertyMetadata that will only apply to this new use of the dependency property.

Reusing dependency properties can lead to some strange side effects in WPF, most notably with styles. For example, if you use a style to set the TextBlock.FontFamily property automatically, your style will also affect the Control.FontFamily property because behind the scenes both classes use the same dependency property. You'll see this phenomenon in action in Chapter 12.

Attached Dependency Properties

Chapter 2 introduced a special type of dependency property called an *attached property*. An attached property is a dependency property, and it's managed by the WPF property system. The difference is that an attached property applies to a class other than the one where it's defined.

The most common example of attached properties is found in the layout containers described in Chapter 4. For example, the Grid class defines the attached properties Row and Column, which you set on the contained elements to indicate where they should be positioned. Similarly, the DockPanel defines the attached property Dock, and the Canvas defines the attached properties Left, Right, Top, and Bottom.

To define an attached property, you use the RegisterAttached() method instead of Register(). Here's an example that registers the Grid.Row property:

```
FrameworkPropertyMetadata metadata = new FrameworkPropertyMetadata(
  0, new PropertyChangedCallback(Grid.OnCellAttachedPropertyChanged));

Grid.RowProperty = DependencyProperty.RegisterAttached("Row", typeof(int),
  typeof(Grid), metadata, new ValidateValueCallback(Grid.IsIntValueNotNegative));
```

As with an ordinary dependency property, you can supply a FrameworkPropertyMetadata object and a ValidateValueCallback.

When creating an attached property, you don't define the .NET property wrapper. That's because attached properties can be set on *any* dependency object. For example, the Grid.Row property may be set on a Grid object (if you have one Grid nested inside another) or on some other element. In fact, the Grid.Row property can be set on an element even if that element isn't in a Grid—and even if there isn't a single Grid object in your element tree.

Instead of using a .NET property wrapper, attached properties require a pair of static methods that can be called to set and get the property value. These methods use the familiar SetValue() and GetValue() methods (inherited from the DependencyObject class). The static methods should be named Set*PropertyName*() and Get*PropertyName*().

Here are the static methods that implement the Grid.Row attached property:

```
public static int GetRow(UIElement element)
{
    if (element == null)
    {
        throw new ArgumentNullException(...);
    }
    return (int)element.GetValue(Grid.RowProperty);
}

public static void SetRow(UIElement element, int value)
```

```
{
    if (element == null)
    {
        throw new ArgumentNullException(...);
    }
    element.SetValue(Grid.RowProperty, value);
}
```

Here's an example that positions an element in the first row of a Grid using code:

```
Grid.SetRow(txtElement, 0);
```

Alternatively, you can call the SetValue() or GetValue() method directly and bypass the static methods:

```
txtElement.SetValue(Grid.RowProperty, 0);
```

The SetValue() method also provides one brain-twisting oddity. Although XAML doesn't allow it, you can use an overloaded version of the SetValue() method in code to attach a value for any dependency property, *even if that property isn't defined as an attached property*. For example, the following code is perfectly legitimate:

```
ComboBox comboBox = new ComboBox();
...
comboBox.SetValue(PasswordBox.PasswordCharProperty, "*");
```

Here, a value for the PasswordBox.PasswordChar property is set for a ComboBox object, even though PasswordBox.PasswordCharProperty is registered as an ordinary dependency property, not an attached property. This action won't change the way the ComboBox works—after all, the code inside the ComboBox won't look for the value of a property that it doesn't know exists—but you could act upon the PasswordChar value in your own code.

Although rarely used, this quirk provides some more insight into the way the WPF property system works, and it demonstrates its remarkable extensibility. It also shows that even though attached properties are registered with a different method than normal dependency properties, in the eyes of WPF there's no real distinction. The only difference is what the XAML parser allows. Unless you register your property as an attached property, you won't be able to set it in on other elements in your markup.

How WPF Uses Dependency Properties

As you'll discover throughout this book, dependency properties are required for a range of WPF features. However, all of these features work through two key behaviors that every dependency property supports—change notification and dynamic value resolution.

As you've already seen, when you change the value of a dependency property, a callback is triggered. This callback is part of the low-level plumbing of WPF, and it takes care of updating data bindings and firing triggers. Contrary to what you might expect, dependency properties do *not* automatically fire events to let you know when a property value changes. Instead, they trigger a protected method named OnPropertyChangedCallback(). This method passes the information along to two WPF services (data binding and triggers) and calls the PropertyChangedCallback, if one is defined.

In other words, if you want to perform an action when a property changes, you have two choices—you can create a binding that uses the property value (Chapter 15), or you can write a trigger that automatically changes another property or starts an animation (Chapter 12). However, dependency properties don't give you a general-purpose way to fire off some code to respond to a property change.

■**Note** If you're dealing with a control that you've created, you can use the property callback mechanism to react to property changes and even raise an event. Many common controls use this technique for properties that correspond to user-supplied information. For example, the TextBox provides a TextChanged event and the ScrollBar provides a ValueChanged event. A control can implement functionality like this using the PropertyChangedCallback, but this functionality isn't exposed from dependency properties in a general way for performance reasons.

The second feature that's key to the way dependency properties work is dynamic value resolution. This means when you retrieve the value from a dependency property, WPF takes several factors into consideration. You've already seen this at work in the ScrollBar example, where the Value property depends on both the value applied locally by code and the Coerce-ValueCallback.

This behavior gives dependency properties their name—in essence, a dependency property *depends* on multiple property providers, each with its own level of precedence. When you retrieve a value from a property value, the WPF property system goes through a series of steps to arrive at the final value. First, it determines the base value for the property by considering the following factors, arranged from lowest to highest precedence:

1. The default value (as set by the FrameworkPropertyMetadata object)

2. The inherited value (if the FrameworkPropertyMetadata.Inherits flag is set and a value has been applied to an element somewhere up the containment hierarchy)

3. The value from a theme style (as discussed in Chapter 15)

4. The value from a project style (as discussed in Chapter 12)

5. The local value (in other words, a value you've set directly on this object using code or XAML)

As this list shows, you override the entire hierarchy by applying a value directly. If you don't, the value is determined by the next applicable item up on the list.

■**Note** One of the advantages of this system is that it's very economical. If the value of a property has not been set locally, WPF will retrieve its value from a style, another element, or the default. In this case, no memory is required to store the value. You can quickly see the savings if you add a few buttons to a form. Each button has dozens of properties which, if they are set through one of these mechanisms, use no memory at all.

WPF follows the previous list to determine the *base value* of a dependency property. However, the base value is not necessarily the final value that you'll retrieve from a property. That's because WPF considers several other providers that can change a property's value.

Here's the five-step process WPF follows to determine a property value:

1. Determine the base value (as described previously).

2. If the property is set using an expression, evaluate that expression. Currently, WPF supports two types of expression: resources (Chapter 11) and data binding (Chapter 15).

3. If this property is the target of animation, apply that animation.

4. Run the CoerceValueCallback to "correct" the value.

5. Run the PropertyChangedCallback to disallow invalid data.

Essentially, dependency properties are hardwired into a small set of WPF services. If it weren't for this infrastructure, these features would add unnecessary complexity and significant overhead.

■**Tip** In future versions of WPF, the dependency property pipeline could be extended to include additional services. When you design custom elements (a topic covered in Chapter 24), you'll probably use dependency properties for most (if not all) of their public properties.

Understanding Routed Events

Every .NET developer is familiar with the idea of *events*—messages that are sent by an object (such as a WPF element) to notify your code when something significant occurs. WPF enhances the .NET event model with a new concept of *event routing*. Event routing allows an event to originate in one element but be raised by another one. For example, event routing allows a click that begins in a toolbar button to rise up to the toolbar and then to the containing window before it's handled by your code.

Event routing gives you the flexibility to write tight, well-organized code that handles events in the most convenient place. It's also a necessity for working with the WPF content model, which allows you to build simple elements (such as a button) out of dozens of distinct ingredients, each of which has its own independent set of events.

Defining and Registering a Routed Event

The WPF event model is quite similar to the WPF property model. As with dependency properties, routed events are represented by read-only static fields, registered in a static constructor, and wrapped by a standard .NET event definition.

For example, the WPF Button class provides the familiar Click event, which is inherited from the abstract ButtonBase class. Here's how the event is defined and registered:

```
public abstract class ButtonBase : ContentControl, ...
{
```

```
// The event definition.
public static readonly RoutedEvent ClickEvent;

// The event registration.
static ButtonBase()
{
    ButtonBase.ClickEvent = EventManager.RegisterRoutedEvent(
      "Click", RoutingStrategy.Bubble,
      typeof(RoutedEventHandler), typeof(ButtonBase));
    ...
}

// The traditional event wrapper.
public event RoutedEventHandler Click
{
    add
    {
        base.AddHandler(ButtonBase.ClickEvent, value);
    }
    remove
    {
        base.RemoveHandler(ButtonBase.ClickEvent, value);
    }
}

...
}
```

While dependency properties are registered with the DependencyProperty.Register() method, routed events are registered with the EventManager.RegisterRoutedEvent() method. When registering an event, you need to specify the name of the event, the type of routine (more on that later), the delegate that defines the syntax of the event handler (in this example, RoutedEventHandler), and the class that owns the event (in this example, ButtonBase).

Usually, routed events are wrapped by ordinary .NET events to make them accessible to all .NET languages. The event wrapper adds and removes registered callers using the AddHandler() and RemoveHandler() methods, both of which are defined in the base FrameworkElement class and inherited by every WPF element.

Of course, like any event, the defining class needs to raise it at some point. Exactly where this takes place is an implementation detail. However, the important detail is that your event is *not* raised through the traditional .NET event wrapper. Instead, you use the RaiseEvent() method that every element inherits from the UIElement class. Here's the appropriate code from deep inside the ButtonBase class:

```
RoutedEventArgs e = new RoutedEventArgs(ButtonBase.ClickEvent, this);
base.RaiseEvent(e);
```

The RaiseEvent() method takes care of firing the event to every caller that's been registered with the AddHandler() method. Because AddHandler() is public, callers have a choice—they can register themselves directly by calling AddHandler(), or they can use the event wrapper. (The following section demonstrates both approaches.) Either way, they'll be notified when the RaiseEvent() method is invoked.

As with dependency properties, the definition of a routed event can be shared between classes. For example, two base classes use the MouseUp event: UIElement (which is the starting point for ordinary WPF elements) and ContentElement (which is the starting point for content elements, which are individual bits of content that can be placed in a flow document). The MouseUp event is defined by the System.Windows.Input.Mouse class. The UIElement and ContentElement classes simply reuse it with the RoutedEvent.AddOwner() method:

```
UIElement.MouseUpEvent = Mouse.MouseUpEvent.AddOwner(typeof(UIElement));
```

All WPF events use the familiar .NET convention for event signatures. That first parameter of every event handler provides a reference to the object that fired the event (the sender). The second parameter is an EventArgs object that bundles together any additional details that might be important. For example, the MouseUp event provides a MouseEventArgs object that indicates what mouse buttons were pressed when the event occurred:

```
private void img_MouseUp(object sender, MouseButtonEventArgs e)
{
}
```

In Windows Forms applications, it was customary for many events to use the base EventArgs class if they didn't need to pass along any extra information. However, the situation is different in WPF applications due to their support for the routed event model.

In WPF, if an event doesn't need to send any additional details, it uses the RoutedEventArgs class, which includes some details about how the event was routed. If the event *does* need to transmit extra information, it uses a more specialized RoutedEventArgs-derived object (such as MouseButtonEventArgs in the previous example). Because every WPF event argument class derives from RoutedEventArgs, every WPF event handler has access to information about event routing.

Attaching an Event Handler

As you learned in Chapter 2, there are several ways to attach an event handler. The most common approach is to add an event attribute to your XAML markup. The event attribute is named after the event you want to handle, and its value is the name of the event handler method. Here's an example that uses this syntax to connect the MouseUp event of the Image to an event handler named img_MouseUp:

```
<Image Source="happyface.jpg" Stretch="None"
 Name="img" MouseUp="img_MouseUp" />
```

Although it's not required, it's a common convention to name event handler methods in the form ElementName_EventName. If the element doesn't have a defined name (presumably because you don't need to interact with it in any other place in your code), consider using the name it *would* have:

```
<Button Click="cmdOK_Click">OK</Button>
```

■Tip It may be tempting to attach an event to a high-level method that performs a task, but you'll have more flexibility if you keep an extra layer of event handling code. For example, when you click a button named cmdUpdate, it shouldn't trigger a method named UpdateDatabase() directly. Instead, it should call an event handler such as cmdUpdate_Click(), which can then call the UpdateDatabase() method that does the real work. This pattern gives you the flexibility to change where your database code is located, replace the update button with a different control, and wire several controls to the same process, all without limiting your ability to change the user interface later on. If you want a simpler way to deal with actions that can be triggered from several different places in a user interface (toolbar buttons, menu commands, and so on), you'll want to add the WPF command feature that's described in Chapter 10.

You can also connect an event with code. Here's the code equivalent of the XAML markup shown previously:

```
img.MouseUp += new MouseButtonEventHandler(img_MouseUp);
```

This code creates a delegate object that has the right signature for the event (in this case, an instance of the MouseButtonEventHandler delegate) and points that delegate to the img_MouseUp() method. It then adds the delegate to the list of registered event handlers for the img.MouseUp event.

C# also allows a more streamlined syntax that creates the appropriate delegate object implicitly:

```
img.MouseUp += img_MouseUp;
```

The code approach is useful if you need to dynamically create a control and attach an event handler at some point during the lifetime of your window. By comparison, the events you hook up in XAML are always attached when the window object is first instantiated. The code approach also allows you to keep your XAML simpler and more streamlined, which is perfect if you plan to share it with nonprogrammers, such as a design artist. The drawback is a significant amount of boilerplate code that will clutter up your code files.

The previous code approach relies on the event wrapper, which calls the UIElement.Add-Handler() method, as shown in the previous section. You can also connect an event directly by calling UIElement.AddHandler() method yourself. Here's an example:

```
img.AddHandler(Image.MouseUpEvent,
  new MouseButtonEventHandler(img_MouseUp));
```

When you use this approach, you always need to create the appropriate delegate type (such as MouseButtonEventHandler). You can't create the delegate object implicitly, as you can when hooking up an event through the property wrapper. That's because the UIElement.AddHandler() method supports all WPF events and it doesn't know the delegate type that you want to use.

Some developers prefer to use the name of the class where the event is defined, rather than the name of the class that is firing the event. Here's the equivalent syntax that makes it clear that the MouseUpEvent is defined in UIElement:

```
img.AddHandler(UIElement.MouseUpEvent,
  new MouseButtonEventHandler(img_MouseUp));
```

■**Note** Which approach you use is largely a matter of taste. However, the drawback to this second approach is that it doesn't make it obvious that the Image class *provides* a MouseUpEvent. It's possible to confuse this code and assume it's attaching an event handler that's meant to deal with the MouseUpEvent in a nested element. You'll learn more about this technique in the section "Attached Events" later in this chapter.

If you want to detach an event handler, code is your only option. You can use the -= operator, as shown here:

```
img.MouseUp -= img_MouseUp;
```

Or you can use the UIElement.RemoveHandler() method:

```
img.RemoveHandler(Image.MouseUpEvent,
  new MouseButtonEventHandler(img_MouseUp));
```

It is technically possible to connect the same event handler to the same event more than once. This is usually the result of a coding mistake. (In this case, the event handler will be triggered multiple times.) If you attempt to remove an event handler that's been connected twice, the event will still trigger the event handler, but just once.

Event Routing

As you learned in the previous chapter, many controls in WPF are content controls, and content controls can hold any type and amount of nested content. For example, you can build a graphical button out of shapes, create a label that mixes text and pictures, or put content in a specialized container to get a scrollable or collapsible display. You can even repeat this nesting process to go as many layers deep as you want.

This ability for arbitrary nesting raises an interesting question. For example, imagine you have a label like this one, which contains a StackPanel that brings together two blocks of text and an image:

```
<Label BorderBrush="Black" BorderThickness="1">
  <StackPanel>
    <TextBlock Margin="3">
     Image and text label</TextBlock>
    <Image Source="happyface.jpg" Stretch="None" />
    <TextBlock Margin="3">
     Courtesy of the StackPanel</TextBlock>
  </StackPanel>
</Label>
```

As you already know, every ingredient you place in a WPF window derives from UIElement at some point, including the Label, StackPanel, TextBlock, and Image. UIElement defines some core events. For example, every class that derives from UIElement provides a MouseDown and MouseUp event.

But consider what happens when you click the image part of the fancy label shown here. Clearly, it makes sense for the Image.MouseDown and Image.MouseUp events to fire. But what if you want to treat all label clicks in the same way? In this case, it shouldn't matter whether the user clicks the image, some of the text, or part of the blank space inside the label border. In every case, you'd like to respond with the same code.

Clearly, you could wire up the same event handler to the MouseDown or MouseUp event of each element, but that would result in a significant amount of clutter and it would make your markup more difficult to maintain. WPF provides a better solution with its routed event model.

Routed events actually come in the following three flavors:

- **Direct events** are like ordinary .NET events. They originate in one element and don't pass to any other. For example, MouseEnter (which fires when the mouse pointer moves over an element) is a direct event.

- **Bubbling events** are events that travel *up* the containment hierarchy. For example, MouseDown is a bubbling event. It's raised first by the element that is clicked. Next, it's raised by that element's parent, and then by *that* element's parent, and so on, until WPF reaches the top of the element tree.

- **Tunneling events** are events that travel *down* the containment hierarchy. They give you the chance to preview (and possibly stop) an event before it reaches the appropriate control. For example, PreviewKeyDown allows you to intercept a key press, first at the window level, and then in increasingly more specific containers until you reach the element that had focus when the key was pressed.

When you register a routed event using the EventManager.RegisterEvent() method, you pass a value from the RoutingStrategy enumeration that indicates the event behavior you want to use for your event.

Because MouseUp and MouseDown are bubbling events, you can now determine what happens in the fancy label example. When the happy face is clicked, the MouseDown event fires in this order:

1. Image.MouseDown

2. StackPanel.MouseDown

3. Label.MouseDown

After the MouseDown event is raised for the label, it's passed on to the next control (which in this case is the Grid that lays out the containing window), and then to its parent (the window). The window is the top level of the containment hierarchy and the final stop in the event bubbling sequence. It's your last chance to handle a bubbling event such as Mouse-Down. If the user releases the mouse button, the MouseUp event fires in the same sequence.

■**Note** In Chapter 9, you'll learn how to create a page-based WPF application. In this situation, the top-level container isn't a window, but an instance of the Page class.

You aren't limited to handling a bubbling event in one place. In fact, there's no reason why you can't handle the MouseDown or MouseUp event at every level. But usually you'll choose the most appropriate level for the task at hand.

The RoutedEventArgs Class

When you handle a bubbling event, the sender parameter provides a reference to the last link in the chain. For example, if an event bubbles up from an image to a label before you handle it, the sender parameter references the label object.

In some cases, you'll want to determine where the event originally took place. You can get that information and other details from the properties of the RoutedEventArgs class (which are listed in Table 6-2). Because all WPF event argument classes inherit from RoutedEventArgs, these properties are available in any event handler.

Table 6-2. *Properties of the RoutedEventArgs Class*

Name	Description
Source	Indicates what object raised the event. In the case of a keyboard event, this is the control that had focus when the event occurred (for example, when the key was pressed). In the case of a mouse event, this is the topmost element under the mouse pointer when the event occurred (for example, when a mouse button was clicked).
OriginalSource	Indicates what object originally raised the event. Usually, the OriginalSource is the same as the source. However, in some cases the OriginalSource goes deeper in the object tree to get a behind-the-scenes element that's part of a higher-level element. For example, if you click close to the border of a window, you'll get a Window object for the event source, but a Border object for the original source. That's because a Window is composed out of individual, smaller components. To take a closer look at this composition model (and learn how to change it), head to Chapter 15, which discusses control templates.
RoutedEvent	Provides the RoutedEvent object for the event triggered by your event handler (such as the static UIElement.MouseUpEvent object). This information is useful if you're handling different events with the same event handler.
Handled	Allows you to halt the event bubbling or tunneling process. When a control sets the Handled property to true, the event doesn't travel any further and isn't raised for any other elements. (As you'll see in the section "Handling a Suppressed Event," there is one way around this limitation.)

Bubbling Events

Figure 6-1 shows a simple window that demonstrates event bubbling. When you click a part of the label, the event sequence is shown in a list box. Figure 6-1 shows the appearance of this window immediately after you click the image in the label. The MouseUp event travels through five levels, ending up at the custom BubbledLabelClick form.

Figure 6-1. *A bubbled image click*

To create this test form, the image and every element above it in the element hierarchy are wired up to the same event handler—a method named SomethingClicked(). Here's the XAML that does it:

```
<Window x:Class="RoutedEvents.BubbledLabelClick"
 xmlns="http://schemas.microsoft.com/winfx/2006/xaml/presentation"
 xmlns:x="http://schemas.microsoft.com/winfx/2006/xaml"
 Title="BubbledLabelClick" Height="359" Width="329"
MouseUp="SomethingClicked">
  <Grid Margin="3" MouseUp="SomethingClicked">
    <Grid.RowDefinitions>
      <RowDefinition Height="Auto"></RowDefinition>
      <RowDefinition Height="*"></RowDefinition>
      <RowDefinition Height="Auto"></RowDefinition>
      <RowDefinition Height="Auto"></RowDefinition>
    </Grid.RowDefinitions>
```

```xml
<Label Margin="5" Grid.Row="0" HorizontalAlignment="Left"
 Background="AliceBlue" BorderBrush="Black" BorderThickness="1"
 MouseUp="SomethingClicked">
  <StackPanel MouseUp="SomethingClicked">
    <TextBlock Margin="3"
     MouseUp="SomethingClicked">
     Image and text label</TextBlock>
    <Image Source="happyface.jpg" Stretch="None"
     MouseUp="SomethingClicked" />
    <TextBlock Margin="3"
     MouseUp="SomethingClicked">
     Courtesy of the StackPanel</TextBlock>
  </StackPanel>
</Label>

<ListBox Grid.Row="1" Margin="5" Name="lstMessages"></ListBox>
<CheckBox Grid.Row="2"  Margin="5" Name="chkHandle">
 Handle first event</CheckBox>
<Button Grid.Row="3" Margin="5" Padding="3" HorizontalAlignment="Right"
 Name="cmdClear" Click="cmdClear_Click">Clear List</Button>
</Grid>
</Window>
```

The SomethingClicked() method simply examines the properties of the RoutedEventArgs object and adds a message to the list box:

```csharp
protected int eventCounter = 0;

private void SomethingClicked(object sender, RoutedEventArgs e)
{
    eventCounter++;
    string message = "#" + eventCounter.ToString() + ":\r\n" +
      " Sender: " + sender.ToString() + "\r\n" +
      " Source: " + e.Source + "\r\n" +
      " Original Source: " + e.OriginalSource;
    lstMessages.Items.Add(message);
    e.Handled = (bool)chkHandle.IsChecked;
}
```

■**Note** Technically, the MouseUp event provides a MouseButtonEventArgs object with additional information about the mouse state at the time of the event. However, the MouseButtonEventArgs object derives from MouseEventArgs, which in turn derives from RoutedEventArgs. As a result, it's possible to use it when declaring the event handler (as shown here) if you don't need additional information about the mouse.

There's one other detail in this example. If you've checked the chkHandle check box, the SomethingClicked() method sets the RoutedEventArgs.Handled property to true, which stops the event bubbling sequence the first time an event occurs. As a result, you'll only see the first event appear in the list, as shown in Figure 6-2.

■Note There's an extra cast required here because the CheckBox.IsChecked property is a nullable Boolean value (a *bool?* rather than a *bool*). The null value represents an indeterminate state for the check box, which means it's neither checked nor unchecked. This feature isn't used in this example, so a simple cast solves the problem.

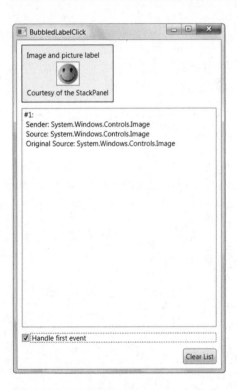

Figure 6-2. *Marking an event as handled*

Because the SomethingClicked() method handles the MouseUp event that's fired by the Window, you'll be able to intercept clicks on the list box and the blank window surface. However, the MouseUp event doesn't fire when you click the Clear button (which removes all the list box entries). That's because the button includes an interesting bit of code that suppresses the MouseUp event and raises a higher-level Click event. At the same time, the Handled flag is set to true, which prevents the MouseUp event from going any further.

Tip Unlike Windows Forms controls, most WPF elements don't expose a Click event. Instead they include the more straightforward MouseDown and MouseUp events. Click is reserved for button-based controls.

Handling a Suppressed Event

Interestingly, there *is* a way to receive events that are marked as handled. Instead of attaching the event handler through XAML, you must use the AddHandler() method described earlier. The AddHandler() method provides an overload that accepts a Boolean value for its third parameter. Set this to true, and you'll receive the event even if the Handled flag has been set:

```
cmdClear.AddHander(UIElement.MouseUpEvent,
  new MouseButtonEventHandler(cmdClear_MouseUp), true);
```

This is rarely a good design decision. The button is designed to suppress the MouseUp event for a reason: to prevent possible confusion. After all, it's a common Windows convention that buttons can be "clicked" with the keyboard in several ways. If you make the mistake of handling the MouseUp event in a Button instead of the Click event, your code will only respond to mouse clicks, not the equivalent keyboard actions.

Attached Events

The fancy label example is a fairly straightforward example of event bubbling because all the elements support the MouseUp event. However, many controls have their own more specialized events. The button is one example—it adds a Click event that isn't defined by any base class.

This introduces an interesting dilemma. Imagine you wrap a stack of buttons in a Stack-Panel. You want to handle all the button clicks in one event handler. The crude approach is to attach the Click event of each button to the same event handler. But the Click event supports event bubbling, which gives you a better option. You can handle all the button clicks by handling the Click event at a higher level (such as the containing StackPanel).

Unfortunately, this apparently obvious code doesn't work:

```
<StackPanel Click="DoSomething" Margin="5">
  <Button Name="cmd1">Command 1</Button>
  <Button Name="cmd2">Command 2</Button>
  <Button Name="cmd3">Command 3</Button>
  ...
</StackPanel>
```

The problem is that the StackPanel doesn't include a Click event, so this is interpreted by the XAML parser as an error. The solution is to use a different attached-event syntax in the form ClassName.EventName. Here's the corrected example:

```
<StackPanel Button.Click="DoSomething" Margin="5">
  <Button Name="cmd1">Command 1</Button>
  <Button Name="cmd2">Command 2</Button>
  <Button Name="cmd3">Command 3</Button>
  ...
</StackPanel>
```

Now your event handler receives the click for all contained buttons.

Note The Click event is actually defined in the ButtonBase class and inherited by the Button class. If you attach an event handler to ButtonBase.Click, that event handler will be used when any ButtonBase-derived control is clicked (including the Button, RadioButton, and CheckBox classes). If you attach an event handler to Button.Click, it's only used for Button objects.

You can wire up an attached event in code, but you need to use the UIElement. AddHandler() method rather than the += operator syntax. Here's an example (which assumes the StackPanel has been given the name pnlButtons):

```
pnlButtons.AddHandler(Button.Click, new RoutedEventHandler(DoSomething));
```

In the DoSomething() event handler you have several options for determining which button fired the event. You can compare its text (which will cause problems for localization) or its name (which is fragile because you won't catch mistyped names when you build the application). The best approach is to make sure each button has a Name property set in XAML, so that you can access the corresponding object through a field in your window class and compare that reference with the event sender. Here's an example:

```
private void DoSomething(object sender, RoutedEventArgs e)
{
    if (sender == cmd1)
    { ... }
    else if (sender == cmd2)
    { ... }
    else if (sender == cmd3)
    { ... }
}
```

Another option is to simply send a piece of information along with the button that you can use in your code. For example, you could set the Tag property of each button, as shown here:

```
<StackPanel Click="DoSomething" Margin="5">
  <Button Name="cmd1" Tag="The first button.">Command 1</Button>
  <Button Name="cmd2" Tag="The second button.">Command 2</Button>
  <Button Name="cmd3" Tag="The third button.">Command 3</Button>
  ...
</StackPanel>
```

You can then access the Tag property in your code:

```
private void DoSomething(object sender, RoutedEventArgs e)
{
    object tag = ((FrameworkElement)sender).Tag;
    MessageBox.Show((string)tag);
}
```

Tunneling Events

Tunneling events work the same as bubbling events, but in the opposite direction. For example, if MouseUp was a tunneled event (which it isn't), clicking the image in the fancy label example would cause MouseUp to fire first in the window, then in the Grid, then in the Stack-Panel, and so on until it reaches the actual source, which is the image in the label.

Tunneling events are easy to recognize because they begin with the work Preview. Furthermore, WPF usually defines bubbling and tunneling events in pairs. That means if you find a bubbling MouseUp event, you can probably also find a tunneling PreviewMouseUp event. The tunneling event always fires before the bubbling event, as shown in Figure 6-3.

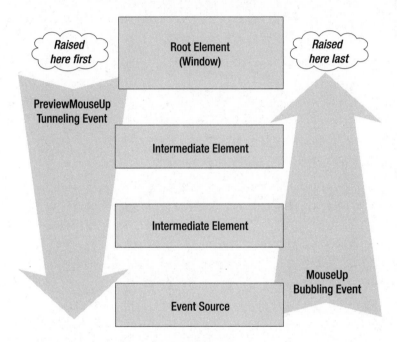

Figure 6-3. *Tunneling and bubbling events*

To make life more interesting, if you mark the tunneling event as handled the bubbling event won't occur. That's because the two events share the same instance of the RoutedEventArgs class.

Tunneling events are useful if you need to perform some preprocessing that acts on certain keystrokes or filters out certain mouse actions. Figure 6-4 shows an example that tests tunneling with the PreviewKeyDown event. When you press a key in the text box, the event is fired first in the window and then down through the hierarchy. And if you mark the PreviewKeyDown event as handled at any point, the bubbling KeyDown event won't occur.

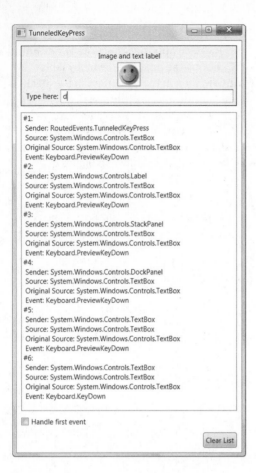

Figure 6-4. *A tunneled key press*

IDENTIFYING THE ROUTING STRATEGY OF AN EVENT

Clearly, the different routing strategies affect how you'll use an event. But how do you determine what type of routing a given event uses?

Tunneling events are straightforward. By .NET convention, a tunneling event always begins with the word Preview (as in *Preview*KeyDown). However, there's no similar mechanism to distinguish bubbling events from direct events. For developers exploring WPF, the easiest approach is to find the event in the class library reference of the help for the .NET Framework SDK (under the .NET Development ➤ .NET Framework SDK ➤ .NET Framework 3.0 Development ➤ Class Library node). You'll see Routed Event Information that indicates the static field for the event, the type of routing, and the event signature.

You can get the same information programmatically by examining the static field for the event. For example, the ButtonBase.ClickEvent.RoutingStrategy property provides an enumerated value that tells you what type of routing the Click event uses.

> **Tip** Be careful about marking a tunneling event as handled. Depending on the way the control is written, this may prevent the control from handling its own event (the related bubbling event) to perform some task or update its state.

WPF Events

Now that you've learned how WPF events work, it's time to consider the rich variety of events that you can respond to in your code. Although every element exposes a dizzying array of events, the most important events usually fall into one of four categories:

- **Lifetime events.** These events occur when the element is initialized, loaded, or unloaded.

- **Mouse events.** These events are the result of mouse actions.

- **Keyboard events.** These events are the result of keyboard actions (such as key presses).

- **Stylus events.** These events are the result of using the penlike stylus, which takes the place of a mouse on a Table PC.

Taken together, mouse, keyboard, and stylus events are known as *input* events.

Lifetime Events

All elements raise events when they are first created and when they are released. You can use these events to initialize a window. Table 6-3 lists these events, which are defined in the FrameworkElement class.

Table 6-3. *Lifetime Events for All Elements*

Name	Description
Initialized	Occurs after the element is instantiated and its properties have been set according to the XAML markup. At this point, the element is initialized, but other parts of the window may not be. Also, styles and data binding haven't been applied yet. At this point, the IsInitialized property is true. Initialized is an ordinary .NET event—not a routed event.
Loaded	Occurs after the entire window has been initialized and styles and data binding have been applied. This is the last stop before the element is rendered. At this point, the IsLoaded property is true.
Unloaded	Occurs when the element has been released, either because the containing window has been closed or the specific element has been removed from the window.

To understand how the Initialized and Loaded events relate, it helps to consider the rendering process. The FrameworkElement implements the ISupportInitialize interface, which provides two methods for controlling the initialization process. The first, BeginInit(), is called immediately after the element is instantiated. After BeginInit() is called, the XAML parser sets all the element properties (and adds any content). The second method, EndInit(), is called when initialization is complete, at which point the Initialized event fires.

■**Note** This is a slight simplification. The XAML parser takes care of calling the BeginInit() and EndInit() methods, as it should. However, if you create an element by hand and add it to a window, it's unlikely that you'll use this interface. In this case, the element raises the Initialized event once you add it to the window, just before the Loaded event.

When you create a window, each branch of elements is initialized in a bottom-up fashion. That means deeply nested elements are initialized before their containers. When the Initialized event fires, you are guaranteed that the tree of elements from the current element down is completely initialized. However, the element that *contains* your element probably isn't initialized, and you can't assume that any other part of the window is initialized.

After each element is initialized, it's also laid out in its container, styled, and bound to a data source, if required. After the Initialized event fires for the window, it's time to go on to the next stage.

Once the initialization process is complete, the Loaded event is fired. The Loaded event follows the reverse path of the Initialized event—in other words, the containing window fires the Loaded event first, followed by more deeply nested elements. When the Loaded event has fired for all elements, the window becomes visible and the elements are rendered.

The lifetime events listed in Table 6-3 don't tell the whole story. The containing window also has its own more specialized lifetime events. These events are listed in Table 6-4.

Table 6-4. *Lifetime Events for the Window Class*

Name	Description
SourceInitialized	Occurs when the HwndSource property of the window is acquired (but before the window is made visible). The HwndSource is a window handle that you may need to use if you're calling legacy functions in the Win32 API.
ContentRendered	Occurs immediately after the window has been rendered for the first time. This isn't a good place to perform any changes that might affect the visual appearance of the window, or you'll force a second render operation. (Use the Loaded event instead.) However, the ContentRendered event does indicate that your window is fully visible and ready for input.
Activated	Occurs when the user switches to this window (for example, from another window in your application or from another application). Activated also fires when the window is loaded for the first time. Conceptually, the Activated event is the window equivalent of a control's GotFocus event.
Deactivated	Occurs when the user switches away from this window (for example, by moving to another window in your application or another application). Deactivated also fires when the window is closed by a user, after the Closing event but before Closed. Conceptually, the Deactivated event is the window equivalent of a control's LostFocus event.
Closing	Occurs when the window is closed, either by a user action or programmatically using the Window.Close() method or the Application.Shutdown() method. The Closing event gives you the opportunity to cancel the operation and keep the window open by setting the CancelEventArgs.Cancel property to true. However, you won't receive the Closing event if your application is ending because the user is shutting down the computer or logging off. To deal with these possibilities, you need to handle the Application.SessionEnding event described in Chapter 3.

Name	Description
Closed	Occurs after the window has been closed. However, the element objects are still accessible, and the Unloaded event hasn't fired yet. At this point, you can perform cleanup, write settings to a persistent storage place (such as a configuration file or the Windows registry), and so on.

If you're simply interested in performing first-time initializing for your controls, the best time to take care of this task is when the Loaded event fires. Usually, you can perform all your initialization in one place, which is typically an event handler for the Window.Loaded event.

Tip You can also use the window constructor to perform your initialization (just add your code immediately after the InitializeComponent() call). However, it's always better to use the Loaded event. That's because if an exception occurs in the constructor of the Window, it's thrown while the XAML parser is parsing the page. As a result, your exception is wrapped in an unhelpful XamlParseException object (with the original exception in the InnerException property).

Input Events

All input events—events that occur due to mouse, keyboard, or stylus actions—pass along extra information in a custom event argument class. In fact, all these classes share a common ancestor: the InputEventArgs class. Figure 6-5 shows the inheritance hierarchy.

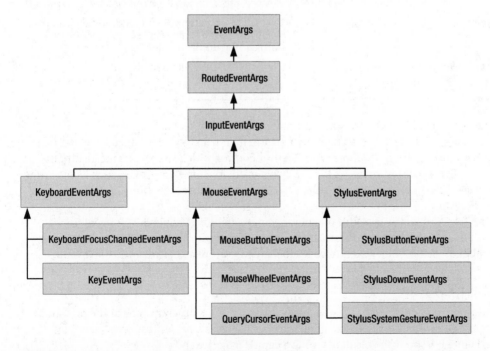

Figure 6-5. *The EventArgs classes for input events*

The InputEventArgs class adds just two properties: Timestamp and Device. The Timestamp provides an integer that indicates when the event occurred as a number of milliseconds. (The actual time that this represents isn't terribly important, but you can compare different time stamp values to determine what event took place first. Larger time stamps signify more recent events.) The Device returns an object that provides more information about the device that triggered the event, which could be the mouse, the keyboard, or the stylus. Each of these three possibilities is represented by a different class, all of which derive from the abstract System.Windows.Input.InputDevice class.

In the rest of this chapter, you'll take a closer look at how you handle mouse and keyboard actions in a WPF application.

Keyboard Input

When the user presses a key, a sequence of events unfolds. Table 6-5 lists these events in the order that they occur.

Table 6-5. *Keyboard Events for All Elements (in Order)*

Name	Routing Type	Description
PreviewKeyDown	Tunneling	Occurs when a key is pressed.
KeyDown	Bubbling	Occurs when a key is pressed.
PreviewTextInput	Tunneling	Occurs when a keystroke is complete and the element is receiving the text input. This event isn't fired for keystrokes that don't result in text being "typed" (for example, it doesn't fire when you press Ctrl, Shift, Backspace, the arrow keys, the function keys, and so on).
TextInput	Bubbling	Occurs when a keystroke is complete and the element is receiving the text input. This event isn't fired for keystrokes that don't result in text.
PreviewKeyUp	Tunneling	Occurs when a key is released.
KeyUp	Bubbling	Occurs when a key is released.

Keyboard handling is never quite as straightforward as it seems. Some controls may suppress some of these events so they can perform their own more specialized keyboard handling. The most notorious example is the TextBox control, which suppresses the TextInput event. The TextBox also suppresses the KeyDown event for some keystrokes, such as the arrow keys. In cases like these, you can usually still use the tunneling events (PreviewTextInput and PreviewKeyDown).

The TextBox control also adds one new event, named TextChanged. This event fires immediately after a keystroke causes the text in the text box to change. At this point, the new text is already visible in the text box, so it's too late to prevent a keystroke you don't want.

Handling a Key Press

The best way to understand the key events is to use a sample program such as the one shown in Figure 6-6. It monitors a text box for all the possible key events and reports when they occur. Figure 6-6 shows the result of typing a capital **S** in a text box.

Figure 6-6. *Watching the keyboard*

This example illustrates an important point. The PreviewKeyDown and KeyDown events fire every time a key is pressed. However, the TextInput event only fires when a character is "typed" into an element. This action may actually involve multiple key presses. In the example in Figure 6-5, two key presses are needed to create the capital letter S. First, the Shift key is pressed, followed by the S key. As a result, you'll see two KeyDown and KeyUp events, but only one TextInput event.

The PreviewKeyDown, KeyDown, PreviewKey, and KeyUp events all provide the same information through the KeyEventArgs object. The most important detail is the Key property, which returns a value from the System.Windows.Input.Key enumeration that identifies the key that was pressed or released. Here's the event handler that handles key events for the example in Figure 6-6:

```
private void KeyEvent(object sender, KeyEventArgs e)
{
    string message = "Event: " + e.RoutedEvent + " " +
      " Key: " + e.Key;
    lstMessages.Items.Add(message);
}
```

The Key value doesn't take into account the state of any other keys. For example, it doesn't matter whether the Shift key is currently pressed when you press the S key; either way you'll get the same Key value (Key.S).

There's one more wrinkle. Depending on your Windows keyboard settings, pressing a key causes the keystroke to be repeated after a short delay. For example, holding down the S key obviously puts a stream of S characters in the text box. Similarly, pressing the Shift key causes multiple keystrokes and a series of KeyDown events. In a real-world test where you type Shift+S, your text box will actually fire a series of KeyDown events for the Shift key, followed by a KeyDown event for the S key, a TextInput event (or TextChanged event in the case of a text box), and then a KeyUp event for the Shift and S keys. If you want to ignore these repeated Shift keys, you can check if a keystroke is the result of a key that's being held down by examining the KeyEventArgs.IsRepeat property, as shown here:

```
if ((bool)chkIgnoreRepeat.IsChecked && e.IsRepeat) return;
```

■Tip The PreviewKeyDown, KeyDown, PreviewKey, and KeyUp events are best for writing low-level keyboard handling (which you'll rarely need outside of a custom control) and handling special keystrokes, such as the function keys.

After the KeyDown event occurs, the PreviewTextInput event follows. (The TextInput event doesn't occur, because the TextBox suppresses this event.) At this point, the text has not yet appeared in the control.

The TextInput event provides your code with a TextCompositionEventArgs object. This object includes a Text property that gives you the processed text that's about to be received by the control. Here's the code that adds this text to the list shown in Figure 6-6:

```
private void TextInput(object sender, TextCompositionEventArgs e)
{
    string message = "Event: " + e.RoutedEvent + " " +
      " Text: " + e.Text;
    lstMessages.Items.Add(message);
}
```

Ideally, you'd use the PreviewTextInput to perform validation in a control like the TextBox. For example, if you're building a numeric-only text box, you could make sure that the current keystroke isn't a letter, and set the Handled flag if it is. Unfortunately, the PreviewTextInput event doesn't fire for some keys that you may need to handle. For example, if you press the space key in a text box, you'll bypass PreviewTextInput altogether. That means you also need to handle the PreviewKeyDown event.

Unfortunately, it's difficult to write robust validation logic in a PreviewKeyDown event handler because all you have is the Key value, which is a fairly low-level piece of information. For example, the Key enumeration distinguishes between the numeric key pad and the number keys that appear just above the letters on a typical keyboard. That means depending on how you press the number 9, you might get a value of Key.D9 or Key.NumPad9. Checking for all the allowed key values is tedious, to say the least.

One option is to use the KeyConverter to convert the Key value into a more useful string. For example, using KeyConverter.ConvertToString() on both Key.D9 and Key.NumPad9 returns "9" as a string. If you just use the Key.ToString() conversion, you'll get the much less useful enumeration name (either "D9" or "NumPad9"):

```
KeyConverter converter = new KeyConverter();
string key = converter.ConvertToString(e.Key);
```

However, even using the KeyConverter is a bit awkward because you'll end up with longer bits of text (such as "Backspace") for keystrokes that don't result in text input.

The best compromise is to handle both PreviewTextInput (which takes care of most of the validation) and use PreviewKeyDown for keystrokes that don't raise PreviewTextInput in the text box (such as the space key). Here's a simple solution that does it:

```
private void pnl_PreviewTextInput(object sender, TextCompositionEventArgs e)
{
    short val;
```

```
        if (!Int16.TryParse(e.Text, out val))
        {
            // Disallow non-numeric keypresses.
            e.Handled = true;
        }
    }

    private void pnl_PreviewKeyDown(object sender, KeyEventArgs e)
    {
        if (e.Key == Key.Space)
        {
            // Disallow the space key, which doesn't raise a PreviewTextInput event.
            e.Handled = true;
        }
    }
```

You can attach these event handlers to a single text box, or you can wire them up to a container (such as a StackPanel that contains several numeric-only text boxes) for greater efficiency.

Note This key handling behavior may seem unnecessarily awkward (and it is). One of the reasons that the TextBox doesn't provide better key handling is because WPF focuses on data binding, a feature that lets you wire up controls such as the TextBox to custom objects. When you use this approach, validation is usually provided by the bound object, errors are signaled by an exception, and bad data triggers an error message that appears somewhere in the user interface. Unfortunately, there's no easy way (at present) to combine the useful, high-level data binding feature with the lower-level keyboard handling that would be necessary to prevent the user from typing invalid characters altogether.

Focus

In the Windows world, a user works with one control at a time. The control that is currently receiving the user's key presses is the control that has *focus*. Sometimes this control is drawn slightly differently. For example, the WPF button uses blue shading to show that it has the focus.

In order for a control to be able to accept the focus, its Focusable property must be set to true. This is the default for all controls.

Interestingly enough, the Focusable property is defined as part of the UIElement class, which means that other noncontrol elements can also be focusable. Usually, in noncontrol classes, Focusable will be false by default. However, you can set it to true. Try this out with a layout container such as the StackPanel—when it receives the focus, a dotted border will appear around the panel's edge.

To move the focus from one element to another, the user can click the mouse or use the Tab and arrow keys. In previous development frameworks, programmers have been forced to take great care to make sure that the Tab key moves focus in a logical manner (generally from left to right and then down the window) and that the right control has focus when the window first appears. In WPF, this extra work is seldom necessary because WPF uses the hierarchical layout of your elements to implement a tabbing sequence. Essentially, when you press the Tab key you'll move to the first child in the current element or, if the current element has no children, to the next child at the same level. For example, if you tab through a window with two StackPanel containers, you'll move through all the controls in the first StackPanel and then through all the controls in the second container.

If you want to take control of tab sequence, you can set the TabIndex property for each control to place it in numerical order. The control with a TabIndex of 0 gets the focus first, followed by the next highest TabIndex value (for example, 1, then 2, then 3, and so on). If more than one element has the same TabIndex value, WPF uses the automatic tab sequence, which means it jumps to the nearest subsequent element.

■**Tip** By default, the TabIndex property for all controls is set to 1. That means you can designate a specific control as the starting point for a window by setting its TabIndex to 0 but rely on automatic navigation to guide the user through the rest of the window from that starting point, according to the order that your elements are defined.

The TabIndex property is defined in the Control class, along with an IsTabStop property. You can set IsTabStop to false to prevent a control from being included in the tab sequence. The difference between IsTabStop and Focusable is that a control with an IsTabStop value of false can still get the focus in another way—either programmatically (when your code calls its Focus() method) or by a mouse click.

Controls that are invisible or disabled ("grayed out") are generally skipped in the tab order and are not activated regardless of the TabIndex, IsTabStop, and Focusable settings. To hide or disable a control, you set the Visibility and IsEnabled properties, respectively.

Getting Key State

When a key press occurs, you often need to know more than just what key was pressed. It's also important to find out what other keys were held down at the same time. That means you might want to investigate the state of other keys, particularly modifiers such as Shift, Ctrl, and Alt.

The key events (PreviewKeyDown, KeyDown, PreviewKeyUp, and KeyUp) make this information easy to get. First, the KeyEventArgs object includes a KeyStates property that reflects the property of the key that triggered the event. More usefully, the KeyboardDevice property provides the same information for any key on the keyboard.

Not surprisingly, the KeyboardDevice property provides an instance of the KeyboardDevice class. Its properties include information about which element currently has the focus (FocusedElement) and what modifier keys were pressed when the event occurred (Modifiers). The modifier keys include Shift, Ctrl, and Alt, and you can check their status using bitwise logic like this:

```
if ((e.KeyboardDevice.Modifiers & ModifierKeys.Control) == ModifierKeys.Control)
{
    lblInfo.Text = "You held the Control key.";
}
```

The KeyboardDevice also provides a few handy methods, as listed in Table 6-6. For each of these methods, you pass in a value from the Key enumeration.

Table 6-6. *KeyboardDevice Methods*

Name	Description
IsKeyDown()	Tells you whether this key was pressed down when the event occurred.
IsKeyUp()	Tells you whether this key was up (not pressed) when the event occurred.
IsKeyToggled()	Tells you whether this key was in a "switched on" state when the event occurred. This only has a meaning for keys that can be toggled on or off, such as Caps Lock, Scroll Lock, and Num Lock.
GetKeyStates()	Returns one or more values from the KeyStates enumeration that tell you whether this key is currently up, pressed, or in a toggled state. This method is essentially the same as calling both IsKeyDown() and IsKeyToggled() on the same key.

When you use the KeyEventArgs.KeyboardDevice property, your code gets the *virtual key state*. This means it gets the state of the keyboard at the time the event occurred. This is not necessarily the same as the current keyboard state. For example, consider what happens if the user types faster than your code executes. Each time your KeyPress event fires, you'll have access to the keystroke that fired the event, not the typed-ahead characters. This is almost always the behavior you want.

However, you aren't limited to getting key information in the key events. You can also get the state of the keyboard at any time. The trick is to use the Keyboard class, which is very similar to KeyboardDevice except it's made up of static members. Here's an example that uses the Keyboard class to check the current state of the left Shift key:

```
if (Keyboard.IsKeyDown(Key.LeftShift))
{
    lblInfo.Text = "The left Shift is held down.";
}
```

■**Note** The Keyboard class also has methods that allow you to attach application-wide keyboard event handlers, such as AddKeyDownHandler() and AddKeyUpHandler(). However, these methods aren't recommended. A better approach to implementing application-wide functionality is to use the WPF command system, as described in Chapter 10.

Mouse Input

Mouse events perform several related tasks. The most fundamental mouse events allow you to react when the mouse is moved over an element. These events are MouseEnter (which fires when the mouse pointer moves over the element) and MouseLeave (which fires when the mouse pointer moves away). Both are *direct events*, which means they don't use tunneling or bubbling. Instead, they originate in one element and are raised by just that element. This makes sense because of the way controls are nested in a WPF window.

For example, if you have a StackPanel that contains a button and you move the mouse pointer over the button, the MouseEnter event will fire first for the StackPanel (once you enter its borders) and then for the button (once you move directly over it). As you move the mouse away, the MouseLeave event will fire first for the button and then for the StackPanel.

You can also react to two events that fire whenever the mouse moves: PreviewMouseMove (a tunneling event) and MouseMove (a bubbling event). All of these events provide your code with the same information: a MouseEventArgs object. The MouseEventArgs object includes properties that tell you the state that the mouse buttons were in when the event fired, and a GetPosition() method that tells you the coordinates of the mouse in relation to an element of your choosing. Here's an example that displays the position of the mouse pointer in device-independent pixels relative to the form:

```
private void MouseMoved(object sender, MouseEventArgs e)
{
    Point pt = e.GetPosition(this);
    lblInfo.Text =
      String.Format("You are at ({0},{1}) in window coordinates",
      pt.X, pt.Y);
}
```

In this case, the coordinates are measured from the top-left corner of the client area (just below the title bar). Figure 6-7 shows this code in action.

Figure 6-7. *Watching the mouse*

You'll notice that the mouse coordinates in this example are not whole numbers. That's because this screen capture was taken on a system running at 120 dpi, not the standard 96 dpi. As explained in Chapter 1, WPF automatically scales up its units to compensate, using more physical pixels. Because the size of a screen pixel no longer matches the size of the WPF unit system, the physical mouse position may be translated to a fractional number of WPF units, as shown here.

■**Tip** The UIElement class also includes two useful properties that can help with mouse hit-testing. Use IsMouseOver to determine whether a mouse is currently over an element or one of its children, and use IsMouseDirectlyOver to find out whether the mouse is over an element but not one of its children. Usually, you won't read and act on these values in code. Instead, you'll use them to build style triggers that automatically change elements as the mouse moves over them. Chapter 12 demonstrates this technique.

Mouse Clicks

Mouse clicks unfold in a similar way to key presses. The difference is that there are distinct events for the left mouse button and the right mouse button. Table 6-7 lists these events in the order they occur. Along with these are two events that react to the mouse wheel: Preview-MouseWheel and MouseWheel.

Table 6-7. *Mouse Click Events for All Elements (in Order)*

Name	Routing Type	Description
PreviewMouseLeftButtonDown and PreviewMouseRightButtonDown	Tunneling	Occurs when a mouse button is pressed
MouseLeftButtonDown	Bubbling	Occurs when a mouse button is pressed
PreviewMouseLeftButtonUp and PreviewMouseRightButtonUp	Tunneling	Occurs when a mouse button is released
MouseLeftButtonUp and MouseRightButtonUp	Bubbling	Occurs when a mouse button is released

All mouse button events provide a MouseButtonEventArgs object. The MouseButton-EventArgs class derives from MouseEventArgs (which means it includes the same coordinate and button state information) and it adds a few members. The less important of these are MouseButton (which tells you which button triggered the event) and ButtonState (which tells you whether the button was pressed or unpressed when the event occurred). The more interesting property is ClickCount, which tells you how many times the button was clicked, allowing you to distinguish single clicks (where ClickCount is 1) from double-clicks (where ClickCount is 2).

■**Tip** Usually, Windows applications react when the mouse key is raised after being clicked (the "up" event rather than the "down" event).

Some elements add higher-level mouse events. For example, the Control class adds a PreviewMouseDoubleClick and MouseDoubleClick event that take the place of the Mouse-LeftButtonUp event. Similarly, the Button class raises a Click event that can be triggered by the mouse or keyboard.

■Note As with key press events, the mouse events provide information about where the mouse was and what buttons were pressed when the mouse event occurred. To get the current mouse position and mouse button state, you can use the static members of the Mouse class, which are similar to those of the Mouse-ButtonEventArgs.

Capturing the Mouse

Ordinarily, every time an element receives a mouse button "down" event, it will receive a corresponding mouse button "up" event shortly thereafter. However, this isn't always the case. For example, if you click an element, hold down the mouse, and then move the mouse pointer off the element, the element won't receive the mouse up event.

In some situations, you may want to have a notification of mouse up events, even if they occur after the mouse has moved off your element. To do so, you need to *capture* the mouse by calling the Mouse.Capture() method and passing in the appropriate element. From that point on, you'll receive mouse down and mouse up events until you call Mouse.Capture() again and pass in a null reference. Other elements won't receive mouse events while the mouse is captured. That means the user won't be able to click buttons elsewhere in the window, click inside text boxes, and so on. Mouse capturing is sometimes used to implement draggable and resizable elements. You'll see an example with the custom drawn resizable window in Chapter 8.

■Tip When you call Mouse.Capture() you can pass in an optional CaptureMode value as the second parameter. Ordinarily, when you call Mouse.Capture() you use CaptureMode.Element, which means your element always receives the mouse events. However, you can use CaptureMode.SubTree to allow mouse events to pass through to the clicked element if that clicked element is a child of the element that's performing the capture. This makes sense if you're already using event bubbling or tunneling to watch mouse events in child elements.

In some cases, you may lose a mouse capture through no fault of your own. For example, Windows may free the mouse if it needs to display a system dialog box. You'll also lose the mouse capture if you don't free the mouse after a mouse up event occurs and the user carries on to click a window in another application. Either way, you can react to losing the mouse capture by handling the LostMouseCapture event for your element.

While the mouse has been captured by an element, you won't be able to interact with other elements. (For example, you won't be able to click another element on your window.) Mouse capturing is generally used for short-term operations such as drag-and-drop.

Drag-and-Drop

Drag-and-drop operations (a technique for pulling information out of one place in a window and depositing it in another) aren't quite as common today as they were a few years ago. Programmers have gradually settled on other methods of copying information that don't require holding down the mouse button (a technique that many users find difficult to master). Programs that do support drag-and-drop often use it as a shortcut for advanced users, rather than a standard way of working.

WPF changes very little about drag-and-drop operations. If you've used them in Windows Forms applications, you'll find the programming interface is virtually unchanged in WPF. The key difference is that the methods and events that are used for drag-and-drop operations are centralized in the System.Windows.DragDrop class and then used by other classes (such as UIElement).

Essentially, a drag-and-drop operation unfolds in three steps:

1. The user clicks an element (or selects a specific region inside it) and holds the mouse button down. At this point, some information is set aside and a drag-and-drop operation begins.

2. The user moves the mouse over another element. If this element can accept the type of content that's being dragged (for example, a bitmap or a piece of text), the mouse cursor changes to a drag-and-drop icon. Otherwise, the mouse cursor becomes a circle with a line drawn through it.

3. When the user releases the mouse button, the element receives the information and decides what to do with it. The operation can be canceled by pressing the Esc key (without releasing the mouse button).

You can try out the way drag-and-drop is supposed to work by adding two TextBox objects to a window that have the built-in logic to support drag-and-drop. If you select some text inside a text box, you can drag it to another text box. When you release the mouse button, the text will be moved. The same technique works between applications—for example, you can drag some text from a Word document and drop it into a WPF TextBox object, or vice versa.

■**Note** Don't confuse a drag-and-drop operation with the ability to "drag" an element around the window. This feature is a technique that drawing and diagramming tools use to allow you to move content around. It's demonstrated in Chapter 14.

Sometimes, you might want to allow drag-and-drop between elements that don't have the built-in functionality. For example, you might want to allow the user to drag content from a text box and drop it in a label. Or you might want to create the example shown in Figure 6-8, which allows a user to drag text from a Label or TextBox object and drop it into a different label. In this situation, you need to handle the drag-and-drop events.

Figure 6-8. *Dragging content from one element to another*

There are two sides to a drag-and-drop operation: the source and target. To create a drag-and-drop source, you need to call the DragDrop.DoDragDrop() method at some point to initiate the drag-and-drop operation. At this point you identify the source of the drag-and-drop operation, set aside the content you want to transfer, and indicate what drag-and-drop effects are allowed (copying, moving, and so on).

Usually, the DoDragDrop() method is called in response to the MouseDown or Preview-MouseDown event. Here's an example that initiates a drag-and-drop operation when a label is clicked. The text content from the label is used for the drag-and-drop operation:

```
private void lblSource_MouseDown(object sender, MouseButtonEventArgs e)
{
    Label lbl = (Label)sender;
    DragDrop.DoDragDrop(lbl, lbl.Content, DragDropEffects.Copy);
}
```

The element that receives the data needs to set its AllowDrop property to true. Additionally, it needs to handle the Drop event to deal with the data:

```
<Label Grid.Row="1" AllowDrop="True" Drop="lblTarget_Drop">To Here</Label>
```

When you set AllowDrop to true, you configure an element to allow any type of information. If you want to be pickier, you can handle the DragEnter event. At this point, you can check the type of data that's being dragged and then determine what type of operation to allow. The following example only allows text content—if you drag something that cannot be converted to text, the drag-and-drop operation won't be allowed and the mouse pointer will change to the forbidding circle-with-a-line cursor:

```
private void lblTarget_DragEnter(object sender, DragEventArgs e)
{
    if (e.Data.GetDataPresent(DataFormats.Text))
      e.Effects = DragDropEffects.Copy;
    else
      e.Effects = DragDropEffects.None;
}
```

Finally, when the operation completes you can retrieve the data and act on it. The following code takes the dropped text and inserts it into the label:

```
private void lblTarget_Drop(object sender, DragEventArgs e)
{
    ((Label)sender).Content = e.Data.GetData(DataFormats.Text);
}
```

You can exchange any type of object through a drag-and-drop operation. However, while this free-spirited approach is perfect for your applications, it isn't wise if you need to communicate with other applications. If you want to drag-and-drop into other applications, you should use a basic data type (such as string, int, and so on), or an object that implements ISerializable or IDataObject (which allows .NET to transfer your object into a stream of bytes and reconstruct the object in another application domain). One interesting trick is to convert a WPF element into XAML and reconstitute it somewhere else. All you need is the XamlWriter and XamlReader objects described in Chapter 2.

■**Note** If you want to transfer data between applications, be sure to check out the System.Windows.Clipboard class, which provides static methods for placing data on the Windows clipboard and retrieving it in a variety of different formats.

The Last Word

In this chapter, you took a deep look at WPF dependency properties and routed events. First, you saw how dependency properties are defined and registered and how they plug into other WPF services. Next, you explored routed events and saw how they allow you to deal with events at different levels—either directly at the source or in a containing element. Finally, you saw how these routing strategies are implemented in the WPF elements to allow you to deal with keyboard and mouse input.

It may be tempting to begin writing event handlers that respond to common events such as mouse movements to apply simple graphical effects or otherwise update the user interface. But don't start writing this logic just yet. As you'll see later in Chapter 12, you can automate many simple program operations with declarative markup using WPF styles and triggers. But before you branch out to this topic, the next chapter takes a short detour to show you how many of the most fundamental graphical widgets (things such as buttons, labels, and text boxes) work in the WPF world.

■**Tip** One of the best ways to learn more about the internals of WPF is to browse the code for basic WPF elements, such as Button, UIElement, and FrameworkElement. One of the best tools to perform this browsing is Lutz Roeder's Reflector, which is available at http://www.aisto.com/roeder/dotnet. Using Reflector, you can see the definitions for dependency properties and routed events, browse through the static constructor code that initializes them, and even explore how the properties and events are used in the class code.

CHAPTER 7

■■■

Classic Controls

Now that you've learned the fundamentals of WPF layout, content, and event handling, you're ready to take a closer look at the elements WPF includes. In this chapter, you'll take a quick tour of the most fundamental WPF controls, including basic ingredients such as labels, buttons, and text boxes. Although Windows developers have been using these items for years, this chapter fills in a few important details about their WPF implementations. Along the way, you'll also take a quick look at the System.Windows.Control class to learn how WPF controls use brushes and fonts.

The Control Class

As you learned in Chapter 5, WPF windows are filled with elements, but only some of these elements are *controls*. Controls are *user-interactive* elements—elements that can take focus and receive input from the keyboard or mouse.

All controls derive from the System.Windows.Control class, which adds a bit of basic infrastructure:

- The ability to set the alignment of content inside the control

- The ability to set the tab order

- Support for painting a background, foreground, and border

- Support for formatting the size and font of text content

You've already learned about the first two points. (Chapter 5 covered content and alignment, while Chapter 6 explored the subtleties of focus and tab order.) The following sections cover brushes and fonts.

Background and Foreground Brushes

All controls include the concept of a background and foreground. Usually, the background is the surface of the control (think of the white or gray area inside the borders of a button), while the foreground is the text. In WPF, you set the color of these two areas (but not the content) using the Background and Foreground properties.

It's natural to expect that the Background and Foreground properties would use color objects, as they do in a Windows Forms application. However, these properties actually use something much more versatile: a Brush object. That gives you the flexibility to fill your background and foreground content with a solid color (by using the SolidColorBrush) or something more exotic (for example, by using a LinearGradientBrush or TileBrush). In this chapter, you'll consider only the simple SolidColorBrush, but you'll try fancier brushwork in Chapter 13.

■**Note** All Brush classes are found in the System.Windows.Media namespace.

Setting Colors in Code

Imagine you want to set a blue surface area inside a button named cmd. Here's the code that does the trick:

```
cmd.Background = new SolidColorBrush(Colors.AliceBlue);
```

This code creates a new SolidColorBrush using a ready-made color via a static property of the handy Colors class. (The names are based on the color names supported by most web browsers.) It then sets the brush as the background brush for the button, which causes its background to be painted a light shade of blue.

■**Note** This method of styling a button isn't completely satisfactory. If you try it, you'll find that it configures the background color for a button in its normal (unpressed) state, but it doesn't change the color that appears when you press the button (which is a darker gray). To really customize every aspect of a button's appearance, you need to delve into templates, as discussed in Chapter 15.

You can also grab system colors (which may be based on user preferences) from the System.Windows.SystemColors enumeration. Here's an example:

```
cmd.Background = new SolidColorBrush(SystemColors.ControlColor);
```

Because system brushes are used frequently, the SystemColors class also provides ready-made properties that return SolidColorBrush objects. Here's how you use them:

```
cmd.Background = SystemColors.ControlBrush;
```

As it's written, both of these examples suffer from a minor problem. If the system color is changed *after* you run this code, your button won't be updated to use the new color. In essence, this code grabs a snapshot of the current color or brush. To make sure your program can update itself in response to configuration changes, you need to use dynamic resources, as described in Chapter 11.

The Colors and SystemColors classes offer handy shortcuts, but they're not the only way to set a color. You can also create a Color object by supplying the R, G, B values (red, green, and blue). Each one of these values is a number from 0 to 255:

```
int red = 0; int green = 255; int blue = 0;
cmd.Foreground = new SolidColorBrush(Color.FromRgb(red, green, blue));
```

You can also make a color partly transparent by supplying an alpha value and calling the Color.FromArgb() method. An alpha value of 255 is completely opaque, while 0 is completely transparent.

RGB AND SCRGB

The RGB standard is useful because it's used in many other programs—for example, you can get the RGB value of a color in a graphic in a paint program and use the same color in your WPF application. However, it's possible that other devices (such as printers) might support a richer range of colors. For this reason, an alternative scRGB standard has been created that represents each color component (alpha, red, green, and blue) using 64-bit values.

The WPF Color structure supports either approach. It includes a set of standard RGB properties (A, R, G, and B) and a set of properties for scRGB (ScA, ScR, ScG, and ScB). These properties are linked, so that if you set the R property, the ScR property is changed accordingly.

The relationship between the RGB values and the scRGB values is not linear. A 0 value in the RGB system is 0 in scRGB, 255 in RGB becomes 1 in scRGB, and all values in between 0 and 255 in RGB are represented as decimal values in between 0 and 1 in scRGB.

Setting Colors in XAML

When you set the background or foreground in XAML, you can use a helpful shortcut. Rather than define a Brush object, you can supply a color name or color value. The WPF parser will automatically create a SolidColorBrush object using the color you specify, and it will use that brush object for the foreground or background. Here's an example that uses a color name:

```
<Button Background="Red">A Button</Button>
```

It's equivalent to this more verbose syntax:

```
<Button>A Button
  <Button.Background>
    <SolidColorBrush Color="Red" />
  </Button.Background>
</Button>
```

You need to use the longer form if you want to create a different type of brush, such as a LinearGradientBrush, and use that to paint the background.

If you want to use a color code, you need to use a slightly less convenient syntax that puts the R, G, and B values in hexadecimal notation. You can use one of two formats—either #rrggbb or #aarrggbb (the difference being that the latter includes the alpha value). You need only two digits to supply the A, R, G, and B values because they're all in hexadecimal notation. Here's an example that creates the same color as in the previous code snippets using #aarrggbb notation:

```
<Button Background="#FFFF0000">A Button</Button>
```

Here the alpha value is FF (255), the red value is FF (255), and the green and blue values are 0.

■**Note** Brushes support automatic change notification. In other words, if you attach a brush to a control and change the brush, the control updates itself accordingly. This works because brushes derive from the System.Windows.Freezable class. The name stems from the fact that all freezable objects have two states— a readable state and a read-only (or "frozen") state.

The Background and Foreground properties aren't the only details you can set with a brush. You can also paint a border around controls (and some other elements, such as the Border element) using the BorderBrush and BorderThickness properties. BorderBrush takes a brush of your choosing, and BorderThickness takes the width of the border in device-independent units. You need to set both properties before you'll see the border.

■**Note** Some controls don't respect the BorderBrush and BorderThickness properties. The Button object ignores them completely because it defines its background and border using the ButtonChrome decorator. However, you can give a button a new face (with a border of your choosing) using templates, as described in Chapter 15.

Transparency

Unlike Windows Forms, WPF supports true transparency. That means if you layer several elements on top of one another and give them all varying layers of transparency, you'll see exactly what you expect. At its simplest, this feature gives you the ability to create graphical backgrounds that "show through" the elements you place on top. At its most complex, this feature allows you to create multilayered animations and other effects that would be extremely difficult in other frameworks.

There are two ways to make an element partly transparent:

- **Set the Opacity property.** *Opacity* is a fractional value from 0 to 1, where 1 is completely solid (the default) and 0 is completely transparent. The Opacity property is defined in the UIElement class (and the base Brush class), so it applies to all elements.

- **Use a semitransparent color.** Any color that has an alpha value less than 255 is semitransparent. If possible, you should use transparent colors rather than the Opacity property because it's likely to perform better. And because you can apply different colors to different parts of a control, you can use transparent colors to create a control that is partly transparent—for example, a semitransparent background with completely opaque text.

Figure 7-1 shows an example that has several semitransparent layers:

- The window has an opaque white background.

- The top-level StackPanel that contains all the elements has an ImageBrush that applies a picture. The Opacity of this brush is reduced to lighten it, allowing the white window background to show through.

- The first button uses a semitransparent red background color. The image shows through in the button background, but the text is opaque.

- The label (under the first button) is used as is. By default, all labels have a completely transparent background color.

- The text box uses opaque text and an opaque border but a semitransparent background color.

- Another StackPanel under the text box uses a TileBrush to create a pattern of happy faces. The TileBrush has a reduced Opacity, so the other background shows through. For example, you can see the sun at the bottom-right corner of the form.

- In the second StackPanel is a TextBlock with a completely transparent background and semitransparent white text. If you look carefully, you can see both backgrounds show through under some letters.

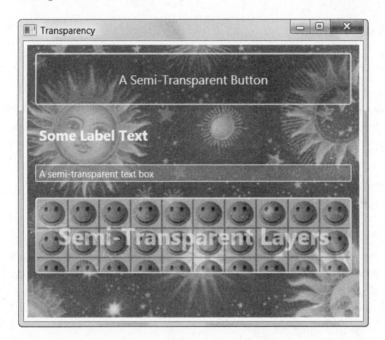

Figure 7-1. *A window with several semitransparent layers*

Here are the contents of the window in XAML. Keep in mind that this example includes one detail you haven't examined yet—the specialized ImageBrush for painting image content. (You'll learn about the ImageBrush class in Chapter 13.)

```
<StackPanel Margin="5">
  <StackPanel.Background>
    <ImageBrush ImageSource="celestial.jpg" Opacity="0.7"/>
  </StackPanel.Background>

  <Button Foreground="White" FontSize="16" Margin="10"
```

```
    BorderBrush="White" Background="#60AA4030"
    Padding="20">A Semi-Transparent Button</Button>
  <Label Margin="10" FontSize="18" FontWeight="Bold" Foreground="White">
   Some Label Text</Label>
  <TextBox Margin="10" Background="#AAAAAAAA" Foreground="White"
    BorderBrush="White">A semi-transparent text box</TextBox>

  <Button Margin="10" Padding="25" BorderBrush="White">
    <Button.Background>
      <ImageBrush ImageSource="happyface.jpg" Opacity="0.6"
      TileMode="Tile" Viewport="0,0,0.1,0.3"/>
    </Button.Background>

    <StackPanel>
      <TextBlock Foreground="#75FFFFFF" TextAlignment="Center"
      FontSize="30" FontWeight="Bold" TextWrapping="Wrap">
      Semi-Transparent Layers</TextBlock>
    </StackPanel>
  </Button>
</StackPanel>
```

Transparency is a popular WPF feature—in fact, it's so easy and works so well that it's a bit of a WPF user-interface cliché. For that reason, be careful not to overuse it.

Fonts

The Control class defines a small set of font-related properties that determine how text appears in a control. These properties are outlined in Table 7-1.

■**Note** The Control class doesn't define any properties that *use* its font. While many controls include a property such as Text, it isn't defined as part of the base control class. Obviously, the font properties don't mean anything unless they're used by the derived class.

Table 7-1. *Font-Related Properties of the Control Class*

Name	Description
FontFamily	The name of the font you want to use.
FontSize	The size of the font in device-independent units (each of which is 1/96 of an inch). This is a bit of a change from tradition that's designed to support WPF's new resolution-independent rendering model. Ordinary Windows applications measure fonts using *points*, which are assumed to be 1/72 of an inch on a standard PC monitor. If you want to turn a WPF font size into a more familiar point size, you can use a handy trick—just multiply by 3/4. For example, a traditional 38-point is equivalent to 48 units in WPF.

Name	Description
FontStyle	The angling of the text, as represented as a FontStyle object. You get the FontStyle preset you need from the static properties of the FontStyles class, which includes Normal, Italic, or Oblique lettering. (*Oblique* is an "artificial" way to create italic text on a computer that doesn't have the required italic font. Letters are taken from the normal font and slanted using a transform. This usually creates a poor result.)
FontWeight	The heaviness of text, as represented as a FontWeight object. You get the FontWeight preset you need from the static properties of the FontWeights class. Bold is the most obvious of these, but some typefaces provide other variations such as Heavy, Light, ExtraBold, and so on.
FontStretch	The amount that text is stretched or compressed, as represented by a FontStretch object. You get the FontStretch preset you need from the static properties of the FontStretches class. For example, UltraCondensed reduces fonts to 50% of their normal width, while UltraExpanded expands them to 200%. Font stretching is an OpenType feature that is not supported by many typefaces. (To experiment with this property, try using the Rockwell font, which does support it.)

Obviously, the most important of these properties is FontFamily. A *font family* is a collection of related typefaces—for example, Arial Regular, Arial Bold, Arial Italic, and Arial Bold Italic are all part of the Arial font family. Although the typographic rules and characters for each variation are defined separately, the operating system realizes they're related. As a result, you can configure an element to use Arial Regular, set the FontWeight property to Bold, and be confident that WPF will switch over to the Arial Bold typeface.

When choosing a font, you must supply the full family name, as shown here:

```
<Button Name="cmd" FontFamily="Times New Roman" FontSize="18">A Button</Button>
```

It's much the same in code:

```
cmd.FontFamily = "Times New Roman";
cmd.FontSize = "18";
```

When identifying a FontFamily, a shortened string is not enough. That means you can't substitute Times or Times New instead of the full name Times New Roman.

Optionally, you can use the full name of a typeface to get italic or bold, as shown here:

```
<Button FontFamily="Times New Roman Bold">A Button</Button>
```

However, it's clearer and more flexible to use just the family name and set other properties (such as FontStyle and FontWeight) to get the variant you want. For example, the following markup sets the FontFamily to Times New Roman and sets the FontWeight to Font-Weights.Bold:

```
<Button FontFamily="Times New Roman" FontWeight="Bold">A Button</Button>
```

Text Decorations and Typography

Some elements also support more advanced text manipulation through the TextDecorations and Typography properties. These allow you to add embellishments to text. For example, you can set the TextDecorations property using a static property from the TextDecorations class. It provides just four decorations, each of which allows you to add some sort of line to your text. They include Baseline, OverLine, Strikethrough, and Underline. The Typography property is more advanced—it lets you access specialized typeface variants that only some fonts will provide. Examples include different number alignments, ligatures (connections between adjacent letters), and small caps.

For the most part, the TextDecorations and Typography features are found only in flow document content—which you use to create rich, readable documents. (Chapter 19 describes documents in detail.) However, the frills also turn up on the TextBox class. Additionally, they're supported by the TextBlock, which is a lighter-weight version of the Label that's perfect for showing small amounts of wrappable text content. Although you're unlikely to use text decorations with the TextBox or change its typography, you may want to use underlining in the TextBlock, as shown here:

```
<TextBlock TextDecorations="Underline">Underlined text</TextBlock>
```

If you're planning to place a large amount of text content in a window and you want to format individual portions (for example, underline important words), you should refer to Chapter 19, where you'll learn about many more flow elements. Although flow elements are designed for use with documents, you can nest them directly inside a TextBlock.

Font Inheritance

When you set any of the font properties, the values flow through to nested objects. For example, if you set the FontFamily property for the top-level window, every control in that window gets the same FontFamily value (unless the control explicitly sets a different font). This feature is similar to the Windows Forms concept of *ambient properties*, but the underlying plumbing is different. It works because the font properties are dependency properties, and one of the features that dependency properties can provide is property value inheritance—the magic that passes your font settings down to nested controls.

It's worth noting that property value inheritance can flow through elements that don't even support that property. For example, imagine you create a window that holds a StackPanel, inside of which are three Label controls. You can set the FontSize property of the window because the Window class derives from the Control class. You *can't* set the FontSize property for the StackPanel because it isn't a control. However, if you set the FontSize property of the window, your property value is still able to flow "through" the StackPanel to get to your labels inside and change their font sizes.

Along with the font settings, several other base properties use property value inheritance. In the Control class, the Foreground property uses inheritance. The Background property does not. However, the default background is a null reference that's rendered by most controls as a transparent background. (That means the parent's background will show through, as shown in Figure 7-1.) In the UIElement class, AllowDrop, IsEnabled, and IsVisible use property inheritance. In the FrameworkElement, the CultureInfo and FlowDirection properties do.

■**Note** A dependency property supports inheritance only if the FrameworkPropertyMetadata.Inherits flag is set to true, which is not the default. Chapter 6 discusses the FrameworkPropertyMetadata class and property registration in detail.

Font Substitution

When you're setting fonts, you need to be careful to choose a font that you know will be present on the user's computer. However, WPF does give you a little flexibility with a font fallback system. You can set FontFamily to a comma-separated list of font options. WPF will then move through the list in order, trying to find one of the fonts you've indicated.

Here's an example that attempts to use Technical Italic font but falls back to Comic Sans MS or Arial if that isn't available:

```
<Button FontFamily="Technical Italic, Comic Sans MS, Arial">A Button</Button>
```

If a font family really does contain a comma in its name, you'll need to escape the comma by including it twice in a row.

Incidentally, you can get a list of all the fonts that are installed on the current computer using the static SystemFontFamilies collection of the System.Windows.Media.Fonts class. Here's an example that uses it to add fonts to a list box:

```
foreach (FontFamily fontFamily in Fonts.SystemFontFamilies)
{
    lstFonts.Items.Add(fontFamily.Source);
}
```

The FontFamily object also allows you to examine other details, such as the line spacing and associated typefaces.

■**Note** One of the ingredients that WPF doesn't include is a dialog box for choosing a font. The WPF Text team has posted two much more attractive WPF font pickers, including a no-code version that uses data binding (http://blogs.msdn.com/text/archive/2006/06/20/592777.aspx) and a more sophisticated version that supports the optional typographic features that are found in some OpenType fonts (http://blogs.msdn.com/text/archive/2006/11/01/sample-font-chooser.aspx).

Font Embedding

Another option for dealing with unusual fonts is to embed them in your application. That way, your application never has a problem finding the font you want to use.

The embedding process is simple. First, you add the font file (typically, a file with the extension .ttf) to your application and set the Build Action to Resource. (You can do this in Visual Studio by selecting the font file in the Solution Explorer and changing its Build Action in the Properties window.)

Next, when you use the font, you need to add the character sequence ./# before the font family name, as shown here:

```
<Label FontFamily="./#Bayern" FontSize="20">This is an embedded font</Label>
```

The ./ characters are interpreted by WPF to mean "the current folder." To understand what this means, you need to know a little more about XAML's packaging system.

As you learned in Chapter 1, you can run stand-alone (known as *loose*) XAML files directly in your browser without compiling them. The only limitation is that your XAML file can't use a code-behind file. In this scenario, the current folder is exactly that, and WPF looks at the font files that are in the same directory as the XAML file and makes them available to your application.

More commonly, you'll compile your WPF application to a .NET assembly before you run it. In this case, the current folder is still the location of the XAML document, only now that document has been compiled and embedded in your assembly. WPF refers to compiled resources using a specialized URI syntax that's discussed in Chapter 11. All application URIs start with pack://application. If you create a project named ClassicControls and add a window named EmbeddedFont.xaml, the URI for that window is this:

```
pack://application:,,,/ClassicControls/embeddedfont.xaml
```

This URI is made available in several places, including through the FontFamily.BaseUri property. WPF uses this URI to base its font search. Thus, when you use the ./ syntax in a compiled WPF application, WPF looks for fonts that are embedded as resources alongside your compiled XAML.

After the ./ character sequence, you can supply the file name, but you'll usually just add the number sign (#) and the font's real family name. In the previous example, the embedded font is named Bayern.

■**Note** Setting up an embedded font can be a bit tricky. You need to make sure you get the font family name exactly right, and you need to make sure you choose the correct build action for the font file. Furthermore, Visual Studio doesn't currently provide design support for embedded fonts (meaning your control text won't appear in the correct font until you run your application). To see an example of the correct setup, refer to the sample code for this chapter.

Embedding fonts raises obvious licensing concerns. Unfortunately, most font vendors allow their fonts to be embedded in documents (such as PDF files) but not applications (such as WPF assemblies) even though an embedded WPF font isn't directly accessible to the end user. WPF doesn't make any attempt to enforce font licensing, but you should make sure you're on solid legal ground before you redistribute a font.

You can check a font's embedding permissions using Microsoft's free font properties extension utility, which is available at http://www.microsoft.com/typography/TrueType-Property21.mspx. Once you install this utility, right-click any font file, and choose Properties to see more detailed information about it. In particular, check the Embedding tab for information about the allowed embedding for this font. Fonts marked with Installed Embedding Allowed are suitable for WPF applications, while fonts with Editable Embedding Allowed may not be. Consult with the font vendor for licensing information about a specific font.

Mouse Cursors

A common task in any application is to adjust the mouse cursor to show when the application is busy or to indicate how different controls work. You can set the mouse pointer for any element using the Cursor property, which is inherited from the FrameworkElement class.

Every cursor is represented by a System.Windows.Input.Cursor object. The easiest way to get a Cursor object is to use the static properties of the Cursors class (from the System.Windows.Input namespace). They include all the standard Windows cursors, such as the hourglass, the hand, resizing arrows, and so on. Here's an example that sets the hourglass for the current window:

```
this.Cursor = Cursors.Wait;
```

Now when you move the mouse over the current window, the mouse pointer changes to the familiar hourglass icon (in Windows XP) or the swirl (in Windows Vista).

■**Note** The properties of the Cursors class draw on the cursors that are defined on the computer. If the user has customized the set of standard cursors, the application you create will use those customized cursors.

If you set the cursor in XAML, you don't need to use the Cursors class directly. That's because the TypeConverter for the Cursor property is able to recognize the property names and retrieve the corresponding Cursor object from the Cursors class. That means you can write markup like this to show the "help" cursor (a combination of an arrow and a question mark) when the mouse is positioned over a button:

```
<Button Cursor="Help">Help</Button>
```

It's possible to have overlapping cursor settings. In this case, the most specific cursor wins. For example, you could set a different cursor on a button and on the window that contains the button. The button's cursor will be shown when you move the mouse over the button, and the window's cursor will be used for every other region in the window.

However, there's one exception. A parent can override the cursor settings of its children using the ForceCursor property. When this property is set to true, the child's Cursor property is ignored, and the parent's Cursor property applies everywhere inside.

If you want to apply a cursor setting to every element in every window of an application, the FrameworkElement.Cursor property won't help you. Instead, you need to use the static Mouse.OverrideCursor property, which overrides the Cursor property of every element:

```
Mouse.OverrideCursor = Cursors.Wait;
```

To remove this application-wide cursor override, set the Mouse.OverrideCursor property to null.

Lastly, WPF supports custom cursors without any fuss. You can use both ordinary .cur cursor files (which are essentially small bitmaps) and .ani animated cursor files. To use a custom cursor, you pass the file name of your cursor file or a stream with the cursor data to the constructor of the Cursor object:

```
Cursor customCursor = new Cursor(Path.Combine(applicationDir, "stopwatch.ani");
this.Cursor = customCursor;
```

The Cursor object doesn't directly support the URI resource syntax that allows other WPF elements (such as the Image) to use files that are stored in your compiled assembly. However, it's still quite easy to add a cursor file to your application as a resource and then retrieve it as a stream that you can use to construct a Cursor object. The trick is using the Application.Get-ResourceStream() method:

```
StreamResourceInfo sri = Application.GetResourceStream(
  new Uri("stopwatch.ani", UriKind.Relative));
Cursor customCursor = new Cursor(sri.Stream);
this.Cursor = customCursor;
```

This code assumes that you've added a file named stopwatch.ani to your project and set its Build Action to Resource. This technique is explained in more detail in Chapter 12.

Content Controls

As you learned in Chapter 5, many of the most fundamental WPF controls are actually content controls. These include the well-worn Label, Button, CheckBox, and RadioButton.

Labels

The simplest of all content controls is the Label control. Like any other content control, it accepts any single piece of content you want to place inside. But what distinguishes the Label control is its support for *mnemonics*—essentially, shortcut keys that set the focus to a linked control.

To support this functionality, the Label control adds a single property, named Target. To set the Target property, you need to use a binding expression that points to another control. Here's the syntax you must use:

```
<Label Target="{Binding ElementName=txtA}">Choose _A</Label>
<TextBox Name="txtA"></TextBox>
<Label Target="{Binding ElementName=txtB}">Choose _B</Label>
<TextBox Name="txtB"></TextBox>
```

The underscore in the label text indicates the shortcut key. (If you really *do* want an underscore to appear in your label, you must add two underscores instead.) All mnemonics work with Alt and the shortcut key you've identified. For example, if the user presses Alt+A in this example, the first label transfers focus to the linked control, which is txtA. Similarly, Alt+B takes the user to txtB.

■**Note** If you've programmed with Windows Forms, you're probably used to using the ampersand (&) character to identify a shortcut key. XAML uses the underscore instead because the ampersand character can't be entered directly in XML—instead, you need to use the clunkier character entity & in its place.

Usually, the shortcut letters are hidden until the user presses Alt, at which point they appear as underlined letters (Figure 7-2). However, this behavior depends on system settings.

Tip If all you need to do is display content without support for mnemonics, you may prefer to use the more lightweight TextBlock element. Unlike the Label, the TextBlock also supports wrapping through its TextWrapping property.

Figure 7-2. *Shortcuts in a label*

Buttons

WPF recognizes three types of button controls: the familiar Button, the CheckBox, and the RadioButton. All of these controls are content controls that derive from ButtonBase.

The ButtonBase class includes only a few members. It defines the Click event and adds support for commands, which allow you to wire buttons to higher-level application tasks (a feat you'll consider in Chapter 10). Finally, the ButtonBase class adds a ClickMode property, which determines when a button fires its Click event in response to mouse actions. The default value is ClickMode.Release, which means the Click event fires when the mouse is clicked and released. However, you can also choose to fire the Click event mouse when the mouse button is first pressed (ClickMode.Press) or, oddly enough, whenever the mouse moves over the button and pauses there (ClickMode.Hover).

Note All button controls support access keys, which work similarly to mnemonics in the Label control. You add the underscore character to identify the access key. If the user presses Alt and the access key, a button click is triggered.

The Button

The Button class represents the ever-present Windows push button. It adds just two writeable properties, IsCancel and IsDefault:

- **When IsCancel is true**, this button is designated as the cancel button for a window. If you press the Escape key while positioned anywhere on the current window, this button is triggered.

- **When IsDefault is true**, this button is designated as the default button (also known as the accept button). Its behavior depends on your current location in the window. If you're positioned on a non-Button control (such as a TextBox, RadioButton, CheckBox, and so on), the default button is given a blue shading, almost as though it has focus. If you press Enter, this button is triggered. However, if you're positioned on another Button control, the current button gets the blue shading, and pressing Enter triggers that button, not the default button.

Many users rely on these shortcuts (particularly the Escape key to close an unwanted dialog box), so it makes sense to take the time to define these details in every window you create. It's still up to you to write the event handling code for the cancel and default buttons, because WPF won't supply this behavior.

In some cases, it may make sense for the same button to be the cancel button *and* the default button for a window. One example is the OK button in an About box. However, there should be only a single cancel button and a single default button in a window. If you designate more than one cancel button, pressing Escape will simply move the focus to the next default button but it won't trigger it. If you have more than one default button, pressing Enter has a somewhat more confusing behavior. If you're on a non-Button control, pressing Enter moves you to the next default button. If you're on a Button control, pressing Enter triggers it.

ISDEFAULT AND ISDEFAULTED

The Button class also includes the horribly confusing IsDefaulted property, which is read-only. IsDefaulted returns true for a default button if another control has focus and that control doesn't accept the Enter key. In this situation, pressing the Enter key will trigger the button.

For example, a TextBox does not accept the Enter key, unless you've set TextBox.AcceptsReturn to true. When a TextBox with an AcceptsReturn value of true has focus, IsDefaulted is false for the default button. When a TextBox with an AcceptsReturns value of false has focus, the default button has IsDefaulted set to true. If this isn't confusing enough, the IsDefaulted property returns false when the button itself has focus, even though hitting Enter at this point will trigger the button.

Although it's unlikely that you'll want to use the IsDefaulted property, it does allow you to write certain types of style triggers, as you'll see in Chapter 12. If not, just add it to your list of obscure WPF trivia, which you can use to puzzle your colleagues.

The ToggleButton and RepeatButton

Alongside Button, three more classes derive from ButtonBase. These include the following:

- GridViewColumnHeader, which represents the clickable header of a column when you use a grid-based ListView. The ListView is described in Chapter 18.

- RepeatButton, which fires Click events continuously, as long as the button is held down. Ordinary buttons fire one Click event per user click.

- ToggleButton, which represents a button that has two states (pushed or unpushed). When you click a ToggleButton, it stays in its pushed state until you click it again to release it. This is sometimes described as "sticky click" behavior.

Both RepeatButton and ToggleButton are defined in the System.Windows.Controls.Primitives namespace, which indicates they aren't often used on their own. Instead, they're used to build more complex controls by composition, or extended with features through inheritance. For example, the RepeatButton is used to build the higher-level ScrollBar control (which, ultimately, is a part of the even higher-level ScrollViewer). The RepeatButton gives the arrow buttons at the ends of the scroll bar their trademark behavior—scrolling continues as long as you hold it down. Similarly, the ToggleButton is used to derive the more useful CheckBox and RadioButton classes described next.

However, neither the RepeatButton nor the ToggleButton is an abstract class, so you can use both of them directly in your user interfaces. The ToggleButton is genuinely useful inside a ToolBar, which you'll use in Chapter 18.

The CheckBox

Both the CheckBox and the RadioButton are buttons of a different sort. They derive from ToggleButton, which means they can be switched on or off by the user, hence their "toggle" behavior. In the case of the CheckBox, switching the control "on" means placing a check mark in it.

The CheckBox class doesn't add any members, so the basic CheckBox interface is defined in the ToggleButton class. Most important, ToggleButton adds an IsChecked property. IsChecked is a nullable Boolean, which means it can be set to true, false, or null. Obviously, true represents a checked box, while false represents an empty one. The null value is a little trickier—it represents an indeterminate state, which is displayed as a shaded box. The indeterminate state is commonly used to represent values that haven't been set or areas where some discrepancy exists. For example, if you have a check box that allows you to apply bold formatting in a text application and the current selection includes both bold and regular text, you might set the check box to null to show an indeterminate state.

To assign a null value in WPF markup, you need to use the null markup extension, as shown here:

```
<CheckBox IsChecked="{x:Null}">A check box in indeterminate state</CheckBox>
```

Along with the IsChecked property, the ToggleButton class adds a property named IsThreeState, which determines whether the user is able to place the check box into an indeterminate state. If IsThreeState is false (the default), clicking the check box alternates its state between checked and unchecked, and the only way to place it in an indeterminate state is through code. If IsThreeState is true, clicking the check box cycles through all three possible states.

The ToggleButton class also defines three events that fire when the check box enters specific states: Checked, Unchecked, and Indeterminate. In most cases, it's easier to consolidate this logic into one event handler by handling the Click event that's inherited from ButtonBase. The Click event fires whenever the button changes state.

The RadioButton

The RadioButton also derives from ToggleButton and uses the same IsChecked property and the same Checked, Unchecked, and Indeterminate events. Along with these, the RadioButton adds a single property named GroupName, which allows you to control how radio buttons are placed into groups.

Ordinarily, radio buttons are grouped by their container. That means if you place three RadioButton controls in a single StackPanel, they form a group from which you can select just one of the three. On the other hand, if you place a combination of radio buttons in two separate StackPanel controls, you have two independent groups on your hands.

The GroupName property allows you to override this behavior. You can use it to create more than one group in the same container or to create a single group that spans multiple containers. Either way, the trick is simple—just give all the radio buttons that belong together the same group name.

Consider this example:

```
<StackPanel>
  <GroupBox Margin="5">
    <StackPanel>
      <RadioButton>Group 1</RadioButton>
      <RadioButton>Group 1</RadioButton>
      <RadioButton>Group 1</RadioButton>
      <RadioButton Margin="0,10,0,0" GroupName="Group2">Group 2</RadioButton>
    </StackPanel>
  </GroupBox>
  <GroupBox Margin="5">
    <StackPanel>
      <RadioButton>Group 3</RadioButton>
      <RadioButton>Group 3</RadioButton>
      <RadioButton>Group 3</RadioButton>
      <RadioButton Margin="0,10,0,0" GroupName="Group2">Group 2</RadioButton>
    </StackPanel>
  </GroupBox>
</StackPanel>
```

Here, there are two containers holding radio buttons, but three groups. The final radio button at the bottom of each group box is part of a third group. In this example it makes for a confusing design, but there may be some scenarios where you want to separate a specific radio button from the pack in a subtle way without causing it to lose its group membership.

■**Tip** You don't need to use the GroupBox container to wrap your radio buttons, but it's a common convention. The GroupBox shows a border and gives you a caption that you can apply to your group of buttons.

Tooltips

WPF has a flexible model for *tooltips* (those infamous yellow boxes that pop up when you hover over something interesting). Because tooltips in WPF are content controls, you can place virtually anything inside a tooltip. You can also tweak various timing settings to control how quickly tooltips appear and disappear.

The easiest way to show a tooltip doesn't involve using the ToolTip class directly. Instead, you simply set the ToolTip property of your element. The ToolTip property is defined in the FrameworkElement class, so it's available on anything you'll place in a WPF window.

For example, here's a button that has a basic tooltip:

```
<Button ToolTip="This is my tooltip">I have a tooltip</Button>
```

When you hover over this button, the text "This is my tooltip" appears in the familiar yellow box.

If you want to supply more ambitious tooltip content, such as a combination of nested elements, you need to break the ToolTip property out into a separate element. Here's an example that sets the ToolTip property of a button using more complex nested content:

```
<Button>
  <Button.ToolTip>
    <StackPanel>
      <TextBlock Margin="3" >Image and text</TextBlock>
      <Image Source="happyface.jpg" Stretch="None" />
      <TextBlock Margin="3" >Image and text</TextBlock>
    </StackPanel>
  </Button.ToolTip>
  <Button.Content>I have a fancy tooltip</Button.Content>
</Button>
```

As in the previous example, WPF implicitly creates a ToolTip object. The difference is that in this case the ToolTip object contains a StackPanel rather than a simple string. Figure 7-3 shows the result.

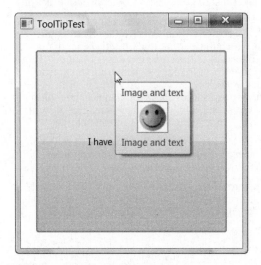

Figure 7-3. *A fancy tooltip*

If more than one tooltip overlaps, the most specific tooltip wins. For example, if you add a tooltip to the StackPanel container in the previous example, this tooltip appears when you hover over an empty part of the panel or a control that doesn't have its own tooltip.

■Note Don't put user-interactive controls in a tooltip because the ToolTip window can't accept focus. For example, if you place a button in a ToolTip, the button will appear, but it isn't clickable. (If you attempt to click it, your mouse click will just pass through to the window underneath.) If you want a tooltip-like window that can hold other controls, consider using the Popup instead, which is discussed shortly, in the section named "The Popup."

Setting ToolTip Properties

The previous example shows how you can customize the content of a tooltip, but what if you want to configure other ToolTip-related settings? You actually have two options. The first technique you can use is to explicitly define the ToolTip object. That gives you the chance to directly set a variety of ToolTip properties.

The ToolTip is a content control, so you can adjust standard properties such as the Background (so it isn't a yellow box), Padding, and Font. You can also modify the members that are defined in the ToolTip class (and listed in Table 7-2). Most of these properties are designed to help you place the tooltip exactly where you want it.

Table 7-2. *ToolTip Properties*

Name	Description
HasDropShadow	Determines whether the tooltip has a diffuse black drop shadow that makes it stand out from the window underneath.
Placement	Determines how the tooltip is positioned, using one of the values from the PlacementMode enumeration. The default value is Mouse, which means that the top-left corner of the tooltip is placed relative to the current mouse position. (The actual position of the tooltip may be offset from this starting point based on the HorizontalOffset and VerticalOffset properties.) Other possibilities allow you to place the tooltip using absolute screen coordinates or place it relative to some element (which you indicate using the PlacementTarget property).
HorizontalOffset and VerticalOffset	Allows you to nudge the tooltip into the exact position you want. You can use positive or negative values.
PlacementTarget	Allows you to place a tooltip relative to another element. In order to use this property, the Placement property must be set to Left, Right, Top, Bottom, or Center. (This is the edge of the element to which the tooltip is aligned.)
PlacementRectangle	Allows you to offset the position of the tooltip. This works in much the same way as the HorizontalOffset and VerticalOffest properties. This property doesn't have an effect if Placement property is set to Mouse.

Name	Description
CustomPopupPlacementCallback	Allows you to position a tooltip dynamically using code. If the Placement property is set to Custom, this property identifies the method that will be called by the ToolTip to get the position where the ToolTip should be placed. Your callback method receives three pieces of information—popupSize (the size of the ToolTip), targetSize (the size of the PlacementTarget, if it's used), and offset (a point that's created based on Horizontal-Offset and VerticalOffset properties). The method returns a CustomPopupPlacement object that tells WPF where to place the tooltip.
StaysOpen	Has no effect in practice. The intended purpose of this property is to allow you to create a tooltip that remains open until the user clicks somewhere else. However, the ToolTipService.ShowDuration property overrides the StaysOpen property. As a result, tooltips always disappear after a configurable amount of time (usually about 5 seconds) or when the user moves the mouse away. If you want to create a tooltip-like window that stays open indefinitely, the easiest approach is to use the Popup control.

Using the ToolTip properties, the following markup creates a tooltip that has no drop shadow but uses a transparent red background that lets the underlying window (and controls) show through:

```
<Button>
  <Button.ToolTip>
    <ToolTip Background="#60AA4030" Foreground="White"
      HasDropShadow="False" >
      <StackPanel>
        <TextBlock Margin="3" >Image and text</TextBlock>
        <Image Source="happyface.jpg" Stretch="None" />
        <TextBlock Margin="3" >Image and text</TextBlock>
      </StackPanel>
    </ToolTip>
  </Button.ToolTip>
  <Button.Content>I have a fancy tooltip</Button.Content>
</Button>
```

In most cases, you'll be happy enough to use the standard tooltip placement, which puts it at the current mouse position. However, the various ToolTip properties give you many more options. Here are some strategies you can use to place a tooltip:

- **Based on the current position of the mouse.** This is the standard behavior, which relies on Placement being set to Mouse. The top-left corner of the tooltip box is lined up with the bottom-left corner of the invisible "bounding box" around the mouse pointer.

- **Based on the position of the moused-over element.** Set the Placement property to Left, Right, Top, Bottom, or Center, depending on the edge of the element you want to use. The top-left corner of the tooltip box will be lined up with that edge.

- **Based on the position of another element (or the window).** Set the Placement property in the same way you would if you were lining the tooltip up with the current element. (Use the value Left, Right, Top, Bottom, or Center.) Then choose the element by setting the PlacementTarget property. Remember to use the {Binding Element-Name=*Name*} syntax to identify the element you want to use.

- **With an offset.** Use any of the strategies described previously, but set the HorizontalOffset and VerticalOffset properties to add a little extra space.

- **Using absolute coordinates.** Set Placement to Absolute and use the HorizontalOffset and VerticalOffset properties (or the PlacementRectangle) to set some space between the tooltip and the top-left corner of the window.

- **Using a calculation at runtime.** Set Placement to Custom. Set the CustomPopupPlacementCallback property to point to a method that you've created.

Figure 7-4 shows how different placement properties stack up. Note that when lining up a tooltip against an element along the tooltip's bottom or right edge, you'll end up with a tiny bit of extra space. That's because of the way that the ToolTip measures its content.

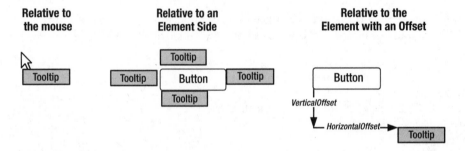

Figure 7-4. *Placing a tooltip explicitly*

Setting ToolTipService Properties

There are some tooltip properties that can't be configured using the properties of the ToolTip class. In this case, you need to use a different class, which is named ToolTipService. ToolTipService allows you to configure the time delays associated with the display of a tooltip. All the properties of the ToolTipService class are attached properties, so you can set them directly in your control tag, as shown here:

```
<Button ToolTipService.InitialShowDelay="1">
  ...
</Button>
```

The ToolTipService class defines many of the same properties as ToolTip. This allows you to use a simpler syntax when you're dealing with text-only tooltips. Rather than adding a nested ToolTip element, you can set everything you need using attributes:

```
<Button ToolTip="This tooltip is aligned with the bottom edge"
  ToolTipService.Placement="Bottom">I have a tooltip</Button>
```

Table 7-3 lists the properties of the ToolTipService class. The ToolTipService class also provides two routed events: ToolTipOpening and ToolTipClosing. You can react to these events to fill a tooltip with just-in-time content or to override the way tooltips work. For example, if you set the handled flag in both events, tooltips will no longer be shown or hidden automatically. Instead, you'll need to show and hide them manually by setting the IsOpen property.

■**Tip** It makes little sense to duplicate the same tooltip settings for several controls. If you plan to adjust the way tooltips are handled in your entire application, use styles so that your settings are applied automatically, as described in Chapter 12. Unfortunately, the ToolTipService property values are not inherited, which means if you set them at the window or container level, they don't flow through to the nested elements.

Table 7-3. *ToolTipService Properties*

Name	Description
InitialShowDelay	Sets the delay (in milliseconds) before this tooltip is shown when the mouse hovers over the element.
ShowDuration	Sets the amount of time (in milliseconds) that this tooltip is shown before it disappears, if the user does not move the mouse.
BetweenShowDelay	Sets a time window (in milliseconds) during which the user can move between tooltips without experiencing the InitialShowDelay. For example, if BetweenShowDelay is 5000, the user has five seconds to move to another control that has a tooltip. If the user moves to another control within that time period, the new tooltip is shown immediately. If the user takes longer, the BetweenShowDelay window expires, and the InitialShowDelay kicks into action. In this case, the second tooltip isn't shown until after the InitialShowDelay period.
ToolTip	Sets the content for the tooltip. Setting ToolTipService.ToolTip is equivalent to setting the FrameworkElement.ToolTip property of an element.
HasDropShadow	Determines whether the tooltip has a diffuse black drop shadow that makes it stand out from the window underneath.
ShowOnDisabled	Determines the tooltip behavior when the associated element is disabled. If true, the tooltip will appear for disabled elements (elements that have their IsEnabled property set to false). The default is false, in which case the tooltip appears only if the associated element is enabled.
Placement, PlacementTarget, PlacementRectangle, and VerticalOffset	Allows you to control the placement of the tooltip. These properties work in the same way as the matching properties of the ToolTip-HorizontalOffset class.
IsEnabled and IsOpen	Allows you to control the tooltip in code. IsEnabled allows you to temporarily disable a ToolTip, and IsOpen allows you to programmatically show or hide a tooltip (or just check whether the tooltip is open).

The Popup

The Popup control has a great deal in common with the ToolTip, although neither one derives from the other.

Like the ToolTip, the Popup can hold a single piece of content, which can include any WPF element. (This content is stored in the Popup.Child property, rather than the ToolTip.Content property.) Also, like the ToolTip, the content in the Popup can extend beyond the bounds of the window. Lastly, the Popup can be placed using the same placement properties and shown or hidden using the same IsOpen property.

The differences between the Popup and ToolTip are more important. They include the following:

- The Popup is never shown automatically. You must set the IsOpen property for it to appear.

- By default, the Popup.StaysOpen property is set to true, and the Popup does not disappear until you explicitly set its IsOpen property to false. If you set StaysOpen to false, the Popup disappears when the user clicks somewhere else.

■**Note** A popup that stays open can be a bit jarring because it behaves like a separate stand-alone window. If you move the window underneath, the popup remains fixed in its original position. You won't witness this behavior with the ToolTip or with a Popup that sets StaysOpen to false because as soon as you click to move the window, the tooltip or popup window disappears.

- The Popup provides a PopupAnimation property that lets you control how it comes into view when you set IsOpen to true. Your options include None (the default), Fade (the opacity of the popup gradually increases), Scroll (the popup slides in from the upper-left corner of the window, space permitting), and Slide (the popup slides down into place, space permitting). In order for any of these animations to work, you must also set the AllowsTransparency property to true.

- The Popup can accept focus. Thus, you can place user-interactive controls in it, such as a Button. This functionality is one of the key reasons to use the Popup instead of the ToolTip.

- The Popup control is defined in the System.Windows.Controls.Primitives namespace because it is most commonly used as a building block for more complex controls. You'll find that the Popup is not quite as polished as other controls—notably, you must set the Background property if you want to see your content because it won't be inherited from your window and you need to add the border yourself (the Border element works perfectly well for this purpose).

Because the Popup must be shown manually, you may choose to create it entirely in code. However, you can define it just as easily in XAML markup—just make sure to include the Name property so you can manipulate it in code.

Figure 7-5 shows an example. Here, when the user moves the mouse over an underlined word, a popup appears with more information and a link that opens an external web browser window.

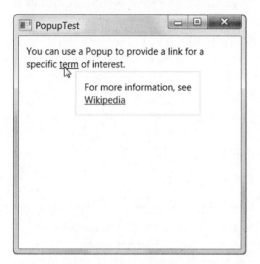

Figure 7-5. *A popup with a hyperlink*

To create this window, you need to include a TextBlock with the initial text and a Popup with the additional content that you'll show when the user moves the mouse into the right place. Technically, it doesn't matter where you define the Popup tag because it's not associated with any particular control. Instead, it's up to you to set the placement properties to position the Popup in the correct spot. In this example, the Popup appears at the current mouse position, which is the simplest option.

```
<TextBlock TextWrapping="Wrap">You can use a Popup to provide a link for a
  specific <Run TextDecorations="Underline" MouseEnter="run_MouseEnter">term</Run>
  of interest.</TextBlock>

<Popup Name="popLink" StaysOpen="False" Placement="Mouse" MaxWidth="200"
  PopupAnimation="Slide" AllowsTransparency="True">
  <Border BorderBrush="Beige" BorderThickness="2" Background="White">
    <TextBlock Margin="10" TextWrapping="Wrap">
      For more information, see
      <Hyperlink NavigateUri="http://en.wikipedia.org/wiki/Term"
       Click="lnk_Click">Wikipedia</Hyperlink>
    </TextBlock>
  </Border>
</Popup>
```

This example presents two elements that you might not have seen before. The Run element allows you to apply formatting to a specific part of a TextBlock—it's a piece of flow content that you'll learn about in Chapter 19 when you consider documents. The Hyperlink allows you to provide a clickable piece of text. You'll take a closer look at it in Chapter 9, when you consider page-based applications.

The only remaining details are the relatively trivial code that shows the Popup when the mouse moves over the right word and the code that launches the web browser when the link is clicked:

```
private void run_MouseEnter(object sender, MouseEventArgs e)
{
    popLink.IsOpen = true;
}

private void lnk_Click(object sender, RoutedEventArgs e)
{
    Process.Start(((Hyperlink)sender).NavigateUri.ToString());
}
```

Note You can show and hide a Popup using a *trigger*—an action that takes place automatically when a specific property hits a specific value. You simply need to create a trigger that reacts when the Popup.IsMouseOver is true and sets the Popup.IsOpen property to true. Chapter 12 has the details.

Text Controls

WPF includes three text-entry controls: TextBox, RichTextBox, and PasswordBox. The PasswordBox derives directly from Control. The TextBox and RichTextBox controls go through another level and derive from TextBoxBase.

Unlike the content controls you've seen, the text boxes are limited in the type of content they can contain. The TextBox always stores a string (provided by the Text property). The PasswordBox also deals with string content (provided by the Password property), although it uses a SecureString internally to mitigate against certain types of attacks. Only the RichTextBox has the ability to store more sophisticated content: a FlowDocument that can contain a complex combination of elements.

In the following sections, you'll consider the core features of the TextBox. You'll end by taking a quick look at the security features of the PasswordBox.

Note The RichTextBox is an advanced control design for displaying FlowDocument objects. You'll learn how to use it when you tackle documents in Chapter 19.

Multiple Lines of Text

Ordinarily, the TextBox control stores a single line of text. (You can limit the allowed number of characters by setting the MaxLength property.) However, there are many cases when you'll want to create a multiline text box for dealing with large amounts of content. In this case, set the TextWrapping property to Wrap or WrapWithOverflow. Wrap always breaks at the edge of the control, even if it means severing an extremely long word in two. WrapWithOverflow allows some lines to stretch beyond the right edge if the line-break algorithm can't find a suitable place (such as a space or a hyphen) to break the line.

To actually see multiple lines in a text box, it needs to be sized large enough. Rather than setting a hard-coded height (which won't adapt to different font sizes and may cause layout problems), you can use the handy MinLines and MaxLines properties. MinLines is the minimum number of lines that must be visible in the text box. For example, if MinLines is 2, the text box will grow to be at least two lines tall. If its container doesn't have enough room, part of the text box may be clipped. MaxLines sets the maximum number of lines that will be displayed. Even if a text box expands to fit its container (for example, a proportionally sized Grid row or the last element in a DockPanel), it won't grow beyond this limit.

Note The MinLines and MaxLines properties have no effect on the amount of content you can place in a text box. They simply help you size the text box. In your code, you can examine the LineCount property to find out exactly how many lines are in a text box.

If your text box supports wrapping, the odds are good that the user can enter more text that can be displayed at once in the visible lines. For this reason, it usually makes sense to add an always-visible or on-demand scroll bar by setting the VerticalScrollBarVisibility property to Visible or Auto. (You can also set the HorizontalScrollBarVisibility property to show a less common horizontal scroll bar.)

You may want to allow the user to enter hard returns in a multiline textbox by pressing the Enter key. (Ordinarily, pressing the Enter key in a text box triggers the default button.) To make sure a text box supports the Enter key, set AcceptsReturn to true. You can also set AcceptsTab to allow the user to insert tabs. Otherwise, the Tab key moves to the next focusable control in the tab sequence.

Tip The TextBox class also includes a host of methods that let you move through the text content programmatically in small or large steps. They include LineUp(), LineDown(), PageUp(), PageDown(), ScrollToHome(), ScrollToEnd(), and ScrollToLine().

Sometimes, you'll create a text box purely for the purpose of displaying text. In this case, set the IsReadOnly property to true to prevent editing. This is preferable to disabling the text box by setting IsEnabled to false because a disabled text box shows grayed-out text (which is more difficult to read), does not support selection (or copying to the clipboard), and does not support scrolling.

Text Selection

As you already know, you can select text in any text box by clicking and dragging with the mouse or holding down Shift while you move through the text with the arrow keys. The

TextBox class also gives you the ability to determine or change the currently selected text programmatically, using the SelectionStart, SelectionLength, and SelectedText properties.

SelectionStart identifies the zero-based position where the selection begins. For example, if you set this property to 10, the first selected character is the 11th character in the text box. The Selection Length indicates the total number of selected characters. (A value of 0 indicates no selected characters.) Finally, the SelectedText property allows you to quickly examine or change the selected text in the text box. You can react to the selection being changed by handling the SelectionChanged event. Figure 7-6 shows an example that reacts to this event and displays the current selection information.

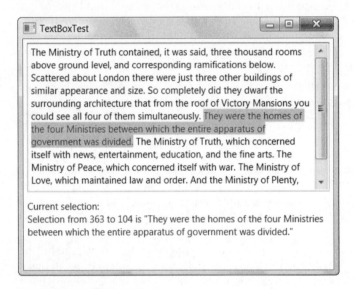

Figure 7-6. *Selecting text*

The TextBox class also includes one property that lets you control its selection behavior: AutoWordSelection. If this is true, the text box selects entire words at a time as you drag through the text.

Miscellaneous TextBox Features

The TextBox includes a few more specialized frills. The most interesting is the spelling-checker feature, which underlines unrecognized words with a red squiggly line. The user can right-click an unrecognized word and choose from a list of possibilities, as shown in Figure 7-7.

To turn on this spelling-checker functionality for the TextBox control, you simply need to set the SpellCheck.IsEnabled dependency property, as shown here:

```
<TextBox SpellCheck.IsEnabled="True">...</TextBox>
```

The spelling checker is WPF-specific and doesn't depend on any other software (such as Office). The spelling checker determines what dictionary to use based on the input language that's configured for the keyboard. You can override this default by setting the Language property of the TextBox, which is inherited from the FrameworkElement class, or you can set the xml:lang attribute on the <TextBox> element.

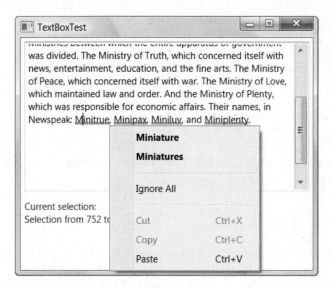

Figure 7-7. *Spell-checking a text box*

Unfortunately, the spelling checker is not customizable in any way. It contains only one additional property (SpellingReform), which determines whether post-1990 spelling rule changes are applied to French and German languages. Another useful feature of the TextBox control is Undo, which allows the user to reverse recent changes. The Undo feature is available programmatically (using the Undo() method), and it's available using the Ctrl+Z keyboard shortcut, as long as the CanUndo property has not been set to false.

Tip When manipulating text in the text box programmatically, you can use the BeginChange() and EndChange() methods to bracket a series of actions that the TextBox will treat as a single "block" of changes. These actions can then be undone in a single step.

The PasswordBox

The PasswordBox looks like a TextBox, but it displays a string of circle symbols to mask the characters it shows. (You can choose a different mask character by setting the PasswordChar property.) Additionally, the PasswordBox does not support the clipboard, so you can't copy the text inside.

Compared to the TextBox class, the PasswordBox has a much simpler, stripped-down interface. Much like the TextBox class, it provides a MaxLength property; a Clear(), a Paste() and a SelectAll() method; and an event that fires when the text is changed (named Password-Changed). But that's it. Still, the most important difference between the TextBox and the PasswordBox is on the inside. Although you can set text and read it as an ordinary string using the Password property, internally the PasswordBox uses a System.Security.SecureString object exclusively.

A SecureString is a text-only object much like the ordinary string. The difference is how it's stored in memory. A SecureString is stored in memory in an encrypted form. The key that's used to encrypt the string is generated randomly and stored in a portion of memory that's never written to disk. The end result is that even if your computer crashes, a malicious user won't be able to examine the paging file to retrieve the password data. At best, he'll find the encrypted form.

The SecureString class also includes on-demand disposal. When you call Secure-String.Dispose(), the in-memory password data is overwritten. This guarantees that all password information has been wiped out of memory and is no longer subject to any kind of exploit. As you'd expect, the PasswordBox is conscientious enough to call Dispose() on the SecureString that it stores internally when the control is destroyed.

List Controls

WPF includes many controls that wrap a collection of items, ranging from the simple ListBox and ComboBox that you'll examine here to more specialized controls such as the ListView, the TreeView, and the ToolBar, which are covered in future chapters. All of these controls derive from the ItemsControl class (which itself derives from Control).

The ItemsControl class fills in the basic plumbing that's used by all list-based controls. Notably, it gives you two ways to fill the list of items. The most straightforward approach is to add them directly to the Items collection, using code or XAML. However, in WPF it's more common to use data binding. In this case, you set the ItemsSource property to the object that has the collection of data items you want to display. (You'll learn more about data binding starting in Chapter 16.)

The class hierarchy that leads from ItemsControls is a bit tangled. One major branch is the *selectors*, which includes the ListBox, the ComboBox, and the TabControl. These controls derive from Selector and have properties that let you track down the currently selected item (SelectedItem) or its position (SelectedIndex). Separate from these are controls that wrap lists of items but don't support selection in the same way. These include the classes for menus, toolbars, and trees—all of which are ItemsControls but aren't selectors.

In order to unlock most of the features of any ItemsControl, you'll need to use data binding. This is true even if you aren't fetching your data from a database or even an external data source. WPF data binding is general enough to work with data in a variety of forms, including custom data objects and collections. But you won't consider the details of data binding just yet. For now, you'll take only a quick look at the ListBox and ComboBox.

The ListBox

The ListBox and ComboBox class represent two common staples of Windows design—variable-length lists that allow the user to select an item.

■**Note** The ListBox class also allows multiple selection if you set the SelectionMode property to Multiple or Extended. In Multiple mode, you can select or deselect any item by clicking it. In Extended mode, you need to hold down the Ctrl key to select additional items or the Shift key to select a range of items. In either type of multiple-selection list, you use the SelectedItems collection instead of the SelectedItem property to get all the selected items.

To add items to the ListBox, you can nest ListBoxItem elements inside the ListBox element. For example, here's a ListBox that contains a list of colors:

```
<ListBox>
  <ListBoxItem>Green</ListBoxItem>
  <ListBoxItem>Blue</ListBoxItem>
  <ListBoxItem>Yellow</ListBoxItem>
  <ListBoxItem>Red</ListBoxItem>
</ListBox>
```

As you'll remember from Chapter 2, different controls treat their nested content in different ways. The ListBox stores each nested object in its Items collection.

The ListBox is a remarkably flexible control. Not only can it hold ListBoxItem objects, but it can also host any arbitrary element. This works because the ListBoxItem class derives from ContentControl, which gives it the ability to hold a single piece of nested content. If that piece of content is a UIElement-derived class, it will be rendered in the ListBox. If it's some other type of object, the ListBoxItem will call ToString() and display the resulting text.

For example, if you decided you want to create a list with images, you could create markup like this:

```
<ListBox>
  <ListBoxItem>
    <Image Source="happyface.jpg"></Image>
  </ListBoxItem>
  <ListBoxItem>
    <Image Source="happyface.jpg"></Image>
  </ListBoxItem>
</ListBox>
```

The ListBox is actually intelligent enough to create the ListBoxItem objects it needs implicitly. That means you can place your objects directly inside the ListBox element. Here's a more ambitious example that uses nested StackPanel objects to combine text and image content:

```
<ListBox>
  <StackPanel Orientation="Horizontal">
    <Image Source="happyface.jpg"  Width="30" Height="30"></Image>
    <Label VerticalContentAlignment="Center">A happy face</Label>
  </StackPanel>
  <StackPanel Orientation="Horizontal">
    <Image Source="redx.jpg" Width="30" Height="30"></Image>
```

```
    <Label VerticalContentAlignment="Center">A warning sign</Label>
  </StackPanel>
  <StackPanel Orientation="Horizontal">
    <Image Source="happyface.jpg"  Width="30" Height="30"></Image>
    <Label VerticalContentAlignment="Center">A happy face</Label>
  </StackPanel>
</ListBox>
```

In this example, the StackPanel becomes the item that's wrapped by the ListBoxItem. This markup creates the rich list shown in Figure 7-8.

Figure 7-8. *A list of images*

■Note One flaw in the current design is that the text color doesn't change when the item is selected. This isn't ideal because it's difficult to read the black text with a blue background. To solve this problem, you need to use a data template, as described in Chapter 17.

This ability to nest arbitrary elements inside list box items allows you to create a variety of list-based controls without needing to use other classes. For example, the Windows Forms toolkit includes a CheckedListBox class that's displayed as a list with a check box next to every item. No such specialized class is required in WPF because you can quickly build one using the standard ListBox:

```
<ListBox Name="lst" SelectionChanged="lst_SelectionChanged"
  CheckBox.Click="lst_SelectionChanged">
  <CheckBox Margin="3">Option 1</CheckBox>
  <CheckBox Margin="3">Option 2</CheckBox>
</ListBox>
```

There's one caveat to be aware of when you use a list with different elements inside. When you read the SelectedItem value (and the SelectedItems and Items collections), you won't see ListBoxItem objects—instead, you'll see whatever objects you placed in the list. In the CheckedListBox example, that means SelectedItem provides a CheckBox object.

For example, here's some code that reacts when the SelectionChanged event fires. It then gets the currently selected CheckBox and displays whether that item has been checked:

```
private void lst_SelectionChanged(object sender, SelectionChangedEventArgs e)
{
    if (lst.SelectedItem == null) return;
    txtSelection.Text = String.Format(
      "You chose item at position {0}.\r\nChecked state is {1}.",
      lst.SelectedIndex,
      ((CheckBox)lst.SelectedItem).IsChecked);
}
```

Tip If you want to find the current selection, you can read it directly from the SelectedItem or SelectedItems property, as shown here. If you want to determine what item (if any) was *unselected*, you can use the RemovedItems property of the SelectionChangedEventArgs object. Similarly, the AddedItems property tells you what items were added to the selection. In single-selection mode, one item is always added and one item is always removed whenever the selection changes. In multiple or extended mode, this isn't necessarily the case.

In the following code snippet, similar code loops through the collection of items to determine which ones are checked. (You could write similar code that loops through the collection of selected items in a multiple-selection list with check boxes.)

```
private void cmd_ExamineAllItems(object sender, RoutedEventArgs e)
{
    StringBuilder sb = new StringBuilder();
    foreach (CheckBox item in lst.Items)
    {
        if (item.IsChecked == true)
        {
            sb.Append(item.Content);
            sb.Append(" is checked.");
            sb.Append("\r\n");
        }
    }
    txtSelection.Text = sb.ToString();
}
```

Figure 7-9 shows the list box that uses this code.

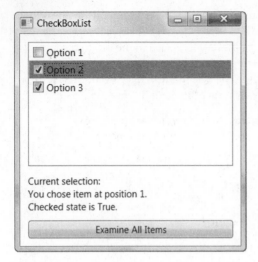

Figure 7-9. *A check box list*

When manually placing items in a list, it's up to you whether you want to place the items in directly or explicitly wrap each one in a ListBoxItem object. The second approach is often cleaner, albeit more tedious. The most important consideration is to be consistent. For example, if you place StackPanel objects in your list, the ListBox.SelectedItem object will be a StackPanel. If you place StackPanel objects wrapped by ListBoxItem objects, the ListBox.SelectedItem object will be a ListBoxItem, so code accordingly.

The ListBoxItem offers a little bit of extra functionality from what you get with directly nested objects. Namely, it defines an IsSelected property that you can read (or set) and a Selected and Unselected event that tells you when that item is highlighted. However, you can get similar functionality using the members of the ListBox class, such as the SelectedItem (or SelectedItems) property, and the SelectionChanged event.

Interestingly, there's a technique to retrieve a ListBoxItem wrapper for a specific object when you use the nested object approach. The trick is the often overlooked Container-FromElement() method. Here's the code that checks whether the first item is selected in a list using this technique:

```
ListBoxItem item = (ListBoxItem)lst.ContainerFromElement(
  (DependencyObject)lst.SelectedItems[0]);
MessageBox.Show("IsSelected: " + item.IsSelected.ToString());
```

The ComboBox

The ComboBox is similar to the ListBox control. It holds a collection of ComboBoxItem objects, which are created either implicitly or explicitly. As with the ListBoxItem, the ComboBoxItem is a content control that can contain any nested element.

The key difference between the ComboBox and ListBox classes is the way they render themselves in a window. The ComboBox control uses a drop-down list, which means only one item can be selected at a time.

If you want to allow the user to type in text in the combo box to select an item, you must set the IsEditable property to true, and you must make sure you are storing ordinary text-only ComboBoxItem objects or an object that provides a meaningful ToString() representation. For example, if you fill an editable combo box with Image objects, the text that appears in the upper portion is simply the fully qualified Image class name, which isn't much use.

One limitation of the ComboBox is the way it sizes itself when you use automatic sizing. The ComboBox widens itself to fit its content, which means that it changes size as you move from one item to the next. Unfortunately, there's no easy way to tell the ComboBox to take the size of its largest contained item. Instead, you may need to supply a hard-coded value for the Width property, which isn't ideal.

Range-Based Controls

WPF includes three controls that use the concept of a *range*. These controls take a numeric value that falls in between a specific minimum and maximum value. These controls—ScrollBar, ProgressBar, and Slider—all derive from the RangeBase class (which itself derives from the Control class). But although they share an abstraction (the range), they work quite differently.

The RangeBase class defines the properties shown in Table 7-4.

Table 7-4. *Properties of the RangeBase Class*

Name	Description
Value	This is the current value of the control (which must fall between the minimum and maximum). By default, it starts at 0. Contrary to what you might expect, Value isn't an integer—it's a double, so it accepts fractional values. You can react to the ValueChanged event if you want to be notified when the value is changed.
Maximum	This is the upper limit (the largest allowed value).
Minimum	This is the lower limit (the smallest allowed value).
SmallChange	This is the amount the Value property is adjusted up or down for a "small change." The meaning of a small change depends on the control (and may not be used at all). For the ScrollBar and Slider, this is the amount the value changes when you use the arrow keys. For the ScrollBar, you can also use the arrow buttons at either end of the bar.
LargeChange	This is the amount the Value property is adjusted up or down for a "large change." The meaning of a large change depends on the control (and may not be used at all). For the ScrollBar and Slider, this is the amount the value changes when you use the Page Up and Page Down keys or when you click the bar on either side of the thumb (which indicates the current position).

Ordinarily, there's no need to use the ScrollBar control directly. The higher-level ScrollViewer control, which wraps two ScrollBar controls, is typically much more useful. (The ScrollViewer was covered in Chapter 5.) However, the Slider and ProgressBar are more valuable on their own.

The Slider

The Slider is a specialized control that's occasionally useful—for example, you might use it to set numeric values in situations where the number itself isn't particularly significant. For example, it makes sense to set the volume in a media player by dragging the thumb in a slider bar from side to side. The general position of the thumb indicates the relative loudness (normal, quiet, loud), but the underlying number has no meaning to the user.

The key Slider properties are defined in the RangeBase class. Along with these, you can use all the properties listed in Table 7-5.

Table 7-5. *Additional Properties in the Slider Class*

Name	Description
Orientation	Switches between a vertical and a horizontal slider.
Delay and Interval	Controls how fast the thumb moves along the track when you click and hold down either side of the slider. Both are millisecond values. The Delay is the time before the thumb moves one (small change) unit after you click, and the Interval is the time before it moves again if you continue holding the mouse button down.
TickPlacement	Determines where the tick marks appear. (Tick marks are notches that appear near the bar to help you visualize the scale.) By default, the TickPlacement is set to None, and no tick marks appear. If you have a horizontal slider, you can place the tick marks above (TopLeft) or below (BottomRight) the track. With a vertical slider, you can place them on the left (TopLeft) and right (BottomRight). (The TickPlacement names are a bit confusing because two values cover four possibilities, depending on the orientation of the slider.)
TickFrequency	Sets the interval in between ticks, which determines how many ticks appear. For example, you could place them every 5 numeric units, every 10, and so on.
Ticks	If you want to place ticks in specific, irregular positions, you can use the Ticks collection. Simply add one number (as a double) to this collection for each tick mark. For example, you could place ticks at the positions 1, 1.5, 2, and 10 on the scale by adding these numbers.
IsSnapToTickEnabled	If true, when you move the slider, it automatically snaps into place, jumping to the nearest tick mark. The default is false.
IsSelectionRangeEnabled	If true, you can use a selection range to shade in a portion of the slider bar. You set the position selection range using the SelectionStart and SelectionEnd properties. The selection range has no intrinsic meaning, but you can use it for whatever purpose makes sense. For example, media players sometimes use a shaded background bar to indicate the download progress for a media file.

Figure 7-10 compares Slider controls with different tick settings.

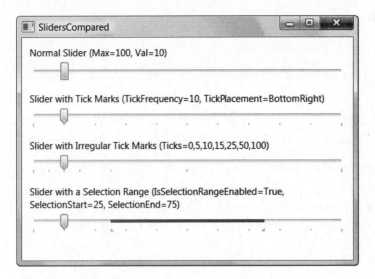

Figure 7-10. *Adding ticks to a slider*

The ProgressBar

The ProgressBar indicates the progress of a long-running task. Unlike the slider, the Progress-Bar isn't user interactive. Instead, it's up to your code to periodically increment the Value property. (Technically speaking, WPF rules suggest the ProgressBar shouldn't be a control because it doesn't respond to mouse actions or keyboard input.) You've already seen one example with the ProgressBar in Chapter 3—a window that uses a background thread to complete a task. The ProgressBar has no natural height of two or three device-independent units. It's up to you to set the Height property (or put it in the appropriate fixed-size container) if you want to see a larger, more traditional bar.

One neat trick that you can perform with the ProgressBar is using it to show a long-running status indicator, even if you don't know how long the task will take. Interestingly (and oddly), you do this by setting the IsIndeterminate property to true:

```
<ProgressBar Height="18"  Width="200" IsIndeterminate="True"></ProgressBar>
```

When setting IsIndeterminate, you no longer use the Minimum, Maximum, and Value properties. Instead, this ProgressBar shows a periodic green pulse that travels from left to right, which is the universal Windows convention indicating that there's work in progress. This sort of indicator makes particular sense in an application's status bar. For example, you could use it to indicate that you're contacting a remote server for information.

The Last Word

In this chapter, you toured the basic WPF controls. You considered several categories:

- Content controls that can contain nested elements, such as the Label, the Button, and the ToolTip

- Text controls that can store ordinary text (the TextBox) or a password (the PasswordBox)

- List controls that contain a collection of items, such as the ListBox and the ComboBox

- Range-based controls that take a numeric value from a range, such as the Slider and the ProgressBar

I'll cover many more essential controls in the chapters to come. In the next two chapters, you'll take a look at the most important top-level controls in WPF controls—the Window and the Page.

■ ■ ■

CHAPTER 8

Windows

Windows are the basic ingredients in any desktop application—so basic that the operating system is named after them. And although WPF has a model for creating navigation applications that divide tasks into separate pages, windows are still the dominant metaphor for creating applications.

In this chapter, you'll explore the Window class. If you've programmed with the Windows Forms toolkit before, much of this material will seem familiar, because the Window class is loosely modeled after the Form class. As a result, you might want to skim through this material, paying attention to details that have changed significantly, such as nonrectangular windows and the Vista-style task dialog box. You can then continue to the next chapter, which tackles a different top-level container (the Page) and a different way to structure applications (using web-style navigation).

The Window Class

As you learned in Chapter 5, the Window class derives from ContentControl. That means it can contain a single child (usually a layout container such as the Grid control), and you can paint the background with a brush by setting the Background property. You can also use the BorderBrush and BorderThickness properties to add a border around your window, but this border is added inside the window frame (around the edge of the client area). You can remove the window frame altogether by setting the WindowStyle property to None, which allows you to create a completely customized window, as you'll see later in the "Nonrectangular Windows" section.

■**Note** The *client area* is the surface inside the window boundaries. This is where you place your content. The nonclient area includes the border and the title bar at the top of the window. The operating system manages this area.

In addition, the Window class adds a small set of members that will be familiar to any Windows programmer. The most obvious are the appearance-related properties that let you change the way the nonclient portion of the window appears. Table 8-1 lists these members.

Table 8-1. *Basic Properties of the Window Class*

Name	Description
AllowsTransparency	If AllowsTransparency is set to true, the Window class allows other windows to show through if the background is set to a transparent color. If set to false (the default), the content behind the window never shows through, and a transparent background is rendered as a black background. This property allows you to create irregularly shaped windows when it's used in combination with a WindowStyle of None, as you'll see in the "Nonrectangular Windows" section.
Icon	Is an ImageSource object that identifies the icon you want to use for your window. Icons appear at the top left of a window (if it has one of the standard border styles), in the taskbar (if ShowInTaskBar is true), and in the selection window that's shown when the user presses Alt+Tab to navigate between running applications. Because these icons are different sizes, your .ico file should include at least a 16×16 pixel image and a 32×32 pixel image. In fact, the Vista icon standard (described at http://www.axialis.com/tutorials/tutorial-vistaicons.html) adds both a 48×48 pixel image and a 256×256 image, which can be sized as needed for other purposes. If Icon is a null reference, the window is given the same icon as the application (which you can set in Visual Studio by double-clicking the Properties node in the Solution Explorer and then choosing the Application tab). If this is omitted, WPF will use a standard but unremarkable icon that shows a window.
Top and Left	Sets the distance between the top-left corner of the window and the top and left edges of the screen, in device-independent pixels. The LocationChanged event fires when either of these details changes. If the WindowStartupPosition property is set to Manual, you can set these properties before the window appears to set its position. You can always use these properties to move the position of a window *after* it has appeared, no matter what value you use for WindowStartupPosition.
ResizeMode	Takes a value from the ResizeMode enumeration that determines whether the user can resize the window. This setting also affects the visibility of the maximize and minimize boxes. Use NoResize to lock a window up completely, CanMinimize to allow minimizing only, CanResize to allow everything, or CanResizeWithGrip to add a visual detail at the bottom-right corner of the window to show that the window is resizable.
RestoreBounds	Gets the bounds of the window. However, if the window is currently maximized or minimized, this property provides the bounds that were last used before the window was maximized or minimized. This is extremely useful if you need to store the position and dimensions of a window, as described later in this chapter.
ShowInTaskbar	If set to true, the window appears in the taskbar and the Alt+Tab list. Usually, you will set this to true only for your application's main window.
SizeToContent	Allows you to create a window that enlarges itself automatically. This property takes a value from the SizeToContent enumeration. Use Manual to disable automatic sizing, or use Height, Width, or WidthAndHeight to allow the window to expand in different dimensions to accommodate dynamic content. When using SizeToContent, the window may be sized larger than the bounds of the screen.
Title	The caption that appears in the title bar for the window (and in the taskbar).

Name	Description
Topmost	When set to true, this window is always displayed on top of every other window in your application (unless these other windows also have TopMost set to true). This is a useful setting for palettes that need to "float" above other windows.
WindowStartupLocation	Takes a value from the WindowStartupLocation enumeration. Use Manual to position a window exactly with the Left and Top properties, CenterScreen to place the window in the center of the screen, or CenterOwner to center the window with respect to the window that launched it. When showing a modeless window with CenterOwner, make sure you set the Owner property of the new window before you show it.
WindowState	Takes a value from the WindowState enumeration. Informs you (and allows you to change) whether the window is currently maximized, minimized, or in its normal state. The StateChanged event fires when this property changes.
WindowStyle	Takes a value from the WindowStyle enumeration, which determines the border for the window. Your options include SingleBorderWindow (the default), ThreeDBorderWindow (which is rendered the same on Windows Vista and almost the same on Windows XP), ToolWindow (a thin border good for floating tool windows, with no maximize or minimize buttons), and None (a very thin raised border with no title bar region). Figure 8-1 shows the difference.

Figure 8-1. *Different values for WindowStyle: (a) Windows Vista, (b) Windows XP*

You've already learned about the lifetime events that fire when a window is created, activated, and unloaded (in Chapter 6). In addition, the Window class includes LocationChanged and WindowStateChanged events, which fire when its position and WindowState change, respectively.

Showing a Window

To display a window, you need to create an instance of the Window class and use the Show() or ShowDialog() method.

The ShowDialog() method shows a *modal* window. Modal windows stop the user from accessing the parent window by blocking any mouse or keyboard input to it, until the modal window is closed. In addition, the ShowDialog() method doesn't return until the modal window is closed, so any code that you've placed after the ShowDialog() call is put on hold. (However, that doesn't mean other code can't run—for example, if you have a timer running, its event handler will still run.) A common pattern in code is to show a modal window, wait until it's closed, and then act on its data.

Here's an example that uses the ShowDialog() method:

```
TaskWindow winTask = new TaskWindow();
winTask.ShowDialog();
// Execution reaches this point after winTask is closed.
```

The Show() method shows a *modeless* window, which doesn't block the user from accessing any other window. The Show() method also returns immediately after the window is shown, so subsequent code statements are executed right away. You can create and show several modeless windows, and the user can interact with them all at once. When using modeless windows, synchronization code is sometimes required to make sure that changes in one window update the information in another window to prevent a user from working with invalid information.

Here's an example that uses the Show() method:

```
MainWindow winMain = new MainWindow();
winMain.Show();
// Execution reaches this point immediately after winMain is shown.
```

Modal windows are ideal for presenting the user with a choice that needs to be made before an operation can continue. For example, consider Microsoft Word, which shows its Options and Print windows modally, forcing you to make a decision before continuing. On the other hand, the windows used to search for text or check the spelling in a document are shown modelessly, allowing the user to edit text in the main document window while performing the task.

Closing a window is equally easy, using the Close() method. Alternatively, you can hide a window from view using Hide() or by setting the Visibility property to Hidden. Either way, the window remains open and available to your code. Generally, it only makes sense to hide modeless windows. That's because if you hide a modal window, your code remains stalled until the window is closed, and the user can't close an invisible window.

Positioning a Window

Usually, you won't need to position a window exactly on the screen. You'll simply use Center-Owner for the WindowState and forget about the whole issue. In other, less common cases, you'll use Manual for the Windows state and set an exact position using the Left and Right properties.

Sometimes you need to take a little more care in choosing an appropriate location and size for your window. For example, you could accidentally create a window that is too large to be accommodated on a low-resolution display. If you are working with a single-window application, the best solution is to create a resizable window. If you are using an application with several floating windows, the answer is not as simple.

You could just restrict your window positions to locations that are supported on even the smallest monitors, but that's likely to frustrate higher-end users (who have purchased better monitors for the express purpose of fitting more information on their screen at a time). In this case, you usually want to make a runtime decision about the best window location. To do this, you need to retrieve some basic information about the available screen real estate using the System.Windows.SystemParameters class.

The SystemParameters class consists of a huge list of static properties that return information about various system settings. For example, you can use the SystemParameters class to determine whether the user has enabled hot tracking and the "drag full windows" option, among many others. With windows, the SystemParameters class is particularly useful because it provides two properties that give the dimensions of the current screen: FullPrimaryScreenHeight and FullPrimaryScreenWidth. Both are quite straightforward, as this bit of code (which centers the window at runtime) demonstrates:

```
double screeHeight = SystemParameters.FullPrimaryScreenHeight;
double screeWidth = SystemParameters.FullPrimaryScreenWidth;
this.Top = (screenHeight - this.Height) / 2;
this.Left = (screenWidth - this.Width) / 2;
```

Although this code is equivalent to using CenterScreen for the WindowState property of the window, it gives you the flexibility to implement different positioning logic and to run this logic at the appropriate time.

An even better choice is to use the SystemParameters.WorkArea rectangle to center the window in the *available* screen area. The work area measurement doesn't include the area where the taskbar is docked (and any other "bands" that are docked to the desktop).

```
double workHeight = SystemParameters.WorkArea.Height;
double workWidth = SystemParameters.WorkArea.Width;
this.Top = (workHeight - this.Height) / 2;
this.Left = (workWidth - this.Width) / 2;
```

■Note Both code examples have one minor drawback. When the Top property is set on a window that's already visible, the window is moved and refreshed immediately. The same process happens when the Left property is set in the following line of code. As a result, keen-eyed users may see the window move twice. Unfortunately, the Window class does not provide a method that allows you to set both position properties at once. The only solution is to position the window after you create it but before you make it visible by calling Show() or ShowDialog().

Saving and Restoring Window Location

A common requirement for a window is to remember its last location. This information can be stored in a user-specific configuration file or in the Windows registry.

If you wanted to store the position of an important window in a user-specific configuration file, you would begin by double-clicking the Properties node in the Solution Explorer and choosing the Settings section. Then, add a user-scoped setting with a data type of System.Windows.Rect, as shown in Figure 8-2.

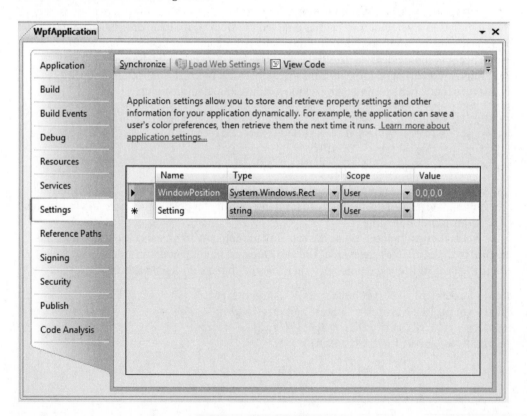

Figure 8-2. *A property for storing a window's position and size*

With this setting in place, it's easy to create code that automatically stores information about a window's size and position, as shown here:

```
Properties.Settings.Default.WindowPosition = win.RestoreBounds;
Properties.Settings.Default.Save();
```

Notice that this code uses the RestoreBounds property, which gives the correct dimensions (the last nonmaximized, nonminimized size) even if the window is currently maximized or minimized. (This handy feature wasn't directly available in Windows Forms, and it necessitated the use of the GetWindowPlacement() unmanaged API function.)

It's just as easy to retrieve this information when you need it:

```
try
{
    Rect bounds = Properties.Settings.Default.WindowPosition;
    win.Top = bounds.Top;
    win.Left = bounds.Left;

    // Restore the size only for a manually sized
    // window.
    if (win.SizeToContent == SizeToContent.Manual)
    {
        win.Width = bounds.Width;
        win.Height = bounds.Height;
    }
}
catch
{
    MessageBox.Show("No settings stored.");
}
```

The only limitation to this approach is that you need to create a separate property for each window that you want to store. If you need to store the position of many different windows, you might want to design a more flexible system. For example, the following helper class stores a position for any window you pass in, using a registry key that incorporates the name of that window. (You could use additional identifying information if you want to store the settings for several windows that will have the same name.)

```
public class WindowPositionHelper
{
    public static string RegPath = @"Software\MyApp\WindowBounds\";

    public static void SaveSize(Window win)
    {
        // Create or retrieve a reference to a key where the settings
        // will be stored.
        RegistryKey key;
        key = Registry.CurrentUser.CreateSubKey(RegPath + win.Name);
```

```
            key.SetValue("Bounds", win.RestoreBounds.ToString());
    }

    public static void SetSize(Window win)
    {
        RegistryKey key;
        key = Registry.CurrentUser.OpenSubKey(RegPath + win.Name);

        if (key != null)
        {
            Rect bounds = Rect.Parse(key.GetValue("Bounds").ToString());
            win.Top = bounds.Top;
            win.Left = bounds.Left;

            // Restore the size only for a manually sized
            // window.
            if (win.SizeToContent == SizeToContent.Manual)
            {
                win.Width = bounds.Width;
                win.Height = bounds.Height;
            }
        }
    }
}
}
```

To use this class in a window, you call the SaveSize() method when the window is closing and call the SetSize() method when the window is first opened. In each case, you pass a reference to the window you want the helper class to inspect. Note that in this example, each window must have a different value for its Name property.

Window Interaction

In Chapter 3, you considered the WPF application model, and you took your first look at how windows interact. As you saw there, the Application class provides you with two tools for getting access to other windows: the MainWindow and Windows properties. If you want to track windows in a more customized way—for example, by keeping track of instances of a certain window class, which might represent documents—you can add your own static properties to the Application class.

Of course, getting a reference to another window is only half the battle. You also need to decide how to communicate. As a general rule, you should minimize the need for window interactions, because they complicate code unnecessarily. If you do need to modify a control in one window based on an action in another window, create a dedicated method in the target window. That makes sure the dependency is well identified, and it adds another layer of indirection, making it easier to accommodate changes to the window's interface.

■**Tip** If the two windows have a complex interaction, are developed or deployed separately, or are likely to change, you can consider going one step further and formalize their interaction by creating an interface with the public methods and implementing that interface in your window class.

Figures 8-3 and 8-4 show two examples for implementing this pattern. Figure 8-3 shows a window that triggers a second window to refresh its data in response to a button click. This window does not directly attempt to modify the second window's user interface; instead, it relies on a custom intermediate method called DoUpdate().

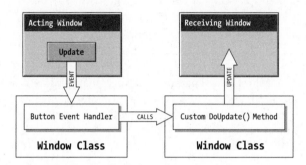

Figure 8-3. *A single window interaction*

The second example, Figure 8-4, shows a case where more than one window needs to be updated. In this case, the acting window relies on a higher-level application method, which calls the required window update methods (perhaps by iterating through a collection of windows). This approach is better because it works at a higher level. In the approach shown Figure 8-3, the acting window doesn't need to know anything specific about the controls in the receiving window. The approach in Figure 8-4 goes one step further—the acting window doesn't need to know anything at all about the receiving window class.

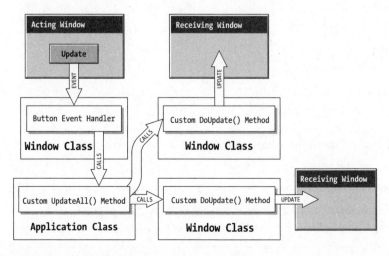

Figure 8-4. *A one-to-many window interaction*

■**Tip** When interacting between windows, the Window.Activate() method often comes in handy. It transfers the activation to the window you want. (You can also use the Window.IsActive property to test whether a window is currently the one and only active window.)

You can do one step further in decoupling this example. Rather than having the Application class trigger a method in the various windows, it could simply fire an event and allow the windows to choose how to respond to that event.

■**Note** WPF can help you abstract your application logic through its support for commands, which are application-specific tasks that can be triggered any way you like. Chapter 10 has the full story.

The examples in Figure 8-3 and Figure 8-4 show how separate windows (usually modeless) can trigger actions in one another. But certain other patterns for window interaction are simpler (such as the dialog model) and supplement this model (such as window ownership). You'll consider these features in the following sections.

Window Ownership

.NET allows a window to "own" other windows. Owned windows are useful for floating toolbox and command windows. One example of an owned window is the Find and Replace window in Microsoft Word. When an owner window is minimized, the owned windows are also minimized automatically. When an owned window overlaps its owner, it is always displayed on top.

To support window ownership, the Window class adds two properties. Owner is a reference that points to the window that owns the current window (if there is one). OwnedWindows is a collection of all the windows that the current window owns (if any).

Setting up ownership is simply a matter of setting the Owner property, as shown here:

```
// Create a new window.
ToolWindow winTool = new ToolWindow();

// Designate the current window as the owner.
winTool.Owner = this;

// Show the owned window.
winTool.Show();
```

Owned windows are always shown modelessly. To remove an owned window, set the Owner property to null.

■**Note** WPF does not include a system for building multiple document interface (MDI) applications. If you want more sophisticated window management, it's up to you to build it (or buy a third-party component).

An owned window can own another window, which can own another window, and so forth (although it's questionable whether this design has any practical use). The only limitations are that a window cannot own itself and two windows cannot own each other.

The Dialog Model

Often, when you show a window modally, you are offering the user some sort of choice. The code that displays the window waits for the result of that choice and then acts on it. This design is known as the *dialog model*. The window you show modally is the dialog box.

You can easily accommodate this design pattern by creating some sort of public property in your dialog window. When the user makes a selection in the dialog window, you would set this property and then close the window. The code that shows the dialog box can then check for this property and determine what to do next based on its value. (Remember, even when a window is closed, the window object, and all its control information, still exists until the variable referencing it goes out of scope.)

Fortunately, some of this infrastructure is already hardwired into the Window class. Every window includes a ready-made DialogResult property, which can take a true, false, or null value. Usually, true indicates the user chose to go forward (for example, clicked OK), while false indicates that the user canceled the operation.

Best of all, once you set the dialog result, it's returned to calling code as the return value of the ShowDialog() method. That means you can create, show, and consider the result of a dialog box window with this lean code:

```
DialogWindow dialog = new DialogWindow();
if (dialog.ShowDialog() == true)
{
    // The user accepted the action. Full speed ahead.
}
else
{
    // The user canceled the action.
}
```

■Note Using the DialogResult property doesn't prevent you from adding custom properties to your window. For example, it's perfectly reasonable to use the DialogResult property to inform the calling code whether an action was accepted or canceled and to provide other important details through custom properties. If the calling code finds a DialogResult of true, it can then check these other properties to get the information it needs.

You can take advantage of another shortcut. Rather than setting the DialogResult by hand after the user clicks a button, you can designate a button as the accept button (by setting IsDefault to true). Clicking that button automatically sets the DialogResult of the window to true. Similarly, you can designate a button as the cancel button (by setting IsCancel to true), in which case clicking it will set the DialogResult to Cancel. (You learned about IsDefault and IsCancel when you considered buttons in Chapter 7.)

■**Note** The dialog model in WPF is different from that of Windows Forms. Buttons do not provide a DialogResult property, so you are limited to creating default and cancel buttons. The DialogResult is more limited—it can be only true, false, or null (which it is initially). Also, clicking a default or cancel button does not automatically close the window—you need to write the code to accomplish that.

Common Dialog Boxes

The Windows operating system includes many built-in dialog boxes that you can access through the Windows API. WPF provides wrappers for just a few of these.

■**Note** There are good reasons that WPF doesn't include wrappers for all the Windows APIs. One of the goals of WPF is to decouple it from the Windows API so it's usable in other environments (like a browser) or portable to other platforms. Also, many of the built-in dialog boxes are showing their age and shouldn't be the first choice for modern applications. Windows Vista also discourages dialog boxes in favor of task-based panes and navigation.

The most obvious of these is the System.Windows.MessageBox class, which exposes a static Show() method. You can use this code to display a standard Windows message box. Here's the most common overload:

```
MessageBox.Show("You must enter a name.", "Name Entry Error",
  MessageBoxButton.OK, MessageBoxImage.Exclamation) ;
```

The MessageBoxButton enumeration allows you to choose the buttons that are shown in the message box. Your options include OK, OKCancel, YesNo, and YesNoCancel. (The less user-friendly AbortRetryIgnore isn't supported.) The MessageBoxImage enumeration allows you to choose the message box icon (Information, Exclamation, Error, Hand, Question, Stop, and so on).

Along with the MessageBox class, WPF includes specialized printing support that uses the PrintDialog (which is described in Chapter 20) and, in the Microsoft.Win32 namespace, OpenFileDialog and SaveFileDialog classes.

The OpenFileDialog and SaveFileDialog classes acquire some additional features (some which are inherited from the FileDialog class). Both support a filter string, which sets the allowed file extensions. The OpenFileDialog also provides properties that let you validate the user's selection (CheckFileExists) and allow multiple files to be selected (Multiselect). Here's an example that shows an OpenFileDialog and displays the selected files in a list box after the dialog box is closed:

```
OpenFileDialog myDialog = new OpenFileDialog();

myDialog.Filter = "Image Files(*.BMP;*.JPG;*.GIF)|*.BMP;*.JPG;*.GIF" +
  "|All files (*.*)|*.*";
myDialog.CheckFileExists = true;
myDialog.Multiselect = true;
```

```
if (myDialog.ShowDialog() == true)
{
    lstFiles.Items.Clear();
    foreach (string file in myDialog.FileNames)
    {
        lstFiles.Items.Add(file);
    }
}
```

You won't find any color pickers, font pickers, or folder browsers (although you can get these ingredients using the System.Windows.Forms classes from .NET 2.0).

Nonrectangular Windows

Irregularly shaped windows are often the trademark of cutting-edge consumer applications such as photo editors, movie makers, and MP3 players, and they're likely to be even more common with WPF applications.

Creating a basic shaped window in WPF is easy. However, creating a slick, professional-looking shaped window takes more work—and, most likely, a talented graphic designer to create the outlines and design the background art.

A Simple Shaped Window

The basic technique for creating a shaped window is to follow these steps:

1. Set the Window.AllowsTransparency property to true.

2. Set the Window.WindowStyle property to None to hide the nonclient region of the window (the blue border). If you don't, you'll get an InvalidOperationException when you attempt to show the window.

3. Set the Background to be transparent (using the color Transparent, which has an alpha value of 0). Or, set the Background to use an image that has transparent areas (regions that are painted with an alpha value of 0).

These three steps effectively remove the standard window appearance (known to WPF experts as the window *chrome*). To get the shaped window effect, you now need to supply some nontransparent content that has the shape you want. You have a number of options:

- Supply background art, using a file format that supports transparency. For example, you can use a PNG file to supply the background of a window. This is a simple, straightforward approach, and it's suitable if you're working with designers who have no knowledge of XAML. However, because the window will be rendered with more pixels at higher system DPIs, the background graphic may become blurry. This is also a problem if you choose to allow the user to resize the window.

- Use the shape-drawing features in WPF to create your background with vector content. This approach ensures that you won't lose quality regardless of the window size and system DPI setting. However, you'll probably want to use a XAML-capable design tool. (Expression Blend is best if you want Visual Studio integration, but even traditional vector drawing may offer XAML export features through a plug-in. One example is Adobe Illustrator with the plug-in at http://www.mikeswanson.com/xamlexport.)

- Use a simpler WPF element that has the shape you want. For example, you can create a nicely rounded window edge with the Border element. This gives you a modern Office-style window appearance with no design work.

Here's a bare-bones transparent window that uses the first approach and supplies a PNG file with transparent regions:

```
<Window x:Class="Windows.TransparentBackground" ...
    WindowStyle="None" AllowsTransparency="True"
    >
  <Window.Background>
    <ImageBrush ImageSource="squares.png"></ImageBrush>
  </Window.Background>
    <Grid>
      <Grid.RowDefinitions>
        <RowDefinition></RowDefinition>
        <RowDefinition></RowDefinition>
        <RowDefinition></RowDefinition>
        <RowDefinition></RowDefinition>
      </Grid.RowDefinitions>
      <Button Margin="20">A Sample Button</Button>
      <Button Margin="20" Grid.Row="2">Another Button</Button>
    </Grid>
</Window>
```

Figure 8-5 shows this window with a Notepad window underneath. Not only does the shaped window (which consists of a circle and square) leave gaps through which you can see the content underneath, some buttons drift off the image and into the transparent region, which means they appear to be floating without a window.

If you've programmed with Windows Forms before, you'll probably notice that shaped windows in WPF have cleaner edges, especially around curves. That's because WPF is able to perform antialiasing between the background of your window and the content underneath to create the smoothened edge.

Figure 8-6 shows another, subtler shaped window. This window uses a rounded Border element to give an easy yet distinctive look. The layout is also simplified, because there's no way your content could accidentally leak outside the border, and the border can be easily resized with no Viewbox required.

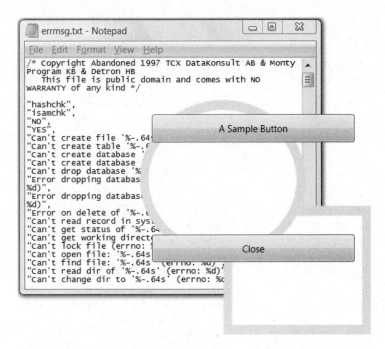

Figure 8-5. *A shaped window that uses a background image*

Figure 8-6. *A shaped window that uses a Border*

This window holds a Grid with three rows, which are used for the title bar, the footer bar, and all the content in between. The content row holds a second Grid, which sets a different background and holds any other elements you want (currently, it holds just a single TextBlock).

Here's the markup that creates the window:

```
<Window x:Class="Windows.ModernWindow" ...
    AllowsTransparency="True" WindowStyle="None"
    Background="Transparent"
    >
  <Border Width="Auto" Height="Auto" Name="windowFrame"
    BorderBrush="#395984" BorderThickness="1"
    CornerRadius="0,20,30,40" >
    <Border.Background>
      <LinearGradientBrush>
        <GradientBrush.GradientStops>
          <GradientStopCollection>
            <GradientStop Color="#E7EBF7" Offset="0.0"/>
            <GradientStop Color="#CEE3FF" Offset="0.5"/>
          </GradientStopCollection>
        </GradientBrush.GradientStops>
      </LinearGradientBrush>
    </Border.Background>

    <Grid>
      <Grid.RowDefinitions>
        <RowDefinition Height="Auto"></RowDefinition>
        <RowDefinition></RowDefinition>
        <RowDefinition Height="Auto"></RowDefinition>
      </Grid.RowDefinitions>

      <TextBlock Text="Title Bar" Margin="1" Padding="5"></TextBlock>

      <Grid Grid.Row="1" Background="#B5CBEF">
        <TextBlock VerticalAlignment="Center" HorizontalAlignment="Center"
          Foreground="White" FontSize="20">Content Goes Here</TextBlock>
      </Grid>

      <TextBlock Grid.Row="2" Text="Footer" Margin="1,10,1,1" Padding="5"
        HorizontalAlignment="Center"></TextBlock>
    </Grid>
  </Border>
</Window>
```

To complete this window, you'd want to create buttons that mimic the standard maximize, minimize, and close buttons in the top-right corner. If you wanted to reuse the window, you'd need to find a way to separate the window style from the window content. The ideal approach is to use a custom control template for your window so that you can apply your customized window look to any window you want. You'll see an example that adapts the window shown here into a reusable template in Chapter 15.

A Transparent Window with Shaped Content

In most cases, WPF windows won't use fixed graphics to create shaped windows. Instead, they'll use a completely transparent background and then place shaped content on this background. (You can see how this works by looking at the button in Figure 8-5, which is hovering over a completely transparent region.)

The advantage of this approach is that it's more modular. You can assemble a window out of many separate components, all of which are first-class WPF elements. But more important, this allows you to take advantage of other WPF features to build truly dynamic user interfaces. For example, you might assemble shaped content that can be resized or use animation to produce perpetually running effects right in your window. This isn't as easy if your graphics are provided in a single static file.

Figure 8-7 shows an example. Here, the window contains a Grid with one cell. Two elements share that cell. The first element is a Path that draws the shaped window border and gives it a gradient fill. The other element is a layout container that holds the content for the window, which overlays the Path. In this case, the layout container is a StackPanel, but you could also use something else (such as another Grid or a Canvas for coordinate-based absolute positioning). This StackPanel holds the close button (with the familiar X icon) and the text.

Figure 8-7. *A shaped window that uses a Path*

■Note Even though Figure 8-5 and Figure 8-6 show different examples, they are interchangeable. In other words, you could create either one using the background-based approach or the shape-drawing approach. However, the shape-drawing approach gives you more abilities if you want to dynamically change the shape later and gives you the best quality if you need to resize the window.

The key piece of this example is the Path element that creates the backgrounds. It's a simple vector-based shape that's composed out of a series of lines and arcs. You'll learn more about the Path element and other WPF shape classes in Chapters 13 and 14. Here's the complete markup for the Path:

```
<Path Stroke="DarkGray" StrokeThickness="2">
  <Path.Fill>
    <LinearGradientBrush StartPoint="0.2,0" EndPoint="0.8,1" >
      <LinearGradientBrush.GradientStops>
```

```
        <GradientStop Color="White" Offset="0"></GradientStop>
        <GradientStop Color="White" Offset="0.45"></GradientStop>
        <GradientStop Color="LightBlue" Offset="0.9"></GradientStop>
        <GradientStop Color="Gray" Offset="1"></GradientStop>
      </LinearGradientBrush.GradientStops>
    </LinearGradientBrush>
  </Path.Fill>

  <Path.Data>
    <PathGeometry>
      <PathGeometry.Figures>
        <PathFigure StartPoint="20,0" IsClosed="True">
          <LineSegment Point="140,0"/>
          <ArcSegment Point="160,20" Size="20,20" SweepDirection="Clockwise"/>
          <LineSegment Point="160,60"/>
          <ArcSegment Point="140,80" Size="20,20" SweepDirection="Clockwise"/>
          <LineSegment Point="70,80"/>
          <LineSegment Point="70,130"/>
          <LineSegment Point="40,80"/>
          <LineSegment Point="20,80"/>
          <ArcSegment Point="0,60" Size="20,20" SweepDirection="Clockwise"/>
          <LineSegment Point="0,20"/>
          <ArcSegment Point="20,0" Size="20,20" SweepDirection="Clockwise"/>
        </PathFigure>
      </PathGeometry.Figures>
    </PathGeometry>
  </Path.Data>
</Path>
```

Currently, the Path is fixed in size (as is the window), although you could make it resizable by hosting it in the Viewbox container that you learned about in Chapter 5. You could also improve this example by giving the close button a more authentic appearance—probably a vector X icon that's drawn on a red surface. Although you could use a separate Path element to represent a button and handle its mouse events, it's better to change the standard Button control using a control template (as described in Chapter 15). You can then make the Path that draws the X icon part of your customized button.

Moving Shaped Windows

One limitation of shaped forms is that they omit the nonclient title bar portion, which allows the user to easily drag the window around the desktop. In Windows Forms, this was a bit of a chore—you either had to react to mouse events such as MouseDown, MouseUp, and Mouse-Move and move the window manually when the user clicks and drags or had to override the WndProc() method and handle the low-level WM_NCHITTEST message. WPF makes the same task much easier. You can initiate window dragging mode at any time by calling the Window.DragMove() method.

So, to allow the user to drag the shaped form you saw in the previous examples, you simply need to handle the MouseLeftButtonDown event for the window (or an element on the window, which will then play the same role as the title bar):

```
<TextBlock Text="Title Bar" Margin="1" Padding="5"
 MouseLeftButtonDown="titleBar_MouseLeftButtonDown"></TextBlock>
```

In your event handler, you need only a single line of code:

```
private void titleBar_MouseLeftButtonDown(object sender,
  MouseButtonEventArgs e)
{
    this.DragMove();
}
```

Now the window follows the mouse around the screen, until the user releases the mouse button.

Resizing Shaped Windows

Resizing a shaped window isn't as easy. If your window is roughly rectangular in shape, the easiest approach is to add a sizing grip to the bottom-right corner by setting the Window.ResizeMode property to CanResizeWithGrip. However, the sizing grip placement assumes that your window is rectangular. For example, if you're creating a rounded window effect using a Border object, as shown earlier in Figure 8-6, this technique may work. The sizing grip will appear in the bottom-right corner, and depending how much you've rounded off that corner, it may appear over the window surface where it belongs. But if you've created a more exotic shape, such as the Path shown earlier in Figure 8-7, this technique definitely won't work—instead, it will create a sizing grip that floats in empty space next to the window.

If the sizing grip placement isn't right for your window or you want to allow the user to size the window by dragging its edges, you'll need to go to a bit more work. You can use two basic approaches. You can use .NET's platform invoke feature (P/Invoke) to send a Win32 message that resizes the window. Or, you can simply track the mouse position as the user drags to one side, and resize the window manually, by setting its Width property. The following example uses the latter approach.

Before you can use either approach, you need a way to detect when the user moves the mouse over the edges of the window. At this point, the mouse pointer should change to a resize cursor. The easiest way to do this in WPF is to place an element along the edge of each window. This element doesn't need to have any visual appearance—in fact, it can be completely transparent and let the window show through. Its sole purpose is to intercept mouse events.

One good candidate is the lowly Rectangle, which is a shape-drawing element you'll study in Chapter 13. A 5-unit wide Rectangle is perfect for the task. Here's how you might place a Rectangle that allows right-side resizing in the rounded-edge window shown in Figure 8-6:

```
<Grid>
    ...
    <Rectangle Grid.RowSpan="3" Width="5"
     VerticalAlignment="Stretch" HorizontalAlignment="Right"
     Cursor="SizeWE" Fill="Transparent"
     MouseLeftButtonDown="window_initiateWiden"
     MouseLeftButtonUp="window_endWiden"
     MouseMove="window_Widen"></Rectangle>
</Grid>
```

The Rectangle is placed in the top row but is given a RowSpan value of 3. That way, it stretches along all three rows and occupies the entire right side of the window. The Cursor property is set to the mouse cursor you want to show when the mouse is over this element. In this case, the "west-east" resize cursor does the trick—it shows the familiar two-way arrow that points left and right.

The Rectangle event handlers toggle the window into resize mode when the user clicks the edge. The only trick is that you need to capture the mouse to ensure you continue receiving mouse events even if the mouse is dragged off the rectangle. The mouse capture is released when the user releases the left mouse button.

```
bool isWiden = false;

private void window_initiateWiden(object sender, MouseEventArgs e)
{
    isWiden = true;
}

private void window_Widen(object sender, MouseEventArgs e)
{
    Rectangle rect = (Rectangle)sender;
    if (isWiden)
    {
        rect.CaptureMouse();
        double newWidth = e.GetPosition(this).X + 5;
        if (newWidth > 0) this.Width = newWidth;
    }
}

private void window_endWiden(object sender, MouseEventArgs e)
{
    isWiden = false;

    // Make sure capture is released.
    Rectangle rect = (Rectangle)sender;
    rect.ReleaseMouseCapture();
}
```

Figure 8-8 shows the code in action.

Figure 8-8. *Resizing a shaped window*

Vista-Style Windows

One of the glaring oversights in WPF is that it doesn't include any managed classes that wrap the new features in Vista. You may have already seen the lack of integration with the UAC security model (which may require you to write a manifest, as described in Chapter 3). Just as conspicuous is the lack of support for extending the "glass blur" effect in window frames and creating dialog boxes using the new task dialog box style.

Fortunately, none of these missing features is truly out of reach. You can gain access to any of them using .NET's P/Invoke feature to make unmanaged calls to the Win32 API. In the following sections, you'll learn how to use Vista's glass effect and new dialog boxes.

But before you go any further, it's worth noting that there's an obvious but significant downside to all of Windows Vista's new features—namely, they won't be available when running WPF applications on that *other* operating system, Windows XP. To avoid problems, you should write code that checks the operating system and degrades gracefully when necessary. For example, you can easily switch between the traditional OpenFileDialog and the Vista equivalent when running on Windows XP. Similarly, you can skip over any code that extends the Vista glass effect.

The easiest way to determine whether you're running on Windows Vista is to read the static OSVersion property from the System.Environment class. Here's how it works:

```
if (Environment.OSVersion.Version.Major >= 6)
{
    // Vista features are supported.
}
```

Using the Windows Vista Glass Effect

One of the most distinctive features in the Windows Vista "look" is the blurred glass window frames, through which you can see other windows and their content. This feature is commonly referred to as Aero Glass (Aero being the name of the Windows Vista user interface).

Applications running under Windows Vista get the Aero Glass effect for free in the nonclient region of the window. If you show a standard window with a standard window frame in WPF and your application is running on an Aero-capable computer (a computer that has any version of Windows Vista other than Home Basic, has the required video card support, and has this feature switched on), you'll get the eye-catching translucent window frame.

Some applications extend this effect into the client area of the window. Two examples are Internet Explorer, which features the glass effect behind the address bar, and Media Player, which uses it behind the playback controls. You can perform the same magic in your own applications. You'll encounter only two limits:

- The blurred glass area of your window always begins at the edges of your window. That means you can't create a glass "patch" in the somewhere in the middle. However, you can place completely opaque WPF elements on the glass frame to create a similar effect.

- The nonglass region inside your window is always defined as a rectangle.

WPF doesn't include classes for performing this effect. Instead, you need to call the DwmExtendFrameIntoClientArea() function from the Win32 API. (The Dwm prefix refers to the *desktop window manager* that controls this effect.) Calling this function allows you to extend the frame into your client area by making one or all of the edges thicker.

Here's how you can import the DwmExtendFrameIntoClientArea() function so it's callable from your application:

```
[DllImport("DwmApi.dll")]
public static extern int DwmExtendFrameIntoClientArea(
  IntPtr hwnd,
  ref Margins pMarInset);
```

You also need to define the fixed Margins structure, as shown here:

```
[StructLayout(LayoutKind.Sequential)]
public struct Margins
{
    public int cxLeftWidth;
    public int cxRightWidth;
    public int cyTopHeight;
    public int cyBottomHeight;
}
```

This has one potential stumbling block. As you already know, the WPF measurement system uses device-independent units that are sized based on the system DPI setting. However, the DwmExtendFrameIntoClientArea() uses physical pixels. To make sure your WPF elements line up with your extended glass frame no matter what the system DPI, you need to take the system DPI into account in your calculations.

The easiest way to retrieve the system DPI is to use the System.Drawing.Graphics class, which exposes two properties—DpiX and DpiY—that indicate the DPI of a window. The following code shows a helper method that takes a handle to a window and a set of WPF units and that returns a Margin object with the correspondingly adjusted measurement in physical pixels:

```
public static Margins GetDpiAdjustedMargins(IntPtr windowHandle,
  int left, int right, int top, int bottom)
{
    // Get the system DPI.
    System.Drawing.Graphics g = System.Drawing.Graphics.FromHwnd(windowHandle);
    float desktopDpiX = g.DpiX;
    float desktopDpiY = g.DpiY;

    // Set the margins.
    VistaGlassHelper.Margins margins = new VistaGlassHelper.Margins();
    margins.cxLeftWidth = Convert.ToInt32(left * (desktopDpiX / 96));
    margins.cxRightWidth = Convert.ToInt32(right * (desktopDpiX / 96));
    margins.cyTopHeight = Convert.ToInt32(top * (desktopDpiX / 96));
    margins.cyBottomHeight = Convert.ToInt32(right * (desktopDpiX / 96));

    return margins;
}
```

■**Note** Unfortunately, the System.Drawing.Graphics is a part of Windows Forms. To gain access to it, you need to add a reference to the System.Drawing.dll assembly.

The final step is to apply the margins to the window using the DwmExtendFrameInto-ClientArea() function. The following code shows an all-in-one helper method that takes the WPF margin measurements and a reference to a WPF window. It then gets the Win32 handle for the window, adjusts the margins, and attempts to extend the glass frame.

```
public static void ExtendGlass(Window win, int left, int right,
  int top, int bottom)
{
    // Obtain the Win32 window handle for the WPF window.
    WindowInteropHelper windowInterop = new WindowInteropHelper(win);
    IntPtr windowHandle = windowInterop.Handle;

    // Adjust the margins to take the system DPI into account.
    Margins margins = GetDpiAdjustedMargins(
      windowHandle, left, right, top, bottom);
```

```
    // Extend the glass frame.
    int returnVal = DwmExtendFrameIntoClientArea(windowHandle, ref margins);
    if (returnVal < 0)
    {
        throw new NotSupportedException("Operation failed.");
    }
}
```

The sample code for this chapter wraps all these ingredients into a single class, called VistaGlassHelper, which you can call from any window. For the code to work, you must call it before the window is shown. The Window.Loaded event provides the perfect opportunity. Additionally, you must remember to set the Background of your window to Transparent so the glass frame shows through the WPF drawing surface.

Figure 8-9 shows an example that thickens the top edge of the glass frame.

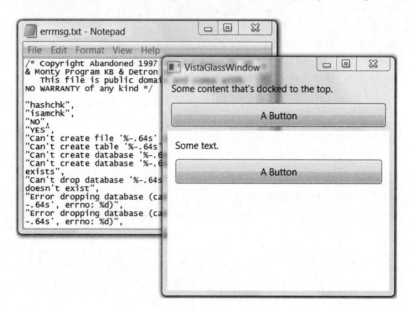

Figure 8-9. *Extending the glass frame*

When creating this window, the content at the top is grouped into a single Border element. That way, you can measure the height of the border and use that measurement to extend the glass frame. (Of course, the glass frame is set only once, when the window is first created. If you change content or resize the window and the Border grows or shrinks, it won't line up with the glass frame any longer.)

Here's the complete markup for the window:

```
<Window x:Class="Windows.VistaGlassWindow2"
    ...
    Loaded="window_Loaded" Background="Transparent"
```

```
      >
  <Grid >
    <DockPanel Name="mainDock" LastChildFill="True">
      <!-- The border is used to compute the rendered height with margins.
           topBar contents will be displayed on the extended glass frame.-->
      <Border Name="topBar" DockPanel.Dock="Top">
        <StackPanel>
          <TextBlock Padding="5">Some content that's docked to the top.</TextBlock>
          <Button Margin="5" Padding="5">A Button</Button>
        </StackPanel>
      </Border>
      <Border Background="White">
        <StackPanel Margin="5">
          <TextBlock Margin="5" >Some text.</TextBlock>
          <Button Margin="5" Padding="5">A Button</Button>
        </StackPanel>
      </Border>
    </DockPanel>
  </Grid>
</Window>
```

Notice that the second Border in this window, which contains the rest of the content, must explicitly set its background to white. Otherwise, this part of the window will be completely transparent. (For the same reason, the second Border shouldn't have any margin space, or you'll see a transparent edge around it.)

When the window is loaded, it calls the ExtendGlass() method and passes in the new coordinates. Ordinarily, the glass frame is 5 units thick, but this code adds to the top edge.

```
private void window_Loaded(object sender, RoutedEventArgs e)
{
    try
    {
        VistaGlassHelper.ExtendGlass(this, 5, 5,
          (int)topBar.ActualHeight + 5, 5);
    }
    catch
    {
        // A DllNotFoundException occurs if you run this on Windows XP.
        // A NotSupportedException is thrown if the
        // DwmExtendFrameIntoClientArea() call fails.
        this.Background = Brushes.White;
    }
}
```

If you want to extend the glass edge so that it covers the entire window, simply pass in margin settings of –1 for each side. Figure 8-10 shows the result.

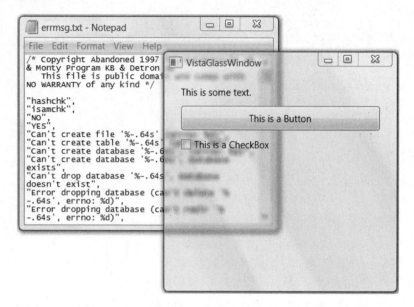

Figure 8-10. *A completely "glassified" window*

When using the Aero Glass effect, you need to consider how the appearance of your content will vary when the window is placed over different backgrounds. For example, if you place black text in a glassified region of a window, it will be easier to read on a light background than on a dark background (although it will be legible on both). To improve the readability of text and make your content stand out against a variety of backgrounds, it's common to add some sort of glow effect. For example, black text with a white glow will be equally legible on light and dark backgrounds. Windows Vista includes its own unmanaged function for drawing glowing text, called DrawThemeTextEx(), but there are a variety of native WPF techniques that can give you a similar (or better) result. Two examples include using a fancy brush to paint your text and adding a bitmap effect to your text. (Both techniques are discussed in Chapter 13.)

MORE DWM MAGIC

In the previous example, you learned how you could create a thicker glass edge (or a completely glassified window) using the DwmExtendFrameIntoClientArea() function. However, DwmExtendFrameIntoClientArea() isn't the only useful function from the Windows API. There are several other API functions that start with *Dwm* and allow you to interact with the desktop window manager.

For example, you can call DwmIsCompositionEnabled() to check that the Aero Glass effect is currently enabled, and you can use DwmEnableBlurBehindWindow() to apply the glass effect to a specific region in a window. There are also a few functions that allow you to get the live thumbnail representation of other applications. For the bare-bones information, check out the MSDN reference for the desktop window manager at http://tinyurl.com/333glv.

The Task Dialog and File Dialog Boxes

Although WPF includes the familiar file dialog boxes, such as OpenFileDialog and OpenSave-Dialog, it doesn't include classes for any of the new dialog boxes that were introduced with Windows Vista. Missing ingredients include the restyled Open and Save dialog boxes and the completely new task dialog box.

The task dialog box is a sort of super-powered MessageBox. It includes a caption, footer space, and a variety of optional controls ranging from a progress bar to a hyperlink. You can use the task dialog box to display a friendlier version of a message box, ask the user a question and collect input, and show a generic "in progress" message while your code is at work. Figure 8-11 shows two simple examples.

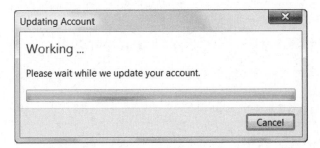

Figure 8-11. *Vista-style dialog boxes*

Although the WPF libraries don't include any support for Vista-style dialog boxes, Microsoft has released an indispensable (but often overlooked) sample that takes care of most of the tedious details. It's available as part of the Windows SDK .NET Framework 3.0 Samples, which you can download at http://tinyurl.com/36s6py. Rather than download the entire package of samples, you can download the group of samples named CrossTechnologySamples.exe, which includes samples that support the new Windows Vista dialog boxes. The specific project you want is named VistaBridge.

This VistaBridge project includes a class library that wraps the required Win32 functions (using P/Invoke) and provides more than 30 higher-level classes. It also includes a test window that demonstrates several ways to use the task dialog box, and it includes a wizard control. A good starting point is the TaskDialog class, which was used to create the windows shown in

Figure 8-11. To use the TaskDialog, you simply create an instance, set the appropriate properties, and call the Show() method. For example, here's how you create the topmost example in Figure 8-11:

```
TaskDialog taskDialog = new TaskDialog();
taskDialog.Content = "Are you sure you want to continue?";
taskDialog.StandardButtons = TaskDialogStandardButtons.YesNo;
taskDialog.MainIcon = TaskDialogStandardIcon.Warning;
taskDialog.Caption = "Confirm Format";
taskDialog.Instruction = "Confirm Drive Format";
taskDialog.FooterText = "NOTE: All data stored on the drive will be lost.";
taskDialog.FooterIcon = TaskDialogStandardIcon.Information;
TaskDialogResult result = taskDialog.Show();
if (result.StandardButtonClicked == TaskDialogStandardButton.Yes)
{ ... }
```

The TaskDialogResult object wraps the information that the user supplied, including any check box or radio button selections (using the CheckBoxChecked and RadioButtonClicked properties). In this example the user has two options (Yes or No), and the clicked button is indicated by the StandardButtonClicked property.

An alternative approach is to define the TaskDialog declaratively in XAML. Because the TaskDialog isn't a WPF element, you need to declare it in the Window.Resources section of your markup, as shown here:

```
<Window ...
  xmlns:v="clr-namespace:Microsoft.SDK.Samples.VistaBridge.Library;assembly=
VistaBridgeLibrary" >
  <Window.Resources>
    <v:TaskDialog x:Key="simpleWait"
     Content="Please wait while we update your account."
     Instruction="Working ..." Caption ="Updating Account"
     Cancelable="True" StandardButtons="Cancel">
      <v:TaskDialogMarquee Name="marquee"/>
    </v:TaskDialog>
  </Window.Resources>
  ...
</Window>
```

You can then retrieve this object by key name in your code and use it:

```
TaskDialog dialog = (TaskDialog)this.Resources["simpleWait"];
TaskDialogResult result = dialog.Show();
```

Chapter 11 covers the WPF resource system in detail.

If you want to take advantage of these Vista-specific APIs, the VistaBridge sample presents the best starting point.

■**Note** At the time of this writing, there's a minor quirk in the VistaBridge sample project. It uses Visual Studio 2005 project files and fails to run properly when converted to Visual Studio 2008. The problem is the manifest file, which needs to be re-created in Visual Studio 2008. To do so, right-click the project in the Solution Explorer, and choose Add ➤ New Item. Pick the Application Manifest File template, and click Add. Then, copy the content from the existing manifest file (which is included as a support file in the project) into the new manifest file that was generated by Visual Studio. Alternatively, you can download a fixed-up version of the VistaBridge project with the samples for this chapter.

The Last Word

In this chapter, you took a quick tour of the WPF window model. Compared to previous technologies such as Windows Forms, the WPF window is a streamlined, slimmed-down entity. In many cases, that's a benefit, because other elements take over the responsibility and allow more flexible application designs (such as the navigation-based systems you'll see in the next chapter). But in other cases, it's a reflection of the fact that WPF is a new, not-quite-mature technology, and it lacks support for the previous generation of Windows staples.

For example, there's no built-in way to create an MDI application, tabbed windows, or docked windows. All these details are possible with a little extra work, but they are often difficult to make absolutely perfect. For that reason, many WPF developers who prefer window-based designs are likely to turn to third-party components, at least in the short term.

CHAPTER 9

Pages and Navigation

Most traditional Windows applications are arranged around a window that contains tool-bars and menus. The toolbars and menus *drive* the application—as the user clicks them, actions happen, and other windows appear. In document-based applications, there may be several equally important "main" windows that are open at once, but the overall model is the same. The user spends most of his time in one place, and jumps to separate windows when necessary.

Windows applications are so common that it's sometimes hard to imagine different ways to design an application. However, desktop developers have spent the past few years watching the developments in the Web—which uses a dramatically different page-based navigation model—and realizing that it's a surprisingly good choice for designing certain types of applications. In a bid to give desktop developers the ability to build web-like desktop applications, WPF includes its own page-based navigation system. And as you'll see in this chapter, it's a remarkably flexible model.

Currently, the page-based model is most commonly used for simple, lightweight applications (or small feature subsets in a more complex window-based application). However, page-based applications are a good choice if you want to streamline application *deployment*. That's because WPF allows you to create a page-based application that runs directly inside Internet Explorer or Firefox, with limited trust. This allows users to run your application with no explicit install step—they simply point their browsers to the right location. You'll learn about this model, called XBAP, in the second half of this chapter.

Understanding Page-Based Navigation

The average web application looks quite a bit different from traditional rich client software. The users of a website spend their time navigating from one page to another. Unless they're unlucky enough to face popup advertising, there's never more than one page visible at a time. When completing a task (such as placing an order or performing a complicated search), the user traverses these pages in a linear sequence from start to finish.

HTML doesn't support the sophisticated windowing capabilities of desktop operating systems, so the best web developers rely on good design and clear, straightforward interfaces. As web design has become increasingly more sophisticated, Windows developers have also begun to see the advantages of this approach. Most important, the web model is simple and streamlined. For that reason, novice users often find websites easier to use than Windows applications, even though Windows applications are obviously much more capable.

In recent years, developers have begun mimicking some of the conventions of the Web in desktop applications. Financial software such as Microsoft Money is a prime example of a web-like interface that leads users through set tasks. However, creating these applications is often *more* complicated than designing a traditional window-based application, because developers need to re-create basic browser features such as navigation.

Note In some cases, developers have built web-like applications using the Internet Explorer browser engine. This is the approach that Microsoft Money takes, but it's one that would be more difficult for non-Microsoft developers. Although Microsoft provides hooks into Internet Explorer, such as the WebBrowser control, building a complete application around these features is far from easy. It also risks sacrificing the best capabilities of ordinary Windows applications.

In WPF, there's no longer any reason to compromise because WPF includes a built-in page model that incorporates navigation. Best of all, this model can be used to create a variety of page-based applications, applications that use some page-based features (for example, in a wizard or help system), or applications that are hosted right in the browser.

Page-Based Interfaces

To create a page-based application in WPF, you need to stop using the Window class as your top-level container for user interfaces. Instead, it's time to switch to the System.Windows.Controls.Page class.

The model for creating pages in WPF is much the same as the model for creating windows. Although you could create page objects with just code, you'll usually create a XAML file and a code-behind file for each page. When you compile that application, the compiler creates a derived page class that combines your code with a bit of automatically generated glue (such as the fields that refer to each named element on your page). This is the same process that you learned about when you considered compilation with a window-based application in Chapter 2.

Note You can add a page to any WPF project. Just choose Project ➤ Add Page in Visual Studio.

Although pages are the top-level user interface ingredient when you're designing your application, they aren't the top-level container when you *run* your application. Instead, your pages are hosted in another container. This is the secret to WPF's flexibility with page-based applications because you can use one of several different containers:

- The NavigationWindow, which is a slightly tweaked version of the Window class
- A Frame that's inside another window
- A Frame that's inside another page
- A Frame that's hosted directly in Internet Explorer or Firefox

You'll consider all of these hosts in this chapter.

A Simple Page-Based Application with NavigationWindow

To try an extremely simple page-based application, create a page like this:

```
<Page x:Class="NavigationApplication.Page1"
    xmlns="http://schemas.microsoft.com/winfx/2006/xaml/presentation"
    xmlns:x="http://schemas.microsoft.com/winfx/2006/xaml"
    WindowTitle="Page1"
    >
  <StackPanel Margin="3">
    <TextBlock Margin="3">
      This is a simple page.
    </TextBlock>
    <Button Margin="2" Padding="2">OK</Button>
    <Button Margin="2" Padding="2">Close</Button>
  </StackPanel>
</Page>
```

Now, modify the App.xaml file so that the startup page is your page file:

```
<Application x:Class="NavigationApplication.App"
    xmlns="http://schemas.microsoft.com/winfx/2006/xaml/presentation"
    xmlns:x="http://schemas.microsoft.com/winfx/2006/xaml"
    StartupUri="Page1.xaml"
    >
</Application>
```

When you run this application, WPF is intelligent enough to realize that you're pointing it to a page rather than a window. It automatically creates a new NavigationWindow object to serve as a container and shows your page inside of it (Figure 9-1). It also reads the page's WindowTitle property and uses that for the window caption.

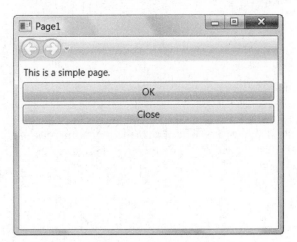

Figure 9-1. *A page in a NavigationWindow*

■**Note** One difference between a page and a window is that you don't typically set the size of a page because it's determined by the host. If you do set the Width and Height properties of the page, the page is made exactly that size, but some content is clipped if the host window is smaller, or it's centered inside the available space if the host window is larger.

The NavigationWindow looks more or less like an ordinary window, aside from the back and forward navigation buttons that appear in the bar at the top. As you might expect, the NavigationWindow class derives from Window, and it adds a small set of navigation-related properties. You can get a reference to the containing NavigationWindow object using code like this:

```
// Get a reference to the window that contains the current page.
NavigationWindow win = (NavigationWindow)Window.GetWindow(this);
```

This code won't work in the page constructor because the page hasn't been placed inside its container yet—instead, wait at least until the Page.Loaded event fires.

■**Tip** It's best to avoid this approach if at all possible and use properties of the Page class (and the navigation service described later in this chapter). Otherwise, your page will be tightly coupled to the NavigationWindow, and you won't be able to reuse it in different hosts.

If you want to create a code-only application, you'd need to create both the navigation window and the page to get the effect shown in Figure 9-1. Here's the code that would do it:

```
NavigationWindow win = new NavigationWindow()
win.Content = new Page1();
win.Show();
```

The Page Class

Like the Window class, the Page class allows a single nested element. However, the Page class isn't a content control—it actually derives directly from FrameworkElement. The Page class is also simpler and more streamlined than the Window class. It adds a small set of properties that allow you to customize its appearance, interact with the container in a limited way, and use navigation. Table 9-1 lists these properties.

Table 9-1. *Properties of the Page Class*

Name	Description
Background	Takes a brush that allows you to set the background fill.
Content	Takes the single element that's shown in the page. Usually, this is a layout container, such as a Grid or a StackPanel.
Foreground, FontFamily, and FontSize	Determines the default appearance of text inside the page. The values of these properties are inherited by the elements inside the page. For example, if you set the foreground fill and font size, by default the content inside the page gets these details.
WindowWidth, WindowHeight, and WindowTitle	Determines the appearance of the window that wraps your page. These properties allow you to take control of the host by setting its width, height, and caption. However, they have an effect only if your page is being hosted in a window (rather than a frame).
NavigationService	Returns a reference to a NavigationService object, which you can use to programmatically send the user to another page.
KeepAlive	Determines whether the page object should be kept alive after the user navigates to another page. You'll take a closer look at this property later in this chapter (in the "Navigation History" section) when you consider how WPF restores the pages in your navigation history.
ShowsNavigationUI	Determines whether the host for this page shows its navigation controls (the forward and back button). By default, it's true.
Title	Sets the name that's used for the page in the navigation history. The host does not use the title to set the caption in the title bar—instead, the WindowTitle property serves that purpose.

It's also important to notice what's not there—namely, there's no equivalent of the Hide() and Show() methods of the Window class. If you want to show a different page, you'll need to use navigation.

Hyperlinks

The easiest way to allow the user to move from one page to another is using hyperlinks. In WPF, hyperlinks aren't separate elements. Instead, they're *inline flow elements*, which must be placed inside another element that supports them. (The reason for this design is that hyperlinks and text are often intermixed. You'll learn more about flow content and text layout in Chapter 19.)

For example, here's a combination of text and links in a TextBlock element, which is the most practical container for hyperlinks:

```
<TextBlock Margin="3" TextWrapping="Wrap">
  This is a simple page.
  Click <Hyperlink NavigateUri="Page2.xaml">here</Hyperlink> to go to Page2.
</TextBlock>
```

When rendered, hyperlinks appear as the familiar blue underlined text (see Figure 9-2).

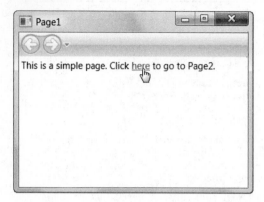

Figure 9-2. *Linking to another page*

You can handle clicks on a link in two ways. You can respond to the Click event and use code to perform some task, or direct the user to another page. However, there's an easier approach. The Hyperlink class also includes a NavigateUri property, which you set to point to any other page in your application. Then, when users click this hyperlink, they travel to the destination page automatically.

■**Note** The NavigateUri property works only if you place the hyperlink in a page. If you want to use a hyperlink in a window-based application to let users perform a task, launch a web page, or open a new window, you need to handle the RequestNavigate event and write the code yourself.

Hyperlinks aren't the only way to move from one page to another. The NavigationWindow includes prominent forward and back buttons (unless you set the Page.ShowsNavigationUI property to false to hide it). Clicking these buttons moves you through the navigation sequence one page at a time. And similar to a browser, you can click the drop-down arrow at the edge of the forward button to examine the complete sequence and jump forward or backward several pages at a time (Figure 9-3).

You'll learn more about how the page history works—and what limitations it has—later in the "Navigation History" section.

■**Note** If you navigate to a new page, and that page doesn't set the WindowTitle property, the window keeps the title it had on the previous page. If you don't set the WindowTitle on any page, the window caption is left blank.

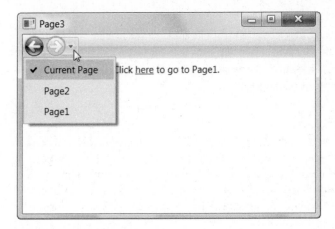

Figure 9-3. *The history of visited pages*

Navigating to Websites

Interestingly, you can also create a hyperlink that points to web content. When the user clicks the link, the target web page loads up in the page area:

```
<TextBlock Margin="3" TextWrapping="Wrap">
  Visit the website
  <Hyperlink NavigateUri="http://www.prosetech.com">www.prosetech.com</Hyperlink>.
</TextBlock>
```

However, if you use this technique, make sure you attach an event handler to the Application.DispatcherUnhandledException or Application.NavigationFailed event. That's because the attempt to navigate to a website could fail if the computer isn't online, the site isn't available, or the web content can't be reached. In this case, the network stack returns an error like "404: File Not Found," which becomes a WebException.

In order to handle this exception gracefully and prevent your application from shutting down unexpectedly, you need to neutralize it with an event handler like this:

```
private void App_NavigationFailed(object sender, NavigationFailedEventArgs e)
{
    if (e.Exception is System.Net.WebException)
    {
        MessageBox.Show("Website " + e.Uri.ToString() + " cannot be reached.");

        // Neutralize the error so the application continues running.
        e.Handled = true;
    }
}
```

NavigationFailed is just one of several navigation events that are defined in the Application class. You'll get the full list later in this chapter, in Table 9-2.

■**Note** Once you lead users to a web page, they'll be able to click its links to travel to other web pages, leaving your content far behind. In fact, they'll return to your WPF page only if they use the navigation history to go back or if you're showing the page in a custom window (as discussed in the next section) and that window includes a control that navigates back to your content.

You can't do a number of things when displaying pages from external websites. You can't prevent the user from navigating to specific pages or sites. Also, you can't interact with the web page using the HTML DOM (document object model). That means you can't scan a page looking for links or dynamically change a page. All of these tasks are possible using the WebBrowser control, which is included with Windows Forms. Chapter 25 has more information about Windows Forms interoperability.

Fragment Navigation

The last trick that you can use with the hyperlink is *fragment navigation*. By adding the number sign (#) at the end of the NavigateUri, followed by an element name, you can jump straight to a specific control on a page. However, this works only if the target page is scrollable. (The target page is scrollable if it uses the ScrollViewer control or if it's hosted in a web browser.) Here's an example:

```
<TextBlock Margin="3">
  Review the <Hyperlink NavigateUri="Page2.xaml#myTextBox">full text</Hyperlink>.
</TextBlock>
```

When the user clicks this link, the application moves to the page named Page2, and scrolls down the page to the element named myTextBox. The page is scrolled down until myTextBox appears at the top of the page (or as close as possible, depending on the size of the page content and the containing window). However, the target element doesn't receive focus.

Hosting Pages in a Frame

The NavigationWindow is a convenient container, but it's not your only option. You can also place pages directly inside other windows or even inside other pages. This makes for an extremely flexible system because you can reuse the same page in different ways depending on the type of application you need to create.

To embed a page inside a window, you simply need to use the Frame class. The Frame class is a content control that can hold any element, but it makes particular sense when used as a container for a page. It includes a property, named Source, that points to a XAML page that you want to display.

Here's an ordinary window that wraps some content in a StackPanel and places a Frame in a separate column:

```xml
<Window x:Class="WindowPageHost.WindowWithFrame"
    xmlns="http://schemas.microsoft.com/winfx/2006/xaml/presentation"
    xmlns:x="http://schemas.microsoft.com/winfx/2006/xaml"
    Title="WindowWithFrame" Height="300" Width="300"
    >
  <Grid Margin="3">
    <Grid.ColumnDefinitions>
      <ColumnDefinition></ColumnDefinition>
      <ColumnDefinition></ColumnDefinition>
    </Grid.ColumnDefinitions>

    <StackPanel>
      <TextBlock Margin="3" TextWrapping="Wrap">
       This is ordinary window content.</TextBlock>
      <Button Margin="3" Padding="3">Close</Button>
    </StackPanel>
    <Frame Grid.Column="1" Source="Page1.xaml"
      BorderBrush="Blue" BorderThickness="1"></Frame>
  </Grid>
</Window>
```

Figure 9-4 shows the result. A border around the frame shows the page content. There's no reason you need to stop at one frame. You can easily create a window that wraps multiple frames, and you can point them all to different pages.

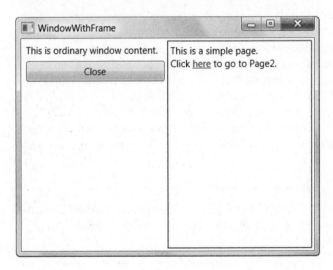

Figure 9-4. *A window with a page embedded in a frame*

As you can see in Figure 9-4, this example doesn't include the familiar navigation buttons. This is because the Frame.NavigationUIVisibility property is (by default) set to Automatic. As a result, the navigation controls appear only once there's something in the forward and back list. To try this, navigate to a new page. You'll see the buttons appear inside the frame, as shown in Figure 9-5.

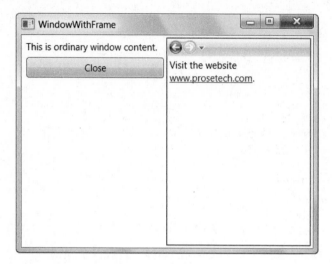

Figure 9-5. *A frame with navigation buttons*

You can change the NavigationUIVisibility property to Hidden if you never want to show the navigation buttons or Visible if you want them to appear right from the start.

Having the navigation buttons inside the frame is a great design if your frame contains content that's separate from the main flow of the application. (For example, maybe you're using it to display context-sensitive help or the content for a walk-through tutorial.) But in other cases, you may prefer to show them at the top of the window. To do this, you need to change your top-level container from Window to NavigationWindow. That way, your window will include the navigation buttons. The frame inside the window will automatically wire itself up to these buttons, so the user gets a similar experience to what's shown in Figure 9-3, except now the window also holds the extra content.

■**Tip** You can add as many Frame objects as you need to a window. For example, you could easily create a window that allows the user to browse through an application task, help documentation, and an external website, using three separate frames.

Hosting Pages in Another Page

Frames give you the ability to create more complex arrangements of windows. As you learned in the previous section, you can use several frames in a single window. You can also place a frame inside another page to create a *nested* page. In fact, the process is exactly the same—you simply add a Frame object inside your page markup.

Nested pages present a more complex navigation situation. For example, imagine you visit a page and then click a link in an embedded frame. What happens when you click the back button?

Essentially, all the pages in a frame are flattened into one list. So the first time you click the back button, you move to the previous page in the embedded frame. The next time you click the back button, you move to the previously visited parent page. Figure 9-6 shows the sequence you follow. Notice that the back navigation button is enabled in the second step.

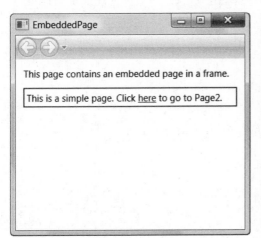 

Figure 9-6. *Navigation with an embedded page*

Most of the time, this navigation model is fairly intuitive because you'll have one item in the back list for each page you visit. However, there are some cases where the embedded frame plays a less important role. For example, maybe it shows different views of the same data or allows you to step through multiple pages of help content. In these cases, stepping through all the pages in the embedded frame may seem awkward or time-consuming. Instead, you may want to use the navigation controls to control the navigation of the parent frame only so that when you click the back button, you move to the previous parent page right away.

To do this, you need to set the JournalOwnership property of the embedded frame to OwnsJournal. This tells the frame to maintain its own distinct page history. By default, the embedded frame will now acquire navigation buttons that allow you to move back and forth through its content (see Figure 9-7). If this isn't what you want, you can use the JournalOwnership property in conjunction with the NavigationUIVisibility property to hide the navigation controls altogether, as shown here:

```
<Frame Source="Page1.xaml"
  JournalOwnership="OwnsJournal" NavigationUIVisibility="Hidden"
  BorderThickness="1" BorderBrush="Blue"></Frame>
```

Now the embedded frame is treated as though it's just a piece of dynamic content inside your page. From the user's point of view, the embedded frame doesn't support navigation.

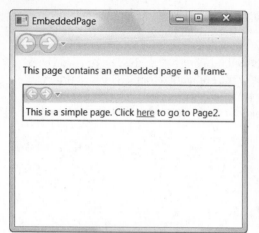
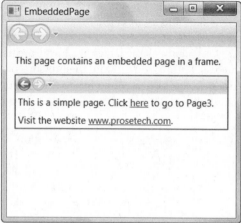

Figure 9-7. *An embedded page that owns its journal and supports navigation*

Hosting Pages in a Web Browser

The final way that you can use page-based navigation applications is in Internet Explorer. However, in order to use this approach, you need to create a *XAML browser application* (which is known as an XBAP). In Visual Studio, the XBAP is a separate project template, and you must select it (rather than the standard WPF Windows application) when creating a project in order to use browser hosting. You'll examine the XBAP model in the latter part of this chapter.

GETTING THE RIGHT SIZE WINDOW

There are really two types of page-based applications:

- Stand-alone Windows applications that use pages for part or all of their user interfaces. You'll use this approach if you need to integrate a wizard into your application or you want a simple task-oriented application. This way, you can use WPF's navigation and journal features to simplify your coding.

- Browser applications (XBAPs) that are hosted by Internet Explorer or Firefox and run with limited permissions. You'll use this approach if you want a lightweight, web-based deployment model.

If you fall into the first category, you probably won't want to set the Application.StartupUri property to point to a page. Instead, you'll create the NavigationWindow manually and then load your first page inside it (as shown earlier), or you'll embed your pages in a custom window using the Frame control. Both of these approaches give you the flexibility to set the size of the application window, which is important for making sure your application looks respectable when it first starts up. On the other hand, if you're creating an XBAP, you have no control over the size of the containing web browser window, and you *must* set the StartupUri property to point to a page.

The Page History

Now that you've learned about pages and the different ways to host them, you're ready to delve deeper into the navigation model that WPF uses. In this section, you'll learn how WPF hyperlinks work and how pages are restored when you navigate back to them.

A Closer Look at URIs in WPF

You might wonder how properties like Application.StartupUri, Frame.Source, and Hyperlink.NavigateUri actually work. In an application that's made up of loose XAML files and run in the browser, it's fairly straightforward—when you click a hyperlink, the browser treats the page reference as a relative URI and looks for the XAML page in the current folder. But in a compiled application, the pages are no longer available as separate resources—instead, they're compiled to BAML and embedded into the assembly. So, how can they be referenced using a URI?

This system works because of the way that WPF addresses application resources (a topic you'll delve into in Chapter 11). When you click a hyperlink in a compiled XAML application, the URI is still treated as a relative path. However, it's relative to the *base URI* for the application. A hyperlink that points to Page1.xaml is actually expanded to this:

```
pack://application:,,,/Page1.xaml
```

This is known as a *pack URI*. It's composed of three parts:

- The **scheme (pack://)** indicates the way that the resource is found.

- The **authority (application:,,,)** indicates the container that holds the resource. In this case, it's an assembly.

- The **path (/Page.1xaml)** indicates the exact location of that resource, relative to the container.

In other words, the pack URI is a path that extracts the compiled XAML resource from the assembly.

This system has several advantages. You can use relative URIs in your hyperlinks, and these relative URIs will work regardless of whether your application is compiled or (less commonly) kept as loose XAML files.

At this point, you might be wondering why it's important to learn how XAML URIs work if the process is so seamless. The chief reason is because you might choose to create an application that navigates to XAML pages that are stored in another assembly. In fact, there are good reasons for this design. Because pages can be used in different containers, you might want to reuse the same set of pages in an XBAP and an ordinary Windows application. That way, you can deploy two versions of your application—a browser-based version and a desktop version. To avoid duplicating your code, you should place all the pages you plan to reuse in a separate class library assembly (DLL), which can then be referenced by both your application projects.

This necessitates a change in your URIs. If you have a page in one assembly that points to a page in another, you need to use the following syntax:

```
pack://application:,,,/PageLibrary;component/Page1.xaml
```

Here, the component is named PageLibrary and the path ,,,PageLibrary;component/ Page1.xaml points to a page named Page1.xaml that's compiled and embedded inside.

Of course, you probably won't use the absolute path. Instead, it makes more sense to use the following slightly shorter relative path in your URIs:

```
/PageLibrary;component/Page1.xaml
```

■**Tip** Use the project template called Custom Control Library (WPF) when you create the SharedLibrary assembly to get the right assembly references, namespace imports, and application settings.

Navigation History

The WPF page history works just like the history in a browser. Every time you navigate to a new page, the previous page is added to the back list. If you click the back button, the page is added to the forward list. If you back out from one page and then navigate to a new page, the forward list is cleared out.

The behavior of the back and forward lists is fairly straightforward, but the plumbing that supports them is more complex. For example, imagine you visit a page with two text boxes, type something in, and move ahead. If you head back to this page, you'll find that WPF restores the state of your text boxes—meaning whatever content you placed in them is still there.

■**Note** There's an important difference between returning to a page through the navigation history and clicking a link that takes you to the same page. For example, if you click links that take you from Page1 to Page2 to Page1, WPF creates three separate page objects. The second time you see Page1, WPF creates it as a separate instance, with its own state. However, if you click the back button twice to return to the first Page1 instance, you'll see that your original Page1 state remains.

You might assume that WPF maintains the state of previously visited pages by keeping the page object in memory. The problem with this design is that the memory overhead may not be trivial in a complex application with many pages. For that reason, WPF can't assume that maintaining the page object is a safe strategy. Instead, when you navigate away from a page, WPF stores the state of all your controls and then destroys the page. When you return to a page, WPF re-creates the page (from the original XAML) and then restores the state of your controls. This strategy has lower overhead because the memory required to save just a few details of control state is far less than the memory required to store the page and its entire visual tree of objects.

This system raises an interesting question. Namely, how does WPF decide what details to store? WPF examines the complete element tree of your page, and it looks at the dependency properties of all your elements. Properties that should be stored have a tiny bit of extra metadata—a *journal* flag that indicates they should be kept in the navigation log known as the *journal*. (The journal flag is set using the FrameworkPropertyMetadata object when registering the dependency property, as described in Chapter 6.)

If you take a closer look at the navigation system, you'll find that many properties don't have the journal flag. For example, if you set the Content property of a content control or the Text property of a TextBlock element using code, neither of these details will be retained when you return to the page. The same is true if you set the Foreground or Background properties dynamically. However, if you set the Text property of a TextBox, the IsSelected property of a CheckBox, or the SelectedIndex property of a ListBox, all these details will remain.

So what can you do if this isn't the behavior you want—in other words, if you set many properties dynamically and you want your pages to retain all of their information? You have several options. The most powerful is to use the Page.KeepAlive property, which is false by default. When set to true, WPF doesn't use the serialization mechanism described previously. Instead, it keeps all your page objects alive. Thus, when you navigate back to a page, it's exactly the way you left it. Of course, this option has the drawback of increased memory overhead, so you should enable only it on the few pages that really need it.

Tip When you use the KeepAlive property to keep a page alive, it won't fire the Initialized event the next time you navigate to it. (Pages that aren't kept alive but are "rehydrated" using WPFs journaling system *will* fire the Initialized event each time the user visits them.) If this behavior isn't what you want, handle the Unloaded and Loaded events of the Page instead, which always fire.

Another solution is to choose a different design that passes information around. For example, you can create page functions (described later in this chapter) that return information. Using page functions, along with extra initialization logic, you can design your own system for retrieving the important information from a page and restoring it when needed.

There's one more wrinkle with the WPF navigation history. As you'll discover later in this chapter, you can write code that dynamically creates a page object and then navigates to it. In this situation, the ordinary mechanism of maintaining the page state won't work. WPF doesn't have a reference to the XAML document for the page, so it doesn't know how to reconstruct the page. (And if the page is created dynamically, there may not even *be* a corresponding XAML document.) In this situation, WPF always keeps the page object alive in memory, no matter what the KeepAlive property says.

Maintaining Custom Properties

Ordinarily, any fields in your page class lose their values when the page is destroyed. If you want to add custom properties to your page class and make sure *they* retain their values, you can set the journal flag accordingly. However, you can't take this step with an ordinary property or a field. Instead, you need to create a dependency property in your page class.

You've already taken a look at dependency properties in Chapter 6. To create a dependency property, you need to follow two steps. First, you need to create the dependency property definition. Second, you need an ordinary property procedure that sets or gets the value of the dependency property.

To define the dependency property, you need to create a static field like this:

```
private static DependencyProperty MyPageDataProperty;
```

By convention, the field that defines your dependency property has the name of your ordinary property, plus the word *Property* at the end.

■**Note** This example uses a private dependency property. That's because the only code that needs to access this property is in the page class where it's defined.

To complete your definition, you need a static constructor that registers your dependency property definition. This is the place where you set the services that you want to use with your dependency property (such as support for data binding, animation, and journaling):

```
static PageWithPersistentData()
{
    FrameworkPropertyMetadata metadata = new FrameworkPropertyMetadata();
    metadata.Journal = true;

    MyPageDataProperty = DependencyProperty.Register(
      "MyPageDataProperty", typeof(string),
      typeof(PageWithPersistentData), metadata, null);
}
```

Now you can create the ordinary property that wraps this dependency property. However, when you write the getter and setter you'll use the GetValue() and SetValue() methods that are defined in the base DependencyObject class:

```
private string MyPageData
{
    set { SetValue(MyPageDataProperty, value); }
    get { return (string)GetValue(MyPageDataProperty); }
}
```

Add all these details to a single page (in this example, one named PageWithPersistent-Data), and the MyPageData property value will be automatically serialized when users navigate away and restored when they return.

The Navigation Service

So far, the navigation you've seen relies heavily on hyperlinks. When this approach works, it's simple and elegant. However, in some cases you'll want to take more control of the navigation process. For example, hyperlinks work well if you're using pages to model a fixed, linear series of steps that the user traverses from start to finish (such as a wizard). However, if you want the user to complete small sequences of steps and return to a common page, or if you want to configure the sequence of steps based on other details (such as the user's previous actions), you need something more.

Programmatic Navigation

You can set the Hyperlink.NavigateUri and Frame.Source properties dynamically. However, the most flexible and powerful approach is to use the WPF navigation service. You can access the navigation service through the container that hosts the page (such as Frame or NavigationWindow), but this approach limits your pages so they can be used only in that type of container. The best approach is to access the navigation service through the static NavigationService.GetNavigationService() method. You pass a reference to your page to the GetNavigationService() method, and it returns a live NavigationService object that lets you perform programmatic navigation:

```
NavigationService nav;
nav = NavigationService.GetNavigationService(this);
```

This code works no matter what container you're using to host your pages.

Note The NavigationService isn't available in page constructor or when the Page.Initialized event fires. Use the Page.Loaded event instead.

The NavigationService class gives you a number of methods you can use to trigger navigation. The most commonly used is the Navigate() method. It allows you to navigate to a page based on its URI:

```
nav.Navigate(new System.Uri("Page1.xaml", UriKind.RelativeOrAbsolute));
```

or by creating the appropriate page object:

```
Page1 nextPage = new Page1();
nav.Navigate(nextPage);
```

If possible, you'll want to navigate by URI because that allows WPF's journaling system to preserve the page data without needing to keep the tree of page objects alive in memory. When you pass a page object to the Navigate() method, the entire object is always retained in memory.

However, you may decide to create the page object manually if you need to pass information into the page. You can pass information in using a custom page class constructor (which is the most common approach), or you can call another custom method in the page class after you've created it. If you add a new constructor to the page, make sure your constructor calls InitializeComponent() to process your markup and create the control objects.

Note If you decide you need to use programmatic navigation, it's up to you whether you use button controls, hyperlinks, or something else. Typically, you'll use conditional code in your event handler to decide which page to navigate to.

WPF navigation is asynchronous. As a result, you can cancel the navigation request before it's complete by calling the NavigationService.StopLoading() method. You can also use the Refresh() method to reload a page.

Finally, the NavigationService also provides GoBack() and GoForward() methods that allow you to move through the back and forward lists. This is useful if you're creating your own navigation controls. Both of these methods raise an InvalidOperationException if you try to navigate to a page that doesn't exist (for example, you attempt to go back when you're on the first page). To avoid these errors, check the Boolean CanGoBack and CanGoForward properties before using the matching methods.

Navigation Events

The NavigationService class also provides a useful set of events that you can use to react to navigation. The most common reason you'll react to navigation is to perform some sort of task when navigation is complete. For example, if your page is hosted inside a frame in a normal window, you might update status bar text in the window when navigation is complete.

Because navigation is asynchronous, the Navigate() method returns before the target page has appeared. In some cases, the time difference could be significant, such as when you're navigating to a loose XAML page on a website (or a XAML page in another assembly that triggers a web download) or when the page includes time-consuming code in its Initialized or Loaded event handler.

The WPF navigation process unfolds like this:

1. The page is located.

2. The page information is retrieved. (If the page is on a remote site, it's downloaded at this point.)

3. Any related resources that the page needs (such as images) are also located and downloaded.

4. The page is parsed and the tree of objects is generated. At this point, the page fires its Initialized event (unless it's being restored from the journal) and its Loaded event.

5. The page is rendered.

6. If the URI includes a fragment, WPF navigates to that element.

Table 9-2 lists the events that are raised by the NavigationService class during the process.

These navigation events are also provided by the Application class and by the navigation containers (NavigationWindow and Frame). If you have more than one navigation container, this gives you the flexibility to handle the navigation in different containers separately. However, there's no built-in way to handle the navigation events for a single *page*. Once you attach an event handler to the navigation service to a navigation container, it continues to fire events as you move from page to page (or until you remove the event handler). Generally, this means that the easiest way to handle navigation is at the application level.

Navigation events can't be suppressed using the RoutedEventArgs.Handled property. That's because navigation events are ordinary .NET events, not routed events.

Tip You can pass data from the Navigate() method to the navigation events. Just look for one of the Navigate() method overloads that take an extra object parameter. This object is made available in the Navigated, NavigationStopped, and LoadCompleted events through the NavigationEventArgs.ExtraData property. For example, you could use this property to keep track of the time a navigation request was made.

Table 9-2. *Events of the NavigationService Class*

Name	Description
Navigating	Navigation is just about to start. You can cancel this event to prevent the navigation from taking place.
Navigated	Navigation has started, but the target page has not yet been retrieved.
NavigationProgress	Navigation is underway, and a chunk of page data has been downloaded. This event is raised periodically to provide information about the progress of navigation. It provides the amount of information that's been downloaded (NavigationProgressEventArgs.BytesRead) and the total amount of information that's required (NavigationProgress-EventArgs.MaxBytes). This event fires every time 1KB of data is retrieved.
LoadCompleted	The page has been parsed. However, the Initialized and Loaded events have not yet been fired.
FragmentNavigation	The page is about to be scrolled to the target element. This event fires only if you use a URI with fragment information.
NavigationStopped	Navigation was canceled with the StopLoading() method.
NavigationFailed	Navigation has failed because the target page could not be located or downloaded. You can use this event to neutralize the exception before it bubbles up to become an unhandled application exception. Just set NavigationFailedEventArgs.Handled to true.

Managing the Journal

Using the techniques you've learned so far, you'll be able to build a linear navigation-based application. You can make the navigation process adaptable (for example, using conditional logic so that users are directed to different steps along the way), but you're still limited to the basic start-to-finish approach. Figure 9-8 shows this navigation topology, which is common when building simple task-based wizards. The dashed lines indicate the steps we're interested in—when the user exits a group of pages that represent a logical task.

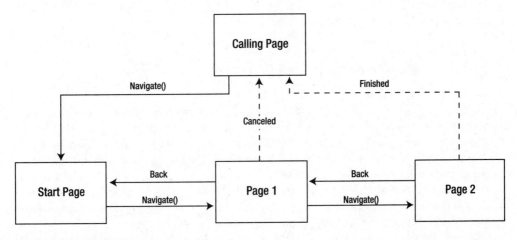

Figure 9-8. *Linear navigation*

If you try to implement this design using WPF navigation, you'll find that there's a missing detail. Namely, when the user is finished with the navigation process (either because they've canceled the operation during one of the steps or because they've completed the task at hand), you need to wipe out the back history. If your application revolves around a main window that isn't navigation-based, this isn't a problem. When the user launches the page-based task, your application simply creates a new NavigationWindow to take the user through it. When the task ends, you can destroy that window. However, if your entire application is navigation-based, this isn't as easy. You need a way to drop the history list when the task is canceled or complete so the user can't step back to one of the intermediary steps.

Unfortunately, WPF doesn't allow you to have much control over the navigation stack. All it gives you is two methods in the NavigationService class: AddBackEntry() and RemoveBackEntry().

RemoveBackEntry() is the one you need in this example. It takes the most recent item from the back list and deletes it. RemoveBackEntry() also returns a JournalEntry object that describes that item. It tells you the URI (through the Source property) and the name that it uses in the navigation history (through the Name property). Remember, the name is set based on the Page.Title property.

If you want to clear several entries after a task is complete, you'll need to call Remove-BackEntry() multiple times. You can use two approaches. If you've decided to remove the entire back list, you can use the CanGoBack property to determine when you've reached the end:

```
while (nav.CanGoBack)
{
    nav.RemoveBackEntry();
}
```

Alternatively, you can continue removing items until you remove the task starting point. For example, if a page launches a task starting with a page named ConfigureAppWizard.xaml, you could use this code when the task is complete:

```
string pageName;
while (pageName != "ConfigureAppWizard.xaml")
{
    JournalEntry entry = nav.RemoveBackEntry();
    pageName = System.IO.Path.GetFileName(entry.Source.ToString());
}
```

This code takes the full URI that's stored in the JournalEntry.Source property and trims it down to just the page name using the static GetFileName() method of the Path class (which works equally well with URIs). Using the Title property would make for more convenient coding, but it isn't as robust. Because the page title is displayed in the navigation history and is visible to the user, it's a piece of information you'd need to translate into other languages when localizing your application. This would break code that expects a hard-coded page title. And even if you don't plan to localize your application, it's not difficult to imagine a scenario where the page title is changed to be clearer or more descriptive.

Incidentally, it is possible to examine all the items in the back and forward lists using the BackStack and ForwardStack properties of the navigation container (such as Navigation-Window or Frame). However, it's not possible to get this information generically through the

NavigationService class. In any case, these properties expose simple read-only collections of JournalEntry objects. They don't allow you to modify the lists, and they're rarely needed.

Adding Custom Items to the Journal

Along with the RemoveBackEntry() method, the NavigationService also gives you an AddBackEntry() method. The purpose of this method is to allow you to save "virtual" entries in the back list. For example, imagine you have a single page that allows the user to perform a fairly sophisticated configuration task. If you want the user to be able to step back to a previous state of that window, you can save it using the AddBackEntry() method. Even though it's only a single page, it may have several corresponding entries in the list.

Contrary to what you might expect, when you call AddBackEntry(), you don't pass in a JournalEntry object. (In fact, the JournalEntry class has a protected constructor and so it can't be instantiated by your code.) Instead, you need to create a custom class that derives from the abstract System.Windows.Navigation.CustomContentState class and stores all the information you need. For example, consider the application shown in Figure 9-9, which allows you to move items from one list to another.

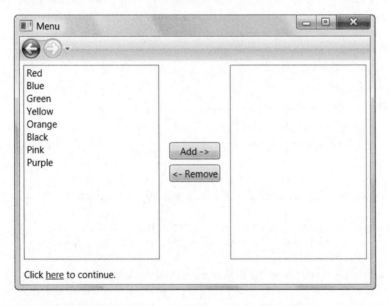

Figure 9-9. *A dynamic list*

Now imagine you want to save the state of this window every time an item is moved from one list to the other. The first thing you need is a class that derives from CustomContentState and keeps track of this information you need. In this case, you simply need to record the contents of both lists. Because this class will be stored in the journal (so your page can be "rehydrated" when needed), it needs to be serializable:

```
[Serializable()]
public class ListSelectionJournalEntry : CustomContentState
{
```

```
private List<String> sourceItems;
private List<String> targetItems;
public List<String> SourceItems
{
    get { return sourceItems; }
}
public List<String> TargetItems
{
    get { return targetItems; }
}
...
```

This gets you off to a good start, but there's still a fair bit more to do. For example, you probably don't want the page to appear with the same title in the navigation history multiple times. Instead, you'll probably want to use a more descriptive name. To make this possible, you need to override the JournalEntryName property.

In this example, there's no obvious, concise way to describe the state of both lists. So it makes sense to let the page choose the name when it saves the entry in the journal. This way, the page can add a descriptive name based on the most recent action (such as Added Blue or Removed Yellow). To create this design, you simply need to make the JournalEntryName depend on a variable, which can be set in the constructor:

```
...
private string _journalName;
public override string JournalEntryName
{
    get { return _journalName; }
}
...
```

The WPF navigation system calls your JournalEntryName property to get the name it should show in the list.

The next step is to override the Replay() method. WPF calls this method when the user navigates to an entry in the back or forward list so that you can apply the previously saved state.

There are two approaches you can take in the Replay() method. You can retrieve a reference to the current page using the NavigationService.Content property. You can then cast that into the appropriate page class and call whatever method is required to implement your change. The other approach, which is used here, is to rely on a callback:

```
...
private ReplayListChange replayListChange;

public override void Replay(NavigationService navigationService,
  NavigationMode mode)
{
    this.replayListChange(this);
```

```
}
...
```

The ReplayListChange delegate isn't shown here, but it's quite simple. It represents a method with one parameter—the ListSelectionJournalEntry object. The page can then retrieve the list information from the SourceItems and TargetItems properties and restore the page.

With this in place, the last step is to create a constructor that accepts all the information you need—namely, the two lists of items, the title to use in the journal, and the delegate that should be triggered when the state needs to be reapplied to the page:

```
...
public ListSelectionJournalEntry(
  List<String> sourceItems, List<String> targetItems,
  string journalName, ReplayListChange replayListChange)
{
    this.sourceItems = sourceItems;
    this.targetItems = targetItems;
    this.journalName = journalName;
    this.replayListChange = replayListChange;
}
}
```

To hook up this functionality into the page, you need to take three steps:

1. You need to call AddBackReference() at the appropriate time to store an extra entry in the navigation history.

2. You need to handle the ListSelectionJournalEntry callback to restore your window when the user navigates through the history.

3. You need to implement the IProvideCustomContentState interface and its single GetContentState() method in your page class. When the user navigates to another page through the history, the GetContentState() method gets called by the navigation service. This allows you to return an instance of your custom class that will be stored as the state of the current page.

Note The IProvideCustomContentState interface is an easily overlooked but essential detail. When the user navigates using the forward or back list, two things need to happen—your page needs to add the current view to the journal (using IProvideCustomContentState) and then needs to restore the selected view (using the ListSelectionJournalEntry callback).

First, whenever the Add button is clicked, you need to create a new ListSelection-JournalEntry object and call AddBackReference() so the previous state is stored in the history.

This process is factored out into a separate method so that you can use it in several places in the page (for example, when either the Add button or the Remove button is clicked):

```
private void cmdAdd_Click(object sender, RoutedEventArgs e)
{
    if (lstSource.SelectedIndex != -1)
    {
        // Determine the best name to use in the navigation history.
        NavigationService nav = NavigationService.GetNavigationService(this);
        string itemText = lstSource.SelectedItem.ToString();
        string journalName = "Added " + itemText;

        // Update the journal (using the method shown below.)
        nav.AddBackEntry(GetJournalEntry(journalName));

        // Now perform the change.
        lstTarget.Items.Add(itemText);
        lstSource.Items.Remove(itemText);
    }
}

private ListSelectionJournalEntry GetJournalEntry(string journalName)
{
    // Get the state of both lists (using a helper method).
    List<String> source = GetListState(lstSource);
    List<String> target = GetListState(lstTarget);

    // Create the custom state object with this information.
    // Point the callback to the Replay method in this class.
    return new ListSelectionJournalEntry(
      source, target, journalName, Replay);
}
```

You can use a similar process when the Remove button is clicked.

The next step is to handle the callback in the Replay() method and update the lists, as shown here:

```
private void Replay(ListSelectionJournalEntry state)
{
    lstSource.Items.Clear();
    foreach (string item in state.SourceItems)
      { lstSource.Items.Add(item); }

    lstTarget.Items.Clear();
    foreach (string item in state.TargetItems)
      { lstTarget.Items.Add(item); }
}
```

And the final step is to implement IProvideCustomContentState in the page:

```
public partial class PageWithMultipleJournalEntries : Page,
 IProvideCustomContentState
```

IProvideCustomContentState defines a single method named GetContentState(). In GetContentState(), you need to store the state for the page in the same way you do when the Add or Remove button is clicked. The only difference is that you don't add it using the AddBackReference() method. Instead, you provide it to WPF through a return value:

```
public CustomContentState GetContentState()
{
    // We haven't stored the most recent action,
    // so just use the page name for a title.
    return GetJournalEntry("PageWithMultipleJournalEntries");
}
```

Remember, the WPF navigation service calls GetContentState() when the user travels to another page using the back or forward buttons. WPF takes the CustomContentState object you return and stores that in the journal for the current page. There's a potential quirk here—if the user performs several actions and then travels back through the navigation history reversing them, the "undone" actions in the history will have the hard-coded page name (PageWithMultipleJournalEntries) rather than the more descriptive original name (such as Added Orange). To improve the way this is handled, you can store the journal name for the page using a member variable in your page class. The downloadable code for this example takes that extra step.

This completes the example. Now, when you run the application and begin manipulating the lists, you'll see several entries appear in the history (Figure 9-10).

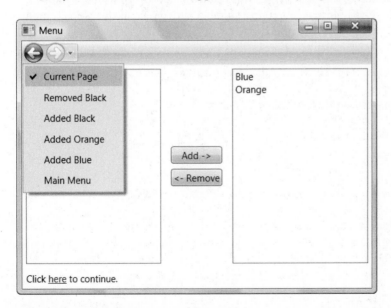

Figure 9-10. *Custom entries in the journal*

Page Functions

So far, you've learned how to pass information to a page (by instantiating the page program-matically, configuring it, and then passing it to the NavigationService.Navigate() method), but you haven't seen how to return information *from* a page. The easiest (and least structured) approach is to store information in some sort of static application variable so that it's accessible to any other class in your program. However, this design isn't the best if you just need a way to transmit simple bits of information one page to another, and you don't want to keep this information in memory for a long time. If you clutter your application with global variables, you'll have a difficult time figuring out the dependencies (what variables are used by which pages), and it will become much more difficult to reuse your pages and maintain your application.

The other approach that WPF provides is the PageFunction class. A PageFunction is a derived version of the Page class that adds the ability to return a result. In a way, a PageFunction is analogous to a dialog box, while a page is analogous to a window.

To create a PageFunction in Visual Studio, right-click your project in the Solution Explorer, and choose Add ➤ New Item. Next, select the WPF category, choose the Page Function (WPF) template, enter a file name, and click Add. The markup for a PageFunction is nearly identical to the markup you use for a Page. The difference is the root element, which is <PageFunction> instead of <Page>.

Technically, the PageFunction is a generic class. It accepts a single type parameter, which indicates the data type that's used for the PageFunction's return value. By default, every new page function is parameterized by string (which means it returns a single string as its return value). However, you can easily modify that detail by changing the TypeArguments attribute in the <PageFunction> element.

In the following example, the PageFunction returns an instance of a custom class named SelectedProduct. In order to support this design, the <PageFunction> element maps the appropriate namespace (NavigationAplication) to a suitable XML prefix (local), which is then used when setting the TypeArguments attribute.

```
<PageFunction
    xmlns="http://schemas.microsoft.com/winfx/2006/xaml/presentation"
    xmlns:x="http://schemas.microsoft.com/winfx/2006/xaml"
    xmlns:local="clr-namespace:NavigationApplication"
    x:Class="NavigationApplication.SelectProductPageFunction"
    x:TypeArguments="local:Product"
    Title="SelectProductPageFunction"
    >
```

This declaration indicates that your page function will return a Product object to the calling page.

Incidentally, as long as you set the TypeArguments attribute in your markup, you don't need to specify the same information in your class declaration. Instead, the XAML parser will generate the correct class automatically. That means this code is enough to declare the page function shown earlier:

```
public partial class SelectProductPageFunction
{ ... }
```

Although this more explicit code works just as well:

```
public partial class SelectProductPageFunction:
  PageFunction<Product>
{ ... }
```

Visual Studio uses this more explicit syntax when you create a PageFunction. By default, all new PageFunction classes that Visual Studio creates derive from PageFunction<string>.

The PageFunction needs to handle all its navigation programmatically. When you click a button or a link that finishes the task, your code must call the PageFunction.OnReturn() method. At this point, you supply the object you want to return, which must be an instance of the class you specified in the declaration. Or you can supply a null value, which indicates that the task was not completed.

Here's an example with two event handlers:

```
private void lnkOK_Click(object sender, RoutedEventArgs e)
{
    // Return the selection information.
    OnReturn(new ReturnEventArgs<Product>(lstProducts.SelectedValue));
}

private  void lnkCancel_Click(object sender, RoutedEventArgs e)
{
    // Indicate that nothing was selected.
    OnReturn(null);
}
```

Using the PageFunction is just as easy. The calling page needs to instantiate the PageFunction programmatically because it needs to hook up an event handler to the PageFunction.Returned event. (This extra step is required because the NavigationService.Navigate() method is asynchronous and returns immediately.)

```
SelectProductPageFunction pageFunction = new SelectProductPageFunction();
pageFunction.Return += new ReturnEventHandler<Product>(
  SelectProductPageFunction_Returned);
this.NavigationService.Navigate(pageFunction);
```

When the user finishes using the PageFunction and clicks a link that calls OnReturn(), the PageFunction.Returned event fires. The returned object is available through the ReturnEventArgs.Result property:

```
private void SelectProductPageFunction_Returned(object sender,
  ReturnEventArgs<Product> e)
{
    Product product = (Product)e.Result;
    if (e != null) lblStatus.Text = "You chose: " + product.Name;
}
```

Usually, the OnReturn() method marks the end of a task, and you don't want the user to be able to navigate back to the PageFunction. You could use the NavigationService.RemoveBackEntry() method to implement this, but there's an easier approach. Every

PageFunction also provides a property named RemoveFromJournal. If you set this to true, the page is automatically removed from the history when it calls OnReturn().

By adding the PageFunction to your application, you now have the ability to use a different sort of navigation topology. You can designate one page as a central hub and allow users to perform various tasks through page functions, as shown in Figure 9-11.

Often, a PageFunction will call another page function. In this case, the recommended way to handle the navigation process once it's complete is to use a chained series of OnReturn() calls. In other words, if PageFunction1 calls PageFunction2, which then calls PageFunction3, when PageFunction3 calls OnReturn() it triggers the Returned event handler in PageFunction2, which then calls OnReturn(), which then fires the Returned event in PageFunction1, which finally calls OnReturn() to end the whole process. Depending on what you're trying to accomplish, it may be necessary to pass your return object up through the whole sequence until it reaches a root page.

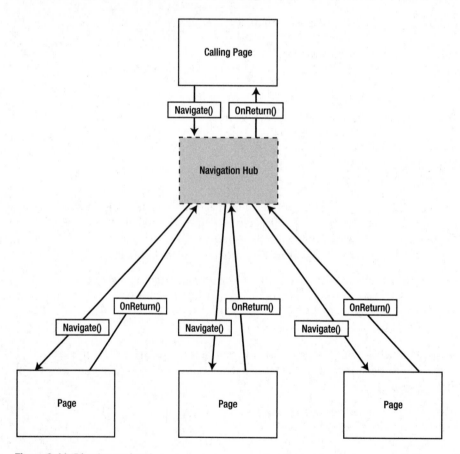

Figure 9-11. *Linear navigation*

XAML Browser Applications

XBAPs are page-based applications that run inside the browser. XBAPs are full-blown WPF applications, with a few key differences:

- **They run inside the browser window.** They can take the entire display area for the web page, or you can place them somewhere inside an ordinary HTML document using the <iframe> tag (as you'll see shortly).

■Note The technical reality is that any type of WPF application, including an XBAP, runs as a separate process managed by the CLR. An XBAP appears to run "inside" the browser simply because it displays all its content in the browser window. This is different from the model used by ActiveX controls (and Silverlight applications), which *are* loaded inside the browser process.

- **They have limited permission.** Although it's possible to configure an XBAP so that it requests full trust permissions, the goal is to use XBAP as a lighter-weight deployment model that allows users to run WPF applications without allowing potentially risky code to execute. The permissions given to an XBAP are the same as the permissions given to a .NET application that's run from the Web or local intranet, and the mechanism that enforces these restrictions (code access security) is the same. That means that by default an XBAP cannot write files, interact with other computer resources (such as the registry), connect to databases, or pop up full-fledged windows.

- **They aren't installed.** When you run an XBAP, the application is downloaded and cached in the browser. However, it doesn't remain installed on the computer. This gives you the instant-update model of the Web—in other words, every time a user returns to use an application, the newest version is downloaded if it doesn't exist in the cache.

The advantage of XBAPs is that they offer a *prompt-free* experience. If .NET 3.5 is installed, a client can surf to an XBAP in the browser and start using it just like a Java applet, a Flash movie, or JavaScript-enhanced web page. There's no installation prompt or security warning. The obvious trade-off is that you need to abide by a stringently limited security model. If your application needs greater capabilities (for example, it needs to read or write arbitrary files, interact with a database, use the Windows registry, and so on), you're far better off creating a stand-alone Windows application. You can then offer a streamlined (but not completely seamless) deployment experience for your application using ClickOnce deployment, which is described in Chapter 27.

XBAP Requirements

The client computer must have the .NET Framework 3.0 or 3.5 in order to run any WPF application, including an XBAP. Windows Vista includes .NET 3.0, so computers running Windows Vista automatically recognize XBAPs. (The version of .NET that you need to run an XBAP— .NET 3.0 or 3.5—depends on the WPF features you're using and the version of .NET you've chosen to target, as described in Chapter 1.)

Currently, two browsers are able to launch XBAP applications: Internet Explorer (version 6 or later) and Firefox (version 2 or later). Internet Explorer 7 has one extra feature—it's able to recognize .xbap files even if .NET 3.0 or 3.5 isn't installed. When the user requests an .xbap file, Internet Explorer gives the user the option to install .NET 3.5 (as shown in Figure 9-12).

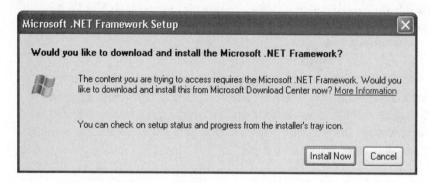

Figure 9-12. *Trying to launch an XBAP without .NET 3.5 on Internet Explorer 7*

Creating an XBAP

Any page-based application can become an XBAP, although Visual Studio forces you to create a new project with the WPF Browser Application template in order to create one. The difference is four key elements in the .csproj project file, as shown here:

```
<HostInBrowser>True</HostInBrowser>
<Install>False</Install>
<ApplicationExtension>.xbap</ApplicationExtension>
<TargetZone>Internet</TargetZone>
```

These tags tell WPF to host the application in the browser (HostInBrowser), to cache it along with other temporary Internet files rather than install it permanently (Install), to use the extension .xbap (ApplicationExtension), and to request the permissions for only the Internet zone (TargetZone). The fourth part is optional—as you'll see shortly, it's technically possible to create an XBAP that has greater permissions. However, XBAPs almost always run with the limited permissions available in the Internet zone, which is the key challenge to programming one successfully.

■**Tip** The .csproj file also includes other XBAP-related tags that ensure the right debugging experience. The easiest way to change an application from an XBAP into a page-based application with a stand-alone window (or vice versa) is to create a new project of the desired type and then import all the pages from the old project.

Once you've created your XBAP, you can design your pages and code them in exactly the same way as if you were using the NavigationWindow. For example, you set the StartupUri in the App.xaml file to one of your pages. When you compile your application, an .xbap file is generated. You can then request that .xbap file in Internet Explorer or Firefox, and (provided the .NET Framework is installed) the application runs in limited trust mode automatically. Figure 9-13 shows an XBAP in Internet Explorer.

Note XBAP projects have a hard-coded debug path. That means if you move an XBAP project from one folder to another, you'll lose the ability to debug it in Visual Studio. To fix the problem, double-click Properties in the Solution Explorer, choose the Debug section, and update the path in the Command Line Arguments text box.

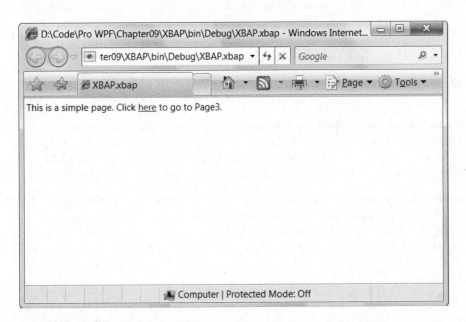

Figure 9-13. *An XBAP in the browser*

The XBAP application runs just the same as an ordinary WPF application, provided you don't attempt to perform any restricted actions (such as showing a stand-alone window). If you're running your application in Internet Explorer 7 (the version that's included with Windows Vista), the browser buttons take the place of the buttons on the NavigationWindow, and they show the back and forward page lists. On previous versions of Internet Explorer and in Firefox, you get a new set of navigation buttons at the top of your page, which isn't quite as nice.

Deploying an XBAP

Although you could create a setup program for an XBAP (and you can run an XBAP from the local hard drive), there's rarely a reason to take this step. Instead, you can simply copy your compiled application to a network share or a virtual directory.

■**Note** You can get a similar effect using loose XAML files. If your application consists entirely of XAML pages with no code-behind files, you don't need to compile it at all. Instead, just place the appropriate .xaml files on your web server and let users browse to them directly. Of course, loose XAML files obviously can't do as much as their compiled counterparts, but they're suitable if you simply need to display a document, a graphic, or an animation, or if you wire up all the functionality you need through declarative binding expressions.

Unfortunately, deploying an XBAP isn't as simple as just copying the .xbap file. You actually need to copy the following three files to the same folder:

- **ApplicationName.exe**. This file has the compiled IL code, just as it does in any .NET application.

- **ApplicationName.exe.manifest**. This file is an XML document that indicates requirements of your application (for example, the version of the .NET assemblies you used to compile your code). If your application uses other DLLs, you can make these available in the same virtual directory as your application and they'll be downloaded automatically.

- **ApplicationName.xbap**. The .xbap file is another XML document. It represents the entry point to your application—in other words, this is the file that the user needs to request in the browser to install your XBAP. The markup in the .xbap file points to the application file and includes a digital signature that uses the key you've chosen for your project.

Once you've transferred these files to the appropriate location, you can run the application by requesting the .xbap file in Internet Explorer or Firefox. It makes no difference whether the files are on the local hard drive or a remote web server—you can request them in the same way.

■**Tip** It's tempting, but don't run the .exe file. If you do, nothing will happen. Instead, double-click the .xbap file in Windows Explorer (or type its path in by hand using Internet Explorer). Either way, all three files must be present, and the browser must be able to recognize the .xbap file extension.

The browser will show a progress page as it begins downloading the .xbap file (Figure 9-14). This downloading process is essentially an installation process that copies the .xbap application to the local Internet cache. When the user returns to the same remote location on subsequent visits, the cached version will be used. (The only exception is if there's a newer version of the XBAP on the server, as described in the next section.)

When you create a new XBAP application, Visual Studio also includes an automatically generated certificate file with a name like ApplicationName_TemporaryKey.pfx. This certificate contains a public/private key pair that's used to add a signature to your .xbap file. If you publish an update to your application, you'll need to sign it with the same key to ensure the digital signature remains consistent.

Rather than using the temporary key, you may want to create a key of your own (which you can then share between projects and protect with a password). To do so, double-click the Properties node under your project in the Solution Explorer and use the options in the Signing tab.

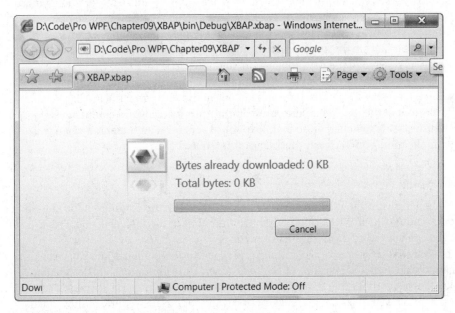

Figure 9-14. *Running an .xbap application for the first time*

Updating an XBAP

When you debug an XBAP application, Visual Studio always rebuilds your XBAP and loads up the latest version in the browser. You don't need to take any extra steps.

This isn't the case if you request an XBAP directly in your browser. When running XBAPs in this fashion, there's a potential problem. If you rebuild the application, deploy it to the same location, and then rerequest it in the browser, you won't necessarily get the updated version. Instead, you'll continue running the older cached copy of the application. This is true even if you close and reopen the browser window, click the browser's Refresh button, and increment the assembly version of your XBAP.

You can manually clear the ClickOnce cache, but this obviously isn't a convenient solution. Instead, you need to update the publication information that's stored in your .xbap file so that the browser recognizes that your newly deployed XBAP represents a new version of your application. Updating the assembly version isn't enough to trigger an update—instead, you need to update the *publish version*.

■**Note** This extra step is required because the download-and-cache functionality of an .xbap is built using the plumbing from ClickOnce, the deployment technology that you'll learn about in Chapter 27. ClickOnce uses the publication version to determine when an update should be applied. This allows you to build an application multiple times for testing (each time with a different assembly version number) but increment the publish version only when you want to deploy a new release.

The easiest way to rebuild your application *and* apply a new publication version is to choose Build ➤ Publish [ProjectName] from the Visual Studio menu (and then click Finish). You don't need to use the publication files (which are placed in the Publish folder under your project directory). That's because the newly generated .xbap file in the Debug or Release folder will indicate the new publish version. All you need to do is deploy this .xbap file (along with the .exe and .manifest files) to the appropriate location. The next time you request the .xbap file, the browser will download the new application files and cache them.

You can see the current publish version by double-clicking the Properties item in the Solution Explorer, choosing the Publish tab, and looking at the settings in the Publish Version section at the bottom of the tab. Make sure you keep the Automatically Increment Revision with Each Publish setting switched on so that the publish version is incremented when you publish your application, which clearly marks it as a new release.

XBAP Security

The most challenging aspect to creating an XBAP is staying within the confines of the limited security model. Ordinarily, an XBAP runs with the permissions of the Internet zone. This is true even if you run your XBAP from the local hard drive.

The .NET Framework uses *code access security* (a core feature that it has had since version 1.0) to limit what your XBAP is allowed to do. In general, the limitations are designed to correspond with what comparable Java or JavaScript code could do in an HTML page. For example, you'll be allowed to render graphics, perform animations, use controls, show documents, and play sounds. You can't access computer resources like files, the Windows registry, databases, and so on.

■**Note** If you've programmed Windows Forms applications with .NET 2.0, you may recall that ClickOnce allows applications to escalate their level of trust through a security prompt. If an application needs more permissions than those provided in the Internet zone, users are prompted with an intimidating security warning and can choose to allow the application. XBAPs don't work the same way. The user is not able to escalate permissions, so an application that needs permissions outside the Internet security zone will fail.

One simple way to find out whether an action is allowed is to write some test code and try it. The WPF documentation also has full details. Table 9-3 provides a quick list of significant supported and disallowed features.

So what's the effect if you attempt to use a feature that's not allowed in the Internet zone? Ordinarily, your application fails as soon as it runs the problematic code with a SecurityException. Alternatively, you can configure your application to request the permission, in which the user receives an error when they first browse to the .xbap file and try to launch your application. (To request a permission, double-click the Properties node in the Visual Studio Solution Explorer, choose the Security tab, and change the permission you want from Zone Default to Include.)

Figure 9-15 shows the result of running an ordinary XBAP that attempts to perform a disallowed action and not handling the resulting SecurityException.

Table 9-3. *Key WPF Features and the Internet Zone*

Allowed	Not Allowed
All core controls, including the RichTextBox	Windows Forms controls (through interop)
Pages, the MessageBox, and the OpenFileDialog	Stand-alone windows and other dialog boxes (such as the SaveFileDialog)
Isolated storage (limited to 512KB)	Access to the file system and access to the registry
2D and 3D drawing, audio and video, flow and XPS documents, and animation	Some bitmap effects (presumably because they rely on unmanaged code)
"Simulated" drag-and-drop (code that responds to mouse-move events)	Windows drag-and-drop
ASP.NET (.asmx) web services and WCF (Windows Communication Foundation) services	Most advanced WCF features (non-HTTP transport, server-initiated connections, and WS-* protocols) and communicating with any server other than the one where the XBAP is hosted

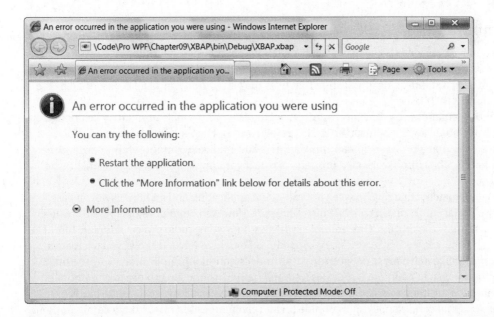

Figure 9-15. *An unhandled exception in an XBAP*

Full-Trust XBAPs

It's possible to create an XBAP that runs with full trust, although this technique isn't recommended. To do so, double-click the Properties node in the Solution Explorer, choose the Security tab, and select This Is a Full Trust Application. However, users won't be able to run your application from a web server or virtual directory anymore. Instead, you'll need to take one of the following steps to ensure that your application is allowed to execute in full trust:

- Run the application from the local hard drive. (You can launch the .xbap file like an executable file by double-clicking it or using a shortcut.) You may want to use a setup program to automate the install process.

- Add the certificate you're using to sign the assembly (by default, it's a .pfx file) to the Trusted Publishers store on the target computer. You can do this using the certmgr.exe tool.

- Assign full trust to the website URL or network computer where the .xbap file is deployed. To do this, you need to use the Microsoft .NET 2.0 Framework Configuration Tool (which you can find in the Administrative Tools section of the Control Panel section in the Start menu).

The first option is the most straightforward. However, all of these steps require an awkward configuration or deployment step that must be performed on everyone else's computer. As a result, they aren't ideal approaches.

■**Note** If your application requires full trust, you should consider building a stand-alone WPF application and deploying it using ClickOnce (as described in Chapter 27). The real goal of the XBAP model is to create a WPF equivalent to the traditional HTML-and-JavaScript website (or Flash applet).

Combination XBAP/Stand-Alone Applications

So far, you've considered how to deal with XBAPs that may run under different levels of trust. However, there's another possibility. You might take the same application and deploy it as both an XBAP *and* a stand-alone application that uses the NavigationWindow (as described in the beginning of this chapter).

In this situation, you don't necessarily need to test your permissions. It may be enough to write conditional logic that tests the static BrowserInteropHelper.IsBrowserHosted property and assumes that a browser-hosted application is automatically running with Internet zone permissions. The IsBrowserHosted property is true if your application is running inside the browser.

Unfortunately, changing between a stand-alone application and an XBAP is not an easy feat because Visual Studio doesn't provide direct support. However, other developers have created tools to simplify the process. One example is the flexible Visual Studio project template found at http://scorbs.com/2006/06/04/vs-template-flexible-application. It allows you to create a single project file and choose between an XBAP and a stand-alone application using the build configuration list. In addition, it provides a compilation constant you can use to conditionally compile code in either scenario and an application property you can use to create binding expressions that conditionally show or hide certain elements based on the build configuration.

Another option is to place your pages in a reusable class library assembly. Then you can create two top-level projects, one that creates a NavigationWindow and loads the first page inside and another that launches the page directly as an XBAP. This makes it easier to maintain your solution but will probably still need some conditional code that tests the IsBrowser-Hosted property and checks specific CodeAccessPermission objects.

Coding for Different Security Levels

In some situations, you might choose to create an application that can function in different security contexts. For example, you may create an XBAP that can run locally (with full trust) or be launched from a website. In this case, it's key to write flexible code that can avoid an unexpected SecurityException.

Every separate permission in the code access security model is represented by a class that derives from CodeAccessPermission. You can use this class to check whether your code is running with the required permission. The trick is to call the CodeAccessPermission.Demand() method, which requests a permission. This demand fails (throwing a SecurityException) if the permission isn't granted to your application.

Here's a simple function that allows you to check for a given permission:

```
private bool CheckPermission(CodeAccessPermission requestedPermission)
{
    try
    {
        // Try to get this permission.
        requestedPermission.Demand();
        return true;
    }
    catch
    {
        return false;
    }
}
```

You can use this function to write code like this, which checks to see whether the calling code has permission to write to a file before attempting the operation:

```
// Create a permission that represents writing to a file.
FileIOPermission permission = new FileIOPermission(
  FileIOPermissionAccess.Write, @"c:\highscores.txt");

// Check for this permission.
if (CheckPermission(permission))
{
    // (It's safe to write to the file.)
}
else
{
    // (It's not allowed. Do nothing or show a message.)
}
```

The obvious disadvantage with this code is that it relies on exception handling to control normal program flow, which is discouraged (both because it leads to unclear code and because it adds overhead). Another alternative would be to simply attempt to perform the operation (such as writing to a file) and then catch any resulting SecurityException. However, this approach makes it more likely that you'll run into a problem halfway through a task, when recovery or cleanup may be more difficult.

Isolated Storage

In many cases, you may be able to fall back on less powerful functionality if a given permission isn't available. For example, although code running in the Internet zone isn't allowed to write to arbitrary locations on the hard drive, it is able to use isolated storage. Isolated storage provides a virtual file system that lets you write data to a small, user-specific and application-specific slot of space. The actual location on the hard drive is obfuscated (so there's no way to know exactly where the data will be written beforehand), and the total space available is 512KB. A typical location on a Windows Vista computer is a path in the form c:\Users\[UserName]\AppData\Local\IsolatedStorage\[GuidIdentifier]. Data in one user's isolated store is restricted from all other nonadministrative users.

■**Note** Isolated storage is the .NET equivalent of persistent cookies in an ordinary web page—it allows small bits of information to be stored in a dedicated location that has specific controls in place to prevent malicious attacks (such as code that attempts to fill the hard drive or replace a system file).

Isolated storage is covered in detail in the .NET reference. However, it's quite easy to use because it exposes the same stream-based model as ordinary file access. You simply use the types in the System.IO.IsolatedStorage namespace. Typically, you'll begin by calling the IsolatedStorageFile.GetUserStoreForApplication() method to get a reference to the isolated store for the current user and application. (Each application gets a separate store.) You can then create a virtual file in that location using the IsolatedStorageFileStream. Here's an example:

```
// Create a permission that represents writing to a file.
string filePath = System.IO.Path.Combine(appPath, "highscores.txt");
FileIOPermission permission = new FileIOPermission(
    FileIOPermissionAccess.Write, filePath);

// Check for this permission.
if (CheckPermission(permission))
{
    // Write to local hard drive.
    try
    {
        using (FileStream fs = File.Create(filePath))
        {
            WriteHighScores(fs);
        }
    }
```

```
    }
    catch { ... }
}
else
{
    // Write to isolated storage.
    try
    {
        IsolatedStorageFile store =
          IsolatedStorageFile.GetUserStoreForApplication();
        using (IsolatedStorageFileStream fs = new IsolatedStorageFileStream(
          "highscores.txt", FileMode.Create, store))
        {
            WriteHighScores(fs);
        }
    }
    catch { ... }
}
```

You can also use methods such as IsolatedStorageFile.GetFileNames() and IsolatedStorageFile.GetDirectoryNames() to enumerate the contents of the isolated store for the current user and application.

Remember, if you've made the decision to create an ordinary XBAP that will be deployed on the Web, you already know that you won't have FileIOPermission for the local hard drive (or anywhere else). If this is the type of application you're designing, there's no reason to use the conditional code shown here. Instead, your code can jump straight to the isolated storage classes.

■**Tip** You can increase the amount of data you can pack into isolated storage by wrapping your file-writing operations with the DeflateStream or GZipStream. Both types are defined in the System.IO.Compression namespace and use compression to reduce the number of bytes required.

Simulating Dialog Boxes with the Popup Control

Another limited feature in XBAPs is the ability to open a secondary window. In many cases, you'll use navigation and multiple pages instead of separate windows, and you won't miss this functionality.

However, sometimes it's convenient to pop open a window to show some sort of a message or collect input. In a stand-alone Windows application, you'd use a modal dialog box for this task. In an XBAP, there's another possibility—you can use the Popup control that was introduced in Chapter 7.

The basic technique is easy. First, you define the Popup in your markup, making sure to set its StaysOpen property to true so it will remain open until you close it. (There's no point in using the PopupAnimation or AllowsTransparency properties, because they won't have any effect in a web page.) Include suitable buttons, such as OK and Cancel, and set the Placement property to Center so the popup will appear in the middle of the browser window.

Here's a simple example:

```
<Popup Name="dialogPopUp" StaysOpen="True" Placement="Center" MaxWidth="200">
  <Border>
    <Border.Background>
      <LinearGradientBrush>
        <GradientStop Color="AliceBlue" Offset="1"></GradientStop>
        <GradientStop Color="LightBlue" Offset="0"></GradientStop>
      </LinearGradientBrush>
    </Border.Background>
    <StackPanel Margin="5" Background="White">
      <TextBlock Margin="10" TextWrapping="Wrap">
       Please enter your name.
      </TextBlock>
      <TextBox Name="txtName" Margin="10"></TextBox>
      <StackPanel Orientation="Horizontal" Margin="10">
        <Button Click="dialog_cmdOK_Click" Padding="3" Margin="0,0,5,0">OK</Button>
        <Button Click="dialog_cmdCancel_Click" Padding="3">Cancel</Button>
      </StackPanel>
    </StackPanel>
  </Border>
</Popup>
```

At the appropriate time (for example, when a button is clicked), disable the rest of your user interface and show the Popup. To disable your user interface, you can set the IsEnabled property of some top-level container, such as a StackPanel or a Grid, to false. (You can also set the Background property of the page to gray, which will draw the user's attention to Popup.) To show the Popup, simply set its IsVisible property to true.

Here's an event handler that shows the previously defined Popup:

```
private void cmdStart_Click(object sender, RoutedEventArgs e)
{
    DisableMainPage();
}

private void DisableMainPage()
{
    mainPage.IsEnabled = false;
    this.Background = Brushes.LightGray;
    dialogPopUp.IsOpen = true;
}
```

When the user clicks the OK or Cancel button, close the Popup by setting its IsVisible property to false, and re-enable the rest of the user interface:

```
private void dialog_cmdOK_Click(object sender, RoutedEventArgs e)
{
    // Copy name from the Popup into the main page.
    lblName.Content = "You entered: " + txtName.Text;
```

```
        EnableMainPage();
}

private void dialog_cmdCancel_Click(object sender, RoutedEventArgs e)
{
        EnableMainPage();
}

private void EnableMainPage()
{
        mainPage.IsEnabled = true;
        this.Background = null;
        dialogPopUp.IsOpen = false;
}
```

Figure 9-16 shows the Popup in action.

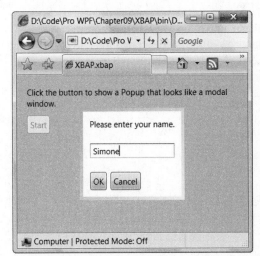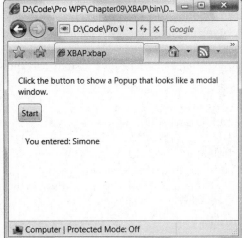

Figure 9-16. *Simulating a dialog box with the Popup*

Using the Popup control to create this workaround has one significant limitation. To ensure that the Popup control can't be used to spoof legitimate system dialog boxes, the Popup window is constrained to the size of the browser window. If you have a large Popup window and a small browser window, this could chop off some of your content. One solution, which is demonstrated with the sample code for this chapter, is to wrap the full content of the Popup control in a ScrollViewer with the VerticalScrollBarVisibility property set to Auto.

There's one other, even stranger option for showing a dialog box in a WPF page. You can use the Windows Forms library from .NET 2.0. You can safely create and show an instance of the System.Windows.Forms.Form class (or any custom form that derives from Form), because it doesn't require unmanaged code permission. In fact, you can even show the form modelessly, so the page remains responsive. The only drawback is that a security balloon automatically appears superimposed over the form and remains until the user clicks the warning message (as shown in Figure 9-17). You're also limited in what you can show *in* the form. Windows Forms controls are acceptable, but WPF content isn't allowed. For an example of this technique, refer to the sample code for this chapter.

Figure 9-17. *Using a .NET 2.0 form for a dialog box*

Embedding an XBAP in a Web Page

Usually, an XBAP is loaded directly in the browser so it takes up all the available space. However, you can have one other option—you can show an XBAP inside a portion of an HTML page, along with other HTML content. All you need to do is create an HTML page that uses the <iframe> tag to point to your .xbap file, as shown here:

```html
<html>
  <head>
    <title>An HTML Page That Contains an XBAP</title>
  </head>
  <body>
    <h1>Regular HTML Content</h1>
    <iframe src="BrowserApplication.xbap"></iframe>
    <h1>More HTML Content</h1>
  </body>
</html>
```

Using an <iframe> is a relatively uncommon technique, but it does allow you to pull off a few new tricks. For example, it allows you to display more than one XBAP in the same browser window. It also allows you to create a WPF-driven gadget for the Windows Vista sidebar.

■**Note** WPF applications don't have direct support for Vista gadgets, but you can embed a WPF application in a gadget using an <iframe>. The key drawback is that the overhead of WPF application is greater than the overhead of an ordinary HTML and JavaScript web page. There are also some quirks with the way that a WPF application handles mouse input. You can find an example of this technique and a good discussion of its limitations at `http://tinyurl.com/38e5se`.

The Last Word

In this chapter, you took a close look at the WPF navigation model. You learned how to build pages, host them in different containers, and use WPF navigation to move from one page to the next.

You also delved into the XBAP model that allows you to create a web-style WPF application that runs in a browser. Because XBAPs still require the .NET Framework, they won't replace the existing web applications and Flash games that we all know and love. However, they just might provide an alternate way to deliver rich content and graphics to Windows users. For example, one could imagine that a company like Microsoft could create an alternate interface to a popular web-based application like Hotmail using an XBAP. To program an XBAP successfully, you need to embrace the limitations of partial trust and code accordingly, which takes some getting used to.

■**Note** If you're planning to build WPF applications that run in a web browser over the Internet, you may want to consider WPF's scaled-down sibling, Silverlight 2.0. Although it's not as powerful as WPF, Silverlight 2.0 borrows a substantial portion of the WPF model and adds support for cross-platform use. (For example, you can run a Silverlight 2.0 application in a Safari browser on a Mac computer.) For more information about Silverlight, refer to `http://silverlight.net`.

CHAPTER 10

■ ■ ■

Commands

In Chapter 6, you learned about routed events, which you can use to respond to a wide range of mouse and keyboard actions. However, events are a fairly low-level ingredient. In a realistic application, functionality is divided into higher-level *tasks*. These tasks may be triggered by a variety of different actions and through a variety of different user-interface elements, including main menus, context menus, keyboard shortcuts, and toolbars.

WPF allows you to define these tasks—known as *commands*—and connect controls to them so you don't need to write repetitive event handling code. Even more important, the command feature manages the state of your user interface by automatically disabling controls when the linked commands aren't available. It also gives you a central place to store (and localize) the text captions for your commands.

In this chapter, you'll learn how to use the prebuilt command classes in WPF, how to wire them up to controls, and how to define your own commands. You'll also consider the limitations of the command model—namely, the lack of a command history and the lack of support for an application-wide Undo feature—and see how you can build your own.

Understanding Commands

In a well-designed Windows application, the application logic doesn't sit in the event handlers but is coded in higher-level methods. Each one of these methods represents a single application "task." Each task may rely on other libraries (such as separately compiled components that encapsulate business logic or database access). Figure 10-1 shows this relationship.

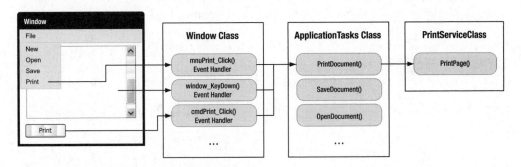

Figure 10-1. *Mapping event handlers to a task*

The most obvious way to use this design is to add event handlers wherever they're needed and use each event handler to call the appropriate application method. In essence, your window code becomes a stripped-down switchboard that responds to input and forwards requests to the heart of the application.

Although this design is perfectly reasonable, it doesn't save you any work. Many application tasks can be triggered through a variety of routes, so you'll often need to code several event handlers that call the same application method. This in itself isn't much of a problem (because the switchboard code is so simple), but life becomes much more complicated when you need to deal with UI *state*.

A simple example shows the problem. Imagine you have a program that includes an application method named PrintDocument(). This method can be triggered in four ways: through a main menu (by choosing File ➤ Print), through a context menu (by right-clicking somewhere and choosing Print), through a keyboard shortcut (Ctrl+P), and through a toolbar button. At certain points in your application's lifetime, you need to temporarily disable the PrintDocument() task. That means you need to disable the two menu commands and the toolbar button so they can't be clicked, and you need to ignore the Ctrl+P shortcut. Writing the code that does this (and adding the code that enables these controls later) is messy. Even worse, if it's not done properly, you might wind up with different blocks of state code overlapping incorrectly, causing a control to be switched on even when it shouldn't be available. Writing and debugging this sort of code is one of the least glamorous aspects of Windows development.

Much to the surprise of many experienced Windows developers, the Windows Forms toolkit didn't provide any features that could help you deal with these issues. Developers could build the infrastructure they needed on their own, but most weren't that ambitious.

Fortunately, WPF fills in the gaps with a new commanding model. It adds two key features:

- It delegates events to the appropriate commands.

- It keeps the enabled state of a control synchronized with the state of the corresponding command.

The WPF command model isn't quite as straightforward as you might expect. To plug into the routed event model, it requires several separate ingredients, which you'll learn about in this chapter. However, the command model is *conceptually* simple. Figure 10-2 shows how a command-based application changes the design shown in Figure 10-1. Now each action that initiates printing (clicking the button, clicking the menu item, or pressing Ctrl+P) is mapped to the same command. A command binding links that command to a single event handler in your code.

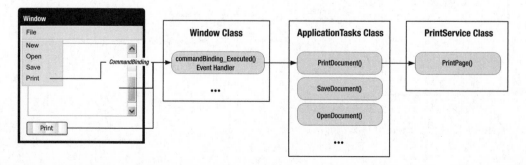

Figure 10-2. *Mapping events to a command*

The WPF command system is a great tool for simplifying application design. However, it still has some fairly significant gaps. Notably, WPF doesn't have any support for the following:

- Command tracking (for example, keeping a history of recent commands)

- "Undoable" commands

- Commands that have state and can be in different "modes" (for example, a command that can be toggled on or off)

The WPF Command Model

The WPF command model consists of a surprising number of moving parts. All together, it has four key ingredients:

- **Commands.** A command *represents* an application task and keeps track of whether it can be executed. However, commands don't actually contain the code that *performs* the application task.

- **Command bindings.** Each command binding links a command to the related application logic, for a particular area of your user interface. This factored design is important, because a single command might be used in several places in your application and have a different significance in each place. To handle this, you use the same command with different command bindings.

- **Command sources.** A command source triggers a command. For example, a MenuItem and a Button can both be command sources. Clicking them executes the bound command.

- **Command targets.** A command target is the element on which the command is being performed. For example, a Paste command might insert text into a TextBox, and an OpenFile command might pop a document into a DocumentViewer. The target may or may not be important, depending on the nature of the command.

In the following sections, you'll dig into the first ingredient—the WPF command.

The ICommand Interface

The heart of the WPF command model is the System.Windows.Input.ICommand interface that defines how commands work. This interface includes two methods and an event:

```
public interface ICommand
{
    void Execute(object parameter);
    bool CanExecute(object parameter);

    event EventHandler CanExecuteChanged;
}
```

In a simple implementation, the Execute() method would contain the application task logic (for example, printing the document). However, as you'll see in the next section, WPF is a bit more elaborate. It uses the Execute() method to fire off a more complicated process that eventually raises an event that's handled elsewhere in your application. This gives you the ability to use ready-made command classes and plug in your own logic. It also gives you the flexibility to use one command (such as Print) in several different places.

The CanExecute() method returns the state of the command—true if it's enabled and false if it's disabled. Both Execute() and CanExecute() accept an additional parameter object that you can use to pass along any extra information you need.

Finally, the CanExecuteChanged event is raised when the state changes. This is a signal to any controls using the command that they should call the CanExecute() method to check the command's state. This is part of the glue that allows command sources (such as a Button or MenuItem) to automatically enable themselves when the command is available and to disable themselves when it's not.

The RoutedCommand Class

When creating your own commands, you won't implement ICommand directly. Instead, you'll use the System.Windows.Input.RoutedCommand class, which implements this interface for you. The RoutedCommand class is the only class in WPF that implements ICommand. In other words, all WPF commands are instances of RoutedCommand (or a derived class).

One of the key concepts behind the command model in WPF is that the RoutedUI-Command class doesn't contain any application logic. It simply *represents* a command. This means one RoutedCommand object has the same capabilities as another.

The RoutedCommand class adds a fair bit of extra infrastructure for event tunneling and bubbling. Whereas the ICommand interface encapsulates the idea of a command—an action that can be triggered and may or may not be enabled—the RoutedCommand modifies the command so that it can bubble through the WPF element hierarchy to get to the right event handler.

To support routed events, the RoutedCommand class implements the ICommand interface privately and then adds slightly different versions of its methods. The most obvious change you'll notice is that the Execute() and CanExecute() methods take an extra parameter. Here are their new signatures:

```
public void Execute(object parameter, IInputElement target)
{...}

public bool CanExecute(object parameter, IInputElement target)
{...}
```

The *target* is the element where the event handling begins. This event begins at the target element and then bubbles up to higher-level containers until your application handles it to perform the appropriate task. (To handle the Executed event, your element needs the help of yet another class—the CommandBinding.)

Along with this shift, the RoutedElement also introduces three properties: the command name (Name), the class that this command is a member of (OwnerType), and any keystrokes or mouse actions that can also be used to trigger the command (in the InputGestures collection).

WHY WPF COMMANDS NEED EVENT BUBBLING

When looking at the WPF command model for the first time, it's tricky to grasp exactly why WPF commands require routed events. After all, shouldn't the command object take care of performing the command, regardless of how it's invoked?

If you were using the ICommand interface directly to create your own command classes, this would be true. The code would be hardwired into the command, so it would work the same way no matter what triggers the command. You wouldn't need event bubbling.

However, WPF uses a number of *prebuilt* commands. These command classes don't contain any real code. They're just conveniently defined objects that represent a common application task (such as printing a document). To act on these commands, you need to use a command binding, which raises an event to your code (as shown in Figure 10-2). To make sure you can handle this event in one place, even if it's fired by different command sources in the same window, you need the power of event bubbling.

This raises an interesting question—namely, why use prebuilt commands at all? Wouldn't it be clearer to have custom command classes do all the work, instead of relying on an event handler? In many ways, this design would be simpler. However, the advantage of prebuilt commands is that they provide much better possibilities for integration. For example, a third-party developer could create a document viewer control that uses the prebuilt Print command. As long as your application uses the same prebuilt command, you won't need to do any extra work to wire up printing in your application. Seen this way, commands are a major piece of WPF's pluggable architecture.

The RoutedUICommand Class

Most of the commands you'll deal with won't be RoutedCommand objects but will be instances of the RoutedUICommand class, which derives from RoutedCommand. (In fact, all the ready-made commands that WPF provides are RoutedUICommand objects.)

RoutedUICommand is intended for commands with text that is displayed somewhere in the user interface (for example, the text of a menu item or the tooltip for a toolbar button). The RoutedUICommand class adds a single property—Text—which is the display text for that command.

The advantage of defining the command text with the command (rather than directly on the control) is that you can perform your localization in one place. However, if your command text never appears anywhere in the user interface, the RoutedCommand class is equivalent.

■**Note** You don't need to use the RoutedUICommand text in your user interface. In fact, there may be good reasons to use something else. For example, you might prefer "Print Document" to just "Print," and in some cases you might replace the text altogether with a tiny graphic.

The Command Library

The designers of WPF realized that every application is likely to have a large number of commands and that many commands are common to many different applications. For example, all document-based applications will have their own versions of the New, Open, and Save commands. To save you the work of creating those commands, WPF includes a basic command library that's stocked with more than 100 commands. These commands are exposed through the static properties of five dedicated static classes:

- **ApplicationCommands.** This class provides the common commands, including clipboard commands (such as Copy, Cut, and Paste) and document commands (such as New, Open, Save, SaveAs, Print, and so on).

- **NavigationCommands.** This class provides commands used for navigation, including some that are designed for page-based applications (such as BrowseBack, BrowseForward, and NextPage) and others that are suitable for document-based applications (such as IncreaseZoom and Refresh).

- **EditingCommands.** This class provides a long list of mostly document-editing commands, including commands for moving around (MoveToLineEnd, MoveLeftByWord, MoveUpByPage, and so on), selecting content (SelectToLineEnd, SelectLeftByWord), and changing formatting (ToggleBold and ToggleUnderline).

- **ComponentCommands.** This includes commands that are used by user-interface components, including commands for moving around and selecting content that are similar to (and even duplicate) some of the commands in the EditingCommands class.

- **MediaCommands.** This class includes a set of commands for dealing with multimedia (such as Play, Pause, NextTrack, and IncreaseVolume).

The ApplicationCommands class exposes a set of basic commands that are commonly used in all types of applications, so it's worth a quick look. Here's the full list:

New	Copy	SelectAll
Open	Cut	Stop
Save	Paste	ContextMenu
SaveAs	Delete	CorrectionList
Close	Undo	Properties
Print	Redo	Help
PrintPreview	Find	
CancelPrint	Replace	

For example, ApplicationCommands.Open is a static property that exposes a RoutedUICommand object. This object represents the "Open" command in an application. Because ApplicationCommands.Open is a static property, there is only one instance of the Open command for your entire application. However, you may treat it differently depending on its source—in other words, where it occurs in the user interface.

The RoutedUICommand.Text property for every command matches its name, with the addition of spaces between words. For example, the text for the ApplicationCommands.SelectAll command is "Select All." (The Name property gives you the same text without the spaces.) The RoutedUICommand.OwnerType property returns a type object for the ApplicationCommands class, because the Open command is a static property of that class.

Tip You can modify the Text property of a command before you bind it in a window (for example, using code in the constructor of your window or application class). Because commands are static objects that are global to your entire application, changing the text affects the command everywhere it appears in your user interface. Unlike the Text property, the Name property cannot be modified.

As you've already learned, these individual command objects are just markers with no real functionality. However, many of the command objects have one extra feature: default input bindings. For example, the ApplicationCommands.Open command is mapped to the keystroke Ctrl+O. As soon as you bind that command to a command source and add that command source to a window, the key combination becomes active, even if the command doesn't appear anywhere in the user interface.

Executing Commands

So far, you've taken a close look at commands, considering both the base classes and interfaces and the command library that WPF provides for you to use. However, you haven't yet seen any examples of how to use these commands.

As explained earlier, the RoutedUICommand doesn't have any hardwired functionality. It simply represents a command. To trigger this command, you need a command *source* (or you can use code). To respond to this command, you need a command *binding* that forwards execution to an ordinary event handler. You'll see both ingredients in the following sections.

Command Sources

The commands in the command library are always available. The easiest way to trigger them is to hook them up to a control that implements the ICommandSource interface, which includes controls that derive from ButtonBase (Button, CheckBox, and so on), individual ListBoxItem objects, the Hyperlink, and the MenuItem.

The ICommandSource interface defines three properties, as listed in Table 10-1.

Table 10-1. *Properties of the ICommandSource Interface*

Name	Description
Command	Points to the linked command. This is the only required detail.
CommandParameter	Supplies any other data you want to send with the command.
CommandTarget	Identifies the element on which the command is being performed.

For example, here's a button that links to the ApplicationCommands.New command using the Command property:

```
<Button Command="ApplicationCommands.New">New</Button>
```

WPF is intelligent enough to search all five command container classes described earlier, which means you can use the following shortcut:

```
<Button Command="New">New</Button>
```

However, you may find that this syntax is less explicit and therefore less clear because it doesn't indicate what class contains the command.

Command Bindings

When you attach a command to a command source, you'll see something interesting. The command source will be automatically disabled.

For example, if you create the New button shown in the previous section, the button will appear dimmed and won't be clickable, just as if you had set IsEnabled to false (see Figure 10-3). That's because the button has queried the state of the command. Because the command has no attached binding, it's considered to be disabled.

Figure 10-3. *A command without a binding*

To change this state of affairs, you need to create a binding for your command that indicates three things:

- What to do when the command is triggered.

- How to determine whether the command can be performed. (This is optional. If you leave out this detail, the command is always enabled as long as there is an attached event handler.)

- Where the command is in effect. For example, the command might be limited to a single button, or it might be enabled over the entire window (which is more common).

Here's a snippet of code that creates a binding for the New command. You can add this code to the constructor of your window:

```
// Create the binding.
CommandBinding binding = new CommandBinding(ApplicationCommands.New);
```

```
// Attach the event handler.
binding.Executed += NewCommand_Executed;

// Register the binding.
this.CommandBindings.Add(binding);
```

Notice that the completed CommandBinding object is added to the CommandBindings collection of the containing window. This works through event bubbling. Essentially, when the button is clicked, the CommandBinding.Executed event bubbles up from the button to the containing elements.

Although it's customary to add all the bindings to the window, the CommandBindings property is actually defined in the base UIElement class. That means it's supported by any element. For example, this example would work just as well if you added the command binding directly to the button that uses it (although then you wouldn't be able to reuse it with another higher-level element). For greatest flexibility, command bindings are usually added to the top-level window. If you want to use the same command from more than one window, you'll need to create a binding in both windows.

■Note You can also handle the CommandBinding.PreviewExecuted event, which is fired first in the highest-level container (the window) and then tunnels down to the button. As you learned in Chapter 6, you use event tunneling to intercept and stop an event before it's completed. If you set the RoutedEvent-Args.Handled property to true, the Executed event will never take place.

The previous code assumes that in the same class you have an event handler named NewCommand_Executed, which is ready to receive the command. Here's an example of some simple code that displays the source of the command:

```
private void NewCommand_Executed(object sender, ExecutedRoutedEventArgs e)
{
    MessageBox.Show("New command triggered by " + e.Source.ToString());
}
```

Now, when you run the application, the button is enabled (see Figure 10-4). If you click it, the Executed event fires, bubbles up to the window, and is handled by the NewCommand() handler shown earlier. At this point, WPF tells you the source of the event (the button). The ExecutedRoutedEventArgs object also allows you to get a reference to the command that was invoked (ExecutedRoutedEventArgs.Command) and any extra information that was passed along (ExecutedRoutedEventArgs.Parameter). In this example, the parameter is null because you haven't passed any extra information. (If you wanted to pass additional information, you would set the CommandParameter property of the command source. And if you wanted to pass a piece of information drawn from another control, you'd need to set CommandParameter using a data binding expression, as shown later in this chapter.)

Figure 10-4. *A command with a binding*

■**Note** In this example, the event handler that responds to the command is still code inside the window where the command originates. The same rules of good code organization still apply to this example—in other words, your window should delegate its work to other components where appropriate. For example, if your command involves opening a file, you may use a custom file helper class that you've created to serialize and deserialize information. Similarly, if you create a command that refreshes a data display, you'll use it to call a method in a database component that fetches the data you need. See Figure 10-2 for a refresher.

In the previous example, the command binding was generated using code. However, it's just as easy to wire up commands declaratively using XAML if you want to streamline your code-behind file. Here's the markup you need:

```
<Window x:Class="Commands.TestNewCommand"
    xmlns="http://schemas.microsoft.com/winfx/2006/xaml/presentation"
    xmlns:x="http://schemas.microsoft.com/winfx/2006/xaml"
    Title="TestNewCommand">
  <Window.CommandBindings>
    <CommandBinding Command="ApplicationCommands.New"
      Executed="NewCommand_Executed"></CommandBinding>
  </Window.CommandBindings>

  <StackPanel Margin="5">
    <Button Padding="5" Command="ApplicationCommands.New">New</Button>
  </StackPanel>
</Window>
```

Unfortunately, Visual Studio does not have any design-time support for defining command bindings. It's also provides relatively feeble support for connecting controls and commands. You can set the Command property of a control using the Properties window, but it's up to you to type the exact name of the command—there's no handy drop-down list of commands from which to choose.

Using Multiple Command Sources

The button example seems like a somewhat roundabout way to trigger an ordinary event. However, the extra command layer starts to make more sense when you add more controls that use the same command. For example, you might add a menu item that also uses the New command:

```
<Menu>
  <MenuItem Header="File">
    <MenuItem Command="New"></MenuItem>
  </MenuItem>
</Menu>
```

Note that this MenuItem object for the New command doesn't set the Header property. That's because the MenuItem is intelligent enough to pull the text out of the command if the Header property isn't set. (The Button control lacks this feature.) This might seem like a minor convenience, but it's an important consideration if you plan to localize your application in different languages. In this case, being able to modify the text in one place (by setting the Text property of your commands) is easier than tracking it down in your windows.

The MenuItem class has another frill. It automatically picks up the first shortcut key that's in the Command.InputBindings collection (if there is one). In the case of the ApplicationsCommands.New command object, that means the Ctrl+O shortcut appears in the menu alongside the menu text (see Figure 10-5).

■**Note** One frill you *don't* get is an underlined access key. WPF has no way of knowing what commands you might place together in a menu, so it can't determine the best access keys to use. This means if you want to use the N key as a quick access key (so that it appears underlined when the menu is opened with the keyboard, and the user can trigger the New command by pressing N), you need to set the menu text manually, preceding the access key with an underscore. The same is true if you want to use a quick access key for a button.

Figure 10-5. *A menu item that uses a command*

Note that you don't need to create another command binding for the menu item. The single command binding you created in the previous section is now being used by two different controls, both of which hand their work off to the same command event handler.

Fine-Tuning Command Text

Based on the ability of the menu to pull out the text of the command item automatically, you might wonder whether you can do the same with other ICommandSource classes, such as the Button control. You can, but it requires a bit of extra work.

You can use two techniques to reuse the command text. One option is to pull the text right out of the static command object. XAML allows you to do this with the Static markup extension. Here's an example that gets the command name "New" and uses that as the text for a button:

```
<Button Command="New" Content="{x:Static ApplicationCommands.New}"></Button>
```

The problem with this approach is that it simply calls ToString() on the command object. As a result, you get the command name but not the command text. (For commands that have multiple words, the command text is nicer because it includes spaces.) You could correct this problem, but it's significantly more work. There's also another issue in the way that one button uses the same command twice, introducing the possibility that you'll inadvertently grab the text from the wrong command.

The preferred solution is to use a data binding expression. This data binding is a bit unusual, because it binds to the current element, grabs the Command object you're using, and pulls out the Text property. Here's the terribly long-winded syntax:

```
<Button Margin="5" Padding="5" Command="ApplicationCommands.New" Content=
  "{Binding RelativeSource={RelativeSource Self}, Path=Command.Text}"
</Button>
```

Chapter 15 covers data binding expressions in detail.

You can use this technique in other, more imaginative ways. For example, you can set the content of a button with a tiny image but use the binding expression to show the command name in a tooltip:

```
<Button Margin="5" Padding="5" Command="ApplicationCommands.New"
  ToolTip="{Binding RelativeSource={RelativeSource Self}, Path=Command.Text}">
<Image ... />
</Button>
```

The content of the button (which isn't shown here) will be a shape or bitmap that appears as a thumbnail icon.

Clearly, this approach is wordier than just putting the command text directly in your markup. However, this approach is worth considering if you are planning to localize your application in different languages. You simply need to set the command text for all your commands when your application starts. (If you change the command text after you've created a command binding, it won't have any effect. That's because the Text property isn't a dependency property, so there's no automatic change notification to update the user interface.)

Invoking a Command Directly

You aren't limited to the classes that implement ICommandSource if you want to trigger a command. You can also call a method directly from any event handler using the Execute()

method. At that point, you need to pass in the parameter value (or a null reference) and a reference to the target element:

```
ApplicationCommands.New.Execute(null, targetElement);
```

The target element is simply the element where WPF begins looking for the command binding. You can use the containing window (which has the command binding) or a nested element (such as the actual element that fired the event).

Incidentally, you can also go through the Execute() method in the associated Command-Binding object. In this case, you don't need to supply the target element, because it's automatically set to the element that exposes the CommandBindings collection that you're using.

```
this.CommandBindings[0].Command.Execute(null);
```

This approach uses only half the command model. It allows you to trigger the command, but it doesn't give you a way to respond to the command's state change. If you want this feature, you may also want to handle the RoutedCommand.CanExecuteChanged to react when the command becomes disabled or enabled. When the CanExecuteChanged event fires, you need to call the RoutedCommand.CanExecute() method to check whether the commands are in a usable state. If not, you can disable or change the content in a portion of your user interface.

COMMAND SUPPORT IN CUSTOM CONTROLS

WPF includes a number of controls that implement ICommandSupport and have the ability to raise commands. (It also includes some controls that have the ability to *handle* commands, as you'll see shortly in the section "Controls with Built-in Commands.") Despite this support, you may come across a control that you'd like to use with the command model, even though it doesn't implement ICommandSource. In this situation, the easiest option is to handle one of the control's events and execute the appropriate command using code. However, another option is to build a new control of your own—one that has the command-executing logic built in.

The downloadable code for this chapter includes an example that uses this technique to create a slider that triggers a command when its value changes. This control derives from the Slider class you learned about in Chapter 8; implements ICommand; defines the Command, CommandTarget, and CommandParameter dependency properties; and monitors the RoutedCommand.CanExecuteChanged event internally. Although the code is straightforward, this solution is a bit over the top for most scenarios. Creating a custom control is a fairly significant step in WPF, and most developers prefer to restyle existing controls with templates (Chapter 14) rather than add an entirely new class. However, if you're designing a custom control from scratch and you want it to provide command support, this example is worth exploring.

Disabling Commands

You'll see the real benefits of the command model when you create a command that varies between an enabled and disabled state. For example, consider the one-window application shown in Figure 10-6, which is a basic text editor that consists of a menu, a toolbar, and a large textbox. It allows you to open files, create new (blank) documents, and save your work.

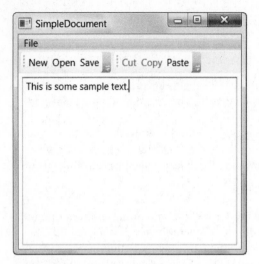

Figure 10-6. *A simple text editor*

In this case, it's perfectly reasonable to make the New, Open, Save, SaveAs, and Close commands perpetually available. But a different design might enable the Save command only if the text has been changed in some way from the original file. By convention, you can track this detail in your code using a simple Boolean value:

```
private bool isDirty = false;
```

You would then set this flag whenever the text is changed:

```
private void txt_TextChanged(object sender, RoutedEventArgs e)
{
    isDirty = true;
}
```

What you need now is a way for the information to make its way from your window to the command binding so that the linked controls can be updated as needed. The trick is to handle the CanExecute event of the command binding. You can attach an event handler to this event through code:

```
CommandBinding binding = new CommandBinding(ApplicationCommands.Save);
binding.Executed += SaveCommand_Executed;
binding.CanExecute += SaveCommand_CanExecute;
this.CommandBindings.Add(binding);
```

or declaratively:

```
<Window.CommandBindings>
  <CommandBinding Command="ApplicationCommands.Save"
    Executed="SaveCommand_Executed" CanExecute="SaveCommand_CanExecute">
  </CommandBinding>
</Window.CommandBindings>
```

In your event handler, you simply need to check the isDirty variable and set the CanExecuteRoutedEventArg.CanExecute property accordingly:

```
private void SaveCommand_CanExecute(object sender, CanExecuteRoutedEventArgs e)
{
    e.CanExecute = isDirty;
}
```

If isDirty is false, the command is disabled. If it's true, the command is enabled. (If you don't set the CanExecute flag, it keeps its most recent value.)

There's one issue to be aware of when using CanExecute. It's up to WPF to call the Routed-Command.CanExecute() method to trigger your event handler and determine the status of your command. The WPF command manager does this when it detects a change it believes is significant—for example, when the focus moves from one control to another, or after you execute a command. Controls can also raise the CanExecuteChanged event to tell WPF to reevaluate a command—for example, this occurs when you press a key in the text box. All in all, the CanExecute event will fire quite frequently, and you shouldn't use time-consuming code inside it.

However, other factors might affect the command state. In the current example, the isDirty flag could be modified in response to another action. If you notice that the command state is not being updated at the correct time, you can force WPF to call CanExecute() on all the commands you're using. You do this by calling the static CommandManager.InvalidateRequerySuggested() method. The command manager then fires the RequerySuggested event to notify the command sources in your window (buttons, menu items, and so on). The command sources will then requery their linked commands and update themselves accordingly.

THE LIMITS OF WPF COMMANDS

Unfortunately, WPF commands are able to change only one aspect of the linked element's state—the value of its IsEnabled property. It's not hard to imagine situations where you need something a bit more sophisticated. For example, you might want to create a PageLayoutView command that can be switched on or off. When switched on, the corresponding controls should be adjusted accordingly. (For example, a linked menu item should be checked, and a linked toolbar button should be highlighted, as a CheckBox is when you add it to a ToolBar.) Unfortunately, there's no way to keep track of the "checked" state of a command. That means you're forced to handle an event for that control and update its state and that of any other linked controls by hand.

There's no easy way to solve this problem. Even if you created a custom class that derives from RoutedUICommand and gave it the functionality for tracking its checked/unchecked state (and raising an event when this detail changes), you'd also need to replace some of the related infrastructure. For example, you'd need to create a custom CommandBinding class that could listen to notifications from your custom command, react when the checked/unchecked state changes, and then update the linked controls.

Checked buttons are an obvious example of user-interface state that falls outside the WPF command model. However, other details might suit a similar design. For example, you might create some sort of a split button that can be switched to different "modes." Once again, there's no way to propagate this change to other linked controls through the command model.

Controls with Built-in Commands

Some input controls handle command events on their own. For example, the TextBox class handles the Cut, Copy, and Paste commands (as well as Undo and Redo commands and some of the commands from the EditingCommands class that select text and move the cursor to different positions).

When a control has its own hardwired command logic, you don't need to do anything to make your command work. For example, if you took the simple text editor shown in Figure 10-6 and added the following toolbar buttons, you would get automatic support for cutting, copying, and pasting text.

```
<ToolBar>
  <Button Command="Cut">Cut</Button>
  <Button Command="Copy">Copy</Button>
  <Button Command="Paste">Paste</Button>
</ToolBar>
```

Now, you can click any of these buttons (while the text box has focus) to copy, cut, or paste text from the clipboard. Interestingly, the text box also handles the CanExecute event. If nothing is currently selected in the text box, the Cut and Copy commands will be disabled. All three commands will be automatically disabled when the focus changes to another control that doesn't support these commands (unless you've attached your own CanExecute event handler that enables them).

This example has an interesting detail. The Cut, Copy, and Paste commands are handled by the text box that has focus. However, the command is triggered by the button in the toolbar, which is a completely separate element. In this example, this process works seamlessly because the button is placed in a toolbar, and the ToolBar class includes some built-in magic that dynamically sets the CommandTarget property of its children to the control that currently has focus. (Technically, the ToolBar looks at the parent, which is the window, and finds the most recently focused control in that context, which is the text box. The ToolBar has a separate *focus scope*, and in that context the button is focused.)

If you place your buttons in a different container (other than a ToolBar or Menu), you won't have this benefit. That means your buttons won't work unless you set the CommandTarget property manually. To do so, you must use a binding expression that names the target element. For example, if the text box is named txtDocument, you would define the buttons like this:

```
<Button Command="Cut"
 CommandTarget="{Binding ElementName=txtDocument}">Cut</Button>
<Button Command="Copy"
 CommandTarget="{Binding ElementName=txtDocument}">Copy</Button>
<Button Command="Paste"
 CommandTarget="{Binding ElementName=txtDocument}">Paste</Button>
```

Another, simpler option is to create a new focus scope using the attached FocusManager.IsFocusScope property. This tells WPF to look for the element in the parent's focus scope when the command is triggered:

```
<StackPanel FocusManager.IsFocusScope="True">
  <Button Command="Cut">Cut</Button>
```

```
    <Button Command="Copy">Copy</Button>
    <Button Command="Paste">Paste</Button>
</StackPanel>
```

This approach has the added advantage that the same commands will apply to multiple controls, unlike the previous example where the CommandTarget was hard-coded. Incidentally, the Menu and ToolBar set the FocusManager.IsFocusScope property to true by default, but you can set it to false if you want the simpler command routing behavior that doesn't hunt down the focused element in the parent's context.

In some rare cases, you might find that a control has built-in command support you don't want to enable. In this situation, you have three options for disabling the command.

Ideally, the control will provide a property that allows you to gracefully switch off the command support. This ensures that the control will remove the feature and adjust itself consistently. For example, the TextBox control provides an IsUndoEnabled property that you can set to false to prevent the Undo feature. (If IsUndoEnabled is true, the Ctrl+Z keystroke triggers it.)

If that fails, you can add a new binding for the command you want to disable. This binding can then supply a new CanExecute event handler that always responds false. Here's an example that uses this technique to remove support for the Cut feature of the text box:

```
CommandBinding commandBinding = new CommandBinding(
    ApplicationCommands.Cut, null, SuppressCommand);
txt.CommandBindings.Add(commandBinding);
```

and here's the event handler that sets the CanExecute state:

```
private void SuppressCommand(object sender, CanExecuteRoutedEventArgs e)
{
    e.CanExecute = false;
    e.Handled = true;
}
```

Notice that this code sets the Handled flag to prevent the text box from performing its own evaluation, which might set CanExecute to true.

This approach isn't perfect. It successfully disables both the Cut keystroke (Ctrl+X) and the Cut command in the context menu for the text box. However, the option will still appear in the context menu in a disabled state.

The final option is to remove the input that triggers the command using the InputBindings collections. For example, you could disable the Ctrl+C keystroke that triggers the Copy command in a TextBox using code like this:

```
KeyBinding keyBinding = new KeyBinding(
    ApplicationCommands.NotACommand, Key.C, ModifierKeys.Control);
txt.InputBindings.Add(keyBinding);
```

The trick is to use the special ApplicationCommands.NotACommand value, which is a command that does nothing. It's specifically intended for disabling input bindings.

When you use this approach, the Copy command is still enabled. You can trigger it through buttons of your own creation (or the context menu for the text box, unless you remove that too by setting the ContextMenu property to null).

■Note You always need to add new command bindings or input bindings to disable features. You can't remove existing bindings. That's because existing bindings don't show up in the public CommandBinding and InputBinding collection. Instead, they're defined through a separate mechanism, called *class bindings*. In Chapter 24 you'll learn how to wire up commands in this way to the custom controls you build.

Advanced Commands

Now that you've seen the basics of commands, it's worth considering a few more sophisticated implementations. In the following sections, you'll learn how to use your own commands, treat the same command differently depending on the target, and use command parameters. You'll also consider how you can support a basic undo feature.

Custom Commands

As well stocked as the five command classes (ApplicationCommands, NavigationCommands, EditingCommands, ComponentCommands, and MediaCommands) are, they obviously can't provide everything your application might need. Fortunately, it's easy to define your own custom commands. All you need to do is instantiate a new RoutedUICommand object.

The RoutedUICommand class provides several constructors. You can create a RoutedUICommand with no additional information, but you'll almost always want to supply the command name, the command text, and the owning type. In addition, you may want to supply a keyboard shortcut for the InputGestures collection.

The best design is to follow the example of the WPF libraries and expose your custom commands through static properties. Here's an example with a command named Requery:

```
public class DataCommands
{
    private static RoutedUICommand requery;

    static DataCommands()
    {
        // Initialize the command.
        InputGestureCollection inputs = new InputGestureCollection();
        inputs.Add(new KeyGesture(Key.R, ModifierKeys.Control, "Ctrl+R"));
        requery = new RoutedUICommand(
           "Requery", "Requery", typeof(DataCommands), inputs);
    }

    public static RoutedUICommand Requery
    {
        get { return requery; }
    }
}
```

■**Tip** You can also modify the RoutedCommand.InputGestures collection of an existing command—for example, by removing existing key bindings or adding new ones. You can even add mouse bindings, so a command is triggered when a combination of a mouse button and modifier key is pressed (although in this case you'll want to place the command binding on just the element where the mouse handling should come into effect).

Once you've defined a command, you can use it in your command bindings just like any of the ready-made commands that are provided by WPF. However, there's one twist. If you want to use your command in XAML, you need to first map your .NET namespace to an XML namespace. For example, if your class is in a namespace named Commands (the default for a project named Commands), you would add this namespace mapping:

```
xmlns:local="clr-namespace:Commands"
```

In this example, local is chosen as the namespace alias. You can use any alias you want, as long as you are consistent in your XAML file.

Now you can access your command through the local namespace:

```
<CommandBinding Command="local:DataCommands.Requery"
  Executed="RequeryCommand_Executed"></CommandBinding>
```

Here's a complete example of a simple window that includes a button that triggers the Requery command:

```
<Window x:Class="Commands.CustomCommand"
    xmlns="http://schemas.microsoft.com/winfx/2006/xaml/presentation"
    xmlns:x="http://schemas.microsoft.com/winfx/2006/xaml"
    Title="CustomCommand" Height="300" Width="300">

  <Window.CommandBindings>
    <CommandBinding Command="local:DataCommands.Requery"
     Executed="RequeryCommand_Executed"></CommandBinding>
  </Window.CommandBindings>

  <Button Margin="5" Command="local:DataCommands.Requery">Requery</Button>
</Window>
```

To complete this example, you simply need to implement the RequeryCommand_ Executed() event handler in your code. Optionally, you can also use the CanExecute event to selectively enable or disable this command.

■**Tip** When using custom commands, you may need to call the static CommandManager.InvalidateRequery-Suggested() method to tell WPF to reevaluate the state of your command. WPF will then trigger the CanExecute event and update any command sources that use that command.

Using the Same Command in Different Places

One of the key ideas in the WPF command model is *scope*. Although there is exactly one copy of every command, the effect of using the command varies depending on where it's triggered. For example, if you have two text boxes, they both support the Cut, Copy, and Paste commands, but the operation happens only in the text box that currently has focus.

You haven't yet learned how to do this with the commands that you wire up yourself. For example, imagine you create a window with space for two documents, as shown in Figure 10-7.

Figure 10-7. *A two-file-at-once text editor*

If you use the Cut, Copy, and Paste commands, you'll find they automatically work on the right text box. However, the commands you've implemented yourself—New, Open, and Save—do not. The problem is that when the Executed event fires for one of these commands, you have no idea whether it pertains to the first or second text box. Although the ExecutedRouted-EventArgs object provides a Source property, this property reflects the element that has the command binding (just like the sender reference). So far, all your command bindings have been attached to the containing window.

The solution to this problem is to bind the command differently in each text box using the CommandBindings collection for the text box. Here's an example:

```
<TextBox.CommandBindings>
  <CommandBinding Command="ApplicationCommands.Save"
    Executed="SaveCommand_Executed"
    CanExecute="SaveCommand_CanExecute"></CommandBinding>
</TextBox.CommandBindings>
```

Now the text box handles the Executed event. In your event handler, you can use this information to make sure the right information is saved:

```
private void SaveCommand_Executed(object sender, ExecutedRoutedEventArgs e)
{
    string text = ((TextBox)sender).Text;
```

```
    MessageBox.Show("About to save: " + text);
    ...
    isDirty = false;
}
```

This implementation has two minor issues. First, the simple isDirty flag no longer works, because you have to keep track of two text boxes. This problem has several solutions. You could use the TextBox.Tag property to store the isDirty flag—that way whenever the CanExecuteSave() method is called, you simply look at the Tag property of the sender. Or, you could create a private dictionary collection that stores the isDirty value, indexed by the control reference. When the CanExecuteSave() method is triggered, you simply look for the isDirty value that belongs to the sender. Here's the full code you'd use:

```
private Dictionary<Object, bool> isDirty = new Dictionary<Object, bool>();

private void txt_TextChanged(object sender, RoutedEventArgs e)
{
    isDirty[sender] = true;
}

private void SaveCommand_CanExecute(object sender, CanExecuteRoutedEventArgs e)
{
    if (isDirty.ContainsKey(sender) && isDirty[sender])
    {
        e.CanExecute = true;
    }
    else
    {
        e.CanExecute = false;
    }
}
```

The other issue with the current implementation is that it creates two command bindings where you really need only one. This adds clutter to your XAML file and makes it more difficult to maintain. This problem is especially bad if you have a large number of commands that are shared between both text boxes.

The solution is to create a single command binding and add that same binding to the CommandBindings collection of both text boxes. This is easy to accomplish in code. If you want to polish it off in XAML, you need to use another feature you haven't considered yet— WPF resources. Although you won't get the full story about WPF resources until Chapter 11, the basics are easy enough. You simply add a section to the top of your window that creates the object you need to use and gives it a key name:

```
<Window.Resources>
  <CommandBinding x:Key="binding" Command="ApplicationCommands.Save"
    Executed="SaveCommand" CanExecute="CanExecuteSave">
  </CommandBinding>
</Window.Resources>
```

The object is then stored in a dictionary collection so you can access it elsewhere. To insert the object into another place in your markup, you use the StaticResource extension and supply the key name:

```
<TextBox.CommandBindings>
  <StaticResource ResourceKey="binding"></StaticResource>
</TextBox.CommandBindings>
```

Using a Command Parameter

So far, the examples you've seen haven't used the command parameter to pass extra information. However, some commands always require some extra information. For example, the NavigationCommands.Zoom command needs a percentage value to use for its zoom. Similarly, you can imagine that some of the commands you're already using might require extra information in certain scenarios. For example, if you use the Save command with the two-file text editor in Figure 10-7, you need to know what file to use when saving the document.

The solution is to set the CommandParameter property. You can set this directly on an ICommandSource control (and you can even use a binding expression that gets a value from another control). For example, here's how you might set the zoom percentage for a button that's linked to the Zoom command by reading the value from another text box:

```
<Button Command="NavigationCommands.Zoom"
  CommandParameter="{Binding ElementName=txtZoom, Path=Text}">
  Zoom To Value
</Button>
```

Unfortunately, that approach doesn't always work. For example, in the two-file text editor, the Save button is reused for each text box, but each text box needs to use a different file name. In situations like these, you're forced to store the information somewhere else (for example, in the TextBox.Tag property or in a separate collection that indexes file names to line up with your text boxes), or you need to trigger the command programmatically like this:

```
ApplicationCommands.New.Execute(theFileName, (Button)sender);
```

Either way, the parameter is made available in the Executed event handler through the ExecutedRoutedEventArgs.Parameter property.

Tracking and Reversing Commands

One feature that the Command model lacks is the ability to make a command reversible. Although there is an ApplicationCommands.Undo command, this command is generally used by edit controls (such as the TextBox) that maintain their own Undo histories. If you want to support an application-wide Undo feature, you need to track the previous state internally and restore it when the Undo command is triggered.

Unfortunately, it's not easy to extend the WPF command system. Relatively few entry points are available for you to connect custom logic, and those that exist are not documented. To create a general-purpose, reusable Undo feature, you'd need to create a whole new set of "undoable" command classes and a specialized type of command binding—in essence, you'd be forced to replace the WPF command system with a new one of your own creation.

A better solution is to design your own system for tracking and reversing commands but to use the CommandManager class to keep a command history. Figure 10-8 shows an example that does exactly that. The window consists of two text boxes, where you can type freely, and a list box that keeps track of every command that's taken place in both text boxes. You can reverse the last command by clicking the Reverse Last Action button.

Figure 10-8. *An application-wide Undo feature*

To build this solution, you need a few new techniques. The first detail is a class for tracking the command history. It might occur to you to build an undo system that stores a list of recent commands. (Perhaps you'd even like to create a derived ReversibleCommand class that exposes a method such as Unexecute() for reversing the task it did previously.) Unfortunately, this system won't work because all WPF commands are treated like singletons. That means there is only one instance of each command in your application.

To understand the problem, imagine you support the EditingCommands.Backspace command, and the user performs several backspaces in a row. You can register that fact by adding the Backspace command to a stack of recent commands, but you're actually adding the same command object several times. As a result, there's no easy way to store other information along with that command, such as the character that's just been deleted. If you want to store this state, you'll need to build your own data structure to do it. This example uses a class named CommandHistoryItem.

Every CommandHistoryItem object tracks several pieces of information:

- The command name.

- The element on which the command was performed. In this example, there are two text boxes, so it could be either one.

- The property that was changed in the target element. In this example, it will be the Text property of the TextBox class.

- An object that you can use to store the previous state of the affected element (for example, the text the text box had before the command was executed).

Note This design is fairly crafty in that it stores the state for one element. If you stored a snapshot of the state in the entire window, you'd use significantly more memory. However, if you have large amounts of data (such as text boxes with dozens of lines), the Undo overhead could be more than trivial. The solution then is to limit the number of items you keep in the history or use a more intelligent (and more complex) routine that stores information about only the changed data, rather than *all* the data.

The CommandHistoryItem also includes one method, an all-purpose Undo() method. This method uses reflection to apply the previous value to the modified property. This works for restoring the text in a TextBox, but in a more complex application you'd need a hierarchy of CommandHistoryItem classes, each of which is able to revert a different type of action in a different way.

Here's the complete code for the CommandHistoryItem class, which conserves some space by using the C# language feature *automatic properties*:

```
public class CommandHistoryItem
{
    public string CommandName
    { get; set; }

    public UIElement ElementActedOn
    { get; set; }

    public string PropertyActedOn
    { get; set; }

    public object PreviousState
    { get; set; }

    public CommandHistoryItem(string commandName)
      : this(commandName, null, "", null)
    { }

    public CommandHistoryItem(string commandName, UIElement elementActedOn,
      string propertyActedOn, object previousState)
    {
        CommandName = commandName;
        ElementActedOn = elementActedOn;
        PropertyActedOn = propertyActedOn;
        PreviousState = previousState;
    }

    public bool CanUndo
    {
```

```
        get { return (ElementActedOn != null && PropertyActedOn != ""); }    }

    public void Undo()
    {
        Type elementType = ElementActedOn.GetType();
        PropertyInfo property = elementType.GetProperty(PropertyActedOn);
        property.SetValue(ElementActedOn, PreviousState, null);
    }
}
```

The next ingredient you need is a command that performs the application-wide Undo action. The ApplicationCommands.Undo command isn't suitable, because it's already used for individual controls for a different purpose (reverting the last editing change). Instead, you need to create a new command, as shown here:

```
private static RoutedUICommand applicationUndo;

public static RoutedUICommand ApplicationUndo
{
    get { return MonitorCommands.applicationUndo; }
}

static MonitorCommands()
{
    applicationUndo = new RoutedUICommand(
      "ApplicationUndo", "Application Undo", typeof(MonitorCommands));
}
```

In this example, the command is defined in a window class named MonitorCommands.

So far, this code is relatively unremarkable (aside from the nifty bit of reflection code that performs the undo operation). The more difficult part is integrating this command history into the WPF command model. An ideal solution would do this in such a way that you can track any command, regardless of how it's triggered and how it's bound. In a poorly designed solution, you'd be forced to rely on a whole new set of custom command objects that have this logic built in or to manually handle the Executed event of every command.

It's easy enough to react to a specific command, but how can you react when *any* command executes? The trick is to use the CommandManager, which exposes a few static events. These events include CanExecute, PreviewCanExecute, Executed, and PreviewCanExecuted. In this example, it's the last two that are most interesting, because they fire whenever any command is executed.

The Executed event is suppressed by the CommandManager, but you can still attach an event handler using the UIElement.AddHandler() method and passing in a value of true for the optional third parameter. This allows you to receive the event even though it's handled, as described in Chapter 6. However, the Executed event fires *after* the event is executed, at which point it's too late to save the state of the affected control in your command history. Instead, you need to respond to the PreviewExecuted event, which fires just before.

Here's the code that attaches the PreviewExecuted event handler in the window constructor and removes it when the window is closed:

```
public MonitorCommands()
{
    InitializeComponent();

    this.AddHandler(CommandManager.PreviewExecutedEvent,
      new ExecutedRoutedEventHandler(CommandExecuted));
}

private void window_Unloaded(object sender, RoutedEventArgs e)
{
    this.RemoveHandler(CommandManager.PreviewExecutedEvent,
      new ExecutedRoutedEventHandler(CommandExecuted));
}
```

When the PreviewExecuted event fires, you need to determine whether it's a command you want to pay attention to. If so, you can create the CommandHistoryItem and add it to the Undo stack. You also need to watch out for two potential problems. First, when you click a toolbar button to perform a command on the text box, the CommandExecuted event is raised twice—once for the toolbar button and once for the text box. This code avoids duplicate entries in the Undo history by ignoring the command if the sender is ICommandSource. Second, you need to explicitly ignore the commands you don't want to add to the Undo history. One example is the ApplicationUndo command, which allows you to reverse the previous action.

```
private void CommandExecuted(object sender, ExecutedRoutedEventArgs e)
{
    // Ignore menu button source.
    if (e.Source is ICommandSource) return;

    // Ignore the ApplicationUndo command.
    if (e.Command == MonitorCommands.ApplicationUndo) return;

    TextBox txt = e.Source as TextBox;
    if (txt != null)
    {
        RoutedCommand cmd = (RoutedCommand)e.Command;
        CommandHistoryItem historyItem = new CommandHistoryItem(
          cmd.Name, txt, "Text", txt.Text);

        ListBoxItem item = new ListBoxItem();
        item.Content = historyItem;
        lstHistory.Items.Add(historyItem);
    }
}
```

This example stores all CommandHistoryItem objects in a ListBox. The ListBox has DisplayMember set to Name so that it shows the CommandHistoryItem.Name property of each item. This code supports the Undo feature only if the command is being fired for a text box. However, it's generic enough to work with any text box on the window. You could extend this code to support other controls and properties.

The last detail is the code that performs the application-wide Undo. Using a CanExecute handler, you can make sure that this code is executed only when there is at least one item in the Undo history:

```
private void ApplicationUndoCommand_CanExecute(object sender,
  CanExecuteRoutedEventArgs e)
{
    if (lstHistory == null || lstHistory.Items.Count == 0)
      e.CanExecute = false;
    else
      e.CanExecute = true;
}
```

To revert the last change, you simply call the Undo() method of the CommandHistoryItem and then remove it from the list:

```
private void ApplicationUndoCommand_Executed(object sender, RoutedEventArgs e)
{
    CommandHistoryItem historyItem = (CommandHistoryItem)
      lstHistory.Items[lstHistory.Items.Count - 1];

    if (historyItem.CanUndo) historyItem.Undo();
    lstHistory.Items.Remove(historyItem);
}
```

Although this example demonstrates the concept and presents a simple application with multiple controls that fully support the Undo feature, you'd need to make many refinements before you would use an approach like this in a real-world application. For example, you'd need to spend considerable time refining the event handler for the Command-Manager.PreviewExecuted event to ignore commands that clearly shouldn't be tracked. (Currently, events such as selecting text with the keyboard and hitting the spacebar raise commands.) Similarly, you'd probably want to add CommandHistoryItem objects for action that should be reversible but aren't represented by commands, such as typing a bunch of text and then navigating to another control. Finally, you'd probably want to limit the Undo history to just the most recent commands.

The Last Word

In this chapter, you explored the WPF command model. You learned how to hook controls to commands, respond when the commands are triggered, and handle commands differently based on where they occur. You also designed your own custom commands and learned how to extend the WPF command system with a basic command history and Undo feature.

Overall, the WPF command model isn't quite as streamlined as other bits of WPF architecture. The way that it plugs into the routed event model requires a fairly complex assortment of classes, and the inner workings aren't extensible. However, the command model is still a great stride forward over Windows Forms, which lacked any sort of command feature.

CHAPTER 11

■ ■ ■

Resources

In WPF applications, there are two very different ingredients that are both described as resources:

- An *assembly resource* is a chunk of binary data that's embedded in your compiled assembly. You can use an assembly resource to make sure your application has an image or sound file it needs.

- An *object resource* is a .NET object that you want to define in one place and use in several others. Although an object resource can be created in code, it's usually defined in XAML markup. This type of resource saves repetitive coding and allows you to store information (such as your application's color scheme) in a central place so it can be modified easily. Object resources are also the basis for reusing WPF styles.

In this chapter, you'll take a look at assembly resources and the pack URI syntax they use. You'll also learn about the emerging support for localization in WPF. Then you'll examine the object resource model and see how it can simplify your XAML markup.

Assembly Resources

Assembly resources in a WPF application work in essentially the same way as assembly resources in other .NET applications. The key difference is the addressing system that you use to refer to them.

Note Assembly resources are also known as *binary resources* because they're embedded in compiled assembly (the EXE or DLL file for your project) as an opaque blob of binary data.

You've already seen binary resources at work in Chapter 2. That's because every time you compile your application, each XAML file in your project is converted to a BAML file that's more efficient to parse. These BAML files are embedded in your assembly as individual resources. It's just as easy to add your own resources.

Adding Resources

You can add your own resources by adding a file to your project and setting its Build Action property (in the Properties window) to Resource. Here's the good news—that's all you need to do.

For better organization, you can create subfolders in your project (right-click the Solution Explorer and choose Add ➤ New Folder) and use these to organize different types of resources. Figure 11-1 shows an example where several image resources are grouped in a folder named Images, and two audio fields appear in a folder named Sounds.

Figure 11-1. *An application with assembly resources*

Resources that you add in this way are easy to update. All you need to do is replace the file and recompile your application. For example, if you create the project shown in Figure 11-1, you could copy all new files to the Images folder using Windows Explorer. As long as you're replacing the contents of files that are included in your project, you don't need to take any special step in Visual Studio (aside from actually compiling your application).

There are a couple of things that you must *not* do in order to use assembly resources successfully:

- Don't make the mistake of setting the Build Action property to Embedded Resource. Even though all assembly resources are embedded resources by definition, the Embedded Resource build action places the binary data in another area where it's more difficult to access. In WPF applications, it's assumed that you always use a build type of Resource.

- Don't use the Resources tab in the Project Properties window. WPF does not support this type of resource URI.

Curious programmers naturally want to know what happens to the resources they embed in their assemblies. WPF merges them all into a single stream (along with BAML resources). This single resource stream is named in this format: AssemblyName.g.resources. In Figure 11-1, the application is named AssemblyResources and the resource stream is named AssemblyResources.g.resources.

If you want to actually *see* the embedded resources in a compiled assembly, you can use a disassembler. Unfortunately, the .NET staple—ildasm—doesn't have this feature. However, you can download the free and much more elegant Reflector tool at `http://www.aisto.com/roeder/DotNet`, which does let you dig into your resources. Figure 11-2 shows the resources for the project shown in Figure 11-1, using Reflector.

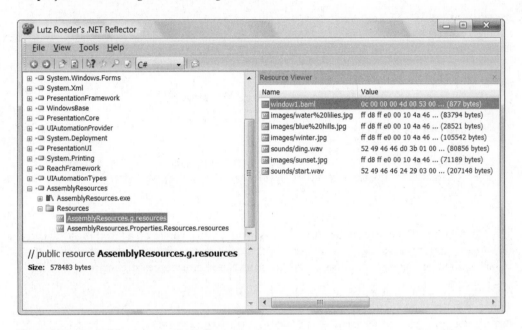

Figure 11-2. *Assembly resources in Reflector*

You'll see the BAML resource for the only window in the application, along with all the images and audio files. The spaces in the file names don't cause a problem in WPF because Visual Studio is intelligent enough to escape them properly. You'll also notice that the file names are changed to lowercase when your application is compiled.

Retrieving Resources

Adding resources is clearly easy enough, but how do you actually *use* them? There's more than one approach that you can use. The low-level choice is to retrieve a StreamResourceInfo object that wraps your data, and then decide what to do with it. You can do this through code, using the static Application.GetResourceStream() method.

For example, here's the code that gets the StreamResourceInfo object for the winter.jpg image:

```
StreamResourceInfo sri = Application.GetResourceStream(
  new Uri("images/winter.jpg", UriKind.Relative));
```

Once you have a StreamResourceInfo object, you can get two pieces of information. The ContentType property returns a string describing the type of data—in this example, it's image/jpg. The Stream property returns an UnmanagedMemoryStream object that you can use to read the data, one byte at a time.

The GetResourceStream() method is really just a helper method that wraps a ResourceManager and ResourceSet classes. These classes are a core part of the .NET Framework resource system, and they've existed since version 1.0. Without the GetResourceStream() method, you'd need to specifically access the AssemblyName.g.resources resource stream (which is where all WPF resources are stored) and search for the object you want. Here's the far uglier code that does the trick:

```
Assembly assembly = Assembly.GetAssembly(this.GetType());
string resourceName = assembly.GetName().Name + ".g";
ResourceManager rm = new ResourceManager(resourceName, assembly);

using (ResourceSet set =
  rm.GetResourceSet(CultureInfo.CurrentCulture, true, true))
{
    UnmanagedMemoryStream s;

    // The second parameter (true) performs a case-insensitive resource lookup.
    s = (UnmanagedMemoryStream)set.GetObject("images/winter.jpg", true);
    ...
}
```

The ResourceManager and ResourceSet classes also allow you to do a few things you can't do with the Application class alone. For example, the following snippet of code shows you the name of all the embedded resources in the AssemblyName.g.resources stream:

```
Assembly assembly = Assembly.GetAssembly(this.GetType());
string resourceName = assembly.GetName().Name + ".g";
ResourceManager rm = new ResourceManager(resourceName, assembly);

using (ResourceSet set =
  rm.GetResourceSet(CultureInfo.CurrentCulture, true, true))
{
    foreach (DictionaryEntry res in set)
    {
        MessageBox.Show(res.Key.ToString());
    }
}
```

Resource-Aware Classes

Even with the help of the GetResourceStream() method, you're unlikely to bother retrieving a resource directly. The problem is that this approach gets you a relatively low-level UnmanagedMemoryStream object, which isn't much use on its own. Instead, you'll want to translate the data into something more meaningful, such as a higher-level object with properties and methods.

WPF provides a few classes that work with resources natively. Rather than forcing you to do the work of resource extraction (which is messy and not typesafe), they take the name of the resource you want to use. For example, if you want to show the Blue hills.jpg image in the WPF Image element, you could use this markup:

```
<Image Source="Images/Blue hills.jpg"></Image>
```

Notice that the backslash becomes a forward slash because that's the convention WPF uses with its URIs. (It actually works *both* ways, but the forward slash is recommended for consistency.)

You can perform the same trick in code. In the case of an Image element, you simply need to set the Source property with a BitmapImage object that identifies the location of the image you want to display as a URI. You could specify a fully qualified file path like this:

```
img.Source = new BitmapImage(new Uri(@"d:\Photo\Backgrounds\arch.jpg"));
```

But if you use a relative URI, you can pull a different resource out of the assembly and pass it to the image, with no UnmanagedMemoryStream object required:

```
img.Source = new BitmapImage(new Uri("images/winter.jpg", UriKind.Relative));
```

This technique constructs a URI that consists of the base application URI with images/winter.jpg added on the end. Most of the time, you don't need to think about this URI syntax—as long as you stick to relative URIs, it all works seamlessly. However, in some cases it's important to understand the URI system in a bit more detail, particularly if you want to access a resource that's embedded in another assembly. The following section digs into WPF's URI syntax.

Pack URIs

As you learned in Chapter 9 when you were dealing with pages, WPF lets you address compiled resources (such as the BAML for a page) using the *pack URI* syntax. The Image and tag in the previous section referenced a resource using a relative URI, like this:

```
images/winter.jpg
```

This is equivalent to the more cumbersome absolute URI shown here:

```
pack://application:,,,/images/winter.jpg
```

You can use this absolute URI when setting the source of an image, although it doesn't provide any advantage:

```
img.Source = new BitmapImage(new Uri("pack://application:,,,/images/winter.jpg"));
```

Tip When using an absolute URI, you can use a file path, a UNC path to a network share, a website URL, or a pack URI that points to an assembly resource. Just be aware that if your application can't retrieve the resource from the expected location, an exception will occur. If you've set the URI in XAML, the exception will happen when the page is being created.

The pack URI syntax is borrowed from the XPS (XML Paper Specification) standard. The reason it looks so strange is because it embeds one URI inside another. The three commas are actually three escaped slashes. In other words, the pack URI shown previously contains an application URI that starts with `application:///`.

Resources in Other Assemblies

Pack URIs also allow you to retrieve resources that are embedded in another library (in other words, in a DLL assembly that your application uses). In this case, you need to use the following syntax:

```
pack://application:,,,/AssemblyName;component/ResourceName
```

For example, if your image is embedded in a referenced assembly named ImageLibrary, you'd use a URI like this:

```
img.Source = new BitmapImage(
  new Uri("pack://application:,,,/ImageLibrary;component/images/winter.jpg"));
```

Or, more practically, you'd use the equivalent relative URI:

```
img.Source = new BitmapImage(
  new Uri("ImageLibrary;component/images/winter.jpg", UriKind.Relative));
```

If you're using a strong-named assembly, you can replace the assembly name with a qualified assembly reference that includes the version, the public key token, or both. You separate each piece of information using a semicolon and precede the version number with the letter *v*. Here's an example with just a version number:

```
img.Source = new BitmapImage(
  new Uri("ImageLibrary;v1.25;component/images/winter.jpg",
  UriKind.Relative));
```

And here's an example with both the version number and the public key token:

```
img.Source = new BitmapImage(
  new Uri("ImageLibrary;v1.25;dc642a7f5bd64912;component/images/winter.jpg",
  UriKind.Relative));
```

Content Files

When you embed a file as a resource, you place it into the compiled assembly and ensure it's always available. This is an ideal choice for deployment, and it side-steps possible problems. However, there are some situations where it isn't practical:

- You want to change the resource file without recompiling the application.

- The resource file is very large.

- The resource file is optional and may not be deployed with the assembly.

- The resource is a sound file.

■**Note** As you'll discover in Chapter 22, the WPF sound classes don't support assembly resources. As a result, there's no way to pull an audio file out of a resource stream and play it—at least not without saving it first. This is a limitation of the underlying bits of technology on which these classes are based (namely, the Win32 API and Media Player).

Obviously, you can deal with this issue by deploying the files with your application and adding code to your application to read these files from the hard drive. However, WPF has a convenient option that can make this process easier to manage. You can specifically mark these noncompiled files as *content* files.

Content files won't be embedded in your assembly. However, WPF adds an Assembly-AssociatedContentFile attribute to your assembly that advertises the existence of each content file. This attribute also records the location of each content file relative to your executable file (indicating whether the content file is in the same folder as the executable file or in a subfolder). Best of all, you can use the same URI system to use content files with resource-aware elements such as the Image class.

To try this out, add a sound file to your project, select it in the Solution Explorer, and change the Build Action in the Properties window to Content. Make sure that the Copy to Output Directory setting is set to Copy Always to make sure the sound file is copied to the output directory when you build your project.

Now you can use a relative URI to point a MediaElement to your content file:

```
<MediaElement Name="Sound" Source="Sounds/start.wav"
  LoadedBehavior="Manual"></MediaElement>
```

To see an application that uses both application resources and content files, check out the downloadable code for this chapter.

Localization

Assembly resources also come in handy when you need to localize a window. Using resources, you allow controls to change according to the current culture settings of the Windows operating system. This is particularly useful with text labels and images that need to be translated into different languages.

In some frameworks, localization is performed by providing multiple copies of user-interface details such as string tables and images. In WPF, localization isn't this fine-grained. Instead, the unit of localization is the XAML file (technically, the compiled BAML resource that's embedded in your application). If you want to support three different languages, you need to include three BAML resources. WPF chooses the right one based on the current culture on the computer that's executing the application. (Technically, WPF bases its decision on the CurrentUICulture property of the thread that's hosting the user interface.)

Of course, this process wouldn't make much sense if you need to create (and deploy) an all-in-one assembly with *all* the localized resources. This wouldn't be much better than creating separate versions of your application for every language because you'd need to rebuild your entire application every time you want to add support for a new culture (or if you need to tweak the text in one of the existing resources). Fortunately, .NET solves this problem using *satellite assemblies*—assemblies that work with your application but are stored in separate subfolders. When you create a localized WPF application, you place each localized BAML resource in a separate satellite assembly. To allow your application to use this assembly, you place it in a subfolder under the main application folder, such as fr-FR for French (France). Your application can then bind to this satellite assembly automatically using a technique called *probing*, which has been a part of the .NET Framework since version 1.0.

The challenge in localizing an application is in the workflow—in other words, how do you pull your XAML files out of your project, get them localized, compile them into satellite assemblies, and then bring them back to your application? This is the shakiest part of the localization story in WPF because there aren't yet any tools (including Visual Studio) that have design support for localization. It's likely that better tools will emerge in the future, but WPF still gives you everything you need to localize your application with a bit more work.

Building Localizable User Interfaces

Before you begin to translate anything, you need to consider how your application will respond to changing content. For example, if you double the length of all the text in your user interface, how will the overall layout of your window be adjusted? If you've built a truly adaptable layout (as described in Chapter 4), you shouldn't have a problem. Your interface should be able to adjust itself to fit dynamic content. Some good practices that suggest you're on the right track include the following:

- Not using hard-coded widths or heights (or at least not using them with elements that contain nonscrollable text content).

- Setting the Window.SizeToContent property to Width, Height, or WidthAndHeight so it can grow as needed. (Again, this isn't always required, depending on the structure of your window, but it's sometimes useful.)

- Using the ScrollViewer to wrap large amounts of text.

OTHER CONSIDERATIONS FOR LOCALIZATION

Depending on the languages in which you want to localize your application, there are other considerations that you might need to take into account. Although a discussion of user interface layout in different languages is beyond the scope of this book, here are some issues to consider:

- If you want to localize your application into a language that has a dramatically different character set, you'll need to use a different font. You can do this by localizing the FontFamily property in your user interface, or you can use a composite font such as Global User Interface, Global Sans Serif, or Global Serif, which support all languages.

- You may also need to think about how your layout works in a right-to-left layout (rather than the standard English left-to-right layout). For example, Arabic and Hebrew use a right-to-left layout. You can control this behavior by setting the FlowDirection property on each page or window in your application. For more information about right-to-left layouts, see the "Bidirectional Features" topic in the Visual Studio help.

Preparing an Application for Localization

The next step is to switch on localization support for your project. This takes just one change—you need to add the following element to the .csproj file for your project anywhere in the first <PropertyGroup> element:

```
<UICulture>en-US</UICulture>
```

This tells the compiler that the default culture for your application is U.S. English (obviously, you could choose something else if that's appropriate). Once you make this change, the build process changes. The next time you compile your application, you'll end up with a subfolder named en-US. Inside that folder is a satellite assembly with the same name as your application and the extension .resources.dll (for example, LocalizableApplication.resources.dll). This assembly contains all the compiled BAML resources for your application, which were previously stored in your main application assembly.

UNDERSTANDING CULTURES

Technically, you don't localize an application for a specific language but for a *culture*, which takes into account regional variation. Cultures are identified by two identifiers separated by a hyphen. The first portion identifies the language. The second portion identifies the country. Thus, fr-CA is French as spoken in Canada, while fr-FR represents French in France. For a full list of culture names and their two-part identifiers, refer to the System.Globalization.CultureInfo class in the Visual Studio help.

This presumes a fine-grained localization that might be more than you need. Fortunately, you can localize an application based just on a language. For example, if you want to define settings that will be used for any French-language region, you could use fr for your culture. This works as long as there isn't a more specific culture available that matches the current computer exactly.

Now, when you run this application, the common language runtime (CLR) automatically looks for satellite assemblies in the right directory based on the computer's regional settings and loads the correct localized resource. For example, if you're running in the fr-FR culture, the CLR will look for an fr-FR subdirectory and use the satellite assemblies it finds there. That means that if you want to add support for more cultures to a localized application, you simply need to add more subfolders and satellite assemblies without disturbing the original application executable.

When the CLR begins probing for a satellite assembly, it follows a few simple rules of precedence:

1. First, it checks for the most specific directory that's available. That means it looks for a satellite assembly that's targeted for the current language and region (such as fr-FR).

2. If it can't find this directory, it looks for a satellite assembly that's targeted for the current language (such as fr).

3. If it can't find this directory, an IOException exception is thrown.

This list is slightly simplified. If you decide to use the global assembly cache (GAC) to share some components over the entire computer, you'll need to realize that .NET actually checks the GAC at the beginning of step 1 and step 2. In other words, in step 1, the CLR checks whether the language- and region-specific version of the assembly is in the GAC and uses it if it is. The same is true for step 2.

The Translation Process

Now you have all the infrastructure you need for localization. All you need to do is create the appropriate satellite assemblies with the alternate versions of your windows (in BAML form), and put these assemblies in the right folders. Doing this by hand would obviously be a lot of work. Furthermore, localization usually involves a third-party translation service that needs to work with your original text. Obviously, it's too much to expect that your translators will be skilled programmers who can find their way around a Visual Studio project (and you're unlikely to trust them with the code anyway). For all these reasons, you need a way to manage the localization process.

Currently, WPF has a partial solution. It works, but it requires a few trips to the command line, and one piece isn't finalized. The basic process works like this:

1. You flag the elements in your application that need to be localized. Optionally, you may add additional comments to help the translator.

2. You extract the localizable details to a .csv file (a comma-separated text file) and send it off to your translation service.

3. Once you receive the translated version of this file, you run locbaml again to generate the satellite assembly you need.

You'll follow these steps in the following sections.

Preparing Markup Elements for Localization

The first step is to add a specialized Uid attribute to all the elements you want to localize. Here's an example:

```
<Button x:Uid="Button_1" Margin="10" Padding="3">A button</Button>
```

The Uid attribute plays a similar role as the Name attribute—it uniquely identifies a button in the context of a single XAML document. That way you can specify localized text for just this button. However, there are a few reasons why WPF uses a Uid instead of just reusing the Name value—including the fact that the name might not be assigned, it might be set according to different conventions and used in code, and so on. In fact, the Name property is itself a localizable piece of information.

■**Note** Obviously, text isn't the only detail you need to localize. You also need to think about fonts, font sizes, margins, padding, other alignment-related details, and so on. In WPF, every property that may need to be localized is decorated with the System.Windows.LocalizabilityAttribute.

Although you don't need to, you should add the Uid to *every* element in every window of a localizable application. This could add up to a lot of extra work, but the msbuild.exe tool can do it automatically. Just use it like this:

```
msbuild /t:updateuid LocalizableApplication.csproj
```

This assumes you wish to add Uids to an application named LocalizableApplication.

And if you want to check whether your elements all have Uids (and make sure you haven't accidentally duplicated one), you can use msbuild.exe like this:

```
msbuild /t:checkuid LocalizableApplication.csproj
```

Tip The easiest way to run msbuild is to launch the Visual Studio Command Prompt (Start ➤ Programs ➤ Microsoft Visual Studio 2005 ➤ Visual Studio Tools ➤ Visual Studio 2005 Command Prompt) so that the path is set to give you easy access. Then you can quickly move to your project folder to run msbuild.exe.

When you generate Uids using msbuild, your Uids are set to match the name of the corresponding control. Here's an example:

```
<Button x:Uid="cmdDoSomething" Name="cmdDoSomething"  Margin="10" Padding="3">
```

If your element doesn't have a name, msbuild creates a less helpful Uid based on the class name, with a numeric suffix:

```
<TextBlock x:Uid="TextBlock_1" Margin="10">
```

Note Technically, this step is how you globalize an application—in other words, prepare it for localization into different languages. Even if you don't plan to localize your application right away, there's an argument to be made that you should prepare it for localization anyway. If you do, you may be able to update your application to a different language simply by deploying a satellite assembly. Of course, globalization's not worth the effort if you haven't taken the time to assess your user interface and make sure it uses an adaptable layout that can accommodate changing content (such as buttons with longer captions, and so on).

Extracting Localizable Content

To extract the localizable content of all your elements, you need to use the locbaml command-line tool. Currently, locbaml isn't included as a compiled tool. Instead, the source code is available as a sample (look for locbaml in the Visual Studio help), and it must be compiled by hand.

When using locbaml, you *must* be in the folder that contains your compiled assembly (for example, LocalizableApplication\bin\Debug). To extract a list of localizable details, you point locbaml to your satellite assembly and use the /parse parameter, as shown here:

```
locbaml /parse en-US\LocalizableApplication.resources.dll
```

The locbaml tool searches your satellite assembly for all its compiled BAML resources and generates a .csv file that has the details. In this example, the .csv file will be named LocalizationApplication.resources.csv.

Each line in the extracted file represents a single localizable property that you've used on an element in your XAML document. Each line consists of the following seven values:

- The name of the BAML resource (for example, LocalizableApplication.g.en-US. resources:window1.baml).

- The Uid of the element and the name of the property to localize. Here's an example: StackPanel_1:System.Windows.FrameworkElement.Margin.

- The localization category. This is a value from the LocalizationCategory enumeration that helps to identify the type of content that this property represents (long text, a title, a font, a button caption, a tooltip, and so on).

- Whether the property is readable (essentially visible as text in the user interface). All readable values always need to be localized, while nonreadable values may or may not require localization.

- Whether the property value can be modified by the translator. This value is always true unless you specifically indicate otherwise.

- Additional comments that you've provided for the translator. If you haven't provided comments, this value is blank.

- The value of the property. This is the detail that needs to be localized.

For example, imagine you have the window shown in Figure 11-3. Here's the XAML markup:

```
<Window x:Uid="Window_1" x:Class="LocalizableApplication.Window1"
    xmlns="http://schemas.microsoft.com/winfx/2006/xaml/presentation"
    xmlns:x="http://schemas.microsoft.com/winfx/2006/xaml"
    Title="LocalizableApplication" Height="300" Width="300"
    SizeToContent="WidthAndHeight"
    >
  <StackPanel x:Uid="StackPanel_1" Margin="10">
    <TextBlock x:Uid="TextBlock_1" Margin="10">One line of text.</TextBlock>
    <Button x:Uid="cmdDoSomething" Name="cmdDoSomething"  Margin="10" Padding="3">
     A button</Button>
    <TextBlock x:Uid="TextBlock_2" Margin="10">
     This is another line of text.</TextBlock>
  </StackPanel>
</Window>
```

Figure 11-3. *A window that can be localized*

When you run this through locbaml, you'll get the information shown in Table 11-1. (For the sake of brevity, the BAML name has been left out because it's always the same window, the resource key has been shortened so it doesn't use fully qualified names, and the comments—which are blank—have been left out.)

Here's where the current tool support is a bit limited. It's unlikely that a translation service will want to work directly with the .csv file because it presents information in a rather awkward way. Instead, another tool is needed that parses this file and allows the translator to review it more efficiently. You could easily build a tool that pulls out all this information, displays the values where Readable and Modifiable are true, and allows the user to edit the corresponding value. However, at the time of this writing WPF doesn't include such a tool.

To perform a simple test, you can open this file directly (use Notepad or Excel) and modify the last piece of information—the value—to supply translated text instead. Here's an example:

```
LocalizableApplication.g.en-US.resources:window1.baml,
TextBlock_1:System.Windows.Controls.TextBlock.$Content,
Text,True,True,,
Une ligne de texte.
```

■**Note** Although this is really a single line of code, it's broken here to fit the bounds of the page.

You don't specify what culture you're using at this point. You do that when you compile the new satellite assembly in the next step.

Table 11-1. *A Sample List of Localizable Properties*

Resource Key	Localization Category	Readable	Modifiable	Value
Window_1:LocalizableApplication.Window1.$Content	None	True	True	#StackPanel_1;
Window_1:Window.Title	Title	True	True	LocalizableApplication
Window_1:FrameworkElement.Height	None	False	True	300
Window_1:FrameworkElement.Width	None	False	True	300
Window_1:Window.SizeToContent	None	False	True	WidthAndHeight
StackPanel_1:FrameworkElement.Margin	None	False	True	10
TextBlock_1:TextBlock.$Content	Text	True	True	One line of text
TextBlock_1:FrameworkElement.Margin	None	False	True	10
cmdDoSomething:Button.$Content	Button	True	True	A button
cmdDoSomething:FrameworkElement.Margin	None	False	True	10
cmdDoSomething:Padding	None	False	True	3
TextBlock_2:TextBlock.$Content	Text	True	True	Another line of text
TextBlock_2:FrameworkElement.Margin	None	False	True	10

Building a Satellite Assembly

Now you're ready to build the satellite assemblies for other cultures. Once again, the locbaml tool takes care of this task, but this time you use the /generate parameter.

Remember, the satellite assembly will contain an alternate copy of each *complete* window as an embedded BAML resource. In order to create these resources, the locbaml tool needs to take a look at the original satellite assembly, substitute all the new values from the translated .csv file, and then generate a new satellite assembly. That means you need to point locbaml to the original satellite assembly and (using the /trans: parameter) the translated list of values. You also need to tell locbaml what culture this assembly represents (using the /cul: parameter). Remember, cultures are defined using two-part identifiers that are listed in the description of the System.Globalization.CultureInfo class.

Here's an example that pulls it all together:

```
locbaml /generate en-US\LocalizableApplication.resources.dll
        /trans:LocalizableApplication.resources.French.csv
        /cul:fr-FR /out:fr-FR
```

This command does the following:

- Uses the original satellite assembly en-US\LocalizedApplication.resources.dll.

- Uses the translates .csv file French.csv.

- Uses the France French culture.

- Outputs to the fr-FR subfolder (which must already exist). Even though this seems implicit based on the culture you're using, you need to supply this detail.

When you run this command line, locbaml creates a new version of the LocalizableApplication.resources.dll assembly with the translated values, and places it in the fr-FR subfolder of the application.

Now when you run the application on a computer that has its culture sent to France French, the alternate version of the window will be shown automatically. You can change the culture using the Regional and Language Options section of the Control Panel. Or for an easier approach to testing, just use code to change the culture of the current thread. You need to do this before you create or show any windows, so it make sense to use an application event or just use your application class constructor as shown here:

```
public partial class App : System.Windows.Application
{
    public App()
    {
        Thread.CurrentThread.CurrentUICulture =
          new CultureInfo("fr-FR");
    }
}
```

Figure 11-4 shows the result.

Figure 11-4. *A window that's localized in French*

Not all localizable content is defined as a localizable property in your user interface. For example, you might need to show an error message when something occurs. The best way to handle this situation with XAML is to use object resources (described in the second half of this chapter). For example, you could store your error message strings as resources in a specific window, in the resources for an entire application, or in a resource dictionary that's shared across multiple applications. Here's an example:

```
<Window.Resources>
  <s:String x:Uid="s:String_1" x:Key="Error">Something bad happened.</s:String>
</ Window.Resources >
```

When you run locbaml, the strings in this file are also added to the content that needs to be localized. When compiled, this information is added to the satellite assembly, ensuring that error messages are in the right language (as shown in Figure 11-5).

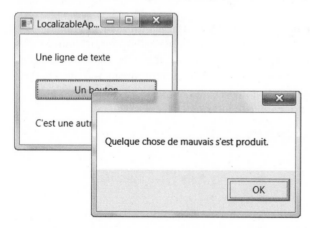

Figure 11-5. *Using a localized string*

Note An obvious weakness in the current system is that it's difficult to keep up with an evolving user interface. The locbaml tool always creates a new file, so if you end up moving controls to different windows or replacing one control with another, you'll probably be forced to create a new list of translations from scratch.

Object Resources

Assembly resources are nothing new to .NET developers. However, WPF also introduces a new resource system that integrates closely with XAML. This system allows you to define resources in a variety of places in your markup (along with specific controls, in specific windows, or across the entire application) and then reuse it easily.

Object resources have a number of important benefits:

- **Efficiency.** Resources let you define an object once and use it in several places in your markup. This streamlines your code and makes it marginally more efficient.

- **Maintainability.** Resources let you take low-level formatting details (such as font sizes) and move them to a central place where they're easy to change. It's the XAML equivalent of creating constants in your code.

- **Adaptability.** Once certain information is separated from the rest of your application and placed in a resource section, it becomes possible to modify it dynamically. For example, you may want to change resource details based on user preferences or the current language.

Note Although it's convenient to refer to WPF resources that are defined in XAML as *object resources* to prevent confusion, usually they're just called *resources*. (Object resources are also sometimes called *logical resources* and *declarative resources*.)

The Resources Collection

Every element includes a Resources property, which stores a dictionary collection of resources. (It's an instance of the ResourceDictionary class.) The resources collection can hold any type of object, indexed by string.

Although every element includes the Resources property (which is defined as part of the FrameworkElement class), the most common way to define resources is at the window-level. That's because every element has access to the resources in its own resource collection and the resources in all of its parents' resource collections.

For example, consider the window with three buttons shown in Figure 11-6. Two of the three buttons use the same brush—an image brush that paints a tile pattern of happy faces.

Figure 11-6. *A window that reuses a brush*

In this case, it's clear that you want both the top and bottom button to have the same styling. However, you might want to change the characteristics of the image brush later on. For that reason, it makes sense to define the image brush in the resources for the window and reuse it as necessary.

Here's how you define the brush:

```
<Window.Resources>
  <ImageBrush x:Key="TileBrush" TileMode="Tile"
    ViewportUnits="Absolute" Viewport="0 0 32 32"
    ImageSource="happyface.jpg" Opacity="0.3">
  </ImageBrush>
</Window.Resources>
```

The details of the image brush aren't terribly important (you'll learn about the specifics in Chapter 13). What *is* important is the first attribute, named Key (and preceded by the x: namespace prefix, which puts it in the XAML namespace rather than the WPF namespace). This assigns the name under which the brush will be indexed in the Window.Resources collection. You can use whatever you want, so long as you use the same name when you need to retrieve the resource.

■**Note** You can instantiate any .NET class in the resources section (including your own custom classes), as long as it's XAML-friendly. That means it needs to have a few basic characteristics, such as a public zero-argument constructor and writeable properties.

To use a resource in your XAML markup, you need a way to refer to it. This is accomplished using a markup extension. In fact, there are two markup extensions that you can use: one for dynamic resources and one for static resources. Static resources are set once, when the window is first created. Dynamic resources are reapplied if the resource is changed. (You'll study the difference more closely a little bit later in this chapter.) In this example, the image brush never changes, so the static resource is fine.

Here's one of the buttons that uses the resource:

```
<Button Background="{StaticResource TileBrush}"
  Margin="5" Padding="5" FontWeight="Bold" FontSize="14">
  A Tiled Button
</Button>
```

In this case, the resource is retrieved and used to assign the Button.Background property. You could perform the exact same feat (with slightly more overhead) by using a dynamic resource:

```
<Button Background="{DynamicResource TileBrush}"
```

Using a simple .NET object for a resource really is this easy. However, there are a few finer points you need to consider. The following sections will fill you in.

The Hierarchy of Resources

Every element has its own resource collection, and WPF performs a recursive search up your element tree to find the resource you want. In the current example, you could move the image brush from the Resources collection of the window to the Resources collection of the Stack-Panel that holds all three buttons without changing the way the application works. You could also put the image brush in Button.Resources collection, but then you'd need to define it twice —once for each button.

There's another issue to consider. When using a static resource, you must always define a resource in your markup *before* you refer to it. That means that even though it's perfectly valid (from a markup perspective) to put the Windows.Resources section after the main content of the form (the StackPanel that contains all the buttons), this change will break the current example. When the XAML parser encounters a static reference to a resource it doesn't know, it throws an exception. (You can get around this problem using a dynamic resource, but there's no good reason to incur the extra overhead.)

As a result, if you want to place your resource in the button element, you need to rearrange your markup a little, so that the resource is defined before the background is set. Here's one way to do it:

```
<Button Margin="5" Padding="5" FontWeight="Bold" FontSize="14">
  <Button.Resources>
    <ImageBrush x:Key="TileBrush" TileMode="Tile"
      ViewportUnits="Absolute" Viewport="0 0 10 10"
      ImageSource="happyface.jpg" Opacity="0.3"></ImageBrush>
  </Button.Resources>

  <Button.Background>
```

```
      <StaticResource ResourceKey="TileBrush"/>
    </Button.Background>

    <Button.Content>Another Tiled Button</Button.Content>
</Button>
```

The syntax for the static resource markup extension looks a bit different in this example because it's set in a nested element (not an attribute). The resource key is specified using the ResourceKey property to point to the right resource.

Interestingly, resource names can be reused as long as you don't use the same resource name more than once in the same collection. That means you could create a window like this, which defines the image brush in two places:

```
<Window x:Class="Resources.TwoResources"
    xmlns="http://schemas.microsoft.com/winfx/2006/xaml/presentation"
    xmlns:x="http://schemas.microsoft.com/winfx/2006/xaml"
    Title="Resources" Height="300" Width="300" >

  <Window.Resources>
    <ImageBrush x:Key="TileBrush" TileMode="Tile"
               ViewportUnits="Absolute" Viewport="0 0 32 32"
               ImageSource="happyface.jpg" Opacity="0.3"></ImageBrush>
  </Window.Resources>

  <StackPanel Margin="5">
    <Button Background="{StaticResource TileBrush}" Padding="5"
      FontWeight="Bold" FontSize="14" Margin="5" >A Tiled Button</Button>

    <Button Padding="5" Margin="5"
      FontWeight="Bold" FontSize="14">A Normal Button</Button>
    <Button Background="{DynamicResource TileBrush}" Padding="5" Margin="5"
      FontWeight="Bold" FontSize="14">
      <Button.Resources>
        <ImageBrush x:Key="TileBrush" TileMode="Tile"
          ViewportUnits="Absolute" Viewport="0 0 32 32"
          ImageSource="sadface.jpg" Opacity="0.3"></ImageBrush>
      </Button.Resources>
      <Button.Content>Another Tiled Button</Button.Content>
    </Button>

  </StackPanel>
</Window>
```

In this case, the button uses the resource it finds first. Because it begins by searching its own Resources collection, the second button uses the sadface.jpg graphic, while the first button gets the brush from the containing window and uses the happyface.jpg image.

Static and Dynamic Resources

You might assume that because the previous example used a static resource it's immune to any changes you make to your resource (in this case, the image brush). However, that's actually not the case.

For example, imagine you execute this code at some point after the resource has been applied and the window has been displayed:

```
ImageBrush brush = (ImageBrush)this.Resources["TileBrush"];
brush.Viewport = new Rect(0, 0, 5, 5);
```

This code retrieves the brush from the Window.Resources collection and manipulates it. (Technically, the code changes the size of each tile, shrinking the happy face and packing the image pattern more tightly.) When you run this code, you probably don't expect any reaction in your user interface—after all, it's a static resource. However, this change does propagate to the two buttons. In fact, the buttons are updated with the new Viewport property setting, *regardless* of whether they use the brush through a static resource or a dynamic resource.

The reason this works is because the Brush class derives from a class named Freezable. The Freezable class has basic-change tracking features (and it can be "frozen" to a read-only state if it doesn't need to change). What that means is whenever you change a brush in WPF, any controls that use that brush refresh themselves automatically. It doesn't matter whether they get their brushes through a resource or not.

At this point, you're probably wondering what the difference is between static and dynamic resource. The difference is that a static resource grabs the object from the resources collection once. Depending on the type of object (and the way it's used), any changes you make to that object may be noticed right away. However, the dynamic resource looks the object up in the resources collection every time it's needed. That means you could place an entirely new object under the same key and the dynamic resource would pick up your change.

To see an example that illustrates the difference, consider the following code, which replaces the current image brush with a completely new (and boring) solid blue brush:

```
this.Resources["TileBrush"] = new SolidColorBrush(Colors.LightBlue);
```

A dynamic resource picks up this change, while a static resource has no idea that its brush has been replaced in the Resources collection by something else. It continues using the original ImageBrush instead.

Figure 11-7 shows this example in a window that includes a dynamic resource (the top button) and a static resource (the bottom button).

Figure 11-7. *Dynamic and static resources*

Usually, you don't need the overhead of a dynamic resource and your application will work perfectly well with a static resource. One notable exception is if you're creating resources that depend on Windows settings (such as system colors). In this situation, you need to use dynamic resources if you want to be able to react to any change in the current color scheme. (Or if you use static resources, you'll keep using the old color scheme until the user restarts the application.) You'll learn more about how this works when you tackle system resources a bit later in this chapter.

As a general guideline, only use dynamic properties when

- Your resource has properties that depend on system settings (such as the current Windows colors or fonts).

- You plan to replace your resource objects programmatically (for example, to implement some sort of dynamic skinning feature, as demonstrated in Chapter 15).

However, you shouldn't get overly ambitious with dynamic resources. The primary issue is that changing a resource doesn't necessarily trigger a refresh in your user interface. (It does in the brush example because of the way brush objects are constructed—namely, they have this notification support built in.) There are a host of occasions where you need to show dynamic content in a control in a way that the control adjusts itself as the content changes, and for that it makes much more sense to use data binding (Chapter 16).

■Note On rare occasions, dynamic resources are also used to improve the first-time-load performance of a form. That's because static resources are always loaded when the window is created, while dynamic resources are loaded when they're first used. However, you won't see any benefit unless your resource is extremely large and complex (in which case parsing its markup takes a nontrivial amount of time).

Nonshared Resources

Ordinarily, when you use a resource in multiple places, you're using the same object instance. This behavior—called *sharing*—is usually what you want. However, it's also possible to tell the parser to create a separate instance of your object each time it's used.

To turn off sharing you use the Shared attribute, as shown here:

```
<ImageBrush x:Key="TileBrush" x:Shared="False" ...></ImageBrush>
```

There are few good reasons for using nonshared resources. You might consider nonshared resources if you want to modify your resource instances separately later on. For example, you could create a window that has several buttons that use the same brush but turn off sharing so that you can change each brush individually. This approach isn't very common because it's inefficient. In this example, it would be better to let all the buttons use the same brush initially, and then create and apply new brush objects as needed. That way you're only incurring the overhead of extra brush objects when you really need to.

Another reason you might use nonshared resources is if you want to reuse an object in a way that otherwise wouldn't be allowed. For example, using this technique, you could define an element (such as an Image or a Button) as a resource, and then display that element in several different places in a window.

Once again, this usually isn't the best approach. For example, if you want to reuse an Image element, it makes more sense to store the relevant piece of information (such as the BitmapImage object that identifies the image source) and share that between multiple Image elements. And if you simply want to standardize controls so they share the same properties, you're far better off using styles, which are described in the next chapter. Styles give you the ability to create identical or nearly identical copies of any element, but they also allow you to override property values when they don't apply and attach distinct event handlers, two features you'd lose if you simply cloned an element using a nonshared resource.

Accessing Resources in Code

Usually, you'll define and use resources in your markup. However, if the need arises, you can work with the resources collection in code.

As you've already seen, you can pull items out of the resources collection by name. However, in order to use this approach you need to use the resource collection of the right element. As you've already seen, this limitation doesn't apply to your markup. A control such as a button can retrieve a resource without specifically knowing where it's defined. When it attempts to assign the brush to its Background property, WPF checks the resources collection of the button for a resource named TileBrush, then it checks the resources collection of the containing StackPanel, and then the containing window. (This process actually continues to look at application and system resources, as you'll see in the next section.)

You can hunt for a resource in the same way using the FrameworkElement.FindResource() method. Here's an example that looks for the resource of a button (or one of its higher-level containers) when a Click event fires:

```
private void cmdChange_Click(object sender, RoutedEventArgs e)
{
    Button cmd = (Button)sender;
    ImageBrush brush = (ImageBrush)sender.FindResource("TileBrush");
    ...
}
```

Instead of FindResource() you can use the TryFindResource() method that returns a null reference if a resource can't be found, rather than throwing an exception.

Incidentally, you can also add resources programmatically. Pick the element where you want to place the resource and use the Add() method of the resources collection. However, it's much more common to define resources in markup.

Application Resources

The Window isn't the last stop in the resource search. If you indicate a resource that can't be found in a control or any of its containers (up to the containing window or page), WPF continues to check the set of resources you've defined for your application. In Visual Studio, these are the resources you've defined in the markup for your App.xaml file, as shown here:

```
<Application x:Class="Resources.App"
    xmlns="http://schemas.microsoft.com/winfx/2006/xaml/presentation"
    xmlns:x="http://schemas.microsoft.com/winfx/2006/xaml"
    StartupUri="Menu.xaml"
    >
    <Application.Resources>
      <ImageBrush x:Key="TileBrush" TileMode="Tile"
        ViewportUnits="Absolute" Viewport="0 0 32 32"
        ImageSource="happyface.jpg" Opacity="0.3">
      </ImageBrush>
    </Application.Resources>
</Application>
```

As you've probably already guessed, application resources give you a great way to reuse an object across your entire application. In this example, it's a good choice if you plan to use the image brush in more than one window.

■**Note** Before creating an application resource, consider the trade-off between complexity and reuse. Adding an application resource gives you better reuse, but it adds complexity because it's not immediately clear which windows use a given resource. (It's conceptually the same as an old-style C++ program with too many global variables.) A good guideline is to use application resources if your object is reused widely (for example, in many windows). If it's used in just two or three, consider defining the resource in each window.

It turns out that application resources *still* aren't the final stop when an element searches for a resource. If the resource can't be found in the application resources, the element continues to look at the system resources.

System Resources

As you learned earlier, dynamic resources are primarily intended to help your application respond to changes in system environment settings. However, this raises a question—how do you retrieve the system environment settings and use them in your code in the first place?

The secret is a set of three classes named SystemColors, SystemFonts, and SystemParameters, all of which are in the System.Windows namespace. SystemColors gives you access to color settings; SystemFonts gives you access to fonts settings; and SystemParameters wraps a huge list of settings that describe the standard size of various screen elements, keyboard and mouse settings, and screen size, and whether various graphical effects (such as hot tracking, drop shadows, and showing window contents while dragging) are switched on.

■**Note** There are two versions of the SystemColors and SystemFonts classes. They're found in the System.Windows namespace and the System.Drawing namespace. Those in the System.Windows namespace are part of WPF. They use the right data types and support the resource system. The ones in the System.Drawing namespace are part of Windows Forms and the .NET Framework 2.0. They aren't useful in a WPF application.

The SystemColors, SystemFonts, and SystemParameters classes expose all their details through static properties. For example, SystemColors.WindowTextColor gets you a Color structure that you can use as you please. Here's an example that uses it to create a brush and fill the foreground of an element:

```
label.Foreground = new SolidBrush(SystemColors.WindowTextColor);
```

Or to be a bit more efficient, you can just use the ready-made brush property:

```
label.Foreground = SystemColors.WindowTextBrush;
```

In WPF, you can access static properties using the static markup extension. For example, here's how you could set the foreground of the same label using XAML:

```
<Label Foreground="{x:Static SystemColors.WindowTextBrush}">
  Ordinary text
</Label>
```

This example doesn't use a resource. It also suffers from a minor failing—when the window is parsed and the label is created, a brush is created based on the current "snapshot" of the window text color. If you change the Windows colors while this application is running (after the window containing the label has been shown), the label won't update itself. Applications that behave this way are considered to be a bit rude.

To solve this problem, you can't set the Foreground property directly to a brush object. Instead, you need to set it to a DynamicResource object that wraps this system resource. Fortunately, all the System*Xxx* classes provide a complementary set of properties that return ResourceKey objects—references that let you pull the resource out of the collection of system resources. These properties have the same name as the ordinary property that returns the object directly, with the word *Key* added to the end. For example, the resource key for the SystemColors.WindowTextBrush is SystemColors.WindowTextBrushKey.

■Note Resource keys aren't simple names—they're references that tell WPF where to look to find a specific resource. The ResourceKey class is opaque, so it doesn't show you the low-level details about how system resources are identified. However, there's no need to worry about your resources conflicting with the system resources because they are in separate assemblies and treated differently.

Here's how you can use a resource from one of the System*Xxx* classes:

```
<Label Foreground="{DynamicResource {x:Static SystemColors.WindowTextBrushKey}}">
  Ordinary text
</Label>
```

This markup is a bit more complex than the previous example. It begins by defining a dynamic resource. However, the dynamic resource isn't pulled out of the resource collection in your application. Instead, it uses a key that's defined by the SystemColors.WindowTextBrushKey property. Because this property is static, you also need to throw in the static markup extension so that the parser understands what you're trying to do.

Now that you've made this change, you have a label that can update itself seamlessly when system settings change.

Organizing Resources with Resource Dictionaries

If you want to share resources between multiple projects, you can create a *resource dictionary*. A resource dictionary is simply a XAML document that does nothing but store the resources you want to use. Here's an example of a resource dictionary that has one resource:

```
<ResourceDictionary
 xmlns="http://schemas.microsoft.com/winfx/2006/xaml/presentation"
 xmlns:x="http://schemas.microsoft.com/winfx/2006/xaml">

  <ImageBrush x:Key="TileBrush" TileMode="Tile"
    ViewportUnits="Absolute" Viewport="0 0 32 32"
    ImageSource="happyface.jpg" Opacity="0.3">
  </ImageBrush>
</ResourceDictionary>
```

When you add a resource dictionary to an application, make sure the Build Action is set to Page (as it is for any other XAML file). This ensures that your resource dictionary is compiled to BAML for best performance. However, it's perfectly allowed to have a resource dictionary with a Build Action of Resource, in which case it's embedded in the assembly but not compiled. Parsing it at runtime is then imperceptibly slower.

In order to use a resource dictionary, you need to merge it into a resource collection somewhere in your application. You could do this in a specific window, but it's more common to merge it into the resources collection for the application, as shown here:

```
<Application x:Class="Resources.App"
    xmlns="http://schemas.microsoft.com/winfx/2006/xaml/presentation"
    xmlns:x="http://schemas.microsoft.com/winfx/2006/xaml"
    StartupUri="Menu.xaml" >
  <Application.Resources>
    <ResourceDictionary>
      <ResourceDictionary.MergedDictionaries>
        <ResourceDictionary Source="AppBrushes.xaml"/>
        <ResourceDictionary Source="WizardBrushes.xaml"/>
      </ResourceDictionary.MergedDictionaries>
    </ResourceDictionary>
  </Application.Resources>
</Application>
```

This markup works by explicitly creating a ResourceDictionary object. The resources collection is always a ResourceDictionary object, but this is one case where you need to specify that detail explicitly so that you can also set the ResourceDictionary.MergedDictionaries property (which is usually null).

The MergedDictionaries collection is a collection of ResourceDictionary objects that you want to use to supplement your resource collection. In this example, there are two: one that's defined in the AppBrushes.xaml resource dictionary and another that's defined in the WizardBrushes.xaml.

If you want to add your own resources *and* merge in resource dictionaries, you simply need to place your resources before or after the MergedProperties section, as shown here:

```
<Application.Resources>
  <ResourceDictionary>
    <ResourceDictionary.MergedDictionaries>
      <ResourceDictionary Source="AppBrushes.xaml"/>
      <ResourceDictionary Source="WizardBrushes.xaml"/>
    </ResourceDictionary.MergedDictionaries>
    <ImageBrush x:Key="GraphicalBrush1" ... ></ImageBrush>
    <ImageBrush x:Key="GraphicalBrush2" ... ></ImageBrush>
  </ResourceDictionary>
</Application.Resources>
```

■**Note** As you learned earlier, it's perfectly reasonable to have resources with the same name stored in different but overlapping resource collections. However, it's not acceptable to merge resource dictionaries that use the same resource names. If there's a duplicate, you'll receive a XamlParseException when you compile your application.

One reason to use resource dictionaries is to define one or more reusable application "skins" that you can apply to your controls. (You'll learn how to develop this technique in Chapter 15.) Another reason is to store content that needs to be localized (such as error message strings).

Sharing Resources Between Assemblies

If you want to share a resource dictionary between multiple applications, you could copy and distribute the XAML file that contains the resource dictionary. This is the simplest approach, but it doesn't give you any version control. A more structured approach is to compile your resource dictionary in a separate class library assembly and distribute that component instead.

When sharing a compiled assembly with one or more resource dictionaries, there's another challenge to face—namely, you need a way to extract the resource you want and use it in your application. There are two approaches you can take. The most straightforward solution is to use code that creates the appropriate ResourceDictionary object. For example, if you have a resource dictionary in a class library assembly named ReusableDictionary.xaml, you could use the following code to create it manually:

```
ResourceDictionary resourceDictionary = new ResourceDictionary();
resourceDictionary.Source = new Uri(
  "ResourceLibrary;component/ReusableDictionary.xaml", UriKind.Relative);
```

This code snippet uses the pack URI syntax you learned about earlier in this chapter. It constructs a relative URI that points to the compiled XAML resource named ReusableDictionary.xaml in the other assembly. Once you've created the ResourceDictionary object, you can manually retrieve the resource you want from the collection:

```
cmd.Background = (Brush)resourceDictionary["TileBrush"];
```

However, you don't need to assign resources manually. Any DynamicResource references you have in your window will be automatically reevaluated when you load a new resource dictionary. You'll see an example of this technique in Chapter 15, when you build a dynamic skinning feature.

If you don't want to write any code, you have another choice. You can use the ComponentResourceKey markup extension, which is designed for just this purpose. You use the ComponentResourceKey to create the key name for your resource. By taking this step, you indicate to WPF that you plan to share your resource between assemblies.

Note Up until this point, you've only seen resources that use strings (such as "TileBrush") for key names. Using a string is the most common way to name a resource. However, WPF has some clever resource extensibility that kicks in automatically when you use certain types of key names that aren't strings. For example, in the next chapter you'll see that you can use a Type object as a key name for a style. This tells WPF to apply the style to the appropriate type of element automatically. Similarly, you can use an instance of ComponentResourceKey as a key name for any resource you want to share between assemblies.

Before you go any further, you need to make sure you've given your resource dictionary the right name. In order for this trick to work, your resource dictionary must be in a file named generic.xaml, and that file must be placed in a Themes subfolder in your application. The resources in the generic.xaml files are considered part of the default theme, and they're always made available. You'll use this trick many more times, particularly when you build custom controls in Chapter 24.

Figure 11-8 shows the proper organization of files. The top project, named ResourceLibrary, includes the generic.xaml file in the correct folder. The bottom project, named Resources, has a reference to ResourceLibrary, so it can use the resources it contains.

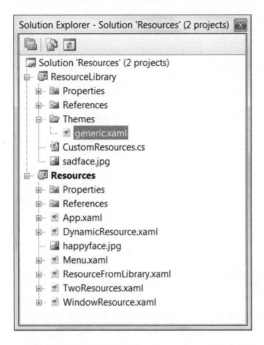

Figure 11-8. *Sharing resources with a class library*

Tip If you have a lot of resources and you want to organize them in the best way possible, you can create individual resource dictionaries, just as you did before. However, make sure you merge these dictionaries into the generic.xaml file, so that they're readily available.

The next step is to create the key name for the resource you want to share, which is stored in the ResourceLibrary assembly. When using a ComponentResourceKey, you need to supply two pieces of information: a reference to a class in your class library assembly, and a descriptive resource ID. The class reference is part of the magic that allows WPF to share your resource with other assemblies. When they use the resource, they'll supply the same class reference and the same resource ID.

It doesn't matter what this class actually looks like, and it doesn't need to contain code. The assembly where this type is defined is the same assembly where ComponentResourceKey will find the resource. The example shown in Figure 11-8 uses a class named CustomResources, which has no code:

```
public class CustomResources
{}
```

Now you can create a key name using this class and a resource ID:

```
x:Key="{ComponentResourceKey TypeInTargetAssembly={x:Type local:CustomResources},
 ResourceId=SadTileBrush}"
```

Here's the complete markup for the generic.xaml file, which includes a single resource—an ImageBrush that uses a different graphic:

```
<ResourceDictionary
 xmlns="http://schemas.microsoft.com/winfx/2006/xaml/presentation"
 xmlns:x="http://schemas.microsoft.com/winfx/2006/xaml"
 xmlns:local="clr-namespace:ResourceLibrary">

  <ImageBrush
   x:Key="{ComponentResourceKey TypeInTargetAssembly={x:Type local:CustomResources},
ResourceId=SadTileBrush}"
    TileMode="Tile" ViewportUnits="Absolute" Viewport="0 0 32 32"
    ImageSource="ResourceLibrary;component/sadface.jpg" Opacity="0.3">
  </ImageBrush>
</ResourceDictionary>
```

Keen eyes will notice one unexpected detail in this example. The ImageSource property is no longer set with the image name (sadface.jpg). Instead, a more complex relative URI is used that clearly indicates the image is a part of the ResourceLibrary component. This is a required step because this resource will be used in the context of another application. If you simply use the image name, that application will search its own resources to find the image. Instead, you need a relative URI that indicates the component where the image is stored.

Now that you've created the resource dictionary, you can use it in another application. First, make sure you've defined a prefix for the class library assembly, as shown here:

```
<Window x:Class="Resources.ResourceFromLibrary"
 xmlns="http://schemas.microsoft.com/winfx/2006/xaml/presentation"
 xmlns:x="http://schemas.microsoft.com/winfx/2006/xaml"
 xmlns:res="clr-namespace:ResourceLibrary;assembly=ResourceLibrary"
 ... >
```

You can then use a DynamicResource that contains a ComponentResourceKey. (This makes sense because the ComponentResourceKey *is* the resource name.) The Component-ResourceKey you use in the consumer is exactly the same as the ComponentResourceKey you use in the class library. You supply a reference to the same class and the same resource ID. The only difference is that you may not use the same XML namespace prefix. This example uses res instead of local, so as to emphasize the fact that the CustomResources class is defined in a different assembly:

```
<Button Background="{DynamicResource {ComponentResourceKey
 TypeInTargetAssembly={x:Type res:CustomResources}, ResourceId=SadTileBrush}}"
 Padding="5" Margin="5" FontWeight="Bold" FontSize="14">
  A Resource From ResourceLibrary
</Button>
```

■**Note** You must use a dynamic resource, not a static resource, when using a ComponentResourceKey.

This completes the example. However, there's one additional step you can take to make it easier to use your resource. You can define a static property that returns the correct Component-ResourceKey that you need to use. Typically, you'll define this property in a class in your component, as shown here:

```
public class CustomResources
{
    public static ComponentResourceKey SadTileBrushKey
    {
        get
        {
            return new ComponentResourceKey(
                typeof(CustomResources), "SadTileBrush");
        }
    }
}
```

Now you use the Static markup extension to access this property and apply the resource without using the long-winded ComponentResourceKey in your markup:

```
<Button
 Background="{DynamicResource {x:Static res:CustomResources.SadTileBrushKey}}"
 Padding="5" Margin="5" FontWeight="Bold" FontSize="14">
  A Resource From ResourceLibrary
</Button>
```

This handy shortcut is essentially the same technique that's used by the System*Xxx* classes that you saw earlier. For example, when you retrieve SystemColors.WindowTextBrushKey, you are receiving the correct resource key object. The only difference is that it's an instance of the private SystemResourceKey rather than ComponentResourceKey. Both classes derive from the same ancestor: an abstract class named ResourceKey.

The Last Word

In this chapter, you took an in-depth look at the WPF resource system. You considered assembly resources that package up binary data with your application, and you looked at object resources that let you reuse the same XAML ingredients in different parts of your application.

You also took a look at localization and learned how satellite assemblies and a few command-line tools (msbuild.exe and locbaml.exe) allow you to provide culture-specific versions of your user interface.

You're not done looking at resources just yet. One of the most practical uses of object resources is to store *styles*—collections of property settings that you can apply to multiple elements. In the next chapter, you'll learn how to define styles and reuse them effortlessly.

CHAPTER 12

■ ■ ■

Styles

In the previous chapter you learned about the WPF resource system, which lets you define objects in one place and reuse them throughout your markup. Although you can use resources to store a wide variety of objects, one of the most common reasons you'll use them is to hold s*tyles*.

A style is a collection of property values that can be applied to an element. The WPF style system plays a similar role to the cascading style sheet (CSS) standard in HTML markup. Like CSS, WPF styles allow you to define a common set of formatting characteristics and apply them throughout your application to ensure consistency. And as with CSS, WPF styles can work automatically, target specific element types, and cascade through the element tree. However, WPF styles are more powerful because they can set *any* dependency property. That means you can use them to standardize nonformatting characteristics, such as the behavior of a control. WPF styles also support *triggers*, which allow you to change the style of a control when another property is changed (as you'll see in this chapter), and they can use *templates* to redefine the built-in appearance of a control (as you'll see in Chapter 15). Once you've learned how to use styles, you'll be sure to include them in all your WPF applications.

Style Basics

As you learned in the previous chapter, resources offer several key benefits, including simpler markup and more maintainable applications. So what do styles add to the picture?

To understand how styles fit in, it helps to consider a simple example. Imagine you need to standardize the font that's used in a window. The simplest approach is to set the font properties of the containing window. These properties, which are defined in the Control class, include FontFamily, FontSize, FontWeight (for bold), FontStyle (for italics), and FontStretch (for compressed and expanded variants). Thanks to the property value inheritance feature, when you set these properties at the window level, all the elements inside the window will acquire the same values, unless they explicitly override them.

Note Property value inheritance is one of the many optional features that dependency properties can provide. Dependency properties are described in Chapter 6.

Now consider a different situation, one in which you want to lock down the font that's used for just a portion of your user interface. If you can isolate these elements in a specific container (for example, if they're all inside one Grid or StackPanel), you can use essentially the same approach and set the font properties of the container. However, life's not usually that easy. For example, you may want to give all buttons a consistent typeface and text size independent from the font settings that are used in other elements. In this case, you need a way to define these details in one place and reuse them wherever they apply.

Resources give you a solution, but it's somewhat awkward. Because there's no Font object in WPF (just a collection of font-related properties), you're stuck defining several related resources, as shown here:

```
<Window.Resources>
  <FontFamily x:Key="ButtonFontFamily">Times New Roman</FontFamily>
  <sys:Double x:Key="ButtonFontSize">18</s:Double>
  <FontWeight x:Key="ButtonFontWeight">Bold</FontWeight>
</Window.Resources>
```

This snippet or markup adds three resources to a window: a FontFamily object with the name of the font you want to use, a double that stores the number 18, and the enumerated value FontWeight.Bold. It assumes you've mapped the .NET namespace System to the XML namespace prefix sys, as shown here:

```
<Window xmlns:sys="clr-namespace:System;assembly=mscorlib" ... >
```

■Tip When setting properties using a resource, it's important that the data types match exactly. WPF won't use a type converter in the same way it does when you set an attribute value directly. For example, if you're setting the FontFamily attribute in an element, you can use the string "Times New Roman" because the FontFamilyConverter will create the FontFamily object you need. However, the same magic won't happen if you try to set the FontFamily property using a string resource—in this situation, the XAML parser throws an exception.

Once you've defined the resources you need, the next step is to actually use these resources in an element. Because the resources are never changed over the lifetime of the application, it makes sense to use static resources, as shown here:

```
<Button Padding="5" Margin="5" Name="cmd"
  FontFamily="{StaticResource ButtonFontFamily}"
  FontWeight="{StaticResource ButtonFontWeight}"
  FontSize="{StaticResource ButtonFontSize}"
  >A Customized Button
</Button>
```

This example works, and it moves the font details (the so-called "magic numbers") out of your markup. However, it also presents two new problems:

- There's no clear indication that the three resources are related (other than the similar resource names). This complicates the maintainability of the application. It's especially a problem if you need to set more font properties or if you decide to maintain different font settings for different types of elements.

- The markup you need to use your resources is quite verbose. In fact, it's less concise than the approach it replaces (defining the font properties directly in the element).

You could improve on the first issue by defining a custom class (such as FontSettings) that bundles all the font details together. You could then create one FontSettings object as a resource and use its various properties in your markup. However, this still leaves you with verbose markup—and it makes for a fair bit of extra work.

Styles provide the perfect solution. You can define a single style that wraps all the properties you want to set. Here's how:

```
<Window.Resources>
  <Style x:Key="BigFontButtonStyle">
    <Setter Property="Control.FontFamily" Value="Times New Roman" />
    <Setter Property="Control.FontSize" Value="18" />
    <Setter Property="Control.FontWeight" Value="Bold" />
  </Style>
</Window.Resources>
```

This markup creates a single resource: a System.Windows.Style object. This style object holds a Setters collection with three Setter objects, one for each property you want to set. Each Setter object names the property that it acts on and the value that it applies to that property. Like all resources, the style object has a key name so you can pull it out of the collection when needed. In this case, the key name is BigFontButtonStyle. (By convention, the key names for styles usually end with "Style.")

Every WPF element can use a single style (or no style). The style plugs into an element through the element's Style property (which is defined in the base FrameworkElement class). For example, to configure a button to use the style you created previously, you'd point the button to the style resource like this:

```
<Button Padding="5" Margin="5" Name="cmd"
  Style="{StaticResource BigFontButtonStyle}"
  >A Customized Button
</Button>
```

Of course, you could also set a style programmatically. All you need to do is pull the style out of the closest Resources collection using the familiar FindResource() method. Here's the code you'd use for a Button object named cmd:

```
cmdButton.Style = (Style)cmd.FindResource("BigFontButtonStyle");
```

Figure 12-1 shows a window with two buttons that use the BigFontButtonStyle.

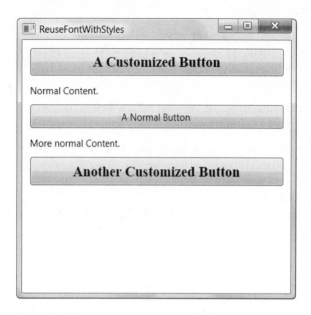

Figure 12-1. *Reusing button settings with a style*

Note Styles set the initial appearance of an element, but you're free to override the characteristics they set. For example, if you apply the BigFontButtonStyle style *and* set the FontSize property explicitly, the Font-Size setting in the button tag overrides the style. Ideally, you won't rely on this behavior—instead, create more styles so that you can set as many details as possible at the style level. This gives you more flexibility to adjust your user interface in the future with minimum disruption.

The style system adds many benefits. Not only does it allow you to create groups of settings that are clearly related, it also streamlines your markup by making it easier to apply these settings. Best of all, you can apply a style without worrying about what properties it sets. In the previous example the font settings were organized into a style named BigFontButtonStyle. If you decide later that your big-font buttons also need more padding and margin space, you can add setters for the Padding and Margin properties as well. All the buttons that use the style automatically acquire the new style settings.

The Setters collection is the most important property of the Style class. But there are five key properties altogether, which you'll consider in this chapter. Table 12-1 shows a snapshot.

Table 12-1. *Properties of the Style Class*

Property	Description
Setters	A collection of Setter or EventSetter objects that set property values and attach event handlers automatically.
Triggers	A collection of objects that derive from TriggerBase and allow you to change style settings automatically. For example, you can modify a style when another property changes or when an event occurs.
Resources	A collection of resources that you want to use with your styles. For example, you might need to use a single object to set more than one property. In that case, it's more efficient to create the object as a resource and then use that resource in your Setter object (rather than create the object as part of each Setter, using nested tags).
BasedOn	A property that allows you to create a more specialized style that inherits (and optionally overrides) the settings of another style.
TargetType	A property that identifies the element type that this style acts upon. This property allows you to create setters that only affect certain elements, and it allows you to create setters that spring into action automatically for the right element type.

Now that you've seen a basic example of a style at work, you're ready to look into the style model more deeply.

Creating a Style Object

In the previous example, the style object is defined at the window level and then reused in two buttons inside that window. Although that's a common design, it's certainly not your only choice.

If you want to create more finely targeted styles, you could define them using the Resources collection of their container, such as a StackPanel or a Grid. If you want to reuse styles across an application, you can define them using the Resources collection of your application. These are also common approaches.

Strictly speaking, you don't need to use styles and resources together. For example, you could define the style of a particular button by filling its Style collection directly, as shown here:

```
<Button Padding="5" Margin="5">
  <Button.Style>
    <Style>
      <Setter Property="Control.FontFamily" Value="Times New Roman" />
      <Setter Property="Control.FontSize" Value="18" />
      <Setter Property="Control.FontWeight" Value="Bold" />
    </Style>
  </Button.Style>
  <Button.Content>A Customized Button</Button.Content>
</Button>
```

This works, but it's obviously a lot less useful. Now there's no way to share this style with other elements.

This approach isn't worth the trouble if you're simply using a style to set some properties (as in this example) because it's easier to set the properties directly. However, this approach is occasionally useful if you're using another feature of styles and you only want to apply it to a single element. For example, you can use this approach to attach triggers to an element. This approach also allows you to modify a part of an element's control template. (In this case, you use the Setter.TargetName property to apply a setter to a specific component inside the element, such as the scroll bar buttons in a list box. You'll learn more about this technique in Chapter 15.)

Setting Properties

As you've seen, every Style object wraps a collection of Setter objects. Each Setter object sets a single property in an element. The only limitation is that a setter can only change a dependency property—other properties can't be modified.

In some cases, you won't be able to set the property value using a simple attribute string. For example, an ImageBrush object (such as the kind you used in the previous chapter to show a tiled pattern) can't be set with a simple string. In this situation, you can use the familiar XAML trick of replacing the attribute with a nested element. Here's an example:

```
<Style x:Key="HappyTiledElementStyle">
  <Setter Property="Control.Background">
    <Setter.Value>
      <ImageBrush TileMode="Tile"
        ViewportUnits="Absolute" Viewport="0 0 32 32"
        ImageSource="happyface.jpg" Opacity="0.3">
      </ImageBrush>
    </Setter.Value>
  </Setter>
</Style>
```

■Tip If you want to reuse the same image brush in more than one style (or in more than one setter in the same style) you can define it as a resource and then use that resource in your style.

To identify the property you want to set, you need to supply both a class and a property name. However, the class name you use doesn't need to be the class where the property is defined. It can also be a derived class that inherits the property. For example, consider the following version of the BigFontButton style, which replaces the references to the Control class with references to the Button class:

```
<Style x:Key="BigFontButtonStyle">
  <Setter Property="Button.FontFamily" Value="Times New Roman" />
  <Setter Property="Button.FontSize" Value="18" />
  <Setter Property="Button.FontWeight" Value="Bold" />
</Style>
```

If you substitute this style in the same example (Figure 12-1), you'll get exactly the same result. So why the difference? In this case, the distinction is how WPF handles other classes that may include the same FontFamily, FontSize, and FontWeight properties but that don't derive from Button. For example, if you apply this version of the BigFontButton style to a Label control, it has no effect. WPF simply ignores the three properties because they don't apply. But if you use the original style, the font properties will affect the label because the Label class derives from Control.

Tip The fact that WPF ignores properties that don't apply means you can also set properties that won't necessarily be available in the element to which you apply the style. For example, if you set the ButtonBase. IsCancel property, it will only have an affect when you set the style on a button.

There are some cases in WPF where the same properties are defined in more than one place in the element hierarchy. For example, the full set of font properties (such as FontFamily) is defined in both the Control class and the TextBlock class. If you're creating a style that applies to TextBlock objects and elements that derive from Control, it might occur to you to create markup like this:

```
<Style x:Key="BigFontStyle">
  <Setter Property="Button.FontFamily" Value="Times New Roman" />
  <Setter Property="Button.FontSize" Value="18" />

  <Setter Property="TextBlock.FontFamily" Value="Arial" />
  <Setter Property="TextBlock.FontSize" Value="10" />
</Style>
```

However, this won't have the desired effect. The problem is that although Button. FontFamily and TextBlock.FontFamily are declared separately in their respective base classes, they are both references to the same dependency property. (In other words, TextBlock.FontSizeProperty and Control.FontSizeProperty are references that point to the same DependencyProperty object. You first learned about this possible issue in Chapter 6.) As a result, when you use this style, WPF sets the FontFamily and FontSize property twice. The last-applied settings (in this case, 10-unit Arial) take precedence and are applied to both Button and TextBlock objects. Although this problem is fairly specific and doesn't occur with many properties, it's important to be on the lookout for it if you often create styles that apply different formatting to different element types.

There's one more trick that you can use to simplify style declarations. If all your properties are intended for the same element type, you can set the TargetType property of the Style object to indicate the class that your properties apply to. For example, if you're creating a button-only style, you could create the style like this:

```
<Style x:Key="BigFontButtonStyle" TargetType="Button">
  <Setter Property="FontFamily" Value="Times New Roman" />
  <Setter Property="FontSize" Value="18" />
  <Setter Property="FontWeight" Value="Bold" />
</Style>
```

This is a relatively minor convenience. As you'll discover later, the TargetType property also doubles as a shortcut that allows you to apply styles automatically if you leave out the style key name.

Attaching Event Handlers

Property setters are the most common ingredient in any style, but you can also create a collection of EventSetter objects that wire up events to specific event handlers. Here's an example that attaches the event handlers for the MouseEnter and MouseLeave events:

```
<Style x:Key="MouseOverHighlightStyle">
  <EventSetter Event="TextBlock.MouseEnter" Handler="element_MouseEnter" />
  <EventSetter Event="TextBlock.MouseLeave" Handler="element_MouseLeave" />
  <Setter Property="TextBlock.Padding" Value="5"/>
</Style>
```

Here's the event handling code:

```
private void element_MouseEnter(object sender, MouseEventArgs e)
{
    ((TextBlock)sender).Background = new
        SolidColorBrush(Colors.LightGoldenrodYellow);
}

private void element_MouseLeave(object sender, MouseEventArgs e)
{
    ((TextBlock)sender).Background = null;
}
```

MouseEnter and MouseLeave use direct event routing, which means they don't bubble up or tunnel down the element tree. If you want to apply a mouseover effect to a large number of elements (for example, you want to change the background color of an element when the mouse moves overtop of it), you need to add the MouseEnter and MouseLeave event handlers to each element. The style-based event handlers simplify this task. Now you simply need to apply a single style, which can include property setters and event setters:

```
<TextBlock Style="{StaticResource MouseOverHighlightStyle}">
  Hover over me.
</TextBlock>
```

Figure 12-2 shows a simple demonstration of this technique with three elements, two of which use the MouseOverHighlightStyle.

Event setters are a rare technique in WPF. If you need the functionality shown here, you're more likely to use event triggers, which define the action you want declaratively (and so require no code). Event triggers are designed to implement animations, which makes them more useful when creating mouseover effects.

Event setters aren't a good choice when handling an event that uses bubbling. In this situation, it's usually easier to handle the event you want on a higher-level element. For example, if you want to link all the buttons in a toolbar to the same event handler for the Click event, the best approach is to attach a single event handler to the Toolbar element that holds all the buttons. In this situation, an event setter is an unnecessary complication.

Figure 12-2. *Handling the MouseEnter and MouseLeave events with a style*

Tip In many cases it's clearer to explicitly define all your events and avoid event setters altogether. If you need to link several events to the same event handler, do it by hand. You can also use tricks such as attaching an event handler at the container level and centralizing logic with commands (Chapter 10).

The Many Layers of Styles

Although you can define an unlimited number of styles at many different levels, each WPF element can only use a single style object at once. Although this might appear to be a limitation at first, it usually isn't because of property value inheritance and style inheritance.

For example, imagine you want to give a group of controls the same font without applying the same style to each one. In this case, you may be able to place them in a single panel (or another type of container) and set the style of the container. As long as you're setting properties that use the property value inheritance feature, these values will flow down to the children. Properties that use this model include IsEnabled, IsVisible, Foreground, and all the font properties.

In other cases, you might want to create a style that builds upon another style. You can use this sort of style inheritance by setting the BasedOn attribute of a style. For example, consider these two styles:

```
<Window.Resources>
  <Style x:Key="BigFontButtonStyle">
    <Setter Property="Control.FontFamily" Value="Times New Roman" />
    <Setter Property="Control.FontSize" Value="18" />
    <Setter Property="Control.FontWeight" Value="Bold" />
  </Style>
```

```
    <Style x:Key="EmphasizedBigFontButtonStyle"
      BasedOn="{StaticResource BigFontButtonStyle}">
      <Setter Property="Control.Foreground" Value="White" />
      <Setter Property="Control.Background" Value="DarkBlue" />
    </Style>
</Window.Resources>
```

The first style (BigFontButtonStyle) defines three font properties. The second style (EmphasizedBigFontButtonStyle) acquires these aspects from BigFontButtonStyle and then supplements them with two more properties that change the foreground and the background brushes. This two-part design gives you the ability to apply just the font settings or the font-and-color combination. This design also allows you to create more styles that incorporate the font or color details you've defined (but not necessarily both).

Note You can use the BasedOn property to create an entire chain of inherited styles. The only rule is that if you set the same property twice, the last property setter (the one in the derived class farthest down the inheritance chain) overrides any earlier definitions.

Figure 12-3 shows style inheritance at work in a simple window that uses both styles.

Figure 12-3. *Creating a style based on another style*

STYLE INHERITANCE ADDS COMPLEXITY

Although style inheritance seems like a great convenience at first glance, it's usually not worth the trouble. That's because style inheritance is subject to the same problems as code inheritance: dependencies that make your application more fragile. For example, if you use the markup shown previously, you're forced to keep the same font characteristics for two styles. If you decide to change BigFontButtonStyle, EmphasizedBigFontButtonStyle changes as well—unless you explicitly add more setters that override the inherited values.

This problem is trivial enough in the two-style example, but it becomes a significant issue if you use style inheritance in a more realistic application. Usually, styles are categorized based on different types of content and the role that the content plays. For example, a sales application might include styles such as ProductTitleStyle, ProductTextStyle, HighlightQuoteStyle, NavigationButtonStyle, and so on. If you base ProductTitleStyle on ProductTextStyle (perhaps because they both share the same font), you'll run into trouble if you apply settings to ProductTextStyle later on that you don't want to apply to ProductTitleStyle

(such as different margins). In this case, you'll be forced to define your settings in ProductTextStyle and explicitly override them in ProductTitleStyle. At the end, you'll be left with a more complicated model and very few style settings that are actually reused.

Unless you have a specific reason to base one style on another (for example, the second style is a special case of the first and changes just a few characteristics out of a large number of inherited settings), don't use style inheritance.

Automatically Applying Styles by Type

So far, you've seen how to create named styles and refer to them in your markup. However, there's another approach. You can apply a style automatically to elements of a certain type.

Doing this is quite easy. You simply need to set the TargetType property to indicate the appropriate type (as described earlier) and leave out the key name altogether. When you do this, WPF actually sets the key name implicitly using the type markup extension, as shown here:

```
x:Key="{x:Type Button}"
```

Now the style is automatically applied to any buttons all the way down the element tree. For example, if you define a style in this way on the window, it applies to every button in that window (unless there's a style farther downstream that replaces it).

Here's an example with a window that sets the button styles automatically to get the same effect you saw in Figure 12-1:

```
<Window.Resources>
  <Style TargetType="Button">
    <Setter Property="FontFamily" Value="Times New Roman" />
    <Setter Property="FontSize" Value="18" />
    <Setter Property="FontWeight" Value="Bold" />
  </Style>
</Window.Resources>
```

```
<StackPanel Margin="5">
  <Button Padding="5" Margin="5">Customized Button</Button>
  <TextBlock Margin="5">Normal Content.</TextBlock>
  <Button Padding="5" Margin="5" Style="{x:Null}">A Normal Button</Button>
  <TextBlock Margin="5">More normal Content.</TextBlock>
  <Button Padding="5" Margin="5">Another Customized Button</Button>
</StackPanel>
```

In this example, the middle button explicitly replaces the style. But rather than supply a new style of its own, this button sets the Style property to a null value, which effectively removes the style.

Although automatic styles are convenient, they can complicate your design. Here are a few reasons why:

- In a complex window with many styles and multiple layers of styles, it becomes difficult to track down whether a given property is set through property value inheritance or a style (and if it's a style, which one). As a result, if you want to change a simple detail, you may need to wade through the markup of your entire window.

- The formatting in a window often starts out more general and becomes increasingly fine-tuned. If you apply automatic styles to the window early on, you'll probably need to override the styles in many places with explicit styles. This complicates the overall design. It's much more straightforward to create named styles for every combination of formatting characteristics you want and apply them by name.

- For example, if you create an automatic style for the TextBlock element, you'll wind up modifying other controls that use the TextBlock (such as a template-driven ListBox control).

To avoid problems, it's best to apply automatic styles judiciously. For example, you might use an automatic style to give a consistent padding to buttons, or control the margin settings of text boxes in a specific container rather than the entire window.

Triggers

One of the themes in WPF is extending what you can do *declaratively*. Whether you're using styles, resources, or data binding, you'll find that you can do quite a bit without resorting to code.

Triggers are another example of this trend. Using triggers, you can automate simple style changes that would ordinarily require boilerplate event-handling logic. For example, you can react when a property is changed and adjust a style automatically.

Triggers are linked to styles through the Style.Triggers collection. Every style can have an unlimited number of triggers, and each trigger is an instance of a class that derives from System.Windows.TriggerBase. WPF gives you the choices listed in Table 12-2.

You can apply triggers directly to elements, without needing to create a style, by using the FrameworkElement.Triggers collection. However, there's a sizeable catch. This Triggers collection only supports event triggers. (There's no technical reason for this limitation; it's simply a feature the WPF team didn't have time to implement and may include in future versions.)

Table 12-2. *Classes That Derive from TriggerBase*

Name	Description
Trigger	This is the simplest form of trigger. It watches for a change in a dependency property and then uses a setter to change the style.
MultiTrigger	This is similar to trigger but combines multiple conditions. All the conditions must be met before the trigger springs into action.
DataTrigger	This trigger works with data binding. It's similar to Trigger, except it watches for a change in any bound data.
MultiDataTrigger	This combines multiple data triggers.
EventTrigger	This is the most sophisticated trigger. It applies an animation when an event occurs.

A Simple Trigger

You can attach a simple trigger to any dependency property. For example, you can create mouseover and focus effects by responding to changes in the IsFocused, IsMouseOver, and IsPressed properties of the Control class.

Every simple trigger identifies the property you're watching and the value that you're waiting for. When this value occurs, the setters you've stored in the Trigger.Setters collection are applied. (Unfortunately, it isn't possible to use more sophisticated trigger logic that compares a value to see how it falls in a range, performs a calculation, and so on. In these situations, you're better off to use an event handler.)

Here's a trigger that waits for a button to get the keyboard focus, at which point it's given a dark red background:

```
<Style x:Key="BigFontButton">
  <Style.Setters>
    <Setter Property="Control.FontFamily" Value="Times New Roman" />
    <Setter Property="Control.FontSize" Value="18" />
  </Style.Setters>

  <Style.Triggers>
    <Trigger Property="Control.IsFocused" Value="True">
      <Setter Property="Control.Foreground" Value="DarkRed" />
    </Trigger>
  </Style.Triggers>
</Style>
```

The nice thing about triggers is that there's no need to write any logic to reverse them. As soon as the trigger stops applying, your element reverts to its normal appearance. In this example that means the button gets its ordinary gray background as soon as the user tabs away.

■Note To understand how this works, you need to remember the dependency property system that you learned about in Chapter 6. Essentially, a trigger is one of the many property providers that can override the value that's returned by a dependency property. However, the original value (whether it is set locally or by a style) still remains. As soon as the trigger becomes deactivated, the pretrigger value is available again.

It's possible to create multiple triggers that may apply to the same element at once. If these triggers set different properties, there's no ambiguity in this situation. However, if you have more than one trigger that modifies the same property, the last trigger in the list wins.

For example, consider the following triggers, which adjust a control depending on whether it is focused, whether the mouse is hovering over it, and whether it's been clicked:

```
<Style x:Key="BigFontButton">
  <Style.Setters>
    ...
  </Style.Setters>
  <Style.Triggers>
    <Trigger Property="Control.IsFocused" Value="True">
      <Setter Property="Control.Foreground" Value="DarkRed" />
    </Trigger>
    <Trigger Property="Control.IsMouseOver" Value="True">
      <Setter Property="Control.Foreground" Value="LightYellow" />
      <Setter Property="Control.FontWeight" Value="Bold" />
    </Trigger>
    <Trigger Property="Button.IsPressed" Value="True">
      <Setter Property="Control.Foreground" Value="Red" />
    </Trigger>
  </Style.Triggers>
</Style>
```

Obviously, it's possible to hover over a button that currently has the focus. This doesn't pose a problem because these triggers modify different properties. But if you click the button, there are two different triggers attempting to set the foreground. Now the trigger for the Button.IsPressed property wins because it's last in the list. It doesn't matter which trigger *occurs* first—for example, WPF doesn't care that a button gets focus before you click it. The order in which the triggers are listed in your markup is all that matters.

■Note In this example, triggers aren't all you need to get a nice-looking button. You're also limited by the button's control template, which locks down certain aspects of its appearance. For best results when customizing elements to this degree, you need to use a control template. However, control templates don't replace triggers—in fact, control templates often use triggers to get the best of both worlds: controls that can be completely customized *and* react to mouseovers, clicks, and other events to change some aspect of their visual appearance.

If you want to create a trigger that only switches on if several criteria are true, you can use a MultiTrigger. It provides a Conditions collection that lets you define a series of property and value combinations. Here's an example that only applies formatting if a button has focus and the mouse is over it:

```
<Style x:Key="BigFontButton">
  <Style.Setters>
    ...
  </Style.Setters>
  <Style.Triggers>
    <MultiTrigger>
      <MultiTrigger.Conditions>
        <Condition Property="Control.IsFocused" Value="True">
        <Condition Property="Control.IsMouseOver" Value="True">
      </MultiTrigger.Conditions>
      <MultiTrigger.Setters>
        <Setter Property="Control.Foreground" Value="DarkRed" />
      </MultiTrigger.Setters>
    </MultiTrigger>
  </Style.Triggers>
</Style>
```

In this case, it doesn't matter what order you declare the conditions in because they must all hold true before the background is changed.

An Event Trigger

While an ordinary trigger waits for a property change to occur, an event trigger waits for a specific event to be fired. You might assume that at this point you use setters to change the element, but that's not the case. Instead, an event trigger requires that you supply a series of actions that modify the control. These actions are used to apply an animation.

Although you won't consider animations in detail until Chapter 21, you can get the idea with a basic example. The following event trigger waits for the MouseEnter event and then animates the FontSize property of the button, enlarging it to 22 units for 0.2 seconds:

```
<Style x:Key="BigFontButtonStyle">
  <Style.Setters>
    ...
  </Style.Setters>

  <Style.Triggers>
    <EventTrigger RoutedEvent="Mouse.MouseEnter">
      <EventTrigger.Actions>
        <BeginStoryboard>
          <Storyboard>
            <DoubleAnimation
              Duration="0:0:0.2"
              Storyboard.TargetProperty="FontSize"
              To="22"  />
```

```
        </Storyboard>
      </BeginStoryboard>
    </EventTrigger.Actions>
  </EventTrigger>
  ...
```

In XAML, every animation must be defined in a storyboard, which provides the timeline for the animation. Inside the storyboard, you define the animation object (or objects) that you want to use. Every animation object performs essentially the same task: it modifies a dependency property over some time period.

In this example, a prebuilt animation class named DoubleAnimation is being used (which is found in the System.Windows.Media.Animation namespace, like all animation classes). DoubleAnimation is able to gradually change any double value (such as FontSize) to a set target over a given period of time. Because the double value is changed in small fractional units, you'll see the font grow gradually. The actual size of the change depends on the total amount of time and the total change you need to make. In this example, the font changes from its current set value to 22 units, over a time period of 0.2 seconds. (You can fine-tune details such as these and create an animation that accelerates or decelerates by tweaking the properties of the DoubleAnimation class.)

Unlike property triggers, you need to reverse event triggers if you want the element to return to its original state. (That's because the default animation behavior is to remain active once the animation is complete, holding the property at the final value. You'll learn more about how this system works in Chapter 21.)

To reverse the font size in this example, the style uses an event trigger that reacts to the MouseLeave event and shrinks the font back to its original size over a full two seconds. You don't need to indicate the target font size in this case—if you don't, WPF assumes you want the original font size that the button had before the first animation kicked in:

```
    ...
    <EventTrigger RoutedEvent="Mouse.MouseLeave">
      <EventTrigger.Actions>
        <BeginStoryboard>
          <Storyboard>
            <DoubleAnimation
              Duration="0:0:1"
              Storyboard.TargetProperty="FontSize"  />
          </Storyboard>
        </BeginStoryboard>
      </EventTrigger.Actions>
    </EventTrigger>
  </Style.Triggers>
</Style>
```

Interestingly, you can also perform an animation when a dependency property hits a specific value. This is useful if you want to perform an animation and there isn't a suitable event to use.

To use this technique you need a property trigger, as described in the previous section. The trick is to not supply any Setter objects for your property trigger. Instead, you set the Trigger.EnterActions and Trigger.ExitActions properties. Both properties take a collection of actions, such as the BeginStoryboard action that starts an animation. The EnterActions are performed when the property reaches the designated value, and ExitActions are performed when the property changes away from the designated value.

You'll learn much more about using event triggers and property triggers to launch animations in Chapter 21.

Last Word

In this chapter, you saw how styles allow you to define named sets of property values and easily apply them to the appropriate element.

Styles are a key ingredient that support many other WPF features. For example, styles give you a way to apply new control templates to a range of controls; use different formatting, depending on the current system theme; dynamically reskin your application; and enhance elements with automatic animations. You'll learn about these techniques in the chapters to come. (In Chapter 15, you'll explore control templates, themes, and application skinning. In Chapter 21, you'll delve into animations.) But first, it's time to tackle another core WPF topic: its rich two-dimensional drawing features.

■ ■ ■

CHAPTER 13

Shapes, Transforms, and Brushes

When you were first introduced to WPF in Chapter 1, you learned that it's powered by an entirely new graphics model—one that handles prebuilt controls and custom-drawn graphics in the same way, uses hardware acceleration with ordinary two-dimensional drawing, and favors scalable vectors over bitmaps.

In this chapter, you'll learn how to draw basic shapes, how to assemble them into more complex graphics, and how to use fancy brushes for painting gradients and creating other image effects. You'll also see how you can use transforms to rotate, skew, and otherwise manipulate just about any piece of user interface, including WPF elements. Not only will this knowledge help you build graphically rich visuals for your user interface, it will also allow you to get the most out of other WPF features such as control templates (Chapter 15) and animation (Chapter 21).

Understanding Shapes

The simplest way to draw 2-D graphical content in a WPF user interface is to use *shapes*: dedicated classes that represent simple lines, ellipses, rectangles, and polygons. Technically, shapes are known as drawing *primitives*. You can combine these basic ingredients to create more complex graphics.

The most important detail about shapes in WPF is the fact that they all derive from FrameworkElement. As a result, shapes *are* elements. This has a number of important consequences:

- **Shapes draw themselves.** You don't need to manage the invalidation and painting process. For example, you don't need to manually repaint a shape when content moves, the window is resized, or the shape's properties change.

- **Shapes are organized in the same way as other elements.** In other words, you can place a shape in any of the layout containers you learned about in Chapter 4. (Although the Canvas is obviously the most useful container because it allows you to place shapes at specific coordinates, which is important when you're building a complex drawing out of multiple pieces.)

- **Shapes support the same events as other elements.** That means you don't need to go to any extra work to deal with focus, key presses, mouse movements, and mouse clicks. You can use the same set of events you'd use with any element, and you have the same support for tooltips, context menus, and drag-and-drop operations.

This model is dramatically different than those in earlier user interface technologies, such as Windows Forms. Those frameworks do most of their work using the traditional windowing model (through User32), which would be incredibly inefficient if applied to pieces of graphical content, such as individual lines and squares. Additionally, the window model requires that each element "own" a small section of screen real estate, which makes it difficult to add transparency and use antialiasing around the edges of a nonrectangular shape.

Because of these limitations, older frameworks use the lower-level GDI/GDI+ model for custom drawing. This requires more work and provides far fewer high-level features.

■Tip As you'll see in Chapter 14, it's still possible to program at a lower level in WPF using the *visual layer*. This lightweight model improves performance if you need to create huge numbers of elements (say, thousands of shapes), and you don't need all the features of the UIElement and FrameworkElement classes (such as data binding and event handling). However, visual layer programming still works at a higher level than GDI/GDI+. Most importantly, WPF still manages the redrawing processing automatically. You simply supply the content.

The Shape Classes

Every shape derives from the abstract System.Windows.Shapes.Shape class. Figure 13-1 shows the inheritance hierarchy for shapes.

As you can see, there's a relatively small set of classes that derive from the Shape class. Line, Ellipse, and Rectangle are all straightforward, while Polyline is a connected series of straight lines, and Polygon is a closed shape made up of a connected series of straight lines. Finally, the Path class is an all-in-one superpower that can combine basic shapes in a single element.

Although the Shape class can't do anything on its own, it defines a small set of important properties, which are listed in Table 13-1.

Table 13-1. *Shape Properties*

Name	Description
Fill	Sets the brush object that paints the surface of the shape (everything inside its borders).
Stroke	Sets the brush object that paints the edge of the shape (its border).
StrokeThickness	Sets the thickness of the border, in device-independent units. When drawing a line, WPF splits the width on each side. So a line that's 10 units wide gets 5 units of space on each side of where a single-unit line would be drawn. If you give a line an odd-number thickness, the line will have a fractional width on each side. For example, an 11-unit line has 5.5 units of space on each side. This pretty much guarantees that the line won't line up evenly with the display pixels of your monitor, even if it's running at 96 dpi resolution, so you'll end up with a slightly fuzzy antialiased edge. You can use the SnapsToDevicePixels property to clean this up if it bothers you (as described in the section "Pixel Snapping" later in this chapter).
StrokeStartLineCap and StrokeEndLineCap	Determine the contour of the edge of the beginning and end of the line. These properties only have an effect for the Line, the Polyline, and (sometimes) the Path shapes. All other shapes are closed, and so have no starting and ending point.

Name	Description
StrokeDashArray, StrokeDashOffset, and StrokeDashCap	Allow you to create a dashed border around a shape. You can control the size and frequency of the dashes and how the edge where each dash line begins and ends is contoured.
StrokeLineJoin and StrokeMiterLimit	Determine the contour of the corners of a shape. Technically, these properties affect the *vertices* where different lines meet, such as the corners of a Rectangle. These properties have no effect for shapes without corners, such as Line and Ellipse.
Stretch	Determines how a shape fills its available space. You can use this property to create a shape that expands to fit its container. You can also force a shape to expand in one direction using a Stretch value for the HorizontalAlignment or VerticalAlignment properties (which are inherited from the FrameworkElement class).
DefiningGeometry	Provides a Geometry object for the shape. A Geometry object describes the coordinates and size of a shape without including the UIElement plumbing, such as the support for keyboard and mouse events. You'll use geometries in Chapter 14.
GeometryTransform	Allows you to apply a Transform object that changes the coordinate system that's used to draw a shape. This allows you to skew, rotate, or displace a shape. Transforms are particularly useful when animating graphics. You'll learn about transforms later in this chapter.
RenderedGeometry	Provides a Geometry object that describes the final, rendered shape. Geometries are described in Chapter 14.

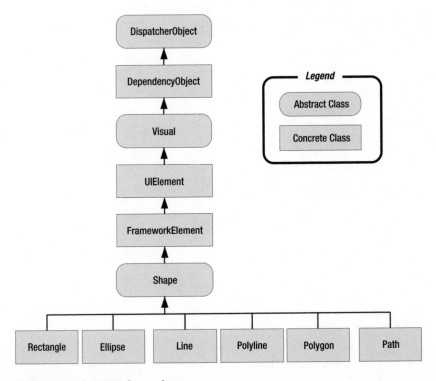

Figure 13-1. *The WPF shape classes*

In the following sections, you'll consider the Rectangle, Ellipse, Line, and Polyline. Along the way, you'll learn the following fundamentals:

- How to size shapes and organize them in a layout container.

- How to control what regions of a complex shape are filled in.

- How to use dashed lines and different line ends (or "caps").

- How to neatly align shape edges along pixel boundaries.

You'll take a look at the more sophisticated Path class in Chapter 14.

Rectangle and Ellipse

The Rectangle and Ellipse are the two simplest shapes. To create either one, set the familiar Height and Width properties (inherited from FrameworkElement) to define the size of your shape, and then set the Fill or Stroke property (or both) to make the shape visible. You're also free to use properties such as MinHeight, MinWidth, HorizontalAlignment, VerticalAlignment, and Margin.

■**Note** If you fail to supply a brush for the Stroke or Fill property, your shape won't appear at all. Both these properties are initially set to use transparent brushes.

Here's a simple example that stacks an ellipse on a rectangle (see Figure 13-2) using a StackPanel:

```
<StackPanel>
  <Ellipse Fill="Yellow" Stroke="Blue"
   Height="50" Width="100" Margin="5" HorizontalAlignment="Left"></Ellipse>
  <Rectangle Fill="Yellow" Stroke="Blue"
   Height="50" Width="100" Margin="5" HorizontalAlignment="Left"></Rectangle>
</StackPanel>
```

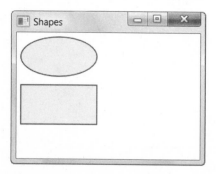

Figure 13-2. *Two simple shapes*

The Ellipse class doesn't add any properties. The Rectangle class adds just two: RadiusX and RadiusY. When set to nonzero values, these properties allow you to create nicely rounded corners.

You can think of RadiusX and RadiusY as describing an ellipse that's used just to fill in the corners of the rectangle. For example, if you set both properties to 10, WPF draws your corners using the edge of a circle that's 10 units wide. As you make your radius larger, more of your rectangle will be rounded off. If you increase RadiusY more than RadiusX, your corners will round off more gradually along the left and right sides and more sharply along the top and bottom edge. If you increase the RadiusX property to match your rectangle's width, and increase RadiusY to match its height, you'll end up converting your rectangle into an ordinary ellipse.

Figure 13-3 shows a few rectangles with rounded corners.

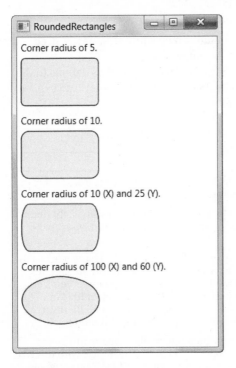

Figure 13-3. *Rounded corners*

Sizing and Placing Shapes

As you already know, hard-coded sizes are usually not the ideal approach to creating user interfaces. They limit your ability to handle dynamic content and they make it more difficult to localize your application into other languages.

When drawing shapes, these concerns don't always apply. Often, you'll need tighter control over shape placement. However, there are many cases where you can make your design a little more flexible. Both the Ellipse and the Rectangle have the ability to size themselves to fill the available space.

If you don't supply the Height and Width properties, the shape is sized based on its container. In the previous example, removing the Height and Width values (and leaving out the MinHeight and MinWidth values) will cause the shapes to shrink to a vanishingly small size, because the StackPanel is sized to fit its content. However, if you force the StackPanel to take the full width of the window (by setting its HorizontalAlignment property to Stretch), then also set the HorizontalAlignment property of the ellipse to Stretch and remove the ellipse's Width property, the ellipse will take the full width of the window.

A better example can be made with the Grid container. If you use the proportional row-sizing behavior (which is the default), you can create an ellipse that fills a window with this stripped-down markup:

```
<Grid>
  <Ellipse Fill="Yellow" Stroke="Blue"></Ellipse>
</Grid>
```

Here, the Grid fills the entire window. The Grid contains a single proportionately sized row, which fills the entire Grid. Finally, the ellipse fills the entire row.

This sizing behavior depends on the value of the Stretch property (which is defined in the Shape class). By default, it's set to Fill, which stretches a shape to fill its container if an explicit size isn't indicated. Table 13-2 lists all your possibilities.

Table 13-2. *Values for the Stretch Enumeration*

Name	Description
Fill	Your shape is stretched in width and height to fit its container exactly. (If you set an explicit height and width, this setting has no effect.)
None	The shape is not stretched. Unless you set a nonzero width and height (using the Height and Width or MinHeight and MinWidth properties), your shape won't appear.
Uniform	The width and height are sized up proportionately until the shape reaches the edge of the container. If you use this with an ellipse, you'll end up with the biggest circle that fits in the window. If you use it with a rectangle, you'll get the biggest possible square. (If you set an explicit height and width, your shape is sized within those bounds. For example, if you set a Width of 10 and a Height of 100 for a rectangle, you'll only get a 10 ×10 square.)
UniformToFill	The width and height are sized proportionately until the shape fills all the available height and width. For example, if you place a rectangle with this size setting into a window that's 100 × 200 units, you'll get a 200 × 200 rectangle, and part of it will be clipped off. (If you set an explicit height and width, your shape is sized within those bounds. For example, if you set a Width of 10 and a Height of 100 for a rectangle, you'll get a 100 × 100 rectangle that's clipped to fit an invisible 10 × 100 box.)

Figure 13-4 shows the difference between Fill, Uniform, and UniformToFill.

Usually, a Stretch value of Fill is the same as setting both HorizontalAlignment and VerticalAlignment to Stretch. The difference occurs if you choose to set a fixed Width or Height on your shape. In this case, the HorizontalAlignment and VerticalAlignment values are simply ignored. However, the Stretch setting still has an effect—it determines how your shape content is sized within the bounds you've given it.

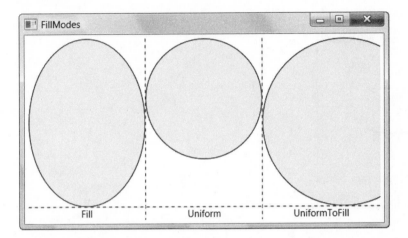

Figure 13-4. *Filling three cells in a Grid*

■**Tip** In most cases, you'll size a shape explicitly or allow it to stretch to fit. You won't combine both approaches.

So far, you've seen how to size a Rectangle and an Ellipse, but what about placing them exactly where you want them? WPF shapes use the same layout system as any other element. However, some layout containers aren't as appropriate. For example, the StackPanel, DockPanel, and WrapPanel often aren't what you want because they're designed to separate elements. The Grid is a bit more flexible because it allows you to place as many elements as you want in the same cell (although it doesn't let you position squares and ellipsis in different parts of that cell). The ideal container is the Canvas, which forces you to specify the coordinates of each shape using the attached Left, Top, Right, or Bottom properties. This gives you complete control over how shapes overlap:

```
<Canvas>
  <Ellipse Fill="Yellow" Stroke="Blue" Canvas.Left="100" Canvas.Top="50"
    Width="100" Height="50"></Ellipse>
    <Rectangle Fill="Yellow" Stroke="Blue" Canvas.Left="30" Canvas.Top="40"
      Width="100" Height="50"></Rectangle>
</Canvas>
```

With a Canvas, the order of your tags is important. In the previous example, the rectangle is superimposed on the ellipse because the ellipse appears first in the list, and so is drawn first (Figure 13-5).

Remember, a Canvas doesn't need to occupy an entire window. For example, there's no reason that you can't create a Grid that uses a Canvas in one of its cells. This gives you the perfect way to lock down fixed bits of drawing logic in a dynamic, free-flowing user interface.

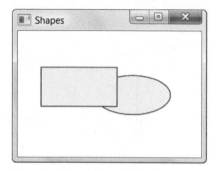

Figure 13-5. *Overlapping shapes in a Canvas*

Sizing Shapes Proportionately with a Viewbox

The only limitation to using the Canvas is that your graphics won't be able to resize themselves to fit larger or smaller windows. This makes perfect sense for buttons (which don't change size in these situations), but not necessarily for other types of graphical content. For example, you might create a complex graphic that you want to be resizable so it can take advantage of the available space.

In situations like these, WPF has an easy solution. If you want to combine the precise control of the Canvas with easy resizability, you can use the Viewbox element. The Viewbox is a simple class that derives from Decorator, which you first considered in Chapter 5. It accepts a single child, which it stretches or shrinks to fit the available space.

Although you could place a single shape in a Decorator, that doesn't provide any real advantage. Instead, the Decorator shines when you need to wrap a group of shapes that make up a drawing. Then you simply place the layout container for your drawing (typically, the Canvas) inside the Viewbox.

The following example puts a Decorator in the second row of a Grid. The Decorator takes the full height and width of the row. The row takes whatever space is left over after the first autosized row is rendered. Here's the markup:

```
<Grid Margin="5">
  <Grid.RowDefinitions>
    <RowDefinition Height="Auto"></RowDefinition>
    <RowDefinition Height="*"></RowDefinition>
  </Grid.RowDefinitions>
```

```
<TextBlock>The first row of a Grid.</TextBlock>

<Viewbox Grid.Row="1" HorizontalAlignment="Left" >
  <Canvas Width="200" Height="150">
    <Ellipse Fill="Yellow" Stroke="Blue" Canvas.Left="10"  Canvas.Top="50"
      Width="100" Height="50" HorizontalAlignment="Left"></Ellipse>
    <Rectangle Fill="Yellow" Stroke="Blue" Canvas.Left="30"  Canvas.Top="40"
      Width="100" Height="50" HorizontalAlignment="Left"></Rectangle>
  </Canvas>
</Viewbox>
</Grid>
```

Figure 13-6 shows how the Viewbox adjusts itself as the window is resized. The first row is unchanged. However, the second row expands to fill the extra space. As you can see, the shape in the Viewbox changes proportionately as the window grows.

Like all shapes, the Viewbox has a Stretch property, but it takes a default value of Uniform. However, you can use any of the other values from Table 13-2. You can also get slightly more control by using the StretchDirection property. By default, this property takes the value Both, but you can use UpOnly to create content that can grow but won't shrink beyond its original size, and DownOnly to create content that can shrink but not grow.

■Note When a shape is resized, WPF resizes its inside area and its border proportionately. That means the larger your shape grows, the thicker its border will be.

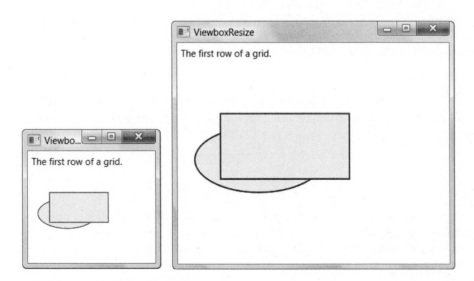

Figure 13-6. *Resizing with a viewbox*

In order for the Viewbox to perform its magic, it needs to be able to determine two pieces of information: the ordinary size that your content would have (if it weren't in a Viewbox) and the new size that you want it to have. The second detail—the new size—is simple enough. The Viewbox gives the inner content all the space that's available, based on its Stretch property. That means the bigger the Viewbox, the bigger your content.

The first detail—the ordinary, non-Viewbox size, is implicit in the way you define the nested content. In the previous example, the Canvas is given an explicit size of 200 by 150 units. Thus, the Viewbox scales the image from that starting point. For example, the ellipse is initially 100 units wide, which means it takes up half the allotted Canvas drawing space. As the Canvas grows larger, the Viewbox respects these proportions and the ellipse continues to take half the available space.

However, consider what happens if you remove the Width and Height properties from the Canvas. Now, the Canvas is given a size of 0 by 0 units, so the Viewbox cannot resize it and your nested content won't appear. (This is different than the behavior you get if you have the Canvas on its own. That's because even though the Canvas is still given a size of 0 by 0, your shapes are allowed to draw outside the Canvas area as long as the Canvas.ClipToBounds property hasn't been set to true. The Viewbox isn't as tolerant of this error.)

Now consider what happens if you wrap the Canvas inside a proportionately sized Grid cell and you don't specify the size of the Canvas. If you aren't using the Viewbox, this approach works perfectly well—the Canvas is stretched to fill the cell and the content inside is visible. But if you place all this content in a Viewbox, this strategy fails. The Viewbox can't determine the initial size, so it can't resize the Grid appropriately.

You can get around this problem by placing certain shapes (such as the Rectangle and Ellipse) directly in an autosized container (such as the Grid). The Viewbox can then evaluate the minimum size the Grid needs to fit its content and then scale it up to fit what's available. However, the easiest way to get the size you really want in a Viewbox is to wrap your content in an element that has a fixed size, whether it's a Canvas, a button, or something else. This fixed size then becomes the initial size that the Viewbox uses for its calculations. Hard-coding a size in this way won't limit the flexibility of your layout because the Viewbox is sized proportionately based on the available space and its layout container.

■**Note** Regardless of whether you use the Viewbox, your graphic will be resized to compensate for different system DPI settings (as described in Chapter 1). In other words, a rectangle on a 96 dpi system will be rendered with fewer pixels than the same rectangle on a 120 dpi system.

Line

The Line shape represents a straight line that connects one point to another. The starting and ending points are set by four properties: X1 and Y1 (for the first point) and X2 and Y2 (for the second). For example, here's a line that stretches from (0, 0) to (10, 100):

```
<Line Stroke="Blue" X1="0" Y1="0" X2="10" Y2="100"></Line>
```

The Fill property has no effect for a line. You must set the Stroke property.

The coordinates you use in a line are relative to the top-left corner where the line is placed. For example, if you place the previous line in a StackPanel, the coordinate (0, 0) points to wherever that item in the StackPanel is placed. It might be the top-left corner of the window, but it probably isn't. If the StackPanel uses a nonzero Margin, or if the line is preceded by other elements, the line will begin at a point (0, 0) some distance down from the top of the window.

However, it's perfectly reasonable to use negative coordinates for a line. In fact, you can use coordinates that take your line out of its allocated space and draw overtop of any other part of the window. This isn't possible with the Rectangle and Ellipse shapes you've seen so far. However, there's also a drawback to this model—namely, lines can't use the flow content model. That means there's no point setting properties such as Margin, HorizontalAlignment, and VerticalAlignment on a line—they won't have any effect. The same limitation applies to the Polyline and Polygon shapes.

Note You can use the Height, Width, and Stretch properties with a line, although it's not terribly common. The basic technique is to use the Height and Width to determine the space that's allocated to the line, and then use the Stretch property to resize the line to fill this area.

If you place a Line in a Canvas, the attached position properties (such as Top and Left) still apply. They determine the starting position of the line. In other words, the two line coordinates are offset by that amount. Consider this line:

```
<Line Stroke="Blue" X1="0" Y1="0" X2="10" Y2="100"
 Canvas.Left="5" Canvas.Top="100"></Line>
```

It stretches from (0, 0) to (10, 100), using a coordinate system that treats the point (5, 100) on the Canvas as (0, 0). That makes it equivalent to this line that doesn't use the Top and Left properties:

```
<Line Stroke="Blue" X1="5" Y1="100" X2="15" Y2="200"></Line>
```

It's up to you whether you use the position properties when you place a Line on a Canvas. Often you can simplify your line drawing by picking a good starting point. You also make it easier to move parts of your drawing. For example, if you draw several lines and other shapes at a specific position in a Canvas, it's a good idea to draw them relative to a nearby point (by using the same Top and Left coordinates). That way, you can shift that entire part of your drawing to a new position as needed.

Note There's no way to create a curved line with Line or Polyline shapes. Instead, you need the more advanced Path class described in Chapter 14.

Polyline

The Polyline class allows you to draw a sequence of connected straight lines. You simply supply a list of X and Y coordinates using the Points property. Technically, the Points property requires a PointCollection object, but you fill this collection in XAML using a lean string-based syntax. You simply need to supply a list of points and add a space or a comma between each coordinate.

A Polyline can have as few as two points. For example, here's a Polyline that duplicates the first line you saw in this section, which stretches from (5, 100) to (15, 200):

```
<Polyline Stroke="Blue" Points="5 100 15 200"></Polyline>
```

For better readability, use commas in between each X and Y coordinate:

```
<Polyline Stroke="Blue" Points="5,100 15,200"></Polyline>
```

And here's a more complex PolyLine that begins at (10, 150). The points move steadily to the right, oscillating between higher Y values such as (50, 160) and lower ones such as (70, 130):

```
<Canvas>
  <Polyline Stroke="Blue" StrokeThickness="5" Points="10,150 30,140 50,160 70,130
90,170 110,120 130,180 150,110 170,190 190,100 210,240" >
  </Polyline>
</Canvas>
```

Figure 13-7 shows the final line.

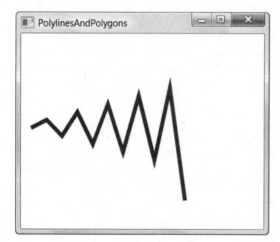

Figure 13-7. *A line with several segments*

At this point, it might occur to you that it would be easier to fill the Points collection programmatically, using some sort of loop that automatically increments X and Y values accordingly. This is true if you need to create highly dynamic graphics—for example, a chart that varies its appearance based on a set of data you extract from a database. But if you simply want to build a fixed piece of graphical content, you won't want to worry about the specific coordinates of your shapes at all. Instead, you (or a designer) will use another tool, such as Expression Design, to draw the appropriate graphics, and then export to XAML.

Polygon

The Polygon is virtually the same as the Polyline. Like the Polyline class, the Polygon class has a Points collection that takes a list of coordinates. The only difference is that the Polygon adds a final line segment that connects the final point to the starting point. (If your final point is already the same as the first point, the Polygon class has no difference.) You can fill the interior of this shape using the Fill brush. Figure 13-8 shows the previous Polyline as a Polygon with a yellow fill.

Note Technically, you can set the Fill property of a Polyline as well. In this situation, the Polyline fills itself as though it were a Polygon—in other words, as though it has an invisible line segment connecting the last point to the first point. This effect is of limited use.

In a simple shape where the lines never cross, it's easy to fill the interior. However, sometimes you'll have a more complex Polygon where it's not necessarily obvious what portions are "inside" the shape (and should be filled) and what portions are outside.

For example, consider Figure 13-9, which features a line that crosses more than one other line, leaving an irregular region at the center that you may or may not want to fill. Obviously, you can control exactly what gets filled by breaking this drawing down into smaller shapes. But you may not need to.

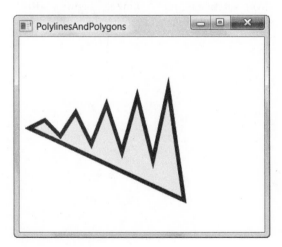

Figure 13-8. *A filled polygon*

Every Polygon and Polyline includes a FillRule property that lets you choose between two different approaches for filling in regions. By default, Fill Rule is set to EvenOdd. In order to decide whether to fill a region, WPF counts the number of lines that must be crossed to reach the outside of the shape. If this number is odd, the region is filled in; if it's even, the region isn't filled. In the center area of Figure 13-9, you must cross two lines to get out of the shape, so it's not filled.

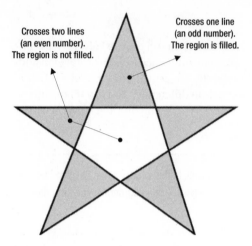

Figure 13-9. *Determining fill areas when FillRule is EvenOdd*

WPF also supports the Nonzero fill rule, which is a little trickier. Essentially, with Nonzero, WPF follows the same line-counting process as EvenOdd, but it takes into account the *direction* that each line flows. If the number of lines going in one direction (say, left to right) is equal to the number going in the opposite direction (right to left), the region is not filled. If the difference between these two counts is not zero, the region *is* filled. In the shape from the previous example, the interior region is filled if you set the FillRule to NonZero. Figure 13-10 shows why. (In this example, the points are numbered in the order they are drawn, and arrows show the direction in which each line is drawn.)

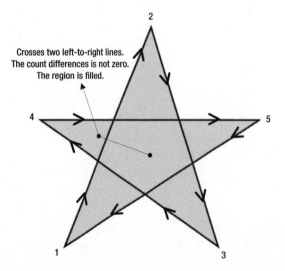

Figure 13-10. *Determining fill areas when FillRule is NonZero*

■Note If there are an odd number of lines, the difference between the two counts can't be zero. Thus, the Nonzero fill rule always fills at least as much as the EvenOdd rule, plus possibly a bit more.

The tricky part about Nonzero is that its fill settings depend on *how* you draw the shape, not what the shape itself looks like. For example, you could draw the same shape in such a way that the center isn't filled (although it's much more awkward, you'd begin by drawing the inner region and then draw the outside spikes in the reverse direction).

Here's the markup that draws the star shown in Figure 13-10:

```
<Polygon Stroke="Blue" StrokeThickness="1" Fill="Yellow"
 Canvas.Left="10" Canvas.Top="175" FillRule="Nonzero"
 Points="15,200 68,70 110,200 0,125 135,125">
</Polygon>
```

Line Caps and Line Joins

When drawing with the Line and Polyline shapes, you can choose how the starting and ending edge of the line is drawn using the StartLineCap and EndLineCap properties. (These properties have no effect on other shapes because they're closed.)

Ordinarily, both StartLineCap and EndLineCap are set to Flat, which means the line ends immediately at its final coordinate. Your other choices are Round (which rounds the corner off gently), Triangle (which draws the two sides of the line together in a point), and Square (which ends the line with a sharp edge). All of these values add length to the line—in other words, they take it beyond the position where it would otherwise end. The extra distance is half the thickness of the line.

■Note The only difference between Flat and Square is the fact that the Square-edged line extends this extra distance. In all other respects, the edge looks the same.

Figure 13-11 shows different line caps at the end of a line.

All shapes except Line allow you to tweak how their corners are shaped using the StrokeLineJoin property. You have three choices. The default value, Miter, uses sharp edges, while Bevel cuts off the point edge, and Round rounds it out gently. Figure 13-12 shows the difference.

When using mitered edges with thick lines and very small angles, the sharp corner can extend an impractically long distance. In this case, you can use Bevel or Round to pare down the corner. Or you could use the StrokeMiterLimit, which automatically bevels the edge when it reaches a certain maximum length. The StrokeMiterLimit is a ratio that compares the length used to miter the corner to half the thickness of the line. If you set this to 1 (which is the default value), you're allowing the corner to extend half the thickness of the line. If you set it to 3, you're allowing the corner to extend to 1.5 times the thickness of the line. The last line in Figure 13-12 uses a higher miter limit with a narrow corner.

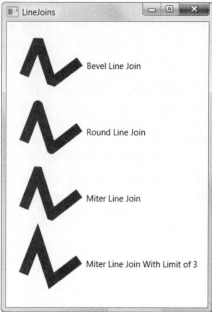

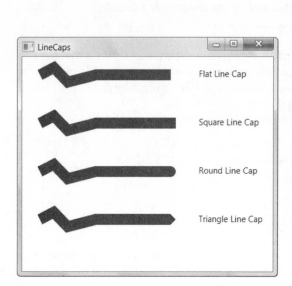

Figure 13-11. *Line caps*　　　　　　　**Figure 13-12.** *Line joins*

Dashes

Instead of drawing boring solid lines for the borders of your shape, you can draw *dashed lines*—lines that are broken with spaces according to a pattern you specify.

When creating a dashed line in WPF, you aren't limited to specific presets. Instead, you choose the length of the solid segment of the line and the length of the broken (blank) segment by setting the StrokeDashArray property. For example, consider this line:

```
<Polyline Stroke="Blue" StrokeThickness="14" StrokeDashArray="1 2"
  Points="10,30 60,0 90,40 120,10 350,10">
</Polyline>
```

It has a line value of 1 and a gap value of 2. These values are interpreted relative to the thickness of the line. So if the line is 14 units thick (as in this example), the solid portion is 14 units, followed by a blank portion of 28 units. The line repeats this pattern for its entirelength.

On the other hand, if you swap these values around like so

```
StrokeDashArray="2 1"
```

you get a line that has 28-unit solid portions broken by 13-unit spaces. Figure 13-13 shows both lines. As you'll notice, when a very thick line segment falls on a corner, it may be broken unevenly.

There's no reason that you need to stick with whole number values. For example, this StrokeDashArray is perfectly reasonable:

```
StrokeDashArray="5 0.2 3 0.2"
```

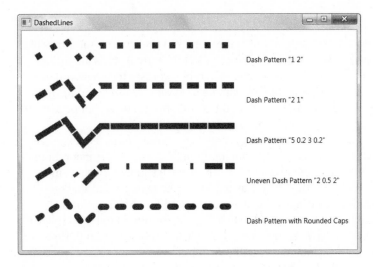

Figure 13-13. *Dashed lines*

It supplies a more complex sequence—a dashed line that's 5 × 14 length, then a 0.2 × 15 break, followed by a 3 × 14 length and another 0.2 × 14 length. At the end of this sequence, the line repeats the pattern from the beginning.

An interesting thing happens if you supply an odd number of values for the StrokeDashArray. Take this one for example:

```
StrokeDashArray="3 0.5 2"
```

When drawing this line, WPF begins with a 3-times-thickness line, followed by a 0.5-times-thickness space, followed by a 2-times-thickness-line. But when it repeats the pattern it starts with a gap, meaning you get a 3-times-thickness *space*, followed by a 0.5-times-thickness line, and so on. Essentially, the dashed line alternates its pattern between line segments and spaces.

If you want to start midway into your pattern, you can use the StrokeDashOffset property, which is a 0-based index number that points to one of the values in your StrokeDashArray. For example, if you set StrokeDashOffset to 1 in the previous example, the line will begin with the 0.5-thickness space. Set it to 2, and the line begins with the 2-thickness segment.

Finally, you can control how the broken edges of your line are capped. Ordinarily, it's a straight edge, but you can set the StrokeDashCap to the Bevel, Square, and Triangle values you considered in the previous section. Remember, all of these settings add one half the line thickness to the end of your dash. If you don't take this into account, you might end up with dashes that overlap one another. The solution is to add extra space to compensate.

Tip When using the StrokeDashCap property with a line (not a shape), it's often a good idea to set the StartLineCap and EndLineCap to the same values. This makes the line look consistent.

Pixel Snapping

As you know, WPF uses a device-independent drawing system. You specify sizes for things like fonts and shapes using "virtual" pixels, which are the same size as normal pixels on ordinary 96 dpi displays but are scaled up on higher dpi displays. In other words, a rectangle you draw that's 50 pixels wide might actually be rendered using more or fewer pixels, depending on the device. This conversion between device-independent units and physical pixels happens automatically, and you usually don't need to think about it at all.

The ratio of pixels between different dpi settings is rarely a whole number. For example, 50 pixels at 96 dpi become 62.4996 pixels on a 120 dpi monitor. (This isn't an error condition—in fact, WPF always allows you to use fractional double values when supplying a value in device-independent units.) Obviously, there's no way to place an edge on a point that's between pixels. WPF compensates by using antialiasing. For example, when drawing a red line that's 62.4992 pixels long, WPF might fill the first 62 pixels normally and then shade the 63rd pixel with a value that's in between the line color (red) and the background. However, there's a catch. If you're drawing straight lines, rectangles, or polygons with square corners, this automatic antialiasing can introduce a tinge of blurriness at the edges of your shape.

You might assume that this problem only appears when you're running an application on a display that has display resolution that's *not* 96 dpi. However, that's not necessarily the case because all shapes can be sized using fractional lengths and coordinates, which causes the same issue. And although you probably won't use fractional values in your shape drawing, *resizable* shapes—shapes that are stretched because they size along with their container or they're placed in a Viewbox—will almost always end up with fractional sizes. Similarly, odd-numbered line thicknesses create a line that has a fractional number of pixels on either side.

The fuzzy edge issue isn't necessarily a problem. In fact, depending on the type of graphic you're drawing it might look quite normal. However, if you don't want this behavior, you can tell WPF not to use antialiasing for a specific shape. Instead, WPF will round the measurement to the nearest device pixel. You turn on this feature, which is called *pixel snapping*, by setting the SnapsToDevicePixels property of a UIElement to true.

To see the difference, look at the magnified window in Figure 13-14, which compares two rectangles. The bottom one uses pixel snapping, while the top one doesn't. If you look carefully, you'll see a thin edge of lighter color along the top and left edges of the unsnapped rectangle.

Not Snapped

Snapped

Figure 13-14. *The effect of pixel snapping*

Transforms

A great deal of drawing tasks can be made simpler with the use of a *transform*—an object that alters the way a shape or element is drawn by secretly shifting the coordinate system it uses. In WPF, transforms are represented by classes that derive from the abstract System.Windows.Media.Transform class, as listed in Table 13-3.

Table 13-3. *Transform Classes*

Name	Description	Important Properties
TranslateTransform	Displaces your coordinate system by some amount. This transform is useful if you want to draw the same shape in different places.	X, Y
RotateTransform	Rotates your coordinate system. The shapes you draw normally are turned around a center point you choose.	Angle, CenterX, CenterY
ScaleTransform	Scales your coordinate system up or down, so that your shapes are drawn smaller or larger. You can apply different degrees of scaling in the X and Y dimensions, thereby stretching or compressing your shape.	ScaleX, ScaleY, CenterX, CenterY
SkewTransform	Warps your coordinate system by slanting it a number of degrees. For example, if you draw a square, it becomes a parallelogram.	AngleX, AngleY, CenterX, CenterX
MatrixTransform	Modifies your coordinate system using matrix multiplication with the matrix you supply. This is the most complex option—it requires some mathematical skill.	Matrix
TransformGroup	Combines multiple transforms so they can all be applied at once. The order in which you apply transformations is important—it affects the final result. For example, rotating a shape (with RotateTransform) and then moving it (with TranslateTransform) sends the shape off in a different direction than if you move it and *then* rotate it.	N/A

Technically, all transforms use matrix math to alter the coordinates of your shape. However, using the prebuilt transforms such as TranslateTransform, RotateTransform, ScaleTransform, and SkewTransform is far simpler than using the MatrixTransform and trying to work out the right matrix for the operation you want to perform. When you perform a series of transforms with the TransformGroup, WPF fuses your transforms together into a single MatrixTransform, ensuring optimal performance.

■Note All transforms derive from Freezable (through the Transform class). That means they have automatic change notification support. If you change a transform that's being used in a shape, the shape will redraw itself immediately.

Transforms are one of those quirky concepts that turn out to be extremely useful in a variety of different contexts. Some examples include the following:

- **Angling a shape.** So far you've been stuck with horizontally aligned rectangles, ellipses, lines, and polygons. Using the RotateTransform, you can turn your coordinate system to create certain shapes more easily.

- **Repeating a shape.** Many drawings are built using a similar shape in several different places. Using a transform, you can take a shape and then move it, rotate it, resize it, and so on.

■Tip In order to use the same shape in multiple places, you'll need to duplicate the shape in your markup (which isn't ideal), use code (to create the shape programmatically), or use the Path shape described in Chapter 14. The Path shape accepts Geometry objects, and you can store a geometry object as a resource so it can be reused throughout your markup.

- **Animation.** You can create a number of sophisticated effects with the help of a transform, such as rotating a shape, moving it from one place to another, and warping it dynamically.

You'll use transforms throughout this book, particularly when you create animations (Chapter 21) and manipulate 3-D content (Chapter 23). For now, you can learn all you need to know by considering how to apply a basic transform to an ordinary shape.

Transforming Shapes

To transform a shape, you assign the RenderTransform property to the transform object you want to use. Depending on the transform object you're using, you'll need to fill in different properties to configure it, as detailed in Table 13-3.

For example, if you're rotating a shape, you need to use the RotateTransform, and supply the angle in degrees. Here's an example that rotates a square by 25 degrees:

```
<Rectangle Width="80" Height="10" Stroke="Blue" Fill="Yellow"
  Canvas.Left="100" Canvas.Top="100">
  <Rectangle.RenderTransform>
    <RotateTransform Angle="25" />
  </Rectangle.RenderTransform>
</Rectangle>
```

When you rotate a shape in this way, you rotate it about the shape's origin (the top-left corner). Figure 13-15 illustrates this by rotating the same square 25, 50, 75, and then 100 degrees.

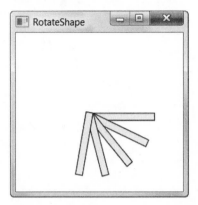

Figure 13-15. *Rotating a rectangle four times*

Sometimes you'll want to rotate a shape around a different point. The RotateTransform, like many other transform classes, provides a CenterX property and a CenterY property. You can use these properties to indicate the center point around which the rotation should be performed. Here's a rectangle that uses this approach to rotate itself 25 degrees around its center point:

```
<Rectangle Width="80" Height="10" Stroke="Blue" Fill="Yellow"
  Canvas.Left="100" Canvas.Top="100">
  <Rectangle.RenderTransform>
    <RotateTransform Angle="25" CenterX="45" CenterY="5" />
  </Rectangle.RenderTransform>
</Rectangle>
```

Figure 13-16 shows the result of performing the same sequence of rotations featured in Figure 13-15, but around the designated center point.

There's a clear limitation to using the CenterX and CenterY properties of the RotateTransform. These properties are defined using absolute coordinates, which means you need to know the exact center point of your content. If you're displaying dynamic content (for example, pictures of varying dimensions or elements that can be resized), this introduces a problem. Fortunately, WPF has a solution with the handy RenderTransformOrigin property, which is supported by all shapes. This property sets the center point using a proportional coordinate system that stretches from 0 to 1 in both dimensions. In other words, the point (0, 0) is designated as the top-left corner and (1, 1) is the bottom-right corner. (If the shape region isn't square, the coordinate system is stretched accordingly.)

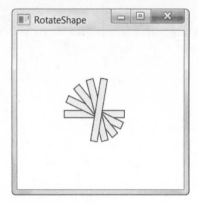

Figure 13-16. *Rotating a rectangle around its middle*

With the help of the RenderTransformOrigin property, you can rotate any shape around its center point using markup like this:

```
<Rectangle Width="80" Height="10" Stroke="Blue" Fill="Yellow"
  Canvas.Left="100" Canvas.Top="100" RenderTransformOrigin="0.5,0.5">
  <Rectangle.RenderTransform>
    <RotateTransform Angle="25" />
  </Rectangle.RenderTransform>
</Rectangle>
```

This works because the point (0.5, 0.5) designates the center of the shape, regardless of its size. In practice, RenderTransformOrigin is generally more useful than the CenterX and CenterY properties, although you can use either one (or both) depending on your needs.

Tip You can use values greater than 1 or less than 0 when setting RenderTransformOrigin property to designate a point that appears outside the bounding box of your shape. For example, you can use this technique with a RotateTransform to rotate a shape in a large arc around a very distant point, such as (5, 5).

Transforming Elements

The RenderTransform and RenderTransformOrigin properties aren't limited to shapes. In fact, the Shape class inherits them from the UIElement class, which means they're supported by all WPF elements, including buttons, text boxes, the TextBlock, entire layout containers full of content, and so on. Amazingly, you can rotate, skew, and scale any piece of WPF user interface (although in most cases you shouldn't).

RenderTransform isn't the only transform-related property that's defined in the base WPF classes. The FrameworkElement also defines a LayoutTransform property. LayoutTransform alters the element in the same way, but it performs its work before the layout pass. This results in slightly more overhead, but it's critical if you're using a layout container to provide automatic layout with a group of controls. (The shape classes also include the LayoutTransform property, but you'll rarely need to use it because you'll usually place your shapes specifically using a container such as the Canvas, rather than using automatic layout.)

To understand the difference, consider Figure 13-17, which includes two StackPanel containers (represented by the shaded areas), both of which contain a rotated button and a normal button. The rotated button in the first StackPanel uses the RenderTransform approach. The StackPanel lays out the two buttons as though the first button is positioned normally, and the rotation happens just before the button is rendered. As a result, the rotated button overlaps the one underneath. In the second StackPanel, the rotated button uses the LayoutTransform approach. The StackPanel gets the bounds that are required for the rotated button and lays out the second button accordingly.

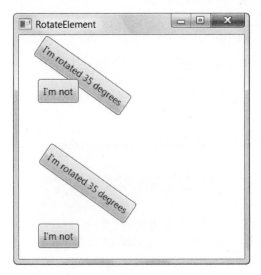

Figure 13-17. *Rotating buttons*

There are a few rare elements that can't be transformed because their rendering work isn't native to WPF. Two examples are the WindowsFormsHost, which lets you place a Windows Forms control in a WPF window (a feat demonstrated in Chapter 25) and the Frame element when it's used to display HTML content (in which case it relies on the COM-based Web-Browser control from Internet Explorer).

To a certain degree, WPF elements aren't aware that they're being modified when you set the LayoutTransform or RenderTransform properties. Notably, transforms don't affect the ActualHeight and ActualWidth properties of the element, which continue to report their untransformed dimensions. This is part of how WPF ensures that features such as flow layout and margins continue to work with the same behavior, even when you apply one or more transforms.

Better Brushes

As you know, brushes fill an area, whether it's the background, foreground, or border of an element, or the fill or stroke of a shape. You've used brushes throughout this book, but so far you've done most of your work with the straightforward SolidColorBrush. You've also learned these fundamental facts about brushes:

- Brushes support change notification because they derive from Freezable. As a result, if you change a brush, any elements that use that brush repaint themselves automatically.

- Brushes support partial transparency. All you need to do is modify the Opacity property to let the background show through.

- The SystemBrushes class provides access to brushes that use the colors defined in the Windows system preferences for the current computer.

Although SolidColorBrush is indisputably useful, there are several other classes that inherit from System.Windows.Media.Brush and give you more exotic effects. Table 13-4 lists them all.

Table 13-4. *Brush Classes*

Name	Description
LinearGradientBrush	Paints an area using a gradient fill, a gradually shaded fill that changes from one color to another (and, optionally, to another and then another, and so on).
RadialGradientBrush	Paints an area using a radial gradient fill, which is similar to a linear gradient except it radiates out in a circular pattern starting from a center point.
ImageBrush	Paints an area using an image that can be stretched, scaled, or tiled.
DrawingBrush	Paints an area using a Drawing object. This object can include shapes you've defined and bitmaps.
VisualBrush	Paints an area using a Visual object. Because all WPF elements derive from the Visual class, you can use this brush to copy part of your user interface (such as the face of a button) to another area. This is useful when creating fancy effects, such as partial reflections.

The DrawingBrush is covered in Chapter 14, when you consider more optimized ways to deal with large numbers of graphics. In this section, you'll learn how to use the brushes that fill areas with gradients, images, and visual content copied from other elements.

The LinearGradientBrush

The LinearGradientBrush allows you to create a blended fill that changes from one color to another.

Here's the simplest possible gradient. It shades a rectangle diagonally from blue (in the top-left corner) to white (in the bottom-right corner):

```
<Rectangle Width="150" Height="100">
  <Rectangle.Fill>
```

```
  <LinearGradientBrush >
    <GradientStop Color="Blue" Offset="0"/>
    <GradientStop Color="White" Offset="1" />
  </LinearGradientBrush>
 </Rectangle.Fill>
</Rectangle>
```

The top gradient in Figure 13-18 shows the result.

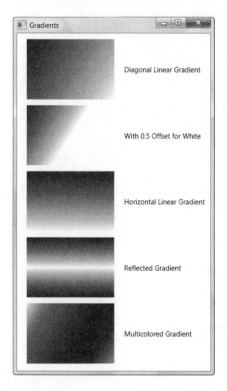

Figure 13-18. *A rectangle with different linear gradients*

To create this gradient, you need to add one GradientStop for each color. You also need to place each color in your gradient using an Offset value from 0 to 1. In this example, the GradientStop for the blue color has an offset of 0, which means it's placed at the very beginning of the gradient. The GradientStop for the white color has an offset of 1, which places it at the end. If you change these values, you could adjust how quickly the gradient switches from one color to the other. For example, if you set the GradientStop for the white color to 0.5, the gradient would blend from blue (in the top-left corner) to white in the middle (the point between the two corners). The right side of the rectangle would be completely white. (The second gradient in Figure 13-18 shows this example.)

The previous markup creates a gradient with a diagonal fill that stretches from one corner to another. However, you might want to create a gradient that blends from top to bottom or side to side, or uses a different diagonal angle. You control these details using the StartPoint and EndPoint properties of the LinearGradientBrush. These properties allow you to choose the point where the first color begins to change and the point where the color change ends with the final color. (The area in between is blended gradually.) However, there's one quirk. The coordinates you use for the starting and ending point aren't real coordinates. Instead, the LinearGradientBrush assigns the point (0, 0) to the top-left corner and (1, 1) to the bottom-right corner of the area you want to fill, no matter how high and wide it actually is.

To create a top-to-bottom horizontal fill, you can use a start point of (0, 0) for the top-left corner, and an end point of (0, 1), which represents the bottom-left corner. To create a side-to-side vertical fill (with no slant), you can use a start point of (0, 0) and an end point of (1, 0) for the bottom-left corner. Figure 13-18 shows a horizontal gradient (it's the third one).

You can get a little craftier by supplying start points and end points that aren't quite aligned with the corners of your gradient. For example, you could have a gradient stretch from (0, 0) to (0, 0.5), which is a point on the left edge, halfway down. This creates a compressed linear gradient—one color starts at the top, blending to the second color in the middle. The bottom half of the shape is filled with the second color. But wait—you can change this behavior using the LinearGradientBrush.SpreadMethod property. It's Pad by default (which means areas outside the gradient are given a solid fill with the appropriate color), but you can also use Reflect (to reverse the gradient, going from the second color back to the first) or Repeat (to duplicate the same color progression). Figure 13-18 shows the Reflect effect (it's the fourth gradient).

The LinearGradientBrush also allows you to create gradients with more than two colors by adding more than two GradientStop objects. For example, here's a gradient that moves through a rainbow of colors:

```
<Rectangle Width="150" Height="100">
  <Rectangle.Fill>
    <LinearGradientBrush StartPoint="0,0" EndPoint="1,1">
      <GradientStop Color="Yellow" Offset="0.0" />
      <GradientStop Color="Red" Offset="0.25" />
      <GradientStop Color="Blue" Offset="0.75" />
      <GradientStop Color="LimeGreen" Offset="1.0" />
    </LinearGradientBrush>
  </Rectangle.Fill>
</Rectangle>
```

The only trick is to set the appropriate offset for each GradientStop. For example, if you want to transition through five colors, you might give your first color an offset of 0, the second 0.25, the third 0.5, the fourth 0.75, and the fifth 1. Or if you want the colors to blend more quickly at the beginning and then end more gradually, you could give the offsets 0, 0.1, 0.2, 0.4, 0.6, and 1.

Remember, Brushes aren't limited to shape drawing. You can substitute the LinearGradientBrush anytime you would use the SolidColorBrush—for example, when filling the background surface of an element (using the Background property), the foreground color of its text (using the Foreground property), or the fill of a border (using the BorderBrush property). Figure 13-19 shows an example of a gradient-filled TextBlock.

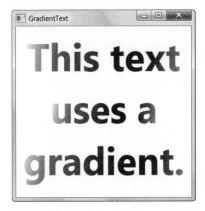

Figure 13-19. *Using the LinearGradientBrush to set the TextBlock.Foreground property*

The RadialGradientBrush

The RadialGradientBrush works similarly to the LinearGradientBrush. It also takes a sequence of colors with different offsets. As with the LinearGradientBrush, you can use as many colors as you want. The difference is how you place the gradient.

To identify the point where the first color in the gradient starts, you use the GradientOrigin property. By default, it's (0.5, 0.5), which represents the middle of the fill region.

Note As with the LinearGradientBrush, the RadialGradientBrush uses a proportional coordinate system that acts as though the top-left corner of your rectangular fill area is (0, 0) and the bottom-right corner is (1, 1). That means you can pick any coordinate from (0, 0) to (1, 1) to place the starting point of the gradient. In fact, you can even go beyond these limits if you want to locate the starting point outside the fill region.

The gradient radiates out from the starting point in a circular fashion. Eventually, your gradient reaches the edge of an inner gradient circle, where it ends. This center of this circle may or may not line up with the gradient origin, depending on the effect you want. The area beyond the edge of the inner gradient circle and the outermost edge of the fill region is given a solid fill using the last color that's defined in RadialGradientBrush.GradientStops collection. Figure 13-20 illustrates.

You set the edge of the inner gradient circle using three properties: Center, RadiusX, and RadiusY. By default, the Center property is (0.5, 0.5), which places the center of the limiting circle in the middle of your fill region and in the same position as the gradient origin.

The RadiusX and RadiusY determine the size of the limiting circle, and by default they're both set to 0.5. These values can be a bit unintuitive—they're measured in relation to the *diagonal* span of your fill area (the length of an imaginary line stretching from the top-left corner to the bottom-right corner of your fill area). That means a radius of 0.5 defines a circle that has a radius that's half the length of this diagonal. If you have a square fill region, you can use a dash of Pythagoras to calculate that this is about 0.7 times the width (or height) of your region. Thus, if you're filling a square region with the default settings, the gradient begins in the center and stretches to its outermost edge at about 0.7 times the width of the square.

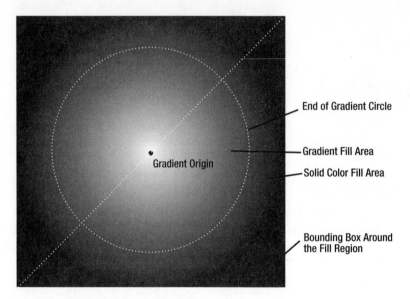

Figure 13-20. *How a radial gradient is filled*

■**Note** If you trace the largest possible ellipse that fits in your fill area, that's the place where the gradient ends with your second color.

The radial gradient fill is a particularly good choice for filling rounded shapes and creating lighting effects. (Master artists use a combination of gradients to create buttons with a glow effect.) A common trick is to offset the GradientOrigin point slightly to create an illusion of depth in your shape. Here's an example:

```
<Ellipse Margin="5" Stroke="Black" StrokeThickness="1" Width="200" Height="200">
  <Ellipse.Fill>
    <RadialGradientBrush RadiusX="1" RadiusY="1" GradientOrigin="0.7,0.3">
      <GradientStop Color="White" Offset="0" />
      <GradientStop Color="Blue" Offset="1" />
    </RadialGradientBrush>
  </Ellipse.Fill>
</Ellipse>
```

Figure 13-21 shows this gradient, along with an ordinary radial gradient that has the standard GradientOrigin (0.5, 0.5).

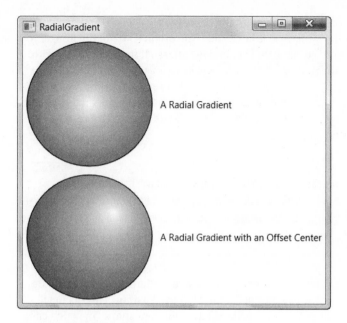

Figure 13-21. *Radial gradients*

The ImageBrush

The ImageBrush allows you to fill an area with a bitmap image. You can use most common file types, including BMP, PNG, GIF, and JPEG files. You identify the image you want to use by setting the ImageSource property. For example, this brush paints the background of a Grid using an image named logo.jpg that's included in the assembly as a resource:

```
<Grid>
  <Grid.Background>
    <ImageBrush ImageSource="logo.jpg"></ImageBrush>
  </Grid.Background>
</Grid>
```

The ImageBrush,ImageSource property works in the same way as the Source property of the Image element, which means you can also set it using a URI that points to a resource, an external file, or a web location. You can also create an ImageBrush that uses XAML-defined vector content by supplying a DrawingImage object for the ImageSource property. You might take this approach to reduce overhead (by avoiding the more costly Shape-derived classes), or if you want to use a vector image to create a tiled pattern. You'll learn more about the DrawingImage class in Chapter 14.

■**Note** WPF respects any transparency information that it finds in an image. For example, WPF supports transparent areas in a GIF file, and transparent or partially transparent areas in a PNG file.

In this example, the ImageBrush is used to paint the background of a cell. As a result, the image is stretched to fit the fill area. If the Grid is larger than the original size of the image, you may see resizing artifacts in your image (such as a general fuzziness). If the shape of the Grid doesn't match the aspect ratio of the picture, the picture will be distorted to fit.

You can control this behavior by modifying the ImageBrush.Stretch property, and assigning one of the values listed in Table 13-2. For example, use Uniform to scale the image to fit the container, but keep the aspect ratio or None to paint the image at its natural size (in which case, part of it may be clipped to fit).

■**Note** Even with a Stretch of None, your image may still be scaled. For example, if you've set your Windows system DPI setting to 120 dpi (also known as *large fonts*), WPF will scale up your bitmap proportionately. This may introduce some fuzziness, but it's a better solution than having your image sizes (and the alignment of your overall user interface) change on monitors with different dpi settings.

If the image is painted smaller than the fill region, the image is aligned according to the AlignmentX and AlignmentY properties. The unfilled area is left transparent. This occurs if you're using Uniform scaling and the region you're filling has a different shape (in which case you'll get blank bars on the top or the sides). It also occurs if you're using None and the fill region is larger than the image.

You can also use the Viewbox property to clip out a smaller portion of the picture that you're interested in using. To do so, you specify four numbers that describe the rectangle you want to clip out of the source picture and use. The first two identify the top-left corner where your rectangle begins, and the following two numbers specify the width and height of the rectangle. The only catch is that the Viewbox uses a relative coordinate system, just like the gradient brushes. This coordinate system designates the top-left corner of your picture as (0, 0) and the bottom-right corner as (1, 1).

To understand how Viewbox works, take a look at this markup:

```
<ImageBrush ImageSource="logo.jpg" Stretch="Uniform"
  Viewbox="0.4,0.5 0.2,0.2"></ImageBrush>
```

Here, the Viewbox starts at (0.4, 0.5), which is almost halfway into the picture. (Technically, the X coordinate is 0.4 × width and the Y coordinate is 0.5 × width.) The rectangle then extends to fill a small box that's 20% as wide and tall as the total image (technically, the rectangle is 0.2 × width long and 0.2 × height tall). The cropped-out portion is then stretched or centered, based on the Stretch, AlignmentX, and AlignmentY properties. Figure 13-22 shows two rectangles that use different ImageBrush objects to fill themselves. The topmost rectangle shows the full image, while the rectangle underneath uses the Viewbox to magnify a small section. Both are given a solid black border.

■**Note** The Viewbox property is occasionally useful when reusing parts of the same picture in different ways to create certain effects. However, if you know in advance that you only need to use a portion of an image, it obviously makes more sense to crop it down in your favorite graphics software.

Figure 13-22. *Different ways to use an ImageBrush*

A Tiled ImageBrush

An ordinary ImageBrush isn't all that exciting. However, you can get some interesting effects by tiling your image across the surface of the brush.

When tiling an image, you have two options:

- **Proportionally sized tiles.** Your fill area always has the same number of tiles. The tiles expand and shrink to fit the fill region.

- **Fixed-sized tiles.** Your tiles are always the same size. The size of your fill area determines the number of tiles that appears.

Figure 13-23 compares the difference when a tile-filled rectangle is resized.

To tile an image, you need to set the ImageSource property (to identify the image you want to tile) and the Viewport, ViewportUnits, and TileMode properties. It's these latter three properties that determine the size of your tile and the way it's arranged.

You use the Viewport property to set the size of each tile. To use proportionately sized tiles, ViewportUnits must be set to RelativeToBoundingBox (which is the default). Then you define the tile size using a proportional coordinate system that stretches from 0 to 1 in both dimensions. In other words, a tile that has a top-left corner at (0, 0) and a bottom-right corner at (1, 1) occupies the entire fill area. To get a tiled pattern, you need to define a Viewport that's smaller than the total size of the fill area, as shown here:

```
<ImageBrush ImageSource="tile.jpg" TileMode="Tile"
  Viewport="0,0 0.5,0.5"></ImageBrush>
```

This creates a Viewport box that begins at the top-left corner of the fill area (0, 0) and stretches down to the midpoint (0.5, 0.5). As a result, the fill region will always hold four tiles, no matter how big or small it is. This behavior is nice because it ensures that there's no danger of having part of a tile chopped off at the edge of a shape. (Of course, this isn't the case if you're using the ImageBrush to fill a nonrectangular area.)

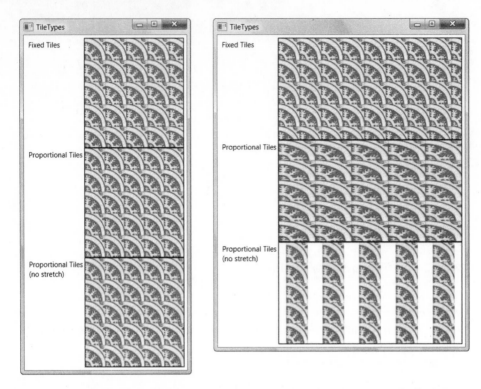

Figure 13-23. *Different ways to tile a rectangle*

Because the tile in this example is relative to the size of the fill area, a larger fill area will use a larger tile, and you may wind up with some blurriness from image resizing. Furthermore, if your fill area isn't perfectly square, the relative coordinate system is squashed accordingly, so each tiled square becomes a rectangle. This behavior is shown in the second tiled pattern in Figure 13-23.

You can alter this behavior by changing the Stretch property (which is Fill by default). Use None to ensure that tiles are never distorted and keep their proper shape. However, if the fill area isn't square, whitespace will appear in between your tiles. This detail is shown in the third tiled pattern in Figure 13-23.

A third option is to use a Stretch value of UniformToFill, which crops your tile image as needed. That way, your tiled image keeps the correct aspect ratio and you don't any have whitespace in between your tiles. However, if your fill area isn't a square, you won't see the complete tile image.

The automatic tile resizing is a nifty feature, but there's a price to pay. Some bitmaps may not resize properly. To some extent, you can prepare for this situation by supplying a bitmap that's bigger than what you need, but this technique can result in a blurrier bitmap when it's scaled down.

An alternate solution is to define the size of your tile in absolute coordinates, based on the size of your original image. To take this step, you set ViewportUnits to Absolute (instead of RelativeToBoundBox). Here's an example that defines a 32 × 32 unit size for each tile and starts them at the top-left corner:

```
<ImageBrush ImageSource="tile.jpg" TileMode="Tile"
  ViewportUnits="Absolute" Viewport="0,0 32,32"></ImageBrush>
```

This type of tiled pattern is shown in the first rectangle in Figure 13-23. The drawback here is that the height and width of your fill area must be divisible by 32. Otherwise, you'll get a partial tile at the edge. If you're using the ImageBrush to fill a resizable element, there's no way around this problem, so you'll need to accept that the tiles won't always line up with the edges of the fill region.

So far, all the tiled patterns you've seen have used a TileMode value of Tile. You can change the TileMode to set how alternate tiles are flipped. Table 13-5 lists your choices.

Table 13-5. *Values from the TileMode Enumeration*

Name	Description
Tile	Copies the image across the available area
FlipX	Copies the image, but flips each second column vertically
FlipY	Copies the image, but flips each second row horizontally
FlipXY	Copies the image, but flips each second column vertically and each second row horizontally

This flipping behavior is often useful if you need to make tiles blend more seamlessly. For example, if you use FlipX, tiles that are side by side will always line up seamlessly. Figure 13-24 compares the different tiling options you can use.

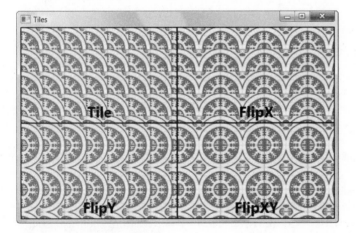

Figure 13-24. *Flipping tiles*

The VisualBrush

The VisualBrush is an unusual brush that allows you to take the visual content of an element and use it to fill any surface. For example, using a VisualBrush you could copy the appearance of a button in a window to a region somewhere else in that same window. However, the button copy won't be clickable or interactive in any way. It's simply a copy of how your element looks.

For example, here's a snippet of markup that defines a button and a VisualBrush that duplicates the button:

```
<Button Name="cmd" Margin="3" Padding="5">Is this a real button?</Button>
<Rectangle Margin="3" Height="100">
  <Rectangle.Fill>
    <VisualBrush Visual="{Binding ElementName=cmd}"></VisualBrush>
  </Rectangle.Fill>
</Rectangle>
```

Although you could define the element you want to use in the VisualBrush itself, it's much more common to use a binding expression to refer to an element in the current window, as in this example. Figure 13-25 shows the original button (at the top of the window) and several differently shaped regions that are painted with a VisualBrush based on that button.

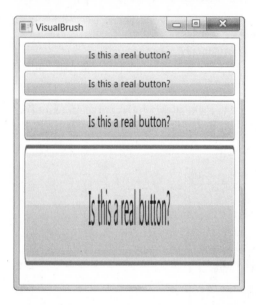

Figure 13-25. *Copying the visual for a button*

A VisualBrush watches for changes in the appearance of your element. For example, if you copy the visual for a button, and that button then receives focus, the VisualBrush repaints its fill area with the new visual—a focused button. The VisualBrush derives from TileBrush, so it also supports all the cropping, stretching, and flipping features you learned about in the previous section. If you combine these details with the transforms you learned about earlier in this chapter, you can easily use a VisualBrush to take element content and manipulate it beyond all recognition.

Because the content of a VisualBrush isn't interactive, you might wonder what purpose it has. In fact, the VisualBrush is useful in a number of situations where you need to create static content that duplicates the "real" content that's featured elsewhere. For example, you can take an element that contains a significant amount of nested content (even an entire window), shrink it down to a smaller size, and use it for a live preview. Some document programs do this to show formatting, Internet Explorer 7 uses it to show previews of the documents in different tabs on the Quick Tabs view (hit Ctrl+Q), and Windows Vista uses it to show previews of different applications in the taskbar.

You can use a VisualBrush in combination with animation to create certain effects (such as a document shrinking down to the bottom of your main application window). The VisualBrush is also the foundation for one of WPF's most notoriously overused effects—the live reflection, which you'll see in the following section (and the even worse live reflection of video content, which you'll see in Chapter 22).

Opacity Masks

In previous chapters, you learned about two ways to make an element (or some of its content) partially transparent:

- **Set the Opacity property to a value less than 1.0**. For example, an opacity of 0.9 creates a 90% visible (10% transparency) effect. Every element and every brush provides an Opacity property.

- **Use a color that has a nonopaque alpha value**. For example, you could use a partially transparent color in a SolidColorBrush, and use that to paint the foreground content or background surface of an element.

All elements also provide another option. You can use the OpacityMask property to make specific regions of an element transparent or partially transparent. The OpacityMask allows you to achieve a variety of common and exotic effects. For example, you can use it to fade a shape gradually into transparency.

The OpacityMask property accepts any brush. The alpha channel of the brush determines where the transparency occurs. For example, if you use a SolidColorBrush that's set to a transparent color for your OpacityMask, your entire element will disappear. If you use a SolidColorBrush that's set to use a nontransparent color, your element will remain completely visible. The other details of the color (the red, green, and blue components) aren't important and are ignored when you set the OpacityMask property.

Using the OpacityMask with a SolidColorBrush doesn't make much sense because you can accomplish the same effect more easily with the Opacity property. However, OpacityMask becomes more useful when you use more exotic types of brushes, such as the LinearGradient or RadialGradientBrush. Using a gradient that moves from a solid to a transparent color, you can create a transparency effect that fades in over the surface of your element, like the one used by this button:

```
<Button FontSize="14" FontWeight="Bold">
  <Button.OpacityMask>
    <LinearGradientBrush StartPoint="0,0" EndPoint="1,0">
      <GradientStop Offset="0" Color="Black"></GradientStop>
      <GradientStop Offset="1" Color="Transparent"></GradientStop>
    </LinearGradientBrush>
  </Button.OpacityMask>
  <Button.Content>A Partially Transparent Button</Button.Content>
</Button>
```

Figure 13-26 shows this button over a window that displays a picture of a grand piano.

Figure 13-26. *A button that fades from solid to transparent*

You can also use the OpacityMask property in conjunction with the VisualBrush to create a reflection effect. For example, the following markup creates one of WPF's most common effects—a text box with mirrored text. As you type, the VisualBrush paints a reflection of the text underneath. The VisualBrush paints a rectangle that uses the OpacityMask property to fade the reflection out, which distinguishes it from the real element above:

```
<TextBox Name="txt" FontSize="30">Here is some reflected text</TextBox>
<Rectangle Grid.Row="1" RenderTransformOrigin="1,0.5">
  <Rectangle.Fill>
    <VisualBrush Visual="{Binding ElementName=txt}"></VisualBrush>
  </Rectangle.Fill>
  <Rectangle.OpacityMask>
    <LinearGradientBrush StartPoint="0,0" EndPoint="0,1">
      <GradientStop Offset="0.3" Color="Transparent"></GradientStop>
      <GradientStop Offset="1" Color="#44000000"></GradientStop>
    </LinearGradientBrush>
  </Rectangle.OpacityMask>
  <Rectangle.RenderTransform>
    <ScaleTransform ScaleY="-1"></ScaleTransform>
  </Rectangle.RenderTransform>
</Rectangle>
```

This example uses a LinearGradientBrush that fades between a completely transparent color and a partially transparent color, to make the reflected content more faded. It also adds a RenderTransform that flips the rectangle so the reflection is upside down. As a result of this transformation, the gradient stops must be defined in the reverse order. Figure 13-27 shows the result.

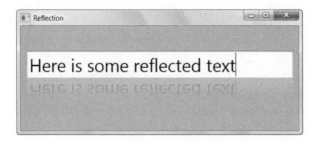

Figure 13-27. *VisualBrush + OpacityMask + RenderTransform = reflection effect*

Along with the gradient brushes and the VisualBrush, the OpacityMask property is often used with the DrawingBrush you'll learn about in the next chapter. This allows you to apply a shaped transparent region to an element.

Bitmap Effects

Shapes, transforms, and brushes are core ingredients in 2-D drawings. Along with these basics (and the geometries and drawings you'll learn about next chapter), WPF also includes a few frills.

One of these frills is a set of *bitmap effects*: ready-made visual effects that you can apply to any element. The goal of bitmap effects is to give you an easy, declarative way to enhance the appearance of text, images, buttons, and other controls. Rather than write your own drawing code, you simply use one of the classes that derives from BitmapEffect (in the System.Windows.Media.Effects namespace) to get instant effects such as blurs, glows, and drop shadows.

There are two key disadvantages to bitmap effects. The first limitation is that bitmap effects are implemented in unmanaged code, and so require a fully trusted application. As a result, you can't use bitmap effects in an XBAP application.

The other disadvantage is that bitmap effects are always rendered in software and don't use the resources of the video card. This makes them slow. As a result, bitmap effects aren't appropriate if you need to restyle a large number of elements in a window. They also aren't ideal for changing the appearance of extremely large elements, because bitmap effects modify the whole visual surface of an element (not just its outer edges). In these situations, you should consider using an alternate approach, such as applying the effects to your graphics in a design tool, or using code to craft a custom-drawn element (Chapter 24).

■Note It's quite possible that future versions of WPF will include better algorithms for bitmap effects that use hardware acceleration. If this is the case, the bitmap effect model won't change, but you'll be able to use bitmap effects more freely throughout your user interface (rather than constraining them to small regions).

Table 13-6 lists all the bitmap effect classes that you can use.

Table 13-6. *Bitmap Effects*

Name	Description	Properties
BlurBitmapEffect	Blurs the content in your element.	Radius, KernelType
BevelBitmapEffect	Adds a beveled (raised) edge around your content.	BevelWidth, EdgeProfile, LightAngle, Relief, Smoothness
EmbossBitmapEffect	Gives your content embossed edges and lines, as though it were stamped or engraved.	LightAngle, Relief
OuterGlowBitmapEffect	Adds a halo of color around your content.	GlowColor, GlowSize, Noise, Opacity
DropShadowBitmapEffect	Adds a rectangular drop shadow behind your element.	Color, Direction, Noise, Opacity, ShadowDepth, Softness
BitmapEffectGroup	Applies a combination of bitmap effects. The order you use is significant, as each effect is applied overtop all the existing effects. The BitmapEffectGroup is rarely used because it multiplies the overhead. In other words, a button with four effects requires four times as much processing as a button with one effect.	Children

Blurs

To apply a bitmap effect, you simply create the appropriate bitmap effect object and assign it to the BitmapEffect property of your element. Here's how you can apply a basic blurring effect to a button:

```
<Button>
  <Button.Content>A Blurred Button</Button.Content>
  <Button.BitmapEffect>
    <BlurBitmapEffect Radius="1"></BlurBitmapEffect>
  </Button.BitmapEffect>
</Button>
```

The BlurBitmapEffect class includes two properties. The Radius property allows you to control the strength of the blur from 0 (no blur) to a blurring level of your choice. A Radius of 1 creates the soft blur shown in the middle button in Figure 13-28. The blurrier button underneath uses the default Radius of 5.

Along with the Radius property, you can also set the KernelType property to change the style of blurring. The default is Gaussian, which creates a smooth blur. Alternatively, you can use Box, which requires fewer calculations. It's less soft, and looks a little bit more like a double image.

Figure 13-28. *Two blurred buttons*

Beveled Edges

The BevelBitmapEffect creates a raised edge around the border of your content. Beveling works well with elements that have a cleanly defined border, the rectangular border that wraps a button, or the crisp edges of text. Figure 13-29 shows the bevel effect with its default settings applied to an ordinary button and a TextBlock. (In order to see the beveling in the text, it's necessary to blow it up to a large font size.)

Figure 13-29. *Two beveled elements*

Note The beveled edge is applied to the outermost border of your element. When using text, the edge of each individual level is beveled (as shown in Figure 13-29), provided your text is placed on a transparent background. If you specify a different background color for your TextBlock, the beveled edge will be added around the rectangle that sets the bounds of the TextBlock—in other words, you'll end up with ordinary text on a beveled, colored rectangle. The same behavior appears when using the DropShadowBitmapEffect and OuterGlowBitmapEffect.

When setting a bevel, you can tweak the effect using a range of properties. BevelWidth controls the width of the beveled edge (which defaults to 5), and EdgeProfile controls how that edge is shaped (possible values are BulgedUp, CurvedIn, CurvedOut, and Linear).

You can change how the beveled edge is shaded by setting the Relief, Smoothness, and LightAngle properties. Relief takes a value from 0 to 1, where 1 applies the strongest shadows (0.3 is the default). Smoothness also takes a value from 0 to 1, where 1 creates the smoothest shadows (0.2 is the default). Finally, LightAngle determines where the shadows appear. It takes a value in degrees, where 0 degrees is the right side (so 90 degrees is at the top, 180 degrees is on the left side, 270 degrees is directly beneath the element, and so on). The default value of 135 degrees puts the light source in the top-left corner and creates the shadows on the bottom and right edges

Embossed Edges

The EmbossBitmapEffect uses an algorithm that detects the edges of content in your element and alters them to give them a textured stand-out effect. If you use this effect on the right content, you'll create the illusion of engraved or stamped content. If you use it on the wrong content, you'll simply end up with distorted patches of color. For example, web-ready graphics often include fuzzy edges or dithered colors that cause artifacts to appear when you apply an embossing effect.

The EmbossBitmapEffect class gives you just two properties to play with: the Relief property for adjusting the amount of embossing (from 0 to 1, with the default being 0.44) and the LightAngle property for choosing the direction that light falls on the embossed edge (which is much like the LightAngle property you used with the BevelBitmapEffect).

Figure 13-30 shows three versions of the same picture with varying levels of embossing. The image on the left has no embossing, the image in the middle has an emboss effect with a Relief of 0.9, and the image on the right has an emboss effect with a Relief of 0.5.

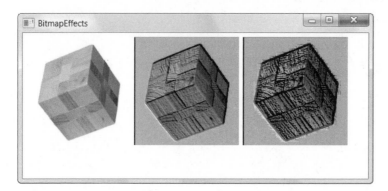

Figure 13-30. *Embossing a picture*

Note Remember, the emboss effect is applied over the entire surface of your element. It mangles most ordinary elements, such as buttons, because it embosses both the outside border and the inner text.

Glows and Shadows

The final two effects are the OuterGlowBitmapEffect and the DropShadowBitmapEffect.

The OuterGlowBitmapEffect adds a diffuse halo of light around your element. You can control the color (GlowColor), the width of the glow effect (GlowSize, which defaults to 5), the sharpness of the glow (Noise, which takes a value between 0 and 1), and whether content underneath shows through the halo (Opacity, which also takes a value between 0 and 1).

The DropShadowBitmapEffect has a similar set of properties, including Color, Noise, Softness, and Opacity. It also includes a Direction property that lets you set the angle from which the light is shining (much as you do with the LightDirection property on the BevelBitmapEffect and EmbossBitmapEffect) and a ShadowDepth that lets you set how far away the shadow appears (although you can't control the actual size of the shadow). Both the OuterGlowBitmapEffect and the DropShadowBitmapEffect cling to the edges of your content, whether it's the rectangular border around a button or the edges of the letters in your text.

Figure 13-31 shows different shadow and glow effects on buttons and text. To create the distant shadows, the ShadowDepth property was increased to 20 and the Color property was changed to a lighter color. To create the thick, grainy glows, the GlowSize property was set to 20 and the Noise property was raised from 0 to 0.5.

Note Bitmap effects are added after the layout pass and don't affect the placement of your controls. That means that the drop shadow or glow around an element may overlap onto another element, if it's large enough.

Figure 13-31. *Shadowns and glows*

DROP SHADOWS WITH LESS OVERHEAD

Many WPF controls use drop shadows, including the Menu, ToolTip, and ComboBox. However, the DropShadowBitmapEffect has too much overhead to be used with these common controls. Instead, these controls simulate the same effect by adding a separate element that looks like a drop shadow. The element that does the work is the SystemDropShadowChrome class, which is found in the Microsoft.Windows.Themes namespace.

The SystemDropShadowChrome is a decorator—a class that wraps a single nested element and adds a visual detail around or behind it. You first learned about decorators in Chapter 5 when you considered the Border and Viewbox. You'll see how decorators are used to paint the background of common controls such as the Button in Chapter 15, and you'll learn how to create your own decorator and use custom drawing code to paint its background in Chapter 24.

If you want to create a drop shadow effect without the overhead of the DropShadowBitmapEffect, you can use the SystemDropShadowChrome. The trick is to add a reference to the Presentation.Framework.Aero.dll assembly, and map the Microsoft.Windows.Themes namespace, as shown here:

```
<Window ... xmlns:theme=
  "clr-namespace:Microsoft.Windows.Themes;assembly=PresentationFramework.Aero">
```

Once you've taken these two steps, you can wrap any element in a SystemDropShadowChrome object:

```
<theme:SystemDropShadowChrome>
  <Button>This Button has an artifical drop shadow</Button>
</theme:SystemDropShadowChrome>
```

SystemDropShadowChrome provides two key properties: Color and CornerRadius. You use Color to set the drop shadow color (as a Color object, not a Brush), and you can use the CornerRadius property to round the edges.

The SystemDropShadowChrome has one limitation. It can only create rectangular drop shadows. It's no help if you want to add a drop shadow behind a different shape or behind text, which clearly makes it less powerful than DropShadowBitmapEffect. The clear benefit is its vastly improved performance.

The Last Word

In this chapter, you took a detailed look at WPF's support for basic 2-D drawing. You began by considering the simple shape classes, and continued to consider transforms, specialized brushes, and even bitmap effects. However, your journey isn't finished yet. In the next chapter you'll take a look at the Path, the most sophisticated of the shape classes, which lets you combine the shapes you've seen so far and add arcs and curves. You'll also consider how you can make more efficient graphics with the help of WPF's Geometry and Drawing objects, and how you can export clip art from other programs. Finally, you'll consider the lower-level visual layer and learn how you can use it to draw large amounts of dynamic content in the most efficient way possible.

■ ■ ■

CHAPTER 14

Geometries, Drawings, and Visuals

In the previous chapter, you started your exploration into WPF's 2-D drawing features. You considered how you can use simple Shape-derived classes in combination with transforms, images, and fancy brushes to create a variety of graphical effects. However, the concepts you learned still fall far short of what you need to create (and manipulate) detailed 2-D scenes made up of vector art. That's because there's a wide gap between rectangles, ellipses, and polygons and the sort of clip art you see in graphically rich applications (such as Flash applets).

In this chapter, you'll extend your skills with a few new concepts. You'll learn how more complex drawings are defined in WPF, how to model arcs and curves, and how you can convert existing vector art to the XAML format you need. You'll also consider the most performant ways to work with complex images—in other words, how you can reduce the overhead involved in managing hundreds or thousands of shapes. This begins with replacing the simple shapes you learned about in the previous chapter with the more powerful Path class, which can wrap complex geometries. At the end of this chapter, you'll consider an even leaner approach—foregoing elements and using the lower-level Visual class to perform your rendering by hand.

Paths and Geometries

In the previous chapter you took a look at a number of classes that derive from Shape, including Rectangle, Ellipse, Polygon, and Polyline. However, there's one Shape-derived class that you haven't considered yet, and it's the most powerful by far. The Path class has the ability to encompass any simple shape, groups of shapes, and more complex ingredients such as curves.

The Path class includes a single property, named Data, that accepts a Geometry object that defines the shape (or shapes) the path includes. You can't create a Geometry object directly because it's an abstract class. Instead, you need to use one of the seven derived classes listed in Table 14-1.

Table 14-1. *Geometry Classes*

Name	Description
LineGeometry	Represents a straight line. The geometry equivalent of the Line shape.
RectangleGeometry	Represents a rectangle (optionally with rounded corners). The geometry equivalent of the Rectangle shape.
EllipseGeometry	Represents an ellipse. The geometry equivalent of the Ellipse shape.
GeometryGroup	Adds any number of Geometry objects to a single path, using the EvenOdd or NonZero fill rule to determine what regions to fill.
CombinedGeometry	Merges two geometries into one shape. The CombineMode property allows you to choose how the two are combined.
PathGeometry	Represents a more complex figure that's composed of arcs, curves, and lines, and can be open or closed.
StreamGeometry	A read-only lightweight equivalent to PathGeometry. The StreamGeometry saves memory because it doesn't hold the individual segments of your path in memory all at once. However, it can't be modified once it's been created.

At this point you might be wondering what the difference is between a path and a geometry. The geometry *defines* a shape. A path allows you to *draw* the shape. Thus, the Geometry object defines details such as the coordinates and size of your shape, while the Path object supplies the Stroke and Fill brushes you'll use to paint it. The Path class also includes the features it inherits from the UIElement infrastructure, such as mouse and keyboard handling.

However, the geometry classes aren't quite as simple as they seem. For one thing, they all inherit from Freezable (through the base Geometry class), which gives them support for change notification. As a result, if you use a geometry to create a path and then modify the geometry after the fact, your path will be redrawn automatically. The geometry classes can also be used to define drawings that you can apply through a brush, which gives you an easy way to paint complex content that doesn't need the user-interactivity features of the Path class. You'll consider this ability in the "Drawings" section later in this chapter.

In the following sections, you'll explore all the classes that derive from Geometry.

Line, Rectangle, and Ellipse Geometries

The LineGeometry, RectangleGeometry, and EllipseGeometry classes map directly to the Line, Rectangle, and Ellipse shapes that you learned about in Chapter 13. For example, you can convert this markup that uses the Rectangle element:

```
<Rectangle Fill="Yellow" Stroke="Blue"
  Width="100" Height="50" ></Rectangle>
```

to this markup that uses the Path element:

```
<Path Fill="Yellow" Stroke="Blue">
  <Path.Data>
    <RectangleGeometry Rect="0,0 100,50"></RectangleGeometry>
  </Path.Data>
</Path>
```

The only real difference is that the Rectangle shape takes Height and Width values, while the RectangleGeometry takes four numbers that describe the size *and* location of the rectangle. The first two numbers describe the X and Y coordinates point where the top-left corner will be placed, while the last two numbers set the width and height of the rectangle. You can start the rectangle out at (0, 0) to get the same effect as an ordinary Rectangle element, or you can offset the rectangle using different values. The RectangleGeometry class also includes the RadiusX and RadiusY properties that let you round the corners (as described earlier).

Similarly, you can convert the following Line:

```
<Line Stroke="Blue" X1="0" Y1="0" X2="10" Y2="100"></Line>
```

to this LineGeometry:

```
<Path Fill="Yellow" Stroke="Blue">
  <Path.Data>
    <LineGeometry StartPoint="0,0" EndPoint="10,100"></LineGeometry>
  </Path.Data>
</Path>
```

and you can convert an Ellipse like this:

```
<Ellipse Fill="Yellow" Stroke="Blue"
  Width="100" Height="50" HorizontalAlignment="Left"></Ellipse>
```

to this EllipseGeometry:

```
<Path Fill="Yellow" Stroke="Blue">
  <Path.Data>
    <EllipseGeometry RadiusX="50" RadiusY="25" Center="50,25"></EllipseGeometry>
  </Path.Data>
</Path>
```

Notice that the two radius values are simply half of the width and height values. You can also use the Center property to offset the location of the ellipse. In this example, the center is placed in the exact middle of the ellipse bounding box, so that it's drawn in exactly the same way as the Ellipse shape.

Overall, these simple geometries work in exactly the same way as the corresponding shapes. You get the added ability to offset rectangles and ellipses, but that's not necessary if you're placing your shapes on a Canvas, which already gives you the ability to position your shapes at a specific position. In fact, if this were all you could do with geometries, you probably wouldn't bother to use the Path element. The difference appears when you decide to combine more than one geometry in the same path, as described in the next section.

Combining Shapes with GeometryGroup

The simplest way to combine geometries is to use the GeometryGroup, and nest the other Geometry-derived objects inside. Here's an example that places an ellipse next to a square:

```
<Path Fill="Yellow" Stroke="Blue" Margin="5" Canvas.Top="10" Canvas.Left="10" >
  <Path.Data>
    <GeometryGroup>
```

```
      <RectangleGeometry Rect="0,0 100,100"></RectangleGeometry>
      <EllipseGeometry Center="150,50" RadiusX="35" RadiusY="25"></EllipseGeometry>
    </GeometryGroup>
  </Path.Data>
</Path>
```

The effect of this markup is the same as if you supplied two Path elements, one with the RectangleGeometry and one with the EllipseGeometry (and that's the same as if you used a Rectangle and Ellipse shape instead). However, there's one advantage to this approach. You've replaced two elements with one, which means you've reduced the overhead of your user interface. In general, a window that uses a smaller number of elements with more complex geometries will perform faster than a window that has a large number of elements with simpler geometries. This effect won't be apparent in a window that has just a few dozen shapes, but it may become significant in one that requires hundreds or thousands.

Of course, there's also a drawback to combining geometries in a single Path element—namely, you won't be able to perform event handling of the different shapes separately. Instead, the Path element will fire all mouse events. However, you can still manipulate the nested RectangleGeometry and EllipseGeometry objects independently to change the overall path. For example, each geometry provides a Transform property that you can set to stretch, skew, or rotate that part of the path.

Another advantage of geometries is that you can reuse the same geometry in several separate Path elements. No code is necessary—you simply need to define the geometry in a Resources collection and refer to it in your path with the StaticExtension or DynamicExtension markup extensions. Here's an example that rewrites the markup shown previously to show instances of the CombinedGeometry, at two different locations on a Canvas and with two different fill colors:

```
<Window.Resources>
  <GeometryGroup x:Key="Geometry">
    <RectangleGeometry Rect="0 ,0 100 ,100"></RectangleGeometry>
    <EllipseGeometry Center="150, 50" RadiusX="35" RadiusY="25"></EllipseGeometry>
  </GeometryGroup>
</Window.Resources>

<Canvas>
  <Path Fill="Yellow" Stroke="Blue" Margin="5" Canvas.Top="10" Canvas.Left="10"
  Data="{StaticResource Geometry}">
  </Path>
  <Path Fill="Green" Stroke="Blue" Margin="5" Canvas.Top="150" Canvas.Left="10"
  Data="{StaticResource Geometry}">
  </Path>
</Canvas>
```

The GeometryGroup becomes more interesting when your shapes intersect. Rather than simply treating your drawing as a combination of solid shapes, the GeometryGroup uses its FillRule property (which can be EvenOdd or Nonzero, as described in Chapter 13) to decide what shapes to fill. Consider what happens if you alter the markup shown earlier like this, placing the ellipse over the square:

```
<Path Fill="Yellow" Stroke="Blue" Margin="5" Canvas.Top="10" Canvas.Left="10" >
  <Path.Data>
    <GeometryGroup>
      <RectangleGeometry Rect="0,0 100,100"></RectangleGeometry>
      <EllipseGeometry Center="50,50" RadiusX="35" RadiusY="25"></EllipseGeometry>
    </GeometryGroup>
  </Path.Data>
</Path>
```

Now this markup creates a square with an ellipse-shaped hole in it. If you change FillRule to Nonzero, you'll get a solid ellipse over a solid rectangle, both with the same yellow fill.

You could create the square-with-a-hole effect by simply superimposing a white-filled ellipse over your square. However, the GeometryGroup class becomes more useful if you have content underneath, which is typical in a complex drawing. Because the ellipse is treated as a hole in your shape (not another shape with a different fill), any content underneath shows through—for example, if you add this line of text:

```
<TextBlock Canvas.Top="50" Canvas.Left="20" FontSize="25" FontWeight="Bold">
  Hello There</TextBlock>
```

Now you'll get the result shown in Figure 14-1.

Figure 14-1. *A path that uses two shapes*

■Note Remember, objects are drawn in the order they are processed. In other words, if you want the text to appear underneath your shape, make sure you add the TextBlock to your markup before the Path element. (Or if you're using a Canvas or Grid to hold your content, you can set the attached Panel.ZIndex property on your elements to place them explicitly, as described in Chapter 4.

Fusing Geometries with CombinedGeometry

The GeometryGroup class is an invaluable tool for building complex shapes out of the basic primitives (rectangle, ellipse, and line). However, it has obvious limitations. It works great for creating a shape by drawing one shape and "subtracting" out other shapes from inside.

However, it's difficult to get the result you want if the shape borders intersect one another, and it's no help if you want to remove part of a shape. To help you out, there's another tool that you can use: the CombinedGeometry class. It's tailor-made for combining shapes that overlap, and where neither shape contains the other completely. Unlike GeometryGroup, CombinedGeometry takes just two geometries, which you supply using the Geometry1 and Geometry2 properties. CombinedGeometry doesn't include the FillRule property—instead, it has the much more powerful GeometryCombineMode property that takes one of four values, as described in Table 14-2.

Table 14-2. *Values from the GeometryCombineMode Enumeration*

Name	Description
Union	Creates a shape that includes all the areas of the two geometries.
Intersect	Creates a shape that contains the area that's shared between the two geometries.
Xor	Creates a shape that contains the area that isn't shared between the two geometries. In other words, it's as if the shapes are combined (using a Union) and then the shared part (the Intersect) is removed.
Exclude	Creates a shape that includes all the area from the first geometry, not including the area that's in the second geometry.

For example, here's how you can merge two shapes to create one shape with the total area using GeometryCombineMode.Union:

```
<Path Fill="Yellow" Stroke="Blue" Margin="5">
  <Path.Data>
    <CombinedGeometry GeometryCombineMode="Union">
      <CombinedGeometry.Geometry1>
        <RectangleGeometry Rect="0,0 100,100"></RectangleGeometry>
      </CombinedGeometry.Geometry1>
      <CombinedGeometry.Geometry2>
        <EllipseGeometry Center="85,50" RadiusX="65" RadiusY="35"></EllipseGeometry>
      </CombinedGeometry.Geometry2>
    </CombinedGeometry>
  </Path.Data>
</Path>
```

Figure 14-2 shows this shape, as well as the result of combining the same shapes in every other way possible.

The fact that a CombinedGeometry can only combine two shapes may seem like a significant limitation, but it's not. You can build a shape that involves dozens of distinct geometries or more—you simply need to use nested CombinedGeometry objects. For example, one CombinedGeometry object might combine two other CombinedGeometry objects, which themselves can combine more geometries. Using this technique, you can build up detailed shapes.

To understand how this works, consider the simple "no" sign (a circle with a slash through it) shown in Figure 14-3. Although there isn't any WPF primitive that resembles this shape, you can assemble it quite quickly using CombinedGeometry objects.

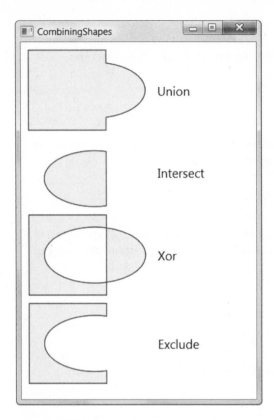

Figure 14-2. *Combining shapes*

Figure 14-3. *Several combined shapes*

It makes sense to start by drawing the ellipse that represents the outer edge of the shape. Then, using a CombinedGeometry with the GeometryCombineMode.Exclude, you can remove a smaller ellipse from the inside. Here's the markup that you need:

```
<Path Fill="Yellow" Stroke="Blue">
  <Path.Data>
    <CombinedGeometry GeometryCombineMode="Exclude">
      <CombinedGeometry.Geometry1>
        <EllipseGeometry Center="50,50" RadiusX="50" RadiusY="50"></EllipseGeometry>
      </CombinedGeometry.Geometry1>
      <CombinedGeometry.Geometry2>
        <EllipseGeometry Center="50,50" RadiusX="40" RadiusY="40"></EllipseGeometry>
      </CombinedGeometry.Geometry2>
    </CombinedGeometry>
  </Path.Data>
</Path>
```

This gets you part of the way, but you still need the slash through the middle. The easiest way to add this element is to use a rectangle that's tilted to the side. You can accomplish this using the RectangleGeometry with a RotateTransform of 45 degrees:

```
<RectangleGeometry Rect="44,5 10,90">
  <RectangleGeometry.Transform>
    <RotateTransform Angle="45" CenterX="50" CenterY="50"></RotateTransform>
  </RectangleGeometry.Transform>
</RectangleGeometry>
```

Note When applying a transform to a geometry, you use the Transform property (not RenderTransform or LayoutTransform). That's because the geometry defines the shape, and any transforms are always applied before the path is used in your layout.

The final step is to combine this geometry with the combined geometry that created the hollow circle. In this case, you need to use GeometryCombineMode.Union to add the rectangle to your shape.

Here's the complete markup for the symbol:

```
<Path Fill="Yellow" Stroke="Blue">
  <Path.Data>
    <CombinedGeometry GeometryCombineMode="Union">
      <CombinedGeometry.Geometry1>
        <CombinedGeometry GeometryCombineMode="Exclude">
          <CombinedGeometry.Geometry1>
            <EllipseGeometry Center="50,50"
             RadiusX="50" RadiusY="50"></EllipseGeometry>
          </CombinedGeometry.Geometry1>
          <CombinedGeometry.Geometry2>
            <EllipseGeometry Center="50,50"
             RadiusX="40" RadiusY="40"></EllipseGeometry>
          </CombinedGeometry.Geometry2>
        </CombinedGeometry>
      </CombinedGeometry.Geometry1>

      <CombinedGeometry.Geometry2>
        <RectangleGeometry Rect="44,5 10,90">
          <RectangleGeometry.Transform>
            <RotateTransform Angle="45" CenterX="50" CenterY="50"></RotateTransform>
          </RectangleGeometry.Transform>
        </RectangleGeometry>
      </CombinedGeometry.Geometry2>
    </CombinedGeometry>
  </Path.Data>
</Path>
```

■**Note** A GeometryGroup object can't influence the fill or stroke brushes used to color your shape. These details are set by the path. As a result, you need to create separate Path objects if you want to color parts of your path differently.

Curves and Lines with PathGeometry

PathGeometry is the superpower of geometries. It can draw anything that the other geometries can, and much more. The only drawback is a lengthier (and somewhat more complex) syntax.

Every PathGeometry object is built out of one or more PathFigure objects (which are stored in the PathGeometry.Figures collection). Each PathFigure is a continuous set of connected lines and curves that can be closed or open. The figure is closed if the end of the last line in the figure connects to the beginning of the first line.

The PathFigure class has four key properties, as described in Table 14-3.

Table 14-3. *PathFigure Properties*

Name	Description
StartPoint	This is a Point that indicates where the line for the figure begins.
Segments	This is a collection of PathSegment objects that are used to draw the figure.
IsClosed	If true, WPF adds a straight line to connect the starting and ending points (if they aren't the same).
IsFilled	If true, the area inside the figure is filled in using the Path.Fill brush.

So far, this all sounds fairly straightforward. The PathFigure is a shape that's drawn using an unbroken line that consists of a number of segments. However, the trick is that there are several type of segments, all of which derive from the PathSegment class. Some are simple, like the LineSegment that draws a straight line. Others, like the BezierSegment, draw curves and are correspondingly more complex.

You can mix and match different segments freely to build your figure. Table 14-4 lists the segment classes you can use.

Table 14-4. *PathSegment Classes*

Name	Description
LineSegment	Creates a straight line between two points.
ArcSegment	Creates an elliptical arc between two points.
BezierSegment	Creates a Bézier curve between two points.
QuadraticBezierSegment	Creates a simpler form of Bézier curve that has one control point instead of two, and is faster to calculate.
PolyLineSegment	Creates a series of straight lines. You can get the same effect using multiple LineSegment objects, but a single PolyLineSegment is more concise.
PolyBezierSegment	Creates a series of Bézier curves.
PolyQuadraticBezierSegment	Creates a series of simpler quadratic Bézier curves.

Straight Lines

It's easy enough to create simple lines using the LineSegment and PathGeometry classes. You simply set the StartPoint and add one LineSegment for each section of the line. The LineSegment.Point property identifies the end point of each segment.

For example, the following markup begins at (10, 100), draws a straight line to (100, 100), and then draws a line from that point to (100, 50). Because the PathFigure.IsClosed property is set to true, a final line segment is adding connection (100, 50) to (0, 0). The final result is a right-angled triangle:

```
<Path Stroke="Blue">
  <Path.Data>
    <PathGeometry>
      <PathFigure IsClosed="True" StartPoint="10,100">
        <LineSegment Point="100,100" />
        <LineSegment Point="100,50" />
      </PathFigure>
    </PathGeometry>
  </Path.Data>
</Path>
```

■**Note** Remember, each PathGeometry can contain an unlimited number of PathFigure objects. That means you can create several separate open or closed figures that are all considered part of the same path.

Arcs

Arcs are a little more interesting than straight lines. You identify the end point of the line using the ArcSegment.Point property, just as you would with a LineSegment. However, the PathFigure draws a curved line from the starting point (or the end point of the previous segment) to the end point of your arc. This curved connecting line is actually a portion of the edge of an ellipse.

Obviously, the end point isn't enough information to draw the arc because there are many curves (some gentle, some more extreme) that could connect two points. You also need to indicate the size of the imaginary ellipse that's being used to draw the arc. You do this using the ArcSegment.Size property, which supplies the X radius and the Y radius of the ellipse. The larger the ellipse size of the imaginary ellipse, the more gradually its edge curves.

■**Note** For any two points, there is a practical maximum and minimum size for the ellipse. The maximum occurs when you create an ellipse so large the line segment you're drawing appears straight. Increasing the size beyond this point has no effect. The minimum occurs when the ellipse is small enough that a full semi-circle connects the two points. Shrinking the size beyond this point also has no effect.

Here's an example that creates the gentle arc shown in Figure 14-4:

```
<Path Stroke="Blue" StrokeThickness="3">
  <Path.Data>
    <PathGeometry>
      <PathFigure IsClosed="False" StartPoint="10,100" >
        <ArcSegment Point="250,150" Size="200,300" />
      </PathFigure>
    </PathGeometry>
  </Path.Data>
</Path>
```

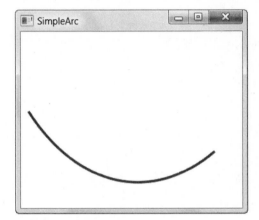

Figure 14-4. *A simple arc*

So far, arcs sound fairly straightforward. However, it turns out that even with the start and end point and the size of the ellipse, you still don't have all the information you need to draw your arc unambiguously. In the previous example, you're relying on two default values that may not be set to your liking.

To understand the problem, you need to consider the other ways that an arc can connect the same two points. If you picture two points on an ellipse, it's clear that you can connect them in two ways—by going around the short side, or by going around the long side. Figure 14-5 illustrates.

You set the direction using the ArcSegment.IsLargeArc property, which can be true or false. The default value is false, which means you get the shorter of the two arcs.

Even once you've set the direction, there is still one point of ambiguity—where the ellipse is placed. For example, imagine you draw an arc that connects a point on the left with a point on the right, using the shortest possible arc. The curve that connects these two points could be stretched down and then up (as it does in Figure 14-4) or it could be flipped so that it curves up and then down. The arc you get depends on the order in which you define the two points in the arc and the ArcSegment.SweepDirection property, which can be Counterclockwise (the default) or Clockwise. Figure 14-6 shows the difference.

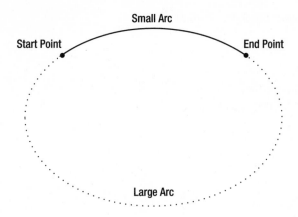

Figure 14-5. *Two ways to trace a curve along an ellipse*

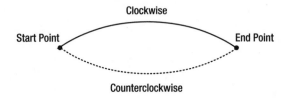

Figure 14-6. *Two ways to flip a curve*

Bézier Curves

Bézier curves connect two line segments using a complex mathematical formula that incorporates two *control points* that determine how the curve is shaped. Bézier curves are an ingredient in virtually every vector drawing application ever created because they're remarkably flexible. Using nothing more than start point, end point, and two control points, you can create a surprisingly wide variety of smooth curves (including loops). Figure 14-7 shows a classic Bézier curve. Two small circles indicate the control points, and a dashed line connects each control point to the end of the line it affects the most.

Even without understanding the math underpinnings, it's fairly easy to get the "feel" of how Bézier curves work. Essentially, the two control points do all the magic. They influence the curve in two ways:

- At the starting point, a Bézier curve runs parallel with the line that connects it to the first control point. At the ending point, the curve runs parallel with the line that connects it to the end point. (In between, it curves.)

- The degree of curvature is determined by the distance to the two control points. If one control point is farther away, it exerts a stronger "pull."

To define a Bézier curve in markup, you supply three points. The first two points (BezierSegment.Point1 and BezierSegment.Point2) are the control points. The third point (BezierSegment.Point3) is the end point of the curve. As always, the starting point is that starting point of the path or wherever the previous segment leaves off.

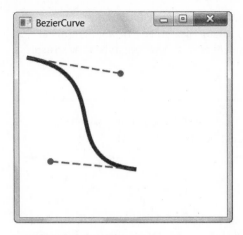

Figure 14-7. *A Bézier curve*

The example shown in Figure 14-7 includes three separate components, each of which uses a different stroke and thus requires a separate Path element. The first path creates the curve, the second adds the dashed lines, and the third applies the circles that indicate the control points. Here's the complete markup:

```
<Canvas>
  <Path Stroke="Blue" StrokeThickness="5" Canvas.Top="20">
    <Path.Data>
      <PathGeometry>
        <PathFigure StartPoint="10,10">
          <BezierSegment Point1="130,30" Point2="40,140"
            Point3="150,150"></BezierSegment>
        </PathFigure>
      </PathGeometry>
    </Path.Data>
  </Path>
  <Path Stroke="Green" StrokeThickness="2" StrokeDashArray="5 2" Canvas.Top="20">
    <Path.Data>
      <GeometryGroup>
        <LineGeometry StartPoint="10,10" EndPoint="130,30"></LineGeometry>
        <LineGeometry StartPoint="40,140" EndPoint="150,150"></LineGeometry>
      </GeometryGroup>
    </Path.Data>
  </Path>
  <Path Fill="Red" Stroke="Red" StrokeThickness="8"  Canvas.Top="20">
    <Path.Data>
      <GeometryGroup>
        <EllipseGeometry Center="130,30"></EllipseGeometry>
        <EllipseGeometry Center="40,140"></EllipseGeometry>
      </GeometryGroup>
    </Path.Data>
  </Path>
</Canvas>
```

Trying to code Bézier paths is a recipe for many thankless hours of trial-and-error computer coding. You're much more likely to draw your curves (and many other graphical elements) in a dedicated drawing program that has an export-to-XAML feature, or Microsoft Expression Blend.

■**Tip** To learn more about the algorithm that underlies the Bézier curve, you can read an informative Wikipedia article on the subject at http://en.wikipedia.org/wiki/Bezier_curve.

The Geometry Mini-Language

The geometries you've seen so far have been relatively concise, with only a few points. More complex geometries are conceptually the same but can easily require hundreds of segments. Defining each line, arc, and curve in a complex path is extremely verbose and unnecessary—after all, it's likely that complex paths will be generated by a design tool rather than written by hand, so the clarity of the markup isn't all that important. With this in mind, the creators of WPF added a more concise alternate syntax for defining geometries that allows you to represent detailed figures with much smaller amounts of markup. This syntax is often described as the *geometry mini-language* (and sometimes the *path mini-language* due to its application with the Path element).

To understand the mini-language, you need to realize that it is essentially a long string holding a series of commands. These commands are read by a type converter that then creates the corresponding geometry. Each command is a single letter and is optionally followed by a few bits of numeric information (such as X and Y coordinates) separated by spaces. Each command is also separated from the previous command with a space.

For example, a bit earlier you created a basic triangle using a closed path with two line segments. Here's the markup that did the trick:

```
<Path Stroke="Blue">
  <Path.Data>
    <PathGeometry>
      <PathFigure IsClosed="True" StartPoint="10,100">
        <LineSegment Point="100,100" />
        <LineSegment Point="100,50" />
      </PathFigure>
    </PathGeometry>
  </Path.Data>
</Path>
```

To duplicate this figure using the mini-language, you'd write this:

```
<Path Stroke="Blue" Data="M 10,100 L 100,100 L 100,50 Z"/>
```

This path uses a sequence of four commands. The first command (M) creates the PathFigure and sets the starting point to (10, 100). The following two commands (L) create line segments. The final command (Z) ends the PathFigure and sets the IsClosed property to true. The commas in this string are optional, as are the spaces between the command and its parameters, but you must leave at least one space between adjacent parameters and commands. That means you can reduce the syntax even further to this less-readable form:

```
<Path Stroke="Blue" Data="M10 100 L100 100 L100 50 Z"/>
```

When creating a geometry with the mini-language, you are actually creating a StreamGeometry object, not a PathGeometry. As a result, you won't be able to modify the geometry later on in your code. If this isn't acceptable, you can create a PathGeometry explicitly but use the same syntax to define its collection of PathFigure objects. Here's how:

```
<Path Stroke="Blue">
  <Path.Data>
    <PathGeometry Figures="M 10,100 L 100,100 L 100,50 Z" />
  </Path.Data>
</Path>
```

The geometry mini-language is easy to grasp. It uses a fairly small set of commands, which are detailed in Table 14-5. Parameters are shown in italics.

Table 14-5. *Commands for the Geometry Mini-Language*

Command	Description
F *value*	Sets the Geometry.FillRule property. Use 0 for EvenOdd, or 1 for NonZero. This command must appear at the beginning of the string (if you decide to use it).
M *x,y*	Creates a new PathFigure for the geometry and sets its start point. This command must be used before any other commands except F. However, you can also use it during your drawing sequence to move the origin of your coordinate system. (The M stands for *move*.)
L *x,y*	Creates a LineSegment to the specified point.
H *x*	Creates a horizontal LineSegment using the specified X value and keeping the Y value constant.
V *y*	Creates a vertical LineSegment using the specified Y value and keeping the X value constant.
A *radiusX, radiusY degrees isLargeArc, isClockwise x,y*	Creates an ArcSegment to the indicated point. You specify the radii of the ellipse that describes the arc, the number of degrees the arc is rotated, and Boolean flags that set the IsLargeArc and SweepDirection properties described earlier.
C x1,y1 x2,y2 x,y	Creates a BezierSegment to the indicated point, using control points at (x1, y1) and (x2, y2).
Q x1, y1 x,y	Creates a QuadraticBezierSegment to the indicated point, with one control point at (x1, y1).
S x2,y2 x,y	Creates a smooth BezierSegment by using the second control point from the previous BezierSegment as the first control point in the new BezierSegment.
Z	Ends the current PathFigure and sets IsClosed to true. You don't need to use this command if you don't want to set IsClosed to true—instead, simply use M if you want to start a new PathFigure or end the string.

■Tip There's one more trick in the geometry mini-language. You can use a command in lowercase if you want its parameters to be evaluated relative to the previous point rather than using absolute coordinates.

Clipping with Geometry

As you've seen, geometries are the most powerful way to create a shape. However, geometries aren't limited to the Path element. They're also used anywhere you need to supply the abstract definition of a shape (rather than draw a real, concrete shape in a window).

Another place geometries are used is to set the Clip property, which is provided by all elements. The Clip property allows you to constrain the outer bounds of an element to fit a specific geometry. You can use the Clip property to create a number of exotic effects. Although it's commonly used to trim down image content in an Image element, you can use the Clip property with any element. The only limitation is that you'll need a closed geometry if you actually want to see anything—individual curves and line segments aren't of much use.

The following example defines a single geometry that's used to clip two elements: an Image element that contains a bitmap, and a standard Button element. The results are shown in Figure 14-8.

Figure 14-8. *Clipping two elements*

Here's the markup for this example:

```
<Window.Resources>
  <GeometryGroup x:Key="clipGeometry" FillRule="Nonzero">
    <EllipseGeometry RadiusX="75" RadiusY="50" Center="100,150"></EllipseGeometry>
    <EllipseGeometry RadiusX="100" RadiusY="25" Center="200,150"></EllipseGeometry>
    <EllipseGeometry RadiusX="75" RadiusY="130" Center="140,140"></EllipseGeometry>
  </GeometryGroup>
</Window.Resources>
<Grid>
  <Grid.ColumnDefinitions>
```

```
    <ColumnDefinition></ColumnDefinition>
    <ColumnDefinition></ColumnDefinition>
  </Grid.ColumnDefinitions>

  <Button Clip="{StaticResource clipGeometry}">A button</Button>
  <Image Grid.Column="1" Clip="{StaticResource clipGeometry}"
    Stretch="None" Source="creek.jpg"></Image>
</Grid>
```

There's one limitation with clipping. The clipping you set doesn't take the size of the element into account. In other words, if the button in Figure 14-8 becomes larger or smaller when the window is resized, the clipped region will remain the same and show a different portion of the button. One possible solution is to wrap the element in a Viewbox to provide automatic rescaling. However, this causes *everything* to resize proportionately, including the details you do want to resize (the clip region and button surface) and those you might not (the button text and the line that draws the button border).

In the next section, you'll go a bit further with Geometry objects and use them to define a lightweight drawing that can be used in a variety of ways.

Drawings

As you've learned, the abstract Geometry class represents a shape or a path. The abstract Drawing class plays a complementary role. It represents a 2-D drawing—in other words, it contains all the information you need to display a piece of vector or bitmap art.

Although there are several types of drawing classes, the GeometryDrawing is the one that works with the geometries you've learned about so far. It adds the stroke and fill details that determine how the geometry should be painted. You can think of a GeometryDrawing as a single shape in a piece of vector clip art. For example, it's possible to convert a standard Windows Metafile (.wmf) into a collection of GeometryDrawing objects that are ready to insert into your user interface. (In fact, you'll learn how to do exactly this in the "Exporting Clip Art" section a little later in this chapter.)

It helps to consider a simple example. Earlier, you saw how to define a simple PathGeometry that represents a triangle:

```
<PathGeometry>
  <PathFigure IsClosed="True" StartPoint="10,100">
    <LineSegment Point="100,100" />
    <LineSegment Point="100,50" />
  </PathFigure>
</PathGeometry>
```

You can use this PathGeometry to build a GeometryDrawing like so:

```
<GeometryDrawing Brush="Yellow">
  <GeometryDrawing.Pen>
    <Pen Brush="Blue" Thickness="3"></Pen>
  </GeometryDrawing.Pen>
<GeometryDrawing.Geometry>
```

```
<PathGeometry>
  <PathFigure IsClosed="True" StartPoint="10,100">
    <LineSegment Point="100,100" />
    <LineSegment Point="100,50" />
  </PathFigure>
</PathGeometry>
    </GeometryDrawing.Geometry>
</GeometryDrawing>
```

Here, the PathGeometry defines the shape (a triangle). The GeometryDrawing defines the shape's appearance (a yellow triangle with a blue outline). Neither the PathGeometry nor the GeometryDrawing is an element, so you can't use either one directly to add your custom-drawn content to a window. Instead, you'll need to use another class that supports drawings, as described in the next section.

Note The GeometryDrawing class introduces a new detail: the System.Windows.Media.Pen class. The Pen class provides the Brush and Thickness properties used in the previous example, along with all the stroke-related properties you learned about with shapes (StartLine, EndLineCap, DashStyle, DashCap, LineJoin, and MiterLimit). In fact, most Shape-derived classes use Pen objects internally in their drawing code but expose pen-related properties directly for ease of use.

GeometryDrawing isn't the only drawing class in WPF (although it is the most relevant one when considering 2-D vector graphics). In fact, the Drawing class is meant to represent *all* types of 2-D graphics, and there's a small group of classes that derive from it. Table 14-6 lists them all.

Table 14-6. *The Drawing Classes*

Class	Description	Properties
GeometryDrawing	Wraps a geometry with the brush that fills it and the pen that outlines it.	Geometry, Brush, Pen
ImageDrawing	Wraps an image (typically, a file-based bitmap image) with a rectangle that defines its bounds.	ImageSource, Rect
VideoDrawing	Combines a MediaPlayer that's used to play a video file with a rectangle that defines its bounds. Chapter 22 has the details about WPF's multimedia support.	Player, Rect
GlyphRunDrawing	Wraps a low-level text object known as a GlyphRun with a brush that paints it.	GlyphRun, ForegroundBrush
DrawingGroup	Combines a collection of Drawing objects of any type. The DrawingGroup allows you to create composite drawings, and apply effects to the entire collection at once, using one of its properties.	BitmapEffect, BitmapEffectInput, Children, ClipGeometry, GuidelineSet, Opacity, OpacityMask, Transform

Displaying a Drawing

Because Drawing-derived classes are not elements, they can't be placed in your user interface. Instead, to display a drawing, you need to use one of three classes listed in Table 14-7.

Table 14-7. *Classes for Displaying a Drawing*

Class	Derives From	Description
DrawingImage	ImageSource	Allows you to host a drawing inside an Image element.
DrawingBrush	Brush	Allows you to wrap a drawing with a brush, which you can then use to paint any surface.
DrawingVisual	Visual	Allows you to place a drawing in a lower-level visual object. Visuals don't have the overhead of true elements but can still be displayed if you implement the required infrastructure. You'll learn more later in this chapter in the "Visuals" section.

There's a common theme in all of these classes—quite simply, they give you a way to display your 2-D content with less overhead.

For example, imagine you want to use a piece of vector art to create the icon for a button. The most convenient (and resource-intensive) way to do this is to place a Canvas inside the button, and place a series of Shape-derived elements inside the Canvas:

```
<Button ... >
  <Canvas ... >
    <Polyline ... >
    <Polyline ... >
    <Rectangle ... >
    <Ellipse ... >
    <Polygon ... >
    ...
  </Canvas>
</Button>
```

As you already know, if you take this approach, each element is completely independent, with its own memory footprint, event handling, and so on.

A better approach is to reduce the number of elements using the Path element. Because each path has a single stroke and fill, you'll still need a large number of Path objects, but you'll probably be able to reduce the number of elements somewhat:

```
<Button ... >
  <Canvas ... >
    <Path ... >
    <Path ... >
    <Path ... >
    ...
  </Canvas>
</Button>
```

Once you start using the Path element, you've made the switch from separate shapes to distinct geometries. You can carry the abstraction one level further by extracting the geometry, stroke, and fill information from the path and turning it into a drawing. You can then fuse your drawings together in a DrawingGroup and place that DrawingGroup in a DrawingImage, which can in turn be placed in an Image element. Here's the new markup this process creates:

```
<Button ... >
  <Image ... >
    <Image.Source>
      <DrawingImage>
        <DrawingImage.Drawing>
          <DrawingGroup>
            <GeometryDrawing ... >
            <GeometryDrawing ... >
            <GeometryDrawing ... >

            ...
          </DrawingGroup>
        </DrawingImage.Drawing>
      </DrawingImage>
    <Image.Source>
  </Image>
</Button>
```

This is a significant change. It hasn't simplified your markup, as you've simply substituted one GeometryDrawing object for each Path object. However, it *has* reduced the number of elements and hence the overhead that's required. The previous example created a Canvas inside the button and added a separate element for each path. But this example requires just one nested element: the Image inside the button. The trade-off is that you no longer have the ability to handle events for each distinct path (for example, you can't detect mouse clicks on separate regions of the drawing). But in a static image that's used for a button, it's unlikely that you want this ability anyway.

■**Note** It's easy to confuse DrawingImage and ImageDrawing, two WPF classes with awkwardly similar names. DrawingImage is used to place a drawing inside an Image element. Typically, you'll use it to put vector content in an Image. ImageDrawing is completely different—it's a Drawing-derived class that accepts bitmap content. This allows you to combine GeometryDrawing and ImageDrawing objects in one DrawingGroup, thereby creating a drawing with vector and bitmap content that you can use however you want.

Although the DrawingImage gives you the majority of the savings, you can still get a tiny bit more efficient and remove one more element with the help of the DrawingBrush. The basic idea is to wrap your DrawingImage in a DrawingBrush, like so:

```
<Button ... >
  <Button.Background>
```

```
    <DrawingBrush>
      <DrawingBrush.Drawing>
        <DrawingGroup>
          <GeometryDrawing ... >
          <GeometryDrawing ... >
          <GeometryDrawing ... >
          ...
        </DrawingGroup>
      </DrawingBrush.Drawing>
    </DrawingBrush>
  </Button.Background>
</Button>
```

One product that uses this approach is Expression Blend.

The DrawingBrush approach isn't exactly the same as the DrawingImage approach shown earlier. That's because the default way that an Image sizes its content is different than the DrawingBrush. The default Image.Stretch property is Uniform, which scales the image up or down to fit the available space. The default DrawingBrush.Stretch property is Fill, which may distort your image.

When changing the Stretch property of a DrawingBrush, you may also want to adjust the Viewport setting to explicitly tweak the location and size of the drawing in the fill region. For example, this markup scales the drawing used by the drawing brush to take 90% of the fill area:

```
<DrawingBrush Stretch="Fill" Viewport="0,0 0.9,0.9">
```

This is useful with the button example because it gives some space for the border around the button. Because the DrawingBrush isn't an element, it won't be placed using the WPF layout process. That means that unlike the Image, the placement of the content in the DrawingBrush won't take the Button.Padding value into account.

One quirk with the DrawingBrush approach is that the content disappears when you move the mouse over the button and a new brush is used to paint its surface. But when you use the Image approach, the picture remains unaffected. To deal with this issue, you need to create a custom control template for the button that doesn't paint its background in the same way. This technique is demonstrated in Chapter 15.

Tip Using DrawingBrush objects also allows you to create some effects that wouldn't otherwise be possible, such as tiling. Because DrawingBrush derives from TileBrush, you can use the TileMode property to repeat a drawing in a pattern across your fill region. Chapter 13 has the full details about tiling with the TileBrush.

Exporting Clip Art

Although all of these examples have declared their drawings inline, a more common approach is to place some portion of this content in a resource dictionary so it can be reused throughout your application (and modified in one place). It's up to you how you break this markup down into resources, but two common choices are to store a dictionary full of DrawingImage objects, or one stocked with DrawingBrush objects. Optionally, you can factor out the Geometry objects and store them as separate resources. (This is handy if you use the same geometry in more than one drawing, with different colors.)

Of course, very few developers will code much (if any) art by hand. Instead, they'll use dedicated design tools that export the XAML content they need. Most design tools don't support XAML export yet, although there are a wide variety of plug-ins and converters that fill the gaps. Here are some examples:

- `http://www.mikeswanson.com/XAMLExport` has a free XAML plug-in for Adobe Illustrator.

- `http://www.mikeswanson.com/swf2xaml` has a free XAML converter for Adobe Flash files.

- Expression Design, Microsoft's illustration and graphic design program, has a built-in XAML export. In can read a variety of vector art file formats, including the .wmf (Windows Metafile Format), which allows you to import existing clip art and export it as XAML.

However, even if you use one of these tools, the knowledge you've learned about geometries and drawings is still important for several reasons.

First, many programs allow you to choose whether you want to export a drawing as a combination of separate elements in a Canvas or as a collection of DrawingBrush or DrawingImage resources. Usually, the first choice is the default choice because it preserves more features. However, if you're using a large number of drawings, your drawings are complex, or you simply want to use the least amount of memory for static graphics like button icons, it's a much better idea to use DrawingBrush or DrawingImage resources. Better still, these formats are separated from the rest of your user interface so it's easier to update them later. (In fact, you could even compile your DrawingBrush or DrawingImage resources in a separate DLL assembly, as described in Chapter 11.)

Tip To save resources in Expression Design, you must explicitly choose Resource Dictionary instead of Canvas in the Document Format list box.

Another reason why it's important to understand the plumbing behind 2-D graphics is because it makes it far easier for you to manipulate them. For example, you can alter a standard 2-D graphic by modifying the brushes used to paint various shapes, applying transforms to individual geometries, or altering the opacity or transform of an entire layer of shapes (through a DrawingGroup object). More dramatically, you can add, remove, or alter individual geometries. These techniques can be easily combined with the animation skills you'll pick up in Chapter 21. For example, it's easy to rotate a Geometry object by modifying the Angle property of a RotateTransform, fade a layer of shapes into existence using DrawingGroup.Opacity, or create a swirling gradient effect by animating a LinearGradientBrush that paints the fill for a GeometryDrawing.

Tip If you're really curious, you can hunt down the resources used by other WPF applications. The basic technique is to use a tool such as Reflector (`http://www.aisto.com/roeder/dotnet`) to find the assembly with the resources. You can then use a Reflector plug-in (`http://www.codeplex.com/reflectoraddins`) to extract one of the BAML resources and decompile it back to XAML. Of course, most companies won't take kindly to developers who steal their handcrafted graphics to use in their own applications!

Visuals

So far, you've learned the best ways to deal with modest amounts of graphical content. By using geometries, drawings, and paths, you reduce the overhead of your 2-D art. Even if you're using complex compound shapes with layered effects and gradient brushes, this is an approach that performs well.

However, this design isn't suitable for drawing-intensive applications that need to render a huge number of graphical elements. For example, consider a mapping program, a physics modeling program that demonstrates particle collisions, or a side-scrolling game. The problem posed by these applications isn't the complexity of the art, but the sheer number of individual graphical elements. Even if you replace your Path elements with lighter weight Geometry objects, the overhead will still hamper the application's performance.

The WPF solution for this sort of situation is to use the lower-level *visual layer* model. The basic idea is that you define each graphical element as a Visual object, which is an extremely lightweight ingredient that has less overhead than a Geometry object or a Path object. You can then use a single element to render all your visuals in a window.

In the following sections, you'll learn how to create visuals, manipulate them, and perform hit testing. Along the way, you'll build a basic vector-based drawing application that lets you add squares to a drawing surface, select them, and drag them around.

Drawing Visuals

Visual is an abstract class, so you can't create an instance of it. Instead, you need to use one of the classes that derive from Visual. These include UIElement (which is the root of WPF's element model), Viewport3DVisual (which allows you to display 3-D content, as described in Chapter 23), and ContainerVisual (which is a basic container that holds other visuals). But the most useful derived class is DrawingVisual, which derives from ContainerVisual and adds the support you need to "draw" the graphical content you want to place in your visual.

To draw content in a DrawingVisual, you call the DrawingVisual.RenderOpen() method. This method returns a DrawingContext that you can use to define the content of your visual. When you're finished, you call DrawingContext.Close(). Here's how it all unfolds:

```
DrawingVisual visual = new DrawingVisual();
DrawingContext dc = visual.RenderOpen();
// (Perform drawing here.)
dc.Close();
```

Essentially, the DrawingContext class is made up of methods that add some graphical detail to your visual. You call these methods to draw various shapes, apply transforms, change the opacity, and so on. Table 14-8 lists the methods of the DrawingContext class.

Table 14-8. *DrawingContext Methods*

Name	Description
DrawLine(), DrawRectangle(), DrawRoundedRectangle(), and DrawEllipse()	Draw the specified shape at the point you specify, with the fill and outline you specify. These methods mirror the shapes you saw in Chapter 13.
DrawGeometry () and DrawDrawing()	Draws more complex Geometry objects and Drawing objects.
DrawText()	Draws text at the specified location. You specify the text, font, fill, and other details by passing a FormattedText object to this method. You can use DrawText() to draw wrapped text if you set the FormattedText.MaxTextWidth property.
DrawImage()	Draws a bitmap image in a specific region (as defined by a Rect).
DrawVideo()	Draws video content (wrapped in a MediaPlayer object) in a specific region. Chapter 22 has the full details about video rendering in WPF.
Pop()	Reverses the last Push*Xxx*() method that was called. You use the Push*Xxx*() method to temporarily apply one or more effects and the Pop() method to reverse them.
PushClip()	Limits drawing to a specific clip region. Content that falls outside of this region isn't drawn.
PushEffect ()	Applies a BitmapEffect to subsequent drawing operations.
PushOpacity() and PushOpacityMask()	Apply a new opacity setting or opacity mask (see Chapter 13) to make subsequent drawing operations partially transparent.
PushTransform()	Sets a Transform object that will be applied to subsequent drawing operations. You can use a transformation to scale, displace, rotate, or skew content.

Here's an example that creates a visual that contains a basic black triangle with no fill:

```
DrawingVisual visual = new DrawingVisual();
using (DrawingContext dc = visual.RenderOpen())
{
    Pen drawingPen = new Pen(Brushes.Black, 3);
    dc.DrawLine(drawingPen, new Point(0, 50), new Point(50, 0));
    dc.DrawLine(drawingPen, new Point(50, 0), new Point(100, 50));
    dc.DrawLine(drawingPen, new Point(0, 50), new Point(100, 50));
}
```

As you call the DrawingContext methods, you aren't actually painting your visual—rather, you're defining its visual appearance. When you finish by calling Close(), the completed drawing is stored in the visual and exposed through the read-only DrawingVisual.Drawing property. WPF retains the Drawing object so that it can repaint the window when needed.

The order of your drawing code is important. Later drawing actions can write content overtop of what already exists. The Push*Xxx*() methods apply settings that will apply to future drawing operations. For example, you can use PushOpacity() to change the opacity level, which will then affect all subsequent drawing operations. You can use Pop() to reverse the most recent Push*Xxx*() method. If you call more than one Push*Xxx*() method, you can switch them off one at a time with subsequent Pop() calls.

Once you've closed the DrawingContext, you can't modify your visual any further. However, you can apply a transform or change a visual's overall opacity (using the Transform and Opacity properties of the DrawingVisual class). If you want to supply completely new content, you can call RenderOpen() again and repeat the drawing process.

Tip Many drawing methods use Pen and Brush objects. If you plan to draw many visuals with the same stroke and fill, or if you expect to render the same visual multiple times (in order to change its content), it's worth creating the Pen and Brush objects you need upfront and holding on to them over the lifetime of your window.

Visuals are used in several different ways. In the remainder of this chapter, you'll learn how to place a DrawingVisual in a window and perform hit testing for it. You can also use a DrawingVisual to define content you want to print, as you'll see in Chapter 20. Finally, you can use visuals to render a custom-drawn element by overriding the OnRender() method, as you'll see in Chapter 24. In fact, that's exactly how the shape classes that you learned about in Chapter 13 do their work. For example, here's the rendering code that the Rectangle element uses to paint itself:

```
protected override void OnRender(DrawingContext drawingContext)
{
    Pen pen = base.GetPen();
    drawingContext.DrawRoundedRectangle(base.Fill, pen, this._rect,
      this.RadiusX, this.RadiusY);
}
```

Wrapping Visuals in an Element

Defining a visual is the most important step in visual-layer programming, but it's not enough to actually show your visual content onscreen. To display a visual, you need the help of a full-fledged WPF element that can add it to the visual tree. At first glance, this seems to reduce the benefit of visual-layer programming—after all, isn't the whole point to avoid elements and their high overhead? However, a single element has the ability to display an unlimited number of elements. Thus, you can easily create a window that holds only one or two elements but hosts thousands of visuals.

To host a visual in an element, you need to perform the following tasks:

- Call the AddVisualChild() and AddLogicalChild() methods of your element to register your visual. Technically speaking, these tasks aren't required to make the visual appear, but they are required to ensure it is tracked correctly, appears in the visual and logical tree, and works with other WPF features such as hit testing.

- Override the VisualChildrenCount property and return the number of visuals you've added.

- Override the GetVisualChild() method and add the code needed to return your visual when it's requested by index number.

When you override VisualChildrenCount and GetVisualChild(), you are essentially hijacking that element. If you're using a content control, decorator, or panel that can hold nested elements, these elements will no longer be rendered. For example, if you override these two methods in a custom window, you won't see the rest of the window content. Instead, you'll only see the visuals that you've added.

For this reason, it's common to create a dedicated custom class that wraps the visuals you want to display. For example, consider the window shown in Figure 14-9. It allows the user to add squares (each of which is a visual) to a custom Canvas.

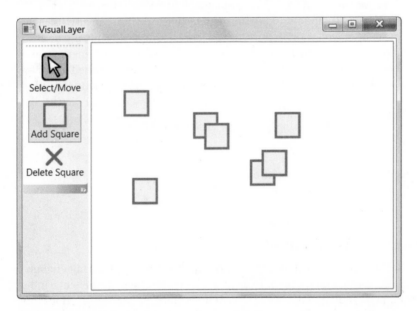

Figure 14-9. *Drawing visuals*

On the left side of the window in Figure 14-9 is a toolbar with three RadioButton objects. As you'll discover in Chapter 18, the ToolBar changes the way some basic controls are rendered, such as buttons. By using a group of RadioButton objects, you can create a set of linked buttons. When you click one of the buttons in this set, it is selected and remains "pushed," while the previously selected button reverts to its normal appearance.

On the right side of the window in Figure 14-9 is a custom Canvas named DrawingCanvas, which stores a collection of visuals internally. DrawingCanvas returns the total number of squares in the VisualChildrenCount property, and uses the GetVisualChild() method to provide access to each visual in the collection. Here's how this details are implemented:

```
public class DrawingCanvas : Canvas
{
    private List<Visual> visuals = new List<Visual>();

    protected override int VisualChildrenCount
    {
        get { return visuals.Count; }
    }

    protected override Visual GetVisualChild(int index)
    {
        return visuals[index];
    }
    ...
```

Additionally, the DrawingCanvas includes an AddVisual() method and a DeleteVisual() method to make it easy for the consuming code to insert visuals into the collection, with the appropriate tracking:

```
    ...
    public void AddVisual(Visual visual)
    {
        visuals.Add(visual);

        base.AddVisualChild(visual);
        base.AddLogicalChild(visual);
    }

    public void DeleteVisual(Visual visual)
    {
        visuals.Remove(visual);

        base.RemoveVisualChild(visual);
        base.RemoveLogicalChild(visual);
    }
}
```

The DrawingCanvas doesn't include the logic for drawing squares, selecting them, and moving them. That's because this functionality is controlled at the application layer. This makes sense because there might be several different drawing tools, all of which work with the same DrawingCanvas. Depending on which button the user clicks, the user might be able to draw different types of shapes or use different stroke and fill colors. All of these details are specific to the window—the DrawingCanvas simply provides the functionality for hosting, rendering, and tracking your visuals.

Here's how the DrawingCanvas is declared in the XAML markup for the window:

```
<local:DrawingCanvas x:Name="drawingSurface" Background="White" ClipToBounds="True"
  MouseLeftButtonDown="drawingSurface_MouseLeftButtonDown"
  MouseLeftButtonUp="drawingSurface_MouseLeftButtonUp"
  MouseMove="drawingSurface_MouseMove" />
```

■Tip By setting the background to white (rather than transparent), it's possible to intercept all mouse clicks on the canvas surface.

Now that you've considered the DrawingCanvas container, it's worth considering the event handling code that creates the squares. The starting point is the event handler for the MouseLeftButton. It's at this point that the code determines what operation is being performed—square creation, square deletion, or square selection. At the moment, we're just interested in the first task:

```
private void drawingSurface_MouseLeftButtonDown(object sender,
  MouseButtonEventArgs e)
{
    Point pointClicked = e.GetPosition(drawingSurface);

    if (cmdAdd.IsChecked == true)
    {
        // Create, draw, and add the new square.
        DrawingVisual visual = new DrawingVisual();
        DrawSquare(visual, pointClicked, false);
        drawingSurface.AddVisual(visual);
    }
    ...
}
```

The actual work is performed by a custom method named DrawSquare(). This approach is useful because the square drawing needs to be triggered at several different points in the code. Obviously, DrawSquare() is required when the square is first created. It's also used when the appearance of the square changes for any reason (such as when it's selected).

The DrawSquare() method accepts three parameters: the DrawingVisual to draw, the point for the top-left corner of the square, and a Boolean flag that indicates whether the square is currently selected, in which case it is given a different fill color.

Here's the modest rendering code:

```
// Drawing constants.
private Brush drawingBrush = Brushes.AliceBlue;
private Brush selectedDrawingBrush = Brushes.LightGoldenrodYellow;
private Pen drawingPen = new Pen(Brushes.SteelBlue, 3);
private Size squareSize = new Size(30, 30);
```

```
private void DrawSquare(DrawingVisual visual, Point topLeftCorner, bool isSelected)
{
    using (DrawingContext dc = visual.RenderOpen())
    {
        Brush brush = drawingBrush;
        if (isSelected) brush = selectedDrawingBrush;

        dc.DrawRectangle(brush, drawingPen,
          new Rect(topLeftCorner, squareSize));
    }
}
```

This is all you need to display a visual in a window: some code that renders the visual, and a container that handles the necessary tracking details. However, there's a bit more work to do if you want to add interactivity to your visuals, as you'll see in the following section.

Hit Testing

The square-drawing application not only allows users to draw squares, it also allows them to move and delete existing squares. In order to perform either of these tasks, your code needs to be able to intercept a mouse click and find the visual at the clicked location. This task is called *hit testing*.

To support hit testing, it makes sense to add a GetVisual() method to the DrawingCanvas class. This method takes a point and returns the matching DrawingVisual. To do its work, it uses the static VisualTreeHelper.HitTest() method. Here's the complete code for the GetVisual() method:

```
public DrawingVisual GetVisual(Point point)
{
    HitTestResult hitResult = VisualTreeHelper.HitTest(this, point);
    return hitResult.VisualHit as DrawingVisual;
}
```

In this case, the code ignores any hit object that isn't a DrawingVisual, including the DrawingCanvas itself. If no squares are clicked, the GetVisual() method returns a null reference.

The delete feature makes use of the GetVisual() method. When the delete command is selected and a square is clicked, the MouseLeftButtonDown event handler uses this code to remove it:

```
else if (cmdDelete.IsChecked == true)
{
    DrawingVisual visual = drawingSurface.GetVisual(pointClicked);
    if (visual != null) drawingSurface.DeleteVisual(visual);
}
```

Similar code supports the dragging feature, but it needs a way to keep track of the fact that dragging is underway. Three fields in the window class serve this purpose—isDragging, selectedVisual, and clickOffset:

```
private bool isDragging = false;
private DrawingVisual selectedVisual;
private Vector clickOffset;
```

When the user clicks a shape, the isDragging field is set to true, the selectedVisual is set to the visual that was clicked, and the clickOffset records the space between the top-left corner of the square and the point where the user clicked. Here's the code from the MouseLeftButtonDown event handler:

```
else if (cmdSelectMove.IsChecked == true)
{
    DrawingVisual visual = drawingSurface.GetVisual(pointClicked);
    if (visual != null)
    {
        // Find the top-left corner of the square.
        // This is done by looking at the current bounds and
        // removing half the border (pen thickness).
        // An alternate solution would be to store the top-left
        // point of every visual in a collection in the
        // DrawingCanvas, and provide this point when hit testing.
        Point topLeftCorner = new Point(
          visual.ContentBounds.TopLeft.X + drawingPen.Thickness / 2,
          visual.ContentBounds.TopLeft.Y + drawingPen.Thickness / 2);
        DrawSquare(visual, topLeftCorner, true);

        clickOffset = topLeftCorner - pointClicked;
        isDragging = true;

        if (selectedVisual != null && selectedVisual != visual)
        {
            // The selection has changed. Clear the previous selection.
            ClearSelection();
        }
        selectedVisual = visual;
    }
}
```

Along with basic bookkeeping, this code also calls DrawSquare() to rerender the DrawingVisual, giving it the new color. The code also uses another custom method, named ClearSelection(), to repaint the previously selected square so it returns to its normal appearance:

```
private void ClearSelection()
{
    Point topLeftCorner = new Point(
      selectedVisual.ContentBounds.TopLeft.X + drawingPen.Thickness / 2,
      selectedVisual.ContentBounds.TopLeft.Y + drawingPen.Thickness / 2);
    DrawSquare(selectedVisual, topLeftCorner, false);
    selectedVisual = null;
}
```

Note Remember, the DrawSquare() method defines the content for the square—it doesn't actually paint it in the window. For that reason, you don't need to worry about inadvertently painting overtop of another square that should be underneath. WPF manages the painting process, ensuring that visuals are painted in the order they are returned by the GetVisualChild() method (which is the order in which they are defined in the visuals collection).

Next, you need to actually move the square as the user drags, and end the dragging operation when the user releases the left mouse button. Both of these tasks are accomplished with some straightforward event handling code:

```
private void drawingSurface_MouseMove(object sender, MouseEventArgs e)
{
    if (isDragging)
    {
        Point pointDragged = e.GetPosition(drawingSurface) + clickOffset;
        DrawSquare(selectedVisual, pointDragged, true);
    }
}

private void drawingSurface_MouseLeftButtonUp(object sender, MouseButtonEventArgs e)
{
    isDragging = false;
}
```

Complex Hit Testing

In the previous example, the hit testing code always returns the topmost visual (or a null reference if the space is empty). However, the VisualTreeHelper class includes two overloads to the HitTest() method that allow you to perform more sophisticated hit testing. Using these methods, you can retrieve all the visuals that are at a specified point, even if they're obscured underneath other visuals. You can also find all the visuals that fall in a given geometry.

To use this more advanced hit testing behavior, you need to create a callback. The VisualTreeHelper will then walk through your visuals from top to bottom (in the reverse order that you created them). Each time it finds a match, it calls your callback with the details. You can then choose to stop the search (if you've dug down enough levels) or continue until no more visuals remain.

The following code implements this technique by adding a GetVisuals() method to the DrawingCanvas. GetVisuals() accepts a Geometry object, which it uses for hit testing. It creates the callback delegate, clears the collection of hit test results, and then starts the hit testing process by calling the VisualTreeHelper.HitTest() method. When the process is finished, it returns a collection with all the visuals that were found:

```
private List<DrawingVisual> hits = new List<DrawingVisual>();

public List<DrawingVisual> GetVisuals(Geometry region)
{
```

```
    // Remove matches from the previous search.
    hits.Clear();

    // Prepare the parameters for the hit test operation
    // (the geometry and callback).
    GeometryHitTestParameters parameters = new GeometryHitTestParameters(region);
    HitTestResultCallback callback =
      new HitTestResultCallback(this.HitTestCallback);

    // Search for hits.
    VisualTreeHelper.HitTest(this, null, callback, parameters);
    return hits;
}
```

Tip In this example, the callback is implemented by a separately defined method named HitTestResultCallback(). Both the HitTestResultCallback() and GetVisuals() use the hits collection, so it must be defined as a member field. However, you could remove this requirement by using an anonymous method for the callback, which you would declare inside the GetVisuals() method.

The callback method implements your hit testing behavior. Ordinarily, the HitTestResult object provides just a single property (VisualHit), but you can cast it to one of two derived types depending on the type of hit test you're performing.

If you're hit testing a point, you can cast HitTestResult to PointHitTestResult, which provides a relatively uninteresting PointHit property that returns the original point you used to perform the hit test. But if you're hit testing a Geometry object, as in this example, you can cast HitTestResult to GeometryHitTestResult and get access to the IntersectionDetail property. This property tells you whether your geometry completely wraps the visual (FullyInside), whether the geometry and visual simply overlap (Intersects), or whether your hit-tested geometry falls within the visual (FullyContains). In this example, hits are only counted if the visual is completely inside the hit-tested region. Finally, at the end of the callback, you can return one of two values from the HitTestResultBehavior enumeration: Continue to keep looking for hits, or Stop to end the process.

```
private HitTestResultBehavior HitTestCallback(HitTestResult result)
{
    GeometryHitTestResult geometryResult = (GeometryHitTestResult)result;
    DrawingVisual visual = result.VisualHit as DrawingVisual;

    // Only include matches that are DrawingVisual objects and
    // that are completely inside the geometry.
    if (visual != null &&
        geometryResult.IntersectionDetail == IntersectionDetail.FullyInside)
    {
        hits.Add(visual);
```

```
    }
    return HitTestResultBehavior.Continue;
}
```

Using the GetVisuals() method, you can create the sophisticated selection box effect shown in Figure 14-10. Here, the user draws a box around a group of squares. The application then reports the number of squares in the region.

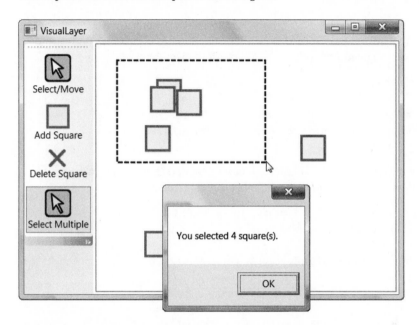

Figure 14-10. *Advanced hit testing*

To create the selection square, the window simply adds another DrawingVisual to the DrawingCanvas. The window also stores a reference to the selection square as a member field, along with a flag named isMultiSelecting that keeps track of when the selection box is being drawn, and a field named selectionSquareTopLeft that tracks the top-left corner of the current selection box:

```
private DrawingVisual selectionSquare;
private bool isMultiSelecting = false;
private Point selectionSquareTopLeft;
```

In order to implement the selection box feature you need to add some code to the event handlers you've already seen. When the mouse is clicked, you need to create the selection box, switch isMultiSelecting to true, and capture the mouse. Here's the code that does this work in the MouseLeftButtonDown event handler:

```
else if (cmdSelectMultiple.IsChecked == true)
{
    selectionSquare = new DrawingVisual();
    drawingSurface.AddVisual(selectionSquare);
```

```
    selectionSquareTopLeft = pointClicked;
    isMultiSelecting = true;

    // Make sure we get the MouseLeftButtonUp event even if the user
    // moves off the Canvas. Otherwise, two selection squares could
    // be drawn at once.
    drawingSurface.CaptureMouse();
}
```

Now, when the mouse moves, you can check if the selection box is currently active, and draw it if it is. To do so, you need this code in the MouseMove event handler:

```
else if (isMultiSelecting)
{
    Point pointDragged = e.GetPosition(drawingSurface);
    DrawSelectionSquare(selectionSquareTopLeft, pointDragged);
}
```

The actual drawing takes place in a dedicated method named DrawSelectionSquare(), which looks a fair bit like the DrawSquare() method you considered earlier:

```
private Brush selectionSquareBrush = Brushes.Transparent;
private Pen selectionSquarePen = new Pen(Brushes.Black, 2);

private void DrawSelectionSquare(Point point1, Point point2)
{
    selectionSquarePen.DashStyle = DashStyles.Dash;

    using (DrawingContext dc = selectionSquare.RenderOpen())
    {
        dc.DrawRectangle(selectionSquareBrush, selectionSquarePen,
            new Rect(point1, point2));
    }
}
```

Finally, when the mouse is released you can perform the hit testing, show the message box, and then remove the selections square. To do so, you need this code in the MouseLeftButtonUp event handler:

```
if (isMultiSelecting)
{
    // Display all the squares in this region.
    RectangleGeometry geometry = new RectangleGeometry(
        new Rect(selectionSquareTopLeft, e.GetPosition(drawingSurface)));
    List<DrawingVisual> visualsInRegion =
        drawingSurface.GetVisuals(geometry);
    MessageBox.Show(String.Format("You selected {0} square(s).",
        visualsInRegion.Count));
```

```
    isMultiSelecting = false;
    drawingSurface.DeleteVisual(selectionSquare);
    drawingSurface.ReleaseMouseCapture();
}
```

The Last Word

In this chapter, you delved deeper into WPF's 2-D drawing model. You began with a thorough look at the Path class, the most powerful of WPF's shape classes, and the geometry model that it uses. Next, you considered how you could use a geometry to build a drawing, and to use that drawing to display lightweight, noninteractive graphics. Finally, you tackled the most efficient way to display graphics in WPF—the lower-level visual layer. Using the visual layer, you saw how you could build a basic drawing application that uses sophisticated hit testing.

In the next chapter you'll consider one of the places where you can put your drawing skills to good use—creating custom control templates.

■ ■ ■

Control Templates

In the past, Windows developers were forced to choose between convenience and flexibility. For maximum convenience, they could use prebuilt controls. These controls worked well enough, but they offered limited customization and almost always had a fixed visual appearance. Occasionally, some controls provided a less than intuitive "owner drawing" mode that allowed developers to paint a portion of the control by responding to a callback. But the basic controls—buttons, text boxes, check boxes, list boxes, and so on—were completely locked down.

As a result, developers who wanted a bit more pizzazz were forced to build custom controls from scratch. This was a problem—not only was it slow and difficult to write the required drawing logic by hand, but custom control developers also needed to implement basic functionality from scratch (such as selection in a text box or key handling in a button). And even once the custom controls were perfected, inserting them into an existing application involved a fairly significant round of editing, which would usually necessitate changes in the code (and more rounds of testing). In short, custom controls were a necessary evil—they were the only way to get a modern, distinctive interface, but they were also a headache to integrate into an application and support.

WPF finally solves the control customization problem with styles (which you considered in Chapter 12), and templates (which you'll begin exploring in this chapter). The reason these features work so well is because of the dramatically different way that controls are implemented in WPF. In previous user interface technologies, such as Windows Forms, commonly used controls aren't actually implemented in .NET code. Instead, the Windows Forms control classes wrap core ingredients from the Win32 API, which are untouchable. But as you've already learned, in WPF every control is composed in pure .NET code, with no Win32 API glue in the background. As a result, it's possible for WPF to expose mechanisms (styles and templates) that allow you to reach into these elements and tweak them. In fact, *tweak* is the wrong word because, as you'll see in this chapter, WPF controls allow the most radical redesigns you can imagine.

Understanding Logical Trees and Visual Trees

Earlier in this book, you spent a great deal of time considering the content model of a window—in other words, how you can nest elements inside other elements to build a complete window.

For example, consider the extremely simple two-button window shown in Figure 15-1. To create this window, you nest a StackPanel control inside a Window. In the StackPanel, you place two Button controls, and inside of each you can add some content of your choice (in this case, two strings). Here's the markup:

```
<Window x:Class="SimpleWindow.Window1"
    xmlns="http://schemas.microsoft.com/winfx/2006/xaml/presentation"
    xmlns:x="http://schemas.microsoft.com/winfx/2006/xaml"
    Title="SimpleWindow" Height="338" Width="356"
    >
    <StackPanel Margin="5">
      <Button Padding="5" Margin="5">First Button</Button>
      <Button Padding="5" Margin="5">Second Button</Button>
    </StackPanel>
</Window>
```

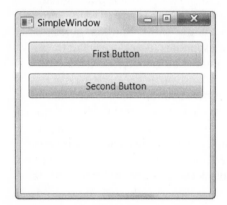

Figure 15-1. *A window with three elements*

The assortment of elements that you've added is called the logical tree, and it's shown in Figure 15-2. As a WPF programmer, you'll spend most of your time building the logical tree and then backing it up with event handling code. In fact, all of the features you've considered so far (such as property value inheritance, event routing, and styling) work through the logical tree.

However, if you want to customize your elements, the logical tree isn't much help. Obviously, you could replace an entire element with another element (for example, you could substitute a custom FancyButton class in place of the current Button), but this requires more work, and it could disrupt your application's interface or its code. For that reason, WPF goes deeper with the *visual tree.*

A visual tree is an expanded version of the logical tree. It breaks elements down into smaller pieces. In other words, instead of seeing a carefully encapsulated black box such as the Button control, you see the visual components of that button—the border that gives buttons their signature shaded background (represented by the ButtonChrome class), the container inside (a ContentPresenter), and the block that holds the button text (represented by the familiar TextBlock). Figure 15-3 shows the visual tree for Figure 15-1.

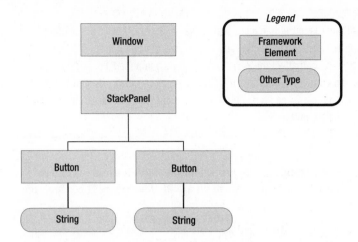

Figure 15-2. *The logical tree for SimpleWindow*

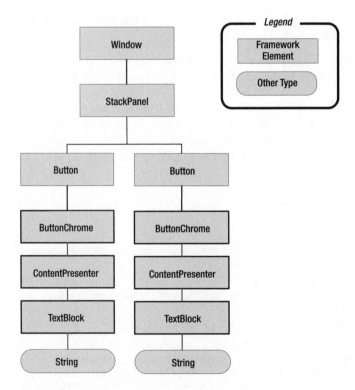

Figure 15-3. *The visual tree for SimpleWindow*

All of these details are themselves elements—in other words, every individual detail in a control such as Button is represented by a class that derives from FrameworkElement.

█Note It's important to realize that there is more than one possible way to expand a logical tree into a visual tree. Details like the styles you've used, the properties you've set, your operating system (Windows XP or Vista), and your current Windows theme can affect the way a visual tree is composed. For instance, in the previous example, the button holds text content, and as a result it automatically creates a nested TextBlock element. But as you know, the Button control is a content control, and so it can hold any other element you wish to use, so long as you nest it inside the button.

So far, this doesn't seem that remarkable. You've just seen that all WPF elements can be decomposed into smaller parts. But what's the advantage for a WPF developer? The visual tree allows you to do two useful things:

- You can alter one of the elements in the visual tree using styles. You can select the specific element you want to modify using the Style.TargetType property. You can even use triggers to make changes automatically when control properties change. However, certain details are difficult or impossible to modify.

- You can create a new template for your control. In this case, your control template will be used to build the visual tree exactly the way you want it.

Interestingly enough, WPF provides two classes that let you browse through the logical and visual trees. These classes are System.Windows.LogicalTreeHelper and System.Windows.Media.VisualTreeHelper.

You've already seen the LogicalTreeHelper in Chapter 2, where it allowed you to hook up event handlers in a WPF application with a noncompiled, dynamically loaded XAML document. The LogicalTreeHelper provides the relatively sparse set of methods listed in Table 15-1. Although these methods are occasionally useful, in most cases you'll use the methods of a specific FrameworkElement instead.

Table 15-1. *LogicalTreeHelper Methods*

Name	Description
FindLogicalNode()	Finds a specific element by name, starting at the element you specify and searching down the logical tree.
BringIntoView()	Scrolls an element into view (if it's in a scrollable container and isn't currently visible). The FrameworkElement.BringIntoView() method performs the same trick.
GetParent()	Gets the parent element of a specific element.
GetChildren()	Gets the child element of a specific element. As you learned in Chapter 2, different elements support different content models. For example, panels support multiple children, while content controls only support a single child. However, the GetChildren() method abstracts away this difference and works with any type of element.

The VisualTreeHelper provides a few similar methods—GetChildrenCount(), GetChild(), and GetParent()—along with a small set of methods that are designed for performing lower-level drawing. (For example, you'll find methods for hit testing and bounds checking, which you considered in Chapter 14.)

The VisualTreeHelper also doubles as an interesting way to study the visual tree in your application. Using the GetChild() method, you can drill down through the visual tree of any window and display it for your consideration. This is a great learning tool, and it requires nothing more than a dash of recursive code.

Figure 15-4 shows one possible implementation. Here, a separate window displays an entire visual tree, starting at any supplied object. In this example, another window (named SimpleWindow), uses the VisualTreeDisplay window to show its visual tree.

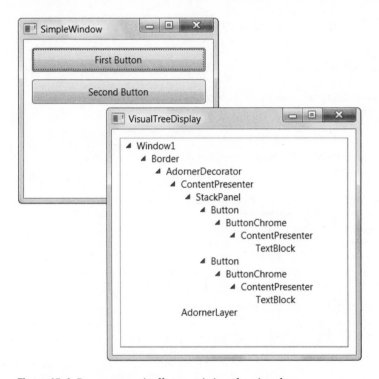

Figure 15-4. *Programmatically examining the visual tree*

Here, a window named Window1 contains a Border, which in turn holds an Adorner-Decorator. (The AdornerDecorator class adds support for drawing content in the adorner layer, which is a special invisible region that overlays your element content. WPF uses the adorner layer to draw details such as focus cues and drag-and-drop indicators.) Inside the AdornerDecorator is a ContentPresenter, which hosts the content of the window. That content includes StackPanel with two Button controls, each of which comprises a ButtonChrome (which draws the standard visual appearance of the button) and a ContentPresenter (which holds the button content). Finally, inside the ContentPresenter of each button is a TextBlock that wraps the text you see in the window.

■Note In this example, the code builds a visual tree in another window. If you place the TreeView in the same window as the one you're examining, you'd inadvertently change the visual tree as you fill the TreeView with items.

Here's the complete code for the VisualTreeDisplay window:

```
public partial class VisualTreeDisplay : System.Windows.Window
{
    public VisualTreeDisplay()
    {
        InitializeComponent();
    }

    public void ShowVisualTree(DependencyObject element)
    {
        // Clear the tree.
        treeElements.Items.Clear();

        // Start processing elements, begin at the root.
        ProcessElement(element, null);
    }

    private void ProcessElement(DependencyObject element,
      TreeViewItem previousItem)
    {
        // Create a TreeViewItem for the current element.
        TreeViewItem item = new TreeViewItem();
        item.Header = element.GetType().Name;
        item.IsExpanded = true;

        // Check whether this item should be added to the root of the tree
        //(if it's the first item), or nested under another item.
        if (previousItem == null)
        {
            treeElements.Items.Add(item);
        }
        else
        {
            previousItem.Items.Add(item);
        }

        // Check whether this element contains other elements.
        for (int i = 0; i < VisualTreeHelper.GetChildrenCount(element); i++)
        {
            // Process each contained element recursively.
            ProcessElement(VisualTreeHelper.GetChild(element, i), item);
        }
    }
}
```

Once you've added this tree to a project, you can use this code from any other window to display its visual tree:

```
VisualTreeDisplay treeDisplay = new VisualTreeDisplay();
treeDisplay.ShowVisualTree(this);
treeDisplay.Show();
```

■**Tip** You can delve into the visual tree of other applications using the remarkable Snoop utility, which is incorporated into Expression Blend and available separately at http://www.blois.us/Snoop. Using Snoop, you can examine the visual tree of any currently running WPF application. You can also zoom in on any element, survey routed events as they're being executed, and explore and even modify element properties.

Understanding Templates

This look at the visual tree raises a few interesting questions. For example, how is a control translated from the logical tree into the expanded representation of the visual tree?

It turns out that every control has a built-in recipe that determines how it should be rendered (as a group of more fundamental elements). That recipe is called a *control template*, and it's defined using a block of XAML markup.

■**Note** Every WPF control is designed to be *lookless*, which means that its visuals (the "look") can be completely redefined. What doesn't change is the control's behavior, which is hardwired into the control class (although it can often be fine-tuned using various properties). When you choose to use a control like the Button, you choose it because you want button-like behavior (in other words, an element that presents content can be clicked to trigger an action and can be used as the default or cancel button on a window.) However, you're free to change the way a button looks and how it reacts when you mouse over it or press it, and any other aspect of its appearance and visual behavior.

Here's a simplified version of the template for the common Button class. It omits the XML namespace declarations, the attributes that set the properties of the nested elements, and the triggers that determine how the button behaves when it's disabled, focused, or clicked:

```
<ControlTemplate ... >
  <mwt:ButtonChrome Name="Chrome" ... >
    <ContentPresenter Content="{TemplateBinding ContentControl.Content}" ... />
  </mwt:ButtonChrome>
  <ControlTemplate.Triggers>
    ...
  </ControlTemplate.Triggers>
</ControlTemplate>
```

Although we haven't yet explored the ButtonChrome and ContentPresenter classes, you can easily recognize that the control template provides the expansion you saw in the visual tree. The ButtonChrome class defines the standard button visuals, while the ContentPresenter holds whatever content you've supplied. If you wanted to build a completely new button (as you'll see later in this chapter), you simply need to create a new control template. In place of ButtonChrome, you'd use something else—perhaps your own custom class, or a drawing class like the ones you considered in Chapter 13.

■Note ButtonChrome derives from Decorator (much like the Border class you learned about in Chapter 5). That means it's designed to add a graphical embellishment around another element—in this case, around the content of a button.

The triggers control how the button changes when it is focused, clicked, and disabled. There's actually nothing particularly interesting in these triggers. Rather than perform the heavy lifting themselves, the focus and click triggers simply modify a property of the ButtonChrome class that provides the visuals for the button:

```
<Trigger Property="UIElement.IsKeyboardFocused">
  <Setter Property="mwt:ButtonChrome.RenderDefaulted" TargetName="Chrome">
    <Setter.Value>
      <s:Boolean>True</s:Boolean>
    </Setter.Value>
  </Setter>
  <Trigger.Value>
    <s:Boolean>True</s:Boolean>
  </Trigger.Value>
</Trigger>
<Trigger Property="ToggleButton.IsChecked">
  <Setter Property="mwt:ButtonChrome.RenderPressed" TargetName="Chrome">
    <Setter.Value>
      <s:Boolean>True</s:Boolean>
    </Setter.Value>
  </Setter>
  <Trigger.Value>
    <s:Boolean>True</s:Boolean>
  </Trigger.Value>
</Trigger>
```

The first trigger ensures that when the button receives focus, the RenderDefaulted property is set to true. The Second trigger ensures that when the button is clicked, the Render-Pressed property is set to true. Either way, it's up to the ButtonChrome class to adjust itself accordingly. The graphical changes that take place are too complex to be represented by a few property setter statements.

Both of the Setter objects in this example use the TargetName property to act upon a specific piece of a control template. This technique is only possible when working with a control template. In other words, you can't write a style trigger that uses the TargetName property to access the ButtonChrome object because the name "Chrome" isn't in scope in your style. This is just one of the ways that templates give you more power than styles alone.

Triggers don't always need to use the TargetName property. For example, the trigger for the IsEnabled property simply adjusts the foreground color of any text content in the button. This trigger does its work by setting the attached TextElement.Foreground property without the help of the ButtonChrome class:

```
<Trigger Property="UIElement.IsEnabled">
  <Setter Property="TextElement.Foreground">
    <Setter.Value>
      <SolidColorBrush>#FFADADAD</SolidColorBrush>
    </Setter.Value>
  </Setter>
  <Trigger.Value>
    <s:Boolean>False</s:Boolean>
  </Trigger.Value>
</Trigger>
```

You'll see the same division of responsibilities when you build your own control templates. If you're lucky enough to be able to do all your work directly with triggers, you may not need to create custom classes and add code. On the other hand, if you need to provide more complex visual tailoring, you may need to derive a custom chrome class of your own. The ButtonChrome class itself provides no customization—it's dedicated to rendering the standard theme-specific appearance of a button on Windows XP and Windows Vista.

Note All the XAML that you see in this section is extracted from the standard Button control template. A bit later, in the "Dissecting Controls" section, you'll learn how to view a control's default control template.

TYPES OF TEMPLATES

This chapter focuses on control templates, which allow you to define the elements that make up a control. However, there are actually three types of templates in the WPF world, all of which derive from the base FrameworkTemplate class. Along with control templates (represented by the ControlTemplate class), there are data templates (represented by DataTemplate and HierarchicalDataTemplate) and the more specialized panel template for an ItemsControl (ItemsPanelTemplate).

Data templates are used to extract data from an object and display it in a content control or in the individual items of a list control. Data templates are ridiculously useful in data binding scenarios, and they're described in detail in Chapter 17. To a certain extent, data templates and control templates overlap. For example, both types of templates allow you to insert additional elements, apply formatting, and so on. However, data templates are used to add elements *inside* an existing control. The prebuilt aspects of that control aren't changed. On the other hand, control templates are a much more drastic approach that allows you to completely rewrite the content model of a control.

Finally, panel templates are used to control the layout of items in a list control (a control that derives from the ItemsControl class). For example, you can use them to create a list box that tiles its items from right to left and then down (rather than the standard top-to-bottom single-line display). Panel templates are described in Chapter 17.

You can certainly combine template types in the same control. For example, if you want to create a slick list control that is bound to a specific type of data, lays its items out in a nonstandard way, and replaces the stock border with something more exciting, you'll want to create your own data templates, panel template, and control template.

The Chrome Classes

The ButtonChrome class is defined in the Microsoft.Windows.Themes namespace, which holds a relatively small set of similar classes that render basic Windows details. Along with ButtonChrome, these classes include BulletChrome (for check boxes and radio buttons), ScrollChrome (for scroll bars), ListBoxChrome, and SystemDropShadowChrome. This is the lowest level of the public control API. At a slightly higher level, you'll find that the System.Windows.Controls.Primitives namespace includes a number of basic elements that you can use independently but are more commonly wrapped into more useful controls. These include ScrollBar, ResizeGrip (for sizing a window), Thumb (the draggable button on a scroll bar), TickBar (the optional set of ticks on a slider), and so on. Essentially, System.Windows.Controls.Primitives provides bare-bones ingredients that can be used in a variety of controls and aren't very useful on their own, while Microsoft.Windows.Themes contains the down-and-dirty drawing logic for rendering these details.

There's one more difference. The types in System.Windows.Controls.Primitives are, like most WPF types, defined in the PresentationFramework.dll assembly. However, those in the Microsoft.Windows.Themes are defined separately in *three* different assemblies: Presentation-Framework.Aero.dll, PresentationFramework.Luna.dll, and PresentationFramework.Royale.dll. Each assembly includes its own version of the ButtonChrome class (and other chrome classes), with slightly different rendering logic. The one that WPF uses depends on your operating system and theme settings.

■**Note** You'll learn more about the internal workings of a chrome class in Chapter 24, and you'll learn to build your own chrome class with custom rendering logic.

Although control templates often draw on the chrome classes, they don't always need to. For example, the ResizeGrip element (which is to create the grid of dots in the bottom-right corner of a resizable window) is simple enough that its template can use the drawing classes you learned about in Chapter 13 and Chapter 14, such as Path, DrawingBrush, and LinearGradientBrush. Here's the (somewhat convoluted) markup that it uses:

```
<ControlTemplate TargetType="ResizeGrip" ... >
  <Grid Background="{TemplateBinding Panel.Background}" SnapsToDevicePixels="True">
    <Path Margin="0,0,2,2" Data="M9,0L11,0 11,11 0,11 0,9 3,9 3,6 6,6 6,3 9,3z"
      HorizontalAlignment="Right" VerticalAlignment="Bottom">
      <Path.Fill>
        <DrawingBrush ViewboxUnits="Absolute" TileMode="Tile" Viewbox="0,0,3,3"
          Viewport="0,0,3,3" ViewportUnits="Absolute">
          <DrawingBrush.Drawing>
            <DrawingGroup>
              <DrawingGroup.Children>
                <GeometryDrawing Geometry="M0,0L2,0 2,2 0,2z">
                  <GeometryDrawing.Brush>
                    <LinearGradientBrush EndPoint="1,0.75" StartPoint="0,0.25">
                      <LinearGradientBrush.GradientStops>
```

```
                    <GradientStop Offset="0.3" Color="#FFFFFFFF" />
                    <GradientStop Offset="0.75" Color="#FFBBC5D7" />
                    <GradientStop Offset="1" Color="#FF6D83A9" />
                  </LinearGradientBrush.GradientStops>
                </LinearGradientBrush>
              </GeometryDrawing.Brush>
            </GeometryDrawing>
          </DrawingGroup.Children>
        </DrawingGroup>
      </DrawingBrush.Drawing>
    </DrawingBrush>
    </Path.Fill>
  </Path>
  </Grid>
</ControlTemplate>
```

> **Note** It's common to see the SnapsToDevicePixels setting in a prebuilt control template (and it's useful in the one you create as well). As you learned in Chapter 13, SnapsToDevicePixels ensures that single-pixel lines aren't placed "between" pixels due to WPF's resolution independence, which creates a fuzzy two-pixel line.

Dissecting Controls

When you create a control template (as you'll see in the next section), your template replaces the existing template completely. This gives you a high level of flexibility, but it also makes life a little more complex. In most cases, you'll need to see the standard template that a control uses before you can create your own adapted version. In some cases, your control template might mirror the standard template with only a minor change.

The WPF documentation doesn't list the XAML for standard control templates. However, you can get the information you need programmatically. The basic idea is to grab a control's template from its Template property (which is defined as part of the Control class) and then serialize it to XAML using the XamlWriter class. Figure 15-5 shows an example with a program that lists all the WPF controls and lets you view each one's control template.

The secret to building this application is a healthy dose of *reflection*, the .NET API for examining types. When the main window in this application is first loaded, it scans all the types in the core PresentationFramework.dll assembly (which is where the Control class is defined). It then adds these types to a collection, which it sorts by type name, and then binds that collection to a list. (You'll learn more about the details of data binding in Chapter 16.)

```
private void Window_Loaded(object sender, EventArgs e)
{
    Type controlType = typeof(Control);
    List<Type> derivedTypes = new List<Type>();

    // Search all the types in the assembly where the Control class is defined.
```

```
    Assembly assembly = Assembly.GetAssembly(typeof(Control));
    foreach (Type type in assembly.GetTypes())
    {
        // Only add a type of the list if it's a Control, a concrete class,
        // and public.
        if (type.IsSubclassOf(controlType) && !type.IsAbstract && type.IsPublic)
        {
            derivedTypes.Add(type);
        }
    }

    // Sort the types. The custom TypeComparer class orders types
    // alphabetically by type name.
    derivedTypes.Sort(new TypeComparer());

    // Show the list of types.
    lstTypes.ItemsSource = derivedTypes;
}
```

Figure 15-5. *Browsing WPF control templates*

Whenever a control is selected from the list, the corresponding control template is shown in the text box on the right. This step takes a bit more work. The first challenge is the fact that a control template is null until the control is actually displayed in a window. Using reflection, the code attempts to create an instance of the control and add it to the current window (albeit with a Visibility of Collapse so it can't be seen). The second challenge is to convert the live ControlTemplate object to the familiar XAML markup. The static XamlWriter.Save() method takes care of this task, although the code uses the XmlWriter and XmlWriterSettings objects to make sure the XAML is indented so that it's easier to read. All of this code is wrapped in an exception handling block, which catches the problems that result from controls that can't be created or can't be added to a Grid (such as another Window or a Page):

```
private void lstTypes_SelectionChanged(object sender, SelectionChangedEventArgs e)
{
    try
    {
        // Get the selected type.
        Type type = (Type)lstTypes.SelectedItem;

        // Instantiate the type.
        ConstructorInfo info = type.GetConstructor(System.Type.EmptyTypes);
        Control control = (Control)info.Invoke(null);

        // Add it to the grid (but keep it hidden).
        control.Visibility = Visibility.Collapsed;
        grid.Children.Add(control);

        // Get the template.
        ControlTemplate template = control.Template;

        // Get the XAML for the template.
        XmlWriterSettings settings = new XmlWriterSettings();
        settings.Indent = true;
        StringBuilder sb = new StringBuilder();
        XmlWriter writer = XmlWriter.Create(sb, settings);
        XamlWriter.Save(template, writer);

        // Display the template.
        txtTemplate.Text = sb.ToString();

        // Remove the control from the grid.
        grid.Children.Remove(control);
    }
    catch (Exception err)
    {
        txtTemplate.Text = "<< Error generating template: " + err.Message + ">>";
    }
}
```

It wouldn't be much more difficult to extend this application so you can edit the template in the text box, convert it back to a ControlTemplate object (using the XamlReader), and then assign that to a control to see its effect. However, you'll have an easier time testing and refining templates by putting them into action in a real window, as described in the next section.

■**Tip** If you're using Expression Blend, you can also use a handy feature that lets you edit the template for any control that you're working with. (Technically, this step grabs the default template, creates a copy of it for your control, and then lets you edit the copy.) To try this out, right-click a control on the design surface and choose Edit Control Parts (Template) ➤ Edit a Copy. Your control template copy will be stored as a resource (see Chapter 11), so you'll be prompted to choose a descriptive resource key, and you'll need to choose between storing your resource in the current window or in the global application resources so you can use your control template throughout your application.

Creating Control Templates

So far, you've learned a fair bit about the way templates work, but you haven't built a template of your own. In the following sections, you'll build a simple custom button and learn a few of the finer details about control templates in the process.

As you've already seen, the basic Button control uses the ButtonChrome class to draw its distinctive background and border. One of the reasons that the Button class uses Button-Chrome instead of the WPF drawing primitives is because a standard button's appearance depends on a few obvious characteristics (whether it's disabled, focused, or in the process of being clicked) and other subtler factors (such as the current Windows theme). Implementing this sort of logic with triggers alone would be awkward.

However, when you build your own custom controls, you're probably not as worried about standardization and theme integration. (In fact, WPF doesn't emphasize user interface standardization nearly as strongly as previous user interface technologies.) Instead, you're more concerned with creating attractive, distinctive controls that blend in with the rest of your user interface. For that reason, you might not need to create classes such as ButtonChrome. Instead, you can use the drawing smarts you picked up in Chapter 13 and Chapter 14 (and the animation skills you'll learn in Chapter 21) to design a self-sufficient control template with no code.

■**Note** For an alternate approach, check out Chapter 24, which explains how to build your own chrome with custom rendering logic and integrate it into a control template.

A Simple Button

To apply a custom control template, you simply set the Template property of your control. Although you can define an inline template (by nesting the control template tag inside the control tag), this approach rarely makes sense. That's because you'll almost always want to reuse your template to skin multiple instances of the same control. To accommodate this design, you need to define your control template as a resource and refer to it using a StaticResource reference, as shown here:

```
<Button Margin="10" Padding="5" Template="{StaticResource ButtonTemplate}">
 A Simple Button with a Custom Template</Button>
```

Not only does this approach make it easier to create a whole host of customized buttons, it also gives you the flexibility to modify your control template later without disrupting the rest of your application's user interface.

In this particular example, the ButtonTemplate resource is placed in the Resources collection of the containing window. However, in a real application you're much more likely to use application resources. The reasons why (and a few design tips) are discussed a bit later in the "Organizing Template Resources" section.

Here's the basic outline for the control template:

```
<Window.Resources>
  <ControlTemplate x:Key="ButtonTemplate" TargetType="{x:Type Button}">
    ...
  </ControlTemplate>
</Window.Resources>
```

You'll notice that this control template sets the TargetType property to explicitly indicate it's designed for buttons. As a matter of style, this is always a good convention to follow. In content controls, such as the button, it's also a requirement, or the ContentPresenter won't work.

To create a template for a basic button, you need to draw your own border and background and then place the content inside the button. Two possible candidates for drawing the border are the Rectangle class and the Border class. The following example uses the Border class to combine a rounded orange outline with an eye-catching red background and white text:

```
<ControlTemplate x:Key="ButtonTemplate" TargetType="{x:Type Button}">
  <Border BorderBrush="Orange" BorderThickness="3" CornerRadius="2"
   Background="Red" TextBlock.Foreground="White">
    ...
  </Border>
</ControlTemplate>
```

This takes care of the background, but you still need a way to display the button content. You may remember from your earlier exploration that the Button class includes a ContentPresenter in its control template. The ContentPresenter is required for all content controls—it's the "insert content here" marker that tells WPF where to stuff the content:

```
<ControlTemplate x:Key="ButtonTemplate" TargetType="{x:Type Button}">
  <Border BorderBrush="Orange" BorderThickness="3" CornerRadius="2"
   Background="Red" TextBlock.Foreground="White">
    <ContentPresenter RecognizesAccessKey="True"></ContentPresenter>
  </Border>
</ControlTemplate>
```

This ContentPresenter sets the RecognizesAccessKey property to true. Although this isn't required, it ensures that the button supports *access keys*—underlined letters that you can use to quickly trigger the button. In this case, if your button has text such as "Click _Me" the user can trigger the button by pressing Alt+M. (Under standard Windows settings, the underscore is hidden and the access key—in this case, *M*—appears underlined as soon as you press the Alt key.) If you don't set RecognizesAccessKey to true, this detail will be ignored and any under-scores will be treated as ordinary underscores and displayed as part of the button content.

Template Bindings

There's still one minor issue with this example. Right now the tag you've added for your button specifies a Margin value of 10 and a Padding of 5. The Margin property is headed by the Stack-Panel but the Padding property is ignored, leaving the contents of your button scrunched up against the sides. The problem here is the fact that the Padding property doesn't have any effect unless you specifically heed it in your template. In other words, it's up to your template to retrieve the padding value and use it to insert some extra space around your content.

Fortunately, WPF has a tool that's designed exactly for this purpose: *template bindings*. By using a template binding, your template can pull out a value from the control to which you're applying the template. In this example, you can use a template binding to retrieve the value of the Padding property and use it to create a margin around the ContentPresenter:

```
<ControlTemplate x:Key="ButtonTemplate" TargetType="{x:Type Button}">
  <Border BorderBrush="Orange" BorderThickness="3" CornerRadius="2"
   Background="Red" TextBlock.Foreground="White">
    <ContentPresenterRecognizesAccessKey="True"
     Margin="{TemplateBinding Padding}"></ContentPresenter>
  </Border>
</ControlTemplate>
```

This achieves the desired effect of adding some space between the border and the content. Figure 15-6 shows your modest new button.

Figure 15-6. *A button with a customized control template*

Template bindings are similar to ordinary data bindings (which you'll consider in Chapter 16), but they're lighter weight because they're specifically designed for use in a control template. They only support one-way data binding (in other words, they can pass information from the control to the template but not the other way around) and they can't be used to draw information from a property of a class that derives from Freezable. If you run into a situation where template bindings won't work, you can use a full-fledged data binding instead. Chapter 24 includes a sample color picker that runs into this problem and uses a combination of template bindings and regular bindings.

Note Template bindings support the WPF change-monitoring infrastructure that's built into all dependency properties. That means that if you modify a property in a control, the template takes it into account automatically. This detail is particularly useful when you're using animations that change a property value repeatedly in a short space of time.

The only way you can anticipate what template bindings are needed is to check the default control template. If you look at the control template for the Button class, you'll find that it uses a template binding in exactly the same way as this custom template—it takes the padding specified on the button and converts it to a margin around the ContentPresenter. You'll also find that the standard button template includes a few more template bindings that aren't used in the simple customized template, such as HorizontalAlignment, VerticalAlignment, and Background. That means if you set these properties on the button, they'll have no effect on the simple custom template.

Note Technically, the ContentPresenter works because it has a template binding that sets the ContentPresenter.Content property to the Button.Content property. However, this binding is implicit, so you don't need to add it yourself.

In many cases, leaving out template bindings isn't a problem. In fact, you don't need to bind a property if you don't plan to use it or don't want it to change your template. For example, it makes sense that the current simple button sets the Foreground property for text to white and ignores any value you've set for the Background property because the foreground and background are intrinsic parts of this button's visual appearance.

There's another reason you might choose to avoid template bindings—your control may not be able to support them adequately. For example, if you've ever set the Background property of a button, you've probably noticed that this background isn't handled consistently when the button is pressed (in fact, it disappears at this point and is replaced with the default visual for pressed buttons). The custom template shown in this example is similar. Although it doesn't yet have any mouseover and mouse-pressed behavior, once you add these details you'll want to take complete control over the colors and how they change in different states.

Template Triggers

If you try out the button that you created in the previous section, you'll find it's a major disappointment. Essentially, it's nothing more than a rounded red rectangle—as you move the mouse over it or click it, there's no visual feedback. The button simply lies there inert.

This problem is easily fixed by adding triggers to your control template. You first considered triggers with styles in Chapter 12. As you know, you can use triggers to change one or more properties when another property changes. The bare minimums that you'll want to respond to in your button are IsMouseOver and IsPressed. Here's a revised version of the control template that changes the colors when these properties change:

```
<ControlTemplate x:Key="ButtonTemplate" TargetType="{x:Type Button}">
  <Border Name="Border" BorderBrush="Orange" BorderThickness="3" CornerRadius="2"
   Background="Red" TextBlock.Foreground="White">
    <ContentPresenter RecognizesAccessKey="True"
     Margin="{TemplateBinding Padding}"></ContentPresenter>
  </Border>
  <ControlTemplate.Triggers>
    <Trigger Property="IsMouseOver" Value="True">
      <Setter TargetName="Border" Property="Background" Value="DarkRed" />
    </Trigger>
    <Trigger Property="IsPressed" Value="True">
      <Setter TargetName="Border" Property="Background" Value="IndianRed" />
      <Setter TargetName="Border" Property="BorderBrush" Value="DarkKhaki" />
    </Trigger>
  </ControlTemplate.Triggers>
</ControlTemplate>
```

There's one other change that makes this template work. The Border element has been given a name, and that name is used to set the TargetName property of each Setter. This way, the Setter can update the Background and BorderBrush properties of the Border that's specified in the template. Using names is the easiest way to make sure a single specific part of a template is updated. You could create an element-typed rule that affects all Border elements (because you know there is only a single border in the button template), but this approach is both clearer and more flexible if you change the template later on.

There's one more required element in any button (and most other controls)—a focus indicator. There's no way to change the existing border to add a focus effect, but you can easily add another element that shows it, and simply show or hide this element based on the Button.IsKeyboardFocused property using a trigger. Although you could create a focus effect in many different ways, the following example simply adds a transparent Rectangle element with a dashed border. The Rectangle doesn't have the ability to hold child content, so you need to make sure the Rectangle overlaps the rest of the content. The easiest way to do this is to wrap the Rectangle and the ContentPresenter in a one-cell Grid, with both elements in the same cell.

Here's the revised template with focus support:

```
<ControlTemplate x:Key="ButtonTemplate" TargetType="{x:Type Button}">
  <Border Name="Border" BorderBrush="Orange" BorderThickness="3" CornerRadius="2"
   Background="Red" TextBlock.Foreground="White">
    <Grid>
      <Rectangle Name="FocusCue" Visibility="Hidden" Stroke="Black"
       StrokeThickness="1" StrokeDashArray="1 2"
       SnapsToDevicePixels="True" ></Rectangle>
      <ContentPresenter RecognizesAccessKey="True"
     Margin="{TemplateBinding Padding}"></ContentPresenter>
    </Grid>
  </Border>
  <ControlTemplate.Triggers>
    <Trigger Property="IsMouseOver" Value="True">
      <Setter TargetName="Border" Property="Background" Value="DarkRed" />
    </Trigger>
    <Trigger Property="IsPressed" Value="True">
      <Setter TargetName="Border" Property="Background" Value="IndianRed" />
      <Setter TargetName="Border" Property="BorderBrush" Value="DarkKhaki" />
    </Trigger>
    <Trigger Property="IsKeyboardFocused" Value="True">
      <Setter TargetName="FocusCue" Property="Visibility" Value="Visible" />
    </Trigger>
  </ControlTemplate.Triggers>
</ControlTemplate>
```

Once again, the Setter finds the element it needs to change using the TargetName property (which points to the FocusCue rectangle in this example).

Note This technique of hiding or showing elements in response to a trigger is a useful building block in many templates. You can use it to replace the visuals of a control with something completely different when its state changes. (For example, a clicked button could change from a rectangle to an ellipse by hiding the former and showing the latter.)

Figure 15-7 shows three buttons that use the revised template. The second button currently has focus (as represented by the dashed rectangle), while the mouse is hovering over the third button.

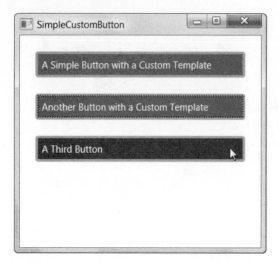

Figure 15-7. *Buttons with focus and mouseover support*

To really round out this button, you'll add an additional trigger that changes the button background (and possibly the text foreground) when the IsEnabled property of the button becomes false:

```
<Trigger Property="IsEnabled" Value="False">
  <Setter TargetName="Border" Property="TextBlock.Foreground" Value="Gray" />
  <Setter TargetName="Border" Property="Background" Value="MistyRose" />
</Trigger>
```

To make sure that this rule takes precedence over any conflicting trigger settings, you should define it at the end of the list of triggers. That way, it doesn't matter if the IsMouseOver property is also true; the IsEnabled property trigger takes precedence and the button remains inactive.

This example shows you all the concepts you need to create your own customized button, but it doesn't show you how to *design* the graphics that make a truly attractive button. At the end of this chapter, you'll find a couple of links to similarly constructed but more elaborate buttons that include the popular glow and glass effects.

TEMPLATES VS. STYLES

It might have occurred to you that there's a similarity between templates and styles. Both allow you to change the appearance of an element, usually throughout your application. However, styles are far more limited in scope. They're able to adjust properties of the control but not replace it with an entirely new visual tree that's made up of different elements.

Already, the simple button you've seen includes features that couldn't be duplicated with styles alone. Although you could use styles to set the background of a button, you'd have more trouble adjusting the background when the button was pressed because the built-in template for the button already includes a trigger for that purpose. You also wouldn't have an easy way to add the focus rectangle.

However, templates also open the door to many more exotic types of buttons that are unthinkable with styles. For example, rather than using a rectangular border, you can create a button that's shaped like an ellipse or uses a path to draw a more complex shape. All you need are the drawing classes from Chapter 13. The rest of your markup—even the triggers that switch the background from one state to another—require relatively few changes.

Organizing Template Resources

When using control templates, you need to decide how broadly you want to share your templates and whether you want to apply them automatically or explicitly.

The first question asks you to think about where you want to use your templates. For example, are they limited to a specific window? In most situations, control templates apply to multiple windows, and possibly even the entire application. To avoid defining them more than once, you can define them in the Resources collection of the Application class, as described in Chapter 11.

However, this raises another consideration. Often, control templates are shared between applications. It's quite possible that a single application might use templates that have been developed separately. However, an application can only have a single App.xaml file and a single Application.Resources collection. For that reason, it's a better idea to define your resources in separate resource dictionaries. That gives you the flexibility to bring them into action in specific windows, or in the entire application. It also allows you to combine styles because any application can hold multiple resource dictionaries. To add a resource dictionary in Visual Studio, right-click your project in the Solution Explorer window, choose Add ➤ New Item, and then select Resource Dictionary (WPF).

You've already learned about resource dictionaries in Chapter 11. Using them is easy. You simply need to add a new XAML file to your application with content like this:

```
<ResourceDictionary
  xmlns="http://schemas.microsoft.com/winfx/2006/xaml/presentation"
  xmlns:x="http://schemas.microsoft.com/winfx/2006/xaml" >
  <ControlTemplate x:Key="ButtonTemplate" TargetType="{x:Type Button}">
    ...
  </ControlTemplate>
</ResourceDictionary>
```

Although you could combine all your templates into a single resource dictionary file, experienced developers prefer to create a separate resource dictionary for each control template. That's because a control template can quickly become quite complex and can draw on a host of other related resources. Keeping these together in one place, but separate from other controls, is good organization.

To use your resource dictionary, you simply add it to the Resources collection of a specific window or, more commonly, your application. You do this using the MergedDictionaries collection. For example, if your button template is in a file named Button.xaml in a project subfolder named Resources, you could use this markup in your App.xaml file:

```
<Application x:Class="SimpleApplication.App"
 xmlns="http://schemas.microsoft.com/winfx/2006/xaml/presentation"
 xmlns:x="http://schemas.microsoft.com/winfx/2006/xaml"
 StartupUri="Window1.xaml">
  <Application.Resources>
    <ResourceDictionary>
      <ResourceDictionary.MergedDictionaries>
        <ResourceDictionary Source="Resources\Button.xaml" />
      </ResourceDictionary.MergedDictionaries>
    </ResourceDictionary>
  </Application.Resources>
</Application>
```

Refactoring the Button Control Template

As you enhance and extend a control template, you may find that it wraps a number of different details, including specialized shapes, geometries, and brushes. It's a good idea to pull these details out of your control template and define them as separate resources. One reason you'll take this step is to make it easier to reuse these brushes among a set of related controls. For example, you might decide that you want to create a customized Button, CheckBox, and RadioButton that use a similar set of colors. To make this easier, you could create a separate resource dictionary for your brushes (named Brushes.xaml) and merge that into the resource dictionary for each of your controls (such as Button.xaml, CheckBox.xaml, and Radio-Button.xaml).

To see this technique in action, consider the following markup. It presents the complete resource dictionary for a button, including the resources that the control template uses, the control template, and the style rule that applies the control template to every button in the application. This is the order that you always need to follow because a resource needs to be defined before it can be used. (If you defined one of the brushes after the template, you'd receive an error because the template wouldn't be able to find the brush it requires.)

```
<ResourceDictionary
    xmlns="http://schemas.microsoft.com/winfx/2006/xaml/presentation"
    xmlns:x="http://schemas.microsoft.com/winfx/2006/xaml">

  <!-- Resources used by the template. -->
  <RadialGradientBrush RadiusX="1" RadiusY="5" GradientOrigin="0.5,0.3"
    x:Key="HighlightBackground">
    <GradientStop Color="White" Offset="0" />
    <GradientStop Color="Blue" Offset=".4" />
  </RadialGradientBrush>

  <RadialGradientBrush RadiusX="1" RadiusY="5" GradientOrigin="0.5,0.3"
    x:Key="PressedBackground">
    <GradientStop Color="White" Offset="0" />
    <GradientStop Color="Blue" Offset="1" />
  </RadialGradientBrush>
```

```
<SolidColorBrush Color="Blue" x:Key="DefaultBackground"></SolidColorBrush>
<SolidColorBrush Color="Gray" x:Key="DisabledBackground"></SolidColorBrush>

<RadialGradientBrush RadiusX="1" RadiusY="5" GradientOrigin="0.5,0.3"
  x:Key="Border">
  <GradientStop Color="White" Offset="0" />
  <GradientStop Color="Blue" Offset="1" />
</RadialGradientBrush>

<!-- The button control template. -->
<ControlTemplate x:Key="GradientButtonTemplate" TargetType="{x:Type Button}">
  <Border Name="Border" BorderBrush="{StaticResource Border}" BorderThickness="2"
   CornerRadius="2" Background="{StaticResource DefaultBackground}"
   TextBlock.Foreground="White">
    <Grid>
      <Rectangle Name="FocusCue" Visibility="Hidden" Stroke="Black"
       StrokeThickness="1" StrokeDashArray="1 2" SnapsToDevicePixels="True">
      </Rectangle>
      <ContentPresenter Margin="{TemplateBinding Padding}"
       RecognizesAccessKey="True"></ContentPresenter>
    </Grid>
  </Border>
  <ControlTemplate.Triggers>
    <Trigger Property="IsMouseOver" Value="True">
      <Setter TargetName="Border" Property="Background"
       Value="{StaticResource HighlightBackground}" />
    </Trigger>
    <Trigger Property="IsPressed" Value="True">
      <Setter TargetName="Border" Property="Background"
       Value="{StaticResource PressedBackground}" />
    </Trigger>
    <Trigger Property="IsKeyboardFocused" Value="True">
      <Setter TargetName="FocusCue" Property="Visibility"
        Value="Visible"></Setter>
    </Trigger>
    <Trigger Property="IsEnabled" Value="False">
      <Setter TargetName="Border" Property="Background"
       Value="{StaticResource DisabledBackground}"></Setter>
    </Trigger>
  </ControlTemplate.Triggers>
</ControlTemplate>
</ResourceDictionary>
```

Figure 15-8 shows the button that this template defines. In this example, a gradient fill is used when the user moves the mouse over the button. However, the gradient is always centered in the middle of the button. If you want to create a more exotic effect, such as a gradient that follows the position of the mouse, you'll need to use an animation or write code. Chapter 24 shows an example with a custom chrome class that implements this effect.

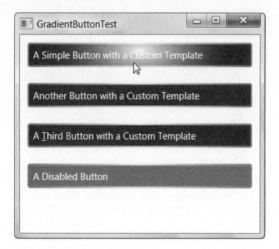

Figure 15-8. *A gradient button*

Applying Templates with Styles

There's one limitation in this design. The control template essentially hard-codes quite a few details, such as the color scheme. That means that if you want to use the same combination of elements in your button (Border, Grid, Rectangle, and ContentPresenter) and arrange them in the same way, but you want to supply a different color scheme, you'll be forced to create a new copy of the template that references different brush resources.

This isn't necessarily a problem (after all, the layout and formatting details may be so closely related that you don't want to separate them anyway). However, it does limit your ability to reuse your control template. If your template uses a complex arrangement of elements that you know you'll want to reuse with a variety of different formatting details (usually colors and fonts), you can pull these details out of your template and put them into a style.

To make this work, you'll need to rework your template. Instead of using hard-coded colors, you need to pull the information out of control properties using template bindings. The following example defines a streamlined template for the fancy button you saw earlier. The control template treats some details as fundamental, unchanging ingredients—namely, the focus box and the rounded 2-unit-thick border. The background and border brushes are configurable. The only trigger that remains is the one that shows the focus box:

```
<ControlTemplate x:Key="CustomButtonTemplate" TargetType="{x:Type Button}">
  <Border Name="Border" BorderThickness="2" CornerRadius="2"
    Background="{TemplateBinding Background}"
    BorderBrush="{TemplateBinding BorderBrush}">
    <Grid>
      <Rectangle Name="FocusCue" Visibility="Hidden" Stroke="Black"
        StrokeThickness="1" StrokeDashArray="1 2" SnapsToDevicePixels="True">
      </Rectangle>
      <ContentPresenter Margin="{TemplateBinding Padding}"
        RecognizesAccessKey="True"></ContentPresenter>
    </Grid>
  </Border>
```

```
      <ControlTemplate.Triggers>
        <Trigger Property="IsKeyboardFocused" Value="True">
          <Setter TargetName="FocusCue" Property="Visibility"
            Value="Visible"></Setter>
        </Trigger>
      </ControlTemplate.Triggers>
</ControlTemplate>
```

The associated style applies this control template, sets the border and background colors, and adds triggers that change the background depending on the state of the button:

```
<Style x:Key="CustomButtonStyle" TargetType="{x:Type Button}">
  <Setter Property="Control.Template"
  Value="{StaticResource CustomButtonTemplate}"></Setter>
  <Setter Property="BorderBrush"
  Value="{StaticResource Border}"></Setter>
  <Setter Property="Background"
     Value="{StaticResource DefaultBackground}"></Setter>
       <Setter Property="TextBlock.Foreground"
        Value="White"></Setter>
  <Style.Triggers>
    <Trigger Property="IsMouseOver" Value="True">
      <Setter Property="Background"
      Value="{StaticResource HighlightBackground}" />
    </Trigger>
    <Trigger Property="IsPressed" Value="True">
      <Setter Property="Background"
      Value="{StaticResource PressedBackground}" />
    </Trigger>
    <Trigger Property="IsEnabled" Value="False">
      <Setter Property="Background"
      Value="{StaticResource DisabledBackground}"></Setter>
    </Trigger>
  </Style.Triggers>
</Style>
```

Ideally, you'd be able to keep all the triggers in the control template because they represent control behavior and use the style simply to set basic properties. Unfortunately, that's not possible here if you want to give the style the ability to set the color scheme.

Note If you set triggers in both the control template and style, the style triggers win out.

To use this new template you need to set the Style property of a button rather than the Template property:

```
<Button Margin="10" Padding="5" Style="{StaticResource CustomButtonStyle}">
 A Simple Button with a Custom Template</Button>
```

You can now create new styles that use the same template but bind to different brushes to apply a new color scheme.

There's one significant limitation in this approach. You can't use the Setter.TargetName property in this style because the style doesn't contain the control template (it simply references it). As a result, your style and its triggers are somewhat limited. They can't reach deep into the visual tree to change the aspect of a nested element. Instead, your style needs to set a property of the control, and the element in the control needs to bind the property using a template binding.

CONTROL TEMPLATES VS. CUSTOM CONTROLS

You can get around both of the problems discussed here—being forced to define control behavior in the style with triggers, and not being able to target specific elements—by creating a custom control. For example, you could build a class that derives from Button and adds properties such as HighlightBackground, DisabledBackground, and PressedBackground. You could then bind to these properties in the control template and simply set them in the style with no triggers required. However, this approach has its own drawback. It forces you to use a different control in your user interface (such as CustomButton instead of just Button). This is more trouble when designing the application.

Usually, you'll switch from custom control templates to custom controls in one of two situations:

- Your control represents a significant change in functionality. For example, you have a custom button, and that button adds new functionality that requires new properties or methods.

- You plan to distribute your control in a separate class library assembly so it can be used in (and customized for) a wide range of applications. In this situation, you need a higher level of standardization than is possible with control templates alone.

If you decide to create a custom control, Chapter 24 has all the information you need.

Applying Templates Automatically

In the current example, each button is responsible for hooking itself up to the appropriate template using the Template or Style property. This makes sense if you're using your control template to create a specific effect in a specific place in your application. It's less convenient if you want to re-skin every button in your entire application with a custom look. In this situation, it's more likely that you want all the buttons in your application to acquire your new template automatically. To make this a reality, you need to apply your control template with a style.

The trick is to use a typed style that affects the appropriate element type automatically and sets the Template property. Here's an example of the style you'd place in the resources collection of your resource dictionary to give your buttons a new look:

```
<Style TargetType="{x:Type Button}">
  <Setter Property="Control.Template" Value="{StaticResource ButtonTemplate}"
</Style>
```

This works because the style doesn't specify a key name, which means the element type (Button) is used instead.

Remember, you can still opt out of this style by creating a button that explicitly sets its Style to a null value:

```
<Button Style="{x:Null}" ... ></Button>
```

Tip This technique works even better if you've followed good design practices and defined your button in a separate resource dictionary. In this situation, the style doesn't sprint into action until you add a Resource-Dictionary tag that imports your resources into the entire application or a specific window, as described earlier.

The possibilities of this approach are remarkable. You can take an existing WPF application and completely re-skin all its controls without touching the user interface at all. All you need to do is add the resource dictionaries to your project and merge them into the Application.Resources collection. This combination of styles and control templates provides an effortless, completely code-free ability to skin any application.

User-Selected Skins

In some applications, you might want to alter templates dynamically, usually in response to user preferences. This is easy enough to accomplish, but it's not well-documented. The basic technique is to load a new resource dictionary at runtime and use it to replace the current resource dictionary. (It's not necessary to replace all your resources, just those that are used for your skin.)

The trick is retrieving the ResourceDictionary object, which is compiled and embedded as a resource in your application. The easiest approach is to use the ResourceManager class described in Chapter 11 to load up the resources you want.

For example, imagine you've created two resources that define alternate versions of the same button control template. One is stored in a file named GradientButton.xaml, while the other is in a file named GradientButtonVariant.xaml. Both files are placed in the Resources subfolder in the current project for better organization.

Now you can create a simple window that uses one of these resources, using a Resources collection like this:

```
<Window.Resources>
  <ResourceDictionary>
    <ResourceDictionary.MergedDictionaries>
      <ResourceDictionary
       Source="Resources/GradientButton.xaml"></ResourceDictionary>
    </ResourceDictionary.MergedDictionaries>
  </ResourceDictionary>
</Window.Resources>
```

Now you can swap in a different resource dictionary using code like this:

```
ResourceDictionary newDictionary = new ResourceDictionary();
newDictionary.Source = new Uri(
  "Resources/GradientButtonVariant.xaml", UriKind.Relative);
this.Resources.MergedDictionaries[0] = newDictionary;
```

This code loads the resource dictionary named GradientButtonVariant and places it into the first slot in the MergedDictionaries collection. It doesn't clear the MergedDictionaries collection (or any other window resources) because it's possible that you might be linking to other resource dictionaries that you want to continue using. It doesn't add a new entry to the MergedDictionaries collection because there could then be conflict between resources with the same name but in different collections.

If you were changing the skin for an entire application, you'd use the same approach but you'd use the resource dictionary of the application. You could update this resource dictionary using code like this:

```
Application.Current.Resources.MergedDictionaries[0] = newDictionary;
```

You can also load a resource dictionary that's defined in another assembly using the URI syntax described in Chapter 11:

```
ResourceDictionary newDictionary = new ResourceDictionary();
newDictionary.Source = new Uri(
  "ControlTemplateLibrary;component/GradientButtonVariant.xaml",
  UriKind.Relative);
this.Resources.MergedDictionaries[0] = newDictionary;
```

When you load a new resource dictionary, all the buttons are automatically updated to use the new template. You can also include basic styles as part of your skin if you don't need to be quite as ambitious when modifying a control.

This example assumes that the GradientButton.xaml and GradientButtonVariant.xaml resources use an element-typed style to change your buttons automatically. As you know, there's another approach—you can opt in to a new template by manually setting the Template or Style property of your Button objects. If you take this approach, make sure you use a DynamicResource reference instead of a StaticResource. If you use a StaticResource, the button template won't be updated when you switch skins.

■**Note** When using a DynamicResource reference, you're making an assumption that the resource you need will appear somewhere in the resource hierarchy. If it doesn't, the resource is simply ignored and the buttons revert to their standard appearance without generating an error.

There's another way to load resource dictionaries programmatically. You can create a code-behind class for your resource dictionary in much the same way you create code-behind classes for windows. You can then instantiate that class directly rather than using the

ResourceDictionary.Source property. This approach has the benefit of being strongly typed (there's no chance of entering an invalid URI for the Source property) and it allows you to add properties, methods, and other functionality to your resource class. For example, you'll use this ability to create a resource that has event handling code in the "Creating a Custom Window" section later in this chapter.

Although it's easy enough to create a code-behind class for your resource dictionary, Visual Studio doesn't do it automatically. Instead, you need to add a code file with a partial class that derives from ResourceDictionary and calls InitializeComponent in the constructor:

```
public partial class GradientButtonVariant : ResourceDictionary
{
    public GradientButtonVariant()
    {
        InitializeComponent();
    }
}
```

Here, the class name GradientButtonVariant is used, and the class is stored in a file named GradientButtonVariant.xaml.cs. The XAML file holding the resource is named GradientButton-Variant.xaml. It's not necessary to make these names consistent, but it's a good idea, and it's in keeping with the convention Visual Studio uses when you create windows and pages.

The next step is to link your class to the resource dictionary. You do that by adding the Class attribute to the root element of your resource dictionary, just as you do with a window, and just as you can do with any XAML class. You then supply the fully qualified class name. In this example, the project is named ControlTemplates; hence the default namespace, so the finished tag looks like this:

```
<ResourceDictionary x:Class="ControlTemplates.GradientButtonVariant" ... >
```

You can now use this code to create your resource dictionary and apply it to a window:

```
GradientButtonVariant newDictionary = new GradientButtonVariant();
this.Resources.MergedDictionaries[0] = newDictionary;
```

If you want your GradientButtonVariant.xaml.cs file to appear nested under the Gradient-ButtonVariant.xaml file in the Solution Explorer, you need to modify the .csproj project file in a text editor. Find the code-behind file in the <ItemGroup> section and change this:

```
<Compile Include="Resources\GradientButtonVariant.xaml.cs" />
```

to this:

```
<Compile Include="Resources\GradientButtonVariant.xaml.cs">
  <DependentUpon> Resources\GradientButtonVariant.xaml</DependentUpon>
</Compile>
```

Building More Complex Templates

In the previous section, you learned how to build a basic template for a button. Using a few straightforward triggers, you were able to create a respectable button without being forced to reimplement any core button functionality (as you would have been forced to do in a Windows Forms application). Best of all, these custom buttons support all the normal button behavior—you can tab from one to the next, you can click them to fire an event, you can use access keys, and so on. Best of all, you can reuse your button template throughout your application and still replace it with a whole new design at a moment's notice.

So what more do you need to know before you can skin all the basic WPF controls? In order to get the snazzy look you probably want, you might need to spend more time studying the details of WPF drawing, including the content in Chapter 13 and Chapter 14. You'll also need a dash of artistic flair. It might surprise you to know that you can use the shapes and brushes you've already learned about to build sophisticated buttons with glass-style blurs and soft glow effects. The secret is in combining multiple layers of shapes, each with a different gradient brush. The best way to get this sort of effect is to learn from the control template examples others have created. (At the end of this chapter, you'll get a list with a few useful links to help you continue your template exploration.)

Another trick that can jazz up your customized controls is animated effects, which you'll learn to use in Chapter 21. For example, you could use an animation to create a button that doesn't abruptly change color when it's clicked and released, but gradually fades from one color to the next.

Finally, along with general drawing skills, you also need to learn a bit more about how complex, multipart templates are built. That's the task you'll tackle in this section.

Multipart Templates

The template for the button control can be decomposed into a few relatively simple pieces. However, many templates aren't so simple. Here are some of the characteristics of more complex templates:

- They include button controls that trigger specific prebuilt commands. Each button is attached to the appropriate command using the Command property.

- They use specifically named elements, which usually have names beginning with "PART_". When creating a custom template, you should make sure that you keep all the named elements because the control class probably includes code that directly manipulates these elements (for example, attaches event handlers).

■Note According to the WPF control guidelines, a control that's missing a named element won't throw an exception. However, it may not work properly.

- They include nested controls, which can have their own templates.

- If they derive from ContentControl, they include a ContentPresenter where the content will be placed. If they derive from ItemsControl, they include an ItemsPresenter that indicates where the panel that contains the list of items will be placed. Scrollable content inside a ScrollViewer control is represented by a ScrollContentPresenter.

- They use the static properties of SystemBrushes, SystemParameters, and SystemFonts to use environment variables (like the current color scheme, the standard height of a scroll bar, and so on).

- More often than not, they arrange their items using a Grid (though a Canvas may be used for precise alignment of different elements).

As always, the best way to get used to these different conventions is to play with the template browser shown earlier to look at the control templates for basic controls. You can then copy and edit the template to use it as a basis for your custom work.

UNDERSTANDING CONTROL TEMPLATE DEPENDENCIES

There is an implicit contract between a control's template and the code that underpins it. If you're replacing a control's standard template with one of your own, you need to make sure your new template meets all the requirements of the control's implementation code.

In simple controls, this process is easy, because there are few (if any) real requirements on the template. In a complex control, the issue is subtler, because it's impossible for the visuals and the implementation to be completely separated. In this situation, the control needs to make some assumptions about its visual display, no matter how well it has been designed.

You've already seen two examples of the requirements a control can place on its control template, with placeholder elements (such as ContentPresenter and ItemsPresenter) and template bindings. In the following sections, you'll see two more: elements with specific names (starting with "PART_") and elements that are specially designed for use in a particular control's template (such as Track in the ScrollBar control). To create a successful control template, you need to look carefully at the standard template for the control in question, make note of how these four techniques are used, and then duplicate them in your own templates.

There's another way to get comfortable with the interaction between controls and control templates. You can create your own custom control. In this case, you'll have the reverse challenge—you'll need to create code that uses a template in a standardized way and that can work equally well with templates supplied by other developers. You'll tackle this challenge in Chapter 24 (which makes a great complement to the perspective you'll get in this chapter).

Control Templates in an ItemsControl

To master the techniques of control template creation, it helps to examine a more advanced example. Imagine you're planning to revamp the familiar ListBox control. In the following sections, you'll see how to alter its appearance, change its selection effect, and replace the scroll bar it uses.

The first step to create this example is to design a template for the ListBox and (optionally) add a style that applies the template automatically. Here are both ingredients rolled into one:

```
<Style TargetType="{x:Type ListBox}">
  <Setter Property="Template">
    <Setter.Value>
      <ControlTemplate TargetType="{x:Type ListBox}">
        <Border
          Name="Border"
          Background="{StaticResource ListBoxBackgroundBrush}"
          BorderBrush="{StaticResource StandardBorderBrush}"
          BorderThickness="1" CornerRadius="3">
          <ScrollViewer Focusable="False">
            <ItemsPresenter Margin="2"></ItemsPresenter>
          </ScrollViewer>
        </Border>
      </ControlTemplate>
    </Setter.Value>
  </Setter>
</Style>
```

This style draws on two brushes for painting the border and the background. The actual template is a simplified version of the standard ListBox template, but it avoids the ListBox-Chrome class in favor of a simpler Border. Inside the Border is the ScrollViewer that provides the list scrolling, and an ItemsPresenter that holds all the items of the list. (Currently, this template lacks a trigger to change its appearance when it's in a disabled state.)

This template is most notable for what it doesn't let you do—namely, configure the appearance of individual items in the list. Without this ability, the selected item is always highlighted with the familiar blue background. To change this behavior, you need to add a control template for the ListBoxItem, which is a content control that wraps the content of each individual item in the list.

As with the ListBox template, you can apply the ListBoxItem template using an element-typed style. The following basic template wraps each item in an invisible border. Because the ListBoxItem is a content control, you use the ContentPresenter to place the item content inside. Along with these basics are triggers that react when an item is moused over or clicked:

```
<Style TargetType="{x:Type ListBoxItem}">
  <Setter Property="Template">
    <Setter.Value>
      <ControlTemplate TargetType="{x:Type ListBoxItem}">
        <Border
          Name="Border" BorderThickness="2" CornerRadius="3" Padding="1" >
          <ContentPresenter />
        </Border>
        <ControlTemplate.Triggers>
          <Trigger Property="IsMouseOver" Value="True">
            <Setter TargetName="Border" Property="BorderBrush"
              Value="{StaticResource HoverBorderBrush}"/>
```

```
                <Setter TargetName="Border" Property="TextBlock.FontSize" Value="20" />
              </Trigger>
              <Trigger Property="IsSelected" Value="True">
                <Setter TargetName="Border" Property="Background"
                 Value="{StaticResource SelectedBackgroundBrush}"/>
                <Setter TargetName="Border" Property="TextBlock.Foreground"
                 Value="{StaticResource SelectedForegroundBrush}"/>
              </Trigger>
            </ControlTemplate.Triggers>
          </ControlTemplate>
        </Setter.Value>
      </Setter>
</Style>
```

Together, these two templates allow you to create the odd list box shown in Figure 15-9, which enlarges the item over which the mouse is currently positioned.

Figure 15-9. *A list box that uses two templates*

Modifying the Scroll Bar

There's one aspect of the list box that's remained out of touch: the scroll bar on the right. It's a part of the ScrollViewer, which is a part of the ListBox template. Even though this example redefines the ListBox template, it doesn't alter the ScrollViewer of the ScrollBar.

To customize this detail, you could create a new ScrollViewer template for use with the ListBox. You could then point the ScrollViewer template to your custom ScrollBar template. However, there's an easier option. You can create an element-typed style that changes the template of all the ScrollBar controls it comes across. This avoids the extra work of creating the ScrollViewer template.

Note In order to ensure that the list box gets the revamped scroll bar, you must place the template for the ScrollBar class before the template for the ListBox class.

The ScrollBar control is surprisingly sophisticated. It's actually built out of a collection of smaller pieces, as shown in Figure 15-10.

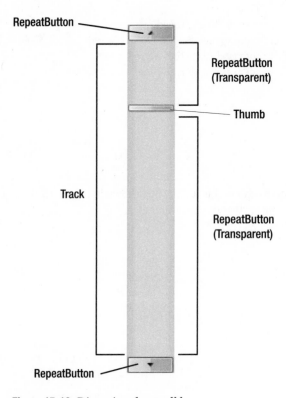

Figure 15-10. *Dissecting the scroll bar*

The background of the scroll bar is represented by the Track class—it's usually a shaded rectangle that's stretched out over the length of the scroll bar. At the far ends of the scroll bar are buttons that allow you to move one increment up or down (or to the left or right). These are instances of the RepeatButton class, which derives from ButtonBase. The key difference between a RepeatButton and the ordinary Button class is that if you hold the mouse down on a RepeatButton, the Click event fires over and over again (which is handy for scrolling).

In the middle of the scroll bar is a Thumb that represents the current position in the scrollable content. And, most interestingly of all, the blank space on either side of the thumb is actually made up of two more RepeatButton objects, which are transparent. When you click either one of these, the scroll bar scrolls an entire *page* (a page is defined as the amount that fits in the visible window of the scrollable content). This gives you the familiar ability to jump quickly through scrollable content by clicking the bar on either side of the thumb.

Here's the template for a vertical scroll bar:

```
<ControlTemplate x:Key="VerticalScrollBar" TargetType="{x:Type ScrollBar}">
  <Grid>
    <Grid.RowDefinitions>
      <RowDefinition MaxHeight="18"/>
      <RowDefinition Height="*"/>
```

```xml
          <RowDefinition MaxHeight="18"/>
      </Grid.RowDefinitions>

      <RepeatButton Grid.Row="0" Height="18"
        Style="{StaticResource ScrollBarLineButtonStyle}"
        Command="ScrollBar.LineUpCommand" >
        <Path Fill="{StaticResource GlyphBrush}"
         Data="M 0 4 L 8 4 L 4 0 Z"></Path>
      </RepeatButton>

      <Track Name="PART_Track" Grid.Row="1"
        IsDirectionReversed="True" ViewportSize="0">
        <Track.DecreaseRepeatButton>
          <RepeatButton Command="ScrollBar.PageUpCommand"
           Style="{StaticResource ScrollBarPageButtonStyle}">
          </RepeatButton>
        </Track.DecreaseRepeatButton>
        <Track.Thumb>
          <Thumb Style="{StaticResource ScrollBarThumbStyle}">
          </Thumb>
        </Track.Thumb>
        <Track.IncreaseRepeatButton>
          <RepeatButton Command="ScrollBar.PageDownCommand"
           Style="{StaticResource ScrollBarPageButtonStyle}">
          </RepeatButton>
        </Track.IncreaseRepeatButton>
      </Track>

      <RepeatButton
        Grid.Row="3" Height="18"
        Style="{StaticResource ScrollBarLineButtonStyle}"
        Command="ScrollBar.LineDownCommand"
        Content="M 0 0 L 4 4 L 8 0 Z">
      </RepeatButton>

      <RepeatButton
        Grid.Row="3" Height="18"
        Style="{StaticResource ScrollBarLineButtonStyle}"
        Command="ScrollBar.LineDownCommand">
        <Path Fill="{StaticResource GlyphBrush}"
          Data="M 0 0 L 4 4 L 8 0 Z"></Path>
      </RepeatButton>
    </Grid>
  </ControlTemplate>
```

This template is fairly straightforward, once you understand the multipart structure of the scroll bar (as shown in Figure 15-9). There are a few key points to note:

- The vertical scroll bar consists of a three-row grid. The top and bottom rows hold the buttons at either end (and appear as arrows). They're fixed at 18 units. The middle section, which holds the track, takes the rest of the space.

- The RepeatButton at both ends use the same style. The only difference is the Content property that contains a Path that draws the arrow because the top button has an up arrow while the bottom button has a down arrow. For conciseness, these arrows are represented using the path mini-language described in Chapter 14. The other details, such as the background fill and the circle that appears around the arrow are defined in the control template, which is set out in the ScrollButtonLineStyle.

- Both buttons are linked to a command in the ScrollBar class (LineUpCommand and LineDownCommand). This is how they do their work. As long as you provide a button that's linked to this command, it doesn't matter what its name is, what it looks like, or what specific class it uses. (Commands are covered in detail in Chapter 10.)

- The Track has the name PART_Track. You must use this name in order for the ScrollBar class to hook up its code successfully. If you look at the default template for the Scroll-Bar class (which is similar, but lengthier), you'll see it appears there as well.

■**Note** If you're examining a control with reflection (or using a tool such as Reflector), you can look for the TemplatePart attributes attached to the class declaration. There should be one TemplatePart attribute for each named part. The TemplatePart attribute indicates the name of the expected element (through the Name property) and its class (through the Type property). In Chapter 21, you'll see how to apply the TemplatePart attribute to your own custom control classes.

- The Track.ViewportSize property is set to 0. This is a specific implementation detail in this template. It ensures that the Thumb always has the same size. (Ordinarily, the thumb is sized proportionately based on the content, so that if you're scrolling through content that mostly fits in the window, the thumb becomes much larger.)

- The Track wraps two RepeatButton objects (whose style is defined separately) and the Thumb. Once again, these buttons are wired up to the appropriate functionality using commands.

You'll also notice that the template uses a key name that specifically identifies it as a vertical scroll bar. As you learned in Chapter 12, when you set a key name on a style, you ensure that it isn't applied automatically, even if you've also set the TargetType property. The reason this example uses this approach is because the template is only suitable for scroll bars in the vertical orientation. Another, element-typed style uses a trigger to automatically apply the control template if the ScrollBar.Orientation property is set to Vertical:

```
<Style TargetType="{x:Type ScrollBar}">
  <Setter Property="SnapsToDevicePixels" Value="True"/>
```

```
    <Setter Property="OverridesDefaultStyle" Value="true"/>
    <Style.Triggers>
      <Trigger Property="Orientation" Value="Vertical">
        <Setter Property="Width" Value="18"/>
        <Setter Property="Height" Value="Auto" />
        <Setter Property="Template" Value="{StaticResource VerticalScrollBar}" />
      </Trigger>
    </Style.Triggers>
  </Style>
```

Although you could easily build a horizontal scroll bar out of the same basic pieces, this
example doesn't take that step (and so retains the normally styled horizontal scroll bar).

The final task is to fill in the styles that format the various RepeatButton objects and the
Thumb. These styles are relatively modest, but they do change the standard look of the scroll
bar. First, the Thumb is shaped like an ellipse:

```
<Style x:Key="ScrollBarThumbStyle" TargetType="{x:Type Thumb}">
  <Setter Property="IsTabStop" Value="False"/>
  <Setter Property="Focusable" Value="False"/>
  <Setter Property="Margin" Value="1,0,1,0" />
  <Setter Property="Background" Value="{StaticResource StandardBrush}" />
  <Setter Property="BorderBrush" Value="{StaticResource StandardBorderBrush}" />
  <Setter Property="Template">
    <Setter.Value>
      <ControlTemplate TargetType="{x:Type Thumb}">
        <Ellipse Stroke="{StaticResource StandardBorderBrush}"
          Fill="{StaticResource StandardBrush}"></Ellipse>
      </ControlTemplate>
    </Setter.Value>
  </Setter>
</Style>
```

Next, the arrows at either end are drawn inside nicely rounded circles. The circles are
defined in the control template, while the arrows are provided from the content of the Repeat-
Button and inserted into the control template using the ContentPresenter:

```
<Style x:Key="ScrollBarLineButtonStyle" TargetType="{x:Type RepeatButton}">
  <Setter Property="Focusable" Value="False"/>
  <Setter Property="Template">
    <Setter.Value>
      <ControlTemplate TargetType="{x:Type RepeatButton}">
        <Grid Margin="1">
          <Ellipse Name="Border" StrokeThickness="1"
            Stroke="{StaticResource StandardBorderBrush}"
            Fill="{StaticResource StandardBrush}"></Ellipse>
          <ContentPresenter HorizontalAlignment="Center"
            VerticalAlignment="Center"></ContentPresenter>
        </Grid>
        <ControlTemplate.Triggers>
```

```
            <Trigger Property="IsPressed" Value="true">
              <Setter TargetName="Border" Property="Fill"
              Value="{StaticResource PressedBrush}" />
            </Trigger>
          </ControlTemplate.Triggers>
        </ControlTemplate>
      </Setter.Value>
    </Setter>
</Style>
```

The RepeatButton objects that are displayed over the track aren't changed. They simply use a transparent background so the track shows through:

```
<Style x:Key="ScrollBarPageButtonStyle" TargetType="{x:Type RepeatButton}">
  <Setter Property="IsTabStop" Value="False"/>
  <Setter Property="Focusable" Value="False"/>
  <Setter Property="Template">
    <Setter.Value>
      <ControlTemplate TargetType="{x:Type RepeatButton}">
        <Border Background="Transparent" />
      </ControlTemplate>
    </Setter.Value>
  </Setter>
</Style>
```

Unlike the normal scroll bar, in this template no background is assigned to the Track, which leaves it transparent. That way, the gently shaded gradient of the list box shows through. The final list box is shown in Figure 15-11.

Figure 15-11. *A list box with a customized scroll bar*

Creating a Custom Window

In Chapter 8, you considered how to build a custom-shaped window that uses WPF drawing elements instead of the standard window frame. Although the technique described there worked well enough, it forced you to manually restyle every window with the shaped border, header region, close buttons, and so on. In this section, you'll see how to adapt that markup into a control template you can use on any window.

The first step is to consult the default control template for the Window class. For the most part, this template is pretty straightforward, but it includes one detail you might not expect: an AdornerDecorator element. This element creates a special drawing area called the *adorner layer* over the rest of the window's client content. WPF controls can use the adorner layer to draw content that should appear superimposed over your elements. This includes small graphical indicators that show focus, flag validation errors, and guide drag-and-drop operations. When you build a custom window, you need to ensure that the adorner layer is present, so that controls that use it continue to function.

With that in mind, it's possible to identify the basic structure that the control template for a window should take:

```
<ControlTemplate x:Key="CustomWindowTemplate" TargetType="{x:Type Window}">
  <Border Name="windowFrame">
    <Grid>
      <Grid.RowDefinitions>
        <RowDefinition Height="Auto"></RowDefinition>
        <RowDefinition></RowDefinition>
        <RowDefinition Height="Auto"></RowDefinition>
      </Grid.RowDefinitions>

      <!-- The title bar. -->
      <TextBlock Text="{TemplateBinding Title}"
       FontWeight="Bold"></TextBlock>
      <Button Style="{StaticResource CloseButton}"
       HorizontalAlignment="Right"></Button>

      <!-- The window content. -->
      <Border Grid.Row="1">
        <AdornerDecorator>
          <ContentPresenter></ContentPresenter>
        </AdornerDecorator>
      </Border>

      <!-- The footer. -->
      <ContentPresenter Grid.Row="2" Margin="10"
       HorizontalAlignment="Center"
       Content="{TemplateBinding Tag}"></ContentPresenter>

      <!-- The resize grip. -->
      <ResizeGrip Name="WindowResizeGrip" Grid.Row="2"
       HorizontalAlignment="Right" VerticalAlignment="Bottom"
```

```
          Visibility="Collapsed" IsTabStop="False" />
      </Grid>
    </Border>

  <ControlTemplate.Triggers>
    <Trigger Property="ResizeMode" Value="CanResizeWithGrip">
      <Setter TargetName="WindowResizeGrip"
       Property="Visibility" Value="Visible"></Setter>
    </Trigger>
  </ControlTemplate.Triggers>
</ControlTemplate>
```

The top-level element in this template is a Border object for the window frame. Inside
that is a Grid with three rows. The contents of the Grid break down as follows:

- The top row holds the title bar, which consists of an ordinary TextBlock that displays the
  window title and a close button. A template binding pulls the window title from the
  Window.Title property.

- The middle row holds a nested Border with the rest of the window content. The
  content is inserted using a ContentPresenter. The ContentPresenter is wrapped in the
  AdornerDecorator, which ensures that the adorner layer is placed over your element
  content.

- The third row holds another ContentPresenter. However, this content presenter doesn't
  use the standard binding to get its content from the Window.Content property. Instead,
  it explicitly pulls its content from the Window.Tag property. Usually, this content is just
  ordinary text, but it could include any element content you want to use.

Note The Tag property is used because the Window class doesn't include any property that's designed to
hold footer text. Another option is to create a custom class that derives from Window and adds a Footer
property you need.

- Also in the third row is a resize grip. A trigger shows the resize grip when the
  Window.ResizeMode property is set to CanResizeWithGrip.

Two details that aren't shown here are the relatively uninteresting style for the resize grip
(which simply creates a small pattern of dots to use as the resize grip), and the close button
(which draws a small *X* on a red square). This markup also doesn't include the formatting
details, such as the gradient brush that paints the background and the properties that create a
nicely rounded border edge. To see the full markup, refer to the sample code provided for this
chapter.

The window template is applied using a simple style. This style also sets three key properties of the Window class that make it transparent. This allows you to create the window border
and background using WPF elements:

```
<Style x:Key="CustomWindowChrome" TargetType="{x:Type Window}">
  <Setter Property="AllowsTransparency" Value="True"></Setter>
  <Setter Property="WindowStyle" Value="None"></Setter>
  <Setter Property="Background" Value="Transparent"></Setter>
  <Setter Property="Template"
   Value="{StaticResource CustomWindowTemplate}"></Setter>
</Style>
```

At this point, you're ready to use your custom window. For example, you could create a window like this that sets the style and fills in some basic content:

```
<Window x:Class="ControlTemplates.CustomWindow"
  xmlns="http://schemas.microsoft.com/winfx/2006/xaml/presentation"
  xmlns:x="http://schemas.microsoft.com/winfx/2006/xaml"
  Title="CustomWindowTest" Height="300" Width="300"
  Tag="This is a custom footer"
  Style="{StaticResource CustomWindowChrome}">

  <StackPanel Margin="10">
    <TextBlock Margin="3">This is a test.</TextBlock>
    <Button Margin="3" Padding="3">OK</Button>
  </StackPanel>
</Window>
```

Figure 15-12 shows the result.

Figure 15-12. *A reusable window template*

There's just one problem. Currently, the window lacks most of the basic behavior windows require. For example, you can't drag the window around the desktop, resize it, or use the close button. To perform these actions, you need code.

There are two possible ways to add the code you need—you could expand your example into a custom Window-derived class, or you could create a code-behind class for your resource dictionary. The custom control approach provides better encapsulation and allows you to extend the public interface of your window (for example, adding useful methods and properties that you can use in your application). However, the code-behind approach is a relatively lightweight alternative that allows you to extend the capabilities of a control template while allowing your application to continue using the base control classes. It's the approach that you'll see in this example. (Chapter 24 presents the custom control alternative.)

You've already learned how to create a code-behind class for your resource dictionary (see the "User-Selected Skins" section earlier). Once you've created the code file, it's easy to add the event handling code you need. The only challenge is that your code runs in the resource dictionary object, not inside your window object. That means you can't use the this keyword to access the current window. Fortunately, there's an easy alternative: the FrameworkElement.TemplatedParent property.

For example, to make the window draggable you need to intercept a mouse event on the title bar and initiate dragging. Here's the revised TextBlock that wires up an event handler when the user clicks with the mouse:

```
<TextBlock Margin="1" Padding="5" Text="{TemplateBinding Title}"
 FontWeight="Bold" MouseLeftButtonDown="titleBar_MouseLeftButtonDown"></TextBlock>
```

Now you can add the following event handler to the code-behind class for the resource dictionary:

```
private void titleBar_MouseLeftButtonDown(object sender, MouseButtonEventArgs e)
{
    Window win = (Window)
      ((FrameworkElement)sender).TemplatedParent;
    win.DragMove();
}
```

To make your window resizable you need to add two invisible rectangles running along the right and bottom edges of the window, respectively. These rectangles can receive mouse events and call event handlers to resize the window.

Here's the markup that you need to configure the Grid in the control template to support resizing:

```
<Rectangle Grid.Row="1" Grid.RowSpan="3"
 Cursor="SizeWE" Fill="Transparent" Width="5"
 VerticalAlignment="Stretch" HorizontalAlignment="Right"
 MouseLeftButtonDown="window_initiateResizeWE"
 MouseLeftButtonUp="window_endResize"
 MouseMove="window_Resize"></Rectangle>

<Rectangle Grid.Row="2"
 Cursor="SizeNS" Fill="Transparent" Height="5"
 HorizontalAlignment="Stretch" VerticalAlignment="Bottom"
 MouseLeftButtonDown="window_initiateResizeNS"
 MouseLeftButtonUp="window_endResize"
 MouseMove="window_Resize"></Rectangle>
```

And here are the event handlers that coordinate the resizing. A Boolean isResizing field keeps track of when resize mode is underway, and the resizeType field tracks the direction in which the window is being resized:

```
private bool isResizing = false;

// Use the Flags attribute to allow simultaneous Width and Height resizing
// (which could be activated using the bottom-right corner of the window.)
[Flags()]
private enum ResizeType
{
    Width, Height
}
private ResizeType resizeType;

private void window_initiateResizeWE(object sender, MouseEventArgs e)
{
    isResizing = true;
    resizeType = ResizeType.Width;
}

private void window_initiateResizeNS(object sender, MouseEventArgs e)
{
    isResizing = true;
    resizeType = ResizeType.Height;
}

private void window_endResize(object sender, MouseEventArgs e)
{
    isResizing = false;

    // Make sure capture is released.
    Rectangle rect = (Rectangle)sender;
    rect.ReleaseMouseCapture();
}

private void window_Resize(object sender, MouseEventArgs e)
{
    Rectangle rect = (Rectangle)sender;
    Window win = (Window)rect.TemplatedParent;

    if (isResizing)
    {
        rect.CaptureMouse();
        if (resizeType == ResizeType.Width)
        {
            double width = e.GetPosition(win).X + 5;
            if (width > 0) win.Width = width;
```

```
        }
        if (resizeType == ResizeType.Height)
        {
            double height = e.GetPosition(win).Y + 5;
            if (height > 0) win.Height = height;
        }
    }
}
```

Finally, similar code handles the click of the close button:

```
private void cmdClose_Click(object sender, RoutedEventArgs e)
{
    Window win = (Window)
      ((FrameworkElement)sender).TemplatedParent;
    win.Close();
}
```

This completes the example, giving you a custom window control template with built-in behavior. You can apply this template to any ordinary WPF window. Of course, there's still a lot of polish needed before this window is attractive enough to suit a modern application. But it demonstrates the sequence of steps you need to follow to build a complex control template and shows how you can achieve results that would have required custom control development in previous user interface frameworks.

The Simple Styles

As you've seen, giving a new template to a common control can be a detailed task. That's because all the requirements of a control template aren't always obvious. For example, a typical ScrollBar requires a combination of two RepeatButton objects and a Track. Other control templates need elements with specific PART_ names. In the case of a custom window, you need to make sure the adorner layer is defined because some controls will require it.

Although you can discover these details by exploring the default template for a control, these default templates are often complicated and include details that aren't important and bindings that you probably won't support anyway. Fortunately, there's a better place to get started: the SimpleStyles sample project.

The SimpleStyles project provides a collection of simple, streamlined templates for all WPF's standard controls, which makes them a useful jumping-off point for any custom control designer. Unlike the default control templates, these use standard colors, perform all their work declaratively (with no chrome classes), and leave out optional parts such as template bindings for less commonly used properties. The goal of SimpleStyles is to give developers a practical starting point that they can use to design their own graphically enhanced control templates. Figure 15-13 shows about half of the controls in the SimpleStyles project.

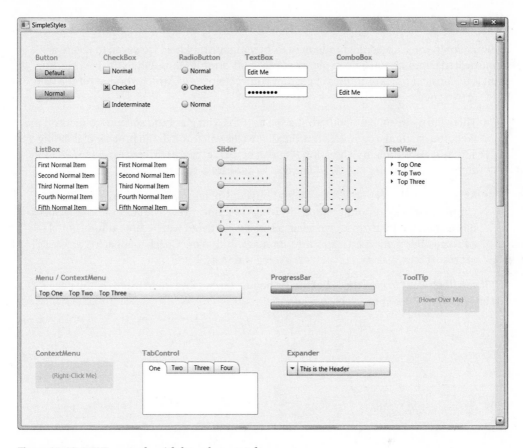

Figure 15-13. *WPF controls with bare-bones styles*

The SimpleStyles examples are included with Visual Studio. To find them, look up "Styling with ControlTemplates sample" in the index of the Visual Studio help. Alternatively, you can get them with the downloadable samples for this chapter.

■**Tip** The SimpleStyles are one of the hidden gems of WPF. They provide templates that are easier to understand and enhance than the default control templates. If you need to enhance a common control with a custom look, this project should be your first stop.

The Last Word

In this chapter, you learned the fundamentals of template building. However, to create a sophisticated template you'll need plenty of trial-and-error fiddling. Often the best starting point is to consider other examples of custom control templates, which abound on the Web. Here are two good examples to check out:

- There are plenty of handcrafted, shaded buttons with glass and soft glow effects on the Web. You can find a complete tutorial that walks you through the process of creating a snazzy glass button in Expression Blend at `http://blogs.msdn.com/mgrayson/archive/2007/02/16/creating-a-glass-button-the-complete-tutorial.aspx`.

- An excellent MSDN Magazine article about control templates provides examples of templates that incorporate simple drawings in innovative ways. For example, a Check-Box is replaced by an up-down lever, a slider is rendered with a three-dimensional tab, a ProgressBar is changed into a thermometer, and so on. Check it out at `http://msdn.microsoft.com/msdnmag/issues/07/01/Foundations`.

If you don't want to type these links in by hand, you can find them listed on the page for this book at `http://www.prosetech.com`.

■ ■ ■

Data Binding

Data binding is the time-honored tradition of pulling information out of an object and displaying it in your application's user interface, without writing the tedious code that does all the work. Often, rich clients use *two-way* data binding, which adds the ability to push information from the user interface back into some object—again, with little or no code. Because many Windows applications are all about data (and all of them need to deal with data some of the time), data binding is a top concern in a user interface technology like WPF.

Developers who are approaching WPF from a Windows Forms background will find that WPF data binding has many similarities. As in Windows Forms, WPF data binding allows you to create bindings that take information from just about any property of any object and stuff it into just about any property of any element. WPF also includes a set of list controls that can handle entire collections of information and allow you to navigate through them. However, there are significant changes in the way that data binding is implemented behind the scenes, some impressive new functionality, and a fair bit of tweaking and fine-tuning. Many of the same concepts apply, but the same code won't.

In this chapter, you'll learn how to use WPF data binding. You'll create declarative bindings that pull the information you need out of elements and other objects. You'll also learn how to plug this system into a back-end database, whether you plan to use the standard ADO.NET data objects or build your own custom data classes.

Data Binding Basics

At its simplest, data binding is a relationship that tells WPF to extract some information from a *source* object and use it to set a property in a *target* object. The target property is always a dependency property, and it's usually in a WPF element—after all, the ultimate goal of WPF data binding is to display some information in your user interface. However, the source object can be just about anything, ranging from another WPF element to an ADO.NET data object (like the DataTable and DataRow) or a data-only object of your own creation. In this chapter, you'll begin your exploration of data binding by considering the simplest approach (element-to-element binding) and then considering how to use data binding with other types of objects.

Binding to the Properties of an Element

The simplest data binding scenario occurs when your source object is a WPF element and your source property is a dependency property. That's because dependency properties have built-in support for change notification, as explained in Chapter 6. As a result, when you change the value of the dependency property in the source object, the bound property in the target object is updated immediately. This is exactly what you want—and it happens without requiring you to build any additional infrastructure.

■Note Although it's nice to know that element-to-element binding is the simplest approach, most developers are more interested in finding out which approach is most common in the real world. Overall, the bulk of your data binding work will be spent binding elements to data objects. This allows you to display the information that you've extracted from an external source (such as a database or file). However, element-to-element binding is often useful. For example, you can use element-to-element binding to automate the way elements interact so that when a user modifies a control, another element is updated automatically. This is a valuable shortcut that can save you from writing boilerplate code (and it's a technique that wasn't possible in the previous generation of Windows Forms applications).

To understand how you can bind an element to another element, consider the simple window shown in Figure 16-1. It contains two controls: a Slider and a TextBlock with a single line of text. If you pull the thumb in the slider to the right, the font size of the text is increased immediately. If you pull it to the left, the font size is reduced.

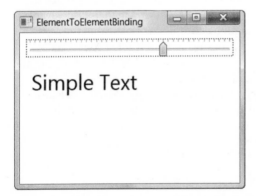

Figure 16-1. *Linked controls through data binding*

Clearly, it wouldn't be difficult to create this behavior using code. You would simply react to the Slider.ValueChanged event and copy the current value from the slider to the TextBlock. However, data binding makes it even easier.

■Tip Data binding also has another benefit—it allows you to create simple XAML pages that you can run in the browser without compiling them into applications. (As you learned in Chapter 1, if your XAML file has a linked code-behind file, it can't be opened in a browser.)

When using data binding, you don't need to make any change to your source object (which is the Slider in this example). Just configure it to take the right range of values, as you would usually:

```
<Slider Name="sliderFontSize" Margin="3"
 Minimum="1" Maximum="40" Value="10"
 TickFrequency="1" TickPlacement="TopLeft">
</Slider>
```

The binding is defined in the TextBlock element. Instead of setting the FontSize using a literal value, you use a binding expression, as shown here:

```
<TextBlock Margin="10" Text="Simple Text" Name="lblSampleText"
 FontSize="{Binding ElementName=sliderFontSize, Path=Value}" >
</TextBlock>
```

Data binding expressions use an XAML markup extension (and hence have curly braces). You begin with the word *Binding*, because you're creating an instance of the System.Windows.Data.Binding class. Although you can configure a Binding object in several ways, in this situation you need to set just two properties: the ElementName that indicates the source element and a Path that indicates the property in the source element.

■**Tip** The name Path is used instead of Property because the Path might point to a property of a property (for example, FontFamily.Source) or an indexer used by a property (for example, Content.Children[0]). You can build up a path with multiple periods to dig into a property of a property of a property, and so on.

If you want to refer to an attached property (a property that's defined in another class but applied to the bound element), you need to wrap the property name in parentheses. For example, if you're binding to an element that's placed in a Grid, the path (Grid.Row) retrieves the row number where you've placed it.

One of the neat features of data binding is that your target is updated automatically, no matter how the source is modified. In this example, the source can be modified in only one way—by the user's interaction with the slider thumb. However, consider a slightly revamped version of this example that adds a few buttons, each of which applies a preset value to the slider. Figure 16-2 shows the new window.

When you click the Set to Large button, this code runs:

```
private void cmd_SetLarge(object sender, RoutedEventArgs e)
{
    sliderFontSize.Value = 30;
}
```

This code sets the value of the slider, which in turn forces a change to the font size of the text through data binding. It's the same as if you had moved the slider thumb yourself.

However, this code doesn't work as well:

```
private void cmd_SetLarge(object sender, RoutedEventArgs e)
{
    lblSampleText.FontSize = 30;
}
```

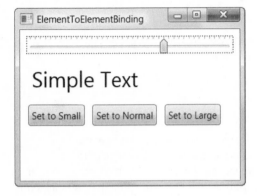

Figure 16-2. *Modifying the data binding source programmatically*

BINDING ERRORS

WPF doesn't raise exceptions to notify you about data binding problems. If you specify an element or a property that doesn't exist, you won't receive any indication—instead, the data will simply fail to appear in the target property.

At first glance, this seems like a debugging nightmare. Fortunately, WPF *does* output trace information that details binding failures. This information appears in Visual Studio's Output window when you're debugging the application. For example, if you try to bind to a nonexistent property, you'll see a message like this in the Output window:

```
System.Windows.Data Error: 35 : BindingExpression path error:
 'Tex' property not found on 'object' ''TextBox' (Name='txtFontSize')'.
 BindingExpression:Path=Tex; DataItem='TextBox' (Name='txtFontSize');
 target element is 'TextBox' (Name='');
 target property is 'Text' (type 'String')
```

WPF also ignores any exception that's thrown when you attempt to read the source property and quietly swallows the exception that occurs if the source data can't be cast to the data type of the target property. However, there is another option when dealing with these problems—you can tell WPF to change the appearance of the source element to indicate that an error has occurred. For example, this allows you to flag invalid input with an exclamation icon or a red outline. The "Validation" section later in this chapter demonstrates this technique.

It sets the font of the text box directly. As a result, the slider position isn't updated to match. Even worse, this has the effect of wiping out your font size binding and replacing it with a literal value. If you move the slider thumb now, the text block won't change at all.

Interestingly, there's a way to force values to flow in both directions: from the source to the target *and* from the target to the source. The trick is to set the Mode property of the Binding. Here's a revised bidirectional binding that allows you to apply changes to either the source or the target and have the other piece of the equation update itself automatically:

```
<TextBlock Margin="10" Text="Simple Text" Name="lblSampleText"
 FontSize="{Binding ElementName=sliderFontSize, Path=Value, Mode=TwoWay}" >
</TextBlock>
```

In this example, you have no reason to use a two-way binding (which requires more overhead) because you can solve the problem by using the right code. However, consider a variation of this example that includes a text box where the user can set the font size precisely. This text box needs to use a two-way binding, so it can both apply the user's changes and display the most recent size value in the text box when it's changed through another avenue. You'll see this example in the next section.

Creating Bindings with Code

When you're building a window, it's usually most efficient to declare your binding expression in the XAML markup using the Binding markup extension. However, it's also possible to create a binding using code.

Here's how you could create the binding for the TextBlock shown in the previous example:

```
Binding binding = new Binding();
binding.Source = sliderFontSize;
binding.Path = new PropertyPath("Value");
binding.Mode = BindingMode.TwoWay;
lblSampleText.SetBinding(TextBlock.TextProperty, binding);
```

You can also remove a binding with code using two static methods of the BindingOperations class. The ClearBinding() method takes a reference to the dependency property that has the binding you want to remove, while ClearAllBindings() removes all the data binding for an element:

```
BindingOperations.ClearAllBindings(lblSampleText);
```

Both ClearBinding() and ClearAllBindings() use the ClearValue() method that every element inherits from the based DependencyObject class. ClearValue() simply removes a property's local value (which, in this case, is a data binding expression).

Markup-based binding is far more common than programmatic binding, because it's cleaner and requires less work. In this chapter, all the examples use markup to create their bindings. However, you will want to use code to create a binding in some specialized scenarios:

- **Creating a dynamic binding.** If you want to tailor a binding based on other runtime information or create a different binding depending on the circumstances, it often makes sense to create your binding in code. (Alternatively, you could define every binding you might want to use in the Resources collection of your window and just add the code that calls SetBinding() with the appropriate binding object.)

- **Removing a binding.** If you want to remove a binding so that you can set a property in the usual way, you need the help of the ClearBinding() or ClearAllBindings() method. It isn't enough to simply apply a new value to the property—if you're using a two-way binding, the value you set is propagated to the linked object, and both properties remain synchronized.

Note You can remove any binding using the ClearBinding() and ClearAllBindings() methods. It doesn't matter whether the binding was applied programmatically or in XAML markup.

- **Creating custom controls.** To make it easier for other people to modify the visual appearance of a custom control you build, you'll need to move certain details (such as event handlers and data binding expressions) into your code and out of your markup. Chapter 24 includes a custom color picking control that uses code to create its bindings.

Multiple Bindings

Although the previous example includes just a single binding, you don't need to stop there. If you wanted, you could set the TextBlock up to draw its text from a text box, its current foreground and background color from separate lists of colors, and so on. Here's an example:

```
<TextBlock Margin="3" Name="lblSampleText"
  FontSize="{Binding ElementName=sliderFontSize, Path=Value}"
  Text="{Binding ElementName=txtContent, Path=Text}"
  Foreground="{Binding ElementName=lstColors, Path=SelectedItem.Tag}" >
</TextBlock>
```

Figure 16-3 shows the triple-bound TextBlock.

Figure 16-3. *A TextBlock that's bound to three elements*

You can also chain data bindings. For example, you could create a binding expression for the TextBox.Text property that links to the TextBlock.FontSize property, which contains a binding expression that links to the Slider.Value property. In this case, when the user drags the slider thumb to a new position, the value flows from the Slider to the TextBlock and then from the TextBlock to the TextBox. Although this works seamlessly, a cleaner approach is to bind your elements as closely as possible to the data they use. In the example described here, you should consider binding both the TextBlock and the TextBox directly to the Slider.Value property.

Life becomes a bit more interesting if you want a target property to be influenced by more than one source—for example, if you want there to be two equally legitimate bindings that set its property. At first glance, this doesn't seem possible. After all, when you create a binding, you can point to only a single target property. However, you can get around this limitation in several ways.

The easiest approach is to change the data binding mode. As you learned in the previous section, the Mode property allows you to change the way a binding works so that values aren't just pushed from the source to the target but also from the target to the source. Using this technique, you can create multiple binding expressions that set the same property. The last-set property is the one that comes into effect.

To understand how this works, consider a variation of the slider bar example that introduces a text box where you can set the exact font size you want. In this example (shown in Figure 16-4), you can set the TextBlock.FontSize property in two ways—by dragging the slider thumb or by typing a font size into the text box. All the controls are synchronized so that if you type a new number in the text box, the font size of the sample text is adjusted *and* the slider thumb is moved to the corresponding position.

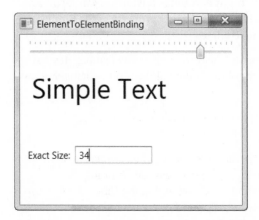

Figure 16-4. *Linking two properties to the font size*

As you know, you can apply only a single data binding to the TextBlock.FontSize property. It makes sense to leave the TextBlock.FontSize property as is so that it binds directly to the slider:

```
<TextBlock Margin="10" Text="Simple Text" Name="lblSampleText"
 FontSize="{Binding ElementName=sliderFontSize, Path=Value, Mode=TwoWay}" >
</TextBlock>
```

Although you can't add another binding to the FontSize property, you *can* bind the new control—the TextBox—to the TextBlock.FontSize property. Here's the markup you need:

```
<TextBox Text="{Binding ElementName=lblSampleText, Path=FontSize, Mode=TwoWay}">
</TextBox>
```

Now, whenever the TextBlock.FontSize property changes, the current value is inserted into the text box. Even better, you can edit the value in the text box to apply a specific size. Notice that in order for this example to work, the TextBox.Text property must use a two-way binding so that values travel both ways. Otherwise, the text box will be able to display the TextBlock.FontSize value but won't be able to change it.

This example has a few quirks:

- Because the Slider.Value property is a double, you'll end up with a fractional font size when you drag the slider thumb. You can constrain the slider to whole numbers by setting the TickFrequency property to 1 (or some other whole number interval) and setting the IsSnapToTickEnabled property to true.

- The text box allows letters and other non-numeric characters. If you enter any, the text box value can no longer be interpreted as a number. As a result, the data binding silently fails, and the font size is set to 0. Another approach would be to handle key presses in the text box to prevent invalid input altogether or to use data binding validation, as discussed later in this chapter.

- The changes you make in the text box aren't applied until the text box loses focus (for example, when you tab to another control). If this isn't the behavior you want, you can get an instantaneous refresh using the UpdateSourceTrigger property of the Binding object, as you'll learn shortly in the "Binding Updates" section.

Interestingly, the solution shown here isn't the only way to connect the text box. It's just as reasonable to configure the text box so that it changes the Slider.Value property instead of the TextBlock.FontSize property:

```
<TextBox Text="{Binding ElementName=sliderFontSize, Path=Value, Mode=TwoWay}">
</TextBox>
```

Now changing the text box triggers a change in the slider, which then applies the new font to the text. Once again, this approach works only if you use two-way data binding.

And lastly, you can swap the roles of the slider and text box so that the slider binds to the text box. To do this, you need to create an unbound TextBox and give it a name:

```
<TextBox Name="txtFontSize" Text="10">
</TextBox>
```

Then you can bind the Slider.Value property, as shown here:

```
<Slider Name="sliderFontSize" Margin="3"
 Minimum="1" Maximum="40"
 Value="{Binding ElementName=txtFontSize, Path=Text, Mode=TwoWay}"
 TickFrequency="1" TickPlacement="TopLeft">
</Slider>
```

Now the slider is in control. When the window is first shown, it retrieves the TextBox.Text property and uses that to set its Value property. When the user drags the slider thumb to a new position, it uses the binding to update the text box. Or, the user can update the slider value (and the font size of the sample text) by typing in the text box.

Note If you bind the Slider.Value property, the text box behaves slightly differently than the previous two examples. Any edits you make in the text box are applied immediately, rather than waiting until the text box loses focus. You'll learn more about controlling when an update takes place in the "Binding Updates" section.

As this example demonstrates, two-way bindings give you remarkable flexibility. You can use them to apply changes from the source to the target and from the target to the source. You can also apply them in combination to create a surprisingly complex code-free window.

Usually, the decision of where to place a binding expression is driven by the logic of your coding model. In the previous example, it probably makes more sense to place the binding in the TextBox.Text property rather than the Slider.Value property, because the text box is an optional add-on to an otherwise complete example, not a core ingredient that the slider relies on. It also makes more sense to bind the text box directly to the TextBlock.FontSize property rather than the Slider.Value property. (Conceptually, you're interested in reporting the current font size, and the slider is just one of the ways this font size can be set. Even though the slider position is the same as the font size, it's an unnecessary extra detail if you're trying to write the cleanest possible markup.) Of course, these decisions are subjective and a matter of coding style. The most important lesson is that all three approaches can give you the same behavior.

In the following sections, you'll explore two details that this example relies on. First, you'll consider your choices for setting the direction of a binding. Then, you'll see how you can tell WPF exactly when it should update the source property in a two-way binding.

Binding Direction

So far, you've seen one-way and two-way data binding. WPF actually allows you to use one of five values from the System.Windows.Data.BindingMode enumeration when setting the Binding.Mode property. Table 16-1 has the full list.

Table 16-1. *Values from the BindingMode Enumeration*

Name	Description
OneWay	The target property is updated when the source property changes.
TwoWay	The target property is updated when the source property changes, and the source property is updated when the target property changes.
OneTime	The target property is set initially based on the source property value. However, changes are ignored from that point onward (unless the binding is set to a completely different object or you call Binding-Expression.UpdateTarget(), as described later in this chapter). Usually, you'll use this mode to reduce overhead if you know the source property won't change.

Continued

Table 16-1. *Continued*

Name	Description
OneWayToSource	Similar to OneWay but in reverse. The source property is updated when the target property changes (which might seem a little backward), but the target property is never updated.
Default	The type of binding depends on the target property. It's either TwoWay (for user-settable properties, such as the TextBox.Text) or OneWay (for everything else). All bindings use this approach unless you specify otherwise.

Figure 16-5 illustrates the difference. You've already seen OneWay and TwoWay. OneTime is fairly straightforward. The other two choices bear some additional investigation.

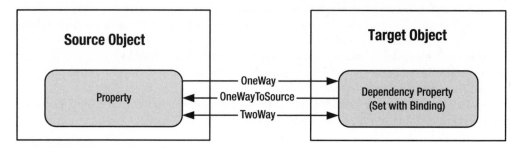

Figure 16-5. *Different ways to bind two properties*

OneWayToSource

You might wonder why there's both a OneWay and a OneWayToSource option—after all, both values create a one-way binding that works in the same way. The only difference is where the binding expression is placed. Essentially, OneWayToSource allows you to flip the source and target by placing the expression in what would ordinarily be considered the binding source.

The most common reason to use this trick is to set a property that isn't a dependency property. As you learned at the beginning of this chapter, binding expressions can be used only to set dependency properties. But by using OneWayToSource, you can overcome this limitation, provided the property that's supplying the value is itself a dependency property.

This technique isn't terribly common when performing element-to-element binding, because almost all element properties are dependency properties. One exception is the set of inline elements that you can use to build documents (as you'll see in Chapter 19). For example, consider the following markup, which creates a FlowDocument that's perfect for displaying nicely formatted regions of static content:

```
<FlowDocumentScrollViewer>
  <FlowDocument>
    <Paragraph>This is a paragraph one.</Paragraph>
    <Paragraph>This is paragraph two.</Paragraph>
  </FlowDocument>
</FlowDocumentScrollViewer>
```

The FlowDocument is placed inside a scrollable container (which is only one of several possible containers you can use) and given two paragraphs with small amounts of text.

Now consider what happens if you want to bind some of the text in a paragraph to another property. The first step is to wrap the text you want to change inside a Run object, which represents any small unit of text inside a FlowDocument. The next step you might attempt is to set the text of the run using a binding expression:

```
<FlowDocumentScrollViewer>
  <FlowDocument>
    <Paragraph>This is a paragraph one.</Paragraph>
    <Paragraph>
      <Run Text="{Binding ElementName=txtParagraph, Path=Text}"
      Name="runParagraphTwo"></Run>
    </Paragraph>
  </FlowDocument>
</FlowDocumentScrollViewer>
```

In this example, the run attempts to pull its text out of a text box named txtParagraph. Unfortunately, this code won't work because Run.Text is not a dependency property, so it doesn't know what to do with your binding expression. The solution is to remove the binding expression from the run and place it in the text box instead:

```
<TextBlock Margin="5">Content for second paragraph: </TextBlock>
<TextBox Margin="5" MinLines="2" TextWrapping="Wrap" Name="txtParagraph"
 Text="{Binding ElementName=runParagraphTwo, Path=Text, Mode=OneWayToSource}">
</TextBox>
```

Now, the text is automatically copied out of the text box and into the run. Of course, you could also use a two-way binding in the text box, which would incur a slight amount of extra overhead. This would be the best way to go if there is some initial text in the run and you want it to appear in the bound text box at the outset.

Default

Initially, it seems logical to assume that all bindings are one-way unless you explicitly specify otherwise. (After all, that's the way the simple slider example works.) However, this actually isn't the case. To demonstrate this fact to yourself, return to the example with the bound text box that allows you to edit the current font size. If you remove the Mode=TwoWay setting, this example still works just as well. That's because WPF uses a different Mode default depending on the property you're binding. (Technically, there's a tiny bit of metadata on every dependency property—the FrameworkPropertyMetadata.BindsTwoWayByDefault flag—that indicates whether that property should use one-way or two-way binding.)

Often, the default is exactly what you want. However, you can imagine an example with a read-only text box that the user can't change. In this case, you can reduce the overhead slightly by setting the mode to use one-way binding.

As a general rule of thumb, it's never a bad idea to explicitly set the mode. Even in the case of a text box, it's worth emphasizing that you want a two-way binding by including the Mode property.

Binding Updates

In the example shown in Figure 16-4 (which binds TextBox.Text to TextBlock.FontSize), there's another quirk. As you change the displayed font size by typing in the text box, nothing happens. It's not until you tab to another control that the change is applied. This behavior is different from the behavior you see with the slider control. There, the new font size is applied as you drag the slider thumb. There's no need to tab away.

To understand this difference, you need to take a closer look at the binding expressions used by these two controls. When you use OneWay or TwoWay binding, the changed value is propagated from the source to the target immediately. In the case of the slider, there's a one-way binding expression in the TextBlock. Thus, changes in the Slider.Value property are immediately applied to the TextBlock.FontSize property. The same behavior takes place in the text box example—changes to the source (which is TextBlock.FontSize) affect the target (TextBox.Text) immediately.

However, changes that flow in the reverse direction—from the target to the source—don't necessarily happen immediately. Instead, their behavior is governed by the Binding.Update-SourceTrigger property (which takes one of the values listed in Table 16-2). When the text is taken from the text box and used to update the TextBlock.FontSize property, you're witnessing an example of a target-to-source update that uses the UpdateSourceTrigger.LostFocus behavior.

Table 16-2. *Values from the UpdateSourceTrigger Enumeration*

Name	Description
PropertyChanged	The source is updated immediately when the target property changes.
LostFocus	The source is updated when the target property changes and the target loses focus.
Explicit	The source is not updated unless you call the Binding-Expression.UpdateSource() method.
Default	The updating behavior is determined by the metadata of the target property (technically, its FrameworkPropertyMetadata.DefaultUpdate-SourceTrigger property). For most properties, the default behavior is PropertyChanged, although the TextBox.Text property has a default behavior of LostFocus.

Remember, the values in Table 16-2 have no effect over how the target is updated. They simply control how the *source* is updated in a TwoWay or OneWayToSource binding.

With this knowledge, you can improve the text box example so that changes are applied to the font size as the user types in the text box. Here's how:

```
<TextBox Text="{Binding ElementName=txtSampleText, Path=FontSize, Mode=TwoWay,
  UpdateSourceTrigger=PropertyChanged}" Name="txtFontSize"></TextBox>
```

■Tip The default behavior of the TextBox.Text property is LostFocus, simply because the text in a text box will change repeatedly as the user types, causing multiple refreshes. Depending on how the source control updates itself, the PropertyChanged update mode can make the application feel more sluggish. Additionally, it might cause the source object to refresh itself before an edit is complete, which can cause problems for validation.

The UpdateSourceTrigger.Explicit behavior is often a good compromise, although it involves writing a bit of code. For example, in the text box example you could add an Apply button that, when clicked, updates the font size. You would then use the BindingExpression.UpdateSource() method to trigger an immediate refresh. Of course, this raises two excellent questions—namely, what is a BindingExpression object, and how do you get it?

A BindingExpression is just a slim package that wraps together two things: the Binding object you've already learned about (provided through the BindingExpression.ParentBinding property) and the object that's being bound from the source (BindingExpression.DataItem). In addition, the BindingExpression object provides two methods for triggering an immediate update for one part of the binding: UpdateSource() and UpdateTarget().

To get a BindingExpression object, you use the GetBindingExpression() method, which every element inherits from the base FrameworkElement class, and pass in the target property that has the binding. Here's an example that changes the font size in the TextBlock based on the current text in the text box:

```
// Get the binding that's applied to the text box.
BindingExpression binding = txtFontSize.GetBindingExpression(TextBox.TextProperty);

// Update the linked source (the TextBlock).
binding.UpdateSource();
```

Binding to Objects That Aren't Elements

So far, you've focused on adding bindings that link two elements. But in data-driven applications, it's more common to create binding expressions that draw their data from a nonvisual object. The only requirement is that the information you want to display must be stored in *public properties*. The WPF data binding infrastructure won't pick up private information or public fields.

When binding to an object that isn't an element, you need to give up the Binding.Element-Name property and use one of the following properties instead:

- **Source.** This is a reference that points to the source object—in other words, the object that's supplying the data.

- **RelativeSource.** This points to the source object using a RelativeSource object, which allows you to base your reference on the current element. This is a specialized tool that's handy when writing control templates and data templates.

- **DataContext.** If you don't specify a source using the Source or RelativeSource property, WPF searches up the element tree starting at the current element. It examines the Data-Context property of each element and uses the first one that isn't null. The DataContext property is extremely useful if you need to bind several properties of the same object to different elements, because you can set the DataContext property of a higher-level container object rather than directly on the target element.

The following sections fill in a few more details about these three options.

Source

The Source property is quite straightforward. The only catch is that you need to have your data object handy in order to bind it. As you'll see, you can use several approaches for getting the data object. You can pull it out of a resource, generate it programmatically, or get it with the help of a data provider.

The simplest option is to point the Source to some static object that's readily available. For example, you could create a static object in your code and use that. Or, you could use an ingredient from the .NET class library, as shown here:

```
<TextBlock Text="{Binding Source={x:Static SystemFonts.IconFontFamily},
 Path=Source}"></TextBlock>
```

This binding expression gets the FontFamily object that's provided by the static SystemFonts.IconFontFamily property. (Notice that you need the help of the static markup extension to set the Binding.Source property.) It then sets the Binding.Path property to the FontFamily.Source property, which gives the name of the font family. The result is a single line of text. In Windows Vista, the font name Segoe UI appears.

Another option is to bind to an object that you've previously created as a resource. For example, this markup creates a FontFamily object that points to the Calibri font:

```
<Window.Resources>
  <FontFamily x:Key="CustomFont">Calibri</FontFamily>
</Window.Resources>
```

And here's a TextBlock that binds to this resource:

```
<TextBlock Text="{Binding Source={StaticResource CustomFont},
 Path=Source}"></TextBlock>
```

Now the text you'll see is *Calibri*.

RelativeSource

The RelativeSource property allows you to point to a source object based on its relation to the target object. For example, you can use RelativeSource property to bind an element to itself or to bind to a parent element that's found an unknown number of steps up the element tree.

To set the Binding.RelativeSource property, you use a RelativeSource object. This makes the syntax a little more convoluted, because you need to create a Binding object and create a nested RelativeSource object inside. One option is to use the property-setting syntax instead of the Binding markup extension. For example, the following code creates a Binding object for the TextBlock.Text property. The Binding object uses a RelativeSource that searches out the parent window and displays the window title.

```
<TextBlock>
  <TextBlock.Text>
    <Binding Path="Title">
      <Binding.RelativeSource>
        <RelativeSource Mode="FindAncestor" AncestorType="{x:Type Window}" />
      </Binding.RelativeSource>
    </Binding>
```

```
    </TextBlock.Text>
</TextBlock>
```

The RelativeSource object uses the FindAncestor mode, which tells it to search up the element tree until it finds the type of element defined by the AncestorType property.

The more common way to write this binding is to combine it into one string using the Binding and RelativeSource markup extensions, as shown here:

```
<TextBlock Text="{Binding Path=Title,
    RelativeSource={RelativeSource FindAncestor, AncestorType={x:Type Window}} }">
</TextBlock>
```

The FindAncestor mode is only one of four options when you create a RelativeSource object. Table 16-3 lists all four modes.

Table 16-3. *Values from the RelativeSourceMode Enumeration*

Name	Description
Self	The expression binds to another property in the same element. (You saw an example of this technique in Chapter 10, where it was used to display the text that's associated with a command in the control that triggers the command.)
FindAncestor	The expression binds to a parent element. WPF will search up the element tree until it finds the parent you want. To specify the parent, you must also set the AncestorType property to indicate the type of parent element you want to find. Optionally, you can use the AncestorLevel property to skip a certain number of occurrences of the specified element. For example, if you want to bind to the third element of type ListBoxItem when going up the tree, you would set AncestorType={x:Type ListBoxItem} and AncestorLevel=3, thereby skipping the first two ListBoxItems. By default, AncestorLevel is 1, and the search stops at the first matching element.
PreviousData	The expression binds to the previous data item in a data-bound list. You would use this in a list item.
TemplatedParent	The expression binds to the element on which the template is applied. This mode works only if your binding is located inside a control template or data template.

At first glance, the RelativeSource property seems like an unnecessary way to complicate your markup. After all, why not bind directly to the source you want using the Source or ElementName property? However, this isn't always possible, usually because the markup the source and target objects are in different chunks of markup. This happens when you're creating control templates and data templates. For example, if you're building a data template that changes the way items are presented in a list, you might need to access the top-level ListBox object to read a property. You'll see several examples that use the RelativeSource binding in Chapter 17 and Chapter 18.

DataContext

In some cases, you'll have a number of elements that bind to the same object. For example, consider the following group of TextBlock elements, each of which uses a similar binding expression to pull out different details about the default icon font, including its line spacing and the style and weight of the first typeface it provides (both of which are simply Regular). You can use the Source property for each one, but this results in fairly lengthy markup:

```
<StackPanel DataContext="{x:Static SystemFonts.IconFontFamily}">
  <TextBlock Text="{Binding Source={x:Static SystemFonts.IconFontFamily},
  Path=Source}"></TextBlock>
  <TextBlock Text="{Binding Source={x:Static SystemFonts.IconFontFamily},
  Path=LineSpacing}"></TextBlock>
  <TextBlock Text="{Binding Source={x:Static SystemFonts.IconFontFamily},
  Path=FamilyTypefaces[0].Style}"></TextBlock>
  <TextBlock Text="{Binding Source={x:Static SystemFonts.IconFontFamily},
  Path=FamilyTypefaces[0].Weight}"></TextBlock>
</StackPanel>
```

In this situation, it's cleaner and more flexible to define the binding source once using the FrameworkElement.DataContext property. In this example, it makes sense to set the DataContext property of the StackPanel that contains all the TextBlock elements. (You could also set the DataContext property at an even higher level—for example, the entire window—but it makes sense to define it as narrowly as possible to make your intentions clear.)

You can set the DataContext property of an element in the same way that you set the Binding.Source property. In other words, you can supply your object inline, pull it out of a static property, or pull it out of a resource, as shown here:

```
<StackPanel DataContext="{x:Static SystemFonts.IconFontFamily}">
```

Now you can streamline your binding expressions by leaving out the source information:

```
<TextBlock Margin="5" Text="{Binding Path=Source}"></TextBlock>
```

When the source information is missing from a binding expression, WPF checks the DataContext property of that element. If it's null, WPF searches up the element tree looking for the first data context that isn't null. (Initially, the DataContext property of all elements is null.) If it finds a data context, it uses that for the binding. If it doesn't, the binding expression doesn't apply any value to the target property.

■**Note** If you create a binding that explicitly specifies a source using the Source property, your element uses that source instead of any data context that might be available.

This example shows you how you can create a basic binding to an object that isn't an element. However, to use this technique in a realistic application, you need to pick up a few more skills. In the next section, you'll learn how to display information drawn from a database by building on these data binding techniques.

Binding to a Database with Custom Objects

When developers hear the term *data binding*, they often think of one specific application—pulling information out of a database and showing it onscreen with little or no code.

As you've already seen, data binding in WPF is a much more general tool. Even if your application never comes into contact with a database, it's still likely to use data binding to automate the way elements interact or translate an object model into a suitable display. However, you can learn a lot about the details of object binding by considering a traditional example that queries and updates a table in a database. But before you get there, you need to consider the custom data access component and data object that this example uses.

Building a Data Access Component

In professional applications, database code is not embedded in the code-behind class for a window but encapsulated in a dedicated class. For even better componentization, these data access classes can be pulled out of your application altogether and compiled in a separate DLL component. This is particularly true when writing code that accesses a database (because this code tends to be extremely performance-sensitive), but it's a good design no matter where your data lives.

DESIGNING DATA ACCESS COMPONENTS

No matter how you plan to use data binding (or even if you don't), your data access code should always be coded in a separate class. This approach is the only way you have the slightest chance to make sure you can efficiently maintain, optimize, troubleshoot, and (optionally) reuse your data access code.

When creating a data class, you should follow a few basic guidelines in this section:

- Open and close connections quickly. Open the database connection in every method call, and close it before the method ends. This way, a connection can't be inadvertently left open. One way to ensure the connection is closed at the appropriate time is with a using block.

- Implement error handling. Use error handling to make sure that connections are closed even if an exception occurs.

- Follow stateless design practices. Accept all the information needed for a method in its parameters, and return all the retrieved data through the return value. This avoids complications in a number of scenarios (for example, if you need to create a multithreaded application or host your database component on a server).

- Store the connection string in one place. Ideally, this is the configuration file for your application.

The database component that's shown in the following example retrieves a table of product information from the Store database, which is a sample database for the fictional IBuySpy store included with some Microsoft case studies. You can get a script to install this database with the online samples for this chapter. Figure 16-6 shows two tables in the Store database and their schemas.

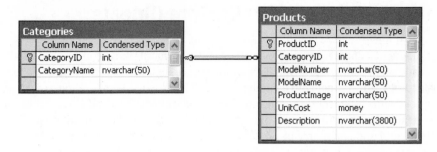

Figure 16-6. *A portion of the Store database*

The data access class is exceedingly simple—it provides just a single method that allows the caller to retrieve one product record. Here's the basic outline:

```
public class StoreDB
{
    // Get the connection string from the current configuration file.
    private string connectionString = Properties.Settings.Default.StoreDatabase;

    public Product GetProduct(int ID)
    {
        ...
    }
}
```

The query is performed through a stored procedure in the database named GetProduct. The connection string isn't hard-coded—instead, it's retrieved through an application setting in the .config file for this application. (To view or set application settings, double-click the Properties node in the Solution Explorer, and then click the Settings tab.)

When other windows need data, they call the StoreDB.GetProduct() method to retrieve a Product object. The Product object is a custom object that has a sole purpose in life—to represent the information for a single row in the Products table. You'll consider it in the next section.

You have several options for making the StoreDB class available to the windows in your application:

- The window could create an instance of StoreDB whenever it needs to access the database.

- You could change the methods in the StoreDB class to be static.

- You could create a single instance of StoreDB and make it available through a static property in another class (following the "factory" pattern).

The first two options are reasonable, but both of them limit your flexibility. The first choice prevents you from caching data objects for use in multiple windows. Even if you don't want to use that caching right away, it's worth designing your application in such a way that it's easy to implement later. Similarly, the second approach assumes you won't have any instance-specific state that you need to retain in the StoreDB class. Although this is a good design principle, you might want to retain some details (such as the connection string) in memory. If you convert the StoreDB class to use static methods, it becomes much more difficult to access different instances of the Store database in different back-end data stores.

Ultimately, the third option is the most flexible. It preserves the switchboard design by forcing all the windows to work through a single property. Here's an example that makes an instance of StoreDB available through the Application class:

```
public partial class App : System.Windows.Application
{
    private static StoreDB storeDB = new StoreDB();
    public static StoreDB StoreDB
    {
        get { return storeDB; }
    }
}
```

In this book, we're primarily interested with how data objects can be bound to WPF elements. The actual process that deals with creating and filling these data objects (as well as other implementation details, such as whether StoreDB caches the data over several method calls, whether it uses stored procedures instead of inline queries, whether it fetches the data from a local XML file when offline, and so on) isn't our focus. However, just to get an understanding of what's taking place, here's the complete code:

```
public class StoreDB
{
    private string connectionString = Properties.Settings.Default.StoreDatabase;

    public Product GetProduct(int ID)
    {
        SqlConnection con = new SqlConnection(connectionString);
        SqlCommand cmd = new SqlCommand("GetProductByID", con);
        cmd.CommandType = CommandType.StoredProcedure;
        cmd.Parameters.AddWithValue("@ProductID", ID);

        try
        {
            con.Open();
            SqlDataReader reader = cmd.ExecuteReader(CommandBehavior.SingleRow);
            if (reader.Read())
            {
                // Create a Product object that wraps the
                // current record.
                Product product = new Product((string)reader["ModelNumber"],
                    (string)reader["ModelName"], (decimal)reader["UnitCost"],
                    (string)reader["Description"] ,
                    (string)reader["ProductImage"]);
                return(product);
            }
            else
```

```
            {
                return null;
            }
        }
        finally
        {
            con.Close();
        }
    }
}
```

■Note Currently, the GetProduct() method doesn't include any exception handling code, so all exceptions will bubble up the calling code. This is a reasonable design choice, but you might want to catch the exception in GetProduct(), perform cleanup or logging as required, and then rethrow the exception to notify the calling code of the problem. This design pattern is called *caller inform*.

Building a Data Object

The data object is the information package that you plan to display in your user interface. Any class works, provided it consists of public properties (fields and private properties aren't supported). In addition, if you want to use this object to make changes (via two-way binding), the properties cannot be read-only.

Here's the Product object that's used by StoreDB:

```
public class Product
{
    private string modelNumber;
    public string ModelNumber
    {
        get { return modelNumber; }
        set { modelNumber = value; }
    }

    private string modelName;
    public string ModelName
    {
        get { return modelName; }
        set { modelName = value; }
    }

    private decimal unitCost;
    public decimal UnitCost
    {
        get { return unitCost; }
        set { unitCost = value; }
    }
```

```
    private string description;
    public string Description
    {
        get { return description; }
        set { description = value; }
    }

    public Product(string modelNumber, string modelName,
      decimal unitCost, string description)
    {
        ModelNumber = modelNumber;
        ModelName = modelName;
        UnitCost = unitCost;
        Description = description;
    }
}
```

Displaying the Bound Object

The final step is to create an instance of the Product object and then bind it to your controls. Although you could create a Product object and store it as a resource or a static property, neither approach makes much sense. Instead, you need to use StoreDB to create the appropriate object at runtime and then bind that to your window.

■**Note** Although the declarative no-code approach sounds more elegant, there are plenty of good reasons to mix a little code into your data-bound windows. For example, if you're querying a database, you probably want to handle the connection in your code so that you can decide how to handle exceptions and inform the user of problems.

Consider the simple window shown in Figure 16-7. It allows the user to supply a product code, and it then shows the corresponding product in the Grid in the lower portion of the window.

When you design this window, you don't have access to the Product object that will supply the data at runtime. However, you can still create your bindings without indicating the data source. You simply need to indicate the property that each element uses from the Product class.

Here's the full markup for displaying a Product object:

```
<Grid Name="gridProductDetails">
  <Grid.ColumnDefinitions>
    <ColumnDefinition Width="Auto"></ColumnDefinition>
    <ColumnDefinition></ColumnDefinition>
  </Grid.ColumnDefinitions>
  <Grid.RowDefinitions>
    <RowDefinition Height="Auto"></RowDefinition>
    <RowDefinition Height="Auto"></RowDefinition>
```

```
    <RowDefinition Height="Auto"></RowDefinition>
    <RowDefinition Height="Auto"></RowDefinition>
    <RowDefinition Height="*"></RowDefinition>
  </Grid.RowDefinitions>

  <TextBlock Margin="7">Model Number:</TextBlock>
  <TextBox Margin="5" Grid.Column="1"
   Text="{Binding Path=ModelNumber}"></TextBox>
  <TextBlock Margin="7" Grid.Row="1">Model Name:</TextBlock>
  <TextBox Margin="5" Grid.Row="1" Grid.Column="1"
   Text="{Binding Path=ModelName}"></TextBox>
  <TextBlock Margin="7" Grid.Row="2">Unit Cost:</TextBlock>
  <TextBox Margin="5" Grid.Row="2" Grid.Column="1"
   Text="{Binding Path=UnitCost}"></TextBox>
  <TextBlock Margin="7,7,7,0" Grid.Row="3">Description:</TextBlock>
  <TextBox Margin="7" Grid.Row="4" Grid.Column="0" Grid.ColumnSpan="2"
   TextWrapping="Wrap" Text="{Binding Path=Description}"></TextBox>
</Grid>
```

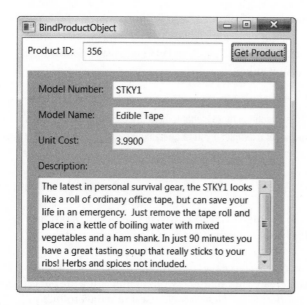

Figure 16-7. *Querying a product*

Notice that the Grid wrapping all these details is given a name so that you can manipulate it in code and complete your data bindings.

When you first run this application, no information will appear. Even though you've defined your bindings, no source object is available.

When the user clicks the button at runtime, you use the StoreDB class to get the appropriate product data. Although you could create each binding programmatically, this wouldn't make much sense (and it wouldn't save much code over just populating the controls by hand). However, the DataContext property provides a perfect shortcut. If you set it for the Grid that contains all your data binding expressions, all your binding expressions will use it to fill themselves with data.

Here's the event handling code that reacts when the user clicks the button:

```
private void cmdGetProduct_Click(object sender, RoutedEventArgs e)
{
    int ID;
    if (Int32.TryParse(txtID.Text, out ID))
    {
        try
        {
            gridProductDetails.DataContext = App.StoreDB.GetProduct(ID);
        }
        catch
        {
            MessageBox.Show("Error contacting database.");
        }
    }
    else
    {
        MessageBox.Show("Invalid ID.");
    }
}
```

Updating the Database

You don't need to do anything extra to enable database updates with this example. As you learned earlier, the TextBox.Text property uses two-way binding by default. As a result, the Product object is modified as you edit the text in the text boxes. (Technically, each property is updated when you tab to a new field, because the default source update mode for the TextBox.Text property is LostFocus.)

You can commit changes to the database at any time. All you need is to add an UpdateProduct() method to the StoreDB class and an Update button the window. When clicked, your code can grab the current Product object from the data context and use it to commit the update:

```
private void cmdUpdateProduct_Click(object sender, RoutedEventArgs e)
{
    Product product = (Product)gridProductDetails.DataContext;
    try
    {
        App.StoreDB.UpdateProduct(product);
    }
    catch
    {
        MessageBox.Show("Error contacting database.");
    }
}
```

This example has one potential stumbling block. When you click the Update button, the focus changes to that button, and any uncommitted edit is applied to the Product object. However, if you set the Update button to be a default button (by setting IsDefault to true), there's another possibility. A user could make a change in one of the fields and hit Enter to trigger the update process without committing the last change. To avoid this possibility, you can explicitly force the focus to change before you execute any database code, like this:

```
FocusManager.SetFocusedElement(this, (Button)sender);
```

Change Notification

The Product binding example works so well because each Product object is essentially fixed—it never changes (except if the user edits the text in one of the linked text boxes).

For simple scenarios, where you're primarily interested in displaying content and letting the user edit it, this behavior is perfectly acceptable. However, it's not difficult to imagine a different situation, where the bound Product object might be modified elsewhere in your code. For example, imagine an Increase Price button that executes this line of code:

```
product.UnitCost *= 1.1M;
```

Note Although you could retrieve the Product object from the data context, this example assumes you're also storing it as a member variable in your window class, which simplifies your code and requires less type casting.

When you run this code, you'll find that even though the Product object has been changed, the old value remains in the text box. That's because the text box has no way of knowing that you've changed a value.

You can use three approaches to solve this problem:

- You can make each property in the Product class a dependency property using the syntax you learned about in Chapter 6. (In this case, your class must derive from DependencyObject.) Although this approach gets WPF to do the work for you (which is nice), it makes the most sense in elements—classes that have a visual appearance in a window. It's not the most natural approach for data classes like Product.

- You can raise an event for each property. In this case, the event must have the name *PropertyName*Changed (for example, UnitCostChanged). It's up to you to fire the event when the property is changed.

- You can implement the System.ComponentModel.INotifyPropertyChanged interface, which requires a single event named PropertyChanged. You must then raise the Property-Changed event whenever a property changes and indicate which property has changed by supplying the property name as a string. It's still up to you to raise this event when a property changes, but you don't need to define a separate event for each property.

The first approach relies on the WPF dependency property infrastructure, while both the second and the third rely on events. Usually, when creating a data object, you'll use the third approach. It's the simplest choice for nonelement classes.

Note You can actually use one other approach. If you suspect a change has been made to a bound object and that bound object doesn't support change notifications in any of the proper ways, you can retrieve the BindingExpression object (using the FrameworkElement.GetBindingExpression() method) and call Binding-Expression.UpdateTarget() to trigger a refresh. Obviously, this is the most awkward solution—you can almost see the duct tape that's holding it together.

Here's the definition for a revamped Product class that uses the INotifyPropertyChanged interface, with the code for the implementation of the PropertyChanged event:

```
public class Product : INotifyPropertyChanged
{
    public event PropertyChangedEventHandler PropertyChanged;
    public void OnPropertyChanged(PropertyChangedEventArgs e)
    {
        if (PropertyChanged != null)
          PropertyChanged(this, e);
    }
}
```

Now you simply need to fire the PropertyChanged event in all your property setters:

```
private decimal unitCost;
public decimal UnitCost
{
    get { return unitCost; }
    set {
        unitCost = value;
        OnPropertyChanged(new PropertyChangedEventArgs("UnitCost"));
    }
}
```

If you use this version of the Product class in the previous example, you'll get the behavior you expect. When you change the current Product object, the new information will appear in the text box immediately.

Tip If several values have changed, you can call OnPropertyChanged() and pass in an empty string. This tells WPF to reevaluate the binding expressions that are bound to any property in your class.

Binding to a Collection of Objects

Binding to a single object is quite straightforward. But life gets more interesting when you need to bind to some collection of objects—for example, all the products in a table.

Although every dependency property supports the single-value binding you've seen so far, collection binding requires an element with a bit more intelligence. In WPF, all the classes that derive from ItemsControl have the ability to show an entire list of items. Data binding possibilities include the ListBox, ComboBox, and ListView (and the Menu and TreeView for hierarchical data).

■**Tip** Although it seems like WPF offers only a small set of list controls, these controls allow you to show your data in a virtually unlimited number of different ways. That's because the list controls support data templates, which allow you to control exactly how items are displayed. You'll learn more about data templates in Chapter 17.

To support collection binding, the ItemsControl class defines the three key properties listed in Table 16-4.

Table 16-4. *Properties in the ItemsControl Class for Data Binding*

Name	Description
ItemsSource	Points to the collection that has all the objects that will be shown in the list.
DisplayMemberPath	Identifies the property that will be used to create the display text for each item.
ItemTemplate	Accepts a data template that will be used to create the visual appearance of each item. This property is far more powerful than DisplayMemberPath, and you'll learn how to use it in Chapter 17.

At this point, you're probably wondering exactly what type of collections you can stuff in the ItemSource property. Happily, you can use just about anything. All you need is support for the IEnumerable interface, which is provided by arrays, all types of collections, and many more specialized objects that wrap groups of items. However, the support you get from a basic IEnumerable interface is limited to read-only binding. If you want to edit the collection (for example, you want to allow inserts and deletions), you need a bit more infrastructure, as you'll see shortly.

Displaying and Editing Collection Items

Consider the window shown in Figure 16-8, which shows a list of products. When you choose a product, the information for that product appears in the bottom section of the window, where you can edit it. (In this example, a GridSplitter lets you adjust the space given to the top and bottom portions of the window.)

To create this example, you need to begin by building your data access logic. In this case, the StoreDB.GetProducts() method retrieves the list of all the products in the database using the GetProducts stored procedure. A Product object is created for each record and added to a generic List collection. (You could use any collection here—for example, an array or a weakly typed ArrayList would work equivalently.)

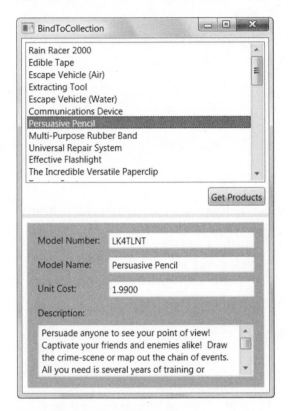

Figure 16-8. *A list of products*

Here's the GetProducts() code:

```
public List<Product> GetProducts()
{
    SqlConnection con = new SqlConnection(connectionString);
    SqlCommand cmd = new SqlCommand("GetProducts", con);
    cmd.CommandType = CommandType.StoredProcedure;

    List<Product> products = new List<Product>();
    try
    {
        con.Open();
        SqlDataReader reader = cmd.ExecuteReader();
        while (reader.Read())
        {
```

```
        // Create a Product object that wraps the
        // current record.
        Product product = new Product((string)reader["ModelNumber"],
          (string)reader["ModelName"], (decimal)reader["UnitCost"],
          (string)reader["Description"], (string)reader["CategoryName"],
          (string)reader["ProductImage"]);

        // Add to collection
        products.Add(product);
    }
}
finally
{
    con.Close();
}
return products;
}
```

When the Get Products button is clicked, the event handling code calls the GetProducts() method and supplies it as the ItemsSource for list. The collection is also stored as a member variable in the window class for easier access elsewhere in your code.

```
private List<Product> products;

private void cmdGetProducts_Click(object sender, RoutedEventArgs e)
{
    products = App.StoreDB.GetProducts();
    lstProducts.ItemsSource = products;
}
```

This successfully fills the list with Product objects. However, the list doesn't know how to display a product object, so it will simply call the ToString() method. Because this method hasn't been overridden in the Product class, this has the unimpressive result of showing the fully qualified class name for every item (see Figure 16-9).

You have three options to solve this problem:

- Set the DisplayMemberPath property of the list. For example, set this to ModelName to get the result shown in Figure 16-9.

- Override the ToString() method to return more useful information. For example, you could return a string with the model number and model name of each item. This approach gives you a way to show more than one property in the list (for example, it's great for combining the FirstName and LastName property in a Customer class). However, you still don't have much control over how the data is presented.

- Supply a data template. This way, you can show any arrangement of property values (and along with fixed text). You'll learn how to use this trick in Chapter 17.

CHAPTER 16 ■ DATA BINDING   519

Once you've decided how to display information in the list, you're ready to move on to the second challenge: displaying the details for the currently selected item in the grid that appears below the list. You could handle this challenge by responding to the SelectionChanged event and manually changing the data context of the grid, but there's a quicker approach that doesn't require any code. You simply need to set a binding expression for the Grid.DataContent property that pulls the selected Product object out of the list, as shown here:

```
<Grid DataContext="{Binding ElementName=lstProducts, Path=SelectedItem}">
  ...
</Grid>
```

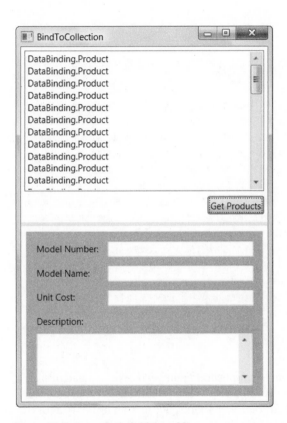

Figure 16-9. *An unhelpful bound list*

When the window first appears, nothing is selected in the list. The ListBox.SelectedItem property is null, and therefore the Grid.DataContext is too, and no information appears. As soon as you select an item, the data context is set to the corresponding object, and all the information appears.

If you try this example, you'll be surprised to see that it's already fully functional. You can edit product items, navigate away (using the list), and then return to see that your edits were successfully committed. In fact, you can even change a value that affects the display text in the list. If you modify the model name and tab to another control, the corresponding entry in the list is refreshed automatically. (Experienced developers will recognize this as a frill that Windows Forms applications lacked.)

■ **Tip** To prevent a field from being edited, set the IsLocked property of the text box to true or, better yet, use a read-only control like a TextBlock.

MASTER-DETAILS DISPLAY

As you've seen, you can bind other elements to the SelectedItem property of your list to show more details about the currently selected item. Interestingly, you can use a similar technique to build a master-details display of your data. For example, you can create a window that shows a list of categories and a list of products. When the user chooses a category in the first list, you can show just the products that belong to that category in the second list.

To pull this off, you need to have a *parent* data object that provides a collection of related *child* data objects through a property. For example, you could build a Category product that provides a property named Category.Products with the products that belong to that category. (In fact, you can find an example of a Category class that's designed like this in Chapter 18.) You can then build a master-details display with two lists. Fill your first list with Category objects. To show the related products, bind your second list—the list that displays products—to the SelectedItem.Products property of the first list. This tells the second list to grab the current Category object, extract its collection of linked Product objects, and display them.

You can find an example that uses related data in Chapter 18, with a TreeView that shows a categorized list of products. You'll see two versions of the example—one that uses Category and Product objects, and one that uses the ADO.NET DataRelation object.

Of course, to complete this example, from an application perspective you'll need to supply some code. For example, you might need an UpdateProducts() method that accepts your collection or products and executes the appropriate statements. Because an ordinary .NET object doesn't provide any change tracking, this is a situation where you might want to consider using the ADO.NET DataSet (as described a little later in this chapter). Alternatively, you might want to force users to update records one at a time. (One option is to disable the list when text is modified in a text box and force the user to then cancel the change by clicking Cancel or apply it immediately by clicking Update.)

Inserting and Removing Collection Items

One limitation of the previous example is that it won't pick up changes you make to the collection. It notices changed Product objects, but it won't update the list if you add a new item or remove one through code.

For example, imagine you add a Delete button that executes this code:

```
private void cmdDeleteProduct_Click(object sender, RoutedEventArgs e)
{
    products.Remove((Product)lstProducts.SelectedItem);
}
```

The deleted item is removed from the collection, but it remains stubbornly visible in the bound list.

To enable collection change tracking, you need to use a collection that implements the INotifyCollectionChanged interface. Most generic collections don't, including the List collection used in the current example. In fact, WPF includes a single collection that uses INotifyCollectionChanged: the ObservableCollection class.

■**Note** If you have an object model that you're porting over from the Windows Forms world, you can use the Windows Forms equivalent of ObservableCollection, which is BindingList. The BindingList collection implements IBindingList instead of INotifyCollectionChanged, which includes a ListChanged event that plays the same role as the INotifyCollectionChanged.CollectionChanged event. In addition, you can derive from BindingList to gain additional features for sorting and item creation in the Windows Forms DataGridView control.

You can derive a custom collection from ObservableCollection to customize the way it works, but that's not necessary. In the current example, it's enough to replace the List<Product> object with an ObservableCollection<Product>, as shown here:

```
public List<Product> GetProducts()
{
    SqlConnection con = new SqlConnection(connectionString);
    SqlCommand cmd = new SqlCommand("GetProducts", con);
    cmd.CommandType = CommandType.StoredProcedure;

    ObservableCollection<Product> products = new ObservableCollection<Product>();
    ...
```

The return type can be left as List<Product>, because the ObservableCollection class derives from the List class. To make this example just a bit more generic, you could use ICollection<Product> for the return type, because the ICollection interface has all the members you need to use.

Now, if you remove or add an item programmatically, the list is refreshed accordingly. Of course, it's still up to you to create the data access code that takes place before the collection is modified—for example, the code that removes the product record from the back-end database.

Binding to the ADO.NET Objects

All the features you've learned about with custom objects also work with the ADO.NET disconnected data objects.

For example, you could create the same user interface you see in Figure 16-9 but use the DataSet, DataTable, and DataRow on the back end, rather than the custom Product class and the ObservableCollection.

To try it, start by considering a version of the GetProducts() method that extracts the same data but packages it into a DataTable:

```
public DataTable GetProducts()
{
    SqlConnection con = new SqlConnection(connectionString);
    SqlCommand cmd = new SqlCommand("GetProducts", con);
    cmd.CommandType = CommandType.StoredProcedure;
    SqlDataAdapter adapter = new SqlDataAdapter(cmd);
    DataSet ds = new DataSet();
    adapter.Fill(ds, "Products");
    return ds.Tables[0];
}
```

You can retrieve this DataTable and bind it to the list in almost the same way you did with the ObservableCollection. The only difference is that you can't bind directly to the DataTable itself. Instead, you need to go through an intermediary known as the DataView. Although you can create a DataView by hand, every DataTable has a ready-made DataView object available through the DataTable.DefaultView property.

■**Note** This limitation is nothing new. Even in a Windows Forms application, all DataTable data binding goes through a DataView. The difference is that the Windows Forms universe can conceal this fact. It allows you to write code that appears to bind directly to a DataTable, when in reality it uses the DataView that's provided by the DataTable.DefaultView property.

Here's the code you need:

```
private DataTable products;

private void cmdGetProducts_Click(object sender, RoutedEventArgs e)
{
    products = App.StoreDB.GetProducts();
    lstProducts.ItemsSource = products.DefaultView;
}
```

Now the list will create a separate entry for each DataRow object in the DataTable.Rows collection. To determine what content is shown in the list, you need to set DisplayMember-Path property with the name of the field you want to show or use a data template (as described in Chapter 17).

The nice aspect of this example is that once you've changed the code that fetches your data, you don't need to make any more modifications. When an item is selected in the list, the Grid underneath grabs the selected item for its data context. The markup you used with the ProductList collection still works, because the property names of the Product class match the field names of the DataRow.

Another nice feature in this example is that you don't need to take any extra steps to implement change notifications. That's because the DataView class implements the IBindingList interface, which allows it to notify the WPF infrastructure if a new DataRow is added or an existing one is removed.

However, you do need to be a little careful when removing a DataRow object. It might occur to you to use code like this to delete the currently selected record:

```
products.Rows.Remove((DataRow)lstProducts.SelectedItem);
```

This code is wrong on two counts. First, the selected item in the list isn't a DataRow object—it's a thin DataRowView wrapper that's provided by the DataView. Second, you probably don't want to remove your DataRow from the collection of rows in the table. Instead, you probably want to mark it as deleted so that when you commit the changes to the database, the corresponding record is removed.

Here's the correct code, which gets the selected DataRowView, uses its Row property to find the corresponding DataRow object, and calls its Delete() method to mark the row for upcoming deletion:

```
((DataRowView)lstProducts.SelectedItem).Row.Delete();
```

At this point, the scheduled-to-be-deleted DataRow disappears from the list, even though it's technically still in the DataTable.Rows collection. That's because the default filtering settings in the DataView hide all deleted records. You'll learn more about filtering in Chapter 17.

Binding to a LINQ Expression

One of the key reasons to prefer .NET 3.5 over .NET 3.0 is its support for Language Integrated Query (LINQ), which is an all-purpose query syntax that works across a variety of data sources and is closely integrated with the C# language. LINQ works with any data source that has a LINQ provider. Using the support that's included with .NET 3.5, you can use similarly structured LINQ queries to retrieve data from an in-memory collection, an XML file, or a SQL Server database. And as with other query languages, LINQ allows you to apply filtering, sorting, grouping, and transformations to the data you retrieve.

Although LINQ is somewhat outside the scope of this chapter, you can learn a lot from a simple example. For example, imagine you have a collection of Product objects, named *products*, and you want to create a second collection that contains only those products that exceed $100 in cost. Using procedural code, you can write something like this:

```
// Get the full list of products.
List<Product> products = App.StoreDB.GetProducts();

// Create a second collection with matching products.
List<Product> matches = new List<Product>();
foreach (Product product in products)
{
    if (product.UnitCost >= 100)
    {
        matches.Add(product);
    }
}
```

Using LINQ, you can use the following *expression*, which is far more concise:

```
// Get the full list of products.
List<Product> products = App.StoreDB.GetProducts();

// Create a second collection with matching products.
IEnumerable<Product> matches = from product in products
        where product.UnitCost >= 100
        select product;
```

This example uses LINQ to Collections, which means it uses a LINQ expression to query the data in an in-memory collection. LINQ expressions use a set of new language keywords, including from, in, where, and select. These LINQ keywords are a genuine part of the C# language.

■Note A full discussion of LINQ is beyond the scope of this book. (For a detailed treatment, refer to the LINQ developer center at `http://msdn.microsoft.com/data/ref/linq` or the huge catalog of LINQ examples at `http://msdn2.microsoft.com/en-us/vcsharp/aa336746.aspx`.)

LINQ revolves around the IEnumerable<T> interface. No matter what data source you use, every LINQ expression returns some object that implements IEnumerable<T>. Because IEnumerable<T> extends IEnumerable, you can bind it in a WPF window just as you bind an ordinary collection:

```
lstProducts.ItemsSource = matches;
```

That said, there are a few quirks worth considering. The following sections give you the details.

Converting IEnumerable<T> to an Ordinary Collection

Unlike ObservableCollection and the DataTable classes, the IEnumerable<T> interface does not provide a way to add or remove items. If you need this capability, you need to first convert your IEnumerable<T> object into an array or List collection using the ToArray() or ToList() method.

Here's an example that uses ToList() to convert the result of a LINQ query (shown previously) into a strongly typed List collection of Product objects:

```
List<Product> productMatches = matches.ToList();
```

■Note ToList() is an extension method, which means it's defined in a different class from the one in which is used. Technically, ToList() is defined in the System.Linq.Enumerable helper class, and it's available to all IEnumerable<T> objects. However, it won't be available if the Enumerable class isn't in scope, which means the code shown here will not work if you haven't imported the System.Linq namespace.

The ToList() method causes the LINQ expression to be evaluated immediately. The end result is an ordinary collection, which you can deal with in all the usual ways. For example, you can wrap it in an ObservableCollection to get notification events, so any changes you make are reflected in bound controls immediately:

```
ObservableCollection<Product> productMatchesTracked =
  new ObservableCollection<Product>(productMatches);
```

You can then bind the productMatchesTracked collection to a control in your window.

Deferred Execution

LINQ uses *deferred execution*. Contrary to what you might expect, the result of a LINQ expression (such as the matches object in the previous example) isn't a straightforward collection. Instead, it's a specialized LINQ object that has the ability to fetch the data when you need it, rather than when the LINQ expression is created.

In this example, the matches object is an instance of the WhereIterator class, which is a private class that's nested inside the System.Linq.Enumerable class:

```
matches = from product in products
          where product.UnitCost >= 100
          select product;
```

Depending on the specific query you use, a LINQ expression might return a different object. For example, a union expression that combines data from two different collections would return an instance of the private UnionIterator class. Or, if you simplify the query by removing the where clause, you'll wind up with a simple SelectIterator. You don't actually need to know the specific iterator class that your code uses because you interact with the results through the IEnumerable<T> interface. (But if you're curious, you can determine the object type at runtime by hovering over the appropriate variable in Visual Studio while in break mode.)

The LINQ iterator objects add an extra layer between defining a LINQ expression and executing it. As soon as you iterate over a LINQ iterator like WhereIterator, it retrieves the data it needs. For example, if you write a foreach block that moves through the matches collection, this action forces the LINQ expression to be evaluated. The same thing happens when you bind an IEnumerable<T> object to a WPF window, in which case the WPF data binding infrastructure iterates over its contents.

■**Note** There's no technical reason why LINQ *needs* to use deferred execution, but there are many reasons why it's a good approach. In many cases, it allows LINQ to use performance optimization techniques that wouldn't otherwise be possible. For example, when using database relationships with LINQ to SQL, you can avoid loading related data that you don't actually use. Deferred execution also allows optimizations when you create LINQ queries that act on top of other LINQ queries.

DEFERRED EXECUTION AND LINQ TO SQL

It's important to understand deferred execution when you're using a data source that may not be available. In the examples you've seen so far, the LINQ expression acts on an in-memory collection, so it's not important (at least to the application developer) to know exactly when the expression is evaluated. However, this isn't the case when you're using LINQ to SQL to perform a just-in-time query against the database. In this situation, enumerating over the IEnumerable<T> results object causes .NET to establish a database connection and execute a query. This is obviously a risky move—if the database server isn't available or can't respond, an exception will occur when you least expect it. For this reason, it's common to use LINQ expressions in two more limited ways:

- After you've retrieved the data (using ordinary data access code), use LINQ to Collections to filter the results. This is handy if you need to provide a variety of different views on the same set of results. This is the approach demonstrated in this section (and in the downloadable examples for this chapter).

- Use LINQ to SQL to get the data you need. This saves you from writing the low-level data access code. Use the ToList() method to force the query to be executed immediately, and return an ordinary collection.

It's generally not a good idea to create a database component that uses LINQ to SQL and returns the IEnumerable<T> result object from a database query. If you allow this, you lose control over when the query will be executed and how potential errors will be handled. (You also lose control over how many times the query will be executed, because the LINQ expression will be re-evaluated every time you iterate over the collection or bind it to a control. Bind the same data to several different controls, and you've just created unnecessary extra work for your database server.)

LINQ to SQL is a significant topic of its own. It provides a flexible, SQL-free way to fetch data from a database and place it into custom objects you've designed. (The cost is learning the LINQ syntax and yet another data access model.) Currently, LINQ to SQL supports SQL Server only. If you're interested in trying it, start with the detailed overview at `http://msdn2.microsoft.com/en-us/library/bb425822.aspx`, or consider a dedicated book about LINQ, such as *Pro LINQ*.

Data Conversion

In an ordinary binding, the information travels from the source to the target without any change. This seems logical, but it's not always the behavior you want. Often, your data source might use a low-level representation that you don't want to display directly in your user interface. For example, you might have numeric codes you want to replace with human-readable strings, numbers that need to be cut down to size, dates that need to be displayed in a long format, and so on. If so, you need a way to convert these values into the right display form. And if you're using a two-way binding, you also need to do the converse—take user-supplied data and convert it to a representation suitable for storage in the appropriate data object.

Fortunately, WPF allows you do to both by creating (and using) a *value converter* class. The value converter is responsible for converting the source data just before it's displayed in the target and (in the case of a two-way binding) converting the new target value just before it's applied back to the source.

■Note This approach to conversion is similar to the way data binding worked in the world of Windows Forms with the Format and Parse binding events. The difference is that in a Windows Forms application, you could code this logic anywhere—you simply needed to attach both events to the binding. In WPF, this logic must be encapsulated in a value converter class, which makes for easier reuse.

Value converters are an extremely useful piece of the WPF data binding puzzle. They can be used in several useful ways:

- **To format data to a string representation.** For example, you can convert a number to a currency string. This is the most obvious use of value converters, but it's certainly not the only one.

- **To create a specific type of WPF object.** For example, you could read a block of binary data and create a BitmapImage object that can be bound to an Image element.

- **To conditionally alter a property in an element based on the bound data.** For example, you might create a value converter that changes the background color of an element to highlight values in a specific range.

In the following sections, you'll consider an example of each of these approaches.

Formatting Strings with a Value Converter

Value converters are the perfect tool for formatting numbers that need to be displayed as text. For example, consider the Product.UnitCost property in the previous example. It's stored as a decimal, and as a result, when it's displayed in a text box, you'll see values like 3.9900. Not only does this display format show more decimal places than you'd probably like, it also leaves out the currency symbol. A more intuitive representation would be the currency-formatted value $3.99, as shown in Figure 16-10.

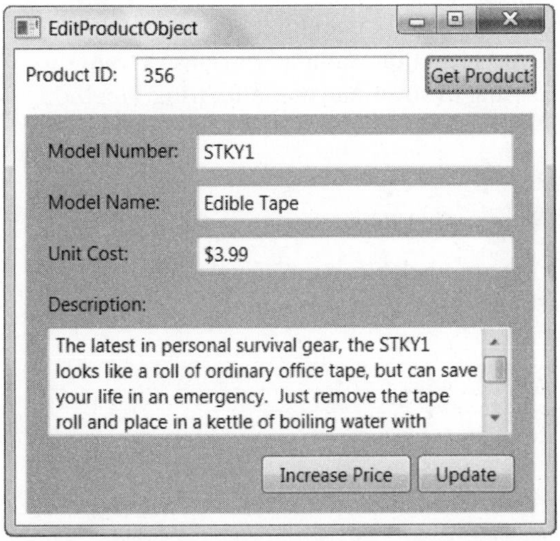

Figure 16-10. *Displaying formatted currency values*

To create a value converter, you need to take four steps:

1. Create a class that implements IValueConverter.

2. Add the ValueConversion attribute to the class declaration, and specify the destination and target data types.

3. Implement a Convert() method that changes data from its original format to its display format.

4. Implement a ConvertBack() method that does the reverse and changes a value from display format to its native format.

Figure 16-11 shows how it works.

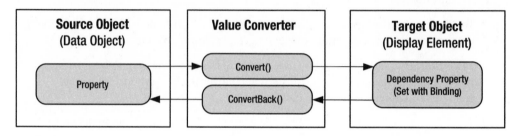

Figure 16-11. *Converting bound data*

In the case of the decimal-to-currency conversion, you can use the Decimal.ToString() method to get the formatted string representation you want. You simply need to specify the currency format string "C", as shown here:

```
string currencyText = decimalPrice.ToString("C");
```

This code uses the culture settings that apply to the current thread. A computer that's configured for the English (United States) region runs with a locale of en-US and displays currencies with the dollar sign ($). A computer that's configured for another local might display a different currency symbol. If this isn't the result you want (for example, you always want the dollar sign to appear), you can specify a culture using the overload of the ToString() method shown here:

```
CultureInfo culture = new CultureInfo("en-US");
string currencyText = decimalPrice.ToString("C", culture);
```

You can learn about all the format strings that are available in the Visual Studio help. However, Table 16-5 and Table 16-6 show some of the most common options you'll use for numeric and date values, respectively.

Table 16-5. *Format Strings for Numeric Data*

Type	Format String	Example
Currency	C	$1,234.50. Parentheses indicate negative values: ($1,234.50). The currency sign is locale-specific.
Scientific (Exponential)	E	1.234.50E+004.
Percentage	P	45.6%.
Fixed Decimal	F?	Depends on the number of decimal places you set. F3 formats values like 123.400. F0 formats values like 123.

Table 16-6. *Format Strings for Times and Dates*

Type	Format String	Format
Short Date	d	M/d/yyyy For example: 10/30/2008
Long Date	D	dddd, MMMM dd, yyyy For example: Wednesday, January 30, 2008
Long Date and Short Time	f	dddd, MMMM dd, yyyy HH:mm aa For example: Wednesday, January 30, 2008 10:00 AM
Long Date and Long Time	F	dddd, MMMM dd, yyyy HH:mm:ss aa For example: Wednesday, January 30, 2008 10:00:23 AM
ISO Sortable Standard	s	yyyy-MM-dd HH:mm:ss For example: 2008-01-30 10:00:23
Month and Day	M	MMMM dd For example: January 30
General	G	M/d/yyyy HH:mm:ss aa (depends on locale-specific settings) For example: 10/30/2008 10:00:23 AM

Converting from the display format back to the number you want is a little trickier. The Parse() and TryParse() methods of the Decimal type are logical choices to do the work, but ordinarily they can't handle strings that include currency symbols. The solution is to use an overloaded version of the Parse() or TryParse() method that accepts a System.Globalization.NumberStyles value. If you supply NumberStyles.Any, you'll be able to successfully strip out the currency symbol, if it exists.

Here's the complete code for the value converter that deals with price values like the Product.UnitCost property:

```
[ValueConversion(typeof(decimal), typeof(string))]
public class PriceConverter : IValueConverter
{
    public object Convert(object value, Type targetType, object parameter,
      CultureInfo culture)
    {
        decimal price = (decimal)value;
        return price.ToString("C", culture);
    }
```

```
    public object ConvertBack(object value, Type targetType, object parameter,
      CultureInfo culture)
    {
        string price = value.ToString(culture);

        decimal result;
        if (Decimal.TryParse(price, NumberStyles.Any, culture, out result))
        {
            return result;
        }
        return value;
    }
}
```

To put this converter into action, you need to begin by mapping your project namespace to an XML namespace prefix you can use in your markup. Here's an example that uses the namespace prefix local and assumes your value converter is in the namespace DataBinding:

```
xmlns:local="clr-namespace:DataBinding"
```

Typically, you'll add this attribute to the <Window> tag that holds all your markup.

Now, you simply need to create an instance of the PriceConverter class and assign it to the Converter property of your binding. To do this, you need the more long-winded syntax shown here:

```
<TextBlock Margin="7" Grid.Row="2">Unit Cost:</TextBlock>
<TextBox Margin="5" Grid.Row="2" Grid.Column="1">
  <TextBox.Text>
    <Binding Path="UnitCost">
      <Binding.Converter>
        <local:PriceConverter></local:PriceConverter>
      </Binding.Converter>
    </Binding>
  </TextBox.Text>
</TextBox>
```

In many cases, the same converter is used for multiple bindings. In this case, it doesn't make sense to create an instance of the converter for each binding. Instead, create one converter object in the Resources collection, as shown here:

```
<Window.Resources>
  <local:PriceConverter x:Key="PriceConverter"></local:PriceConverter>
</Window.Resources>
```

Then, you can point to it in your binding using a StaticResource reference, as described in Chapter 11:

```
<TextBox Margin="5" Grid.Row="2" Grid.Column="1"
 Text={Binding Path=UnitCost, Converter={StaticResource PriceConverter}">
</TextBox>
```

Creating Objects with a Value Converter

Value converters are indispensable when you need to bridge the gap between the way data is stored in your classes and the way it's displayed in a window. For example, imagine you have picture data stored as a byte array in a field in a database. You could convert the binary data into a System.Windows.Media.Imaging.BitmapImage object and store that as part of your data object. However, this design might not be appropriate.

For example, you might need the flexibility to create more than one object representation of your image, possibly because your data library is used in both WPF applications and Windows Forms applications (which use the System.Drawing.Bitmap class instead). In this case, it makes sense to store the raw binary data in your data object and convert it to a WPF BitmapImage object using a value converter. (To bind it to a form in a Windows Forms application, you'd use the Format and Parse events of the System.Windows.Forms.Binding class.)

■**Tip** To convert a block of binary data into an image, you must first create a BitmapImage object and read the image data into a MemoryStream. Then, you can call the BitmapImage.BeginInit() method, set its StreamSource property to point to your MemoryStream, and call EndInit() to finish loading the image.

The Products table from the Store database doesn't include binary picture data, but it does include a ProductImage field that stores the file name of an associated product image. In this case, there's even more reason to delay creating the image object. First, the image might not be available depending on where the application's running. Second, there's no point in incurring the extra memory overhead storing the image unless it's going to be displayed.

The ProductImage field includes the file name but not the full path of an image file, which gives you the flexibility to put the image files in any suitable location. The value converter has the task of creating a URI that points to the image file based on the ProductImage field and the directory you want to use. The directory is stored using a custom property named ImageDirectory, which defaults to the current directory.

Here's the complete code for the ImagePathConverter that performs the conversion:

```
public class ImagePathConverter : IValueConverter
{
    private string imageDirectory = Directory.GetCurrentDirectory();
    public string ImageDirectory
    {
        get { return imageDirectory; }
        set { imageDirectory = value; }
    }

    public object Convert(object value, Type targetType, object parameter,
      System.Globalization.CultureInfo culture)
    {
        string imagePath = Path.Combine(ImageDirectory,
          (string)value);
        return new BitmapImage(new Uri(imagePath));
    }
```

```
    public object ConvertBack(object value, Type targetType, object parameter,
      System.Globalization.CultureInfo culture)
    {
        throw new NotSupportedException();
    }
}
```

To use this converter, begin by adding it to the Resources. In this example, the ImageDirectory property is not set, which means the ImagePathConverter defaults to the current application directory:

```
<Window.Resources>
  <local:ImagePathConverter x:Key="ImagePathConverter"></local:ImagePathConverter>
</Window.Resources>
```

Now it's easy to create a binding expression that uses this value converter:

```
<Image Margin="5" Grid.Row="2" Grid.Column="1" Stretch="None"
 HorizontalAlignment="Left" Source=
 "{Binding Path=ProductImagePath, Converter={StaticResource ImagePathConverter}}">
</Image>
```

This works because the Image.Source property expects an ImageSource object, and the BitmapImage class derives from ImageSource.

Figure 16-12 shows the result.

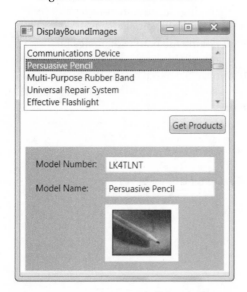

Figure 16-12. *Displaying bound images*

You might improve this example in a couple of ways. First, attempting to create a BitmapImage that points to a nonexistent file causes an exception, which you'll receive when setting the DataContext, ItemsSource, or Source property. Alternatively, you can add properties to the ImagePathConverter class that allow you to configure this behavior. For example, you might introduce a Boolean SuppressExceptions property. If set to true, you could catch exceptions in the Convert() method and then return the Binding.DoNothing value (which tells WPF to temporarily act as though no data binding is set). Or, you could add a DefaultImage property that takes a placeholder BitmapImage. The ImagePathConverter could then return the default image if an exception occurs.

You'll also notice that this converter supports only one-way conversion. That's because it's not possible to change the BitmapImage object and use that to update the image path. However, you could take an alternate approach. Rather than return a BitmapImage from the ImagePathConverter, you could simply return the fully qualified URI from the Convert() method, as shown here:

```
return new Uri(imagePath);
```

This works just as successfully, because the Image element uses a type converter to translate the Uri to the ImageSource object it really wants. If you take this approach, you could then allow the user to choose a new file path (perhaps using a TextBox that's set with the help of the OpenFileDialog class). You could then extract the file name in the ConvertBack() method and use that to update the image path that's stored in your data object.

Applying Conditional Formatting

Some of the most interesting value converters aren't designed to format data for presentation. Instead, they're intended to format some other appearance-related aspect of an element based on a data rule.

For example, imagine you want to flag high-priced items by giving them a different background color. You can easily encapsulate this logic with the following value converter:

```
public class PriceToBackgroundConverter : IValueConverter
{
    public decimal MinimumPriceToHighlight
    {
        get; set;
    }

    public Brush HighlightBrush
    {
        get; set;
    }

    public Brush DefaultBrush
    {
        get; set;
    }

    public object Convert(object value, Type targetType, object parameter,
      System.Globalization.CultureInfo culture)
    {
        decimal price = (decimal)value;
        if (price >= MinimumPriceToHighlight)
```

```
        return HighlightBrush;
    else
        return DefaultBrush;
}

public object ConvertBack(object value, Type targetType, object parameter,
    System.Globalization.CultureInfo culture)
{
    throw new NotSupportedException();
}
}
```

Once again, the value converter is carefully designed with reusability in mind. Rather than hard-coding the color highlights in the converter, they're specified in the XAML by the code that *uses* the converter:

```
<local:PriceToBackgroundConverter x:Key="PriceToBackgroundConverter"
  DefaultBrush="{x:Null}" HighlightBrush="Orange" MinimumPriceToHighlight="50">
</local:PriceToBackgroundConverter>
```

Brushes are used instead of colors so that you can create more advanced highlight effects using gradients and background images. And if you want to keep the standard, transparent background (so the background of the parent elements is used), just set the DefaultBrush or HighlightBrush property to null, as shown here.

Now all that's left is to use this converter to set the background of some element, like the Border that contains all the other elements:

```
<Border Background=
  "{Binding Path=UnitCost, Converter={StaticResource PriceToBackgroundConverter}}"
  ... >
```

OTHER WAYS TO APPLY CONDITIONAL FORMATTING

Using a custom IValueConverter is only one of the ways to apply conditional formatting based on your data object. You can also use data triggers in a style, style selector, and template selector, all of which are described in the next chapter. Each one of these approaches has its own advantages and disadvantages.

The IValueConverter approach works best when you need to set a single property in an element based on the bound data object. It's easy, and it's automatically synchronized. If you make changes to the bound data object, the linked property is changed immediately.

Data triggers are similarly straightforward, but they support only extremely simple logic that tests for equality. For example, a data trigger can apply formatting that applies to products in a specific category, but it can't apply formatting that kicks in when the price is greater than a specific minimum value. The key advantage of data triggers is that you can use them to apply certain types of formatting and selection effects without writing any code.

Style selectors and template selectors are the most powerful option. They allow you to change multiple properties in the target element at once and change the way items are presented in the list. However, they introduce additional complexity. Also, you need to add code that reapplies your styles and templates if the bound data changes.

Evaluating Multiple Properties

You can pull off one last trick with a value converter—evaluating several distinct fields and using them to create a single converted value. For example, you could use this to fuse together different pieces of information (such as a FirstName and LastName field), perform calculations (such as multiplying UnitPrice by UnitsInStock), and apply formatting that takes several details into consideration (such as highlighting all high-priced products in a specific category).

To perform this trick, you need two ingredients:

- A MultiBinding that defines the binding (instead of an ordinary Binding object)

- A converter that implements IMultiValueConverter (rather than IValueConverter)

The MultiBinding groups a sequence of Binding objects. Here's an example where a MultiBinding uses two properties in the data object:

```
<TextBlock>Total Stock Value: </TextBlock>
<TextBox>
  <TextBox.Text>
    <MultiBinding Converter="{StaticResource ValueInStockConverter}">
      <Binding Path="UnitCost"></Binding>
      <Binding Path="UnitsInStock"></Binding>
    </MultiBinding>
  </TextBox.Text>
</TextBox>
```

The IMultiValueConverter interface defines similar Convert() and ConvertBack() methods as the IValueConverter interface. The main difference is that you're provided with an array of values rather than a single value. These values are placed in the same order that they're defined in your markup. Thus, in the previous example you can expect UnitCost to appear first, followed by UnitsInStock.

Here's the code for the ValueInStockConverter:

```
public class ValueInStockConverter : IMultiValueConverter
{
    public object Convert(object[] values, Type targetType, object parameter,
      System.Globalization.CultureInfo culture)
    {
        // Return the total value of all the items in stock.
        decimal unitCost = (decimal)values[0];
        int unitsInStock = (int)values[1];
        return unitCost * unitsInStock;
    }

    public object[] ConvertBack(object value, Type[] targetTypes,
      object parameter, System.Globalization.CultureInfo culture)
    {
        throw new NotSupportedException();
    }
}
```

Validation

Another key ingredient in any two-binding scenario is *validation*—in other words, logic that catches incorrect values and refuses them. You can build validation directly into your controls (for example, by responding to input in the text box and refusing invalid characters), but this low-level approach limits your flexibility.

Fortunately, WPF provides a validation feature that works closely with the data binding system you've explored. Validation gives you two more options to catch invalid values:

- **You can raise errors in your data object.** To notify WPF of an error, simply throw an exception from a property set procedure. Ordinarily, WPF ignores any exceptions that are thrown when setting a property, but you can configure it to show a more helpful visual indication. Another option is to implement the IDataErrorInfo interface in your data class, which gives you the ability to indicate errors without throwing exceptions.

- **You can define validation at the binding level.** This gives you the flexibility to use the same validation regardless of the input control. Even better, because you define your validation in a distinct class, you can easily reuse it with multiple bindings that store similar types of data.

In general, you'll use the first approach if your data objects already have hardwired validation logic in their property set procedures and you want to take advantage of that logic. You'll use the second approach when you're defining validation logic for the first time and you want to reuse it in different contexts and with different controls. However, some developers choose to use both techniques. They use validation in the data object to defend against a small set of fundamental errors and use validation in the binding to catch a wider set of user-entry errors.

■Note Validation applies only when a value from the target is being used to update the source—in other words, when you're using a TwoWay or OneWayToSource binding.

Validation in the Data Object

Some developers build error checking directly into their data objects. For example, here's a modified version of the Product.UnitPrice property that disallows negative numbers:

```
public decimal UnitCost
{
    get { return unitCost; }
    set
    {
        if (value < 0)
            throw new ArgumentException("UnitCost cannot be negative.");
        else
        {
            unitCost = value;
            OnPropertyChanged(new PropertyChangedEventArgs("UnitCost"));
```

```
      }
   }
}
```

The validation logic shown in this example prevents negative price values, but it doesn't give the user any feedback about the problem. As you learned earlier, WPF quietly ignores data binding errors that occur when setting or getting properties. In this case, the user won't have any way of knowing that the update has been rejected. In fact, the incorrect value will remain in the text box—it just won't be applied to the bound data object. To improve this situation, you need the help of the ExceptionValidationRule, which is described next.

DATA OBJECTS AND VALIDATION

Whether or not it's a good approach to place validation logic in a data object is a matter of never-ending debate.

This approach has some advantages—for example, it catches all errors all the time, whether they occur because of an invalid user edit, a programming mistake, or a calculation that's based on other invalid data. However, this has the disadvantage of making the data objects more complex and moving validation code that's intended for an application's front end deeper into the back-end data model.

If applied carelessly, property validation can inadvertently rule out perfectly reasonable uses of the data object. They can also lead to inconsistencies and actually *compound* data errors. (For example, it might not make sense for the UnitsInStock to hold a value of −10, but if the underlying database stores this value, you might still want to create the corresponding Product object so you can edit it in your user interface.) Sometimes, problems like these are solved by creating yet another layer of objects—for example, in a complex system developers might build a rich business object model overtop the bare-bones data object layer.

In the current example, the StoreDB and Product classes are designed to be part of a back-end data access component. In this context, the Product class is simply a glorified package that lets you pass information from one layer of code to another. For that reason, validation code really doesn't belong in the Product class.

The ExceptionValidationRule

The ExceptionValidationRule is a prebuilt validation rule that tells WPF to report all exceptions. To use the ExceptionValidationRule, you must add it to the Binding.ValidationRules collection, as shown here:

```
<TextBox Margin="5" Grid.Row="2" Grid.Column="1">
  <TextBox.Text>
    <Binding Path="UnitCost">
      <Binding.Converter>
        <local:PriceConverter></local:PriceConverter>
      </Binding.Converter>
      <Binding.ValidationRules>
        <ExceptionValidationRule></ExceptionValidationRule>
      </Binding.ValidationRules>
    </Binding>
  </TextBox.Text>
</TextBox>
```

This example uses both a value converter and a validation rule. Usually, validation is performed before the value is converted, but the ExceptionValidationRule is a special case. It catches exceptions that occur at any point, including exceptions that occur if the edited value can't be cast to the correct data type, exceptions that are thrown by the property setter, and exceptions that are thrown by the value converter.

So, what happens when validation fails? Validation errors are recorded using the attached properties of the System.Windows.Controls.Validation class. For each failed validation rule, WPF takes three steps:

- It sets the attached Validation.HasError property to true on the bound element (in this case, the TextBox control).

- It creates a ValidationError object with the error details (as returned from the ValidationRule.Validate() method) and adds that to the attached Validation.Errors collection.

- If the Binding.NotifyOnValidationError property is set to true, WPF raises the Validation.Error attached event on the element.

The visual appearance of your bound control also changes when an error occurs. WPF automatically switches the template that a control uses when its Validation.HasError property is true to the template that's defined by the attached Validation.ErrorTemplate property. In a text box, the new template changes the outline of the box to a thin red border.

In most cases, you'll want to augment the error indication in some way and give specific information about the error that caused the problem. You can use code that handles the Error event, or you can supply a custom control template that provides a different visual indication. But before you tackle either of these tasks, it's worth considering two other ways WPF allows you to catch errors—by using IDataErrorInfo in your data objects and by writing custom validation rules.

The DataErrorValidationRule

Many object-orientation purists prefer not to raise exceptions to indicate user input errors. There are several possible reasons, including the following: a user input error isn't an exceptional condition, error conditions may depend on the interaction between multiple property values, and it's sometimes worthwhile to hold on to incorrect values for further processing rather than reject them outright.

In the Windows Forms world, developers could use the IDataErrorInfo interface (from the System.ComponentModel namespace) to avoid exceptions but still place the validation code in the data class. The IDataErrorInfo interface was originally designed to support grid-based display controls such as the DataGridView, but it also works as an all-purpose solution for reporting errors. Although IDataErrorInfo wasn't supported in the first release of WPF, it is supported in WPF 3.5.

The IDataErrorInfo interface requires two members: a string property named Error and a string indexer. The Error property provides an overall error string that describes the entire object (which could be something as simple as "Invalid Data"). The string indexer accepts a property name and returns the corresponding detailed error information. For example, if you pass "UnitCost" to the string indexer, you might receive a response such as "The UnitCost cannot be negative." The key idea here is that properties are set normally, without any fuss, and the indexer allows the user interface to check for invalid data. The error logic for the entire class is centralized in one place.

Here's a revised version of the Product class that implements IDataErrorInfo. Although you could use IDataErrorInfo to provide validation messages for a range of validation problems, this validation logic checks just one property—ModelNumber—for errors:

```
public class Product : INotifyPropertyChanged, IDataErrorInfo
{
    ...

    private string modelNumber;
    public string ModelNumber
    {
        get { return modelNumber; }
        set {
            modelNumber = value;
            OnPropertyChanged(new PropertyChangedEventArgs("ModelNumber"));
        }
    }

    // Error handling takes place here.
    public string this[string propertyName]
    {
        get
        {
            if (propertyName == "ModelNumber")
            {
                bool valid = true;
                foreach (char c in ModelNumber)
                {
                    if (!Char.IsLetterOrDigit(c))
                    {
                        valid = false;
                        break;
                    }
                }
                if (!valid)
                    return "The ModelNumber can only contain letters and numbers.";
            }
            return null;
        }
    }

    // WPF doesn't use this property.
    public string Error
    {
        get { return null; }
    }
}
```

To tell WPF to use the IDataErrorInfo interface, and use it to check for errors when a property is modified, you must add the DataErrorValidationRule to the collection of Binding.ValidationRules, as shown here:

```
<TextBox Margin="5" Grid.Column="1">
  <TextBox.Text>
    <Binding Path="ModelNumber">
      <Binding.ValidationRules>
        <DataErrorValidationRule></DataErrorValidationRule>
      </Binding.ValidationRules>
    </Binding>
  </TextBox.Text>
</TextBox>
```

Incidentally, you can combine both approaches by creating a data object that throws exceptions for some types of errors and uses IDataErrorInfo to report others. You just need to make sure you use both the ExceptionValidationRule and the DataErrorValidationRule.

Tip .NET 3.5 provides a shortcut. Rather than adding the ExceptionValidationRule to the binding, you can set the Binding.ValidatesOnExceptions property to true. Rather than adding the DataErrorValidationRule, you can set the Binding.ValidatesOnDataErrors property to true.

Custom Validation Rules

The approach for applying a custom validation rule is similar to applying a custom converter. You define a class that derives from ValidationRule (in the System.Windows.Controls namespace), and you override the Validate() method to perform your validation. If desired, you can add properties that accept other details that you can use to influence your validation (for example, a validation rule that examines text might include a Boolean CaseSensitive property).

Here's a complete validation rule that restricts decimal values to fall between some set minimum and maximum. By default, the minimum is set at 0, and the maximum is the largest number that will fit in the decimal data type, because this validation rule is intended for use with currency values. However, both these details are configurable through properties for maximum flexibility.

```
public class PositivePriceRule : ValidationRule
{
    private decimal min = 0;
    private decimal max = Decimal.MaxValue;

    public decimal Min
    {
        get { return min; }
        set { min = value; }
    }
```

```
public decimal Max
{
    get { return max; }
    set { max = value; }
}

public override ValidationResult Validate(object value,
  CultureInfo cultureInfo)
{
    decimal price = 0;

    try
    {
        if (((string)value).Length > 0)
            price = Decimal.Parse((string)value, NumberStyles.Any, culture);
    }
    catch
    {
        return new ValidationResult(false, "Illegal characters.");
    }

    if ((price < Min) || (price > Max))
    {
        return new ValidationResult(false,
          "Not in the range " + Min + " to " + Max + ".");
    }
    else
    {
        return new ValidationResult(true, null);
    }
}
}
```

Notice that the validation logic uses the overloaded version of the Decimal.Parse() method that accepts a value from the NumberStyles enumeration. That's because validation is always performed *before* conversion. If you've applied both the validator and the converter to the same field, you need to make sure that your validation will succeed if there's a currency symbol present. The success or failure of the validation logic is indicated by returning a ValidationResult object. The IsValid property indicates whether the validation succeeded, and if it didn't, the ErrorContent property provides an object that describes the problem. In this example, the error content is set to a string that will be displayed in the user interface, which is the most common approach.

Once you've perfected your validation rule, you're ready to attach it to an element by adding it to the Binding.ValidationRules collection. Here's an example that uses the PositivePriceRule and sets the Maximum at 999.99:

```
<TextBlock Margin="7" Grid.Row="2">Unit Cost:</TextBlock>
  <TextBox Margin="5" Grid.Row="2" Grid.Column="1">
```

```
        <TextBox.Text>
          <Binding Path="UnitCost">
            <Binding.ValidationRules>
              <local:PositivePriceRule Max="999.99" />
            </Binding.ValidationRules>
          </Binding>
        </TextBox.Text>
</TextBox>
```

Often, you'll define a separate validation rule object for each element that uses the same type of rule. That's because you might want to adjust the validation properties (such as the minimum and maximum in the PositivePriceRule) separately. If you know that you want to use *exactly* the same validation rule for more than one binding, you can define the validation rule as a resource and simply point to it in each binding using the StaticResource markup extension.

As you've probably gathered, the Binding.ValidationRules collection can take an unlimited number of rules. When the value is committed to the source, WPF checks each validation rule, in order. (Remember, a value in a text box is committed to the source when the text box loses focus, unless you specify otherwise with the UpdateSourceTrigger property.) If all the validation succeeds, WPF then calls the converter (if one exists) and applies the value to the source.

■**Note** If you add the PositivePriceRule followed by the ExceptionValidationRule, the PositivePriceRule will be evaluated first. It will capture errors that result from an out-of-range value. However, the ExceptionValidationRule will catch type-casting errors that result if you type an entry that can't be cast to a decimal value (such as a sequence of letters).

When you perform validation with the PositivePriceRule, the behavior is the same as when you use the ExceptionValidationRule—the text box is outlined in red, the HasError and Errors properties are set, and the Error event fires. To provide the user with some helpful feedback, you need to add a bit of code or customize the ErrorTemplate. You'll learn how to take care of both approaches in the following sections.

■**Tip** Custom validation rules can be extremely specific so that they target a specific constraint for a specific property or much more general so that they can be reused in a variety of scenarios. For example, you could easily create a custom validation rule that validates a string using a regular expression you specify, with the help of .NET's System.Text.RegularExpressions.Regex class. Depending on the regular expression you use, you could use this validation rule with a variety of pattern-based text data, such as email addresses, phone numbers, IP addresses, and ZIP codes.

Reacting to Validation Errors

In the previous example, the only indication the user receives about an error is a red outline around the offending text box. To provide more information, you can handle the Error event, which fires whenever an error is stored or cleared. However, you must first make sure you've set the Binding.NotifyOnValidationError property to true:

```
<Binding Path="UnitCost" NotifyOnValidationError="True">
```

The Error event is a routed event that uses bubbling, so you can handle the Error event for multiple controls by attaching an event handler in the parent container, as shown here:

```
<Grid Name="gridProductDetails" Validation.Error="validationError">
```

Here's the code that reacts to this event and displays a message box with the error information. (A less disruptive option would be to show a tooltip or display the error information somewhere else in the window.)

```
private void validationError(object sender, ValidationErrorEventArgs e)
{
    // Check that the error is being added (not cleared).
    if (e.Action == ValidationErrorEventAction.Added)
    {
        MessageBox.Show(e.Error.ErrorContent.ToString());
    }
}
```

The ValidationErrorEventArgs.Error property provides a ValidationError object that bundles together several useful details, including the exception that caused the problem (Exception), the validation rule that was violated (ValidationRule), the associated Binding object (BindingInError), and any custom information that the ValidationRule object has returned (ErrorContent).

If you're using custom validation rules, you'll almost certainly choose to place the error information in the ValidationError.ErrorContent property. If you're using the ExceptionValidationRule, the ErrorContent property will return the Message property of the corresponding exception. However, there's a catch. If an exception occurs because the data type cannot be cast to the appropriate value, the ErrorContent works as expected and reports the problem. However, if the property setter in the data object throws an exception, this exception is wrapped in a TargetInvocationException, and the ErrorContent provides the text from the TargetInvocationException.Message property, which is the much less helpful warning "Exception has been thrown by the target of an invocation."

Thus, if you're using your property setters to raise exceptions, you'll need to add code that checks the InnerException property of the TargetInvocationException. If it's not null, you can retrieve the original exception object and use its Message property instead of the ValidationError.ErrorContent property.

Getting a List of Exceptions

At certain times, you might want to get a list of all the outstanding errors in your current window (or a given container in that window). This task is relatively straightforward—all you need to do is walk through the element tree testing the Validation.HasError property of each element.

The following code routine demonstrates an example that specifically searches out invalid data in TextBox objects. It uses recursive code to dig down through the entire element hierarchy. Along the way, the error information is aggregated into a single message that's then displayed to the user.

```
private void cmdOK_Click(object sender, RoutedEventArgs e)
{
    string message;
    if (FormHasErrors(message))
    {
        // Errors still exist.
        MessageBox.Show(message);
    }
    else
    {
        // There are no errors. You can continue on to complete the task
        // (for example, apply the edit to the data source.).
    }
}

private bool FormHasErrors(out string message)
{
    StringBuilder sb = new StringBuilder();
    GetErrors(sb, gridProductDetails);
    message = sb.ToString();
    return message != "";
}

private void GetErrors(StringBuilder sb, DependencyObject obj)
{
    foreach (object child in LogicalTreeHelper.GetChildren(obj))
    {
        TextBox element = child as TextBox;
        if (element == null) continue;

        if (Validation.GetHasError(element))
        {
            sb.Append(element.Text + " has errors:\r\n");
            foreach (ValidationError error in Validation.GetErrors(element))
            {
                sb.Append("  " + error.ErrorContent.ToString());
                sb.Append("\r\n");
            }
```

```
        }
        // Check the children of this object for errors.
        GetErrors(sb, element);
      }
    }
}
```

In a more complete implementation, the FormHasErrors() method would probably create a collection of objects with error information. The cmdOK_Click() event handler would then be responsible for constructing an appropriate message.

Showing a Different Error Indicator

To get the most out of WPF validation, you'll want to create your own error template that flags errors in an appropriate way. At first glance, this seems like a fairly low-level way to go about reporting an error—after all, a standard control template gives you the ability to customize the composition of a control in minute detail. However, an error template isn't like an ordinary control template.

Error templates use the *adorner layer*, which is a drawing layer that exists just above ordinary window content. Using the adorner layer, you can add a visual embellishment to indicate an error without replacing the control template of the control underneath or changing the layout in your window. The standard error template for a text box works by adding a red Border element that floats just above the corresponding text box (which remains unchanged underneath). You can use an error template to add other details, like images, text, or some other sort of graphical detail that draws attention to the problem.

The following markup shows an example. It defines an error template that uses a green border and adds an asterisk next to the control with the invalid input. The template is wrapped in a style rule so that it's automatically applied to all the text boxes in the current window:

```
<Style TargetType="{x:Type TextBox}">
  <Setter Property="Validation.ErrorTemplate">
    <Setter.Value>
      <ControlTemplate>
        <DockPanel LastChildFill="True">
          <TextBlock DockPanel.Dock="Right" Foreground="Red"
           FontSize="14" FontWeight="Bold">*</TextBlock>
          <Border BorderBrush="Green" BorderThickness="1">
            <AdornedElementPlaceholder></AdornedElementPlaceholder>
          </Border>
        </DockPanel>
      </ControlTemplate>
    </Setter.Value>
  </Setter>
</Style>
```

The AdornedElementPlaceholder is the glue that makes this technique work. It represents the control itself, which exists in the element layer. By using the AdornedElementPlaceholder, you're able to arrange your content in relation to the text box underneath.

As a result, the border in this example is placed directly overtop of the text box, no matter what its dimensions are. The asterisk in this example is placed just to the right (as shown in Figure 16-13). Best of all, the new error template content is superimposed on top of the existing content without triggering any change in the layout of the original window. (In fact, if you're careless and include too much content in the adorner layer, you'll end up overwriting other portions of the window.)

Figure 16-13. *Flagging an error with an error template*

Tip If you want your error template to appear superimposed over the element (rather than positioned around it), you can place both your content and the AdornerElementPlaceholder in the same cell of a Grid. Alternatively, you can leave out the AdornerElementPlaceholder altogether, but then you lose the ability to position your content precisely in relation to the element underneath.

This error template still suffers from one problem—it doesn't provide any additional information about the error. To show these details, you need to extract them using data binding. One good approach is to take the error content of the first error and use it for tooltip text of your error indicator. Here's a template that does exactly that:

```
<ControlTemplate>
  <DockPanel LastChildFill="True">
    <TextBlock DockPanel.Dock="Right"
     Foreground="Red" FontSize="14" FontWeight="Bold"
     ToolTip="{Binding ElementName=adornerPlaceholder,
             Path=AdornedElement.(Validation.Errors)[0].ErrorContent}"
    >*</TextBlock>
```

```
  <Border BorderBrush="Green" BorderThickness="1">
    <AdornedElementPlaceholder Name="adornerPlaceholder">
    </AdornedElementPlaceholder>
  </Border>
 </DockPanel>
</ControlTemplate>
```

The Path of the binding expression is a little convoluted and bears closer examination. The source of this binding expression is the AdornedElementPlaceholder, which is defined in the control template:

```
ToolTip="{Binding ElementName=adornerPlaceholder, ...
```

The AdornedElementPlaceholder class provides a reference to the element underneath (in this case, the TextBox object with the error) through a property named AdornedElement:

```
ToolTip="{Binding ElementName=adornerPlaceholder,
         Path=AdornedElement ...
```

To retrieve the actual error, you need to check the Validation.Errors property of this element. However, you need to wrap the Validation.Errors property in parentheses to indicate that it's an attached property, rather than a property of the TextBox class:

```
ToolTip="{Binding ElementName=adornerPlaceholder,
         Path=AdornedElement.(Validation.Errors) ...
```

Finally, you need to use an indexer to retrieve the first ValidationError object from the collection and then extract its Error content property:

```
ToolTip="{Binding ElementName=adornerPlaceholder,
         Path=AdornedElement.(Validation.Errors)[0].ErrorContent}"
```

Now you can see the error message when you move the mouse over the asterisk.

Alternatively, you might want to show the error message in a ToolTip for the Border or TextBox itself so that the error message appears when the user moves the mouse over any portion of the control. You can perform this trick without the help of a custom error template—all you need is a trigger on the TextBox control that reacts when Validation.HasError becomes true and applies the ToolTip with the error message. Here's an example:

```
<Style TargetType="{x:Type TextBox}">
  ...
  <Style.Triggers>
    <Trigger Property="Validation.HasError" Value="True">
      <Setter Property="ToolTip"
       Value="{Binding RelativeSource={RelativeSource Self},
       Path=(Validation.Errors)[0].ErrorContent}" />
    </Trigger>
  </Style.Triggers>
</Style>
```

Figure 16-14 shows the result.

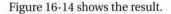

Figure 16-14. *Turning a validation error message into a tooltip*

The Last Word

This chapter took a thorough look at data binding. You learned how to create data binding expressions that draw information from other elements and custom objects and how to push changes back to the source. You also learned how to use change notification, bind entire collections, and bind to the ADO.NET disconnected data objects.

In many ways, WPF data binding is designed to be an all-purpose solution for automating the way that elements interact and mapping the object model of an application to its user interface. Although WPF applications are still new, those that exist today use data binding much more frequently and thoroughly than their Windows Forms counterparts. In WPF, data binding is much more than an optional frill, and every professional WPF developer needs to master it.

You haven't reached the end of your data exploration yet. You still have several topics to tackle. In the following two chapters, you'll build on the data binding basics you've learned here and tackle these new topics:

- **Data views.** In every application that uses data binding, there's a data view at work. Often, you can ignore this piece of background plumbing. But if you take a closer look, you can use it to write navigation logic and apply filtering and sorting.

- **Data templates.** If you want to really customize the information that's shown for each record in an ItemsControl like the ListBox, you need to use a data template. Doing so gives you the ability to combine fields; lay them out in a predetermined way; add formatting; and even throw in other shapes, elements, and controls.

- **Data providers.** Data providers are objects that make it easier to bind to certain data sources declaratively. WPF includes two data providers: one for easy display of XML data and one for binding to the data returned by an object. These providers are somewhat limited, but they're occasionally useful for quick, straightforward data binding scenarios.

- **Advanced data controls.** Although WPF isn't nearly as mature in this area as Windows Forms, the two staples of modern windows design—the ListView and TreeView—support data binding in a flexible and remarkably powerful way.

CHAPTER 17

■ ■ ■

Data Templates, Data Views, and Data Providers

In Chapter 16, you learned the essentials of WPF data binding—how to pull information out of an object and display it in a window, with little or no code. Along the way, you considered how to make that information editable, how to format it, how to convert it to the representation you need, and how to incorporate more advanced features such as validation. However, you still have more to learn.

In this chapter, you'll continue your exploration by tackling three subjects that will allow you to build better bound windows. First, you'll look at *data templates*, which let you customize the way each item is shown in an ItemsControl. Data templates are the secret to converting a basic list into a rich data presentation tool complete with custom formatting, picture content, and additional WPF controls. Once you've mastered data templates, you'll consider *data views*, which work behind the scenes to coordinate collections of bound data. Using data views, you can add navigation logic to implement filtering, sorting, and grouping. Finally, you'll end with a look at *data providers*, which allow you to pull information from a data source with less code.

Data Binding Redux

In most data binding scenarios, you aren't binding to a single object but to an entire collection or DataTable. Figure 17-1 shows a familiar example—a form with a list of products. When the user selects a product, its details appear on the right.

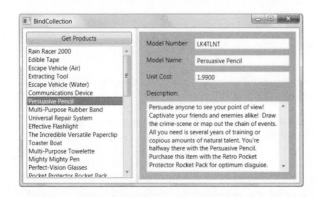

Figure 17-1. *Browsing a collection of products*

In Chapter 16, you learned to build exactly this sort of form. Here's a quick review of the basic steps:

1. First you need to create the list of items, which you can show in an ItemsControl. Set the DisplayMemberPath to indicate the property (or field) you want to show for each item in the list. This list shows the model name of each item:

```
<ListBox Name="lstProducts" DisplayMemberPath="ModelName"></ListBox>
```

2. To fill the list with data, set the ItemsSource property to your collection (or DataTable). Typically, you'll perform this step in code when your window loads or the user clicks a button. In this example, the ItemsControl is bound to an ObservableCollection of Product objects.

```
ObservableCollection<Product> products = App.StoreDB.GetProducts();
lstProducts.ItemsSource = products;
```

3. To show item-specific information, add as many elements as you need, each with a binding expression that identifies the property or field you want to display. In this example, each item in the collection is a Product object. Here's an example that shows the model number of an item by binding to the Product.ModelNumber property:

```
<TextBox Text="{Binding Path=ModelNumber}"></TextBox>
```

4. The easiest way to connect the item-specific elements to the currently selected item is to wrap them in a single container. Set the DataContext property of the container to refer to the selected item in the list:

```
<Grid DataContext="{Binding ElementName=lstProducts, Path=SelectedItem}">
```

So far, this is all review. However, what you haven't yet considered is how to tailor the list of items—how to filter it, sort it, and create a more detailed representation of each data item.

The last task is the one you'll consider first. In the previous series of steps, the Display-MemberPath property indicates the property of each data item that you want to show in the list. If you leave out the DisplayMemberPath, the list simply calls ToString() on each object to get its string representation. But what if you want to use a combination of properties from the bound object, lay them out in a specific way, or display a visual representation that's more sophisticated than a simple string? To use any of these techniques, you need to create a data template.

Data Templates

A *data template* is a chunk of XAML markup that defines how a bound data object should be displayed. Two types of controls support data templates:

- Content controls support data templates through the ContentTemplate property. The content template is used to display whatever you've placed in the Content property.

- List controls (controls that derive from ItemsControl) support data templates through the ItemTemplate property. This template is used to display each item from the collection (or each row from a DataTable) that you've supplied as the ItemsSource.

The list-based template feature is actually based on content control templates. That's because each item in a list is wrapped by a content control, such as ListBoxItem for the ListBox, ComboBoxItem for the ComboBox, and so on. Whatever template you specify for the ItemTemplate property of the list is used as the ContentTemplate of each item in the list.

So, what can you put inside a data template? It's actually quite simple. A data template is an ordinary block of XAML markup. Like any other block of XAML markup, the template can include any combination of elements. It should also include one or more data binding expressions that pull out the information that you want to display. (After all, if you don't include any data binding expressions, each item in the list will appear the same, which isn't very helpful.)

The best way to see how a data template works is to start with a basic list that doesn't use them. For example, consider this list box, which was shown previously:

```
<ListBox Name="lstProducts" DisplayMemberPath="ModelName"></ListBox>
```

You can get the same effect with this list box that uses a data template:

```
<ListBox Name="lstProducts">
  <ListBox.ItemTemplate>
    <DataTemplate>
      <TextBlock Text="{Binding Path=ModelName}"></TextBlock>
    </DataTemplate>
  </ListBox.ItemTemplate>
</ListBox>
```

When the list is bound to the collection of products (by setting the ItemsSource property), a single ListBoxItem is created for each Product. The ListBoxItem.Content property is set to the appropriate Product object, and the ListBoxItem.ContentTemplate is set to the data template shown earlier, which extracts the value from the Product.ModelName property and displays it in a TextBlock.

So far, the results are underwhelming. But now that you've switched to a data template, there's no limit to how you can creatively present your data. Here's an example that wraps each item in a rounded border, shows two pieces of information, and uses bold formatting to highlight the model number:

```
<ListBox Name="lstProducts" HorizontalContentAlignment="Stretch">
  <ListBox.ItemTemplate>
    <DataTemplate>
      <Border Margin="5" BorderThickness="1" BorderBrush="SteelBlue"
       CornerRadius="4">
        <Grid Margin="3">
          <Grid.RowDefinitions>
            <RowDefinition></RowDefinition>
            <RowDefinition></RowDefinition>
          </Grid.RowDefinitions>
          <TextBlock FontWeight="Bold"
           Text="{Binding Path=ModelNumber}"></TextBlock>
          <TextBlock Grid.Row="1"
           Text="{Binding Path=ModelName}"></TextBlock>
        </Grid>
      </Border>
```

```
      </DataTemplate>
    </ListBox.ItemTemplate>
  </ListBox>
```

When this list is bound, a separate Border object is created for each product. Inside the Border element is a Grid with two pieces of information, as shown in Figure 17-2.

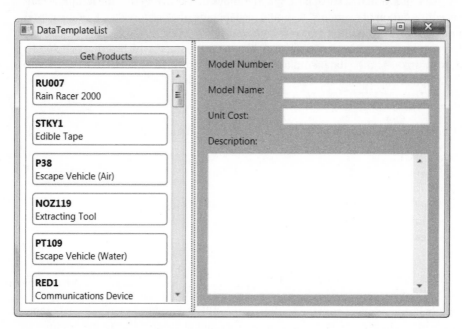

Figure 17-2. *A list that uses a data template*

■**Tip**   When using Grid objects to lay out individual items in a list, you may want to use the SharedSizeGroup property described in Chapter 4. You can apply the SharedSizeGroup property (with a descriptive group name) to individual rows or columns to ensure that those rows and columns are made the same size for every item. Chapter 18 includes an example that builds a rich list that combines text and image content using this approach.

Separating and Reusing Templates

Like styles, templates are often declared as a window or application resource rather than defined in the list where you use them. This separation is often clearer, especially if you use long, complex templates or multiple templates in the same control (as described in the next section). It also gives you the ability to reuse your templates in more than one list or content control if you want to present your data the same way in different places in your user interface.

To make this work, all you need to do is to define your data template in a resources collection and give it a key name (as described in Chapter 11). Here's an example that extracts the template shown in the previous example:

```
<Window.Resources>
  <DataTemplate x:Key="ProductDataTemplate">
    <Border Margin="5" BorderThickness="1" BorderBrush="SteelBlue"
     CornerRadius="4">
      <Grid Margin="3">
        <Grid.RowDefinitions>
          <RowDefinition></RowDefinition>
          <RowDefinition></RowDefinition>
        </Grid.RowDefinitions>
        <TextBlock FontWeight="Bold"
         Text="{Binding Path=ModelNumber}"></TextBlock>
        <TextBlock Grid.Row="1"
         Text="{Binding Path=ModelName}"></TextBlock>
      </Grid>
    </Border>
  </DataTemplate>
</Window.Resources>
```

Now you can use your data template using a StaticResource reference:

```
<ListBox Name="lstProducts" HorizontalContentAlignment="Stretch"
 ItemTemplate="{StaticResourceProductDataTemplate }"></ListBox>
```

You can use another interesting trick if you want to reuse the same data template in different types of controls automatically. You can set the DataTemplate.DataType property to identify the type of bound data for which your template should be used. For example, you could alter the previous example by removing the key and specifying that this template is intended for bound Product objects, no matter where they appear:

```
<Window.Resources>
  <DataTemplate DataType="{x:Type local:Product}">
  </DataTemplate>
</Window.Resources>
```

This assumes you've defined an XML namespace prefix named *local* and mapped it your project namespace.

Now this template will be used with any list or content control in this window that's bound to Product objects. You don't need to specify the ItemTemplate setting.

Note Data templates don't require data binding. In other words, you don't need to use the ItemsSource property to fill a template list. In the previous examples, you're free to add Product objects declaratively (in your XAML markup) or programmatically (by calling the ListBox.Items.Add() method). In both cases, the data template works in the same way.

More Advanced Templates

Data templates can be remarkably self-sufficient. Along with basic elements such as the TextBlock and data binding expressions, they can also use more sophisticated controls, attach event handlers, convert data to different representations, use animations, and so on.

It's worth considering a couple of quick examples that show how powerful data templates are. First, you can use IValueConverter objects in your data binding to convert your data to a more useful representation. Consider, for example, the ImagePathConverter demonstrated in Chapter 16. It accepts a picture file name and uses it to create a BitmapImage object with the corresponding image content. This BitmapImage object can then be bound directly to the Image element.

You can use the ImagePathConverter to build the following data template that displays the image for each product:

```
<Window.Resources>
  <local:ImagePathConverter x:Key="ImagePathConverter"></local:ImagePathConverter>
  <DataTemplate x:Key="ProductTemplate">
    <Border Margin="5" BorderThickness="1" BorderBrush="SteelBlue"
      CornerRadius="4">
      <Grid Margin="3">
        <Grid.RowDefinitions>
          <RowDefinition></RowDefinition>
          <RowDefinition></RowDefinition>
          <RowDefinition></RowDefinition>
        </Grid.RowDefinitions>
        <TextBlock FontWeight="Bold" Text="{Binding Path=ModelNumber}"></TextBlock>
        <TextBlock Grid.Row="1" Text="{Binding Path=ModelName}"></TextBlock>
        <Image Grid.Row="2" Grid.RowSpan="2" Source=
"{Binding Path=ProductImagePath, Converter={StaticResource ImagePathConverter}}">
        </Image>
      </Grid>
    </Border>
  </DataTemplate>
</Window.Resources>
```

Although this markup doesn't involve anything exotic, the result is a much more interesting list (see Figure 17-3).

Another useful technique is to place controls directly inside a template. For example, Figure 17-4 shows a list of categories. Next to each category is a View button that you can use to launch another window with just the matching products in that category.

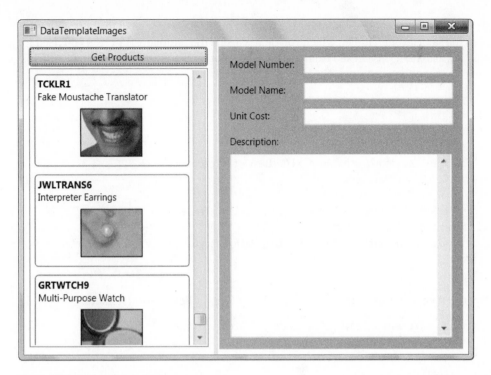

Figure 17-3. *A list with image content*

Figure 17-4. *A list with button controls*

The trick in this example is handling the button clicks. Obviously, all of the buttons will be linked to the same event handler, which you define inside the template. However, you need to determine which item was clicked from the list. One solution is to store some extra identifying information in the Tag property of the button, as shown here:

```
<DataTemplate>
  <Grid Margin="3">
    <Grid.ColumnDefinitions>
      <ColumnDefinition></ColumnDefinition>
      <ColumnDefinition Width="Auto"></ColumnDefinition>
    </Grid.ColumnDefinitions>

    <TextBlock Text="{Binding Path=CategoryName}"></TextBlock>
    <Button Grid.Column="2" HorizontalAlignment="Right" Padding="2"
      Click="cmdView_Clicked" Tag="{Binding Path=CategoryID}">View ...</Button>
  </Grid>
</DataTemplate>
```

You can then retrieve the Tag property in the cmdView_Clicked event handler:

```
private void cmdView_Clicked(object sender, RoutedEventArgs e)
{
    Button cmd = (Button)sender;
    int categoryID = (int)cmd.Tag;
    ...
}
```

You can use this information to take another action. For example, you might launch another window that shows products and pass the CategoryID value to that window, which can then use filtering to show only the products in that category. (One easy way to implement filtering is with data views, as described later in this chapter.)

If you want all the information about the selected data item, you can grab the entire data object by leaving out the Path property when you define the binding:

```
<Button HorizontalAlignment="Right" Padding="1"
  Click="cmdView_Clicked" Tag="{Binding}">View ...</Button>
```

Now your event handler will receive the Product object (if you're binding a collection of Products). If you're binding to a DataTable, you'll receive a DataRowView object instead, which you can use to retrieve all the field values exactly as you would with a DataRow object.

Passing the entire object has another advantage: it makes it easier to update the list selection. In the current example, it's possible to click a button in any item, regardless of whether that item is currently selected. This is potentially confusing, because the user could select one item and click the View button of another item. When the user returns to the list window, the first item remains selected even though the second item was the one that was used by the previous operation. To remove the possibility for confusion, it's a good idea to move the selection to the new list item when the View button is clicked, as shown here:

```
Button cmd = (Button)sender;
Product product = (Product)cmd.Tag;
lstCategories.SelectedItem = product;
```

Another option is to show the View button only in a selected item. This technique involves modifying or replacing the template you're using in this list, which is described in the "Templates and Selection" section a bit later in this chapter.

Varying Templates

One limitation with the templates you've seen so far is that you're limited to one template for the entire list. But in many situations, you'll want the flexibility to present different data items in different ways.

You can achieve this goal in several ways. Here are some common techniques:

- **Use a data trigger.** You can use a trigger to change a property in the template based on the value of a property in the bound data object. Data triggers work like the property triggers you learned about with styles in Chapter 12, except they don't require dependency properties.

- **Use a value converter.** A class that implements IValueConverter can convert a value from your bound object to a value you can use to set a formatting-related property in your template.

- **Use a template selector.** A template selector examines the bound data object and chooses between several distinct templates.

Data triggers offer the simplest approach. The basic technique is to set a property of one of the elements in your template based on a property in your data item. For example, you could change the background of the custom border that wraps each list item based on the CategoryName property of the corresponding Product object. Here's an example that highlights products in the Tools category with boldface lettering:

```
<DataTemplate x:Key="DefaultTemplate">
  <DataTemplate.Triggers>
    <DataTrigger Binding="{Binding Path=CategoryName}" Value="Tools">
      <Setter Property="ListBoxItem.Foreground" Value="Red"></Setter>
    </DataTrigger>
  </DataTemplate.Triggers>
  <Border Margin="5" BorderThickness="1" BorderBrush="SteelBlue"
   CornerRadius="4">
    <Grid Margin="3">
      <Grid.RowDefinitions>
        <RowDefinition></RowDefinition>
        <RowDefinition></RowDefinition>
      </Grid.RowDefinitions>
      <TextBlock FontWeight="Bold"
       Text="{Binding Path=ModelNumber}"></TextBlock>
      <TextBlock Grid.Row="1"
       Text="{Binding Path=ModelName}"></TextBlock>
    </Grid>
  </Border>
</DataTemplate>
```

Because the Product object implements the INotifyPropertyChanged interface (as described in Chapter 16), any changes are picked up immediately. For example, if you modify the CategoryName property to move a product out of the Tools category, its text in the list changes at the same time.

This approach is useful but inherently limited. It doesn't allow you to change complex details about your template, only tweak individual properties of the elements in the template (or the container element). Also, as you learned in Chapter 12, triggers can test only for equality—they don't support more complex comparison conditions. That means you can't use this approach to highlight prices that exceed a certain value, for example. And if you need to choose between a range of possibilities (for example, giving each product category a different background color), you'll need to write one trigger for each possible value, which is messy.

Another option is to create one template that's intelligent enough to adjust itself based on the bound object. To pull this trick off, you usually need to use a value converter that examines a property in your bound object and returns a more suitable value. For example, you could create a CategoryToColorConverter that examines a product's category and returns a corresponding Color object. That way, you can bind directly to the CategoryName property in your template, as shown here:

```
<Border Margin="5" BorderThickness="1" BorderBrush="SteelBlue" CornerRadius="4"
  Background=
  "{Binding Path=CategoryName, Converter={StaticResource CategoryToColorConverter}">
```

You saw how to create a value converter and use it to apply conditional formatting in Chapter 16. You also saw a value converter example in the previous section, which was used to display images in a list.

Like the trigger approach, the value converter approach also prevents you from making dramatic changes, such as replacing a portion of your template with something completely different. However, it allows you to implement more sophisticated formatting logic. Also, it allows you to base a single formatting property on several properties from the bound data object. (To pull off this trick, use the IMultiValueConverter interface described in Chapter 16 instead of the ordinary IValueConverter.)

■Tip Value converters are a good choice if you might want to reuse your formatting logic with other templates.

Template Selectors

Another, more powerful option is to give different items a completely different template. Unfortunately, there's no way to do this declaratively. Instead, you need to build a specialized class that derives from DataTemplateSelector. This class has the responsibility of examining each data item and choosing the appropriate template. This work is performed in the Select-Template() method, which you must override.

Here's a rudimentary template selector that chooses between two templates:

```
public class ProductByCategoryTemplateSelector : DataTemplateSelector
{
    public override DataTemplate SelectTemplate(object item,
```

```
    DependencyObject container)
{
    Product product = (Product)item;
    Window window = Application.Current.MainWindow;

    if (product.CategoryName == "Travel")
    {
        return (DataTemplate)window.FindResource("TravelProductTemplate");
    }
    else
    {
        return (DataTemplate)window.FindResource("DefaultProductTemplate");
    }
}
}
```

In this example, products that are in the Travel category get one template, while all other products get another. Both the templates you want to use must be defined in the Resources collection of the window, with the key names TravelProductTemplate and DefaultProduct-Template.

This template selector works, but it's not perfect. One problem is that your code depends on details that are in the markup, which means there's a dependency that isn't enforced at compile time and could easily be disrupted (for example, if you give your templates the wrong resource keys). The other problem is that this template selector hard-codes the value it's looking for (in this case, the category name), which limits reuse.

A better idea is to create a template selector that uses one or more properties to allow you to specify some of these details, such as the criteria you're using to evaluate your data items and the templates you want to use. The following template selector is still quite simple but extremely flexible. It's able to examine any data object, look for a given property, and compare that property against another value to choose between two templates. The property, property value, and templates are all specified as properties. The SelectTemplate() method uses reflection to find the right property in a manner similar to the way data bindings work when digging out bound values.

Here's the complete code:

```
public class SingleCriteriaHighlightTemplateSelector : DataTemplateSelector
{
    public DataTemplate DefaultTemplate
    {
        get; set;
    }

    public DataTemplate HighlightTemplate
    {
        get; set;
    }

    public string PropertyToEvaluate
```

```
    {
        get; set;
    }

    public string PropertyValueToHighlight
    {
        get; set;
    }

    public override DataTemplate SelectTemplate(object item,
      DependencyObject container)
    {
        Product product = (Product)item;

        // Use reflection to get the property to check.
        Type type = product.GetType();
        PropertyInfo property = type.GetProperty(PropertyToEvaluate);

        // Decide if this product should be highlighted
        // based on the property value.
        if (property.GetValue(product, null).ToString() == PropertyValueToHighlight)
        {
            return HighlightTemplate;
        }
        else
        {
            return DefaultTemplate;
        }
    }
}
```

To make this work, you'll need to create the two styles you want to use, and you'll need to create and initialize an instance of the SingleCriteriaHighlightTemplateSelector.

Here are two similar templates, which are distinguished only by the background color, the use of bold formatting, and an extra line of text:

```
<Window.Resources>
  <DataTemplate x:Key="DefaultTemplate">
    <Border Margin="5" BorderThickness="1" BorderBrush="SteelBlue"
      CornerRadius="4">
      <Grid Margin="3">
        <Grid.RowDefinitions>
          <RowDefinition></RowDefinition>
          <RowDefinition></RowDefinition>
        </Grid.RowDefinitions>
        <TextBlock
```

```
        Text="{Binding Path=ModelNumber}"></TextBlock>
        <TextBlock Grid.Row="1"
         Text="{Binding Path=ModelName}"></TextBlock>
      </Grid>
    </Border>
  </DataTemplate>

  <DataTemplate x:Key="HighlightTemplate">
    <Border Margin="5" BorderThickness="1" BorderBrush="SteelBlue"
     Background="LightYellow" CornerRadius="4">
      <Grid Margin="3">
        <Grid.RowDefinitions>
          <RowDefinition></RowDefinition>
          <RowDefinition></RowDefinition>
          <RowDefinition></RowDefinition>
        </Grid.RowDefinitions>
        <TextBlock FontWeight="Bold"
         Text="{Binding Path=ModelNumber}"></TextBlock>
        <TextBlock Grid.Row="1" FontWeight="Bold"
         Text="{Binding Path=ModelName}"></TextBlock>
        <TextBlock Grid.Row="2" FontStyle="Italic" HorizontalAlignment="Right">
         *** Great for vacations ***</TextBlock>
      </Grid>
    </Border>
  </DataTemplate>
</Window.Resources>
```

When you create the SingleCriteriaHighlightTemplateSelector, you point it to these two templates. You can also create the SingleCriteriaHighlightTemplateSelector as a resource (which is useful if you want to reuse it in more than one place), or you can define it inline in your list control, as in this example:

```
<ListBox Name="lstProducts" HorizontalContentAlignment="Stretch">
  <ListBox.ItemTemplateSelector>
    <local:SingleCriteriaHighlightTemplateSelector
      DefaultTemplate="{StaticResource DefaultTemplate}"
      HighlightTemplate="{StaticResource HighlightTemplate}"
      PropertyToEvaluate="CategoryName"
      PropertyValueToHighlight="Travel"
    >
    </local:SingleCriteriaHighlightTemplateSelector>
  </ListBox.ItemTemplateSelector>
</ListBox>
```

Here, the SingleCriteriaHighlightTemplateSelector looks for a Category property in the bound data item and uses the HighlightTemplate if it contains the text *Travel*. Figure 17-5 shows the result.

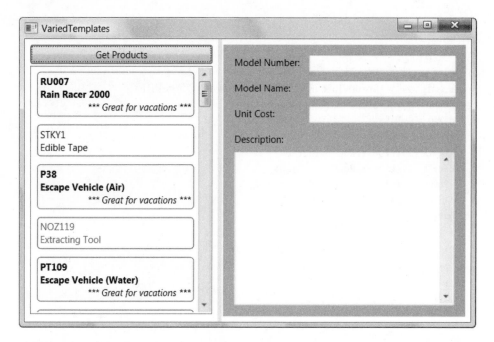

Figure 17-5. *A list with two data templates*

■**Tip** One disadvantage with this approach is that you'll probably be forced to create multiple templates that are similar, which causes a bit of duplication. For best maintainability, you shouldn't create more than a few templates for a single list—instead, use triggers and styles to apply different formatting to your templates. (The ItemsControl.ItemContainerStyleSelector property is a particular help here, as described in the "Style Selectors" section later in this chapter.)

The template selection process is performed once, when you first bind the list. This is a problem if you're displaying editable data and it's possible for an edit to move the data item from one template category to another. In this situation, you need to force WPF to reapply the templates, and there's no graceful way to do it. The brute-force approach is to remove the template selector by setting the ItemTemplateSelector property to null and then to reassign it:

```
DataTemplateSelector selector = lstProducts.ItemTemplateSelector;
lstProducts.ItemTemplateSelector = null;
lstProducts.ItemTemplateSelector = selector;
```

You may choose to run this code automatically in response to certain changes by handling events such as PropertyChanged (which is raised by all classes that implement INotifyPropertyChanged, including Product), DataTable.RowChanged (if you're using the ADO.NET data objects), and, more generically, Binding.SourceUpdated (which fires only when Binding.NotifyOnSourceUpdated is true). When you reassign the template selector, WPF examines and updates every item in the list—a process that's quick for small-to-medium lists.

Templates and Selection

There's a small but irritating quirk in the current template example. The problem is that the templates you've seen don't take selection into account.

If you select an item in the list, WPF automatically sets the Foreground and Background properties of the item container (in this case, the ListBoxItem object). The foreground is white, and the background is blue. The Foreground property uses property inheritance, so any elements you've added to your template automatically acquire the new white color, unless you've explicitly specified a new color. The Background color doesn't use property inheritance, but the default Background value is Transparent. If you have a transparent border, for example, the new blue background shows through. Otherwise, the color you've set in the template still applies.

This mishmash can alter your formatting in a way you might not intend. Figure 17-6 shows an example.

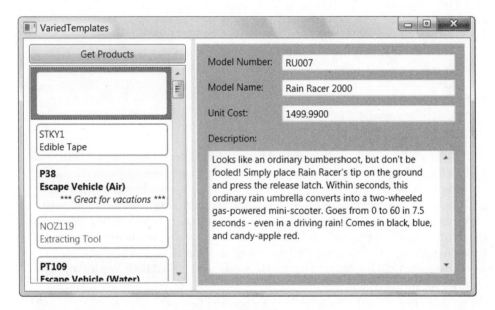

Figure 17-6. *Unreadable text in a highlighted item*

You could hard-code all your colors to avoid this problem, but then you'll face another challenge. The only indication that an item is selected will be the blue background around your curved border.

Obviously, a better solution would be to modify your template or supply a completely new template for selected items. After all, you might want to make a wide range of changes when an item becomes selected. (For example, you might want to fill in additional information, expanding it in the list so the user doesn't need to look to another control to get the full details about an item. Or, you might want to replace the bound elements with editable controls such as the TextBox so the item can be edited in place.)

Unfortunately, modifying the template of a selected item isn't as easy as you'd expect. The ItemsControl class doesn't provide a SelectedItemDataTemplate property. The DataTemplate-Selector class you learned about in the previous section isn't any help either, because it generates templates when the list is first bound. It's no help if you want to change the template when an item is selected or deselected.

So, how can you solve this problem? In a list that doesn't use templates, you can use style triggers to modify the selected item. You use these styles to modify the container that holds each item in the list. (In the case of the ListBox, it's a ListBoxItem; in the case of a ComboBox, it's a ComboBoxItem, and so on.)

You can apply these styles in two ways. You can apply a style by type to all ListBoxItem controls, or you can use the ListBox.ItemContainerStyle property (as in the following example), which allows you to set a style that's used to affect every ListBoxItem object that's created for that list. Both approaches work equally well.

```
<ListBox Name="lstProducts" HorizontalContentAlignment="Stretch">
  <ListBox.ItemContainerStyle>
    <Style>
      <Setter Property="Control.Padding" Value="0"></Setter>
      <Style.Triggers>
        <Trigger Property="ListBoxItem.IsSelected" Value="True">
          <Setter Property="ListBoxItem.Background" Value="DarkRed" />
        </Trigger>
      </Style.Triggers>
    </Style>
  </ListBox.ItemContainerStyle>
</ListBox>
```

This trigger applies a dark red background to the selected item. Unfortunately, this code doesn't have the desired effect for a list that uses templates. That's because these templates include elements with a different background color that's displayed over the dark red background. Unless you make everything transparent (and allow the red color to wash through your entire template), you're left with a thin red edge around the margin area of your template.

The solution is to explicitly bind the background in part of your template to the value of the ListBoxItem.Background property. This makes sense—after all, you've now gone to the work of choosing the right background color to highlight the selected item. You just need to make sure it appears in the right place.

The markup you need to implement this solution is a bit messy. That's because you can't make do with an ordinary binding expression, which can simply bind to a property in the current data object (in this case, the Product object). Instead, you need to grab the background from the item container (in this case, the ListBoxItem). This involves using the Binding.RelativeSource property to search up the element tree for the first matching ListBoxItem object. Once that element is found, you can grab its background color and use it accordingly.

Here's the finished template, which uses the selected background in the curved border region. The Border element is placed inside a Grid with a white background, which ensures that the selected color does not appear in the margin area outside the curved border. The result is the much slicker selection style shown in Figure 17-7.

```
<DataTemplate>
  <Grid Margin="0" Background="White">
    <Border Margin="5" BorderThickness="1"
      BorderBrush="SteelBlue" CornerRadius="4"
      Background="{Binding Path=Background, RelativeSource={
                          RelativeSource
                          Mode=FindAncestor,
                          AncestorType={x:Type ListBoxItem}
                        }}" >
      <Grid Margin="3">
        <Grid.RowDefinitions>
          <RowDefinition></RowDefinition>
          <RowDefinition></RowDefinition>
        </Grid.RowDefinitions>
        <TextBlock FontWeight="Bold" Text="{Binding Path=ModelNumber}"></TextBlock>
        <TextBlock Grid.Row="1" Text="{Binding Path=ModelName}"></TextBlock>
      </Grid>
    </Border>
  </Grid>
</DataTemplate>
```

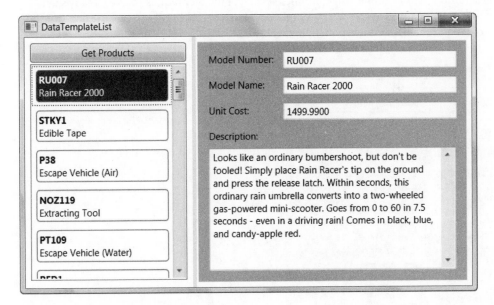

Figure 17-7. *Highlighting a selected item*

SELECTION AND SNAPSTODEVICEPIXELS

You should make one other change to ensure your template displays perfectly on computers with different system DPI settings (such as 120 dpi rather than the standard 96 dpi). You should set the ListBox.SnapsTo-DevicePixels property to true. This ensures that the edge of the list doesn't use antialiasing if it falls in between pixels.

If you don't set SnapsToDevicePixels to true, it's possible that you'll get a trace of the familiar blue border creeping in between the edge of your template and the edge of the containing ListBox control. (For more information about fractional pixels and why they occur when the system DPI is set to a value other than 96 dpi, see the discussion about WPF's device-independent measuring system in Chapter 1.)

This approach—using a binding expression to alter a template—works well if you can pull the property value you need out of the item container. For example, it's a great technique if you want to get the background and foreground color of a selected item. However, it isn't as useful if you need to alter the template in a more profound way.

For example, consider the list of product shown in Figure 17-8. When you select a product from this list, that item is expanded from a single-line text display to a box with a picture and full description. This example also combines several of the techniques you've already seen, including showing image content in a template and using data binding to set the background color of the Border element when an item is selected.

Figure 17-8. *Expanding a selected item*

To create this sort of list, you need to use a variation of the technique used in the previous example. You still need to use the RelativeSource property of a Binding to search for the current ListBoxItem. However, now you don't want to pull out its background color. Instead, you want to examine whether it's selected. If it isn't, you can hide the extra information by setting its Visibility property.

This technique is similar to the previous example but not exactly the same. In the previous example, you were able to bind directly to the value you wanted so that the background of the ListBoxItem became the background of the Border object. But in this case, you need to consider the ListBoxItem.IsSelected property and set the Visibility property of another element. The data types don't match—IsSelected is a Boolean value, while Visibility takes a value from the Visibility enumeration. As a result, you can't bind the Visibility property to the IsSelected property (at least, not without the help of a custom IValueConverter). The solution is to use a data trigger so that when the IsSelected property is changed in the ListBoxItem, you modify Visibility property of your container.

The place in your markup where you put the trigger is also different. It's no longer convenient to place the trigger in the ItemContainerStyle, because you don't want to change the visibility of the entire item. Instead, you want to hide just a single section, so the trigger needs to be part of a style that applies to just one container.

Here's a slightly simplified version of the template that doesn't have the automatically expanding behavior yet. Instead, it shows all the information (including the picture and description) for every product in the list.

```
<DataTemplate>
  <Border Margin="5" BorderThickness="1" BorderBrush="SteelBlue"
  CornerRadius="4">
    <StackPanel Margin="3">
      <TextBlock Text="{Binding Path=ModelName}"></TextBlock>
      <StackPanel>
        <TextBlock Margin="3" Text="{Binding Path=Description}"
         TextWrapping="Wrap" MaxWidth="250" HorizontalAlignment="Left"></TextBlock>
        <Image Source=
"{Binding Path=ProductImagePath, Converter={StaticResource ImagePathConverter}}">
        </Image>
        <Button FontWeight="Regular" HorizontalAlignment="Right" Padding="1"
         Tag="{Binding}">View Details...</Button>
      </StackPanel>
    </StackPanel>
  </Border>
</DataTemplate>
```

Inside the Border is a StackPanel that holds all the content. Inside that StackPanel is a second StackPanel that holds the content that should be shown only for selected items, which includes the description, image, and button. To hide this information, you need to set the style of the inner StackPanel using a trigger, as shown here:

```
<StackPanel>
  <StackPanel.Style>
    <Style>
      <Style.Triggers>
        <DataTrigger
          Binding="{Binding Path=IsSelected, RelativeSource={
                            RelativeSource
                            Mode=FindAncestor,
                            AncestorType={x:Type ListBoxItem}
                        }}"
          Value="False">
          <Setter Property="StackPanel.Visibility" Value="Collapsed" />
        </DataTrigger>
      </Style.Triggers>
    </Style>
  </StackPanel.Style>

  <TextBlock Margin="3" Text="{Binding Path=Description}"
    TextWrapping="Wrap" MaxWidth="250" HorizontalAlignment="Left"></TextBlock>
  <Image Source=
"{Binding Path=ProductImagePath, Converter={StaticResource ImagePathConverter}}">
  </Image>
  <Button FontWeight="Regular" HorizontalAlignment="Right" Padding="1"
    Tag="{Binding}">View Details...</Button>
</StackPanel>
```

In this example, you need to use a DataTrigger instead of an ordinary trigger, because the property you need to evaluate is in an ancestor element (the ListBoxItem), and the only way to access it is using a data binding expression.

Now, when the ListBoxItem.IsSelected property changes to False, the StackPanel.Visibility property is changed to Collapsed, hiding the extra details.

■**Note** Technically, the expanded details are always present, just hidden. As a result, you'll experience the extra overhead of generating these elements when the list is first created, not when an item is selected. This doesn't make much difference in the current example, but this design could have a performance effect if you use it for an extremely long list with a complex template.

Style Selectors

Data templates are the most powerful tools for changing the appearance of the items in a list. However, sometimes they're a little excessive. For example, you may not need to radically alter the layout and content of each item in a list. Instead, you may simply be interested in applying some basic formatting—for example, changing the foreground and background colors or the text in the list. In this case, it makes more sense to use a style.

In the previous section, you saw how you can define a style that's automatically applied to each item container (such as the ListBoxItem, ComboBoxItem, and so on). All you need to do is set the ListBox.ItemContainerStyle property. Like any style, you can use a combination of Setter elements to set properties in the ListBoxItem. The formatting you set is applied to every item in the list, although you can use triggers to change the formatting based on other details, such as whether the item is currently selected. You also saw this technique in the previous example.

One additional feature that you can use is a style selector, which works analogously to a template selector. The style selector is a dedicated class with the simple task of evaluating each item and supplying the correct style. This allows you to vary the style that's used for each data object based on specific information about that object. For example, you could easily create a style selector that highlights high-priced products with a different text color. And although the same feat is possible with a template selector, the style selector is a better choice in this case. That's because the template selector approach requires that you build an entirely separate template for high-priced products, which forces you to duplicate some details from the standard template and makes it more difficult to modify these details later. The style selector allows you to use a single template and simply tweak a few properties to suit.

Style selectors are often used to apply an alternating row style—in other words, a set of formatting characteristics that distinguish every second item in a list. Usually, alternating rows are given subtly different backgrounds colors so that the rows are clearly separated, as shown in Figure 17-9.

Figure 17-9. *Alternating row highlighting with a style selector*

To create a style selector, you build a class that derives from the base System.Windows.Controls.StyleSelector class and overrides the SelectStyle() method. SelectStyle() works in the same way as SelectTemplate() in a template selector, except it returns a Style object instead of a DataTemplate.

The following style selector applies one style to odd rows and another one to even rows. For maximum reusability, both styles are supplied through properties rather than hard-coded.

```
public class AlternatingRowStyleSelector : StyleSelector
{
    public Style DefaultStyle
```

```
    {
        get; set;
    }

    public Style AlternateStyle
    {
        get; set;
    }

    // Track the row index.
    private int i = 0;

    public override Style SelectStyle(object item, DependencyObject container)
    {
        // Reset the counter if this is the first item.
        ItemsControl ctrl = ItemsControl.ItemsControlFromItemContainer(container);
        if (item == ctrl.Items[0])
        {
            i = 0;
        }
        i++;

        // Choose between the two styles based on the current position.
        if (i % 2 == 1)
        {
            return DefaultStyle;
        }
        else
        {
            return AlternateStyle;
        }
    }
}
```

To complete the example shown in Figure 17-9, you simply need to define the styles you want to use. In this example, every odd-numbered item keeps the standard style settings. Thus, you need to supply only the style that should be used for even items:

```
<Style x:Key="AlternateStyle">
  <Setter Property="ListBoxItem.Background" Value="GoldenrodYellow" ></Setter>
</Style>
```

Now you can use this style to configure the AlternatingRowStyleSelector that's applied to the list:

```
<ListBox Grid.Row="1" Margin="7,3,7,10" Name="lstProducts"
 DisplayMemberPath="ModelName">
  <ListBox.ItemContainerStyleSelector>
    <local:AlternatingRowStyleSelector
     AlternateStyle="{StaticResource AlternateStyle}" />
  </ListBox.ItemContainerStyleSelector>
</ListBox>
```

As with template selectors, style selectors are evaluated only when an item is added to the list is filled for the first time. If you add new items to the list between existing items, the alternating row formatting will be thrown off. The solution is to manually clear the style selector (by setting ItemContainerStyleSelector to null) and then reapply it.

Changing Item Layout

Data templates and style selectors give you remarkable control over every aspect of item presentation. However, they don't allow you to change how the items are organized with respect to each other. No matter what templates and styles you use, the ListBox puts each item into a separate horizontal row and stacks each row to create the list.

You can change this layout by replacing the container that the list uses to lay out its children. To do so, you set the ItemsPanelTemplate property with a block of XAML that defines the panel you want to use. This panel can be any class that derives from System.Windows.Controls.Panel.

The following uses a WrapPanel to wrap items across the available width of the ListBox control (as shown in Figure 17-10):

```
<ListBox Margin="7,3,7,10" Name="lstProducts"
 ItemTemplate="{StaticResource ItemTemplate}"
 ScrollViewer.HorizontalScrollBarVisibility="Disabled">
  <ListBox.ItemsPanel>
    <ItemsPanelTemplate>
      <WrapPanel></WrapPanel>
    </ItemsPanelTemplate>
  </ListBox.ItemsPanel>
</ListBox>
```

For this approach to work, you must also set the attached ScrollViewer.HorizontalScroll-BarVisibility property to Disabled. This ensures that the ScrollViewer (which the ListBox uses automatically) never uses a horizontal scroll bar. Without this detail, the WrapPanel will be given infinite width in which to lay out its items, and this example becomes equivalent to a horizontal StackPanel.

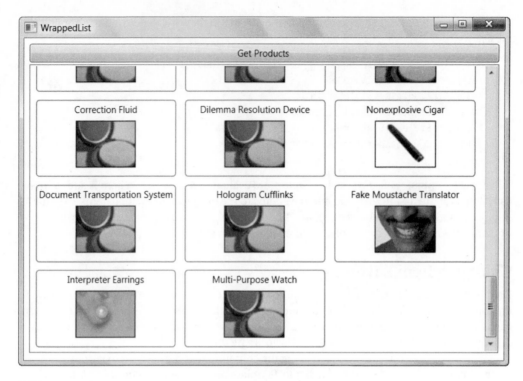

Figure 17-10. *Tiling items in the display area of a list*

Data Views

Now that you've explored the art of building data templates, you're ready to move on to another part of the data binding picture: data views.

When you bind a collection (or a DataTable) to an ItemsControl, a data view is quietly created behind the scenes. This view sits between your data source and the bound control. The data view is a window into your data source. It tracks the current item, and it supports features such as sorting, filtering, and grouping. These features are independent of the data object itself, which means you can bind the same data in different ways in different portions of a window (or different parts of your application). For example, you could bind the same collection of products to two different lists but filter them to show different records.

The view object that's used depends on the type of data object. All views derive from CollectionView, but two specialized implementations derive from CollectionView: ListCollectionView and BindingListCollectionView. Here's how it works:

- If your data source implements IBindingList, a BindingListCollectionView is created. This happens when you bind an ADO.NET DataTable.

- If your data source doesn't implement IBindingList but it implements IList, a ListCollectionView is created. This happens when you bind an ObservableCollection, like the list of products.

- If your data source doesn't implement IBindingList or IList but it implements IEnumerable, you get a basic CollectionView.

Tip Ideally, you'll avoid the third scenario. The CollectionView offers poor performance for large items and operations that modify the data source (such as insertions and deletions). As you learned in Chapter 16, if you're not binding to an ADO.NET data object, it's almost always easiest to use the ObservableCollection class (or derive a custom class from ObservableCollection).

Retrieving a View Object

To get ahold of a view object that's currently in use, you use the static GetDefaultView() method of the System.Windows.Data.CollectionViewSource class. When you call GetDefault-View(), you pass in the data source—the collection or DataTable that you're using. Here's an example that gets the view for the collection of products that's bound to the list:

```
ICollectionView view = CollectionViewSource.GetDefaultView(lstProducts.ItemsSource);
```

The GetDefaultView() method always returns an ICollectionView reference. It's up to you to cast the view object to the appropriate class, such as a ListCollectionView or BindingList-CollectionView, depending on the data source.

```
ListCollectionView view =
  (ListCollectionView)CollectionViewSource.GetDefaultView(lstProducts.ItemsSource);
```

In the following sections, you'll learn how to use the view object to add filtering, sorting, and grouping.

Filtering Collections

Filtering allows you to show a subset of records that meet specific conditions. When working with a collection as a data source, you set the filter using the Filter property of the view object.

The implementation of the Filter property is a little awkward. It accepts a Predicate delegate that points to a custom filtering method (that you create). Here's an example of how you can connect a view to a method named FilterProduct():

```
ListCollectionView view = (ListCollectionView)
  CollectionViewSource.GetDefaultView(lstProducts.ItemsSource);
view.Filter = new Predicate<object>(FilterProduct);
```

The filtering examines a single data item from the collection and returns true if it should be allowed in the list or false if it should be excluded. When you create the Predicate object, you specify the type of object that it's meant to examine. The awkward part is that the view expects you to use a Predicate<object> instance—you can't use something more useful (such as Predicate<Product>) to save yourself the type casting code.

Here's a simple method that shows products only if they exceed $100:

```
public bool FilterProduct(Object item)
{
    Product product = (Product)item;
    return (product.UnitCost > 100);
}
```

Obviously, it makes little sense to hard-code values in your filter condition. A more realistic application would filter dynamically based on other information, like the user-supplied criteria shown in Figure 17-11.

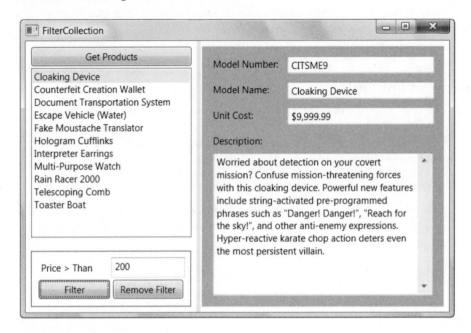

Figure 17-11. *Filtering the product list*

You can use two strategies to make this scenario work. If you use an anonymous delegate, you can define an inline filtering method, which gives you access to any local variables that are in scope in the current method. Here's an example:

```
ListCollectionView view = (ListCollectionView)
  CollectionViewSource.GetDefaultView(lstProducts.ItemsSource);
view.Filter = delegate(object item)
            {
                Product product = (Product)item;
                return (product.UnitCost > 100);
            }
```

Although this is a neat, elegant approach, in more complex filtering scenarios you're more likely to use a different strategy and create a dedicated filtering class. That's because in these situations, you often need to filter using several different criteria, and you may want the ability to modify the filtering criteria later.

The filtering class wraps the filtering criteria and the callback method that performs the filtering. Here's an extremely simple filtering class that filters products that fall below a minimum price:

```
public class ProductByPriceFilter
{
    public decimal MinimumPrice
```

```
    {
        get; set;
    }

    public ProductByPriceFilter(decimal minimumPrice)
    {
        MinimumPrice = minimumPrice;
    }

    public bool FilterItem(Object item)
    {
        Product product = item as Product;
        if (product != null)
        {
            return (product.UnitCost > MinimumPrice);
        }
        return false;
    }
}
```

Here's the code that creates the ProductByPriceFilterer and uses it to apply minimum price filtering:

```
private void cmdFilter_Click(object sender, RoutedEventArgs e)
{
    decimal minimumPrice;
    if (Decimal.TryParse(txtMinPrice.Text, out minimumPrice))
    {
        ListCollectionView view =
          CollectionViewSource.GetDefaultView(lstProducts.ItemsSource)
          as ListCollectionView;

        if (view != null)
        {
            ProductByPriceFilter filter =
              new ProductByPriceFilter(minimumPrice);
            view.Filter = new Predicate<object>(filter.FilterItem);
        }
    }
}
```

It might occur to you to create different filters for filtering different types of data. For example, you might plan to create (and reuse) a MinMaxFilter, a StringFilter, and so on. However, it's usually more helpful to create a single filtering class for each window where you want to apply filtering. That's because you can't chain more than one filter together.

> **Note** Of course, you could create a custom implementation that solves this problem—for example, a FilterChain class that wraps a collection of IFilter objects and calls the FilterItem() method of each one to find out whether to exclude an item. However, this extra layer may be more code and complexity than you need.

If you want to modify the filter later without re-creating the ProductByPriceFilter object, you'll need to store a reference to the filter object as a member variable in your window class. You can then modify the filter properties. However, you'll also need to call the Refresh() method of the view object to force the list to be refiltered. Here's some code that adjusts the filter settings whenever the TextChanged event fires in the text box that contains the minimum price:

```
private void txtMinPrice_TextChanged(object sender, TextChangedEventArgs e)
{
    ListCollectionView view =
      CollectionViewSource.GetDefaultView(lstProducts.ItemsSource)
      as ListCollectionView;
    if (view != null)
    {
        decimal minimumPrice;
        if (Decimal.TryParse(txtMinPrice.Text, out minimumPrice) &&
          (filter != null))
        {
            filter.MinimumPrice = minimumPrice;
            view.Refresh();
        }
    }
}
```

> **Tip** It's a common convention to let the user choose to apply different types of conditions using a series of check boxes. For example, you could create a check box for filtering by price, by name, by model number, and so on. The user can then choose which filter conditions to apply by checking the appropriate check boxes.

Finally, you can completely remove a filter by setting the Filter property to null:

```
view.Filter = null;
```

Filtering the DataTable

Filtering works differently with the DataTable. If you've worked with ADO.NET before, you probably already know that every DataTable works in conjunction with a DataView object (which is, like the DataTable, defined in the System.Data namespace along with the other core ADO.NET data objects). The ADO.NET DataView plays much the same role as the WPF view object. Like a WPF view, it allows you to filter records (by field content using the RowFilter property or by row state using the RowStateFilter property). It also supports sorting through the Sort property. Unlike the WPF view object, the DataView doesn't track the position in a set of data. It also provides additional properties that allow you to lock down editing capabilities (AllowDelete, AllowEdit, and AllowNew).

It's quite possible to change the way a list of data is filtered by retrieving the bound DataView and modifying its properties directly. (Remember, you can get the default DataView from the DataTable.DefaultView property.) However, it would be nicer if you had a way to adjust the filtering through the WPF view object so that you can continue to use the same model.

It turns out that this is possible, but there are some limitations. Unlike the ListCollection-View, the BindingListCollectionView that's used with the DataTable doesn't support the Filter property. (BindingListCollectionView.CanFilter returns false, and attempting to set the Filter property causes an exception to be thrown.) Instead, the BindingListCollectionView provides a CustomFilter property. The CustomFilter property doesn't do any work of its own—it simply takes the filter string that you specify and uses it to set the underlying DataView.RowFilter property.

The DataView.RowFilter is easy enough to use but a little messy. It takes a string-based filter expression, which is modeled after the snippet of SQL you'd use to construct the WHERE clause in a SELECT query. As a result, you need to follow all the conventions of SQL, such as bracketing string and date values with single quotes ('). And if you want to use multiple conditions, you need to string them all together using the OR and AND keywords.

Here's an example that duplicates the filtering shown in the earlier, collection-based example so that it works with a DataTable of product records:

```
decimal minimumPrice;
if (Decimal.TryParse(txtMinPrice.Text, out minimumPrice))
{
    BindingListCollectionView view =
      CollectionViewSource.GetDefaultView(lstProducts.ItemsSource)
      as BindingListCollectionView;
    if (view != null)
    {
        view.CustomFilter = "UnitCost > " + minimumPrice.ToString();
    }
}
```

Notice that this example takes the roundabout approach of converting the text in the txtMinPrice text box to a decimal value and then back to a string to use for filtering. This requires a bit more work, but it avoids possible injection attacks and errors with invalid characters. If you simply concatenate the text from the txtMinPrice text box to build your filter string, it could contain filter operations (=, <, >) and keywords (AND, OR) that apply completely different filtering than what you intend. This could happen as part of a deliberate attack or because of user error.

Sorting

You can also use a view to implement sorting. The easiest approach is to sort based on the value of one or more properties in each data item. You identify the fields you want to use using System.ComponentModel.SortDescription objects. Each SortDescription identifies the field you want to use for sorting and the sort direction (ascending or descending). You add the SortDescription objects in the order that you want to apply them. For example, you could sort first by category and then by model name.

Here's an example that applies a simple ascending sort by model name:

```
ICollectionView view = CollectionViewSource.GetDefaultView(lstProducts.ItemsSource);
view.SortDescriptions.Add(
  new SortDescription("ModelName", ListSortDirection.Ascending));
```

Because this code uses the ICollectionView interface rather than a specific view class, it works equally well no matter what type of data source you're binding. In the case of a BindingListCollectionView (when binding a DataTable), the SortDescription objects are used to build a sorting string that's applied to the underlying DataView.Sort property.

■**Note** In the rare case that you have more than one BindingListCollectionView working with the same DataView, both will share the same filtering and sorting settings, because these details are stored in the DataView, not the BindingListCollectionView. If this isn't the behavior you want, you can create more than one DataView to wrap the same DataTable.

As you'd expect, when sorting strings, values are ordered alphabetically. Numbers are ordered numerically. To apply a different sort order, begin by clearing the existing SortDescriptions collection.

You also have the ability to perform a custom sort, but only if you're using the ListCollectionView (not the BindingListCollectionView). The ListCollectionView provides a CustomSort property that accepts an IComparer object that performs the comparison between any two data items and indicates which one should be considered greater than the other. This approach is handy if you need to build a sorting routine that combines properties to get a sorting key. It also makes sense if you have nonstandard sorting rules. For example, you may want to ignore the first few characters of a product code, perform a calculation on a price, convert your field to a different data type or a different representation before sorting, and so on. Here's an example that counts the number of letters in the model name and uses that to determine sort order:

```
public class SortByModelNameLength : IComparer
{
    public int Compare(object x, object y)
    {
        Product productX = (Product)x;
        Product productY = (Product)y;
        return productX.ModelName.Length.CompareTo(productY.ModelName.Length);
    }
}
```

Here's the code that connects the IComparer to a view:

```
ListCollectionView view = (ListCollectionView)
  CollectionViewSource.GetDefaultView(lstProducts.ItemsSource);
view.CustomSort = new SortByModelNameLength();
```

In this example, the IComparer is designed to fit a specific scenario. If you have an IComparer that you need to reuse with similar data in different places, you can generalize it. For example, you could change the SortByModelNameLength class to a SortByTextLength class. When creating a SortByTextLength instance, your code would need to supply the name of the property to use (as a string), and your Compare() method could then use reflection to look it up in the data object (as with the SingleCriteriaHighlightTemplateSelector earlier in this chapter).

Grouping

In much the same way that they support sorting, views also allow you to apply grouping. As with sorting, you can group the easy way (based on a single property value) or the hard way (using a custom callback).

To perform grouping, you add System.ComponentModel.PropertyGroupDescription objects to the CollectionView.GroupDescriptions collection. Here's an example that groups products by category name:

```
ICollectionView view = CollectionViewSource.GetDefaultView(lstProducts.ItemsSource);
view.GroupDescriptions.Add(new PropertyGroupDescription("CategoryName"));
```

■**Note** This example assumes that the Product class has a property named CategoryName. It's more likely that you have a property named Category (which returns a linked Category object) or CategoryID (which identifies the category with a unique ID number. You can still use grouping in these scenarios, but you'll need to add a value converter that examines the grouping information (such as the Category object or CategoryID property) and returns the correct category text to use for the group. You'll see how to use a value converter with grouping in the next example.

This example has one problem. Although your items will now be arranged into separate groups based on their categories, it's difficult to see that any grouping has been applied when you look at the list. In fact, the result is the same as if you simply sorted by category name.

There's actually more taking place—you just can't see it with the default settings. When you use grouping, your list creates a separate GroupItem object for each group, and it adds these GroupItem objects to the list. The GroupItem is a content control, so each GroupItem holds the appropriate container (like ListBoxItem objects) with your actual data. The secret to showing your groups is formatting the GroupItem element so it stands out.

You could use a style that applies formatting to all the GroupItem objects in a list. However, you probably want more than just formatting—for example, you might want to display a group header, which requires the help of a template. Fortunately, the ItemsControl class makes both tasks easy through its ItemsControl.GroupStyle property, which provides a collection of GroupStyle objects. Despite the name, GroupStyle class is not a style. It's simply a convenient package that wraps a few useful settings for configuring your GroupItem objects. Table 17-1 lists the properties of the GroupStyle class.

Table 17-1. *GroupStyle Properties*

Name	Description
ContainerStyle	Sets the style that's applied to the GroupItem that's generated for each group.
ContainerStyleSelector	Instead of using ContainerStyle, you can use ContainerStyleSelector to supply a class that chooses the right style to use, based on the group.
HeaderTemplate	Allows you to create a template for displaying content at the beginning of each group.
HeaderTemplateSelector	Instead of using HeaderTemplate, you can use HeaderTemplateSelector to supply a class that chooses the right header template to use, based on the group.
Panel	Allows you to change the template that's used to hold groups. For example, you could use a WrapPanel instead of the standard StackPanel to create a list that tiles groups from left to right and then down.

In this example, all you need is a header before each group. You can use this to create the effect shown in Figure 17-12.

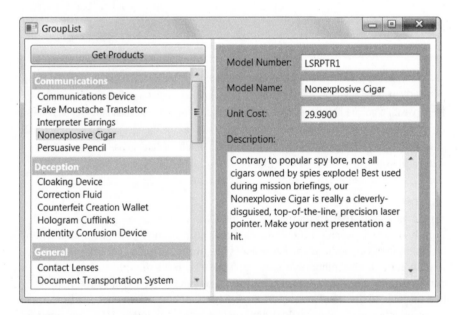

Figure 17-12. *Grouping the product list*

To add a group header, you need to set the GroupStyle.HeaderTemplate. You can fill this property with an ordinary data template, like the ones you saw earlier in this chapter. You can use any combination of elements and data binding expressions inside your template.

However, there's one trick. When you write your binding expression, you aren't binding against the data object from your list (in this case, the Product object). Instead, you're binding against the PropertyGroupDescription object for that group. That means if you want to display the field value for that group (as shown in Figure 17-12), you need to bind the Property-GroupDescription.Name property rather than Product.CategoryName.

Here's the complete template:

```
<ListBox Name="lstProducts" DisplayMemberPath="ModelName">
  <ListBox.GroupStyle>
    <GroupStyle>
      <GroupStyle.HeaderTemplate>
        <DataTemplate>
          <TextBlock Text="{Binding Path=Name}" FontWeight="Bold"
            Foreground="White" Background="LightGreen"
            Margin="0,5,0,0" Padding="3"/>
        </DataTemplate>
      </GroupStyle.HeaderTemplate>
    </GroupStyle>
  </ListBox.GroupStyle>
</ListBox>
```

■ **Tip** The ListBox.GroupStyle property is actually a collection of GroupStyle objects. This allows you to add multiple levels of grouping. To do so, you need to add more than one PropertyGroupDescription (in the order that you want your grouping and subgrouping applied) and then add a matching GroupStyle object to format each level.

You'll probably want to use grouping in conjunction with sorting. If you want to sort your groups, just make sure that the first SortDescription you use sorts based on the grouping field. The following code sorts the categories alphabetically by category name and then sorts each product within the category alphabetically by model name.

```
view.SortDescriptions.Add(new SortDescription("CategoryName",
  ListSortDirection.Ascending));
view.SortDescriptions.Add(new SortDescription("ModelName",
  ListSortDirection.Ascending));
```

One limitation with the simple grouping approach you see here is that it requires a field with duplicate values in order to perform its grouping. The previous example works because many products share the same category and have duplicate values for the CategoryName property. However, this approach doesn't work as well if you try to group by another piece of information, such as the UnitCost field. In this situation, you'll end up with a separate group for each product.

This problem has a solution. You can create a class that examines some piece of information and places it into a conceptual group for display purposes. This technique is commonly used to group data objects using numeric or date information that fall into specific ranges. For example, you could create a group for products that are less than $50, another for products that fall between $50 and $100, and so on. Figure 17-13 shows this example.

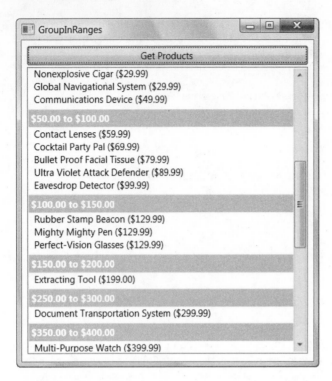

Figure 17-13. *Grouping in ranges*

To create this solution, you need to supply a value converter that examines a field in your data source (or multiple fields if you implement IMultiValueConverter) and returns the group header. As long as you use the same group header for multiple data objects, these objects are placed into the same logical group.

The following code shows the converter that creates the price ranges shown in Figure 17-13. It's designed to have some flexibility—namely, you can specify the size of the grouping ranges. (In Figure 17-13, the group range is 50 units big.)

```
public class PriceRangeProductGrouper : IValueConverter
{
    public int GroupInterval
    {
        get; set;
    }

    public object Convert(object value, Type targetType, object parameter,
      CultureInfo culture)
    {
        decimal price = (decimal)value;
        if (price < GroupInterval)
        {
            return String.Format(culture, "Less than {0:C}", GroupInterval);
        }
```

```
    else
    {
        int interval = (int)price / GroupInterval;
        int lowerLimit = interval * GroupInterval;
        int upperLimit = (interval + 1) * GroupInterval;
        return String.Format(culture, "{0:C} to {1:C}", lowerLimit, upperLimit);
    }
}

public object ConvertBack(object value, Type targetType, object parameter,
  CultureInfo culture)
{
    throw new NotSupportedException("This converter is for grouping only.");
}
}
```

To make this class even more flexible so that it can be used with other fields, you could add other properties that allow you to set the fixed part of the header text and a format string to use when converting the numeric values to header text. (The current code assumes the numbers should be treated as currencies, so 50 becomes $50.00 in the header.)

Here's the code that uses the converter to apply the range grouping. Note that the products must first be sorted by price, or you'll end up grouping them based on where they fall in the list.

```
ICollectionView view =
  CollectionViewSource.GetDefaultView(lstProducts.ItemsSource);
view.SortDescriptions.Add(new SortDescription("UnitCost",
  ListSortDirection.Ascending));

PriceRangeProductGrouper grouper = new PriceRangeProductGrouper();
grouper.GroupInterval = 50;
view.GroupDescriptions.Add(new PropertyGroupDescription("UnitCost", grouper));
```

This example does its work in code, but you can also create the converter and the view declaratively by placing them both in the Resources collection of the window. You'll see how this works in the next section.

Creating Views Declaratively

So far, the examples you've seen work the same way. They retrieve the view you want to use with code and then modify it programmatically. However, you have another choice—you can construct a CollectionViewSource declaratively in XAML markup and then bind the CollectionViewSource to your controls (such as the list).

■**Note** Technically, the CollectionViewSource is not a view. It's a helper class that allows you to retrieve a view (using the GetDefaultView() method you've seen in the previous examples) and a factory that can create a view when you need it (as you'll see in this section).

The two most important properties of the CollectionViewSource class are View, which wraps the view object, and Source, which wraps the data source. The CollectionViewSource also adds the SortDescriptions and GroupDescriptions properties, which mirror the identically named view properties you've already learned about. When the CollectionViewSource creates a view, it simply passes the value of these properties to the view.

The CollectionViewSource also includes a Filter event, which you can handle to perform filtering. This filtering works in the same way as the Filter callback that's provided by the view object, except it's defined as an event so you can easily hook up your event handler in XAML.

For example, consider the previous example, which placed products in groups using price ranges. Here's how you would define the converter and CollectionViewSource you need for this example declaratively:

```
<local:PriceRangeProductGrouper x:Key="Price50Grouper" GroupInterval="50"/>
  <CollectionViewSource x:Key="GroupByRangeView">
    <CollectionViewSource.SortDescriptions>
      <component:SortDescription PropertyName="UnitCost" Direction="Ascending"/>
    </CollectionViewSource.SortDescriptions>
    <CollectionViewSource.GroupDescriptions>
      <PropertyGroupDescription PropertyName="UnitCost"
      Converter="{StaticResource Price50Grouper}"/>
  </CollectionViewSource.GroupDescriptions>
</CollectionViewSource>
```

Notice that the SortDescription class isn't one of the WPF namespaces. To use it, you need to add the following namespace alias:

```
xmlns:component="clr-namespace:System.ComponentModel;assembly=WindowsBase"
```

Once you've set up the CollectionViewSource, you can bind to it in your list:

```
<ListBox ItemsSource="{Binding Source={StaticResource GroupByRangeView}}" ... >
```

At first glance, this looks a bit odd. It seems as though the ListBox control is binding to the CollectionViewSource, not the view exposed by the CollectionViewSource (which is stored in the CollectionViewSource.View property). However, WPF data binding makes a special exception for the CollectionViewSource. When you use it in a binding expression, WPF asks the CollectionViewSource to create its view and then binds that view to the appropriate element.

The declarative approach doesn't really save you any work. You still need code that retrieves the data at runtime. The difference is that now your code must pass the data along to the CollectionViewSource rather than supply it directly to the list:

```
ICollection<Product> products = App.StoreDB.GetProducts();
CollectionViewSource viewSource = (CollectionViewSource)
  this.FindResource("GroupByRangeView");
viewSource.Source = products;
```

Alternatively, you could create the products collection as a resource using XAML markup. You could then bind the CollectionViewSource to your products collection declaratively. However, you still need to use code to populate your products collection.

■**Note** People use a few dubious tricks to create code-free data binding. Sometimes, the data collection is defined and filled using XAML markup (with hard-coded values). In other cases, the code for populating the data object is hidden away in the data object's constructor. Both these approaches are severely impractical. I mention them only because they're often used to create quick, off-the-cuff data binding examples.

Now that you've seen the code-based and markup-based approaches for configuring a view, you're probably wondering which one is the better design decision. Both are equally valid. The choice you make depends on where you want to centralize the details for your data view.

However, the choice becomes more significant if you want to use *multiple* views. In this situation, there's a good case to be made for defining all your views in markup and then using code to swap in the appropriate view.

■**Tip** Creating multiple views makes sense if your views are dramatically different. (For example, they group on completely different criteria.) In many cases, it's simpler to modify the sorting or grouping information for the current view. For example, if you want to extend the window shown in Figure 17-13 so that you can create larger or smaller groups, the most efficient approach is to dynamically modify the PriceRange-ProductGrouper.GroupInterval property.

Navigating with a View

One of the simplest things you can do with a view object is determine the number of items in the list (through the Count property) and get a reference to the current data object (CurrentItem) or current position index (CurrentPosition). You can also use a handful of methods to move from one record to another, such as MoveCurrentToFirst(), MoveCurrentToLast(), MoveCurrent-ToNext(), MoveCurrentToPrevious(), and MoveCurrentToPosition(). So far, you haven't needed these details because all the examples you've seen have used the list to allow the user to move from one record to the next. But if you want to create a record browser application, you might want to supply your own navigation buttons. Figure 17-14 shows one example.

The bound text boxes that show the data for the bound product stay the same. They need only to indicate the appropriate property, as shown here:

```
<TextBlock Margin="7">Model Number:</TextBlock>
<TextBox Margin="5" Grid.Column="1" Text="{Binding Path=ModelNumber}"></TextBox>
```

However, this example doesn't include any list control, so it's up to you to take control of the navigation. To simplify life, you can store a reference to the view as a member variable in your window class:

```
private ListCollectionView view;
```

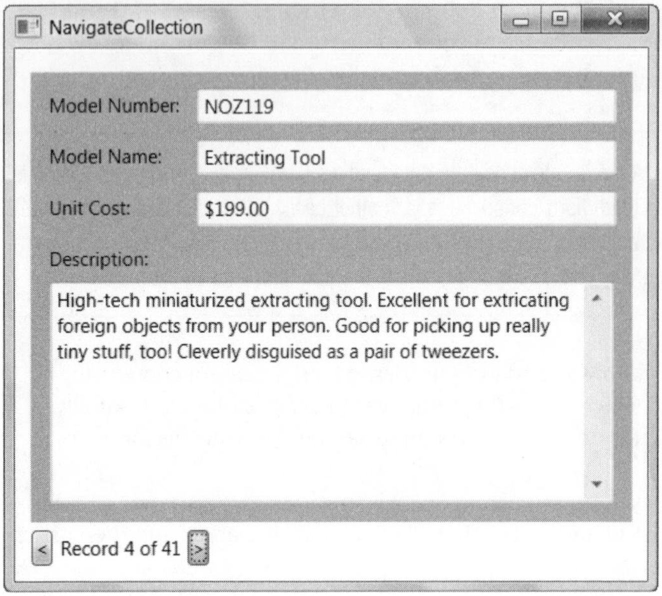

Figure 17-14. *A record browser*

In this case, the code casts the view to the appropriate view type (ListCollectionView) rather than using the ICollectionView interface. The ICollectionView interface provides most of the same functionality, but it lacks the Count property that gives the total number of items in the collection.

When the window first loads up you can get the data, place it in the DataContext of the window, and store a reference to the view:

```
ICollection<Products> products = App.StoreDB.GetProducts();
this.DataContext = products;

view = (ListCollectionView)CollectionViewSource.GetDefaultView(this.DataContext);
view.CurrentChanged += new EventHandler(view_CurrentChanged);
```

The second line does all the magic needed to show your collection of items in the window. It places the whole collection of Product objects in the DataContext. The bound controls on the form will search up the element tree until they find this object. Of course, you want the binding expressions to bind to the current item in the collection, not the collection itself, but WPF is smart enough to figure this out automatically. It automatically supplies them with the current item, so you don't need a stitch of extra code.

The previous example has one additional code statement. It connects an event handler to the CurrentChanged event of the view. When this event fires, you can perform a few useful actions, such as enabling or disabling the previous and next buttons depending on the current position and displaying the current position in a TextBlock at the bottom of the window.

```
private void view_CurrentChanged(object sender, EventArgs e)
{
    lblPosition.Text = "Record " + (view.CurrentPosition + 1).ToString() +
```

```
        " of " + view.Count.ToString();
    cmdPrev.IsEnabled = view.CurrentPosition > 0;
    cmdNext.IsEnabled = view.CurrentPosition < view.Count - 1;
}
```

This code seems like a candidate for data binding and triggers. However, the logic is just a bit too complex (partly because you need to add 1 to the index to get the record position number that you want to display).

The final step is to write the logic for the previous and next buttons. Because these buttons are automatically disabled when they don't apply, you don't need to worry about moving before the first item or after the last item.

```
private void cmdNext_Click(object sender, RoutedEventArgs e)
{
    view.MoveCurrentToNext();
}

private void cmdPrev_Click(object sender, RoutedEventArgs e)
{
    view.MoveCurrentToPrevious();
}
```

For an interesting frill, you can add a list control to this form so the user has the option of stepping through the records one at a time with the buttons or using the list to jump directly to a specific item (as shown in Figure 17-15).

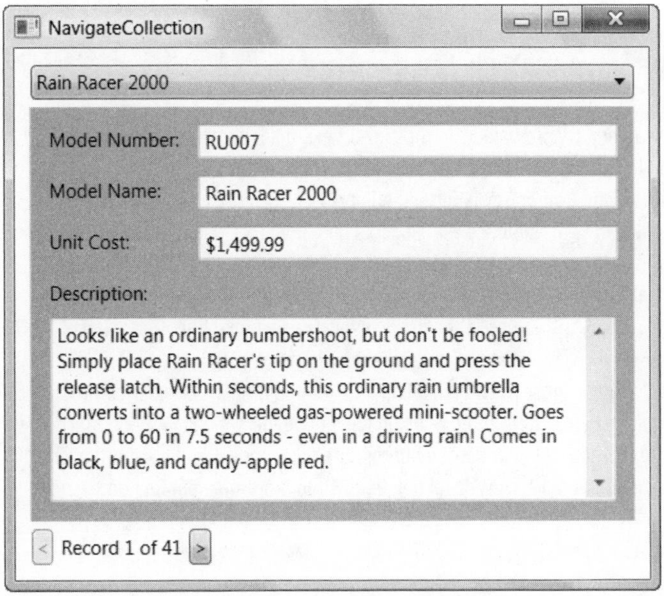

Figure 17-15. *A record browser with a drop-down list*

In this case, you need a ComboBox that uses the ItemsSource property (to get the full list of products) and uses a binding on the Text property (to show the right item):

```
<ComboBox Name="lstProducts" DisplayMemberPath="ModelName"
 Text="{Binding Path=ModelName}"
 SelectionChanged="lstProducts_SelectionChanged"></ComboBox>
```

When you first retrieve the collection of products, you'll bind the list:

```
lstProducts.ItemsSource = products;
```

This might not have the effect you expect. By default, the selected item in an ItemsControl is not synchronized with the current item in the view. That means that when you make a new selection from the list, you aren't directed to the new record—instead, you end up modifying the ModelName property of the current record. Fortunately, there are two easy approaches to solve the problem.

The brute-force approach is to simply move to the new record whenever an item is selected in the list. Here's the code that does it:

```
private void lstProducts_SelectionChanged(object sender, RoutedEventArgs e)
{
    view.MoveCurrentTo(lstProducts.SelectedItem);
}
```

A simpler solution is to set the ItemsControl.IsSynchronizedWithCurrentItem to true. That way, the currently selected item is automatically synchronized to match the current position of the view with no code required.

USING A LOOKUP LIST FOR EDITING

The ComboBox provides a handy way to edit record values. In the current example, it doesn't make much sense—after all, there's no reason to give one product the same name as another product. However, it's not difficult to think of other scenarios where the ComboBox is a great editing tool.

For example, you might have a field in your database that accepts one of a small set of preset values. In this case, use a ComboBox, and bind it to the appropriate field using a binding expression for the Text property. However, fill the ComboBox with the allowable values by setting its ItemsSource property to point to the list you've defined. And if you want to display the values in the list one way (say, as text) but store them another way (as numeric codes), just add a value converter to your Text property binding.

Another case where a lookup list makes sense is when dealing with related tables. For example, you might want to allow the user to pick the category for a product using a list of all the defined categories. The basic approach is the same: set the Text property to bind to the appropriate field, and fill in the list of options with the ItemsSource property. If you need to convert low-level unique IDs into more meaningful names, use a value converter.

Data Providers

In most of the examples you've seen, the top-level data source has been supplied by programmatically setting the DataContext of an element or the ItemsSource property of a list control.

In general, this is the most flexible approach, particularly if your data object is constructed by another class (such as StoreDB). However, you have other options.

As you saw in the previous chapter, you can define your data object as a resource of your window (or some other container). This works well if you can construct your object declaratively, but it makes less sense if you need to connect to an outside data store (such as a database) at runtime. However, some developers still use this approach (often in a bid to avoid writing event handling code). The basic idea is to create a wrapper object that fetches the data you need in its constructor. For example, you could create a resource section like this:

```
<Window.Resources>
  <ProductListSource x:Key="products"></ProductListSource>
</Window.Resources>
```

Here, ProductListSource is a class that derives from ObservableCollection<Products>. Thus, it has the ability to store a list of products. It also has some basic logic in the constructor that calls StoreDB.GetProducts() to fill itself.

Now, other elements can use this in their binding:

```
<ListBox ItemsSource="{StaticResource products}"
```

This approach seems tempting at first, but it's a bit risky. When you add error handling, you'll need to place it in the ProductListSource class. You may even need to show a message explaining the problem to the user. As you can see, this approach mingles the data model, the data access code, and the user interface code in a single muddle, so it doesn't make much sense for this example. This approach *could* make sense if you're constructing your data without needing to access any outside resources (files, databases, and so on), but even then it's a bit risky.

Data providers are, in some ways, an extension of this limited model. A data provider gives you the ability to bind directly to an object that you define in the resources section of your markup. However, instead of binding directly to the data object itself, you bind to a data provider that's able to retrieve or construct that object. This approach makes sense if the data provider is full-featured—for example, if it has the ability to raise events when exceptions occur and provides properties that allow you to configure other details about its operation. Unfortunately, the data providers that are included in WPF aren't yet up to this standard. They're too limited to be worth the trouble in a situation with external data (for example, when fetching the information from a database or a file). They may make sense in simpler scenarios—for example, you could use a data provider to glue together some controls that supply input to a class that calculates a result. However, they add relatively little in this situation except the ability to reduce event handling code in favor of markup.

All data providers derive from the System.Windows.Data.DataSourceProvider class. Currently, WPF provides just two data providers:

- **ObjectDataProvider**, which gets information by calling a method in another class

- **XmlDataProvider**, which gets information directly from an XML file

The goal of both of these objects is to allow you to instantiate your data object in XAML, without resorting to event handling code.

The ObjectDataProvider

The ObjectDataProvider allows you to get information from another class in your application. It adds the following features:

- It can create the object you need and pass parameters to the constructor.

- It can call a method in that object and pass method parameters to it.

- It can create the data object asynchronously. (In other words, it can wait until after the window is loaded and then perform the work in the background.)

For example, here's a basic ObjectDataProvider that creates an instance of the StoreDB class, calls its GetProducts() method, and makes the data available to the rest of your window:

```
<Window.Resources>
  <ObjectDataProvider x:Key="productsProvider" ObjectType="{x:Type local:StoreDB}"
    MethodName="GetProducts"></ObjectDataProvider>
</Window.Resources>
```

You can now create a binding that gets the source from the ObjectDataProvider:

```
<ListBox Name="lstProducts" DisplayMemberPath="ModelName"
 ItemsSource="{Binding Source={StaticResource productsProvider}}"></ListBox>
```

This tag looks like it binds to the ObjectDataProvider, but the ObjectDataProvider is intelligent enough to know you really want to bind to the product list that it returns from the GetProducts() method.

■**Note** The ObjectDataProvider, like all data providers, is designed to retrieve data but not update it. In other words, there's no way to force the ObjectDataProvider to call a different method in the StoreDB class to trigger an update. This is just one example of how the data provider classes in WPF are less mature than other implementations in other frameworks, such as the data source controls in ASP.NET.

Error Handling

As written, this example has a giant limitation. When you create this window, the XAML parser creates the window and calls the GetProducts() method so it can set up the binding. Everything runs smoothly if the GetProducts() method returns the data you want, but the result isn't as nice if an unhandled exception is thrown (for example, if the database is too busy or isn't reachable). At this point, the exception bubbles up from the InitializeComponent() call in the window constructor. The code that's showing this window needs to catch this error, which is conceptually confusing. And there's no way to continue and show the window—even if you catch the exception in the constructor, the rest of the window won't be initialized properly.

Unfortunately, there's no easy way to solve this problem. The ObjectDataProvider class includes an IsInitialLoadEnabled property that you can set to false to prevent it from calling GetProducts() when the window is first created. If you set this, you can call Refresh() later to trigger the call. Unfortunately, if you use this technique, your binding expression will fail, because the list won't be able to retrieve its data source. (This is unlike most data binding errors, which fail silently without raising an exception.)

So, what's the solution? You can construct the ObjectDataProvider programmatically, although you'll lose the benefit of declarative binding, which is the reason you probably used the ObjectDataProvider in the first place. Another solution is to configure the ObjectDataProvider to perform its work asynchronously, as described in the next section. In this situation, exceptions cause a silent failure (although a trace message will still be displayed in the Debug window detailing the error).

Asynchronous Support

Most developers will find that there aren't many reasons for using the ObjectDataProvider. Usually, it's easier to simply bind directly to your data object and add the tiny bit of code that calls the class that queries the data (such as StoreDB). However, there is one reason that you might use the ObjectDataProvider—to take advantage of its support for asynchronous data querying.

```
<ObjectDataProvider IsAsynchronous="True" ... >
```

It's deceptively simple. As long as you set the ObjectDataProvider.IsAsynchronous property to true, the ObjectDataProvider performs its work on a background thread. As a result, your interface isn't tied up while the work is underway. Once the data object has been constructed and returned from the method, the ObjectDataProvider makes it available to all bound elements.

■Tip If you don't want to use the ObjectDataProvider, you can still launch your data access code asynchronously. The trick is to use WPF's support for multithreaded applications. One useful tool is the Background-Worker component that's described in Chapter 3. When you use the BackgroundWorker, you gain the benefit of optional cancellation support and progress reporting. However, incorporating the BackgroundWorker into your user interface is more work than simply setting the ObjectDataProvider.IsAsynchronous property.

ASYNCHRONOUS DATA BINDINGS

WPF also provides asynchronous support through the IsAsync property of each Binding object. However, this feature is far less useful than the asynchronous support in the ObjectDataProvider. When you set Binding.IsAsync to true, WPF retrieves the bound property from the data object asynchronously. However, the data object itself is still created synchronously.

For example, imagine you create an asynchronous binding for the StoreDB example that looks like this:

```
<TextBox Text="{Binding Path=ModelNumber, IsAsync=True}" />
```

Even though you're using an asynchronous binding, you'll still be forced to wait while your code queries the database. Once the product collection is created, the binding will query the Product.ModelNumber property of the current product object asynchronously. This behavior has little benefit, because the property procedures in the Product class take a trivial amount of time to execute. In fact, all well-designed data objects are built out of lightweight properties such as this, which is one reason that the WPF team had serious reservations about providing the Binding.IsAsync property at all!

The only way to take advantage of Binding.IsAsync is to build a specialized class that includes time-consuming logic in a property get procedure. For example, consider an analysis application that binds to a data model. This data object might include a piece of information that's calculated using a time-consuming algorithm. You could bind to this property using an asynchronous binding but bind to all the other properties with synchronous bindings. That way, some information will appear immediately in your application, and the additional information will appear once it's ready.

WPF also includes a priority binding feature that builds on asynchronous bindings. Priority binding allows you to supply several asynchronous bindings in a prioritized list. The highest-priority binding is preferred, but if it's still being evaluated, a lower-priority binding is used instead. Here's an example:

```
<TextBox>
  <TextBox.Text>
    <PriorityBinding>
      <Binding Path="SlowSpeedProperty" IsAsync="True" />
      <Binding Path="MediumSpeedProperty" IsAsync="True" />
      <Binding Path="FastSpeedProperty" />
    </PriorityBinding>
  </TextBox.Text>
</TextBox>
```

This assumes that the current data context contains an object with three properties named SlowSpeedProperty, MediumSpeedProperty, and FastSpeedProperty. The bindings are placed in their order of importance. As a result, SlowSpeedProperty is always used to set the text, if it's available. But if the first binding is still in the midst of reading SlowSpeedProperty (in other words, there is time-consuming logic in the property get procedure), MediumSpeedProperty is used instead. If that's not available, FastSpeedProperty is used. For this approach to work, you must make all the binding asynchronous, except the fastest, lowest-priority binding at the end of the list. This binding can be asynchronous (in which case the text box will appear empty until the value is retrieved) or synchronous (in which case the window won't be frozen until the synchronous binding has finished its work).

The XmlDataProvider

The XmlDataProvider provides a quick and straightforward way to extract XML data from a separate file, web location, or application resource and make it available to the elements in your application. The XmlDataProvider is designed to be read-only (in other words, it doesn't provide the ability to commit changes), and it isn't able to deal with XML data that may come from other sources (such as a database record, a web service message, and so on). As a result, it's a fairly specific tool.

If you've used .NET to work with XML in the past, you already know that .NET provides a rich set of libraries for reading, writing, and manipulating XML. You can use streamlined reader and writer classes that allow you to step through XML files and handle each element with custom code, you can use XPath or the DOM to hunt for specific bits of content, and you can use serializer classes to convert entire objects to and from an XML representation. Each of these approaches has advantages and disadvantages, but all of them are more powerful than the XmlDataProvider.

If you foresee needing the ability to modify XML or to convert XML data into an object representation that you can work with in your code, you're better off using the extensive XML support that already exists in .NET. The fact that your data is stored in an XML representation then becomes a low-level detail that's irrelevant to the way you construct your user interface. (Your user interface can simply bind to data objects, as in the database-backed examples you've seen in this chapter.) However, if you absolutely must have a quick way to extract XML content and your requirements are relatively light, the XmlDataProvider is a reasonable choice.

To use the XmlDataProvider, you begin by defining it and pointing it to the appropriate file by setting the Source property.

```
<XmlDataProvider x:Key="productsProvider" Source="store.xml"></XmlDataProvider>
```

You can also set the Source programmatically (which is important if you aren't sure what the file name is that you need to use). By default, the XmlDataProvider loads the XML content asynchronously, unless you explicitly set XmlDataProvider.IsAsynchronous to false.

Here's a portion of the simple XML file used in this example. It wraps the entire document in a top-level Products element and places each product in a separate Product element. The individual properties for each product are provided as nested elements.

```
<Products>
  <Product>
    <ProductID>355</ProductID>
    <CategoryID>16</CategoryID>
    <ModelNumber>RU007</ModelNumber>
    <ModelName>Rain Racer 2000</ModelName>
    <ProductImage>image.gif</ProductImage>
    <UnitCost>1499.99</UnitCost>
    <Description>Looks like an ordinary bumbershoot ... </Description>
  </Product>
  <Product>
    <ProductID>356</ProductID>
    <CategoryID>20</CategoryID>
    <ModelNumber>STKY1</ModelNumber>
    <ModelName>Edible Tape</ModelName>
    <ProductImage>image.gif</ProductImage>
    <UnitCost>3.99</UnitCost>
    <Description>The latest in personal survival gear ... </Description>
  </Product>
  ...
</Products>
```

To pull information from your XML, you use XPath expressions. XPath is a powerful standard that allows you to retrieve the portions of a document that interest you. Although a full discussion of XPath is beyond the scope of this book, it's easy to sketch out the essentials.

XPath uses a pathlike notation. For example, the path / identifies the root of an XML document, and /Products identifies a root element named <Products>. The path /Products/Product selects every <Product> element inside the <Products> element.

When using XPath with the XmlDataProvider, your first task is to identify the root node. In this case, that means selecting the <Products> element that contains all the data. (If you wanted to focus on a specific section of the XML document, you would use a different top-level element.)

```
<XmlDataProvider x:Key="productsProvider" Source="store.xml"
 XPath="/Products"></XmlDataProvider>
```

The next step is to bind your list. When working the XmlDataProvider, you use the Binding.XPath property instead of the Binding.Path property. This gives you the flexibility to dig into your XML as deeply as you need.

Here's the markup that pulls out all the <Product> elements:

```
<ListBox Name="lstProducts" Margin="5" DisplayMemberPath="ModelName"
 ItemsSource="{Binding Source={StaticResource products}, XPath=Product}" ></ListBox>
```

When setting the XPath property in a binding, you need to remember that your expression is relative to the current position in the XML document. For that reason, you don't need to supply the full path /Products/Product in the list binding. Instead, you can simply use the relative path Product, which starts from the <Products> node that was selected by the XmlDataProvider.

Finally, you need to wire up each of the elements that displays the product details. Once again, the XPath expression you write is evaluated relative to the current node (which will be the <Product> element for the current product). Here's an example that binds to the <ModelNumber> element:

```
<TextBox Text="{Binding XPath=ModelNumber}"></TextBox>
```

Once you make these changes, you'll be left with an XML-based example that's nearly identical to the object-based bindings you've seen so far. The only difference is that all the data is treated as ordinary text. To convert it to a different data type or a different representation, you'll need to use a value converter.

The Last Word

In this chapter, you delved deeper into data binding, one of the key pillars of WPF. In the past, many of the scenarios you've considered in this chapter would be handled using code. In WPF, the data binding model (in conjunction with styles and templates) allows you to do much more work declaratively. In fact, data binding is nothing less than an all-purpose way to display any type of information, regardless of where it's stored, how you want to displayed, or whether it's editable.

Although you've now considered all the key principles of data binding (and a bit more besides), the following chapters cover a few more topics that will allow you to expand the way you present complex data. First up is Chapter 18, which takes a closer look at a few specialized controls that derive from ItemsControl, including the ListView and TreeView.

CHAPTER 18

■■■

Lists, Trees, Toolbars, and Menus

So far, you've learned a wide range of techniques and tricks for using WPF data binding to display information in the form you need. Along the way, you've seen many examples that revolve around the lowly ListBox control.

Thanks to the extensibility provided by styles, data templates, and control templates, even the ListBox (and it's similarly equipped sibling, the ComboBox) can serve as remarkably powerful tools for displaying data in a variety of ways. However, some types of data presentation would be difficult to implement with the ListBox alone. Two important examples include the following:

- Showing a tabular grid of information

- Showing a hierarchical tree of information

Although you could build these controls from scratch using the basic plumbing in the ItemsControl, WPF has two much more helpful starting points: the ListView and TreeView controls. Longtime Windows developers will recognize these as two of the most familiar "modern" Windows controls, and they turn up everywhere from file-browsing tools such as Windows Explorer to management utilities.

In this chapter, you'll take a closer look at the ListView and TreeView controls, and you'll learn how to use them to create a variety of commonly used designs. Then, you'll consider a few more specialized classes that derive from ItemsControl, including the WPF Menu, ToolBar, and StatusBar.

■Note The WPF ListView and TreeView are far different from the lists and trees you may have used in previous user interface frameworks like Windows Forms. In previous frameworks, the ListView and TreeView have provided only limited customizability. However, the WPF versions are among the most flexible controls in the entire WPF toolkit, and you can fine-tune every aspect of their display (and many aspects of their behavior).

The ItemsControl Class

As you know, the ItemsControl class defines the basic functionality for controls that wrap a list of items. Those items can be entries in a list, nodes in a tree, commands in a menu, buttons in a toolbar, and so on. Figure 18-1 provides an at-a-glance overview of all the ItemsControl classes in WPF.

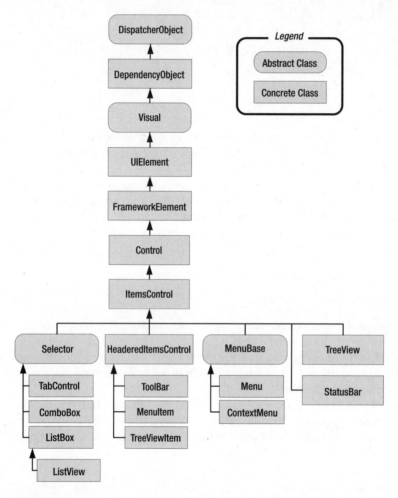

Figure 18-1. *Classes that derive from ItemsControl*

■**Note** You'll notice that some item wrappers appear in the class hierarchy of classes that derive from ItemsControl. For example, you'll not only see the expected Menu and TreeView classes, but you'll also see MenuItem and TreeViewItem. That's because these classes have the ability to contain their own collection of items—that's what gives trees and menus their nested, hierarchical structure. On the other hand, you won't find ComboBoxItem or ListBoxItem in this list, because they don't need to hold a child collection of items and so don't derive from ItemsControl.

The most important plumbing appears in the ItemsControl class, which all list-based controls derive from. The ItemsControl defines the properties that support data binding, data templating, and configurable styling (through style and template selectors). Although you've seen all these features in the previous two chapters, it's worth reviewing. Table 18-1 summarizes the key properties of the ItemsControl class.

Table 18-1. *Properties of the ItemsControl Class*

Name	Description
ItemsSource	The bound data source (the collection or DataView that you want to display in the list).
DisplayMemberPath	The property that you want to display for each data item. For a more sophisticated representation or to use a combination of properties, use the ItemTemplate instead.
ItemTemplate	A template that defines the elements (complete with the formatting and binding expressions you want to use to display each item).
ItemTemplateSelector	A DataTemplateSelector that uses code to choose a template for each item in the list. This allows you to give different templates to different items. You must create a custom DataTemplateSelector class yourself.
ItemContainerStyle	A style that allows you to set the properties of the container that wraps each item. The container depends on the type of list (for example, it's ListBoxItem for the ListBox class and ComboBoxItem for the ComboBox class). These wrapper objects are created automatically as the list is filled.
ItemContainerStyleSelector	A StyleSelector that uses code to choose a style for the wrapper of each item in the list. This allows you to give different styles to different items in the list. You must create a custom StyleSelector yourself.
ItemContainerGenerator	Provides a reference to an ItemContainerGenerator helper object. Using this object, you can use a small set of methods that get the item wrapper (ListBoxItem, ComboBoxItem, and so on) for a given list item or list index (ContainerFromItem() and ContainerFromIndex()), or vice versa (ItemFromContainer() and IndexFromContainer()).
ItemsPanel	Defines the panel that's created to hold the items of the list. All the item wrappers are added to this container. Usually, a StackPanel is used with a vertical (top-to-bottom) orientation.
GroupStyle	If you're using grouping, this is a style that defines how each group should be formatted. When using grouping, the item wrappers (ListBoxItem, ComboBoxItem, and so on) are added in GroupItem wrappers that represent each group, and these groups are then added to the list.
GroupStyleSelector	A StyleSelector that uses code to choose a style for each group. This allows you to give different styles to different groups. You must create a custom StyleSelector yourself.

The next rung in the ItemsControl inheritance hierarchy is the Selector class, which adds a straightforward set of properties for determining (and setting) a selected item. Not all ItemsControls support selection. For example, selection doesn't have any meaning for the ToolBar or Menu, so these classes derive from ItemsControl but not Selector.

The properties that the Selector class adds include SelectedItem (the selected data object), SelectedIndex (the position of the selected item), and SelectedValue (the "value" property of the selected data object, which you designate by setting SelectedValuePath). Notice that the Selector class doesn't provide support for multiple selection—that's added to the ListBox through its SelectionMode and SelectedItems properties (which is essentially all the ListBox class adds to this model).

■Note Even though the TreeView supports selection, its hierarchical structure makes it different from other selectors and prevents it from deriving directly from the Selector class. However, the TreeView class does define the same SelectedItem, SelectedValue, and SelectedValue path properties. It omits the SelectedIndex property, which has no meaning because tree nodes can be found at different levels in the tree hierarchy. Finally, the Selector provides a SelectionChanged event to notify you when the current selection changes, while the TreeView uses the SelectedItemChanged event for the same purpose. (The naming difference reflects that the SelectionChanged event will indicate whether *multiple* items have been selected or unselected, which is possible in a multiselect ListBox.)

In most of the data binding examples you've considered so far, this chapter has focused on the ListBox and used it to explore the features that are built into the ItemsControl and Selector classes. However, you still haven't considered a few points about ItemsControls. The following sections fill in a few of these blanks. First, you'll learn how to use ComboBox editing and autocomplete. Next, you'll see how to use the ListBox to get a list of check boxes or radio buttons.

The ComboBox

Like the ListBox, the ComboBox is a descendant of the Selector class. Unlike the ListBox, the ComboBox is built out of two pieces: a selection box that shows the currently selected item and a drop-down list where you can choose that item. The drop-down list appears when you click the drop-down arrow at the edge of the combo box. Or, if your combo box is in read-only mode (the default), you can open the drop-down list by clicking anywhere in the selection box. Finally, you can programmatically open or close the drop-down list by setting the IsDropDownOpen property.

Ordinarily, the ComboBox control shows a read-only combo box, which means you can use it to select an item but you can type in arbitrary text of your own. However, you can change this behavior by setting the IsReadOnly property to false and the IsEditable property to true. Now, the selection box becomes a text box, and you can type in whatever text you want.

The ComboBox control provides a rudimentary form of AutoComplete that completes entries as you type. (This shouldn't be confused with the fancier AutoComplete that you see in programs such as Internet Explorer, which shows a whole *list* of possibilities under the current text box.) Here's how it works—as you type in the ComboBox control, WPF fills in the remainder of the selection box with the first matching AutoComplete suggestion. For example, if you type **Gr** and your list contains the string Green, the combo box will fill in the letters *een*. The AutoComplete text is selected, so you'll automatically overwrite it if you keep typing.

If you don't want the AutoComplete behavior, simply set the ComboBox.IsTextSearch-Enabled property to false. This property is inherited from the base ItemsControl class, and it applies to many other list controls. For example, if IsTextSearchEnabled is set to true in a ListBox, you can type the first level of an item to jump to that position.

■**Note** WPF doesn't include any features for using the system-tracked AutoComplete lists, like the list of recent URLs and files. It also doesn't provide support for drop-down AutoComplete lists.

Lists of Complex Objects

So far, the behavior of the ComboBox is quite straightforward. However, it changes a bit if your list contains more complex objects rather than simple strings of text.

You can place more complex objects in a ComboBox in two ways. The first option is to add them manually. As with the ListBox, you can place any content you want in a ComboBox. For example, if you want a list of images and text, you'd simply place the appropriate elements in a StackPanel and wrap that StackPanel in a ComboBoxItem object. More practically, you can use data templates to insert the data from an object into a predefined group of elements. You explored this approach in detail in Chapter 17.

When using nontext content, it's not as obvious what the selection box should contain. If the IsEditable property is false (the default), the selection box will show an exact visual copy of the item. For example, Figure 18-2 shows a ComboBox that uses a data template that incorporates text and image content.

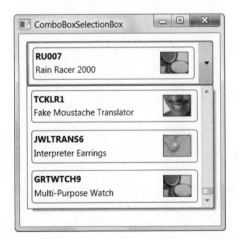

Figure 18-2. *A read-only ComboBox that uses templates*

■**Note** The important detail is what the combo box is displaying as its content, not what it has as its data source. For example, imagine you fill a ComboBox control with Product objects and set the DisplayMemberPath property to ModelName so the combo box shows the ModelName property of each item. Even though the combo box retrieves its information from a group of Product objects, your markup creates an ordinary text list. As a result, the selection box will behave the way you expect it to behave. It will show the ModelName of the current product, and if IsEditable is true and IsReadOnly is false, it will allow you to edit that value.

The user won't be able to interact with the content that appears in the selection box. For example, if the content of the currently selected item includes a text box, you won't be able to type in it. If the currently selected item includes a button, you won't be able to click it. Instead, clicking the selection box will simply open the drop-down list. (Of course, there are countless good usability reasons not to put user-interactive controls in a drop-down list in the first place.)

If the IsEditable property is true, the behavior of the ComboBox control changes. Instead of showing a copy of the selected item, the selection box displays a textual representation of it. To create this textual representation, WPF simply calls ToString() on the item. Figure 18-3 shows an example with the same combo box that's shown in Figure 18-2. In this case, the display text DataBinding.Product is simply the fully qualified class name of the currently selected Product object, which is the default ToString() implementation unless you override it in your data class.

Figure 18-3. *An editable ComboBox that uses templates*

The easiest option to correct this problem is to set the attached TextSearch.TextPath property to indicate the property that should be used for the content of the selection box. Here's an example:

```
<ComboBox IsEditable="True" IsReadOnly="True" TextSearch.TextPath="ModelName" ...>
```

Although IsEditable must be true, it's up to you whether you set IsReadOnly to false (to allow editing of that property) or true (to prevent the user from typing in arbitrary text). Figure 18-4 shows the result.

■**Tip** What if you want to show richer content than a simple piece of text but you still want the content in the selection box to be different from the content in the drop-down list? The ComboBox includes a Selection-BoxItemTemplate property that defines the template that's used for the selection box. Unfortunately, the SelectionBoxItemTemplate is read-only. It's automatically set to match the current item, and you can't supply a different template. However, you could create an entirely new ComboBox control template that doesn't use the SelectionBoxItemTemplate at all. Instead, this control template could hard-code the selection box template or could retrieve it from the Resources collection in the window.

Figure 18-4. *Displaying a property in the selection box*

Improving the Performance of the ComboBox

The ComboBox has a well-known limitation. If you pack it with thousands of items, there will be a noticeable delay when you click the down arrow to open the drop-down portion of the combo box. That's because even though the combo box shows only a subset of the total list of items, it still iterates over the entire list and creates an element for each item.

Fortunately, this problem is easy to fix. The solution is to explicitly insert a Virtualizing-StackPanel container for hosting the items in the ComboBox control. Doing so is easy. You simply need to modify the ComboBox.ItemsPanel property, as shown here:

```
<ComboBox>
  <ComboBox.ItemsPanel>
    <ItemsPanelTemplate>
      <VirtualizingStackPanel></VirtualizingStackPanel>
    </ItemsPanelTemplate>
  </ComboBox.ItemsPanel>
</ComboBox>
```

Now, a different set of steps happens when you click the down arrow in the combo box. First, the VirtualizingStackPanel calculates how many items will fit in the display area that's given to the combo box drop-down. Then, it generates elements for just this subset of the list. As you scroll through the list, additional elements are generated without any noticeable hesitation. The end result is a much more responsive user interface.

Incidentally, the ListBox control automatically uses a VirtualizingStackPanel to hold its items. If you override this behavior by supplying a standard StackPanel for the ListBox.ItemsPanel property and you add a very large number of items to the ListBox, you'll see essentially the same delay. In this case, the delay will occur when the window is first created and the list is displayed for the first time.

A ListBox with Check Boxes or Radio Buttons

New WPF developers sometimes look for popular controls that have gone missing. One example is the CheckedListBox from Windows Forms, which displays a check box next to each item that can be checked or cleared.

At first glance, the value of a single CheckedListBox seems small. After all, it's easy enough to solve the problem by composition. All you need to do is fill a ScrollViewer with a series of CheckBox objects. However, this implementation doesn't provide the same programming model. There's no easy way to iterate through all the check boxes, and, more important, there's no way to use this implementation with data binding. (Ideally, you'd be able to fill the Scroll-Viewer with CheckBox controls simply by supplying a collection of data objects.)

The solution is to use an ordinary ListBox but use control templates to change the appearance of each item. Figure 18-5 and Figure 18-6 show two examples—one with a list filled with RadioButton elements (only one of which can be chosen at a time) and one with a list of CheckBox elements. The two solutions are similar, but the list with radio buttons is easier.

Figure 18-5. *A radio button list using a template*

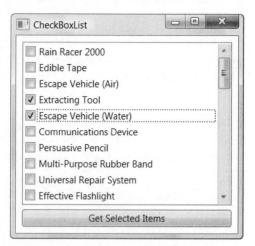

Figure 18-6. *A check box list using a template*

The basic technique is to change the control template used as the container for each list item. You don't want to modify the ListBox.Template property, because this provides the template for the ListBox. Instead, you need to modify the ListBoxItem.Template property. Here's the template you need to wrap each item in a RadioButton element:

```
<ControlTemplate TargetType="{x:Type ListBoxItem}">
  <RadioButton Focusable="False" IsChecked="{Binding Path=IsSelected,
RelativeSource={RelativeSource TemplatedParent},Mode=TwoWay}">
    <ContentPresenter></ContentPresenter>
  </RadioButton>
</ControlTemplate>
```

This works because a RadioButton is a content control and can contain any content. Although you could use a binding expression to get the content, it's far more flexible to use the ContentPresenter element, as shown here. The ContentPresenter grabs whatever would ordinarily appear in the item, which might be property text (if you're using the ListBox.DisplayMemberPath property) or a more complex representation of the data (if you're using the ListBox.ItemTemplate property).

The real trick is the binding expression for the RadioButton.IsChecked property. This expression retrieves the value of the ListBoxItem.IsSelected property using the Binding.RelativeSource property. That way, when you click a RadioButton to select it, the corresponding ListBoxItem is marked as selected. At the same time, all other items are deselected. This binding expression also works in the other direction, which means you can set the selection in code and the right RadioButton will be filled in.

To complete this template, you need to set the RadioButton.Focusable property to false. Otherwise, you'll be able to tab to the currently selected ListBoxItem (which is focusable) and then into the RadioButton itself, which doesn't make much sense.

The ListBoxItem.Template property isn't exposed through the ListBox class. To set this property, you need a style rule that can dig down to the right level. Fortunately, this part is easy, because the ListBox class includes an ItemContainerStyle property that allows you to supply a style that's used for individual list items. The following markup shows the style rule, with its control template:

```
<Window.Resources>
  <Style x:Key="RadioButtonListStyle" TargetType="{x:Type ListBox}">
    <Setter Property="ItemContainerStyle">
      <Setter.Value>
        <Style TargetType="{x:Type ListBoxItem}" >
          <Setter Property="Margin" Value="2" />
          <Setter Property="Template">
            <Setter.Value>
              <ControlTemplate TargetType="{x:Type ListBoxItem}">
                <RadioButton Focusable="False"
                 IsChecked="{Binding Path=IsSelected, Mode=TwoWay,
                            RelativeSource={RelativeSource TemplatedParent} }">
                  <ContentPresenter></ContentPresenter>
                </RadioButton>
```

```
            </ControlTemplate>
          </Setter.Value>
        </Setter>
      </Style>
    </Setter.Value>
  </Setter>
</Style>
</Window.Resources>
```

Although you could set the ListBox.ItemContainerStyle property directly, this example factors it out one more level. The style that sets the ListBoxItem.Control template is wrapped in another style that applies this style to the ListBox.ItemContainerStyle property. This makes the template reusable, allowing you to connect it to as many ListBox objects as you want:

```
<ListBox Style="{StaticResource RadioButtonListStyle}" Name="lstProducts"
 DisplayMemberPath="ModelName">
```

You could also use the same style to adjust other properties of the ListBox.

Creating a ListBox that shows check boxes is just as easy. In fact, you have to make only two changes. First, replace the RadioButton element with an identical CheckBox element. Then, change the ListBox.SelectionMode property to allow simple multiple selection. Now, the user can check as many or as few items as desired.

Here's the style rule that transforms an ordinary ListBox into a list of check boxes:

```
<Style x:Key="CheckBoxListStyle" TargetType="{x:Type ListBox}">
  <Setter Property="SelectionMode" Value="Multiple"></Setter>
  <Setter Property="ItemContainerStyle">
    <Setter.Value>
      <Style TargetType="{x:Type ListBoxItem}" >
        <Setter Property="Margin" Value="2" />
        <Setter Property="Template">
          <Setter.Value>
            <ControlTemplate TargetType="{x:Type ListBoxItem}">
              <CheckBox Focusable="False"
                IsChecked="{Binding Path=IsSelected, Mode=TwoWay,
                          RelativeSource={RelativeSource TemplatedParent} }">
                <ContentPresenter></ContentPresenter>
              </CheckBox>
            </ControlTemplate>
          </Setter.Value>
        </Setter>
      </Style>
    </Setter.Value>
  </Setter>
</Style>
```

The ListView

The ListView is a specialized list class that's designed for displaying different *views* of the same data. The ListView is particularly useful if you need to build a multicolumn view that displays several pieces of information about each data item.

The ListView derives from the ListBox class and extends it with a single detail: the View property. The View property is yet another extensibility point for creating rich list displays. If you don't set the View property, the ListView behaves just like its lesser-powered ancestor, the ListBox. However, the ListView becomes much more interesting when you supply a view object that indicates how data items should be formatted and styled.

Technically, the View property points to an instance of any class that derives from View-Base (which is an abstract class). The ViewBase class is surprisingly simple—in fact, it's little more than a package that binds together two styles. One style applies to the ListView control (and is referenced by the DefaultStyleKey property), while the other style applies to the items in the ListView (and is referenced by the ItemContainerDefaultStyleKey property). The Default-StyleKey and ItemContainerDefaultStyleKey properties don't actually provide the style; instead, they return a ResourceKey object that points to it.

At this point, you might wonder why you need a View property—after all, the ListBox already offers powerful data template and styling features (as do all classes that derive from ItemsControls). Ambitious developers can rework the visual appearance of the ListBox by supplying a different data template, layout panel, and control template.

In truth, you don't need a ListView class with a View property in order to create customizable multicolumned lists. In fact, you could achieve much the same thing on your own using the template and styling features of the ListBox. However, the View property is a useful abstraction. Here are some of its advantages:

- **Reusable views.** The ListView separates all the view-specific details into one object. That makes it easier to create views that are data-independent and can be used on more than one list.

- **Multiple views.** The separation between the ListView control and the View objects also makes it easier to switch between multiple views with the same list. (For example, you use this technique in Windows Explorer to get a different perspective on your files and folders.) You could build the same feature by dynamically changing templates and styles, but it's easier to have just one object that encapsulates all the view details.

- **Better organization.** The view object wraps two styles: one for the root ListView control and one that applies to the individual items in the list. Because these styles are packaged together, it's clear that these two pieces are related and may share certain details and interdependencies. For example, this makes a lot of sense for a column-based ListView, because it needs to keep its column headers and column data lined up.

Using this model, there's a great potential to create a number of useful prebuilt views that all developers can use. Unfortunately, the first version of WPF includes just one view: the Grid-View. Although the GridView is extremely useful for creating multicolumn lists, you'll need to create your own custom view if you have other needs. The following sections show you how to do both.

THE GRIDVIEW VS. THE DATAGRIDVIEW

The GridView can't compete with the specialized features provided by more mature data controls, such as the DataGridView from Windows Forms. Some of the features that are lacking include the following:

- Individual cell selection. You must select entire rows in the GridView.

- Automatic sorting. You can respond to cell header clicks in a GridView and perform sorting using the techniques described in Chapter 17. Unfortunately, it's not so easy to determine what field to sort by (particularly if your field names don't match your column headers) and what to do with formatted numbers. The only solution is to keep track of extra information about your data source and write some messy conditional code.

- Cell styling. The GridView lets you give different templates to different columns and different styles to different rows. However, these features aren't nearly as fine-grained as those of the DataGridView, which lets you format individual cells.

- Freezable columns. This DataGridView feature allows you to make sure some columns always remain in view when scrolling from side to side in a wide grid.

- Virtualization. This DataGridView feature allows you to query just a subset of the information for a list that could contain tens of thousands of items.

- Editing support. You can use control templates and triggers to provide editing behavior in a GridView, but it's not easy; you'll face quirks aplenty, and you won't have support for keyboard navigation. You can find a sample implementation of an editable GridView column at http://blogs.msdn.com/atc_avalon_team/archive/2006/03/14/550934.aspx.

If you need DataGridView-like functionality, the best approach is to take advantage of Windows Forms interoperability to use the DataGridView control in your WPF applications. Other options are to build it yourself, purchase a third-party control, or wait, because the architects of WPF are actively considered a more capable grid control for future versions. At the time of this writing, Xceed Software (http://xceed.com) offers a free DataGrid control for WPF.

Creating Columns with the GridView

The GridView is a class that derives from ViewBase and represents a list view with multiple columns. You define those columns by adding GridViewColumn objects to the GridView.Columns collection.

Both GridView and GridViewColumn provide a small set of useful methods that you can use to customize the appearance of your list. To create the simplest, most straightforward list (which resembles the details view in Windows Explorer), you need to set just two properties for each GridViewColumn: the Header and the DisplayMemberBinding. The Header property supplies the text that's placed at the top of the column, while the DisplayMemberBinding property contains a binding that extracts the piece of information you want to display from each data item.

Figure 18-7 shows a straightforward example with three columns of information about a product.

Figure 18-7. *A grid-based ListView*

Here's the markup that defines the three columns used in this example:

```
<ListView Margin="5" Name="lstProducts">
  <ListView.View>
    <GridView>
      <GridView.Columns>
        <GridViewColumn Header="Name"
         DisplayMemberBinding="{Binding Path=ModelName}" />
        <GridViewColumn Header="Model"
         DisplayMemberBinding="{Binding Path=ModelNumber}" />
        <GridViewColumn Header="Price" DisplayMemberBinding=
"{Binding Path=UnitCost, Converter={StaticResource PriceConverter} }" />
      </GridView.Columns>
    </GridView>
  </ListView.View>
</ListView>
```

This example has a few important points worth noticing. First, none of the columns has a hard-coded size. Instead, the GridView sizes its columns just large enough to fit the widest visible item (or the column header, if it's wider), which makes a lot of sense in the flow layout world of WPF. (Of course, this leaves you in a bit of trouble if you have huge columns values. In this case, you may choose to wrap your text, as described in the upcoming "Cell Templates" section.)

Also, notice how the DisplayMemberBinding property is set using a full-fledged binding expression, which supports all the tricks you learned about in Chapter 16. For example, you can use an IValueConverter, such as the PriceConverter that changes decimal values into more readable currency strings in this example. (For the full code for the PriceConverter, refer to Chapter 16, or refer to the downloadable code for this chapter.)

Resizing Columns

Initially, the GridView makes each column just wide enough to fit the largest visible value. However, you can easily resize any column by clicking and dragging the edge of the column header. Or, you can double-click the edge of the column header to force the GridViewColumn to resize itself based on whatever content is currently visible. For example, if you scroll down the list and find an item that's truncated because it's wider than the column, just double-click the right edge of that column's header. The column will automatically expand itself to fit.

For more micromanaged control over column size, you set a specific width when you declare the column:

```
<GridViewColumn Width="300" ... />
```

This simply determines the initial size of the column. It doesn't prevent the user from resizing the column using either of the techniques described previously. Unfortunately, the GridViewColumn class doesn't define properties like MaxWidth and MinWidth, so there's no way to constrain how a column can be resized. Your only option is to supply a new template for the GridViewColumn's header if you want to disable resizing altogether.

Note The user can also reorder columns by dragging a header to a new position.

Cell Templates

The GridViewColumn.DisplayMemberBinding property isn't the only option for showing data in a cell. Your other choice is the CellTemplate property, which takes a data template. This is exactly like the data templates you learned about in Chapter 17, except it applies to just one column. If you're ambitious, you can give each column its own data template.

Cell templates are a key piece of the puzzle when customizing the GridView. One feature that they allow is text wrapping. Ordinarily, the text in a column is wrapped in a single-line TextBlock. However, it's easy to change this detail using a data template of your own devising:

```
<GridViewColumn Header="Description" Width="300">
  <GridViewColumn.CellTemplate>
    <DataTemplate>
      <TextBlock Text="{Binding Path=Description}" TextWrapping="Wrap"></TextBlock>
    </DataTemplate>
  </GridViewColumn.CellTemplate>
</GridViewColumn>
```

Notice that in order for the wrapping to have an effect, you need to constrain the width of the column using the Width property. If the user resizes the column, the text will be rewrapped to fit. You *don't* want to constrain the width of the TextBlock, because that would ensure that your text is limited to a single specific size, no matter how wide or narrow the column becomes.

The only limitation in this example is that the data template needs to bind explicitly to the property you want to display. For that reason, you can't create a template that enables wrapping and reuse it for every piece of content you want to wrap. Instead, you need to create a separate template for each field. This isn't a problem in this simple example, but it's annoying if you create a more complex template that you'd like to apply to other lists (for example, a template that converts data to an image and displays it in an Image element, or a template that uses a TextBox control to allow editing). There's no easy way to reuse any template on multiple columns—instead, you'll be forced to cut and paste the template and then modify the binding.

Note It would be nice if you created a data template that uses the DisplayMemberBinding property. That way, you could use DisplayMemberBinding to extract the specific property you want and use CellTemplate to format that content into the right visual representation. Unfortunately, this just isn't possible. If you set both DisplayMember and CellTemplate, the GridViewColumn uses the DisplayMember property to set the content for the cell and ignores the template altogether.

Data templates aren't limited to tweaking the properties of a TextBlock. You can also use date templates to supply completely different elements. For example, the following column uses a data template to show an image. The ProductImagePath converter (shown in Chapter 16) helps by loading the corresponding image file from the file system.

```
<GridViewColumn Header="Picture" >
  <GridViewColumn.CellTemplate>
    <DataTemplate>
      <Image Source=
"{Binding Path=ProductImagePath,Converter={StaticResource ImagePathConverter}}">
      </Image>
    </DataTemplate>
  </GridViewColumn.CellTemplate>
</GridViewColumn>
```

Figure 18-8 shows a ListView that uses both templates to show wrapped text and a product image.

Tip When creating a data template, you have the choice of defining it inline (as in the previous two examples) or referring to a resource that's defined elsewhere. Because column templates can't be reused for different fields, it's usually clearest to define them inline.

As you learned in Chapter 17, you can vary templates so that different data items get different templates. To do this, you need to create a template selector that chooses the appropriate template based on the properties of the data object at that position. To use this feature, create your selector, and use it to set the GridViewColumn.CellTemplateSelector property. For a full template selector example, see Chapter 17.

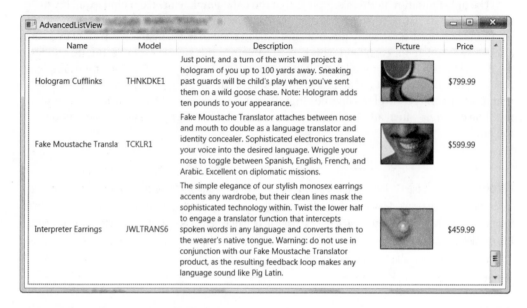

Figure 18-8. *Columns that use templates*

CUSTOMIZING COLUMN HEADERS

Cell templates aren't the only templates you can use with the ListView. You can also use column header templates to change how the column header appears if the standard gray box doesn't excite you.

So far, you've seen how to customize the appearance of the values in every cell. However, you haven't done anything to fine-tune the column headers. If the standard gray boxes don't excite you, you'll be happy to find out that you can change the content and appearance of the column headers just as easily as the column values. In fact, you can use several approaches.

If you want to keep the gray column header boxes but you want to fill them with your own content, you can simply set the GridViewColumn.Header property. The previous examples have the Header property using ordinary text, but you can supply an element instead. Use a StackPanel that wraps a TextBlock and Image to create a fancy header that combines text and image content.

If you want to fill the column headers with your own content but you don't want to specify this content separately for each column, you can use the GridViewColumn.HeaderTemplate property to define a data template. This data template binds to whatever object you've specified in the GridViewColumn.Header property and presents it accordingly.

If you want to reformat a specific column header, you can use the GridViewColumn.HeaderContainerStyle property to supply a style. If you want to reformat all the column headers in the same way, use the GridView.ColumnHeaderContainerStyle property instead.

If you want to completely change the appearance of the header (for example, replacing the gray box with a rounded blue border), you can supply a completely new control template for the header. Use GridView-Column.HeaderTemplate to change a specific column, or use GridView.ColumnHeaderTemplate to change them all in the same way. You can even use a template selector to choose the right template for a given header by setting the GridViewColumn.HeaderTemplateSelector or GridView.ColumnHeaderTemplateSelector properties.

Creating a Custom View

So far, you've focused on how the ListView works in conjunction with the GridView. The Grid-View is the only view object that's provided in the first version of WPF, but you can create your own to extend the ListView's capabilities. Unfortunately, it's far from straightforward.

To understand the problem, you need to understand a little more about the way a view works. Views do their work by overriding two protected properties: DefaultStyleKey and Item-ContainerDefaultKeyStyle. Each property returns a specialized object called a ResourceKey, which points to a style that you've defined in XAML. The DefaultStyleKey property points to the style that should be applied to configure the overall ListView, while the Item-Container.DefaultKeyStyle property points to the style that should be used to configure each ListViewItem in the ListView. Although these styles are free to tweak any property, they usually do their work by replacing the ControlTemplate that's used for the ListView and the DataTemplate that's used for each ListViewItem.

Here's where the problems occur. The DataTemplate you use to display items is defined in XAML markup. Imagine you want to create a ListView that shows a tiled image for each item. This is easy enough using a DataTemplate—you simply need to bind the Source property of an Image to the right property of your data object. But how do you know what data object the user will supply? If you hard-code property names as part of your view, you'll limit its usefulness, making it impossible to reuse your custom view in other scenarios. The alternative—forcing the user to supply the DataTemplate—means you can't pack as much functionality into the view, which means reusing it won't be as useful.

Tip Before you begin creating a custom view, consider whether you could get the same result by simply using the right DataTemplate with a ListBox or a ListView and GridView combination.

So why go to all the effort of designing a custom view if you can already get all the functionality you need by restyling the ListView (or even the ListBox)? The primary reason is if you want a list that can dynamically change views. For example, you might want a product list that can be viewed in different modes, depending on the user's selection. You could implement this by dynamically swapping in different DataTemplate objects (and this is a reasonable approach), but often a view needs to change both the DataTemplate of the ListViewItem and the layout or overall appearance of the ListView itself. A view helps clarify the relationship between these details in your source code.

The following example shows you how to create a grid that can be switched seamlessly from one view to another. The grid begins in the familiar column-separated view but also supports two tiled image views, as shown in Figure 18-9 and Figure 18-10.

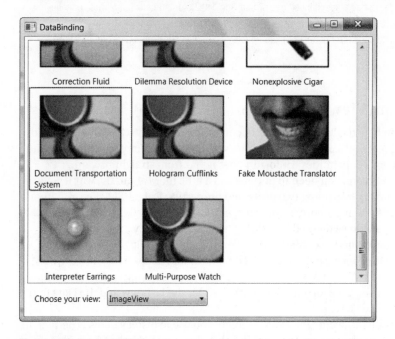

Figure 18-9. *An image view*

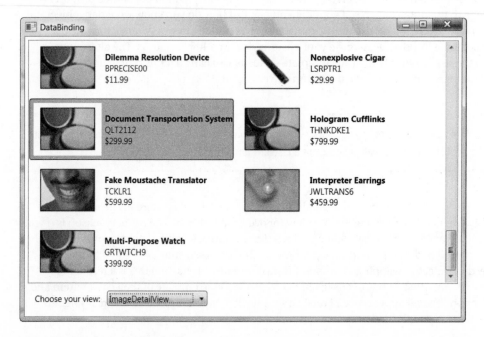

Figure 18-10. *A detailed image view*

The View Class

The first step that's required to build this example is the class representing the custom view. This class must derive from ViewBase. In addition, it usually (although not always) overrides the DefaultStyleKey and ItemContainerDefaultStyleKey properties to supply style references.

In this example, the view is named TileView, because its key characteristic is that it tiles its items in the space provided. It uses a WrapPanel to lay out the contained ListViewItem objects. This view is not named ImageView, because the tile content isn't hard-coded and may not include images at all. Instead, the tile content is defined using a template that the developer supplies when using the TileView.

The TileView class applies two styles, named TileView (which applies to the ListView) and TileViewItem (which applies to the ListViewItem). Additionally, the TileView defines a property named ItemTemplate so the developer using the TileView can supply the right data template. This template is then inserted inside each ListViewItem and used to create the tile content.

```
public class TileView : ViewBase
{
    private DataTemplate itemTemplate;
    public DataTemplate ItemTemplate
    {
        get { return itemTemplate; }
        set { itemTemplate = value; }
    }

    protected override object DefaultStyleKey
    {
        get { return new ComponentResourceKey(GetType(), "TileView"); }
    }

    protected override object ItemContainerDefaultStyleKey
    {
        get { return new ComponentResourceKey(GetType(), "TileViewItem"); }
    }
}
```

As you can see, the TileView class doesn't do much. It simply provides a ComponentResourceKey reference that points to the right style. You first learned about the ComponentResourceKey in Chapter 11, when considering how you could retrieve shared resources from a DLL assembly.

The ComponentResourceKey wraps two pieces of information: the type of class that owns the style, and a descriptive ResourceId string that identifies the resource. In this example, the type is obviously the TileView class for both resource keys. The descriptive ResourceId names aren't as important, but you'll need to be consistent. In this example, the default style key is named TileView, and the style key for each ListViewItem is named TileViewItem. In the following section, you'll dig into both these styles and see how they're defined.

The View Styles

For the TileView to work as written, WPF needs to be able to find the styles that you want to use. The trick to making sure styles are automatically available is creating a resource dictionary named generic.xaml. This resource dictionary must be placed in a project subfolder named Themes. WPF uses the generic.xaml file to get the default styles that are associated with a class. (You'll learn more about this system when you consider custom control development in Chapter 24.)

In this example, the generic.xaml file defines the styles that are associated with the TileView class. To set up the association between your styles and the TileView, you need to give your style the correct key in the generic.xaml resource dictionary. Rather than using an ordinary string key, WPF expects your key to be a ComponentResourceKey object, and this ComponentResourceKey needs to match the information that's returned by the DefaultStyleKey and ItemContainerDefaultStyleKey properties of the TileView class.

Here's the basic structure of the Generic.xaml resource dictionary, with the correct keys:

```
<ResourceDictionary
    xmlns="http://schemas.microsoft.com/winfx/2006/xaml/presentation"
    xmlns:x="http://schemas.microsoft.com/winfx/2006/xaml"
    xmlns:local="clr-namespace:DataBinding">

  <Style x:Key="{ComponentResourceKey TypeInTargetAssembly={x:Type local:TileView},
ResourceId=TileView}"
    TargetType="{x:Type ListView}"
    BasedOn="{StaticResource {x:Type ListBox}}">
    ...
  </Style>

  <Style x:Key="{ComponentResourceKey TypeInTargetAssembly={x:Type local:TileView},
ResourceId=TileViewItem}"
    TargetType="{x:Type ListViewItem}"
    BasedOn="{StaticResource {x:Type ListBoxItem}}">
    ...
  </Style>

</ResourceDictionary>
```

As you can see, the key of each style is set to match the information provided by the TileView class. Additionally, the styles also set the TargetType property (to indicate what element the style modifies) and the BasedOn property (to inherit basic style settings from more fundamental styles used with the ListBox and ListBoxItem). This saves some work, and it allows you to focus on extending these styles with custom settings.

Because these two styles are associated with the TileView, they'll be used to configure the ListView whenever you've set the View property to a TileView object. If you're using a different view object, these styles will be ignored. This is the magic that makes the ListView work the way you want so that it seamlessly reconfigures itself every time you change the View property.

The TileView style that applies to the ListView makes three changes:

• It adds a slightly different border around the ListView.

- It sets the attached Grid.IsSharedSizeScope property to true. This allows different list items to use shared column or row settings if they use the Grid layout container (a feature first explained in Chapter 4). In this example, it makes sure each item has the same dimensions in the detailed tile view.

- It changes the ItemsPanel from a StackPanel to a WrapPanel, allowing the tiling behavior. The WrapPanel width is set to match the width of the ListView.

Here's the full markup for this style:

```
<Style x:Key="{ComponentResourceKey TypeInTargetAssembly={x:Type local:TileView},
 ResourceId=TileView}"
 TargetType="{x:Type ListView}" BasedOn="{StaticResource {x:Type ListBox}}">
  <Setter Property="BorderBrush" Value="Black"></Setter>
  <Setter Property="BorderThickness" Value="0.5"></Setter>
  <Setter Property="Grid.IsSharedSizeScope" Value="True"></Setter>

  <Setter Property="ItemsPanel">
    <Setter.Value>
      <ItemsPanelTemplate>
        <WrapPanel Width="{Binding (FrameworkElement.ActualWidth),
                          RelativeSource={RelativeSource
                          AncestorType=ScrollContentPresenter}}">
        </WrapPanel>
      </ItemsPanelTemplate>
    </Setter.Value>
  </Setter>
</Style>
```

These are relatively minor changes. A more ambitious view could link to a style that changes the control template that's used for the ListView, changing it much more dramatically. This is where you begin to see the benefits of the view model. By changing a single property in the ListView, you can apply a combination of related settings through two styles. The TileView style that applies to the ListViewItem changes a few other details. It sets the padding and content alignment and, most important, sets the DataTemplate that's used to display content.

Here's the full markup for this style:

```
<Style x:Key="{ComponentResourceKey TypeInTargetAssembly={x:Type local:TileView},
 ResourceId=TileViewItem}"
 TargetType="{x:Type ListViewItem}"
 BasedOn="{StaticResource {x:Type ListBoxItem}}">
  <Setter Property="Padding" Value="3"/>
  <Setter Property="HorizontalContentAlignment" Value="Center"></Setter>
  <Setter Property="ContentTemplate" Value="{Binding Path=View.ItemTemplate,
    RelativeSource={RelativeSource Mode=FindAncestor, AncestorType={x:Type ListView}
                }}"></Setter>
</Style>
```

Remember, to ensure maximum flexibility, the TileView is designed to use a data template that's supplied by the developer. To apply this template, the TileView style needs to retrieve the TileView object (using the ListView.View property) and then pull the data template from the Tile-View.ItemTemplate property. This step is performed using a binding expression that searches up the element tree (using the FindAncestor RelativeSource mode) until it finds the containing ListView.

Note Rather than setting the ListViewItem.ContentTemplate property, you could achieve the same result by setting the ListView.ItemTemplate property. It's really just a matter of preference.

Using the ListView

Once you've built your view class and the supporting styles, you're ready to put them to use in a ListView control. To use a custom view, you simply need to set the ListView.View property to an instance of your view object, as shown here:

```
<ListView Name="lstProducts">
  <ListView.View>
    <TileView ... >
  </ListView.View>
</ListView>
```

However, this example demonstrates a ListView that can switch between three views. As a result, you need to instantiate three distinct view objects. The easiest way to manage this is to define each view object separately in the Windows.Resources collection. You can then load the view you want when the user makes a selection from the ComboBox control using this code:

```
private void lstView_SelectionChanged(object sender, SelectionChangedEventArgs e)
{
    ComboBoxItem selectedItem = (ComboBoxItem)lstView.SelectedItem;
    lstProducts.View = (ViewBase)this.FindResource(selectedItem.Content);
}
```

The first view is simple enough—it uses the familiar GridView class that you considered earlier to create a multicolumn display. Here's the markup it uses:

```
<GridView x:Key="GridView">
  <GridView.Columns>
    <GridViewColumn Header="Name"
     DisplayMemberBinding="{Binding Path=ModelName}" />
    <GridViewColumn Header="Model"
     DisplayMemberBinding="{Binding Path=ModelNumber}" />
    <GridViewColumn Header="Price"
      DisplayMemberBinding="{Binding Path=UnitCost,
           Converter={StaticResource PriceConverter} }" />
  </GridView.Columns>
</GridView>
```

The two TileView objects are more interesting. Both of them supply a template to determine what the tile looks like. The ImageView (shown in Figure 18-6) uses a StackPanel that
stacks the product image above the product title:

```
<local:TileView x:Key="ImageView">
  <local:TileView.ItemTemplate>
    <DataTemplate>
      <StackPanel Width="150" VerticalAlignment="Top">
        <Image Source="{Binding Path=ProductImagePath,
                         Converter={StaticResource ImagePathConverter}}">
        </Image>
        <TextBlock TextWrapping="Wrap" HorizontalAlignment="Center"
         Text="{Binding Path=ModelName}"></TextBlock>
      </StackPanel>
    </DataTemplate>
  </local:TileView.ItemTemplate>
</local:TileView>
```

The ImageDetailView uses a two-column grid. A small version of the image is placed on
the left, and more detailed information is placed on the right. The second column is placed
into a shared size group so that all the items have the same width (as determined by the
largest text value).

```
<local:TileView x:Key="ImageDetailView">
  <local:TileView.ItemTemplate>
    <DataTemplate>
      <Grid>
        <Grid.ColumnDefinitions>
          <ColumnDefinition Width="Auto"></ColumnDefinition>
          <ColumnDefinition Width="Auto" SharedSizeGroup="Col2"></ColumnDefinition>
        </Grid.ColumnDefinitions>

        <Image Margin="5"  Width="100"
         Source="{Binding Path=ProductImagePath,
                   Converter={StaticResource ImagePathConverter}}">
        </Image>
        <StackPanel Grid.Column="1" VerticalAlignment="Center">
          <TextBlock FontWeight="Bold" Text="{Binding Path=ModelName}"></TextBlock>
          <TextBlock Text="{Binding Path=ModelNumber}"></TextBlock>
          <TextBlock Text="{Binding Path=UnitCost,
                         Converter={StaticResource PriceConverter} }">
          </TextBlock>
        </StackPanel>
      </Grid>
    </DataTemplate>
  </local:TileView.ItemTemplate>
</local:TileView>
```

This is undoubtedly more code than you wanted to generate to create a ListView with multiple viewing options. However, the example is now complete, and you can easily create additional views (based on the TileView class) that supply different item templates and give you even more viewing options.

Passing Information to a View

You can make your view classes more flexible by adding properties that the consumer can set when using the view. Your style can then retrieve these values using data binding and use them to configure the Setter objects.

For example, the TileView currently highlights selected items with an unattractive blue color. The effect is all the more jarring because it makes the black text with the product details more difficult to read. As you probably remember from Chapter 15, you can fix these details by using a customized control template with the right triggers.

But rather than hard-code a set of pleasing colors, it makes sense to let the view consumer specify this detail. To do with the TileView, you could add a set of properties like these:

```
private Brush selectedBackground = Brushes.Transparent;
public Brush SelectedBackground
{
    get { return selectedBackground; }
    set { selectedBackground = value; }
}

private Brush selectedBorderBrush = Brushes.Black;
public Brush SelectedBorderBrush
{
    get { return selectedBorderBrush; }
    set { selectedBorderBrush = value; }
}
```

Now you can set these details when instantiating a view object:

```
<local:TileView x:Key="ImageDetailView" SelectedBackground="LightSteelBlue">
  ...
</local:TileView>
```

The final step is to use these colors in the ListViewItem style. To do so, you need to add a Setter that replaces the ControlTemplate. In this case, a simple rounded border is used with a ContentPresenter. When the item is selected, a trigger fires and applies the new border and background colors:

```
<Style x:Key="{ComponentResourceKey TypeInTargetAssembly={x:Type local:TileView},
 ResourceId=TileViewItem}"
 TargetType="{x:Type ListViewItem}"
 BasedOn="{StaticResource {x:Type ListBoxItem}}">
  ...
  <Setter Property="Template">
    <Setter.Value>
      <ControlTemplate TargetType="{x:Type ListBoxItem}">
```

```xml
      <Border Name="Border" BorderThickness="1" CornerRadius="3">
        <ContentPresenter />
      </Border>
      <ControlTemplate.Triggers>
        <Trigger Property="IsSelected" Value="True">
          <Setter TargetName="Border" Property="BorderBrush"
           Value="{Binding Path=View.SelectedBorderBrush,
                   RelativeSource={RelativeSource Mode=FindAncestor,
                   AncestorType={x:Type ListView}}}"></Setter>
          <Setter TargetName="Border" Property="Background"
           Value="{Binding Path=View.SelectedBackground,
                   RelativeSource={RelativeSource Mode=FindAncestor,
                   AncestorType={x:Type ListView}}}"></Setter>
        </Trigger>
      </ControlTemplate.Triggers>
    </ControlTemplate>
  </Setter.Value>
  </Setter>
</Style>
```

Figure 18-9 and Figure 18-10 show this selection behavior. Figure 18-9 uses a transparent background, while Figure 18-10 uses a light blue highlight color.

■**Note** Unfortunately, this technique of passing information to a view still doesn't help you make a truly generic view. That's because there's no way to modify the data templates based on this information.

The TreeView

The TreeView is a Windows staple, and it's a common ingredient in everything from the Windows Explorer file browser to the .NET help library. WPF's implementation of the TreeView is impressive, because it has full support for data binding.

■**Note** The Windows Forms toolkit beats WPF with its rich DataGridView control for displaying and browsing data. However, it falls behind with weaker implementations of the ListView and TreeView, neither of which supports data binding.

The TreeView is, at its heart, a specialized ItemsControl that hosts TreeViewItem objects. But unlike the ListViewItem, the TreeViewItem is not a content control. Instead, each TreeViewItem is a separate ItemsControl, with the ability to hold more TreeViewItem objects. This flexibility allows you to create a deeply layered data display.

■**Note** Technically, the TreeViewItem derives from HeaderedItemsControl, which derives from ItemsControl. The HeaderedItemsControl class adds a Header property, which holds the content (usually text) that you want to display for that item in the tree. WPF includes two other HeaderedItemsControls: the MenuItem and the ToolBar.

Here's the skeleton of a very basic TreeView, which is declared entirely in markup:

```
<TreeView>
  <TreeViewItem Header="Fruit">
    <TreeViewItem Header="Orange"/>
    <TreeViewItem Header="Banana"/>
    <TreeViewItem Header="Grapefruit"/>
  </TreeViewItem>
  <TreeViewItem Header="Vegetables">
    <TreeViewItem Header="Aubergine"/>
    <TreeViewItem Header="Squash"/>
    <TreeViewItem Header="Spinach"/>
  </TreeViewItem>
</TreeView>
```

It's not necessary to construct a TreeView out of TreeViewItem objects. In fact, you have the ability to add virtually any element to a TreeView, including buttons, panels, and images. However, if you want to display nontext content, the best approach is to use a TreeViewItem wrapper and supply your content through the TreeViewItem.Header property. This gives you the same effect as adding non-TreeViewItem elements directly to your TreeView but makes it easier to manage a few TreeView-specific details, such as selection and node expansion. If you want to display a non-UIElement object, you can format it using data templates with the HeaderTemplate or HeaderTemplateSelector property.

A Data-Bound TreeView

Usually, you won't fill a TreeView with fixed information that's hard-coded in your markup. Instead, you'll construct the TreeViewItem objects you need programmatically, or you'll use data binding to display a collection of objects.

Filling a TreeView with data is easy enough—as with any ItemsControl, you simply set the ItemsSource property. However, this technique fills only the first level of the TreeView. A more interesting use of the TreeView incorporates *hierarchical data* that has some sort of nested structure.

For example, consider the TreeView shown in Figure 18-11. The first level consists of Category objects, while the second level shows the Product objects that fall into each category.

The TreeView makes hierarchical data display easy, whether you're working with hand-crafted classes or the ADO.NET DataSet. You simply need to specify the right data templates. Your templates indicate the relationship between the different levels of the data.

For example, imagine you want to build the example shown in Figure 18-11. You've already seen the Products class that's used to represent a single Product. But to create the example shown in Figure 18-9, you also need a Category class. Like the Product class, the

Category class implements the INotifyPropertyChanged to provide change notifications. The only new detail is that the Category class exposes a collection of Product objects through its Product property.

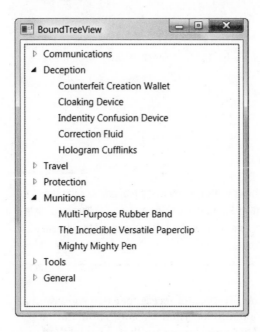

Figure 18-11. *A TreeView of categories and products*

```
public class Category : INotifyPropertyChanged
{
    private string categoryName;
    public string CategoryName
    {
        get { return categoryName; }
        set { categoryName = value;
            OnPropertyChanged(new PropertyChangedEventArgs("CategoryName"));
            }
    }

    private ObservableCollection<Product> products;
    public ObservableCollection<Product> Products
    {
        get { return products; }
        set { products = value;
            OnPropertyChanged(new PropertyChangedEventArgs("Products"));
        }
    }

    public event PropertyChangedEventHandler PropertyChanged;
```

```
    public void OnPropertyChanged(PropertyChangedEventArgs e)
    {
        if (PropertyChanged != null)
            PropertyChanged(this, e);
    }

    public Category(string categoryName, ObservableCollection<Product> products)
    {
        CategoryName = categoryName;
        Products = products;
    }
}
```

■**Tip** This trick—creating a collection that exposes another collection through a property—is the secret to navigating parent-child relationships with WPF data binding. For example, you can bind a collection of Category objects to one list control and then bind another list control to the Products property of the currently selected Category object to show the related Product objects.

To use the Category class, you also need to modify the data access code that you saw in Chapter 17. Now, you'll query the information about products and categories from the database. In this example, the window calls the StoreDB.GetCategoriesAndProducts() method to get a collection of Category objects, each of which has a nested collection of Product objects. The Category collection is then bound to the tree so that it will appear in the first level:

```
treeCategories.ItemsSource = App.StoreDB.GetCategoriesAndProducts();
```

To display the categories, you need to supply a TreeView.ItemTemplate that can process the bound objects. In this example, you need to display the CategoryName property of each Category object. Here's the data template that does it:

```
<TreeView Name="treeCategories" Margin="5">
  <TreeView.ItemTemplate>
    <HierarchicalDataTemplate>
      <TextBlock Text="{Binding Path=CategoryName}" />
    </HierarchicalDataTemplate>
  </TreeView.ItemTemplate>
</TreeView>
```

The only unusual detail here is that the TreeView.ItemTemplate is set using a Hierarchical-DataTemplate object instead of a DataTemplate. The HierarchicalDataTemplate has the added advantage that it can wrap a second template. The HierarchicalDataTemplate can then pull a collection of items from the first level and provide that to the second-level template. You simply set the ItemsSource property to identify the property that has the child items, and you set the ItemTemplate property to indicate how each object should be formatted.

Here's the revised date template:

```
<TreeView Name="treeCategories" Margin="5">
  <TreeView.ItemTemplate>
    <HierarchicalDataTemplate ItemsSource="{Binding Path=Products}">
      <TextBlock Text="{Binding Path=CategoryName}" />
      <HierarchicalDataTemplate.ItemTemplate>
        <DataTemplate>
          <TextBlock Text="{Binding Path=ModelName}" />
        </DataTemplate>
      </HierarchicalDataTemplate.ItemTemplate>
    </HierarchicalDataTemplate>
  </TreeView.ItemTemplate>
</TreeView>
```

Essentially, you now have two templates, one for each level of the tree. The second template uses the selected item from the first template as its data source.

Although this markup works perfectly well, it's common to factor out each data template and apply it to your data objects by data type instead of by position. To understand what that means, it helps to consider a revised version of the markup for the data-bound TreeView:

```
<Window x:Class="DataBinding.BoundTreeView" ...
    xmlns:local="clr-namespace:DataBinding">
  <Window.Resources>
    <HierarchicalDataTemplate DataType="{x:Type local:Category}"
     ItemsSource="{Binding Path=Products}">
      <TextBlock Text="{Binding Path=CategoryName}"/>
    </HierarchicalDataTemplate>

    <HierarchicalDataTemplate DataType="{x:Type local:Product}">
      <TextBlock Text="{Binding Path=ModelName}" />
    </HierarchicalDataTemplate>
  </Window.Resources>

  <Grid>
    <TreeView Name="treeCategories" Margin="5">
    </TreeView>
  </Grid>
</Window>
```

In this example, the TreeView doesn't explicitly set its ItemTemplate. Instead, the appropriate ItemTemplate is used based on the data type of the bound object. Similarly, the Category template doesn't specify the ItemTemplate that should be used to process the Products collection. It's also chosen automatically by data type. This tree is now able to show a list of products or a list of categories that contain groups of products.

In the current example, these changes don't add anything new. This approach simplifies the markup and makes it easier to reuse your templates, but it doesn't change the way your data is displayed. However, if you have deeply nested trees that have looser structures, this design is invaluable. For example, imagine you're creating a tree of Manager objects, and each

Manager object has an Employees collection. This collection might contain ordinary Employee objects or other Manager objects, which would in turn contain more Employees. If you use the type-based template system shown earlier, each object automatically gets the template that's right for its data type.

Binding a DataSet to a TreeView

You can also use a TreeView to show a multilayered DataSet—one that has relationships linking one DataTable to another.

For example, here's a code routine that creates a DataSet, fills it with a table of products and a separate table of categories, and links the two tables together with a DataRelation object:

```
public DataSet GetCategoriesAndProductsDataSet()
{
    SqlConnection con = new SqlConnection(connectionString);
    SqlCommand cmd = new SqlCommand("GetProducts", con);
    cmd.CommandType = CommandType.StoredProcedure;
    SqlDataAdapter adapter = new SqlDataAdapter(cmd);

    DataSet ds = new DataSet();
    adapter.Fill(ds, "Products");
    cmd.CommandText = "GetCategories";
    adapter.Fill(ds, "Categories");

    // Set up a relation between these tables.
    DataRelation relCategoryProduct = new DataRelation("CategoryProduct",
      ds.Tables["Categories"].Columns["CategoryID"],
      ds.Tables["Products"].Columns["CategoryID"]);
      ds.Relations.Add(relCategoryProduct);

    return ds;
}
```

To use this in a TreeView, you begin by binding to the DataTable you want to use for the first level:

```
DataSet ds = App.StoreDB.GetCategoriesAndProductsDataSet();

treeCategories.ItemsSource = ds.Tables["Categories"].DefaultView;
```

But how do you get the related rows? After all, you can't call a method like GetChildRows() from XAML. Fortunately, the WPF data binding system has built-in support for this scenario. The trick is to use the name of your DataRelation as the ItemsSource for your second level. In this example, the DataRelation was created with the name CategoryProduct, so this markup does the trick:

```
<TreeView Name="treeCategories" Margin="5">
  <TreeView.ItemTemplate>
    <HierarchicalDataTemplate ItemsSource="{Binding CategoryProduct}">
      <TextBlock Text="{Binding CategoryName}" Padding="2" />
        <HierarchicalDataTemplate.ItemTemplate>
          <DataTemplate>
            <TextBlock Text="{Binding ModelName}" Padding="2" />
          </DataTemplate>
        </HierarchicalDataTemplate.ItemTemplate>
    </HierarchicalDataTemplate>
  </TreeView.ItemTemplate>
</TreeView>
```

Now this example works in the same way as the previous example, which used custom Product and Category objects.

Just-in-Time Node Creation

TreeView controls are often used to hold huge amounts of data. As you learned earlier, data-laden ListView objects are a problem, because the ListView doesn't include any virtualization or paging feature. As a result, all your data needs to be loaded at once and submitted to the ListView as a single in-memory object. The situation with the TreeView is a bit better. That's because the TreeView display is collapsible. Even if the user scrolls from top to bottom, not all the information is necessarily visible. The information that isn't visible can be omitted from the TreeView altogether, reducing its overhead (and the amount of time required to fill the tree). Even better, each TreeViewItem fires an Expanded event when it's opened and a Collapsed event when it's closed. You can use this point in time to fill in missing nodes or discard one that you don't need. This technique is called *just-in-time node creation*.

Just-in-time node creation can be applied to applications that pull their data from a database, but the classic example is a directory-browsing application. In current times, most people have huge, sprawling hard drives. Although you could fill a TreeView with the directory structure of a hard drive, the process is aggravatingly slow. A better idea is to begin with a partially collapsed view and allow the user to dig down into specific directories (as shown in Figure 18-12). As each node is opened, the corresponding subdirectories are added to the tree—a process that's nearly instantaneous.

Using a just-in-time TreeView to display the folders on a hard drive is nothing new. (In fact, the technique is demonstrated in my book *Pro .NET 2.0 Windows Forms and Custom Controls in C#* [Apress, 2005].) However, event routing makes the WPF solution just a bit more elegant.

The first step is to add a list of drives to the TreeView when the window first loads. Initially, the node for each drive is collapsed. The drive letter is displayed in the header, and the DriveInfo object is stored in the TreeViewItem.Tag property to make it easier to find the nested directories later without re-creating the object. (This increases the memory overhead of the application, but it also reduces the number of file access security checks. The overall effect is small, but it improves performance slightly and simplifies the code.)

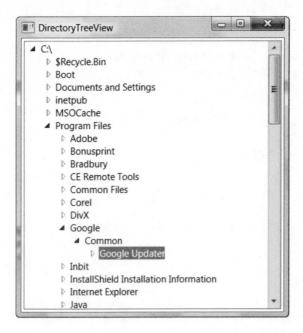

Figure 18-12. *Digging into a directory tree*

Here's the code that fills the TreeView with a list of drives, using the System.IO.DriveInfo class:

```
foreach (DriveInfo drive in DriveInfo.GetDrives())
{
    TreeViewItem item = new TreeViewItem();
    item.Tag = drive;
    item.Header = drive.ToString();

    item.Items.Add("*");
    treeFileSystem.Items.Add(item);
}
```

This code adds a placeholder (a string with an asterisk) under each drive node. The placeholder is not shown, because the node begins in a collapsed state. As soon as the node is expanded, you can remove the placeholder and add the list of subdirectories in its place.

___

■**Note** The placeholder is a useful tool that can allow you to determine whether the user has expanded this folder to view its contents yet. However, the primary purpose of the placeholder is to make sure the expand icon appears next to this item. Without that, the user won't be able to expand the directory to look for subfolders. If the directory doesn't include any subfolders, the expand icon will simply disappear when the user attempts to expand it—which is similar to the behavior of Windows Explorer when viewing network folders.

___

To perform the just-in-time node creation, you must handle the TreeViewItem.Expanded event. Because this event uses bubbling, you can attach an event handler directly on the Tree-View to handle the Expanded event for any TreeViewItem inside:

```
<TreeView Name="treeFileSystem" TreeViewItem.Expanded="item_Expanded">
</TreeView>
```

Here's the code that handles the event and fills in the missing next level of the tree using the System.IO.DirectoryInfo class:

```
private void item_Expanded(object sender, RoutedEventArgs e)
{
    TreeViewItem item = (TreeViewItem)e.OriginalSource;
    item.Items.Clear();

    DirectoryInfo dir;
    if (item.Tag is DriveInfo)
    {
        DriveInfo drive = (DriveInfo)item.Tag;
        dir = drive.RootDirectory;
    }
    else
    {
        dir = (DirectoryInfo)item.Tag;
    }

    try
    {
        foreach (DirectoryInfo subDir in dir.GetDirectories())
        {
            TreeViewItem newItem = new TreeViewItem();
            newItem.Tag = subDir;
            newItem.Header = subDir.ToString();
            newItem.Items.Add("*");
            item.Items.Add(newItem);
        }
    }
    catch
    {
        // An exception could be thrown in this code if you don't
        // have sufficient security permissions for a file or directory.
        // You can catch and then ignore this exception.
    }
}
```

Currently, this code performs a refresh every time the item is expanded. Optionally, you could perform this only the first time it's expanded, when the placeholder is found. This reduces the work your application needs to do but increases the chance of out-of-date information. Alternatively, you could perform a refresh every time an item is selected by handling

the TreeViewItem.Selected event, or you could use a component such as the System.IO.File-
SystemWatcher to wait for operating system notifications when a folder is added, removed, or
renamed. The FileSystemWatcher is the only way to ensure that you update the directory tree
immediately when a change happens, but it also has the greatest overhead.

CREATING ADVANCED TREEVIEW CONTROLS

There's a lot you can accomplish when you combine the power of control templates (discussed in Chapter 15)
with the TreeView. In fact, you can create a control that looks and behaves in a radically different way simply
by replacing the templates for the TreeView and TreeViewItem controls.

    Making these adjustments requires some deeper template exploration. You can get started with some
eye-opening examples. Visual Studio includes a sample of a multicolumned TreeView that unites a tree with
a grid. To browse it, look for the index entry "TreeListView sample [WPF]" in the Visual Studio help. Another
intriguing example is Josh Smith's layout experiment, which transforms the TreeView into something that
more closely resembles an organization chart. You can view the full code at `http://www.codeproject.`
`com/KB/WPF/CustomTreeViewLayout.aspx`.

Menus

WPF provides two menu controls: Menu (for main menus) and ContextMenu (for popup
menus that are attached to other elements). Like all the WPF classes, WPF performs the rendering for the Menu and ContextMenu controls. That means these controls aren't simple
Win32 wrappers, and they have the flexibility to be used in some unusual ways.

■**Note** If you use the Menu class in a browser-hosted application, it appears at the top of the page. The
browser window wraps your page, and it may or may not include a menu of its own, which will be completely separate.

The Menu Class

WPF doesn't make any assumption about where a stand-alone menu should be placed. Ordinarily, you'll dock it at the top of your window using a DockPanel or the top row of a Grid, and
you'll stretch it across the entire width of your window. However, you can place a menu anywhere, even alongside other controls (as shown in Figure 18-13). Furthermore, you can add as
many menus in a window as you want. Although it might not make much sense, you have the
ability to stack menu bars or scatter them throughout your user interface.

    This freedom provides some interesting possibilities. For example, if you create a menu
with one top-level heading and style it to look like button, you'll end up with a one-click
popup menu (like the menu that's activated in Figure 18-13). This sort of user interface trick-
ery might help you get the exact effect you want in a highly customized interface. Or, it might
just be a more powerful way to confuse users.

Figure 18-13. *Mixed menus*

The Menu class adds a single new property: IsMainMenu. When true (which is the default value), pressing the Alt key or F10 gives the menu focus, just as in any other Windows application. Along with this small detail, the Menu container has a few of the familiar ItemsControl properties for you to play with. That means you can create data-bound menus using the ItemsSource, DisplayMemberPath, ItemTemplate, and ItemTemplateSelector properties. You can also apply grouping, change the layout of menu items inside the menu, and apply styles to your menu items.

For example, Figure 18-14 shows a scrollable sidebar menu. You can create it by supplying a StackPanel for the ItemsPanel property, changing its background, and wrapping the entire Menu in a ScrollViewer. Obviously, you can make more radical changes to the visual appearance of menus and submenus using triggers and control templates. The bulk of the styling logic is in the default control template for the MenuItem.

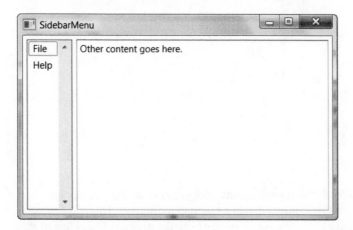

Figure 18-14. *A Menu in a StackPanel*

Menu Items

Menus are composed of MenuItem objects and Separator objects. The MenuItem class derives from HeaderedItemsControl, because each menu item has a header (which contains the text for that item) and can hold a collection of MenuItem objects (which represents a submenu). The Separator simply displays a horizontal line separating menu items.

Here's a straightforward combination of MenuItem objects that creates the rudimentary menu structure shown in Figure 18-15:

```
<Menu>
  <MenuItem Header="File">
    <MenuItem Header="New"></MenuItem>
    <MenuItem Header="Open"></MenuItem>
    <MenuItem Header="Save"></MenuItem>
    <Separator></Separator>
    <MenuItem Header="Exit"></MenuItem>
  </MenuItem>
  <MenuItem Header="Edit">
    <MenuItem Header="Undo"></MenuItem>
    <MenuItem Header="Redo"></MenuItem>
    <Separator></Separator>
    <MenuItem Header="Cut"></MenuItem>
    <MenuItem Header="Copy"></MenuItem>
    <MenuItem Header="Paste"></MenuItem>
  </MenuItem>
</Menu>
```

As with buttons, you can use the underscore to indicate an Alt+ shortcut key combination. Whereas this is often considered an optional feature in buttons, most menu users expect to have keyboard shortcuts.

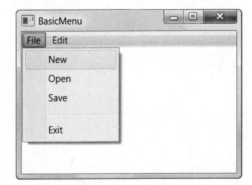

Figure 18-15. *A basic menu*

WPF allows you to break most of the common sense rules of structuring a menu. For example, you can have non-MenuItem objects inside a Menu or MenuItem. This allows you to create menus that hold ordinary WPF elements, ranging from the ordinary CheckBox to a DocumentViewer. For a variety of reasons, placing non-MenuItem objects in a menu is almost always a bad way to go. If you place non-MenuItem objects in a menu, they'll exhibit a few oddities that you'll need to track down and correct. For example, a TextBox in a MenuItem will lose focus as soon as you move the mouse out of the bounds of the MenuItem. If you really want a user interface that includes some sort of drop-down menu with controls, consider using another element (such as the Expander) and styling it to suit your needs. Use menus only when you really want the behavior of a menu—in other words, a group of clickable commands.

■Note Set the MenuItem.StaysOpenOnClick property to true if you want submenus to remain visible when opened until the user clicks somewhere else.

MenuItem objects can also be used *outside* the standard Menu, ContextMenu, and Menu-Item containers. These items behave just like ordinary menu items—they glow blue when you hover over them, and they can be clicked to trigger actions. However, any submenus they include won't be accessible. Again, this is an aspect of Menu flexibility you probably won't want to use.

To react when a MenuItem is clicked, you may choose to handle the MenuItem.Click event. You can handle it for individual items, or you can attach an event handler to the root Menu tag. Your other alternative is to use the Command, CommandParameter, and CommandTarget properties to connect a MenuItem to a Command object, as you learned to do with buttons in Chapter 10. This is particularly useful if your user interface includes multiple menus (for example, a main menu and a context menu) that use the same commands or includes a menu and a toolbar that do.

Along with text content (which is supplied through the Header property), MenuItem objects can actually show several more details:

- A thumbnail icon in the margin area just to the left of the menu command.

- A check mark in the margin area. If you set the check mark and an icon, only the check mark appears.

- Shortcut text to the right of the menu text. For example, you might see Ctrl+O to indicate the shortcut key for the Open command.

Setting all these ingredients is easy. To show a thumbnail icon, you set the MenuItem.Icon property. Interestingly, the Icon property accepts any object, which gives you the flexibility to construct a miniature vector drawing. This way, you can take full advantage of WPF's resolution-independent scaling to show more detail at higher system DPI settings. If you want to use an ordinary icon, simply use an Image element with a bitmap source.

To show a check mark next to a menu item, you simply need to set the MenuItem.Is-Checked property to true. Additionally, if IsCheckable is true, clicking the menu item will toggle back and forth between its checked and unchecked state. However, there's no way to associate a group of checked menu items. If that's the effect you want, you need to write the code to clear the other check boxes when an item is checked.

You can set the shortcut text for a menu item using the MenuItem.InputGestureText property. However, simply displaying this text doesn't make it active. It's up to you to watch for the key presses you want. This is almost always too much work, so menu items are commonly used with commands, which gives you the shortcut key behavior and the InputGestureText in one step.

For example, the following MenuItem is linked to the ApplicationsCommands.Open command:

```
<MenuItem Command="ApplicationCommands.Open"></MenuItem>
```

This command already has the Ctrl+O keystroke defined in the RoutedUICommand.InputGestures command collection. As a result, Ctrl+O appears for the shortcut text, and the Ctrl+O keystroke triggers the command (assuming you've wired up the appropriate event handler). If a keystroke wasn't defined, you could add it to the Input-Gestures collection yourself.

■Tip Several useful properties indicate the current state of the MenuItem, including IsChecked, IsHighlighted, IsPressed, and IsSubmenuOpen. You can use these to write triggers that apply different styling in response to certain actions.

The ContextMenu Class

Like the Menu, the ContextMenu class holds a collection of MenuItem objects. The difference is that a ContextMenu can't be placed in a window. Instead, it can be used only to set the ContextMenu property of another element:

```
<TextBox>
  <TextBox.ContextMenu>
    <MenuItem ... >
      ...
    </MenuItem>
  </TextBox.ContextMenu>
</TextBox>
```

The ContextMenu property is defined in the FrameworkElement class, so it's supported by virtually all WPF elements. If you set the ContextMenu property of an element that ordinarily has its own context menu, your menu replaces the standard menu. If you simply want to remove an existing context menu, just set it to a null reference.

When you attach a ContextMenu object to an element, it appears automatically when the user right-clicks that control (or presses Shift+F10 while it has focus). The context menu won't appear if the element has IsEnabled set to false, unless you explicitly allow this with the ContextMenuService.ShowOnDisabled attached property:

```
<TextBox ContextMenuService.ShowOnDisabled="True">
  <TextBox.ContextMenu>
    ...
  </TextBox.ContextMenu>
</TextBox>
```

Menu Separators

The Separator is a standard element for dividing menus into groups of related commands. However, the content of the separator is completely fluid, thanks to control templates. By taking a separator and supplying a new template, you can add other, nonclickable elements to your menus, such as subheadings.

You might expect that you could add a subheading simply by adding a non-MenuItem object to a menu, such as a TextBlock with some text. However, if you take this step, the newly added element keeps the menu selection behavior; this means you can step through it with the keyboard, and when you hover over it with the mouse, the edges glow blue. The Separator doesn't exhibit this behavior—it's a fixed piece of content that doesn't react to keyboard or mouse actions.

Here's an example of a Separator that defines a text title:

```
<Separator>
  <Separator.Template>
    <ControlTemplate>
      <Border CornerRadius="2" Padding="5" Background="PaleGoldenrod"
       BorderBrush="Black" BorderThickness="1">
        <TextBlock FontWeight="Bold">
         Editing Commands
        </TextBlock>
      </Border>
    </ControlTemplate>
  </Separator.Template>
</Separator>
```

Figure 18-16 shows the title this creates.

Figure 18-16. *A menu that includes a fixed subheading*

Unfortunately, the Separator isn't a content control, so it's not possible to separate the content you want to show (for example, the string of text) from the formatting you want to use. That means you'll be forced to define the same template each time you use the separator if you want to vary its text. To make this process a bit simpler, you can create a separator style that bundles together all the properties you want to set on the TextBlock inside the Separator, except for the text.

Toolbars and Status Bars

Toolbars and status bars are two staples of the Windows world. Both are specialized containers that hold a collection of items. Traditionally, a toolbar holds buttons, and a status bar consists primarily of text and other noninteractive indicators (like a progress bar). However, both toolbars and status bars are used with a variety of different controls.

In Windows Forms, toolbars and status bars have their own content model. Although it's still possible to place arbitrary controls inside a toolbar and status bar using a wrapper, the process isn't seamless. Thanks to the new content model in WPF, this situation has improved dramatically. The WPF ToolBar and StatusBar classes support all WPF elements, giving you unparalleled flexibility. In fact, there are no toolbar-specific or status bar–specific elements. Everything you need is already available in the basic collection of WPF elements.

The ToolBar

A typical WPF ToolBar is filled with Button, ComboBox, CheckBox, RadioButton, and Separator objects. Because these elements are all content controls (except for the Separator), you can place text and image content inside. Although you can use other elements, such as Label and Image to put noninteractive elements into the ToolBar, the effect is often confusing.

At this point, you might be wondering how you can place these common controls in a toolbar without creating an odd visual effect. After all, the content that appears in standard Windows toolbars looks quite a bit different from similar content that appears in a window. For example, the buttons in a toolbar are displayed with a flat, streamlined appearance that removes the border and the shaded background. The toolbar surface shows through underneath, and the button glows blue when you hover over it with the mouse.

In the WPF way of thinking, the button in a toolbar is the same as a button in a window—both are clickable regions you can use to perform an action. The only difference is the visual appearance. Thus, the perfect solution is to use the existing Button class but adjust various properties or change the control template. This is exactly what the ToolBar class does—it overrides the default style of some types of children, including the buttons. You can still have the last word by manually setting the Button.Style property if you want to create your own customized toolbar button, but usually you'll get all the control you need by setting the button content.

Not only does the ToolBar change the appearance of many of the controls its holds, but it also changes the behavior of the ToggleButton and the CheckBox and RadioButton that derive from it. A ToggleButton or CheckBox in a ToolBar is rendered like an ordinary button, but when you click it, the button remains highlighted (until you click it again). The RadioButton has a similar appearance, but you must click another RadioButton in a group to clear the highlighting. (To prevent confusion, it's always best to separate a group of RadioButton objects in a toolbar using the Separator.)

To demonstrate what this looks like, consider the simple markup shown here:

```
<ToolBar>
  <Button Content="{StaticResource DownloadFile}"></Button>
  <CheckBox FontWeight="Bold">Bold</CheckBox>
  <CheckBox FontStyle="Italic">Italic</CheckBox>
  <CheckBox>
    <TextBlock TextDecorations="Underline">Underline</TextBlock>
  </CheckBox>
  <Separator></Separator>
  <ComboBox SelectedIndex="0">
    <ComboBoxItem>100%</ComboBoxItem>
    <ComboBoxItem>50%</ComboBoxItem>
    <ComboBoxItem>25%</ComboBoxItem>
  </ComboBox>
  <Separator></Separator>
</ToolBar>
```

Figure 18-17 shows this toolbar in action, with two CheckBox controls in the checked state and the drop-down list on display.

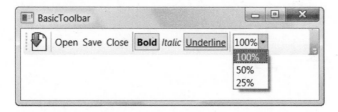

Figure 18-17. *Different controls in a toolbar*

Although the example in Figure 18-17 is limited to buttons that contain text, ToolBar buttons usually hold image content. (You can also combine both by wrapping an Image element and a TextBlock or Label in a horizontal StackPanel.) If you're using image content, you need to decide whether you want to use bitmap images (which may show scaling artifacts at different resolutions), icons (which improve this situation somewhat because you can supply several differently sized images in one file), or vector images (which require the most markup but provide flawless resizing).

The ToolBar control has a few oddities. First, unlike other controls that derive from Items-Control, it doesn't supply a dedicated wrapper class. (In other words, there is a ToolBarItem class.) The ToolBar simply doesn't require this wrapper to manage items, track selection, and so on, as other list controls. Another quirk in the ToolBar is that it derives from HeaderedItems-Control even though the Header property has no effect. It's up to you to use this property in some interesting way. For example, if you have an interface that uses several ToolBar objects, you could allow users to choose which ones to display from a context menu. In that menu, you could use the toolbar name that's set in the Header property.

The ToolBar has one more interesting property: Orientation. You can create a top-to-bottom toolbar that's docked to one of the sides of your window by setting the ToolBar.Orientation property to Vertical. However, each element in the toolbar will still be oriented horizontally (for example, text won't be turned on its side), unless you use a LayoutTransform to rotate it.

The Overflow Menu

If a toolbar has more content than it can fit in a window, it removes items until the content fits. These extra items are placed into an overflow menu, which you can see by clicking the drop-down arrow at the end of the toolbar. Figure 18-18 shows the same toolbar shown in Figure 18-17 but in a smaller window that necessitates an overflow menu.

The ToolBar control adds items to the overflow menu automatically, starting with the last item. However, you can configure the way this behavior works to a limited degree by applying the attached ToolBar.OverflowMode property to the items in the toolbar. Use Overflow-Mode.Never to ensure that an important item is never placed in the overflow menu, Overflow-Mode.AsNeeded (the default) to allow it to be placed in the overflow menu when space is scarce, or OverflowMode.Always to force an item to remain permanently in the overflow menu. (For example, Visual Studio keeps the customization command Add or Remove buttons in the overflow menu of its toolbars, and the main Excel 2003 and Word 2003 toolbars include a command named Show Buttons on Two Rows or Show Buttons on One Row that's always in the overflow menu.)

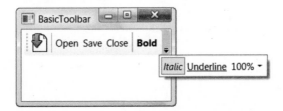

Figure 18-18. *The automatic overflow menu*

■**Note** If the toolbar's container (usually, a window) is smaller than the required space to display all the OverflowMode.Always items, the items that don't fit will be clipped off at the bounds of the container and will be inaccessible to the user.

If your toolbar contains more than one OverflowMode.AsNeeded item, the ToolBar removes items that are at the end of the toolbar first. Unfortunately, there's no way to assign relative priorities to toolbar items. For example, there's no way to create an item that's allowed in the overflow menu but won't be placed there until every other relocatable item has already been moved. There's also no way to create buttons that adapt their sizes based on the available space, as in the Office 2007 ribbon. Look for third-party controls to bridge these gaps.

The ToolBarTray

Although you're free to add multiple ToolBar controls to your window and manage them using a layout container, WPF has a class that's designed to take care of some of the work: the

ToolBarTray. Essentially, the ToolBarTray holds a collection of ToolBar objects (which are exposed through a property named ToolBars).

The ToolBarTray makes it easier for toolbars to share the same row, or *band*. You can configure the ToolBarTray so that toolbars share a band, while others are placed on other bands. The ToolBarTray provides the shaded background behind the entire ToolBar area. But most important, the ToolBarTray adds support for toolbar drag-and-drop functionality. Unless you set the ToolBarTray.IsLocked property to true, the user can rearrange your toolbars in a ToolBar tray by clicking the grip at the left side. Toolbars can be repositioned in the same band or moved to a different band. However, the user is not able to drag a toolbar from one ToolBarTray to another. If you want to lock down individual toolbars, simply set the ToolBarTray.IsLocked attached property on the appropriate ToolBar objects.

■**Note** When moving toolbars, it's possible that some content may be obscured. For example, the user may move a toolbar to a position that leaves very little room for another adjacent toolbar. In this situation, the missing items are added to the overflow menu.

You can place as many ToolBar objects as you want in a ToolBarTray. By default, all your toolbars will be placed in left-to-right order on the topmost band. Initially, each toolbar is given its full desired width. (If a subsequent toolbar doesn't fit, some or all of its buttons are moved to the overflow menu.) To get more control, you can specify which band a toolbar should occupy by setting the Band property using a numeric index (where 0 is the topmost band). You can also set the placement inside the band explicitly by using the BandIndex property. A BandIndex of 0 puts the toolbar at the beginning of the band.

Here's some sample markup that creates several toolbars in a ToolBarTray. Figure 18-19 shows the result.

```
<ToolBarTray>
  <ToolBar>
    <Button>One</Button>
    <Button>Two</Button>
    <Button>Three</Button>
  </ToolBar>
  <ToolBar>
    <Button>A</Button>
    <Button>B</Button>
    <Button>C</Button>
  </ToolBar>
  <ToolBar Band="1">
    <Button>Red</Button>
    <Button>Blue</Button>
    <Button>Green</Button>
    <Button>Black</Button>
  </ToolBar>
</ToolBarTray>
```

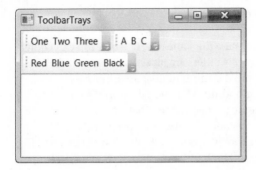

Figure 18-19. *Grouping toolbars in the ToolBarTray*

The StatusBar

Compared to the ToolBar, the StatusBar is a much less glamorous control class. Like the Tool-Bar, it holds any content (which it wraps implicitly in StatusBarItem objects), and it overrides the default styles of some elements to provide more suitable rendering. However, the Status-Bar control doesn't have the support for draggable rearranging or an overflow menu. It's primarily used to display text and image indicators (and the occasional progress bar).

The StatusBar doesn't work very well if you want to use one of the ButtonBase-derived elements or the ComboBox. It doesn't override the styles of any of these controls, so they look out of place in the status bar. If you need to create a status bar that includes these controls, you might consider docking an ordinary ToolBar control to the bottom of your window. It's probably as a result of this general lack of features that the StatusBar is found in the System.Windows.Controls.Primitives namespace rather than in the more mainstream System.Windows.Controls namespace where the ToolBar control exists.

There's one tip worth noting if you're using a status bar. Ordinarily, the StatusBar control lays its children out from left to right using a horizontal StackPanel. However, applications often use proportionately sized status bar items or keep items locked to the right side of the status bar. You can implement this design by specifying that the status bar should use a different panel. (This is a technique you saw earlier in this chapter with the tile-based ListView.) One way to get proportionally or right-aligned items is to use a Grid for your layout container. The only trick is that you must wrap the child element in a StatusBarItem object in order to set the Grid.Column property appropriately.

Here's an example that places one TextBlock on the left side of a StatusBar and another on the right side:

```
<StatusBar Grid.Row="1">
  <StatusBar.ItemsPanel>
    <ItemsPanelTemplate>
      <Grid>
        <Grid.ColumnDefinitions>
          <ColumnDefinition Width="*"></ColumnDefinition>
          <ColumnDefinition Width="Auto"></ColumnDefinition>
        </Grid.ColumnDefinitions>
      </Grid>
    </ItemsPanelTemplate>
  </StatusBar.ItemsPanel>
```

```
  </StatusBar.ItemsPanel>
  <TextBlock>Left Side</TextBlock>
  <StatusBarItem Grid.Column="1">
    <TextBlock>Right Side</TextBlock>
  </StatusBarItem>
</StatusBar>
```

This highlights one of the key advantages of WPF—other controls can benefit from the core layout model without needing to re-create it. By contrast, Windows Forms included several controls that wrapped some sort of proportionally sized items, including the StatusBar and the DataGridView. Despite the conceptual scenario, these controls were forced to include their own layout model and add their own layout-specific properties to manage child items. In WPF, this isn't the case—every control that derives from ItemsControl can use any panel to arrange its child items.

The Last Word

In this chapter, you took a closer look at the ItemsControl classes provided by WPF. You started out with the basic ComboBox and ListBox, and then you considered how to use the ListView to create lists with multiple viewing modes and the TreeView to show hierarchical data. Finally, you considered three more specialized list controls: the Menu, ToolBar, and StatusBar.

The most impressive aspect of all these classes is that they derive from a single base class—the ItemsControl—that defines their essential functionality. The fact that all these controls share the same content model, the same data binding ability, and the same styling and templating features is one of WPF's small miracles. Remarkably, the ItemsControl defines all the basics for any WPF list control, even those that wrap hierarchical data, like the TreeView and Menu. The only change in the model is that the children of these controls (TreeViewItem and MenuItem objects) are *themselves* ItemsControl objects, with the ability to host their own children.

The next chapter shifts away from the data binding story to tackle WPF's document features. You'll learn how to show richly formatted, reflowable document content in your applications and how to use the RichTextBox to allow users to edit it.

■ ■ ■

CHAPTER 19

Documents

Using the WPF skills you've picked up so far, you can craft windows and pages that include a wide variety of elements. Displaying fixed text is easy—you simply need to add the TextBlock and Label elements to the mix.

However, the Label and TextBlock aren't a good solution if you need to display large volumes of text (such as a newspaper article or detailed instructions for online help). Large amounts of text are particularly problematic if you want your text to fit in a resizable window in the best possible way. For example, if you pile a large swath of text into a TextBlock and stretch it to fit a wide window, you'll end up with long lines that are difficult to read. Similarly, if you combine text and pictures using the ordinary TextBlock and Image elements, you'll find that they no longer line up correctly when the window changes size.

To deal with these issues, WPF includes a set of higher-level features that work with *documents*. These features allow you to display large amounts of content in a way that makes them easy to read regardless of the size of the containing window. For example, WPF can hyphenate words (if you only have a narrow space available) or place your text into multiple columns (if you have a wide space to work with).

In this chapter, you'll learn how to use *flow documents* to display content. You'll also learn how to let users edit flow document content with the RichTextBox control. Once you've mastered flow documents, you'll take a quick look at XPS, Microsoft's new technology for creating print-ready documents. Finally, you'll consider WPF's annotation feature, which allows users to add comments and other markers to documents and store them permanently.

Understanding Documents

WPF separates documents into two broad categories:

- **Fixed documents.** These are typeset, print-ready documents. The positioning of all content is fixed (for example, the way text is wrapped over multiple lines and hyphenated can't change). Although you might choose to read a fixed document on a computer monitor, fixed documents are intended for print output. Conceptually, they're equivalent to Adobe PDF files. WPF includes a single type of fixed document, which uses Microsoft's XPS (XML Paper Specification) standard.

- **Flow documents.** These are documents that are designed for viewing on a computer. Like fixed documents, flow documents support rich layout. However, WPF can optimize a flow document based on the way you want to view it. It can lay out the content dynamically based on details such as the size of the view window, the display resolution, and so on. Conceptually, flow documents are used for many of the same reasons as HTML documents, but they have more advanced text layout features.

Although flow documents are obviously more important from an application-building point of view, fixed documents are important for documents that need to be printed without alteration (such as forms and publications).

WPF provides support for both types of documents using different containers. The DocumentViewer allows you to show fixed documents in a WPF window. The FlowDocument-Reader, FlowDocumentPageViewer, and FlowDocumentScrollViewer give you different ways to look at flow documents. All of these containers are read-only. However, WPF includes APIs for creating fixed documents programmatically, and you can use the RichTextBox to allow the user to edit flow content.

In this chapter, you'll spend most of your time exploring flow documents and the ways they can be used in a WPF application. Toward the end of this chapter, you'll take a look at fixed documents, which are more straightforward.

Flow Documents

In a flow document, the content adapts itself to fit the container. Flow content is ideal for onscreen viewing. In fact, it avoids many of the pitfalls of HTML.

Ordinary HTML content uses flow layout to fill the browser window. (This is the same way WPF organizes elements if you use a WrapPanel.) Although this approach is very flexible, it only gives a good result for a small range of window sizes. If you maximize a window on a high-resolution monitor (or, even worse, a widescreen display), you'll end up with long lines that are extremely difficult to read. Figure 19-1 shows this problem with a portion of a web page from Wikipedia.

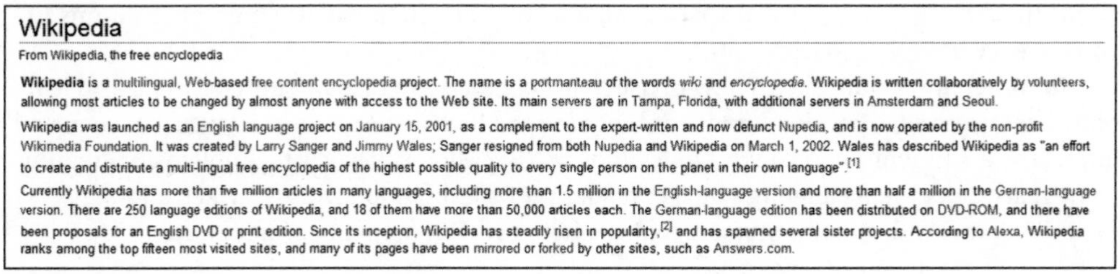

Wikipedia

From Wikipedia, the free encyclopedia

Wikipedia is a multilingual, Web-based free content encyclopedia project. The name is a portmanteau of the words *wiki* and *encyclopedia*. Wikipedia is written collaboratively by volunteers, allowing most articles to be changed by almost anyone with access to the Web site. Its main servers are in Tampa, Florida, with additional servers in Amsterdam and Seoul.

Wikipedia was launched as an English language project on January 15, 2001, as a complement to the expert-written and now defunct Nupedia, and is now operated by the non-profit Wikimedia Foundation. It was created by Larry Sanger and Jimmy Wales; Sanger resigned from both Nupedia and Wikipedia on March 1, 2002. Wales has described Wikipedia as "an effort to create and distribute a multi-lingual free encyclopedia of the highest possible quality to every single person on the planet in their own language".[1]

Currently Wikipedia has more than five million articles in many languages, including more than 1.5 million in the English-language version and more than half a million in the German-language version. There are 250 language editions of Wikipedia, and 18 of them have more than 50,000 articles each. The German-language edition has been distributed on DVD-ROM, and there have been proposals for an English DVD or print edition. Since its inception, Wikipedia has steadily risen in popularity,[2] and has spawned several sister projects. According to Alexa, Wikipedia ranks among the top fifteen most visited sites, and many of its pages have been mirrored or forked by other sites, such as Answers.com.

Figure 19-1. *Long lines in flow content*

Many websites avoid this problem by using some sort of fixed layout that forces content to fit a narrow column. (In WPF, you can create this sort of design by placing your content in a column inside a Grid container and setting the ColumnDefinition.MaxWidth property.) This prevents the readability problem, but it results in a fair bit of wasted screen space in large windows. Figure 19-2 shows this problem on a portion of a page from the New York Times website.

Figure 19-2. *Wasted space in flow content*

Flow document content in WPF improves upon these current-day approaches by incorporating better pagination, multicolumn display, sophisticated hyphenation and text flow algorithms, and user-adjustable viewing preferences. The end result is that WPF gives the user a much better experience when reading large amounts of content.

The Flow Elements

You build a WPF flow document using a combination of flow elements. Flow elements have an important difference from the elements you've seen so far. They don't inherit from the familiar UIElement and FrameworkElement classes. Instead, they form an entirely separate branch of classes that derive from ContentElement and FrameworkContentElement.

The content element classes are simpler than the non-content element classes that you've seen throughout this book. However, content elements support a similar set of basic events, including events for keyboard and mouse handling, drag-and-drop operations, tooltip display, and initialization. The key difference between content and non-content elements is that content elements do not handle their own rendering. Instead, they require a container that can render all its content elements. This deferred rendering allows the container to introduce various optimizations. For example, it allows the container to choose the best way to wrap lines of text in a paragraph, even though a paragraph is a single element.

■Note Content elements can accept focus, but ordinarily they don't (because the Focusable property is set to false by default). You can make a content element focusable by setting Focusable to true on individual elements, by using an element type style that changes a whole group of elements, or by deriving your own custom element that sets Focusable to true. The Hyperlink is an example of a content element that sets its Focusable property to true.

Figure 19-3 shows the inheritance hierarchy of content elements.

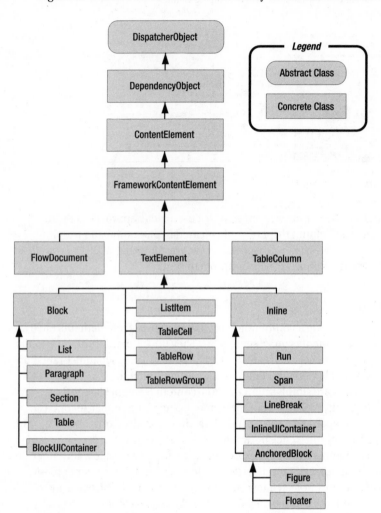

Figure 19-3. *Content elements*

There are two key branches of content elements:

- **Block elements.** These elements can be used to group other content elements. For example, a Paragraph is a block element. It can hold text that's formatted in various different ways. Each section of separately formatted text is a distinct element in the paragraph.

- **Inline elements.** These elements are nested inside a block element (or another inline element). For example, the Run element wraps a bit of text, which can then be nested in a Paragraph element.

The content model allows multiple layers of nesting. For example, you can place a Bold element inside an Underline element to create text that's both bold and underlined. Similarly, you might create a Section element that wraps together multiple Paragraph elements, each of which contains a variety of inline elements with the actual text content. All of these elements are defined in the System.Windows.Documents namespace.

■**Tip** If you're familiar with HTML, this model will seem more than a little familiar. WPF adopts many of the same conventions (such as the distinction between block and inline elements). If you're an HTML pro, you might consider using the surprisingly capable HTML-to-XAML translator at `http://wpf.netfx3.com/files/folders/developer/entry816.aspx`. With the help of this translator, which is implemented in C# code, you can use an HTML page as the starting point for a flow document.

Formatting Content Elements

Although the content elements don't share the same class hierarchy as non-content elements, they feature many of the same formatting properties as ordinary elements. Table 19-1 lists some properties that you'll recognize from your work with non-content elements.

Table 19-1. *Basic Formatting Properties for Content Elements*

Name	Description
Foreground and Background	Accept brushes that will be used to paint the foreground text and the background surface. You can also set the Background property on the FlowDocument object that contains all your markup.
FontFamily, FontSize, FontStretch, FontStyle, and FontWeight	Allow you to configure the font that's used to display text. You can also set these properties on the FlowDocument object that contains all your markup.
ToolTip	Allows you to set a tooltip that will appear when the user hovers over this element. You can use a string of text, or a full ToolTip object, as described in Chapter 7.
Style	Identifies the style that should be used to set the properties of an element automatically.

Block elements also add the properties shown in Table 19-2.

Table 19-2. *Additional Formatting Properties for Block Elements*

Name	Description
BorderBrush and BorderThickness	Allow you to create a border that will be shown around the edge of an element.
Margin	Sets the spacing between the current element and its container (or any adjacent elements). When the margin is not set, flow containers add a default space of about 18 units in between block elements and the edges of the container. If you don't want this spacing, you can explicitly set smaller margins. However, to reduce the space between two paragraphs you'll need to shrink both the bottom margin of the first paragraph and the top margin of the second paragraph. If you want all paragraphs to start out with reduced margins, consider using an element-type style rule that acts on all paragraphs.

Continued

Table 19-2. *Continued*

Name	Description
Padding	Sets the spacing between its edges and any nested elements inside. The default padding is 0.
TextAlignment	Sets the horizontal alignment of nested text content (which can be Left, Right, Center, or Justify). Ordinarily, content is justified.
LineHeight	Sets the spacing between lines in the nested text content. Line height is specified as a number of device-independent pixels. If you don't supply this value, the text is single-spaced based on the characteristics of the font you're using.
LineStackingStrategy	Determines how lines are spaced if they contain mixed font sizes. The default option, MaxHeight, makes the line as tall as the largest text inside. The alternative, BlockLineHeight, uses the height configured in the LineHeight property for all lines, which means the text is spaced based on the font of the paragraph. If this font is smaller than the largest text in the paragraph, the text in some lines may overlap. If it's equal or larger, you'll get a consistent spacing that leaves extra whitespace between some lines.

Along with the properties described in these two tables, there are some additional details that you can tweak in specific elements. Some of these pertain to pagination and multicolumn displays and are discussed in the "Pages and Columns" section later in this chapter. A few other properties of interest include the following:

- TextDecorations, which is provided by the Paragraph and all Inline-derived elements. It takes a value of strikethrough, overline, or (most commonly) underline. You can combine these values to draw multiple lines on a block of text, although it's not common.

- Typography, which is provided by the top-level FlowDocument element, as well as TextBlock and all TextElement-derived types. It provides a Typography object that you can use to alter a variety of details about the way text is rendered (most of which only apply to OpenType fonts).

Constructing a Simple Flow Document

Now that you've taken a look at the content element model, you're ready to assemble some content elements into a simple flow document.

You create a flow document using the FlowDocument class. Visual Studio allows you to create a new flow document as a separate file, or you can define it inside an existing window by using one of the supported containers. For now, start building a simple flow document using the FlowDocumentScrollViewer as a container. Here's how your markup should start:

```
<Window x:Class="Documents.FlowContent"
    xmlns="http://schemas.microsoft.com/winfx/2006/xaml/presentation"
    xmlns:x="http://schemas.microsoft.com/winfx/2006/xaml"
    Title="FlowContent" Height="381" Width="525" >
```

```
<FlowDocumentScrollViewer>
  <FlowDocument>
    ...
  </FlowDocument>
</FlowDocumentScrollViewer>

</Window>
```

■Tip Currently, there's no WYSIWYG interface for creating flow documents. Some developers are creating tools that can transform files written in Word 2007 XML (known as WordML) to XAML files with flow document markup. However, these tools aren't production ready. In the meantime, you can create a basic text editor using a RichTextBox (as described in the "Editing a Flow Document" section later in this chapter) and use it to create flow document content.

You might assume that you could begin typing your text inside the FlowDocument element, but you can't. Instead, the top-level of a flow document must use a block-level element. Here's an example with a Paragraph:

```
<FlowDocumentScrollViewer>
  <FlowDocument>
    <Paragraph>Hello, world of documents.</Paragraph>
  </FlowDocument>
</FlowDocumentScrollViewer>
```

There's no limit on the number of top-level elements you can use. So this example with two paragraphs is also acceptable:

```
<FlowDocumentScrollViewer>
  <FlowDocument>
    <Paragraph>Hello, world of documents.</Paragraph>
    <Paragraph>This is a second paragraph.</Paragraph>
  </FlowDocument>
</FlowDocumentScrollViewer>
```

Figure 19-4 shows the modest result.

The scroll bar is added automatically. The font (Segoe UI) is picked up from the Windows system settings, not the containing window.

■Note Ordinarily, the FlowDocumentScrollViewer allows text to be selected (as in a web browser). This way, a user can copy portions of a document to the Windows clipboard and paste them in other applications. If you don't want this behavior, set the FlowDocumentScrollViewer.IsSelectionEnabled property to false.

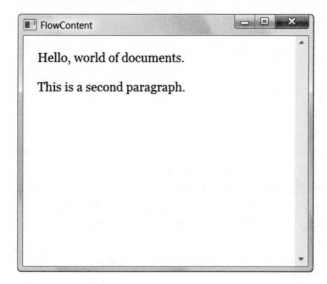

Figure 19-4. *A bare-bones flow document*

Block Elements

Creating a basic document is easy, but to get the result you really want you need to master a range of different elements. Among them are the five block elements described in the following sections.

Paragraph

You've already seen the Paragraph element, which represents a paragraph of text. Technically, paragraph doesn't contain text—instead, it contains a collection of inline elements, which are stored in the Paragraph.Inlines collection.

There are two consequences of this fact. First, it means a paragraph can contain a whole lot more than text. Second, it means that in order for a paragraph to contain text, the paragraph needs to contain an inline Run element. The Run element contains the actual text, as shown here:

```
<Paragraph>
  <Run>Hello, world of documents.</Run>
</Paragraph>
```

This long-winded syntax wasn't required in the previous example. That's because the Paragraph class is intelligent enough to create a Run implicitly when you place text directly inside.

However, in some cases it's important to understand the behind-the-scenes reality of how a paragraph works. For example, imagine you want to retrieve the text from a paragraph programmatically and you have the following markup:

```
<Paragraph Name="paragraph">Hello, world of documents.</Paragraph>
```

You'll quickly discover that the Paragraph class doesn't contain a Text property. In fact, there's no way to get the text from the paragraph. Instead, to retrieve the text (or change it), you need to grab the nested Run object, as shown here:

```
((Run)paragraph.Inlines.FirstInline).Text = "Hello again.";
```

■**Tip** You can improve the readability of this code by using a Span element to wrap the text you want to modify. You can then give the Span element a name and access it directly. The Span element is described in the "Inline Elements" section.

The Paragraph class includes a TextIndent property that allows you to set the amount that the first line should be indented. (By default, it's 0.) You supply a value in device-independent units.

The Paragraph class also includes a few properties that determine how it splits lines over column and page breaks. You'll consider these details in the "Pages and Columns" section later in this chapter.

■**Note** Unlike HTML, WPF doesn't have block elements for headings. Instead, you simply use paragraphs with different font sizes.

List

The List element represents a bulleted or numeric list. You choose by setting the MarkerStyle property. Table 19-3 lists your options. You can also set the distance between each list item and its marker using the MarkerOffset property.

Table 19-3. *Values from the TextMarkerStyle Enumeration*

Name	Appears As . . .
Disc	A solid bullet. This is the default.
Box	A solid square box.
Circle	A bullet with no fill.
Square	A square box with no fill.
Decimal	An incrementing number (1, 2, 3). Ordinarily, it starts at 1, but you can adjust the StartingIndex to begin counting at a higher number. Despite the name, a MarkerStyle of Decimal will not show fractional values, just integral numbers.
LowerLatin	A lowercase letter that's incremented automatically (a, b, c).
UpperLatin	An uppercase letter that's incremented automatically (A, B, C).
LowerRoman	A lowercase Roman numeral that's incremented automatically (i, ii, iii, iv).
UpperRoman	An uppercase Roman numeral that's incremented automatically (I, II, III, IV).
None	Nothing.

You nest ListItem elements inside the List element to represent individual items in the list. However, each ListItem must itself include a suitable block element (such as a Paragraph). Here's an example that creates two lists, one with bullets and one with numbers:

```
<Paragraph>Top programming languages:</Paragraph>
<List>
  <ListItem>
    <Paragraph>C#</Paragraph>
  </ListItem>
  <ListItem>
    <Paragraph>C++</Paragraph>
  </ListItem>
  <ListItem>
    <Paragraph>Perl</Paragraph>
  </ListItem>
  <ListItem>
    <Paragraph>Logo</Paragraph>
  </ListItem>
</List>

<Paragraph Margin="0,30,0,0">To-do list:</Paragraph>
<List MarkerStyle="Decimal">
  <ListItem>
    <Paragraph>Program a WPF application</Paragraph>
  </ListItem>
  <ListItem>
    <Paragraph>Bake bread</Paragraph>
  </ListItem>
</List>
```

Figure 19-5 shows the result.

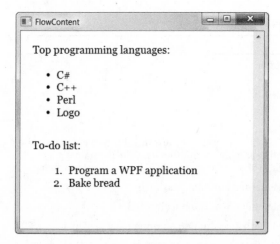

Figure 19-5. *Two lists*

Table

The Table element is designed to display tabular information. It's modeled after the HTML <table> element.

To create a table, you must follow these steps:

1. Place a TableRowGroup element inside the Table. The TableRowGroup holds a group of rows, and every table consists of one or more TableRowGroup elements. On its own, the TableRowGroup doesn't do anything. However, if you use multiple groups and give them each different formatting, you get an easy way to change the overall look of your table without setting repetitive formatting properties on each row.

2. Place a TableRow element inside your TableRowGroup for each row.

3. Place a TableCell element inside each TableRow to represent each column in the row.

4. Place a block element (typically a Paragraph) in each TableCell. This is where you'll add your content for that cell.

Here are the first two rows of the simple table shown in Figure 19-6:

```
<Paragraph FontSize="20pt">Largest Cities in the Year 100</Paragraph>
<Table>
  <TableRowGroup Paragraph.TextAlignment="Center">
    <TableRow FontWeight="Bold" >
      <TableCell>
        <Paragraph>Rank</Paragraph>
      </TableCell>
      <TableCell>
        <Paragraph>Name</Paragraph>
      </TableCell>
      <TableCell>
        <Paragraph>Population</Paragraph>
      </TableCell>
    </TableRow>
    <TableRow>
      <TableCell>
        <Paragraph>1</Paragraph>
      </TableCell>
      <TableCell>
        <Paragraph>Rome</Paragraph>
      </TableCell>
      <TableCell>
        <Paragraph>450,000</Paragraph>
      </TableCell>
    </TableRow>
    ...
  </TableRowGroup>
</Table>
```

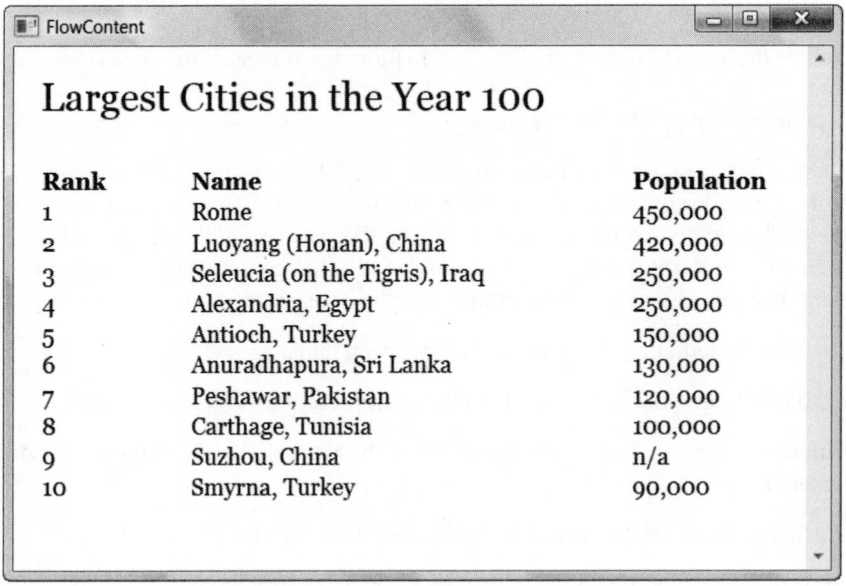

Largest Cities in the Year 100

Rank	Name	Population
1	Rome	450,000
2	Luoyang (Honan), China	420,000
3	Seleucia (on the Tigris), Iraq	250,000
4	Alexandria, Egypt	250,000
5	Antioch, Turkey	150,000
6	Anuradhapura, Sri Lanka	130,000
7	Peshawar, Pakistan	120,000
8	Carthage, Tunisia	100,000
9	Suzhou, China	n/a
10	Smyrna, Turkey	90,000

Figure 19-6. *A basic table*

■Note Unlike a Grid, cells in a Table are filled by position. You must include a TableCell element for each cell in the table, and you must place each row and value in the correct display order.

If you don't supply explicit column widths, WPF splits the space evenly between all its columns. You can override this behavior by supplying a set of TableColumn objects for the Table.Rows property and setting the Width of each one. Here's the markup that the previous example uses to make the middle column three times as big as the first and last columns:

```
<Table.Columns>
  <TableColumn Width="*"></TableColumn>
  <TableColumn Width="3*"></TableColumn>
  <TableColumn Width="*"></TableColumn>
</Table.Columns>
```

There are a few more tricks you can perform with a table. You can set the ColumnSpan and RowSpan properties of a cell to make it stretch over multiple rows. You can also use the CellSpacing property of the table to set the number of units of space that's used to pad in between cells. You can also apply individual formatting (such as different text and background colors) to different cells. However, don't expect to find good support for table borders. You can use the BorderThickness and BorderBrush properties of the TableCell, but this forces you to draw a separate border around the edge of each cell with separate borders. These borders don't look quite right when you use them on a group of contiguous cells. Although the Table element provides the BorderThickness and BorderBrush properties, these only allow you to draw a border around the entire table. If you're hoping for a more sophisticated effect (for example, adding lines in between columns), you're out of luck.

Another limitation is the fact that columns must be sized explicitly or proportionately (using the asterisk syntax shown previously). However, you can't combine the two approaches. For example, there's no way to create two fixed-width columns and one proportional column to receive the leftover space, as you can with the Grid.

■**Note** Some content elements are similar to other non-content elements. However, the content elements are designed solely for use inside a flow document. For example, there's no reason to try to swap a Grid with a Table. The Grid is designed to be the most efficient option when laying out the controls in a window, while a Table is optimized to present text in the most readable way possible in a document.

Section

The Section element doesn't have any built-in formatting of its own. Instead, it's used to wrap other block elements in a convenient package. By grouping elements in a Section element, you can apply common formatting to an entire portion of a document. For example, if you want the same background color and font in several contiguous paragraphs, you can place these paragraphs in a section and then set the Section.Background property, as shown here:

```
<Section FontFamily="Palatino" Background="LightYellow">
  <Paragraph>Lorem ipsum dolor sit amet... </Paragraph>
  <Paragraph>Ut enim ad minim veniam...</Paragraph>
  <Paragraph>Duis aute irure dolor in reprehenderit...</Paragraph>
</Section>
```

This works because the font settings are inherited by the contained paragraphs. The background value is not inherited, but because the background of every paragraph is transparent by default, the section background shows through.

Even better, you can set the Section.Style property to format your section using a style:

```
<Section Style="IntroText">
```

The Section element is analogous to the <div> element in HTML.

■**Tip** Many flow documents use style extensively to categorize content formatting based on its type. For example, a book reviewing site might create separate styles for review titles, review text, emphasized pull quotes, and bylines. These styles could then define whatever formatting is appropriate.

BlockUIContainer

The BlockUIContainer allows you to place non-content elements (classes that derive from UIElement) inside a document, where a block element would otherwise go. For example, you can use the BlockUIContainer to add buttons, check boxes, and even entire layout containers such as the StackPanel and Grid to a document. The only rule is that the BlockUIContainer is limited to a single child.

You might wonder why you would ever want to place controls inside a document. After all, isn't the best rule of thumb to use layout containers for user-interactive portions of your interface, and flow layout for length, read-only blocks of content? However, in real-world applications there are many types of documents that need to provide some sort of user inter-action (beyond what the Hyperlink content element provides). For example, if you're using the flow layout system to create online help pages, you might want to include a button that trig-gers an action.

Here's an example that places a button under a paragraph:

```
<Paragraph>
  You can configure the foof feature using the Foof Options dialog box.
</Paragraph>
<BlockUIContainer>
  <Button HorizontalAlignment="Left" Padding="5">Open Foof Options</Button>
</BlockUIContainer>
```

You can connect an event handler to the Button.Click event in the usual way.

■**Tip** Mingling content elements and ordinary non-content elements makes sense if you have a user-interactive document. For example, if you're creating a survey application that lets users fill out different surveys, it may make sense to take advantage of the advanced text layout provided by the flow document model, without sacrificing the user's ability to enter values and make choices using common controls.

Inline Elements

WPF provides a larger set of inline elements, which can be placed inside block elements or other inline elements. Most of the inline elements are quite straightforward. Table 19-4 lists your options.

Table 19-4. *Inline Content Elements*

Name	Description
Run	Contains ordinary text. Although you can apply formatting to a Run element, it's generally preferred to use a Span element instead. Run elements are often created implicitly (such as when you add text to a paragraph).
Span	Wraps any amount of other inline elements. Usually, you'll use a span to specifically format a piece of text. To do so, you wrap the Span element around a Run element and set the properties of the Span element. (For a shortcut, just place text inside the Span element, and the nested Run element will be created automatically.) Another reason to use a Span is to make it easy for your code to find and manipulate a specific piece of text. The Span element is analogous to the <span> element in HTML.

Name	Description
Bold, Italic, and Underline	Apply bold, italic, and underline formatting. These elements derive from Span. Although you can use these tags, it usually makes more sense to wrap the text you want to format inside a Span element and then set the Span.Style property to point to a style that applies the formatting you want. That way, you have the flexibility to easily adjust the formatting characteristics later on, without altering the markup of your document.
Hyperlink	Represents a clickable link inside a flow document. In a window-based application, you can respond to the Click event to perform an action (for example, showing a different document). In a page-based application, you can use the NavigateUri property to let the user browse directly to another page (as explained in Chapter 9).
LineBreak	Adds a line break inside a block element. Before using a line break, consider whether it would be clearer to use increased Margin or Padding values to add whitespace between elements.
InlineUIContainer	Allows you to place non-content elements (classes that derive from UIElement) where an inline element would otherwise go (for example, in a Paragraph element). The InlineUIContainer is similar to the BlockUIElement, but it's an inline element rather than a block element.
Floater and Figure	Allow you to embed a floating box of content that you can use to highlight important information, display a figure, or show related content (such as advertisements, links, code listings, and so on).

Preserving Whitespace

Ordinarily, whitespace in XML is collapsed. Because XAML is an XML-based language, it follows the same rules.

As a result, if you include a string of spaces in your content, it's converted to single space. That means this markup

```
<Paragraph>hello     there</Paragraph>
```

is equivalent to this:

```
<Paragraph>hello there</Paragraph>
```

Spaces between content and tags are also collapsed. So this line of markup

```
<Paragraph>     Hello there</Paragraph>
```

becomes

```
<Paragraph>Hello there</Paragraph>
```

For the most part, this behavior makes sense. It allows you to indent your document markup using line breaks and tabs where convenient without altering the way that content is interpreted.

Tabs and line breaks are treated in the same way as spaces. They're collapsed to a single space when they appear inside your content, and ignored when they appear on the edges of your content. However, there's one exception to this rule. If you have a space before an inline element, WPF preserves that space. (And if you have several spaces, WPF collapses these spaces to a single space.) That means you can write markup like this:

```
<Paragraph>A common greeting is <Bold>hello</Bold>.</Paragraph>
```

Here, the space between the content "A common greeting is" and the nested Bold element is retained, which is what you want. However, if you rewrote the markup like this, you'd lose the space:

```
<Paragraph>A common greeting is<Bold> hello</Bold>.</Paragraph>
```

In this case, you'll see the text "A common greeting ishello" in your user interface. Incidentally, Visual Studio 2005 incorrectly ignores the space in both examples when you're viewing flow document content in a design window. However, when you run your application you'll get the correct behavior.

In some situations, you might want to add space where it would ordinarily be ignored or include a series of spaces. In this situation, you need to use the xml:space attribute with the value *preserve*, which is an XML convention that tells an XML parser to keep all the whitespace characters in nested content:

```
<Paragraph xml:space="preserve">This    text    is    spaced    out</Paragraph>
```

This seems like the perfect solution, but there are still a few headaches. Now that the XML parser is paying attention to whitespace, you can no longer use line breaks and tabs to indent your content for easier reading. In a long paragraph, this is a significant trade-off that makes the markup more difficult to understand. (Of course, this won't be an issue if you're using another tool to generate the markup for your flow document, in which case you really don't care what the serialized XAML looks like.)

Because you can use the xml:space attribute on any element, you can pay attention to whitespace more selectively. For example, the following markup preserves whitespace in the nested Run element only:

```
<Paragraph>
  <Run xml:space="preserve">This       text      </Run> is spaced out.
</Paragraph>
```

Floater

The Floater element gives you a way to set some content off from the main document. Essentially, this content is placed in a "box" that floats somewhere in your document. (Often, it's displayed off to one side.) Figure 19-7 shows an example with a single line of text.

Figure 19-7. *A floating pull quote*

To create this floater, you simply insert a Floater element somewhere inside another block element (such as a paragraph). The Floater itself can contain one or more block elements. Here's the markup used to create the example in Figure 19-7. (The ellipses indicate omitted text.)

```
<Paragraph>
  It was a bright cold day in April, and the clocks were striking thirteen ...
</Paragraph>
<Paragraph>The hallway smelt of boiled cabbage and old rag mats.
  <Run xml:space="preserve"> </Run>
  <Floater Style="{StaticResource PullQuote}">
    <Paragraph>"The hallway smelt of boiled cabbage"</Paragraph>
  </Floater>
  At one end of it a coloured poster, too large for indoor display ...
</Paragraph>
```

Here's the style that this Floater uses:

```
<Style x:Key="PullQuote">
  <Setter Property="Paragraph.FontSize" Value="30"></Setter>
  <Setter Property="Paragraph.FontStyle" Value="Italic"></Setter>
  <Setter Property="Paragraph.Foreground" Value="Green"></Setter>
  <Setter Property="Paragraph.Padding" Value="5"></Setter>
  <Setter Property="Paragraph.Margin" Value="5,10,15,10"></Setter>
</Style>
```

Ordinarily, the flow document widens the floater so that all its content fits on one line or, if that's not possible, so that it takes the full width of one column in the document window. (In the current example, there's only one column, so the Floater takes the full width of the document window.)

If this isn't what you want, you can specify the width in device-independent units using the Width property. You can also use the HorizontalAlignment property to choose whether the floater is centered, placed on the left edge, or placed on the right edge of the line where the Floater element is placed. Here's how you can create the left-aligned floater shown in Figure 19-8:

```
<Floater Style="{StaticResource PullQuote}" Width="205" HorizontalAlignment="Left">
  <Paragraph>"The hallway smelt of boiled cabbage"</Paragraph>
</Floater>
```

The Floater will use the specified width, unless it stretches beyond the bounds of the document window (in which case the floater gets the full width of the window).

Figure 19-8. *A left-aligned floater*

By default, the floating box that's used for the Floater is invisible. However, you can set a shaded background (through the Background property) or a border (through the BorderBrush and BorderThickness properties) to clearly separate this content from the rest of your document. You can also use the Margin property to add space between the floating box and the document, and the Padding property to add space between the edges of the box and its contents.

Note Ordinarily, the Background, BorderBrush, BorderThickness, Margin, and Padding properties are only available to block elements. However, they're also defined in the Floater and Figure classes, which are inline elements.

You can also use a floater to show a picture. But oddly enough, there is no flow content element that's up to the task. Instead, you'll need to use the Image element in conjunction with the BlockUIContainer or the InlineUIContainer.

However, there's a catch. When inserting a floater that wraps an image, the flow document assumes the figure should be as wide as a full column of text. The Image inside will then stretch to fit, which could result in problems if you're displaying a bitmap and it has to be scaled up or down a large amount. You could change the Image.Stretch property to disable this image resizing feature, but in that case the floater will still take the full width of the column—it simply leaves extra blank space at the sides of the figure.

The only reasonable solution when embedding a bitmap in a flow document is to set a fixed size for the floater box. You can then choose how the image sizes itself in that box using the Image.Stretch property. Here's an example:

```
<Paragraph>
  It was a bright cold day in April,
  <Floater Width="100" Padding="5,0,5,0" HorizontalAlignment="Right">
    <BlockUIContainer>
      <Image Source="BigBrother.jpg"></Image>
    </BlockUIContainer>
  </Floater>
  and the clocks ...
</Paragraph>
```

Figure 19-9 shows the result. Notice that the image actually stretches out over two paragraphs, but this doesn't pose a problem. The flow document wraps the text around all the floaters.

Figure 19-9. *A floater with an image*

Note Using a fixed-size floater also gives the most sensible result when you use zooming. As the zoom percentage changes, so does the size of your floater. The image inside the floater can then stretch itself as needed (based on the Image.Stretch property) to fill or center itself in the floater box.

Figure

The Figure element is similar to the Floater element, but it gives a bit more control over positioning. Usually, you'll use floaters and give WPF a little more control to arrange your content. But if you have a complex, rich document, you might prefer to use figures to make sure your floating boxes aren't bumped too far away as the window is resized, or to put boxes in specific positions.

So what does the Figure class offer that the Floater doesn't? Table 19-5 describes the properties you have to play with. However, there's one caveat: many of these properties (including HorizontalAnchor, VerticalOffset, and HorizontalOffset) aren't supported by the FlowDocumentScrollViewer that you've been using to display your flow document. Instead, they need one of the more sophisticated containers you'll learn about later in the "Read-Only Flow Document Containers" section. For now, replace the FlowDocumentScrollViewer tags with tags for the FlowDocumentReader if you want to use the figure placement properties.

Table 19-5. *Figure Properties*

Name	Description
Width	Sets the width of the figure. You can size a figure just as you size a floater, using device-independent pixels. However, you have the additional ability of sizing the figure proportionately, respective to the overall window or the current column. For example, in your XAML, you can supply the text "0.25 content" to create a box that takes 25% of the width of the window, or "2 Column" to create a box that's two columns wide.
Height	Sets the height of the figure. You can also set the exact height of a figure in device-independent units. (By comparison, a floater makes itself as tall as required to fit all its content in the specified width.) If your use of the Width and Height properties creates a floating box that's too small for all of its content, some content will be truncated.
HorizontalAnchor	Replaces the HorizontalAlignment property in the Floater class. However, along with three equivalent options (ContentLeft, ContentRight, and ContentCenter), it also includes options that allow you to orient the figure relative to the current page (such as PageCenter) or column (such as ColumnCenter).
VerticalAnchor	Allows you to align the image vertically with respect to the current line of text, the current column, or the current page.

Name	Description
HorizontalOffset and VerticalOffset	Set the figure alignment. These properties allow you to move the figure from its anchored position. For example, a negative VerticalOffset will shift the figure box up the number of units you specify. If you use this technique to move a figure away from the edge of the containing window, text will flow into the space you free up. (If you want to increase spacing on one side of a figure but you don't want text to enter that area, adjust the Figure.Padding property instead.)
WrapDirection	Determines whether text is allowed to wrap on one side or both sides (space permitting) of a figure.

Interacting with Elements Programmatically

So far, you've seen examples of how to create the markup required for flow documents. It should come as no surprise that flow documents can also be constructed programmatically. (After all, that's what the XAML parser does when it reads your flow document markup.)

Creating a flow document programmatically is fairly tedious because of a number of disparate elements that need to be created. As with all XAML elements, you must create each element and then set all its properties, as there are no constructors to help you out. You also need to create a Run element to wrap every piece of text, as it won't be generated automatically.

Here's a snippet of code that creates a document with a single paragraph and some bolded text. It then displays the document in an existing FlowDocumentScrollViewer named docViewer:

```
// Create the first part of the sentence.
Run runFirst = new Run();
runFirst.Text = "Hello world of ";

// Create bolded text.
Bold bold = new Bold();
Run runBold = new Run();
runBold.Text = "dynamically generated";
bold.Inlines.Add(runBold);

// Create last part of sentence.
Run runLast = new Run();
runLast.Text = " documents";

// Add three parts of sentence to a paragraph, in order.
Paragraph paragraph = new Paragraph();
paragraph.Inlines.Add(runFirst);
paragraph.Inlines.Add(bold);
paragraph.Inlines.Add(runLast);

// Create a document and add this paragraph.
FlowDocument document = new FlowDocument();
document.Blocks.Add(paragraph);
```

```
// Show the document.
docViewer.Document = document;
```

The result is the sentence "Hello world of **dynamically generated** documents."

Most of the time, you won't create flow documents programmatically. However, you might want to create an application that browses through portions of a flow document and modifies them dynamically. You can do this in the same way that you interact with any other WPF elements: by responding to element events, and by attaching a name to the elements that you want to change. However, because flow documents use deeply nested content with a free-flowing structure, you may need to dig through several layers to find the actual content you want to modify. (Remember, this content is always stored in a Run element, even if the run isn't declared explicitly.)

There are some properties that can help you navigate the structure of a flow document:

- To get the block elements in a flow document, use the FlowDocument.Blocks collection. Use FlowDocument.Blocks.FirstBlock or FlowDocument.Blocks.LastBlock to jump to the first or last block element.

- To move from one block element to the next (or previous) block, use the Block.NextBlock property (or Block.PreviousBlock). You can also use the Block.SiblingBlocks collection to browse all the block elements that are at the same level.

- Many block elements can contain other elements. For example, the List element provides a ListItem collection, the Section provides a Blocks collection, and the Paragraph provides an Inlines collection.

If you need to modify the text inside a flow document, the easiest way is to isolate exactly what you want to change (and no more) using a Span element. For example, the following flow document highlights selected nouns, verbs, and adverbs in a block of text so they can be modified programmatically. The type of selection is indicated with an extra bit of information—a string that's stored in the Span.Tag property.

■**Tip** Remember, the Tag property in any element is reserved for your use. It can store any value or object that you want to use later on.

```
<FlowDocument Name="document">
  <Paragraph FontSize="20" FontWeight="Bold">
    Release Notes
  </Paragraph>
  <Paragraph>
    These are the release <Span Tag="Plural Noun">notes</Span>
    for <Span Tag="Proper Noun">Linux</Span> version 1.2.13.
  </Paragraph>
  <Paragraph>
    Read them <Span Tag="Adverb">carefully</Span>, as they
    tell you what this is all about, how to <Span Tag="Verb">boot</Span>
    the <Span Tag="Noun">kernel</Span>, and what to do if
```

```
    something goes wrong.
  </Paragraph>
</FlowDocument>
```

This design allows you to create the straightforward Mad Libs game shown in Figure 19-10. In this game, the user gets the chance to supply values for all the span tags before seeing the source document. These user-supplied values are then substituted for the original values to humorous effect.

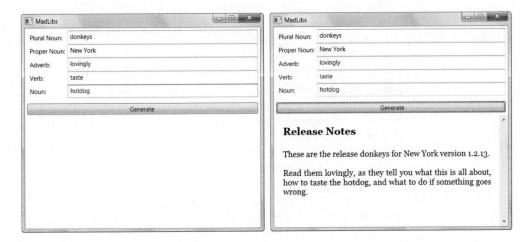

Figure 19-10. *Dynamically modifying a flow document*

To make this example as generic as possible, the code doesn't have any specific knowledge about the document that you're using. Instead, it's written generically so that it can pull the named Span elements out of all the top-level paragraphs in any document. It simply walks through the Blocks collection looking for paragraphs and then walks through the Inlines collection of each paragraph looking for spans. Each time it finds a Span object, it creates the text box that the user can use to supply a new value and adds it to a grid above the document (along with a descriptive label). And to make the substitution process easier, each text box stores a reference (through the TextBox.Tag property) to the Run element with the text inside the corresponding Span element:

```
private void WindowLoaded(Object sender, RoutedEventArgs e)
{
    // Clear grid of text entry controls.
    gridWords.Children.Clear();

    // Look at paragraphs.
    foreach (Block block in document.Blocks)
    {
        Paragraph paragraph = block as Paragraph;

        // Look for spans.
        foreach (Inline inline in paragraph.Inlines)
```

```
            {
                Span span = inline as Span;
                if (span != null)
                {
                    // Create a slot in the row for this term.
                    RowDefinition row = new RowDefinition();
                    gridWords.RowDefinitions.Add(row);

                    // Add the descriptive label for this term.
                    Label lbl = new Label();
                    lbl.Content = inline.Tag.ToString() + ":";
                    Grid.SetColumn(lbl, 0);
                    Grid.SetRow(lbl, gridWords.RowDefinitions.Count - 1);
                    gridWords.Children.Add(lbl);

                    // Add the text box where the user can supply a value for this term.
                    TextBox txt = new TextBox();
                    Grid.SetColumn(txt, 1);
                    Grid.SetRow(txt, gridWords.RowDefinitions.Count - 1);
                    gridWords.Children.Add(txt);

                    // Link the text box to the run where the text should appear.
                    txt.Tag = span.Inlines.FirstInline;
                }
            }
        }
    }
}
```

When the user clicks the Generate button, the code walks through all the text boxes that were added dynamically in the previous step. It then copies the text from the text box to the related Run in the flow document:

```
private void cmdGenerate_Click(Object sender, RoutedEventArgs e)
{
    foreach (UIElement child in gridWords.Children)
    {
        if (Grid.GetColumn(child) == 1)
        {
            TextBox txt = (TextBox)child;
            if (txt.Text != "") ((Run)txt.Tag).Text = txt.Text;
        }
    }
    docViewer.Visibility = Visibility.Visible;
}
```

It might occur to you to do the reverse—in other words, walk through the document again, inserting the matching text each time you find a Span. However, this approach is more problematic because you can't enumerate through the collections of inline elements in a paragraph at the same time that you're modifying its content.

Text Justification

You may have already noticed that text content in a flow document is, by default, justified so that every line stretches from the left to the right margin. You can change this behavior using the TextAlignment property, but most flow documents in WPF are justified.

To improve the readability of justified text, you can use a WPF feature called *optimal paragraph layout* that ensures that whitespace is distributed as evenly as possible. This avoids the distracting rivers of whitespace and oddly spaced out words that can occur with more primitive line-justification algorithms (such as those provided by web browsers).

■**Note** Basic line justification algorithms work on one line at a time. WPF's optimal paragraph justification uses a total-fit algorithm that looks ahead at the lines to come. It then chooses line breaks that balance the word spacing throughout the entire paragraph and result in the minimal cost over all lines.

Ordinarily, WPF's optimal paragraph feature isn't enabled. Presumably, this is because of the additional overhead in the total-fit algorithm. However, in most cases you'll find that the responsiveness of your application (how it "feels" as you resize the window) is the same with optimal paragraphs enabled.

To enable optimal paragraphs, set the FlowDocument.IsOptimalParagraphEnabled property to true. Figure 19-11 compares the difference by placing a flow document that uses normal paragraphs on top, and one that uses the total-fit algorithm below.

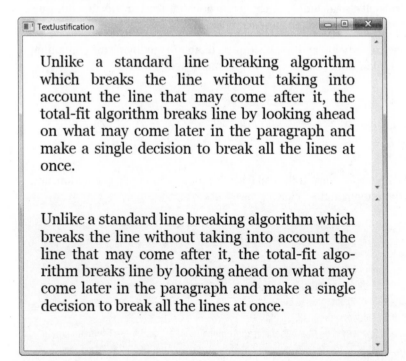

Figure 19-11. *Comparing ordinary justification (top) with optimal paragraphs (bottom)*

To further improve text justification, particularly in narrow windows, set the FlowDocument.IsHyphenationEnabled property to true. This way, WPF will break long words where necessary to keep the space between words small. Hyphenation works well with the optimal paragraph feature, and it's particularly important when using multicolumn displays. WPF uses a hyphenating dictionary to make sure that hyphens fall in the appropriate places (between syllables, as in "algo-rithm" rather than "algori-thm").

Read-Only Flow Document Containers

WPF provides three read-only containers that you can use to display flow documents:

- **FlowDocumentScrollViewer** shows the entire document with a scroll bar to let you move through it if the document exceeds the size of the FlowDocumentScrollViewer. The FlowDocumentScrollViewer doesn't support pagination or multicolumn displays (although it does support printing and zooming, as all containers do). All of the examples you've seen up to this point have used the FlowDocumentScrollViewer.

- **FlowDocumentPageViewer** splits a flow document into multiple pages. Each page is as large as the available space and the user can step from one page to the next. The Flow-DocumentPageViewer has more overhead than the FlowDocumentScrollViewer (due to the additional calculations required for breaking content into pages).

- **FlowDocumentReader** combines the features of the FlowDocumentScrollViewer and FlowDocumentPageViewer. It lets the user choose whether to read content in a scrollable or paginated display. It also includes searching functionality. The FlowDocumentReader has the most overhead of any flow document container.

Switching from one container to another is simply a matter of modifying the containing tag. For example, here's a flow document in a FlowDocumentPageViewer:

```
<FlowDocumentPageViewer>
  <FlowDocument>
    <Paragraph>Hello, world of documents.</Paragraph>
  </FlowDocument>
</FlowDocumentPageViewer>
```

Each of these containers provides additional features, such as zooming, pagination, and printing. You'll learn about them in the following sections.

THE TEXTBLOCK

You can display small amounts of flow content using the familiar TextBlock, a text display element that you've seen extensively over the past chapters. Although the TextBlock is often used to hold ordinary text (in which case the TextBlock creates a Run object to wrap that text), you can actually place any combination of inline elements inside. They'll all be added to the TextBlock.Inlines collection.

The TextBlock provides text wrapping (through the TextWrapping property), and a TextTrimming property that allows you to control how text is treated when it can't fit in the bounds of the TextBlock. When this occurs, the extra text is trimmed off, but you can choose whether an ellipse is used to indicate that trimming has taken place. Your options are the following:

- None. The text is trimmed with no ellipse. "This text is too big" might become "This text is to".

- WordEllipse. The ellipse is inserted after the last word that fits (as in "This text is . . .").

- CharacterEllipse. The ellipse is inserted after the last character that fits (as in "This text is t . . .").

The TextBlock can't match the scrolling and paging features of the more sophisticated FlowDocument containers. For that reason, the TextBlock is best for displaying small amounts of flow content, such as control labels and hyperlinks. The TextBlock can't accommodate block elements at all.

Zooming

All three document containers support *zooming*: the ability for you to shrink or magnify the displayed content. The Zoom property of the container (for example, FlowDocumentScrollViewer.Zoom) sets the size of the content as a percentage value. Ordinarily, the Zoom value begins at 100, and the FontSize values correspond to any other elements in your window. If you increase the Zoom value to 200, the text size is doubled. Similarly, if you reduce it to 50, the text size is halved (although you can use any value in between).

Obviously, you can set the zoom percentage by hand. You can also change the zoom programmatically using IncreaseZoom() and DecreaseZoom(), which change the Zoom value by the amount specified by the ZoomIncrement property. You can also wire up other controls to these features using commands (Chapter 10). But there's no need to go to any of this trouble. The simplest approach is to let users set the zoom percentage to match their preferences. The FlowDocumentScrollViewer includes a toolbar with a zoom slider bar for just this purpose. To make it visible, set IsToolbarVisible to true, as shown here:

```
<FlowDocumentScrollViewer MinZoom="50" MaxZoom="1000"
  Zoom="100" ZoomIncrement="5" IsToolbarVisible="True">
```

Figure 19-12 shows a flow document with a zoom slider bar at the bottom.

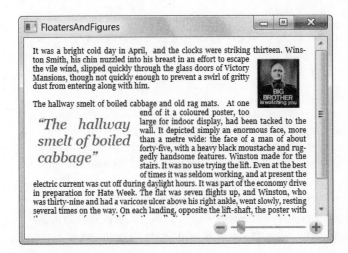

Figure 19-12. *Scaling down a document*

If you're using the FlowDocumentPageViewer or FlowDocumentReader, the zoom slider is always visible (although you can still configure the zoom increment and the minimum and maximum allowed zoom values).

Tip Zooming affects the size of anything that's set in device-independent units (not just font sizes). For example, if your flow document uses floater or figure boxes with explicit widths, these widths are also sized proportionately.

Pages and Columns

The FlowDocumentPageViewer can split a long document into separate pages. This makes it easier to read long content. (When scrolling, readers are constantly forced to stop reading, scroll down, and then find the point where they left off. But when readers browse through a series of pages, they know exactly where to start reading—at the top of each page.)

The number of pages depends on the size of the window. For example, if you allow a FlowDocumentPageViewer to take the full size of a window, you'll notice that the number of pages changes as you resize the window, as shown in Figure 19-13.

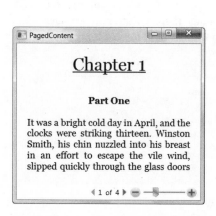
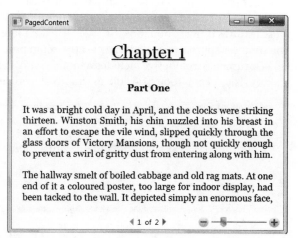

Figure 19-13. *Dynamically repaginated content*

If you make the window wide enough, the FlowDocumentPageViewer splits the text into multiple columns to make it easier to read (Figure 19-14). Figure 19-13 and Figure 19-14 show the same window. This window simply adjusts itself to make the best use of the available space.

Note Remember, Floater elements like to make themselves as wide as a single column. You can make them smaller by setting an explicit width, but not wider. On the other hand, Figure elements can easily span multiple columns.

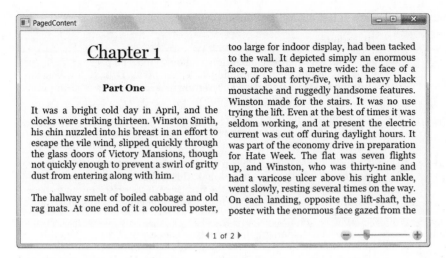

Figure 19-14. *Automatic columns*

Although the standard settings give good page breaking and column breaking, you can tweak them in a number of ways to get exactly the result you want. There are two key extensibility points that you can use: the FlowDocument class that contains the content (which provides the properties listed in Table 19-6) and individual Paragraph elements in the document (which provide the properties listed in Table 19-7).

Table 19-6. *FlowDocument Properties for Controlling Columns*

Name	Description
ColumnWidth	Specifies the preferred size of text columns. This acts as a minimum size, and the FlowDocumentPageViewer adjusts the width to make sure all the space is used on the page.
IsColumnWidthFlexible	Determines whether the document container can adjust the column size. If false, the exact column width specified by the ColumnWidth property is used. The FlowDocumentPageViewer will not create partial columns, so this may leave some blank space at the right edge of the page (or on either side if FlowDocumentMaxPageWidth is less than the width of the document window). If true (the default), the FlowDocumentPageViewer splits the space evenly to create columns, respecting the ColumnWidth property as a minimum.
ColumnGap	Sets the blank space in between columns.
ColumnRuleWidth and ColumnRuleBrush	Allow you to draw a vertical line in between columns. You can choose the width and fill of that line.

Table 19-7. *Paragraph Properties for Controlling Columns*

Name	Description
KeepTogether	Determines whether a paragraph can be split over a page break. If true, this paragraph will not be split over a page break. Usually, it will all be bumped to the next page. (This setting makes sense for small amounts of text that need to be read in one piece.)
KeepWithNext	Determines whether a pair of paragraphs can be separated by a page break. If true, this paragraph will not be divided from the following paragraph over a page break. (This setting makes sense for headings.)
MinOrphanLines	Controls how a paragraph can be split over a page break. When this paragraph is split over a page break, this is the minimum number of lines that needs to appear on the first page. If there isn't enough space for this number of lines, the entire paragraph will be bumped to the next page.
MinWindowLines	Controls how a paragraph can be split over a page break. When this paragraph is split over a page break, this is the minimum number of lines that needs to appear on the second page. The FlowDocument-PageViewer will move lines from the first page to the second to meet this criteria.

■**Note** Obviously, there are situations when the column-break properties of the Paragraph element can't be met. For example, if a paragraph is too large to fit on a single page, it doesn't matter whether you set KeepTogether to true, as the paragraph must be broken.

The FlowDocumentPageViewer isn't the only container that supports pagination. The FlowDocumentReader allows the user to choose between a scroll mode (which works exactly like the FlowDocumentScrollViewer) and two page modes. You can choose to see one page at a time (which works exactly like the FlowDocumentPageViewer), or two pages side by side. To switch between viewing modes, you simply click one of the icons in the bottom-right corner of the FlowDocumentReader toolbar.

Loading Documents from a File

So far, the examples you've seen declare the FlowDocument inside its container. However, it's no stretch to imagine that once you've created the perfect document viewer, you might want to reuse it to show different document content. (For example, you might show different topics in a help window.) To make this possible, you need to dynamically load content into the container using the XamlReader class in the System.Windows.Markup namespace.

Fortunately, it's a fairly easy task. Here's the code you need (without the obligatory error-handling you'd use to catch file access problems):

```
using (FileStream fs = File.Open(documentFile, FileMode.Open))
{
    FlowDocument document = XamlReader.Load(fs) as FlowDocument;

    if (document == null)
```

```
    {
        MessageBox.Show("Problem loading document.");
    }
    else
    {
        flowContainer.Document = document;
    }
}
```

It's just as easy to take the current content of a FlowDocument and save it to a XAML file using the XamlWriter class. This functionality is less useful (after all, the containers you've seen so far don't allow the user to make changes). However, it's a worthwhile technique if you need to make programmatic changes to a document based on user actions (for example, you want to save the text from the completed Mad Libs game shown earlier), or you want to construct a FlowDocument programmatically and save it directly to disk.

Here's the code that serializes a FlowDocument object to XAML:

```
using (FileStream fs = File.Open(documentFile, FileMode.Create))
{
    XamlWriter.Save(flowContainer.Document, fs);
}
```

Printing

If you want to print a flow document, it's easy. Just use the Print() method of the container. (All flow document containers support printing.) The Print() method shows the Windows Print dialog box where the user can choose the printer and other printing preferences, such as the number of copies, before choosing to cancel the operation or to go ahead and send the job to the printer.

Printing, like many of the features in the flow document containers, works through commands. As a result, if you want to wire a control up to this functionality, you don't need to write code that calls the Print() method. Instead, you can simply use the appropriate command, as shown here:

```
<Button Command="ApplicationCommands.Print" CommandTarget="docViewer">Print</Button>
```

Along with printing, the flow document containers also support commands for searching, zooming, and page navigation.

Commands may also have key bindings. For example, the Print command has a default key binding that maps the Ctrl+P keystroke. As a result, even if you don't include a button or code to call the Print() method, the user can still hit Ctrl+P to trigger it and show the Print window. If you don't want this behavior, you need to remove the key binding from the command.

■Note It's possible to customize the printout of a flow document. You'll learn how to do this, and how to print other types of content, in Chapter 20.

Editing a Flow Document

All the flow document containers you've seen so far are read-only. They're ideal for displaying document content, but they don't allow the user to make changes. Fortunately, there's another WPF element that fills the gap: the RichTextBox control.

Programming toolkits have included rich text controls, in some form or another, for more than a decade. However, the RichTextBox control that WPF includes is significantly different than its predecessors. It's no longer bound to the dated RTF standard that's found in word processing programs. Instead, it now stores its content as a FlowDocument object.

The consequences of this change are significant. Although you can still load RTF content into a RichTextBox control, internally the RichTextBox uses the much more straightforward flow content model that you've studied in this chapter. That makes it far easier to manipulate document content programmatically.

The RichTextBox control also exposes a rich programming model that provides plenty of extensibility points so you can plug in your own logic, which allows you to use the Rich-TextBox as a building block for your own customized text editor. The one drawback is speed. The WPF RichTextBox, like most of the rich text controls that have preceded it, can be a bit sluggish. If you need to hold huge amounts of data, use intricate logic to handle key presses, or add effects such as automatic formatting (for example, Visual Studio's syntax highlighting or Word's spelling-checker underlining), the WPF RichTextBox probably won't provide the performance you need.

■Note The RichTextBox doesn't support all the features that read-only flow document containers do. Zooming, pagination, multicolumn displays, and search are all features that the RichTextBox doesn't provide.

Loading a File

To try out the RichTextBox, you can declare one of the flow documents you've already seen inside a RichTextBox element, as shown here:

```
<RichTextBox>
  <FlowDocument>
    <Paragraph>Hello, world of editable documents.</Paragraph>
  </FlowDocument>
</RichTextBox>
```

More practically, you may choose to retrieve a document from a file and then insert it in the RichTextBox. To do this, you can use the same approach that you used to load and save the content of a FlowDocument before displaying it in a read-only container—namely, the static XamlReader.Load() method. However, you might want the additional ability to load and save files in other formats (namely, .rtf files). To do this, you need to use the System.Windows.Documents.TextRange class, which wraps a chunk of text. The TextRange is a miraculously useful container that allows you to convert text from one format to another and apply formatting (as described in the next section).

Here's a simple code snippet that translates an .rtf document into a selection of text in a TextRange and then inserts it into a RichTextBox:

```
OpenFileDialog openFile = new OpenFileDialog();
openFile.Filter = "RichText Files (*.rtf)|*.rtf|All Files (*.*)|*.*";

if (openFile.ShowDialog() == true)
{
    TextRange documentTextRange = new TextRange(
      richTextBox.Document.ContentStart, richTextBox.Document.ContentEnd);

    using (FileStream fs = File.Open(openFile.FileName, FileMode.Open))
    {
        documentTextRange.Load(fs, DataFormats.Rtf);
    }
}
```

Notice that before you can do anything, you need to create a TextRange that wraps the portion of the document you want to change. Even though there's currently no document content, you still need to specify the starting point and ending point of the selection. To select the whole document, you can use the FlowDocument.ContentStart and FlowDocument.ContentEnd properties, which provide the TextPointer objects the TextRange requires.

Once the TextRange has been created, you can fill it with data using the Load() method. However, you need to supply a string that identifies the type of data format you're attempting to convert. You can use one of the following:

- DataFormat.Xaml for XAML flow content

- DataFormats.Rtf for rich text (as in the previous example)

- DataFormats.XamlPackage for XAML flow content with embedded images

- DataFormats.Text for plain text

Note The DataFormats.XamlPackage format is essentially the same as DataFormats.Xaml. The only difference is that DataFormats.XamlPackage stores the binary data for any embedded images (which is left out if you use the ordinary DataFormats.Xaml serialization). The XAML package format is not a true standard—it's just a feature that WPF provides to make it easier to serialize document content and support other features you might want to implement, such as cut-and-paste or drag-and-drop.

Although the DataFormats class provides many additional fields, the rest aren't supported. For example, you won't have any luck attempting to convert an HTML document to flow content using DataFormats.Html. Both the XAML package format and RTF require unmanaged code permission, which means you can't use them in a limited-trust scenario (such as a browser-based application).

The TextRange.Load() method only works if you specify the correct file format. However, it's quite possible that you might want to create a text editor that supports both XAML (for best fidelity) and RTF (for compatibility with other programs, such as word processors). In this situation, the standard approach is to let the user specify the file format or make an assumption about the format based on the file extension, as shown here:

```
using (FileStream fs = File.Open(openFile.FileName, FileMode.Open))
{
    if (Path.GetExtension(openFile.FileName).ToLower() == ".rtf")
    {
        documentTextRange.Load(fs, DataFormats.Rtf);
    }
    else
    {
        documentTextRange.Load(fs, DataFormats.Xaml);
    }
}
```

This code will encounter an exception if the file isn't found, can't be accessed, or can't be loaded using the format you specify. For all these reasons, you should wrap this code in an exception handler.

Remember, no matter how you load your document content, it's converted to a Flow-Document in order to be displayed by the RichTextBox. To study exactly what's taking place, you can write a simple routine that grabs the content from the FlowDocument and converts it to a string text using the XamlWriter or a TextRange. Here's an example that displays the markup for the current flow document in another text box:

```
// Copy the document content to a MemoryStream.
using (MemoryStream stream = new MemoryStream())
{
    TextRange range = new TextRange(richTextBox.Document.ContentStart,
      richTextBox.Document.ContentEnd);
    range.Save(stream, DataFormats.Xaml);
    stream.Position = 0;

    // Read the content from the stream and display it in a text box.
    using (StreamReader r = new StreamReader(stream))
    {
        txtFlowDocumentMarkup.Text = r.ReadToEnd();
    }
}
```

This trick is extremely useful as a debugging tool for investigating how the markup for a document changes after it's been edited.

Saving a File

You can also save your document using a TextRange object. You need to supply two Text-Pointer objects—one that identifies the start of the content, and one that demarcates the end. You can then call the TextRange.Save() method and specify the desired export format (text, XAML, XAML package, or RTF) using a field from the DataFormats class. Once again, the XAML package and RTF formats require unmanaged code permission.

The following block of code saves the document using the XAML format unless the file name has an .rtf extension. (Another, more explicit approach is to give the user the choice of using a save feature that uses XAML and an export feature that uses RTF.)

```
SaveFileDialog saveFile = new SaveFileDialog();
saveFile.Filter =
  "XAML Files (*.xaml)|*.xaml|RichText Files (*.rtf)|*.rtf|All Files (*.*)|*.*";

if (saveFile.ShowDialog() == true)
{
    // Create a TextRange around the entire document.
    TextRange documentTextRange = new TextRange(
      richTextBox.Document.ContentStart, richTextBox.Document.ContentEnd);

    // If this file exists, it's overwritten.
    using (FileStream fs = File.Create(saveFile.FileName))
    {
        if (Path.GetExtension(saveFile.FileName).ToLower() == ".rtf")
        {
            documentTextRange.Save(fs, DataFormats.Rtf);
        }
        else
        {
            documentTextRange.Save(fs, DataFormats.Xaml);
        }
    }
}
```

When you use the XAML format to save a document, you probably assume that the document is stored as an ordinary XAML file with a top-level FlowDocument element. This is close, but not quite right. Instead, the top-level element must be a Section element.

As you learned earlier in this chapter, the Section is an all-purpose container that wraps other block elements. This makes sense—after all, the TextRange object represents a section of selected content. However, make sure that you don't try to use the TextRange.Load() method with other XAML files, including those that have a top-level FlowDocument, Page, or Window element, as none of these files will be parsed successfully. (Similarly, the document file can't link to code-behind file or attach any event handlers.) If you have a XAML file that has a top-level FlowDocument element, you can create a corresponding FlowDocument object using the XamlReader.Load() method, as you did with the other FlowDocument containers.

■**Tip** If you want to convert your document to other popular formats, such as the WordML format used by Word 2007, be sure to check out the serialization sample at http://msdn2.microsoft.com/en-us/library/ms771375.aspx. Although the XML processing code is lengthy and tedious, you can reuse it to get the same functionality in your own applications.

Formatting Selected Text

You can learn a fair bit about the RichTextBox control by building a simple rich text editor, like the one shown in Figure 19-15. Here, toolbar buttons allow the user to quickly apply bold formatting, italic formatting, and underlining. But the most interesting part of this example is the ordinary TextBox control underneath, which shows the XAML markup for the FlowDocument object that's currently displayed in the RichTextBox. This allows you to study how the RichTextBox modifies the FlowDocument object as you make edits.

■**Note** Technically, you don't need to code the logic for bolding, italicizing, and underlining selected text. That's because the RichTextBox supports the ToggleBold, ToggleItalic, and ToggleUnderline commands from the EditingCommands class. You can wire your buttons up to these commands directly. However, it's still worth considering this example to learn more about how the RichTextBox works. The knowledge you gain is indispensable if you need to process text in another way. (The downloadable code for this chapter demonstrates both the code-based approach and the command-based approach.)

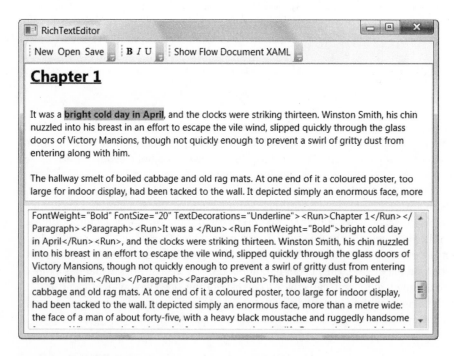

Figure 19-15. *Editing text*

All of the buttons work in a similar way. They use the RichTextBox.Selection property, which provides a TextSelection object that wraps the currently selected text. (TextSelection is a slightly more advanced class that derives from the TextRange class you saw in the previous section.)

Making changes with the TextSelection object is easy enough, but not obvious. The simplest approach is to use the ApplyPropertyValue() to change a dependency property in the selection. For example, you could apply bold formatting to any text elements in the selection using this code:

```
richTextBox.Selection.ApplyPropertyValue(
  TextElement.FontWeightProperty, FontWeights.Bold);
```

There's more happening here than meets the eye. For example, if you try this out on a small piece of text inside a larger paragraph, you'll find that this code automatically creates an inline Run element to wrap the selection and then applies the bold formatting to just that run. This way, you can use the same line of code to format individual words, entire paragraphs, and irregular selections that involve more than one paragraph (in which case you'll end up with a separate run being created in each affected paragraph).

Of course, this code as written isn't a complete solution. If you want to toggle the bold formatting, you'll also need to use the TextSelection.GetPropertyValue() to check whether bold formatting is already applied:

```
Object obj = richTextBox.Selection.GetPropertyValue(
  TextElement.FontWeightProperty);
```

This method is a little trickier. If your selection encloses text that is all unambiguously bold or unambiguously normal, you'll receive the FontWeights.Bold or FontWeights.Normal property. However, if your selection contains some bold text and some normal text, you'll get a DependencyProperty.UnsetValue instead.

It's up to you how you want to handle a mixed selection. You might want to do nothing, always apply the formatting, or decide based on the first character (which is what the EditingCommands.ToggleBold command does). To do this, you'd need to create a new TextRange that wraps just the starting point of the selection. Here's the code that implements the latter approach and checks the first letter in ambiguous cases:

```
Object obj = richTextBox.Selection.GetPropertyValue(
  TextElement.FontWeightProperty);

if (obj == DependencyProperty.UnsetValue)
{
    TextRange range = new TextRange(richTextBox.Selection.Start,
      richTextBox.Selection.Start);

    obj = range.GetPropertyValue(TextElement.FontWeightProperty).ToString();
}

FontWeight fontWeight = (FontWeight)obj;

if (fontWeight == FontWeights.Bold)
  fontWeight = FontWeights.Normal;
else
  fontWeight = FontWeights.Bold;
```

```
richTextBox.Selection.ApplyPropertyValue(
  TextElement.FontWeightProperty, fontWeight);
```

In some cases, a user might trigger the bold command without any selected text at all. Just for fun, here's a code routine that checks for this condition and then checks the formatting that's applied to the entire paragraph that contains this text. The font weight of that paragraph is then flipped from bold to normal or from normal to bold:

```
if (richTextBox.Selection.Text == "")
{
    FontWeight fontWeight = richTextBox.Selection.Start.Paragraph.FontWeight;
    if (fontWeight == FontWeights.Bold)
      fontWeight = FontWeights.Normal;
    else
      fontWeight = FontWeights.Bold;

    richTextBox.Selection.Start.Paragraph.FontWeight = fontWeight;
}
```

Tip To get the plain, unformatted text in a selection, use the TextRange.Text property.

There are many more methods for manipulating text in a RichTextBox. For example, the TextRange class and RichTextBox class both include a range of properties that let you get character offsets, count lines, and navigate through the flow elements in a portion of a document. To get more information, consult the Visual Studio help.

Getting Individual Words

One frill that the RichTextBox lacks is the ability to isolate specific words in a document. Although it's easy enough to find the flow document element that exists in a given position (as you saw in the previous section), the only way to grab the nearest word is to move character by character, checking for whitespace. This type of code is tedious and extremely difficult to write without error.

Prajakta Joshi of the WPF editing team has posted a reasonably complete solution at http://blogs.msdn.com/prajakta/archive/2006/11/01/navigate-words-in-richtextbox.aspx that detects word breaks. Using this code, you can quickly create a host of interesting effects, such as the following routine that grabs a word when the user right-clicks, and then displays that word in a separate text box. Another option might be to show a popup with a dictionary definition, launch an e-mail program or a web browser to follow a link, and so on:

```
private void richTextBox_MouseDown(object sender, MouseEventArgs e)
{
    if (e.RightButton == MouseButtonState.Pressed)
    {
        // Get the nearest TextPointer to the mouse position.
```

```
        TextPointer location = richTextBox.GetPositionFromPoint(
            Mouse.GetPosition(richTextBox), true);

        // Get the nearest word using this TextPointer.
        TextRange word = WordBreaker.GetWordRange(location);

        // Display the word.
        txtSelectedWord.Text = word.Text;
    }
}
```

Note This code doesn't actually connect to the MouseDown event because the RichTextBox intercepts and suppresses MouseUp and MouseDown. Instead, this event handler is attached to the PreviewMouse-Down event, which occurs just before MouseDown.

PLACING UIELEMENT OBJECTS IN A RICHTEXTBOX

As you learned earlier in this chapter, you can use the BlockUIContainer and InlineUIContainer classes to place non-content elements (classes that derive from UIElement) inside a flow document. However, if you use this technique to add interactive controls (such as text boxes, buttons, check boxes, hyperlinks, and so on) to a RichTextBox, they'll be disabled automatically and will appear grayed out.

You can opt out of this behavior and force the RichTextBox to enable embedded controls, much like the read-only FlowDocument containers do. To do so, simply set the RichTextBox.IsDocumentEnabled property to true. (It's worth noting that this property was added in .NET 3.5. You could get the same result in .NET 3.0, but it required an awkward workaround.)

Although it's easy, you may want to think twice before you set IsDocumentEnabled to true. Including element content inside a RichTextBox introduces all sorts of odd usability quirks. For example, controls can be deleted and undeleted (using Ctrl+Z or the Undo command), but undeleting them loses their event handlers. Furthermore, text can be inserted in between adjacent containers, but if you attempt to cut and paste a block of content that includes UIElement objects, they'll be discarded. For reasons like these, it's probably not worth the trouble to use embedded controls inside a RichTextBox.

Fixed Documents

Flow documents allow you to dynamically lay out complex, text-heavy content in a way that's naturally suited to onscreen reading. Fixed documents—those that use XPS (the XML Paper Specification)—are much less flexible. They serve as print-ready documents that can be distributed and printed on any output device with full fidelity to the original source. Toward that end, they use a precise, fixed layout, have support for font embedding, and can't be casually rearranged.

XPS isn't just a part of WPF. It's a standard that's tightly integrated into Windows Vista. Windows Vista includes a print driver that can create XPS documents (in any application) and a viewer that allows you to display them. These two pieces work similarly to Adobe Acrobat, allowing users to create, review, and annotate print-ready electronic documents. Additionally, Microsoft Office 2007 includes a free downloadable add-in (available at `http://tinyurl.com/v46jc`) that allows the creation of XPS and PDF documents.

■**Note** Under the hood, XPS files are actually ZIP files that contain a library of compressed files, including fonts, images, and text content for individual pages (using a XAML-like XML markup). To browse the inner contents of an XPS file, just rename the extension to .zip and open it. You can also refer to `http://msdn.microsoft.com/msdnmag/issues/06/01/XMLPaperSpecification` for an overview of the XPS file format.

You can display an XPS document just as easily as you display a flow document. The only difference is the viewer. Instead of using one of the FlowDocument containers (FlowDocument-Reader, FlowDocumentScrollViewer, or FlowDocumentPageViewer), you use the simply named DocumentViewer. It includes controls for searching and zooming (Figure 19-16). It also provides a similar set of properties, methods, and commands as the FlowDocument containers.

Here's the code you might use to load an XPS file into memory and show it in a Document-Viewer:

```
XpsDocument doc = new XpsDocument("filename.xps", FileAccess.Read);
docViewer.Document = doc.GetFixedDocumentSequence();
doc.Close();
```

The XpsDocument class isn't terribly exciting. It provides the GetFixedDocument-Sequence() method used previously, which returns a reference to the document root with all its content. It also includes an AddFixedDocument() method for creating the document sequence in a new document, and two methods for managing digital signatures (SignDigitally() and RemoveSignature()).

XPS documents are closely associated with the concept of printing. A single XPS document is fixed at a particular page size and lays its text out to fit the available space. As with flow documents, you can get straightforward support for printing a fixed document using the ApplicationCommands.Print command. In Chapter 20, you'll learn how to get fine-grained control of printing, and you'll see how the XPS model allows you to create a straightforward print preview feature.

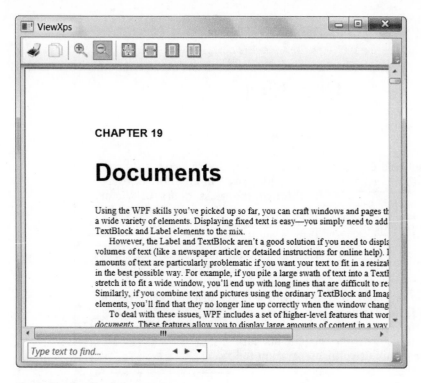

Figure 19-16. *A fixed document*

Annotations

WPF provides an annotation feature that allows you to add comments and highlights to flow documents and fixed documents. These annotations can be used to suggest revisions, highlight errors, or flag important pieces of information.

Many products provide a wide range of annotation types. For example, Adobe Acrobat allows you to draw revision marks and shapes on a document. WPF isn't quite as flexible. It allows you to use two types of annotations:

- **Highlighting.** You can select some text and give it a colored background of your choice. (Technically, WPF highlighting applies a partially transparent color *over* your text, but the effect makes it seem as if you were changing the background.)

- **Sticky notes.** You can select some text and attach a floating box that contains additional text information or ink content.

Figure 19-17 shows the sample you'll learn how to build in this section. It shows a flow document with a highlighted text region and two sticky notes, one with ink content and one with text content.

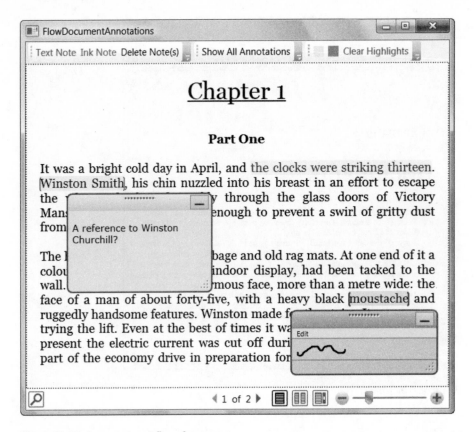

Figure 19-17. *Annotating a flow document*

All four of the WPF document containers—FlowDocumentReader, FlowDocumentScroll-
Viewer, FlowDocumentPageViewer, and DocumentViewer—support annotations. But in order
to use annotations, you need to take two steps. First, you need to manually enable the annotation service using a bit of initialization code. Second, you need to add controls (such as
toolbar buttons) that allow users to add the types of annotations you want to support.

The Annotation Classes

WPF's annotation system relies on several classes from the System.Windows.Annotations and
System.Windows.Annotations.Storage namespace. Here are the key players:

- **AnnotationService.** This class manages the annotations feature. In order to use annotations, it's up to you to create this object.

- **AnnotationStore.** This class manages the storage of your annotations. It defines several
  methods that you can use to create and delete individual annotations. It also includes
  events that you can use to react to annotations being created or changed. Annotation-
  Store is an abstract class, and there's currently just one class that derives from it:
  XmlStreamStore. XmlStreamStore serializes annotations to an XML-based format and
  allows you to store your annotation XML in any stream.

- **AnnotationHelper.** This class provides a small set of static methods for dealing with annotations. These methods bridge the gap between the stored annotations and the document container. Most of the AnnotationHelper methods work with the currently selected text in the document container (allowing you to highlight it, annotate it, or remove its existing annotations). The AnnotationHelper also allows you to find where a specific annotation is placed in a document.

In the following sections, you'll use all three of these key ingredients.

■**Tip** Both the AnnotationStore and the AnnotationHelper provide methods for creating and deleting annotations. However, the methods in the AnnotationStore class work with the currently selected text in a document container. For that reason, the AnnotationStore methods are best for programmatically manipulating annotations without user interaction, while the AnnotationHelper methods are best for implementing user-initiated annotation changes (for example, adding an annotation when the user selects some text and clicks a button).

Enabling the Annotation Service

Before you can do anything with annotations, you need to enable the annotation service with the help of an AnnotationService and AnnotationStream object.

In the example shown in Figure 19-17, it makes sense to create the AnnotationService when the window first loads. Creating the service is simple enough—you just need to create an AnnotationService object for the document reader and call AnnotationService.Enable(). However, when you call Enable() you need to pass in an AnnotationStore object. The Annotation-Service manages the information for your annotations, while the AnnotationStore manages the storage of these annotations.

Here's the code that creates and enables annotations:

```
// A stream for storing annotation.
private MemoryStream annotationStream;

// The service that manages annotations.
private AnnotationService service;

protected void window_Loaded(object sender, RoutedEventArgs e)
{
    // Create the AnnotationService for your document container.
    service = new AnnotationService(docReader);

    // Create the annotation storage.
    annotationStream = new MemoryStream();
    AnnotationStore store = new XmlStreamStore(annotationStream);

    // Enable annotations.
    service.Enable(store);
}
```

Notice that in this example, annotations are stored in a MemoryStream. As a result, they'll be discarded as soon as the MemoryStream is garbage collected. If you want to store annotations so they can be reapplied to the original document, you have two choices. You can create a FileStream instead of a MemoryStream, which ensures the annotation data is written as the user applies it. Or you can copy the data in the MemoryStream to another location (such as a file or a database record) after the document is closed.

■Tip If you aren't sure whether annotations have been enabled for your document container, you can use the static AnnotationService.GetService() method and pass in a reference to the document container. This method returns a null reference if annotations haven't been enabled yet.

At some point, you'll also need to close your annotation stream and switch off the AnnotationService. In this example, these tasks are performed when the user closes the window:

```
protected void window_Unloaded(object sender, RoutedEventArgs e)
{
    if (service != null && service.IsEnabled)
    {
        // Flush annotations to stream.
        service.Store.Flush();

        // Disable annotations.
        service.Disable();
        annotationStream.Close();
    }
}
```

This is all you need to enable annotations in a document. If there are any annotations defined in the stream object when you call AnnotationService.Enable(), these annotations will appear immediately. However, you still need to add the controls that will allow the user to add or remove annotations. That's the topic of the next section.

■Tip Every document container can have one instance of the AnnotationService. Every document should have its own instance of the AnnotationStore. When you open a new document, you should disable the AnnotationService, save and close the current annotation stream, create a new AnnotationStore, and then reenable the AnnotationService.

Creating Annotations

There are two ways to manipulate annotations. You can use one of the methods of the AnnotationHelper class that allows you to create annotations (CreateTextStickyNoteForSelection() and CreateInkStickyNoteForSelection()), delete them (DeleteTextStickyNotesForSelection() and DeleteInkStickyNotesForSelection()), and apply highlighting (CreateHighlightsForSelection() and ClearHighlightsForSelection()). The "ForSelection" part of the method name indicates that these methods apply the annotation to whatever text is currently selected.

Although the AnnotationHelper methods work perfectly well, it's far easier to use the corresponding commands that are exposed by the AnnotationService class. You can wire these commands directly to the buttons in your user interface. That's the approach we'll take in this example.

Before you can use the AnnotationService class in XAML you need to map the System.Windows.Annotations namespace to an XML namespace, as it isn't one of the core WPF namespaces. You can add a mapping like this:

```
<Window x:Class="XpsAnnotations.FlowDocumentAnnotations"
  xmlns:annot=
  "clr-namespace:System.Windows.Annotations;assembly=PresentationFramework" ... >
```

Now you can create a button like this, which creates a text note for the currently selected portion of the document:

```
<Button Command="annot:AnnotationService.CreateTextStickyNoteCommand">
  Text Note
</Button>
```

Now when the user clicks this button, a green note window will appear. The user can type text inside this note. (If you create an ink sticky note with the CreateInkStickyNoteCommand, the user can draw inside the note window instead.)

■Note This Button element doesn't set the CommandTarget property. That's because the button is placed in a toolbar. As you learned in Chapter 10, the Toolbar class is intelligent enough to automatically set the CommandTarget to the element that has focus. Of course, if you use the same command in a button outside of a toolbar, you'll need to set the CommandTarget to point to your document viewer.

Sticky notes don't need to remain visible at all times. If you click the minimize button in the top-right corner of the note window, it will disappear. All you'll see is the highlighted portion of the document where the note is set. If you hover over this highlighted region with the mouse, a note icon appears (see Figure 19-18)—click this to restore the sticky note window. The AnnotationService stores the position of each note window, so if you drag one somewhere specific in your document, close it and then reopen it; it will reappear in its previous place.

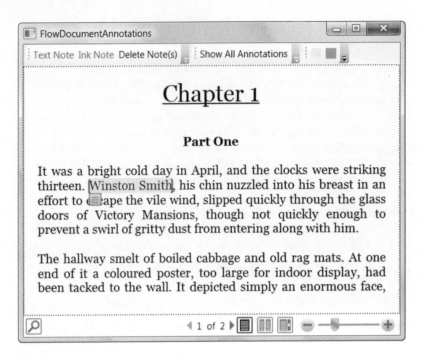

Figure 19-18. *A "hidden" annotation*

In the previous example, the annotation is created without any author information. If you plan to have multiple users annotating the same document, you'll almost certainly want to store some identifying information. Just pass a string that identifies the author as a parameter to the command, as shown here:

```
<Button Command="annot:AnnotationService.CreateTextStickyNoteCommand"
 CommandParameter="{StaticResource AuthorName}">
  Text Note
</Button>
```

This markup assumes the author name is set as a resource:

```
<sys:String x:Key="AuthorName">[Anonymous]</sys:String>
```

This allows you to set the author name when the window first loads, at the same time as you initialize the annotation service. You can use a name that the user supplies, which you'll probably want to store in a user-specific .config file as an application setting. Alternatively, you can use the following code to grab the current user's Windows user account name with the help of the System.Security.Principal.WindowsIdentity class:

```
WindowsIdentity identity = WindowsIdentity.GetCurrent();
this.Resources["AuthorName"] = identity.Name;
```

To create the window shown in Figure 19-17, you'll also want to create buttons that use the CreateInkStickyNoteCommand (to create a note window that accepts hand-drawn ink content) and DeleteStickyNotesCommand (to remove previously created sticky notes):

```
<Button Command="annot:AnnotationService.CreateInkStickyNoteCommand"
 CommandParameter="{StaticResource AuthorName}">
   Ink Note
</Button>
<Button Command="annot:AnnotationService.DeleteStickyNotesCommand">
   Delete Note(s)
</Button>
```

The DeleteStickyNotesCommand removes all the sticky notes in the currently selected text. Even if you don't provide this command, the user can still remove annotations using the Edit menu in the note window (unless you've given the note window a different control template that doesn't include this feature).

The final detail is to create the buttons that allow you to apply highlighting. To add a highlight, you use the CreateHighlightCommand and you pass the Brush object that you want to use as the CommandParameter. However, it's important to make sure you use a brush that has a partially transparent color. Otherwise, your highlighted content will be completely obscured, as shown in Figure 19-19.

For example, if you want to use the solid color #FF32CD32 (for lime green) to highlight your text, you should reduce the alpha value, which is stored as a hexadecimal number in the first two characters. (The alpha value ranges from 0 to 255, where 0 is fully transparent and 255 is fully opaque.) For example, the color #**54**FF32CD32 gives you a semitransparent version of the lime green color, with an alpha value of 84 (or 54 in hexadecimal notation).

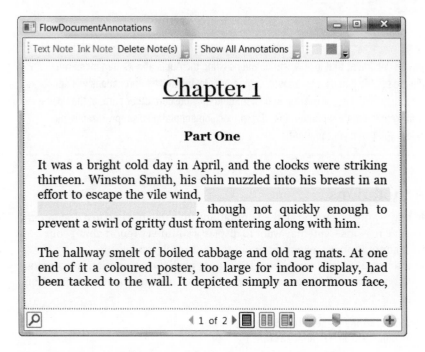

Figure 19-19. *Highlighting content with a nontransparent color*

The following markup defines two highlighting buttons, one for applying yellow high-lights and one for green highlights. The button itself doesn't include any text. It simply shows a 15-by-15 square of the appropriate color. The CommandParameter defines a SolidColorBrush that uses the same color but with reduced opacity so the text is still visible:

```
<Button Background="Yellow" Width="15" Height="15" Margin="2,0"
 Command="annot:AnnotationService.CreateHighlightCommand">
  <Button.CommandParameter>
    <SolidColorBrush Color="#54FFFF00"></SolidColorBrush>
  </Button.CommandParameter>
</Button>

<Button Background="LimeGreen" Width="15" Height="15" Margin="2,0"
 Command="annot:AnnotationService.CreateHighlightCommand">
  <Button.CommandParameter>
    <SolidColorBrush Color="#5432CD32"></SolidColorBrush>
  </Button.CommandParameter>
</Button>
```

You can add a final button to remove highlighting in the selected region:

```
<Button Command="annot:AnnotationService.ClearHighlightsCommand">
  Clear Highlights
</Button>
```

■**Note** When you print a document that includes annotations using the ApplicationCommands.Print command, the annotations are printed just as they appear. In other words, minimized annotations will appear minimized, visible annotations will appear overtop of content (and may obscure other parts of the document), and so on. If you want to create a printout that doesn't include annotations, simply disable the annotation service before you begin your printout.

Examining Annotations

At some point, you may want to examine all the annotations that are attached to a document. There are many possible reasons—you may want to display a summary report about your annotations, print an annotation list, export annotation text to a file, and so on.

The AnnotationStore makes it relatively easy to get a list of all the annotations it contains using the GetAnnotations() method. You can then examine each annotation as an Annotation object:

```
IList<Annotation> annotations = service.Store.GetAnnotations();
foreach (Annotation annotation in annotations)
{
    ...
}
```

In theory, you can find annotations in a specific portion of a document using the overloaded version of the GetAnnotations() method that takes a ContentLocator object. In practice, however, this is tricky, because the ContentLocator object is difficult to use correctly and you need to match the starting position of the annotation precisely.

Once you've retrieved an Annotation object, you'll find that it provides the properties listed in Table 19-8.

Table 19-8. *Annotation Properties*

Name	Description
Id	A global identifier (GUID) that uniquely identifies this annotation. If you know the GUID for an annotation, you can retrieve the corresponding Annotation object using the AnnotationStore.GetAnnotation() method. (Of course, there's no reason you'd know the GUID of an existing annotation unless you had previously retrieved it by calling GetAnnotations(), or you had reacted to an AnnotationStore event when the annotation was created or changed.)
AnnotationType	The XML element name that identifies this type of annotation, in the format namespace:localname.
Anchors	A collection of zero, one, or more AnnotationResource objects that identify what text is being annotated.
Cargos	A collection of zero, one, or more AnnotationResource objects that contain the user data for the annotation. This includes the text of a text note, or the ink strokes for an ink note.
Authors	A collection of zero, one, or more strings that identify who created the annotation.
CreationTime	The date and time when the annotation was created.
LastModificationTime	The date and time the annotation was last updated.

The Annotation object is really just a thin wrapper over the XML data that's stored for the annotation. One consequence of this design is that it's difficult to pull information out of the Anchors and Cargos properties. For example, if you want to get the actual text of an annotation, you need to look at the second item in the Cargos selection. This contains the text, but it's stored as a Base64-encoded string (which avoids problems if the note contains characters that wouldn't otherwise be allowed in XML element content). If you want to actually view this text, it's up to you to write tedious code like this to crack it open:

```
// Check for text information.
if (annotation.Cargos.Count > 1)
{
    // Decode the note text.
    string base64Text = annotation.Cargos[1].Contents[0].InnerText;
    byte[] decoded = Convert.FromBase64String(base64Text);

    // Write the decoded text to a stream.
    MemoryStream m = new MemoryStream(decoded);

    // Using the StreamReader, convert the text bytes into a more
```

```
    // useful string.
    StreamReader r = new StreamReader(m);
    string annotationXaml = r.ReadToEnd();
    r.Close();

    // Show the annotation content.
    MessageBox.Show(annotationXaml);
}
```

This code gets the text of the annotation, wrapped in the XAML <Section> element. The opening <Section> tag includes attributes that specify a wide range of typography details. Inside the <Section> element are more <Paragraph> and <Run> elements.

■Note Like a text annotation, an ink annotation will also have a Cargos collection with more than one item. However, in this case the Cargos collection will contain the ink data but no decodable text. If you use the previous code on an ink annotation, you'll get an empty message box. Thus, if your document contains both text and ink annotations, you should check the Annotation.AnnotationType property to make sure you're dealing with a text annotation before you use this code.

If you just want to get the text without the surrounding XML, you can use the XamlReader to deserialize it (and avoid using the StreamReader). The XML can be deserialized into a Section object, using code like this:

```
if (annotation.Cargos.Count > 1)
{
    // Decode the note text.
    string base64Text = annotation.Cargos[1].Contents[0].InnerText;
    byte[] decoded = Convert.FromBase64String(base64Text);

    // Write the decoded text to a stream.
    MemoryStream m = new MemoryStream(decoded);

    // Deserialize the XML into a Section object.
    Section section = XamlReader.Load(m) as Section;
    m.Close();

    // Get the text inside the Section.
    TextRange range = new TextRange(section.ContentStart, section.ContentEnd);

    // Show the annotation content.
    MessageBox.Show(range.Text);
}
```

As Table 19-8 shows, text isn't the only detail you can recover from an annotation. It's easy to get the annotation author, the time it was created, and the time it was last modified.

You can also retrieve information about where an annotation is anchored in your document. However, the Anchors collection isn't much help for this task, because it provides a low-level collection of AnnotationResource objects that wrap additional XML data. To make life easier, .NET 3.5 adds a GetAnchorInfo() method to the AnnotationHelper class. This method takes an annotation and returns an object that implements IAnchorInfo.

```
IAnchorInfo anchorInfo = AnnotationHelper.GetAnchorInfo(service, annotation);
```

IAnchorInfo combines the AnnotationResource (the Anchor property), the annotation (Annotation), and an object that represents the location of the annotation in the document tree (ResolvedAnchor), which is the most useful detail. Although the ResolvedAnchor property is typed as an object, text annotations and highlights always return a TextAnchor object. The TextAnchor describes the starting point of the anchored text (BoundingStart) and the ending point (BoundingEnd).

Here's how you could determine the highlighted text for an annotation using the IAnchorInfo:

```
IAnchorInfo anchorInfo = AnnotationHelper.GetAnchorInfo(service, annotation);
TextAnchor resolvedAnchor = anchorInfo.ResolvedAnchor as TextAnchor;
if (resolvedAnchor != null)
{
    TextPointer startPointer = (TextPointer)resolvedAnchor.BoundingStart;
    TextPointer endPointer = (TextPointer)resolvedAnchor.BoundingEnd;

    TextRange range = new TextRange(startPointer, endPointer);
    MessageBox.Show(range.Text);
}
```

You can also use the TextAnchor objects as a jumping-off point to get to the rest of the document tree, as shown here:

```
// Scroll the document so the paragraph with the annotated text is displayed.
TextPointer textPointer = (TextPointer)resolvedAnchor.BoundingStart;
textPointer.Paragraph.BringIntoView();
```

The samples for this chapter include an example that uses this technique to create an annotation list. When an annotation is selected in the list, the annotated portion of the document is shown automatically.

In both cases, the AnnotationHelper.GetAnchorInfo() method allows you to travel from the annotation to the annotated text, much as the AnnotationStore.GetAnnotations() method allows you to travel from the document content to the annotations.

Although it's relatively easy to examine existing annotations, the WPF annotation feature isn't as strong when it comes to manipulating these annotations. It's easy enough for the user to open a sticky note, drag it to a new position, change the text, and so on, but it's not easy for you to perform these tasks programmatically. In fact, all the properties of the Annotation object are read-only. There are no readily available methods to modify an annotation, so annotation editing involves deleting and re-creating the annotation. You can do this using the methods of the AnnotationStore or the AnnotationHelper (if the annotation is attached to the currently selected text). However, both approaches require a fair bit of grunt work. If you use the AnnotationStore, you need to construct an Annotation object by hand. If you use the AnnotationHelper, you need to explicitly set the text selection to include the right text before you create the annotation. Both approaches are tedious and unnecessarily error-prone.

Reacting to Annotation Changes

You've already() learned how the AnnotationStore allows you to retrieve the annotations in a document (with GetAnnotations()) and manipulate them (with DeleteAnnotation() and AddAnnotation()). The AnnotationStore provides one additional feature—it raises events that inform you when annotations are changed.

The AnnotationStore provides four events: AnchorChanged (which fires when an annotation is moved), AuthorChanged (which fires when the author information of an annotation changes), CargoChanged (which fires when annotation data, including text, is modified), and StoreContentChanged (which fires when an annotation is created, deleted, or modified in any way).

The online samples for this chapter include an annotation-tracking example. An event handler for the StoreContentChanged event reacts when annotation changes are made. It retrieves all the annotation information (using the GetAnnotations() method) and then displays the annotation text in a list.

■**Note** The annotation events occur after the change has been made. That means there's no way to plug in custom logic that extends an annotation action. For example, you can't add just-in-time information to an annotation or selectively cancel a user's attempt to edit or delete an annotation.

Storing Annotations in a Fixed Document

The previous examples used annotations on a flow document. In this scenario, annotations can be stored for future use, but they must be stored separately—for example, in a distinct XML file.

When using a fixed document, you can use the same approach, but you have an additional option—you can store annotations directly in the XPS document file. In fact, you could even store multiple sets of distinct annotations, all in the same document. You simply need to use the package support in the System.IO.Packaging namespace.

As you learned earlier, every XPS document is actually a ZIP archive that includes several files. When you store annotations in an XPS document, you are actually creating another file inside the ZIP archive.

The first step is to choose a URI to identify your annotations. Here's an example that uses the name AnnotationStream:

```
Uri annotationUri = PackUriHelper.CreatePartUri(
  new Uri("AnnotationStream", UriKind.Relative));
```

Now you need to get the Package for your XPS document using the static Package-Store.GetPackage() method:

```
Package package = PackageStore.GetPackage(doc.Uri);
```

You can then create the package part that will store your annotations inside the XPS document. However, you need to check if the annotation package part already exists (in case you've loaded the document before and already added annotations). If it doesn't exist, you can create it now:

```
PackagePart annotationPart = null;
if (package.PartExists(annotationUri))
{
    annotationPart = package.GetPart(annotationUri);
}
else
{
    annotationPart = package.CreatePart(annotationUri, "Annotations/Stream");
}
```

The last step is to create an AnnotationStore that wraps the annotation package part, and then enable the AnnotationService in the usual way:

```
AnnotationStore store = new XmlStreamStore(annotationPart.GetStream());
service = new AnnotationService(docViewer);
service.Enable(store);
```

In order for this technique to work, you must open the XPS file using FileMode.ReadWrite mode rather than FileMode.Read, so the annotations can be written to the XPS file. For the same reason, you need to keep the XPS document open while the annotation service is at work. You can close the XPS document when the window is closed (or you choose to open a new document).

Customizing the Appearance of Sticky Notes

The note windows that appear when you create a text note or ink note are instances of the StickyNoteControl class, which is found in the System.Windows.Controls namespace. Like all WPF controls, you can customize the visual appearance of the StickyNoteControl using style setters or applying a new control template.

For example, you can easily create a style that applies to all StickyNoteControl instances using the Style.TargetType property. Here's an example that gives every StickyNoteControl a new background color:

```
<Style TargetType="{x:Type StickyNoteControl}">
  <Setter Property="Background" Value="LightGoldenrodYellow"/>
</Style>
```

To make a more dynamic version of the StickyNoteControl, you can write a style trigger that responds to the StickyNoteControl.IsActive property, which is true when the sticky note has focus.

For more control, you can use a completely different control template for your StickyNoteControl. The only trick is that the StickyNoteControl template varies depending on whether it's used to hold an ink note or a text note. If you allow the user to create both types of notes, you need a trigger that can choose between two templates. Ink notes must include an

InkCanvas, and text notes must contain a RichTextBox. In both cases, this element should be named PART_ContentControl.

Here's a style that applies the bare minimum control template for both ink and text sticky notes. It sets the dimensions of the note window and chooses the appropriate template based on the type of note content:

```xml
<Style x:Key="MinimumStyle" TargetType="{x:Type StickyNoteControl}">
  <Setter Property="OverridesDefaultStyle" Value="true" />
  <Setter Property="Width" Value="100" />
  <Setter Property="Height" Value ="100" />
  <Style.Triggers>
    <Trigger Property="StickyNoteControl.StickyNoteType"
     Value="{x:Static StickyNoteType.Ink}">
      <Setter Property="Template">
        <Setter.Value>
          <ControlTemplate>
            <InkCanvas Name="PART_ContentControl" Background="LightYellow" />
          </ControlTemplate>
        </Setter.Value>
      </Setter>
    </Trigger>
    <Trigger Property="StickyNoteControl.StickyNoteType"
     Value="{x:Static StickyNoteType.Text}">
      <Setter Property="Template">
        <Setter.Value>
          <ControlTemplate>
            <RichTextBox Name="PART_ContentControl" Background="LightYellow"/>
          </ControlTemplate>
        </Setter.Value>
      </Setter>
    </Trigger>
  </Style.Triggers>
</Style>
```

Last Word

Most developers already know that WPF offers a new model for drawing, layout, and animation. However, its rich document features are often overlooked.

In this chapter, you've seen how to create flow documents, lay out text inside them in a variety of ways, and control how that text is displayed in different containers. You also learned how to use the FlowDocument object model to change portions of the document dynamically, and you considered the RichTextBox, which provides a solid base for advanced text editing features.

Lastly, you took a quick look at fixed documents and the XpsDocument class. The XPS model provides the plumbing for WPF's new printing feature, which is the subject of the next chapter.

CHAPTER 20

■ ■ ■

Printing

Printing in WPF is vastly more powerful than it was with Windows Forms. Tasks that weren't possible using the .NET libraries and that would have forced you to use the Win32 API or WMI (such as checking a print queue) are now fully supported using the classes in the new System. Printing namespace.

Even more dramatic is the thoroughly revamped printing model that organizes all your coding around a single ingredient: the PrintDialog class in the System.Windows.Controls namespace. Using the PrintDialog class, you can show a Print dialog box where the user can pick a printer and change its setting, and you can send elements, documents, and low-level visuals directly to the printer. In this chapter, you'll learn how to use the PrintDialog class to create properly scaled and paginated printouts.

Basic Printing

Although WPF includes dozens of print-related classes (most of which are found in the System. Printing namespace), there's a single starting point that makes life easy: the PrintDialog class.

The PrintDialog wraps the familiar Print dialog box that lets the user choose the printer and a few other standard print options, such as the number of copies (Figure 20-1). However, the PrintDialog class is more than just a pretty window—it also has the built-in ability to trigger a printout.

To submit a print job with the PrintDialog class, you need to use one of two methods:

- **PrintVisual()** works with any class that derives from System.Windows.Media.Visual. This includes any graphic you draw by hand and any element you place in a window.

- **PrintDocument()** works with any DocumentPaginator object. This includes the ones that are used to split a FlowDocument (or XpsDocument) into pages and any custom DocumentPaginator you create to deal with your own data.

In the following sections, you'll consider a variety of strategies that you can use to create a printout.

Figure 20-1. *The PrintDialog in Windows Vista*

Printing an Element

The simplest approach to printing is to take advantage of the model you're already using for onscreen rendering. Using the PrintDialog.PrintVisual() method, you can send any element in a window (and all its children) straight to the printer.

To see an example in action, consider the window shown in Figure 20-2. It contains a Grid that lays out all the elements. In the topmost row is a Canvas, and in that Canvas is a drawing that consists of a TextBlock and a Path (which renders itself as a rectangle with an elliptic hole in the middle).

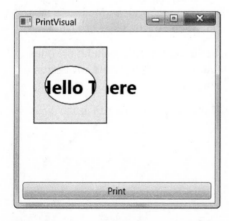

Figure 20-2. *A simple drawing*

To send the Canvas to the printer, complete with all the elements it contains, you can use this snippet of code when the Print button is clicked:

```
PrintDialog printDialog = new PrintDialog();
if (printDialog.ShowDialog() == true)
{
    printDialog.PrintVisual(canvas, "A Simple Drawing");
}
```

The first step is to create a PrintDialog object. The next step is to call ShowDialog() to show the Print dialog box. ShowDialog returns a nullable Boolean value. A return value of true indicates that the user clicked OK, a return value of false indicates that the user clicked Cancel, and a null value indicates that the dialog box was closed without either button being clicked.

When calling the PrintVisual() method, you pass two arguments. The first is the element that you want to print, and the second is a string that's used to identify the print job. You'll see it appear in the Windows print queue (under the Document Name column).

When printing this way, you don't have much control over the output. The element is always lined up with the top-left corner of the page. If your element doesn't include nonzero Margin values, the edge of your content might land in the nonprintable area of the page, which means it won't appear in the printed output.

The lack or margin control is only the beginning of the limitations that you'll face using this approach. You also can't paginate your content if it's extremely long, so if you have more content than can fit on a single page, some will be left out at the bottom. Finally, you have no control over the scaling that's used to render your job to the printing. Instead, WPF uses the same device-independent rendering system based on $1/96^{th}$-inch units. For example, if you have a rectangle that's 96 units wide, that rectangle will appear to be an inch wide on your monitor (assuming you're using the standard 96 dpi Windows system setting) and an inch wide on the printed page. Often, this results in a printout that's quite a bit smaller than what you want.

Note Obviously, WPF will fill in much more detail in the printed page, because virtually no printer has a resolution as low as 96 dpi (600 dpi and 1200 dpi are much more common printer resolutions). However, WPF will keep your content the same size in the printout as it is on your monitor.

Figure 20-3 shows the full-page printout of the Canvas from the window shown in Figure 20-2.

Figure 20-3. *A printed element*

PRINTDIALOG QUIRKS

The PrintDialog class wraps a lower-level internal .NET class named Win32PrintDialog, which in turns wraps the Print dialog box that's exposed by the Win32 API. Unfortunately, these extra layers remove a little bit of your flexibility.

One potential problem is the way that the PrintDialog class works with modal windows. Buried in the inaccessible Win32PrintDialog code is a bit of logic that always makes the Print dialog box modal with respect to your application's *main* window. This leads to an odd problem if you show a modal window from your main window and then call the PrintDialog.ShowDialog() method from that window. Although you'd expect the Print dialog box to be modal to your second window, it will actually be modal with respect to your main window, which means the user can return to your second window and interact with it (even clicking the Print button to show multiple instances of the Print dialog box)! The somewhat clumsy solution is to manually change your application's main window to the current window before you call PrintDialog.ShowDialog() and then switch it back immediately afterward.

There's another limitation to the way the PrintDialog class works. Because your main application thread owns the content you're printing, it's not possible to perform your printing on a background thread. This becomes a concern if you have time-consuming printing logic. Two possible solutions exist. If you construct the visuals you want to print on the background thread (rather than pulling them out of an existing window), you'll be able to perform your printing on the background thread. However, a simpler solution is to use the PrintDialog box to let the user specify the print settings and then use the XpsDocumentWriter class to actually print the content instead of the printing methods of the PrintDialog class. The XpsDocumentWriter includes the ability to send content to the printer asynchronously, and it's described in the "Printing Through XPS" section later in this chapter.

Transforming Printed Output

You may remember (from Chapter 13) that you can attach the Transform object to the Render-Transform or LayoutTransform property of any element to change the way it's rendered. Transform objects could solve the problem of inflexible printouts, because you could use them to resize an element (ScaleTransform), move it around the page (TranslateTransform), or both (TransformGroup). Unfortunately, visuals have the ability to lay themselves out only one way at a time. That means there's no way to scale an element one way in a window and another way in a printout—instead, any Transform objects you apply will change both the printed output and the onscreen appearance of your element.

If you aren't intimidated by a bit of messy compromise, you can work around this issue in several ways. The basic idea is to apply your transform objects just before you create the print-out and then remove them. To prevent the resized element from appearing in the window, you can temporarily hide it.

You might expect to hide your element by changing its Visibility property, but this will hide your element from both the window and the printout, which obviously isn't what you want. One possible solution is to change the Visibility of the parent (in this example, the layout Grid). This works because the PrintVisual() method considers only the element you specify and its children, not the details of the parent.

Here's the code that puts it all together and prints the Canvas shown in Figure 20-2, but five times bigger in both dimensions:

```
PrintDialog printDialog = new PrintDialog();
if (printDialog.ShowDialog() == true)
{
    // Hide the Grid.
    grid.Visibility = Visibility.Hidden;

    // Magnify the output by a factor of 5.
    canvas.LayoutTransform = new ScaleTransform(5, 5);

    // Print the element.
    printDialog.PrintVisual(canvas, "A Scaled Drawing");

    // Remove the transform and make the element visible again.
    canvas.LayoutTransform = null;
    grid.Visibility = Visibility.Visible;
}
```

This example has one missing detail. Although the Canvas (and its contents) is stretched, the Canvas is still using the layout information from the containing Grid. In other words, the Canvas still believes it has an amount of space to work with that's equal to the dimensions of the Grid cell in which it's placed. In this example, this oversight doesn't cause a problem, because the Canvas doesn't limit itself to the available space (unlike some other containers). However, you will run into trouble if you have text and you want it to wrap to fit the bounds of the printed page or if your Canvas has a background (which, in this example, will occupy the smaller size of the Grid cell rather than the whole area behind the Canvas).

The solution is easy. After you set the LayoutTransform (but before you print the Canvas), you need to trigger the layout process manually using the Measure() and Arrange() methods that every element inherits from the UIElement class. The trick is that when you call these methods, you'll pass in the size of the page, so the Canvas stretches itself to fit. (Incidentally, this is also why you set the LayoutTransform instead of the RenderTransform property, because you want the layout to take the newly expanded size into account.) You can get the page size from the PrintableAreaWidth and PrintableAreaHeight properties.

Note Based on the property names, it's reasonable to assume that PrintableAreaWidth and PrintableArea-Height reflect the *printable* area of the page—in other words, the part of the page on which the printer can actually print. (Most printers can't reach the very edges, usually because that's where the rollers grip onto the page.) But in truth, PrintableAreaWidth and PrintableAreaHeight simply return the *full* width and height of the page in device-independent units. For a sheet of 8.5×11 paper, that's 816 and 1056. (Try dividing these numbers by 96 dpi, and you'll get the full paper size.)

The following example demonstrates how to use the PrintableAreaWidth and Printable-AreaHeight properties. To be a bit nicer, it leaves off 10 units (about 0.1 of an inch) as a border around all edges of the page.

```
PrintDialog printDialog = new PrintDialog();
if (printDialog.ShowDialog() == true)
{
    // Hide the Grid.
    grid.Visibility = Visibility.Hidden;

    // Magnify the output by a factor of 5.
    canvas.LayoutTransform = new ScaleTransform(5, 5);

    // Define a margin.
    int pageMargin = 5;

    // Get the size of the page.
    Size pageSize = new Size(printDialog.PrintableAreaWidth - pageMargin * 2,
    printDialog.PrintableAreaHeight - 20);

    // Trigger the sizing of the element.
    canvas.Measure(pageSize);
    canvas.Arrange(new Rect(pageMargin, pageMargin,
      pageSize.Width, pageSize.Height));

    // Print the element.
    printDialog.PrintVisual(canvas, "A Scaled Drawing");
```

```
    // Remove the transform and make the element visible again.
    canvas.LayoutTransform = null;
    grid.Visibility = Visibility.Visible;
}
```

The end result is a way to print any element and scale it to suit your needs (see the full-page printout in Figure 20-4). This approach works perfectly well, but you can see the (somewhat messy) glue that's holding it all together.

Figure 20-4. *A scaled printed element*

Printing Elements Without Showing Them

Because the way you want to show data in your application and the way you want it to appear in a printout are often different, it sometimes makes sense to create your visual programmatically (rather than using one that appears in an existing window). For example, the following code creates an in-memory TextBlock object, fills it with text, sets it to wrap, sizes it to fit the printed page, and then prints it:

```
PrintDialog printDialog = new PrintDialog();
if (printDialog.ShowDialog() == true)
{
    // Create the text.
    Run run = new Run("This is a test of the printing functionality " +
      "in the Windows Presentation Foundation.");

    // Wrap it in a TextBlock.
    TextBlock visual = new TextBlock();
    TextBlock.Inlines.Add(run);

    // Use margin to get a page border.
    visual.Margin = new Thickness(15);
```

```
// Allow wrapping to fit the page width.
    visual.TextWrapping = TextWrapping.Wrap;

    // Scale the TextBlock up in both dimensions by a factor of 5.
    // (In this case, increasing the font would have the same effect,
    // because the TextBlock is the only element.)
    visual.LayoutTransform = new ScaleTransform(5, 5);

    // Size the element.
    Size pageSize = new Size(printDialog.PrintableAreaWidth,
      printDialog.PrintableAreaHeight);
    visual.Measure(pageSize);
    visual.Arrange(new Rect(0,0, pageSize.Width, pageSize.Height));

    // Print the element.
    printDialog.PrintVisual(visual, "A Scaled Drawing");
}
```

Figure 20-5 shows the printed page that this code creates.

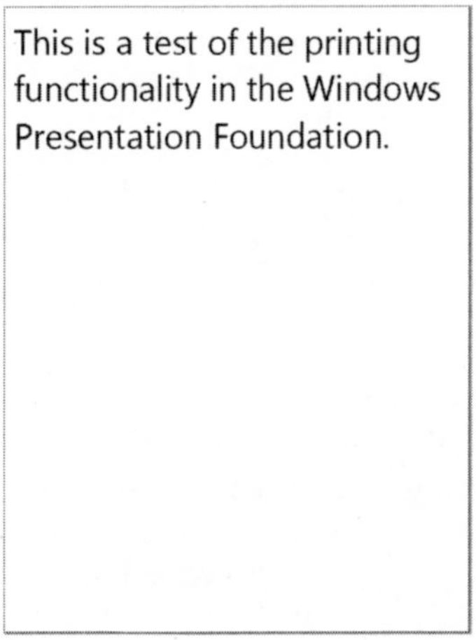

> This is a test of the printing functionality in the Windows Presentation Foundation.

Figure 20-5. *Wrapped text using a TextBlock*

This approach allows you to grab the content you need out of a window but customize its printed appearance separately. However, it's of no help if you have content that needs to span more than one page (in which case you'll need the printing techniques described in the following sections).

Printing a Document

The PrintVisual() method may be the most versatile printing method, but the PrintDialog class also includes another option. You can use PrintDocument() to print the content from a flow document. The advantage of this approach is that a flow document can handle a huge amount of complex content and can split that content over multiple pages (just as it does onscreen).

You might expect that the PrintDialog.PrintDocument() method would require a Flow-Document object, but it actually takes a DocumentPaginator object. The DocumentPaginator is a specialized class whose sole role in life is to take content, split it into multiple pages, and supply each page when requested. Each page is represented by a DocumentPage object, which is really just a wrapper for a single Visual object with a little bit of sugar on top. You'll find just three more properties in the DocumentPage class. Size returns the size of the page, ContentBox is the size of the box where content is placed on the page after margins are added, and BleedBox is the area where print production-related bleeds, registration marks, and crop marks appear on the sheet, outside the page boundaries.

What this means is that PrintDocument() works in much the same way as PrintVisual(). The difference is that it prints several visuals—one for each page.

■**Note** Although you could split your content into separate pages without using a DocumentPaginator and make repeated calls to PrintVisual(), this isn't a good approach. If you do, each page will become a separate print job.

So how do you get a DocumentPaginator object for a FlowDocument? The trick is to cast the FlowDocument to an IDocumentPaginatorSource and then use the DocumentPaginator property. Here's an example:

```
PrintDialog printDialog = new PrintDialog();
if (printDialog.ShowDialog() == true)
{
    printDialog.PrintDocument(
        ((IDocumentPaginatorSource)docReader.Document).DocumentPaginator,
        "A Flow Document");
}
```

This code may or may not produce the desired result, depending on the container that's currently housing your document. If your document is in-memory (but not in a window) or if it's stored in RichTextBox or FlowDocumentScrollViewer, this codes works fine. You'll end up with a multipaged printout with two columns (on a standard sheet of 8.5×11 paper in portrait orientation). This is the same result you'll get if you use the ApplicationCommands.Print command.

■**Note** As you learned in Chapter 10, some controls include built-in command wiring. The FlowDocument containers (like the FlowDocumentScrollViewer used here) is one example. It handles the Application-Commands.Print command to perform a basic printout. This hardwired printing code is similar to the code shown previously, although it uses the XpsDocumentWriter, which is described in the "Printing Through XPS" section of this chapter.

However, if your document is stored in a FlowDocumentPageViewer or a FlowDocument-Reader, the result isn't as good. In this case, your document is paginated the same way as the current view in the container. So if there are 24 pages required to fit the content into the current window, you'll get 24 pages in the printed output, each with a tiny window worth of data. Again, the solution is a bit messy, but it works. (It's also essentially the same solution that the ApplicationCommands.Print command takes.) The trick is to force the FlowDocument to paginate itself for the printer. You can do this by setting the FlowDocument.PageHeight and FlowDocument.PageWidth properties to the boundaries of the page, not the boundaries of the container. (In containers such as the FlowDocumentScrollViewer, these properties aren't set because pagination isn't used. That's why the printing feature works without a hitch—it paginates itself automatically when you create the printout.)

```
FlowDocument doc = docReader.Document;

doc.PageHeight = printDialog.PrintableAreaHeight;
doc.PageWidth = printDialog.PrintableAreaWidth;
printDialog.PrintDocument(
  ((IDocumentPaginatorSource)doc).DocumentPaginator,
    "A Flow Document");
```

You'll probably also want to set properties such as ColumnWidth and ColumnGap so you can get the number of columns you want. Otherwise, you'll get whatever is used in the current window.

The only problem with this approach is that once you've changed these properties, they apply to the container that displays your document. As a result, you'll end up with a compressed version of your document that's probably too small to read in the current window. A proper solution takes this into account by storing all these values, changing them, and then reapplying the original values.

Here's the complete code printing a two-column printout with a generous margin (added through the FlowDocument.PagePadding property):

```
PrintDialog printDialog = new PrintDialog();
if (printDialog.ShowDialog() == true)
{
    FlowDocument doc = docReader.Document;

    // Save all the existing settings.
    double pageHeight = doc.PageHeight;
    double pageWidth = doc.PageWidth;
    Thickness pagePadding = doc.PagePadding;
    double columnGap = doc.ColumnGap;
    double columnWidth = doc.ColumnWidth;

    // Make the FlowDocument page match the printed page.
    doc.PageHeight = printDialog.PrintableAreaHeight;
    doc.PageWidth = printDialog.PrintableAreaWidth;
    doc.PagePadding = new Thickness(50);

    // Use two columns.
    doc.ColumnGap = 25;
```

```
doc.ColumnWidth = (doc.PageWidth - doc.ColumnGap
  - doc.PagePadding.Left - doc.PagePadding.Right) / 2;

printDialog.PrintDocument(
  ((IDocumentPaginatorSource)doc).DocumentPaginator, "A Flow Document");

// Reapply the old settings.
doc.PageHeight = pageHeight;
doc.PageWidth = pageWidth;
doc.PagePadding = pagePadding;
doc.ColumnGap = columnGap;
doc.ColumnWidth = columnWidth;
}
```

This approach has a few limitations. Although you're able to tweak properties that adjust the margins and number of columns, you don't have much control. Of course, you can modify the FlowDocument programmatically (for example, temporarily increasing its FontSize), but you can't tailor the printout with details such as page numbers. You'll learn one way to get around this restriction in the next section.

PRINTING ANNOTATIONS

WPF includes two classes that derive from DocumentPaginator. FlowDocumentPaginator paginates flow documents—it's what you get when you examine the FlowDocument.DocumentPaginator property. Similarly, FixedDocumentPaginator paginates XPS documents, and it's used automatically by the XpsDocument class. However, both of these classes are marked internal and aren't accessible to your code. Instead, you can interact with these paginators by using the members of the base DocumentPaginator class.

WPF includes just one public, concrete paginator class, AnnotationDocumentPaginator, which is used to print a document with its associated annotations. (Chapter 19 discussed annotations.) AnnotationDocument-Paginator is public so that you can create it, if necessary, to trigger a printout of an annotated document.

To use the AnnotationDocumentPaginator, you must wrap an existing DocumentPaginator in a new AnnotationDocumentPaginator object. To do so, simply create an AnnotationDocumentPaginator, and pass in two references. The first reference is the original paginator for your document, and the second reference is the annotation store that contains all the annotations. Here's an example:

```
// Get the ordinary paginator.
FlowDocument doc = ((IDocumentPaginatorSource)doc).DocumentPaginator;

// Get the (currently running) annotation service for a
// specific document container.
AnnotationService service = AnnotationService.GetService(docViewer);

// Create the paginator.
AnnotationDocumentPaginator paginator = new AnnotationDocumentPaginator(
  doc, service.Store);
```

Now, you can print the document with the superimposed annotations (in their current minimized or maximized state) by calling PrintDialog.PrintDocument() and passing in the AnnotationDocumentPaginator object.

Manipulating the Pages in a Document Printout

You can gain a bit more control over how a FlowDocument is printed by creating your own DocumentPaginator. As you might guess from its name, a DocumentPaginator divides the content of a document into distinct pages for printing (or displaying in a page-based Flow-Document viewer). The DocumentPaginator is responsible for returning the total number of pages based on a given page size and providing the laid-out content for each page as a DocumentPage object.

Your DocumentPaginator doesn't need to be complex—in fact, it can simply wrap the DocumentPaginator that's provided by the FlowDocument and allow it to do all the hard work of breaking the text up into individual pages. However, you can use your DocumentPaginator to make minor alterations, such as adding a header and a footer. The basic trick is to intercept every request the PrintDialog makes for a page and then alter that page before passing it along.

The first ingredient of this solution is building a HeaderedFlowDocumentPaginator class that derives from DocumentPaginator. Because DocumentPaginator is an abstract class, HeaderedFlowDocument needs to implement several methods. However, HeaderedFlow-Document can pass most of the work on to the standard DocumentPaginator that's provided by the FlowDocument.

Here's the basic skeleton of the HeaderedFlowDocumentPaginator class:

```
public class HeaderedFlowDocumentPaginator : DocumentPaginator
{
    // The real paginator (which does all the pagination work).
    private DocumentPaginator flowDocumentPaginator;

    // Store the FlowDocument paginator from the given document.
    public HeaderedFlowDocumentPaginator(FlowDocument document)
    {
        flowDocumentPaginator =
          ((IDocumentPaginatorSource)document).DocumentPaginator;
    }

    public override bool IsPageCountValid
    {
        get { return flowDocumentPaginator.IsPageCountValid;  }
    }

    public override int PageCount
    {
        get { return flowDocumentPaginator.PageCount; }
    }

    public override Size PageSize
    {
        get { return flowDocumentPaginator.PageSize; }
        set { flowDocumentPaginator.PageSize = value; }
    }
```

```
public override IDocumentPaginatorSource Source
{
    get { return flowDocumentPaginator.Source; }
}

public override DocumentPage GetPage(int pageNumber)
{ ... }
}
```

Because the HeaderedFlowDocumentPaginator hands off its work to its private DocumentPaginator, this code doesn't indicate how the PageSize, PageCount, and IsPageCountValid properties work. The PageSize is set by the DocumentPaginator consumer (the code that's using the DocumentPaginator). This property tells the DocumentPaginator how much space is available in each printed page (or onscreen). The PageCount and IsPageCountValid properties are provided *to* the DocumentPaginator consumer to indicate the pagination result. Whenever PageSize is changed, the DocumentPaginator will recalculate the size of each page. (Later in this chapter, you'll see a more complete DocumentPaginator that was created from scratch and includes the implementation details for these properties.)

The GetPage() method is where the action happens. This code calls the GetPage() method of the real DocumentPaginator and then gets to work on the page. The basic strategy is to pull the Visual object out of the page and place it in a new ContainerVisual object. You can then add the text you want to that ContainerVisual. Finally, you can create a new DocumentPage that wraps the ContainerVisual, with its newly inserted header.

■Note This code uses visual-layer programming (Chapter 14). That's because you need a way to create visuals that represent your printed output. You don't need the full overhead of elements, which include event handling, dependency properties, and other plumbing. Custom print routines (as described in the next section) will almost always use visual-layer programming and the ContainerVisual, DrawingVisual, and DrawingContext classes.

Here's the complete code:

```
public override DocumentPage GetPage(int pageNumber)
{
    // Get the requested page.
    DocumentPage page = flowDocumentPaginator.GetPage(pageNumber);

    // Wrap the page in a Visual object. You can then apply transformations
    // and add other elements.
    ContainerVisual newVisual = new ContainerVisual();
    newVisual.Children.Add(page.Visual);

    // Create a header.
    DrawingVisual header = new DrawingVisual();
    using (DrawingContext dc = header.RenderOpen())
```

```
    {
        Typeface typeface = new Typeface("Times New Roman");
        FormattedText text = new FormattedText("Page " +
          (pageNumber + 1).ToString(), CultureInfo.CurrentCulture,
          FlowDirection.LeftToRight, typeface, 14, Brushes.Black);

        // Leave a quarter inch of space between the page edge and this text.
        dc.DrawText(text, new Point(96*0.25, 96*0.25));
    }

    // Add the title to the visual.
    newVisual.Children.Add(header);

    // Wrap the visual in a new page.
    DocumentPage newPage = new DocumentPage(newVisual);
    return newPage;
}
```

This implementation assumes the page size doesn't change because of the addition of your header. Instead, the assumption is that there's enough empty space in the margin to accommodate the header. If you use this code with a small margin, the header will be printed overtop of your document content. This is the same way headers work in programs such as Microsoft Word. Headers aren't considered part of the main document, and they're positioned separately from the main document content.

There's one minor messy bit. You won't be able to add the Visual object for the page to the ContainerVisual while it's displayed in a window. The workaround is to temporarily remove it from the container, perform the printing, and then add it back.

```
FlowDocument document = docReader.Document;
docReader.Document = null;

HeaderedFlowDocumentPaginator paginator =
  new HeaderedFlowDocumentPaginator(document);
printDialog.PrintDocument(paginator, "A Headered Flow Document");

docReader.Document = document;
```

The HeaderedFlowDocumentPaginator is used for the printing, but it's not attached to the FlowDocument, so it won't change the way the document appears onscreen.

Custom Printing

By this point, you've probably realized the fundamental truth of WPF printing. You can use the quick-and-dirty techniques described in the previous section to send content from a window to your printer and even tweak it a bit. But if you want to build a first-rate printing feature for your application, you'll need to design it yourself.

Printing with the Visual Layer Classes

The best way to construct a custom printout is to use the visual-layer classes. Two classes are particularly useful:

- **ContainerVisual** is a stripped-down visual that can hold a collection of one or more other Visual objects (in its Children collection).

- **DrawingVisual** derives from ContainerVisual and adds a RenderOpen() method and a Drawing property. The RenderOpen() method creates a DrawingContext object that you can use to draw content in the visual (such as text, shapes, and so on), and the Drawing property lets you retrieve the final product as a DrawingGroup object.

Once you understand how to use these classes, the process for creating a custom printout is fairly straightforward.

1. Create your DrawingVisual. (You can also create a ContainerVisual in the less common case that you want to combine more than one separate drawn DrawingVisual object on the same page.)

2. Call DrawingVisual.RenderOpen() to get the DrawingContext object.

3. Use the methods of the DrawingContext to create your output.

4. Close the DrawingContext. (If you've wrapped the DrawingContext in a using block, this step is automatic.)

5. Using PrintDialog.PrintVisual() to send your visual to the printer.

Not only does this approach give you more flexibility than the print-an-element techniques you've used so far, it also has less overhead.

Obviously, the key to making this work is knowing what methods the DrawingContext class has for you to create your output. Table 20-1 describes the methods you can use. The Push*Xxx*() methods are particularly interesting, because they apply settings that will apply to future drawing operations. You can use Pop() to reverse the most recent Push*Xxx*() method. If you call more than one Push*Xxx*() method, you can switch them off one at a time with subsequent Pop() calls.

Table 20-1. *DrawingContext Methods*

Name	Description
DrawLine(), DrawRectangle(), DrawRoundedRectangle(), and DrawEllipse()	Draws the specified shape at the point you specify, with the fill and outline you specify. These methods mirror the shapes you saw in Chapter 13.
DrawGeometry () and DrawDrawing()	Draws more complex Geometry and Drawing objects. You saw these in Chapter 14.
DrawText()	Draws text at the specified location. You specify the text, font, fill, and other details by passing a FormattedText object to this method. You can use DrawText() to draw wrapped text if you set the FormattedText.MaxTextWidth property.
DrawImage()	Draws a bitmap image in a specific region (as defined by a Rect).

Continued

Table 20-1. *Continued*

Name	Description
Pop()	Reverse the last Push*Xxx*() method that was called. You use the Push*Xxx*() method to temporarily apply one or more effects and the Pop() method to reverse them.
PushClip()	Limits drawing to a specific clip region. Content that falls outside this region isn't drawn.
PushEffect ()	Applies a BitmapEffect to subsequent drawing operations.
PushOpacity()	Applies a new opacity setting to make subsequent drawing operations partially transparent.
PushTransform()	Sets a Transform object that will be applied to subsequent drawing operations. You can use a transformation to scale, displace, rotate, or skew content.

These are all the ingredients that are required to create a respectable printout (along with a healthy dash of math to work out the optimum placement of all your content). The following code uses this approach to center a block of formatted text on a page and add a border around the page:

```
PrintDialog printDialog = new PrintDialog();
if (printDialog.ShowDialog() == true)
{
    // Create a visual for the page.
    DrawingVisual visual = new DrawingVisual();

    // Get the drawing context.
    using (DrawingContext dc = visual.RenderOpen())
    {
        // Define the text you want to print.
        FormattedText text = new FormattedText(txtContent.Text,
          CultureInfo.CurrentCulture, FlowDirection.LeftToRight,
          new Typeface("Calibri"), 20, Brushes.Black);

        // You must pick a maximum width to use text wrapping.
        text.MaxTextWidth = printDialog.PrintableAreaWidth / 2;

        // Get the size required for the text.
        Size textSize = new Size(text.Width, text.Height);

        // Find the top-left corner where you want to place the text.
        double margin = 96*0.25;
        Point point = new Point(
          (printDialog.PrintableAreaWidth - textSize.Width) / 2 - margin,
          (printDialog.PrintableAreaHeight - textSize.Height) / 2 - margin);

        // Draw the content.
        dc.DrawText(text, point);
```

```
        // Add a border (a rectangle with no background).
        dc.DrawRectangle(null, new Pen(Brushes.Black, 1),
          new Rect(margin, margin, printDialog.PrintableAreaWidth - margin * 2,
          printDialog.PrintableAreaHeight - margin * 2));
    }

    // Print the visual.
    printDialog.PrintVisual(visual, "A Custom-Printed Page");
}
```

Tip To improve this code, you'll probably want to move your drawing logic to a separate class (possibly the document class that wraps the content you're printing). You can then call a method in that class to get your visual and pass the visual to the PrintVisual() method in the event handling in your window code.

Figure 20-6 shows the output.

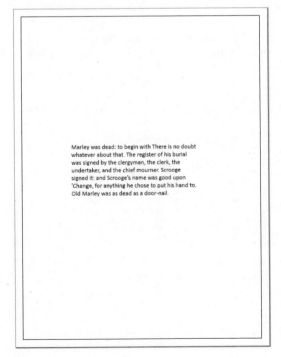

Figure 20-6. *A custom printout*

Custom Printing with Multiple Pages

A visual can't span pages. If you want a multipage printout, you need to use the same class you used when printing a FlowDocument: the DocumentPaginator. The difference is that you need to create the DocumentPaginator yourself from scratch. And this time you won't have a private DocumentPaginator on the inside to take care of all the heavy lifting.

Implementing the basic design of a DocumentPaginator is easy enough. You need to add a method that splits your content into pages, and you need to store the information about those pages internally. Then, you simply respond to the GetPage() method to provide the page that the PrintDialog needs. Each page is generated as a DrawingVisual, but the DrawingVisual is wrapped by the DocumentPage class.

The tricky part is separating your content into pages. There's no WPF magic here—it's up to you to decide how to divide your content. Some content is relatively easy to separate (like the long table you'll see in the next example), while some types of content are much more problematic. For example, if you want to print a long, text-based document, you'll need to move word by word through all your text, adding words to lines and lines to pages. You'll need to measure each separate piece of text to see whether it fits in the line. And that's just to split text content using ordinary left justification—if you want something comparable to the best-fit justification used for the FlowDocument, you're better off using the PrintDialog.PrintDocument() method, as described earlier, because there's a huge amount of code to write and some very specialized algorithms to use.

The following example demonstrates a typical not-too-difficult pagination job. The contents of a DataTable are printed in a tabular structure, putting each record on a separate row. The rows are split into pages based on how many lines fit on a page using the chosen font. Figure 20-7 shows the final result.

Model Number	Model Name
RU007	Rain Racer 2000
STKY1	Edible Tape
P38	Escape Vehicle (Air)
NOZ119	Extracting Tool
PT109	Escape Vehicle (Water)
RED1	Communications Device
LK4TLNT	Persuasive Pencil
NTMBS1	Multi-Purpose Rubber Band
NE1RPR	Universal Repair System
BRTLGT1	Effective Flashlight
INCPPRCLP	The Incredible Versatile Paperclip
DNTRPR	Toaster Boat
TGFDA	Multi-Purpose Towelette
WOWPEN	Mighty Mighty Pen
ICNCU	Perfect-Vision Glasses
LKARCKT	Pocket Protector Rocket Pack
DNTGCGHT	Counterfeit Creation Wallet
WRLD00	Global Navigational System
CITSME9	Cloaking Device
BME007	Indentity Confusion Device
SHADE01	Ultra Violet Attack Defender
SQUKY1	Guard Dog Pacifier
CHEW99	Survival Bar
COOLCMB1	Telescoping Comb
FF007	Eavesdrop Detector
LNGWADN	Escape Cord
1MOR4ME	Cocktail Party Pal
SQRTME1	Remote Foliage Feeder
ICUCLRLY00	Contact Lenses
OPNURMIND	Telekinesis Spoon

Model Number	Model Name
ULOST007	Rubber Stamp Beacon
BSUR2DUC	Bullet Proof Facial Tissue
NOBOOBOO4U	Speed Bandages
BHONST93	Correction Fluid
BPRECISE00	Dilemma Resolution Device
LSRPTR1	Nonexplosive Cigar
QLT2112	Document Transportation System
THNKDKE1	Hologram Cufflinks
TCKLR1	Fake Moustache Translator
JWLTRANS6	Interpreter Earrings
GRTWTCH9	Multi-Purpose Watch

Figure 20-7. *A table of data split over two pages*

In this example, the custom DocumentPaginator contains the code for splitting the data into pages and the code for printing each page to a Visual object. Although you could factor this into two classes (for example, if you want to allow the same data to be printed in the same way but paginated differently), usually you won't because the code required to calculate the page size is tightly bound to the code that actually prints the page.

The custom DocumentPaginator implementation is fairly long, so I'll break it down piece by piece. First, the StoreDataSetPaginator stores a few important details in private variables, including the DataTable that you plan to print and the chosen typeface, font size, page size, and margin:

```
public class StoreDataSetPaginator : DocumentPaginator
{
    private DataTable dt;

    private Typeface typeface;
    private double fontSize;
    private double margin;

    private Size pageSize;
    public override Size PageSize
    {
        get { return pageSize; }
        set
        {
            pageSize = value;
            PaginateData();
        }
    }

    public StoreDataSetPaginator(DataTable dt, Typeface typeface,
      double fontSize, double margin, Size pageSize)
    {
        this.dt = dt;
        this.typeface = typeface;
        this.fontSize = fontSize;
        this.margin = margin;
        this.pageSize = pageSize;
        PaginateData();
    }
    ...
```

Notice that these details are supplied in the constructor and then can't be changed. The only exception is the PageSize property, which is a required abstract property from the DocumentPaginator class. You could create properties to wrap the other details if you wanted to allow your code to alter these details after creating the paginator. You'd simply need to make sure you call PaginateData() when any of these details are changed.

The PaginateData() isn't a required member. It's just a handy place to calculate how many pages are needed. The StoreDataSetPaginator paginates its data as soon as the DataTable is supplied in the constructor.

When the PaginateData() method runs, it measures the amount of space required for a line of text and compares that against the size of the page to find out how many lines will fit on each page. The result is stored in a field named rowsPerPage.

```
...
private int rowsPerPage;
private int pageCount;

private void PaginateData()
{
    // Create a test string for the purposes of measurement.
    FormattedText text = GetFormattedText("A");

    // Count the lines that fit on a page.
    rowsPerPage = (int)((pageSize.Height-margin*2) / text.Height);

    // Leave a row for the headings
    rowsPerPage -= 1;

    pageCount = (int)Math.Ceiling((double)dt.Rows.Count / rowsPerPage);
}
...
```

This code assumes that a capital letter *A* is sufficient for calculating the line height. However, this might not be true for all fonts, in which case you'd need to pass a string that includes a complete list of all characters, numbers, and punctuation to GetFormattedText().

■Note To calculate the number of lines that fit on a page, you use the FormattedText.Height property. You *don't* use FormattedText.LineHeight, which is 0 by default. The LineHeight property is provided for you to override the default line spacing when drawing a block with multiple lines of text. However, if you don't set it, the FormattedText class uses its own calculation, which uses the Height property.

In some cases, you'll need to do a bit more work and store a custom object for each page (for example an array of strings with the text for each line). However, this isn't required in the StoreDataSetPaginator example because all the lines are the same, and there isn't any text wrapping to worry about.

The PaginateData() uses a private helper method named GetFormattedText(). When printing text, you'll find that you need to construct a great number of FormattedText objects. These FormattedText objects will always share the same culture and left-to-right text flow options. In many cases, they'll also use the same typeface. The GetFormattedText() encapsulates these details and so simplifies the rest of your code. The StoreDataSetPaginator uses two overloaded versions of GetFormattedText(), one of which accepts a different typeface to use:

```
...
private FormattedText GetFormattedText(string text)
{
    return GetFormattedText(text, typeface);
}
private FormattedText GetFormattedText(string text, Typeface typeface)
{
    return new FormattedText(
        text, CultureInfo.CurrentCulture, FlowDirection.LeftToRight,
        typeface, fontSize, Brushes.Black);
}
...
```

Now that you have the number of pages, you can implement the remainder of the required DocumentPaginator properties:

```
...
// Always returns true, because the page count is updated immediately,
// and synchronously, when the page size changes.
// It's never left in an indeterminate state.
public override bool IsPageCountValid
{
    get { return true; }
}

public override int PageCount
{
    get { return pageCount; }
}

public override IDocumentPaginatorSource Source
{
    get { return null; }
}
...
```

There's no factory class that can create this custom DocumentPaginator, so the Source property returns null.

The last implementation detail is also the longest. The GetPage() method returns a DocumentPage object for the requested page, with all the data.

The first step is to find the position where the two columns will begin. This example sizes the columns relative to the width of one capital letter *A*, which is a handy shortcut when you don't want to perform more detailed calculations.

```
...
public override DocumentPage GetPage(int pageNumber)
{
    // Create a test string for the purposes of measurement.
    FormattedText text = GetFormattedText("A");
```

```
double col1_X = margin;
double col2_X = col1_X + text.Width * 15;
...
```

The next step is to find the offsets that identify the range of records that belong on this page:

```
...

// Calculate the range of rows that fits on this page.
int minRow = pageNumber * rowsPerPage;
int maxRow = minRow + rowsPerPage;
...
```

Now the print operation can begin. There are three elements to print: column headers, a separating line, and the rows. The underlined header is drawn using DrawText() and Draw-Line() methods from the DrawingContext class. For the rows, the code loops from the first row to the last row, drawing the text from the corresponding DataRow in the two columns and then increasing the Y-coordinate position by an amount equal to the line height of the text.

```
...
// Create the visual for the page.
DrawingVisual visual = new DrawingVisual();

// Initial, set the position to the top-left corner of the printable area.
Point point = new Point(margin, margin);

using (DrawingContext dc = visual.RenderOpen())
{
    // Draw the column headers.
    Typeface columnHeaderTypeface = new Typeface(
      typeface.FontFamily, FontStyles.Normal, FontWeights.Bold,
      FontStretches.Normal);
    point.X = col1_X;
    text = GetFormattedText("Model Number", columnHeaderTypeface);
    dc.DrawText(text, point);
    text = GetFormattedText("Model Name", columnHeaderTypeface);
    point.X = col2_X;
    dc.DrawText(text, point);

    // Draw the line underneath.
    dc.DrawLine(new Pen(Brushes.Black, 2),
      new Point(margin, margin + text.Height),
      new Point(pageSize.Width - margin, margin + text.Height));

    point.Y += text.Height;

    // Draw the column values.
    for (int i = minRow; i < maxRow; i++)
```

```
    {
        // Check for the end of the last (half-filled) page.
        if (i > (dt.Rows.Count - 1)) break;

        point.X = col1_X;
        text = GetFormattedText(dt.Rows[i]["ModelNumber"].ToString());
        dc.DrawText(text, point);

        // Add second column.
        text = GetFormattedText(dt.Rows[i]["ModelName"].ToString());
        point.X = col2_X;
        dc.DrawText(text, point);
        point.Y += text.Height;
    }
    }
    return new DocumentPage(visual);
}
```

Now that the StoreDateSetDocumentPaginator is complete, you can use it whenever you want to print the contents of the DataTable with the product list, as shown here:

```
PrintDialog printDialog = new PrintDialog();
if (printDialog.ShowDialog() == true)
{
    StoreDataSetPaginator paginator = new StoreDataSetPaginator(ds.Tables[0],
        new Typeface("Calibri"), 24, 96*0.75,
        new Size(printDialog.PrintableAreaWidth, printDialog.PrintableAreaHeight));

    printDialog.PrintDocument(paginator, "Custom-Printed Pages");
}
```

The StoreDataSetPaginator has a certain amount of flexibility built in—for example, it can work with different fonts, margins, and paper sizes—but it can't deal with data that has a different schema. Clearly, there's still room in the WPF library for a handy class that could accept data, column and row definitions, headers and footers, and so on, and then print a properly paginated table. WPF doesn't have anything like this currently, but you can expect third-party vendors to provide components that fill the gaps.

Print Settings and Management

So far, you've focused all your attention on two methods of the PrintDialog class: PrintVisual() and PrintDocument(). This is all you need to use to get a decent printout, but you have more to do if you want to manage printer settings and jobs. Once again, the PrintDialog class is your starting point.

Maintaining Print Settings

In the previous examples, you saw how the PrintDialog class allows you to choose a printer and its settings. However, if you've used these examples to make more than one printout, you may have noticed a slight anomaly. Each time you return to the Print dialog box, it reverts to the default print settings. You need to pick the printer you want and adjust it all over again.

Life doesn't need to be this difficult. You have the ability to store this information and reuse it. One good approach is to store the PrintDialog as a member variable in your window. That way, you don't need to create the PrintDialog before each new print operation—you just keep using the existing object. This works because the PrintDialog encapsulates the printer selection and printer settings through two properties: PrintQueue and PrintTicket.

The PrintQueue property refers to a System.Printing.PrintQueue object, which represents the print queue for the selected printer. And as you'll discover in the next section, the Print-Queue also encapsulates a good deal of features for managing your printer and its jobs.

The PrintTicket property refers to a System.Printing.PrintTicket object, which defines the settings for a print job. It includes details such as print resolution and duplexing. If you want, you're free to tweak the settings of a PrintTicket programmatically. The PrintTicket class even has a GetXmlStream() method and a SaveTo() method, both of which let you serialize the ticket to a stream, and a constructor that lets you re-create a PrintTicket object based on the stream. This is an interesting option if you want to persist specific print settings between application sessions. (For example, you could use this ability to create a "print profile" feature.)

As long as these PrintQueue and PrintTicket properties remain consistent, the selected printer and its properties will remain the same each time you show the Print dialog box. So even if you need to create the PrintDialog box multiple times, you can simply set these properties to keep the user's selections.

Printing Page Ranges

You haven't yet considered one of the features in the PrintDialog class. You can allow the user to choose to print only a subset of a larger printout using the Pages text box in the Page Range box. The Pages text box lets the user specify a group of pages by entering the starting and ending page (for example, *4–6*) or pick a specific page (for example, *4*). It doesn't allow multiple page ranges (such as *1–3,5*).

The Pages text box is disabled by default. To switch it on, you simply need to set the Print-Dialog.UserPageRangeEnabled property to true before you call ShowDialog(). The Selection and Current Page options will remain disabled, because they aren't supported by the Print-Dialog class. You can also set the MaxPage and MinPage properties to constrain the pages that the user can pick.

After you've shown the Print dialog box, you can determine whether the user entered a page range by checking the PageRangeSelection property. If it provides a value of UserPages, there's a page range present. The PageRange property provides a PageRange property that indicates the starting page (PageRange.PageFrom) and ending page (PageRange.PageTo). It's up to your printing code to take these values into account and print only the requested pages.

Managing a Print Queue

Typically, a client application has a limited amount of interaction with the print queue. After a job is dispatched, you may want to display its status or (rarely) provide the option to pause, resume, or cancel the job. The WPF print classes go far beyond this level and allow you to build tools that can manage local or remote print queues.

The classes in the System.Printing namespace provide the support for managing print queues. You can use a few key classes to do most of the work, and they're outlined in Table 20-2.

Table 20-2. *Key Classes for Print Management*

Name	Description
PrintServer and LocalPrintServer	Represents a computer that provides printers or another device that does. (This "other device" might include a printer with built-in networking or a dedicated piece of network hardware that acts as a print server.) Using the PrintServer class, you can get a collection of PrintQueue objects for that computer. You can also use the LocalPrintServer class, which derives from PrintServer and always represents the current computer. It adds a DefaultPrintQueue property that you can use to get (or set) the default printer and a static GetDefault-PrintQueue() method that you can use without creating a LocalPrintServer instance.
PrintQueue	Represents a configured printer on a print server. The PrintQueue class allows you to get information about that printer's status and manage the print queue. You can also get a collection of PrintQueueJobInfo objects for that printer.
PrintSystemJobInfo	Represents a job that's been submitted to a print queue. You can get information about its status and modify its state or delete it.

Using these basic ingredients, you can create a program that launches a printout without any user intervention.

```
PrintDialog dialog = new PrintDialog();

// Pick the default printer.
dialog.PrintQueue = LocalPrintServer.GetDefaultPrintQueue();

// Print something.
dialog.PrintDocument(someContent, "Automatic Printout");
```

You can also create and apply a PrintTicket object to the PrintDialog to configure other print-related settings. More interestingly, you can delve deeper in the PrintServer, PrintQueue, and PrintSystemJobInfo classes to study what's taking place.

Figure 20-8 shows a simple program that allows you to browse the print queues on the current computer and see the outstanding jobs for each one. This program also allows you to perform some basic printer management tasks, such as suspending a printer (or a print job), resuming the printer (or print job), and canceling one job or all the jobs in a queue. By considering how this application works, you can learn the basics of the WPF print management model.

Figure 20-8. *Browsing printer queues and jobs*

This example uses a single PrintServer object, which is created as member field in the window class:

```
private PrintServer printServer = new PrintServer();
```

When you create a PrintServer object without passing any arguments to the constructor, the PrintServer represents the current computer. Alternatively, you could pass the UNC path that points to a print server on the network, like this:

```
private PrintServer printServer = new PrintServer(\\Warehouse\PrintServer);
```

Using the PrintServer object, the code grabs a list of print queues that represent the printers that are configured on the current computer. This step is easy—all you need to do is call the PrintServer.GetPrintQueues() method when the window is first loaded:

```
private void Window_Loaded(object sender, EventArgs e)
{
    lstQueues.DisplayMemberPath = "FullName";
```

```
    lstQueues.SelectedValuePath = "FullName";
    lstQueues.ItemsSource = printServer.GetPrintQueues();
}
```

The only piece of information this code snippet uses is the PrintQueue.FullName property. However, the PrintQueue class is stuffed with properties you can examine. You can get the default print settings (using properties such as DefaultPriority, DefaultPrintTicket, and so on), you can get the status and general information (using properties such as QueueStatus and NumberOfJobs), and you can isolate specific problems using Boolean Is*Xxx* and Has*Xxx* properties (such as IsManualFeedRequired, IsWarmingUp, IsPaperJammed, IsOutOfPaper, HasPaperProblem, and NeedUserIntervention).

The current example reacts when a printer is selected in the list by displaying the status for that printer and then fetching all the jobs in the queue. The PrintQueue.GetPrintJobInfoCollection() performs this task.

```
private void lstQueues_SelectionChanged(object sender, SelectionChangedEventArgs e)
{
    try
    {
        PrintQueue queue =
            printServer.GetPrintQueue(lstQueues.SelectedValue.ToString());
        lblQueueStatus.Text = "Queue Status: " + queue.QueueStatus.ToString();
        lstJobs.DisplayMemberPath = "JobName";
        lstJobs.SelectedValuePath = "JobIdentifier";

        lstJobs.ItemsSource = queue.GetPrintJobInfoCollection();
    }
    catch (Exception err)
    {
        MessageBox.Show(err.Message,
            "Error on " + lstQueues.SelectedValue.ToString());
    }
}
```

Each job is represented as a PrintSystemJobInfo object. When a job is selected in the list, this code shows its status:

```
private void lstJobs_SelectionChanged(object sender, SelectionChangedEventArgs e)
{
    if (lstJobs.SelectedValue == null)
    {
        lblJobStatus.Text = "";
    }
    else
    {
        PrintQueue queue =
            printServer.GetPrintQueue(lstQueues.SelectedValue.ToString());
        PrintSystemJobInfo job = queue.GetJob((int)lstJobs.SelectedValue);
```

```
        lblJobStatus.Text = "Job Status: " + job.JobStatus.ToString();
    }
}
```

The only remaining detail is the event handlers that manipulate the queue or job when you click one of the buttons in the window. This code is extremely straightforward. All you need to do is get a reference to the appropriate queue or job and then call the corresponding method. For example, here's how to pause a PrintQueue:

```
PrintQueue queue = printServer.GetPrintQueue(lstQueues.SelectedValue.ToString());
queue.Pause();
```

And here's how to pause a print job:

```
PrintQueue queue = printServer.GetPrintQueue(lstQueues.SelectedValue.ToString());
PrintSystemJobInfo job = queue.GetJob((int)lstJobs.SelectedValue);
job.Pause();
```

■**Note** It's possible to pause (and resume) an entire printer or a single job. You can do both tasks using the Printers icon in the Control Panel. Right-click a printer to pause or resume a queue, or double-click a printer to see its jobs, which you can manipulate individually.

Obviously, you'll need to add error handling when you perform this sort of task, because it won't necessarily succeed. For example, Windows security might stop you from attempting to cancel someone else's print job or an error might occur if you try to print to a networked printer after you've lost your connection to the network.

WPF includes quite a bit of print-related functionality. If you're interested in using this specialized functionality (perhaps because you're building some sort of tool or creating a long-running background task), check out the classes in the System.Printing namespace in the .NET SDK.

Printing Through XPS

As you learned in Chapter 19, WPF supports two complementary types of documents. Flow documents handle flexible content that flows to fit any page size you specify. XPS documents store print-ready content that's based on a fixed-page size. The content is frozen in place and preserved in its precise, original form.

As you'd expect, printing an XpsDocument is easy. The XpsDocument class exposes a DocumentPaginator, just like the FlowDocument. However, the DocumentPaginator of an XpsDocument has little to do, because the content is already laid out in fixed, unchanging pages.

Here's the code you might use to load an XPS file into memory, show it in a Document-Viewer, and then send it to the printer:

```
// Display the document.
XpsDocument doc = new XpsDocument("filename.xps", FileAccess.ReadWrite);
docViewer.Document = doc.GetFixedDocumentSequence();
doc.Close();

// Print the document.
if (printDialog.ShowDialog() == true)
{
    printDialog.PrintDocument(docViewer.Document.DocumentPaginator,
      "A Fixed Document");
}
```

Obviously, you don't need to show a fixed document in a DocumentViewer before you print it. This code includes that step because it's the most common option. In many scenarios, you'll load up the XpsDocument for review and print it after the user clicks a button.

As with the viewers for FlowDocument objects, the DocumentViewer also handles the ApplicationCommands.Print command, which means you can send an XPS document from the DocumentViewer to the printer with no code required.

XPS SUPPORT ON WINDOWS XP

XPS document support is a built-in part of the .NET Framework 3.0. However, the ability to print XPS content directly is a Windows Vista feature, because it requires the XPS printing model. Furthermore, the XPS print path requires an XPS-enabled print driver, and these aren't broadly available for older printers.

Fortunately, WPF includes an interoperability layer that ensures you can print XPS content on either operating system without any noticeable differences. When printing XPS content on Windows Vista with an XPS-enabled print driver, WPF uses the XPS print path. When printing without an XPS-enabled print driver, WPF performs some behind-the-scenes translation that seamlessly converts the XPS content to the GDI model used by traditional printer drivers.

Creating an XPS Document for a Print Preview

WPF also includes all the support you need to programmatically create XPS documents. Creating an XPS document is conceptually similar to printing some content—once you've built your XPS document, you've chosen a fixed page size and frozen your layout. So why bother taking this extra step? There are two good reasons:

- **Print preview.** You can use your generated XPS document as a print preview by displaying it in a DocumentViewer. The user can then choose whether to go ahead with the printout.

- **Asynchronous printing.** The XpsDocumentWriter class includes both a Write() method for synchronous printing and a WriteAsync() method that lets you send content to the printer asynchronously. For a long, complex print operation, the asynchronous option is preferred. It allows you to create a more responsive application.

The only limitation when creating an XPS document is that you need to write it to a file. You can't simply create an XPS document in memory. You may want to use a method like Path.GetTempFileName() to get a suitable temporary file path.

The basic technique for creating an XPS document is create an XpsDocumentWriter object using the static XpsDocument.CreateXpsDocumentWriter () method. Here's an example:

```
XpsDocument xpsDocument = new XpsDocument("filename.xps", FileAccess.ReadWrite);
XpsDocumentWriter writer = XpsDocument.CreateXpsDocumentWriter(xpsDocument);
```

The XpsDocumentWriter is a stripped-down class—its functionality revolves around the Write() and WriteAsync() methods that write content to your XPS document. Both of these methods are overloaded multiple times, allowing you to write different types of content, including another XPS document, a page that you've extracted from an XPS document, a visual (which allows you to write any element), and a DocumentPaginator. The last two options are the most interesting, because they duplicate the options you have with printing. For example, if you've created a DocumentPaginator to enable custom printing (as described earlier in this chapter), you can also use it to write an XPS document.

Here's an example that opens an existing flow document and then writes it in the XpsDocumentWriter using the Write() method. The newly created XPS document is then displayed in a DocumentViewer, which acts as a print preview.

```
using (FileStream fs = File.Open("FlowDocument1.xaml", FileMode.Open))
{
    FlowDocument flowDocument = (FlowDocument)XamlReader.Load(fs);
    writer.Write((((IDocumentPaginatorSource)flowDocument).DocumentPaginator);

    // Display the new XPS document in a viewer.
    docViewer.Document = xpsDocument.GetFixedDocumentSequence();
    xpsDocument.Close();
}
```

You can get a visual or paginator in a WPF application in an endless variety of ways. Because the XpsDocumentWriter supports these classes, it allows you to write any WPF content to an XPS document.

Printing Directly to the Printer via XPS

As you've learned in this chapter, the printing support in WPF is built on the XPS print path. If you use the PrintDialog class, you might not see any sign of this low-level reality. If you use the XpsDocumentWriter, it's impossible to miss.

So far, you've been funneling all your printing through the PrintDialog class. This isn't necessary—in fact, the PrintDialog delegates the real work to the XpsDocumentWriter. The trick is to create an XpsDocumentWriter that wraps a PrintQueue rather than a FileStream. The actual code for writing the printed output is identical—you simply rely on the Write() and WriteAsync() methods.

Here's a snippet of code that shows the Print dialog box, gets the selected printer, and uses it to create an XpsDocumentWriter that submits the print job:

```
string filePath = Path.Combine(appPath, "FlowDocument1.xaml");

if (printDialog.ShowDialog() == true)
{
    PrintQueue queue = printDialog.PrintQueue;
    XpsDocumentWriter writer = PrintQueue.CreateXpsDocumentWriter(queue);

    using (FileStream fs = File.Open(filePath, FileMode.Open))
    {
        FlowDocument flowDocument = (FlowDocument)XamlReader.Load(fs);
        writer.Write((((IDocumentPaginatorSource)flowDocument).DocumentPaginator);
    }
}
```

Interestingly, this example still uses the PrintDialog class. However, it simply uses it to display the standard Print dialog box and allow the user to choose a printer. The actual printing is performed through the XpsDocumentWriter.

Asynchronous Printing

The XpsDocumentWriter makes asynchronous printing easy. In fact, you can convert the previous example to use asynchronous printing by simply replacing the call to the Write() method with a call to WriteAsync().

Note In Windows, all print jobs are printed asynchronously. However, the process of *submitting* the print job takes place synchronously if you use Write() and asynchronously if you use WriteAsync(). In many cases, the time taken to submit a print job won't be significant, and you won't need this feature. Another consideration is that if you want to build (and paginate) the content you want to print asynchronously, this is often the most time-consuming stage of printing, and if you want this ability, you'll need to write the code that runs your printing logic on a background thread. You can use the techniques described in Chapter 3 (such as the BackgroundWorker) to make this process relatively easy.

The signature of the WriteAsync() method matches the signature of the Write() method—in other words, WriteAsync() accepts a paginator, visual, or one of a few other types of objects. Additionally, the WriteAsync() method includes overloads that accept an optional second parameter with state information. This state information can be any object you want to use to identify the print job. This object is provided through the WritingCompletedEventArgs object when the WritingCompleted event fires. This allows you to fire off multiple print jobs at once, handle the WritingCompleted event for each one with the same event handler, and determine which one has been submitted each time the event fires.

When an asynchronous print job is underway, you can cancel it by calling the Cancel-Async() method. The XpsDocumentWriter also includes a small set of events that allow you to react as a print job is submitted, including WritingProgressChanged, WritingCompleted, and WritingCancelled. Keep in mind that the WritingCompleted event fires when the print job has been written to the print queue, but this doesn't mean the printer has printed it yet.

The Last Word

In this chapter, you learned about the new printing model that's introduced in WPF. First you considered the easiest entry point: the all-in-one PrintDialog class that allows users to configure print settings and allows your application to send a document or visual to the printer. After considering a variety of ways to extend the PrintDialog and use it with onscreen and dynamically generated content, you looked at the lower-level XPS printing model. You then learned about the XpsDocumentWriter, which supports the PrintDialog and can be used independently. The XpsDocumentWriter gives you an easy way to create a print preview (because WPF doesn't include any print preview control), and it allows you to submit your print job asynchronously.

CHAPTER 21

■■■

Animation

Animation allows you to create truly *dynamic* user interfaces. It's often used to apply effects—for example, icons that grow when you move over them, logos that spin, text that scrolls into view, and so on. Sometimes, these effects seem like excessive glitz. But used properly, animations can enhance an application in a number of ways. They can make an application seem more responsive, natural, and intuitive. (For example, a button that slides in when you click it feels like a real, physical button—not just another gray rectangle.) Animations can also draw attention to important elements and guide the user through transitions to new content. (For example, an application could advertise newly downloaded content with a twinkling, blinking, or pulsing icon in the status bar.)

Animations are a core part of the WPF model. That means you don't need to use timers and event handling code to put them into action. Instead, you can create them declaratively, configure them using one of a handful of classes, and put them into action without writing a single line of C# code. Animations also integrate themselves seamlessly into ordinary WPF windows and pages. For example, if you animate a button so it drifts around the window, the button still behaves like a button. It can be styled, it can receive focus, and it can be clicked to fire off the typical event handling code. This is what separates animation from traditional media files, such as video. (In Chapter 22, you'll learn how to put a video window in your application. A video window is a completely separate region of your application—it's able to play video content, but it's not user interactive.)

In this chapter, you'll consider the rich set of animation classes that WPF provides. You'll see how to use them in code and (more commonly) how to construct and control them with XAML. Along the way, you'll see a wide range of animation examples, including fading pictures, rotating buttons, and expanding elements.

Understanding WPF Animation

In previous Windows-based platforms (such as Windows Forms and MFC), developers had to build their own animation systems from scratch. The most common technique was to use a timer in conjunction with some custom painting logic. WPF changes the game with a new *property-based* animation system. The following two sections describe the difference.

Timer-Based Animation

Imagine you need to make a piece of text spin in the About box of a Windows Forms application. Here's the traditional way you would structure your solution:

1. Create a timer that fires periodically (say, every 50 milliseconds).

2. When the timer fires, use an event handler to calculate some animation-related details, such as the new degree of rotation. Then, invalidate part or all of the window.

3. Shortly thereafter, Windows will ask the window to repaint itself, triggering your custom painting code.

4. In your painting code, render the rotated text.

Although this timer-based solution isn't very difficult to implement, integrating it into an ordinary application window is more trouble than it's worth. Here are some of the problems:

- **It paints pixels, not controls.** To rotate text in Windows Forms, you need the lower-level GDI+ drawing support. It's easy enough to use, but it doesn't mix well with ordinary window elements, such as buttons, text boxes, labels, and so on. As a result, you need to segregate your animated content from your controls, and you can't incorporate any user-interactive elements into an animation. If you want a rotating button, you're out of luck.

- **It assumes a single animation.** If you decide you want to have two animations running at the same time, you need to rewrite all your animation code—and it could become much more complex. WPF is much more powerful in this regard, allowing you to build more complex animations out of individual, simpler animations.

- **The animation frame rate is fixed.** It's whatever the timer is set at. And if you change the timer interval, you might need to change your animation code (depending on how your calculations are performed). Furthermore, the fixed frame rate you choose is not necessarily the ideal one for the computer's video hardware.

- **Complex animations require exponentially more complex code.** The spinning text example is easy enough, but moving a small vector drawing along a path is quite a bit more difficult. In WPF, even intricate animations can be defined in XAML (and generated with a third-party design tool).

Even without WPF's animation support, you can already simplify the spinning text example. That's because WPF provides a retained graphics model, which ensures that a window is automatically rerendered when it changes. This means you don't need to worry about invalidating and repainting it yourself. Instead, the following steps work just fine:

1. Create a timer that fires periodically. (WPF provides a System.Windows.Threading.DispatcherTimer that works on the user interface thread.)

2. When the timer fires, use an event handler to calculate some animation-related details, such as the new degree of rotation. Then, modify the corresponding elements.

3. WPF notices the changes you've made to the elements in your window. It then repaints (and caches) the new window content.

With this new solution, you don't need to fiddle with low-level drawing classes, and you don't need to segregate your animated content from ordinary elements in the same window.

Although this is an improvement, timer-based animation still suffers from several flaws: it results in code that isn't very flexible, it becomes horribly messy for complex effects, and it doesn't get the best possible performance. Instead, WPF includes a higher-level model that allows you to focus on *defining* your animations, without worrying about the way they're rendered. This model is based on the dependency property infrastructure, which is described in the next section.

Property-Based Animation

Often, an animation is thought of as a series of frames. To perform the animation, these frames are shown one after the other, like a stop-motion video. WPF animations use a dramatically different model. Essentially, a WPF animation is simply a way to modify the value of a dependency property over an interval of time.

For example, to make a button that grows and shrinks, you can modify its Width property in an animation. To make it shimmer, you could change the properties of the LinearGradientBrush that it uses for its background. The secret to creating the right animation is determining what properties you need to modify.

If you want to make other changes that can't be made by modifying a property, you're out of luck. For example, you can't add or remove elements as part of animation. Similarly, you can't ask WPF to perform a transition between a starting scene and an ending scene (although some crafty workarounds can simulate this effect). And finally, you can use animation only with a dependency property, because only dependency properties use the dynamic property resolution system (described in Chapter 6) that takes animations into account.

At first glance, the property-focused nature of WPF animations seems terribly limiting. However, as you work with WPF, you'll find that it's surprisingly capable. In fact, you can create a wide range of animated effects using common properties that every element supports.

That said, there are many cases where the property-based animation system won't work. As a rule of thumb, the property-based animation is a great way to add dynamic effects to otherwise ordinary Windows applications. For example, if you want a slick front end for your interactive shopping tool, property-based animations will work perfectly well. However, if you need to use animations as part of the core purpose of your application and you want them to continue running over the lifetime of your application, you probably need something more flexible and more powerful. For example, if you're creating a basic arcade game or using complex physics calculations to model collisions, you'll need greater control over the animation. In these situations, you'll be forced to do most of the work yourself using WPF's lower-level frame-based rendering support, which is described at the end of this chapter.

Basic Animation

You've already learned the first rule of WPF animation—every animation acts on a single dependency property. However, there's another restriction. To animate a property (in other words, change its value in a time-dependent way), you need to have an animation class that supports its data type. For example, the Button.Width property uses the double data type. To animate it, you use the DoubleAnimation class. However, Button.Padding uses the Thickness structure, so it requires the ThicknessAnimation class.

This requirement isn't as absolute as the first rule of WPF animation, which limits animations to dependency properties. That's because you can animate a dependency property that doesn't have a corresponding animation class by creating your *own* animation class for that data type. However, you'll find that the System.Windows.Media.Animation namespace includes animation classes for most of the data types that you'll want to use.

Many data types don't have a corresponding animation class because it wouldn't be practical. A prime example is enumerations. For example, you can control how an element is placed in a layout panel using the HorizontalAlignment property, which takes a value from the HorizontalAlignment enumeration. However, the HorizontalAlignment enumeration allows you to choose between only four values (Left, Right, Center, and Stretch), which greatly limits its use in an animation. Although you can swap between one orientation and another, you can't smoothly transition an element from one alignment to another. For that reason, there's no animation class for the HorizontalAlignment data type. You can build one yourself, but you're still constrained by the four values of the enumeration.

Reference types are not usually animated. However, their subproperties are. For example, all content controls sport a Background property that allows you to set a Brush object that's used to paint the background. It's rarely efficient to use animation to switch from one brush to another, but you can use animation to vary the properties of a brush. For example, you could vary the Color property of a SolidColorBrush (using the ColorAnimation class) or the Offset property of a GradientStop in a LinearGradientBrush (using the DoubleAnimation class). This extends the reach of WPF animation, allowing you to animate specific aspects of an element's appearance.

The Animation Classes

Based on the animation types mentioned so far—DoubleAnimation and ColorAnimation—you might assume all animation classes are named in the form *TypeName*Animation. This is close but not exactly true.

There are actually two types of animations—those that vary a property incrementally between the starting and finishing values (a process called *linear interpolation*) and those that abruptly change a property from one value to another. DoubleAnimation and ColorAnimation are examples of the first category; they use interpolation to smoothly change the value. However, interpolation doesn't make sense when changing certain data types, such as strings and reference type objects. Rather than use interpolation, these data types are changed abruptly at specific times using a technique called *key frame animation*. All key frame animation classes are named in the form *TypeName*AnimationUsingKeyFrames, as in StringAnimationUsing-KeyFrames and ObjectAnimationUsingKeyFrames.

Some data types have a key frame animation class but no interpolation animation class. For example, you can animate a string using key frames, but you can't animate a string using interpolation. However, *every* data type supports key frame animations, unless they have no animation support at all. In other words, every data type that has a normal animation class that uses interpolation (such as DoubleAnimation and ColorAnimation) also has a corresponding animation type for key frame animation (such as DoubleAnimationUsingKeyFrames and ColorAnimationUsingKeyFrames).

Truthfully, there's still one more type of animation. The third type is called a *path-based animation*, and it's much more specialized than animation that uses interpolation or key frames. A path-based animation modifies a value to correspond with the shape that's described by a PathGeometry object, and it's primarily useful for moving an element along a path. The classes for path-based animations have names in the form *TypeName*Animation-UsingPath, such as DoubleAnimationUsingPath and PointAnimationUsingPath.

■**Note** Although WPF currently uses three approaches to animation (linear interpolation, key frames, and paths), there's no reason you can't create more animation classes that modify values using a completely different approach. The only requirement is that your animation class must modify values in a time-dependent way.

All in all, you'll find the following in the System.Windows.Media.Animation namespace:

- Seventeen *TypeName*Animation classes, which use interpolation

- Twenty-two *TypeName*AnimationUsingKeyFrames classes, which use key frame animation

- Three *TypeName*AnimationUsingPath classes, which use path-based animation

Every one of these animation classes derives from an abstract *TypeName*AnimationBase class that implements a few fundamentals. This gives you a shortcut to creating your own animation classes. If a data type supports more than one type of animation, both animation classes derive from the abstract animation base class. For example, DoubleAnimation and DoubleAnimationUsingKeyFrames both derive from DoubleAnimationBase.

■**Note** These 42 classes aren't the only things you'll find in the System.Windows.Media.Animation namespace. Every key frame animation also works with its own key frame class and key frame collection classes, which adds to the clutter. In total, there are more than 100 classes in System.Windows.Media.Animation.

You can quickly determine what data types have native support for animation by reviewing these 42 classes. The following is the complete list:

BooleanAnimationUsingKeyFrames	PointAnimationUsingKeyFrames
ByteAnimation	PointAnimationUsingPath
ByteAnimationUsingKeyFrames	Point3DAnimation
CharAnimationUsingKeyFrames	Point3DAnimationUsingKeyFrames
ColorAnimation	QuarternionAnimation
ColorAnimationUsingKeyFrames	QuarternionAnimationUsingKeyFrames
DecimalAnimation	RectAnimation
DecimalAnimationUsingKeyFrames	RectAnimationUsingKeyFrames
DoubleAnimation	Rotation3DAnimation
DoubleAnimationUsingKeyFrames	Rotation3DAnimationUsingKeyFrames
DoubleAnimationUsingPath	SingleAnimation
Int16Animation	SingleAnimationUsingKeyFrames
Int16AnimationUsingKeyFrames	SizeAnimation
Int32Animation	SizeAnimationUsingKeyFrames
Int32AnimationUsingKeyFrames	StringAnimationUsingKeyFrames
Int64Animation	ThicknessAnimation
Int64AnimationUsingKeyFrames	ThicknessAnimationUsingKeyFrames
MatrixAnimationUsingKeyFrames	VectorAnimation
MatrixAnimationUsingPath	VectorAnimationUsingKeyFrames
ObjectAnimationUsingKeyFrames	Vector3DAnimation
PointAnimation	Vector3DAnimationUsingKeyFrames

Many of these types are self-explanatory. For example, once you master the DoubleAnimation class, you won't think twice about SingleAnimation, Int16Animation, Int32Animation, and all the other animation classes for simple numeric types, which work in the same way. Along with the animation classes for numeric types, you'll find a few that work with other basic data types (byte, bool, string, and char) and many more that deal with two-dimensional and three-dimensional Drawing primitives (Point, Size, Rect, Vector, and so on). You'll also find an animation class for the Margin and Padding properties of any element (ThicknessAnimation), one for color (ColorAnimation), and one for any reference type object (ObjectAnimationUsingKeyFrames). You'll consider many of these animation types as you work through the examples in this chapter.

THE CLUTTERED ANIMATION NAMESPACE

If you look in the System.Windows.Media.Animation namespace, you may be a bit shocked. It's packed full with different animation classes for different data types. The effect is a bit overwhelming. It would be nice if there were a way to combine all the animation features into a few core classes. And what developer wouldn't appreciate a generic Animate<T> class that could work with any data type? However, this model isn't currently possible, for a variety of reasons. First, different animation classes may perform their work in slightly different ways, which means the code required will differ. For example, the way a color value is blended from one shade to another by the ColorAnimation class differs from the way a single numeric value is modified by the DoubleAnimation class. In other words, although the animation classes expose the same public interface for you to use, their internal workings may differ. Their interface is standardized through inheritance, because all animation classes derive from the same base classes (beginning with Animatable).

However, this isn't the full story. Certainly, many animation classes *do* share a significant amount of code, and a few areas absolutely cry out for a dash of generics, such as the 100 or so classes used to represent key frames and key frame collections. In an ideal world, animation classes would be distinguished by the type of animation they perform, so you could use classes such as NumericAnimation<T>, KeyFrame-Animation<T>, or LinearInterpolationAnimation<T>. One can only assume that the deeper reason that prevents solutions like these is that XAML lacks direct support for generics.

Animations in Code

As you've already learned, the most common animation technique is linear interpolation, which modifies a property smoothly from its starting point to its end point. For example, if you set a starting value of 1 and an ending value of 10, your property might be rapidly changed from 1 to 1.1, 1.2, 1.3, and so on, until the value reaches 10.

At this point, you're probably wondering how WPF determines the increments it will use when performing interpolation. Happily, this detail is taken care of automatically. WPF uses whatever increment it needs to ensure a smooth animation at the currently configured frame rate. The standard frame rate WPF uses is 60 frames per second. (You'll learn how to tweak this detail later in this chapter.) In other words, every $1/60^{th}$ of a second WPF calculates all animated values and updates the corresponding properties.

The simplest way to use an animation is to instantiate one of the animation classes listed earlier, configure it, and then use the BeginAnimation() of the element you want to modify. All WPF elements inherit BeginAnimation(), which is part of the IAnimatable interface, from the base UIElement class. Other classes that implement IAnimatable include ContentElement (the base class for bits of document flow content) and Visual3D (the base class for 3D visuals).

Note This isn't the most common approach—it most situations, you'll create animations declaratively using XAML, as described later in the "Declarative Animation and Storyboards" section. However, using XAML is slightly more involved because you need another object—called a *storyboard*—to connect the animation to the appropriate property. Code-based animations are also useful in certain scenarios where you need to use complex logic to determine the starting and ending values for your animation.

Figure 21-1 shows an extremely simple animation that widens a button. When you click the button, WPF smoothly extends both sides until the button fills the window.

Figure 21-1. *An animated button*

To create this effect, you use an animation that modifies the Width property of the button. Here's the code that creates and launches this animation when the button is clicked:

```
DoubleAnimation widthAnimation = new DoubleAnimation();
widthAnimation.From = 160;
widthAnimation.To = this.Width - 30;
widthAnimation.Duration = TimeSpan.FromSeconds(5);
cmdGrow.BeginAnimation(Button.WidthProperty, widthAnimation);
```

Three details are the bare minimum of any animation that uses linear interpolation: the starting value (From), the ending value (To), and the time that the entire animation should take (Duration). In this example, the ending value is based on the current width of the containing window. These three properties are found in all the animation classes that use interpolation.

The From, To, and Duration properties seem fairly straightforward, but you should note a few important details. The following sections explore these properties more closely.

From

The From value is the starting value for the Width property. If you click the button multiple times, each time you click it the Width is reset to 160, and the animation runs again. This is true even if you click the button while an animation is already underway.

■Note This example exposes another detail about WPF animations; namely, every dependency property can be acted on by only one animation at a time. If you start a second animation, the first one is automatically discarded.

In many situations, you don't want an animation to begin at the original From value. There are two common reasons:

- **You have an animation that can be triggered multiple times in a row for a cumulative effect.** For example, you might want to create a button that grows a bit more each time it's clicked.

- **You have animations that may overlap.** For example, you might use the MouseEnter event to trigger an animation that expands a button and the MouseLeave event to trigger a complementary animation that shrinks it back. (This is often known as a "fish-eye" effect.) If you move the mouse over and off this sort of button several times in quick succession, each new animation will interrupt the previous one, causing the button to "jump" back to the size that's set by the From property.

The current example falls into the second category. If you click the button while it's already growing, the width is reset to 160 pixels—which can be a bit jarring. To correct the problem, just leave out the code statement that sets the From property:

```
DoubleAnimation widthAnimation = new DoubleAnimation();
widthAnimation.To = this.Width - 30;
widthAnimation.Duration = TimeSpan.FromSeconds(5);
cmdGrow.BeginAnimation(Button.WidthProperty, widthAnimation);
```

There's one catch. For this technique to work, the property you're animating must have a previously set value. In this example, that means the button must have a hard-coded width (whether it's defined directly in the button tag or applied through a style setter). The problem is that in many layout containers, it's common not to specify a width and to allow the container to control it based on the element's alignment properties. In this case, the default width applies, which is the special value Double.NaN (where NaN stands for "not a number"). You can't animate a property that has this value using linear interpolation.

So, what's the solution? In many cases, the answer is to hard-code the button's width. As you'll see, animations often require a more fine-grained control of element sizing and positioning than you'd otherwise use. In fact, the most common layout container for "animatable" content is the Canvas, because it makes it easy to move content around (with possible overlap) and resize it. The Canvas is also the most lightweight layout container, because no extra layout work is needed when a property like Width is changed.

In the current example, there's another option. You could retrieve the current value of the button using its ActualWidth property, which indicates the current rendered width. You can't animate ActualWidth (it's read-only), but you can use it to set the From property of your animation:

```
widthAnimation.From = cmdGrow.ActualWidth;
```

This technique works for both code-based animations (like the current example) and the declarative animations you'll see later (which require the use of a binding expression to get the ActualWidth value).

■**Note** It's important to use the ActualWidth property in this example rather than the Width property. That's because Width reflects the desired width that you choose, while ActualWidth indicates the rendered width that was used. If you're using automatic layout, you probably won't set a hard-coded Width at all, so the Width property will simply return Double.NaN, and an exception will be raised when you attempt to start the animation.

You need to be aware of another issue when you use the current value as a starting point for an animation—it may change the speed of your animation. That's because the duration isn't adjusted to take into account that there's a smaller spread between the initial value and the final value. For example, imagine you create a button that doesn't use the From value and instead animates from its current position. If you click the button when it has almost reached its maximum width, a new animation begins. This animation is configured to take five seconds (through the Duration property), even though there are only a few more pixels to go. As a result, the growth of the button will appear to slow down.

This effect appears only when you restart an animation that's almost complete. Although it's a bid odd, most developers don't bother trying to code around it. Instead, it's considered to be an acceptable quirk.

■**Note** You could compensate for this problem by writing some custom logic that modifies the animation duration, but it's seldom worth the effort. To do so, you'd need to make assumptions about the standard size of the button (which limits the reusability of your code), and you'd need to create your animations programmatically so that you could run this code (rather than declaratively, which is the more common approach you'll see a bit later).

To

Just as you can omit the From property, you can omit the To property. In fact, you could leave out both the From and To properties to create an animation like this:

```
DoubleAnimation widthAnimation = new DoubleAnimation();
widthAnimation.Duration = TimeSpan.FromSeconds(5);
cmdGrow.BeginAnimation(Button.WidthProperty, widthAnimation);
```

At first glance, this animation seems like a long-winded way to do nothing at all. It's logical to assume that because both the To and From properties are left out, they'll both use the same value. But there's a subtle and important difference.

When you leave out From, the animation uses the current value and takes animation into account. For example, if the button is midway through a grow operation, the From value uses the expanded width. However, when you leave out To, the animation uses the current value *without taking animation into account*. Essentially, that means the To value becomes the *original* value—whatever you last set in code, on the element tag, or through a style. (This works thanks to WPF's property resolution system, which is able to calculate a value for a property based on several overlapping property providers, without discarding any information. Chapter 6 describes this system in more detail.)

In the button example, that means if you start a grow animation and then interrupt it with the animation shown previously (perhaps by clicking another button), the button will shrink from its half-grown size until it reaches the original width that's set in the XAML markup. On the other hand, if you run this code while no other animation is underway, nothing will happen. That's because the From value (the animated width) and the To value (the original width) are the same.

By

Instead of using To, you can use the By property. The By property is used to create an animation that changes a value *by* a set amount, rather than *to* a specific target. For example, you could great an animation that enlarges a button by 10 units more than its current size, as shown here:

```
DoubleAnimation widthAnimation = new DoubleAnimation();
widthAnimation.By = 10;
widthAnimation.Duration = TimeSpan.FromSeconds(0.5);
cmdGrowIncrementally.BeginAnimation(Button.WidthProperty, widthAnimation);
```

This approach isn't necessary in the button example, because you could achieve the same result using a simple calculation to set the To property, like this:

```
widthAnimation.To = cmdGrowIncrementally.Width + 10;
```

However, the By value makes more sense when you're defining your animation in XAML, because XAML doesn't provide a way to perform simple calculations.

■Note You can use By and From in combination, but it doesn't save you any work. The By value is simply added to the From value to arrive at the To value.

The By property is offered by most, but not all, animation classes that use interpolation. For example, it doesn't make sense with non-numeric data types, such as a Color structure (as used by ColorAnimation).

There's one other way to get similar behavior without using the By property—you can create an *additive* animation by setting the IsAdditive property. When you do, the current value is added to both the From and To values automatically. For example, consider this animation:

```
DoubleAnimation widthAnimation = new DoubleAnimation();
widthAnimation.From = 0;
widthAnimation.To = -10;
widthAnimation.Duration = TimeSpan.FromSeconds(0.5);
widthAnimation.IsAdditive = true;
```

It starts from the current value and finishes at a value that's reduced by 10 units. On the other hand, if you use this animation:

```
DoubleAnimation widthAnimation = new DoubleAnimation();
widthAnimation.From = 10;
widthAnimation.To = 50;
widthAnimation.Duration = TimeSpan.FromSeconds(0.5);
widthAnimation.IsAdditive = true;
```

the property jumps to the new value (which is 10 units greater than the current value) and then increases until it reaches a final value that is 50 more units than the current value before the animation began.

Duration

The Duration property is straightforward enough—it takes the time interval (in milliseconds, minutes, hours, or whatever else you'd like to use) between the time the animation starts and the time it ends. Although the duration of the animations in the previous examples is set using a TimeSpan, the Duration property actually requires a Duration object. Fortunately, Duration and TimeSpan are quite similar, and the Duration structure defines an implicit cast that can convert System.TimeSpan to System.Windows.Duration as needed. That's why this line of code is perfectly reasonable:

```
widthAnimation.Duration = TimeSpan.FromSeconds(5);
```

So, why bother introducing a whole new type? The Duration also includes two special values that can't be represented by a TimeSpan object—Duration.Automatic and Duration.Forever. Neither of these values is useful in the current example. (Automatic simply sets the animation to a 1-second duration, and Forever makes the animation infinite in length, which prevents it from having any effect.) However, these values become useful when creating more complex animations.

Simultaneous Animations

You can use BeginAnimation() to launch more than one animation at a time. The Begin-Animation() method returns almost immediately, allowing you to use code like this to animate two properties simultaneously:

```
DoubleAnimation widthAnimation = new DoubleAnimation();
widthAnimation.From = 160;
widthAnimation.To = this.Width - 30;
widthAnimation.Duration = TimeSpan.FromSeconds(5);

DoubleAnimation heightAnimation = new DoubleAnimation();
heightAnimation.From = 40;
```

```
heightAnimation.To = this.Height - 50;
heightAnimation.Duration = TimeSpan.FromSeconds(5);

cmdGrow.BeginAnimation(Button.WidthProperty, widthAnimation);
cmdGrow.BeginAnimation(Button.HeightProperty, heightAnimation);
```

In this example, the two animations are not synchronized. That means the width and height won't grow at exactly the same intervals. (Typically, you'll see the button grow wider and then grow taller just after.) You can overcome this limitation by creating animations that are bound to the same timeline. You'll learn this technique later in this chapter, when you consider storyboards.

Animation Lifetime

Technically, WPF animations are *temporary*, which means they don't actually change the value of the underlying property. While an animation is active, it simply overrides the property value. This is because of the way that dependency properties work (as described in Chapter 6), and it's an often overlooked detail that can cause significant confusion.

A one-way animation (like the button growing animation) remains active after it finishes running. That's because the animation needs to hold the button's width at the new size. This can lead to an unusual problem—namely, if you try to modify the value of the property using code after the animation has completed, your code will appear to have no effect. That's because your code simply assigns a new local value to the property, but the animated value still takes precedence.

You can solve this problem in several ways, depending on what you're trying to accomplish:

- Create an animation that resets your element to its original state. You do this by not setting the To property. For example, the button shrinking animation reduces the width of the button to its last set size, after which you can change it in your code.

- Create a reversible animation. You do this by setting the AutoReverse property to true. For example, when the button growing animation finishes widening the button, it will play out the animation in reverse, returning it to its original width. The total duration of your animation will be doubled.

- Change the FillBehavior property. Ordinarily, FillBehavior is set to HoldEnd, which means that when an animation ends, it continues to apply its final value to the target property. If you change FillBehavior to Stop, as soon as the animation ends the property reverts to its original value.

- Remove the animation object when the animation is complete by handling the Completed event of the animation object.

The first three options change the behavior of your animation. One way or another, they return the animated property to its original value. If this isn't what you want, you need to use the last option.

First, before you launch the animation, attach an event handler that reacts when the animation finishes:

```
widthAnimation.Completed += animation_Completed;
```

■**Note** The Completed event is a normal .NET event that takes an ordinary EventArgs object with no additional information. It's not a routed event.

When the Completed event fires, you can render the animation inactive by calling the BeginAnimation() method. You simply need to specify the property and pass in a null reference for the animation object:

```
cmdGrow.BeginAnimation(Button.WidthProperty, null);
```

When you call BeginAnimation(), the property returns to the value it had before the animation started. If this isn't what you want, you can take note of the current value that's being applied by the animation, remove the animation, and then manually set the new property, like so:

```
double currentWidth = cmdGrow.Width;
cmdGrow.BeginAnimation(Button.WidthProperty, null);
cmdGrow.Width = currentWidth;
```

Keep in mind that this changes the local value of the property. That may affect how other animations work. For example, if you animate this button with an animation that doesn't specify the From property, it uses this newly applied value as a starting point. In most cases, this is the behavior you want.

The Timeline Class

As you've seen, every animation revolves around a few key properties. You've seen several of these properties: From and To (which are provided in animation classes that use interpolation) and Duration and FillBehavior (which are provided in all animation classes). Before going any further, it's worth taking a closer look at the properties you have to work with.

Figure 21-2 shows the inheritance hierarchy of the WPF animation types. It includes all the base classes, but it leaves out the full 42 animation types (and the corresponding *TypeName*AnimationBase classes).

The class hierarchy includes three main branches that derive from the abstract Timeline class. MediaTimeline is used when playing audio or video files—it's described in Chapter 22. AnimationTimeline is used for the property-based animation system you've considered so far. And TimelineGroup allows you to synchronize timelines and control their playback. It's described later in this chapter in the "Simultaneous Animations" section, when you tackle storyboards.

The first useful members appear in the Timeline class, which defines the Duration property you've already considered and a few more. Table 21-1 lists its properties.

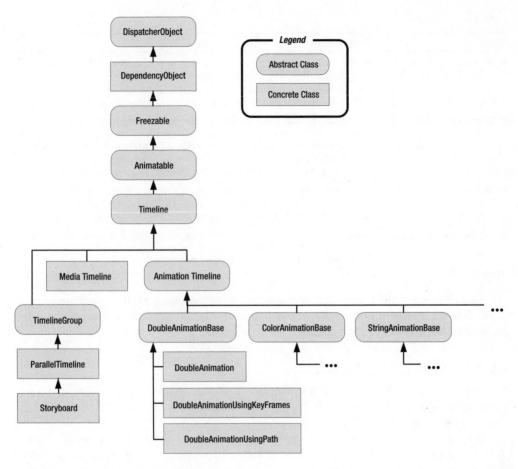

Figure 21-2. *The animation class hierarchy*

Table 21-1. *Timeline Properties*

Name	Description
BeginTime	Sets a delay that will be added before the animation starts (as a TimeSpan). This delay is added to the total time, so a five-second animation with a five-second delay takes ten seconds. BeginTime is useful when synchronizing different animations that start at the same time but should apply their effects in sequence.
Duration	Sets the length of time the animation runs, from start to finish, as a Duration object.
SpeedRatio	Increases or decreases the speed of the animation. Ordinarily, SpeedRatio is 1. If you increase it, the animation completes more quickly (for example, a SpeedRatio of 5 completes five times faster). If you decrease it, the animation is slowed down (for example, a SpeedRatio of 0.5 takes twice as long). You can change the Duration of your animation for an equivalent result. The SpeedRatio is not taken into account when applying the BeginTime delay.

Continued

Table 21-1. *Continued*

Name	Description
AccelerationRatio and DecelerationRatio	Makes an animation nonlinear, so it starts off slow and then speeds up (by increasing the AccelerationRatio) or slows down at the end (by increasing the DecelerationRatio). Both values are set from 0 to 1 and begin at 0. Furthermore, the total of both values cannot exceed 1.
AutoReverse	If true, the animation will play out in reverse once it's complete, reverting to the original value. This also doubles the time the animation takes. If you've increased the SpeedRatio, it applies to both the initial playback of the animation and the reversal. The BeginTime applies only to the very beginning of the animation—it doesn't delay the reversal.
FillBehavior	Determines what happens when the animation ends. Usually, it keeps the property fixed at the ending value (FillBehavior.HoldEnd), but you can also choose to return it to its original value (FillBehavior.Stop).
RepeatBehavior	Allows you to repeat an animation a specific number of times or for a specific time interval. The RepeatBehavior object that you use to set this property determines the exact behavior.

Although BeginTime, Duration, SpeedRatio, and AutoReverse are all fairly straightforward, some of the other properties warrant closer examination. The following sections delve into AccelerationRatio, DecelerationRatio, and RepeatBehavior.

AccelerationRatio and DecelerationRatio

AccelerationRatio and DecelerationRatio allow you to compress part of the timeline so it passes by more quickly. The rest of the timeline is stretched to compensate so that the total time is unchanged.

Both of these properties represent a percentage value. For example, an AccelerationRatio of 0.3 indicates that you want to spend the first 30% of the duration of the animation accelerating. For example, in a ten-second animation, the first three seconds would be taken up with acceleration, and the remaining seven seconds would pass at a consistent speed. (Obviously, the speed in the last seven seconds is faster than the speed of a nonaccelerated animation, because it needs to make up for the slow start.) If you set AccelerationRatio to 0.3 and DecelerationRatio to 0.3, acceleration takes place for the first three seconds, the middle four seconds are at a fixed maximum speed, and deceleration takes place for the last three seconds. Viewed this way, it's obvious that the total of AccelerationRatio and DecelerationRatio can't top 1, because then it required more than 100% of the available time to perform the requested acceleration and deceleration. Of course, you could set AccelerationRatio to 1 (in which case the animation speeds up from start to finish) or DecelerationRatio to 1 (in which case the animation slows down from start to finish).

Animations that accelerate and decelerate are often used to give a more natural appearance. However, the AccelerationRatio and DecelerationRatio give you only relatively crude control. For example, they don't let you vary the acceleration or set it specifically. If you want to have an animation that uses varying degrees of acceleration, you'll need to define a series of animations, one after the other, and set the AccelerationRatio and DecelerationRatio property of each one, or you'll need to use a key frame animation with key spline frames (as described at the end of this chapter). Although this technique gives you plenty of flexibility, keeping track of all the details is a headache, and it's a perfect case for using a design tool to construct your animations.

RepeatBehavior

The RepeatBehavior property allows you to control how an animation is repeated. If you want to repeat it a fixed number of times, pass the appropriate number of times the RepeatBehavior constructor. For example, this animation repeats twice:

```
DoubleAnimation widthAnimation = new DoubleAnimation();
widthAnimation.To = this.Width - 30;
widthAnimation.Duration = TimeSpan.FromSeconds(5);
widthAnimation.RepeatBehavior = new RepeatBehavior(2);
cmdGrow.BeginAnimation(Button.WidthProperty, widthAnimation);
```

When you run this animation, the button will increase in size (over five seconds), jump back to its original value, and then increase in size again (over five seconds), ending at the full width of the window. If you've set AutoReverse to true, the behavior is slightly different—the entire animation is completed forward and backward (meaning the button expands and then shrinks), and *then* it's repeated again.

■**Note** Animations that use interpolation provide an IsCumulative property, which tells WPF how to deal with each repetition. If IsCumulative is true, the animation isn't repeated from start to finish. Instead, each subsequent animation adds to the previous one. For example, if you use IsCumulative with the animation shown earlier, the button will expand twice as wide over twice as much time. To put it another way, the first iteration is treated normally, but every repetition after that is treated as though you set IsAdditive to true.

Rather than using RepeatBehavior to set a repeat count, you can use it to set a repeat *interval*. To do so, simply pass a TimeSpan to the RepeatBehavior constructor. For example, the following animation repeats itself for 13 seconds:

```
DoubleAnimation widthAnimation = new DoubleAnimation();
widthAnimation.To = this.Width - 30;
widthAnimation.Duration = TimeSpan.FromSeconds(5);
widthAnimation.RepeatBehavior = new RepeatBehavior(TimeSpan.FromSeconds(13));
cmdGrow.BeginAnimation(Button.WidthProperty, widthAnimation);
```

In this example, the Duration property specifies that the entire animation takes five seconds. As a result, the RepeatBehavior of 13 seconds will trigger two repeats and then leave the button halfway through a third repeat (at the three-second mark).

■**Tip** You can use RepeatBehavior to perform just part of an animation. To do so, use a fractional number of repetitions, or use a TimeSpan that's less than the duration.

Finally, you can cause an animation to repeat itself endlessly with the RepeatBehavior.Forever value:

```
widthAnimation.RepeatBehavior = RepeatBehavior.Forever;
```

Declarative Animation and Storyboards

As you've seen, WPF animations are represented by a group of animation classes. You set the relevant information, such as the starting value, ending value, and duration, using a handful of properties. This obviously makes them a great fit for XAML. What's less clear is how you wire an animation up to a particular element and property and how you trigger it at the right time.

It turns out that two ingredients are at work in any declarative animation:

- **A storyboard.** It's the XAML equivalent of the BeginAnimation() method. It allows you to direct an animation to the right element and property.

- **An event trigger.** It responds to a property change or event (such as the Click event of a button) and controls the storyboard. For example, to start an animation, the event trigger must *begin* the storyboard.

You'll learn how both pieces work in the following sections.

The Storyboard

A storyboard is an enhanced timeline. You can use it to group multiple animations, and it also has the ability to control the playback of animation—pausing it, stopping it, and changing its position. However, the most basic feature provided by the Storyboard class is its ability to point to a specific property and specific element using the TargetProperty and TargetName properties. In other words, the storyboard bridges the gap between your animation and the property you want to animate.

Here's how you might define a storyboard that manages a DoubleAnimation:

```
<Storyboard TargetName="cmdGrow" TargetProperty="Width">
  <DoubleAnimation From="160" To="300" Duration="0:0:5"></DoubleAnimation>
</Storyboard>
```

Both TargetName and TargetProperty are attached properties. That means you can apply them directly to the animation, as shown here:

```
<Storyboard>
  <DoubleAnimation
    Storyboard.TargetName="cmdGrow" Storyboard.TargetProperty="Width"
    From="160" To="300" Duration="0:0:5"></DoubleAnimation>
</Storyboard>
```

This syntax is more common, because it allows you to put several animations in the same storyboard but allow each animation to act on a different element and property.

Defining a storyboard is the first step to creating an animation. To actually put this storyboard into action, you need an event trigger.

Event Triggers

You first learned about event triggers in Chapter 12, when you considered styles. Styles give you one way to attach an event trigger to an element. However, you can define an event trigger in four places:

- In a style (the Styles.Triggers collection)

- In a data template (the DataTemplate.Triggers collection)

- In a control template (the ControlTemplate.Triggers collection)

- In an element directly (the FrameworkElement.Triggers collection)

When creating an event trigger, you need to indicate the routed event that starts the trigger and the action (or actions) that are performed by the trigger. With animations, the most common action is BeginStoryboard, which is equivalent to calling BeginAnimation().

The following example uses the Triggers collection of a button to attach an animation to the Click event. When the button is clicked, it grows.

```
<Button Padding="10" Name="cmdGrow" Height="40" Width="160"
 HorizontalAlignment="Center" VerticalAlignment="Center">
  <Button.Triggers>
    <EventTrigger RoutedEvent="Button.Click">
      <EventTrigger.Actions>
        <BeginStoryboard>
          <Storyboard>
            <DoubleAnimation Storyboard.TargetProperty="Width"
              To="300" Duration="0:0:5"></DoubleAnimation>
          </Storyboard>
        </BeginStoryboard>
      </EventTrigger.Actions>
    </EventTrigger>
  </Button.Triggers>

  <Button.Content>
    Click and Make Me Grow
  </Button.Content>
</Button>
```

■Tip To create an animation that fires when the window first loads, add an event trigger in the Window.Triggers collection that responds to the Window.Loaded event.

The Storyboard.TargetProperty property identifies the property you want to change (in this case, Width). If you don't supply a class name, the storyboard uses the parent element, which is the button you want to expand. If you want to set an attached property (for example, Canvas.Left or Canvas.Top), you need to wrap the entire property in brackets, like this:

```
<DoubleAnimation Storyboard.TargetProperty="(Canvas.Left)" ... />
```

The Storyboard.TargetName property isn't required in this example. When you leave it out, the storyboard uses the parent element, which is the button.

> **Note** All an event trigger is able to do is launch *actions*. All actions are represented by classes that derive from System.Windows.TriggerAction. Currently, WPF includes a very small set of actions that are designed for interacting with a storyboard and controlling media playback.

There's one difference between the declarative approach shown here and the code-only approach demonstrated earlier. Namely, the To value is hard-coded at 300 units, rather than set relative to the size of the containing window. If you wanted to use the window width, you'd need to use a data binding expression, like so:

```
<DoubleAnimation Storyboard.TargetProperty="Width"
  To="{Binding ElementName=window,Path=Width}" Duration="0:0:5">
</DoubleAnimation>
```

This still doesn't get exactly the result you need. Here, the button grows from its current size to full width of the window. The code-only approach enlarges the button to 30 units less than the full size, using a trivial calculation. Unfortunately, XAML doesn't support inline calculations. One solution is to build an IValueConverter that does the work for you. Fortunately, this odd trick is easy to implement (and many developers have). You can find one example at http://blogs.msdn.com/llobo/archive/2006/11/13/Arithmetic-operations-in-Xaml.aspx or check out the downloadable examples for this chapter.

> **Note** Another option is to create a custom dependency property in your window class that performs the calculation. You can then bind your animation to the custom dependency property. For more information about creating dependency properties, see Chapter 6.

You can now duplicate all the examples you've seen so far by creating triggers and storyboards and setting the appropriate properties of the DoubleAnimation object.

Attaching Triggers with a Style

The FrameworkElement.Triggers collection is a bit of an oddity. It supports only event triggers. The other trigger collections (Styles.Triggers, DataTemplate.Triggers, and ControlTemplate.Triggers) are more capable. They support the three basic types of WPF triggers: property triggers, data triggers, and event triggers.

> **Note** There's no technical reason why the FrameworkElement.Triggers collection shouldn't support additional trigger types, but this functionality wasn't implemented in time for the first version of WPF.

Using an event trigger is the most common way to attach an animation. However, it's not your only option. If you're using the Triggers collection in a style, data template, or control template, you can also create a property trigger that reacts when a property value changes. For example, here's a style that duplicates the example shown earlier. It triggers a storyboard when IsPressed is true:

```
<Window.Resources>
  <Style x:Key="GrowButtonStyle">
    <Style.Triggers>
      <Trigger Property="Button.IsPressed" Value="True">
        <Trigger.EnterActions>
          <BeginStoryboard>
            <Storyboard>
              <DoubleAnimation Storyboard.TargetProperty="Width"
                To="250" Duration="0:0:5"></DoubleAnimation>
            </Storyboard>
          </BeginStoryboard>
        </Trigger.EnterActions>
      </Trigger>
    </Style.Triggers>
  </Style>
</Window.Resources>
```

You can attach actions to a property trigger in two ways. You can use Trigger.EnterActions to set actions that will be performed when the property changes to the value you specify (in the previous example, when IsPressed becomes true) and use Trigger.ExitActions to set actions that will be performed when the property changes back (when the value of IsPressed returns to false). This is a handy way to wrap together a pair of complementary animations.

Here's the button that uses the style shown earlier:

```
<Button Padding="10" Name="cmdGrow" Height="40" Width="160"
  Style="{StaticResource GrowButtonStyle}"
  HorizontalAlignment="Center" VerticalAlignment="Center">
  Click and Make Me Grow
</Button>
```

Remember, you don't need to use property triggers in a style. You can also use event triggers, as you saw in the previous section. Finally, you don't need to define a style separately from the button that uses it (you can set the Button.Style property with an inline style), but this two-part separation is more common, and it gives you the flexibility to apply the same animation to multiple elements.

Attaching Triggers with a Template

One of the most powerful ways to reuse an animation is by defining it in a template. In Chapter 15, you saw a stylized ListBox that used curved borders and a shaded background. This ListBox also used property triggers to change the font size of a ListBoxItem when you hovered over it with the mouse. This effect was a little jarring, because the text would jump immediately from its initial size to the new, larger size. Using animation, you can create a much smoother experience and increase the text size gradually over a short interval of time. And because each ListBoxItem can have its own animation, when you run your mouse up and down the list, you'll see several items start to grow and then shrink back again, creating an intriguing "fish-eye" effect. (A more extravagant fish-eye effect would enlarge and warp the item over which you're hovering. This is also possible in WPF using animated transforms, as you'll see later.)

Although it's not possible to capture this effect in a single image, Figure 21-3 shows a snapshot of this list after the mouse has moved rapidly over several items.

Figure 21-3. *Individual animations on each ListBoxItem*

You won't reconsider the entire template ListBoxItem example here, because it's built from many different pieces that style the ListBox, the ListBoxItem, and the various constituents of the ListBox (such as the scroll bar). The important piece is the style that changes the ListBoxItem template.

You can add the mouseover animation in two equivalent ways—by creating an event trigger that responds to the MouseEnter and MouseLeave events or by creating a property trigger that adds enter and exit actions when the IsMouseOver property changes. The following example uses the event trigger approach:

```
<Style TargetType="{x:Type ListBoxItem}">
  <Setter Property="Template">
    <Setter.Value>
      <ControlTemplate TargetType="{x:Type ListBoxItem}">
        <Border ... >
          <ContentPresenter />
        </Border>
<ControlTemplate.Triggers>
        <EventTrigger RoutedEvent="ListBoxItem.MouseEnter">
```

```
            <EventTrigger.Actions>
              <BeginStoryboard>
                <Storyboard>
                  <DoubleAnimation Storyboard.TargetProperty="FontSize"
                    To="20" Duration="0:0:1"></DoubleAnimation>
                </Storyboard>
              </BeginStoryboard>
            </EventTrigger.Actions>
          </EventTrigger>
          <EventTrigger RoutedEvent="ListBoxItem.MouseLeave">
            <EventTrigger.Actions>
              <BeginStoryboard>
                <Storyboard>
                  <DoubleAnimation Storyboard.TargetProperty="FontSize"
                    BeginTime="0:0:0.5" Duration="0:0:0.2"></DoubleAnimation>
                </Storyboard>
              </BeginStoryboard>
            </EventTrigger.Actions>
          </EventTrigger>

          <Trigger Property="IsMouseOver" Value="True">
            <Setter TargetName="Border" Property="BorderBrush" ... />
          </Trigger>
          <Trigger Property="IsSelected" Value="True">
            <Setter TargetName="Border" Property="Background" ... />
            <Setter TargetName="Border" Property="TextBlock.Foreground" ... />
          </Trigger>
        </ControlTemplate.Triggers>
      </ControlTemplate>
    </Setter.Value>
  </Setter>
</Style>
```

In this example, the ListBoxItem enlarges relatively slowly (over one second) and then decreases much more quickly (in 0.2 seconds). However, there is a 0.5-second delay before the shrinking animation begins.

Note that the shrinking animation leaves out the From and To properties. That way, it always shrinks the text from its current size to its original size, as described earlier in this chapter. If you move the mouse on and off a ListBoxItem, you'll get the result you expect—it appears as though the item simply continues expanding while the mouse is overtop and continues shrinking when the mouse is moved away.

■ Tip This example works well, but it's not the snappiest animation you'll see. Every time the size of a List-BoxItem changes, WPF must perform a layout pass to arrange the items in the ListBox. It's for reasons like these that animations often take place outside automatic layout containers and use the simpler (and more performant) Canvas instead.

Overlapping Animations

The storyboard gives you the ability to change the way you deal with animations that over-lap—in other words, when a second animation is applied to a property that is already being animated. You do this using the BeginStoryboard.HandoffBehavior property.

Ordinarily, when two animations overlap, the second animation overrides the first one immediately. This behavior is known as *snapshot-and-replace* (and represented by the SnapshotAndReplace value in the HandoffBehavior enumeration). When the second anima-tion starts, it takes a snapshot of the property as it currently is (based on the first animation), stops the animation, and replaces it with the new animation.

The only other HandoffBehavior option is Compose, which fused the second animation into the first animation's timeline. For example, consider a revised version of the ListBox example that uses HandoffBehavior.Compose when shrinking the button:

```
<EventTrigger RoutedEvent="ListBoxItem.MouseLeave">
  <EventTrigger.Actions>
    <BeginStoryboard HandoffBehavior="Compose">
      <Storyboard>
        <DoubleAnimation Storyboard.TargetProperty="FontSize"
          BeginTime="0:0:0.5" Duration="0:0:0.2"></DoubleAnimation>
      </Storyboard>
    </BeginStoryboard>
  </EventTrigger.Actions>
</EventTrigger>
```

Now, if you move the mouse onto a ListBoxItem and off it, you'll see a different behavior. When you move the mouse off the item, it will continue expanding, which will be clearly visi-ble until the second animation reaches its begin time delay of 0.5 seconds. Then, the second animation will shrink the button. Without the Compose behavior, the button would simply wait, fixed at its current size, for the 0.5-second time interval before the second animation kicks in.

Using a HandoffBehavior of compose requires more overhead. That's because the clock that's used to run the original animation won't be released when the second animation starts. Instead, it will stay alive until the ListBoxItem is garbage collected or a new animation is used on the same property.

Tip If performance becomes an issue, the WPF team recommends that you manually release the anima-tion clock for your animations as soon as they are complete (rather than waiting for the garbage collector to find them). To do this, you need to handle an event like Storyboard.Completed. Then, call BeginAnimation() on the element that has just finished its animation, supplying the appropriate property and a null reference in place of an animation.

Simultaneous Animations

The Storyboard class derives indirectly from TimelineGroup, which gives it the ability to hold more than one animation. Best of all, these animations are managed as one group—meaning they're started at the same time.

To see an example, consider the following storyboard. It starts two animations, one that acts on the Width property of a button and the other that acts on the Height property. Because the animations are grouped into one storyboard, they increment the button's dimensions in unison, which gives a more synchronized effect than simply calling BeginAnimation() multiple times in your code.

```
<EventTrigger RoutedEvent="Button.Click">
  <EventTrigger.Actions>
    <BeginStoryboard>
      <Storyboard>
        <DoubleAnimation Storyboard.TargetProperty="Width"
          To="300" Duration="0:0:5"></DoubleAnimation>
        <DoubleAnimation Storyboard.TargetProperty="Height"
          To="300" Duration="0:0:5"></DoubleAnimation>
      </Storyboard>
    </BeginStoryboard>
  </EventTrigger.Actions>
</EventTrigger>
```

In this example, both animations have the same duration, but this isn't a requirement. The only consideration with animations that end at different times is their FillBehavior. If an animation's FillBehavior property is set to HoldEnd, it holds the value until all the animations in the storyboard are completed. If the storyboard's FillBehavior property is HoldEnd, the final animated values are held indefinitely (until a new animation replaces this one or until you manually remove the animation).

It's at this point that the Timeline properties you learned about in Table 21-1 start to become particularly useful. For example, you can use SpeedRatio to make one animation in a storyboard run faster than the other. Or, you can use BeginTime to offset one animation relative to another so that it starts at a specific point.

■**Note** Because Storyboard derives from Timeline, you can use all the properties that were described in Table 21-1 to configure its speed, use acceleration or deceleration, introduce a delay time, and so on. These properties will affect all the contained animations, and they're cumulative. For example, if you set the Storyboard.SpeedRatio to 2 and the DoubleAnimation.SpeedRatio to 2, that animation will run four times faster than usual.

Controlling Playback

So far, you've been using one action in your event triggers—the BeginStoryboard action that launches an animation. However, you can use several other actions to control a storyboard once it's created. These actions, which derive from the ControllableStoryboardAction class, are listed in Table 21-2.

Table 21-2. *Action Classes for Controlling a Storyboard*

Name	Description
PauseStoryboard	Stops playback of an animation and keeps it at the current position.
ResumeStoryboard	Resumes playback of a paused animation.
StopStoryboard	Stops playback of an animation and resets the animation clock to the beginning.
SeekStoryboard	Jumps to a specific position in an animation's timeline. If animation is currently playing, it continues playback from the new position. If the animation is currently paused, it remains paused.
SetStoryboardSpeedRatio	Changes the SpeedRatio of the entire storyboard (rather than just one animation inside).
SkipStoryboardToFill	Moves the storyboard to the end of its timeline. Technically, this period is known as the *fill region*. For a standard animation, with FillBehavior set to HoldEnd, the animation continues to hold the final value.
RemoveStoryboard	Removes a storyboard, halting any in-progress animation and returning the property to its original, last-set value. This has the same effect as calling BeginAnimation() on the appropriate element with a null animation object.

■**Note** Stopping an animation is not equivalent to completing an animation (unless FillBehavior is set to Stop). That's because even when an animation reaches the end of its timeline, it continues to apply its final value. Similarly, when an animation is paused, it continues to apply the most recent intermediary value. However, when an animation is stopped, it no longer applies any value, and the property reverts to its preanimation value.

There's an undocumented stumbling block to using these actions. For them to work successfully, you must define all the triggers in one Triggers collection. If you place the BeginStoryboard action in a different trigger collection than the PauseStoryboard action, the PauseStoryboard action won't work. To see the design you need to use, it helps to consider an example.

For example, consider the window shown in Figure 21-4. It superimposes two Image elements in exactly the same position, using a grid. Initially, only the topmost image—which shows a day scene of a Toronto city landmark—is visible. But as the animation runs, it reduces the opacity from 1 to 0, eventually allowing the night scene to show through completely. The effect is as if the image is changing from day to night, like a sequence of time-lapse photography.

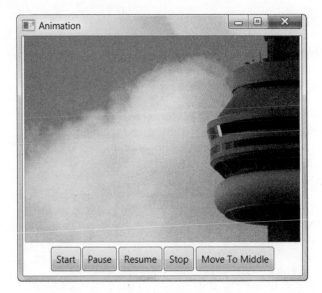

Figure 21-4. *A controllable animation*

Here's the markup that defines the Grid with its two images:

```
<Grid>
  <Image Source="night.jpg"></Image>
  <Image Source="day.jpg" Name="imgDay"></Image>
</Grid>
```

and here's the animation that fades from one to the other:

```
<DoubleAnimation
  Storyboard.TargetName="imgDay" Storyboard.TargetProperty="Opacity"
  From="1" To="0" Duration="0:0:10">
</DoubleAnimation>
```

To make this example more interesting, it includes several buttons at the bottom that allow you to control the playback of this animation. Using these buttons, you can perform the typical media player actions, such as pausing, resuming, and stopping. (You could add other buttons to change the speed ratio and seek out specific times.)

Here's the markup that defines these buttons:

```
<StackPanel Orientation="Horizontal" HorizontalAlignment="Center" Margin="5">
  <Button Name="cmdStart">Start</Button>
  <Button Name="cmdPause">Pause</Button>
  <Button Name="cmdResume">Resume</Button>
  <Button Name="cmdStop">Stop</Button>
  <Button Name="cmdMiddle">Move To Middle</Button>
</StackPanel>
```

Ordinarily, you might choose to place the event trigger in the Triggers collection of each individual button. However, as explained earlier, that doesn't work for animations. The easiest solution is to define all the event triggers in one place, such as the Triggers collection of a containing element, and wire them up using the EventTrigger.SourceName property. As long as the SourceName matches the Name property you've given the button, the trigger will be applied to the appropriate button.

In this example, you could use the Triggers collection of the StackPanel that holds the buttons. However, it's often easier to use the Triggers collection of the top-level element, which is the window in this case. That way, you can move your buttons to different places in your user interface without disabling their functionality.

```
<Window.Triggers>
  <EventTrigger SourceName="cmdStart" RoutedEvent="Button.Click">
    <BeginStoryboard Name="fadeStoryboardBegin">
      <Storyboard>
        <DoubleAnimation
          Storyboard.TargetName="imgDay" Storyboard.TargetProperty="Opacity"
          From="1" To="0" Duration="0:0:10">
        </DoubleAnimation>
      </Storyboard>
    </BeginStoryboard>
  </EventTrigger>

  <EventTrigger SourceName="cmdPause" RoutedEvent="Button.Click">
    <PauseStoryboard BeginStoryboardName="fadeStoryboardBegin"></PauseStoryboard>
  </EventTrigger>
  <EventTrigger SourceName="cmdResume" RoutedEvent="Button.Click">
    <ResumeStoryboard BeginStoryboardName="fadeStoryboardBegin"></ResumeStoryboard>
  </EventTrigger>
  <EventTrigger SourceName="cmdStop" RoutedEvent="Button.Click">
    <StopStoryboard BeginStoryboardName="fadeStoryboardBegin"></StopStoryboard>
  </EventTrigger>
  <EventTrigger SourceName="cmdMiddle" RoutedEvent="Button.Click">
    <SeekStoryboard BeginStoryboardName="fadeStoryboardBegin"
      Offset="0:0:5"></SeekStoryboard>
  </EventTrigger>
</Window.Triggers>
```

Notice that you must give a name to the BeginStoryboard action. (In this example, it's fadeStoryboardBegin). The other triggers specify this name in the BeginStoryboardName property to link up to the same storyboard.

You'll encounter one limitation when using storyboard actions. The properties they provide (such as SeekStoryboard.Offset and SetStoryboardSpeedRatio.SpeedRatio) are not dependency properties. That limits your ability to use data binding expressions. For example, you can't automatically read the Slider.Value property and apply it to the SetStoryboard-SpeedRatio.SpeedRatio action, because the SpeedRatio property doesn't accept a data binding expression. You might think you could code around this problem by using the SpeedRatio property of the Storyboard object, but this won't work. When the animation starts, the SpeedRatio value is read and used to create an animation clock. If you change it after that point, the animation continues at its normal pace.

If you want to adjust the speed or position dynamically, the only solution is to use code. The Storyboard class exposes methods that provide the same functionality as the triggers described in Table 21-2, including Begin(), Pause(), Resume(), Seek(), Stop(), SkipToFill(), SetSpeedRatio(), and Remove().

To access the Storyboard object, you need to make sure you set its Name property in the markup:

```
<Storyboard Name="fadeStoryboard">
```

■Note Don't confuse the name of the Storyboard object (which is required to use the storyboard in your code) with the name of the BeginStoryboard action (which is required to wire up other trigger actions that manipulate the storyboard). To prevent confusion, you may want to adopt a convention like adding the word *Begin* to the end of the BeginStoryboard name.

Now you simply need to write the appropriate event handler and use the methods of the Storyboard object. (Remember, simply changing storyboard properties such as SpeedRatio won't have any effect. They simply configure the settings that will be used when the animation starts.)

Here's an event handler that reacts when you drag the thumb on a Slider. It then takes the value of the slider (which ranges from 0 to 3) and uses it to apply a new speed ratio:

```
private void sldSpeed_ValueChanged(object sender, RoutedEventArgs e)
{
    fadeStoryboard.SetSpeedRatio(this, sldSpeed.Value);
}
```

Notice that the SetSpeedRatio() requires two arguments. The first argument is the top-level animation container (in this case, the current window). All the storyboard methods require this reference. The second argument is the new speed ratio.

THE WIPE EFFECT

The previous example provides a gradual transition between the two images you're using by varying the Opacity of the topmost image. Another common way to transition between images is to perform a "wipe" that unveils the new image overtop the existing one.

The trick to using this technique is to create an opacity mask for the topmost image. Here's an example:

```
<Image Source="day.jpg" Name="imgDay">
  <Image.OpacityMask>
    <LinearGradientBrush StartPoint="0,0" EndPoint="1,0">
      <GradientStop Offset="0" Color="Transparent" x:Name="transparentStop" />
      <GradientStop Offset="0" Color="Black" x:Name="visibleStop" />
    </LinearGradientBrush>
  </Image.OpacityMask>
</Image>
```

This opacity mask uses a gradient that defines two gradient stops, Black (where the image will be completely visible) and Transparent (where the image will be completely transparent). Initially, both stops are positioned at the left edge of the image. Because the visible stop is declared last, it takes precedence, and the image will be completely opaque. Notice that both stops are named so they can be easily accessed by your animation.

Next, you need to perform your animation on the offsets of the LinearGradientBrush. In this example, both offsets are moved from the left side to the right side, allowing the image underneath to appear. To make this example a bit fancier, the offsets don't occupy the same position while they move. Instead, the visible offset leads the way, followed by the transparent offset after a short delay of 0.2 seconds. This creates a blended fringe at the edge of the wipe while the animation is underway.

```
<Storyboard>
  <DoubleAnimation
    Storyboard.TargetName="visibleStop"
    Storyboard.TargetProperty="Offset"
    From="0" To="1.2" Duration="0:0:1.2" ></DoubleAnimation>
  <DoubleAnimation
    Storyboard.TargetName="transparentStop"
    Storyboard.TargetProperty="Offset" BeginTime="0:0:0.2"
    From="0" To="1" Duration="0:0:1" ></DoubleAnimation>
</Storyboard>
```

There's one odd detail here. The visible stop moves to 1.2 rather than simply 1, which denotes the right edge of the image. This ensures that both offsets move at the same speed, because the total distance each one must cover is proportional to the duration of its animation.

Wipes commonly work from left to right or top to bottom, but more creative effects are possible by using difference opacity masks. For example, you could use a DrawingBrush for your opacity mask and modify its geometry to let the content underneath show through in a tiled pattern. You'll see more examples that animate brushes later in this chapter.

Monitoring Progress

The animation player shown in Figure 21-4 still lacks one feature that's common in most media players—the ability to determine your current position. To make it a bit fancier, you can add some text that shows the time offset and a progress bar that provides a visual indication of how far you are in the animation. Figure 21-5 shows a revised animation player with both details (along with the Slider for controlling speed that was explained in the previous section).

Figure 21-5. *Displaying position and progress in an animation*

Adding these details is fairly straightforward. First you need a TextBlock element to show the time and a ProgressBar control to show the graphical bar. You might assume you could set the TextBlock value and the ProgressBar content using a data binding expression, but this isn't possible. That's because the only way to retrieve the information about the current animation clock from the Storyboard is to use methods such as GetCurrentTime() and GetCurrent-Progress(). There isn't any way to get the same information from properties.

The easiest solution is to react to one of the storyboard events listed in Table 21-3.

Table 21-3. *Storyboard Events*

Name	Description
Completed	The animation has reached its ending point.
CurrentGlobalSpeedInvalidated	The speed has changed, or the animation has been paused, resumed, stopped, or moved to a new position. This event also occurs when the animation clock reverses (at the end of a reversible animation) and when it accelerates or decelerates.

Continued

Table 21-3. *Continued*

Name	Description
CurrentStateInvalidated	The animation has started or ended.
CurrentTimeInvalidated	The animation clock has moved forward an increment, changing the animation. This event also occurs when the animation starts, stops, or ends.
RemoveRequested	The animation is being removed. The animated property will subsequently return to its original value.

In this case, the event you need is CurrentTimeInvalidated, which fires every time the animation clock moves forward. (Typically, this will be 60 times per second, but if your code takes more time to execute, you may miss clock ticks.)

When the CurrentTimeInvalidated event fires, the sender is a Clock object (from the System.Windows.Media.Animation namespace). The Clock object allows you to retrieve the current time as a TimeSpan and the current progress as a value from 0 to 1.

Here's the code that updates the label and the progress bar:

```
private void storyboard_CurrentTimeInvalidated(object sender, EventArgs e)
{
    Clock storyboardClock = (Clock)sender;

    if (storyboardClock.CurrentProgress == null)
    {
        lblTime.Text = "[[ stopped ]]";
        progressBar.Value = 0;
    }
    else
    {
        lblTime.Text = storyboardClock.CurrentTime.ToString();
        progressBar.Value = (double)storyboardClock.CurrentProgress;
    }
}
```

■**Tip** If you use the Clock.CurrentProgress property, you don't need to perform any calculation to determine the value for your progress bar. Instead, simply configure your progress bar with a minimum of 0 and a maximum of 1. That way, you can simply use the Clock.CurrentProgress to set the ProgressBar.Value, as in this example.

Desired Frame Rate

As you learned earlier in this chapter, WPF attempts to keep animations running at 60 frames per second. This ensures smooth, fluid animations from start to finish. Of course, WPF might not be able to deliver on its intentions. If you have multiple complex animations running at once and the CPU or video card can't keep up, the overall frame rate may drop (in the best-case scenario), or it may jump to catch up (in the worst-case scenario).

Although it's rare to increase the frame rate, you may choose to *decrease* the frame rate. You might take this step for one of two reasons:

- Your animation looks good at a lower frame rate, so you don't want to waste the extra CPU cycles.

- Your application is running on a less powerful CPU or video card, and you know your complete animation won't be rendered as well at a high frame rate as it would at a lower rate.

Note Developers sometimes assume that WPF includes code that scales the frame rate down based on the video card hardware. It does not. Instead, WPF always attempts 60 frames per second, unless you tell it otherwise.

Adjusting the frame rate is easy. You simply use the Timeline.DesiredFrameRate attached property on the storyboard that contains your animations. Here's an example that halves the frame rate:

```
<Storyboard Timeline.DesiredFrameRate="30">
```

Figure 21-6 shows a simple test application that animates a circle so that it arcs across a Canvas.

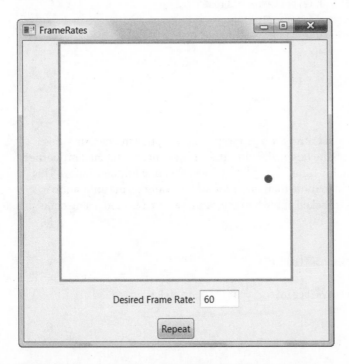

Figure 21-6. *Testing frame rates with a simple animation*

The application begins with an Ellipse object in a Canvas. The Canvas.ClipToBounds property is set to true so the edges of the circle won't leak over the edge of the Canvas into the rest of the window.

```
<Canvas ClipToBounds="True">
  <Ellipse Name="ellipse" Fill="Red" Width="10" Height="10"></Ellipse>
</Canvas>
```

To move the circle across the Canvas, two animations take place at once—one that updates the Canvas.Left property (moving it from left to right) and one that changes the Canvas.Top property (causing it to rise up and then fall back down). The Canvas.Top animation is reversible—once the circle reaches its highest point, it falls back down. The Canvas.Left animation is not, but it takes twice as long, so both animations move the circle simultaneously. The final trick is using the DecelerationRatio property on the Canvas.Top animation. That way, the circle rises more slowly as it reaches the summit, which creates a more realistic effect.

Here's the complete markup for the animation:

```
<Window.Resources>
  <BeginStoryboard x:Key="beginStoryboard">
    <Storyboard Timeline.DesiredFrameRate=
     "{Binding ElementName=txtFrameRate,Path=Text}">
      <DoubleAnimation Storyboard.TargetName="ellipse"
       Storyboard.TargetProperty="(Canvas.Left)"
       From="0" To="300" Duration="0:0:5">
      </DoubleAnimation>
      <DoubleAnimation Storyboard.TargetName="ellipse"
       Storyboard.TargetProperty="(Canvas.Top)"
       From="300" To="0" AutoReverse="True" Duration="0:0:2.5"
       DecelerationRatio="1">
      </DoubleAnimation>
    </Storyboard>
  </BeginStoryboard>
</Window.Resources>
```

Notice that the Canvas.Left and Canvas.Top properties are wrapped in brackets—this indicates that they aren't found on the target element (the ellipse) but are attached properties. You'll also see that the animation is defined in the Resources collection for the window. This allows the animation to be started in more than one way. In this example, the animation is started when the Repeat button is clicked and when the window is first loaded, using code like this:

```
<Window.Triggers>
  <EventTrigger RoutedEvent="Window.Loaded">
    <EventTrigger.Actions>
      <StaticResource ResourceKey="beginStoryboard"></StaticResource>
    </EventTrigger.Actions>
  </EventTrigger>
</Window.Triggers>
```

The real purpose of this example is to try different frame rates. To see the effect of a particularly frame rate, you simply need to type the appropriate number in the text box and click Repeat. The animation is then triggered with the new frame rate (which it picks up through a data binding expression), and you can watch the results. At lower frame rates, the ellipse won't appear to move evenly—instead, it will hop across the Canvas.

You can also adjust the Timeline.DesiredFrame property in code. For example, you may want to read the static RenderCapability.Tier to determine the level of video card support.

■**Note** With a little bit of work, you can also create a helper class that lets you put the same logic into work in your XAML markup. You'll find one example at `http://blogs.msdn.com/henryh/archive/2006/08/23/719568.aspx`, which demonstrates how you can lower the frame rate declaratively based on the tier.

Animation Types Revisited

You now know the fundamentals of WPF's property animation system—how animations are defined, how they're connected to elements, and how you can control playback with a storyboard. Now is a good time to take a step back and take a closer look at the animation classes for different data types, and consider how you can use them to achieve the effect you want.

The first challenge in creating any animation is choosing the right property to animate. Making the leap between the result you want (for example, an element moving across the window) and the property you need to use (in this case, Canvas.Left and Canvas.Top) isn't always intuitive. Here are a few guidelines:

- If you want to use an animation to make an element appear or disappear, don't use the Visibility property (which allows you to switch only between completely visible or completely invisible). Instead, use the Opacity to fade it in or out.

- If you want to animate the position of an element, consider using a Canvas. It provides the most direct properties (Canvas.Left and Canvas.Top) and requires the least overhead. Alternatively, you can get similar effects in other layout containers by animating properties such as Margin and Padding using the ThicknessAnimation class. You can also animate the MinWidth or MinHeight or a column or row in a Grid.

■**Tip** Many animation effects are designed to progressively "reveal" an element. Common options include making an element fade into visibility, slide into view, or expand from a tiny point. However, there are many alternatives. For example, you could blur out an element using the BlurBitmapEffect described in Chapter 13 and animate the Radius property to reduce the blur and allow the element to come gradually into focus.

- The most common properties to animate are transforms. You can use them to move or flip an element (TranslateTransform), rotate it (RotateTransform), resize or stretch it (ScaleTransform), and more. Used carefully, they can sometimes allow you to avoid hard-coding sizes and positions in your animation.

- One good way to change the surface of an element through an animation is to modify the properties of the brush. You can use a ColorAnimation to change the color or another animation object to transform a property of a more complex brush, like the offset in a gradient.

The following examples demonstrate how to animate transforms and brushes and how to use a few more animation types. You'll also learn how to create multisegmented animations with key frames, path-based animations, and frame-based animations.

Animating Transforms

Transforms offer one of the most powerful ways to customize an element. When you use transforms, you don't simply change the bounds of an element. Instead, the entire visual appearance of the element is moved, flipped, skewed, stretched, enlarged, shrunk, or rotated. For example, if you animate the size of a button using a ScaleTransform, the entire button is resized, including its border and its inner content. The effect is much more impressive than if you animate its Width and Height or the FontSize property that affects its text.

As you learned in Chapter 13, every element has the ability to use transform in two different ways: the RenderTransform property and the LayoutTransform property. RenderTransform is more efficient, because it's applied after the layout pass and used to transform the final rendered output. LayoutTransform is applied before the layout pass, and as a result, other controls are rearranged to fit. Changing the LayoutTransform property triggers a new layout operation (unless you're using your element in a Canvas, in which case RenderTransform and LayoutTransform are equivalent).

To use a transform in animation, the first step is to define the transform. (An animation can change an existing transform but not create a new one.) For example, imagine you want to allow a button to rotate. This requires the RotateTransform:

```
<Button>
  <Button.Content>A Button</Button.Content>
  <RenderTransform>
    <RotateTransform></RotateTransform>
  </RenderTransform>
</Button>
```

Now here's an event trigger that makes the button rotate when the mouse moves over it. It uses the target property RenderTransform.Angle—in other words, it reads the button's RenderTransform property and modifies the Angle property of the RotateTransform object that's defined there. The fact that the RenderTransform property can hold a variety of different transform objects, each with different properties, doesn't cause a problem. As long as you're using a transform that has an angle property, this trigger will work.

```
<EventTrigger RoutedEvent="Button.MouseEnter">
  <EventTrigger.Actions>
    <BeginStoryboard>
      <Storyboard>
        <DoubleAnimation Storyboard.TargetProperty="RenderTransform.Angle"
          To="360" Duration="0:0:0.8" RepeatBehavior="Forever"></DoubleAnimation>
      </Storyboard>
```

```
      </BeginStoryboard>
    </EventTrigger.Actions>
  </EventTrigger>
```

The button rotates one revolution every 0.8 seconds and continues rotating perpetually. While the mouse is rotating, it's still completely usable—for example, you can click it and handle the Click event.

To make sure the button rotates around its center point (not the top-left corner), you need to set the RenderTransformOrigin property as shown here:

```
<Button RenderTransformOrigin="0.5,0.5">
```

Remember, the RenderTransformOrigin property uses relative units from 0 to 1, so 0.5 represents a midpoint.

To stop the rotation, you can use a second trigger that responds to the MouseLeave event. At this point, you could remove the storyboard that performs the rotation, but this causes the button to jump back to its original orientation in one step. A better approach is to start a second animation that replaces the first. This animation leaves out the To and From properties, which means it seamlessly rotates the button back to its original orientation in a snappy 0.2 seconds:

```
<EventTrigger RoutedEvent="Button.MouseLeave">
  <EventTrigger.Actions>
    <BeginStoryboard>
      <Storyboard>
        <DoubleAnimation Storyboard.TargetProperty="LayoutTransform.Angle"
          Duration="0:0:0.2"></DoubleAnimation>
      </Storyboard>
    </BeginStoryboard>
  </EventTrigger.Actions>
 </EventTrigger>
```

To create your rotating button, you'll need to add both these triggers to the Button.Triggers collection. Or, you could pull them (and the transform) into a style and apply that style to as many buttons as you want. For example, here's the markup for the window full of "rotatable" buttons shown in Figure 21-7:

```
<Window x:Class="Animation.RotateButton" ... >
  <Window.Resources>
    <Style TargetType="{x:Type Button}">
      <Setter Property="HorizontalAlignment" Value="Center"></Setter>
      <Setter Property="RenderTransformOrigin" Value="0.5,0.5"></Setter>
      <Setter Property="Padding" Value="20,15"></Setter>
      <Setter Property="Margin" Value="2"></Setter>
      <Setter Property="LayoutTransform">
        <Setter.Value>
          <RotateTransform></RotateTransform>
        </Setter.Value>
      </Setter>
      <Style.Triggers>
```

```
        <EventTrigger RoutedEvent="Button.MouseEnter">
          ...
        </EventTrigger>
        <EventTrigger RoutedEvent="Button.MouseLeave">
          ...
        </EventTrigger>
      </Style.Triggers>
    </Style>

  </Window.Resources>
  <StackPanel Margin="5" Button.Click="cmd_Clicked">
    <Button>One</Button>
    <Button>Two</Button>
    <Button>Three</Button>
    <Button>Four</Button>
    <TextBlock Name="lbl" Margin="5"></TextBlock>
  </StackPanel>
</Window>
```

When any button is clicked, a message is displayed in the TextBlock.

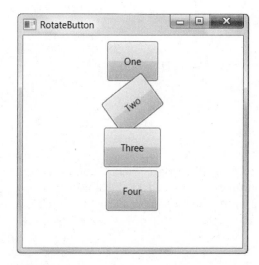

Figure 21-7. *Using a render transform*

This example also gives you a great chance to consider the difference between the RenderTransform and the LayoutTransform. If you modify the code to use a LayoutTransform, you'll see that the other buttons are pushed out of the way as a button spins (see Figure 21-8). For example, if the topmost button turns, the buttons underneath bounce up and down to avoid it.

Of course, to get a sense of how the buttons "feel," it's worth trying this example with the downloadable code.

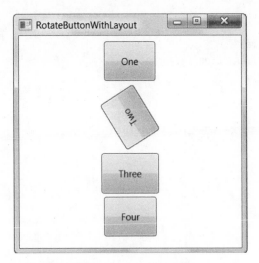

Figure 21-8. *Using a layout transform*

Animating Multiple Transforms

You can easily use transforms in combination. In fact, it's easy—you simply need to use the TransformGroup to set the LayoutTransform or RenderTransform property. You can nest as many transforms as you need inside the TransformGroup.

Figure 21-9 shows an interesting effect that was created using two transforms. A document window begins as a small thumbnail in the top-left corner of the window. When the window appears, this content rotates, expands, and fades into view rapidly. This is conceptually similar to the effect that Windows uses when you maximize a window. In WPF, you can use this trick with any element using transforms.

To create this effect, two transforms are defined in a TransformGroup and used to set the RenderTransform property of a Border object that contains all the content.

```
<Border.RenderTransform>
  <TransformGroup>
    <ScaleTransform></ScaleTransform>
      <RotateTransform></RotateTransform>
    </TransformGroup>
</Border.RenderTransform>
```

Your animation can interact with both of these transform objects by specifying a numeric offset (0 for the ScaleTransform that appears first and 1 for the RotateTransform that's next). For example, here's the animation that enlarges the content:

```
<DoubleAnimation Storyboard.TargetName="element"
  Storyboard.TargetProperty="RenderTransform.Children[0].ScaleX"
  From="0" To="1" Duration="0:0:2" AccelerationRatio="1">
</DoubleAnimation>
<DoubleAnimation Storyboard.TargetName="element"
  Storyboard.TargetProperty="RenderTransform.Children[0].ScaleY"
  From="0" To="1" Duration="0:0:2" AccelerationRatio="1">
</DoubleAnimation>
```

and here's the animation in the same storyboard that rotates it:

```
<DoubleAnimation Storyboard.TargetName="element"
  Storyboard.TargetProperty="RenderTransform.Children[1].Angle"
  From="70" To="0" Duration="0:0:2" >
</DoubleAnimation>
```

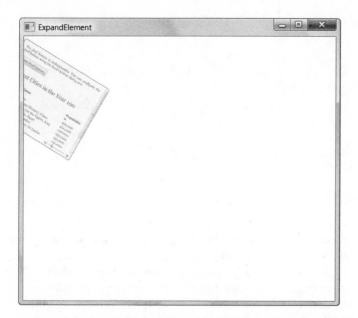

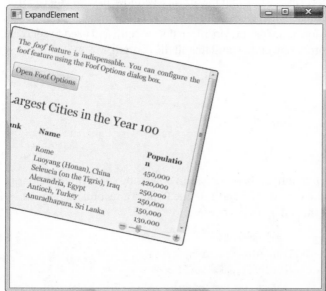

Figure 21-9. *Content that "jumps" into view*

The animation is slightly more involved than shown here. For example, there's an animation that increases the Opacity property at the same time, and when the Border reaches full size, it briefly "bounces" back, creating a more natural feel. Creating the timeline for this animation and tweaking the various animation object properties takes time—ideally, you'll perform tasks like this using a design tool such as Expression Blend rather than code them by hand. An even better scenario would be if a third-party developer grouped this logic into a single custom animation that you could then reuse and apply to your objects as needed. (As it currently stands, you could reuse this animation by storing the Storyboard as an application-level resource.)

This effect is surprisingly practical. For example, you could use it to draw attention to new content—such as a file that the user has just opened. The possible variations are endless. For example, a retail company could create a product catalog that slides a panel with product details or rolls a product image into view when you hover over the corresponding product name.

Animating Brushes

Animating brushes is another common technique in WPF animations, and it's just as easy as animating transforms. Once again, the technique is to dig into the particular subproperty you want to change, using the appropriate animation type.

Figure 21-10 shows an example that tweaks a RadialGradientBrush. As the animation runs, the center point of the radial gradient drifts along the ellipse, giving it a three-dimensional effect. At the same time, the outer color of the gradient changes from blue to black.

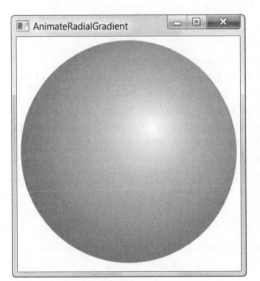 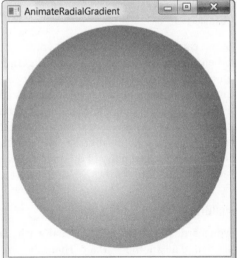

Figure 21-10. *Altering a radial gradient*

To perform this animation, you need to use two animation types that you haven't considered yet. ColorAnimation blends gradually between two colors, creating a subtle color-shift effect. PointAnimation allows you to move a point from one location to another. (It's essentially the same as if you modified both the X coordinate and the Y coordinate using a separate

DoubleAnimation, with linear interpolation.) You can use a PointAnimation to deform a figure that you've constructed out of points or to change the location of the radial gradient's center point, as in this example.

Here's the markup that defines the ellipse and its brush:

```
<Ellipse Name="ellipse" Margin="5" Grid.Row="1" Stretch="Uniform">
  <Ellipse.Fill>
    <RadialGradientBrush
     RadiusX="1" RadiusY="1" GradientOrigin="0.7,0.3">
        <GradientStop Color="White" Offset="0"></GradientStop>
        <GradientStop Color="Blue" Offset="1"></GradientStop>
    </RadialGradientBrush>
  </Ellipse.Fill>
</Ellipse>
```

and here are the two animations that move the center point and change the second color:

```
<PointAnimation Storyboard.TargetName="ellipse"
 Storyboard.TargetProperty="Fill.GradientOrigin"
 From="0.7,0.3" To="0.3,0.7" Duration="0:0:10" AutoReverse="True"
 RepeatBehavior="Forever">
</PointAnimation>
<ColorAnimation Storyboard.TargetName="ellipse"
 Storyboard.TargetProperty="Fill.GradientStops[1].Color"
 To="Black" Duration="0:0:10" AutoReverse="True"
 RepeatBehavior="Forever">
</ColorAnimation>
```

You can create a huge range of hypnotic effects by varying the colors and offsets in Linear-GradientBrush and RadialGradientBrush. And if that's not enough, gradient brushes also have their own RelativeTransform property that you can use to rotate, scale, stretch, and skew them. The WPF team has a fun tool called Gradient Obsession for building gradient-based animations. You can find it (and the source code) at http://wpf.netfx3.com/files/folders/designer/entry7718.aspx. For some additional ideas, check out the animation examples Charles Petzold provides at http://www.charlespetzold.com/blog/2006/07/230620.html, which change the geometry of different DrawingBrush objects, creating tiled patterns that morph into different shapes.

VisualBrush

As you learned in Chapter 13, a VisualBrush allows you to take the appearance of any element and use it to fill another surface. That other surface can be anything from an ordinary rectangle to letters of text.

Figure 21-11 shows a basic example. On top sits a real, live button. Underneath, a VisualBrush is used to fill a rectangle with a picture of the button that stretches and rotates under the effect of various transforms.

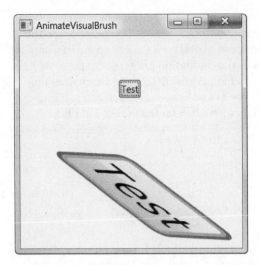

Figure 21-11. *Animating an element that's filled with a VisualBrush*

The VisualBrush also opens up some interesting possibilities for animation. For example, instead of animating the live, real element, you can animate a simple rectangle that has the same fill.

To understand how this works, consider the example shown earlier in Figure 21-9, which pops an element into view. While this animation is underway, the animated element is treated the same as any other WPF element, which means it's possible to click the button inside or scroll through the content with the keyboard (if you're fast enough). In some situations, this could cause confusion. In other situations, it might result in worse performance because of the extra overhead required to transform input (like mouse clicks) and pass it along to the original element.

Replacing this effect with a VisualBrush is easy. First you need to create another element that fills itself using a VisualBrush. That VisualBrush must draw its visual from the element you want to animate (which, in this example, is the border named element).

```
<Rectangle Name="rectangle">
  <Rectangle.Fill>
    <VisualBrush Visual="{Binding ElementName=element}">
    </VisualBrush>
  </Rectangle.Fill>
  <Rectangle.RenderTransform>
    <TransformGroup>
      <ScaleTransform></ScaleTransform>
      <RotateTransform></RotateTransform>
    </TransformGroup>
  </Rectangle.RenderTransform>
</Rectangle>
```

To place the rectangle into the same position as the original element, you can place them both into the same cell of a Grid. The cell is sized to fit original element (the border), and the rectangle is stretched along to match. Another option is to overlay a Canvas on top of your real application layout container. (You could then bind your animation properties to the Actual-Width and ActualHeight properties of the real element underneath to make sure it lines up.)

Once you've added the rectangle, you simply need to adjust your animations to animate its transforms. The final step is to hide the rectangle when the animations are complete:

```
private void storyboardCompleted(object sender, EventArgs e)
{
    rectangle.Visibility = Visibility.Collapsed;
}
```

Key Frame Animation

All the animations you've seen so far have used linear interpolation to move from a starting point to an ending point. But what if you need to create an animation that has multiple segments and moves less regularly? For example, you might want to create an animation that slides an element into view quickly and then slowly moves it the rest of the way into place. You could achieve this effect by creating a sequence of two animations and using the BeginTime property to start the second animation after the first one. However, there's an easier approach—you can use a key frame animation.

A *key frame animation* is an animation that's made up of many short segments. Each segment represents an initial, final, or intermediary value in the animation. When you run the animation, it moves smoothly from one value to another.

For example, consider the Point animation that allowed you to move the center point of a RadialGradientBrush from one spot to another:

```
<PointAnimation Storyboard.TargetName="ellipse"
 Storyboard.TargetProperty="Fill.GradientOrigin"
 From="0.7,0.3" To="0.3,0.7" Duration="0:0:10" AutoReverse="True"
 RepeatBehavior="Forever">
</PointAnimation>
```

You can replace this PointAnimation object with an equivalent PointAnimationUsing-KeyFrames object, as shown here:

```
<PointAnimationUsingKeyFrames Storyboard.TargetName="ellipse"
 Storyboard.TargetProperty="Fill.GradientOrigin"
 AutoReverse="True" RepeatBehavior="Forever" >
  <LinearPointKeyFrame Value="0.7,0.3" KeyTime="0:0:0"></LinearPointKeyFrame>
  <LinearPointKeyFrame Value="0.3,0.7" KeyTime="0:0:10"></LinearPointKeyFrame>
</PointAnimationUsingKeyFrames>
```

This animation includes two key frames. The first sets the Point value when the animation first starts. (If you want to use the current value that's set in the RadialGradientBrush, you can leave out this key frame.) The second key frame defines the end value, which is reached after ten seconds. The PointAnimationUsingKeyFrames object performs linear interpolation to

move smoothly from the first key frame value to the second, just as the PointAnimation does
with the From and To values.

■Note Every key frame animation uses its own key frame animation object (like LinearPointKeyFrame).
For the most point, these classes are the same—they include a Value property that stores the target value
and a KeyTime property that indicates when the frame reaches the target value. The only difference is the
data type of the Value property. In a LinearPointKeyFrame it's a Point, in a DoubleKeyFrame it's a double, and
so on.

You can create a more interesting example using a series of key frames. The following animation walks the center point through a series of positions that are reached at different times.
The speed that the center point moves will change depending on how long the duration is
between key frames and how much distance needs to be covered.

```
<PointAnimationUsingKeyFrames Storyboard.TargetName="ellipse"
 Storyboard.TargetProperty="Fill.GradientOrigin"
 RepeatBehavior="Forever" >
  <LinearPointKeyFrame Value="0.7,0.3" KeyTime="0:0:0"></LinearPointKeyFrame>
  <LinearPointKeyFrame Value="0.3,0.7" KeyTime="0:0:5"></LinearPointKeyFrame>
  <LinearPointKeyFrame Value="0.5,0.9" KeyTime="0:0:8"></LinearPointKeyFrame>
  <LinearPointKeyFrame Value="0.9,0.6" KeyTime="0:0:10"></LinearPointKeyFrame>
  <LinearPointKeyFrame Value="0.8,0.2" KeyTime="0:0:12"></LinearPointKeyFrame>
  <LinearPointKeyFrame Value="0.7,0.3" KeyTime="0:0:14"></LinearPointKeyFrame>
</PointAnimationUsingKeyFrames>
```

This animation isn't reversible, but it does repeat. To make sure there's no jump between
the final value of one iteration and the starting value of the next iteration, the animation ends
at the same center point that it began.

Chapter 23 shows another key frame example. It uses a Point3DAnimationUsingKeyFrames
animation to move the camera through a 3D scene and a Vector3DAnimationUsingKeyFrames
to rotate the camera at the same time.

■Note Using a key frame animation isn't quite as powerful as using a sequence of multiple animations.
The most important difference is that you can't apply different AccelerationRatio and DecelerationRatio
values to each key frame. Instead, you can apply only a single value to the entire animation.

Discrete Key Frame Animations

The key frame animation you saw in the previous example uses *linear* key frames. As a result,
it transitions smoothly between the key frame values. Another option is to use *discrete* key
frames. In this case, no interpolation is performed. When the key time is reached, the property
changes abruptly to the new value.

Linear key frame classes are named in the form Linear*DataType*KeyFrame. Discrete key frame classes are named in the form Discrete*DataType*KeyFrame. Here's a revised version of the RadialGradientBrush example that uses discrete key frames:

```
<PointAnimationUsingKeyFrames Storyboard.TargetName="ellipse"
 Storyboard.TargetProperty="Fill.GradientOrigin"
 RepeatBehavior="Forever" >
  <DiscretePointKeyFrame Value="0.7,0.3" KeyTime="0:0:0"></DiscretePointKeyFrame>
  <DiscretePointKeyFrame Value="0.3,0.7" KeyTime="0:0:5"></DiscretePointKeyFrame>
  <DiscretePointKeyFrame Value="0.5,0.9" KeyTime="0:0:8"></DiscretePointKeyFrame>
  <DiscretePointKeyFrame Value="0.9,0.6" KeyTime="0:0:10"></DiscretePointKeyFrame>
  <DiscretePointKeyFrame Value="0.8,0.2" KeyTime="0:0:12"></DiscretePointKeyFrame>
  <DiscretePointKeyFrame Value="0.7,0.3" KeyTime="0:0:14"></DiscretePointKeyFrame>
</PointAnimationUsingKeyFrames>
```

When you run this animation, the center point will jump from one position to the next at the appropriate time. It's a dramatic (but jerky) effect.

All key frame animation classes support discrete key frames, but only some support linear key frames. It all depends on the data type. The data types that support linear key frames are the same ones that support linear interpolation and provide a *DataType*Animation class. Examples include Point, Color, and double. Data types that don't support linear interpolation include string and object. You'll see an example in Chapter 22 that uses the StringAnimation-UsingKeyFrames class to display different pieces of text as an animation progresses.

■**Tip** You can combine both types of key frame—linear and discrete—in the same key frame animation.

Spline Key Frame Animations

There's one more type of key frame: a *spline* key frame. Every class that supports linear key frames also supports spline key frames, and they're named in the form Spline*DataType*-KeyFrame.

Like linear key frames, spline key frames use interpolation to move smoothly from one key value to another. The difference is that every spline key frame sports a KeySpline property. Using the KeySpline property, you define a cubic Bézier curve that influences the way interpolation is performed. Although it's tricky to get the effect you want (at least without an advanced design tool to help you), this technique gives the ability to create more seamless acceleration and deceleration and more lifelike motion.

As you may remember from Chapter 14, a Bézier curve is defined by a start point, an end point, and two control points. In the case of a key spline, the start point is always (0,0), and the end point is always (1,1). You simply supply the two control points. The curve that you create describes the relationship between time (in the X axis) and the animated value (in the Y axis).

Here's an example that demonstrates a key spline animation by comparing the motion of two ellipses across a Canvas. The first ellipse uses a DoubleAnimation to move slowly and evenly across the window. The second ellipse uses a DoubleAnimationUsingKeyFrames with two SplineDoubleKeyFrame objects. It reaches the destination at the same times (after ten seconds), but it accelerates and decelerates during its travel, pulling ahead and dropping behind the other ellipse.

```
<DoubleAnimation Storyboard.TargetName="ellipse1"
 Storyboard.TargetProperty="(Canvas.Left)"
 To="500" Duration="0:0:10">
</DoubleAnimation>

<DoubleAnimationUsingKeyFrames Storyboard.TargetName="ellipse2"
 Storyboard.TargetProperty="(Canvas.Left)" >
  <SplineDoubleKeyFrame KeyTime="0:0:5" Value="250"
   KeySpline="0.25,0 0.5,0.7"></SplineDoubleKeyFrame>
  <SplineDoubleKeyFrame KeyTime="0:0:10" Value="500"
   KeySpline="0.25,0.8 0.2,0.4"></SplineDoubleKeyFrame>
</DoubleAnimationUsingKeyFrames>
```

The fastest acceleration occurs shortly after the five-second mark, when the second SplineDoubleKeyFrame kicks in. Its first control point matches a relatively large Y axis value, which represents the animation progress (0.8) against a correspondingly smaller X axis value, which represents the time. As a result, the ellipse increases its speed over a small distance, before slowing down again.

Figure 21-12 shows a graphical depiction of the two curves that control the movement of the ellipse. To interpret these curves, remember that they chart the progress of the animation from top to bottom. Looking at the first curve, you can see that it follows a fairly even progress downward, with a short pause at the beginning and a gradual leveling off at the end. However, the second curve plummets downward quite quickly, achieving the bulk of its progress, and then levels off for the remainder of the animation.

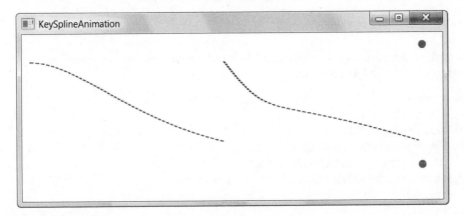

Figure 21-12. *Charting the progress of a key spline animation*

Path-Based Animation

A path-based animation uses a PathGeometry object to set a property. Although a path-based animation can, in principle, be used to modify any property that has the right data type, it's most useful when animating position-related properties. In fact, the path-based animation classes are primarily intended to help you move a visual object along a path.

As you learned in Chapter 14, a PathGeometry object describes a figure that can include lines, arcs, and curves. Figure 21-13 shows an example with a PathGeometry object that consists of two arcs and a straight line segment that joins the last defined point to the starting point. This creates a closed routed over which a small vector image travels at a constant rate.

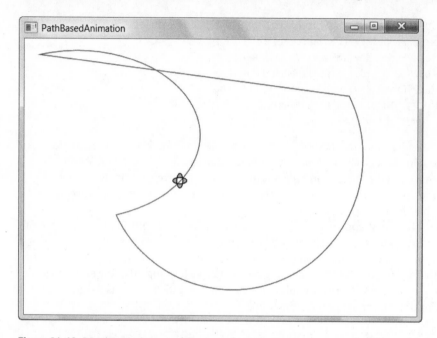

Figure 21-13. *Moving an image along a path*

Creating this example is easy. The first step is to build the path you want to use. In this example, the path is defined as a resource:

```
<Window.Resources>
  <PathGeometry x:Key="path">
    <PathFigure IsClosed="True">
      <ArcSegment Point="100,200" Size="15,10"
       SweepDirection="Clockwise"></ArcSegment>
      <ArcSegment Point="400,50" Size="5,5" ></ArcSegment>
    </PathFigure>
  </PathGeometry>
</Window.Resources>
```

Although it's not necessary, this example displays the path. That way, you can clearly see that the image follows the route you've defined. To show the path, you simply need to add a Path element that uses the geometry you've defined:

```
<Path Stroke="Red" StrokeThickness="1" Data="{StaticResource path}"
 Canvas.Top="10" Canvas.Left="10">
</Path>
```

The Path element is placed in a Canvas, along with the Image element that you want to move around the path:

```
<Image Name="image">
  <Image.Source>
    <DrawingImage>
      <DrawingImage.Drawing>
        <GeometryDrawing Brush="LightSteelBlue">
          <GeometryDrawing.Geometry>
            <GeometryGroup>
              <EllipseGeometry Center="10,10" RadiusX="9" RadiusY="4" />
              <EllipseGeometry Center="10,10" RadiusX="4" RadiusY="9" />
            </GeometryGroup>
          </GeometryDrawing.Geometry>
          <GeometryDrawing.Pen>
            <Pen Thickness="1" Brush="Black" />
          </GeometryDrawing.Pen>
        </GeometryDrawing>
      </DrawingImage.Drawing>
    </DrawingImage>
  </Image.Source>
</Image>
```

The final step is to create the animations that move the image. To move the image, you need to adjust the Canvas.Left and Canvas.Top properties. The DoubleAnimationUsingPath does the trick, but you'll need two—one to work on the Canvas.Left property and one to deal with the Canvas.Top property. Here's the complete storyboard:

```
<Storyboard>
  <DoubleAnimationUsingPath Storyboard.TargetName="image"
    Storyboard.TargetProperty="(Canvas.Left)"
    PathGeometry="{StaticResource path}"
    Duration="0:0:5" RepeatBehavior="Forever" Source="X" />
  <DoubleAnimationUsingPath Storyboard.TargetName="image"
    Storyboard.TargetProperty="(Canvas.Top)"
    PathGeometry="{StaticResource path}"
    Duration="0:0:5" RepeatBehavior="Forever" Source="Y" />
</Storyboard>
```

As you can see, when creating a path-based animation, you don't supply starting and ending values. Instead, you indicate the PathGeometry that you want to use with the Path-Geometry property. Some path-based animation classes, such as PointAnimationUsingPath, apply both the X and Y components to the destination property. The DoubleAnimationUsing-Path class doesn't have this ability, because it sets just one double value. As a result, you also need to set the Source property to X or Y to indicate whether you're using the X coordinate or the Y coordinate from the path.

Although a path-based animation can use a path that includes a Bézier curve, it's quite a bit different from the key spline animations you learned about in the previous section. In a key spline animation, the Bézier curve describes the relationship between animation progress and time, allowing you to create an animation that changes speed. But in a path-based animation, the collection of lines and curves that constitutes the path determines the *values* that will be used for the animated property.

■Note A path-based animation always runs at a continuous speed. WPF considers the total length of the path and the duration you've specified to determine that speed.

Frame-Based Animation

Along with the property-based animation system, WPF provides a way to create frame-based animation using nothing but code. All you need to do is respond to the static Composition-Target.Rendering event, which is fired to get the content for each frame. This is a far lower-level approach, which you won't want to tackle unless you're sure the standard property-based animation model won't work for your scenario (for example, if you're building a simple side-scrolling game, creating physics-based animations, or modeling particle effects such as fire, snow, and bubbles).

The basic technique for building a frame-based animation is easy. You simply need to attach an event handler to the static CompositionTarget.Rendering event. Once you do, WPF will begin calling this event handler continuously. (As long as your rendering code executes quickly enough, WPF will call it 60 times each second.) In the rendering event handler, it's up to you to create or adjust the elements in the window accordingly. In other words, you need to manage all the work yourself. When the animation has ended, detach the event handler.

Figure 21-14 shows a straightforward example. Here, a random number of circles fall from the top of a Canvas to the bottom. They fall at different speeds (based on a random starting velocity), but they accelerate downward at the same rate. The animation ends when all the circles reach the bottom.

In this example, each falling circle is represented by an Ellipse element. A custom class named EllipseInfo keeps a reference to the ellipse and tracks the details that are important for the physics model. In this case, there's only one piece of information—the velocity at which the ellipse is moving along the X axis. (You could easily extend this class to include a velocity along the Y axis, additional acceleration information, and so on.)

```
public class EllipseInfo
{
    private Ellipse ellipse;
    public Ellipse Ellipse
    {
        get { return ellipse; }
        set { ellipse = value; }
    }

    private double velocityY;
    public double VelocityY
    {
        get { return velocityY; }
```

```
        set { velocityY = value; }
    }

    public EllipseInfo(Ellipse ellipse, double velocityY)
    {
        VelocityY = velocityY;
        Ellipse = ellipse;
    }
}
```

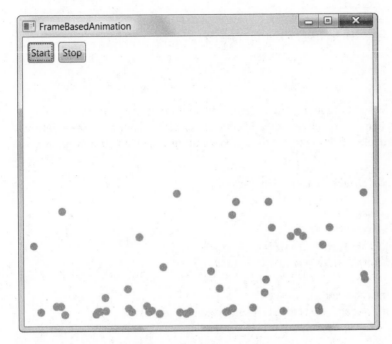

Figure 21-14. *A frame-based animation of falling circles*

The application keeps track of the EllipseInfo object for each ellipse using a collection. There are several more window-level fields, which record various details that are used when calculating the fall of the ellipse. You could easily make these details configurable.

```
private List<EllipseInfo> ellipses = new List<EllipseInfo>();

private double accelerationY = 0.1;
private int minStartingSpeed = 1;
private int maxStartingSpeed = 50;
private double speedRatio = 0.1;
private int minEllipses = 20;
private int maxEllipses = 100;
private int ellipseRadius = 10;
```

When a button is clicked, the collection is cleared, and the event handler is attached to the CompositionTarget.Rendering event:

```
private bool rendering = false;

private void cmdStart_Clicked(object sender, RoutedEventArgs e)
{
    if (!rendering)
    {
        ellipses.Clear();
        canvas.Children.Clear();

        CompositionTarget.Rendering += RenderFrame;
        rendering = true;
    }
}
```

If the ellipses don't exist, the rendering code creates them automatically. It creates a random number of ellipses (currently, between 20 and 100) and gives each of them the same size and color. The ellipses are placed at the top of the Canvas, but they're offset randomly along the X axis.

```
private void RenderFrame(object sender, EventArgs e)
{
    if (ellipses.Count == 0)
    {
        // Animation just started. Create the ellipses.
        int halfCanvasWidth = (int)canvas.ActualWidth / 2;

        Random rand = new Random();
        int ellipseCount = rand.Next(minEllipses, maxEllipses+1);
        for (int i = 0; i < ellipseCount; i++)
        {
            // Create the ellipse.
            Ellipse ellipse = new Ellipse();
            ellipse.Fill = Brushes.LimeGreen;
            ellipse.Width = ellipseRadius;
            ellipse.Height = ellipseRadius;

            // Place the ellipse.
            Canvas.SetLeft(ellipse, halfCanvasWidth +
                rand.Next(-halfCanvasWidth, halfCanvasWidth));
            Canvas.SetTop(ellipse, 0);
            canvas.Children.Add(ellipse);

            // Track the ellipse.
            EllipseInfo info = new EllipseInfo(ellipse,
                speedRatio * rand.Next(minStartingSpeed, maxStartingSpeed));
```

```
            ellipses.Add(info);
        }
    }
    ...
```

If the ellipses already exist, the code tackles the more interesting job of animating them. Each ellipse is moved slightly using the Canvas.SetTop() method. The amount of movement depends on the assigned velocity.

```
    ...
    else
    {
        for (int i = ellipses.Count-1; i >= 0; i--)
        {
            EllipseInfo info = ellipses[i];
            double top = Canvas.GetTop(info.Ellipse);
            Canvas.SetTop(info.Ellipse, top + 1 * info.VelocityY);
            ...
```

To improve performance, the ellipses are removed from the tracking collection as soon as they've reached the bottom of the Canvas. That way, you don't need to process them again. To allow this to work without causing you to lose your place while stepping through the collection, you need to iterate backward, from the end of the collection to the beginning.

If the ellipse hasn't yet reached the bottom of the Canvas, the code increases the velocity. (Alternatively, you could set the velocity based on how close the ellipse is to the bottom of the Canvas for a magnet-like effect.)

```
            ...
            if (top >= (canvas.ActualHeight - ellipseRadius*2))
            {
                // This circle has reached the bottom.
                // Stop animating it.
                ellipses.Remove(info);
            }
            else
            {
                // Increase the velocity.
                info.VelocityY += accelerationY;
            }
            ...
```

Finally, if all the ellipses have been removed from the collection, the event handler is removed, allowing the animation to end:

```
            ...
            if (ellipses.Count == 0)
            {
                // End the animation.
                // There's no reason to keep calling this method
                // if it has no work to do.
```

```
              CompositionTarget.Rendering -= RenderFrame;
              rendering = false;
          }
      }
   }
}
```

Obviously, you could extend this animation to make the circles bounce, scatter, and so on. The technique is the same—you simply need to use more complex formulas to arrive at the velocity.

There's one caveat to consider when building frame-based animations: they aren't time-dependent. In other words, your animation may run faster on fast computers, because the frame rate will increase and your CompositionTarget.Rendering event will be called more frequently. To compensate for this effect, you need to write code that takes the current time into account.

The best way to get started with frame-based animations is to check out the surprisingly detailed per-frame animation sample included with the WPF SDK (and also provided with the sample code for this chapter). It demonstrates several particle effects and uses a custom Time-Tracker class to implement time-dependent frame-based animations.

The Last Word

In this chapter, you explored WPF's animation support in detail. Now that you've mastered the basics, you can spend more time with the art of animation—deciding what properties to animate and how to modify them to get the effect you want. You'll find countless examples on the Web, including several that are referred to in this chapter. (If you want to avoid tired fingers from typing in long URLs, refer to the book page at www.prosetech.com to get a list with all the links.)

THE FUTURE OF WPF ANIMATION

The animation model in WPF is surprisingly full-featured. However, getting the result you want isn't always easy. If you want to animate separate portions of your interface as part of a single animated "scene," you're often forced to write a fair bit of markup with interdependent details that aren't always clear. In more complex animations, you may be forced to hard-code details and fall back to code to perform calculations for the ending value of animation. And if you need fine-grained control over an animation, such as when modeling a physical particle system, you'll need to control every step of the way using frame-based animation.

The future of WPF animation promises higher-level classes that are built on the basic plumbing you've learned about in this chapter. Ideally, you'll be able to plug animations into your application simply by using prebuilt animation classes, wrapping your elements in specialized containers, and setting a few attached properties. The actual implementation that generates the effect you want—whether it's a smooth dissolve between two images or a series of animated fly-ins that builds a window—will be provided for you.

To see an example of this future direction, check out the open source Animation Behaviors project at http://www.codeplex.com/AnimationBehaviors, which provides an easy way to attach a small set of prebuilt animation effects to your user interface elements. Although this is just one early example (which may or may not flourish), the WPF team has indicated that prebuilt animations are a hotly requested feature and one that they want to support in the future.

CHAPTER 22

■ ■ ■

Sound and Video

In this chapter, you'll tackle two more areas of WPF functionality: audio and video.

The support WPF provides for audio is a significant step up from previous versions of .NET, but it's far from groundbreaking. WPF gives you the ability to play a wide variety of sound formats, including MP3 files and anything else supported by Windows Media Player. However, WPF's sound capabilities still fall far short of DirectSound (the advanced audio API in DirectX), which allows you to apply dynamic effects and place sounds in a simulated 3D space. WPF also lacks a way to retrieve spectrum data that tells you the highs and lows of sound, which is useful for creating some types of synchronized effects and sound-driven animations.

WPF's video support is more impressive. Although the ability to play video (such as MPEG and WMV files) isn't earth-shattering, the way it integrates into the rest of the WPF model is dramatic. For example, you can use video to fill thousands of elements at once and combine it with effects, animation, transparency, and even 3D objects.

In this chapter, you'll see how to integrate video and audio content into your applications. You'll even take a quick look at WPF's support for speech synthesis and speech recognition. But before you get to the more exotic examples, you'll begin by considering the basic code required to play humble WAV audio.

Playing WAV Audio

The .NET Framework has a sketchy history of sound support. Versions 1.0 and 1.1 didn't include any managed way to play audio, and when the long-delayed support finally appeared in .NET 2.0, it was in the form of the rather underwhelming SoundPlayer class (which you can find in the underpopulated System.Media namespace). The SoundPlayer is severely limited: it can play only WAV audio files, it doesn't support playing more than one sound at once, and it doesn't provide the ability to control any aspect of the audio playback (for example, details such as volume and balance). To get these features, developers using the Windows Forms toolkit had to work with the unmanaged quartz.dll library.

> **■Note** The quartz.dll library is a key part of DirectX, and it's included with Windows Media Player and the Windows operating system. (Sometimes, the same component is known by the more marketing-friendly term DirectShow, and previous versions were called ActiveMovie.) For the gory details that describe how to use quartz.dll with Windows Forms, refer to my book *Pro .NET 2.0 Windows Forms and Custom Controls in C#* (Apress, 2005).

The SoundPlayer class is supported in WPF applications. If you can live with its significant limitations, it still presents the easiest, most lightweight way to add audio to an application. The SoundPlayer class is also wrapped by the SoundPlayerAction class, which allows you to play sounds through a declarative trigger (rather than writing a few lines of C# code in an event handler). In the following sections, you'll take a quick look at both classes, before you move on to WPF's much more powerful MediaPlayer and MediaElement classes.

The SoundPlayer

To play a sound with the SoundPlayer class, you follow several steps:

1. Create a SoundPlayer instance.

2. Specify the sound content by setting either the Stream property or the SoundLocation property. If you have a Stream-based object that contains WAV audio content, use the Stream property. If you have a file path or URL that points to a WAV file, use the Sound-Location property.

3. Once you've set the Stream or SoundLocation property, you can tell SoundPlayer to actually load the audio data by calling the Load() or LoadAsync() method. The Load() method is the simplest—it stalls your code until all the audio is loaded into memory. LoadAsync() quietly carries its work out on another thread and fires the LoadCompleted event when it's finished.

> **■Note** Technically, you don't need to use Load() or LoadAsync(). The SoundPlayer will load the audio data if needed when you call Play() or PlaySync(). However, it's a good idea to explicitly load the audio—not only does that save you the overhead if you need to play it multiple times, but it also makes it easy to handle exceptions related to file problems separately from exceptions related to audio playback problems.

4. Now, you can call PlaySync() to pause your code while the audio plays, or you can use Play() to play the audio on another thread, ensuring that your application's interface remains responsive. Your only other option is PlayLooping(), which plays the audio asynchronously in an unending loop (perfect for those annoying soundtracks). To halt the current playback at any time, just call Stop().

■Tip If you're hunting for WAV files to test with the SoundPlayer, look for the Media directory in the Windows directory, which holds WAV files for all the Windows system sounds.

The following code snippet shows the simplest approach to load and play a sound asynchronously:

```
SoundPlayer player = new SoundPlayer();
player.SoundLocation = "test.wav";
try
{
    player.Load();
    player.Play();
}
catch (System.IO.FileNotFoundException err)
{
    // An error will occur here if the file can't be found.
}
catch (FormatException err)
{
    // A FormatException will occur here if the file doesn't
    // contain valid WAV audio.
}
```

So far, the code has assumed that the audio is present in the same directory as the compiled application. However, you don't need to load the SoundPlayer audio from a file. If you've created small sounds that are played in several points in your application, it may make more sense to embed the sound files into your compiled assembly as a binary resource (not to be confused with the declarative resources, which are the resources you define in XAML markup). This technique, which was discussed in Chapter 11, works just as well with sound files as it does with images. For example, if you add the ding.wav audio file with the resource name Ding (just browse to the Properties ➤ Resources node in the Solution Explorer and use the designer support), you could use this code to play it:

```
SoundPlayer player = new SoundPlayer();
player.Stream = Properties.Resources.Ding;
player.Play();
```

■Note The SoundPlayer class doesn't deal well with large audio files, because it needs to load the entire file into memory at once. You might think that you can resolve this problem by submitting a large audio file in smaller chunks, but the SoundPlayer wasn't designed with this technique in mind. There's no easy way to synchronize the SoundPlayer so that it plays multiple audio snippets one after the other, because it doesn't provide any sort of queuing feature. Each time you call PlaySync() or Play(), the current audio playback stops. Workarounds are possible, but you'll be far better off using the MediaElement class discussed later in this chapter.

The SoundPlayerAction

The SoundPlayerAction is a new feature that WPF introduces to make it more convenient to use the SoundPlayer class. The SoundPlayerAction class derives from TriggerAction, which allows you to use it in response to any event.

■**Note** You first considered event triggers in Chapter 12. Additionally, Chapter 21 shows several examples that use event triggers with animations.

The SoundPlayerAction uses a single property, Source, which maps to the SoundPlayer. Source property. Here's a button that uses a SoundPlayerAction to connect the Click event to a sound. The trigger is wrapped in a style that you could apply to multiple buttons (if you pulled it out of the button and placed it in a Resources collection).

```
<Button>
  <Button.Content>Play Sound</Button.Content>
  <Button.Style>
    <Style>
      <Style.Triggers>
        <EventTrigger RoutedEvent="Button.Click">
          <EventTrigger.Actions>
            <SoundPlayerAction Source="test.wav"></SoundPlayerAction>
          </EventTrigger.Actions>
        </EventTrigger>
      </Style.Triggers>
    </Style>
  </Button.Style>
</Button>
```

When using the SoundPlayerAction, the sound is always played asynchronously. You're also limited to the Source property—there's no handy Stream property to play the audio in an embedded resource. That means the only place you can grab your audio from is a nearby file. (Unfortunately, the application pack URI system that's described in Chapter 11 doesn't apply to the SoundPlayer class, because it's not part of WPF.)

System Sounds

One of the shameless frills of the Windows operating system is its ability to map audio files to specific system events. Along with SoundPlayer, .NET 2.0 also introduced a System.Media. SystemSounds class that allows you to access the most common of these sounds and use them in your own applications. This technique works best if all you want is a simple chime to indicate the end of a long-running operation or an alert sound to indicate a warning condition.

Unfortunately, the SystemSounds class is based on the MessageBeep Win32 API, and as a result, it provides access only to the following generic system sounds:

• Asterisk

• Beep

- Exclamation

- Hand

- Question

The SystemSounds class provides a property for each of these sounds, which returns a SystemSound object you can use to play the sound through its Play() method. For example, to sound a beep in your code, you simply need to execute this line of code:

```
SystemSounds.Beep.Play();
```

To configure what WAV files are used for each sound, head to the Control Panel, and select the Sounds and Audio Devices icon (in Windows XP) or the Sound icon (in Windows Vista).

The MediaPlayer

The SoundPlayer, SoundPlayerAction, and SystemSounds classes are easy to use but relatively underpowered. In today's world, it's much more common to use compressed MP3 audio for everything except the simplest of sounds, instead of the original WAV format. But if you want to play MP3 audio or MPEG video, you need to turn to two different classes: MediaPlayer and MediaElement. Both classes depend on key pieces of technology that are provided through Windows Media Player. However, there's a catch—they require Windows Media Player version 10 or later. Windows Vista makes the cut easily, because it includes Windows Media Player 11, but existing Windows XP installations have no such guarantee.

■**Note** Windows XP introduces another catch for 64-bit programmers—namely, the 64-bit version of Windows XP includes a 32-bit version of Media Player. As a result, you must compile your WPF application in 32-bit to ensure that you have audio and video support. (This is the default for any new WPF project, unless you explicitly configure it as a 64-bit application, which will run only on 64-bit versions of Windows.)

The MediaPlayer class (found in the WPF-specific System.Windows.Media namespace) is the WPF equivalent to the SoundPlayer class. Although it's clearly not as lightweight, it works in a similar way—namely, you create a MediaPlayer object, call the Open() method to load your audio file, and call Play() to begin playing it asynchronously. (There's no option for synchronous playback.) Here's a barebones example:

```
private MediaPlayer player = new MediaPlayer();

private void cmdPlayWithMediaPlayer_Click(object sender, RoutedEventArgs e)
{
    player.Open(new Uri("test.mp3", UriKind.Relative));
    player.Play();
}
```

There are a few important details to notice in this example:

- The MediaPlayer is created outside the event handler, so it lives for the lifetime of the window. That's because the MediaPlayer.Close() method is called when the MediaPlayer object is disposed from memory. If you create a MediaPlayer object in the event handler, it will be released from memory almost immediately and probably garbage collected shortly after, at which point the Close() method will be called and playback will be halted.

Tip You should create a Window.Unloaded event handler to call Close() to stop any currently playing audio when the window is closed.

- You supply the location of your file as a URI. Unfortunately, this URI doesn't use the application pack syntax that you learned about in Chapter 11, so it's not possible to embed an audio file and play it using the MediaPlayer class. This limitation is because the MediaPlayer class is built on functionality that's not native to WPF—instead, it's provided by a distinct, unmanaged component of the Windows Media Player.

- There's no exception handling code. Irritatingly, the Open() and Play() methods don't throw exceptions (the asynchronous load and playback process is partly to blame). Instead, it's up to you to handle the MediaOpened and MediaFailed events if you want to determine whether your audio is being played.

The MediaPlayer is fairly straightforward but still more capable than SoundPlayer. It provides a small set of useful methods, properties, and events. Table 22-1 has the full list.

Table 22-1. *Key MediaPlayer Members*

Member	Description
Balance	Sets the balance between the left and right speaker as a number from –1 (left speaker only) to 1 (right speaker only).
Volume	Sets the volume as a number from 0 (completely muted) to 1 (full volume). The default value is 0.5.
SpeedRatio	Sets a speed multiplier to play audio (or video) at faster than normal speed. The default value of 1 is normal speed, while 2 is two-times normal speed, 10 is ten-times speed, 0.5 is half-times speed, and so on. You can use any positive double value.
HasAudio and HasVideo	Indicates whether the currently loaded media file includes audio or video, respectively. To show video, you need to use the MediaElement class described next.
NaturalDuration, NaturalVideoHeight, NaturalVideoWidth	Indicates the play duration at normal speed and the size of the video window. (As you'll discover later, you can scale or stretch a video to fit different window sizes.)
Position	A TimeSpan indicating the current location in the media file. You can set this property to skip to a specific time position.

Member	Description
DownloadProgress and BufferingProgress	Indicates the percentage of a file that has been downloaded (useful if the Source is a URL pointing to a web or remote computer) or buffered (if the media file you're using is encoded in a streaming format so it can be played before it's entirely downloaded). The percentage is represented as a number from 0 to 1.
Clock	Gets or sets the MediaClock that's associated with this player. The MediaClock is used only when you're synchronizing audio to a timeline (in much the same way that you learned to synchronize an animation to a timeline in Chapter 21). If you're using the methods of the MediaPlayer to perform manual playback, this property is null.
Open()	Loads a new media file.
Play()	Begins playback. Has no effect if the file is already being played.
Pause()	Pauses playback but doesn't change the position. If you call Play() again, playback will begin at the current position. Has no effect if the audio is not playing.
Stop()	Stops playback and resets the position to the beginning of the file. If you call Play() again, playback will begin at the beginning of the file. Has no effect if the audio has already been stopped.

Using these members, you could build a basic but full-featured media player. However, WPF programmers usually use another quite similar element, which is defined in the next section: the MediaElement class.

The MediaElement

The MediaElement is a WPF element that wraps all the functionality of the MediaPlayer class. Like all elements, the MediaElement is placed directly in your user interface. If you're using the MediaElement to play audio, this fact isn't important, but if you're using the MediaElement for video, you place it where the video window should appear.

A simple MediaElement tag is all you need to play a sound. For example, if you add this markup to your user interface:

```
<MediaElement Source="test.mp3"></MediaElement>
```

the test.mp3 audio will be played as soon as it's loaded (which is more or less as soon as the window is loaded).

Playing Audio Programmatically

Usually, you'll want the ability to control playback more precisely. For example, you might want it to be triggered at a specific time, repeated indefinitely, and so on. One way to achieve this result is to use the methods of the MediaElement class at the appropriate time.

The startup behavior of the MediaElement is determined by its LoadedBehavior property, which is one of the few properties that the MediaElement class adds, which isn't found in the MediaPlayer class. The LoadedBehavior takes any value from the MediaState enumeration.

The default value is Play, but you can also use Manual, in which case the audio file is loaded, and your code takes responsibility for starting the playback at the right time. Another option is Pause, which also suspends playback but doesn't allow you to use the playback methods. (Instead, you'll need to start playback using triggers and a storyboard, as described in the next section.)

■**Note** The MediaElement class also provides an UnloadedBehavior property, which determines what should happen when the element is unloaded. In this case, Close is really the only sensible choice, because it closes the file and releases all system resources.

So to play audio programmatically, you must begin by changing the LoadedBehavior, as shown here:

```
<MediaElement Source="test.mp3" LoadedBehavior="Manual" Name="media"></MediaElement>
```

You must also choose a name so that you can interact with the media element in code. Generally, interaction consists of the straightforward Play(), Pause(), and Stop() methods. You can also set Position to move through the audio. Here's a simple event handler that seeks to the beginning and starts playback:

```
private void cmdPlay_Click(object sender, RoutedEventArgs e)
{
    media.Position = TimeSpan.Zero;
    media.Play();
}
```

If this code runs while playback is already underway, the first line will reset the position to the beginning, and playback will continue from that point. The second line will have no effect, because the media file is already being played. If you try to use this code on a MediaElement that doesn't have the LoadedBehavior property set to Manual, you'll receive an exception.

■**Note** In a typical media player, you can trigger basic commands like play, pause, and stop in more than one way. Obviously, this is a great place to use the WPF command model. In fact, there's a command class that already includes some handy infrastructure, the System.Windows.Input.MediaCommands class. However, the MediaElement does not have any default command bindings that support the MediaCommands class. In other words, it's up to you to write the event handling logic that implements each command and calls the appropriate MediaElement method. The savings to you is that multiple user interface elements can be hooked up to the same command, reducing code duplication. Chapter 10 has more about commands.

Handling Errors

The MediaElement doesn't throw an exception if it can't find or load a file. Instead, it's up to you to handle the MediaFailed event. Fortunately, this task is easy. Just tweak your Media-Element tag:

```
<MediaElement ... MediaFailed="media_MediaFailed"></MediaElement>
```

And, in the event handler, use the ExceptionRoutedEventArgs.ErrorException property to get an exception object that describes the problem:

```
private void media_MediaFailed(object sender, ExceptionRoutedEventArgs e)
{
    lblErrorText.Content = e.ErrorException.Message;
}
```

Playing Audio with Triggers

So far, you haven't received any advantage by switching from the MediaPlayer to the Media-Element class (other than support for video, which is discussed later in this chapter). However, by using a MediaElement, you also gain the ability to control audio declaratively, through XAML markup rather than code. You do this using triggers and storyboards, which you first saw when you considered animation in Chapter 21. The only new ingredient is the Media-Timeline, which controls the timing of your audio or video file and works with MediaElement to coordinates its playback. MediaTimeline derives from Timeline and adds a Source property that identifies the audio file you want to play.

The following markup demonstrates a simple example. It uses the BeginStoryboard action to begin playing a sound when the mouse clicks a button. (Obviously, you could respond equally well to other mouse and keyboard events.)

```
<Grid>
 <Grid.RowDefinitions>
   <RowDefinition Size="Auto"></RowDefinition>
   <RowDefinition Size="Auto"></RowDefinition>
 </Grid.RowDefinitions>
 <MediaElement x:Name="media"></MediaElement>

 <Button>
   <Button.Content>Click me to hear a sound.</Button.Content>
   <Button.Triggers>
     <EventTrigger RoutedEvent="Button.Click">
       <EventTrigger.Actions>
       <BeginStoryboard>
         <Storyboard>
           <MediaTimeline Source="soundA.wav"
             Storyboard.TargetName="media"></MediaTimeline>
         </Storyboard>
```

```
        </BeginStoryboard>
      </EventTrigger.Actions>
    </EventTrigger>
  </Button.Triggers>
 </Button>
</Grid>
```

Because this example plays audio, the positioning of the MediaElement isn't important. In this example, it's placed inside a Grid, behind a Button. (The ordering isn't important, because the MediaElement won't have any visual appearance at runtime.) When the button is clicked, a Storyboard is created with a MediaTimeline. Notice that the source isn't specified in the MediaElement.Source property. Instead, the source is passed along through the MediaTimeline.Source property.

Note When you use MediaElement as the target of a MediaTimeline, it no longer matters what you set the LoadedBehavior and UnloadedBehavior to. Once you use a MediaTime, your audio or video is driven by a WPF animation clock (technically, an instance of the MediaClock class, which is exposed through the MediaElement.Clock property).

You can use a single Storyboard to control the playback of a single MediaElement—in other words, not only stopping it but also pausing, resuming, and stopping it at will. For example, consider the extremely simple four-button media player shown in Figure 22-1.

Figure 22-1. *A window for controlling playback*

This window uses a single MediaElement, MediaTimeline, and Storyboard. The Storyboard and MediaTimeline are declared in the Window.Resources collection:

```
<Window.Resources>
  <Storyboard x:Key="MediaStoryboardResource">
    <MediaTimeline Storyboard.TargetName="media" Source="test.mp3"></MediaTimeline>
  </Storyboard>
</Window.Resources>
```

The only challenge is that you must remember to define all the triggers for managing the storyboard in one collection. You can then attach them to the appropriate controls using the EventTrigger.SourceName property.

In this example, the triggers are all declared inside the StackPanel that holds the buttons. Here are the triggers and the buttons that use them to manage the audio:

```
<StackPanel Orientation="Horizontal">
  <StackPanel.Triggers>
    <EventTrigger RoutedEvent="ButtonBase.Click" SourceName="cmdPlay">
      <EventTrigger.Actions>
        <BeginStoryboard Name="MediaStoryboard"
         Storyboard="{StaticResource MediaStoryboardResource}"/>
      </EventTrigger.Actions>
    </EventTrigger>
    <EventTrigger RoutedEvent="ButtonBase.Click" SourceName="cmdStop">
      <EventTrigger.Actions>
        <StopStoryboard BeginStoryboardName="MediaStoryboard"/>
      </EventTrigger.Actions>
    </EventTrigger>
    <EventTrigger RoutedEvent="ButtonBase.Click" SourceName="cmdPause">
      <EventTrigger.Actions>
        <PauseStoryboard BeginStoryboardName="MediaStoryboard"/>
      </EventTrigger.Actions>
    </EventTrigger>
    <EventTrigger RoutedEvent="ButtonBase.Click" SourceName="cmdResume">
      <EventTrigger.Actions>
        <ResumeStoryboard BeginStoryboardName="MediaStoryboard"/>
      </EventTrigger.Actions>
    </EventTrigger>
  </StackPanel.Triggers>

  <MediaElement  Name="media"></MediaElement>
  <Button Name="cmdPlay">Play</Button>
  <Button Name="cmdStop">Stop</Button>
  <Button Name="cmdPause">Pause</Button>
  <Button Name="cmdResume">Resume</Button>
</StackPanel>
```

Notice that even though the implementation of MediaElement and MediaPlayer allows you to resume playback after pausing by calling Play(), the Storyboard doesn't work in the same way. Instead, a separate ResumeStoryboard action is required. If this isn't the behavior you want, you can consider adding some code for your play button instead of using the declarative approach.

■Note The downloadable code samples for this chapter include a declarative media player window and a more flexible code-driven media player window.

Playing Multiple Sounds

Although the previous example showed you how to control the playback of a single media file, there's no reason you can't extend it to play multiple audio files. The following example includes two buttons, each of which plays its own sound. When the button is clicked, a new Storyboard is created, with a new MediaTimeline, which is used to play a different audio file through the same MediaElement.

```
<Grid>
 <Grid.RowDefinitions>
   <RowDefinition Size="Auto"></RowDefinition>
   <RowDefinition Size="Auto"></RowDefinition>
 </Grid.RowDefinitions>
 <MediaElement x:Name="media"></MediaElement>

 <Button>
   <Button.Content>Click me to hear a sound.</Button.Content>
   <Button.Triggers>
     <EventTrigger RoutedEvent="Button.Click">
       <EventTrigger.Actions>
       <BeginStoryboard>
         <Storyboard>
           <MediaTimeline Source="soundA.wav"
            Storyboard.TargetName="media"></MediaTimeline>
         </Storyboard>
       </BeginStoryboard>
       </EventTrigger.Actions>
     </EventTrigger>
   </Button.Triggers>
 </Button>

 <Button Grid.Row="1">
   <Button.Content >Click me to hear a different sound.</Button.Content>
   <Button.Triggers>
     <EventTrigger RoutedEvent="Button.Click">
       <EventTrigger.Actions>
         <BeginStoryboard>
          <Storyboard>
            <MediaTimeline Source="soundB.wav"
             Storyboard.TargetName="media"></MediaTimeline>
          </Storyboard>
         </BeginStoryboard>
       </EventTrigger.Actions>
     </EventTrigger>
   </Button.Triggers>
 </Button>
</Grid>
```

In this example, if you click both buttons in quick succession, you'll see that the second sound interrupts the playback of the first. This is a consequence of using the same Media-Element for both timelines. A slicker (but more resource-heavy) approach is to use a separate MediaElement for each button and point the MediaTimeline to the corresponding Media-Element. (In this case, you can specify the Source directly in the MediaElement tag, because it doesn't change.) Now, if you click both buttons in quick succession, both sounds will play at the same time.

The same applies to the MediaPlayer class—if you want to play multiple audio files, you need multiple MediaPlayer objects. If you decide to use the MediaPlayer or MediaElement with code, you have the opportunity to use more intelligent optimization that allows exactly two simultaneous sounds, but no more. The basic technique is to define two MediaPlayer objects and flip between them each time you play a new sound. (You can keep track of which object you used last using a Boolean variable.) To make this technique really effortless, you can store the audio file names in the Tag property of the appropriate element, so all your event handling code needs to do is find the right MediaPlayer to use, set its Source property, and call its Play() method.

Changing Volume, Balance, Speed, and Position

The MediaElement exposes the same properties as the MediaPlayer (detailed in Table 22-1) for controlling the volume, the balance, the speed, and the current position in the media file. Figure 22-2 shows a simple window that extends the sound player example from Figure 22-1 with additional controls for adjusting these details.

Figure 22-2. *Controlling more playback details*

The volume and balance sliders are the easiest to wire up. Because Volume and Balance are dependency properties, you can connect the slider to the MediaElement with a two-way binding expression. Here's what you need:

```
<Slider Grid.Row="1" Minimum="0" Maximum="1"
 Value="{Binding ElementName=media, Path=Volume, Mode=TwoWay}"></Slider>
<Slider Grid.Row="2" Minimum="-1" Maximum="1"
 Value="{Binding ElementName=media, Path=Balance, Mode=TwoWay}"></Slider>
```

Although two-way data binding expressions incur slightly more overhead, they ensure that if the MediaElement properties are changed some other way, the slider controls remain synchronized.

The SpeedRatio property can be connected in the same way:

```
<Slider Grid.Row="3" Minimum="0" Maximum="2"
  Value="{Binding ElementName=media, Path=SpeedRatio}"></Slider>
```

However, this has a few quirks. First, SpeedRatio isn't used in a clock-driven audio (one that uses a MediaTimeline). To use it, you need to set the LoadedBehavior property of SpeedRatio to Manual and take control of its playback manually through the playback methods.

■**Tip** If you're using a MediaTimeline, you can get the same effect from the SetStoryboardSpeedRatio action as setting the MediaElement.SpeedRatio property. You learned about these details in Chapter 21.

Second, SpeedRatio isn't a dependency property, and WPF doesn't receive change notifications when it's modified. That means if you include code that modifies the SpeedRatio property, the slider won't be updated accordingly. (One workaround is to modify the slider in your code, rather than modify the MediaElement directly.)

■**Note** Changing the playback speed of audio can distort the audio and cause sound artifacts, such as echoes.

The last detail is the current position, which is provided by the Position property. Once again, the MediaElement needs to be in Manual mode before you can set the Position property, which means you can't use the MediaTimeline. (If you're using a MediaTimeline, consider using the BeginStoryboard action with an Offset to the position you want, as described in Chapter 21.)

To make this work, you don't use any data binding in the slider:

```
<Slider Minimum="0" Name="sliderPosition"
  ValueChanged="sliderPosition_ValueChanged"></Slider>
```

You use code like this to set up the position slider when you open a media file:

```
private void media_MediaOpened(object sender, RoutedEventArgs e)
{
    sliderPosition.Maximum = media.NaturalDuration.TimeSpan.TotalSeconds;
}
```

You can then jump to a specific position when the slider tab is moved:

```
private void sliderPosition_ValueChanged(object sender, RoutedEventArgs e)
{
    // Pausing the player before moving it reduces audio "glitches"
    // when the value changes several times in quick succession.
    media.Pause();
    media.Position = TimeSpan.FromSeconds(sliderPosition.Value);
    media.Play();
}
```

The drawback here is that the slider isn't updated as the media advances. If you want this feature, you need to cook up a suitable workaround (like a DispatcherTimer that triggers a periodic check while playback is taking place and updates the slider then). The same is true if you're using the MediaTimeline. For various reasons you can't bind directly to the MediaElement. Clock information. Instead, you'll need to handle the Storyboard.CurrentTimeInvalidated event, as demonstrated in the AnimationPlayer example in Chapter 21.

Synchronizing an Animation with Audio

In some cases, you may want to synchronize another animation to a specific point in a media file (audio or video). For example, if you have a lengthy audio file that features a person describing a series of steps, you might want to fade in different images after each pause.

Depending on your needs, this design may be overly complex, and you may be able to achieve better performance and simpler design by segmenting the audio into separate files. That way, you can load the new audio and perform the correlated action all at once, simply by responding to the MediaEnded event. In other situations, you need to synchronize something with continuous, unbroken playback of a media file.

One technique that allows you to pair playback with other actions is a key frame animation (which was introduced in Chapter 21). You can then wrap this key frame animation and your MediaTimeline into a single storyboard. That way you can supply specific time offsets for your animation, which will then correspond to precise times in the audio file. In fact, you can even use a third-party program that allows you to annotate audio and export a list of important times. You can then use this information to set up the time for each key frame.

When using a key frame animation, it's important to set the Storyboard.SlipBehavior property to Slip. This specifies that your key frame animation should not creep ahead of the MediaTimeline, if the media file is delayed. This is important because the MediaTimeline could be delayed by buffering (if it's being streamed from a server) or, more commonly, by load time.

The following markup demonstrates a basic example of an audio file with two synchronized animations. The first varies the text in a label as specific parts of the audio file are
reached. The second shows a small circle halfway through the audio and pulses it in time to
the beat by varying the value of the Opacity property.

```
<Window.Resources>
  <Storyboard x:Key="Board" SlipBehavior="Slip">
    <MediaTimeline Source="sq3gm1.mid"
      Storyboard.TargetName="media"/>

      <StringAnimationUsingKeyFrames
        Storyboard.TargetName="lblAnimated"
        Storyboard.TargetProperty="(Label.Content)" FillBehavior="HoldEnd">
        <DiscreteStringKeyFrame Value="First note..." KeyTime="0:0:3.4" />
        <DiscreteStringKeyFrame Value="Introducing the main theme..."
          KeyTime="0:0:5.8" />
        <DiscreteStringKeyFrame Value="Irritating bass begins..."
          KeyTime="0:0:28.7" />
        <DiscreteStringKeyFrame Value="Modulation!" KeyTime="0:0:53.2" />
        <DiscreteStringKeyFrame Value="Back to the original theme."
          KeyTime="0:1:8" />
      </StringAnimationUsingKeyFrames>

      <DoubleAnimationUsingKeyFrames
        Storyboard.TargetName="ellipse"
        Storyboard.TargetProperty="Opacity" BeginTime="0:0:29.36"
        RepeatBehavior="30x">
        <LinearDoubleKeyFrame Value="1" KeyTime="0:0:0" />
        <LinearDoubleKeyFrame Value="0" KeyTime="0:0:0.64" />
      </DoubleAnimationUsingKeyFrames>
    </Storyboard>
</Window.Resources>

<Window.Triggers>
  <EventTrigger RoutedEvent="MediaElement.Loaded">
    <EventTrigger.Actions>
      <BeginStoryboard Name="mediaStoryboard" Storyboard="{StaticResource Board}">
      </BeginStoryboard>
    </EventTrigger.Actions>
  </EventTrigger>
</Window.Triggers>
```

To make this example even more interesting, it also includes a slider that allows you to change your position. You'll see that even if you change the position using the slider, the three animations are adjusted automatically to the appropriate point by the MediaTimeline. (The slider is kept synchronized using the Storyboard.CurrentTimeInvalidated event, and the ValueChanged event is handled to seek to a new position after the user drags the slider thumb. You saw both of these techniques in Chapter 21, with the AnimationPlayer example.)

Figure 22-3 shows the program in action.

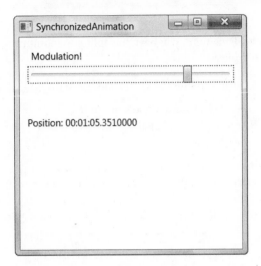

Figure 22-3. *Synchronized animations*

Playing Video

Everything you've learned about using the MediaElement class applies equally well when you use a video file instead of an audio file. As you'd expect, the MediaElement class supports all the video formats that are supported by Windows Media Player. Although support depends on the codecs you've installed, you can't count on basic support for WMV, MPEG, and AVI files.

The key difference with video files is that the visual and layout-related properties of the MediaElement are suddenly important. Most important, the Stretch and StretchDirection properties determine how the video window is scaled to fit its container (and work in the same way as the Stretch and StretchDirection properties that you learned about on all Shape-derived classes). When setting the Stretch value, you can use None to keep the native size, Uniform to stretch it to fit its container without changing its aspect ratio, Uniform to stretch it to fit its container in both dimensions (even if that means stretching the picture), and UniformToFill to resize the picture to fit the largest dimension of its container while preserving its aspect ratio (which guarantees that part of the video window will be clipped out if the container doesn't have the same aspect ratio as the video).

Tip The MediaElement's preferred size is based on the native video dimensions. For example, if you create a MediaElement with a Stretch value of Uniform (the default) and place it inside a Grid row with a Height value of Auto, the row will be sized just large enough to keep the video at its standard size, so no scaling is required.

Video Effects

Because the MediaElement works like any other WPF element, you have the ability to manipulate it in some surprising ways. Here are some examples:

- You can use a MediaElement as the content inside a content control, such as a button.

- You can set the content for thousands of content controls at once with multiple MediaElement objects—although your CPU probably won't bear up very well under the strain.

- You can also combine video with transformations through the LayoutTransform or RenderTransform property. This allows you to move your video window, stretch it, skew it, or rotate it.

Tip Generally, RenderTransform is preferred over LayoutTransform for the MediaElement, because it's lighter weight. It also takes the value of the handy RenderTransformOrigin property into account, allowing you to use relative coordinates for certain transforms (such as rotation).

- You can set the Clipping property of the MediaElement to cut down the video window to a specific shape or path and show only a portion of the full window.

- You can set the Opacity property to allow other content to show through behind your video window. In fact, you can even stack multiple semitransparent video windows on top of each other (with dire consequences for performance).

- You can use an animation to change a property of the MediaElement (or one of its transforms) dynamically.

- You can copy the current content of the video window to another place in your user interface using a VisualBrush, which allows you to create specific effects like reflection.

- You can place a video window on a three-dimensional surface and use an animation to move it as the video is being played (as described in Chapter 23).

For example, the following markup creates the reflection effect shown in Figure 22-4. It does so by creating a Grid with two rows. The top row holds a MediaElement that plays a video file. The bottom row holds a Rectangle that's painted with a VisualBrush. The trick is that the VisualBrush takes its content from the video window above it, using a binding expression. The video content is then flipped over by using the RelativeTransform property and then faded out gradually toward the bottom using an OpacityMask gradient.

```
<Grid Margin="15" HorizontalAlignment="Center">
  <Grid.RowDefinitions>
    <RowDefinition Height="Auto"></RowDefinition>
    <RowDefinition></RowDefinition>
  </Grid.RowDefinitions>
  <Grid.ColumnDefinitions>
    <ColumnDefinition Width="Auto"></ColumnDefinition>
  </Grid.ColumnDefinitions>

  <Border BorderBrush="DarkGray" BorderThickness="1" CornerRadius="2">
    <MediaElement x:Name="video" Source="test.mpg" LoadedBehavior="Manual"
     Stretch="Fill"></MediaElement>
  </Border>

  <Border Grid.Row="1" BorderBrush="DarkGray" BorderThickness="1" CornerRadius="2">
    <Rectangle VerticalAlignment="Stretch" Stretch="Uniform">
    <Rectangle.Fill>
      <VisualBrush Visual="{Binding ElementName=video}">
        <VisualBrush.RelativeTransform>
          <ScaleTransform ScaleY="-1" CenterY="0.5"></ScaleTransform>
        </VisualBrush.RelativeTransform>
      </VisualBrush>
    </Rectangle.Fill>

    <Rectangle.OpacityMask>
      <LinearGradientBrush StartPoint="0,0" EndPoint="0,1">
        <GradientStop Color="Black" Offset="0"></GradientStop>
        <GradientStop Color="Transparent" Offset="0.6"></GradientStop>
      </LinearGradientBrush>
    </Rectangle.OpacityMask>
    </Rectangle>
  </Border>
</Grid>
```

This example performs fairly well. The reflection effect has a similar rendering overhead to two video windows, because each frame must be copied to the lower rectangle. In addition, each frame needs to be flipped and faded to create the reflection effect. (WPF uses an intermediary rendering surface to perform these transformations.) But on a modern computer, the extra overhead is barely noticeable.

This isn't the case with other video effects. In fact, video is one of the few areas in WPF where it's extremely easy to overtask the CPU and create interfaces that perform poorly. Average computers can't handle more than a few simultaneous video windows (depending, obviously, on the size of your video file—higher resolutions and higher frame rates obviously mean more data, which is more time-consuming to process).

The downloadable examples for this chapter include another example that demonstrates video effects: an animation that rotates a video window as it plays. The need to wipe out each video frame and redraw a new one at a slightly different angle runs relatively well on modern video cards but causes a noticeable flicker on lower-tier cards. If in doubt, you should profile your user interface plans on a lesser-powered computer to see whether they stand up and should provide a way to opt out of the more complex effects your application provides or gracefully disable them on lower-tier cards.

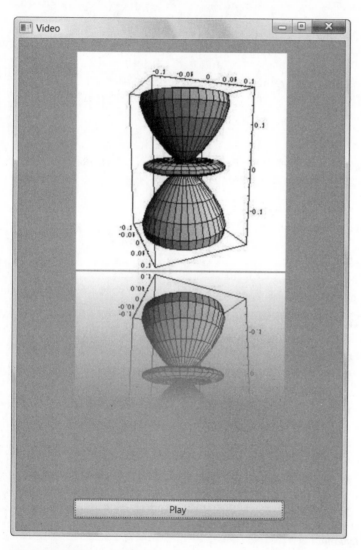

Figure 22-4. *Reflected video*

THE VIDEODRAWING CLASS

WPF includes a VideoDrawing class that derives from the Drawing class you learned about in Chapter 14. The VideoDrawing can be used to create a DrawingBrush, which can then be used to fill the surface of an element, creating much the same effect as demonstrated in the previous example with the VisualBrush.

However, there's a difference that may make the VideoDrawing approach more efficient. That's because VideoDrawing uses the MediaPlayer class, while the VisualBrush approach requires the use of the MediaElement class. The MediaPlayer class doesn't need to manage layout, focus, or any other element details, so it's more lightweight than the MediaElement class. In some situations, using the VideoDrawing and DrawingBrush instead of the MediaElement and VisualBrush can avoid the need for an intermediary rendering surface and thus improve performance (although in my information testing, I didn't notice much of a difference between the two approaches).

Using the VideoDrawing takes a fair bit more work, because the MediaPlayer needs to be started in code (by calling its Play() method). Usually, you'll create all three objects—the MediaPlayer, VideoDrawing, and DrawingBrush—in code. Here's a basic example that paints the video on the background of the current window:

```
// Create the timeline.
// This isn't required, but it allows you to configure details
// that wouldn't otherwise be possible (like repetition).
MediaTimeline timeline = new MediaTimeline(
  new Uri("test.mpg", UriKind.Relative));
timeline.RepeatBehavior = RepeatBehavior.Forever;

// Create the clock, which is shared with the MediaPlayer.
MediaClock clock = timeline.CreateClock();
MediaPlayer player = new MediaPlayer();
player.Clock = clock;

// Create the VideoDrawing.
VideoDrawing videoDrawing = new VideoDrawing();
videoDrawing.Rect = new Rect(150, 0, 100, 100);
videoDrawing.Player = player;

// Assign the DrawingBrush.
DrawingBrush brush = new DrawingBrush(videoDrawing);
this.Background = brush;

// Start the timeline.
clock.Controller.Begin();
```

Speech

Audio and video support is a core pillar of the WPF platform. However, WPF also includes libraries that wrap two less commonly used multimedia features: speech synthesis and speech recognition.

Both of these features are supported through classes in the System.Speech.dll assembly. By default, Visual Studio doesn't add a reference to this assembly in a new WPF project, so it's up to you to add one to your project.

■**Note** Speech is a peripheral part of WPF. Although the speech support is technically considered to be part of WPF and it was released with WPF in the .NET Framework 3.0, the speech namespaces start with System. Speech, not System.Windows.

Speech Synthesis

Speech synthesis is a feature that generates spoken audio based on text you supply. Speech synthesis isn't built into WPF—instead, it's a Windows accessibility feature. System utilities such as Narrator, a lightweight screen reader included with Windows XP and Windows Vista, use speech synthesis to help blind users to navigate basic dialog boxes. More generally, speech synthesis can be used to create audio tutorials and spoken instructions, although prerecorded audio provides better quality.

■**Note** Speech synthesis makes sense when you need to create audio for *dynamic* text—in other words, when you don't know at compile time what words need to be spoken at runtime. But if the audio is fixed, prerecorded audio is easier to use, is more efficient, and sounds better. The only other reason you might consider speech synthesis is if you need to narrate a huge amount of text and prerecording it all would be impractical.

Although both Windows XP and Windows Vista have speech synthesis built in, the computerized voice they use is different. Windows XP uses the robotic-sounding Sam voice, while Windows Vista includes a more natural female voice named Anna. You can download and install additional voices on either operating system.

Playing speech is deceptively simple. All you need to do is create an instance of the SpeechSynthesizer class from the System.Speech.Synthesis namespace and call its Speak() method with a string of text. Here's an example:

```
SpeechSynthesizer synthesizer = new SpeechSynthesizer();
synthesizer.Speak("Hello, world");
```

When using this approach—passing plain text to the SpeechSynthesizer—you give up a fair bit of control. You may run into words that aren't pronounced properly, emphasized appropriately, or spoken at the correct speed. To get more control over spoken text, you need to use the PromptBuilder class to construct a definition of the speech. Here's how you could replace the earlier example with completely equivalent code that uses the PromptBuilder:

```
PromptBuilder prompt = new PromptBuilder();
prompt.AppendText("Hello, world");

SpeechSynthesizer synthesizer = new SpeechSynthesizer();
synthesizer.Speak(prompt);
```

This code doesn't provide any advantage. However, the PromptBuilder class has a number of other methods that you can use to customize the way text is spoken. For example, you can emphasize a specific word (or several words) by using an overloaded version of the Append-Text() method that takes a value from the PromptEmphasis enumeration. Although the precise effect of emphasizing a word depends on the voice you're using, the following code stresses the *are* in the sentence "How are you?"

```
PromptBuilder prompt = new PromptBuilder();
prompt.AppendText("How ");
prompt.AppendText("are ", PromptEmphasis.Strong);
prompt.AppendText("you");
```

The AppendText() method has two other overloads—one that takes a PromptRate value that lets you increase or decrease speed and one that takes a PromptVolume value that lets you increase or decrease the volume.

If you want to change more than one of these details at the same time, you need to use a PromptStyle object. The PromptStyle wraps PromptEmphasis, PromptRate, and Prompt-Volume values. You can supply values for all three details or just the one or two you want to use.

To use a PromptStyle object, you call PromptBuilder.BeginStyle(). The PromptStyle you've created is then applied to all the spoken text until you can EndStyle(). Here's a revised example that uses emphasis and a change in speed to put the stress on the word *are*:

```
PromptBuilder prompt = new PromptBuilder();
prompt.AppendText("How ");
PromptStyle style = new PromptStyle();
style.Rate = PromptRate.ExtraSlow;
style.Emphasis = PromptEmphasis.Strong;
prompt.StartStyle(style);
prompt.AppendText("are ");
prompt.EndStyle();
prompt.AppendText("you");
```

■**Note** If you call BeginStyle(), you must call EndStyle() later in your code. If you fail to do so, you'll receive a runtime error.

The PromptEmphasis, PromptRate, and PromptVolume enumerations provide relatively crude ways to influence a voice. There's no way to get finer-grained control or introduce nuances or subtler specific speech patterns into spoken text. However, the PromptBuilder includes a AppendTextWithHind() method that allows you to deal with telephone numbers, dates, times, and words that need to spelled out. You supply your choice using the SayAs enumeration. Here's an example:

```
prompt.AppendText("The word laser is spelt ");
prompt.AppendTextWithHint("laser", SayAs.SpellOut);
```

This produces the narration "The word laser is spelt l-a-s-e-r."

Along with the AppendText() and AppendTextWithHint() methods, the PromptBuilder also includes a small collection of additional methods for adding ordinary audio to the stream (AppendAudio()), creating pauses of a specified duration (AppendBreak()), switching voices (StartVoice() and EndVoice()), and speaking text according to a specified phonetic pronunciation (AppendTextWithPronounciation()).

The PromptBuilder is really a wrapper for the Synthesis Markup Language (SSML) standard, which is described at http://www.w3.org/TR/speech-synthesis. As such, it shares the limitations of that standard. As you call the PromptBuilder methods, the corresponding SSML markup is generated behind the scenes. You can see the final SSML representation of your code by calling PromptBuilder.ToXml() at the end of your work, and you can call Prompt-Builder.AppendSsml() to take existing SSML markup and read it into your prompt.

Speech Recognition

Speech recognition is a feature that translates user-spoken audio into text. As with speech synthesis, speech recognition is a feature of the Windows operating system. Speech recognition is built into Windows Vista but not Windows XP. Instead, it's available to Windows XP users through Office XP or later, the Windows XP Plus! Pack, or the free Microsoft Speech Software Development Kit (which is downloadable at http://www.microsoft.com/speech/download/sdk51).

■**Note** If speech recognition isn't currently running, the speech recognition toolbar will appear when you instantiate the SpeechRecognizer class. If you attempt to instantiate the SpeechRecognizer class and you haven't configured speech recognition for your voice, Windows will automatically start a wizard that leads you through the process.

Speech recognition is also a Windows accessibility feature. For example, it allows users with disabilities to interact with common controls by voice. Speech recognition also allows hands-free computer use, which is useful in certain environments.

The most straightforward way to use speech recognition is to create an instance of the SpeechRecognizer class from the System.Speech.Recognition namespace. You can then attach an event handler to the SpeechRecognized event, which is fired whenever spoken words are successfully converted to text:

```
SpeechRecognizer recognizer = new SpeechRecognizer();
recognizer.SpeechRecognized += recognizer_SpeechReconized;
```

You can then retrieve the text in the event handler from the SpeechRecognizedEvent-Args.Result property:

```
private void recognizer_SpeechReconized(object sender, SpeechRecognizedEventArgs e)
{
    MessageBox.Show("You said:" + e.Result.Text);
}
```

The SpeechRecognizer wraps a COM object. To avoid unseemly glitches, you should declare it as a member variable in your window class (so the object remains alive as long as the window exists) and you should call its Dispose() method when the window is closed (to remove your speech recognition hooks).

Note The SpeechRecognizer class actually raises a sequence of events when audio is detected. First, SpeechDetected is raised if the audio appears to be speech. SpeechHypothesized then fires one or more times, as the words are tentatively recognized. Finally, the SpeechRecognizer raises a SpeechRecognized if it can successfully process the text or SpeechRecognitionRejected event if it cannot. The SpeechRecognition-Rejected event includes information about what the SpeechRecognizer believes the spoken input might have been, but its confident level is not high enough to accept the input.

It's generally not recommended that you use speech recognition in this fashion. That's because WPF has its own UI Automation feature that works seamlessly with the speech recognition engine. When configured, it allows users to enter text in text controls and trigger button controls by speaking their automation names. However, you could use the SpeechRecognition class to add support for more specialized commands to support specific scenarios. You do this by specifying a *grammar* based on the Speech Recognition Grammar Specification (SRGS).

The SRGS grammar identifies what commands are valid for your application. For example, it may specify that commands can use only one of a small set of words (*in* or *off*) and that these words can be used only in specific combinations (*blue on, red on, blue off*, and so on).

You can construct an SRGS grammar in two ways. You can load it from an SRGS document, which specifies the grammar rules using an XML-based syntax. To do this, you need to use the SrgsDocument from the System.Speech.Recognition.SrgsGrammar namespace:

```
SrgsDocument doc = new SrgsDocument("app_grammar.xml");
Grammar grammar = new Grammar(doc);
recognizer.LoadGrammar(grammar);
```

Alternatively, you can construct your grammar declaratively using the GrammarBuilder. The GrammarBuilder plays an analogous role the PromptBuilder you considered in the previous section—it allows you to append grammar rules bit by bit to create a complete grammar. For example, here's a declaratively constructed grammar that accepts two-word input, where the first words has five possibilities and the second word has just two:

```
GrammarBuilder grammar = new GrammarBuilder();
grammar.Append(new Choices("red", "blue", "green", "black", "white"));
grammar.Append(new Choices("on", "off"));

recognizer.LoadGrammar(new Grammar(grammar));
```

This markup allows commands like *red on* and *green off*. Alternate input like *yellow on* or *on red* won't be recognized.

The Choices object represents the SRGS *one-of* rule, which allows the user to speak one word out of a range of choices. It's the most versatile ingredient when building a grammar. Several more overloads to the GrammarBuilder.Append() method accept different input. You can pass an ordinary string, in which case the grammar will require the user to speak exactly that word. You can pass a string followed by a value from the SubsetMatchingMode enumeration to require the user to speak some part of a word or phrase. Finally, you can pass a string followed by a number of minimum and maximum repetitions. This allows the grammar to ignore the same word if it's repeated multiple times, and it also allows you to make a word optional (by giving it a minimum repetition of 0).

Grammars that use all these features can become quite complex. For more information about the SRGS standard and its grammar rules, refer to http://www.w3.org/TR/speech-grammar.

The Last Word

In this example, you explored how to integrate sound and video into a WPF application. You learned about two different ways to control the playback of media files—either programmatically using the methods of the MediaPlayer or MediaTimeline classes or declaratively using a storyboard.

As always, the best approach depends on your requirements. The code-based approach gives you more control and flexibility, but it also forces you to manage more details and introduces additional complexity. As a general rule, the code-based approach is best if you need fine-grained control over audio playback. However, if you need to combine media playback with animations, the declarative approach is far easier.

CHAPTER 23

∎∎∎

3-D Drawing

Developers have used DirectX and OpenGL to build three-dimensional interfaces for many years. However, the difficult programming model and the substantial video card requirements have kept 3-D programming out of most mainstream consumer applications and business software.

WPF introduces a new expansive 3-D model that promises to change all that. Using WPF, you can build complex 3-D scenes out of straightforward markup. Helper classes provide hit-testing, mouse-based rotation, and other fundamental building blocks. And virtually any computer running Windows XP or Windows Vista can display the 3-D content, thanks to WPF's ability to fall back on software rendering when video card support is lacking.

The most remarkable part of WPF's libraries for 3-D programming is that they are designed to be a clear, consistent extension of the WPF model you've already learned about. For example, you use the same set of brush classes to paint 3-D surfaces as you use to paint 2-D shapes. You use a similar transform model to rotate, skew, and move 3-D objects, and a similar geometry model to define their contours. More dramatically, you can use the same styling, data binding, and animation features on 3-D objects as you use with 2-D content. It's this support of high-level WPF features that makes WPF's 3-D graphics suitable for everything from eye-catching effects in simple games to charting and data visualization in a business application. (The one situation where WPF's 3-D model *isn't* sufficient is high-powered real-time games. If you're planning to build the next Halo, you're much better off with the raw power of DirectX.)

Even though WPF's model for 3-D drawing is surprisingly clear and consistent, creating rich 3-D interfaces is still difficult. In order to code 3-D animations by hand (or just under-stand the underlying concepts), you need to master more than a little math. And modeling anything but a trivial 3-D scene with handwritten XAML is a huge, error-prone chore—it's far more involved than the 2-D equivalent of creating a XAML vector image by hand. For that rea-son, you're much more likely to rely on a third-party tool to create 3-D objects, export them to XAML, and then add them to your WPF applications.

Entire books have been written about all these issues—3-D programming math, 3-D design tools, and the 3-D libraries in WPF. In this chapter, you'll learn enough to understand the WPF model for 3-D drawing, create basic 3-D shapes, design more advanced 3-D scenes with a 3-D modeling tool, and use some of the invaluable code released by the WPF team and other third-party developers.

3-D Drawing Basics

A 3-D drawing in WPF involves four ingredients:

- A viewport, which hosts your 3-D content

- A 3-D object

- A light source that illuminates part or all of your 3-D scene

- A camera, which provides the vantage point from which you view the 3-D scene

Of course, more complex 3-D scenes will feature multiple objects and may include multiple light sources. (It's also possible to create a 3-D object that doesn't require a light source, if the 3-D object itself gives off light.) However, these basic ingredients provide a good starting point.

Compared to 2-D graphics, it's the second and third points that really make a difference. Programmers who are new to 3-D programming sometimes assume that 3-D libraries are just a simpler way to create an object that has a 3-D appearance, such as a glowing cube or a spinning sphere. But if that's all you need, you're probably better off creating a 3-D drawing using the 2-D drawing classes you've already learned about. After all, there's no reason that you can't use the shapes, transforms, and geometries you learned about in Chapter 13 and Chapter 14 to construct a shape that appears to be 3-D—in fact, it's usually easier than working with the 3-D libraries.

So what's the advantage of using the 3-D support in WPF? The first advantage is that you can create effects that would be extremely complex to calculate using a simulated 3-D model. One good example is light effects such as reflection, which become very involved when working with multiple light sources and different materials with different reflective properties. The other advantage to using a 3-D drawing model is that it allows you to interact with your drawing as a set of 3-D objects. This greatly extends what you can do programmatically. For example, once you build the 3-D scene you want, it becomes almost trivially easy to rotate your object or rotate the camera around your object. Doing the same work with 2-D programming would require an avalanche of code (and math).

Now that you know what you need, it's time to build an example that has all these pieces. This is the task you'll tackle in the following sections.

The Viewport

If you want to work with 3-D content, you need a container that can host it. This container is the Viewport3D class, which is found in the System.Windows.Controls namespace. Viewport3D derives from FrameworkElement, and so it can be placed anywhere you'd place a normal element. For example, you can use it as the content of a window or a page, or you can place it inside a more complex layout.

The Viewport3D class only hints at the complexity of 3-D programming. It adds just two properties—Camera, which defines your lookout onto the 3-D scene, and Children, which holds all the 3-D objects you want to place in the scene. Interestingly enough, the light source that illuminates your 3-D scene is itself an object in the viewport.

Note Among the inherited properties in the Viewport3D class, one is particularly significant: ClipToBounds. If set to true (the default), content that stretches beyond the bounds of the viewport is trimmed out. If set to false, this content appears overtop of any adjacent elements. This is the same behavior you get from the ClipToBounds property of the Canvas. However, there's an important difference when using the Viewport3D: performance. Setting Videport3D.ClipToBounds to false can dramatically improve performance when rendering a complex, frequently refreshed 3-D scene.

3-D Objects

The viewport can host any 3-D object that derives from Visual3D (from the System.Windows.Media.Media3D namespace, where the vast majority of the 3-D classes live). However, you'll need to perform a bit more work than you might expect to create a 3-D visual. In version 1.0, the WPF library lacks a collection of 3-D shape primitives. If you want a cube, a cylinder, a torus, and so on, you'll need to build it yourself.

One of the nicest design decisions that the WPF team made when building the 3-D drawing classes was to structure them in a similar way as the 2-D drawing classes. That means you'll immediately be able to understand the purpose of a number of core 3-D classes (even if you don't yet know how to use them). Table 23-1 spells out the relationships.

Table 23-1. *2-D Classes and 3-D Classes Compared*

2-D Class	3-D Class	Notes
Visual	Visual3D	Visual3D is the base class for all 3-D objects (objects that are rendered in a Viewport3D container). Like the Visual class, you could use the Visual3D class to derive lightweight 3-D shapes or to create more complex 3-D controls that provide a richer set of events and framework services. However, you won't get much help. You're more likely to use one of the classes that derive from Visual3D, such as ModelVisual3D or ModelUIElement3D.
Geometry	Geometry3D	The Geometry class is an abstract way to define a 2-D figure. Often geometries are used to define complex figures that are composed out of arcs, lines, and polygons. The Geometry3D class is the 3-D analogue—it represents a 3-D surface. However, while there are several 2-D geometries, WPF includes just a single concrete class that derives from Geometry3D: MeshGeometry3D. The MeshGeometry3D has a central importance in 3-D drawing because you'll use it to define all your 3-D objects.
GeometryDrawing	GeometryModel3D	There are several ways to use a 2-D Geometry object. You can wrap it in a GeometryDrawing and use that to paint the surface of an element or the content of a Visual. The GeometryModel3D class serves the same purpose—it takes a Geometry3D, which can then be used to fill your Visual3D.

Continued

Table 23-1. *Continued*

2-D Class	3-D Class	Notes
Transform	Transform3D	You already know that 2-D transforms are incredibly useful tools for manipulating elements and shapes in all kinds of ways, including moving, skewing, and rotating them. Transforms are also indispensable when performing animations. Classes that derive from Transform3D perform the same magic with 3-D objects. In fact, you'll find surprisingly similar transform classes such as Rotate-Transform3D, ScaleTransform3D, Translate-Transform3D, Transform3DGroup, and Matrix-Transform3D. Of course, the options provided by an extra dimension are considerable, and 3-D transforms are able to warp and distort visuals in ways that look quite different.

At first, you may find it a bit difficult to untangle the relationships between these classes. Essentially, the Viewport3D holds Visual3D objects. To actually give a Visual3D some content, you'll need to define a Geometry3D that describes the shape and wrap it in a Geometry-Model3D. You can then use that as the content for your Visual3D. Figure 23-1 shows this relationship.

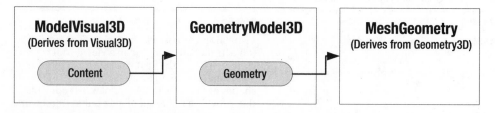

Figure 23-1. *How a 3-D object is defined*

This two-step process—defining the shapes you want to use in abstract and then fusing them with a visual—is an optional approach for 2-D drawing. However, it's mandatory for 3-D drawing because there are no prebuilt 3-D classes in the library. (The members of the WPF team and others have released some sample code online that starts to fill this gap, but it's still evolving.)

The two-step process is also important because 3-D models are a bit more complex than 2-D models. For example, when you create a Geometry3D object, you not only specify the vertexes of your shape, you also specify the *material* out of which it's composed. Different materials have different properties for reflecting and absorbing light.

Geometry

To build a 3-D object, you need to start by building the geometry. As you've already learned, there's just one class that fills this purpose: MeshGeometry3D.

Unsurprisingly, a MeshGeometry3D object represents a *mesh*. If you've ever dealt with 3-D drawing before (or if you've read a bit about the technology that underlies modern-day video cards), you may already know that computers prefer to build 3-D drawings out of triangles. That's because a triangle is the simplest, most granular way to define a surface. Triangles are simple because every triangle is defined by just three points (the vertexes at the corner). Arcs and curved surfaces are obviously more complex. Triangles are granular because other straight-edged shapes (squares, rectangles, and more complex polygons) can be broken down into a collection of triangles. For better or worse, modern-day graphics hardware and graphics programming is built on this core abstraction.

Obviously, most of the 3-D objects you want won't look like simple, flat triangles. Instead you'll need to combine triangles—sometimes just a few, but often hundreds or thousands that line up with one another at varying angles. A mesh is this combination of triangles. With enough triangles, you can ultimately create the illusion of anything, including a complex surface. (Of course, there are performance considerations involved, and 3-D scenes often map some sort of bitmap or 2-D content onto a triangle in a mesh to create the illusion of a complex surface with less overhead. WPF supports this technique.)

Understanding how a mesh is defined is one of the first keys to 3-D programming. If you look at the MeshGeometry3D class, you'll find that it adds the four properties listed in Table 23-2.

Table 23-2. *Properties of the MeshGeometry3D Class*

Name	Description
Positions	Contains a collection of all the points that define the mesh. Each point is a vertex in a triangle. For example, if your mesh has 10 completely separate triangles, you'll have 30 points in this collection. More commonly, some of your triangles will join at their edges, which means one point will become the vertex of several triangles. For example, a cube requires 12 triangles (two for each side), but only 8 distinct points. Making matters even more complicated, you may choose to define the same shared vertex multiple times, so that you can better control how separate triangles are shaded with the Normals property.
TriangleIndices	Defines the triangles. Each entry in this collection represents a single triangle by referring to three points from the Positions collection.
Normals	Provides a vector for each vertex (each point in the Positions collection). This vector indicates how the point is angled for lighting calculations. When WPF shades the face of a triangle, it measures the light at each of the three vertexes using the normal vector. Then, it interpolates between these three points to fill the surface of the triangle. Getting the right normal vectors makes a substantial difference to how a 3-D object is shaded—for example, it can make the divisions between triangles blend together or appear as sharp lines.
TextureCoordinates	Defines how a 2-D texture is mapped onto your 3-D object when you use a VisualBrush to paint it. The TextureCoordinates collection provides a 2-D point for each 3-D point in the Positions collection.

You'll consider shading with normals and texture mapping later in this chapter. But first, you'll learn how to build a basic mesh.

The following example shows the simplest possible mesh, which consists of a single triangle. The units you use aren't important because you can move the camera closer or farther away, and you can change the size or placement of individual 3-D objects using transforms. What *is* important is the coordinate system, which is shown in Figure 23-2. As you can see, the X and Y axes have the same orientation as in 2-D drawing. What's new is the Z axis. As the Z axis value decreases, the point moves farther away. As it increases, the point moves closer.

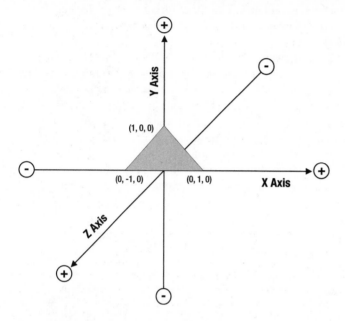

Figure 23-2. *A triangle in 3-D space*

Here's the MeshGeometry element that you can use to define this shape inside a 3-D visual. The MeshGeometry3D object in this example doesn't use the Normals property or the TextureCoordinates property because the shape is so simple and will be painted with a Solid-ColorBrush:

```
<MeshGeometry3D Positions="-1,0,0  0,1,0  1,0,0" TriangleIndices="0,2,1" />
```

Here, there are obviously just three points, which are listed one after the other in the Positions property. The order you use in the Positions property isn't important because the TriangleIndices property clearly defines the triangle. Essentially, the TriangleIndices property states that there is a single triangle made of point #0, #2, and #1. In other words, the TriangleIndices property tells WPF to draw the triangle by drawing a line from (-1, 0 ,0) to (1, 0, 0) and then to (0, 1, 0).

Note that 3-D programming has several subtle, easily violated rules. When defining a shape, you'll face the first one—namely, you must list the points in a counterclockwise order around the Z axis. This example follows that rule. However, you could easily violate it if you changed the TriangleIndices to 0, 1, 2. In this case, you'd still define the same triangle, but that triangle would be backward—in other words, if you look at it down the Z axis (as in Figure 23-2), you'll actually be looking at the *back* of the triangle.

■Note The difference between the back of a 3-D shape and the front is not a trivial one. In some cases, you may paint both with a different brush. Or you may choose not to paint the back at all in order to avoid using any resources for a part of the scene that you'll never see. If you inadvertently define the points in a clockwise order, and you haven't defined the material for the back of your shape, it will disappear from your 3-D scene.

Geometry Model and Surfaces

Once you have the properly configured MeshGeometry3D that you want, you need to wrap it in a GeometryModel3D.

The GeometryModel3D class has just three properties: Geometry, Material, and Back-Material. The Geometry property takes the MeshGeometry3D that defines the shape of your 3-D object. In addition, you can use the Material and BackMaterial properties to define the surface out of which your shape is composed.

The surface is important for two reasons. First, it defines the color of the object (although you can use more complex brushes that paint textures rather than solid colors). Second, it defines how that material responds to light.

WPF includes four material classes, all of which derive from the abstract Material class in the System.Windows.Media.Media3D namespace). They're listed in Table 23-3. In this example, we'll stick with DiffuseMaterial, which is the most common choice because its behavior is closest to a real-world surface.

Table 23-3. *Material Classes*

Name	Description
DiffuseMaterial	Creates a flat, matte surface. It diffuses light evenly in all directions.
SpecularMaterial	Creates a glossy, highlighted look (think metal or glass). It reflects light back directly, like a mirror.
EmissiveMaterial	Creates a glowing look. It generates its own light (although this light does not reflect off other objects in the scene).
MaterialGroup	Lets you combine more than one material. The materials are then layered overtop of one another in the order they're added to the MaterialGroup.

DiffuseMaterial offers a single Brush property that takes the Brush object you want to use to paint the surface of your 3-D object. (If you use anything other than a SolidColorBrush, you'll need to set the MeshGeometry3D.TextureCoordinates property to define the way it's mapped onto the object, as you'll see later in this chapter.)

Here's how you can configure the triangle to be painted with a yellow matte surface:

```
<GeometryModel3D>
  <GeometryModel3D.Geometry>
    <MeshGeometry3D Positions="-1,0,0  0,1,0  1,0,0" TriangleIndices="0,2,1" />
  </GeometryModel3D.Geometry>

  <GeometryModel3D.Material>
    <DiffuseMaterial Brush="Yellow" />
  </GeometryModel3D.Material>
</GeometryModel3D>
```

In this example, the BackMaterial property is not set, so the triangle will disappear if viewed from behind.

All that remains is to use this GeometryModel3D to set the Content property of a Model-Visual3D and then place that ModelVisual3D in a viewport. But in order to see your object, you'll also need two more details: a light source and a camera.

Light Sources

In order to create realistically shaded 3-D objects, WPF uses a lighting model. The basic idea is that you add one (or several) light sources to your 3-D scene. Your objects are then illuminated based on the type of light you've chosen, its position, direction, and intensity.

Before you delve into WPF lighting, it's important that you realize that the WPF lighting model doesn't behave like light in the real world. Although the WPF lighting system is constructed to emulate the real world, calculating true light reflections is a processor-intensive task. WPF makes use of a number of simplifications that ensure the lighting model is practical, even in animated 3-D scenes with multiple light sources. These simplifications include the following:

- Light effects are calculated for objects *individually*. Light reflected from one object will not reflect off another object. Similarly, an object will not cast a shadow on another object, no matter where it's placed.

- Lighting is calculated at the vertexes of each triangle and then interpolated over the surface of the triangle. (In other words, WPF determines the light strength at each corner and blends that to fill in the triangle.) As a result of this design, objects that have relatively few triangles may not be illuminated correctly. To achieve better lighting, you'll need to divide your shapes into hundreds or thousands of triangles.

Depending on the effect you're trying to achieve, you may need to work around these issues by combining multiple light sources, using different materials, and even adding extra shapes. In fact, getting the precise result you want is part of the art of 3-D scene design.

■**Note** Even if you don't provide a light source, your object will still be visible. However, without a light source, all you'll see is a solid black silhouette.

WPF provides four light classes, all of which derive from the abstract Light class. Table 23-4 lists them all. In this example, we'll stick with a single DirectionalLight, which is the most common type of lighting.

Table 23-4. *Light Classes*

Name	Description
DirectionalLight	Fills the scene with parallel rays of light traveling in the direction you specify.
AmbientLight	Fills the scene with scattered light.
PointLight	Radiates light in all directions, beginning at a single point in space.
SpotLight	Radiates light outward in a cone, starting from a single point.

Here's how you can define a white DirectionalLight:

```
<DirectionalLight Color="White" Direction="-1,-1,-1" />
```

In this example, the vector that determines the path of the light starts at the origin (0, 0, 0) and goes to (-1, -1, -1). That means that each ray of light is a straight line that travels from top-right front toward the bottom-left back. This makes sense in this example because the triangle (shown in Figure 23-2) is angled to face this light.

When calculating the light direction, it's the angle that's important, not the length of your vector. That means a light direction of (-2, -2, -2) is equivalent to the normalized vector (-1, -1, -1) because the angle it describes is the same.

In this example, the direction of the light doesn't line up exactly with the triangle's surface. If that's the effect you want, you'll need a light source that sends its beams straight down the Z axis, using a direction of (0, 0, -1). This distinction is deliberate. Because the beams strike the triangle at an angle, the triangle's surface will be shaded, which creates a more pleasing effect.

Figure 23-3 shows an approximation of the (-1, -1, -1) directional light as it strikes the triangle. Remember, a directional light fills the entire 3-D space.

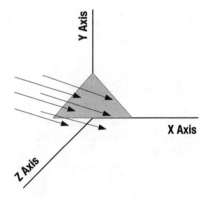

Figure 23-3. *The path of a (-1, -1, -1) directional light*

Note Directional lights are sometimes compared to sunlight. That's because the light rays received from a faraway light source (such as the sun) become almost parallel.

All light objects derive indirectly from GeometryModel3D. That means that you treat them exactly like 3-D objects by placing them inside a ModelVisual3D and adding them to a viewport. Here's a viewport that includes both the triangle you saw earlier and the light source:

```
<Viewport3D>
  <Viewport3D.Camera>...</Viewport3D.Camera>

  <ModelVisual3D>
    <ModelVisual3D.Content>
      <DirectionalLight Color="White" Direction="-1,-1,-1" />
```

```
        </ModelVisual3D.Content>
      </ModelVisual3D>

      <ModelVisual3D>
        <ModelVisual3D.Content>
          <GeometryModel3D>
            <GeometryModel3D.Geometry>
              <MeshGeometry3D Positions="-1,0,0 0,1,0 1,0,0" TriangleIndices="0,2,1" />
            </GeometryModel3D.Geometry>
            <GeometryModel3D.Material>
              <DiffuseMaterial Brush="Yellow" />
            </GeometryModel3D.Material>
          </GeometryModel3D>
        </ModelVisual3D.Content>
      </ModelVisual3D>

</Viewport3D>
```

There's one detail that's left out of this example—the viewport doesn't include a camera that defines your vantage point on the scene. That's the task you'll tackle in the next section.

A CLOSER LOOK AT 3-D LIGHTING

Along with DirectionalLight, AmbientLight is another all-purpose lighting class. Using AmbientLight on its own gives 3-D shapes a flat look, but you can combine it with another light source to add some illumination that brightens up otherwise darkened areas. The trick is to use an AmbientLight that's less than full strength. Instead of using a white AmbientLight, use one-third white (set the Color property to #555555) or less. You can also set the DiffuseMaterial.AmbientColor property to control how strongly an AmbientLight affects the material in a given mesh. Using white (the default) gives the strongest effect, while using black creates a material that doesn't reflect any ambient light.

The DirectionalLight and AmbientLight are the most useful lights for simple 3-D scenes. The PointLight and SpotLight only give the effect you want if your mesh includes a large number of triangles—typically hundreds. This is due to the way that WPF shades surfaces.

As you've already learned, WPF saves time by calculating the lighting intensity only at the vertexes of a triangle. If your shape uses a small number of triangles, this approximation breaks down. Some points will fall inside the range of the SpotLight or PointLight, while others won't. The result is that some triangles will be illuminated while others will remain in complete darkness. Rather than getting a soft rounded circle of light on your object, you'll end up with a group of illuminated triangles, giving the illuminated area a jagged edge.

The problem here is that PointLight and SpotLight are used to create soft, circular lighting effects, but you need a very large number of triangles to create a circular shape. (To create a perfect circle, you need one triangle for each pixel that lies on the perimeter of the circle.) If you have a 3-D mesh with hundreds or thousands of triangles, the pattern of partially illuminated triangles can more easily approximate a circle, and you'll get the lighting effect you want.

The Camera

Before a 3-D scene can be rendered, you need to place a camera at the correct position and orient it in the correct direction. You do this by setting the Viewport3D.Camera property with a Camera object.

In essence, the camera determines how a 3-D scene is projected onto the 2-D surface of a Viewport. WPF includes three camera classes: the commonly used PerspectiveCamera and the more exotic OrthographicCamera and MatrixCamera. The PerspectiveCamera renders the scene so that objects that are farther away appear smaller. This is the behavior that most people expect in a 3-D scene. The OrthographicCamera flattens 3-D objects so that the exact scale is preserved, no matter where a shape is positioned. This looks a bit odd, but it's useful for some types of visualization tools. For example, technical drawing applications often rely on this type of view. (Figure 23-4 shows the difference between the PerspectiveCamera and the OrthographicCamera.) Finally, the MatrixCamera allows you to specify a matrix that's used to transform the 3-D scene to 2-D view. It's an advanced tool that's intended for highly specialized effect and for porting code from other frameworks (such as Direct3D) that use this type of camera.

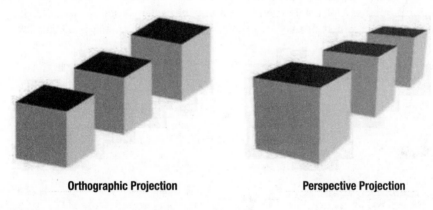

Orthographic Projection   **Perspective Projection**

Figure 23-4. *Perspective in different types of cameras*

Choosing the right camera is relatively easy, but placing and configuring it is a bit trickier. The first detail is to specify a point in 3-D space where the camera will be positioned by setting its Position property. The second step is to set a 3-D vector in the LookDirection property that indicates how the camera is oriented. In a typical 3-D scene, you'll place the camera slightly off to one corner using the Position property, and then tilt it to survey the view using the LookDirection property.

▇Note The position of the camera determines how large your scene appears in the viewport. The closer the camera, the larger the scale. In addition, the viewport is stretched to fit its container and the content inside is scaled accordingly. For example, if you create a viewport that fills a window, you can expand or shrink your scene by resizing the window.

You need to set the Position and LookDirection properties in concert. If you use Position to offset the camera but fail to compensate by turning the camera back in the right direction using LookDirection, you won't see the content you've created in your 3-D scene. To make sure you're correctly oriented, pick a point that you want to see square on from your camera. You can then calculate the look direction using this formula:

```
CameraLookDirection = CenterPointOfInterest - CameraPosition
```

In the triangle example, the camera is placed in the top-left corner using a position of (-2, 2, 2). Assuming you want to focus on the origin point (0, 0, 0), which falls in the middle of the triangle's bottom edge, you would use this look direction:

```
CameraLookDirection = (0, 0, 0) - (-2, 2, 2)
                    = (2, -2, -2)
```

This is equivalent to the normalized vector (1, -1, -1) because the direction it describes is the same. As with the Direction property of a DirectionalLight, it's the direction of the vector that's important, not its magnitude.

Once you've set the Position and LookDirection properties, you may also want to set the UpDirection properties. UpDirection determines how the camera is titled. Ordinarily, UpDirection is set to (0, 1, 0), which means the up direction is straight up, as shown in Figure 23-5.

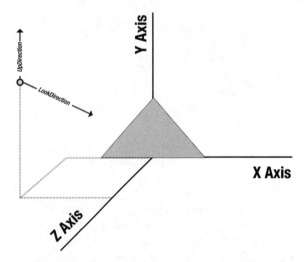

Figure 23-5. *Positioning and angling the camera*

If you offset this slightly—say to (0.25, 1, 0)—the camera is tilted around the X axis, as shown in Figure 23-6. As a result, the 3-D objects will appear to be tilted a bit in the other direction. It's just as if you'd cocked your head to one side while surveying the scene.

With these details in mind, you can define the PerspectiveCamera for the simple one-triangle scene that's been described over the previous sections:

```
<Viewport3D>
  <Viewport3D.Camera>
    <PerspectiveCamera Position="-2,2,2" LookDirection="2,-2,-2"
```

```
        UpDirection="0,1,0" />
    </Viewport3D.Camera>
    ...
</Viewport3D>
```

Figure 23-7 shows the final scene.

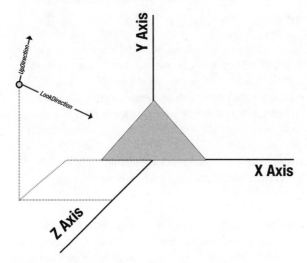

Figure 23-6. *Another way to angle the camera*

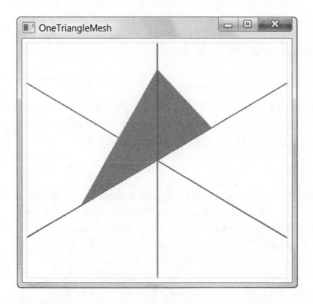

Figure 23-7. *A complete 3-D scene with one triangle*

AXIS LINES

There's one added detail in Figure 23-7: the axis lines. These lines are a great testing tool, as they make it easy to see where your axes are placed. If you render a 3-D scene and nothing appears, the axis lines can help you isolate the potential problem, which could include a camera pointing the wrong direction or positioned off to one side, or a shape that's flipped backward (and thus invisible). Unfortunately, WPF doesn't include any class for drawing straight lines. Instead, you need to render long, vanishingly narrow triangles.

Fortunately, there's a tool that can help. The WPF 3-D team has created a handy ScreenSpaceLines3D that solves the problem in a freely downloadable class library that's available (with complete source code) at `http://www.codeplex.com/3DTools`. This project includes several other useful code ingredients, including the Trackball described later in this chapter in the "Interactivity and Animations" section.

The ScreenSpaceLines3D class allows you to draw straight lines with an invariant width. In other words, these lines have the fixed thickness that you choose no matter where you place the camera. (They do not become thicker as the camera gets closer, and thinner as it recedes.) This makes these lines useful to create wireframes, boxes that indicate content regions, vector lines that indicate the normal for lighting calculations, and so on. These applications are most useful when building a 3-D design tool or when debugging an application. The example in Figure 23-5 uses the ScreenSpaceLines3D class to draw the axis lines.

There are a few other camera properties that are often important. One of these is FieldOfView, which controls how much of your scene you can see at once. FieldOfView is comparable to a zoom lens on a camera—as you decrease the FieldOfView, you see a smaller portion of the scene (which is then enlarged to fit the Viewport3D). As you increase the FieldOfView, you see a larger part of the scene. However, it's important to remember that changing the field of view is *not* the same as moving the camera closer or farther away from the objects in your scene. Smaller fields of view tend to compress the distance between near and far objects, while wider fields of view exaggerate the perspective difference between near and far objects. (If you've played with camera lenses before, you may have noticed this effect.)

Note The FieldOfView property only applies to the PerspectiveCamera. The OrthographicCamera includes a Width property that's analogous. The Width property determines the viewable area but it doesn't change the perspective because no perspective effect is used for the OrthographicCamera.

The camera classes also include NearPlaneDistance and FarPlaneDistance properties that set the blind spots of the camera. Objects closer than the NearPlaneDistance won't appear at all, and objects farther than the FarPlaneDistance are similarly invisible. Ordinarily, NearPlaneDistance defaults to 0.125, and FarPlaneDistance defaults to Double.PositiveInfinity, which renders both effects negligible. However, there are some cases where you'll need to change these values to prevent rendering artifacts. The most common example is when a complex mesh is extremely close to the camera, which can cause z-fighting (also known as *stitching*). In this situation, the video card is unable to correctly determine which triangles are closest to the camera and should be rendered. The result is a pattern of artifacts of the surface of your mesh.

Z-fighting usually occurs because of floating point round-off errors in the video card. To avoid this problem, you can increase the NearPlaneDistance to clip objects that are extremely close to the camera. Later in this chapter, you'll see an example that animates the camera so it flies through the center of a torus. To create this effect without causing z-fighting, it's necessary to increase the NearPlaneDistance.

Note Rendering artifacts are almost always the result of objects close to the camera and a NearPlaneDistance that's too large. Similar problems with very distant objects and the FarPlaneDistance are much less common.

Deeper into 3-D

Going to the trouble of cameras, lights, materials, and mesh geometries is a lot of work for an unimpressive triangle. However, you've now seen the bare bones of WPF's 3-D support. In this section, you'll learn how to use it to introduce more complex shapes.

Once you've mastered the lowly triangle, the next step up is to create a solid, faceted shape by assembling a small group of triangles. In the following example, you'll create the markup for the cube shown in Figure 23-8.

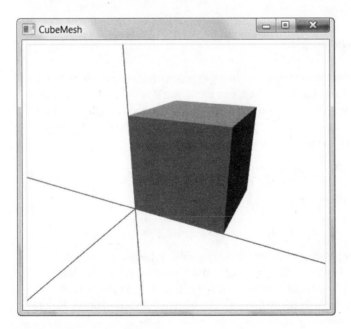

Figure 23-8. *A 3-D cube*

■**Note** You'll notice that the edges of the cube in Figure 23-8 have smooth, anti-aliased edges. Unfortunately, if you're rendering 3-D on Windows XP you won't get this level of quality. Due to sketchy support in XP video drivers, WPF doesn't attempt to perform anti-aliasing with the edges of 3-D shapes, leaving them jagged.

The first challenge to building your cube is determining how to break it down into the triangles that the MeshGeometry object recognizes. Each triangle acts like a flat, 2-D shape.

A cube consists of six square sides. Each square side needs two triangles. Each square side can then be joined to the adjacent side at an angle. Figure 23-9 shows how a cube breaks down into triangles.

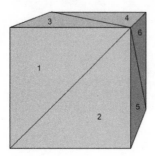

Figure 23-9. *Breaking the cube into triangles*

To reduce overhead and improve performance in a 3-D program it's common to avoid rendering shapes that you won't see. For example, if you know you'll never look at the underside of the cube shown in Figure 23-8, there's no reason to define the two triangles for that side. However, in this example you'll define every side so you can rotate the cube freely.

Here's a MeshGeometry3D that creates a cube:

```
<MeshGeometry3D Positions="0,0,0   10,0,0   0,10,0   10,10,0
                           0,0,10  10,0,10  0,10,10  10,10,10"
             TriangleIndices="0,2,1   1,2,3   0,4,2   2,4,6
                              0,1,4   1,5,4   1,7,5   1,3,7
                              4,5,6   7,6,5   2,6,3   3,6,7" />
```

First, the Positions collection defines the corners of the cube. It begins with the four points in the back (where z = 0) and then adds the four in the front (where z = 10). The TriangleIndices property maps these points to triangles. For example, the first entry in the collection is 0, 2, 1. It creates a triangle from the first point (0, 0, 0) to the second point (0, 0, 10) to the third point (0, 10, 0). This is one of the triangles required for the back side of the square. (The index 1, 2, 3 fills in the other backside triangle.)

Remember, when defining triangles, you must define them in counterclockwise order to make their front side face forward. However, the cube appears to violate that rule. The squares on the front side are defined in counterclockwise order (see the index 4, 5, 6 and 7, 6, 5, for instance), but those on the back side are defined in clockwise order, including the index 0, 2, 1 and 1, 2, 3. This is because the back side of the cube must have its triangle facing backward. To better visualize this, imagine rotating the cube around the Y axis so that the back side is facing forward. Now, the backward-facing triangles will be facing forward, making them completely visible, which is the behavior you want.

Shading and Normals

There's one issue with the cube mesh demonstrated in the previous section. It doesn't create the faceted cube shown in Figure 23-8. Instead, it gives you the cube shown in Figure 23-10, with clearly visible seams where the triangles meet.

Figure 23-10. *A cube with lighting artifacts*

This problem results from the way that WPF calculates lighting. In order to simplify the calculation process, WPF computes the amount of light that reaches each vertex in a shape—in other words, it only pays attention to the corners of your triangles. It then blends the lighting over the surface of the triangle. While this ensures that every triangle is nicely shaded, it may cause other artifacts. For example, in this situation it prevents the adjacent triangles that share a cube side from being shaded evenly.

To understand why this problem occurs, you need to know a little more about normals. Each normal defines how a vertex is oriented toward the light source. In most cases, you'll want your normal to be perpendicular to the surface of your triangle.

Figure 23-11 illustrates the front face of a cube. The front face has two triangles and a total of four vertexes. Each of these four vertexes should have a normal that points outward at a right angle to the square's surface. In other words, each normal should have a direction of (0, 0, 1).

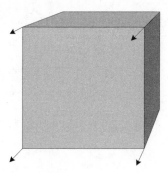

Figure 23-11. *Normals on the front side of a cube*

Tip Here's another way to think about normals. When the normal vector lines up with the light direction vector, but in opposite directions, the surface will be fully illuminated. In this example, that means a directional light with a direction of (0, 0, -1) will completely light up the front surface of the cube, which is what you expect.

The triangles on the other sides of the square need their own normals as well. In each case, the normals should be perpendicular to the surface. Figure 23-12 fills in the normals on the front, top, and right sides of the cube.

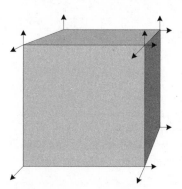

Figure 23-12. *Normals on the visible faces of a cube*

The cube diagrammed in Figure 23-12 is the same cube shown in Figure 23-8. When WPF shades this cube, it examines it one triangle at a time. For example, consider the front surface. Each point faces the directional light in exactly the same way. For that reason, each point will have exactly the same illumination. As a result, when WPF blends the illumination at the four corners, it creates a flat, consistently colored surface with no shading.

So why doesn't the cube you've just created exhibit this lighting behavior? The culprit is the shared points in the Positions collection. Although normals apply to the way triangles are shaded, they're only defined on the vertexes of the triangle. Each point in the Positions collection has just a single normal defined for it. That means if you share points between two different triangles, you also end up sharing normals.

That's what's happened in Figure 23-10. The different points on the same side are illuminated differently because they don't all have the same normal. WPF then blends the illumination from these points to fill in the surface of each triangle. This is a reasonable default behavior, but because the blending is performed on each triangle, different triangles won't line up exactly, and you'll see the seams of color where the separate triangles meet.

One easy (but tedious) way to solve this problem is to make sure no points are shared between triangles by declaring each point several times (once for each time it's used). Here's the lengthier markup that does this:

```
<MeshGeometry3D Positions="0,0,0    10,0,0    0,10,0    10,10,0
                0,0,0    0,0,10    0,10,0    0,10,10
                0,0,0    10,0,0    0,0,10    10,0,10
                10,0,0   10,10,10  10,0,10   10,10,0
                0,0,10   10,0,10   0,10,10   10,10,10
                0,10,0   0,10,10   10,10,0   10,10,10"
                TriangleIndices="0,2,1     1,2,3
                4,5,6     6,5,7
                8,9,10    9,11,10
                12,13,14  12,15,13
                16,17,18  19,18,17
                20,21,22  22,21,23" />
```

In this example, this step saves you from needing to code the normals by hand. WPF correctly generates them for you, making each normal perpendicular to the triangle surface, as shown in Figure 23-11. The result is the faceted cube shown in Figure 23-8.

Note Although this markup is much longer, the overhead is essentially unchanged. That's because WPF always renders your 3-D scene as a collection of distinct triangles, whether or not you share points in the Positions collection.

It's important to realize that you don't always want your normals to match. In the cube example, it's a requirement to get the faceted appearance. However, you might want a different lighting effect. For example, you might want a blended cube that avoids the seam problem shown earlier. In this case, you'll need to define your normal vectors explicitly.

Choosing the right normals can be a bit tricky. However, to get the result you want, keep these two principles in mind:

- To calculate a normal that's perpendicular to a surface, calculate the cross product of the vectors that make up any two sides of your triangle. However, make sure to keep the points in counterclockwise order so that the normal points out from the surface (instead of into it).

- If you want the blending to be consistent over a surface that includes more than one triangle, make sure all the points in all the triangles share the same normal.

To calculate the normal you need for a surface, you can use a bit of C# code. Here's a simple code routine that can help you calculate a normal that's perpendicular to the surface of a triangle based on its three points:

```csharp
private Vector3D CalculateNormal(Point3D p0, Point3D p1, Point3D p2)
{
    Vector3D v0 = new Vector3D(p1.X - p0.X, p1.Y - p0.Y, p1.Z - p0.Z);
    Vector3D v1 = new Vector3D(p2.X - p1.X, p2.Y - p1.Y, p2.Z - p1.Z);
    return Vector3D.CrossProduct(v0, v1);
}
```

Next, you need to set the Normals property by hand by filling it with vectors. Remember, you must add one normal for each position.

The following example smoothens the blending between adjacent triangles on the same side of a rectangle by sharing normals. The adjacent triangles on a cube face share two of the same points. Therefore it's only the two nonshared points that need to be adjusted. As long as they match, the shading will be consistent over the entire surface:

```xml
<MeshGeometry3D Positions="0,0,0 10,0,0 0,10,0 10,10,0
                           0,0,10 10,0,10 0,10,10 10,10,10"
               TriangleIndices="0,2,1 1,2,3 0,4,2 2,4,6
                                0,1,4 1,5,4 1,7,5 1,3,7
                                4,5,6 7,6,5 2,6,3 3,6,7"
               Normals="0,1,0 0,1,0 1,0,0 1,0,0
                        0,1,0 0,1,0 1,0,0 1,0,0" />
```

This creates the smoother cube shown in Figure 23-13. Now large portions of the cube end up sharing the same normal. This causes an extremely smooth effect that blends the edges of the cube, making it more difficult to distinguish the sides.

Figure 23-13. *An extremely smooth cube*

This effect isn't correct or incorrect—it simply depends on the effect you're trying to achieve. For example, faceted sides create a more geometric look, while blended sides look more organic. One common trick is to use blending with a large multifaceted polygon to make it look like a sphere, a cylinder, or another sort of curved shape. Because the blending hides the edges of the shape, this effect works remarkably well.

More Complex Shapes

Realistic 3-D scenes usually involve hundreds or thousands of triangles. For example, one approach to building a simple sphere is to split the sphere into bands and then split each band into a faceted series of squares, as shown in the leftmost example in Figure 23-14. Each square then requires two triangles.

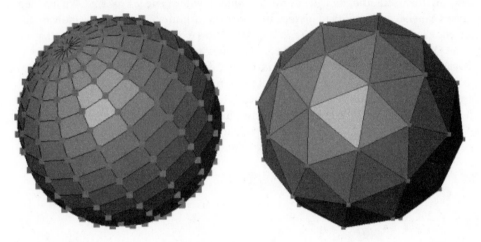

Figure 23-14. *Two ways to model a basic sphere*

To build this sort of nontrivial mesh, you need to construct it in code or use a dedicated 3-D modeling program. The code-only approach requires significant math. (For a WPF example that builds a sphere in code, see `http://www.codeproject.com/WPF/XamlUVSphere.asp`.) The design approach requires a sophisticated application.

Fortunately, there are plenty of tools for building 3-D scenes that you can use in WPF applications. Here are a few:

- ZAM 3D is a 3-D modeling tool designed explicitly for XAML. It's available at `http://www.erain.com/Products/ZAM3D`.

- Blender is an open source toolkit for 3-D modeling. It's available at `http://www.blender.org`, and there's an experimental XAML export script at `http://codeplex.com/xamlexporter`. Taken together, this provides a sophisticated and completely free platform for building 3-D content for WPF applications.

- Export plug-ins are beginning to appear for a range of professional 3-D modeling programs such as Maya and LightWave. For a list of some, check out `http://blogs.msdn.com/mswanson/articles/WPFToolsAndControls.aspx`.

All 3-D modeling programs include basic primitives, such as the sphere, that are built out of smaller triangles. You can then use these primitives to construct a scene. 3-D modeling programs also let you add and position your light sources and apply textures. Some, such as ZAM 3D, also allow you to define animations you want to perform on the objects in your 3-D scene.

Model3DGroup Collections

When working with complex 3-D scenes, you'll usually need to arrange multiple objects. As you already know, a Viewport3D can hold multiple Visual3D objects, each of which uses a different mesh. However, this isn't the best way to build a 3-D scene. You'll get far better performance by creating as few meshes as possible and combining as much content as possible into each mesh.

Obviously, there's another consideration: flexibility. If your scene is broken down into separate objects, you have the ability to hit test, transform, and animate these pieces individually. However, you don't need to create distinct Visual3D objects to get this flexibility. Instead, you can use the Model3DGroup class to place several meshes in a single Visual3D.

Model3DGroup derives from Model3D (as do the GeometryModel3D and Light classes). However, it's designed to group together a combination of meshes. Each mess remains a distinct piece of your scene that you can manipulate individually.

For example, consider the 3-D character shown in Figure 23-15. This character was created in ZAM 3D and exported to XAML. His individual body parts—head, torso, belt, arm, and so on—are separate meshes grouped into a single Model3DGroup object.

Figure 23-15. *A 3-D character*

The following is a portion of the markup, which draws the appropriate meshes from a resource dictionary:

```
<ModelVisual3D>
  <ModelVisual3D.Content>
    <Model3DGroup x:Name="Scene" Transform="{DynamicResource SceneTR20}">
      <AmbientLight ... />
      <DirectionalLight ... />
      <DirectionalLight ... />
      <Model3DGroup x:Name="CharacterOR22">
        <Model3DGroup x:Name="PelvisOR24">
          <Model3DGroup x:Name="BeltOR26">
            <GeometryModel3D x:Name="BeltOR26GR27"
             Geometry="{DynamicResource BeltOR26GR27}"
             Material="{DynamicResource ER_Vector___Flat_Orange___DarkMR10}"
             BackMaterial="{DynamicResource ER_Vector___Flat_Orange___DarkMR10}" />
          </Model3DGroup>
          <Model3DGroup x:Name="TorsoOR29">
            <Model3DGroup x:Name="TubesOR31">
              <GeometryModel3D x:Name="TubesOR31GR32"
               Geometry="{DynamicResource TubesOR31GR32}"
               Material="{DynamicResource ER___Default_MaterialMR1}"
               BackMaterial="{DynamicResource ER___Default_MaterialMR1}"/>
            </Model3DGroup>

            ...


  </ModelVisual3D.Content>
</ModelVisual3D>
```

The entire scene is defined in a single ModelVisual3D, which contains a Model3DGroup. That Model3DGroup contains other nested Model3DGroup objects. For example, the top-level Model3DGroup contains the lights and the character, while the Model3DGroup for the character contains another Model3DGroup that contains the torso, and that Model3DGroup contains details such as the arms, which contain the palms, which contain the thumbs, and so on, leading eventually to the GeometryModel3D objects that actually define the objects and their material. As a result of this carefully segmented, nested design (which is implicit in the way you create these objects in a design tool such as ZAM 3D), you can animate these body parts individually, making the character walk, gesture, and so on. (You'll take a look at animating 3-D content a bit later in this chapter in the "Interactivity and Animations" section.)

Note Remember, the lowest overhead is achieved by using the fewest number of meshes and the fewest number of ModelVisual3D objects. The Model3DGroup allows you to reduce the number of ModelVisual3D objects you use (there's no reason to have more than one) while retaining the flexibility to manipulate parts of your scene separately.

Materials Revisited

So far, you've used just one of the types of material that WPF supports for constructing 3-D objects. The DiffuseMaterial is by far the most useful material type—it scatters light in all directions, like a real-world object.

When you create a DiffuseMaterial, you supply a Brush. So far, the examples you've seen have used solid color brushes. However, the color you see is determined by the brush color and the lighting. If you have direct, full-strength lighting, you'll see the exact brush color. But if your lighting hits a surface at an angle (as in the previous triangle and cube examples), you'll see a darker, shaded color.

■**Note** Interestingly, WPF does allow you to make partially transparent 3-D objects. The easiest approach is to set the Opacity property of the brush that you use with the material to a value less than 1.

The SpecularMaterial and EmissiveMaterial types work a bit differently. Both are additively blended into any content that appears underneath. For that reason, the most common way to use both types of material is in conjunction with a DiffuseMaterial.

Consider the SpecularMaterial. It reflects light much more sharply than DiffuseMaterial. You can control how sharply the light is reflected using the SpecularPower property. Use a low number, and light is reflected more readily, no matter at what angle it strikes the surface. Use a higher number, and direct light is favored more strongly. Thus, a low SpecularPower produces a washed-out, shiny effect, while a high SpecularPower produces sharply defined highlights.

On its own, placing a SpecularMaterial over a dark surface creates a glasslike effect. However, SpecularMaterial is more commonly used to add highlights to a DiffuseMaterial. For example, using a white SpecularMaterial overtop of a DiffuseMaterial creates a plastic-like surface, while a darker SpecularMaterial and DiffuseMaterial produce a more metallic effect. Figure 23-16 shows two versions of a torus (a 3-D ring). The version on the left uses an ordinary DiffuseMaterial. The version on the right adds a SpecularMaterial overtop. The highlights appear in several places because the scene includes two directional lights that are pointed in different directions.

To combine two surfaces, you need to wrap them in a MaterialGroup. Here's the markup that creates the highlights shown in Figure 23-16:

```
<GeometryModel3D>
  <GeometryModel3D.Material>
    <MaterialGroup>
      <DiffuseMaterial>
        <DiffuseMaterial.Brush>
          <SolidColorBrush Color="DarkBlue" />
        </DiffuseMaterial.Brush>
      </DiffuseMaterial>
      <SpecularMaterial SpecularPower="24">
        <SpecularMaterial.Brush>
          <SolidColorBrush Color="LightBlue" />
        </SpecularMaterial.Brush>
```

```
    </SpecularMaterial>
  </GeometryModel3D.Material>

  <GeometryModel3D.Geometry>...</GeometryModel3D.Geometry>
<GeometryModel3D>
```

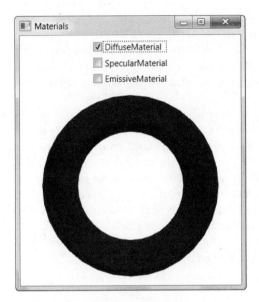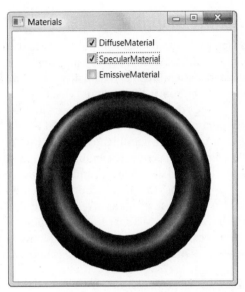

Figure 23-16. *Adding a SpecularMaterial*

■**Note** If you place a SpecularMaterial or an EmissiveMaterial on a white surface, you won't see anything at all. That's because the SpecularMaterial and EmissiveMaterial contribute their color additively, and the color white is already maxed out with the maximum possible red, green, and blue contributions. To see the full effect of SpecularMaterial or EmissiveMaterial, place them on a black surface (or use them over a black DiffuseMaterial).

The EmissiveMaterial is stranger still. It emits light, which means that a green Emissive-Material that's displayed over a dark surface shows up as a flat green silhouette, regardless of whether your scene includes any light sources.

Once again, you can get a more interesting effect by layering an EmissiveMaterial over a DiffuseMaterial. Because of the additive nature of EmissiveMaterial, the colors are blended. For example, if you place a red EmissiveMaterial over a blue DiffuseMaterial, your shape will acquire a purple tinge. The EmissiveMaterial will contribute the same amount of red over the entire surface of the shape, while the DiffuseMaterial will be shaded according to the light sources in your scene.

■**Tip** The light "radiated" from an EmissiveMaterial doesn't reach other objects. To create the effect of a glowing object that illuminates other nearby objects, you may want to place a light source (such as Point-Light) near your EmissiveMaterial.

Texture Mapping

So far, you've used the SolidColorBrush to paint your objects. However, WPF allows you to paint a DiffuseMaterial object using any brush. That means you can paint it with gradients (LinearGradientBrush and RadialGradientBrush), vector or bitmap images (ImageBrush), or the content from a 2-D element (VisualBrush).

There's one catch. When you use anything other than a SolidColorBrush, you need to supply additional information that tells WPF how to map the 2-D content of the brush onto the 3-D surface you're painting. You supply this information using the MeshGeometry.Texture-Coordinates collection. Depending on your choice, you can tile the brush content, extract just a part of it, and stretch, warp, and otherwise mangle it to fit curved and angular surfaces.

So how does the TextureCoordinates collection work? The basic idea is that each coordinate in your mesh needs a corresponding point in TextureCoordinates. The coordinate in the mesh is a point in 3-D space, while the point in the TextureCoordinates collection is a 2-D point because the content of a brush is always 2-D. The following sections show you how to use texture mapping to display image and video content on a 3-D shape.

Mapping the ImageBrush

The easiest way to understand how TextureCoordinates work is to use an ImageBrush that allows you to paint a bitmap. Here's an example that uses a misty scene of a tree at dawn:

```
<GeometryModel3D.Material>
  <DiffuseMaterial>
    <DiffuseMaterial.Brush>
      <ImageBrush ImageSource="Tree.jpg"></ImageBrush>
    </DiffuseMaterial.Brush>
  </DiffuseMaterial>
</GeometryModel3D.Material>
```

In this example, the ImageBrush is used to paint the content of the cube you created earlier. Depending on the TextureCoordinates you choose, you could stretch the image, wrapping it over the entire cube, or you could put a separate copy of it on each face (as we do in this example). Figure 23-17 shows the end result.

■**Note** This example adds one extra detail. It uses a Slider at the bottom of the window that allows the user to rotate the cube, viewing it from all angles. This is made possible by a transform, as you'll learn in the next section.

Figure 23-17. *A textured cube*

Initially, the TextureCoordinates collection is empty and your image won't appear on the 3-D surface. To get started with the cube example, you may want to concentrate on mapping just a single face. In the current example, the cube is oriented so that its left side is facing the camera. Here is the mesh for the cube. The two triangles that make up the left (front-facing) side are in bold:

```
<MeshGeometry3D
   Positions="0,0,0    10,0,0    0,10,0    10,10,0
              0,0,0     0,0,10    0,10,0    0,10,10
              0,0,0    10,0,0     0,0,10   10,0,10
             10,0,0    10,10,10  10,0,10   10,10,0
              0,0,10   10,0,10    0,10,10  10,10,10
              0,10,0    0,10,10  10,10,0   10,10,10"
   TriangleIndices="
              0,2,1      1,2,3
              4,5,6      6,5,7
              8,9,10     9,11,10
             12,13,14   12,15,13
             16,17,18   19,18,17
             20,21,22   22,21,23"   />
```

Most of the mesh points aren't mapped at all. In fact, the only points that are mapped are these four, which define the face of the cube that's oriented toward the camera:

(0,0,0) (0,0,10) (0,10,0) (0,10,10)

Because this is actually a flat surface, mapping is relatively easy. You can choose a set of TextureCoordinates for this face by removing the dimension that has a value of 0 in all four points. (In this example, that's the X coordinate because the visible face is actually on the left side of the cube.)

Here's the TextureCoordinates that fill this requirement:

```
(0,0) (0,10) (10,0) (10,10)
```

The TextureCoordinates collection uses relative coordinates. To keep things simple, you may want to use 1 to indicate the maximum value. In this example, that transformation is easy:

```
(0,0) (0,1) (1,0) (1,1)
```

This set of TextureCoordinates essentially tells WPF to take the point (0, 0) at the bottom left of the rectangle that represents the brush content, and map that to the corresponding point (0, 0, 0) in 3-D space. Similarly, take the bottom-right corner (0, 1) and map that to (0, 0, 10), make the top-left corner (1, 0) map to (0, 10, 0), and make the top-right corner (1, 1) map to (0, 10, 10).

Here's the cube mesh that uses this texture mapping. All the other coordinates in the Positions collection are mapped to (0, 0), so that the texture is not applied to these areas:

```
<MeshGeometry3D
   Positions="0,0,0    10,0,0    0,10,0    10,10,0
              0,0,0     0,0,10    0,10,0    0,10,10
              0,0,0    10,0,0     0,0,10   10,0,10
             10,0,0    10,10,10  10,0,10   10,10,0
              0,0,10   10,0,10    0,10,10  10,10,10
              0,10,0    0,10,10  10,10,0   10,10,10"
   TriangleIndices="..."
   TextureCoordinates="
             0,0  0,0  0,0  0,0
             0,0  0,1  1,0  1,1
             0,0  0,0  0,0  0,0
             0,0  0,0  0,0  0,0
             0,0  0,0  0,0  0,0
             0,0  0,0  0,0  0,0" />
```

This markup maps the texture to a single face on the cube. Although it is mapped successfully, the image is turned on its side. To get a top-up image, you need to rearrange your coordinates to use this order:

```
1,1 0,1 1,0 0,0
```

You can extend this process to map each face of the cube. Here's a set of TextureCoordinates that does exactly that and creates the multifaceted cube shown in Figure 23-17:

```
TextureCoordinates="0,0 0,1 1,0 1,1
                    1,1 0,1 1,0 0,0
                    0,0 1,0 0,1 1,1
                    0,0 1,0 0,1 1,1
                    1,1 0,1 1,0 0,0
                    1,1 0,1 1,0 0,0"
```

There are obviously many more effects you can create by tweaking these points. For example, you could stretch your texture around a more complex object like a sphere. Because the meshes required for this sort of object typically include hundreds of points, you won't fill the TextureCoordinates collection by hand. Instead, you'll rely on a 3-D modeling program (or a math-crunching code routine that does it at runtime). If you want to apply different brushes to different portions of your mesh, you'll need to split your 3-D object into multiple meshes, each of which will have a different material that uses a different brush. You can then combine those meshes into one Model3DGroup for the lowest overhead.

Video and the VisualBrush

Ordinary images aren't the only kind of content you can map to a 3-D surface. You can also map content that changes, such as gradient brushes that have animated values. One common technique in WPF is to map a video to a 3-D surface. As the video plays, its content is displayed in real time on the 3-D surface.

Achieving this somewhat overused effect is surprisingly easy. In fact, you can map a video brush to the faces of a cube, with different orientations, using the exact same set of Texture-Coordinates you used in the previous example to map the image. All you need to do is replace the ImageBrush with a more capable VisualBrush and use a MediaElement for your visual. With the help of an event trigger, you can even start a looping playback of your video without requiring any code.

The following markup creates a VisualBrush that performs looping playback and rotates the cube at the same time, displaying its different axes. (You'll learn more about how you can use animation and rotation to achieve this effect in the next section.)

```
<GeometryModel3D.Material>
  <DiffuseMaterial>
    <DiffuseMaterial.Brush>
      <VisualBrush>
        <VisualBrush.Visual>
          <MediaElement>
            <MediaElement.Triggers>
              <EventTrigger RoutedEvent="MediaElement.Loaded">
                <EventTrigger.Actions>
                  <BeginStoryboard>
                    <Storyboard >
                      <MediaTimeline Source="test.mpg"
                        RepeatBehavior="Forever" />
                      <DoubleAnimation Storyboard.TargetName="rotate"
                        Storyboard.TargetProperty="Angle"
                        To="360" Duration="0:0:5" RepeatBehavior="Forever" />
                    </Storyboard>
                  </BeginStoryboard>
                </EventTrigger.Actions>
              </EventTrigger>
            </MediaElement.Triggers>
          </MediaElement>
        </VisualBrush.Visual>
```

```
      </VisualBrush>
    </DiffuseMaterial.Brush>
  </DiffuseMaterial>
</GeometryModel3D.Material>
```

Figure 23-18 shows a snapshot of this example in action.

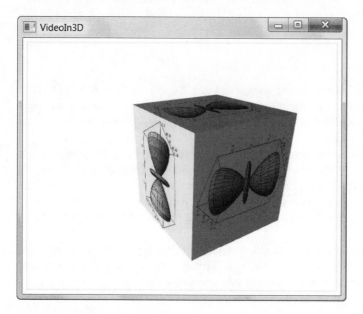

Figure 23-18. *Displaying video on several 3-D surfaces*

Interactivity and Animations

To get the full value out of your 3-D scene, you need to make it *dynamic*. In other words, you need to have some way to modify part of the scene, either automatically or in response to user actions. After all, if you don't need a dynamic 3-D scene, you'd be better off creating a 3-D image in your favorite illustration program and then exporting it as an ordinary XAML vector drawing. (Some 3-D modeling tools, such as ZAM 3D, provide exactly this option.)

In the following sections, you'll learn how to manipulate 3-D objects using transforms and how to add animation and move the camera. You'll also consider a separately released tool: a Trackball class that allows you to rotate a 3-D scene interactively. Finally, you'll learn how to perform hit testing in a 3-D scene and how to place interactive 2-D elements, such as buttons and text boxes, on a 3-D surface.

Transforms

As with 2-D content, the most powerful and flexible way to change an aspect of your 3-D scene is to use transforms. This is particularly the case with 3-D, as the classes you work with are relatively low-level. For example, if you want to scale a sphere, you need to construct the appropriate geometry and use the ScaleTransform3D to animate it. If you had a 3-D sphere primitive to work with, this might not be necessary because you might be able to animate a higher-level property like Radius.

Transforms are obviously the answer to creating dynamic effects. However, before you can use transforms, you need to decide how you want to apply them. There are several possible approaches:

- Modify a transform that's applied to your Model3D. This allows you to change a single aspect of a single 3-D object. You can also use this technique on a Model3DGroup, as it derives from Model3D.

- Modify a transform that's applied to your ModelVisual3D. This allows you to change an entire scene.

- Modify a transform that's applied to your light. This allows you to change the lighting of your scene (for example, to create a "sunrise" effect).

- Modify a transform that's applied to your camera. This allows you to move the camera through your scene.

Transforms are so useful in 3-D drawing that it's a good idea to get into the habit of using a Transform3DGroup whenever you need a transform. That way, you can add additional transforms afterward without being forced to change your animation code. The ZAM 3D modeling program always adds a set of four placeholder transforms to every Model3DGroup, so that the object represented by that group can be manipulated in various ways:

```
<Model3DGroup.Transform>
  <Transform3DGroup>
    <TranslateTransform3D OffsetX="0" OffsetY="0" OffsetZ="0"/>
    <ScaleTransform3D ScaleX="1" ScaleY="1" ScaleZ="1"/>
    <RotateTransform3D>
      <RotateTransform3D.Rotation>
        <AxisAngleRotation3D Angle="0" Axis="0 1 0"/>
      </RotateTransform3D.Rotation>
    </RotateTransform3D>
    <TranslateTransform3D OffsetX="0" OffsetY="0" OffsetZ="0"/>
  </Transform3DGroup>
</Model3DGroup.Transform>
```

Notice that this set of transforms includes two TranslateTransform3D objects. That's because translating an object before it's been rotated produces a different result than translating it after it's been rotated, and you may want to use both effects.

Another handy technique is to name your transform objects in XAML using the x:Name attribute. Even though the transform objects don't have a name property, this creates a private member variable you can use to access them more easily without being forced to dig through a deep hierarchy of objects. This is particularly important because complex 3-D scenes often have multiple layers of Model3DGroup objects, as described earlier. Walking down this element tree from the top-level ModelVisual3D is awkward and error-prone.

Rotations

To get a taste of the ways you might use transforms, consider the following markup. It applies a RotateTransform3D, which allows you to rotate a 3-D object around an axis you specify. In this case, the axis of rotation is set to line up exactly with the Y axis in your coordinate system:

```
<ModelVisual3D.Transform>
  <RotateTransform3D>
    <RotateTransform3D.Rotation>
      <AxisAngleRotation3D x:Name="rotate" Axis="0 1 0" />
    </RotateTransform3D.Rotation>
  </RotateTransform3D>
</ModelVisual3D.Transform>
```

Using this named rotation, you can create a databound Slider that allows the user to spin the cube around its axis:

```
<Slider Grid.Row="1"  Minimum="0" Maximum="360" Orientation="Horizontal"
  Value="{Binding ElementName=rotate, Path=Angle}" ></Slider>
```

Just as easily, you can use this rotation in an animation. Here's an animation that spins a torus (a 3-D ring) simultaneously along two different axes. It all starts when a button is clicked:

```
<Button>
  <Button.Content>Rotate Torus</Button.Content>
    <Button.Triggers>
      <EventTrigger RoutedEvent="Button.Click">
        <BeginStoryboard>
          <Storyboard RepeatBehavior="Forever">
            <DoubleAnimation Storyboard.TargetName="ring"
              Storyboard.TargetProperty="rotate1" To="360" Duration="0:0:2.5"/>
            <DoubleAnimation Storyboard.TargetName="ring"
              Storyboard.TargetProperty="rotate2" To="360" Duration="0:0:2.5"/>
          </Storyboard>
        </BeginStoryboard>
      </EventTrigger>
    </Button.Triggers>
</Button>
```

Figure 23-19 shows four snapshots of the torus in various stages of rotation.

■**Note** WPF masters are exploring ways to provide reusable 3-D effects that other developers can apply to their content with a minimum of fuss. One early example is the Planerator, a Decorator that rotates the 2-D element content you place inside. (You can download it at `http://tinyurl.com/2j6thq`.) Similar work is underway to create reusable 3-D transitions (for example, creating content that flies in to view or duplicating the Mac OS X "Genie" effect, which warps a window and funnels it down to the bottom of the screen when it's minimized).

Figure 23-19. *A rotating 3-D shape*

A Fly Over

A common effect in 3-D scenes is to move the camera around the object. This task is conceptually quite easy in WPF. You simply need a TranslateTransform to move the camera. However, two considerations apply:

- Usually, you'll want to move the camera along a route rather than in a straight line from a start point to an end point. There are two ways to solve this challenge—you can use a path-based animation to follow a geometrically defined route, or you can use a key frame animation that defines several smaller segments.

- As the camera moves, it also needs to adjust the direction in which it's looking. You'll also need to animate the LookDirection property to keep focused on the object.

The following markup shows an animation that flies through the center of a torus, spins around its outer edge, and eventually drifts back to the starting point. To see this animation in action, check out the samples for this chapter:

```
<StackPanel Orientation="Horizontal">
  <Button>
    <Button.Content>Begin Fly-Through</Button.Content>
    <Button.Triggers>
      <EventTrigger RoutedEvent="Button.Click">
        <BeginStoryboard>
          <Storyboard>
            <Point3DAnimationUsingKeyFrames
             Storyboard.TargetName="camera"
             Storyboard.TargetProperty="Position">
              <LinearPoint3DKeyFrame Value="0,0.2,-1" KeyTime="0:0:10"/>
              <LinearPoint3DKeyFrame Value="-0.5,0.2,-1" KeyTime="0:0:15"/>
              <LinearPoint3DKeyFrame Value="-0.5,0.5,0" KeyTime="0:0:20"/>
              <LinearPoint3DKeyFrame Value="0,0,2" KeyTime="0:0:23"/>
            </Point3DAnimationUsingKeyFrames>
```

```
            <Vector3DAnimationUsingKeyFrames
             Storyboard.TargetName="camera"
             Storyboard.TargetProperty="LookDirection">
              <LinearVector3DKeyFrame Value="-1,-1,-3" KeyTime="0:0:4"/>
              <LinearVector3DKeyFrame Value="-1,-1,3" KeyTime="0:0:10"/>
              <LinearVector3DKeyFrame Value="1,0,3" KeyTime="0:0:14"/>
              <LinearVector3DKeyFrame Value="0,0,-1" KeyTime="0:0:22"/>
            </Vector3DAnimationUsingKeyFrames>
          </Storyboard>
        </BeginStoryboard>
      </EventTrigger>
    </Button.Triggers>
  </Button>
</StackPanel>
```

For a bit more fun, you can start both animations (the rotation shown earlier and the fly-over effect shown here), which will cause the camera to pass through the edge of the ring as it rotates. You can also animate the UpDirection property of the camera to wiggle it as it moves:

```
<Vector3DAnimation
  Storyboard.TargetName="camera" Storyboard.TargetProperty="UpDirection"
  From="0,0,-1" To="0,0.1,-1" Duration="0:0:0.5" AutoReverse="True"
  RepeatBehavior="Forever" />
```

3-D PERFORMANCE

Rendering a 3-D scene requires much more work than rendering a 2-D scene. When you animate a 3-D scene, WPF attempts to refresh the parts that have changed 60 times per second. Depending on the complexity of your scene, this can easily use up the memory resources on your video card, which will cause the frame rate to fall and the animation to become choppy.

There are a few basic techniques you can use to get better 3-D performance. Here are some strategies for tweaking the viewport to reduce the 3-D rendering overhead:

- If you don't need to crop content that extends beyond the bounds of your viewport, set Viewport3D.ClipToBounds to false.

- If you don't need to provide hit testing in your 3-D scene, set Viewport3D.IsHitTestVisible to false.

- If you don't mind lower quality—jagged edges on 3-D shapes—set the attached property Render-Options.EdgeMode to Aliased on the Viewport3D.

- If your Viewport3D is larger than it needs to be, resize it to be smaller.

It's also important to ensure that your 3-D scene is as lightweight as possible. Here are a few critical tips for creating the most efficient meshes and models:

- Whenever possible, create a single complex mesh rather than several smaller meshes.

- If you need to use different materials for the same mesh, define the MeshGeometry object once (as a resource) and then reuse it to create multiple GeometryModel3D objects.

- Whenever possible, wrap a group of GeometryModel3D objects in a Model3DGroup, and place that group in a single ModelVisual3D object. Don't create a separate ModelVisual3D object for each GeometryModel3D.

- Don't define a back material (using GeometryModel3D.BackMaterial) unless the user will actually see the back of the object. Similarly, when defining meshes, consider leaving out triangles that won't be visible (for example, the bottom surface of a cube).

- Prefer solid brushes, gradient brushes, and the ImageBrush over the DrawingBrush and VisualBrush, both of which have more overhead. When using the DrawingBrush and VisualBrush to paint static content, you can cache the brush content to improve performance. To do so, use the attached property RenderOptions.CachingHint on the brush and set it to Cache.

If you keep these guidelines in mind, you'll be well on the way to ensuring the best possible 3-D drawing performance, and the highest possible frame rate for 3-D animation.

The Trackball

One of the most commonly requested behaviors in a 3-D scene is the ability to rotate an object using the mouse. One of the most common implementations is called a *virtual trackball*, and it's found in many 3-D graphics and 3-D design programs. Although WPF doesn't include a native implementation of a virtual trackball, the WPF 3-D team has released a free sample class that performs this function. This virtual trackball is a robust, extremely popular piece of code that finds its way into most of the 3-D demo applications that are provided by the WPF team.

The basic principle of the virtual trackball is that the user clicks somewhere on the 3-D object and drags it around an imaginary center axis. The amount of rotation depends on the distance the mouse is dragged. For example, if you click in the middle of the right side of a Viewport3D and drag the mouse to the left, the 3-D scene will appear to rotate around an imaginary vertical line. If you move the mouse all the way to the left side, the 3-D scene will be flipped 180 degrees to expose its back, as shown in Figure 23-20.

Although the virtual trackball appears to rotate the 3-D scene, it actually works by moving the camera. The camera always remains equally distant from the center point of the 3-D scene—essentially, the camera is moved along the contour of a big sphere that contains the entire scene. For a description of how the WPF virtual trackball works and the calculations that are involved, refer to http://viewport3d.com/trackball.htm. You can download the virtual trackball code with the 3-D tools projects described earlier at http://www.codeplex.com/3DTools.

■**Note** Because the virtual trackball moves the camera, you shouldn't use it in conjunction with your own camera-moving animation. However, you can use it in conjunction with an animated 3-D scene (for example, a 3-D scene that contains a rotating torus like the one described earlier).

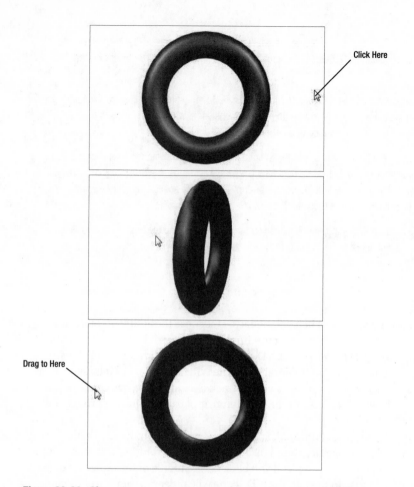

Figure 23-20. *Changing your viewpoint with the virtual trackball*

Using the virtual trackball is absurdly easy. All you need to do is wrap your Viewport3D in the TrackballDecorator class. The TrackballDecorator class is included with the 3-D tools project, so you'll need to begin by adding an XML alias for the namespace:

```
<Window xmlns:tools="clr-namespace:_3DTools;assembly=3DTools"    ...    >
```

Then you can easily add the TrackballDecorator to your markup:

```
<tools:TrackballDecorator>
  <Viewport3D>
    ...
  </Viewport3D>
</tools:TrackballDecorator>
```

Once you take this step, the virtual trackball functionality is automatically available—just click with the mouse and drag.

Hit Testing

Sooner or later, you'll want to create an interactive 3-D scene—one where the user can click 3-D shapes to perform different actions. The first step to implementing this design is *hit testing*, the process by which you intercept a mouse click and determine what region was clicked. Hit testing is easy in the 2-D world, but it's not quite as straightforward in a Viewport3D.

Fortunately, WPF provides sophisticated 3-D hit-testing support. You have three options for performing hit-testing in a 3-D scene:

- You can handle the mouse events of the viewport (such as MouseUp or MouseDown). Then you can call the VisualTreeHelper.HitTest() method to determine what object was hit. In the first version of WPF (released with .NET 3.0), this was the only possible approach.

- You can create your own 3-D control by deriving a custom class from the abstract UIElement3D class. This approach works, but it requires a lot of work. You need to implement all the UIElement-type plumbing on your own.

- You can replace one of your ModelVisual3D objects with a ModelUIElement3D object. The ModelUIElement3D class is derived from UIElement3D. It fuses the all-purpose 3-D model you've used so far with the interactive capabilities of a WPF element, including mouse handling.

To understand how 3-D hit testing works, it helps to consider a simple example. In the following section, you'll add hit testing to the familiar torus.

Hit Testing in the Viewport

To use the first approach to hit testing, you need to attach an event handler to one of the mouse events of the Viewport3D, such as MouseDown:

```
<Viewport3D MouseDown="viewport_MouseDown">
```

The MouseDown event handler uses hit-testing code at its simplest. It takes the current position of the mouse and returns a reference for the topmost ModelVisual3D that the point intercepts (if any):

```
private void viewport_MouseDown(object sender, MouseButtonEventArgs e)
{
    Viewport3D viewport = (Viewport3D)sender;
    Point location = e.GetPosition(viewport);
    HitTestResult hitResult = VisualTreeHelper.HitTest(viewport, location);

    if (hitResult != null && hitResult.VisualHit == ringVisual)
    {
        // The click hit the ring.
    }
}
```

Although this code works in simple examples, it's usually not sufficient. As you learned earlier, it's almost always better to combine multiple objects in the same ModelVisual3D. In many cases, all the objects in your entire scene will be placed in the same ModelVisual3D, so the hit doesn't provide enough information.

Fortunately, if the click intercepts a mesh, you can cast the HitTestResult to the more capable RayMeshGeometry3DHitTestResult object. You can find out which ModelVisual3D was hit using the RayMeshGeometry3DHitTestResult:

```
RayMeshGeometry3DHitTestResult meshHitResult =
  hitResult as RayMeshGeometry3DHitTestResult;
if (meshHitResult != null && meshHitResult.ModelHit == ringModel)
{
    // Hit the ring.
}
```

Or for even more fine-grained hit testing, you can use the MeshHit property to determine which specific mesh was hit. In the following example, the code determines whether the mesh representing the torus was hit. If it has been hit, the code creates and starts a new animation that rotates the torus. Here's the trick—the rotation axis is set so that it runs through the center of the torus, perpendicular to an imaginary line that connects the center of the torus to the location where the mouse was clicked. The effect makes it appear that the torus has been "hit" and is rebounding away from the click by twisting slightly away from the foreground and in the opposite direction.

Here's the code that implements that effect:

```
private void viewport_MouseDown(object sender, MouseButtonEventArgs e)
{
    Viewport3D viewport = (Viewport3D)sender;
    Point location = e.GetPosition(viewport);
    HitTestResult hitResult = VisualTreeHelper.HitTest(viewport, location);
    RayMeshGeometry3DHitTestResult meshHitResult =
      hitResult as RayMeshGeometry3DHitTestResult;

    if (meshHitResult != null && meshHitResult.MeshHit == ringMesh)
    {
      // Set the axis of rotation.
      axisRotation.Axis = new Vector3D(
        -meshHitResult.PointHit.Y, meshHitResult.PointHit.X, 0);

      // Start the animation.
      DoubleAnimation animation = new DoubleAnimation();
      animation.To = 40;
      animation.DecelerationRatio = 1;
      animation.Duration = TimeSpan.FromSeconds(0.15);
      animation.AutoReverse = true;
      axisRotation.BeginAnimation(AxisAngleRotation3D.AngleProperty, animation);
    }
}
```

This approach to hit testing works perfectly well. However, if you have a scene with a large number of 3-D objects and the interaction you require with these objects is straightforward (for example, you have a dozen buttons), this approach to hit testing makes for more work than necessary. In this situation, you're better off using the ModelUIElement3D class, which is introduced in the next section.

The ModelUIElement3D

The ModelUIElement3D is a type of Visual3D. Like all the Visual3D objects, it can be placed in a Viewport3D container.

Figure 23-21 shows the inheritance hierarchy for all the classes that derive from Visual3D. The three key classes that derive from Visual3D are ModelVisual3D (which you've used up to this point), UIElement3D (which defines the 3-D equivalent of the WPF element), and Viewport2DVisual3D (which allows you to place 2-D content in a 3-D scene, as described in the section "2-D Elements on 3-D Surfaces" later in this chapter).

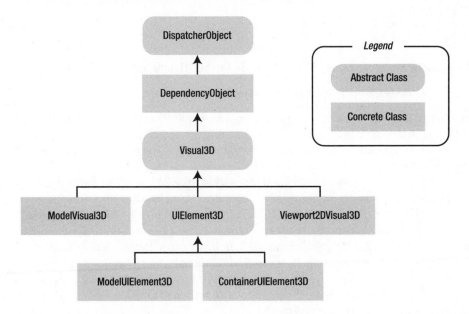

Figure 23-21. *The 3-D visual classes*

The UIElement3D class plays an analogous role to the UIElement class in the 2-D world, by adding support for mouse, keyboard, and stylus events, along with focus tracking. However, UIElement3D doesn't support any sort of layout system. The UIElement3D class, its descendants, and the Viewport2DVisual3D class are all new in WPF 3.5.

Although you can create a custom 3-D element by deriving from UIElement3D, it's far easier to use the ready-made classes that derive from UIElement3D: ModelUIElement3D and ContainerUIElement3D.

Using a ModelUIElement3D is not much different from using the ModelVisual3D class with which you're already familiar. The ModelUIElement3D class supports transforms (through the Transform property) and allows you to define its shape with a GeometryModel3D object (by setting the Model property, not the Content property as you do with ModelVisual3D).

Hit Testing with the ModelUIElement3D

Right now, the torus consists of a single ModelVisual3D, which contains a Model3DGroup. This group includes the torus geometry and the light sources that illuminate it. To change the torus example so that it uses the ModelUIElement3D, you simply need to replace the Model-Visual3D that represents the torus with a ModelUIElement3D:

```
<Viewport3D x:Name="viewport">
  <Viewport3D.Camera>...</Viewport3D.Camera>

  <ModelUIElement3D>
    <ModelUIElement3D.Model>
      <Model3DGroup>...<Model3DGroup>
    </ModelUIElement3D.Model>
  </ModelUIElement3D>

</Viewport3D>
```

Now you can perform hit testing directly with the ModelUIElement3D:

```
<ModelUIElement3D MouseDown="ringVisual_MouseDown">
```

The difference between this example and the previous one is that now the MouseDown event will fire only when the ring is clicked (rather than any time a point inside the viewport is clicked). However, the event-handling code still needs a bit of tweaking to get the result you want in this example.

The MouseDown event provides a standard MouseButtonEventArgs object to the event handler. This object provides the standard mouse event details, such as the exact time the event occurred, the state of the mouse buttons, and a GetPosition() method that allows you to determine the clicked coordinates relative to any element that implements IInputElement (such as the Viewport3D or the MouseUIElement3D). In many cases, these 2-D coordinates are exactly what you need. (For example, they are a requirement if you're using 2-D content on a 3-D surface, as described in the next section. In this case, any time you move, resize, or create elements, you're positioning them in 2-D space, which is then mapped to a 3-D surface based on a preexisting set of texture coordinates.)

However, in the current example it's important to get the 3-D coordinates on the torus mesh so that the appropriate animation can be created. That means you still need to use the VisualTreeHelper.HitTest() method, as shown here:

```
private void ringVisual_MouseDown(object sender, MouseButtonEventArgs e)
{
    // Get the 2-D coordinates relative to the viewport.
    Point location = e.GetPosition(viewport);

    // Get the 3-D coordinates relative to the mesh.
    RayMeshGeometry3DHitTestResult meshHitResult =
      (RayMeshGeometry3DHitTestResult)VisualTreeHelper.HitTest(
        viewport, location);
```

```
    // Create the animation.
    axisRotation.Axis = new Vector3D(
      -meshHitResult.PointHit.Y, meshHitResult.PointHit.X, 0);
    DoubleAnimation animation = new DoubleAnimation();
    animation.To = 40;
    animation.DecelerationRatio = 1;
    animation.Duration = TimeSpan.FromSeconds(0.15);
    animation.AutoReverse = true;
    axisRotation.BeginAnimation(AxisAngleRotation3D.AngleProperty, animation);
}
```

Using this sort of realistic 3-D behavior, you could create a true 3-D "control," such as a button that deforms when you click it.

If you simply want to react to clicks on a 3-D object and you don't need to perform calculations that involve the mesh, you won't need to use the VisualTreeHelper at all. The fact that the MouseDown event fired tells you that the torus was clicked.

■Tip In most cases, the ModelUIElement3D provides a simpler approach to hit testing than using the mouse events of the viewport. If you simply want to detect when a given shape is clicked (for example, you have a 3-D shape that represents a button and triggers an action), the ModelUIElement3D class is perfect. On the other hand, if you want to perform more complex calculations with the clicked coordinates or examine *all* the shapes that exist at a clicked location (not just the topmost one), you'll need more sophisticated hit testing code, and you'll probably want to respond to the mouse events of the viewport.

The ContainerUIElement3D

The ModelUIElement3D class is intended to represent a single control-like object. If you want to place more than one ModelUIElement3D in a 3-D scene and allow the user to interact with them independently, you need to create ModelUIElement3D objects and wrap them in a single ContainerUIElement3D. You can then add that ContainerUIElement3D to the viewport.

The ContainerUIElement3D has one other advantage. It supports any combination of objects that derive from Visual3D. That means it can hold ordinary ModelVisual3D objects, interactive ModelUIElement3D objects, and Viewport2DVisual3D objects, which represent 2-D elements that have been placed in 3-D space. You'll learn more about this trick in the next section.

2-D Elements on 3-D Surfaces

As you learned earlier in this chapter, you can use texture mapping to place 2-D brush content on a 3-D surface. You can use this to place images or videos in a 3-D scene. Using a Visual-Brush, you can even take the visual appearance of an ordinary WPF element (such as a button), and place it in your 3-D scene.

However, the VisualBrush is inherently limited. As you already know, the VisualBrush can copy the visual appearance of an element, but it doesn't actually duplicate the element. If you use the VisualBrush to place the visual for a button in a 3-D scene, you'll end up with a 3-D picture of a button. In other words, you won't be able to click it.

WPF 3.5 includes the solution to this problem: the Viewport2DVisual3D class. The Viewport2DVisual3D class wraps another element and maps it to a 3-D surface using texture mapping. You can place the Viewport2DVisual3D directly in a Viewport3D, alongside other Visual3D objects (such as ModelVisual3D objects and ModelUIElement3D objects). However, the element inside the Viewport2DVisual3D retains its interactivity and has all the WPF features you're accustomed to, including layout, styling, templates, mouse events, drag-and-drop, and so on.

■**Note** The Viewport2DVisual3D class was introduced in WPF 3.5. You can find an earlier solution in the 3-D tools project that you've already learned about (http://www.codeplex.com/3DTools). It includes two classes (Interactive3DDecorator and InteractiveVisual3D) which provide a similar but subtly different 2-D to 3-D mapping service. If you're working with WPF applications that target .NET 3.0, you might still use these classes. Otherwise, you'll have no need for them (although you'll find other goodies in the 3-D tools project).

Figure 23-22 shows an example. A StackPanel containing a TextBlock, Button, and TextBox is placed on one of the faces of a 3-D cube. The user is in the process of typing text into the TextBox, and you can see the I-beam cursor that shows the insertion point.

Figure 23-22. *Interactive WPF elements in 3-D*

In your Viewport3D, you can place all the usual ModelVisual3D objects. In the example shown in Figure 23-22, there's a ModelVisual3D for the cube. To place your 2-D element content in the scene, you use a Viewport2DVisual3D object instead. The Viewport2DVisual3D class provides the properties listed in Table 23-5.

Table 23-5. *Properties of the InteractiveVisual3D*

Name	Description
Geometry	The mesh that defines the 3-D surface.
Visual	The 2-D element that will be placed on the 3-D surface. You can use only a single element, but it's perfectly legitimate to use a container panel to wrap multiple elements together. The example in Figure 23-22 uses a Border that contains a StackPanel with three child elements.
Material	The material that will be used to render the 2-D content. Usually, you'll use a DiffuseMaterial. You must set the attached Viewport2DVisual3D.IsVisualHost-Material on the DiffuseMaterial to true so that the material is able to show element content.
Transform	A Transform3D or Transform3DGroup that determines how your mesh should be altered (rotated, scaled, skewed, and so on).

Using the 2-D on 3-D technique is relatively straightforward, provided you're already familiar with texture mapping (as described in the "Texture Mapping" section earlier in this chapter). Here's the markup that creates the WPF elements shown in Figure 23-22:

```
<Viewport2DVisual3D>
  <Viewport2DVisual3D.Geometry>
    <MeshGeometry3D
      Positions="0,0,0 0,0,10 0,10,0 0,10,10"
      TriangleIndices="0,1,2 2,1,3"
      TextureCoordinates="0,1 1,1 0,0 1,0"
    />
  </Viewport2DVisual3D.Geometry>

  <Viewport2DVisual3D.Material>
    <DiffuseMaterial Viewport2DVisual3D.IsVisualHostMaterial="True" />
  </Viewport2DVisual3D.Material>

  <Viewport2DVisual3D.Visual>
    <Border BorderBrush="Yellow" BorderThickness="1">
      <StackPanel Margin="10">
        <TextBlock Margin="3">This is 2D content on a 3D surface.</TextBlock>
        <Button Margin="3">Click Me</Button>
        <TextBox Margin="3">[Enter Text Here]</TextBox>
      </StackPanel>
    </Border>
  </Viewport2DVisual3D.Visual>
```

```
  <Viewport2DVisual3D.Transform>
    <RotateTransform3D>
      <RotateTransform3D.Rotation>
        <AxisAngleRotation3D
          Angle="{Binding ElementName=sliderRotate, Path=Value}"
          Axis="0 1 0" />
      </RotateTransform3D.Rotation>
    </RotateTransform3D>
  </Viewport2DVisual3D.Transform>
</Viewport2DVisual3D>
```

In this example, the Viewport2DVisual3D.Geometry property supplies a mesh that mirrors a single face of the cube. The TextureCoordinates of the mesh define how the 2-D content (the Border that wraps the StackPanel) should be mapped to the 3-D surface (the cube face). The texture mapping that you use with the Viewport2DVisual3D works in the same way as the texture mapping you used earlier with the ImageBrush and VisualBrush.

■**Note** When defining the TextureCoordinates, it's important to make sure you have the element facing the camera. WPF does not render anything for the back surface of Viewport2DVisual3D, so if you flip it around and stare at its back, the element will disappear. (If this isn't the result you want, you can use another Viewport2DVisual3D to create content for the back side.)

This example also uses a RotateTransform3D to allow the user to turn the cube around using a slider underneath the Viewport3D. The ModelVisual3D that represents the cube includes the same RotateTransform3D, so the cube and 2-D element content move together.

Currently, this example doesn't use any event handling in the Viewport2DVisual3D content. However, it's easy enough to add an event handler:

```
<Button Margin="3" Click="cmd_Click">Click Me</Button>
```

WPF handles mouse events in a clever way. It uses texture mapping to translate the virtual 3-D coordinates (where the mouse is) to ordinary, non-texture-mapped 2-D coordinates. From the element's point of view, the mouse events are exactly the same in the 3-D world as they are in the 2-D world. This is part of the magic that holds the solution together.

■**Tip** For a more elaborate example of 2-D content on a 3-D surface, refer to http://tinyurl.com/3cnfxx. You'll find a spinning globe example that lets you plant markers (with descriptive text) at arbitrary locations. All the content in this example consists of 2-D elements that are mapped to 3-D space.

The Last Word

3-D support is one of the gems of the WPF platform. Previous high-level development toolkits, such as Windows Forms, have avoided 3-D support altogether, leaving it to hard-core DirectX junkies. In fact, the most impressive part of WPF's 3-D features is their ease of use. Although it's possible to create complex code that creates and modifies 3-D meshes using intense math, it's just as possible to export 3-D models from a design tool and manipulate them using straightforward transformations. And key features such as a virtual trackball implementation and 2-D element interactivity are provided by high-level classes that take no expertise at all.

This chapter provided a tour of the core pillars of WPF's 3-D support and introduced some of the indispensable tools that have emerged since WPF 1.0 was released. However, 3-D programming is a detailed topic, and it's certainly possible to delve much more deeply into 3-D theory. If you want to brush up on the math that underlies 3-D development, you may want to consider the book *3D Math Primer for Graphics and Game Development* by Fletcher Dunn (Wordware Publishing, 2002). You're also certain to find complete books on 3-D programming with WPF.

The easiest way to continue your exploration into the world of 3-D is to head to the Web and check out the resources and sample code provided by the WPF team and other independent developers. Here's a short list of useful links, including some that have already been referenced in this chapter:

- `http://www.codeplex.com/3DTools` provides an essential library of tools for developers doing 3-D work in WPF, including the virtual trackball and the ScreenSpaceLines3D class discussed in this chapter.

- `http://blogs.msdn.com/mswanson/articles/WPFToolsAndControls.aspx` provides a list of WPF tools, including 3-D design programs that use XAML natively and export scripts that can transform other 3-D formats (including Maya, LightWave, Blender, and 3ds) to XAML.

- `http://www.therhogue.com/WinFX` includes samples that demonstrate several common 3-D effects (such as a carousel of images) and some more complex techniques (such as an animated mesh).

- `http://blogs.msdn.com/danlehen/archive/2005/10/16/481597.aspx` includes classes that wrap the meshes required for three common 3-D primitives: a cone, a sphere, and a cylinder.

- `http://wpf.netfx3.com/files/folders/applications/entry3377.aspx` provides a Sand-Box3D project that allows you to load simple 3-D meshes and manipulate them with transforms.

If you're in no mood to type in lengthy links, or you want to find out if these addresses have changed, check out the link page for this book at `http://www.prosetech.com`.

CHAPTER 24

■ ■ ■

Custom Elements

In previous Windows development frameworks, custom controls played a central role. But in WPF, the emphasis has shifted. Custom controls are still a useful way to build custom widgets that you can share between applications, but they're no longer a requirement when you want to enhance and customize core controls. (To understand how remarkable this change is, it helps to point out that this book's predecessor, *Pro .NET 2.0 Windows Forms and Custom Controls*, had nine complete chapters about custom controls and additional examples in other chapters. But in this book, you've made it to Chapter 24 without a single custom control sighting!)

WPF de-emphasizes custom controls because of its support for styles, content controls, and templates. These features give every developer several ways to refine and extend standard controls without deriving a new control class. Here are your possibilities:

- **Styles.** You can use a style to painlessly reuse a combination of control properties. You can even apply effects using triggers. To get the same effect in Windows Forms, developers needed to copy and paste code (which was impractical) or derive a custom control with hardwired property setting logic in the constructor.

- **Content controls.** Any control that derives from ContentControl supports nested content. Using content controls, you can quickly create compound controls that aggregate other elements. (For example, you can transform a button into an image button or a list box into an image list.)

- **Control templates.** All WPF controls are *lookless*, which means they have hardwired functionality but the appearance is defined separately through the control template. Replace the default template with something new, and you can revamp basic controls such as buttons, check boxes, radio buttons, and even windows.

- **Data templates.** All ItemsControl-derived classes support data templates, which allow you to create a rich list representation of some type of data object. Using the right data template, you can display each item using a combination of text, images, and even editable controls, all in a layout container of your choosing.

If possible, you should pursue these avenues before you decide to create a custom control or another type of custom element. That's because these solutions are simpler, easier to implement, and often easier to reuse.

So, when *should* you create a custom element? Custom elements aren't the best choice when you want to fine-tune the appearance of an element, but they do make sense when you want to change its underlying functionality. For example, there's a reason that WPF has separate classes for the TextBox and PasswordBox classes. They handle key presses differently, store their data internally in a different way, interact with other components such as the clipboard differently, and so on. Similarly, if you want to design a control that has its own distinct set of properties, methods, and events, you'll need to build it yourself.

In this chapter, you'll learn how to create custom elements and how to make them into first-class WPF citizens. That means you'll outfit them with dependency properties and routed events to get support for essential WPF services such as data binding, styles, and animation. You'll also learn how to create a *lookless* control—a template-driven control that allows the control consumer to supply different visuals for greater flexibility.

■**Note** Although you can create a custom element that isn't a control, most custom elements you create in WPF will be controls—that is to say they'll be able to receive focus, and they'll interact with the user's key presses and mouse actions. For that reason, the terms *custom elements* and *custom controls* are sometimes used interchangeably in WPF development.

Understanding Custom Elements in WPF

Although you can code a custom element in any WPF project, you'll usually want to place custom elements in a dedicated class library (DLL) assembly. That way, you can share your work with multiple WPF applications.

To make sure you have the right assembly references and namespace imports, you should choose the Custom Control Library (WPF) project type when you create your application in Visual Studio. Inside your class library, you can create as many or as few controls as you like.

■**Tip** As with all class library development, it's often a good practice to place both your class library and the application that uses your class library in the same Visual Studio solution. That way you can easily modify and debug both pieces at once.

The first step in creating a custom control is choosing the right base class to inherit from. Table 24-1 lists some commonly used classes for creating custom controls, and Figure 24-1 shows where they fit into the element hierarchy.

Table 24-1. *Base Classes for Creating a Custom Element*

Name	Description
FrameworkElement	This is the lowest level you'll typically use when creating a custom element. Usually, you'll take this approach only if you want to draw your content from scratch by overriding OnRender() and using the System.Windows.Media.DrawingContext. It's similar to the approach you saw in Chapter 14, where a user interface was constructed using Visual objects. The FrameworkElement class provides the basic set of properties and events for elements that aren't intended to interact with the user.

Name	Description
Control	This is the most common starting point when building a control from scratch. It's the base class for all user-interactive widgets. The Control class adds properties for setting the background and foreground, as well as the font and alignment of content. The control class also places itself into the tab order (through the IsTabStop property) and introduces the notion of double-clicking (through the MouseDoubleClick and PreviewMouseDoubleClick events). But most important, the Control class defines the Template property that allows its appearance to be swapped out with a customized element tree for endless flexibility.
ContentControl	This is the base class for controls that can display a single piece of arbitrary content. That content can be an element or a custom object that's used in conjunction with a template. (The content is set through the Content property, and an optional template can be provided in the ContentTemplate property.) Many controls wrap a specific, limited type of content (like a string of text in a text box). Because these controls don't support all elements, they shouldn't be defined as content controls.
UserControl	This is a content control that can be configured using a design-time surface. Although a user control isn't that different from an ordinary content control, it's typically used when you want to quickly reuse an unchanging block of user interface in more than one window (rather than create a true stand-alone control that can be transported from one application to another).
ItemsControl or Selector	ItemsControl is the base class for controls that wrap a list of items but don't support selection, while Selector is the more specialized base class for controls that do support selection. These classes aren't often used to create custom controls, because the data templating features of the ListBox, ListView, and TreeView provide a great deal of flexibility.
Panel	This is the base class for controls with layout logic. A layout control can hold multiple children and arranges them according to specific layout semantics. Often, panels include attached properties that can be set on the children to configure how the children are arranged.
Decorator	This is the base class for elements that wrap another element and provide a graphical effect or specific feature. Two prominent examples are the Border, which draws a line around an element, and the Viewbox, which scales its content dynamically using a transform. Other decorators include the chrome classes used to give the familiar border and background to common controls like the button.
A specific control class	If you want to introduce a refinement to an existing control, you can derive directly from that control. For example, you can create a TextBox with built-in validation logic (as demonstrated later in this chapter). However, before you take this step, consider whether you could accomplish the same thing using event handling code or a separate component. Both approaches allow you to decouple your logic from the control and reuse it with other controls.

In this chapter, you'll see a user control, a lookless color picker that derives directly from the Control class, a custom text box, a custom layout panel, and a custom-drawn element that derives from FrameworkElement and overrides OnRender().

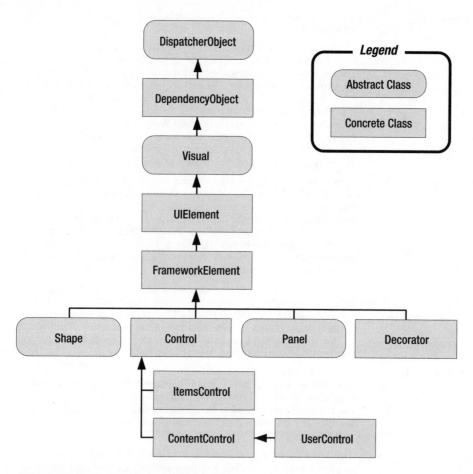

Figure 24-1. *Element and control base classes*

Building a Basic User Control

A good way to get started with custom controls is to take a crack at creating a straightforward user control. In this section, we'll begin by creating a basic color picker. Later, you'll see how to refactor this control into a more capable template-based control.

Creating a basic color picker is easy—in fact, several examples are available online, one with the .NET Framework SDK and another with the Bag-O-Tricks custom control library that's provided by the WPF team. However, creating a custom color picker is still a worthy exercise. Not only does it demonstrate a variety of important control building concepts, but it also gives you a practical piece of functionality.

You could create a custom dialog box for your color picker, such as the kind that's included with Windows Forms. But if you want to create a color picker that you can integrate into different windows, a custom control is a far better choice. The most straightforward type of custom control is a *user control*, which allows you to assemble a combination of elements in the same way as when you design a window or page. Because the color picker appears to be little more than a fairly straightforward grouping of existing controls with added functionality, a user control seems like a perfect choice.

A typical color picker allows a user to select a color by clicking somewhere in a color gradient or specifying individual red, green, and blue components. Figure 24-2 shows the basic color picker you'll create in this section (at the top of the window). It consists of three Slider controls for adjusting color components, along with a Rectangle that shows a preview of the selected color.

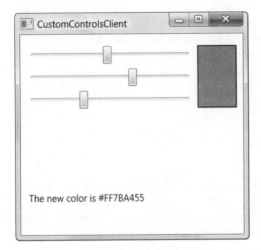

Figure 24-2. *A color picker user control*

■Note The user control approach has one significant flaw—it limits your ability to customize the appearance of your color picker to suit different windows, applications, and uses. Fortunately, it's not much harder to step up to a more template-based control, as you'll see a bit later.

Defining Dependency Properties

The first step you need to create the color picker is to add a user control to your custom control library project. When you do, Visual Studio creates a XAML markup file and a corresponding custom class to hold your initialization and event handling code. This is the same experience as when you create a new window or page—the only difference is that the top-level container is the UserControl class:

```
public partial class ColorPicker : System.Windows.Controls.UserControl
{ ... }
```

The easiest starting point is to design the public interface that the user control exposes to the outside world. In other words, it's time to create the properties, methods, and events that the control consumer (the application that uses the control) will rely on to interact with the color picker.

The most fundamental detail is the Color property—after all, the color picker is nothing more than a specialized tool for displaying and choosing a color value. To support WPF features such as data binding, styles, and animation, writeable control properties are almost always dependency properties.

As you learned in Chapter 6, the first step to creating a dependency property is to define a static field for it, with the word *Property* added to the end of your property name:

```
public static DependencyProperty ColorProperty;
```

The Color property will allow the control consumer to set or retrieve the color value programmatically. However, the sliders in the color picker also allow the user to modify one aspect of the current color. To implement this design, you could use event handlers that respond when a slider value is changed and update the Color property accordingly. But it's cleaner to wire the sliders up using data binding. To make this possible, you need to define each of the color components as a separate dependency property:

```
public static DependencyProperty RedProperty;
public static DependencyProperty GreenProperty;
public static DependencyProperty BlueProperty;
```

Although the Color property will store a System.Windows.Media.Color object, the Red, Green, and Blue properties will store individual byte values that represent each color component. (You could also add a slider and a property for managing the alpha value, which allows you to create a partially transparent color, but this example doesn't add this detail.)

Defining the static fields for your properties is just the first step. You also need a static constructor in your user control that registers them, specifying the property name, the data type, and the control class that owns the property. As you learned in Chapter 6, this is the point where you can opt in to specific property features (such as value inheritance) by passing a FrameworkPropertyMetadata object with the right flags set. It's also the point where you can attach callbacks for validation, value coercion, and property change notifications.

In the color picker, you have just one consideration—you need to attach callbacks that respond when the various properties are changed. That's because the Red, Green, and Blue properties are really a different representation of the Color property, and if one property changes, you need to make sure the others stay synchronized.

Here's the static constructor code that registers the four dependency properties of the color picker:

```
static ColorPicker()
{
    ColorProperty = DependencyProperty.Register(
      "Color", typeof(Color), typeof(ColorPicker),
      new FrameworkPropertyMetadata(Colors.Black,
        new PropertyChangedCallback(OnColorChanged)));

    RedProperty = DependencyProperty.Register(
      "Red", typeof(byte), typeof(ColorPicker),
      new FrameworkPropertyMetadata(
        new PropertyChangedCallback(OnColorRGBChanged)));

    GreenProperty = DependencyProperty.Register(
```

```
        "Green", typeof(byte), typeof(ColorPicker),
      new FrameworkPropertyMetadata(
        new PropertyChangedCallback(OnColorRGBChanged)));

    BlueProperty = DependencyProperty.Register(
      "Blue", typeof(byte), typeof(ColorPicker),
    new FrameworkPropertyMetadata(
      new PropertyChangedCallback(OnColorRGBChanged)));
}
```

Now that you have your dependency properties defined, you can add standard property wrappers that make them easier to access and usable in XAML.

```
public Color Color
{
    get { return (Color)GetValue(ColorProperty); }
    set { SetValue(ColorProperty, value); }
}

public byte Red
{
    get { return (byte)GetValue(RedProperty); }
    set { SetValue(RedProperty, value); }
}

public byte Green
{
    get { return (byte)GetValue(GreenProperty); }
    set { SetValue(GreenProperty, value); }
}

public byte Blue
{
    get { return (byte)GetValue(BlueProperty); }
    set { SetValue(BlueProperty, value); }
}
```

Remember, the property wrappers shouldn't contain any logic, because properties may be set and retrieved directly using the SetValue() and GetValue() methods of the base DependencyObject class. For example, the property synchronization logic in this example is implemented using callbacks that fire when the property changes through the property wrapper or a direct SetValue() call.

The property change callbacks are responsible for keeping the Color property consistent with the Red, Green, and Blue properties. Whenever the Red, Green, or Blue property is changed, the Color property is adjusted accordingly:

```
private static void OnColorRGBChanged(DependencyObject sender,
  DependencyPropertyChangedEventArgs e)
{
```

```
    ColorPicker colorPicker = (ColorPicker)sender;
    Color color = colorPicker.Color;

    if (e.Property == RedProperty)
        color.R = (byte)e.NewValue;
    else if (e.Property == GreenProperty)
        color.G = (byte)e.NewValue;
    else if (e.Property == BlueProperty)
        color.B = (byte)e.NewValue;

    colorPicker.Color = color;
}
```

and when the Color property is set, the Red, Green, and Blue values are also updated:

```
private static void OnColorChanged(DependencyObject sender,
  DependencyPropertyChangedEventArgs e)
{
    Color newColor = (Color)e.NewValue;

    ColorPicker colorPicker = (ColorPicker)sender;
    colorPicker.Red = newColor.R;
    colorPicker.Green = newColor.G;
    colorPicker.Blue = newColor.B;
}
```

Despite its appearances, this code won't cause an infinite series of calls as each property tries to change the other. That's because WPF doesn't allow reentrancy in the property change callbacks. For example, if you change the Color property, the OnColorChanged() method will be triggered. The OnColorChanged() method will modify the Red, Green, and Blue properties, triggering the OnColorRGBChanged() callback three times (once for each property). However, the OnColorRBGChanged() will not trigger the OnColorChanged() method again.

■ **Tip** It might occur to you to use the coercion callbacks discussed in Chapter 6 to deal with the color properties. However, this approach isn't appropriate. Property coercion callbacks are designed for properties that are interrelated and may override or influence one other. They don't make sense for properties that expose the same data in different ways. If you used property coercion in this example, it would be possible to set different values in the Red, Green, and Blue properties and have that color information *override* the Color property. The behavior you really want is to set the Red, Green, and Blue properties and use that color information to permanently *change* the value of the Color property.

Defining Routed Events

You might also want to add routed events that can be used to notify the control consumer when something happens. In the color picker example, it's useful to have an event that fires when the color is changed. Although you could define this event as an ordinary .NET event, using a routed event allows you to provide event bubbling and tunneling, so the event can be handled in a higher-level parent, such as the containing window.

As with the dependency properties, the first step to defining a routed event is to create a static property for it, with the word *Event* added to the end of the event name:

```
public static readonly RoutedEvent ColorChangedEvent;
```

You can then register the event in the static constructor. At this point you specify the event name, the routing strategy, the signature, and the owning class:

```
ColorChangedEvent = EventManager.RegisterRoutedEvent(
  "ColorChanged", RoutingStrategy.Bubble,
  typeof(RoutedPropertyChangedEventHandler<Color>), typeof(ColorPicker));
```

Rather than going to the work of creating a new delegate for your event signature, you can sometimes reuse existing delegates. The two useful delegates are RoutedEventHandler (for a routed event that doesn't pass along any extra information) and RoutedPropertyChangedEventHandler (for a routed event that provides the old and new values after a property has been changed). The RoutedPropertyChangedEventHandler, which is used in the previous example, is a generic delegate that's parameterized by type. As a result, you can use it with any property data type without sacrificing type safety.

Once you've defined and registered the event, you need to create a standard .NET event wrapper that exposes your event. This event wrapper can be used to attach (and remove) event listeners:

```
public event RoutedPropertyChangedEventHandler<Color> ColorChanged
{
    add { AddHandler(ColorChangedEvent, value); }
    remove { RemoveHandler(ColorChangedEvent, value); }
}
```

The final detail is the code that raises the event at the appropriate time. This code must call the RaiseEvent() method that's inherited from the base DependencyObject class.

In the color picker example, you simply need to add these lines of code to the end of the OnColorChanged() method:

```
RoutedPropertyChangedEventArgs<Color> args =
  new RoutedPropertyChangedEventArgs<Color>(oldColor, newColor);
args.RoutedEvent = ColorPicker.ColorChangedEvent;

colorPicker.RaiseEvent(args);
```

Remember, the OnColorChanged() callback is triggered whenever the Color property is modified, either directly or by modifying the Red, Green, and Blue color components.

Adding Markup

Now that your user control's public interface is in place, all you need is the markup that creates the control's appearance. In this case, a basic Grid is all that's needed to bring together the three Slider controls and the Rectangle with the color preview. The trick is the data binding expressions that tie these controls to the appropriate properties, with no event handling code required.

All in all, four data binding expressions are at work in the color picker. The three sliders are bound to the Red, Green, and Blue properties and are allowed to range from 0 to 255 (the acceptable values for a byte). The Rectangle.Fill property is set using a SolidColorBrush, and the Color property of that brush is bound to the Color property of the user control.

Here's the complete markup:

```
<UserControl x:Class="CustomControls.ColorPicker"
    xmlns="http://schemas.microsoft.com/winfx/2006/xaml/presentation"
    xmlns:x="http://schemas.microsoft.com/winfx/2006/xaml" Name="colorPicker">
  <Grid>
    <Grid.RowDefinitions>
      <RowDefinition Height="Auto"></RowDefinition>
      <RowDefinition Height="Auto"></RowDefinition>
      <RowDefinition Height="Auto"></RowDefinition>
    </Grid.RowDefinitions>
    <Grid.ColumnDefinitions>
      <ColumnDefinition></ColumnDefinition>
      <ColumnDefinition Width="Auto"></ColumnDefinition>
    </Grid.ColumnDefinitions>

    <Slider Name="sliderRed" Minimum="0" Maximum="255"
     Value="{Binding ElementName=colorPicker,Path=Red}"></Slider>
    <Slider Grid.Row="1" Name="sliderGreen" Minimum="0" Maximum="255"
     Value="{Binding ElementName=colorPicker,Path=Green}"></Slider>
    <Slider Grid.Row="2" Name="sliderBlue" Minimum="0" Maximum="255"
     Value="{Binding ElementName=colorPicker,Path=Blue}"></Slider>

    <Rectangle Grid.Column="1" Grid.RowSpan="3"
     Width="50" Stroke="Black" StrokeThickness="1">
      <Rectangle.Fill>
        <SolidColorBrush Color="{Binding ElementName=colorPicker,Path=Color}">
        </SolidColorBrush>
      </Rectangle.Fill>
    </Rectangle>

  </Grid>
</UserControl>
```

The markup for a user control plays the same role as the control template for a lookless control. If you want to make some of the details in your markup configurable, you can use binding expressions that link them to control properties. For example, currently the Rectangle's width is hard-coded at 50 units. However, you could replace this detail with a data binding expression that pulls the value from a dependency property in your user control. That way, the control consumer could modify that property to choose a different width. Similarly, you could make the stroke color and thickness variable. However, if you want to make a control with real flexibility, you're much better off to create a lookless control and define the markup in a template, as described later in this chapter.

Occasionally, you might choose to use binding expressions to repurpose one of the core properties that's already defined in your control. For example, the UserControl class uses its Padding property to add space between the outer edge and the inner content that you define. (This detail is implemented through the control template for the UserControl.) However, you could also use the Padding property to set the spacing around each slider, as shown here:

```
<Slider Name="sliderRed" Minimum="0" Maximum="255"
  Margin="{Binding ElementName=colorPicker,Path=Padding}"
  Value="{Binding ElementName=colorPicker,Path=Red}"></Slider>
```

Similarly, you could grab the border settings for the Rectangle from the BorderThickness and BorderBrush properties of the UserControl. Once again, this is a shortcut that may make perfect sense for creating simple controls but can be improved by introducing additional properties (for example, SliderMargin, PreviewBorderBrush, and PreviewBorderThickness) or creating a full-fledged template-based control.

NAMING A USER CONTROL

In the example shown here, the top-level UserControl is assigned a name (colorPicker). This allows you to write straightforward data binding expressions that bind to properties in the custom user control class. However, this technique raises an obvious question. Namely, what happens when you create an instance of the user control in a window (or page) and assign a new name to it?

Fortunately, this situation works without a hitch, because the user control performs its initialization before that of the containing window. First, the user control is initialized, and its data bindings are connected. Next, the window is initialized, and the name that's set in the window markup is applied to the user control. The data binding expressions and event handlers in the window can now use the window-defined name to access the user control, and everything works the way you'd expect.

Although this sounds straightforward, you might notice a couple of quirks if you use code that examines the UserControl.Name property directly. For example, if you examine the Name property in an event handler in the user control, you'll see the new name that was applied by the window. Similarly, if you don't set a name in the window markup, the user control will retain the original name from the user control markup. You'll then see this name if you examine the Name property in the window code.

Neither of these quirks represents a problem, but a better approach would be to avoid naming the user control in the user control markup and use the Binding.RelativeSource property to search up the element tree until you find the UserControl parent. Here's the lengthier syntax that does this:

```
<Slider Name="sliderRed" Minimum="0" Maximum="255"
      Value="{Binding Path=Red,
            RelativeSource={RelativeSource FindAncestor,
                      AncestorType={x:Type UserControl}}
            }">
</Slider>
```

You'll see this approach later, when you build a template-based control in the section "Refactoring the Color Picker Markup."

Using the Control

Now that you've completed the control, using it is easy. To use the color picker in another window, you need to begin by mapping the assembly and .NET namespace to an XML namespace, as shown here:

```
<Window x:Class="CustomControlsClient.ColorPickerUserControlTest"
  xmlns:lib="clr-namespace:CustomControls;assembly=CustomControls" ... >
```

Using the XML namespace you've defined and the user control class name, you can create your user control exactly as you create any other type of object in XAML markup. You can also set its properties and attach event handlers directly in the control tag, as shown here:

```
<lib:ColorPickerUserControl Name="colorPicker" Color="Beige"
  ColorChanged="colorPicker_ColorChanged"></lib:ColorPickerUserControl>
```

Because the Color property uses the Color data type and the Color data type is decorated with a TypeConverter attribute, WPF knows to use the ColorConverter to change the string color name into the corresponding Color object before setting the Color property.

The code that handles the ColorChanged event is straightforward:

```
private void colorPicker_ColorChanged(object sender,
  RoutedPropertyChangedEventArgs<Color> e)
{
    lblColor.Text = "The new color is " + e.NewValue.ToString();
}
```

This completes your custom control. However, there's still one frill worth adding. In the next section, you'll enhance the color picker with support for WPF's command feature.

Command Support

Many controls have baked-in command support. You can add this to your controls in two ways:

- Add command bindings that link your control to specific commands. That way, your control can respond to a command without the help of any external code.

- Create a new RoutedUICommand object for your command as a static field in your control. Then, add a command binding for that command. This allows your control to automatically support commands that aren't already defined in the basic set of command classes that you learned about in Chapter 10.

In the following example, you'll use the first approach to add support for the ApplicationCommands.Undo command.

■**Tip** For more information about commands and how to create custom RoutedUICommand objects, refer to Chapter 10.

To support an Undo feature in the color picker, you need to track the previous color in a member field:

```
private Color? previousColor;
```

It makes sense to make this field nullable, because when the control is first created, there shouldn't be a previous color set. (You can also clear the previous color programmatically after an action that you want to make irreversible.)

When the color is changed, you simply need to record the old value. You can take care of this task by adding this line to the end of the OnColorChanged() method:

```
colorPicker.previousColor = (Color)e.OldValue;
```

Now you have the infrastructure in place that you need to support the Undo command. All that's left is to create the command binding that connects your control to the command and handle the CanExecute and Executed events.

The best place to create command bindings is when the control is first created. For example, the following code uses the color picker's constructor to add a command binding to the ApplicationCommands.Undo command:

```
public ColorPicker()
{
    InitializeComponent();
    SetUpCommands();
}

private void SetUpCommands()
{
    // Set up command bindings.
    CommandBinding binding = new CommandBinding(ApplicationCommands.Undo,
      UndoCommand_Executed, UndoCommand_CanExecute);

    this.CommandBindings.Add(binding);
}
```

To make your command functional, you need to handle the CanExecute event and allow the command as long as there is a previous value:

```
private void UndoCommand_CanExecute(object sender, CanExecuteRoutedEventArgs e)
{
    e.CanExecute = previousColor.HasValue;
}
```

Finally, when the command is executed, you can swap in the new color.

```
private void UndoCommand_Executed(object sender, ExecutedRoutedEventArgs e)
{
    this.Color = (Color)previousColor;
}
```

You can trigger the Undo command in two different ways. You can use the default Ctrl+Z key binding when an element in the user control has focus, or you can add a button to the client that triggers the command, like this one:

```
<Button Command="Undo" CommandTarget="{Binding ElementName=colorPicker}">
  Undo
</Button>
```

Either way, the current color is abandoned and the previous color is applied.

Tip The current example stores just one level of undo information. However, it's easy to create an undo stack that stores a series of values. You just need to store Color values in the appropriate type of collection. The Stack<T> collection in the System.Collections.Generic namespaces is a good choice, because it implements a last-in first-out approach that makes it easy to grab the most recent Color object when performing an undo operation.

More Robust Commands

The technique described earlier is a perfectly legitimate way to connect commands to controls, but it's not the technique that's used in WPF elements and professional controls. These elements use a more robust approach and attach static command handlers using the CommandManager.RegisterClassCommandBinding() method.

The problem with the implementation shown in the previous example is that it uses the public CommandBindings collection. This makes it a bit fragile, because the client can modify the CommandBindings collection freely. This isn't possible if you use the RegisterClassCommandBinding() method. This is the approach that WPF controls use. For example, if you look at the CommandBindings collection of a TextBox, you won't find any of the bindings for hardwired commands such as Undo, Redo, Cut, Copy, and Paste, because these are registered as class bindings.

The technique is fairly straightforward. Instead creating the command binding in the instance constructor, you must create the command binding in the static constructor, using code like this:

```
CommandManager.RegisterClassCommandBinding(typeof(ColorPicker),
  new CommandBinding(ApplicationCommands.Undo,
    UndoCommand_Executed, UndoCommand_CanExecute));
```

Although this code hasn't changed much, there's an important shift. Because the UndoCommand_Executed() and UndoCommand_CanExecute() methods are referred to in the constructor, they must both be static methods. To retrieve instance data (such as the current color and the previous color information), you need to cast the event sender to a ColorPicker object and use it.

Here's the revised command handling code:

```
private static void UndoCommand_CanExecute(object sender,
  CanExecuteRoutedEventArgs e)
{
```

```
    ColorPicker colorPicker = (ColorPicker)sender;
    e.CanExecute = colorPicker.previousColor.HasValue;
}

private static void UndoCommand_Executed(object sender,
  ExecutedRoutedEventArgs e)
{
    ColorPicker colorPicker = (ColorPicker)sender;
    Color currentColor = colorPicker.Color;
    colorPicker.Color = (Color)colorPicker.previousColor;
}
```

Incidentally, this technique isn't limited to commands. If you want to hardwire event handling logic into your control, you can use a class event handler with the EventManager.RegisterClassHandler() method. Class event handlers are always invoked before instance event handlers, allowing you to easily suppress events.

A Closer Look at User Controls

User controls provide a fairly painless but somewhat limited way to create a custom control. To understand why, it helps to take a closer look at how user controls work.

Behind the scenes, the UserControl class works a lot like the ContentControl class from which it derives. In fact, it has just a few key differences:

- The UserControl class changes some default values. Namely, it sets IsTabStop and Focusable to false (so it doesn't occupy a separate place in the tab order), and it sets HorizontalAlignment and VerticalAlignment to Stretch (rather than Left and Top) so it fills the available space.

- The UserControl class applies a new control template that consists of a Border element that wraps a ContentPresenter. The ContentPresenter holds the content you add using markup.

- The UserControl class changes the source of routed events. When events bubble or tunnel from controls inside the user control to elements outside the user control, the source changes to point to the user control rather than the original element. This gives you a bit more encapsulation. (For example, if you handle the UIElement.MouseLeftButtonDown event in the layout container that holds the color picker, you'll receive an event when you click the Rectangle inside. However, the source of this event won't be the Rectangle element but the ColorPicker object that contains the Rectangle. If you create the same color picker as an ordinary content control, this isn't the case—it's up to you to intercept the event in your control, handle it, and reraise it.)

The most significant difference between user controls and other types of custom controls is the way that a user control is designed. Like all controls, user controls have a control template. However, you'll rarely change this template—instead, you'll supply the markup as part of your custom user control class, and this markup is processed using the InitializeComponent() method when the control is created. On the other hand, a lookless control has no markup—everything it needs is in the template.

An ordinary ContentControl has the following stripped-down template:

```
<ControlTemplate TargetType="ContentControl">
  <ContentPresenter
   ContentTemplate="{TemplateBinding ContentControl.ContentTemplate}"
   Content="{TemplateBinding ContentControl.Content}" />
</ControlTemplate>
```

This template does little more than fill in the supplied content and apply the optional content template. Properties such as Padding, Background, HorizontalAlignment, and VerticalAlignment won't have any effect unless you explicitly bind to it.

The UserControl has a similar template with a few more niceties. Most obviously, it adds a Border element and binds its properties to the BorderBrush, BorderThickness, Background, and Padding properties of the user control to make sure they have some meaning. Additionally, the ContentPresenter inside binds to the alignment properties.

```
<ControlTemplate TargetType="UserControl">
  <Border BorderBrush="{TemplateBinding Border.BorderBrush}"
   BorderThickness="{TemplateBinding Border.BorderThickness}"
   Background="{TemplateBinding Panel.Background}" SnapsToDevicePixels="True"
   Padding="{TemplateBinding Control.Padding}">

    <ContentPresenter
     HorizontalAlignment="{TemplateBinding Control.HorizontalContentAlignment}"
     VerticalAlignment="{TemplateBinding Control.VerticalContentAlignment}"
     SnapsToDevicePixels="{TemplateBinding UIElement.SnapsToDevicePixels}"
     ContentTemplate="{TemplateBinding ContentControl.ContentTemplate}"
     Content="{TemplateBinding ContentControl.Content}" />

  </Border>
</ControlTemplate>
```

Technically, you could change the template of a user control. In fact, you could move all your markup into the template, with only slight readjusting. But there's really no reason to take this step—if you want a more flexible control that separates the visual look from the interface that's defined by your control class, you'd be much better off creating a custom lookless control, as described in the next section.

Lookless Controls

The goal of user controls is to provide a design surface that supplements the control template, giving you a quicker way to define the control at the price of future flexibility. This causes a problem if you're happy with the functionality of a user control, but you need to tailor its visual appearance. For example, imagine you want to use the same color picker but give it a different "skin" that blends better into an existing application window. You may be able to change some aspects of the user control through styles, but parts of it are locked away inside, hard-coded into the markup. For example, there's no way to move the preview rectangle to the left side of the sliders.

The solution is to create a lookless control—a control that derives from one of the control base classes but doesn't have a design surface. Instead, this control places its markup into a default template that can be replaced at will without disturbing the control logic.

Refactoring the Color Picker Code

Changing the color picker into a lookless control isn't too difficult. The first step is easy—you simply need to change the class declaration, as shown here:

```
public class ColorPicker : System.Windows.Controls.Control
{ ... }
```

In this example, the ColorPicker class derives from Control. FrameworkElement isn't suitable, because the color picker does allow user interaction and the other higher-level classes don't accurately describe the color picker's behavior. For example, the color picker doesn't allow you to nest other content inside, so the ContentControl class isn't appropriate.

The code inside the ColorPicker class is the same as the code for the user control (aside from the fact that you must remove the call to InitializeComponent() in the constructor). You follow the same approach to define dependency properties and routed events. The only difference is that you need to tell WPF that you will be providing a new style for your control class. This style will provide the new control template. (If you don't take this step, you'll continue whatever template is defined in the base class.)

To tell WPF that you're providing a new style, you need to call the OverrideMetadata() method in the static constructor your class. You call this method on the DefaultStyleKeyProperty, which is a dependency property that defines the default style for your control. The code you need is as follows:

```
DefaultStyleKeyProperty.OverrideMetadata(typeof(ColorPicker),
  new FrameworkPropertyMetadata(typeof(ColorPicker)));
```

You could supply a different type if you want to use the template of another control class, but you'll almost always create a specific style for each one of your custom controls.

Refactoring the Color Picker Markup

Once you've added the added the call to OverrideMetadata, you simply need to plug in the right style. This style needs to be placed in a resource dictionary named generic.xaml, which must be placed in a Themes subfolder in your project. That way, your style will be recognized as the default style for your control. Additionally, you can create different styles for different theme settings by giving the resource dictionaries the right name. (You'll learn more about this system a little later in this chapter, in the "Theme-Specific Styles and the Default Style" section.)

Often, a custom control library has several controls. To keep their styles separate for easier editing, the generic.xaml file often uses resource dictionary merging. The following markup shows a generic.xaml file that pulls in the resources from the ColorPicker.xaml resource dictionary in the same Themes subfolder of a control library named CustomControls:

```
<ResourceDictionary
  xmlns="http://schemas.microsoft.com/winfx/2006/xaml/presentation"
  xmlns:x="http://schemas.microsoft.com/winfx/2006/xaml" >
```

```
    <ResourceDictionary.MergedDictionaries>
      <ResourceDictionary Source="/CustomControls;component/themes/ColorPicker.xaml">
      </ResourceDictionary>
    </ResourceDictionary.MergedDictionaries>

</ResourceDictionary>
```

Your custom control style must use the TargetType attribute to attach itself to the color picker automatically. Here's the basic structure of the markup that appears in the ColorPicker.xaml file:

```
<ResourceDictionary
 xmlns="http://schemas.microsoft.com/winfx/2006/xaml/presentation"
 xmlns:x="http://schemas.microsoft.com/winfx/2006/xaml"
 xmlns:local="clr-namespace:CustomControls">
  <Style TargetType="{x:Type local:ColorPicker}">

    ...
  </Style>
</ResourceDictionary>
```

You can use your style to set any properties in the control class (whether they're inherited from the base class or new properties you've added). However, the most useful task that your style performs is to apply a new template that defines the default visual appearance of your control.

It's fairly easy to convert ordinary markup (like that used by the color picker) into a control template. Keep these considerations in mind:

- When creating binding expressions that link to properties in the parent control class, you can't use the ElementName property. Instead, you need to use the RelativeSource property to indicate that you want to bind to the parent control. If one-way data binding is all that you need, you can usually use the lightweight TemplateBinding markup extension instead of the full-fledged Binding.

- You can't attach event handlers in the control template. Instead, you'll need to give your elements recognizable names and attach event handlers to them programmatically in the control constructor.

- Don't name an element in a control template unless you want to attach an event handler or interact with it programmatically. When naming an element you want to use, give it a name in the form PART_*ElementName*.

With these considerations in mind, you can create the following template for the color picker. The most important changed details are highlighted in bold.

```
<Style TargetType="{x:Type local:ColorPicker}">
  <Setter Property="Template">
    <Setter.Value>
      <ControlTemplate TargetType="{x:Type local:ColorPicker}">
        <Grid>
          <Grid.RowDefinitions>
            <RowDefinition Height="Auto"></RowDefinition>
```

```xml
          <RowDefinition Height="Auto"></RowDefinition>
          <RowDefinition Height="Auto"></RowDefinition>
        </Grid.RowDefinitions>
        <Grid.ColumnDefinitions>
          <ColumnDefinition></ColumnDefinition>
          <ColumnDefinition Width="Auto"></ColumnDefinition>
        </Grid.ColumnDefinitions>

        <Slider Minimum="0" Maximum="255"
         Margin="{TemplateBinding Padding}"
         Value="{Binding Path=Red,
                 RelativeSource={RelativeSource TemplatedParent}}">
        </Slider>
        <Slider Grid.Row="1" Minimum="0" Maximum="255"
         Margin="{ TemplateBinding Padding}"
         Value="{Binding Path=Red,
                 RelativeSource={RelativeSource TemplatedParent}}">
        </Slider>
        <Slider Grid.Row="2" Minimum="0" Maximum="255"
         Margin="{ TemplateBinding Padding}"
         Value="{Binding Path=Red,
                 RelativeSource={RelativeSource TemplatedParent}}">
        </Slider>

        <Rectangle Grid.Column="1" Grid.RowSpan="3"
         Margin="{ TemplateBinding Padding}"
         Width="50" Stroke="Black" StrokeThickness="1">
          <Rectangle.Fill>
            <SolidColorBrush
             Color="{Binding Path=Color,
                 RelativeSource={RelativeSource TemplatedParent}}">
            </SolidColorBrush>
          </Rectangle.Fill>
        </Rectangle>
      </Grid>
    </ControlTemplate>
  </Setter.Value>
 </Setter>
</Style>
```

As you'll notice, some binding expressions have been replaced with the TemplateBinding extension. Others still use the Binding extension but have the RelativeSource set to point to the template parent (the custom control). Although both TemplateBinding and Binding with a RelativeSource of TemplatedParent are for the same purpose—extracting data from the properties of your custom control—the lighter-weight TemplateBinding is always appropriate. It won't work if you need two-way binding (as with the sliders) or when binding to the property of a class that derives from Freezable (like the SolidColorBrush).

Streamlining the Control Template

As it stands, the color picker control template fills in everything you need, and you can use it in the same way that you use the color picker user control. However, it's still possible to simplify the template by removing some of the details.

Currently, any control consumer that wants to supply a custom template will be forced to add a slew of data binding expressions to ensure that the control continues to work. This isn't difficult, but it is tedious. Another option is to configure all the binding expressions in the initialization code of the control itself. This way, the template doesn't need to specify these details.

■**Note** This is the same technique you use when attaching event handlers to the elements that make up a custom control. You attach each event handler programmatically, rather than use event attributes in the template.

Adding Part Names

For this system to work, your code needs to be able to find the elements it needs. WPF controls locate the elements they need by name. As a result, your element names become part of the public interface of your control and need suitably descriptive names. By convention, these names begin with the text *PART_* followed by the element name. The element name uses initial caps, just like a property name. PART_RedSlider is a good choice for a required element name, while PART_sldRed, PART_redSlider, and RedSlider are all poor choices.

For example, here's how you would prepare the three sliders for programmatic binding, by removing the binding expression from the Value property and adding a PART_ name:

```
<Slider Name="PART_RedSlider" Minimum="0" Maximum="255"
 Margin="{TemplateBinding Padding}"></Slider>
<Slider Grid.Row="1" Name="PART_GreenSlider" Minimum="0" Maximum="255"
 Margin="{TemplateBinding Padding}"></Slider>
<Slider Grid.Row="2" Name="PART_BlueSlider" Minimum="0" Maximum="255"
 Margin="{TemplateBinding Padding}"></Slider>
```

Notice that the Margin property still uses a binding expression to add padding, but this is an optional detail that can easily be left out of custom template (which may choose to hard-code the padding or use a different layout).

To ensure maximum flexibility, the Rectangle isn't given a name. Instead, the SolidColorBrush inside is given a name. That way, the color preview feature can be used with any shape or an arbitrary element, depending on the template.

```
<Rectangle Grid.Column="1" Grid.RowSpan="3"
 Margin="{TemplateBinding Padding}"
 Width="50" Stroke="Black" StrokeThickness="1">
  <Rectangle.Fill>
    <SolidColorBrush x:Name="PART_PreviewBrush"></SolidColorBrush>
  </Rectangle.Fill>
</Rectangle>
```

Manipulating Template Parts

You could connect your binding expressions when the control is initialized, but there's a better approach. WPF has a dedicated OnApplyTemplate() method that you should override if you need to search for elements in the template and attach event handlers or add data binding expressions. In that method, you can use the GetTemplateChild() method (which is inherited from FrameworkElement) to find the elements you need.

If you don't find an element that you want to work with, the recommended pattern is to do nothing. Optionally, you can add code that checks that the element, if present, is the correct type and raises an exception if it isn't. (The thinking here is that a missing element represents a conscious opting out of a specific feature, whereas an incorrect element type represents a mistake.)

Here's how you can connect the data binding expression for a single slider in the OnApplyTemplate() method:

```
public override void OnApplyTemplate()
{
    base.OnApplyTemplate();

    RangeBase slider = GetTemplateChild("PART_RedSlider") as RangeBase;
    if (slider != null)
    {
        // Bind to the Red property in the control, using a two-way binding.
        Binding binding = new Binding("Red");
        binding.Source = this;
        binding.Mode = BindingMode.TwoWay;
        slider.SetBinding(RangeBase.ValueProperty, binding);
    }
    ...
}
```

Notice that the code uses the System.Windows.Controls.Primitives.RangeBase class (from which Slider derives) instead of the Slider class. That's because the RangeBase class provides the minimum required functionality—in this case, the Value property. By making the code as generic as possible, the control consumer gains more freedom. For example, it's now possible to supply a custom template that uses a different RangeBase-derived control in place of the color sliders.

The code for binding the other two sliders is virtually identical. The code for binding the SolidColorBrush is slightly different, because the SolidColorBrush does not include the SetBinding() method (which is defined in the FrameworkElement class). One easy workaround is to create a binding expression for the ColorPicker.Color property, which uses the one-way-to-source direction. That way, when the color picker's color is changed, the brush is updated automatically.

```
SolidColorBrush brush = GetTemplateChild("PART_PreviewBrush") as SolidColorBrush;
if (brush != null)
{
    Binding binding = new Binding("Color");
    binding.Source = brush;
```

```
    binding.Mode = BindingMode.OneWayToSource;
    this.SetBinding(ColorPicker.ColorProperty, binding);
}
```

To see the benefit of this change in design, you need to create a control that uses the color picker but supplies a new control template. Figure 24-3 shows one possibility.

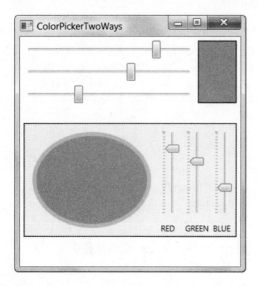

Figure 24-3. *A color picker custom control with two different templates*

Documenting Template Parts

There's one last refinement that you should make to the previous example. Good design guidelines suggest that you add the TemplatePart attribute to your control declaration to document what part names you use in your template and what type of control you use for each part. Technically, this step isn't required, but it's a piece of documentation that can help others who are using your class (and it can also be inspected by design tools that let you build customized control templates, such as Expression Blend).

Here are the TemplatePart attributes you should add to the ColorPicker control class:

```
[TemplatePart(Name="PART_RedSlider", Type=typeof(RangeBase))]
[TemplatePart(Name = "PART_BlueSlider", Type=typeof(RangeBase))]
[TemplatePart(Name="PART_GreenSlider", Type=typeof(RangeBase))]
public class ColorPicker : System.Windows.Controls.Control
{ ... }
```

Theme-Specific Styles and the Default Style

As you've seen, the ColorPicker gets its default control template from a file named generic.xaml, which is placed in a project folder named Themes. This slightly strange convention is actually part of the theme support that's built into WPF.

The Themes folder holds the default styles for the controls you create, customized for the different versions and themes of the Windows operating system. If you aren't interested in creating theme-specific styles, all you need is the generic.xaml file. This resource dictionary holds the fallback styles that are used for your controls if no theme-specific files are available.

If you *do* want to create controls that are aware of the current theme and vary themselves in minor or major ways, you simply need to add the right files to the Themes folder. Table 24-2 lists the themes you can set, and the file name you need to use for your resource dictionary. If you choose not the supply a file for a specific theme, your control falls back to the generic.xaml dictionary when that theme is active.

Note The theme-specific resource dictionaries are used to set the default control style (which should contain the default control template). However, no matter what default or theme-specific styles you use, you're always free to replace the control template by setting the Template property of a control object.

Table 24-2. *File Names for Theme-Specific Resource Dictionaries*

Operating System	Base Theme Name	Theme Color Name	File Name
Windows Vista (default)	Aero	NormalColor	Aero.NormalColor.xaml
Windows XP (blue, the default)	Luna	NormalColor	Luna.NormalColor.xaml
Windows XP (olive green)	Luna	Homestead	Luna.Homestead.xaml
Windows XP (silver)	Luna	Metallic	Luna.Metallic.xaml
Window XP Media Center Edition 2005	Royale	Normal	Royale.NormalColor.xaml
Windows XP (Zune, released separately)	Zune	NormalColor	Zune.NormalColor.xaml
Windows XP or Windows Vista	Classic		Classic.xaml

The set of defined themes is relatively small (although new ones may be added to this list in the future). Currently, Windows Vista supports only two themes—the standard Aero theme and the legacy Windows Classic look.

Tip It doesn't matter if the user has saved a custom theme under a new name or applied a custom color scheme. All user-created themes are based on one of the themes in the list shown in Table 24-2. This detail determines the style for your control. If needed, you can access the currently configured current system colors (and even use them in your template) using the system resources that are exposed by the SystemColors class, as described in Chapter 11.

If you decide to create a theme-specific look for one of your controls, you need to start by creating the appropriate resource dictionaries with the right file names. However, this step isn't quite enough to get these styles working in your application. You also need to use the ThemeInfo attribute on your assembly to enable theme support.

The ThemeInfo attribute is an assembly-level attribute that takes two parameters in its constructor. The first configures theme-specific style support, and the second configures support for the generic.xaml fallback. When you create a new WPF project in Visual Studio, the ThemeInfo attribute is added to the AssemblyInfo.cs file that configures generic.xaml support but not theme-specific style. (You can find the AssemblyInfo.cs file under the Properties node in the Solution Explorer.)

By default, the ThemeInfo attribute looks like this:

```
[assembly: ThemeInfo(ResourceDictionaryLocation.None,
 ResourceDictionaryLocation.SourceAssembly)]
```

To enable theme-specific style support, you need to change the ThemeInfo attribute to this:

```
[assembly: ThemeInfo(ResourceDictionaryLocation.SourceAssembly,
 ResourceDictionaryLocation.SourceAssembly)]
```

Although None and SourceAssembly are the two most commonly used values from the ResourceDictionaryLocation enumeration, you can also use ExternalAssembly. In this case, WPF looks for an assembly with the file name *AssemblyName.ThemeName*.dll in the same folder as your application. For example, if you've created a library named CustomControls.dll, the resources for the Windows Vista styles will be found in an assembly named CustomControls.Aero.dll. Windows XP styles will be in CustomControls.Luna.dll, CustomControls.Royale.dll, and so on. (Notice that the color part of the theme name isn't used. Instead, it's assumed that you'll put all the color-specific themes in one assembly for each base theme.) You've already seen this system when you considered the chrome classes in Chapter 15 that support controls like the Button. They use resources from assemblies with names like PresentationFramework.Aero.dll and PresentationFramework.Luna.dll.

THEME STYLES VERSUS APPLICATION STYLES

Every control has a default style (or several theme-dependent default styles). You call DefaultStyleKeyProperty.OverrideMetadata() in the static constructor of your control class to indicate what default style your custom control should use. If you don't your control will simply use the default style that's defined for the control that your class derives from.

Contrary to what you might expect, the default theme style is not exposed through the Style property. All the controls in the WPF library return a null reference for their Style property.

Instead, the Style property is reserved for an *application style* (the type you learned to build in Chapter 12). If you set an application style, it's merged into the default theme style. If you set an application style that conflicts with the default style, the application style wins and overrides the property setter or trigger in the default style. However, the details you don't override remain. This is the behavior you want. It allows you to create an application style that changes just a few properties (for example, the text font in a button), without removing the other essential details that are supplied in the default theme style (like the control template).

Incidentally, you can retrieve the default style programmatically. To do so, you can use the FindResource() method to search up the resource hierarchy for a style that has the right element-type key. For example, if you want to find the default style that's applied to the Button class, you can use this code statement:

```
Style style = Application.Current.FindResource(typeof(Button));
```

Extending an Existing Control

Most of the time when you build a custom element, you'll derive from one of the base classes listed in Table 24-1, such as FrameworkElement, Control, ContentControl, or Panel. In some cases, however, you might be able to tweak an existing control so that it does what you want.

One example is the basic WPF TextBox, which can be enhanced it countless ways. In this section, you'll learn how to create a text box that approximates the MaskedTextBox from the Windows Forms world, which has no WPF equivalent.

Understanding Masked Edit Controls

A *masked* text box is a text box that automatically formats input as it's entered. For example, if you type 1234567890 into a masked edit control that uses a U.S. telephone number mask, the number will be displayed as the string (123) 456-7890. Masked edit controls have numerous advantages:

- **They provide more guidance.** When empty, a masked edit control shows all the literal values, along with placeholders where the user supplied values need to go. For example, the phone number control shows the text string (__) ___-____ when it's empty, clearly indicating what type of information it needs.

- **They make data easier to understand.** Many values are easier to read and interpret when formatted a certain way. Examples include Social Security numbers, phone numbers, ZIP codes, and IP addresses.

- **They prevent errors.** Masks not only enforce details such as data length and format, but they also reject invalid characters (such as letters in a phone number or a second decimal place in a number).

One of the most interesting aspects of a masked edit control is the way it avoids *canonicalization errors*, which occur when there is more than one way of representing the same information. One example of a canonicalization error is when a date is entered in day-month format when your code expects month-day. Phone numbers can also suffer from canonicalization errors. For example, your code might assume that the user will enter a series of ordinary numbers and fail if the user adds dashes or forgets to include the area code. Masked edit controls neatly sidestep many of these problems.

The Windows Forms toolkit includes a MaskedTextBox that uses masking to prompt the user and reject invalid characters. However, the MaskedTextBox control doesn't actually include the functionality needed to validate masks. Instead, the MaskedTextBox control relies on a more generic service provided by another class—the MaskedTextProvider class in the System.ComponentModel namespace. You can use the MaskedTextProvider to implement a WPF masked edit control. However, the process isn't easy because you need to have fine-grained control over the display and keyboard handling of the control.

Mask Syntax

Every mask is built out of two types of characters: *placeholders*, which designate where the user must supply a character, and *literals*, which are used to format the value.

For example, the mask 990.990.990.990 represents an IP address. The periods (.) are literals that are always displayed. They can't be deleted, modified, or moved by the user. In fact, as the user types, the cursor automatically jumps over the literal characters. The 0 and 9 characters are placeholders; 0 represents a required number, and 9 represents an optional number. Thus, the IP address mask requires four numbers separated by periods, each with one to three digits.

A masked edit control displays all the literal characters and puts a *prompt character* where each placeholder is defined. For example, if you have the mask 990.990.990.990 and you are using the underscore for your prompt character (which is the default), a masked text box will show ___.___.___.___ initially.

Table 24-3 shows the characters you can use to build a mask.

Table 24-3. *Basic Properties of the MaskedTextBox*

Character	Description
0	Required digit (0–9).
9	Optional digit or space. If left blank, a space is inserted automatically.
#	Optional digit, space, or plus/minus symbol. If left blank, a space is inserted automatically.
L	Required ASCII letter (a–z or A–Z).
?	Optional ASCII letter.
&	Required Unicode character. Allows anything that isn't a control key, including punctuation and symbols.
C	Optional Unicode character.
A	Required alphanumeric character (allows letter or number but not punctuation or symbols).
a	Optional alphanumeric character.
.	Decimal placeholder.
,	Thousands placeholder.
:	Time separator.
/	Date separator.
$	Currency symbol.
<	All the characters that follow will be converted automatically to lowercase as the user types them. (There is no way to switch back to mixed-case entry mode once you use this character.)
>	All the characters that follow will be converted automatically to uppercase as the user types them.
\	Escapes a masked character, turning it into a literal. Thus, if you use \&, it is interpreted as the literal character &, which will be inserted in the text box.
All other characters	All other characters are treated as literals and are shown in the text box.

The MaskedTextProvider

Behind the scenes, the MaskedTextBox that's provided with Windows Forms relies on another component: the System.ComponentModel.MaskedTextProvider. Although the System.Windows.Forms.MaskedTextBox control is specific to Windows Forms, the MaskedTextProvider can be used to implement masked editing with any display technology, so long as you're able to intercept key presses before the editing control.

To create a custom masked control, you need to follow these guidelines:

- Create a control that maintains an instance of MaskedTextProvider internally. The MaskedTextProvider is stateful—it maintains the text that the user has entered into the mask so far.

- Whenever the custom control receives a key press, you need to determine the attempted action and pass it on to the MaskedTextProvider using methods such as Add(), Insert(), Remove(), and Replace(). The MaskedTextProvider will automatically ignore invalid characters.

- After you've sent a change to the MaskedTextProvider, you need to call MaskedTextProvider.ToDisplayString() to get the latest text. You can then refresh your custom control. Ideally, you'll update just those characters that have changed, although that often isn't when you're deriving from other controls, in which case you may need to replace all the text in one operation, which might cause flicker.

The difficulty in using the MaskedTextProvider is keeping track of all the low-level details, such as the user's current position in the input string.

Implementing a WPF Masked Text Box

To create the most robust text-based control in WPF, you would derive from the lower-level System.Windows.Controls.Primitives.TextBoxBase class (from which TextBox and PasswordBox inherit). However, you can make a relatively well-rounded masked edit control with a lot less effort by deriving directly from TextBox, as in this example.

The MaskedTextBox begins by declaring the all-important Mask property. This dependency property stores a string that uses the masking syntax explained earlier. The Mask property is connected to a property change callback that resets the text in the control when the mask changes.

```
public class MaskedTextBox : System.Windows.Controls.TextBox
{
    public static DependencyProperty MaskProperty;

    static MaskedTextBox()
    {
        MaskProperty = DependencyProperty.Register("Mask",
            typeof(string), typeof(MaskedTextBox),
            new FrameworkPropertyMetadata(MaskChanged));
    }

    public string Mask
    {
        get { return (string)GetValue(MaskProperty); }
        set { SetValue(MaskProperty, value); }
    }
    ...
}
```

The next step is to add two important private methods. The first, GetMaskProvider(), creates a MaskedTextProvider using the current mask and then applies the text from the control.

```
private MaskedTextProvider GetMaskProvider()
{
    MaskedTextProvider maskProvider = new MaskedTextProvider(Mask);
    maskProvider.Set(Text);
    return maskProvider;
}
```

The second, RefreshText(), gets the most recent text from the MaskedTextProvider, displays it in the current control, and resets the cursor to the correct position.

```
private void RefreshText(MaskedTextProvider maskProvider, int pos)
{
    // Refresh string.
    this.Text = maskProvider.ToDisplayString();

    // Position cursor.
    this.SelectionStart = pos;
}
```

With these details in place, you're ready to begin working with the masked text. For example, it's easy to add a read-only property that evaluates the current mask and text and determines whether the mask has been completely filled in using the MaskedText-Provider.MaskCompleted property:

```
public bool MaskCompleted
{
    get
    {
        MaskedTextProvider maskProvider = GetMaskProvider();
        return maskProvider.MaskCompleted;
    }
}
```

It's just as easy to write the property change callback that updates the text when the mask changes:

```
private static void MaskChanged(DependencyObject d,
  DependencyPropertyChangedEventArgs e)
{
    MaskedTextBox textBox = (MaskedTextBox)d;
    MaskedTextProvider maskProvider = textBox.GetMaskProvider();
    textBox.RefreshText(maskProvider, 0);
}
```

Before you go any further, you can simplify your life by coding one more handy private function. This method, named SkipToEditableCharacter(), returns the edit position where the cursor should be positioned. You need to call this at various times as the user moves through the mask to make sure you skip over mask characters. The

MaskedTextProvider.FindEditPositionFrom() performs the hard work, finding the next valid insertion point to the right of the current cursor position.

```
private int SkipToEditableCharacter(int startPos)
{
    MaskedTextProvider maskProvider = GetMaskProvider();

    int newPos = maskProvider.FindEditPositionFrom(startPos, true);
    if (newPos == -1)
    {
        // Already at the end of the string.
        return startPos;
    }
    else
    {
        return newPos;
    }
}
```

As you learned in Chapter 6, handling key presses in the TextBox is a somewhat awkward affair. To receive all the key events you need, you'll be forced to handle two events: PreviewKeyDown and PreviewTextInput. Rather than attaching event handlers to these events, you can override the corresponding On*Event*() method.

■ **Tip** There's no guarantee that a given event will have a corresponding On*Event*() method that you can override. However, this is a convention that many control developers follow, and it's respected in all WPF elements.

You can use OnPreviewTextInput to react to ordinary characters and the Backspace key. However, when inserting a character, you need to take special care to find out whether the insert key is currently on. Notice the code sets the e.Handled property to true so that the key won't be processed any further by other event handlers.

```
protected override void OnPreviewTextInput(TextCompositionEventArgs e)
{
    MaskedTextProvider maskProvider = GetMaskProvider();
    int pos = this.SelectionStart;

    // Adding a character.
    if (pos < this.Text.Length)
    {
        pos = SkipToEditableCharacter(pos);

        // Overwrite mode is on.
        if (Keyboard.IsKeyToggled(Key.Insert))
```

```
        {
            if (maskProvider.Replace(e.Text, pos))
            {
                pos++;
            }
        }
        // Insert mode is on.
        else
        {
            if (maskProvider.InsertAt(e.Text, pos))
            {
                pos++;
            }
        }

        // Find the new cursor position.
        pos = SkipToEditableCharacter(pos);
    }
    RefreshText(maskProvider, pos);
    e.Handled = true;

    base.OnPreviewTextInput(e);
}
```

The OnPreviewKeyDown() method allows you to handle special extended keys, such as Delete.

```
protected override void OnPreviewKeyDown(KeyEventArgs e)
{
    base.OnKeyDown(e);

    MaskedTextProvider maskProvider = GetMaskProvider();
    int pos = this.SelectionStart;

    // Deleting a character (Delete key).
    // This does nothing if you try to delete
    // a format character.
    if (e.Key == Key.Delete && pos < (this.Text.Length))
    {
        if (maskProvider.RemoveAt(pos))
        {
            RefreshText(maskProvider, pos);
        }
        e.Handled = true;
    }
```

```
    // Deleting a character (backspace).
    // This steps over a format character, but doesn't
    // delete the next character.
    else if (e.Key == Key.Back)
    {
        if (pos > 0)
        {
            pos--;
            if (maskProvider.RemoveAt(pos))
            {
                RefreshText(maskProvider, pos);
            }
        }
        e.Handled = true;
    }
}
```

Figure 24-4 shows the MaskedTextBox at work. Editing with the MaskedTextBox is quite intuitive. The user can move to any position in the text box and delete or insert characters (in which case existing characters are moved to the right or left, provided they are allowed in their new positions). Optional characters can be ignored (the user can just skip over them using the arrow keys), or space characters can be inserted in their place.

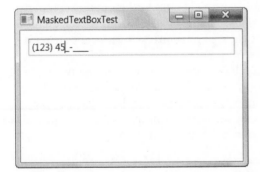

Figure 24-4. *Entering data in a masked text box*

Improving the MaskedTextBox

This lengthy code still doesn't provide all the functionality you probably want. Currently, the masked text box exhibits some odd behavior when you cut or paste text. Either one of these actions can mangle the mask, and it won't be stored until the next keystroke. Similarly, setting the Text property programmatically provides another way to submit values that aren't allowed by the mask.

Correcting these problems requires some slightly messy workarounds. Ideally, you'd create a custom masked text box by deriving from TextBoxBase and implementing a significant amount of the functionality yourself. However, even with the current design it's possible to sidestep the problems that appear.

The easiest way to deal with the paste and cut problems is to disable these features altogether. As you learned in Chapter 10, you can accomplish this by adding a new command binding that overrides the class command binding and marks the command as handled. Here's the code you need:

```
public MaskedTextBox() : base()
{
    CommandBinding commandBinding1 = new CommandBinding(
      ApplicationCommands.Paste, null, SuppressCommand);
    this.CommandBindings.Add(commandBinding1);
    CommandBinding commandBinding2 = new CommandBinding(
      ApplicationCommands.Cut, null, SuppressCommand);
    this.CommandBindings.Add(commandBinding2);
}

private void SuppressCommand(object sender, CanExecuteRoutedEventArgs e)
{
    e.CanExecute = false;
    e.Handled = true;
}
```

You can close the backdoor provided by the Text property in several ways. One obvious approach is to use dependency property features such as a validation callback. (Truthfully, property value *coercion* makes more sense, because you might want to allow the Text property to be set before the Mask property, while the previous mask is still in effect.) However, there's a problem—the Text property is defined in the base class, so you don't have the chance to register it and set the appropriate metadata.

Fortunately, there's an easy solution. You can call the OverrideMetadata property on TextProperty to supply new metadata that will apply exclusively to the MaskedTextBox. This technique is conceptually the same as the technique you use to override the DefaultStyleKey property when specifying the default style for a template-driven control.

To use this technique, you need to add this code to the static constructor:

```
FrameworkPropertyMetadata metadata = new FrameworkPropertyMetadata();
metadata.CoerceValueCallback = CoerceText;
TextProperty.OverrideMetadata(typeof(MaskedTextBox), metadata);
```

Then you can use the following callback method to coerce the Text property:

```
private static object CoerceText(DependencyObject d, object value)
{
    MaskedTextBox textBox = (MaskedTextBox)d;
    MaskedTextProvider maskProvider = new MaskedTextProvider(textBox.Mask);
    maskProvider.Set((string)value);
    return maskProvider.ToDisplayString();
}
```

The MaskedTextProvider.Set() method automatically discards the input you supply if there are characters that contradict the mask. However, placeholders aren't required, so both of the following assignment statements are equivalent:

```
maskedTextBox.Text = "(123) 456-7890";
maskedTextBox.Text = "1234567890";
```

Lastly, to make sure the Text property is reinterpreted when the Mask property is changed, your MaskChanged() callback should trigger the Text property coercion, as shown here. This is also enough to update the display text in the control.

```
private static void MaskChanged(DependencyObject d,
  DependencyPropertyChangedEventArgs e)
{
    MaskedTextBox textBox = (MaskedTextBox)d;
    d.CoerceValue(TextProperty);
}
```

Custom Panels

One common type of custom element is a custom panel. As you learned in Chapter 4, panels host one or more children and implement specific layout logic to arrange them appropriately. Custom panels are an essential ingredient if you want to build your own system for tear-off toolbars or dockable windows. Custom panels are often useful when creating composite controls that need a specific nonstandard layout. For example, you could create a custom panel as part of an Office 2007–style "ribbon" that rearranges and resizes its buttons dynamically as the available space changes.

You're already familiar with the basic types of panels that WPF includes for organizing content (such as the StackPanel, DockPanel, WrapPanel, Canvas, and Grid). You've also seen that some WPF elements use their own custom panels (such as the TabPanel, ToolBarOverflowPanel, and VirtualizingPanel). You can find many more examples of custom panels online. Here are some worth exploring:

- A RadialPanel that organizes items in a circular fashion around a center point (in the help that's included with the .NET 3.0 SDK)

- A custom Canvas that allows its children to be dragged with no extra event handling code (http://www.codeproject.com/WPF/DraggingElementsInCanvas.asp)

- Two panels that implements fisheye and fanning effects on a list of items (http://www.codeproject.com/WPF/Panels.asp)

- A panel that uses a frame-based animation to transition from one layout to another (http://wpf.netfx3.com/files/folders/controls/entry8196.aspx)

In the next sections, you'll learn how to create a custom panel, and you'll consider two straightforward examples—a basic Canvas clone and an enhanced version of the WrapPanel.

The Two-Step Layout Process

Every panel uses the same plumbing: a two-step process that's responsible for sizing and arranging children. The first stage is the *measure* pass, and it's at this point that the panel determines how large its children want to be. The second stage is the *layout* pass, and it's at this point that each control is assigned its bounds. Two steps are required because the panel might need to take into account the desires of all its children before it decides how to partition the available space.

You add the logic for these two steps by overriding the oddly named MeasureOverride() and ArrangeOverride() methods, which are defined in the FrameworkElement class as part of the WPF layout system. The odd names represent that the MeasureOverride() and ArrangeOverride() methods replace the logic that's defined in the MeasureCore() and ArrangeCore() methods that are defined in the UIElement class. These methods are *not* overridable.

MeasureOverride()

The first step is to determine how much space each child wants using the MeasureOverride() method. However, even in the MeasureOverride() method children aren't given unlimited room. At a bare minimum, children are confined to fit in the space that's available to the panel. Optionally, you might want to limit them more stringently. For example, a Grid with two proportionally sized rows will give children half the available height. A StackPanel will offer the first element all the space that's available, then offer the second element whatever's left, and so on.

Every MeasureOverride() implementation is responsible for looping through the collection of children and calling the Measure() method of each one. When you call the Measure() method, you supply the bounding box—a Size object that determines the maximum available space for the child control. At the end of the MeasureOverride() method, the panel returns the space it needs to display all its children and their desired sizes.

Here's the basic structure of the MeasureOverride() method, without the specific sizing details:

```
protected override Size MeasureOverride(Size constraint)
{
    // Examine all the children.
    foreach (UIElement element in base.InternalChildren)
    {
        // Ask each child how much space it would like, given the
        // availableSize constraint.
        Size availableSize = new Size(...);
        element.Measure(availableSize);
        // (You can now read element.DesiredSize to get the requested size.)
    }

    // Indicate how much space this panel requires.
    // This will be used to set the DesiredSize property of the panel.
    return new Size(...);
}
```

The Measure() method doesn't return a value. After you call Measure() on a child, that child's DesiredSize property provides the requested size. You can use this information in your calculations for future children (and to determine the total space required for the panel).

You *must* call Measure() on each child, even if you don't want to constrain the child's size or use the DesiredSize property. Many elements will not render themselves until you've called

Measure(). If you want to give a child free reign to take all the space it wants, pass a Size object with a value of Double.PositiveInfinity for both dimensions. (The ScrollViewer is one element that uses this strategy, because it can handle any amount of content.) The child will then return the space it needs for all its content. Otherwise, the child will normally return the space it needs for its content or the space that's available—whichever is smaller.

At the end of the measuring process, the layout container must return its desired size. In a simple panel, you might calculate the panel's desired size by combining the desired size of every child.

Note You can't simply return the constraint that's passed to the MeasureOverride() method for the desired size of your panel. Although this seems like a good way to take all the available size, it runs into trouble if the container passes in a Size object with Double.PositiveInfinity for one or both dimensions (which means "take all the space you want"). Although an infinite size is allowed as a sizing constraint, it's not allowed as a sizing result, because WPF won't be able to figure out how large your element should be. Furthermore, you really shouldn't take more space than you need. Doing so can cause extra whitespace and force elements that occur after your layout panel to be bumped further down the window.

Attentive readers may have noticed that there's a close similarity between the Measure() method that's called on each child and the MeasureOverride() method that defines the first step of the panel's layout logic. In fact, the Measure() method triggers the MeasureOverride() method. Thus, if you place one layout container inside another, when you call Measure(), you'll get the total size required for the layout container and all its children.

Tip One reason the measuring process goes through two steps (a Measure() method that triggers the MeasureOverride() method) is to deal with margins. When you call Measure(), you pass in the total available space. When WPF calls the MeasureOverride() method, it automatically reduces the available space to take margin space into account (unless you've passed in an infinite size).

ArrangeOverride()

Once every element has been measured, it's time to lay them out in the space that's available. The layout system calls the ArrangeOverride() method of your panel, and the panel calls the Arrange() method of each child to tell it how much space it's been allotted. (As you can probably guess, the Arrange() method triggers the ArrangeOverride() method, much as the Measure() method triggers the MeasureOverride() method.)

When measuring items with the Measure() method, you pass in a Size object that defines the bounds of the available space. When placing an item with the Arrange() method, you pass in a System.Windows.Rect object that defines the size *and* position of the item. At this point, it's as though every element is placed with Canvas-style X and Y coordinates that determine the distance between the top-left corner of your layout container and the element.

■Note Elements (and layout panels) are free to break the rules and attempt to draw outside of their allocated bounds. For example, in Chapter 13 you saw how the Line can overlap adjacent items. However, ordinary elements should respect the bounds they're given. Additionally, most containers will clip children that extend outside their bounds.

Here's the basic structure of the ArrangeOverride() method, without the specific sizing details:

```
protected override Size ArrangeOverride(Size arrangeSize)
{
    // Examine all the children.
    foreach (UIElement element in base.InternalChildren)
    {
        // Assign the child it's bounds.
        Rect bounds = new Rect(...);
        element.Arrange(bounds);
        // (You can now read element.ActualHeight and element.ActualWidth
        //  to find out the size it used..)
    }

    // Indicate how much space this panel occupies.
    // This will be used to set the ActualHeight and ActualWidth properties
    // of the panel.
    return arrangeSize;
}
```

When arranging elements, you can't pass infinite sizes. However, you can give an element its desired size by passing in the value from its DesiredSize property. You can also give an element *more* space than it requires. In fact, this happens frequently. For example, a vertical StackPanel gives a child as much height as it requests but gives it the full width of the panel itself. Similarly, a Grid might use fixed or proportionally sized rows that are larger than the desired size of the element inside. And even if you've placed an element in a size-to-content container, that element can still be enlarged if an explicit size has been set using the Height and Width properties.

When an element is made larger than its desired size, the HorizontalAlignment and VerticalAlignment properties come into play. The element content is placed somewhere inside the bounds that it has been given.

Because the ArrangeOverride() method always receives a defined size (not an infinite size), you can return the Size object that's passed in to set the final size of your panel. In fact, many layout containers take this step to occupy all the space that's been given. (You aren't in danger of taking up space that could be needed for another control, because the measure step of the layout system ensures that you won't be given more space than you need unless that space is available.)

The Canvas Clone

The quickest way to get a grasp of these two methods is to explore the inner workings of the Canvas class, which is the simplest layout container. To create your own Canvas-style panel, you simply need to derive from Panel and add the MeasureOverride() and ArrangeOverride() methods shown next:

```
public class CanvasClone : System.Windows.Controls.Panel
{ ... }
```

The Canvas places children where they want to be placed and gives them the size they want. As a result, it doesn't need to calculate how the available space should be divided. That makes its MeasureOverride() method extremely simple. Each child is given infinite space to work with:

```
protected override Size MeasureOverride(Size constraint)
{
    Size size = new Size(double.PositiveInfinity, double.PositiveInfinity);
    foreach (UIElement element in base.InternalChildren)
    {
        element.Measure(size);
    }
    return new Size();
}
```

Notice that the MeasureOverride() returns an empty Size object, which means the Canvas doesn't request any space at all. It's up to you to specify an explicit size for the Canvas or place it in a layout container that will stretch it to fill the available space.

The ArrangeOverride() method is only slightly more involved. To determine the proper placement of each element, the Canvas uses attached properties (Left, Right, Top, and Bottom). As you learned in Chapter 6 (and as you'll see in the WrapBreakPanel next), attached properties are implemented with two helper methods in the defining class: a Get*Property*() and a Set*Property*() method.

The Canvas clone that you're considering is a bit simpler—it respects only the Left and Top attached properties (not the redundant Right and Bottom properties). Here's the code it uses to arrange elements:

```
protected override Size ArrangeOverride(Size arrangeSize)
{
    foreach (UIElement element in base.InternalChildren)
    {
        double x = 0;
        double y = 0;
        double left = Canvas.GetLeft(element);
        if (!DoubleUtil.IsNaN(left))
        {
            x = left;
        }
        double top = Canvas.GetTop(element);
        if (!DoubleUtil.IsNaN(top))
```

```
        {
            y = top;
        }
        element.Arrange(new Rect(new Point(x, y), element.DesiredSize));
    }
    return arrangeSize;
}
```

A Better Wrapping Panel

Now that you've examined the panel system in a fair bit of detail, it's worth creating your own layout container that adds something you can't get with the basic set of WPF panels. In this section, you'll see an example that extends the capabilities of the WrapPanel.

The WrapPanel performs a simple function that's occasionally quite useful. It lays out its children one after the other, moving to the next line once the width in the current line is used up. Windows Forms included a similar layout tool, called the FlowLayoutPanel. Unlike the WrapPanel, the FlowLayoutPanel added one extra ability—an attached property that children could use to force an immediate line break. (Technically, this wasn't an attached property but a property that's added through an extender provider, but the two concepts are analogous.)

Although the WrapPanel doesn't provide this capability, it's fairly easy to add one. All you need is a custom panel that adds the necessary attached property. The following listing shows a WrapBreakPanel that adds an attached LineBreakBeforeProperty. When set to true, this property causes an immediate line break before the element.

```
public class WrapBreakPanel : Panel
{
    public static DependencyProperty LineBreakBeforeProperty;

    static WrapBreakPanel()
    {
        FrameworkPropertyMetadata metadata = new FrameworkPropertyMetadata();
        metadata.AffectsArrange = true;
        metadata.AffectsMeasure = true;
        LineBreakBeforeProperty = DependencyProperty.RegisterAttached(
           "LineBreakBefore", typeof(bool), typeof(WrapBreakPanel), metadata);
    }
    ...
}
```

As with any dependency property, the LineBreakBefore property is defined as a static field and then registered in the static constructor for your class. The only difference is that you use the RegisterAttached() method rather than Register().

The FrameworkPropertyMetadata object for the LineBreakBefore property specifically indicates that it affects the layout process. As a result, a new layout pass will be triggered whenever this property is set.

Attached properties aren't wrapped by normal property wrappers, because they aren't set in the same class that defines them. Instead, you need to provide two static methods that can use the DependencyObject.SetValue() method to set this property on any arbitrary element. Here's the code that you need for the LineBreakBefore property:

```
public static void SetLineBreakBefore(UIElement element, Boolean value)
{
    element.SetValue(LineBreakBeforeProperty, value);
}
public static Boolean GetLineBreakBefore(UIElement element)
{
    return (bool)element.GetValue(LineBreakBeforeProperty);
}
```

The only remaining detail is to take this property into account when performing the layout logic. The layout logic of the WrapBreakPanel is based on the WrapPanel. During the measure stage, elements are arranged into lines so that the panel can calculate the total space it needs. Each element is added into the current line unless it's too large or the LineBreakBefore property is set to true. Here's the full code:

```
protected override Size MeasureOverride(Size constraint)
{
    Size currentLineSize = new Size();
    Size panelSize = new Size();

    foreach (UIElement element in base.InternalChildren)
    {
        element.Measure(constraint);
        Size desiredSize = element.DesiredSize;

        if (GetLineBreakBefore(element) ||
          currentLineSize.Width + desiredSize.Width > constraint.Width)
        {
            // Switch to a new line (either because the element has requested it
            // or space has run out).
            panelSize.Width = Math.Max(currentLineSize.Width, panelSize.Width);
            panelSize.Height += currentLineSize.Height;
            currentLineSize = desiredSize;

            // If the element is too wide to fit using the maximum width
            // of the line, just give it a separate line.
            if (desiredSize.Width > constraint.Width)
            {
                panelSize.Width = Math.Max(desiredSize.Width, panelSize.Width);
                panelSize.Height += desiredSize.Height;
                currentLineSize = new Size();
            }
        }
        else
        {
            // Keep adding to the current line.
            currentLineSize.Width += desiredSize.Width;
```

```
          // Make sure the line is as tall as its tallest element.
          currentLineSize.Height = Math.Max(desiredSize.Height,
            currentLineSize.Height);
      }
  }

  // Return the size required to fit all elements.
  // Ordinarily, this is the width of the constraint, and the height
  // is based on the size of the elements.
  // However, if an element is wider than the width given to the panel,
  // the desired width will be the width of that line.
  panelSize.Width = Math.Max(currentLineSize.Width, panelSize.Width);
  panelSize.Height += currentLineSize.Height;
  return panelSize;
}
```

The key detail in this code is the test that checks the LineBreakBefore property. This implements the additional logic that's not provided in the ordinary WrapPanel.

The code for the ArrangeOverride() is almost the same but slightly more tedious. The difference is that the panel needs to determine the maximum height of the line (which is determined by the tallest element) before it begins laying out that line. That way, each element can be given the full amount of available space, which takes into account the full height of the line. This is the same process that's used to lay out an ordinary WrapPanel. To see the full details, refer to the downloadable code examples for this chapter.

Using the WrapBreakPanel is easy. Here's some markup that demonstrates that the WrapBreakPanel correctly separates lines and calculates the right desired size based on the size of its children:

```
<StackPanel>
  <StackPanel.Resources>
    <Style TargetType="{x:Type Button}">
      <Setter Property="Margin" Value="3"></Setter>
      <Setter Property="Padding" Value="3"></Setter>
    </Style>
  </StackPanel.Resources>

  <TextBlock Padding="5" Background="LightGray">
    Content above the WrapBreakPanel.
  </TextBlock>
  <lib:WrapBreakPanel>
    <Button>No Break Here</Button>
    <Button>No Break Here</Button>
    <Button>No Break Here</Button>
    <Button>No Break Here</Button>
    <Button lib:WrapBreakPanel.LineBreakBefore="True" FontWeight="Bold">
     Button with Break
    </Button>
    <Button>No Break Here</Button>
```

```
    <Button>No Break Here</Button>
    <Button>No Break Here</Button>
    <Button>No Break Here</Button>
  </lib:WrapBreakPanel>
  <TextBlock Padding="5" Background="LightGray">
    Content below the WrapBreakPanel.
  </TextBlock>
</StackPanel>
```

Figure 24-5 shows how this markup is interpreted.

Figure 24-5. *The WrapBreakPanel*

Custom-Drawn Elements

In the previous section, you began to explore the inner workings of WPF elements—namely, the MeasureOverride() and ArrangeOverride() methods that allow every element to plug into WPF's layout system. In this section, you'll delve a bit deeper and consider how elements render themselves.

Most WPF elements use *composition* to create their visual appearance. In other words, a typical element builds itself out of other, more fundamental elements. You've seen this pattern at work throughout this chapter. For example, you define the composite elements of a user control using markup that's processed in the same way as the XAML in a custom window. You define the visual tree for a custom control using a control template. And when creating a custom panel, you don't need to define any visual details at all. The composite elements are provided by the control consumer and added to the Children collection.

This emphasis is different from what you see in previous user interface technologies such as Windows Forms. In Windows Forms, some controls draw themselves using the User32 library that's part of the Windows API, but most custom controls rely on the GDI+ drawing classes to render themselves from scratch. Because Windows Forms doesn't provide high-level graphical primitives that can be added directly to a user interface (like WPF's rectangles, ellipses, and paths), any control that needs a nonstandard visual appearance requires custom rendering code.

Of course, composition can take you only so far. Eventually, some class needs to take responsibility for drawing content. In WPF, this point is a long way down the element tree. In a typical window, the rendering is performed by individual bits of text, shapes, and bitmaps, rather than high-level elements.

The OnRender() Method

To perform custom rendering, an element must override the OnRender() method, which is inherited from the base UIElement class. The OnRender() method doesn't necessarily replace composition—some controls use OnRender() to paint a visual detail and use composition to layer other elements over it. Two examples are the Border class, which draws its border in the OnRender() method, and the Panel class, which draws its background in the OnRender() method. Both the Border and Panel support child content, and this content is rendered over-top the custom-drawn details.

The OnRender() method receives a DrawingContext object, which provides a set of useful methods for drawing content. You first learned about the DrawingContext class in Chapter 14, when you used it to draw the content for a Visual object. The key difference when performing drawing in the OnRender() method is that you don't explicitly create and close the Drawing-Context. That's because several different OnRender() methods could conceivable use the same DrawingContext. For example, a derived element might perform some custom drawing and call the OnRender() implementation in the base class to draw additional content. This works because WPF automatically creates the DrawingContext object at the beginning of this process and closes it when it's no longer needed.

■Note Technically, the OnRender() method doesn't actually *draw* your content to the screen. Instead, it draws your content to the DrawingContext object, and WPF then caches that information. WPF determines when your element needs to be repainted and paints the content that you created with the DrawingContext. This is the essence of WPF's retained graphics system—you define the content, and it manages the painting and refreshing process seamlessly.

The most surprising detail about WPF rendering is that so few classes actually do it. Most classes are built out of other simpler classes, and you need to dig quite a way down the element tree of a typical control before you discover a class that actually overrides OnRender(). Here are some that do:

- **The TextBlock class.** Wherever you place text, there's TextBlock object using OnRender() to draw it.

- **The Image class.** The Image class overrides OnRender() to paint its image content using the DrawingContext.DrawImage() method.

- **The MediaElement class.** The MediaElement overrides OnRender() to draw a frame of video, if it's being used to play a video file.

- **The shape classes.** The base Shape class overrides OnRender() to draw its internally stored Geometry object, with the help of the DrawingContext.DrawGeometry() method. This Geometry object could represent an ellipse, a rectangle, or a more complex path composed of lines and curves, depending on the specific Shape-derived class. Many elements use shapes to draw small visual details.

- **The chrome classes.** Classes such as ButtonChrome and ListBoxChrome draw the outer appearance of a common control and place the content you specify inside. Many other Decorator-derived classes, such as Border, also override OnRender().

- **The panel classes.** Although the content of a panel is supplied by its children, the OnRender() method takes care of drawing a rectangle with the background color if the Background property is set.

Often, the OnRender() implementation is deceptively simple. For example, here's the rendering code for any Shape-derived class:

```
protected override void OnRender(DrawingContext drawingContext)
{
    this.EnsureRenderedGeometry();
    if (this._renderedGeometry != Geometry.Empty)
    {
        drawingContext.DrawGeometry(this.Fill, this.GetPen(),
          this._renderedGeometry);
    }
}
```

Remember, overriding OnRender() isn't the only way to render content and add it to your user interface. You can also create a DrawingVisual object and add that visual to a UIElement using the AddVisualChild() method (and implementing a few other details, as described in Chapter 14). You can then call DrawingVisual.RenderOpen() to retrieve a DrawingContext for your DrawingVisual and use it to render its content.

Some elements use this strategy in WPF to display some graphical detail overtop other element content. For example, you'll see it with drag-and-drop indicators, error indicators, and focus boxes. In all these cases, the DrawingVisual approach allows the element to draw content *over* other content, rather than *under* it. But for the most part, rendering takes place in the dedicated OnRender() method.

Evaluating Custom Drawing

When you create your own custom elements, you may choose to override OnRender() to draw custom content. You might override OnRender() in an element that contains content (most commonly, a Decorator-derived class) so you can add a graphical embellishment around that content. Or, you might override OnRender() in an element that doesn't have any nested content so that you can draw its full visual appearance. For example, you might create a custom element that draws a small graphical detail, which you can then use in another control through composition. One example in WPF is the TickBar element, which draws the tick marks for a Slider. The TickBar is embedded in the visual tree of a Slider through the Slider's default control template (along with a Border and a Track that includes two RepeatButton controls and a Thumb).

The obvious question is when to use the comparatively low-level OnRender() approach and when to use composition with other classes (such as the Shape-derived elements) to draw what you need. To decide, you need to evaluate the complexity of the graphics you need and the interactivity you want to provide.

For example, consider the ButtonChrome class. In WPF's implementation of the ButtonChrome class, the custom rendering code takes various properties into account, including RenderDefaulted, RenderMouseOver, and RenderPressed. The default control template for the Button uses triggers to set these properties at the appropriate time, as you saw in Chapter 15. For example, the when the mouse moves over the button, the Button class uses a trigger to set the ButtonChrome.RenderMouseOver property to true.

Whenever the RenderDefaulted, RenderMouseOver, or RenderPressed property is changed, the ButtonChrome calls the base InvalidateVisual() method to indicate that its current appearance is no longer valid. WPF then calls the ButtonChrome.OnRender() method to get its new graphical representation.

If the ButtonChrome class used composition, this behavior would be more difficult to implement. It's easy enough to create the standard appearance for the ButtonChrome class using the right elements, but it's more work to modify it when the button's state changes. You'd need to dynamically change the nested elements that compose the ButtonChrome class or—if the appearance changes more dramatically—you'd be forced to hide one element and show another one in its place.

Most custom elements won't need custom rendering. But if you need to render complex visuals that change significantly when properties are changed or certain actions take place, the custom rendering approach just might be easier to use and more lightweight.

A Custom-Drawn Element

Now that you know how the OnRender() method works and when to use it, the last step is to consider a custom control that demonstrates it in action.

The following code defines an element named CustomDrawnElement that demonstrates a simple effect. It paints a shaded background uses the RadialGradientBrush. The trick is the highlight point where the gradient starts is set dynamically so it follows the mouse. Thus, as the user moves the mouse over the control, the white glowing center point follows, as shown in Figure 24-6.

The CustomDrawnElement doesn't need to contain any child content, so it derives directly from FrameworkElement. It allows only a single property to be set—the background color of the gradient. (The foreground color is hard-coded to be white, although you could easily change this detail.)

```
public class CustomDrawnElement : FrameworkElement
{
    public static DependencyProperty BackgroundColorProperty;

    static CustomDrawnElement()
    {
        FrameworkPropertyMetadata metadata =
          new FrameworkPropertyMetadata(Colors.Yellow);
        metadata.AffectsRender = true;
        BackgroundColorProperty = DependencyProperty.Register("BackgroundColor",
```

```
        typeof(Color), typeof(CustomDrawnElement), metadata);
}

public Color BackgroundColor
{
    get { return (Color)GetValue(BackgroundColorProperty); }
    set { SetValue(BackgroundColorProperty, value); }
}
...
```

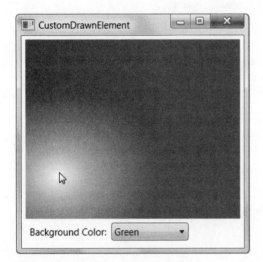

Figure 24-6. *A custom-drawn element*

The BackgroundColor dependency property is specifically marked with the
FrameworkPropertyMetadata.AffectRender flag. As a result, WPF will automatically
call OnRender() whenever the color is changed. However, you also need to make sure
OnRender() is called when the mouse moves to a new position. This is handled by calling
the InvalidateVisual() method at the right times:

```
...
protected override void OnMouseMove(MouseEventArgs e)
{
    base.OnMouseMove(e);
    this.InvalidateVisual();
}

protected override void OnMouseLeave(MouseEventArgs e)
{
    base.OnMouseLeave(e);
    this.InvalidateVisual();
}
...
```

The only remaining detail is the rendering code. It uses the DrawingContext.Draw-Rectangle() method to paint the element's background. The ActualWidth and ActualHeight properties indicate the final rendered dimensions of the control.

```
...
protected override void OnRender(DrawingContext dc)
{
    base.OnRender(dc);

    Rect bounds = new Rect(0, 0, base.ActualWidth, base.ActualHeight);
    dc.DrawRectangle(GetForegroundBrush(), null, bounds);
}
...
```

Finally, a private helper method named GetForegroundBrush() constructs the correct RadialGradientBrush based on the current position of the mouse. To calculate the center point, you need to convert the current position of the mouse over the element to a relative position from 0 to 1, which is what the RadialGradientBrush expects.

```
...
private Brush GetForegroundBrush()
{
    if (!IsMouseOver)
    {
        return new SolidColorBrush(BackgroundColor);
    }
    else
    {
        RadialGradientBrush brush = new RadialGradientBrush(
          Colors.White, BackgroundColor);

        // Get the position of the mouse in device-independent units,
        // relative to the control itself.
        Point absoluteGradientOrigin = Mouse.GetPosition(this);

        // Convert the point coordinates to proportional (0 to 1) values.
        Point relativeGradientOrigin = new Point(
          absoluteGradientOrigin.X / base.ActualWidth,
          absoluteGradientOrigin.Y / base.ActualHeight);

        // Adjust the brush.
        brush.GradientOrigin = relativeGradientOrigin;
        brush.Center = relativeGradientOrigin;

        return brush;
    }
}
}
```

This completes the example.

A Custom Decorator

As a general rule, you should never use custom drawing in a control. If you do, you violate the premise of WPF's lookless controls. The problem is that once you hardwire in some drawing logic, you've ensured that a portion of your control's visual appearance cannot be customized through the control template.

A much better approach is to design a separate element that draws your custom content (such as the CustomDrawnElement class in the previous example) and then use that element inside the default control template for your control. That's the approach used in both of the controls that you've considered in this chapter—the Button and the Slider.

It's worth quickly considering how you can adapt the previous example so that it can function as part of a control template. Custom-drawn elements usually play two roles in a control template:

- They draw some small graphical detail (like the arrow on a scroll button).

- They provide a more detailed background or frame around another element.

The second approach requires a custom decorator. You can change the CustomDrawnElement into a custom-drawn element by making two small changes. First, derive it from Decorator:

```
public class CustomDrawnDecorator : Decorator
```

Next, override the OnMeasure() method to specify the required size. It's the responsibility of all decorators to consider their children, add the extra space required for their embellishments, and then return the combined size. The CustomDrawnDecorator doesn't need any extra space to draw a border. Instead, it simply makes itself as large as the content warrants using this code:

```
protected override Size MeasureOverride(Size constraint)
{
    UIElement child = this.Child;
    if (child != null)
    {
        child.Measure(constraint);
        return child.DesiredSize;
    }
    else
    {
        return new Size();
    }
}
```

Once you've created your custom decorator, you can use it in a custom control template. For example, here's a button template that places the mouse-tracking gradient background behind the button content. It uses template bindings to make sure the properties for alignment and padding are respected.

```
<ControlTemplate x:Key="ButtonWithCustomChrome">
  <lib:CustomDrawnDecorator BackgroundColor="LightGreen">
    <ContentPresenter Margin="{TemplateBinding Padding}"
```

```
         HorizontalAlignment="{TemplateBinding HorizontalContentAlignment}"
         VerticalAlignment="{TemplateBinding VerticalContentAlignment}"
         ContentTemplate="{TemplateBinding ContentControl.ContentTemplate}"
         Content="{TemplateBinding ContentControl.Content}"
         RecognizesAccessKey="True" />
    </lib:CustomDrawnDecorator>
</ControlTemplate>
```

You can now use this template to restyle your buttons with a new look. Of course, to make your decorator more practical, you'd probably want to make it vary its appearance when the mouse button is clicked. You can do this using triggers that modify properties in your chrome class. Chapter 15 has a complete discussion of this design.

The Last Word

In this chapter, you took a detailed look at custom control development in WPF. You saw how to build basic user controls and extend existing WPF controls and how to create the WPF gold standard—a template-based lookless control. Finally, you considered custom drawing and how you can use custom-drawn content with a lookless control.

If you're planning to dive deeper into the world of custom control development, you'll find some excellent samples online. One good starting point is the Bag-O-Tricks sample project provided by Kevin Moore (a program manager on the WPF team) at http://wpf.netfx3.com/ files/folders/controls/entry8196.aspx. This sample includes a variety of custom controls that range from simple to complex, including date controls, an up-down numeric text box, a color picker, and a panel with built-in animation.

CHAPTER 25

■ ■ ■

Interacting with Windows Forms

In an ideal world, once developers master a new technology such as WPF they'd leave the previous framework behind. Everything would be written using the latest, most capable toolkit, and no one would ever worry about legacy code. Of course, this ideal world is nothing like the real world, and there are two reasons why most WPF developers will need to interact with the Windows Forms platform at some point: to leverage existing code investments and to compensate for missing features in WPF.

In this chapter, you'll look at different strategies for integrating Windows Forms and WPF content. You'll consider how to use both types of windows in a single application, and you'll explore the more impressive trick of mixing content from both platforms in a single window. But before you delve into WPF and Windows Forms interoperability, it's worth taking a step back and assessing the reasons you should (and shouldn't) use WPF interoperability.

Assessing Interoperability

If you've spent the past few years programming in Windows Forms, you probably have more than a few applications and a library of custom code that you rely on. Currently, there's no tool to transform Windows Forms interfaces into similar WPF interfaces (and even if there were, such a tool would be only a starting point of a long and involved migration process). Of course, there's no *need* to transplant a Windows Forms application into the WPF environment—most of the time, you're better off keeping your application as is and moving to WPF for new projects. However, life isn't always that simple. You might decide that you want to add a WPF feature (such as an eye-catching 3-D animation) to an existing Windows Forms application. Or you might decide that you want to eventually move an existing Windows Forms application to WPF by gradually migrating it piece by piece as you release updated versions. Either way, the interoperability support in WPF can help you make the transition gradually and without sacrificing all the work you've done before.

The other reason to consider integration is to get features that are missing in WPF. Although WPF extends its feature set into areas that Windows Forms never touched (such as animation, 3-D drawing, and rich document display), there are still some Windows Forms features that are missing in WPF or have more mature implementations in Windows Forms. This doesn't mean you should fill the gap using Windows Forms controls—after all, it may be simpler to rebuild these features, use alternatives, or just wait for future WPF releases—but it is a compelling option.

Before you toss WPF elements and Windows Forms controls together, it's important to assess your overall goals. In many situations, developers are faced with a decision between incrementally enhancing a Windows Forms application (and gradually moving it into the WPF world) or replacing it with a newly rewritten WPF masterpiece. Obviously, the first approach is faster and easier to test, debug, and release. However, in a suitably complex application that needs a major WPF injection, there may come a point where it's simpler to start over in WPF and import the legacy bits that you need.

■**Note** As always, when moving from one user interface platform to another, you should only be forced to migrate the user interface. Other details, such as data access code, validation rules, file access, and so on, should be abstracted away in separate classes (and possibly even separate assemblies), which you can plug into a WPF front-end just as easily as a Windows Forms application. Of course, this level of componentization isn't always possible, and sometimes other details (such as data binding considerations and validation strategies) can lead you to shape your classes a certain way and inadvertently limit their reusability.

Missing Features in WPF

You might turn to WPF to use a control you know and love from Windows Forms if there's no equivalent in WPF. As always, you need to evaluate your options carefully and check for possible alternatives before using the interoperability layer. Table 25-1 presents an overview of missing controls and where to the find equivalent functionality.

Table 25-1. *Missing Controls and Features in WPF*

Windows Forms Control	Closest WPF Equivalent	Consider Windows Forms?
LinkLabel	Use the inline Hyperlink in a TextBlock. Chapter 9 shows how.	No
MaskedTextBox	There is no equivalent control (although you can build one yourself using the System.ComponentModel.MaskedTextProvider class, as described in Chapter 24).	Yes
DateTimePicker and MonthCalendar	The Windows Forms versions of these controls wrap Win32 controls that are far from perfect. (For example, they do not always display correctly depending on the properties you've set, and they don't support null values.) Although native WPF versions of these controls aren't included in .NET 3.5, you can download them at http://j832.com/BagOTricks.	No
DomainUpDown and NumericUpDown	Use a TextBox with two RepeatButton controls to emulate these controls.	No
CheckedListBox	If you don't use data binding, you can place multiple CheckBox elements in a ScrollViewer. If you need binding support, you can use the ListBox with a custom control template. See Chapter 18 for an example (and for a RadioButtonList).	No

Windows Forms Control	Closest WPF Equivalent	Consider Windows Forms?
DataGridView	The ListView and GridView provide a different way to get some of the same features as the DataGridView, but not all of them. For example, only the DataGridView provides column freezing, virtualization, and a multilayered style system that allows you to format different types of cells in different ways.	Yes
WebBrowser	There is no equivalent control, but you can use the Frame control to host HTML pages (as described in Chapter 9). However, the Frame doesn't provide access to the HTML object model of the page. That means you'll need to use the WebBrowser if you want to interact with the page programmatically.	Yes
PropertyGrid	There is no equivalent control.	Yes
ColorDialog, FolderBrowserDialog, FontDialog, PageSetupDialog	You can use these components in WPF. However, most of these common dialog boxes are easily re-created in WPF, without the old-fashioned look. You can find examples with the sample code or search online. (And Chapter 24 demonstrates a basic color-picking custom control.)	No
PrintPreviewControl and PrintPreviewDialog	There are several do-it-yourself approaches. The easiest is to construct a FlowDocument programmatically, which you can then display in a document viewer and send to the printer. Although the PrintPreviewControl and PrintPreviewDialog are a more mature solution and require less work, using them in WPF is not recommended. That's because you'd need to switch to the older Windows Forms printing model. Of course, if you have existing printing code that uses the Windows Forms libraries, interoperability avoids a lot of work.	Maybe
ErrorProvider, HelpProvider	There is no support in WPF for Windows Forms extender providers. If you have forms that use these features, you may continue using them in a WPF application through interoperability. However, you can't use these providers to display error messages or context-sensitive help for WPF controls.	Yes
AutoComplete	Although WPF includes AutoComplete functionality in the ComboBox (Chapter 18) through the IsTextSearching-enabled property, it's a simple AutoComplete feature that fills in a single suggestion from the current list. It doesn't provide the full list of suggestions that Windows Forms does with its AutoComplete feature, and it doesn't provide access to the recent URLs recorded by the operating system. Using Windows Forms to get this support is generally overkill—it's better to leave this feature out or dig in and build it yourself.	Maybe
MDI	WPF does not support MDI windows. However, the layout system is flexible to accommodate a wide range of different custom-built approaches, including do-it-yourself tabbed windows. However, this involves significant work. If you need MDI, it's best to build a full Windows Forms application, rather than try to combine WPF and Windows Forms.	Yes

---

■**Note** For more information about Windows Forms specifics, including AutoComplete, its support for MDI, and its print model and extender providers, refer to my book *Pro .NET 2.0 Windows Forms and Custom Controls in C#* (Apress, 2005).

As you can see from Table 25-1, a few Windows Forms controls are good candidates for integration because they can be easily inserted into WPF windows and would take considerable work to re-create. These include the MaskedTextBox, DataGridView, PropertyGrid, and WebBrowser (if you need to interact with the HTML object model of a page). If you've created your own custom Windows Forms controls, they probably also belong to this list—in other words, they're easier to port to WPF than re-create from scratch.

There's a broader set of controls that aren't available in WPF but have reasonable (or sometimes improved) equivalents. These include the DateTimePicker, CheckedListBox, and ImageList. Finally, there are some features that are out of reach in WPF, which means they aren't provided in WPF and there isn't a viable interoperability strategy. If you need to build or update an application that makes heavy use of an extender provider (such as the ErrorProvider, HelpProvider, or a custom provider of your own creation) or uses MDI windows, it's better to stick with a Windows Forms application. You may choose to integrate WPF content into your Windows Forms application, but the reverse tasks—migrating to WPF—will require more work.

Mixing Windows and Forms

The cleanest way to integrate WPF and Windows Forms content is to place each in a separate window. That way your application consists of well-encapsulated window classes, each of which deals with just a single technology. Any interoperability details are handled in the *glue* code—the logic that creates and shows your windows.

Adding Forms to a WPF Application

The easiest approach to mixing windows and forms is to add one or more forms (from the Windows Forms toolkit) to an otherwise ordinary WPF application. Visual Studio makes this easy—just right-click the project name in the Solution Explorer and choose Add ➤ New Item. Then, select the Windows Forms category on the left side, and choose the Windows Form template. Lastly, give your form a file name, and click Add. The first time you add a form, Visual Studio adds references to all the required Windows Forms assemblies, including System.Windows.Forms.dll and System.Drawing.dll.

You can design a form in a WPF project in the same way that you design it in a Windows Forms project. When you open a form, Visual Studio loads the normal Windows Forms designer and fills the Toolbox with Windows Forms controls. When you open the XAML file for a WPF window, you get the familiar WPF design surface instead.

■**Tip** For better separation between WPF and Windows Forms content, you might choose to place the "foreign" content in a separate class library assembly. For example, a Windows Forms application might use the WPF windows defined in a separate assembly. This approach makes especially good sense if you plan to reuse some of these windows in both Windows Forms and WPF applications.

Adding WPF Windows to a Windows Forms Application

The reverse trick is a bit more awkward. Visual Studio doesn't directly allow you to create a new WPF window in a Windows Forms application. (In other words, you won't see it as one of the available templates when you right-click your project and choose Add ➤ New Item.) However, you can add the existing .cs and .xaml files that define a WPF window from another WPF project. To do so, right-click your project in the Solution Explorer, choose Add ➤ Existing Item, and find both these files. You'll also need to add references to the core WPF assemblies (PresentationCore.dll, PresentationFramework.dll, and WindowsBase.dll).

■Tip There's a shortcut to adding the WPF references you need. You can add a WPF user control (which Visual Studio *does* support), which causes Visual Studio to add these references automatically. You can then delete the user control from your project. To add a WPF user control, right-click the project, choose Add ➤ New Item, pick the WPF category, and select the User Control (WPF) template.

Once you add a WPF window to a Windows Forms application, it's treated correctly. When you open it, you'll be able to use the WPF designer to modify it. When you build the project, the XAML will be compiled and the automatically generated code will be merged with your code-behind class, just as it is in a full-fledged WPF application.

Creating a project that uses forms and windows isn't too difficult. However, there are a few extra considerations when you show these forms and windows at runtime. If you need to show a window or form modally (as you would with a dialog box), the task is straightforward and your code is essentially unchanged. But if you want to show a window modelessly, you need a bit of extra code to ensure proper keyboard support, as you'll see in the following sections.

Showing Modal Windows and Forms

Showing a modal form from a WPF application is effortless. You use exactly the same code you'd use in a Windows Forms project. For example, if you have a form class named Form1, you'd use code like this to show it modally:

```
Form1 frm = new Form1();
if (frm.ShowDialog() == System.Windows.Forms.DialogResult.OK)
{
    MessageBox.Show("You clicked OK in a Windows Forms form.");
}
```

You'll notice that the Form.ShowDialog() method works in a slightly different way than WPF's Window.ShowDialog() method (described in Chapter 8). While Window.ShowDialog() returns true, false, or null, Form.ShowDialog() returns a value from the DialogResult enumeration.

The reverse trick—showing a WPF window from a form—is just as easy. Once again, you simply interact with the public interface of your Window class, and WPF takes care of the rest:

```
Window1 win = new Window1();
if (win.ShowDialog() == true)
{
    MessageBox.Show("You clicked OK in a WPF window.");
}
```

Showing Modeless Windows and Forms

It's not quite as straightforward if you want to show windows or forms modelessly. The challenge is that keyboard input is received by the root application and needs to be delivered to the appropriate window. In order for this to work between WPF and Windows Forms content, you need a way to forward these messages along to the right window or form.

If you want to show a WPF window modelessly from inside a Windows Forms application, you must use the static ElementHost.EnableModelessKeyboardInterop() method. You'll also need a reference to the WindowsFormsIntegration.dll assembly, which defines the Element-Host class in the System.Windows.Forms.Integration namespace. (You'll learn more about the ElementHost class later in this chapter.)

You call the EnableModelessKeyboardInterop() method after you create the window, but before you show it. When you call it, you pass in a reference to the new WPF window, as shown here:

```
Window1 win = new Window1();
ElementHost.EnableModelessKeyboardInterop(win);
win.Show();
```

When you call EnableModelessKeyboardInterop(), the ElementHost adds a message filter to the Windows Forms application. This message filter intercepts keyboard messages when your WPF window is active and forwards them to your window. Without this detail, your WPF controls won't receive any keyboard input.

If you need to show a modeless Windows Forms application inside a WPF application, you use the similar WindowsFormsHost.EnableWindowsFormsInterop() method. However, you don't need to pass in a reference to the form you plan to show. Instead, you simply need to call this method once before you show any form. (One good choice is to call this method at application startup.)

```
WindowsFormsHost.EnableWindowsFormsInterop();
```

Now you can show your form modelessly without a hitch:

```
Form1 frm = new Form1();
frm.Show();
```

Without the call to EnableWindowsFormsInterop(), your form will still appear, but it won't recognize all keyboard input. For example, you won't be able to use the Tab key to move from one control to the next.

You can extend this process to multiple levels. For example, you could create a WPF window that shows a form (modally or modelessly), and that form could then show a WPF window. Although you won't need to do this very often, it's more powerful than the element-based interoperability support you'll learn about later. This support allows you to integrate different types of content in the same window but doesn't allow you to nest more than one layer deep (for example, creating a WPF window that contains a Windows Forms control which, in turn, hosts a WPF control).

Visual Styles for Windows Forms Controls

When you show a form in a WPF application, that form uses the old fashioned (pre–Windows XP) styles for buttons and other common controls. That's because support for the newer styles must be explicitly enabled by calling the Application.EnableVisualStyles() method. Ordinarily, Visual Studio adds this line of code to the Main() method of every new Windows Forms application. However, when you create a WPF application, this detail isn't included.

To resolve this issue, just call the EnableVisualStyles() method once before showing any Windows Forms content. A good place to do this is when the application is first started, as shown here:

```
public partial class App : System.Windows.Application
{
    protected override void OnStartup(StartupEventArgs e)
    {
        // Raises the Startup event.
        base.OnStartup(e);

        System.Windows.Forms.Application.EnableVisualStyles();
    }
}
```

Notice that the EnableVisualStyles() method is defined in the System.Windows.Forms.Application class, *not* the System.Windows.Application class that forms the core of your WPF application.

Windows Forms Classes That Don't Need Interoperability

As you know, Windows Forms controls have a different inheritance hierarchy than WPF elements. These controls can't be used in a WPF window without interoperability. However, there are some Windows Forms *components* that don't have this limitation. Provided you have a reference to the necessary assembly (usually System.Windows.Forms.dll), you can use these types without any special considerations.

For example, you can use the dialog classes (such as ColorDialog, FontDialog, PageSetupDialog, and so on) directly. In practice, this isn't terribly useful because these dialog boxes are slightly outdated and because they wrap structures that are a part of Windows Forms, not WPF. For example, if you use the ColorDialog, you'll get a System.Drawing.Color object rather than the System.Windows.Media.Color object you really want. The same is true when you use the FontDialog and the PageSetupDialog and PrintPreviewDialog that are designed to work with the older Windows Forms printing model. In fact, the only Windows Forms dialog box that's of any use and that doesn't have a WPF equivalent in the Microsoft.Win32 namespace is FolderBrowserDialog, which lets the user pick a folder.

More useful Windows Forms components include the SoundPlayer (described in Chapter 22), which you can use as a lightweight equivalent to WPF's MediaPlayer and MediaElement; the BackgroundWorker (described in Chapter 3), which you can use to manage an asynchronous task safely; and the NotifyIcon (described next), which allows you to show a system tray icon.

The only disadvantage to using the NotifyIcon in a WPF window is that there's no design-time support. It's up to you to create the NotifyIcon by hand, attach event handlers, and so on.

Once you supply an icon using the Icon property and set Visible to true, your icon will appear in the system tray (shown in Figure 25-1). When your application ends, you should call Dispose() on the NotifyIcon to remove it from the system tray immediately.

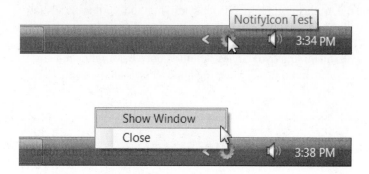

Figure 25-1. *A system tray icon*

The NotifyIcon does use some Windows Forms–specific bits. For example, it uses a Windows Forms context menu, which is an instance of the System.Windows.Forms.Context-MenuStrip class. Thus, even if you're using the NotifyIcon with a WPF application, you need to define its context menu using the Windows Forms model.

Creating all the objects for a menu in code and attaching event handlers is more than a little tedious. Fortunately, there's a simpler solution when building a WPF application that uses the NotifyIcon—you can create a *component* class. A component class is a custom class that derives from System.ComponentModel.Component. It provides two features that ordinary classes lack: support for deterministically releasing resources (when its Dispose() method is called) and design-time support in Visual Studio.

Every custom component gets a design surface (technically known as the *component tray*) where you can drag and configure other classes that implement IComponent, including Windows Forms. In other words, you can use the component tray to build and configure a NotifyIcon, complete with a context menu and event handlers. Here's what you need to do to build a custom component that wraps an instance of the NotifyIcon and includes a context menu:

1. Open or create a new WPF project.

2. Right-click the project name in the Solution Explorer and choose Add ➤ New Item. Pick the Component Class template, supply a name for your custom component class, and click Add.

3. Drop a NotifyIcon onto the design surface of your component. (You'll find the NotifyIcon in the Common Controls section of the Toolbox.)

4. At this point, Visual Studio adds the reference you need to the System.Windows.Forms.dll assembly. However, it won't add a reference to the System.Drawing.dll namespace, which has many core Windows Forms types. You must add a reference to System.Drawing.dll manually.

5. Drop a ContextMenuStrip onto the design surface of your component (from the Menus & Toolbars section of the Toolbox). This will represent the context menu for your NotifyIcon. Figure 25-2 shows both ingredients in Visual Studio.

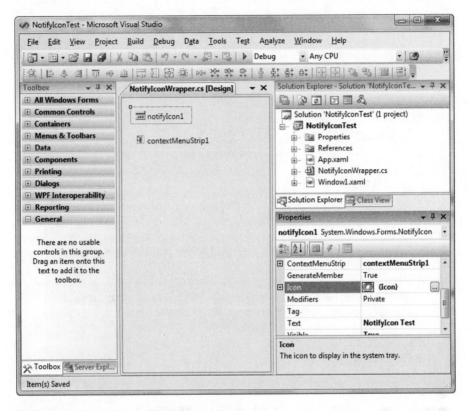

Figure 25-2. *The design surface of a component*

6. Select the NotifyIcon and configure it using the Properties window. You'll want to set the following properties: Text (the tooltip text that appears when you hover over the NotifyIcon), Icon (the icon that appears in the system tray), and ContextMenuStrip (the ContextMenuStrip you added in the previous step).

7. To build the context menu, right-click the ContextMenuStrip and choose Edit Items. You'll see a collection editor that you can use to add the menu items (which you should place after the root menu item). Give them easily recognizable names because you'll need to connect the event handlers yourself.

8. To see your component class code, right-click the component in the Solution Explorer and choose View Code. (Don't open the .Designer.cs code file. This file contains the code that Visual Studio generates automatically, which is combined with the rest of the component code using partial classes.)

9. Add the code that connects your menu's event handlers. Here's an example that adds the event handler for two menu commands—a Close button and a Show Window button:

```
public partial class NotifyIconWrapper : Component
{
    public NotifyIconWrapper()
    {
        InitializeComponent();

        // Attach event handlers.
        cmdClose.Click += cmdClose_Click;
        cmdShowWindow.Click += cmdShowWindow_Click;
    }

    // Use just one instance of this window.
    private Window1 win = new Window1();

    private void cmdShowWindow_Click(object sender, EventArgs e)
    {
        // Show the window (and bring it to the forefront if it's already visible).
        if (win.WindowState == System.Windows.WindowState.Minimized)
            win.WindowState = System.Windows.WindowState.Normal;

        win.Show();
        win.Activate();
    }

    private void cmdClose_Click(object sender, EventArgs e)
    {
        System.Windows.Application.Current.Shutdown();
    }

    // Clean up when this component is released by releasing all
    // contained components (including the NotifyIcon).
    protected override void Dispose(bool disposing)
    {
        if (disposing && (components != null)) components.Dispose();
        base.Dispose(disposing);
    }

    // (Designer code omitted.)
}
```

Now that you've created the custom component class, you simply need to create an instance of it when you want to show the NotifyIcon. This triggers the designer code in your component, which creates the NotifyIcon object, making it visible in the system tray.

Removing the system tray icon is just as easy—you just need to call Dispose() on your component. This step forces the component to call Dispose() on all contained components, including the NotifyIcon.

Here's a custom application class that shows the icon when the application starts and removes it when the application ends:

```
public partial class App : System.Windows.Application
{
    private NotifyIconWrapper component;

    protected override void OnStartup(StartupEventArgs e)
    {
        base.OnStartup(e);

        this.ShutdownMode = ShutdownMode.OnExplicitShutdown;
        component = new NotifyIconWrapper();
    }

    protected override void OnExit(ExitEventArgs e)
    {
        base.OnExit(e);
        component.Dispose();
    }
}
```

To complete this example, make sure you remove the StartupUri attribute from the App.xaml file. This way, the application starts by showing the NotifyIcon but doesn't show any additional windows until the user clicks an option from the menu.

This example relies on one more trick. A single main window is kept alive for the entire application and shown whenever the user chooses Show Window from the menu. However, this runs into trouble if the user closes the window. There are two possible solutions—you can re-create the window as needed the next time the user clicks Show Window, or you can intercept the Window.Closing event and quietly conceal the window instead of destroying it. Here's how:

```
private void window_Closing(object sender, CancelEventArgs e)
{
    e.Cancel = true;
    this.WindowState = WindowState.Minimized;
    this.ShowInTaskbar = false;
}
```

Notice that this code doesn't change the Visibility property of the window or call its Hide() method because neither action is allowed when the window is closing. Instead, it minimizes it and removes it from the taskbar. When restoring the window you'll need to check the window state and return the window to its normal state along with its taskbar button.

Creating Windows with Mixed Content

In some cases the clean window-by-window separation isn't suitable. For example, you might want to place WPF content in an existing form alongside Windows Form content. Although this model is conceptually messier, WPF handles it quite gracefully.

In fact, including Windows Forms content in a WPF application (or vice versa) is more straightforward than adding ActiveX content to a Windows Forms application. In the latter scenario, Visual Studio must generate a wrapper class that sits between the ActiveX control and your code, which manages the transition from managed to unmanaged code. This wrapper is *component-specific*, which means each ActiveX control you use requires a separate customized wrapper. And because of the quirks of COM, the interface exposed by the wrapper might not match the interface of the underlying component exactly.

When integrating Windows Forms and WPF content, you don't need a wrapper class. Instead, you use one of a small set of containers, depending on the scenario. These containers work with any class, so there's no code generation step. This simpler model is possible because even though Windows Forms and WPF are dramatically different technologies, they are both firmly grounded in the world of managed code.

The most significant advantage of this design is that you can interact with Windows Forms controls and WPF elements in your code directly. The interoperability layer only comes into effect when this content is rendered in the window. This part takes place automatically without requiring any developer intervention. You also don't need to worry about keyboard handling in modeless windows because the interoperability classes you'll use (ElementHost and WindowsFormsHost) handle that automatically.

WPF and Windows Forms "Airspace"

In order to integrate WPF and Windows Forms content in the same window, you need to be able to segregate a portion of your window for "foreign" content. For example, it's completely reasonable to throw a 3-D graphic into a Windows Forms application because you can place that 3-D graphic in a distinct region of a window (or even make it take up the entire window). However, it's not easy or worthwhile to reskin all the buttons in your Windows Forms application by making them WPF elements because you'll need to create a separate WPF region for each button.

Along with the considerations of complexity, there are also some things that just aren't possible with WPF interoperability. For example, you can't *combine* WPF and Windows Forms content by overlapping it. That means you can't have a WPF animation send an element flying over a region that's rendered with Windows Forms. Similarly, you can't overlap partially transparent Windows Forms content over a WPF region to blend them together. Both of these violate what's known as the *airspace rule*, which dictates that WPF and Windows Forms must always have their own distinct window regions, which they manage exclusively. Figure 25-3 shows what's allowed and what isn't.

Technically, the airspace rule results from the fact that in a window that includes WPF content and Windows Forms content, both regions have a separate window handle, or *hwnd*. Each hwnd is managed, rendered, and refreshed separately.

Window handles are managed by the Windows operating system. In classic Windows applications, every control is a separate window, which means each control has ownership of a distinct piece of screen real estate. Obviously, this type of "window" isn't the same as the top-level windows that float around your screen—it's simply a self-contained region (rectangular or otherwise). In WPF, the model is dramatically different—there's a single, top-level hwnd, and the WPF engine does the compositing for the entire window, which allows more pleasing rendering (for example, effects such as dynamic antialiasing) and far greater flexibility (for example, visuals that render content outside their bounds).

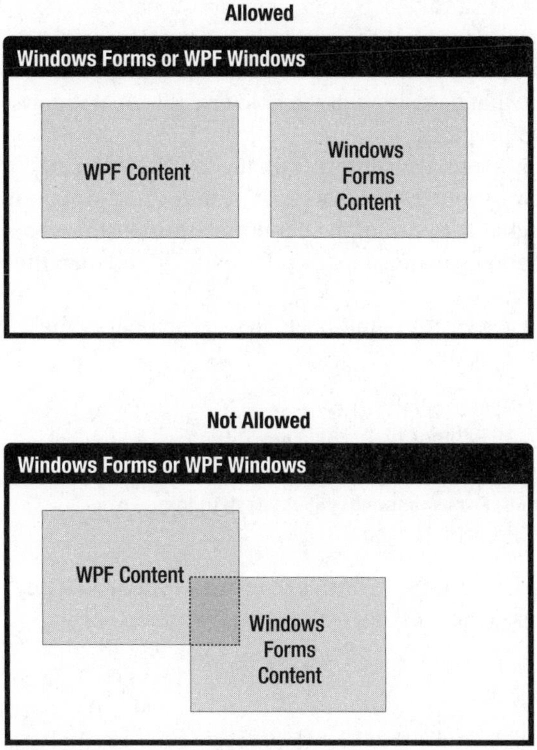

Allowed

Windows Forms or WPF Windows

WPF Content

Windows
Forms
Content

Not Allowed

Windows Forms or WPF Windows

WPF Content

Windows
Forms
Content

Figure 25-3. *The airspace rule*

■**Note** There are a few WPF elements that use separate window handles. These include menus, tooltips, and the drop-downs portion of a combo box, all of which need the ability to extend beyond the bounds of the window.

The implementation of the airspace rule is fairly straightforward. If you place Windows Forms content overtop of WPF content, you'll find that the Windows Forms content is always overtop, no matter where it's declared in the markup or what layout container you use. That's because the WPF content is a single window, and the container with Windows Forms content is implemented as a separate window that's displayed overtop of a portion of the WPF window.

If you place WPF content in a Windows Forms form, the result is a bit different. Every control in Windows Forms is a distinct window and therefore has its own hwnd. So WPF content can be layered anywhere with relation to other Windows Forms controls in the same window, depending on its z-index. (The z-index is determined by the order in which you add controls to the parent's Controls collection, so that controls added later appear on top of those added before.) However, the WPF content still has its own completely distinct region. That means you can't use transparency or any other technique to partially overwrite (or combine your element with) Windows Forms content. Instead, the WPF content exists in its own self-contained region.

Hosting Windows Forms Controls in WPF

To show a Windows Forms control in a WPF window, you use the WindowsFormsHost class in the System.Windows.Forms.Integration namespace. The WindowsFormsHost is a WPF element (it derives from FrameworkElement) that has the ability to hold exactly one Windows Forms control, which is provided in the Child property.

It's easy enough to create and use WindowsFormsHost programmatically. However, in most cases it's easiest to create it declaratively in your XAML markup. The only disadvantage is that Visual Studio doesn't include much designer support for the WindowsFormsHost control. Although you can drag and drop it onto a window, you need to fill in its content (and map the required namespace) by hand.

The first step is to map the System.Windows.Forms namespace, so you can refer to the Windows Forms control you want to use:

```
<Window x:Class="InteroperabilityWPF.HostWinFormControl"
    xmlns="http://schemas.microsoft.com/winfx/2006/xaml/presentation"
    xmlns:x="http://schemas.microsoft.com/winfx/2006/xaml"
    xmlns:wf="clr-namespace:System.Windows.Forms;assembly=System.Windows.Forms"
    Title="HostWinFormControl" Height="300" Width="300" >
```

Now you can create the WindowsFormsHost and the control inside just as you would any other WPF element. Here's an example that uses the MaskedTextBox from Windows Forms:

```
<Grid>
  <WindowsFormsHost>
    <wf:MaskedTextBox x:Name="maskedTextBox"></wf:MaskedTextBox>
  </WindowsFormsHost>
</Grid>
```

Note The WindowsFormsHost can hold any Windows Forms control (that is, any class that derives from System.Windows.Forms.Control). It can't hold Windows Forms components that aren't controls, such as the HelpProvider or the NotifyIcon.

Figure 25-4 shows a MaskedTextBox in a WPF window.

You can set most of the properties of your MaskedTextBox directly in your markup. That's because Windows Forms uses the same TypeConverter infrastructure (discussed in Chapter 2) to change strings into property values of a specific type. This isn't always convenient—for example, the string representation of a type may be awkward to enter by hand—but it usually allows you to configure your Windows Forms controls without resorting to code. For example, here's a MaskedTextBox equipped with a mask that shapes user input into a seven-digit phone number with an optional area code:

```
<wf:MaskedTextBox x:Name="maskedTextBox" Mask="(999)-000-0000"></wf:MaskedTextBox>
```

Figure 25-4. *A masked text box for a phone number*

You can also use ordinary XAML markup extensions to fill in null values, use static properties, create type objects, or use objects that you've defined in the Resources collection of the window. Here's an example that uses the type extension to set the MaskedTextBox.Validating-Type property. This specifies that the MaskedTextBox should change the supplied input (a phone number string) into an Int32 when the Text property is read or the focus changes:

```
<wf:MaskedTextBox x:Name="maskedTextBox" Mask="(999)-000-0000"
  ValidatingType="{x:Type sys:Int32}"></wf:MaskedTextBox>
```

One markup extension that won't work is a data binding expression because it requires a dependency property. (Windows Forms controls are constructed out of normal .NET properties.) If you want to bind a property of a Windows Forms control to the property of a WPF element, there's an easy workaround—just set the dependency property on the WPF element and adjust the BindingDirection as required. (Chapter 16 has the full details.)

Finally, it's important to note that you can hook events up to your Windows Forms control using the familiar XAML syntax. Here's an example that attaches an event handler for the MaskInputRejected event, which occurs when a keystroke is discarded because it doesn't suit the mask:

```
<wf:MaskedTextBox x:Name="maskedTextBox" Mask="(999)-000-0000"
  MaskInputRejected="maskedTextBox_MaskInputRejected"></wf:MaskedTextBox>
```

Obviously, these aren't routed events, so you can't define them at higher levels in the element hierarchy.

When the event fires, your event handler responds by showing an error message in another element. In this case, it's a WPF label that's located elsewhere on the window:

```
private void maskedTextBox_MaskInputRejected(object sender,
  System.Windows.Forms.MaskInputRejectedEventArgs e)
{
    lblErrorText.Content = "Error: " + e.RejectionHint.ToString();
}
```

■**Tip** Don't import the Windows Forms namespaces (such as System.Windows.Forms) in a code file that already uses WPF namespaces (such as System.Windows.Controls). The Windows Forms classes and the WPF classes share many names. Basic ingredients (such as Brush, Pen, Font, Color, Size, and Point) and common controls (such as Button, TextBox, and so on) are found in both libraries. To prevent naming clashes, it's best to import just one set of namespaces in your window (WPF namespaces for a WPF window, Windows Forms namespaces for a form) and use fully qualified names or a namespace alias to access the others.

This example illustrates the nicest feature about WPF and Windows Forms interoperability: it doesn't affect your code. Whether you're manipulating a Windows Forms control or a WPF element, you use the familiar class interface for that object. The interoperability layer is simply the magic that lets both ingredients coexist in the window. It doesn't require any extra code.

■**Note** In order to have Windows Forms controls use more up-to-date control styles introduced with Windows XP, you must call EnableVisualStyles() when your application starts, as described in the "Visual Styles for Windows Forms Controls" section earlier in this chapter.

Windows Forms content is rendered by Windows Forms, not WPF. Therefore, display-related properties of the WindowsFormsHost container (properties such as Transform, Clip, and Opacity) have no effect on the content inside. That means that even if you set a rotational transform, set a narrow clipping region, and make your content 50% transparent, you'll see no change. Similarly, Windows Forms uses a different coordinate system that sizes controls using physical pixels. As a result, if you increase the system DPI setting of your computer, you'll find that the WPF content resizes cleanly to be more detailed, but the Windows Forms content does not.

WPF and Windows Forms User Controls

One of the most significant limitations of the WindowsFormsHost element is the fact that it can only hold a single Windows Forms control. To compensate, you could use a Windows Forms container control. Unfortunately, Windows Forms container controls don't support XAML content models, so you'll need to fill in the contents of the container control programmatically.

A much better approach is to create a Windows Forms user control. This user control can be defined in a separate assembly that you reference, or you can add it directly to your WPF project (using the familiar Add ➤ New Item command). This gives you the best of both worlds—you have full design support to build your user control, and an easy way to integrate it into your WPF window.

In fact, using a user control gives you an extra layer of abstraction similar to using separate windows. That's because the containing WPF window won't be able to access the individual controls in your user control. Instead, it will interact with the higher-level properties you've added to your user control, which can then modify the controls inside. This makes your code better encapsulated and simpler because it limits the points of interaction between the WPF window and your Windows Forms content. It also makes it easier to migrate to a WPF-only solution in the future, simply by creating a WPF user control that has the same properties and swapping that in place of the WindowsFormsHost. (And once again, you can further improve the design and flexibility of your application by moving the user control into a separate class library assembly.)

■**Note** Technically, your WPF window can access the controls in a user control by accessing the Controls collection of the user control. However, in order to use this back door you need to write error-prone lookup code that searches for specific controls using a string name. That's always a bad idea.

As long as you're creating a user control, it's a good idea to make it behave as much like WPF content as possible so it's easier to integrate into your WPF window layout. For example, you may want to consider using the FlowLayoutPanel and TableLayoutPanel container controls so that the content inside your user controls flows to fit its dimensions. Simply add the appropriate control and set its Dock property to DockStyle.Fill. Then place the controls you want to use inside. For more information about using the Windows Forms layout controls (which are subtly different than the WPF layout panels), refer to my book *Pro .NET 2.0 Windows Forms and Custom Controls in C#* (Apress, 2005).

ACTIVEX INTEROPERABILITY

WPF has no direct support for ActiveX interoperability. However, Windows Forms has extensive support in the form of *runtime callable wrappers* (RCWs), dynamically generated interop classes that allow a managed Windows Forms application to host an Active component. Although there are .NET-to-COM quirks that can derail some controls, this approach works reasonably well for most scenarios, and it works seamlessly if the person who creates the component also provides a *primary interop assembly*, which is a handcrafted, fine-tuned RCW that's guaranteed to dodge interop issues.

So how does this help you if you need to design a WPF application that uses an ActiveX control? In this case, you need to layer two levels of interoperability. First, you place the ActiveX control in a Windows Forms user control or form. You then place that user control in your WPF window, or show the form from your WPF application.

Hosting WPF Controls in Windows Forms

The reverse approach—hosting WPF content in a form built with Windows Forms—is just as easy. In this situation, you don't need the WindowsFormsHost class. Instead, you use the System.Windows.Forms.Integration.ElementHost class, which is part of the WindowsForms-Integration.dll assembly.

The ElementHost has the ability to wrap any WPF element. However, the ElementHost is a genuine Windows Forms control, which means you can place it in a form alongside other Windows Forms content. In some respects, the ElementHost is more straightforward than the WindowsFormsHost, because every control in Windows Forms is displayed as a separate hwnd. Thus, it's not terribly difficult for one of these windows to be rendered with WPF instead of User32/GDI+.

Visual Studio provides some design-time support for the ElementHost control, but only if you place your WPF content in a WPF user control. Here's what to do:

1. Right-click the project name in the Solution Explorer, and choose Add ➤ New Item. Pick the User Control (WPF) template, supply a name for your custom component class, and click Add.

Note This example assumes you're placing the WPF user control directly in your Windows Forms project. If you have a complex user control, you must choose to use a more structured approach and place it in a separate class library assembly.

---

2. Add the WPF controls you need to your new WPF user control. Visual Studio gives you the usual level of design-time support for this step, so you can drag WPF controls from the Toolbox, configure them with the Properties window, and so on.

3. When you're finished, rebuild your project (choose Build ➤ Build Solution). You can't use your WPF user control in a form until you've compiled it.

4. Open to the Windows Forms form where you want to add your WPF user control (or create a new form by right-clicking the project in the Solution Explorer and choosing Add ➤ Windows Form).

5. To place the WPF user control in a form, you need the help of the ElementHost control. The ElementHost control appears on the WPF Interoperability tab of the Toolbox. Drag it onto your form, and size it accordingly.

Tip For better separation, it's a good idea to add the ElementHost to a specific container rather than directly to the form. This makes it easier to separate your WPF content from the rest of the window. Typically, you'll use the Panel, FlowLayoutPanel, or TableLayoutPanel.

---

6. To choose the content for the ElementHost, you use the smart tag. If the smart tag isn't visible, you can show it by selecting the ElementHost and clicking the arrow in the top-right corner. In the smart tag you'll find a drop-down list named Select Hosted Content. Using this list, you can pick the WPF user control you want to use, as shown in Figure 25-5.

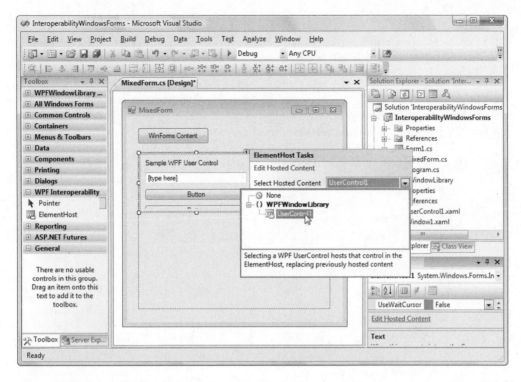

Figure 25-5. *Selecting WPF content for an ElementHost*

7. Although the WPF user control will appear in your form, you can't edit its content there. To jump to the corresponding XAML file in a hurry, click the Edit Hosted Content link in the ElementHost smart tag.

Technically, the ElementHost can hold any type of WPF element. However, the Element-Host smart tag expects you to choose a user control that's in your project (or a referenced assembly). If you want to use a different type of control, you'll need to write code that adds it to the ElementHost programmatically.

Access Keys, Mnemonics, and Focus

The WPF and Windows Forms interoperability works because the two types of content can be rigorously separated. Each region handles its own rendering and refreshing and interacts with the mouse independently. However, this segregation isn't always appropriate. For example, it runs into potential problems with keyboard handling, which sometimes needs to be global across an entire form. Here are some examples:

- When you tab from the last control in one region, you expect focus to move to the first control in the next region.

- When you use a shortcut key to trigger a control (such as a button), you expect that button to respond no matter what region of the window it's located in.

- When you use a label mnemonic, you expect the focus to move to the linked control.

- Similarly, if you suppress a keystroke using a preview event, you don't expect the corresponding key event to occur in either region, no matter what control currently has focus.

The good news is that all these expected behaviors work without any customization needed. For example, consider the WPF window shown in Figure 25-6. It includes two WPF buttons (top and bottom) and a Windows Forms button (in the middle).

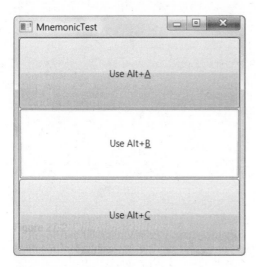

Figure 25-6. *Three buttons with shortcut keys*

Here's the markup:

```
<Grid>
  <Grid.RowDefinitions>
    <RowDefinition></RowDefinition>
    <RowDefinition></RowDefinition>
    <RowDefinition></RowDefinition>
  </Grid.RowDefinitions>
  <Button Click="cmdClicked">Use Alt+_A</Button>
  <WindowsFormsHost Grid.Row="1">
    <wf:Button Text="Use Alt+&amp;B" Click="cmdClicked"></wf:Button>
  </WindowsFormsHost>
  <Button Grid.Row="2" Click="cmdClicked">Use Alt+_C</Button>
</Grid>
```

Note The syntax for identifying accelerator keys is slightly different in WPF (which uses an underscore) than in Windows Forms. Windows Forms uses the & character, which must be escaped as & in XML because it's a special character.

When this window first appears, the text in all buttons is normal. When the user presses and holds the Alt key, all three shortcuts are underlined. The user can then trigger any one of the three buttons by pressing the A, B, or C key (while holding down Alt).

The same magic works with mnemonics, which allows labels to forward the focus to a nearby control (typically a text box). You can also tab through the three buttons in this window as though they were all WPF-defined controls, moving from top to bottom. Finally, the same example continues to work if you host a combination of Windows Forms and WPF content in a Windows Forms form.

Keyboard support isn't always this pretty, and there are a few focus-related quirks that you may run into. Here's a list of issues to watch out for:

- Although WPF supports a keystroke forwarding system to make sure every element and control gets a chance to handle keyboard input, the keyboard handling models of WPF and Windows Forms still differ. For that reason, you won't receive keyboard events from the WindowsFormsHost when the focus is in the Windows Forms content inside. Similarly, if the user moves from one control to another inside a WindowsFormsHost, you won't receive the GotFocus and LostFocus events from the WindowsFormsHost.

■Note Incidentally, the same is true for WPF mouse events. For example, the MouseMove event won't fire for the WindowsFormsHost while you move the mouse inside its bounds.

- Windows Forms validation won't fire when you move the focus from a control inside the WindowsFormsHost to an element outside the WindowsFormsHost. Instead, it will only fire when you move from one control to another inside the WindowsFormsHost. (When you remember that the WPF content and the Windows Forms content are essentially separated windows, this makes perfect sense because it's the same behavior you experience if you switch between different applications.)

- If the window is minimized while the focus is somewhere inside a WindowsFormsHost, the focus may not be restored when the window is restored.

Property Mapping

One of the most awkward details in interoperability between WPF and Windows Forms is the way they use similar but different properties. For example, WPF controls have a Background property that allows you to supply a brush that paints the background. Windows Forms controls use a simpler BackColor property that fills the background with a color based on an ARGB value. Obviously, there's a disconnect between these two properties, even though they're often used to set the same aspect of a control's appearance.

Most of the time, this isn't a problem. As a developer, you'll simply be forced to switch between both APIs, depending on the object you're working with. However, WPF adds a little bit of extra support through a feature called *property translators*.

Property translators won't allow you to write WPF-style markup and have it work with Windows Forms controls. In fact, property translators are quite modest. They simply convert a few basic properties of the WindowsFormsHost (or ElementHost) from one system to another, so that they can be applied on the child control.

For example, if you set the WindowsFormsHost.IsEnabled property, the Enabled property of the control inside is modified accordingly. This isn't a necessary feature (you could do much the same thing by modifying the Enabled property of the child directly, instead of the IsEnabled property of the container), but it can often make your code a bit clearer.

To make this work, the WindowsFormsHost and ElementHost classes both have a PropertyMap collection, which is responsible for associating a property name with a delegate that identifies a method that performs the conversion. By using a method, the property map system is able to handle sticky conversions such as BackColor to Background and vice versa. By default, each is filled with a default set of associations. (You're free to create your own or replace the existing ones, but this degree of low-level fiddling seldom makes sense).

Table 25-2 lists the standard property map conversions that are provided by the Windows-FormHost and ElementHost classes.

Table 25-2. *Property Maps*

WPF Property	Windows Forms Property	Comments
Foreground	ForeColor	Converts any ColorBrush into the corresponding Color object. In the case of a GradientBrush, the color of the GradientStop with the lowest offset value is used instead. For any other type of brush, the ForeColor is not changed and the default is used.
Background	BackColor or BackgroundImage	Converts any SolidColorBrush to the corresponding Color object. Transparency is not supported. If a more exotic brush is used, the WindowsFormsHost creates a bitmap and assigns it to the Background-Image property instead.
Cursor	Cursor	
FlowDirection	RightToLeft	
FontFamily, FontSize, FontStretch, FontStyle, FontWeight	Font	
IsEnabled	Enabled	
Padding	Padding	
Visibility	Visible	Converts a value from the Visibility enumeration into a Boolean value. If Visibility is Hidden, the Visible property is set to true, so that the content size can be used for layout calculations but the WindowsFormsHost does not draw the content. If Visibility is Collapsed, the Visible property is not changed (so it remains with its currently set or default value) and the WindowsFormsHost does not draw the content.

■**Note** Property maps work dynamically. For example, if the WindowsFormsHost.FontFamily property is changed, a new Font object is constructed and applied to the Font property of the child control.

WIN32 INTEROPERABILITY

With Windows Forms entering its twilight years and no major feature enhancements planned, it's hard to remember that Windows Forms was a new kid on the block just a few years ago. WPF certainly doesn't limit its interoperability to Windows Forms application—if you want to work with the Win32 API or place WPF content in a C++ MFC application, you can do that too.

You can host Win32 in WPF using the System.Windows.Interop.HwndHost class, which works analogously to the WindowsFormsHost class. The same limitations that apply to WindowsFormsHost apply to HwndSource (for example, the airspace rule, focus quirks, and so on). In fact, WindowsFormsHost derives from HwndHost.

The HwndHost is your gateway to the traditional world of C++ and MFC applications. However, it also allows you to integrate managed DirectX content. Currently, WPF does not include any DirectX interoperability features, and you can't use the DirectX libraries to render content in a WPF window. However, you can use DirectX to build a separate window and then host that inside a WPF window using the HwndHost. Although DirectX is far beyond the scope of this book (and an order of magnitude more complex than WPF programming), you can download the managed DirectX libraries at http://msdn.microsoft.com/directx.

The complement of HwndHost is the HwndSource class. While HwndHost allows you to place any hwnd in a WPF window, HwndSource wraps any WPF visual or element in an hwnd so it can be inserted in a Win32-based application, such as an MFC application. The only limitation is that your application needs a way to access the WPF libraries, which are managed .NET code. This isn't a trivial task. If you're using a C++ application, the simplest approach is to use the Managed Extensions for C++. You can then create your WPF content, create an HwndSource to wrap it, set the HwndHost.RootVisual property to the top-level element, and then place the HwndSource into your window.

You'll find much more content to help you with complex integration projects and legacy code online and in the Visual Studio help.

The Last Word

In this chapter you considered the interoperability support that allows WPF applications to show Windows Forms content (and vice versa). Then you examined the WindowsFormsHost element, which lets you embed a Windows Forms control in a WPF window, and the Element-Host, which lets you embed a WPF element in a form. Both of these classes provide a simple, effective way to manage the transition from Windows Forms to WPF.

CHAPTER 26

■■■

Multithreading and Add-Ins

As you've discovered over the previous 25 chapters, WPF revolutionizes almost all the conventions of Windows programming. It introduces a new approach to everything from defining the content in a window to rendering 3D graphics. WPF even introduces a few new concepts that aren't obviously UI-focused, such as dependency properties and routed events.

Of course, a great number of coding tasks fall outside the scope of user interface programming and haven't changed in the WPF world. For example, WPF applications use the same classes as other .NET applications when contacting databases, manipulating files, and performing diagnostics. Also, a few features fall somewhere between traditional .NET programming and WPF. These features aren't strictly limited to WPF applications, but they have specific WPF considerations. In this chapter, you'll take a look at the two notable examples.

First, you'll look at *multithreading*, which allows your WPF application to perform background work while keeping a responsive user interface. To design a safe and stable multithreading application, you need to understand WPF's threading rules. Next, you'll try the new *add-in model*, which allows your WPF application to dynamically load and use separately compiled components with useful bits of functionality.

Note Both multithreading and the add-in model are advanced topics that could occupy an entire book worth of material; therefore, you won't get an exhaustive examination of either feature in this chapter. However, you will get the basic outline you need to use them with WPF, and you'll establish a solid foundation for future exploration.

Multithreading

Multithreading is the art of executing more than one piece of code at once. The goal of multithreading is usually to create a more responsive interface—one that doesn't freeze up while it's in the midst of other work—although you can also use multithreading to take better advantage of dual-core CPUs when executing a processor-intensive algorithm or to perform other work during a high-latency operation (for example, to perform some calculations while waiting for a response from a web service).

Early in the design of WPF, the creators considered a new threading model. This model—called *thread rental*—allowed user interface objects to be accessed on any thread. To reduce the cost of locking, groups of related objects could be grouped under a single lock (called a *context*). Unfortunately, this design introduced additional complexity for single-threaded applications (which needed to be context-aware) and made it more difficult to interoperate with legacy code (like the Win32 API). Ultimately, the plan was abandoned.

The result is that WPF supports a *single-threaded apartment* model that's very much like the one used in Windows Forms applications. It has a few core rules:

- WPF elements have *thread affinity*. The thread that creates them owns them, and other threads can't interact with them directly. (An *element* is a WPF object that's displayed in a window.)

- WPF objects that have thread affinity derive from DispatcherObject at some point in their class hierarchy. DispatcherObject includes a small set of members that allow you to verify whether code is executing on the right thread to use a specific object and (if not) switch it over.

- In practice, one thread runs your entire application and owns all WPF objects. Although you could use separate threads to show separate windows, this design is rare.

In the following sections, you'll explore the DispatcherObject class and learn the simplest way to perform an asynchronous operation in a WPF application.

The Dispatcher

A *dispatcher* manages the work that takes place in a WPF application. The dispatcher owns the application thread and manages a queue of work items. As your application runs, the dispatcher accepts new work requests and executes one at a time.

Technically, a dispatcher is created the first time you instantiate a class that derives from DispatcherObject on a new thread. If you create separate threads and use them to show separate windows, you'll wind up with more than one dispatcher. However, most applications keep things simple and stick to one user interface thread and one dispatcher. They then use multithreading to manage data operations and other background tasks.

■Note The dispatcher is an instance of the System.Windows.Threading.Dispatcher class. All the dispatcher-related objects are also found in the small System.Windows.Threading namespace, which is new to WPF. (The core threading classes that have existed since .NET 1.0 are found in System.Threading.)

You can retrieve the dispatcher for the current thread using the static Dispatcher.CurrentDispatcher property. Using this Dispatcher object, you can attach event handlers that respond to unhandled exceptions or respond when the dispatcher shuts down. You can also get a reference to the System.Threading.Thread that the dispatcher controls, shut down the dispatcher, or marshal code to the correct thread (a technique you'll see in the next section).

The DispatcherObject

Most of the time, you won't interact with a dispatcher directly. However, you'll spend plenty of time using instances of DispatcherObject, because every visual WPF object derives from this class. A DispatcherObject is simply an object that's linked to a dispatcher—in other words, an object that's bound to the dispatcher's thread.

The DispatcherObject introduces just three members, as listed in Table 26-1.

Table 26-1. *Members of the DispatcherObject Class*

Name	Description
Dispatcher	Returns the dispatcher that's managing this object
CheckAccess()	Returns true if the code is on the right thread to use the object; returns false otherwise
VerifyAccess()	Does nothing if the code is on the right thread to use the object; throws an InvalidOperationException otherwise

WPF objects call VerifyAccess() frequently to protect themselves. They don't call VerifyAccess() in response to every operation (because that would impose too great a performance overhead), but they do call it often enough that you're unlikely to use an object from the wrong thread for very long.

For example, the following code responds to a button click by creating a new System.Threading.Thread object. It then uses that thread to launch a small bit of code that changes a text box in the current window.

```
private void cmdBreakRules_Click(object sender, RoutedEventArgs e)
{
    Thread thread = new Thread(UpdateTextWrong);
    thread.Start();
}


private void UpdateTextWrong()
{
    // Simulate some work taking place with a five-second delay.
    Thread.Sleep(TimeSpan.FromSeconds(5));

    txt.Text = "Here is some new text.";
}
```

This code is destined to fail. The UpdateTextWrong() method will be executed on a new thread, and that thread isn't allowed to access WPF objects. In this case, the TextBox object catches the violation by calling VerifyAccess(), and an InvalidOperationException is thrown.

To correct this code, you need to get a reference to the dispatcher that owns the TextBox object (which is the same dispatcher that owns the window and all the other WPF objects in the application). Once you have access to that dispatcher, you can call Dispatcher.BeginInvoke() to marshal some code to the dispatcher thread. Essentially, BeginInvoke() schedules your code as a task for the dispatcher. The dispatcher then executes that code.

Here's the corrected code:

```
private void cmdFollowRules_Click(object sender, RoutedEventArgs e)
{
    Thread thread = new Thread(UpdateTextRight);
    thread.Start();
}
```

```
private void UpdateTextRight()
{
    // Simulate some work taking place with a five-second delay.
    Thread.Sleep(TimeSpan.FromSeconds(5));

    // Get the dispatcher from the current window, and use it to invoke
    // the update code.
    this.Dispatcher.BeginInvoke(DispatcherPriority.Normal,
      (ThreadStart) delegate() {
                    txt.Text = "Here is some new text.";
                }
    );
}
```

The Dispatcher.BeginInvoke() method takes two parameters. The first indicates the priority of the task. In most cases, you'll use DispatcherPriority.Normal, but you can also use a lower priority if you have a task that doesn't need to be completed immediately and that should be kept on hold until the dispatcher has nothing else to do. For example, this might make sense if you need to display a status message about a long-running operation somewhere in your user interface. You can use DispatcherPriority.ApplicationIdle to wait until the application is finished all other work or the even more laid-back DispatcherPriority.SystemIdle to wait until the entire system is at rest and the CPU is idle.

You can also use an above-normal priority to get the dispatcher's attention right away. However, it's recommended that you leave higher priorities to input messages (such as key presses). These need to be handled nearly instantaneously, or the application will feel sluggish. On the other hand, adding a few milliseconds of extra time to a background operation won't be noticeable, so a priority of DispatcherPriority.Normal makes more sense in this situation.

The second BeginInvoke() parameter is a delegate that points to the method with the code you want to execute. This could be a method somewhere else in your code, or you can use an anonymous method to define your code inline (as in this example). The inline approach works well for simple operations, like this single-line update. However, if you need to use a more complex process to update the user interface, it's a good idea to factor this code into a separate method.

■**Note** The BeginInvoke() method also has a return value, which isn't used in the earlier example. BeginInvoke() returns a DispatcherOperation object, which allows you to follow the status of your marshaling operation and determine when your code has actually been executed. However, the DispatcherOperation is rarely useful, because the code you pass to BeginInvoke() should take very little time.

Remember, if you're performing a time-consuming background operation, you need to perform this operation on a separate thread and *then* marshal its result to the dispatcher thread (at which point you'll update the user interface or change a shared object). It makes no sense to perform your time-consuming code in the method that you pass to BeginInvoke().

For example, this slightly rearranged code still works but is impractical:

```
private void UpdateTextRight()
{
    // Get the dispatcher from the current window.
    this.Dispatcher.BeginInvoke(DispatcherPriority.Normal,
      (ThreadStart) delegate() {
                    // Simulate some work taking place.
                    Thread.Sleep(TimeSpan.FromSeconds(5));

                    txt.Text = "Here is some new text.";
                }
    );
}
```

The problem here is that all the work takes place on the dispatcher thread. That means this code ties up the dispatcher in the same way a non-multithreaded application would.

■**Note** The dispatcher also provides an Invoke() method. Like BeginInvoke(), Invoke() marshals the code you specify to the dispatcher thread. But unlike BeginInvoke(), Invoke() stalls your thread until the dispatcher executes your code. You might use Invoke() if you need to pause an asynchronous operation until the user has supplied some sort of feedback. For example, you could call Invoke() to run a snippet of code that shows an OK/Cancel dialog box. After the user clicks a button and your marshaled code completes, the Invoke() method will return, and you can act upon the user's response.

The BackgroundWorker

You can perform asynchronous operations in many ways. You've already seen one no-frills approach—creating a new System.Threading.Thread object by hand, supplying your asynchronous code, and launching it with the Thread.Start() method. This approach is powerful, because the Thread object doesn't hold anything back. You can create dozens of threads at will, set their priorities, control their status (for example, pausing, resuming, and aborting them), and so on. However, this approach is also a bit dangerous. If you access shared data, you need to use locking to prevent subtle errors. If you create threads frequently or in large numbers, you'll generate additional, unnecessary overhead.

The techniques to write good multithreading code—and the .NET classes you'll use—aren't WPF-specific. If you've written multithreaded code in a Windows Forms application, you can use the same techniques in the WPF world. In the remainder of this chapter, you'll consider one of the simplest and safest approaches: the System.ComponentModel.BacgroundWorker component.

■**Tip** To see several different approaches, ranging from simple to more complex, you may want to refer to my book *Programming .NET 2.0 Windows Forms and Custom Controls in C#* (Apress, 2005).

The BackgroundWorker was introduced in .NET 2.0 to simplify threading considerations in Windows Forms applications. However, the BackgroundWorker is equally at home in WPF. The BackgroundWorker component gives you a nearly foolproof way to run a time-consuming task on a separate thread. It uses the dispatcher behind the scenes and abstracts away the marshaling issues with an event-based model.

As you'll see, the BackgroundWorker also supports two frills: progress events and cancel messages. In both cases the threading details are hidden, making for easy coding.

■**Note** The BackgroundWorker is perfect if you have a single asynchronous task that runs in the background from start to finish (with optional support for progress reporting and cancellation). If you have something else in mind—for example, an asynchronous task that runs throughout the entire life of your application or an asynchronous task that communicates with your application while it does its work, you'll need to design a customized solution using .NET's threading support.

A Simple Asynchronous Operation

To try the BackgroundWorker, it helps to consider a sample application. The basic ingredient for any test is a time-consuming process. The following example uses a common algorithm for finding prime numbers in a given range called the *sieve of Eratosthenes*, which was invented by Eratosthenes himself in about 240 BC. With this algorithm, you begin by making a list of all the integers in a range of numbers. You then strike out the multiples of all primes less than or equal to the square root of the maximum number. The numbers that are left are the primes.

In this example, I won't go into the theory that proves the sieve of Eratosthenes works or show the fairly trivial code that performs it. (Similarly, don't worry about optimizing it or comparing it against other techniques.) However, you will see how to perform the sieve of Eratosthenes algorithm asynchronously.

The full code is available with the online examples for this chapter. It takes this form:

```
public class Worker
{
    public static int[] FindPrimes(int fromNumber, int toNumber)
    {
        // Find the primes between fromNumber and toNumber,
        // and return them as an array of integers.
    }
}
```

The FindPrimes() method takes two parameters that delimit a range of numbers. The code then returns an integer array with all the prime numbers that occur in that range.

Figure 26-1 shows the example we're building. This window allows the user to choose the range of numbers to search. When the user clicks Find Primes, the search begins, but it takes place in the background. When the search is finished, the list of prime numbers appears in the list box.

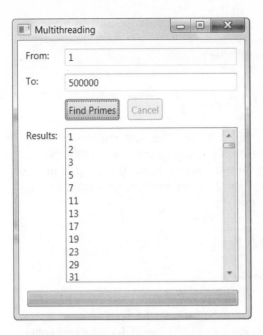

Figure 26-1. *A completed prime number search*

Creating the BackgroundWorker

To use the BackgroundWorker, you begin by creating an instance. Here, you have two options:

- You can create the BackgroundWorker in your code and attach all the event handlers programmatically.

- You can declare the BackgroundWorker in your XAML. The advantage of this approach is that you can hook up your event handlers using attributes. Because the Background-Worker isn't a visible WPF element, you can't place it just anywhere. Instead you need to declare it as a resource for your window. (You'll learn all about resources in Chapter 11.)

Both approaches are equivalent. The downloadable sample uses the second approach. The first step is to make the System.ComponentModel namespace accessible in your XAML document through a namespace import. To do this, you need to use the namespace mapping technique you learned about in Chapter 2:

```
<Window x:Class="Multithreading.BackgroundWorkerTest"
    xmlns="http://schemas.microsoft.com/winfx/2006/xaml/presentation"
    xmlns:x="http://schemas.microsoft.com/winfx/2006/xaml"
    xmlns:cm="clr-namespace:System.ComponentModel;assembly=System"
    ... >
```

Now you can create an instance of the BackgroundWorker in the Window.Resources collection. When doing this, you need to supply a key name so the object can be retrieved later. In this example, the key name is backgroundWorker:

```
<Window.Resources>
  <cm:BackgroundWorker x:Key="backgroundWorker"></cm:BackgroundWorker>
</Window.Resources>
```

The advantage of declaring the BackgroundWorker in the Window.Resources section is that you can set its properties and attach its event handlers using attributes. For example, here's the BackgroundWorker tag you'll end up with at the end of this example, which enables support for progress notification and cancellation and attaches event handlers to the DoWork, ProgressChanged, and RunWorkerCompleted events:

```
<cm:BackgroundWorker x:Key="backgroundWorker"
  WorkerReportsProgress="True" WorkerSupportsCancellation="True"
  DoWork="backgroundWorker_DoWork"
  ProgressChanged="backgroundWorker_ProgressChanged"
  RunWorkerCompleted="backgroundWorker_RunWorkerCompleted">
</cm:BackgroundWorker>
```

To get access to this resource in your code, you need to pull it out of the Resources collection. In this example, the window performs this step in its constructor so that all your event handling code can access it more easily:

```
public partial class BackgroundWorkerTest : Window
{
    private BackgroundWorker backgroundWorker;

    public BackgroundWorkerTest()
    {
        InitializeComponent();
        backgroundWorker =
          ((BackgroundWorker)this.FindResource("backgroundWorker"));
    }

    ...
}
```

■**Note** You'll learn much more about the Resources collection in Chapter 11.

Running the BackgroundWorker

The first step to using the BackgroundWorker with the prime number search example is to create a custom class that allows you to transmit the input parameters to the Background-Worker. When you call BackgroundWorker.RunWorkerAsync(), you can supply any object, which will be delivered to the DoWork event. However, you can supply only a single object, so you need to wrap the to and from numbers into one class, as shown here:

```
public class FindPrimesInput
{
    public int From
    { get; set; }

    public int To
    { get; set; }

    public FindPrimesInput(int from, int to)
    {
        From = from;
        To = to;
    }
}
```

To start the BackgroundWorker on its way, you need to call the BackgroundWorker.Run-WorkerAsync() method and pass in the FindPrimesInput object. Here's the code that does this when the user clicks the Find Primes button:

```
private void cmdFind_Click(object sender, RoutedEventArgs e)
{
    // Disable this button and clear previous results.
    cmdFind.IsEnabled = false;
    cmdCancel.IsEnabled = true;
    lstPrimes.Items.Clear();

    // Get the search range.
    int from, to;
    if (!Int32.TryParse(txtFrom.Text, out from))
    {
        MessageBox.Show("Invalid From value.");
        return;
    }
    if (!Int32.TryParse(txtTo.Text, out to))
    {
        MessageBox.Show("Invalid To value.");
        return;
    }

    // Start the search for primes on another thread.
    FindPrimesInput input = new FindPrimesInput(from, to);
    backgroundWorker.RunWorkerAsync(input);
}
```

When the BackgroundWorker begins executing, it grabs a free thread from the CLR thread pool and then fires the DoWork event from this thread. You handle the DoWork event and begin your time-consuming task. However, you need to be careful not to access shared data (such as fields in your window class) or user interface objects. Once the work is complete, the BackgroundWorker fires the RunWorkerCompleted event to notify your application. This event fires on the dispatcher thread, which allows you to access shared data and your user interface, without incurring any problems.

Once the BackgroundWorker acquires the thread, it fires the DoWork event. You can handle this event to call the Worker.FindPrimes() method. The DoWork event provides a DoWorkEventArgs object, which is the key ingredient for retrieving and returning information. You retrieve the input object through the DoWorkEventArgs.Argument property and return the result by setting the DoWorkEventArgs.Result property.

```
private void backgroundWorker_DoWork(object sender, DoWorkEventArgs e)
{
    // Get the input values.
    FindPrimesInput input = (FindPrimesInput)e.Argument;

    // Start the search for primes and wait.
    // This is the time-consuming part, but it won't freeze the
    // user interface because it takes place on another thread.
    int[] primes = Worker.FindPrimes(input.From, input.To);

    // Return the result.
    e.Result = primes;
}
```

Once the method completes, the BackgroundWorker fires the RunWorkerCompleted-EventArgs on the dispatcher thread. At this point, you can retrieve the result from the RunWorkerCompletedEventArgs.Result property. You can then update the interface and access window-level variables without worry.

```
private void backgroundWorker_RunWorkerCompleted(object sender,
  RunWorkerCompletedEventArgs e)
{
    if (e.Error != null)
    {
        // An error was thrown by the DoWork event handler.
        MessageBox.Show(e.Error.Message, "An Error Occurred");
    }
    else
    {
        int[] primes = (int[])e.Result;
        foreach (int prime in primes)
        {
            lstPrimes.Items.Add(prime);
        }
    }
```

```
    cmdFind.IsEnabled = true;
    cmdCancel.IsEnabled = false;
    progressBar.Value = 0;
}
```

Notice that you don't need any locking code, and you don't need to use the Dispatcher.BeginInvoke() method. The BackgroundWorker takes care of these issues for you.

Behind the scenes, the BackgroundWorker uses a few multithreading classes that were introduced in .NET 2.0, including AsyncOperationManager, AsyncOperation, and SynchronizationContext. Essentially, the BackgroundWorker uses AsyncOperationManager to manage the background task. The AsyncOperationManager has some built-in intelligence—namely, it's able to get the synchronization context for the current thread. In a Windows Forms application, the AsyncOperationManager gets a WindowsFormsSynchronizationContext object, whereas a WPF application gets a DispatcherSynchronizationContext object. Conceptually, these classes do the same job, but their internal plumbing is different.

Tracking Progress

The BackgroundWorker also provides built-in support for tracking progress, which is useful for keeping the client informed about how much work has been completed in a long-running task.

To add support for progress, you need to first set the BackgroundWorker.WorkerReportsProgress property to true. Actually, providing and displaying the progress information is a two-step affair. First, the DoWork event handling code needs to call the BackgroundWorker.ReportProgress() method and provide an estimated percent complete (from 0% to 100%). You can do this as little or as often as you like. Every time you call ReportProgress(), the BackgroundWorker fires the ProgressChanged event. You can react to this event to read the new progress percentage and update the user interface. Because the ProgressChanged event fires from the user interface thread, there's no need to use Dispatcher.BeginInvoke().

The FindPrimes() method reports progress in 1% increments, using code like this:

```
int iteration = list.Length / 100;
for (int i = 0; i < list.Length; i++)
{
    ...

    // Report progress only if there is a change of 1%.
    // Also, don't bother performing the calculation if there
    // isn't a BackgroundWorker or if it doesn't support
    // progress notifications.
    if ((i % iteration == 0) &&
      (backgroundWorker != null) && backgroundWorker.WorkerReportsProgress)
    {
        backgroundWorker.ReportProgress(i / iteration);
    }
}
```

Once you've set the BackgroundWorker.WorkerReportsProgress property, you can respond to these progress notifications by handling the ProgressChanged event. In this example, a progress bar is updated accordingly:

```
private void backgroundWorker_ProgressChanged(object sender,
  ProgressChangedEventArgs e)
{
    progressBar.Value = e.ProgressPercentage;
}
```

Figure 26-2 shows the progress meter while the task is in progress.

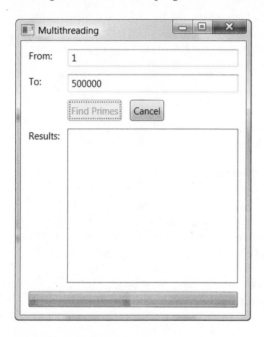

Figure 26-2. *Tracking progress for an asynchronous task*

Supporting Cancellation

It's just as easy to add support for canceling a long-running task with the BackgroundWorker. The first step is to set the BackgroundWorker.WorkerSupportsCancellation property to true.

To request a cancellation, your code needs to call the BackgroundWorker.CancelAsync() method. In this example, the cancellation is requested when a Cancel button is clicked:

```
private void cmdCancel_Click(object sender, RoutedEventArgs e)
{
    backgroundWorker.CancelAsync();
}
```

Nothing happens automatically when you call CancelAsync(). Instead, the code that's performing the task needs to explicitly check for the cancel request, perform any required cleanup, and return. Here's the code in the FindPrimes() method that checks for cancellation requests just before it reports progress:

```
for (int i = 0; i < list.Length; i++)
{
    ...
    if ((i % iteration) && (backgroundWorker != null))
    {
        if (backgroundWorker.CancellationPending)
        {
            // Return without doing any more work.
            return;
        }

        if (backgroundWorker.WorkerReportsProgress)
        {
            backgroundWorker.ReportProgress(i / iteration);
        }
    }
}
```

The code in your DoWork event handler also needs to explicitly set the DoWork-
EventArgs.Cancel property to true to complete the cancellation. You can then return from
that method without attempting to build up the string of primes.

```
private void backgroundWorker_DoWork(object sender, DoWorkEventArgs e)
{
    FindPrimesInput input = (FindPrimesInput)e.Argument;
    int[] primes = Worker.FindPrimes(input.From, input.To,
      backgroundWorker);

    if (backgroundWorker.CancellationPending)
    {
        e.Cancel = true;
        return;
    }

    // Return the result.
    e.Result = primes;
}
```

Even when you cancel an operation, the RunWorkerCompleted event still fires. At this
point, you can check whether the task was cancelled and handle it accordingly.

```
private void backgroundWorker_RunWorkerCompleted(object sender,
  RunWorkerCompletedEventArgs e)
{
    if (e.Cancelled)
    {
        MessageBox.Show("Search cancelled.");
    }
    else if (e.Error != null)
```

```
    {
        // An error was thrown by the DoWork event handler.
        MessageBox.Show(e.Error.Message, "An Error Occurred");
    }
    else
    {
        int[] primes = (int[])e.Result;
        foreach (int prime in primes)
        {
            lstPrimes.Items.Add(prime);
        }
    }
    cmdFind.IsEnabled = true;
    cmdCancel.IsEnabled = false;
    progressBar.Value = 0;
}
```

Now the BackgroundWorker component allows you to start a search and end it prematurely.

Application Add-Ins

Add-ins (also known as *plug-ins*) are separately compiled components that your application can find, load, and use dynamically. Often, an application is designed to use add-ins so that it can be enhanced in the future without needing to be modified, recompiled, and retested. Add-ins also give you the flexibility to customize separate instances of an application for a particular market or client. But the most common reason to use the add-in model is to allow third-party developers to extend the functionality of your application. For example, add-ins in Adobe Photoshop provide a wide range of picture-processing effects. Add-ins in Firefox provide enhanced web surfing features and entirely new functionality. In both cases, the add-ins are created by third-party developers.

Since .NET 1.0, developers have had all the technology they need to create their own add-in system. The two basic ingredients are *interfaces* (which allow you to define the contracts through which the application interacts with the add-in and the add-in interacts with the application) and *reflection* (which allows your application to dynamically discover and load add-in types from a separate assembly). However, building an add-in system from scratch requires a fair bit of work. You need to devise a way to locate add-ins, and you need to ensure that they're managed correctly (in other words, that they execute in a restricted security context and can be unloaded when necessary).

.NET 3.5 introduces a prebuilt add-in model that uses the same infrastructure of interfaces and reflection. The key advantage of the add-in model is that you don't need to write the underlying plumbing for tasks such as discovery. The key disadvantage is the add-in model's sheer complexity. The designers of .NET have taken great care to make the add-in model flexible enough to handle a wide range of versioning and hosting scenarios. The end result is that you must create at least seven (!) separate components to implement the add-in model in an application, even if you don't need to use its most sophisticated features.

The Add-in Pipeline

The heart of the add-in model is the add-in *pipeline*, which is a chain of components that allows the hosting application to interact with an add-in (see Figure 26-3). At one end of the pipeline is the hosting application. At the other end is the add-in. In between are the five components that govern the interaction.

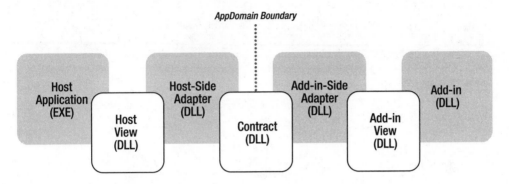

Figure 26-3. *Communicating through the add-in pipeline*

At first glance, this model seems a bit excessive. A simpler scenario would put a single layer (the contract) between the application and the add-in. However, the additional layers (the views and adapters) allow the add-in model to be much more flexible in certain situations (as described in the sidebar "More Advanced Adapters").

How the Pipeline Works

The *contract* is the cornerstone of the add-in pipeline. It includes one or more interfaces that define how the host application can interact with its add-ins and how the add-ins can interact with the host application. The contract assembly can also include custom serializable types that you plan to use to transmit data between the host application and the add-in.

The add-in pipeline is designed with extensibility and flexibility in mind. It's for this reason that the host application and the add-in don't directly use the contract. Instead, they use their own respective versions of the contract, called *views*. The host application uses the host view, while the add-in uses the add-in view. Typically, the view includes abstract classes that closely match the interfaces in the contract.

Although they're usually quite similar, the contracts and views are completely independent. It's up to the *adapters* to link these two pieces together. The adapters perform this linkage by providing classes that simultaneously inherit from the view classes and implement the contract interfaces. Figure 26-4 shows this design.

Essentially, the adapters bridge the gap between the views and the contract interface. They map calls on a view to calls on the contract interface. They also map calls on the contract interface to the corresponding method on the view. This complicates the design somewhat but adds an all-important extra layer of flexibility.

To understand how the adapters work, consider what happens when an application uses an add-in. First, the host application calls one of the methods in the host view. But remember, the host view is an abstract class. Behind the scenes, the application is actually calling a method on the host adapter *through* the host view. (This is possible because the host adapter class derives from the host view class.) The host adapter then calls the corresponding method in the contract interface, which is implemented by the add-in adapter. Finally, the add-in adapter calls a method in the add-in view. This method is implemented by the add-in, which performs the actual work.

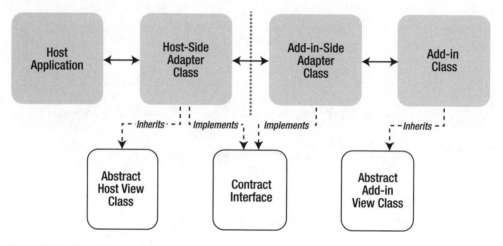

Figure 26-4. *Class relationships in the pipeline*

MORE ADVANCED ADAPTERS

If you don't have any specialized versioning or hosting needs, the adapters are fairly straightforward. They simply pass the work along through the pipeline. However, the adapters are also an important extensibility point for more sophisticated scenarios. One example is versioning. Obviously, you can independently update an application or its add-ins without changing the way they interact, as long as you continue to use the same interfaces in the contract. However, in some cases you might need to change the interfaces to expose new features. This causes a bit of a problem, because the old interfaces must still be supported for backward compatibility with old add-ins. After a few revisions, you'll end up with a complex mess of similar yet different interfaces, and the application will need to recognize and support them all.

With the add-in model, you can take a different approach to backward compatibility. Instead of providing multiple interfaces, you can provide a single interface in your contract and use adapters to create different views. For example, a version 1 add-in can work with a version 2 application (which exposes a version 2 contract) as long as you have an add-in adapter that spans the gap. Similarly, if you develop an add-in that uses the version 2 contract, you can use it with the original version 1 application (and version 1 contract) by using a different add-in adapter.

It's possible to work similar magic if you have specialized hosting needs. For example, you can use adapters to load add-ins with different isolation levels or even share them between applications. The hosting application and the add-in don't need to be aware of these details, because the adapters handle all the details.

Even if you don't need to create custom adapters to implement specialized versioning and hosting strategies, you still need to include these components. However, all your add-ins can use the same view and adapter components. In other words, once you've gone to the trouble of setting up the complete pipeline for one add-in, you can add more add-ins without much work, as illustrated in Figure 26-5.

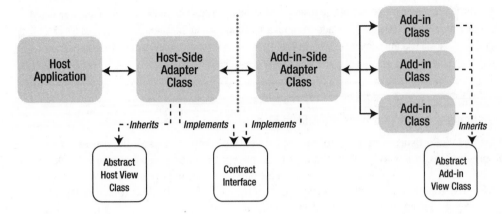

Figure 26-5. *Multiple add-ins that use the same pipeline*

In the following sections, you'll learn how to implement the add-in pipeline for a WPF application.

The Add-in Folder Structure

To use the add-in pipeline, you must follow a strict directory structure. This directory structure is separate from the application. In other words, it's perfectly acceptable to have your application residing at one location and all the add-ins and pipeline components residing at another location. However, the add-in components must be arranged in specifically named subdirectories with respect to one another. For example, if your add-in system uses the root directory c:\MyApp, you need the following subdirectories:

c:\MyApp\AddInSideAdapters

c:\MyApp\AddInViews

c:\MyApp\Contracts

c:\MyApp\HostSideAdapters

c:\MyApp\AddIns

Finally, the AddIns directory (shown last in this list) must have a separate subdirectory for each add-in your application is using, such as c:\MyApp\AddIns\MyFirstAddIn, c:\MyApp\AddIns\MySecondAddIn, and so on.

In this example, it's assumed that the application executable is deployed in the c:\MyApp subdirectory. In other words, the same directory does double duty as the application folder and as the add-in root. This is a common deployment choice, but it's certainly not a requirement.

■**Note** If you've been paying close attention to the pipeline diagrams, you may have noticed that there's a subdirectory for each component except the host-side views. That's because the host views are used directly by the host application, so they're deployed alongside the application executable. (In this example, that means they are in c:\MyApp.) The add-in views aren't deployed in the same way, because it's likely that several add-ins will use the same add-in view. Thanks to the dedicated AddInViews folder, you need to deploy (and update) just one copy of each add-in view assembly.

Preparing a Solution That Uses the Add-In Model

The add-in folder structure is mandatory. If you leave out one of the subdirectories listed in the previous section, you'll encounter a runtime exception when you search for add-ins.

Currently, Visual Studio doesn't have a template for creating applications that use add-ins. Thus, it's up to you to create these folders and set up your Visual Studio project to use them.

Here's the easiest approach to follow:

1. Create a top-level directory that will hold all the projects you're about to create. For example, you might name this directory c:\AddInTest.

2. Create a new WPF project for the host application in this directory. It doesn't matter what you name the project, but you must place it in the top-level directory you created in step 1 (for example, c:\AddInTest\HostApplication).

3. Add a new class library project for each pipeline component, and place them all in the same solution. At a bare minimum, you'll need to create a project for one add-in (for example, c:\AddInTest\MyAddIn), one add-in view (c:\AddInTest\MyAddInView), one add-in side adapter (c:\AddInTest\MyAddInAdapter), one host view (c:\AddInTest\HostView), and one host-side adapter (c:\AddInTest\HostAdapter). Figure 26-6 shows an example from the downloadable code for this chapter, which you'll consider in the following sections. It includes an application (named HostApplication) and two add-ins (named FadeImageAddIn and NegativeImageAddIn).

Figure 26-6. *A solution that uses the add-in pipeline*

Note Technically, it doesn't matter what project names and directory names you use when you create the pipeline components. The required folder structure, which you learned about in the previous section, will be created when you build the application (provided you configure your project settings properly, as described in the following two steps). However, to simplify the configuration process, it's strongly recommended that you create all the project directories in the top-level directory you established in step 1.

4. Now you need to create a build directory inside the top-level directory. This is where your application and all the pipeline components will be placed once they're compiled. It's common to name this directory Output (as in c:\AddInTest\Output).

5. As you design the various pipeline components, you'll modify the build path of each one so that the component is placed in the right subdirectory. For example, your add-in adapter should be compiled to a directory like c:\AddInTest\Output\ AddInSideAdapters. To modify the build path, double-click the Properties node in the Solution Explorer. Then, click the Build tab. In the Output section (at the bottom), you'll find a text box named Output Path. You need to use a relative output path that travels one level up the directory tree and then uses the Output directory. For example, the output path for an add-in adapter would be ..\Output\AddInSideAdapters. As you build each component in the following sections, you'll learn which build path to use. Figure 26-7 shows a preview of the final result, based on the solution shown in Figure 26-6.

Figure 26-7. *The folder structure for a solution that uses the add-in pipeline*

There's one more consideration when developing with the add-in model in Visual Studio: references. Some pipeline components need to reference other pipeline components. However, you don't want the referenced assembly to be copied with the assembly that contains the reference. Instead, you rely on the add-in model's directory system.

To prevent a referenced assembly from being copied, you need to select the assembly in the Solution Explorer (it appears under the References node). Then, set Copy Local to False in the Properties window. As you build each component in the following sections, you'll learn which references to add.

■**Tip** Correctly configuring an add-in project can take a bit of work. To start off on the right foot, you can use the add-in example that's discussed in this chapter, which is available with the downloadable code for this book.

An Application That Uses Add-Ins

In the following sections, you'll create an application that uses the add-in model to support different ways of processing a picture (Figure 26-8). When the application starts, it lists all the add-ins that are currently present. The user can then select one of the add-ins from the list and use it to modify the currently displayed picture.

Figure 26-8. *An application that uses add-ins to manipulate a picture*

The Contract

The starting point for defining the add-in pipeline for your application is to create a contract assembly. The contract assembly defines two things:

- The interfaces that determine how the host will interact with the add-in and how the add-in will interact with the host.

- Custom types that you use to exchange information between the host and add-in. These types must be serializable.

The example shown in Figure 26-8 uses an exceedingly simple contract. Plug-ins provide a method named ProcessImageBytes() that accepts a byte array with image data, modifies it, and returns the modified byte array. Here's the contract that defines this method:

```
[AddInContract]
public interface IImageProcessorContract : IContract
{
    byte[] ProcessImageBytes(byte[] pixels);
}
```

When creating a contract, you must derive from the IContract interface, and you must decorate the class with the AddInContract attribute. Both the interface and the attribute are found in the System.AddIn.Contract namespace. To have access to them in your contract assembly, you must add a reference to the System.AddIn.Contract.dll assembly.

Because the image-processing example doesn't use custom types to transmit data (just ordinary byte arrays), no types are defined in the contract assembly. Byte arrays can be transmitted between the host application and add-in because arrays and bytes are serializable.

The only additional step you need is to configure the build directory. The contract assembly must be placed in the Contracts subdirectory of the add-in root, which means you can use an output path of ..\Output\Contracts in the current example.

■**Note** In this example, the interfaces are kept as simple as possible to avoid clouding the code with extra details. In a more realistic image-processing scenario, you might include a method that returns a list of configurable parameters that affect how the add-in processes the image. Each add-in would have its own parameters. For example, a filter that darkens a picture might include an Intensity setting, a filter that skews a picture might have an Angle setting, and so on. The host application could then supply these parameters when calling the ProcessImageBytes() method.

The Add-in View

The add-in view provides an abstract class that mirrors the contract assembly and is used on the add-in side. Creating this class is easy:

```
[AddInBase]
public abstract class ImageProcessorAddInView
{
    public abstract byte[] ProcessImageBytes(byte[] pixels);
}
```

Notice that the add-in view class must be decorated with the AddInBase attribute. This attribute is found in the System.AddIn.Pipeline namespace. The add-in view assembly requires a reference to the System.AddIn.dll assembly in order to access it.

The add-in view assembly must be placed in the AddInViews subdirectory of the add-in root, which means you can use an output path of ..\Output\AddInViews in the current example.

The Add-In

The add-in view is an abstract class that doesn't provide any functionality. To create a usable add-in, you need a concrete class that derives from the abstract view class. This class can then add the code that actually does the work (in this case, processing the image).

The following add-in inverts the color values to create an effect that's similar to a photo negative. Here's the complete code:

```
[AddIn("Negative Image Processor", Version = "1.0.0.0",
 Publisher = "Imaginomics",
 Description = "Inverts colors to look like a photo negative")]
public class NegativeImageProcessor : AddInView.ImageProcessorAddInView
{
    public override byte[] ProcessImageBytes(byte[] pixels)
    {
        for (int i = 0; i < pixels.Length - 2; i++)
        {
            // Assuming 24-bit, color, each pixel has three bytes of data.
            pixels[i] = (byte)(255 - pixels[i]);
            pixels[i + 1] = (byte)(255 - pixels[i + 1]);
            pixels[i + 2] = (byte)(255 - pixels[i + 2]);
        }
        return pixels;
    }
}
```

■**Note** In this example, the byte array is passed into the ProcessImageBytes() method through a parameter, modified directly, and then passed back to the calling code as the return value. However, when you call ProcessImageBytes() from a different application domain, this behavior isn't as simple as it seems. The add-in infrastructure actually makes a *copy* of the original byte array and passes that copy to the add-in's application domain. Once the byte array is modified and has been returned from the method, the add-in infrastructure copies it back into the host's application domain. If ProcessImageBytes() didn't return the modified byte array in this way, the host would never see the changed picture data.

To create an add-in, you simply need to derive a class from the abstract view class and decorate it with the AddIn attribute. Additionally, you can use the properties of the AddIn attribute to supply an add-in name, version, publisher, and description, as done here. This information is made available to the host during add-in discovery.

The add-in assembly requires two references: one to the System.AddIn.dll assembly and one to the add-in view project. However, you must set the Copy Local property of the add-in view reference to False (as described earlier in the section "Preparing a Solution That Uses the Add-in Model"). That's because the add-in view isn't deployed with the add-in—instead, it's placed in the designated AddInViews subdirectory.

The add-in must be placed in its own subdirectory in the AddIns subdirectory of the add-in root. In the current example, you would use an output path like ..\Output\AddIns\ NegativeImageAddIn.

The Add-in Adapter

The current example has all the add-in functionality that you need, but there's still a gap between the add-in and the contract. Although the add-in view is modeled after the contract, it doesn't implement the contract interface that's used for communication between the application and the add-in.

The missing ingredient is the add-in adapter. It implements the contract interface. When a method is called in the contract interface, it calls the corresponding method in the add-in view. Here's the code for the most straightforward add-in adapter that you can create:

```
[AddInAdapter]
public class ImageProcessorViewToContractAdapter :
  ContractBase, Contract.IImageProcessorContract
{
    private AddInView.ImageProcessorAddInView view;

    public ImageProcessorViewToContractAdapter(
      AddInView.ImageProcessorAddInView view)
    {
        this.view = view;
    }

    public byte[] ProcessImageBytes(byte[] pixels)
    {
        return view.ProcessImageBytes(pixels);
    }
}
```

All add-in adapters must derive from ContractBase (from the System.AddIn.Pipeline namespace). ContractBase derives from MarshalByRefObject, which allows the adapter to be called over an application domain boundary. All add-in adapters must also be decorated with the AddInAdapter attribute (from the System.AddIn.Pipeline namespace). Furthermore, the add-in adapter must include a constructor that receives an instance of the appropriate view as an argument. When the add-in infrastructure creates the add-in adapter, it automatically uses this constructor and passes in the add-in itself. (Remember, the add-in derives from the abstract add-in view class expected by the constructor.) Your code simply needs to store this view for later use.

The add-in adapter requires three references: one to System.AddIn.dll, one to System.AddIn.Contract.dll, and one to the contract project. You must set the Copy Local property of the contract reference to False (as described earlier in the section "Preparing a Solution That Uses the Add-in Model").

The add-in adapter assembly must be placed in the AddInSideAdapters subdirectory of the add-in root, which means you can use an output path of ..\Output\AddInSideAdapters in the current example.

The Host View

The next step is to build the host side of the add-in pipeline. The host interacts with the host view. Like the add-in view, the host view is an abstract class that closely mirrors the contract interface. The only difference is that it doesn't require any attributes.

```
public abstract class ImageProcessorHostView
{
    public abstract byte[] ProcessImageBytes(byte[] pixels);
}
```

The host view assembly must be deployed along with the host application. You can adjust the output path manually (for example, so the host view assembly is placed in the ..\Output folder in the current example). Or, when you add the host view reference to the host application, you can leave the Copy Local property set to True. This way, the host view will be copied automatically to the same output directory as the host application.

The Host Adapter

The host-side adapter derives from the host view. It receives an object that implements the contract, which it can then use when its methods are called. This is the same forwarding process that the add-in adapter uses, but in reverse. In this example, when the host application calls the ProcessImageBytes() method of the host view, it's actually calling ProcessImageBytes() in the host adapter. The host adapter calls ProcessImageBytes() on the contract interface (which is then forwarded across the application boundary and transformed into a method call on the add-in adapter).

Here's the complete code for the host adapter:

```
[HostAdapter]
public class ImageProcessorContractToViewHostAdapter :
 HostView.ImageProcessorHostView
{
    private Contract.IImageProcessorContract contract;
    private ContractHandle contractHandle;

    public ImageProcessorContractToViewHostAdapter(
      Contract.IImageProcessorContract contract)
    {
        this.contract = contract;
        contractHandle = new ContractHandle(contract);
    }

    public override byte[] ProcessImageBytes(byte[] pixels)
    {
        return contract.ProcessImageBytes(pixels);
    }
}
```

You'll notice the host adapter actually uses two member fields. It stores a reference to the current contract object, and it stores a reference to a System.AddIns.Pipeline.ContractHandle object. The ContractHandle object manages the lifetime of the add-in. If the host adapter doesn't create a ContractHandle object (and keep a reference to it), the add-in will be released immediately after the constructor code ends. When the host application attempts to use the add-in, it will receive an AppDomainUnloadedException.

The host adapter project needs references to System.Add.dll and System.AddIn.Contract.dll. It also needs references to the contract assembly and the host view assembly (both of which must have Copy Local set to false). The output path is the HostSideAdapters subdirectory in the add-in root (in this example it's ..\Output\HostSideAdapters).

The Host

Now that the infrastructure is in place, the final step is to create the application that uses the add-in model. Although any type of executable .NET application could be a host, this example uses a WPF application.

The host needs just one reference that points to the host view project. The host view is the entry point to the add-in pipeline. In fact, now that you've done the heavy lifting in implementing the pipeline, the host doesn't need to worry about how it's managed. It simply needs to find the available add-ins, activate the ones it wants to use, and then call the methods that are exposed by the host view.

The first step—finding the available add-ins—is called *discovery*. It works through the static methods of the System.AddIn.Hosting.AddInStore class. To load add-ins, you simply supply the add-in root path and call AddInStore.Update(), as shown here:

```
// In this example, the path where the application is running
// is also the add-in root.
string path = Environment.CurrentDirectory;
AddInStore.Update(path);
```

After calling Update(), the add-in system will create two files with cached information. A file named PipelineSegments.store will be placed in the add-in root. This file includes information about the different views and adapters. A file named AddIns.store will be placed in the AddIns subdirectory, with information about all the available add-ins. If new views, adapters, or add-ins are added, you can update these files by calling AddInStore.Update() again. (This method returns quite quickly if there are no new add-ins or pipeline components.) If there is reason to expect that there is a problem with existing add-in files, you can call AddInStore.Rebuild() instead, which always rebuilds the add-in files from scratch.

Once you've created the cache files, you can search for the specific add-ins. You can use the FindAddIn() method to find a single specific add-in, or you can use the FindAddIns() method to find all the add-ins that match a specified host view. The FindAddIns() method returns a collection of tokens, each of which is an instance of the System.AddIn.Hosting.AddInToken class.

```
IList<AddInToken> tokens = AddInStore.FindAddIns(
   typeof(HostView.ImageProcessorHostView), path);
lstAddIns.ItemsSource = tokens;
```

You can get information about the add-in through a few key properties (Name, Description, Publisher, and Version). In the image-processing application (shown in Figure 26-8), the token list is bound to a ListBox control, and some basic information is shown about each add-in using the following data template:

```
<ListBox Name="lstAddIns" Margin="3">
  <ListBox.ItemTemplate>
    <DataTemplate>
      <StackPanel Margin="3,3,0,8" HorizontalAlignment="Stretch">
        <TextBlock Text="{Binding Path=Name}" FontWeight="Bold" />
        <TextBlock Text="{Binding Path=Publisher}" />
        <TextBlock Text="{Binding Path=Description}"
         FontSize="10" FontStyle="Italic" />
      </StackPanel>
    </DataTemplate>
  </ListBox.ItemTemplate>
</ListBox>
```

You can create an instance of the add-in by calling the AddInToken.Activate<T> method. In the current application, the user clicks the Go button to activate an add-in. The information is then pulled out of the current image (which is shown in the window) and passed to the ProcessImageBytes() method of the host view. Here's how it works:

```
private void cmdProcessImage_Click(object sender, RoutedEventArgs e)
{
    // Copy the image information from the image to a byte array.
    BitmapSource source = (BitmapSource)img.Source;
    int stride = source.PixelWidth * source.Format.BitsPerPixel/8;
    stride = stride + (stride % 4) * 4;
    int arraySize = stride * source.PixelHeight *
      source.Format.BitsPerPixel / 8;
    byte[] originalPixels = new byte[arraySize];
    source.CopyPixels(originalPixels, stride, 0);

    // Get the selected add-in token.
    AddInToken token = (AddInToken)lstAddIns.SelectedItem;

    // Get the host view.
    HostView.ImageProcessorHostView addin =
      token.Activate<HostView.ImageProcessorHostView>(
        AddInSecurityLevel.Internet);

    // Use the add-in.
    byte[] changedPixels = addin.ProcessImageBytes(originalPixels);

    // Create a new BitmapSource with the changed image data, and display it.
    BitmapSource newSource = BitmapSource.Create(source.PixelWidth,
```

```
    source.PixelHeight, source.DpiX, source.DpiY, source.Format,
    source.Palette, changedPixels, stride);
  img.Source = newSource;
}
```

When you call the AddInToken.Activate<T> method, quite a few steps unfold behind the scenes:

1. A new application domain is created for the add-in. Alternatively, you can load the add-in into the application domain of the host application or into a completely separate process. However, the default is to place it in a distinct application domain in the current process, which usually gives the best compromise between stability and performance. You can also choose the level of permissions that are given to the new application domain. (In this example, they're limited to the Internet set of permissions, which is a heavily restricted permission set that's applied to code that's executed from the Web.)

2. The add-in assembly is loaded into the new application domain. The add-in is then instantiated through reflection, using its no-argument constructor. As you've already seen, the add-in derives from an abstract class in the add-in view assembly. As a result, loading the add-in also loads the add-in view assembly into the new application domain.

3. The add-in adapter is instantiated in the new application domain. The add-in is passed to the add-in adapter as a constructor argument. (The add-in is typed as the add-in view.)

4. The add-in adapter is made available to the host's application domain (through a remoting proxy). However, it's typed as the contract that it implements.

5. In the host application domain, the host adapter is instantiated. The add-in adapter is passed to the host adapter through its constructor.

6. The host adapter is returned to the host application (typed as the host view). The application can now call the methods of the host view to interact with the add-in through the add-in pipeline.

There are other overloads for the Activate<T> method that allow you to supply a custom permission set (to fine-tune security), a specific application domain (which is useful if you want to run several add-ins in the same application domain), and an outside process (which allows you to host the add-in in a completely separate EXE application for even greater isolation). All of these examples are illustrated in the Visual Studio help.

This code completes the example. The host application can now discover its add-ins, activate them, and interact with them through the host view.

ADD-IN LIFETIME

You don't need to manage the lifetime of your add-ins by hand. Instead, the add-in system will automatically release an add-in and shut down its application domain. In the previous example, the add-in is released when the variable that points to the host view goes out of scope. If you want to keep the same add-in active for a longer time, you could assign it to a member variable in the window class.

In some situations, you might want more control over the add-in lifetime. The add-in model gives the host application the ability to shut down an add-in automatically using the AddInController class (from the System.AddIn.Hosting namespace), which tracks all the currently active add-ins. The AddInControls provides a static method named GetAddInController(), which accepts a host view and returns an AddInController for that add-in. You can then use the AddInController.Shutdown() method to end it, as shown here:

```
AddInController controller = AddInController.GetAddInController(addin);
controller.Shutdown();
```

At this point, the adapters will be disposed, the add-in will be released, and the add-in's application domain will be shut down if it doesn't contain any other add-ins.

Adding More Add-Ins

Using the same add-in view, it's possible to create an unlimited number of distinct add-ins. In this example there are two, which process images in two different ways. The second add-in uses a crude algorithm to darken the picture by removing part of the color from random pixels:

```
[AddIn("Fade Image Processor", Version = "1.0.0.0", Publisher = "SupraImage",
 Description = "Darkens the picture")]
public class FadeImageProcessor : AddInView.ImageProcessorAddInView
{
    public override byte[] ProcessImageBytes(byte[] pixels)
    {
        Random rand = new Random();
        int offset = rand.Next(0, 10);
        for (int i = 0; i < pixels.Length - 1 - offset; i++)
        {
            if ((i + offset) % 5 == 0)
            {
                pixels[i] = 0;
            }
        }
        return pixels;
    }
}
```

In the current example, this add-in builds to the output path ..\Output\AddIns\FadeImageAddIn. There's no need to create additional views or adapters. Once you deploy this add-in (and then call the Rebuild() or Update() method of the AddInStore class), your host application will find both add-ins.

Interacting with the Host

In the current example, the host is in complete control of the add-in. However, the relationship is often reversed. A common example is an add-in that drives an area of application functionality. This is particularly common with visual add-ins (the subject of the next section), such as custom toolbars. Often, this process of allowing the add-in to call the host is called *automation.*

From a conceptual standpoint, automation is quite straightforward. The add-in simply needs a reference to an object in the host's application domain, which it can manipulate through a separate interface. However, the add-in system's emphasis on versioning flexibility makes the implementation of this technique a bit more complicated. A single host interface is not enough, because it tightly binds the host and the add-in together. Instead, you'll need to implement a pipeline with views and adapters.

To see this challenge, consider the slightly updated version of the image-processing application, which is shown in Figure 26-9. It features a progress bar at the bottom of the window that's updated as the add-in processes the image data.

Figure 26-9. *An add-in that reports progress*

■**Tip** The rest of this section explores the changes you need to make to the image processor to support host automation. To see how these pieces fit together and examine the full code, download the code samples for this chapter.

For this application to work, the add-in needs a way to pass progress information to the host while it works. The first step in implementing this solution is to create the interface that defines how the add-in can interact with the host. This interface should be placed in the contract assembly (or in a separate assembly in the Contracts folder).

Here's the interface that describes how the add-in should be allowed to report progress, by calling a method named ReportProgress() in the host application:

```
public interface IHostObjectContract : IContract
{
    void ReportProgress(int progressPercent);
}
```

As with the add-in interface, the host interface must inherit from IContract. Unlike the add-in interface, the host interface does not use the AddInContract attribute, because it isn't implemented by an add-in.

The next step is to create the add-in view and host view. As when designing an add-in, you simply need an abstract class that closely corresponds to the interface you're using. To use the IHostObjectContract interface shown earlier, you simply need to add the following class definition to both the add-in view and host view projects.

```
public abstract class HostObject
{
    public abstract void ReportProgress(int progressPercent);
}
```

Notice that the class definition does not use the AddInBase attribute in either project.

The actual implementation of the ReportProgress() method is in the host application. It needs a class that derives from the HostObject class (in the host view assembly). Here's a slightly simplified example that uses the percentage to update a ProgressBar control:

```
public class AutomationHost : HostView.HostObject
{
    private ProgressBar progressBar;

    public Host(ProgressBar progressBar)
    {
        this.progressBar = progressBar;
    }

    public override void ReportProgress(int progressPercent)
    {
        progressBar.Value = progressPercent;
    }
}
```

You now have a mechanism that the add-in can use to send progress information to the host application. However, there's one problem—the add-in doesn't have any way to get a reference to the HostObject. This problem doesn't occur when the host application is using an add-in, because it has a discovery feature that it can use to search for add-ins. There's no comparable service for add-ins to locate their host.

The solution is for the host application to pass the HostObject reference to the add-in. Typically, this step will be performed when the add-in is first activated. By convention, the method that the host application uses to pass this reference is often called Initialize().

Here's the updated contract for image processor add-ins:

```
[AddInContract]
public interface IImageProcessorContract : IContract
{
    byte[] ProcessImageBytes(byte[] pixels);
    void Initialize(IHostObjectContract hostObj);
}
```

When Initialize() is called, the add-in will simply store the reference for later use. It can then call the ReportProgress() method whenever is appropriate, as shown here:

```
[AddIn]
public class NegativeImageProcessor : AddInView.ImageProcessorAddInView
{
    private AddInView.HostObject host;
    public override void Initialize(AddInView.HostObject hostObj)
    {
        host = hostObj;
    }

    public override byte[] ProcessImageBytes(byte[] pixels)
    {
        int iteration = pixels.Length / 100;

        for (int i = 0; i < pixels.Length - 2; i++)
        {
            pixels[i] = (byte)(255 - pixels[i]);
            pixels[i + 1] = (byte)(255 - pixels[i + 1]);
            pixels[i + 2] = (byte)(255 - pixels[i + 2]);

            if (i % iteration == 0)
                host.ReportProgress(i / iteration);
        }
        return pixels;
    }
}
```

So far, the code hasn't posed any real challenges. However, the last piece—the adapters—is a bit more complicated. Now that you've added the Initialize() method to the add-in contract, you need to also add it to the host view and add-in view. However, the signature of the method can't match the contract interface. That's because the Initialize() method in the interface expects an IHostObjectContract as an argument. The views, which are not linked the contract in any way, have no knowledge of the IHostObjectContract. Instead, they use the abstract HostObject class that was described earlier:

```
public abstract class ImageProcessorHostView
{
    public abstract byte[] ProcessImageBytes(byte[] pixels);

    public abstract void Initialize(HostObject host);
}
```

The adapters are the tricky part. They need to bridge the gap between the abstract HostObject view classes and the IHostObjectContract interface.

For example, consider the ImageProcessorContractToViewHostAdapter on the host side. It derives from the abstract ImageProcessorHostView class, and as a result it implements the version of Initialize() that receives a HostObject instance. This Initialize() method needs to convert this view to the contract and then call the IHostObjectContract.Initialize() method.

The trick is to create an adapter that performs this transformation (much like the adapter that performs the same transformation with the add-in view and add-in interface). The following code shows the new HostObjectViewToContractHostAdapter that does the work and the Initialize() method that uses it to make the jump from the view class to the contract interface:

```
public class HostObjectViewToContractHostAdapter : ContractBase,
  Contract.IHostObjectContract
{
    private HostView.HostObject view;

    public HostObjectViewToContractHostAdapter(HostView.HostObject view)
    {
        this.view = view;
    }

    public void ReportProgress(int progressPercent)
    {
        view.ReportProgress(progressPercent);
    }
}


[HostAdapter]
public class ImageProcessorContractToViewHostAdapter :
  HostView.ImageProcessorHostView
{
    private Contract.IImageProcessorContract contract;
    private ContractHandle contractHandle;

    ...

    public override void Initialize(HostView.HostObject host)
    {
        HostObjectViewToContractHostAdapter hostAdapter =
          new HostObjectViewToContractHostAdapter(host);
        contract.Initialize(hostAdapter);
    }
}
```

A similar transformation takes place in the add-in adapter, but in reverse. Here, the ImageProcessorViewToContractAdapter implements the IImageProcessorContract interface. It needs to take the IHostObjectContract object that it receives in its version of the Initialize()

method and then convert the contract to a view. Next, it can pass the call along by calling the Initialize() method in the view. Here's the code:

```
[AddInAdapter]
public class ImageProcessorViewToContractAdapter : ContractBase,
  Contract.IImageProcessorContract
{
    private AddInView.ImageProcessorAddInView view;
    ...

    public void Initialize(Contract.IHostObjectContract hostObj)
    {
        view.Initialize(new HostObjectContractToViewAddInAdapter(hostObj));
    }
}

public class HostObjectContractToViewAddInAdapter : AddInView.HostObject
{
    private Contract.IHostObjectContract contract;
    private ContractHandle handle;

    public HostObjectContractToViewAddInAdapter(
      Contract.IHostObjectContract contract)
    {
        this.contract = contract;
        this.handle = new ContractHandle(contract);
    }

    public override void ReportProgress(int progressPercent)
    {
        contract.ReportProgress(progressPercent);
    }
}
```

Now, when the host calls Initialize() on an add-in, it can flow through the host adapter (ImageProcessorContractToViewHostAdapter) and the add-in adapter (ImageProcessor-ViewToContractAdapter), before being called on the add-in. When the add-in calls the ReportProgress() method, it flows through similar steps, but in reverse. First, it flows through the add-in adapter (HostObjectContractToViewAddInAdapter) and then it passes to the host adapter (HostObjectViewToContractHostAdapter).

This walk-through completes the example—sort of. The problem is that the host application calls the ProcessImageBytes() method on the main user interface thread. As a result, the user interface is effectively locked up. Although the calls to ReportProgress() are handled and the progress bar is updated, the window isn't refreshed until the operation is complete.

A far better approach is to perform the time-consuming call to ProcessImageBytes() on a background thread, either by creating a Thread object by hand or by using the Background-Worker. Then, when the user interface needs to be updated (when ReportProgress() is called and when the final image is returned), you must use the Dispatcher.BeginInvoke() method to marshal the call back to the user interface thread. All of these techniques were demonstrated earlier in this chapter. To see the threading code in action in this example, refer to the downloadable code for this chapter.

Visual Add-Ins

Considering that the WPF is a display technology, you've probably started to wonder whether there's a way to have an add-in generate a user interface. This isn't a small challenge. The problem is that the user interface elements in WPF aren't serializable. Thus, they can't be passed between the host application and the add-in.

Fortunately, the designers of the add-in system created a sophisticated workaround. The solution is to allow WPF applications to display user interface content that's hosted in separate application domains. In other words, your host application can display controls that are actually running in the application domain of an add-in. If you interact with these controls (clicking them, typing in them, and so on), the events are fired in the add-in's application domain. If you need to pass information from the add-in to the application, or vice versa, you use the contract interfaces, as you've explored in the previous sections.

Figure 26-10 shows this technique in action in a modified version of the image-processing application. When an add-in is selected, the host application asks the add-in to provide a control with suitable content. That control is then displayed at the bottom of the window.

Figure 26-10. *A visual add-in*

In this example, the negative image add-in has been selected. It provides a user control that wraps an Image control (with a preview of the effect) and a Slider control. As the slider is adjusted, the intensity of the effect is changed, and the preview is updated. (The update process is sluggish, because of the poorly optimized image-processing code. Much better algorithms could be used, possibly incorporating unsafe code blocks for maximum performance.)

Although the plumbing that makes this work is fairly sophisticated, it's surprisingly easy to use. The key ingredient is the INativeHandleContract interface from the System.AddIn.Contract namespace. It allows a window handle to be passed between an add-in and the host application.

Here's the revised IImageProcessorContract from the contract assembly. It replaces the ProcessImageBytes() method with a GetVisual() method that accepts similar image data but returns a chunk of user interface:

```
[AddInContract]
public interface IImageProcessorContract : IContract
{
    INativeHandleContract GetVisual(Stream imageStream);
}
```

You don't use the INativeHandlerContract in the view classes, because it isn't directly usable in your WPF applications. Instead, you use the type you expect to see—a FrameworkElement. Here's the host view:

```
public abstract class ImageProcessorHostView
{
    public abstract FrameworkElement GetVisual(Stream imageStream);
}
```

And here's the nearly identical add-in view:

```
[AddInBase]
public abstract class ImageProcessorAddInView
{
    public abstract FrameworkElement GetVisual(Stream imageStream);
}
```

This example is surprisingly similar to the automation challenge in the previous section. Once again, you have a different type being passed in the contract from the one that's used in the views. And once again, you need to use the adapters to perform the contract-to-view and view-to-contract conversion. However, this time the work is done for you by a specialized class called FrameworkElementAdapters.

FrameworkElementAdapters is found in the System.AddIn.Pipeline namespace, but it's actually part of WPF, and it's part of the System.Windows.Presentation.dll assembly. The FrameworkElementAdapters class provides two static methods that perform the conversion work: ContractToViewAdapter() and ViewToContractAdapter().

Here's how the FrameworkElementAdapters.ContractToViewAdapter() method bridges the gap in the host adapter:

```
[HostAdapter]
public class ImageProcessorContractToViewHostAdapter :
  HostView.ImageProcessorHostView
{
    private Contract.IImageProcessorContract contract;
    private ContractHandle contractHandle;

    ...
```

```
    public override FrameworkElement GetVisual(Stream imageStream)
    {
        return FrameworkElementAdapters.ContractToViewAdapter(
          contract.GetVisual(imageStream));
    }
}
```

And here's how the FrameworkElementAdapters.ViewToContractAdapter() method bridges the gap in the add-in adapter:

```
[AddInAdapter]
public class ImageProcessorViewToContractAdapter : ContractBase,
  Contract.IImageProcessorContract
{
    private AddInView.ImageProcessorAddInView view;
    ...

    public INativeHandleContract GetVisual(Stream imageStream)
    {
        return FrameworkElementAdapters.ViewToContractAdapter(
          view.GetVisual(imageStream));
    }
}
```

Now the final detail is to implement the GetVisual() method in the add-in. In the negative image processor, a new user control named ImagePreview is created. The image data is passed to the ImagePreview control, which sets up the preview image and handles slider clicks. (The user control code is beside the point for this example, but you can see the full details by downloading the samples for this chapter.)

```
[AddIn]
public class NegativeImageProcessor : AddInView.ImageProcessorAddInView
{
    public override FrameworkElement GetVisual(System.IO.Stream imageStream)
    {
        return new ImagePreview(imageStream);
    }
}
```

Now that you've seen how to return a user interface object from an add-in, there's no limit to what type of content you can generate. The basic infrastructure—the INativeHandleContract interface and the FrameworkElementAdapters class—remains the same.

The Last Word

In this chapter, you took a look at two advanced topics that could occupy entire books of their own. First you considered the multithreading considerations of WPF applications (which are essentially the same as the considerations for any other type of Windows application) and saw how to safely update controls from other threads and make multithreading easy with BackgroundWorker. Next you dove into the deeply layered add-in model. You learned how its pipeline works, why it works the way it does, and how to create basic add-ins that support host automation and provide visual content.

There's quite a bit more you can learn about the add-in model. If you plan to make add-ins a key part of a professional application, you'll want to take a closer look at specialized versioning and hosting scenarios and deployment, best practices for dealing with unhandled add-in exceptions, and how to allow more complex interactions between the host and add-in and between separate add-ins. You can find some additional information in the Visual Studio help (look under the index entry "add-ins [.NET Framework]"), but you won't find much advanced content. To get the real details, you'll need to visit the team blog for the Microsoft developers who created the add-in system at `http://blogs.msdn.com/clraddins`. You may also be interested in Jason He's blog (`http://blogs.msdn.com/zifengh`). He's a member of the add-in team who has written about his experience adapting Paint.NET to use the add-in model.

■ ■ ■

ClickOnce Deployment

Sooner or later, you'll want to unleash your WPF applications on the world. Although you can use dozens of different ways to transfer an application from your development computer to an end user's desktop, most WPF applications use one of the following deployment strategies:

- **Run in the browser.** If you create a page-based WPF application, you can run it right in the browser. You don't need to install anything. However, your application needs to be able to function with a very limited set of privileges. (For example, you won't be allowed to access arbitrary files, use the Windows registry, pop up new windows, and so on.) You learned about this approach in Chapter 9.

- **Deploy via the browser.** WPF applications integrate closely with the ClickOnce setup feature, which allows users to launch a setup program from a browser page. Best of all, applications that are installed through ClickOnce can be configured to check for updates automatically. On the negative side, you have little ability to customize your setup and no way to perform system configuration tasks (such as registering file types, creating a database, and so on).

- **Deploy via a traditional setup program.** This approach still lives on in the WPF world. If you choose this option, it's up to you whether you want to create a full-fledged Microsoft Installer (MSI) setup or a more streamlined (but more limited) ClickOnce setup. Once you've built your setup, you can choose to distribute it by placing it on a CD, in an e-mail attachment, on a network share, and so on.

In this chapter, you'll consider the second approach: deploying your application with the ClickOnce deployment model.

Application Deployment

Although it's technically possible to move a .NET application from one computer to another just by copying the folder that contains it, professional applications often require a few more frills. For example, you might need to add shortcuts to the Start menu or desktop, register file types, and set up additional resources (such as a custom event log or a database). To get these features, you need to create a custom setup program.

You have many options for creating a setup program. You can use a retail product like InstallShield, or you can create an MSI setup using the Setup Project template in Visual Studio. Traditional setup programs give you a familiar setup wizard, with plenty of features for transferring files and performing a variety of configuration actions.

Your other choice is to use the ClickOnce deployment system that's closely integrated in WPF. ClickOnce has plenty of limitations (most of them by design), but it offers two important advantages:

- Support for automatically downloading updates from the Web.

- Support for installing and running applications in limited trust scenarios. This feature is available only if you create a XAML browser application (XBAP), as described in Chapter 9.

In the near term, these two features might not be enough to entice developers to give up the features of a full-fledged setup program. But in the future, as it becomes more common to run Windows using an account with limited trust (for example, in Windows Vista) and as browser-based WPF applications become more widespread, ClickOnce will gain in importance. And if browser-based WPF applications ever begin to displace today's generation of web-only applications, ClickOnce will be a key piece of the puzzle.

If you've worked with Windows Forms in .NET 2.0, you'll notice that ClickOnce is actually scaled back in WPF. In .NET 2.0, ClickOnce was the preferred way to deploy an application over the Web and the only way to compete with traditional websites. In WPF, browser-based applications offer a more effective way to build a WPF-powered web application, and they don't need to be explicitly deployed. In WPF, you'll use ClickOnce to deploy stand-alone applications only.

There's another change in the mix. In .NET 2.0, a Windows Forms application could be configured to use partial trust and then deployed using ClickOnce. This isn't possible in WPF, because unmanaged code permission is required to create a WPF window. To have unmanaged code permission, your application must run with full trust. That means installing a stand-alone WPF application using ClickOnce presents the same security roadblock as installing any type of application from the Web—namely, Internet Explorer will present a security warning. If the user goes ahead, the installed application will have the ability to do anything that the current user can do.

Understanding ClickOnce

Although ClickOnce allows some customization, some details never change. Before you start using ClickOnce, it's important to get an understanding of the basic model and its limitations.

ClickOnce is designed with simple, straightforward applications in mind. It's particularly suitable for line-of-business applications and internal company software. Typically, these applications perform their work with the data and services on middle-tier server computers. As a result, they don't need privileged access to the local computer. These applications are also deployed in enterprise environments that may include thousands of workstations. In these environments, the cost of application deployment and updating isn't trivial, especially if it needs to be handled by an administrator. As a result, it's more important to provide a simple, streamlined setup process than to pack in features.

ClickOnce may also make sense for consumer applications that are deployed over the Web, particularly if these applications are updated frequently and don't have extensive installation requirements. However, the limitations of ClickOnce (such as the lack of flexibility for customizing the setup wizard) don't make it practical for sophisticated consumer applications that have detailed setup requirements or need to guide the user through a set of proprietary configuration steps. In these cases, you'll need the more sophisticated setup applications you can create using MSI.

■**Note** For ClickOnce to install a WPF application, the computer must already have the .NET Framework 3.0 or 3.5 runtime, depending on the version that you're targeting (as described in Chapter 1). When you first launch a ClickOnce setup, a bootstrapper runs that verifies this requirement. If the .NET Framework runtime isn't installed, the bootstrapper shows a message box that explains the issue and prompts the user to install .NET from Microsoft's website.

The ClickOnce Installation Model

Although ClickOnce supports several types of deployment, the overall model is designed to make web deployment practical and easy. Here's how it works: You use Visual Studio to publish your ClickOnce application to a web server. Then, the user surfs to an automatically generated web page (named publish.htm) that provides a link to install the application. When the user clicks that link, the application is downloaded, installed, and added to the Start menu. Figure 27-1 shows this process.

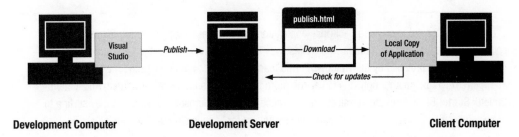

Development Computer   **Development Server**   **Client Computer**

Figure 27-1. *Installing a ClickOnce application*

Although ClickOnce is ideal for web deployment, the same basic model lends itself to other scenarios, including the following:

- Deploying your application from a network file share

- Deploying your application from a CD or DVD

- Deploying your application to a web server or network file share and then sending a link to the setup program via e-mail

The installation web page isn't created when deploying to a network share, a CD, or a DVD. Instead, in these cases users must install the application by running the setup.exe program directly.

■Note These options aren't as compelling as the deploy-from-the-Web approach. After all, if you've already distributed a CD or directed users to run a specific setup program, it's safe to assume they've decided to trust your application. In this case, it may make more sense to use a full-fledged setup program that offers more features. However, you may still choose to use ClickOnce if you're deploying an application in more than one way (including a web-based deployment), if you have relatively modest setup requirements, or if you want to use the automatic update feature.

The most interesting part of a ClickOnce deployment is the way it supports updating. Essentially, you (the developer) have control over several update settings. For example, you can configure the application to check for updates automatically or periodically at certain intervals. When users launch your application, they actually run a shim that checks for newer versions and offers to download them.

You can even configure your application to use a web-like online-only mode. In this situation, the application must be launched from the ClickOnce web page. The application is still cached locally for optimum performance, but users won't be able to run the application unless they're able to connect to the site where the application was published. This ensures that users always run the latest, most up-to-date version of your application.

■Tip You don't need to create a ClickOnce application to get the automatic updating feature. You could build a similar feature yourself. The easiest way is to adapt the code for the Application Updater Component that's provided by the Windows Forms team at `http://windowsclient.net/articles/appupdater.aspx`. Another option is to use the more flexible (but somewhat convoluted) Application Updater Starter Block from the Practices and Guidance Group at Microsoft. You can find it by surfing to `http://www.microsoft.com/downloads` and searching for "Application Updater Block."

ClickOnce Limitations

ClickOnce is designed to be a lighter setup option than MSI-based setups. As a result, ClickOnce deployment doesn't allow for much configuration. Many aspects of its behavior are completely fixed, either to guarantee a consistent user experience or to encourage enterprise-friendly security policies.

The limitations of ClickOnce include the following:

- ClickOnce applications are installed for a single user. You cannot install an application for all users on a workstation.

- ClickOnce applications are always installed in a system-managed user-specific folder. You cannot change or influence the folder where the application is installed.

- If ClickOnce applications are installed in the Start menu, they show up as a single short-cut in the form [Publisher Name] ➤ [Product Name]. You can't change this, and you can't add other shortcuts, such as a shortcut for a help file, related website, or an unin-stall feature. Similarly, you can't add a ClickOnce application to the Startup group, the Favorites menu, and so on.

- You can't change the user interface of the setup wizard. That means you can't add new dialog boxes, change the wording of existing ones, and so on.

- You can't change the installation page that ClickOnce applications generate. However, you can edit the HTML by hand after it's generated.

- A ClickOnce setup can't install shared components in the global assembly cache (GAC).

- A ClickOnce setup can't perform custom actions (such as creating a database, register-ing file types, or configuring registry settings).

You can work around some of these issues. For example, you could configure your appli-cation to register custom file types or set registry defaults the first time it's launched on a new computer. However, if you have complex setup requirements, you're much better off creating a full-fledged MSI setup program. You can use a third-party tool, or you can create a Setup Project in Visual Studio. Both of these options are beyond the scope of this book.

A Simple ClickOnce Publication

The easiest way to publish an application through ClickOnce is to choose Build ➤ Publish [ProjectName] from the Visual Studio menu, which walks you through a short wizard. This wizard doesn't give you access to all the ClickOnce features you'll learn about in this chapter, but it's a quick way to get started.

CREATING A CLICKONCE SETUP ON WINDOWS VISTA

Before you get started, there are some additional considerations for Windows Vista users who want to publish their applications to a local web server. If you're publishing your application to a virtual directory on the local computer, you'll need to ensure that Internet Information Services (IIS) 7 is installed using the Programs and Features entry in the Control Panel, which allows you to turn Windows features on or off. When you choose to install IIS 7, make sure you include the .NET Extensibility option and the IIS 6 Management Compatibility option (which allows Visual Studio to interact with IIS).

If you're publishing to a virtual directory in Visual Studio. However, the User Account Control (UAC) security feature restricts administrator privileges unless they're specifically requested. In order to get admin-istrator privileges in Visual Studio so you can access IIS, you need to explicitly run Visual Studio as an administrator. The easiest way to do this is to right-click the Microsoft Visual Studio 2008 shortcut in the Start menu and choose Run As Administrator. You can also configure your computer to always run Visual Studio as an administrator, which is a trade-off between convenience and security that needs to be weighed carefully. To put this in place, right-click the Visual Studio shortcut, choose Properties, and then head to the Compatibility tab, where you'll find an option named Run This Program As An Administrator.

UAC can also cause some problems when *installing* a ClickOnce application. See the sidebar "ClickOnce Setups and UAC" later in this chapter for more details.

The first choice you're faced with in the publishing wizard is choosing the location where you want to publish the application (see Figure 27-2).

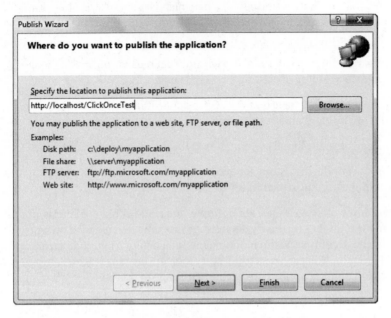

Figure 27-2. *Choosing a publish location*

There's nothing particularly important about the location where you first publish your application, because this isn't necessarily the same location you'll use to host the setup files later. In other words, you could publish to a local directory and then transfer the files to a web server. The only caveat is that you need to know the ultimate destination of your files when you run the publishing wizard, because you need to supply this information. Without it, the automatic update feature won't work.

Of course, you could choose to publish the application directly to its final destination, but it's not necessary. In fact, building the installation locally is often the easiest option.

Choosing a Location

To get a better sense for how this works, start by choosing a local file path location (such as c:\Temp\ClickOnceApp). Then click Next. You're now faced with the real question—where users will go to install this application (see Figure 24-3).

This bit is important, because it influences your update strategy. The choices you make are stored in a manifest file that's deployed with your application.

Note There is one case in which you won't see the dialog box in Figure 27-3. If you enter a virtual directory to a web server for the publish location (in other words, a URL starting with http://), the wizard assumes this is the final installation location.

In Figure 27-3, you have essentially three choices. You can create an installation for a network file share, a web server, or CD or DVD media. The following sections explain each approach.

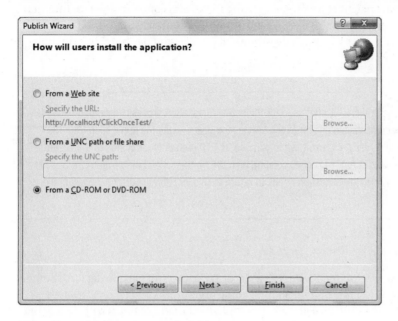

Figure 27-3. *Choosing the installation type*

Publishing for a Network File Share

In this case, all the users in your network will access the installation by browsing to a specific UNC path and running a file named setup.exe at that location.

A UNC path is a network path in the form \\ComputerName\ShareName. You can't use a networked drive, because networked drives depend on system settings (so different users might have their drives mapped differently). To provide automatic updates, the ClickOnce infrastructure needs to know exactly where it can find the installation files, because this is also the location where you'll deploy updates.

Publishing for a Web Server

You can create an installation for a web server on a local intranet or the Internet. Visual Studio will generate an HTML file named publish.htm that simplifies the process. Users request this page in a browser and click a link to download and install the application.

You have several options for transferring your files to a web server. If you want to take a two-step approach (publish the files locally and then transfer them to the right location), you simply need to copy the files from the local directory to your web server using the appropriate mechanism (such as FTP). Make sure you preserve the directory structure.

If you want to publish your files straight to the web server without any advance testing, you have two choices. If you are using IIS and the current account you're running has the necessary permissions to create a new virtual directory on the web server (or upload files to an existing one), you can publish files straight to your web server. Just supply the virtual directory path in the first step of the wizard. For example, you could use the publish location `http://ComputerName/VirtualDirectoryName` (in the case of an intranet) or `http://DomainName/VirtualDirectoryName` (for a server on the Internet).

You can also publish straight to a web server using FTP. This is often required in Internet (rather than intranet) scenarios. In this case, Visual Studio will contact your web server and transfer the ClickOnce files over FTP. You'll be prompted for user and password information when you connect.

■Note FTP is used to transfer files—it's not used for the actual installation process. Instead, the idea is that the files you upload become visible on some web server, and users install the application from the publish.htm file on that web server. As a result, when you use an FTP path in the first step of the wizard (Figure 27-2), you'll still need to supply the corresponding web URL in the second step (Figure 27-3). This is important, because the ClickOnce publication needs to return to this location to perform its automatic update checks.

Publishing for a CD or DVD

If you choose to publish to setup media such as a CD or DVD, you still need to decide whether you plan to support the automatic update feature. Some organizations will use CD-based deployment exclusively, while others will use it to supplement their existing web-based or networked-based deployment. You choose which option applies for use in the third step of the wizard (see Figure 27-4).

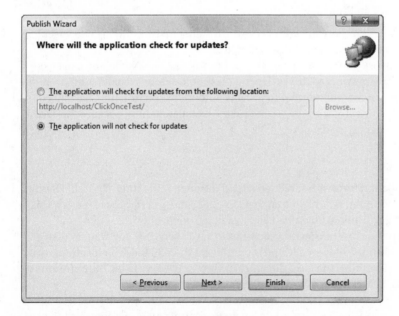

Figure 27-4. *Support for automatic updates*

Here, you have a choice. You can supply a URL or UNC path that the application will check for updates. This assumes that you plan to publish the application to that location. Alternatively, you can omit this information and bypass the automatic update feature altogether.

■**Note** The publishing wizard doesn't give you an option for how often to check for updates. By default, ClickOnce applications check for an update whenever they're launched. If a new version is found, .NET prompts the user to install it before launching the application. You'll learn how to change these settings later in this chapter.

Online or Offline

If you're creating a deployment for a web server or network share, you'll get one additional option, as shown in Figure 27-5.

Figure 27-5. *Support for offline use*

The default choice is to create an online/offline application that runs whether or not the user can connect to the published location. In this case, a shortcut for the application is added to the Start menu.

If you choose to create an online-only application, the user needs to return to the published location to run the application. (To help make this clear, the publish.htm web page will show a button labeled Run instead of Install.) This ensures that an old version of the application can't be used after you roll out an update. This part of the deployment model is analogous to a web application.

When you create an online-only application, the application will still be downloaded (into a locally cached location) the first time it's launched. Thus, while startup times may be longer (because of the initial download), the application will still run as quickly as any other installed Windows application. However, the application can't be launched when the user isn't connected to the network or Internet, which makes it unsuitable for mobile users (such as laptop users who don't always have an Internet connection available).

If you choose to create an application that supports offline use, the setup program will add a Start menu shortcut. The user can launch the application from this shortcut, regardless of whether the computer is online or offline. If the computer is online, the application will check for new versions in the location where the application was published. If an update exists, the application will prompt the user to install it. You'll learn how to configure this policy later.

Note If you choose to publish for a CD installation, you don't have the option of creating an online-only application.

This is the final choice in the publishing wizard. Click Next to see the final summary, and click Finish to generate the deployment files and copy them to the location you chose in step 1.

Deployed Files

ClickOnce uses a fairly straightforward directory structure. It creates a setup.exe file in the location you chose and a subdirectory for the application.

For example, if you deployed an application named ClickOnceTest to the location c:\ClickOnceTest, you'll end up with files like these:

c:\ClickOnceTest\setup.exe

c:\ClickOnceTest\publish.htm

c:\ClickOnceTest\ClickOnceTest.application

c:\ClickOnceTest\ClickOnceTest_1_0_0_0.application

c:\ClickOnceTest\ClickOnceTest_1_0_0_0\ClickOnceTest.exe.deploy

c:\ClickOnceTest\ClickOnceTest_1_0_0_0\ClickOnceTest.exe.manifest

The publish.htm file is present only if you're deploying to a web server. The .manifest and .application files store information about required files, update settings, and other details. (You can get a low-level look at these files and their XML file in the MSDN Help.) The .manifest and .application files are digitally signed at the time of publication, so these files can't be modified by hand. If you do make a change, ClickOnce will notice the discrepancy and refuse to install the application.

As you publish newer versions of your application, ClickOnce adds new subdirectories for each new version. For example, if you change the publish version of your application to 1.0.0.1, you'll get a new directory like this:

c:\ClickOnceTest\ClickOnceTest_1_0_0_1\ClickOnceTest.exe.deploy

c:\ClickOnceTest\ClickOnceTest_1_0_0_1\ClickOnceTest.exe.manifest

When you run the setup.exe program, it handles the process of installing any prerequisites (such as the .NET Framework) and then installs the most recent version of your application.

Installing a ClickOnce Application

To see ClickOnce in action with a web deployment, follow these steps:

1. Make sure you have the optional IIS web server component installed. In Windows XP, choose Settings ➤ Control Panel ➤ Add or Remove Programs from the Start menu, choose the Add/Remove Windows Components section, and scroll through the list until you find Internet Information Services (IIS). This option must be checked. In Windows Vista, follow the instructions in the "Using ClickOnce on Windows Vista" sidebar earlier in this chapter.

2. Using Visual Studio, create a basic Windows application, and compile it.

3. Launch the publishing wizard (by choosing Build ➤ Publish), and select `http://localhost/ClickOnceTest` for the publish location. The localhost portion of the URL points to the current computer. As long as IIS is installed and you are running with sufficient privileges, Visual Studio will be able to create this virtual directory.

4. Choose to create an online and offline application, and then click Finish to end the wizard. The files will be deployed to a folder named ClickOnceTest in the IIS web server root (by default, the directory c:\Inetpub\wwwroot).

5. Run the setup.exe program directly, or load up the publish.htm page (shown in Figure 27-6) and click Install. You'll receive a security message asking whether you want to trust the application (similar to when you download an ActiveX control in a web browser).

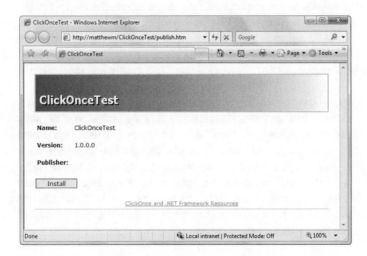

Figure 27-6. *The publish.htm installation page*

6. If you choose to continue, the application will be downloaded, and you'll be asked to verify that you want to install it.

7. Once the application is installed, you can run it from the Start menu shortcut or uninstall it using the Add/Remove Programs dialog box.

The shortcut for ClickOnce applications isn't the standard shortcut to which you're probably accustomed. Instead, it's an application reference—a text file with information about the application name and the location of the deployment files. The actual program files for your application are stored in a location that's difficult to find and impossible to control. The location follows this pattern:

```
c:\Documents and Settings\[UserName]\Local Settings\Apps\2.0\[...]\[...]\[...]
```

The final three portions of this path are opaque, automatically generated strings like C6VLXKCE.828. Clearly, you aren't expected to access this directory directly.

CLICKONCE SETUPS AND UAC

As you no doubt already know, Windows Vista includes a feature called User Account Control (UAC), which restricts administrator privileges to reduce the damage that can be caused by a malicious application. If the current user attempts to perform a task that requires administrator privileges, a special UAC dialog box appears that asks the user to confirm the permission elevation before continuing. This step can be performed only when a new process is started. Once the process is running, it cannot elevate its permissions.

When designing UAC, Microsoft was faced with the challenge of ensuring that most existing programs would work correctly most of the time. One of the compromises it made was with installation programs. Because many setup programs require administrator privileges, Windows Vista prompts the user to elevate to administrator level when a setup program is launched. Windows Vista "detects" a setup program based on the file name, so a file named setup.exe is automatically treated as an installation program and running it triggers permission elevation.

The problem is that not all setup programs require this permission elevation. The setup applications used by ClickOnce applications are perfect examples. However, if you run a ClickOnce setup, you'll be faced with the unnecessary UAC prompt. Even worse, if you're running under an account that doesn't have administrator privileges, you'll be forced to supply administrator credentials, and the ClickOnce application will be installed for that administrator account, *not* the current user account. As a result, it won't appear in your Start menu.

A few solutions are possible. One option is to direct users to launch the setup by double-clicking the .application file (like ClickOnceTest.application) rather than using the setup.exe application or the publish.htm page (which also uses setup.exe). Unfortunately, this breaks web-based deployment unless you create your own installation page that points to the .application file. This approach also won't work if the user doesn't at least have .NET 2.0 runtime—without it, the .application extension won't be recognized. Another option is to rename the setup.exe file to something else (like MyApp.exe). Unfortunately, this approach doesn't work because Vista still detects that the executable uses an internal resource named setup. You can use a resource editor to manually change this detail, but this approach is an awkward workaround at best. Microsoft plans to fix these limitations in the next build of Visual Studio.

Updating a ClickOnce Application

To see how a ClickOnce application can update itself automatically, follow these steps with the installation from the previous example:

1. Make a minor but noticeable change in the application (for example, adding a button).

2. Recompile the application, and republish it to the same location.

3. Run the application from the Start menu. The application will detect the new version and ask you whether you'd like to install it (see Figure 27-7).

4. Once you accept the update, the new version of the application will install and start.

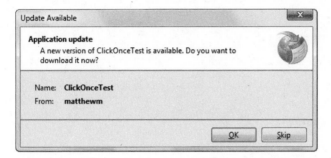

Figure 27-7. *Detecting a newer version of a ClickOnce application*

In the following sections, you'll learn how to customize some additional ClickOnce options.

■Note The ClickOnce engine, dfsvc.exe, handles updates and downloads.

ClickOnce Options

The publishing wizard is a quick way to create a ClickOnce deployment, but it doesn't allow you to adjust all the possible options. To get access to more ClickOnce settings, double-click the Properties node in the Solution Explorer, and then click the Publish tab. You'll see the settings shown in Figure 27-8.

Some of these settings duplicate details you've already seen in the wizard. For example, the first two text boxes allow you to choose the publishing location (the place where the Click-Once files will be placed, as set in step 1 of the wizard) and the installation location (the place from which the user will run the setup, as set in step 2 of the wizard). The Install Mode setting allows you to choose whether the application should be installed on the local computer or run in an online-only mode, as described earlier in this chapter. At the bottom of the window, the Publish Wizard button launches the wizard you saw earlier, and the Publish Now button publishes the project using the previous settings.

The following sections discuss the settings you haven't already seen.

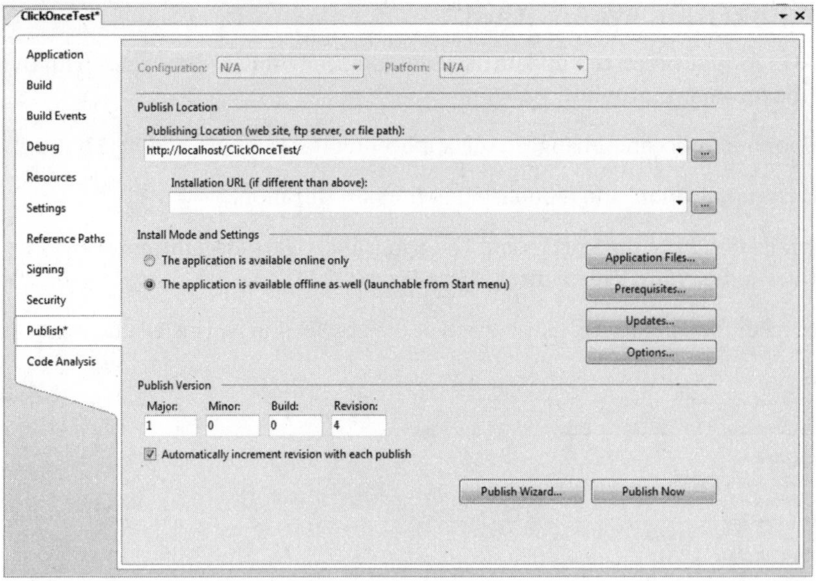

Figure 27-8. *ClickOnce project settings*

Publish Version

The Publish Version section sets the version of your application that's stored in the ClickOnce manifest file. This isn't the same as the assembly version, which you can set on the Application tab, although you might set both to match.

The key difference is that the publish version is the criteria that are used to determine whether a new update is available. If a user launches version 1.5.0.0 of an application and version 1.5.0.1 is available, the ClickOnce infrastructure will show the update dialog box shown in Figure 27-7.

By default, the Automatically Increment Revision with Each Publish check box is set, in which case the final part of the publish version (the revision number) is incremented by 1 after each publication, so 1.0.0.0 becomes 1.0.0.1, then 1.0.0.2, and so on. If you want to publish the same version of your application to multiple locations using Visual Studio, you should switch off this option. However, keep in mind that the automatic update feature springs into action only if it finds a higher version number. The date stamp on the deployed files has no effect (and isn't reliable).

It may seem horribly inelegant to track separate assembly and publication version numbers. However, sometimes it makes sense. For example, while testing an application, you may want to keep the assembly version number fixed without preventing testers from getting the latest version. In this case, you can use the same assembly version number but keep the autoincrementing publish version number. When you're ready to release an official update, you can set the assembly version and the publish version to match. Also, a published application might contain multiple assemblies with different version numbers. In this case, it wouldn't be realistic to use the assembly version number—instead, the ClickOnce infrastructure needs to consider a single version number to determine whether an update is warranted.

Updates

Click the Updates button to show the Application Updates dialog box (Figure 27-9), where you can choose your update strategy.

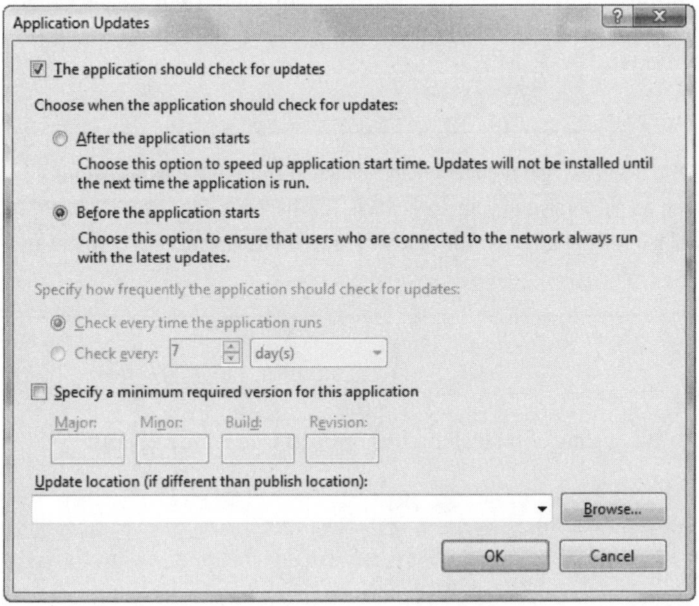

Figure 27-9. *Setting update options*

■Note The Updates button isn't available if you're creating an online-only application. An online-only application always runs from its published location on a website or network share.

You first choose whether the application performs update checking. If it does, you can choose when updates are performed. You have two options:

- **Before the application starts.** If you use this model, the ClickOnce infrastructure checks for an application update (on the website or network share) every time the user runs the application. If an update is detected, it's installed, and *then* the application is launched. This option is a good choice if you want to make sure the user gets an update as soon as it's available.

- **After the application starts.** If you use this model, the ClickOnce infrastructure checks for a new update after the application is launched. If an updated version is detected, this version is installed the *next* time the user starts the application. This is the recommended option for most applications, because it improves load times.

If you choose to perform checks after the application starts, the check is performed in the background. You can choose to perform it every time the application is run (the default option) or in less frequent intervals. For example, you can limit checks to once per number of hours, days, or weeks.

You can also specify a minimum required version. You can use this to make updates mandatory. For example, if you set the publish version to 1.5.0.1 and the minimum version to 1.5.0.0 and then publish your application, any user who has a version older than 1.5.0.0 will be forced to update before being allowed to run the application. (By default there is no minimum version, and all updates are optional.)

■**Note** Even if you specify a minimum version and require the application to check for updates before starting, a user could end up running an old version of your application. This happens if the user is offline, in which case the update check will fail without an error. The only way around this limitation is to create an online-only application.

Publish Options

The Publish Options dialog box has a slew of miscellaneous options (see Figure 27-10).

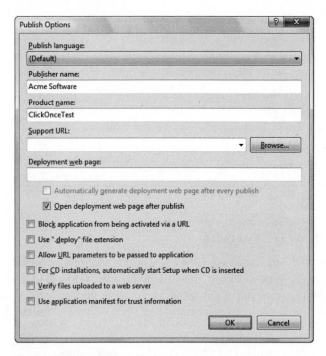

Figure 27-10. *Miscellaneous ClickOnce options*

The publisher and product names are used to create the Start menu hierarchy. In the example shown in Figure 27-10, the shortcut will be generated as Start ➤ Acme Software ➤ ClickOnceTest. This information also turns up with the application information in the Add/Remove Programs dialog box, along with the support URL.

You can also use the Publish Options dialog box to change the name of the installation page in web deployments (which is publish.htm by default), and you can choose whether you want Visual Studio to launch this page automatically after a successful publication (presumably so you can test it). Two more options give you control over how the setup works—allowing you to set whether the application is launched automatically once it's installed and whether an autorun.inf file should be generated to tell CD players to launch the setup program immediately when the CD is inserted into the CD drive.

The Last Word

This chapter gave a quick tour of the ClickOnce deployment model, which was introduced in .NET 2.0 and remains a good choice for deploying stand-alone WPF applications. As with XBAPs, ClickOnce entails certain compromises—for example, you need to accept compromises about certain client configuration details you can't control. You also need to resign yourself to the fact that ClickOnce won't truly be a preferred way to deploy applications until it becomes more established, which means computers need to be running Windows Vista or the .NET 2.0 Framework. However, it's likely that ClickOnce will be a key deployment technology in the future and will continue to gain importance.

Index

■Numbers

2-D element, placing on 3-D surfaces, 12

3-D drawing
  2-D and 3-D drawing classes, table of, 811
  adjusting camera's blind spots, 822
  advantages of, 810
  AmbientLight class, 818
  animation that flies around torus, 841
  avoiding z-fighting (stitching), 822
  Blender, 829
  breaking cube down into triangles, 824
  brush color and lighting, 832
  building basic mesh, 813
  building geometry for 3-D object, 812
  calculating light direction, 817
  calculating normal that's perpendicular to triangle's surface, 828
  changing 3-D scene using virtual trackball, 843
  changing FieldOfView property, 822
  combining two surfaces by wrapping them in MaterialGroup, 832
  coordinate system for describing 3-D objects, 814
  creating 3-D fly-over scene, 841
  creating solid and faceted cube, 823
  declaring each Position point several times, 827
  defining back and front of 3-D shape, 815
  defining geometry model and surfaces, 815
  defining Geometry3D and wrapping it in GeometryModel3D, 812
  defining PerspectiveCamera, 820
  defining white DirectionalLight, 817
  DiffuseMaterial class, 815, 832
  DirectionalLight class, 818
  downloading virtual trackball code, 843
  Dunn, Fletcher, 853
  EmissiveMaterial class, 832
  faceted vs. blended sides, 829
  FarPlaneDistance property, 822
  formula for calculating LookDirection, 820
  four ingredients of, 810
  guidelines for choosing right normals, 827
  hit-testing
    with ModelUIElement3D, 848–849
    overview, 845
    in Viewport, 845–847

HitTestResult, 846
how light and shadow effects are calculated, 816
Interactive3DDecorator class, 850
Light class, 816
light classes, table of, 816
light source as object in viewport, 810
LightWave, 829
listing points in counterclockwise order around Z axis, 814
making 3-D scene dynamic, 838
making partially transparent 3-D objects, 832
manipulating 3-D objects using transforms, 838
mapping video to 3-D surface, 837
markup for 3-D character, 831
markup for creating VisualBrush that loops video playback, 837
Material class, 815
material classes, table of, 815
MatrixCamera class, 819
Maya, 829
MeshGeometry3D class, table of properties, 813
MeshGeometry3D for creating cube, 824
MeshGeometry3D object as representing mesh of triangles, 813
MeshGeometry.TextureCoordinates collection, 834
MeshHit property, 846
Model3DGroup class, 830
ModelVisual3D class, 845–851
NearPlaneDistance property, 822
no WPF collection of 3-D shape primitives, 811
normal, defined, 825
Normals property, 828
not rendering unseen shapes, 824
OrthographicCamera class, 819
painting 3-D object with yellow matte surface, 815
PerspectiveCamera class, 819
placing and configuring camera, 819
placing light objects inside ModelVisual3D, 817
PointLight class, 818
preventing rendering artifacts, 822

3-D drawing (continued)
 problem of sharing Position points and sharing normals, 827
 RayMeshGeometry3DHitTestResult, 846
 relying on third-party 3-D design tools, 809
 setting camera's LookDirection property, 819
 setting camera's Position property, 819
 setting camera's UpDirection property, 820
 setting Viewport3D.Camera property with Camera object, 819
 SpecularMaterial class, 832
 SpotLight class, 818
 techniques for building basic sphere, 829
 texture mapping, 834
 tools for building 3-D scenes, 829
 TrackballDecorator class, 844
 TriangleIndices property, 824
 two-step process for creating 3-D models, 812
 unequal shading of cube sides, 825
 useful links on 3-D programming with WPF, 853
 using axis lines as testing tool, 822
 using texture mapping to place 2-D brush content on 3-D surface, 849
 using viewport to host 3-D content, 810
 viewport, camera position, and window size, 819
 viewport with triangle and light source, 817
 Viewport3D class, 810
 VisualBrush, limitations of, 849
 VisualTreeHelper.HitTest(), 845
 WPF lighting model, 816
 WPF's libraries for 3-D programming, 809
 WPF's three camera classes, 819
 ZAM 3D, 829
3-D surfaces, placing 2-D elements on, 12

A

AccelerationRatio property, 744
accelerator keys, 922
AcceptsReturn property, 203
AcceptsTab property, 203
Activate<T> method, 953
ActiveEditingMode property, 108
ActiveMovie (DirectShow), 784
ActiveX, 914
ActualHeight property, 86
ActualWidth property, 86
adapters, 941
 add-in, 949
 host, 950–951
AddBackEntry() method, 264–265
AddBackReference() method, 267–269

AddFixedDocument() method, 682
AddHandler() method, 150, 159, 313
add-in adapters, 949
AddIn attribute, 948
add-in model, 12
add-in view, 947
AddInAdapter attribute, 949
AddInBase attribute, 947, 956
AddInContract attribute, 947, 956
AddInController class, 954
AddInController.Shutdown() method, 954
add-ins, 940–963
 creating applications that use, 946–954
  add-in adapter, 949
  add-in view, 947
  adding more add-ins, 954
  contract assemblies, 946–947
  host, 951–954
  host adapter, 950–951
  host view, 950
  overview, 946
 interacting with host, 955–960
 overview, 940
 pipeline, 941–946
  folder structure, 943–944
  how works, 941–943
  overview, 941
  preparing solution, 944–946
 visual, 960–962
AddIns directory, 943, 951
AddInSideAdapters subdirectory, 949
AddInStore.Rebuild() method, 951
AddInStore.Update() method, 951
AddInToken.Activate<T> method, 952–953
AddInViews subdirectory, 947
AddLogicalChild() method, 434
AddOwner() method, 145
AddVisual() method, 435
AddVisualChild() method, 434, 897
Adjust Font Size (DPI), 9
Adobe Flash, 1, 430
Adobe Illustrator, 430
ADO.NET
 data objects, 491
  binding to, 521
  creating DataView, 522
  DataTable.DefaultView property, 522
  DisplayMemberPath property, 522
 DataTables and DataView objects, 578
AdornedElementPlaceholder, 545–547
adorner layer, 449, 483, 545
AdornerDecorator class, 449, 483
Aero Glass effect, 236–240
airspace rule, 914
AllowDrop property, 176
AllowsTransparency property, 200, 227, 283
ambient properties, 186

AmbientColor property, 818
AmbientLight class, 818
AncestorType property, 505
anchoring, 75
animation, 5
    3-D, that flies around torus, 841
    accelerating and decelerating, 744
    AccelerationRatio property, 744
    accessing Storyboard object, 757
    adding mouseover animation, 750
    adding standard playback buttons for
        animation, 755
    animating element that's filled with
        VisualBrush, 770
    Animation Behaviors project, 782
    animation classes, complete list of, 734
    AnimationTimeline class, 742
    applying same animation to multiple
        elements, 749
    applying second animation to already
        animated property, 752
    attaching animation to Click event, 747
    attaching event handler to
        CompositionTarget.Rendering event,
        778
    attaching triggers with style, 748
    attaching triggers with template, 750
    AutoReverse property, 741–745
    BeginStoryboard action, 747
    BeginStoryboard.HandoffBehavior
        property, 752
    brushes, 769
    building gradient-based animations, 770
    canvas as most common layout container
        for animation, 737
    causing animation to repeat itself
        endlessly, 745
    changing 3-D scene using virtual trackball,
        843
    changing FillBehavior property, 741, 753
    code-based animations, 735
    ColorAnimation class, 769
    comparing key frame animation and
        sequence of multiple animations,
        773
    comparing RenderTransform and
        LayoutTransform, 766
    comparing Visibility and Opacity
        properties, 763
    ControllableStoryboardAction class, 754
    controlling how animation is repeated,
        745
    controlling playback, 754
    creating 3-D fly-over scene, 841
    creating additive animation by setting
        IsAdditive property, 739

creating animation
    that fires when window first loads, 747
    that widens button, 736
creating animation class for data type, 732
creating document window that jumps
    into view, 767
creating dynamic user interfaces, 729
creating event trigger for MouseEnter and
    MouseLeave events, 750
creating fish-eye effect, 750
creating frame-based animation using
    nothing but code, 778
creating property trigger that triggers
    storyboard, 749
creating reversible animation, 741
CurrentTimeInvalidated event, 760
data types and key frame animation,
    732–774
DataTypeAnimation class, 774
DecelerationRatio property, 744
declarative animation, 746
decreasing frame rate, 761
defining, 22
defining storyboard, 746
defining transform, 764
defining with declarative tags, 5
determining increment size when
    performing interpolation, 735
determining whether torus mesh has been
    hit, 846
differentiating from traditional media
    files, 729
discrete key frame classes, naming format,
    774
discrete key frames, 773
displaying position and progress in
    animation, 759
DoubleAnimation class, 770
DoubleAnimationUsingPath, 777
downloading virtual trackball code, 843
Duration property, 740
EventTrigger.SourceName property, 756
Expression Blend design tool, 769
frame-based animation
    of falling circles, 778
    as not time-dependent, 782
From, To, and Duration properties, 736
fusing second animation into first
    animation's timeline, 752
future of WPF animation, 782
gradient brushes and RelativeTransform
    property, 770
Gradient Obsession tool, 770
guidelines for choosing right property to
    animate, 763
handling Completed event of animation
    object, 741

animation *(continued)*
    handling one-way animations that remain
        active after finishing, 741
    HandoffBehavior.Compose, 752
    IAnimatable interface, 735
    inheritance hierarchy of WPF animation
        types, 742
    IsCumulative property, 745
    key frame animation
        defined, 772
        naming format, 732
    KeySpline property, 774
    LayoutTransform property, 764
    linear interpolation, naming format, 732
    linear key frame classes, naming format,
        774
    linear key frames, 773
    LinearGradientBrush, 758, 770
    managing simultaneous animations as
        one group, 753
    manipulating 3-D objects using
        transforms, 838
    moving camera along route rather than
        straight line, 841
    moving element along path, 733
    moving image along path, 776
    multiple transforms, 767
    nesting transforms inside
        TransformGroup, 767
    omitting both From and To properties, 738
    omitting From property, 737
    omitting To property, 738
    path-based animation, naming format,
        733
    PathGeometry object, 733
    performing linear interpolation between
        key frames, 772
    performing wipe transition, 758
    Petzold, Charles, 770
    Point3DAnimationUsingKeyFrames, 773
    PointAnimation class, 769
    PointAnimationUsingKeyFrames object,
        772
    PointAnimationUsingPath class, 777
    position-related properties, 775
    procedure for creating timer-based
        animation, 730
    progressively revealing element, 763
    property with special value of
        Double.NaN, 737
    property-based animation, defined, 731
    radial gradient along ellipse, 769
    RadialGradientBrush, 769–770
    reference types as not usually animated,
        732
    rendering animation inactive by calling
        BeginAnimation(), 742

RenderTransform property, 764
RepeatBehavior property, 745
resetting animated element to its original
    state, 741
reusing animation by defining it in
    template, 750
RotateTransform, 763–764, 767
rotating 3-D object around specified axis,
    840, 852
rotating button on mouseover, 764
ScaleTransform, 763, 767
setting RenderTransform property of
    Border object, 767
setting RenderTransformOrigin property,
    765
similarity of Duration property and
    TimeSpan object, 740
snapshot-and-replace behavior, 752
specific aspects of element's appearance,
    732
spline key frames, 774
stopping vs. completing animation, 754
storyboard
    actions and properties, 757
    defined, 746
    table of events, 759
style to change ListBoxItem template, 750
TargetName property, 746
TargetProperty property, 746
Timeline class, table of properties, 742
TimelineGroup class, 742
TranslateTransform, 763
two properties simultaneously, 740
TypeNameAnimationBase class, 733
using animation class that supports
    dependency property's data type, 731
using BeginAnimation(), 735, 740
using brush properties to animate
    element's surface, 764
using By property instead of To property,
    739
using Canvas to animate position, 763
using discrete key frames in
    RadialGradientBrush example, 774
using event trigger to control storyboard,
    746
using event triggers to attach animation,
    749
using opacity masks, 758
using PathGeometry object to set
    property, 775
using RepeatBehavior property to set
    repeat interval, 745
using series of key frames, 773
using transforms to animate element's
    visual appearance, 764

using Trigger.EnterActions and
 Trigger.ExitActions, 749
Vector3DAnimationUsingKeyFrames, 773
working with Bézier curves, 774
working with overlapping animations, 752
working with various animation classes
 for different data types, 735
with WPF dependency property only, 731
WPF's standard frame rate, 735
Animation Behaviors project, 782
AnimationTimeline class, 742
Annotation class
 properties as read-only, 693
 retrieving information from Anchors and
  Cargos properties, 691
 table of properties, 691
Annotation.AnnotationType property, 692
AnnotationDocumentPaginator class, 707
AnnotationHelper class, 685–693
annotations
 accepting hand-drawn ink content in note
  window, 688
 adding comments and highlights to
  flow/fixed documents, 683
 Annotation class, 691
 AnnotationHelper class, 685–687
 AnnotationService class, 684
 AnnotationStore class, 684
 attaching sticky notes to selected text, 683
 CreateHighlightCommand, 689
 CreateInkStickyNoteCommand, 688
 creating, deleting, and highlighting
  annotations, 687
 creating FileStream, 686
 customizing appearance of sticky notes,
  695
 DeleteStickyNotesCommand, 688
 enabling Annotation Service, 685
 examining and manipulating existing
  annotations, 693
 GetAnnotations() method, 690
 giving every StickyNoteControl new
  background color, 695
 having multiple users annotate same
  document, 688
 hiding and restoring sticky notes, 687
 highlighting content with semitransparent
  color, 689
 highlighting text, 683
 mapping System.Windows.Annotations
  namespace, 687
 printing document that includes
  annotations, 690
 procedure for storing annotations in XPS
  document file, 694
 reacting to annotation changes, 694
 StickyNoteControl class, 695

storing annotations in MemoryStream,
 686
storing position of each note window in
 AnnotationService, 687
support for, in WPF document containers,
 684
System.IO.Packaging namespace, 694
using different control template for
 StickyNoteControl, 695
XmlStreamStore class, 684
Annotations classes, WPF, 684–685
AnnotationService class, Enable() method,
 685
AnnotationStore class, 684, 690
AnnotionService class, 686
antialiasing, 2, 3, 8
App_Startup() method, 64
AppDomainUnloadedException attribute,
 951
AppendSsml() method, 806
AppendText() method, 805
AppendTextWithHind() method, 806
application add-ins. *See* add-ins
Application class, 251, 262
 accessing current application instance, 65
 allowing interactions between windows,
  66
 App_Startup() method, 64
 Application events, table of, 61
 Application.g.vb App.g.cs file, 59
 Application.xaml.vb App.xaml.cs file, 61
 App.xaml, 59
 calling base class implementation, 63
 casting window object to right type, 65
 creating dedicated method in target
  window, 222
 Current property, 65
 custom Application class overriding
  OnSessionEnding, 63
 deriving custom class from, 58
 DispatcherExceptionUnhandled event, 62
 DoUpdate() method, 223
 examining contents of
  Application.Windows collection, 65
 function of, 57
 Main() method, 58–61
 MainWindow property, 58, 222
 minimizing need for window interactions,
  222
 one-to-many window interaction, 223
 reading command-line arguments, 64
 ReasonSessionEnding property, 61
 Run() method, 58, 61
 Shutdown() method, 61
 ShutdownMode property, enumeration
  values, 60
 single window interaction, 223

Application class *(continued)*
    Startup event, 58
    storing references to important windows,
        66
    Visual Studio and, 58
Application element, 25
application life cycle
    application events, 61–63
    creating application object, 57–58
    deriving custom application class, 58–60
    overview, 57
    shutdown, 60–61
application resources, considering trade-off
        between complexity and reuse, 340
Application tag, 59
application tasks, 64–65
Application Updater Component, 968
Application Updater Starter Block
        (Microsoft), 968
Application Updates dialog box, 979
application windows, determining size of, 6
ApplicationCommands class, 294, 310
ApplicationCommands.Print command, 705,
        725
ApplicationCommands.Undo command, 866
ApplicationExtension tag, 274
Application.GetResourceStream() method,
        190
Application.g.vb App.g.cs file, 59
ApplicationName.exe.manifest, 276
ApplicationName.xbap, 276
applications, single-instance
    Application.Startup event, 68
    creating, 68
    FileRegistrationHelper class, 72
    Microsoft Word, 68
    registering file extension using
        Microsoft.Win32 namespace, 72
    ShowDocument() method, 70
    SingleInstanceApplicationWrapper class,
        70
    using systemwide mutex, 68
    Windows Communication Foundation
        (WCF), 69
    WpfApp class, 70
    wrapping WPF application with
        WindowsFormsApplicationBase
        class, 69
Application.Startup event, 68
Application.StartupUri property, 64
Application.Windows collection, 65
Application.xaml.vb App.xaml.cs file, 61
ApplyPropertyValue() method, 679
App.xaml, 59, 913
architecture of WPF
    core WPF namespaces, 17
    DependencyObject class, 16

Direct3D, 16
dispatcher, 18
DispatcherObject class, 16–18
elements and controls compared, 19
Media Integration Layer (MIL), 16
milcore.dll, 16
PresentationCore.dll, 16
PresentationFramework.dll, 16
single-thread affinity (STA), 18
UIElement class, 16
User32, 16
Visual class, 16
WindowsBase.dll, 16
WindowsCodecs.dll, 16
ArcSegment class, 418–419
Arrange() method, 702, 889
arrange stage, 77
ArrangeCore() method, 888
ArrangeOverride() method, 78, 888–891, 894
    basic structure of, 890
    DesiredSize property, 890
    giving element its desired size, 890
    giving element more space than it
        requires, 890
    making element larger than its desired
        size, 890
asInvoker application, 73
ASP.NET, similarity of tagging syntax to
        HTML, 23
assembly resources
    accessing AssemblyName.g.resources
        resource stream, 320
    adding resources, 318
    AssemblyAssociatedContentFile attribute,
        323
    binary resources, 317
    BitmapImage object, 321
    Build Action property, 318
    ContentType property, 320
    defined, 317
    Embedded Resource build action, 318
    GetResourceStream() method, 319–320
    grouping and organizing, 318
    marking noncompiled files as content
        files, 323
    Reflector, 319
    resource stream, naming convention, 319
    resource-aware classes, 320
    ResourceManager class, 320
    Resources tab, Project Properties window,
        318
    ResourceSet class, 320
    retrieving, 319
    retrieving resources embedded in another
        library, 322
    Stream property, 320
    StreamResourceInfo object, 319

syntax in WPF, 321
UnmanagedMemoryStream object, 320
using build type of Resource, 318
using disassembler, 319
using strong-named assembly, 322
when deploying resource files isn't
        practical, 322
working with resources natively, 321
AssemblyAssociatedContentFile attribute,
        323
AssemblyName, 45
asynchronous printing, 728
AsyncOperation class, 937
AsyncOperationManager class, 937
attached events, 159
attached properties, 36, 82, 146
attributes
    Class, 27
    ContentProperty, 37–39
    Name, 29
    RuntimeNameProperty, 29
    setting XAML class properties through
            attributes, 25
    TypeConverter, 32
    using to attach event handlers, 42
    XAML start tag, 26
    x:Key, 37
    xmlns, 26
    xml:space="preserve", 41
audio
    audio file with two synchronized
            animations, code example, 798
    MediaElement class, 789
    MediaPlayer class, 787
    playing WAV audio, 783
    SoundPlayer class, 784
    SoundPlayerAction class, 786
authority, 257
AutoComplete feature, 600
automation, 955
AutoReverse property, 741–745
AutoWordSelection, 204
axis lines, using as testing tool, 822

■ **B**

Background property, 215
BackgroundWorker class, 909
BackgroundWorker component
    adding support for canceling long-
            running task, 938
    adding support for tracking progress, 937
    AsyncOperation class, 937
    AsyncOperationManager class, 937
    calling ReportProgresss() method, 937
    cancel messages, 932
    CancelAsync() method, 938
    creating, 933

declaring in XAML, 933
DoWork event, 936
executing, 934
FindPrimes() method, 932
performing sieve of Eratosthenes
        algorithm asynchronously, 932
progress events, 932
ProgressChanged event, 937
RunWorkerCompleted event, 936–939
SynchronizationContext class, 937
System.ComponentModel namespace,
        933
using with single asynchronous
        background task, 932
Window.Resources collection, 934
WorkerReportsProgress property, 937–938
WorkerSupportsCancellation property,
        938
BackMaterial property, 815–816
BackStack property, 264
Bag-O-Tricks custom control library, 858
Balance property, 796
BAML (Binary Application Markup
        Language), 24, 47, 51
Band property, 639
BandIndex property, 639
BasedOn attribute, 357
BasedOn property, 616
BeginAnimation() method, 735–742
BeginChange() method, 205
BeginInit() method, 163
BeginInvoke() method, 929–930
BeginStoryboard action, 747
BeginStoryboard.HandoffBehavior property,
        752
BeginStyle() method, 805
Bevel line join, 381
BevelBitmapEffect class, 406
BevelWidth property, 406
Bézier curves, 774, 777
BezierSegment class, 420
Binary Application Markup Language
        (BAML), 24, 47, 51
binary resources, 317
Binding class, 493, 498
Binding markup extension, 493–495
BindingExpression class, 503
BindingExpression.UpdateSource() method,
        502–503
BindingList collection, 521
BindingListCollectionView, 574, 579
BindingMode enumeration, 499
BindingOperations class, 495
Binding.RelativeSource property, 566–569,
        865
Binding.ValidatesOnDataErrors property, 540
Binding.ValidatesOnExceptions property, 540

Binding.ValidationRules collection, 541
Binding.XPath property, 596
bi-pane proportional resizing, 75
bitmap effects
    adding diffuse halo of light around
        element, 407
    applying blur effect to button, 404
    BevelBitmapEffect class, 405
    BitmapEffect class, 403
    BlurBitmapEffect class, 404
    creating glows and shadows, 407
    creating raised edge (bevel) around
        element's border, 405
    disadvantages of, 403
    DropShadowBitmapEffect class, 407
    EmbossBitmapEffect class, 406
    embossing edges, 406
    Gaussian blur, 404
    goal of, 403
    implementing only in unmanaged code,
        403
    OuterGlowBitmapEffect class, 407
    rendering in software and not on video
        card, 403
    simulating drop shadow effect, 408
bitmap scaling, 10
BitmapEffect class, 404
BitmapImage class, 321, 532, 556
BleedBox property, 705
Blender, 829
block elements
    BlockUIContainer class, 655
    defined, 646
    List element, 651
    Paragraph element, 650
    Section element, 655
    Table element, 653
    table of formatting properties, 647
Blocks collection, 664
BlockUIContainer class, 655, 656, 681
BlurBitmapEffect class, 404
Border class, 133, 459, 896
Border element, 869
BorderBrush property, 182, 215, 654
BorderThickness property, 133, 182, 215, 654
Bottom property, 105
Brush class
    classes deriving from, 390
    Opacity property, 182
Brush object, 179
brushes
    adding more than two GradientStops, 392
    adding one GradientStop for each blended
        color, 391
    animating, 769
    animating element that's filled with
        VisualBrush, 770

    animating radial gradient along ellipse,
        769
    automatic change notification, 182
    background and foreground, 179
    BorderBrush property, 182
    BorderThickness property, 182
    Brush object, 179
    building gradient-based animations, 770
    ColorAnimation class, 769
    comparing proportionally sized and fixed-
        sized tiles, 397
    creating gradients with more than two
        colors, 392
    creating radial gradient with offset center,
        394
    deriving from Freezable, 390
    DoubleAnimation class, 770
    gradient brushes and RelativeTransform
        property, 770
    Gradient Obsession tool, 770
    ImageBrush, 182, 395
    LinearGradientBrush, 181, 390, 770
    markup for button that fades from solid to
        transparent, 401
    markup for shading rectangle diagonally,
        390
    Opacity property, 390
    OpacityMask property, 401
    painting border around controls, 182
    PointAnimation class, 769
    RadialGradientBrush, 393, 769–770
    setting button's surface color, 180
    SolidColorBrush, 180
    support for change notification, 390
    support for partial transparency, 390
    SystemBrushes class, 390
    TileBrush, 183
    tiling image across surface of brush, 397
    using color that has nonopaque alpha
        value, 401
    using tiled ImageBrush, 397
    VisualBrush, 399
bubbling events, 154–156, 161
Build Action property, 318
BulletChrome class, 454
Button class, 192, 459
Button control, 119, 191
Button object, 182
<Button> element, 25
ButtonBase class, 191
ButtonChrome class, 451–454, 898–899
ButtonChrome decorator, 133, 182
ButtonState event, 173
By property
    not using with non-numeric data types,
        739
    using instead of To property, 739

using when defining animation in XAML, 739
byte arrays, 947

■C

C#, partial classes, 28
caller inform design pattern, 510
camera
   3-D animation that flies around torus, 841
   animating camera's LookDirection property, 841
   animating camera's UpDirection property, 842
   changing 3-D scene using virtual trackball, 843
   creating 3-D fly-over scene, 841
   downloading virtual trackball code, 843
   moving along route rather than straight line, 841
   placing and configuring, 819
   setting Viewport3D.Camera property with Camera object, 819
Camera property, 810
CancelAsync() method, 728, 938
CanContentScroll property, 126
CanExecute() method, 292, 301, 303
CanExecute property, 303
CanExecuteChanged event, 292, 301–303
CanExecuteRoutedEventArg class, 303
CanGoBack property, 262–264
CanGoForward property, 262
canonicalization errors, 879
CanUndo property, 205
Canvas
   animation and, 737
   Bottom property, 105
   ClipToBounds property, 106, 376, 762
   code example with four buttons, 105
   controlling layering of overlapping elements, 106
   controlling shape placement and overlap, 373
   description of, 78
   Height property, 105
   Left property, 104
   lightweight features of, 105
   nesting inside user interface, 106
   placing elements using exact coordinates, 104
   placing Line in Canvas, 377
   promoting element by increasing its ZIndex, 106
   Right property, 105
   SetZIndex(), 106
   tag order and overlapping shapes, 374
   Top property, 104
   using to animate position, 763

using Viewbox element to resize shapes proportionally, 374
Width property, 105
ZIndex property, 106
Canvas class, 891
Cargos collection, 692
CellSpacing property, 654
CellTemplate property, 610
CellTemplateSelector property, 612
Center property, 393, 411
CenterOwner, 219
CenterX property, 387
CenterY property, 387
certmgr.exe tool, 280
change notification, 147
CheckBox class, 193
CheckBox control, 119
CheckBox element, 604–606
CheckBox.IsChecked property, 158
CheckedListBox, 906
CheckFileExists property, 226
Child property, 200
Children property, 810
chrome classes, 454
Class attribute, 27, 59
class bindings, 306
class hierarchy, 18, 19
ClearAllBindings() method, 495
ClearHighlightsForSelection() method, 687
ClearSelection() method, 438
ClearValue() method, 141–145, 495
Click event, 159, 191, 633
ClickCount event, 173
ClickMode property, 191
clickOffset field, 437
ClickOnce
   accessing advanced project settings, 977
   accessing installation from UNC path, 971
   adding subdirectories for each new application version, 974
   advantages and disadvantages of, 965–966
   automatically downloading application updates from Web, 966
   bypassing automatic update feature, 973
   choosing installation type, 971
   choosing publishing location, 970
   choosing update options in Application Updates dialog box, 979
   choosing when application updates are performed, 979
   configuring application for web-like online-only mode, 968
   consumer applications deployed over Web, 966
   contents of .manifest and .application files, 974

ClickOnce *(continued)*
    creating application that supports offline use, 974
    creating online-only application, 973
    deploying stand-alone WPF applications only, 966
    deployment scenarios and options, 967
    developer control over update settings, 968
    dfsvc.exe, 977
    entering virtual directory on web server for publish location, 970
    enterprise environments and, 966
    handling permission elevation on Windows Vista installations, 976
    inability to install shared components in GAC, 969
    Install Mode setting, 977
    installation and configuration limitations, 968
    installation model, 967
    installing and running applications in limited trust scenarios, 966
    link to publish.htm website for application downloading and installation, 967
    location of setup.exe and other deployed files, 974
    making application updates mandatory, 980
    procedure for installing ClickOnce application, 975–976
    publication considerations for Windows Vista users, 969
    Publish Now button, 977
    Publish Options dialog box, 980
    Publish Wizard button, 977
    publishing application, 969
    publishing application to virtual directory in Visual Studio, 969
    publishing straight to web server using FTP, 972
    publishing to CD or DVD, 972
    publishing to network file share, 971
    publishing to web server or local intranet, 971
    running setup.exe program, 975
    running WPF applications with unmanaged code permission and full trust, 966
    scaling back of, from .NET 2.0 to WPF, 966
    setting miscellaneous options, 980
    setting publish version, 978
    shortcut for ClickOnce applications, 976
    tracking separate assembly and publication version numbers, 978
    transferring application files to web server, 971
    understanding basic deployment model, 966
    unsuitability for sophisticated consumer applications, 966
    updating ClickOnce application automatically, 977
    using Visual Studio publishing wizard, 969
    using Visual Studio to publish ClickOnce application to web server, 967
    verifying that .NET Framework 3.0 runtime is installed, 967
ClickOnce cache, 277
client area, defined, 215
clip art, exporting, 429
Clip property, 424, 425
clipboard, 205
Clipping property, 800
ClipToBounds property, 106, 376, 762, 811
Clock class, 760
Clock property, 792
Close() method, 218
CLR (common language runtime), 16
    global assembly cache (GAC), 326
    probing for satellite assembly, 325
Code DOM model, 52
code only development, 46, 47
CodeAccessPermission class, 281
code-based animations, 735
code-behind class, 27
CoerceValueCallback, 142–149
coercion, 140–142
    examples of property coercion, 143
    WPF dependency property system and, 144
CollectionView, 574–588
CollectionView.GroupDescriptions collection, 581
CollectionViewSource class
    example of defining converter and CollectionViewSource declaratively, 586
    Filter event, 586
    GetDefaultView() method, 575
    GroupDescriptions property, 586
    as helper class and factory, 586
    SortDescriptions property, 586
    Source property, 586
    View property, 586
color picker
    adding basic Grid, 863
    adding command bindings, 866
    adding command support to controls, 866
    adding standard property wrappers, 861
    adding support for ApplicationCommands.Undo command, 866

adding TemplatePart attribute to control declaration, 876

adding user control to custom control library project, 859

adjusting color components with Slider controls, 859

attaching callbacks that respond to changed properties, 860

calling OverrideMetadata() method, 871

calling RaiseEvent() method, 863

changing color picker into lookless control, 871

checking for correct type of element, 875

code for binding SolidColorBrush, 875

Color property, 860, 866

ColorChanged event, 866

complete markup, 864

connecting data binding expression using OnApplyTemplate(), 875

control consumer, 859

converting ordinary markup into control template, 872

creating basic color picker, 858

creating different styles for different theme settings, 871

creating standard .NET event wrapper, 863

creating template for, 872

DefaultStyleKeyProperty, 871

defined, 859

defining and adding routed events, 862

defining static fields for properties, 860

designing public interface, 859

generic.xaml resource dictionary, 871

handling CanExecute and Executed events, 867

mapping assembly and .NET namespace to XML namespace, 866

markup structure for ColorPicker.xaml, 872

not using coercion callbacks with color properties, 862

OnColorChanged(), 863

overriding OnApplyTemplate() method, 875

property change callbacks for updating properties, 861

providing descriptive names for element names, 874

Red, Green, and Blue properties, 860

revised command handling code, 868

RoutedEventHandler, 863

RoutedPropertyChangedEventHandler, 863

SetValue(), 861

static constructor code for registering dependency properties, 860

streamlining color picker control template, 874

tracking previous color in member field, 867

triggering Undo command, 868

UserControl class, 859

using binding expressions to repurpose core property, 865

using data binding for color sliders, 860

using in another window, 866

using TargetType attribute, 872

Color property, 408, 860, 862

ColorAnimation class, 732, 769

ColorChanged event, 866

ColorDialog class, 909

Color.FromArgb() method, 181

Colors class, 180–181

Column property, 92

ColumnDefinition element, 92–110

ColumnDefinition object, 94

ColumnGap property, 706

ColumnHeaderContainerStyle property, 612

ColumnSpan property, 96, 111, 654

ColumnWidth property, 706

CombinedGeometry class

applying transform to geometry, 416

building up distinct shapes with many geometries, 414

combining overlapping shapes, 414

creating simple "No" sign (circle with slash through it), 414–417

GeometryCombineMode property, enumeration values, 414

merging two shapes to create one shape, 414

using Geometry1 and Geometry2 properties, 414

ComboBox control

adding complex objects to, 601

AutoComplete feature, 600

ComboBoxItem object, 210

components of, 600

DisplayMemberPath property, 602

hard-coding value for Width property, 211

improving performance of, 603–604

IsEditable property, 211, 600–602

IsReadOnly property, 600–602

IsTextSearchEnabled property, 601

not placing user-interactive controls in drop-down list, 602

SelectionBoxItemTemplate property, 603

setting IsDropDownOpen property, 600

setting TextSearch.TextPath property, 602

use of drop-down list, 211

using automatic sizing, 211

using nontext content in, 601

ComboBoxItem object, 210

Command class, 299
Command property, 633
CommandBinding class, 297
CommandBindings collection, 308, 868
CommandHistoryItem class, 311, 312
command-line arguments, 64–65
CommandManager class
    InvalidateRequerySuggested(), 303, 307
    keeping command history, 311
    RegisterClassCommandBinding(), 868
CommandParameter property, 297, 310, 633
commands
    adding command bindings to top-level
        window, 297
    adding new binding for command you
        want to disable, 305
    adding new command bindings or input
        bindings to disable features, 306
    ApplicationCommands class, 294
    basic command library, 294
    binding custom command differently in
        two places, 308
    calling static
        CommandManager.Invalidate-
        RequerySuggested(), 303
    calling Undo() method of
        CommandHistoryItem, 315
    CanExecute(), 292
    CanExecuteChanged event, 292
    class bindings, 306
    command binding, defined, 291
    command sources, 291, 292, 295
    command target, defined, 291
    CommandBinding class, 297
    CommandHistoryItem class, 311, 312
    commands as static objects global to
        application, 295
    ComponentCommands class, 294
    controls raising CanExecuteChanged
        event, 303
    controls with built-in commands, 304
    creating all-purpose, application-wide
        Undo() command, 312–313
    creating command binding, 296
    custom commands, 306
    dealing with user-interface state, 290
    default input bindings and command
        objects, 295
    defined, 224, 291–292
    disabling commands, 296, 301
    disabling input bindings, 305
    EditingCommands class, 294
    Execute(), 292
    features of, 289
    forcing WPF to call CanExecute() on all
        used commands, 303

handling commands that vary between
    enabled and disabled state, 301
ICommand interface, 291
ICommandSource interface, table of
    properties, 295
instantiating new RoutedUICommand
    object, 306
localization and setting Text property, 299
mapping events to same command, 290
mapping .NET namespace to XML
    namespace, 307
MediaCommands class, 294
modifying
    RoutedCommand.InputGestures
    collection of command, 307
namespace requirement for using custom
    command in XAML, 307
NavigationCommands class, 294
not adding unwanted commands to Undo
    history, 314
pulling text out of static command object,
    300
reacting to executed commands using
    CommandManager, 313
refining Undo feature for real-world
    application, 315
Requery command, 307
RequerySuggested event, 303
responding to PreviewExecuted event, 313
RoutedCommand class, 292
RoutedUICommand class, 292–293
setting Boolean isDirty flag, 302
setting CommandParameter property,
    297, 310
setting text for menu access keys, 299
storing CommandHistoryItem objects in
    ListBox, 315
supplying keyboard shortcut for
    InputGestures collection, 306
supporting application-wide Undo
    feature, 310
switching off control's built-in command
    support, 305
techniques for reusing command text, 300
tracking and reversing commands, 310
using ApplicationCommands.NotA-
    Command value, 305
using command parameter to pass extra
    information, 310
using CommandManager class to keep
    command history, 311
using data binding expression to pull out
    Text property, 300
using event handlers to call appropriate
    application methods, 289

using Execute() to invoke command directly, 300
using multiple command sources, 299
using same command in different places, 308
using WPF resources, 309
when user-interface state falls outside WPF command model, 303
why WPF commands require routed events, 293
wiring up commands declaratively using XAML, 298
WPF command model, 290, 291, 293
CommandTarget property, 304, 633
common language runtime. *See* CLR
Community Technology Preview (CTP), 11
component class, 910
component tray, 910
ComponentCommands class, 294
ComponentResourceKey, 345, 347, 615–616
CompositionTarget.Rendering event, 778
Connect() method, 52
container controls, 39
ContainerFromElement() method, 210
containers, 75, 78
ContainerVisual class, 431, 711
content controls
    button controls and access keys, 191
    ButtonBase class, 191
    CheckBox class, 193
    CheckBox control, 193
    Escape key, 192
    GridViewColumnHeader class, 192
    Label control, 190
    mnemonics, 190
    Popup control, 200
    RadioButton control, 193–194
    RepeatButton class, 193
    ToggleButton class, 193
    ToolTip class, 195
    ToolTip property, 195
    Tooltips control, 194
content elements, 647
Content property, 40, 119, 266, 552
ContentBox property, 705
ContentControl class, 19, 40
    aligning content relative to its borders, 121
    Button control, 119
    CheckBox control, 119
    class hierarchy of, 118
    combining text and images in StackPanel, 120
    content controls and content nesting, 123
    content controls, defined, 117
    Content property, 119, 857
    ContentTemplate property, 121, 857
    description of, 857

differentiating content controls from layout containers, 117
displaying text string on button surface, 119
drawing vector image inside button, 122
HasContent property, 121
HeaderedContentControl class, 119
Label, 119
OnRender(), 119
placing image inside button, 119
RadioButton control, 119
ScrollViewer, 119, 123
System.Windows.Shapes namespace, 122
TextBlock element, 120
ToolTip, 119
ToString(), 119, 121
UserControl class, 119
using Image class, 119
Window class, 118–119, 215
WPF windows and, 65
ContentElement class, 151, 645, 735
ContentEnd property, 675
ContentLocator object, 691
ContentPresenter, 451, 459, 605, 620, 869–870
ContentProperty attribute, 37–39
ContentStart property, 675
ContentTemplate property, 121, 552
ContentType property, 320
context, 927
ContextMenu class, 634
ContextMenuStrip class, 910–911
contract assemblies, 946–947
ContractBase attribute, 948
ContractHandle object, 951
Contracts subdirectory, 947
ContractToViewAdapter() method, 961
Control class
    automatic change notification in brushes, 182
    Background and Foreground properties, 179
    BorderBrush property, 182
    BorderThickness property, 182
    Brush object, 179
    brushes, 179
    Cursor property, 189
    Cursors class, 189
    description of, 857
    font embedding, procedure for, 187
    font family, defined, 185
    font inheritance, 186
    font properties as dependency properties, 186
    font substitution, 187
    font-related properties of, 184
    FontStretches class, 185
    FontStyles class, 185

Control class (continued)
    FontWeights class, 185
    ForceCursor property, 189
    functions of, 179
    HorizontalContentAlignment property, 121
    identifying FontFamily, 185
    ImageBrush, 182
    IsTabStop property, 857
    LinearGradientBrush, 181
    making element partly transparent, 182–184
    mouse cursors, 189
    MouseDoubleClick event, 173, 857
    Opacity property, 182
    OpenType, 185
    OverrideCursor property, 189
    padding content of button, 121
    Padding property, 121
    painting border around controls, 182
    PreviewMouseDoubleClick event, 173, 857
    property value inheritance, 186
    scRGB standard, 181
    setting background and foreground colors in XAML, 181
    setting button's surface color, 180
    setting FontFamily to list of font options, 187
    SolidColorBrush, 180
    template support, 19
    TextDecorations class, 185
    TextDecorations property, 185
    TileBrush, 183
    Typography property, 185
    using custom cursor, 189
    using transparent colors, 182
    VerticalContentAlignment property, 121
    WPF Color structure, 181
    WPF font size compared to Windows point size, 184
control classes, 877
control consumer, 859
control templates
    adapting custom-window markup into reusable control template, 483
    adding basic window behaviors to window template, 485
    adding control template for ListBoxItem, 476
    adding trigger to change button's background, 464
    adding triggers to, 462
    applying custom control template by setting Template property, 458
    applying templates automatically, 470
    applying window template using simple style, 484
    basic markup for Button control template, 459
    basic structural markup for window's control template, 483–484
    Border class, 459
    browsing WPF control templates, 455
    building complex, multipart templates, 474
    Button class example, 451
    ButtonChrome class, 451
    characteristics of complex templates, 474
    chrome classes, 454
    comparing template bindings to data bindings, 461
    comparing to custom controls, 470
    ContentPresenter, 451
    converting live ControlTemplate object to XAML markup, 457
    creating, 458
    creating code-behind class for resource dictionary, 472, 486
    creating focus indicator for button, 462
    creating new styles that use same template, 469
    creating separate resource dictionary for each control template, 465
    creating template for revamped ListBox control, 475
    custom controls and user interface standardization, 458
    customizing template for vertical ScrollBar, 477–480
    deciding where to apply your templates, 465
    defining, 22
    defining control template as resource, 458
    defining resources in separate resource dictionaries, 465
    defining template details as separate resources, 466
    defining templates in Resources collection of Application class, 465
    dependencies, 475
    dissecting controls, 455
    handling click of window's close button, 488
    IsMouseOver property, 462
    IsPressed property, 462
    isResizing field, 487
    jazzing up customized controls, 474
    keeping all triggers in control template, 469
    loading resource dictionary defined in another assembly, 472
    making window draggable, 486
    making window resizable, 486
    MergedDictionaries collection, 465, 472

obtaining XAML for standard control templates, 455

organizing template resources, 465

practical examples of other custom control templates, 490

problems in giving new template to common control, 488

providing user-selectable skins, 471

putting template details into associated style, 468

reasons to avoid template bindings, 461

Rectangle class, 459

refactoring Button control template, 466

reflection, 455

RepeatButton class, 478

replacing current resource dictionary at runtime, 471

ResizeGrip element, markup example, 454

resizeType field, 487

resource dictionary for button, complete markup, 466

retrieving control's template and serializing it to XAML, 455

retrieving Padding property using template binding, 460

ScrollBar class, 480

Setter.TargetName property, 470

setting key name on style, 480

setting sequential order for conflicting trigger settings, 464

setting TargetName property of each Setter, 462

similarity between templates and styles, 464

SimpleStyles project, 488

styling ScrollBar's RepeatButton objects and Thumb, 481–482

template bindings, 460

Track class, 478

using adorner layer to draw superimposed content, 483

using DynamicResource reference, 472

using focus and click triggers, 452

using FrameworkElement.Templated-Parent property, 486

using resource dictionary, 465

using ResourceManager class, 471

using StaticResource reference, 458

using styles and control templates to skin any application, 470

using TargetName property, 452

using template bindings to pull details out of control properties, 468

when to switch from custom control templates to custom controls, 470

XamlReader class, 457

XamlWriter class, 455

XamlWriter.Save(), 457

ControllableStoryboardAction class, 754, 757

controls

arranging based on their content, 4

base classes for creating custom element, 856

choosing Custom Control Library project type, 856

choosing right base class to inherit from, 856

concept of background and foreground in, 179

content controls, defined, 117

control templates, 451

creating custom control, 856

creating undo stack that stores series of values, 868

defined, 19, 179

Label, 117

logical tree, building, 446

lookless controls, 855

lookless controls, defined, 451

mnemonics, 117

never using custom drawing in control, 901

past problems in control customization, 445

placing custom controls in dedicated class library (DLL) assembly, 856

ToolTip, 117

visual tree, defined, 446

writeable control properties as usually dependency properties, 860

ControlTemplate, 613

ConvertToString() method, 168

Copy Local property, 950

Copy to Output Directory, 323

CornerRadius property, 133, 408

Count property, 587

CreateHighlightCommand, 689

CreateHighlightsForSelection() method, 687

CreateInkStickyNoteCommand, 688

CreateInkStickyNoteForSelection() method, 687

CreateTextStickyNoteForSelection() method, 687

CreateXpsDocumentWriter () method, 726

CrossTechnologySamples.exe, 241

CTP (Community Technology Preview), 11

CultureInfo class, 331

Currency data type, 529

Current property, 65

CurrentChanged event, 588

CurrentDispatcher property, 928

CurrentProgress property, 760

CurrentTimeInvalidated event, 760
CurrentUICulture property, 323
Cursor property, 189
Cursors class, 189
Custom Control Library, 258, 856
custom controls, alternatives to, 855
Custom DPI Setting dialog box, 10
custom panels
    adding attached LineBreakBeforeProperty
        to WrapBreakPanel, 892
    Arrange() as triggering ArrangeOverride(),
        889
    ArrangeCore(), 888
    ArrangeOverride(), 888–891
    basing WrapBreakPanel on WrapPanel, 893
    Canvas class, 891
    creating Canvas-style panel, 891
    examples of, 887
    extending capabilities of WrapPanel, 892
    layout pass, 887
    Measure() as triggering
        MeasureOverride(), 889
    measure pass, 887
    MeasureCore(), 888
    MeasureOverride(), 888–891
    overriding MeasureOverride() and
        ArrangeOverride(), 888
    RegisterAttached(), 892
    two-step layout process, 887
    uses for, 887
CustomContentState class, 265, 269
CustomDrawnDecorator, 901
CustomDrawnElement
    BackgroundColor property, 898
    creating, 898
    RadialGradientBrush, 898
CustomFilter property, 579
CustomPopupPlacementCallback property,
    198
CustomSort property, 580

∎D
dashed lines, 382–383
data binding, 917
    adding validation rule to
        Binding.ValidationRules collection,
        541
    ADO.NET data objects, 491
    AdornedElementPlaceholder, 545–547
    AncestorType property, 505
    automatic target updating, 493
    Binding class, 493
    binding elements closely to their data, 497
    binding markup extension, 493–495
    binding to ADO.NET data objects, 521
    binding to collection of objects, 516
    binding to LINQ expression

converting IEnumerable(Of T)
    IEnumerable<T> to ordinary
    collection, 524–525
deferred execution, 525–526
overview, 523–524
binding to non-element objects, 503
binding to nonexistent property, 494
binding updates, 502
BindingExpression class, 503
BindingExpression.UpdateSource(),
    502–503
BindingMode enumeration, table of
    values, 499
BindingOperations class, 495
Binding.RelativeSource property, 566–569
bubbling, 543
building data access components, 507
building data object, 510
building validation directly into controls,
    536
caller inform design pattern, 510
chaining bindings, 497
change notification and dependency
    properties, 491
checking InnerException property of
    TargetInvocationException, 543
ClearAllBindings(), 495
ClearValue(), 495
collection items, displaying and editing,
    516
collection items, inserting and removing,
    520
contents of ValidationError object, 543
creating and using value converter class,
    526
creating Binding object with nested
    RelativeSource object inside, 504
creating binding using code, 495
creating custom controls, 496
creating DataView, 522
creating dynamic binding, 495
creating error templates, 545
creating multiple binding expressions that
    set same property, 497
creating multiple bindings, 496
creating XAML pages to run in browser,
    492
data conversion, defined, 526
data templates and, 555
DataContent property, 519
DataContext property, 503, 505, 512
DataErrorValidationRule, 539–540
DataTable.DefaultView property, 522
defined, 491
defining validation at binding level, 536
displaying bound object, 511
displaying error content in ToolTip, 546

DisplayMemberPath property, 518, 522, 552
element-to-element binding, 491
enabling database updates, 513
ErrorContent property, 541–543
ExceptionValidationRule, 537–542
Explicit update mode, 503
FindAncestor mode, 505
forcing values to flow bidirectionally between source and target, 495
FormHasErrors(), 545
getting list of all outstanding errors, 544
guidelines for designing data access components, 507
handling change notification, 514
handling Error event, 543
HasError property, 538
how WPF handles validation failures, 538
IEnumerable interface, 516
INotifyCollectionChanged interface, 521
INotifyPropertyChanged interface, 514
IsValid property, 541
ItemsControl class, 516, 551–552, 566
ItemsSource property, 552–555
linking controls through, 492
LostFocus update mode, 502
markup-based vs. programmatic binding, 495
modifying data binding source programmatically, 493
NotifyOnValidationError property, 538
OnPropertyChanged(), 515
options for binding two properties, 499
options for catching invalid values, 536
outputting trace information on binding failures, 494
preventing field from being edited, 520
PropertyChanged event, 514
PropertyChanged update mode, 502
raising errors in data object, 536
reacting to validation errors, 543
reducing overhead by setting mode to one-way binding, 501
RelativeSource property, 503–504
RelativeSourceMode enumeration, table of values, 505
removing binding with code, 495
setting DataContext property of container, 552
setting ElementName property, 493
setting Mode property of Binding, 495
setting NotifyOnValidationError property, 543
setting Path property, 493
setting property that isn't dependency property, 500
Source property, 503–504

StoreDB class, 508
summary of data-binding procedure, 552
support for IDataErrorInfo, 11
support for LINQ, 11
TargetInvocationException, 543
TemplateBinding, 872–873
two-way bindings, 491–499
understanding OneWayToSource BindingMode, 500
UpdateSourceTrigger property, 502–542
using same validation rule for more than one binding, 542
Validation class, 538
validation rule for restricting decimal values, 540
ValidationError object, 538
Validation.ErrorTemplate property, 538
ValidationResult object, 541
ValidationRules collection, 537
ValidationRule.Validate(), 538
visual indication of errors in bound controls, 538
writing custom validation rules, 540
writing data binding expressions, 22, 493
data conversion
    applying conditional formatting, 533
    BitmapImage class, 532
    converting from display format back to number, 529
    converting raw binary data into WPF BitmapImage object, 531
    creating converter object in Resources collection, 530
    creating objects with value converter, 531
    creating value converter class, 526
    data triggers, 534
    Decimal.ToString(), 528
    defined, 526
    evaluating multiple properties, 535
    format strings, 528
    formatting strings with data converter, 527
    ImagePathConverter, code example, 531
    IMultiValueConveter interface, 535
    mapping project namespace to XML namespace prefix, 530
    MultiBinding, 535
    Parse(), 529
    PriceConverter class, 530
    SuppressExceptions property, 533
    System.Globalization.NumberStyles value, 529
    TryParse(), 529
    using custom IValueConverter, 533
Data property, 409
data providers, 591, 594

data templates
　adding elements inside existing control, 453
　binding Visibility property to IsSelected property, 569
　building specialized class deriving from DataTemplateSelector, 560
　changing item layout by setting ItemsPanelTemplate property, 573
　code examples, 553
　comparing template selectors and style selectors, 571
　composition of, 553
　Content property, 552
　ContentTemplate property, 552
　creating template selector, 560
　creating template that adjusts to bound object, 560
　creating value converter that applies conditional formatting, 560
　data binding and, 555
　data triggers, 559
　defined, 552
　defining in resources collection, 554
　functions of, 453
　ItemContainerStyle property, 571
　ItemTemplate property, 552
　list-based and content-control templates, 553
　modifying template of selected or deselected item, 565
　placing controls directly inside template, 556
　presenting different data items in different ways, 559
　retrieving all information about selected data item, 558
　reusing same data template in different types of controls, 555
　SelectStyle(), 571
　SelectTemplate(), 560–561
　setting DataType property, 555
　setting SnapsToDevicePixels property, 568
　setting style of inner StackPanel using trigger, 569
　setting template's element property based on data-item property, 559
　SingleCriteriaHighlightTemplateSelector class, 562–564, 581
　style selectors, defined, 571
　StyleSelector class, 571
　template selection and displaying editable data, 564
　template selectors, 559
　using binding expression to alter template, 566
　using ImagePathConverter, code example, 556
　using IValueConverter objects in data binding, 556
　using style triggers to modify selected item, 566
　using with StaticResource reference, 555
　value converters, 559
data triggers, 534, 559, 560
data types
　data binding format string, 529
　DataTypeAnimation class, 774
　having or not having corresponding animation class, 732
　key frame vs. interpolation animation classes, 732
　linear and discrete key frames, 774
　setting properties using resource, 350
data views
　adding group header, 582
　adding multiple levels of grouping, 583
　adjusting filtering through WPF view object, 579
　ADO.NET DataView, function of, 578
　applying grouping, 581
　binding ObservableCollection, 574
　binding same data in different ways within window, 574
　clearing existing SortDescriptions collection, 580
　code for connecting IComparer to view, 581
　combining grouping with sorting, 583
　constructing CollectionViewSource declaratively in XAML, 585
　Count property, 587
　creating filtering class, 576
　creating more than one DataView to wrap same DataTable, 580
　creating multiple views, 587
　creating Predicate object, 575
　creating separate GroupItem object for each group, 581
　creating single filtering class for each window, 577
　creating views declaratively, 585
　CurrentChanged event, 588
　defined, 574
　defining inline filtering method, 576
　filtering collections, 575
　filtering DataTable, 578
　filtering dynamically, 576
　forcing list to be refiltered, 578
　GetDefaultView(), 575
　grouping data objects in ranges, 583
　ICollectionView interface, 588
　implementing IBindingList, 574

implementing IEnumerable, 574
implementing IList, 574
navigating data objects and records with
    view, 587
removing filter, 578
retrieving bound DataView and modifying
    its properties directly, 579
retrieving view object, 575
setting GroupStyle.HeaderTemplate
    property, 582
sorting based on property values in each
    data item, 580
storing reference to filter object as
    member variable, 578
using Filter property of view object, 575
using lookup list for editing, 590
using SortDescription to identify sort field
    and sort direction, 580
using value converter to apply range
    grouping, 585
using view to implement sorting, 580
view objects and CollectionView, 574
writing logic for previous and next
    buttons, 589
DataContent property, 519
DataContext property, 503, 505, 512, 552
DataFormats class, 675–676
DataGridView control, 13, 608, 621, 906
DataTable, 578, 579
DataTable.DefaultView property, 522
DataTemplate, 613
DataTemplateSelector class, 560–566
DataType property, 555
DataTypeAnimation class, 774
DataView, 522, 579
Date data types, 529
DateTimePicker, 906
DecelerationRatio property, 744, 762
Decimal.ToString(), 528
declarative resources, 333
declarative user interfaces, 5, 20
Decorator class, 857
decorators, 133, 134
DecreaseZoom() method, 669
default constructor, 28
DefaultStyleKey property, 607, 613, 871
DefaultView property, 579
DeflateStream, 283
DeleteInkStickyNotesForSelection() method,
    687
DeleteStickyNotesCommand, 688
DeleteTextStickyNotesForSelection()
    method, 687
DeleteVisual() method, 435
Demand() method, 281
dependency properties, 36
    AddOwner(), 145

attached properties, 146
calling static
    DependencyProperty.Register()
    method, 139
change notification, 147
classes sharing same dependency
    property, 145
ClearValue(), 141, 145
CoerceValueCallback, 142–143, 148–149
coercion, 140–142
creating custom dependency properties,
    138
defining DependencyProperty object as
    static field, 138
defining object that represents property,
    138
defining static field, 860
defining with readonly keyword, 138
DependencyObject class, 140
DependencyProperty class, 138
DependencyProperty.Register(), 142
DependencyProperty.UnsetValue, 142
Dependency.Register(), 141
determining base value of, 149
determining property value, 149
differentiating from normal properties,
    138
dynamic value resolution, 148
events not automatically fired, 147
FrameworkPropertyMetadata object,
    139–146
GetValue(), 146
handling interrelated properties, 143
IsMarginValid property, 140
naming convention, 138
OnPropertyChangedCallback(), 147
PasswordChar property, 147
performing action when property
    changes, 148
property metadata, 141
property validation, 139
property value inheritance, 349
property wrapper, 140
PropertyChangedCallback, 141–149
RegisterAttached(), 146
registering with WPF, 138
retrieving value from property value, 148
reusing, 146
rules of precedence, 141
SetValue(), 146
triggering callback, 147
using overloaded version of SetValue(),
    147
ValidateValueCallback, 141–143, 146
validation callback, 139
WPF's property resolution system, 145
WPF's use of, 147

dependency properties *(continued)*
  wrapped by .NET property procedures, 138
  writeable control properties as usually dependency properties, 860
DependencyObject class, 16–18, 36, 50, 140
  ClearValue(), 495
  GetValue(), 861
  SetValue(), 861
  using GetValue() and SetValue() methods, 260
DependencyProperty class, 138, 679
DependencyProperty.Register() method, 139, 142
DependencyProperty.UnsetValue, 142
Dependency.Register() method, 141
design tools, 429–430
DesiredSize property, 85, 888–890
Device property, 166
device-independent units, 7, 26
dfsvc.exe, 977
dialog model, 225
DialogResult enumeration, 907
DialogResult property, 225
DiffuseMaterial class
  AmbientColor property, 818
  Brush property, 815, 832
  comparing two versions of torus, 832
  MeshGeometry.TextureCoordinates collection, 834
  painting DiffuseMaterial object with any brush, 834
direct events, 154, 171
Direct3D, 16
Direction property, 407
DirectionalLight class, 818
DirectShow (ActiveMovie), 784
DirectX, 20, 809, 925
  3-D graphics, 2
  antialiasing, 2
  comparison to WPF, 14
  downloading managed .NET libraries for, 14
  games and hardware acceleration, 2
  GPU (graphics processing unit), 2
  origins of, 2
  programming API, 2
  quartz.dll library, 783
  rendering tiers, 4
  transparency, 2
Disable Display Scaling on High DPI Settings, 10
discovery, 951
discrete key frames, 773
dispatcher, 18, 928
Dispatcher.BeginInvoke() method, 959
DispatcherExceptionUnhandled event, 62

DispatcherObject class, 16–18, 928, 929
DispatcherOperation object, 930
DispatcherPriority, 930
DispatcherUnhandledException event, 251
DisplayMemberBinding property, 608–610
DisplayMemberPath property, 518, 522, 602, 605, 631
Dispose() method, 206, 910, 913
Dock property, 88
docking, 75
DockPanel, 51, 78, 90
Document class, 67
DocumentPage class, 705
DocumentPaginator class, 697
  building HeaderedFlowDocumentPaginator class, 708–710
  creating custom DocumentPaginator from scratch, 714
  FixedDocumentPaginator class, 707
  FlowDocumentPaginator class, 707
  function of, 705
  GetFormattedText(), 716
  GetPage(), 709, 717
  IsPageCountValid property, 709
  PageCount property, 709
  PageSize property, 709, 715
  PaginateData(), 715–716
  rowsPerPage field, 716
  StoreDataSetPaginator class, 715–719
  XpsDocument class, 707
documents
  displaying large amounts of text, 643
  DocumentViewer, 644
  fixed documents, defined, 643, 681
  flow documents, defined, 643
  FlowDocumentPageViewer, 644
  FlowDocumentReader, 644
  FlowDocumentScrollViewer, 644, 663
  read-only containers for displaying flow documents, 668
  RichTextBox, 644
  System.Windows.Documents namespace, 647
  using XAML format to save document, 677
  XPS (XML Paper Specification), 643, 681
DocumentViewer, 682
DoDragDrop() method, 176
DoubleAnimation class, 732–734, 770
DoubleAnimationUsingPath, 777
Double.NaN, 737
DoUpdate() method, 223
DoWork event, 936
DpiX property, 237
DpiY property, 237
drag-and-drop operations, 174
DragDrop class, 175

DragEnter event, 176
DragIncrement property, 99
DragMove() method, 232
DrawGeometry() method, 897
DrawImage() method, 896
Drawing class
   classes deriving from, 426
   classes for displaying drawing, 427
   differentiating DrawingImage and
      ImageDrawing classes, 428
   displaying 2-D piece of vector or bitmap
      art, 425
   fusing drawings together in
      DrawingGroup, 428
   GeometryDrawing class, 425
Drawing property, 432
DrawingBrush class, 427, 428, 429
DrawingCanvas class
   AddVisual(), 435
   casting HitTestResult to
      GeometryHitTestResult, 440
   ClearSelection(), 438
   clickOffset field, 437
   code from MouseLeftButtonDown event
      handler, 438
   creating callback, 439
   creating square-drawing application, 434
   DeleteVisual(), 435
   deleting square, 437
   dragging square, 437–439
   DrawSelectionSquare(), 442
   DrawSquare() rendering code, 436
   GetVisual(), 437
   GetVisualChild(), 435
   GetVisuals(), 439–441
   hit testing, defined, 437
   HitTestResultCallback(), 440
   isDragging field, 437
   isMultiSelecting flag, 441
   markup for creating squares, 436
   performing more sophisticated hit testing,
      439
   reporting number of squares in user-
      selected region, 441
   selectedVisual field, 437
   selectionSquareTopLeft field, 441
   VisualChildrenCount property, 435
   XAML markup for declaring
      DrawingCanvas in window, 436
DrawingContext class, 896
   Close(), 431
   DrawGeometry(), 897
   DrawImage(), 896
   DrawLine(), 718
   DrawRectangle(), 900
   DrawText(), 718
   Pop(), 433, 711

PushOpacity(), 433
   table of methods, 432, 711
DrawingContext object, 711
DrawingGroup class, 428
DrawingImage class, 427, 428
DrawingImage object, 395
DrawingVisual class, 427
   calling methods in DrawingContext class,
      431
   drawing content over other content, not
      under it, 897
   Drawing property, 432, 711
   Opacity property, 433
   RenderOpen(), 431–433, 711, 897
   Transform property, 433
DrawLine() method, 718
DrawRectangle() method, 900
DrawSelectionSquare() method, 442
DrawText() method, 718
DrawThemeTextEx() function, 240
Dreamweaver, 23
DropShadowBitmapEffect class, 407
dual-core CPUs, 927
Dunn, Fletcher, 853
Duration property, 736, 740
DwmEnableBlurBehindWindow() function,
      240
DwmExtendFrameIntoClientArea() function,
      236–237, 240
DwmIsCompositionEnabled() function, 240
dynamic resources, 335
   guidelines for using, 338
   improving first-time-load performance of
      form, 339
   responding to changes in system
      environment settings, 341
dynamic value resolution, 148

■ E

EdgeProfile property, 406
EditingCommands class, 304
   ToggleBold, ToggleItalic, and ToggleItalic
      commands, 678
   types of included commands, 294
EditingMode property, 107
eight ball example, 43
ElementHost class, 908, 914, 924
ElementName property, 493, 872
elements
   AddLogicalChild(), 434
   AddVisualChild(), 434
   base classes for creating custom element,
      856
   compared to controls, 19
   convention for naming element, 872
   creating custom decorator, 901
   creating CustomDrawnElement, 898

elements *(continued)*
  custom rendering, benefits of, 898
  custom-drawn, 895
  CustomDrawnDecorator, 901
  defined, 117, 928
  evaluating when to use OnRender(), 897
  GetForegroundBrush(), 900
  overriding GetVisualChild(), 434
  overriding VisualChildrenCount property, 434
  performing custom rendering by overriding OnRender(), 896
  placing custom elements in DLL assembly, 856
  registering and hosting visual in element, 434
  role of custom-drawn elements in control template, 901
  using composition to build more complex elements, 895
  when to create custom element, 855
Ellipse class, 368
  creating ellipse, 370
  creating ellipse that fills window, 372
  sizing to fill available space, 371
EllipseGeometry class, 411
Embedded Resource build action, 318
EmbossBitmapEffect class, 406
EmissiveMaterial class, 832, 833
Enable() method, 685
EnableModelessKeyboardInterop() method, 908
EnableVisualStyles() method, 909, 918
EnableWindowsFormsInterop() method, 908
EndChange() method, 205
EndInit() method, 163
EndLineCap property, 381
EndPoint property, 391
EndStyle() method, 805
entity references, 40
enumerations, 32
Environment class, 235
error messages, 332
error templates
  AdornedElementPlaceholder, 545–547
  displaying error content in ToolTip, 546
  using adorner layer, 545
ErrorContent property, 541–543
ErrorException property, 791
ErrorProvider, 906
Escape key, 192
event handlers, 22, 42
event routing, 42
  AddHandler(), 150, 159
  attached events, 159
  attaching event handler, 151
  bubbled image click, code example, 156
  bubbling events, 154–156
  button control and Click event, 159
  connecting event directly by calling AddHandler(), 152
  connecting event with delegates and code, 152
  ContentElement class, 151
  creating appropriate delegate type, 152
  creating delegate object with right signature, 152
  defined, 149
  defining and registering, 149
  detaching event handler, 153
  direct events, 154
  ensuring each button has Name property set in XAML, 160
  event signatures, 151
  event wrapper, 150
  firing sequence for tunneling and bubbling events, 161
  handling suppressed events, 159
  identifying routing strategy of event, 162
  KeyDown event, 161
  marking tunneling event as handled, 163
  MouseDown event, 154
  MouseEnter event, 154
  MouseEventArgs object, 151
  MouseUp event, 151
  naming event handler methods, 151
  PreviewKeyDown event, 154, 161
  RaiseEvent(), 150
  RegisterEvent(), 154
  RegisterRoutedEvent(), 150
  RemoveHandler(), 150
  RoutedEventArgs class, 151, 155
  sharing between classes, 151
  three types of routed events, 154
  tunneling events, 154, 161, 297
  UIElement class, 151
  understanding, 149
  using -= operator, 153
  using event wrapper, 151
  using RemoveHandler() helper method, 153
  wiring up attached event in code, 160
  WPF event model, 149
  wrapping of routed events by .NET events, 150
event signatures, 151
event triggers
  attaching actions to property trigger, 749
  attaching triggers with style, 748
  BeginStoryboard action, 747
  creating event trigger for MouseEnter and MouseLeave events, 750
  creating property trigger that triggers storyboard, 749

defining, 747
EventTrigger.SourceName property, 756
launching animation, 363
returning element to its original state, 364
supplying series of actions to modify
    control, 363
Triggers collection, 748
using to attach animation, 749
using to control animation storyboard,
    746
using Trigger.EnterActions and
    Trigger.ExitActions, 749
waiting for specific event to be fired, 363
event wrapper, 150
EventManager class, 869
events, defined, 149
EventTrigger class, 792
EventTrigger.SourceName property, 756
ExceptionValidationRule, 538
Execute() method, 292
Executed event, 297
ExecutedRoutedEventArgs, 297
ExpandDirection property, 131
Expanded event, 629
Expander control, 119
    combining with ScrollViewer, 132
    ExpandDirection property, 131
    implementing lazy load, 132
    IsExpanded property, 130
    synchronizing other controls with, 132
    use in online help and on web pages, 129
    window size and expanding content, 132
Explicit update mode, 503
Exponential data type, 529
Expression Blend design tool, 23, 227, 379,
    422, 429, 430, 458, 490, 769
extender providers, 37
ExtendGlass() method, 239
Extensible Application Markup Language.
    See XAML
extension classes, 35
ExtraData property, 262

F

FarPlaneDistance property, 822
FieldOfView property, 822
Figure element, 662
FileDialog class, 226
FileRegistrationHelper class, 72
FileStream class, 46, 686
FileViewer class, 64
FillBehavior property, 741, 753
FillRule property, 379, 412
Filter event, 586
Filter property, 575
FindAddIn() method, 951
FindAncestor mode, 505

FindEditPositionFrom() method, 883
FindPrimes() method, 932
FindResource() method, 351
Firefox, support for XBAPs, 11
Fixed Decimal data type, 529
fixed documents
    browsing inner contents of XPS file, 682
    creating and viewing XPS documents, 682
    defined, 643, 681
    DocumentViewer, 644
    features of, 681
    printing documents without alteration,
        644
    printing fixed document using
        ApplicationCommands.Print, 682
    using DocumentViewer to display XPS
        document, 682
    XPS (XML Paper Specification), 643, 681
    XpsDocument class, 682
FixedDocumentPaginator class, 707
Flash, Adobe, 1, 430
Floater element, 658
flow documents
    benefits of using, 645
    block elements, 646, 647
    building from flow elements, 645
    changing text justification, 667
    collapsing whitespace, tabs, and line
        breaks in XAML, 657
    comparing content and noncontent
        elements, 645
    constructing, 648, 663
    content elements, 646, 647
    ContentElement class, 645
    creating Floater, 659
    creating Mad Libs game, 665
    creating simple document, code example,
        663
    creating table, procedure and markup for,
        653–654
    defined, 643
    distinguishing block and inline elements,
        646
    editing flow document using RichTextBox
        control, 674
    embedding bitmap in flow document, 661
    enabling optimal paragraph layout, 667
    Figure element, table of properties, 662
    Floater element, 658
    FlowDocument class, 648
    FlowDocumentPageViewer, 644, 668
    FlowDocumentReader, 644, 668
    FlowDocumentScrollViewer, 644, 663, 668
    Focusable property, 645
    FrameworkContentElement class, 645
    function of, 724

flow documents *(continued)*
  getting block elements in flow document, 664
  HTML content and flow layout, 644
  HTML-to-XAML translator, 647
  improving readability of justified text, 667
  inline elements, 646, 656
  IsHyphenationEnabled property, 668
  IsOptimalParagraphEnabled property, 667
  laying out content dynamically, 643
  List element, 651
  making content element focusable, 645
  modifying text inside flow document, 664
  moving from one block element to next, 664
  navigating structure of, 664
  no WYSIWYG interface for creating, 649
  onscreen viewing of, 644
  Paragraph element, 650
  printing flow document using Print(), 673
  readability problems and window size, 644
  read-only containers for displaying flow documents, 668
  reusing created document viewer, 672
  RichTextBox, 644
  Run element, 650, 664
  Section element, 655
  sizing table columns explicitly or proportionately, 655
  Span.Tag property, 664
  supplying TableColumn objects for Table.Rows property, 654
  System.Windows.Documents namespace, 647
  Table element, 653
  TextAlignment property, 667
  TextDecorations, 648
  total-fit algorithm, 667
  Typography object, 648
  using block-level element inside FlowDocument element, 649
  using BlockUIContainer to place noncontent elements inside flow document, 655, 681
  using fixed-size Floater, 662
  using FlowDocument.Blocks collection, 664
  using FlowDocumentScrollViewer as container, 648
  using hyphenation to improve text justification, 668
  using XAML format to save document, 677
  using XamlReader class, 672
  using XamlWriter class, 673
  using xml:space attribute with value preserve, 658
flow layout, 4

FlowDirection property, 324
FlowDocument class, 202, 648, 697
  ColumnGap property, 706
  ColumnWidth property, 706
  ContentStart and ContentEnd properties, 675
  FlowDocument properties for controlling columns, table of, 671
  PageHeight property, 706
  PagePadding property, 706
  PageWidth property, 706
  Paragraph properties for controlling columns, table of, 671
FlowDocumentPageViewer
  repaginating content dynamically, 670
  splitting flow document into separate pages, 668–670
  splitting text into multiple columns, 670
  support for zooming, 669
  using IncreaseZoom() and DecreaseZoom(), 669
FlowDocumentPaginator class, 707
FlowDocumentReader, 662
  choosing between scroll mode and two page modes, 672
  reading content in scrollable or paginated display, 668
  support for zooming, 669
  using IncreaseZoom() and DecreaseZoom(), 669
FlowDocumentScrollViewer
  displaying entire document with scroll bar, 668
  IsSelectionEnabled property, 649
  no support for pagination or multicolumn displays, 668
  support for zooming, 669
  using as container for flow document, 648
  using IncreaseZoom() and DecreaseZoom(), 669
FlowDocumentScrollViewer container, 705–706
FlowLayoutPanel, 75, 892, 919
focus, 169
Focusable property, 169, 645, 869
FocusManager.IsFocusScope property, 304
folder structure, 943–944
FolderBrowserDialog class, 909
font family, 185
FontDialog class, 909
FontFamily property, 324
fonts
  Control class, font-related properties, 184
  embedded fonts and licensing permissions, 188
  font family, defined, 185

font properties as dependency properties, 186
FontStretches class, 185
FontStyles class, 185
FontWeights class, 185
identifying FontFamily, 185
inheritance of, 186
OpenType, 185–187
procedure for embedding, 187
property value inheritance, 186
setting FontFamily to list of font options, 187
substitution of, 187
TextDecorations class, 185
TextDecorations property, 185
Typography property, 185
WPF font size compared to Windows point size, 184
FontStretches class, 185
FontStyles class, 185
FontWeights class, 185
ForceCursor property, 189
Form class, 215
format strings, 528
FormattedText class, 716
FormHasErrors() method, 545
Form.ShowDialog() method, 907
ForwardStack property, 264
fragment navigation, 252
Frame class
    controlling navigation of parent frame only, 255
    creating nested page, 254
    creating XBAP, 256
    embedding page inside window, 252
    handling back button, 255
    hosting pages, 252, 254, 256
    including navigation buttons inside frame, 254
    setting JournalOwnership property of embedded frame, 255
    Source property, 252
    using several frames in single window, 253
Frame element, 119, 389
frame rate
    decreasing, 761
    testing frame rates with simple animation, 761
    Timeline.DesiredFrameRate attached property, 761
    using fixed frame rate, 730
    viewing effect of different frame rates, 763
frame-based animation
    animation of falling circles, 778
    animations not time-dependent, 782

attaching event handler to CompositionTarget.Rendering event, 778
    creating using nothing but code, 778
    uses for, 778
FrameworkContentElement class, 645
FrameworkElement class, 18, 29, 82
    Cursor property, 189
    defining Margin property as dependency property, 138
    description of, 856
    GetTemplateChild(), 875
    TemplatedParent property, 486
    ToolTip property, 195
    Triggers collection, 748
FrameworkElementAdapters class, 961–962
FrameworkElementAdapters.ContractTo-ViewAdapter() method, 961
FrameworkElementAdapters.ViewTo-ContractAdapter() method, 962
FrameworkElement.FindResource() method, 340
FrameworkElement.Triggers collection, 360
FrameworkPropertyMetadata class, 186
FrameworkPropertyMetadata object, 146, 892
    configuring dependency property features, 141
    creating, 139
    setting journal flag, 258
    table of available properties, 141
FrameworkTemplate class, 453
Freezable class, 337
From property, 737, 738
FrontPage, 23
FullName property, 723
FullPrimaryScreenHeight, 219
FullPrimaryScreenWidth, 219

■**G**

GAC (global assembly cache), 326, 969
garbage collector, 752
Gaussian blur, 404
GDI/GDI+, 1, 6, 20, 368
generic.xaml, 345–346, 616, 871
geometry, building for 3-D object, 812
Geometry class, 409, 410, 424
geometry mini-language
    command sequences in, 422
    creating StreamGeometry object, not PathGeometry, 423
    representing detailed figures with less markup, 422
    table of commands and parameters, 423
    using relative vs. absolute coordinates, 424
Geometry property, 815, 852
GeometryCombineMode property, 414

GeometryDrawing class, 425, 426
GeometryGroup class
  advantages and disadvantages of, 412
  creating square-with-a-hole effect, 413
  determining fills of intersecting shapes,
    412
  FillRule property, 412
  nesting Geometry-derived objects inside,
    411
  reducing overhead of user interface, 412
  reusing same geometry in several separate
    Path elements, 412
GeometryModel3D class, 815–816
GetAddInController() method, 954
GetAnchorInfo() method, 693
GetAnnotation() method, 691
GetAnnotations() method, 690, 691
GetChild() method, 449
GetContentState() method, 267–269
GetDefaultView() method, 575
GetFileName() method, 264
GetFixedDocumentSequence() method, 682
GetForegroundBrush() method, 900
GetFormattedText() method, 716
GetMaskProvider() method, 882
GetNavigationService() method, 261
GetPackage() method, 694
GetPage() method, 709, 717
GetPosition() method, 172
GetPrintJobInfoCollection() method, 723
GetPrintQueues() method, 722
GetProduct() method, 508
GetProducts() method, 517
GetProperty() method, 891
GetPropertyValue() method, 679
GetResourceStream() method, 319–320
GetService() method, 686
GetTempFileName() method, 726
GetTemplateChild() method, 875
GetUserStoreForApplication() method, 282
GetValue() method, 140, 146
GetVisual() method, 437, 961–962
GetVisualChild() method, 434–435
GetVisuals() method, 439–441
GetXmlStream() method, 720
global assembly cache (GAC), 326, 969
Global Sans Serif, 324
Global Serif, 324
Global User Interface, 324
GlowColor property, 407
GlowSize property, 407
glue code, 906
GoBack() method, 262
GoForward() method, 262
GPU (graphics processing unit), 2
Gradient Obsession tool, 770
GradientOrigin property, 393

GradientStop, 391, 392
GrammarBuilder class, 808
Graphics class, 237
graphics processing unit (GPU), 2
Grid
  absolute sizes, 94
  assigning weight for dividing space
    unequally, 95
  automatic sizes, 94
  changing row and column sizes, 94
  Column property, 92
  ColumnDefinition object, Width property,
    94
  ColumnSpan property, 96
  creating Grid-based layout, 92
  creating shared group, code example, 103
  defining controls row by row and from
    right to left, 93
  description of, 78
  filling ColumnDefinition and
    RowDefinition elements, 92
  giving same proportions to separate Grid
    controls, 101
  GridSplitter class, 97
  IsSharedSizeScope property, 103, 617
  nesting one Grid inside another, code
    example, 100
  placing individual elements into cells, 92
  proportional sizes, 94
  resizing rows or columns, 97
  Row property, 92
  RowDefinition object, Height property, 94
  RowSpan property, 96
  separating elements into invisible grid of
    rows and columns, 91
  shared size groups, 101
  shared size groups as not global to
    application, 103
  SharedSizeGroup property, 103, 554
  ShowGridLines property, 92
  spanning rows and columns, 96
  splitting window into two rows, code
    example, 95
  using in Visual Studio, 94
  using mix of proportional and other sizing
    modes, 95
  using nested Grid containers, 96
GridSplitter class, 98, 99
GridView
  adding GridViewColumn objects to
    GridView.Columns collection, 608
  advantages of DataGridView over, 608
  cell templates, 610
  changing content and appearance of
    column headers, 612
  ColumnHeaderContainerStyle property,
    612

creating columns with, 608
customizing column headers, 612
defining three-column, grid-based
    ListView, 609
ProductImagePath converter, 611
reordering columns, 610
sizing and resizing columns, 609–610
supplying new control template for
    header, 613
using column header templates, 612
using date templates to supply different
    elements, 611
wrapping text in columns, 610
GridViewColumn
    CellTemplate property, 610
    CellTemplateSelector property, 612
    DisplayMemberBinding property, 608–610
    Header property, 608, 612
    HeaderContainerStyle property, 612
    HeaderTemplate property, 612
GridViewColumnHeader class, 192
GroupBox control, 119, 127
GroupDescriptions property, 586
GroupItem object, 581
GroupName property, 194
GroupStyle class, 582
GroupStyle.HeaderTemplate property, 582
GZipStream, 283

■H
Handled property, 262, 297
Handles statement, 157–158
hardware acceleration, 2, 20
    rendering tiers, 4
    running rich WPF applications on older
        video cards, 3
    WDDM and XPDM drivers, 3
HasContent property, 121
HasError property, 538
Header property, 608, 612, 622
HeaderContainerStyle property, 612
HeaderedContentControl class
    Expander control, 119, 129
    GroupBox control, 119, 127
    TabItem control, 119, 128
HeaderedFlowDocumentPaginator class,
    708–710
HeaderedItemsControl class, 622
HeaderTemplate property, 612
Height property, 84, 213, 716
HelpProvider, 13, 906
Hide() method, 218
HierarchicalDataTemplate, 624
highestAvailable application, 73
hit testing
    creating callback, 439
    defined, 437

performing more sophisticated hit testing,
    439
    square-drawing application, 437
HitTest() method, 437–439, 845
HitTestResult, 846
HitTestResultCallback() method, 440
HorizontalAlignment property, 82, 869
HorizontalContentAlignment property, 121
HorizontalScrollBarVisibility property, 125,
    203
host adapters, 950–951
host view, 950
HostInBrowser tag, 274
HostObject class, 956–957
HostObjectViewToContractHostAdapter
    class, 958
hosts, 951–954, 955–960
HostSideAdapters subdirectory, 951
HTML, 1
HTML-to-XAML translator, 647
hwnd, 914
HwndSource class, 925
HwndSource property, 164
Hyperlink class, 250
Hyperlink element, 201
hyperlinks
    directing user to another page, 250
    DispatcherUnhandledException event,
        251
    fragment navigation, 252
    handling clicks on, 250
    handling WebException, 251
    as inline flow elements in WPF, 249
    jumping to specific control on page, 252
    navigating to websites, 251
    NavigationFailed event, 251
    responding to Click event to perform task,
        250
    TextBlock elements and, 249
    using relative URIs in, 257

■I
IAnimatable interface, 735
IBindingList, 574
.ico (icon) files, 216
ICollectionView interface, 588
ICommand interface, 291
ICommandSource interface, 295
IComponent, 910
icon (.ico) files, 216
Icon property, 633, 910
IContract interface, 947
IDataErrorInfo interface, 11, 536
IDictionary, 37
IEnumerable interface, 516, 574
IEnumerable(Of T) IEnumerable<T>,
    524–525

<iframe> tag, 286
IHostObjectContract argument, 957
IHostObjectContract interface, 956–958
IHostObjectContract.Initialize() method, 958
IImageProcessorContract interface, 958–961
IIS (Internet Information Services) 7, 969
ildasm, 319
IList, 37, 574
Illustrator, Adobe, 430
Image class, 119
ImageBrush, 182
    changing TileMode property, 399
    comparing proportionally sized and fixed-
        sized tiles, 397
    filling area with bitmap image, 395
    flipping tiles, 399
    ImageSource property, 395
    Stretch property, 396–398
    supplying DrawingImage object for
        ImageSource property, 395
    tiling image across surface of brush, 397
    using Viewbox property, 396
    Viewport property, 397
    ViewportUnits property, 397
ImageDetailView object, 619
ImageList, 906
ImagePathConverter, 531, 556
ImagePreview control, 962
ImageProcessorContractToViewHostAdapter
        class, 958
ImageProcessorViewToContractAdapter
        class, 958
ImageSource class, 427
ImageSource property, 346, 395
ImageView object, 619
IMultiValueConverter interface, 535, 560
INativeHandleContract interface, 961–962
IncreaseZoom() method, 669
Initialize() method, 956
InitializeComponent() method, 28, 47, 165,
        261, 869
Initialized event, 163
InkCanvas
    ActiveEditingMode property, 108
    annotating content with user-drawn
        strokes, 107
    description of, 79, 106
    EditingMode property, enumeration
        values, 107
    FrameworkElement class, 107
    predefined gestures, 108
    Stroke objects, 107
    Strokes collection, 107
    stylus input and tablet PCs, 107
inline elements
    collapsing whitespace, tabs, and line
        breaks in XAML, 657

creating Floater, 659
defined, 646
embedding bitmap in flow document, 661
Figure element, table of properties, 662
Floater element, 658
table of, 656
using fixed-size Floater, 662
using xml:space attribute with value
        preserve, 658
Inlines collection, 650, 668
InlineUIContainer class, 681
InnerException property, 165
INotifyCollectionChanged interface, 521
INotifyPropertyChanged interface, 514, 560
input events, 163, 165
InputBindings collection, 299
InputDevice class, 166
InputEventArgs class, 166
InputGestures collection, 292, 634
InputGestureText property, 633
Install Mode setting, 977
Install tag, 274
InstallShield, 965
interactive controls, 11
Interactive3DDecorator class, 850
InteractiveVisual3D class, 852
interfaces, 940
Internet Explorer
    IE 7's ability to launch .xbap files, 274
    opening loose XAML files in, 53
    page-based applications and, 245
    Quick Tabs view, 401
    StartupUri property, 256
    WebBrowser control, 246
Internet Information Services (IIS) 7, 969
Internet zone, 278
InvalidateRequerySuggested() method, 303,
        307
InvalidateVisual() method, 898–899
InvalidOperationException, 262, 929
Invoke() method, 931
IOException, 325
IProvideCustomContentState interface,
        267–269
IsAdditive property, 739
IsAsync property, 593
IsAsynchronous property, 593–595
IsBrowserHosted property, 280
IsCancel property, 192, 225
IsChecked property, 193, 633
IScrollInfo, 126
IsCumulative property, 745
IsDefault property, 192, 225
IsDefaulted property, 192
isDragging field, 437
IsDropDownOpen property, 600
IsEditable property, 211, 600–602

IsEnabled property, 170
IsExpanded property, 130
IsHyphenationEnabled property, 668
IsIndeterminate property, 213
IsInitialized property, 163
IsInitialLoadEnabled property, 592
IsLargeArc property, 419
IsLoaded property, 163
IsLocked property, 639
IsMainMenu property, 631
IsMarginValid property, 140
IsMouseDirectlyOver property, 173
IsMouseOver property, 173, 462
isMultiSelecting flag, 441
IsolatedStorageFile.GetDirectoryNames()
        method, 283
IsolatedStorageFile.GetFileNames() method,
        283
IsolatedStorageFileStream, 282
IsOpen property, 199–200
IsOptimalParagraphEnabled property, 667
IsPageCountValid property, 709
IsPressed property, 462
IsReadOnly property, 203, 600–602
IsRepeat property, 167
isResizing field, 487
IsSelected property, 128, 210
IsSelectionEnabled property, 649
IsSharedSizeScope property, 103, 617
IsSingleInstance property, 69
IsSnapToTickEnabled property, 498
IsSynchronizedWithCurrentItem, 590
IsTabStop property, 170, 869
IsTextSearchEnabled property, 601
IsThreeState property, 193
IsToolbarVisible property, 669
ISupportInitialize interface, 145, 163
IsValid property, 541
IsVisible property, 284
ItemContainerDefaultKeyStyle property, 613
ItemContainerDefaultStyleKey property, 607
ItemContainerStyle property, 571, 605–606
Items collection, 207
ItemsControl, 78
ItemsControl class, 19, 40, 551–552, 566
    classes deriving from, 598
    description of, 857
    GroupStyle property, 581
    IsSynchronizedWithCurrentItem, 590
    ItemSource property, 516
    ItemsSource property, 206
    list-based controls and, 598
    Selector class, 600
    selectors, 206
    table of properties, 516, 599
    using with data binding, 206
ItemSource property, 516

ItemsPanelTemplate property, 573
ItemsSource property, 552–555, 590, 622–624,
        631
ItemTemplate property, 552, 605, 615, 624,
        631
ItemTemplateSelector property, 631
IValueConverter objects, 556

■J
Joshi, Prajakta, 680
journal, 258, 265
journal flag, setting, 258
JournalEntry class, 265
JournalEntryName property, 266
JournalOwnership property, 255
just-in-time node creation, 627

■K
KeepAlive property, 259
Key attribute, 334
key frame animation
    audio file with two synchronized
        animations, 798
    comparing with sequence of multiple
        animations, 773
    data types and, 774
    DataTypeAnimation class, 774
    defined, 772
    discrete key frame classes, naming format,
        774
    discrete key frames, 773
    key frame class and key frame collection
        classes, 733
    KeySpline property, 774
    linear key frames, 773, 774
    naming format, 732
    pairing playback with other actions, 797
    performing linear interpolation between
        key frames, 772
    Point3DAnimationUsingKeyFrames, 773
    PointAnimationUsingKeyFrames object,
        772
    setting Storyboard.SlipBehavior property
        to Slip, 797
    spline key frames, 774
    supplying specific time offsets for
        animation, 797
    using discrete key frames in
        RadialGradientBrush example, 774
    using series of key frames, 773
    Vector3DAnimationUsingKeyFrames, 773
    working with Bézier curves, 774
Key property, 167
Keyboard class, 171
keyboard events, 163, 166
KeyboardDevice class, 170, 171
KeyboardDevice property, 170

KeyConverter, 168
KeyDown event, 161, 168
KeyEventArgs object, 167, 170
KeySpline property, 774
KeyStates property, 170
keystroke forwarding, 923

■L

Label control, 117–119, 190
Language Integrated Query. *See* LINQ
Language property, 204
LastChildFill, 88–90
layout in WPF
    ActualHeight property, 86
    ActualWidth property, 86
    adding elements through containers, 76
    adding whitespace using Margin property,
        76
    adjusting when content changes, 76
    arrange stage, 77
    arranging window components in tabular
        structure, 109
    building layout structure easy to maintain
        and enhance, 97
    Canvas, 78, 104
    containers, 75
    core layout containers, table of, 78
    creating dialog box with OK and Cancel
        buttons, 90
    creating Grid-based layout, 92
    creating modular user interfaces, 112
    creating resolution-independent, size-
        independent interfaces, 76
    DesiredSize property, 85
    displaying dynamic content, 111
    Dock property, 88
    DockPanel, 78–90
    elements growing to fit their content, 76
    elements not positioned using screen
        coordinates, 76
    flow-based layout as standard, 76
    Grid, 78, 91
    guidelines for layout containers, 76
    handling localized text, 111
    handling transition to other languages, 76
    Height property, 84
    hiding and showing individual panels, 113
    HorizontalAlignment property, 82
    InkCanvas, 79, 106
    LastChildFill, 90
    layout containers and attached properties,
        82
    layout containers as nested, 76
    layout containers as sharing and
        distributing space, 76
    layout model in .NET 1.x, 75
    layout model in .NET 2.0, 75
    layout properties, table of, 81
    Margin property, 83
    measure stage, 77
    nesting layout containers, 90
    no scrolling support in layout containers,
        77
    Padding property, 90
    Panel class, table of public properties, 77
    Panel-derived classes for arranging layout,
        78
    principles of, 76
    rudimentary support for coordinate-
        based layout, 75–76
    ScrollViewer, 77
    SizeToContent property, 86
    StackPanel, 78–90
    stages of, 77
    TabPanel, 79
    Thickness structure, 83
    ToolbarOverflowPanel, 79
    ToolbarPanel, 79
    UniformGrid, 78, 104
    use of automatic layout in most layout
        containers, 82
    using maximum and minimum size
        properties to lock control, 84
    VerticalAlignment property, 82
    VirtualizingStackPanel, 79
    Visibility property, 113
    Width property, 84
    window sizing, hard-coded vs. automatic,
        86
    Windows Forms layout model, 76
    WrapPanel, 78, 86
    WrapPanel class, 112
layout pass, 887
LayoutTransform property, 388, 701–702,
    764, 800
LCD monitors, 7
Left property, 104, 220
LIFE, 18
lifetime events, 163, 164
Light class, 816
light sources, 816
LightAngle property, 406
LightWave, 829
line caps, 381
Line class, 368
    inability to use flow content model, 377
    placing Line in Canvas, 377
    setting starting and ending points, 376
    Stroke property, 376
    understanding line caps, 381
    using negative coordinates for line, 377
    using StartLineCap and EndLineCap
        properties, 381
line joins, 381

linear interpolation
    animating property with special value of
        Double.NaN, 737
    animating two properties simultaneously,
        740
    Canvas as most common layout container
        for animation, 737
    creating additive animation by setting
        IsAdditive property, 739
    creating animation that widens button,
        736
    Duration property, 740
    From, To, and Duration properties, 736
    IsCumulative property, 745
    naming format, 732
    omitting both From and To properties, 738
    similarity of Duration property and
        TimeSpan object, 740
    using BeginAnimation() to launch more
        than one animation at time, 740
    using By property instead of To property,
        739
linear key frames, 773
LinearGradientBrush, 181, 758, 770
    creating blended fill, 390
    markup for shading rectangle diagonally,
        390
    proportional coordinate system, 391
    SpreadMethod property, 392
    using StartPoint and EndPoint properties,
        391
LineBreakBefore property, 892
LineCount property, 203
LineDown() method, 125
LineGeometry class, 411
LineHeight property, 716
LineLeft() method, 125
LineRight() method, 125
LineSegment class, 418
LineUp() method, 125
LINQ (Language Integrated Query)
    binding to LINQ expression
        converting IEnumerable(Of T)
            IEnumerable<T> to ordinary
            collection, 524–525
        deferred execution, 525–526
        overview, 523–524
    data binding support for, 11
list controls
    ComboBox control, 210
    ItemsControl class, 206
    ListBox control, 206
List element, 651–652
ListBox class, 207
ListBox control, 952
    binding expression for
        RadioButton.IsChecked property, 605

changing control template for each list
    item, 604
changing SelectionMode property to allow
    multiple selection, 606
CheckBox element, 604–606
combining text and image content in, 207
ContainerFromElement(), 210
ContentPresenter element, 605
displaying check boxes in, 606
DisplayMemberPath property, 605
IsSelected property, 210
ItemContainerStyle property, 605–606
Items collection, 207
ItemTemplate property, 605
ListBoxItem.Control template, 606
manually placing items in list, 210
modifying ListBoxItem.Template property,
    605
nesting arbitrary elements inside list box
    items, 208
RadioButton element, 604–606
RemovedItems property, 209
retrieving ListBoxItem wrapper for specific
    object, 210
Selected event, 210
SelectedItem property, 209
SelectedItems property, 600
SelectionChanged event, 209–210
SelectionMode property, 600
setting RadioButton.Focusable property,
    605
Unselected event, 210
ListBoxChrome class, 454
ListBoxChrome decorator, 133
ListBoxItem elements, 207
ListBox.ItemsPanel property, 604
ListCollectionView, 574, 580, 588
ListSelectionJournalEntry callback, 267
ListView class
    ControlTemplate, 613
    creating custom view, 613
    creating customizable multicolumned
        lists, 607
    creating grid that can switch views, 614
    DataTemplate, 613
    DefaultStyleKey property, 613
    function of, 607
    ItemContainerDefaultKeyStyle property,
        613
    ResourceKey, 613
    separating ListView control from View
        objects, 607
    switching between multiple views with
        same list, 607
    TileView class, 615
    View property, 607
    View property, advantages of, 607

ListView class *(continued)*
  ViewBase class, 607
ListView control
  adding properties to view classes, 620
  adding Setter to replace ControlTemplate, 620
  defining view objects in Windows.Resources collection, 618
  GridView class, 618
  ImageDetailView object, 619
  ImageView object, 619
  passing information to view, 620
  setting ListView.View property, 618
  using custom view, 618
literals, 879
Load() method, 784
LoadAsync() method, 784
LoadCompleted event, 784
LoadComponent() method, 28
Loaded event, 163–164, 238
LoadedBehavior property, 789
LoadFile() method, 64
LocalizabilityAttribute, 326
localization
  adding <PropertyGroup> element to .csproj file, 325
  adding specialized Uid attribute to elements, 326
  adding support for more than one culture to application, 325
  building localizable user interfaces, 324
  building satellite assembly, 331
  culture names and their two-part identifiers, 325
  CultureInfo class, 331
  CurrentUICulture property, 323
  extracting localizable content, 327
  global assembly cache (GAC), 326
  Global Sans Serif, 324
  Global Serif, 324
  Global User Interface, 324
  LocalizabilityAttribute, 326
  localizing FontFamily property in user interface, 324
  managing localization process, 326
  placing localized BAML resources in satellite assemblies, 324
  preparing application for, 325
  preparing markup elements for, 326
  probing, 324
  setting FlowDirection property for right-to-left layouts, 324
  using locbaml.exe command-line tool, 327
  using msbuild.exe to generate Uid attributes, 327
  XAML file as unit of localization, 323

localized text, 111
LocalPrintServer class, 721
LocationChanged event, 218
locbaml.exe
  building satellite assembly, 331
  compiling by hand, 327
  /cul: parameter, 331
  /generate parameter, 331
  /parse parameter, 327
  table of localizable properties, 329
  /trans: parameter, 331
logical resources, 333
logical scrolling, 126
logical tree, 446, 448
LogicalTreeHelper class, 51, 448
Long Date data types, 529
lookless controls, 20
  adding TemplatePart attribute to control declaration, 876
  calling OverrideMetadata() method, 871
  changing color picker into lookless control, 871
  checking for correct type of element, 875
  code for binding SolidColorBrush, 875
  connecting data binding expression using OnApplyTemplate(), 875
  converting ordinary markup into control template, 872
  creating, 870
  creating different styles for different theme settings, 871
  creating template for color picker, 872
  DefaultStyleKeyProperty, 871
  defined, 451, 871
  ElementName property, 872
  generic.xaml resource dictionary, 871
  markup structure for ColorPicker.xaml, 872
  providing descriptive names for element names, 874
  RelativeSource property, 872
  streamlining color picker control template, 874
  TemplateBinding, 872–873
  using TargetType attribute, 872
LostFocus event, 164
LostFocus update mode, 502
LostMouseCapture event, 174

■M

Mad Libs game, creating, 665
Main() method, 58–61
MainWindow property, 58, 222
manifests, 73
margins, 83
MarkerStyle property, 651
markup extensions, 35

MarshalByRefObject attribute, 949
Mask property, 881
MaskCompleted property, 882
masked edit controls
    adding read-only property to evaluate
        mask and text, 882
    advantages of, 879
    avoiding canonicalization errors, 879
    calling OverrideMetadata property on
        TextProperty, 886
    calling SkipToEditableCharacter(), 882
    guidelines for creating custom masked
        control, 881
    handling key events, 883
    handling special extended keys, 884
    handling text cut-and-paste problems, 886
    having MaskChanged() callback trigger
        Text property, 887
    implementing WPF masked text box, 881
    improving MaskedTextBox, 885
    literals, 879
    mask characters, table of, 880
    mask syntax, 879
    masked text box, defined, 879
    OnPreviewKeyDown(), 884
    OnPreviewTextInput event, 883
    overriding OnEvent() method, 883
    phone number control, 879
    placeholders, 879
    PreviewKeyDown event, 883
    PreviewTextInput event, 883
    prompt character, 880
    using MaskedTextProvider, 880
    writing property change callback to
        update text, 882
MaskedTextBox, 906
    GetMaskProvider(), 882
    improving, 885
    Mask property, 881
    RefreshText(), 882
    ValidatingType property, 917
MaskedTextProvider
    FindEditPositionFrom(), 883
    MaskCompleted property, 882
    Set(), 886
    ToDisplayString(), 881
    tracking user's current position in input
        string, 881
MaskedTextProvider class, 879
Material class, 815
Material property, 815
MatrixCamera, 819
MaxLength property, 202, 205
MaxLines property, 203
Maya, 829
MDI (multiple document interface), 224
MDI windows, 906

Measure() method, 702, 888
measure stage, 77
MeasureCore() method, 888
MeasureOverride() method, 78, 891
    allowing child to take all space it wants,
        889
    basic structure of, 888
    calling Measure() method of each child,
        888
    DesiredSize property, 888
    determining how much space each child
        wants, 888
    passing Size object with value of
        Double.PositiveInfinity, 889
Media Integration Layer (MIL), 16
MediaClock class, 792
MediaCommands class, 294
MediaElement class, 323, 909
    adding MediaElement tag for playing
        sound, 789
    Balance property, 796
    Clock property, 792
    controlling additional playback details,
        795
    controlling audio declaratively through
        XAML markup, 791
    controlling audio playback
        programmatically, 789
    creating video-reflection effect, code
        example, 800
    error handling, 791
    ErrorException property, 791
    LayoutTransform property, 800
    LoadedBehavior property, 789
    Manual mode, 796
    MediaState enumeration, 789
    Pause() method, 790
    placement of, for audio and video, 789
    Play() method, 790
    playing audio with triggers, 791
    playing multiple audio files, code
        example, 794
    playing video, 799
    Position property, 796
    RenderTransform property, 800
    RenderTransformOrigin property, 800
    requirement for Windows Media Player
        version 10 or later, 787
    setting Clipping property, 800
    setting Opacity property, 800
    setting Position to move through audio
        file, 790
    SpeedRatio property, 796
    Stop() method, 790
    Stretch property, 799
    StretchDirection property, 799
    support for WMV, MPEG, and AVI files, 799

MediaElement class *(continued)*
  synchronizing animation with audio or
    video file, 797
  types of video effects, 800
  using separate ResumeStoryboard action
    after pausing playback, 793
  using single Storyboard to control audio
    playback, 792
  Volume property, 796
MediaFailed event, 788
MediaOpened event, 788
MediaPlayer class, 909
  creating Window.Unloaded event handler
    to call Close(), 788
  lack of exception handling code, 788
  MediaFailed event, 788
  MediaOpened event, 788
  no option for synchronous playback, 787
  Open(), 787
  Play(), 787
  playing multiple audio files, 795
  requirement for Windows Media Player
    version 10 or later, 787
  supplying location of audio file as URI,
    788
  table of useful methods, properties, and
    events, 788
MediaState enumeration, 789
MediaTimeline class, 742, 791
MemoryStream, 686
Menu class
  creating scrollable sidebar menu, 631
  DisplayMemberPath property, 631
  dividing menus into groups of related
    commands, 635
  example of Separator that defines text
    title, 635
  IsMainMenu property, 631
  ItemsSource property, 631
  ItemTemplate property, 631
  ItemTemplateSelector property, 631
  Separator as not content control, 636
  using menu separators, 635
MenuItem class
  Command property, 633
  CommandParameter property, 633
  CommandTarget property, 633
  creating rudimentary menu structure, 632
  displaying check mark next to menu item,
    633
  handling Click event, 633
  having non-MenuItem objects inside
    Menu or MenuItem, 632
  Icon property, 633
  including keyboard shortcuts, 632
  InputGestureText property, 633
  IsChecked property, 633

Separator objects, 632
  setting shortcut text for menu item, 633
  showing thumbnail icon, 633
  StaysOpenOnClick property, 633
MergedDictionaries collection, 465, 472
MergedDictionaries property, 343
mesh, 813
MeshGeometry class, 834
MeshGeometry3D class
  Normals property, 813–814
  Positions property, 813–814
  table of properties, 813
  TextureCoordinates property, 813–815
  TriangleIndices property, 813–814
MeshHit property, 846
MessageBeep Win32 API, 786
MessageBox class, 226
MessageBoxButton enumeration, 226
MessageBoxImage enumeration, 226
Microsoft Application Updater Starter Block,
  968
Microsoft Expression Blend, 21
Microsoft Installer (MSI), 965
Microsoft Money, 246
Microsoft .NET 2.0 Framework Configuration
  Tool, 280
Microsoft Office 2007, 682
Microsoft Speech Software Development Kit,
  806
Microsoft Word, 68, 677
Microsoft XPS (XML Paper Specification), 24,
  322, 643, 681, 682
Microsoft.Win32 namespace, 226, 909
Microsoft.Windows.Themes, 408, 454
MIL (Media Integration Layer), 16
milcore.dll, 16
MinLines property, 203
Miter line join, 381
mnemonics, 117, 190, 923
modal windows, 218
Mode property, 495
Model3D class, 839
Model3DGroup class, 830, 831
modeless windows, 218
ModelUIElement3D class, 845–849
ModelVisual3D class, 839, 845, 851
modifier keys, 170
Money, Microsoft, 246
Mouse class, 174
mouse cursors, 189
mouse events, 163
  AllowDrop property, 176
  ButtonState event, 173
  capturing mouse by calling
    Mouse.Capture(), 174
  ClickCount event, 173
  creating drag-and-drop source, 176

direct events, defined, 171
DoDragDrop(), 176
drag-and-drop operations, 174
DragDrop class, 175
DragEnter event, 176
dragging-and-dropping into other
    applications, 176
GetPosition(), 172
getting mouse coordinates, 172
IsMouseDirectlyOver property, 173
IsMouseOver property, 173
losing mouse capture, 174
LostMouseCapture event, 174
Mouse class, 174
mouse click events for all elements, 173
MouseButton event, 173
MouseButtonEventArgs object, 173
MouseDoubleClick event, 173
MouseEnter event, 171
MouseLeave event, 171
MouseMove event, 172
PreviewMouseDoubleClick event, 173
PreviewMouseMove event, 172
MouseButton event, 173
MouseButtonEventArgs object, 157, 173, 848
Mouse.Capture() method, 174
MouseDoubleClick event, 173, 857
MouseDown event, 154
MouseEnter event, 154, 171, 356
MouseEventArgs object, 151, 172
MouseLeave event, 171, 356, 765
MouseLeftButtonDown event, 232
MouseMove event, 172
MouseUp event, 151
MouseUp() method, 152
msbuild.exe, 327
MSDN Magazine, 490
MSI (Microsoft Installer), 965
MultiBinding, 535
multiple document interface (MDI), 224
Multiselect property, 226
multitargeting, 12
multithreading
    BackgroundWorker component, 931
    BeginInvoke(), 929–930
    context, 927
    CurrentDispatcher property, 928
    defined, 927
    dispatcher, 928
    DispatcherObject class, 928
    DispatcherOperation object, 930
    DispatcherPriority, 930
    dual-core CPUs, 927
    Invoke(), 931
    performing asynchronous operations, 931
    performing time-consuming background
        operation, 930

single-threaded apartment model, 928
    System.Threading.Thread, 931
    thread affinity, 928
    thread rental, 927
    VerifyAccess(), 929
    writing good multithreading code, 931
MultiTrigger, 363
MustInherit abstract classes, 941
MustInherit abstract view class, 948
mutex, defined, 68

■N
Name attribute, 29
Name property, 292, 865
namespaces
    core WPF namespace, 27
    core XAML namespace, 27
    declaring in XML, 26
    defining in XAML, 26
    .NET and, 27
    System.Windows.Shapes, 122
    using namespace prefixes, 45
    in WPF, 27
    XML namespaces as URIs, 27
Narrator screen reader, 804
native resolution, 7
Navigate() method, 261, 262
NavigateUri property, 250, 657
NavigationCommands class, 294
NavigationFailed event, 251
NavigationService class
    AddBackEntry(), 264–265
    AddBackReference(), 267–269
    adding custom items to journal, 265
    Application class, 262
    building linear navigation-based
        application, 263
    CanGoBack property, 262–264
    CanGoForward property, 262
    Content property, 266
    creating page object manually, 261
    ExtraData property, 262
    GetContentState(), 267–269
    GoBack(), 262
    GoForward(), 262
    Handled property, 262
    how WPF navigation occurs, 262
    InitializeComponent(), 261
    IProvideCustomContentState interface,
        267–269
    JournalEntryName property, 266
    ListSelectionJournalEntry callback, 267
    methods for controlling navigation stack,
        264
    Navigate(), 261–262
    navigating to page based on its URI, 261
    RemoveBackEntry(), 264

NavigationService class *(continued)*
  Replay(), 266–268
  ReplayListChange delegate, 267
  returning information from page, 270
  SourceItems property, 267
  StopLoading(), 261
  suppressing navigation events, 262
  table of navigation events, 262
  TargetItems property, 267
  using Refresh() to reload page, 261
  WPF navigation as asynchronous, 261
NavigationUIVisibility property, 254–255
NavigationWindow class
  creating page-based application with, 247
  forward and back buttons, 250
NearPlaneDistance property, 822
.NET
  Code DOM model, 52
  global assembly cache (GAC), 326
  ildasm, 319
  mapping .NET namespace to XML
      namespace, 44
  namespaces in, 27
  p/invoke, 233–235
  probing, 324
  replacing .NET properties with
      dependency properties, 137
  ResourceManager class, 320
  ResourceSet class, 320
  satellite assemblies, 324
  type converters, 32
  window ownership, 224
  XML capabilities in, 594
.NET 1.x
  anchoring, 75
  docking, 75
  fixed controls using hard-coded
      coordinates, 75
  lack of bi-pane proportional resizing, 75
  layout system as fairly primitive, 75
.NET 2.0, 1
  BackgroundWorker component, 931
  coordinate-based layout, 76
  enhancing Button and Label classes, 123
  flow-based layout panels, 76
  FlowLayoutPanel, 75
  SoundPlayer class, 783
  System.Drawing namespace, 341
  System.Media.SystemSounds class, 786
  TableLayoutPanel, 75
.NET 2.0 Framework Configuration Tool, 280
.NET 3.0
  XBAPs and, 273
  XPS document support, 725
.NET Framework 3.0, 11
no fixed control appearance, 20
no-argument constructors, 45

Noise property, 407
nonclient area, defined, 215
nonrectangular windows
  adding sizing grip to shaped window, 233
  comparing background-based and shape-
      drawing approaches, 231
  creating shaped window with rounded
      Border element, 228
  creating simple transparent window, 228
  creating transparent window with shaped
      content, 231
  detecting mouse movements over edges of
      window, 233
  Expression Blend design tool, 227
  initiating window dragging mode by
      calling Window.DragMove(), 232
  moving shaped windows, 232
  placing Rectangle that allows right-side
      window resizing, 233
  placing sizing grip correctly, 233
  procedure for creating shaped window,
      227
  providing background art, 227
  removing standard window appearance
      (window chrome), 227
  resizing shaped windows, 233
  resizing window manually by setting its
      Width property, 233
  setting Window.ResizeMode property, 233
  using Path element to create background,
      231
Nonzero fill rule, 380
normal
  defined, 825
  guidelines for choosing right normals, 827
  problem of sharing Position points and
      sharing normals, 827
  that's perpendicular to triangle's surface,
      calculating, 828
  understanding, 825
Normals property, 813–814, 828
NotifyIcon class, 909
NotifyOnValidationError property, 538, 543
null markup extension, 193
NullExtension, 35

■O
object resources
  accessing resources in code, 339
  adding resources programmatically, 340
  advantages of, 333
  application resources, 340
  ComponentResourceKey, 345
  creating resource dictionary, 342
  declarative resources, 333
  defined, 317
  defining image brush as resource, 334

defining resources at window level, 333
FrameworkElement.FindResource(), 340
Freezable class, 337
generic.xaml file, code example, 346
hierarchy of resources, 335
ImageSource property, 346
Key attribute, 334
logical resources, 333
nonshared resources, reasons for using, 339
resource keys, 342
ResourceDictionary class, 333
ResourceKey property, 336
resources collection, 333
Resources property, 333
reusing resource names, 336
sharing resources among assemblies, 344
static vs. dynamic resources, 335–338
system resources, 341
TryFindResource(), 340
using markup extension, 335
using .NET object for resource, 335
using Shared attribute to turn off sharing, 339
object-based drawing, 20
ObjectDataProvider, 591
error handling, 592
features of, 592
getting information from another class in application, 592
IsAsynchronous property, 593
IsInitialLoadEnabled property, 592
retrieving data but not updating it, 592
support for asynchronous data querying, 593
ObservableCollection, 574
ObservableCollection class, 521
Office 2007, 682
OnApplyTemplate() method, 875
OnColorChanged() method, 862–863
OnColorRGBChanged() method, 862
OnEvent() method, 883
OneWayToSource option, 500
OnPreviewKeyDown() method, 884
OnPreviewTextInput event, 883
OnPropertyChanged() method, 515
OnPropertyChangedCallback() method, 147
OnRender() method, 119, 856, 896, 897
OnReturn() method, 271
OnStartup() method, 69
OnStartupNextInstance() method, 69
opacity masks, 758
Opacity property, 182, 390, 401, 407, 433, 800
OpacityMask property, 401, 402
Open() method, 787
OpenFileDialog class, 226, 533
OpenGL, 809

OpenType, 185–187
Orientation property, 638
OrthographicCamera class, 819
OSVersion property, 235
OuterGlowBitmapEffect class, 407
OverflowMode property, 638
OverrideCursor property, 189
OverrideMetadata() method, 871
owned windows, 224
OwnedWindows property, 224
Owner property, 224
owner-drawn controls, 20
OwnerType property, 292

■**P**

pack URIs, 257, 321
PackageStore class, 694
Padding property, 90, 121, 865
Page class
comparison to PageFunction class, 270
comparison to Window class, 248
table of properties, 248
using navigation to show different page, 249
Page element, 25
page functions, 259
page-based navigation
accessing WPF navigation service, 261
browser applications (XBAPs) and, 256
controlling navigation of parent frame only, 255
creating dependency property in page class, 259
creating nested page, 254
creating new NavigationWindow object as container, 247
creating page-based application with NavigationWindow, 247
creating XBAP, 256
differences between page and window, 248
DispatcherUnhandledException event, 251
embedding page inside window, 252
fragment navigation, 252
GetNavigationService(), 261
handling back button, 255
handling WebException, 251
hosting pages
in another container, 246
in another page, 254
in frame, 252
in Web browser, 256
Hyperlink class, 250
hyperlinks as inline flow elements, 249
maintaining state of previously visited pages, 258

page-based navigation *(continued)*
   Microsoft Money and its weblike interface, 246
   NavigationFailed event, 251
   NavigationUIVisibility property, 254–255
   operation of WPF page history, 258
   Page class, table of properties, 248
   programmatic navigation, 261
   RequestNavigate event, 250
   returning information from page, 270
   setting JournalOwnership property of embedded frame, 255
   ShowsNavigationUI property, 250
   stand-alone Windows applications, 256
   StartupUri property, 256
   understanding, 245
   understanding XAML URIs, 257
   using hyperlinks to navigate to websites, 251
   using KeepAlive property, 259
   using navigation to show different page, 249
   using several frames in single window, 253
   web model of application design, 245
   WindowTitle property, 250
PageCount property, 709
PageDown() method, 125
PageFunction class
   comparison to Page class, 270
   creating PageFunction in Visual Studio, 270
   OnReturn() method, 271
   RemoveFromJournal property, 272
   returning SelectedProduct object to calling page, 270
   using PageFunction, 271
PageFunction classes, 271
PageHeight property, 706
Page.Initialized event, 261
PageLeft() method, 125
Page.Loaded event, 261
PagePadding property, 706
PageRangeSelection property, 720
PageRight() method, 125
Pages text box, 720
PageSetupDialog class, 909
PageSize property, 709, 715
PageUp() method, 125
PageWidth property, 706
PaginateData() method, 715–716
Panel class, 19, 39–40, 896
   description of, 857
   IsItemsHost, 78
   layout containers as deriving from, 118
   overriding MeasureOverride() and ArrangeOverride(), 78
   public properties, table of, 77

panel templates, 453
<Paragraph> element, 650, 651, 692
parameterized constructors, 45
Parse() method, 529
partial classes, 28, 51
Password property, 202
PasswordBox control, 202, 205, 206
PasswordChanged property, 205
PasswordChar property, 147, 205
Path class, 368
   Data property, 409
   differentiating Geometry and Path objects, 410
   GetFileName(), 264
   switching from separate shapes to distinct geometries, 428
Path element, 231
Path property, 493
path-based animation
   animating position-related properties, 775
   Bézier curves in, 777
   DoubleAnimationUsingPath, 777
   moving image along path, 776
   naming format, 733
   PointAnimationUsingPath class, 777
   running at continuous speed, 778
   using PathGeometry object to set property, 775
PathFigure class, 417
PathGeometry class, 417, 733, 775
PathSegment class, 417
Pause() method, 790
Pen class, 426
Percentage data type, 529
PerspectiveCamera class, 819, 822
Petzold, Charles, 770
phone number control, 879
p/invoke, 233–235
pipelines, add-in, 941–946
   folder structure, 943–944
   how works, 941–943
   overview, 941
   preparing solution, 944–946
PipelineSegments.store file, 951
pixel shaders, defined, 4
pixel snapping, 384
placeholders, 879
Placement property, 197, 283
PlacementTarget property, 198
Play() method, 784–790
PlayLooping() method, 784
PlaySync() method, 784–785
plug-ins. *See* add-ins
Point property, 418
Point3DAnimationUsingKeyFrames, 773
PointAnimation class, 769
PointAnimationUsingPath class, 777

PointLight class, 818
Points property, 378
Polygon class, 368
    determining fill areas in complex
        Polygons, 379
    FillRule property, 379
    markup for drawing star, 381
    setting FillRule to NonZero, 380
    using Fill brush to fill interior shape, 379
Polyline class, 368
    drawing sequence of connected straight
        lines, 378
    Points property, 378
    understanding line caps, 381
    using StartLineCap and EndLineCap
        properties, 381
Pop() method, 433, 711
Popup control
    accepting focus, 200
    AllowsTransparency property, 200, 283
    characteristics of, 200
    Child property, 200
    defining in XAML, 200
    IsOpen property, 200
    IsVisible property, 284
    opening secondary window in XBAP, 283
    Placement property, 283
    PopupAnimation property, 200, 283
    StaysOpen property, 200, 283
PopupAnimation property, 200, 283
Position property, 796
Positions property, 813–814
PresentationCore.dll, 16
PresentationFramework.Aero.dll assembly,
    454
PresentationFramework.dll assembly, 16,
    454–455
PresentationFramework.Luna.dll assembly,
    454
PresentationFramework.Royale.dll assembly,
    454
PreviewExecuted event, 297, 313
PreviewKeyDown event, 154, 161, 168, 883
PreviewMouseDoubleClick event, 173, 857
PreviewMouseMove event, 172
PreviewTextInput event, 168, 883
PriceConverter class, 530
primary interop assembly, 919
primitives, 5
Print dialog box, 697
Print() method, 673
PrintableAreaHeight property, 702
PrintableAreaWidth property, 702
PrintDialog class, 226
    Arrange(), 702
    calling ShowDialog(), 699

checking PageRangeSelection property,
    720
creating PrintDialog object, 699
DocumentPage class, 705
DocumentPaginator class, 697, 705–708
FlowDocument class, 697, 706
handling of modal windows, 700
hiding element by changing its Visibility
    property, 701
inability to print on background thread,
    700
limitations of, 699
maintaining and reusing your printer
    settings, 720
managing printer settings and jobs, 719
manipulating pages in document
    printout, 708
margin and header positions, 710
Measure(), 702
Print dialog box, 697
PrintableAreaHeight property, 702
PrintableAreaWidth property, 702
PrintDocument(), 697, 704, 714
printing content of FlowDocument, 704
printing document with its associated
    annotations, 707
printing elements without showing them,
    703
printing range of pages, 720
printing two-column printout with
    margin, 706
PrintQueue property, 720
PrintTicket property, 720
PrintVisual(), 697, 711
storing PrintDialog as member variable,
    720
submitting print job, 697
System.Printing.PrintQueue object, 720
Transform object and inflexible printouts,
    701
triggering printout, 697
using Pages text box, 720
Win32PrintDialog, 700
Windows print queue, 699
XpsDocument class, 697
XpsDocumentWriter class, 700
PrintDocument() method, 697, 704, 714
printing
    browsing and managing jobs in print
        queue, 722
    centering block of formatted text on page,
        712
    constructing custom printout using
        visual-layer classes, 710
    creating multipage printout, 714
    launching printout without user
        intervention, 721

printing *(continued)*
  managing local or remote print queues, 721
  managing printer settings and jobs, 719
  pausing PrintQueue or print job, 724
  PrintDialog class, 697
  separating content into pages, 714
  setting column positions, 717
  System.Printing namespace, 697, 724
  System.Windows.Controls namespace, 697
  Windows print queue, 699
PrintPreviewDialog class, 909
PrintQueue class, 721, 723
PrintQueue property, 720
PrintServer class, 722
PrintSystemJobInfo class, 721–723
PrintTicket class, 720
PrintTicket property, 720
PrintVisual() method, 698, 699, 711
priority binding, 594
probing, 324
ProcessImageBytes() method, 947–952, 959, 961
Product object, 510
ProductImagePath converter, 611
ProgressBar control, 213, 956
ProgressChanged event, 937
prompt character, 880
PromptBuilder class, 805, 806
PromptEmphasis enumeration, 805
PromptRate value, 805
PromptVolume value, 805
properties
  attached, 36
  complex, 32
  Content, 40
  ContentProperty attribute, 39
  dependency properties, 36
  distinguishing from other types of nested content, 33
  NullExtension, 35
  property-element syntax, 33
  ProvideValue(), 35
  setting complex property, 33
  setting property value dynamically, 35
  similarity of attached properties to extender providers, 37
  simple, and type converters, 31
  StaticExtension, 35
  supporting more than one type of collection, 38
  System.Windows.Markup.MarkupExtension, 35
  Text, 40
  TypeExtension, 35
  using markup extension, 35

property mapping, 923
property metadata, 141
property resolution system, 731–739
property translators, 923
property value inheritance, 186, 349
property wrapper, 140
property-based animation, 731
PropertyChanged event, 514
PropertyChanged update mode, 502
PropertyChangedCallback, 141–149
property-element syntax, 33
PropertyGrid, 906
<PropertyGroup> element, 325
ProvideValue() method, 35
public key token, 322
Publish Now button, 977
Publish Options dialog box, 980
Publish Wizard button, 977
PushOpacity() method, 433

■Q

quartz.dll library, 783
Quick Tabs view (IE 7), 401

■R

RadialGradientBrush, 393, 394, 769–770, 898
RadioButton control, 119, 194
RadioButton element, 604–606
RadioButton.Focusable property, 605
RadiusX property, 371, 393, 411
RadiusY property, 371, 393, 411
RaiseEvent() method, 150, 863
RangeBase class
  table of properties, 211–212
  Value property, 211, 875
  ValueChanged event, 211
range-based controls
  ProgressBar control, 213
  ScrollBar control, 211
  Slider control, 212
RayMeshGeometry3DHitTestResult, 846
RCWs (runtime callable wrappers), 919
ReasonSessionEnding property, 61
RecognizesAccessKey property, 459
Rectangle class, 368, 370, 371, 459
RectangleGeometry class, 411
reflection, 455, 940
Reflector, 177
  using Reflector plug-in, 431
  viewing embedded resources, 319
Refresh() method, 261
RefreshText() method, 882
Register() method, 139
RegisterAttached() method, 146, 892
RegisterClassCommandBinding() method, 868
RegisterClassHandler() method, 869

RegisterEvent() method, 154
RegisterRoutedEvent() method, 150
RelativeSource property, 503–504, 872
RelativeSourceMode enumeration, 505
Relief property, 406
RemoveBackEntry() method, 264
RemovedItems property, 209
RemoveFromJournal property, 272
RemoveHandler() method, 150
RemoveSignature() method, 682
RenderCapability class, 4
RenderCapability.Tier property, 3–4
RenderDefaulted property, 452
rendering artifacts (3-D), 822
RenderOpen() method, 431–433, 711, 897
RenderPressed property, 452
RenderTransform property, 386, 701–702, 764, 800
RenderTransformOrigin property, 387, 765, 800
RepeatBehavior property, 745
RepeatButton class, 193, 478
Replay() method, 266–268
ReplayListChange delegate, 267
ReportProgress() method, 937, 956–959
Requery command, 307
RequerySuggested event, 303
RequestNavigate event, 250
requireAdministrator application, 73
ResizeBehavior property, 98
ResizeDirection property, 98
ResizeGrip element, 454
ResizeMode property, 233, 484
resizeType field, 487
resolution independence, 6, 20
ResolvedAnchor property, 693
resource dictionaries
    adding resource dictionary in Visual Studio, 465
    creating, 342
    generic.xaml, 345
    MergedDictionaries property, 343
    merging individual dictionaries into generic.xaml file, 345
    merging it into application's resource collection, 343
    naming correctly, 345
    reasons for using, 344
    ResourceDictionary object, 343
    setting application's Build Action, 342
    using in other applications, 346
ResourceDictionary class, 333, 473
ResourceDictionary object, 343
ResourceId, 615
ResourceKey property, 336, 613
ResourceManager class, 320, 471

resources
    accessing in code, 339
    adding programmatically, 340
    application resources, 340
    assembly resources, defined, 317
    benefits of, 349
    binary resources, 317
    ComponentResourceKey, 345
    creating resource dictionary, 342
    defining, 22
    FrameworkElement.FindResource(), 340
    generic.xaml file, code example, 346
    object resources, defined, 317
    resource keys, 342
    sharing resources among assemblies, 344
    static vs. dynamic, 337
    storing error message strings as resources, 332
    system resources, 341
    TryFindResource(), 340
Resources property, 333
Resources tab, Project Properties window, 318
ResourceSet class, 320
RestoreBounds property, 221
retained graphics model, 730
RichTextBox control
    building simple rich text editor, 678
    declaring FlowDocument, 674
    detecting word breaks and grabbing word, code example, 680
    displaying markup for current flow document, 676
    FlowDocument, 202
    formatting selected text, 678
    loading and saving files in different formats, 674–675
    not using embedded controls inside of, 681
    placing interactive controls inside, 11
    RTF content and, 674
    saving document using TextRange object, 676
    Section element, 677
    setting MaxLength property, 202
    sluggish performance as drawback, 674
    storing content as FlowDocument object, 674
    TextSelection class, 678
    unsupported features, 674
    using XAML format to save document, 677
    using XamlReader.Load(), 674
Right property, 105
Roeder, Lutz, 177
RotateTransform class, 386, 387, 763–767
RotateTransform3D, 840, 852
Round line join, 381

routed events, 18
  defined, 137
  defining and adding, 862
  providing event bubbling and tunneling, 863
RoutedCommand class, 292, 301–303
RoutedEventArgs class, 151, 155, 297
RoutedEventArgs.Handled property, 158
RoutedEventHandler, 863
RoutedPropertyChangedEventHandler, 863
RoutedUICommand class, 292, 293
Row property, 92
RowDefinition element, 92
RowDefinition object, 94
RowFilter property, 579
RowSpan property, 96, 654
rowsPerPage field, 716
RowStateFilter property, 579
Run element, 201, 650, 664
Run() method, 58, 61
<Run> element, 692
runtime callable wrappers (RCWs), 919
RuntimeNameProperty attribute, 29
RunWorkerCompleted event, 936, 939

■S

satellite assemblies, 324
SaveFileDialog class, 226
SaveSize() method, 222
SaveTo() method, 720
ScaleTransform, 763, 767
ScaleTransform3D, 838
scheme, 257
scope, 308
ScreenSpaceLines3D class, 822
scRGB standard, 181
ScrollBar class, 144, 480
ScrollBar control, 211
ScrollBar element, 454
ScrollBarVisibility enumeration, 125
ScrollChrome class, 454
ScrollToXxx() method, 125
ScrollViewer, 77, 119
  CanContentScroll property, 126
  combining with Expander, 132
  custom scrolling, 126
  Grid layout container and, 133
  HorizontalScrollBarVisibility property, 125
  IScrollInfo, 126
  ScrollBarVisibility enumeration, 125
  scrolling content programmatically, 125
  using ScrollToXxx() methods, 125
  VerticalScrollBarVisibility property, 125
  wrapping layout container in, 124
Section element, 655, 677
<Section> element, 692
SecureString object, 202, 205, 206

Selected event, 210
SelectedIndex property, 600
SelectedItem property, 209, 600
SelectedItemChanged event, 600
SelectedItems property, 600
SelectedProduct object, 270
SelectedText property, 204
SelectedValue property, 600
selectedVisual field, 437
SelectionBoxItemTemplate property, 603
SelectionChanged event, 204, 209–210, 600
SelectionEnd property, 212
SelectionLength property, 204
SelectionMode property, 207, 600
selectionSquareTopLeft field, 441
SelectionStart property, 204, 212
Selector class, 600, 857
selectors, 206
SelectStyle() method, 571
SelectTemplate() method, 560–561
Separator objects, 632
SetContent() method, 67
SetProperty() method, 891
SetSize() method, 222
SetSpeedRatio() method, 757
Setter objects, 351
Setter.TargetName property, 354, 470
Setup Project template, 965
SetValue() method, 140, 147, 861
SetZIndex() method, 106
ShadowDepth property, 407
Shape class, 19
  angling shape, 386
  animating shape, 386
  Bevel line join, 381
  choosing layout containers for shapes, 373
  comparing RenderTransform and LayoutTransform, 389
  creating ellipse, 370
  creating rectangle, 370
  drawing dashed lines, 382
  Ellipse class, 368
  Geometry object, 369
  LayoutTransform property, 388
  Line class, 368, 376
  markup for rotating square, 386
  Miter line join, 381
  not using antialiasing for specific shape, 384
  Path class, 368, 409
  pixel snapping, 384
  placing certain shapes in autosized container, 376
  Polygon class, 368, 379
  Polyline class, 368, 378
  Rectangle class, 368
  RenderTransformOrigin property, 387

repeating shape, 386
resizing to compensate for different
    system DPI settings, 376
Round line join, 381
setting line joins, 381
setting shape's center point, 387
setting SnapsToDevicePixels property of
    UIElement, 384
shape resizing and border thickness, 375
shapes (primitives) as elements, 367
Stretch property, table of enumeration
    values, 372
StretchDirection property, 375
StrokeDashArray property, 382
StrokeDashCap, 383
StrokeDashOffset property, 383
StrokeLineJoin property, 381
StrokeMiterLimit, 381
supplying brush for Stroke or Fill property,
    370
table of properties, 368
Transform class, 385
Transform object, 369
using Canvas to control shape placement
    and overlap, 373
using Viewbox element to resize shapes
    proportionally, 374
Shared attribute, 339
shared size groups, 101
SharedSizeGroup property, 103, 554
Short Date data type, 529
Show() method, 218, 226
ShowDialog() method, 218, 225, 699
ShowDocument() method, 70
ShowGridLines property, 92
ShowsNavigationUI property, 250
ShowsPreview property, 99
Shutdown() method, 61
ShutdownMode property, 60
sieve of Eratosthenes, 932
SignDigitally() method, 682
Silverlight, 14, 24, 287
SimpleStyles project, 488
SingleCriteriaHighlightTemplateSelector
    class, 562–564, 581
SingleInstanceApplicationWrapper class, 70
SingleInstanceApplicationWrapper.On-
    StartupNextInstance() method, 72
single-thread affinity (STA), 18
Size property, 418, 705
SizeToContent property, 86, 132, 324
SkipToEditableCharacter() method, 882
Slider control, 960
    IsSnapToTickEnabled property, 498
    RangeBase class, table of properties, 212
    SelectionEnd property, 212
    SelectionStart property, 212

setting position selection range, 212
    TickFrequency property, 498
    Ticks collection, 212
    uses for, 212
    using in color picker, 859
Smoothness property, 406
snapshot-and-replace behavior, 752
SnapsToDevicePixels property, 384, 455, 568
Snoop utility, 451
SolidColorBrush, 180
Solution Explorer, 58, 323
Sort property, 579
SortDescription objects, 580
SortDescriptions property, 586
Sound icon, 787
SoundLocation property, 784
SoundPlayer class, 909
    embedding sound files into compiled
        assembly as binary resource, 785
    limitations of, 783
    Load(), 784
    LoadAsync(), 784
    LoadCompleted event, 784
    loading and playing sound
        asynchronously, 785
    no queueing feature for playing multiple
        audio snippets, 785
    Play(), 784–785
    PlayLooping(), 784
    PlaySync(), 784–785
    procedure for playing sound, 784
    SoundLocation property, 784
    Stream property, 784
    WAV audio files, 783
SoundPlayerAction class, 784, 786
Sounds and Audio Devices icon, 787
Source property, 252, 473, 503–504, 586, 595,
    786, 791
SourceItems property, 267
SourceName property, 792
Span.Tag property, 664
Speak() method, 804
SpecularMaterial class, 832
SpecularPower property, 832
speech recognition, 806, 807
Speech Recognition Grammar Specification
    (SRGS), 807, 808
Speech Software Development Kit, Microsoft,
    806
speech synthesis, 804
SpeechDetected event, 807
SpeechHypothesized event, 807
SpeechRecognitionRejected event, 807
SpeechRecognized event, 807
SpeechRecognizer class, 807, 808
SpeechSynthesizer class, 804
SpeedRatio property, 796

SpellCheck.IsEnabled property, 204
SpellingReform property, 205
spline key frames, 774
splitter bars, 97
SpotLight class, 818
SpreadMethod property, 392
square-drawing application, 434
SRGS (Speech Recognition Grammar
    Specification), 807, 808
SrgsDocument, 807
SSML (Synthesis Markup Language), 806
STA (single-thread affinity), 18
StackPanel, 90
    arranging elements vertically or
        horizontally, 80
    button stack example, 79
    changing alignment defaults, 82
    considerations when sizing button, 85
    description of, 78
    DesiredSize property, 85
    Height property, 84
    HorizontalAlignment property, 82
    IScrollInfo and logical scrolling, 126
    layout properties, table of, 81
    Margin property, 83
    setting control margins, 83
    Thickness structure, 83
    using in Visual Studio, 80
    VerticalAlignment property, 82
    Width property, 84
StartLineCap property, 381
StartPoint property, 391, 418
Startup event, 58
StartupUri attribute, 913
StartupUri property, 59, 256
static resources, 335
StaticExtension, 35
StaticResource, 458, 555
StatusBar class, 636, 640
StatusBarItem object, 640
StaysOpen property, 200, 283
StaysOpenOnClick property, 633
StickyNoteControl class, 695
stitching (z-fighting), 822
Stop() method, 790
StopLoading() method, 261
Store database
    installing, 507
    ProductImage field, 531
    two tables and their schemas, 507
StoreDataSetPaginator class, 715–719
StoreDB class
    adding UpdateProduct(), 513
    binding to ADO.NET data objects, 521
    binding to collection of objects, 516
    building data object, 510
    caller inform design pattern, 510

collection items, displaying and editing,
    516
collection items, inserting and removing,
    520
DataContent property, 519
DataContext property, 512
displaying bound object, 511
DisplayMemberPath property, 518
enabling database updates, 513
GetProduct(), 508
GetProducts(), 517
handling change notification, 514
IEnumerable interface, 516
INotifyCollectionChanged interface, 521
INotifyPropertyChanged interface, 514
ItemsControl class, table of properties, 516
making instance available through
    Application class, 509
OnPropertyChanged(), 515
options for making it available to
    application windows, 508
preventing field from being edited, 520
Product object, 510
PropertyChanged event, 514
Storyboard class
    BeginStoryboard action, 747
    BeginStoryboard.HandoffBehavior
        property, 752
    creating property trigger that triggers
        storyboard, 749
    defining storyboard, 746
    fusing second animation into first
        animation's timeline, 752
    HandoffBehavior.Compose, 752
    managing simultaneous animations as
        one group, 753
    SetSpeedRatio(), 757
    snapshot-and-replace behavior, 752
    storyboard, defined, 746
    TargetName property, 746–748
    TargetProperty property, 746–748
Stream property, 320, 784
StreamResourceInfo object, 319
Stretch property, 121, 136, 372, 375, 396, 398,
    799
StretchDirection property, 136, 375, 799
Stroke objects, 107
Stroke property, 376
StrokeDashArray property, 382
StrokeDashCap, 383
StrokeDashOffset property, 383
StrokeLineJoin property, 381
StrokeMiterLimit, 381
Strokes collection, 107
Style class
    creating Style object, 353
    table of properties, 352

TargetType property, 448
Style property, 351
style selectors, 571
styles, 5
   adding Setter objects, 351
   advantages of, 339
   applying different style formats to
      different element types, 355
   applying only one Style object to element
      at once, 357
   applying style-based event handlers, 356
   attaching event handlers for MouseEnter
      and MouseLeave events, 356
   automatically applying styles by type, 359
   benefits of, 352
   comparing event setters and event
      triggers, 356
   comparing to CSS, 349
   complications arising from automatic
      styles, 360
   creating collection of EventSetter objects,
      356
   creating Style object, 353
   creating style that builds upon another
      style, 357
   creating System.Windows.Style object as
      resource, 351
   defined, 349
   defining style to wrap various font
      properties, 351
   disadvantages of style inheritance, 359
   example of standardizing font properties
      of window, 349
   identifying property to be set, 354
   linking triggers to styles through
      Style.Triggers collection, 360
   naming convention, 351
   not using styles and resources together,
      353
   omitting key name when setting
      TargetType property, 359
   overriding style characteristics, 352
   pulling style out of Resources collection
      using FindResource(), 351
   setters as only changing dependency
      property, 354
   setting BasedOn attribute of, 357
   setting element's Style property, 351
   setting style programmatically, 351
   setting TargetType property of Style object,
      355
   Style class, table of properties, 352
   Style objects as wrapping collection of
      Setter objects, 354
   support for triggers and templates, 349
   using BasedOn property to create chain of
      inherited styles, 358
   using resources to hold styles, 349
   using Setter.TargetName property, 354
   using styles and resources together, 353
   using to set any dependency property, 349
   wiring up events to event handlers, 356
StyleSelector class, 571
Style.Triggers collection, 360
stylus events, 163
SuppressExceptions property, 533
SweepDirection property, 419
SynchronizationContext class, 937
Synthesis Markup Language (SSML), 806
system DPI setting, 6–9
System.Add.dll assembly, 951
System.AddIn.Contract namespace, 947, 961
System.AddIn.Contract.dll assembly, 951
System.AddIn.dll assembly, 948
System.AddIn.Hosting namespace, 954
System.AddIn.Hosting.AddInStore class, 951
System.AddIn.Hosting.AddInToken class, 951
System.AddIn.Pipeline namespace, 947, 961
System.AddIns.Pipeline.ContractHandle
   object, 951
SystemBrushes class, 390
System.Collections.Generic namespace, 868
SystemColors class, 180
System.ComponentModel namespace, 879,
   933
System.ComponentModel.Component class,
   910
System.ComponentModel.MaskedText-
   Provider, 880
System.ComponentModel.PropertyGroup-
   Description, 581
System.ComponentModel.SortDescription,
   580
System.Data namespace, 578
System.Drawing namespace, 341
System.Drawing.dll, 906, 910
System.Drawing.Graphics class, 237
SystemDropShadowChrome class, 408, 454
System.Environment class, 235
System.Globalization.NumberStyles value,
   529
System.IO.Compression namespace, 283
System.IO.DriveInfo class, 628
System.IO.FileSystemWatcher, 630
System.IO.IsolatedStorage namespace, 282
System.IO.Packaging namespace, 694
System.Linq.Enumerable class, 525
System.Media namespace, 783
SystemParameters class, 219
System.Printing namespace, 697, 721, 724
System.Printing.PrintQueue object, 720
System.Security.Principal.WindowsIdentity
   class, 688
SystemSounds class, 786, 787

System.Speech.dll assembly, 804
System.Speech.Recognition namespace, 807
System.Speech.Recognition.SrgsGrammar
    namespace, 807
System.Speech.Synthesis namespace, 804
System.Threading.DispatcherObject, 18
System.Threading.Thread, 928–931
System.TimeSpan, 740
System.Windows namespace, 341
System.Windows.Annotations namespace,
    684–685
System.Windows.Application class, 909
System.Windows.Clipboard class, 177
System.Windows.Controls namespace, 540,
    695, 697, 810
System.Windows.Controls.ContentControl,
    19
System.Windows.Controls.Control, 19, 117
System.Windows.Controls.Decorator, 133
System.Windows.Controls.ItemsControl, 19
System.Windows.Controls.Page class, 246
System.Windows.Controls.Panel, 19, 573
System.Windows.Controls.Primitives
    namespace, 193, 200, 454–455, 640
System.Windows.Controls.Primitives.Range-
    Base class, 875
System.Windows.Controls.Primitives.TextBox
    Base class, 881
System.Windows.Data.CollectionViewSource
    class, 575
System.Windows.Data.DataSourceProvider
    class, 591
System.Windows.DependencyObject, 18
System.Windows.Documents namespace,
    647
System.Windows.Documents.TextRange
    class, 674
System.Windows.Forms.Application class,
    57, 909
System.Windows.Forms.Control class, 916
System.Windows.Forms.dll, 906, 910
System.Windows.Forms.Integration
    namespace, 916
System.Windows.FrameworkElement, 18
System.Windows.Freezable class, 182
System.Windows.Input.Cursor, 189
System.Windows.Input.ICommand interface,
    291
System.Windows.Input.RoutedCommand
    class, 292
System.Windows.Interop.HwndHost class,
    925
System.Windows.LogicalTreeHelper, 448
System.Windows.Markup, 672
System.Windows.Markup.MarkupExtension,
    35
System.Windows.Media namespace, 787

System.Windows.Media.Animation
    namespace, 732–733, 735, 760
System.Windows.Media.Brush, 390
System.Windows.Media.Color, 860
System.Windows.Media.DrawingContext,
    856
System.Windows.Media.Effects namespace,
    403
System.Windows.Media.Fonts class, 187
System.Windows.Media.Media3D
    namespace, 811
System.Windows.Media.Pen class, 426
System.Windows.Media.Transform class, 385
System.Windows.Media.Visual, 18, 697
System.Windows.Media.VisualTreeHelper,
    448
System.Windows.MessageBox class, 226
System.Windows.Presentation.dll assembly,
    961
System.Windows.Rect, 220
System.Windows.Shapes namespace, 122
System.Windows.Shapes.Shape, 19
System.Windows.Shapes.Shape class, 368
System.Windows.Threading namespace, 928
System.Windows.Threading.DispatcherTimer,
    730
System.Windows.TriggerAction, 748
System.Windows.TriggerBase, 360
System.Windows.UIElement, 18

■T

TabControl, 128
TabIndex property, 170
TabItem control, 119, 128
Table element
    CellSpacing property, 654
    creating table, procedure and markup for,
        653–654
    sizing table columns explicitly or
        proportionately, 655
    supplying TableColumn objects for
        Table.Rows property, 654
    TableCell element, 653
    TableRow element, 653
    TableRowGroup element, 653
TableCell element, 654
TableLayoutPanel, 75, 919
TableRow element, 653
TableRowGroup element, 653
TabletPC, 79
TabPanel, 79
TabStripPlacement property, 128
Tag property, 484, 627
Target property, 190
TargetInvocationException, 543
TargetItems property, 267
TargetName property, 452, 462, 746–748

TargetProperty property, 746–748
TargetType attribute, 872
TargetType property, 355, 448, 616
TargetZone tag, 274
TaskDialog class, 241
TaskDialogResult object, 242
template selectors, 559
TemplateBinding, 872–873
TemplatedParent property, 486
TemplatePart attributes, 480
templates, 5
    attaching triggers with template, 750
    building complex, multipart templates,
        474
    characteristics of complex templates, 474
    combining template types in same
        control, 453
    control template dependencies, 475
    control templates, 453
    data templates, 453
    FrameworkTemplate class, 453
    hiding or showing elements in response to
        trigger, 463
    panel templates, 453
    retrieving control's template and
        serializing it to XAML, 455
    reusing, 554
    setting sequential order for conflicting
        trigger settings, 464
    similarity between templates and styles,
        464
    template bindings, 460
    types of, 453
text controls, 202
text handling, 5
Text property, 40, 202, 293
TextAlignment property, 667
TextBlock, 120, 668, 669
TextBox class, 31, 36, 40, 186, 203
TextBox control
    AcceptsReturn property, 203
    AcceptsTab property, 203
    AutoWordSelection, 204
    BeginChange(), 205
    CanUndo property, 205
    creating multiline text box, 202
    EndChange(), 205
    IsReadOnly property, 203
    Language property, 204
    LineCount property, 203
    pressing Enter key in, 203
    SelectedText property, 204
    selecting text, 203
    SelectionChanged event, 204
    SelectionLength property, 204
    SelectionStart property, 204

setting HorizontalScrollBarVisibility
    property, 203
setting VerticalScrollBarVisibility property,
    203
SpellCheck.IsEnabled property, 204
spelling-checker feature, 204
SpellingReform property, 205
Text property, 202
TextBox class, 203
TextChanged event, 166
TextWrapping property, 203
Undo feature, 205
using MinLines and MaxLines properties,
    203
TextChanged event, 166
TextCompositionEventArgs object, 168
TextDecorations class, 185, 648
TextDecorations property, 185
TextIndent property, 651
TextInput event, 166–168
TextMarkerStyle enumeration, 651
TextPointer objects, 676
TextRange class, 675, 676
TextSearch.TextPath property, 602
TextSelection class, 678, 679
TextTrimming property, 668
texture mapping, 834
TextureCoordinates collection
    creating multifaceted cube, 836
    markup for creating VisualBrush that
        loops video playback, 837
    markup for mapping one face of cube, 835
    using ImageBrush to paint bitmap, 834
    using relative coordinates in, 836
TextureCoordinates property, 813–815
TextWrapping property, 203, 668
Thickness structure, 83
ThicknessAnimation class, 731, 763
this keyword, 486
thread affinity, 928
Thread object, 959
thread rental, 927
Thumb element, 454
TickBar element, 454, 897
TickFrequency property, 498
Ticks collection, 212
TileBrush, 183
TileMode property, 399, 429
TileView class
    adding set of properties to, 620
    BasedOn property, 616
    changes to, after selecting TileView style,
        616
    ComponentResourceKey, 615–616
    ItemTemplate property, 615
    markup for TileView style, 617

TileView class *(continued)*
    retrieving default styles using
        generic.xaml, 616
    TargetType property, 616
    TileView style, 615
    TileViewItem style, 615
Time data types, 529
Timeline class
    AccelerationRatio property, 744
    BeginTime property, 753
    DecelerationRatio property, 744, 762
    DesiredFrameRate attached property, 761
    RepeatBehavior property, 745
    SpeedRatio property, 753
    table of properties, 742
TimelineGroup class, 742
timer-based animation, 730
Timestamp property, 166
Title property, 484
To property, 736, 738
ToggleButton class, 193
ToList() method, 525
ToolBar class
    adding items automatically to overflow
        menu, 638
    changing behavior of ToggleButton, 636
    components of, 636
    configuring OverflowMode property, 638
    holding image content in buttons, 637
    lack of dedicated wrapper class, 637
    overriding default style of some types of
        children, 636
    setting Orientation property, 638
    toolbar, function of, 636
ToolbarOverflowPanel, 79
ToolbarPanel, 79
ToolBarTray class, 639
ToolTip, 117–119
ToolTip class, 195
ToolTip property, 195
Tooltips control
    configuring ToolTip-related settings, 196
    CustomPopupPlacementCallback
        property, 198
    inability of ToolTip window to accept
        focus, 196
    options for placing ToolTip, 197
    Placement property, 197
    PlacementTarget property, 198
    ToolTip class, 195
    ToolTip properties, table of, 196
    ToolTipService class, 198
ToolTipService class, 199
Top property, 104, 220
top-level elements in XAML, 25
ToString() method, 119, 121, 168, 207, 211,
    518

total-fit algorithm, 667
ToXml() method, 806
Track class, 478, 480
TrackballDecorator class, 844
Transform class, 385
Transform object, 701–702
Transform property, 433
Transform3DGroup class, 839
transforms
    animating element's visual appearance,
        764
    approaches for creating dynamic 3-D
        effects, 839
    assigning RenderTransform property to
        transform object, 386
    comparing RenderTransform and
        LayoutTransform, 389, 766
    creating databound Slider for rotating 3-D
        objects, 840
    creating document window that jumps
        into view, 767
    defined, 385
    deriving from Freezable, 386
    Expression Blend design tool, 769
    Frame element, 389
    LayoutTransform property, 388, 764
    manipulating 3-D objects using, 838
    Model3D class, 839
    Model3DGroup class, 839
    ModelVisual3D class, 839
    multiple, animating, 767
    naming transform objects using x:Name
        attribute, 839
    nesting inside TransformGroup, 767
    RenderTransform property, 764
    RenderTransformOrigin property, 387
    RotateTransform, 763–764, 767
    RotateTransform class, 386
    RotateTransform3D, 840, 852
    rotating button on mouseover, 764
    ScaleTransform, 763, 767
    ScaleTransform3D, 838
    setting RenderTransform property of
        Border object, 767
    setting RenderTransformOrigin property,
        765
    setting shape's center point, 387
    Transform3DGroup class, 839
    transforming any element, 388
    TranslateTransform, 763
    TranslateTransform3D class, 839
    use of matrix math to alter shape
        coordinates, 385
    WindowsFormsHost, 389
TranslateTransform, 763
TranslateTransform3D class, 839
transparency, 2, 182–184

TreeView class, 78, 600

TreeView control

adding non-TreeViewItem elements to
TreeView, 622

adding placeholder under each drive
node, 628

applying data templates by data type
instead of by position, 625

constructing TreeViewItem objects
programmatically, 622

displaying CategoryName property of
each Category object, 624

displaying folders on hard drive using
just-in-time TreeView, 627

displaying non-UIElement object, 622

filling TreeView with data, 622

handling TreeViewItem.Expanded event,
629

HierarchicalDataTemplate, 624

implementing Category class and
INotifyPropertyChanged, 623

incorporating hierarchical data with
nested structure, 622

ItemsSource property, 624

ItemTemplate property, 624

just-in-time node creation, 627

markup for basic TreeView, 622

setting ItemsSource property, 622

as specialized ItemsControl that hosts
TreeViewItem objects, 621

specifying right data templates for
different levels of data, 622

System.IO.DriveInfo class, 628

System.IO.FileSystemWatcher, 630

TreeViewItem objects, 622

using name of DataRelation as
ItemsSource, 626

using TreeView to show multilayered
DataSet, 626

TreeViewItem, 627, 629

TriangleIndices property, 813–814, 824

Trigger.EnterActions, 749

Trigger.ExitActions, 749

triggers

applying event triggers using
FrameworkElement.Triggers
collection, 360

attaching simple trigger to dependency
property, 361

automating simple style changes, 360

Conditions collection, 363

considering trigger order when modifying
elements, 362

creating multiple triggers that apply to
same element, 362

event triggers, 363

linking to styles through Style.Triggers
collection, 360

performing animation when dependency
property hits specific value, 364

returning to pre-trigger appearance of
element, 361

setting sequential order for conflicting
trigger settings, 464

setting Trigger.EnterActions and
Trigger.ExitActions properties, 365

System.Windows.TriggerBase, classes
deriving from, 360

TargetName property and, 452

using MultiTrigger, 363

waiting for button to get keyboard focus,
361

Triggers collection, 748

Trusted Publishers store, 280

TryFindResource() method, 340

TryParse() method, 529

tunneling events, 154, 161

type converters, 32

TypeArguments attribute, 270

TypeConverter attribute, 32

TypeExtension, 35

TypeNameAnimationBase class, 733

Typography object, 648

Typography property, 185

∎U

UAC (User Account Control), 73, 969, 976

Uid attribute, 326

UIElement class, 16–18, 151, 431

AddHandler(), 313

Arrange(), 702

IsMouseDirectlyOver property, 173

IsMouseOver property, 173

Label, 120

Measure(), 702

OnRender(), 896

Opacity property, 182

TextBlock, 120

Visibility property, enumeration values,
113

UIElement3D class, 847

UIElement.AddHandler() method, 152

UNC path, 971

Undo feature, 205, 310

UndoCommand_CanExecute() method, 868

UndoCommand_Executed() method, 868

UniformGrid, 78, 104

UnionIterator class, 525

UnmanagedMemoryStream object, 320

Unselected event, 210

Update() method, 951

UpdateProduct() method, 513

UpdateSourceTrigger property, 498, 502, 542

URIs, 321–322
Use Windows XP Style DPI Scaling, 9–10
User Account Control (UAC), 73, 969, 976
user controls
    adding command bindings, 866
    adding command support to controls, 866
    adding user control to custom control
        library project, 859
    Color property, 860
    ContentControl template, 870
    control consumer, 859
    control template, 869
    creating basic color picker, 858
    creating lookless control, 870
    creating new RoutedUICommand object
        for command, 866
    creating undo stack that stores series of
        values, 868
    defining and adding routed events, 862
    designing public interface, 859
    goal of, 870
    InitializeComponent(), 869
    naming, 865
    property coercion callbacks, role of, 862
    UserControl class, 859, 869
    using binding expressions to repurpose
        core property, 865
    writeable control properties as usually
        dependency properties, 860
user interface
    accommodating large monitors and high-
        resolution displays, 23
    bitmap-based interfaces as resolution-
        dependent, 23
    building localizable interfaces, 324
    creating modular interfaces, 112
    creating resolution-independent, size-
        independent interfaces in WPF, 76
    handling localized text, 111
    integrating video content into, 5
    localizing FontFamily property, 324
    migrating from Windows Forms to WPF,
        904
    separating completely from code, 5
    vector graphics and, 10
    window as only holding single element, 76
User32, 1, 16, 20
    lack of support for graphical scaling, 6
    windowing model, 368
    WPF and, 2
UserControl class, 119, 859
    Binding.RelativeSource property, 865
    Border element, 869
    changing source of routed events, 869
    ContentPresenter, 869–870
    description of, 857

differentiating user controls and custom
    controls, 869
Focusable property, 869
HorizontalAlignment property, 869
InitializeComponent(), 869
IsTabStop property, 869
Name property, 865
Padding property, 865
VerticalAlignment property, 869
UserPageRangeEnabled property, 720

■V

ValidateValueCallback, 141–143, 146
ValidatingType property, 917
validation
    adding it to Binding.ValidationRules
        collection, 541
    AdornedElementPlaceholder, 545–547
    applying property validation carelessly,
        537
    applying when using TwoWay or
        OneWayToSource binding, 536
    bubbling, 543
    building validation directly into controls,
        536
    checking InnerException property of
        TargetInvocationException, 543
    code example for disallowing negative
        numbers, 536
    contents of ValidationError object, 543
    creating error templates, 545
    DataErrorValidationRule, 539–540
    defining at binding level, 536
    displaying error content in ToolTip, 546
    ErrorContent property, 541–543
    ExceptionValidationRule, 537–542
    FormHasErrors(), 545
    getting list of all outstanding errors, 544
    handling Error event, 543
    HasError property, 538
    how WPF handles validation failures, 538
    IsValid property, 541
    NotifyOnValidationError property, 538
    options for catching invalid values, 536
    raising errors in data object, 536
    reacting to validation errors, 543
    setting NotifyOnValidationError property,
        543
    TargetInvocationException, 543
    using same validation rule for more than
        one binding, 542
    Validation class, 538
    validation rule for restricting decimal
        values, 540
    ValidationError object, 538
    Validation.ErrorTemplate property, 538
    ValidationResult object, 541

ValidationRules collection, 537
ValidationRule.Validate(), 538
visual indication of errors in bound
        controls, 538
writing custom validation rules, 540
validation callback, 139, 140
Validation class, 538
ValidationError object, 538, 543
Validation.ErrorTemplate property, 538
ValidationResult object, 541
ValidationRules collection, 537
ValidationRule.Validate(), 538
validator controls, 877
value converters, 559
    applying conditional formatting, 533
    BitmapImage class, 532
    converting from display format back to
            number, 529
    converting raw binary data into WPF
            BitmapImage object, 531
    creating, 528
    creating converter object in Resources
            collection, 530
    creating objects with, 531
    data triggers, 534
    Decimal.ToString(), 528
    evaluating multiple properties, 535
    format strings, 528
    formatting strings, 527
    ImagePathConverter, code example, 531
    IMultiValueConveter interface, 535
    mapping project namespace to XML
            namespace prefix, 530
    MultiBinding, 535
    Parse(), 529
    PriceConverter class, 530
    reusing your formatting logic with other
            templates, 560
    SuppressExceptions property, 533
    System.Globalization.NumberStyles value,
            529
    TryParse(), 529
    uses for, 527
    using custom IValueConverter, 533
Value property, 211, 875
ValueChanged event, 211
vbc.exe csc.exe compiler, 53
.vbproj .csproj file, 274
vector graphics, 10
Vector3DAnimationUsingKeyFrames, 773
VerifyAccess() method, 929
vertex shaders, defined, 4
VerticalAlignment property, 82, 869
VerticalContentAlignment property, 121
VerticalScrollBarVisibility property, 125, 203
video cards, 3–4
video, mapping to 3-D surface, 837

VideoDrawing class, 803
View property, 586, 607
ViewBase class, 607
Viewbox class
    determining shape's ordinary, non-
            Viewbox size, 376
    resizing shapes proportionally in canvas,
            374
    Stretch property, 375
Viewport, 397, 845–847
Viewport2DVisual3D class, 850–851
Viewport3D class
    Camera property, 810, 819
    Children property, 810
    ClipToBounds inherited property, 811
    hosting any 3-D object that derives from
            Visual3D, 811
    light source as object in viewport, 810
    using as content of window or page, 810
Viewport3DVisual class, 431
ViewportSize property, 480
ViewportUnits property, 397
views, 941
    add-in, 947
    host, 950
ViewToContractAdapter() method, 961
virtual key state, 171
VirtualizingStackPanel, 79, 604
Visibility property, 113, 170, 218, 913
visual add-ins, 960–962
Visual Basic C#, 22
Visual class, 16–18
    AddLogicalChild(), 434
    AddVisualChild(), 434
    ContainerVisual class, 431
    defining graphical element as Visual
            object, 431
    DrawingVisual class, 427, 431
    overriding GetVisualChild(), 434
    overriding VisualChildrenCount property,
            434
    UIElement class, 431
    Viewport3DVisual class, 431
visual layer model, 431
Visual Studio, 5, 21, 318
    adding resource dictionary, 465
    Application class and, 58
    App.xaml, 59
    automatically creating partial class for
            event handling code, 28
    Automatically Increment Revision with
            Each Publish setting, 278
    choosing Custom Control Library (WPF)
            project type, 856
    choosing Run As Administrator option,
            969
    creating PageFunction in, 270

Visual Studio *(continued)*
  creating XAML with, 21–22
  debugging XBAP projects in, 275
  format strings, 528
  Main(), creating, 58
  procedure for installing ClickOnce
      application, 975–976
  publishing application to virtual directory
      in, 969
  publishing ClickOnce application to web
      server, 967
  setting Build Action to Resource, 187
  Setup Project template, 965
  Solution Explorer, 58, 906, 910, 920
  two-stage compilation process for WPF
      applications, 51
  updating ClickOnce application
      automatically, 977
  using Grid in, 94
  using StackPanel in, 80
  using XAML Browser Application
      template, 274
  Windows Forms designer, 906
  wrapper class as component-specific, 914
visual tree
  defined, 446
  examining programmatically, 449
  expanding upon logical tree, 446
  Snoop utility, 451
  using with styles and templates, 448
  VisualTreeDisplay window, code example,
      450
  VisualTreeHelper class, list of methods, 448
Visual3D class, 735
VisualBrush
  animating special effects, 401
  animation possibilities of, 770
  creating reflection effect using
      OpacityMask property, 402
  filling surface with element's visual
      content, 399
  markup for copying button's appearance,
      400
  markup for creating VisualBrush that
      loops video playback, 837
  markup for painting text box with
      mirrored text, 402
VisualChildrenCount property, 434–435
visual-layer classes, 711
VisualTreeHelper class
  drilling down through visual tree of
      window, 449
  GetChild(), 449
  HitTest(), 437, 439, 845
  list of methods, 448
VisualTreeHelper.HitTest() method, 848
Volume property, 796

■W

WAV audio, 783
WCF (Windows Communication
    Foundation), 11, 69
WDDM (Windows Vista Display Driver
    Model), 3
WebBrowser control, 13, 246, 252
WebException, 251
weight, 95
WF (Windows Workflow Foundation), 11, 24
WF XAML, 24
WhereIterator class, 525
whitespace, handling, 40–41
Width property, 84
Win32, hosting in WPF, 925
Win32PrintDialog, 700
Window class, 118–119, 248
  adding sizing grip to shaped window, 233
  AdornerDecorator class, 483
  allowing single nested element, 121
  AllowsTransparency property, 227
  Background property, 215
  BorderBrush property, 215
  BorderThickness property, 215
  calling SaveSize() when window is closing,
      222
  calling SetSize() when window is first
      opened, 222
  centering window in available screen area,
      219
  checking result of dialog box window, 225
  client and nonclient areas defined, 215
  Close(), 218
  closing window, 218
  comparison to Page class, 248
  creating and displaying several modeless
      windows, 218
  creating public property in dialog window,
      225
  creating resizable window, 219
  deciding window location at runtime, 219
  designating accept and cancel buttons in
      dialog window, 225
  dialog model, defined, 225
  DialogResult property, 225
  displaying modal window, 218
  displaying modeless window, 218
  DragMove(), 232
  Hide(), 218
  hiding window from view, 218
  icon (.ico) files, 216
  Left property, 220
  Loaded event, 238
  LocationChanged event, 218
  modeless windows and synchronization
      code, 218

MouseLeftButtonDown event, 232
obtaining dimensions of current screen, 219
owned windows as displayed modelessly, 224
OwnedWindows property, 224
positioning window on screen, 219
removing owned windows, 224
removing window frame, 215
ResizeMode property, 233, 484
RestoreBounds property, 221
saving and restoring window location, 220
setting exact window position, 219
setting Owner property, 224
setting Visibility property to Hidden, 218
Show(), 218
ShowDialog(), 218, 225
storing current position of several windows, 221
storing window position in user-specific configuration file, 220
SystemParameters class, 219
System.Windows.Rect, 220
table of properties, 215
Tag property, 484
Title property, 484
Top property, 220
using CenterOwner for WindowState, 219
using Left and Right properties, 219
window ownership, 224
Windows property, 222
WindowStartupPosition property, 216
WindowStateChanged event, 218
WindowStyle property, 215, 227
Window element, 25
window handles, 914
Window.Loaded event, 67
Window.Owner property, 67
Window.Resources collection, 934
windows
    enabling automatic sizing, 86
    hard-coding of sizes, 86
    SizeToContent property, 86
Windows 3.0, 1
Windows Communication Foundation (WCF), 11, 69
Windows Forms, 75
    accelerator keys, 922
    adding ActiveX content to Windows Forms application, 914
    advantages of DataGridView over GridView, 608
    airspace rule, 914
    ambient properties, 186
    Application Updater Component, 968
    assessing interoperability with WPF, 903
    BackgroundWorker class, 909

BindingList collection, 521
CheckedListBox, 906
CheckedListBox control, 604
classes not needing interoperability, 909
ColorDialog class, 909
comparing dialog model to that in WPF, 226
comparison to WPF, 13
ContextMenuStrip class, 910–911
coordinate system for sizing controls, 918
creating user controls, 918
data binding, 917
DataGridView, 906
DataGridView control, 13, 621
DateTimePicker, 906
DialogResult enumeration, 907
ElementHost class, 908, 914, 924
EnableModelessKeyboardInterop(), 908
EnableVisualStyles(), 909, 918
EnableWindowsFormsInterop(), 908
ErrorProvider, 906
extender providers, 37
FlowLayoutPanel, 892
FolderBrowserDialog class, 909
FontDialog class, 909
Form class, 215
Form.ShowDialog(), 907
glue code, 906
having WPF controls receive keyboard input, 908
HelpProvider, 906
HelpProvider component, 13
hooking events up to control using XAML, 917
hosting Windows Forms controls in WPF, 916
hosting WPF controls in, 919
Icon property, 910
ImageList, 906
incorporating lower-level GDI+ drawing support in animation, 730
interoperability problems with keyboard handling, 921
ISupportInitialize interface, 145
MaskedTextBox, 906
MaskedTextBox control, 879–880
MaskedTextProvider class, 879
MDI windows, 906
migrating applications to WPF, 903
missing WPF controls and features, table of, 904
mixing windows and forms, 906–909
mnemonics, 923
no need for wrapper class, 914
NotifyIcon class, 909
overlapping of WPF and Windows Forms content, 914

Windows Forms *(continued)*
  PageSetupDialog class, 909
  preventing naming clashes among Windows Forms and WPF namespaces, 918
  primary interop assembly, 919
  PrintPreviewDialog class, 909
  property map conversions, table of, 924
  property mapping, 923
  property translators, 923
  PropertyGrid, 906
  quartz.dll library, 783
  runtime callable wrappers (RCWs), 919
  SoundPlayer class, 909
  System.ComponentModel.MaskedText-Provider, 880
  System.Drawing namespace, 341
  System.Drawing.dll, 906, 910
  System.Drawing.Graphics class, 237
  System.Windows.Forms.dll, 906, 910
  TypeConverter infrastructure, 916
  User32 library, 895
  using ampersand character to identify shortcut key, 190
  using separate window handle (hwnd), 914
  Visual Basic C# and, 22
  visual styles for controls and, 909
  visual styles for Windows Forms controls, 909
  WebBrowser, 906
  WebBrowser control, 13
  Windows Forms toolkit, 906
  WindowsFormsHost class, 914, 916, 918, 924
  z-index, 915
Windows Forms toolkit, 208
Windows graphics, 1
Windows Media Player, 5, 783, 784
Windows print queue, 699
Windows property, 222
Windows SDK .NET Framework 3.0 Samples, 241
Windows Vista
  Adjust Font Size (DPI), 9
  adjusting system DPI setting, 9
  bitmap scaling, 10
  built-in support for speech recognition, 806
  creating and viewing XPS documents, 682
  Custom DPI Setting dialog box, 10
  Desktop Window Manager (DWM), 16
  Disable Display Scaling on High DPI Settings, 10
  Internet Information Services (IIS) 7, 969
  milcore.dll, 16
  Narrator screen reader, 804

  new task dialog box, functions of, 241
  no WPF support for Vista-style dialog boxes, 241
  printing XPS content, 725
  publishing applications to local web server, 969
  Sound icon, 787
  taking advantage of Vista-specific APIs, 242
  Use Windows XP Style DPI Scaling, 9–10
  User Account Control (UAC), 73, 969, 976
  using Aero Glass effect, 236
Windows Vista Display Driver Model (WDDM), 3
Windows Workflow Foundation (WF), 11, 24
Windows XP
  lack of support for speech recognition, 806
  MediaPlayer and 64-bit version of, 787
  Narrator screen reader, 804
  no antialiasing on edges of 3-D shapes, 824
  Sounds and Audio Devices icon, 787
Windows XP Display Driver Model (XPDM), 3
WindowsBase.dll, 16
WindowsCodecs.dll, 16
WindowsFormsApplicationBase class, 69
WindowsFormsHost, 389
WindowsFormsHost class, 914, 916, 918, 924
Window.ShowDialog() method, 907
WindowStartupPosition property, 216
WindowStateChanged event, 218
WindowStyle property, 215, 227
WindowTitle property, 249–250
Word 2007 XML (WordML), 649
Word, Microsoft, 68, 677
WordML (Word 2007 XML), 649
WorkArea property, 219
WorkerReportsProgress property, 937–938
WorkerSupportsCancellation property, 938
WPF browser-hosted applications (XBAPs), 11
WPF Everywhere (WPF/E), 14
WPF XAML, 24
WpfApp class, 70
WPF/E (WPF Everywhere), 14
WrapBreakPanel, 892, 894
WrapPanel, 96
  basing WrapBreakPanel on, 893
  code example for series of buttons, 87
  controlling small-scale details in user interface, 87
  default settings, 86
  description of, 78
  Dock property, 88
  extending capabilities of, 892
  LastChildFill, 88
  setting order of docking controls, 89

wrapper classes, 46, 914
Write() method, 725–727
WriteAsync() method, 725–727
WritingCompleted event, 727–728

■X

XAML, 47–49
<Button> element, 25
Adobe Illustrator plug-in for, 430
advantages of, 20
Application element, 25
Application tag, 59
Application.g.vb App.g.cs file, 59
Application.xaml.vb App.xaml.cs file, 61
AssemblyName, 45
attached properties, translating into
    method calls, 36
attached properties, two-part naming
    syntax, 36
attached properties, using to control
    layout, 36
attaching name to Grid element, 29
automatically creating partial class for
    event handling code, 28
BAML, 24
basics of, 25
bridging gap between string values and
    nonstring properties, 32
building simple no-code XAML files, 53
C# and, 20
case-insensitivity of type converters, 32
case-sensitivity of, 32
Class attribute, 27, 59
classes that define their own Name
    property, 29
code-behind class, 27
coding styles for creating WPF application,
    46
collapsing whitespace, tabs, and line
    breaks in XAML, 657
compiling, 24
complex properties, 32
Connect(), 52
connecting event handlers, 27
container controls, 39
containment, 25
Content property, 40
ContentControl class, 40
ContentProperty attribute, 37–39
controls containing collection of visual
    items, 39
controls containing singular content, 39
converter for Adobe Flash files, 430
core WPF namespace, 27
core XAML namespace, 27
creating blank window with, 25
creating custom wrapper classes, 46

creating with Visual Studio, 21–22
declarative animation, 746
default constructor, 28
defined, 24
dependency properties, 36
DependencyObject class, 36, 50
design tools and, 23
designing WPF application in Visual
    Studio, 23
distinguishing properties from other types
    of nested content, 33
DockPanel object, 51
eight ball example, full window definition,
    43
eight ball window and its controls, 30
element attributes as setting element
    properties, 31
embedding BAML as resource into DLL or
    EXE assembly, 24
entity references, 40
enumerations, 32
event model in WPF, 42
event routing, 42
example of bare-bones XAML document,
    25
Expression Design's built-in XAML export,
    430
extension classes, 35
FileStream class, 46
FrameworkElement class, 29
graphical user interfaces before WPF, 22
Grid element, 25
IDictionary, 37
IList, 37
including Name attribute in control, 29
InitializeComponent(), 47
InitializeComponent() method, 28
instantiating .NET objects, 21
integrating workflow between developers
    and designers, 21
ItemsControl class, 40
lack of public fields or call methods in, 45
lack of support for inline calculations, 748
LoadComponent(), 28
loading and compiling, 46
loading XAML dynamically vs. compiling
    XAML to BAML, 51
LogicalTreeHelper, 51
loose XAML files, 53
mapping element to instance of .NET
    class, 25
mapping .NET namespace to XML
    namespace, 44
merging code with designer-generated
    file, 28
Microsoft Expression Blend, 21
namespace prefixes, 45

XAML *(continued)*

namespaces, defining, 26

nesting elements, 25, 37

.NET objects and, 24

no one-to-one mapping between XML and .NET namespaces, 27

no support for parameterized constructors, 45

no-argument constructors, 45

NullExtension, 35

Page element, 25

Panel class, 39–40

parser, 26

parser error due to no associated type converter, 32

parser's procedure for finding type converter, 32

parsing and validation of at compile time, 32

partial classes, contents of, 51

problems in exporting content to bitmap format, 22

properties supporting more than one type of collection, 38

property-element syntax, 33

ProvideValue(), 35

replacing attribute with nested element, 354

replacing XAML tags with set of code statements, 34

RuntimeNameProperty attribute, 29

separating graphical content from code, 22

setting background and foreground colors in, 181

setting class properties through attributes, 25

setting complex property, 33

setting mouse cursor in, 189

setting property value dynamically, 35

setting type converter at class level, 32

setting x:Key attribute, 37

Silverlight XAML, 24

similarity of attached properties to extender providers, 37

simple properties and type converters, 31

special characters, 40

start tag attributes, 26

StartupUri property, 59

StaticExtension, 35

subsets of, 24

System.Windows.Markup.Markup-Extension, 35

Text property, 40

TextBox class, 31, 36, 40

top-level elements, 25

type converters, 32

TypeConverter attribute, 32

TypeExtension, 35

using code-behind class to manipulate controls programmatically, 29

using device-independent units in measurements, 26

using dictionary collection, 37

using markup extension, 35

using markup extensions as nested properties, 35

using to construct WPF user interfaces, 21

using TypeConverter attribute on property declaration, 32

using types from other namespaces, 44

using underscore to identify shortcut key, 190

using without compiling, 24

using xml:space="preserve" attribute on element, 41

Visual Studio, 21

WF XAML, 24

whitespace, handling, 40–41

Window element, 25

Windows Workflow Foundation (WF), 24

WPF XAML, 24

xamlc.exe compiler, 51

XamlReader class, 47–49

XML character entities, table of, 40

XML Paper Specification (XPS), 24

xmlns attribute, 26

XPS XAML, 24

XAML browser application (XBAP)

advantages of, 273

ApplicationExtension tag, 274

ApplicationName.exe, 276

ApplicationName.exe.manifest, 276

ApplicationName.xbap, 276

automatically generated certificate file, 277

CodeAccessPermission class, 281

coding for different security levels, 281

combining XBAP and stand-alone applications, 280

creating, 256, 274

creating XBAP that runs with full trust, 280

debugging, 277

defined, 273

Demand(), 281

deploying, 276

designing and coding pages, 275

displaying more than one XBAP in same browser window, 286

as downloaded but not installed, 273

embedding XBAP in web page, 286

four key elements in .csproj project file, 274

GetUserStoreForApplication(), 282

HostInBrowser tag, 274
Install tag, 274
Internet Explorer 6 or 7, 274
IsBrowserHosted property, 280
IsolatedStorageFile.GetDirectoryNames(),
     283
IsolatedStorageFile.GetFileNames(), 283
IsolatedStorageFileStream, 282
key supported and disallowed features,
     table of, 278
limited permissions and stringent security
     of, 273
manually clearing ClickOnce cache, 277
.NET 3.0, 273
.NET Framework and code access security,
     278
not having FileIOPermission for local hard
     drive, 283
opening secondary window using Popup
     control, 283
performing disallowed action, 279
rebuilding application and applying new
     publication version, 278
requirements, 273
running inside browser window, 273
running with permissions of Internet
     zone, 278
security, 278
setting IsEnabled property to disable user
     interface, 284
TargetZone tag, 274
updating publish version, 277
using <iframe> tag, 286
using isolated storage to provide virtual
     file system, 282
using .xbap extension, 274
XAML URIs, 257
xamlc.exe compiler, 51
XamlParseException, 165, 343
XamlReader class, 47–49, 457, 672, 674
XamlWriter class, 455, 457, 673
XBAP (XAML browser application)
   advantages of, 273
   ApplicationExtension tag, 274
   ApplicationName.exe, 276
   ApplicationName.exe.manifest, 276
   ApplicationName.xbap, 276
   automatically generated certificate file,
        277
   CodeAccessPermission class, 281
   coding for different security levels, 281
   combining XBAP and stand-alone
        applications, 280
   creating, 256, 274
   creating XBAP that runs with full trust, 280
   debugging, 277
   defined, 273

Demand(), 281
deploying, 276
designing and coding pages, 275
displaying more than one XBAP in same
     browser window, 286
as downloaded but not installed, 273
embedding XBAP in web page, 286
four key elements in .csproj project file,
     274
GetUserStoreForApplication(), 282
HostInBrowser tag, 274
Install tag, 274
Internet Explorer 6 or 7, 274
IsBrowserHosted property, 280
IsolatedStorageFile.GetDirectoryNames(),
     283
IsolatedStorageFile.GetFileNames(), 283
IsolatedStorageFileStream, 282
key supported and disallowed features,
     table of, 278
limited permissions and stringent security
     of, 273
manually clearing ClickOnce cache, 277
.NET 3.0, 273
.NET Framework and code access security,
     278
not having FileIOPermission for local hard
     drive, 283
opening secondary window using Popup
     control, 283
performing disallowed action, 279
rebuilding application and applying new
     publication version, 278
requirements, 273
running inside browser window, 273
running with permissions of Internet
     zone, 278
security, 278
setting IsEnabled property to disable user
     interface, 284
TargetZone tag, 274
updating publish version, 277
using <iframe> tag, 286
using isolated storage to provide virtual
     file system, 282
using .xbap extension, 274
.xbap extension, 274
XBAPs (WPF browser-hosted applications),
     11
Xceed Software, 608
x:Key attribute, setting, 37
XML
   character entities, table of, 40
   declaring namespaces in, 26
   namespaces as URIs, 27
   xmlns attribute, 26

XML Paper Specification (Microsoft XPS), 24,
    322, 643, 681, 682
XmlDataProvider, 591, 594, 595, 596
xmlns attribute, 26
xml:space attribute, 658
xml:space="preserve" attribute, 41
XmlStreamStore class, 684
XPath expressions, 595
XPDM (Windows XP Display Driver Model), 3
XpsDocument class, 697, 707
    AddFixedDocument(), 682
    CreateXpsDocumentWriter (), 726
    GetFixedDocumentSequence(), 682
    GetTempFileName(), 726
    loading, displaying, and printing XPS file,
        724
    RemoveSignature(), 682
    role of DocumentPaginator in printing,
        724
    SignDigitally(), 682
    using XPS document as print preview, 725

XpsDocumentWriter class
    CancelAsync(), 728
    printing directly to printer via XPS, 726
    sending content to printer
        asynchronously, 700
    using asynchronous printing, 727
    Write(), 725–727
    WriteAsync(), 725–727
    WritingCompleted event, 727–728

■Z
ZAM 3D, 829
z-fighting (stitching), 822
z-index, 915
ZIndex property, 106

You Need the Companion eBook

Your purchase of this book entitles you to buy the companion PDF-version eBook for only $10. Take the weightless companion with you anywhere.

We believe this Apress title will prove so indispensable that you'll want to carry it with you everywhere, which is why we are offering the companion eBook (in PDF format) for $10 to customers who purchase this book now. Convenient and fully searchable, the PDF version of any content-rich, page-heavy Apress book makes a valuable addition to your programming library. You can easily find and copy code—or perform examples by quickly toggling between instructions and the application. Even simultaneously tackling a donut, diet soda, and complex code becomes simplified with hands-free eBooks!

Once you purchase your book, getting the $10 companion eBook is simple:

❶ Visit **www.apress.com/promo/tendollars/**.

❷ Complete a basic registration form to receive a randomly generated question about this title.

❸ Answer the question correctly in 60 seconds, and you will receive a promotional code to redeem for the $10.00 eBook.

THE EXPERT'S VOICE™

233 Spring Street, New York, NY 10013

Offer valid through 4/10.